THE PAINTING HANDBOOK

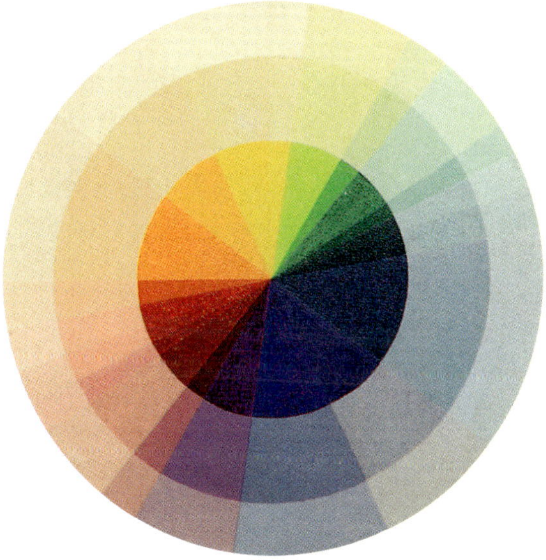

THE PAINTING HANDBOOK

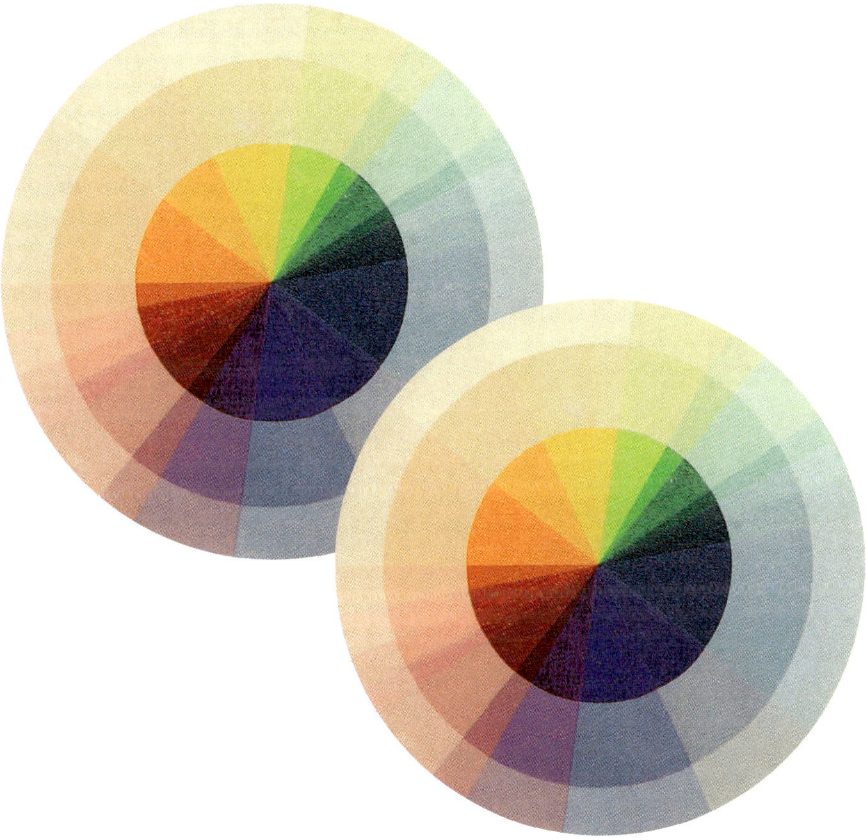

Oceana

AN OCEANA BOOK

Produced and Published by
Oceana Books
The Old Brewery
6 Blundell Street
London N7 9BH

This edition printed 2003

ISBN 1-86160-756-3

QUMTPHB

Manufactured in Singapore by
Pica Digital Pte Ltd
Printed in Singapore by
Star Standard Industries Pte Ltd

CONTENTS

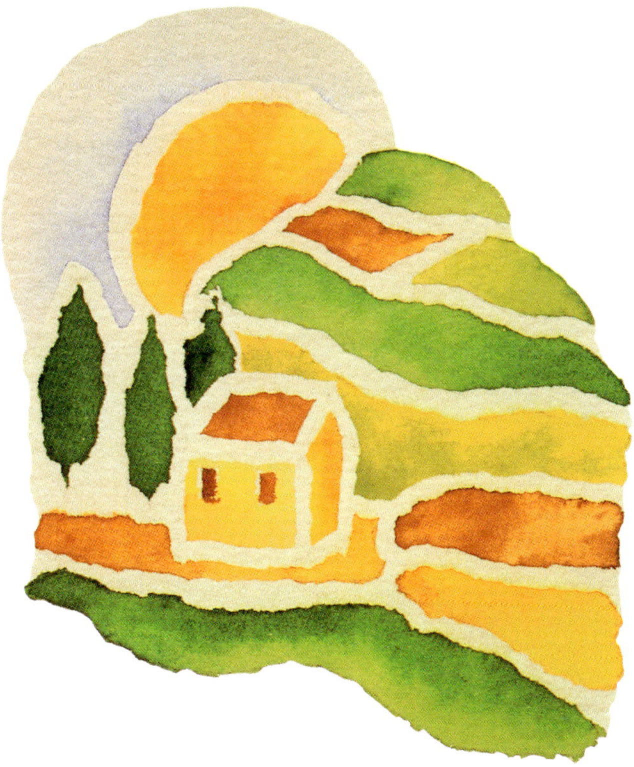

There is a theory that anyone can paint a good picture given the correct advice and a little encouragement. In *The Painting Handbook* we look at painting and drawing in detail from the basic drawing techniques, the starting block of painting, through to more complex painting skills. A handy reference book, whether you are a fledgling artist or a more accomplished practitioner you will benefit from the expert advice given at every stage of the painting process.

Each painting medium has its own characteristics, that are shown to their best advantage by examining the most appropriate surfaces, paints, tools, and techniques with which to work. By fully understanding a medium you can begin to manipulate it to create your own personal style of painting.

Using color theory, the principles of drawing can be brought to life. Some basic rules of color will enable you to make your images realistic and add dimension with shade and light, tone and hues. Having mastered your preferred medium there are step-by-step projects for inspiration and practice. Try painting a portrait or building, discover the techniques, that bring birds and animals to life and add emotion to your work with the strength and movement displayed by the weather.

INTRODUCTION

Throughout the world, more and more people have taken up painting and drawing, and this book is a complete practical guide whether you are a student of art, or simply interested in learning and improving your technique and approach. This book is crammed with indispensable information. As well as dealing with all the traditional areas of art, such as oil and watercolor painting, the book's comprehensive coverage includes some less well-known fields, such as airbrushing, spattering, and scumbling.

The book also aims to help the artist answer questions like – what do I need to know, how do I go about it, and what materials and equipment do I need? The book does this by providing a clear introduction to each medium, showing the range of available equipment and demonstrating a comprehensive range of techniques in a clear step-by-step format showing photographs with informative captions.

The extensive range of illustrated materials includes, for example, watercolor papers, drawing inks, oil paints and brushes, technical pens, and drawing equipment.

Every technique is broken down into a number of steps, that are photographed. Each individual step is numbered and given an extensive explanatory caption. By following the numbers through, a complete technique can be built up.

The techniques covered range from laying washes in watercolor, applying size and grounds in oil painting, and pastel techniques, to masking in acrylic painting, and using airbrushes, and sprayguns.

LEARNING FROM ARTISTS

Learning how to draw and paint from the example and work of other artists has a long tradition, stretching back into prehistoric times. The earliest known examples are to be found in the cave paintings of southern France and Spain. The artists involved in making these images of bison and other game certainly learned their craft from example and no one would have been better qualified to give this than their more experienced elders.

The process has continued over the centuries, even though the demands of art have naturally changed. In the Middle Ages, for instance, the Church was the dominant influence on the artist, who spent much of his working life creating images to illustrate Biblical legends. Primitive man, on the other hand, probably painted as a type of magical process, hunting the beasts captured successfully on cave walls as a preparation for the actual events of the hunt. Between these two extremes came many others, from the decoration of buildings to the gratification of aristocratic whims. But, within all these approaches, there is a common core – the interpretation of the visual world.

LEARNING TO SEE

Painting and drawing are an extension of the art of seeing. It therefore follows that learning to look and see in an aware, intelligent manner is a prerequisite of good picture making. When the first attempts to draw a portrait or paint a still life prove unsatisfactory, this is just as likely to be the result of inadequate initial observation as the result of a lack of knowledge of the actual practical techniques. In any event, the cultivation of a vision of the world about you is a most rewarding and exciting experience, as well as a yardstick against which to measure the success or failure of drawings or paintings. In undertaking the process, you will be in the company of artists throughout the centuries. All of them have learned to interpret the visual world through painstaking looking, as well as through the development of basic technical skills. Study the world about you; observe the relationships of colors and the scale of things one to

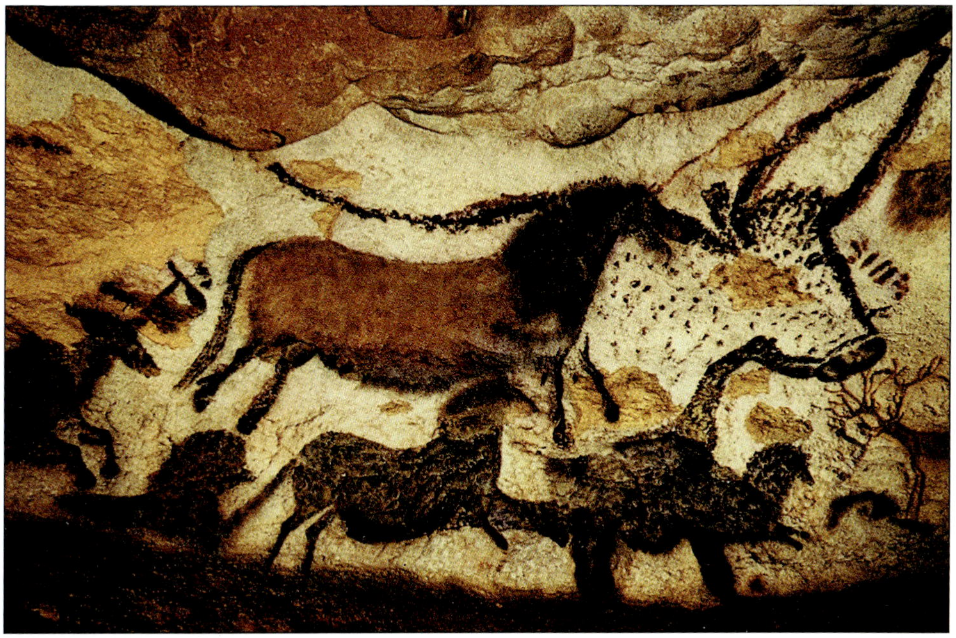

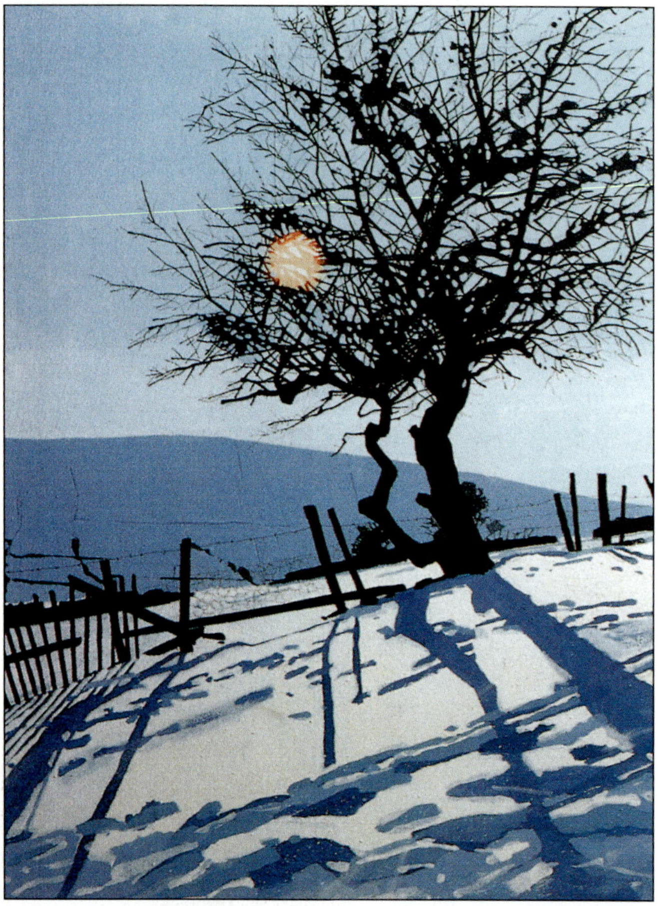

certainly can be frustrating – but it is surprising how soon the combination of a cultivated eye and a learning hand make improvements.

The eventual rewards of making telling, well-drawn and constructed drawings and paintings are great. Much pleasure and endless joy to others can ensue; the greater your experience and the wider the range of projects undertaken, the better the results. Another great benefit that springs from picture making is that you soon learn to see the world in different ways from others. The dull, olive green tone of a tree in the foreground, alongside the acid yellow greens of fresh spring foliage, will be seen to contrast well with the sun-bathed sea, shimmering turquoise blue in the middle distance. So much more can be gleaned from seeing in this way than by a casual observer.

The criterion for anything you may produce should be quality. If color is involved, then it should be harmonious, or disruptive by choice, not by accident. Balance should be aimed for in the design, but it should satisfy the viewer's need for completeness. Areas of relative inactivity can be balanced against small, tightly focused areas, where a great deal is happening. Dimensional suggestion is a further important element. The use of linear perspective and what is called atmosphere, or "aerial perspective," to create illusions of space will also bring rewards from applied study.

another – large to small, grand to insignificant. Look also at the way artists of the past saw and painted what they observed.

This process, of necessity, must be a subjective one, even though we are all part of an endless stream of development and much common ground exists from which we can learn. What will be a "good" picture to one artist will not necessarily be so to another; a careful depiction in great detail of a favorite landscape, for instance, will be beautiful to some, but anathema to others. However, as long as the essential discipline of looking, seeing, and interpreting is observed, the basic foundations are laid for future development. The initial technological steps themselves are not always easy – and

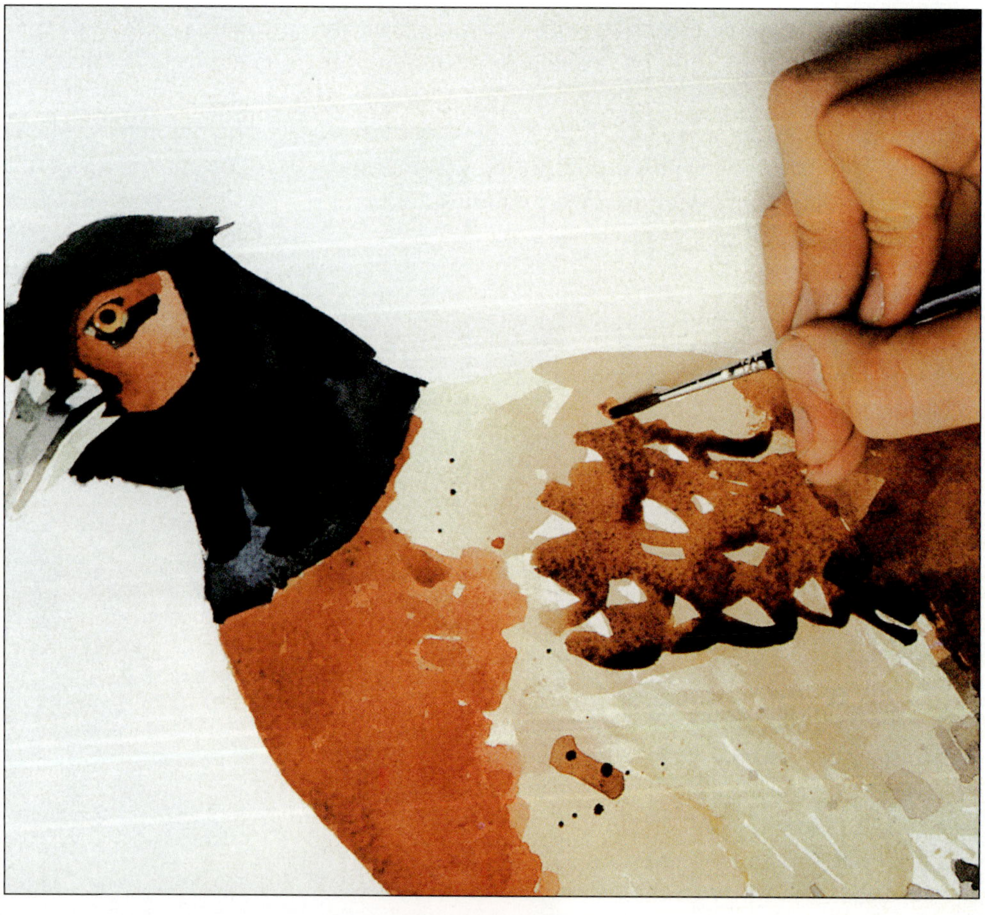

PRINCIPLES OF DRAWING AND PAINTING

The first step to learning to paint is to familiarize yourself with the basic principles of drawing. Use proportion, color, and perspective to understand how to transfer what the eye sees onto paper. These are the tools of painting that provide the foundation on which personal style can develop.

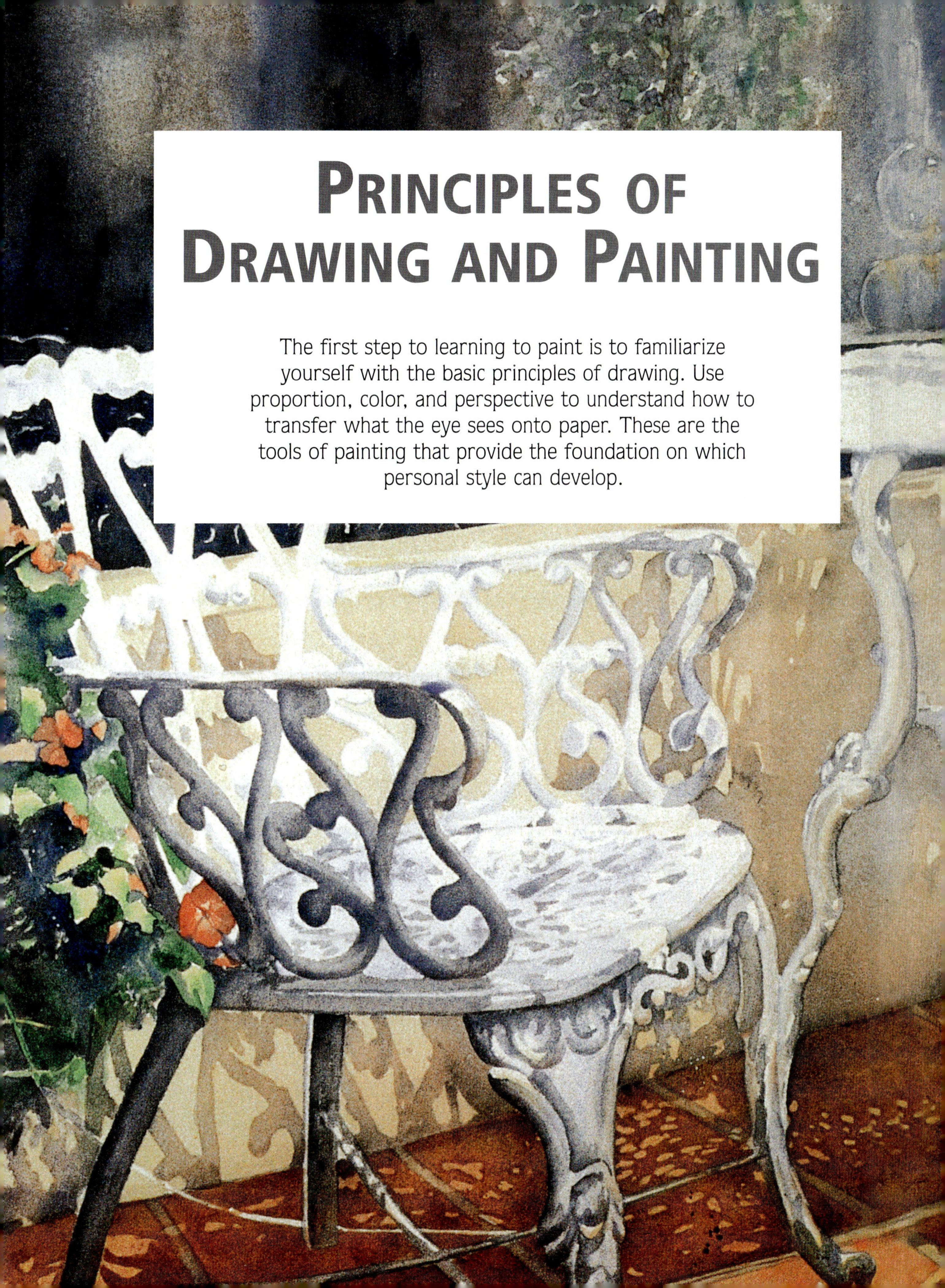

SHAPES and FORMS

The Components of Shape

Not all the objects we draw are one simple shape. Often they are composed of many smaller ones, and we have to understand how they fit together.

The old saying about "not seeing the woods for the trees" expresses just what can happen when there are other shapes within a main one. You concentrate on the components and lose sight of the overall outline, or find you can't fit the smaller shapes into it. It is relatively easy to manage when two-dimensional shapes are imposed onto a three-dimensional surface, such as in a printed pattern. The design on a dish won't interfere with your perception of the shape, so you would begin with an outline and add the pattern. But sometimes the components are themselves three-dimensional, and this can be considerably trickier.

Obvious examples of multi-part shapes are a cauliflower, composed of several florets, a summer tree with its clusters of foliage, and a bunch of grapes. Less obvious would be a clump of trees, or flowers in a vase. In both these cases, particularly the second, it is hard to concentrate on the outline of the whole because the eye naturally registers the smaller shapes. But you should always look for the main shape first. If you have trouble identifying the larger shapes, look at the subject with your eyes half-closed. This cuts out much of the distracting detail and lets you perceive the main masses as dark against light or vice versa.

DIVERSITY OF SHAPES

But sometimes there is no clear outline that defines a shape; instead, what you see is a collection of different shapes seemingly – or actually – stuck together. Some man-made objects come into this category: chairs, for example, can include many shapes, from a circle or square (the seat) to tapering cylinders (the legs), to curves (arms or backrest). Here you would have to begin with the outline of one or two "key" shapes, such as the seat or back, and fit the arms and legs into them in a logical way.

SIMPLIFYING THE SHAPES

Floral groups are a potential pitfall. Because flowers are so eye-catching, as well as being complex shapes in themselves, it is natural to begin with them, but it is not wise. If you draw each flower separately, you will often find that they don't fit properly, or sit convincingly in the vase. For this exercise you will need a massed group of daisy-like blooms, either cut flowers or a houseplant such as a chrysanthemum. Outline the entire main shape lightly with pencil, treating it as a silhouette. When you are sure the shape is correct, work into the drawing, defining the vase and the chief flowerheads, but trying to see them as simple shapes – circles or ellipses.

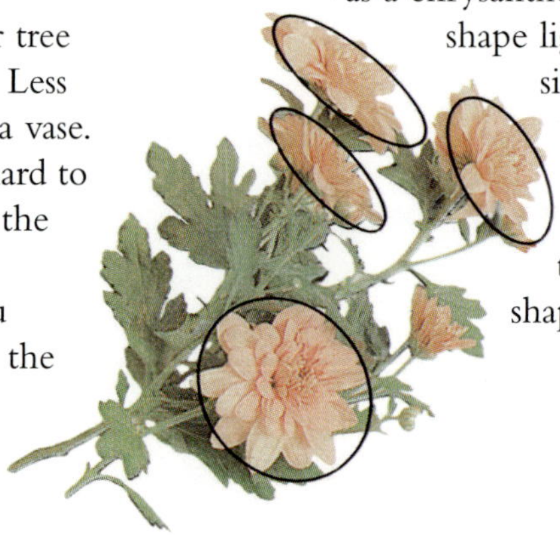

PAINTING A FLOWERHEAD

Each flowerhead can be seen as a basic circle, changing shape according to the angle from which it is viewed.

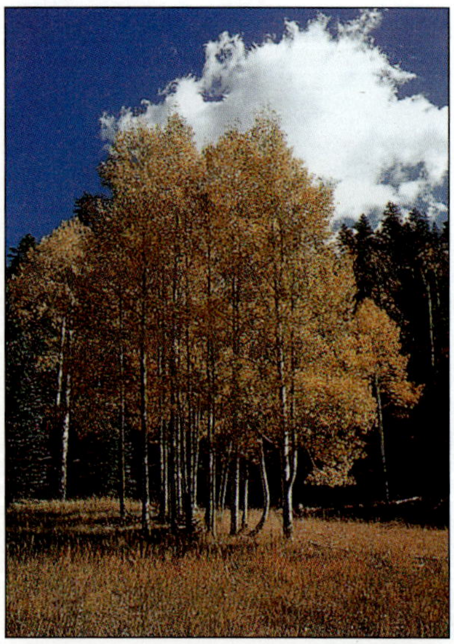

PAINTING TREES

Because of the darker background, the overall shape of the pale trees can be read clearly.

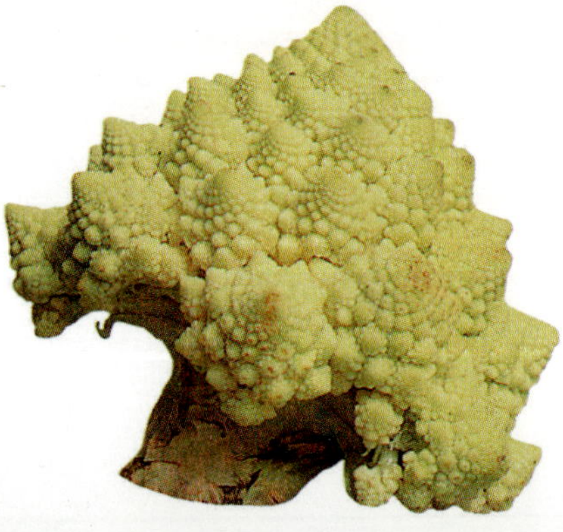

PAINTING A CAULIFLOWER

Take note that when painting or drawing a cauliflower that the florets become smaller at the top, but still retain the same shape throughout.

COMPARING SHAPES

Most painting subjects, whether landscape, figure, or still life, contain a number of different shapes of varying sizes, that you must learn to assess against one another. Drawing a single object composed of different shapes helps you to acquire these analytical skills. A chair, preferably one with a circular seat, is an ideal subject, since you will have to identify each shape as well as seeing how they fit together. Use any drawing medium you like, and begin with an outline of the largest component. Keep the lines light so that you can erase or draw over them if they are wrong – or use charcoal, which can be erased simply by rubbing. Once you have established the main shape, look carefully at the way the others relate to it, assessing the proportions by asking yourself questions such as "Are the legs longer, shorter, or wider than the backrest"?

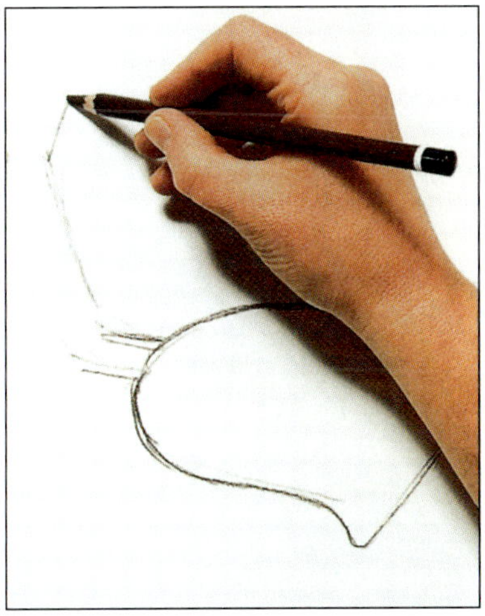

1 The largest shape, that of the seat, was drawn first, and the shape, angle, and relative size of the backrest is assessed against this.

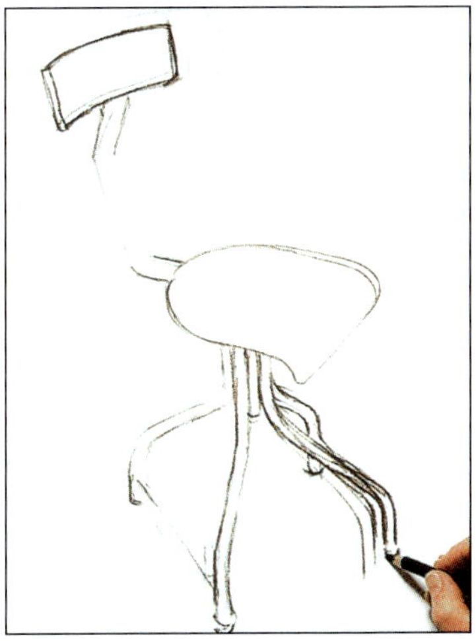

2 The legs and the bars joining them are complex and hard to draw, and have necessitated some reworking.

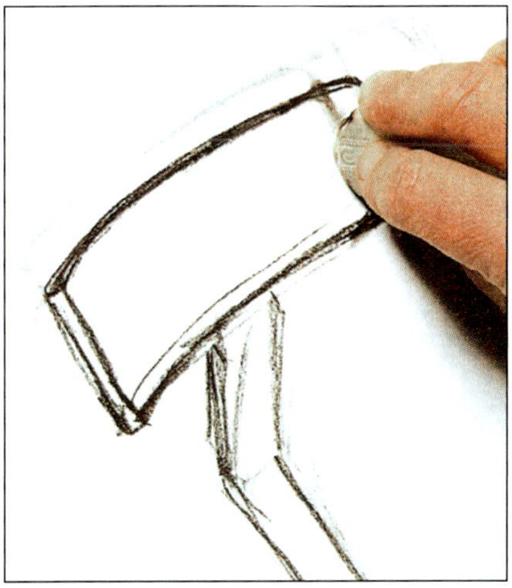

3 As the drawing progressed, one shape was checked against another. The backrest was too large, so some lines are erased and redrawn.

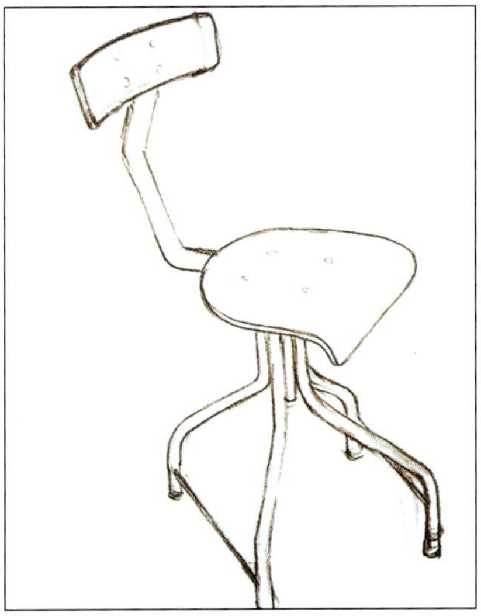

4 As important final touches, the lines showing the exact thickness of the seat and backrest, and the small studs on the seat, were added.

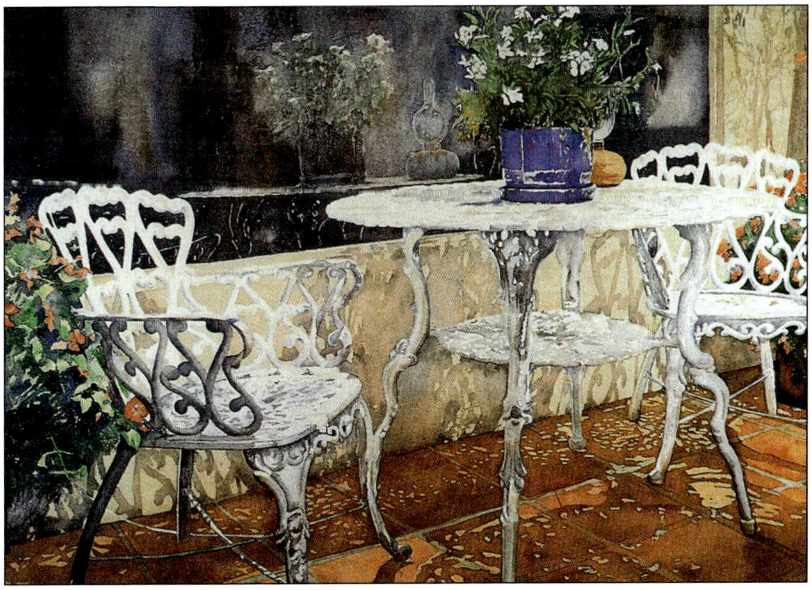

A SUNNY GARDEN by Joan I. Roche (watercolor)

The delicate ironwork of the furniture and its corresponding shadows have given the artist an opportunity to create a lively and unusual outdoor still life. Complex shapes like these are not easy to draw, but if you begin by outlining it, making sure the proportions are correct, you will be able to build up the smaller shapes gradually.

DRAWING IN TONE

Because it is difficult to think about tone when you are worrying about how to analyze and mix colors, it is a good idea to practise tonal modeling in monochrome first. Set up a still life group with a variety of shapes, including an item with a reflective surface and one or two organic objects, such as fruit or vegetables. Make sure that the group is in a good light so that you can see the forms clearly; light coming from one side and slightly above is best. Using conté crayon, soft pencil, or pastel, build up the drawing by shading, trying to avoid outline altogether if you can, or using it just to establish the shapes.

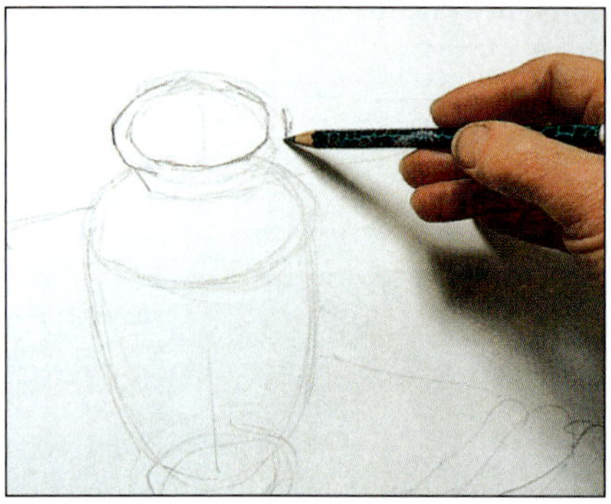

1 A light drawing is made to establish the shapes and proportions of the objects. This is a wise precaution, as it is more difficult to correct a heavily shaded drawing than an outline.

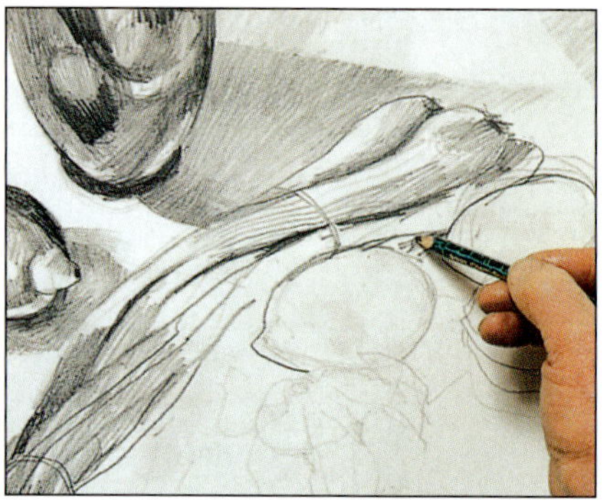

2 The artist is using a very soft pencil, so she is working from the top down to avoid smudging completed areas and messing up the paper.

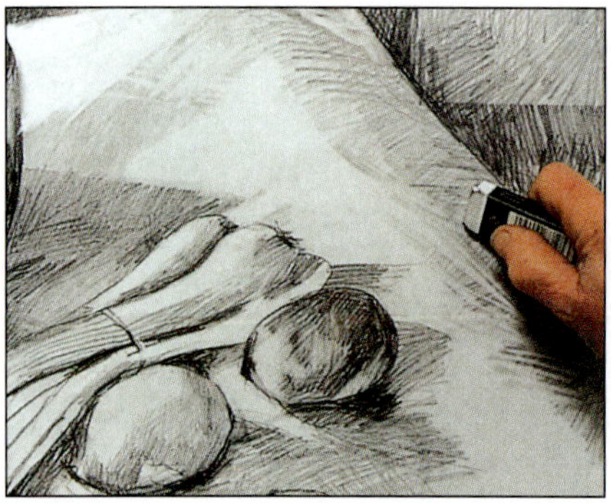

3 An eraser is used to soften the shading at the edge of the tablecloth. Erasers are an essential tool for tonal drawings in charcoal or pencil, as they can be used to pick out highlights or lighten areas that have become too dark.

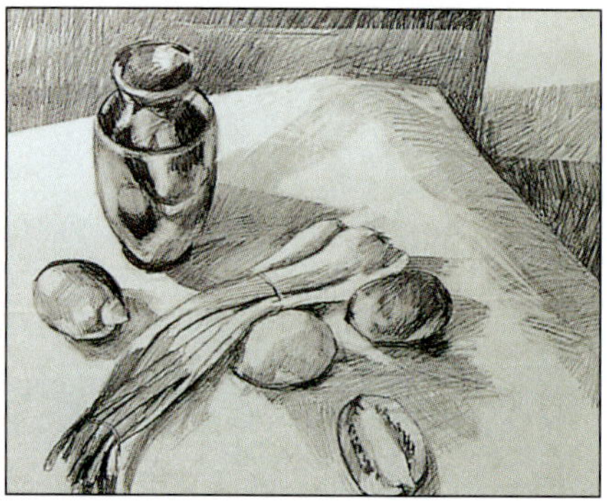

4 Soft pencil can be rubbed with a finger to create gentle gradations, but this artist prefers a linear approach, using hatching and crosshatching to impart energy to the drawing.

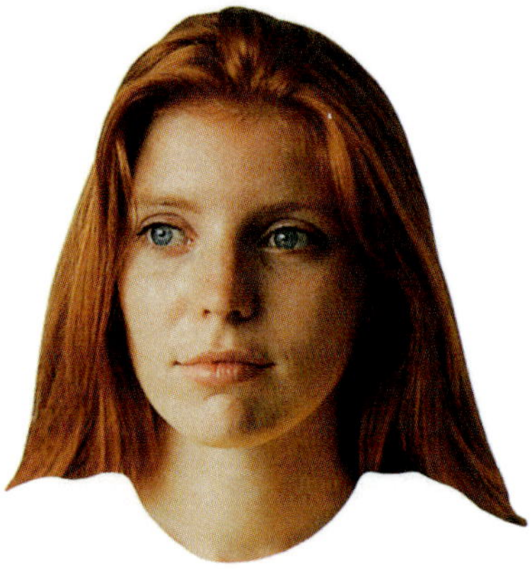

TONE CHANGES

Tone changes are gradual on cheeks and forehead, but they are far more abrupt on the nose and chin.

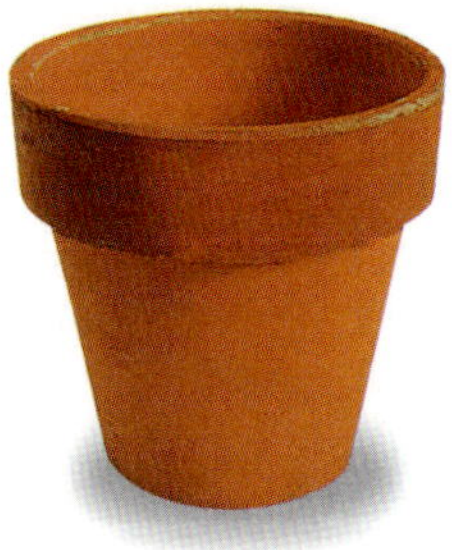

BLENDING TONES

Tones blend into one another on the body of the pot, but the rim produces clear highlight.

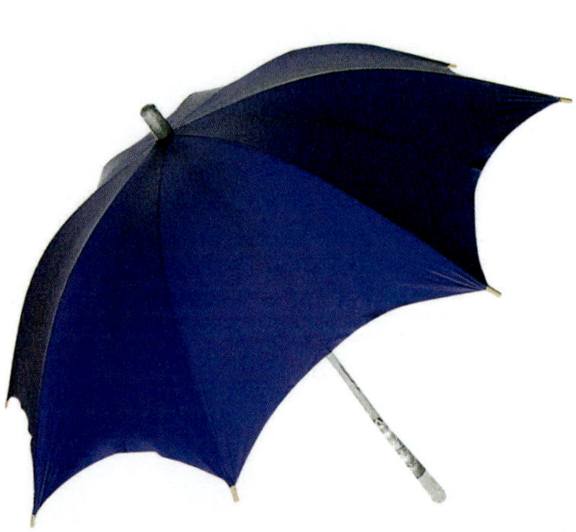

SHARP DIVISIONS

Sharp divisions between tones on this umbrella, mark the interlocking planes.

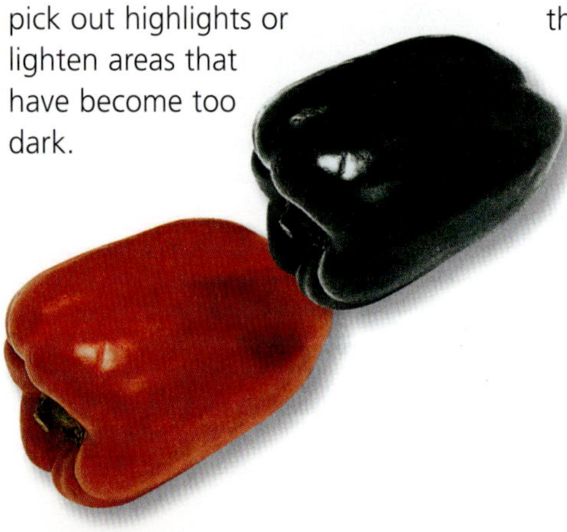

TONAL VARIATIONS

The tonal variations can be seen most clearly in the black and red versions of these peppers.

Proportion

Art rules and principles have been formulated after much experiment and of course they must be known before they can be broken or ignored to satisfy personal aesthetic values. The subject and the artist's intuition and instinct – not the rules – should always be the guiding force.

The division of space known as the Golden Section is perhaps the best known system of proportion in pictorial composition. The simplest method of finding the Golden Section in any given rectangle is to take a sheet of paper of the size one is working to and fold it in half three times in succession (do this for both the length and width of the paper). The folds will divide the paper into eight equal parts, from which a 3:5 ratio can be determined. (Alternative ratios might be 2:3, 5:8 or 8:13). In the work of artists such as Piero della Francesca, the vertical division of the Golden Section is used to determine the placement of the central figure of Christ.

Similarly, in the work of other painters, it is used to place the most important element in the composition. As we develop our powers of observation, however, we sometimes unconsciously place the most significant vertical element in our drawing on that same division in the painting. In landscape the horizon presents a natural division of the total area of the painting. In lowland areas, where the sky is dominant, the horizon will be quite low, as in the work of Rembrandt and other Dutch painters. Where there are hills and mountains, the horizon might be placed high in the composition to give emphasis to rising forms.

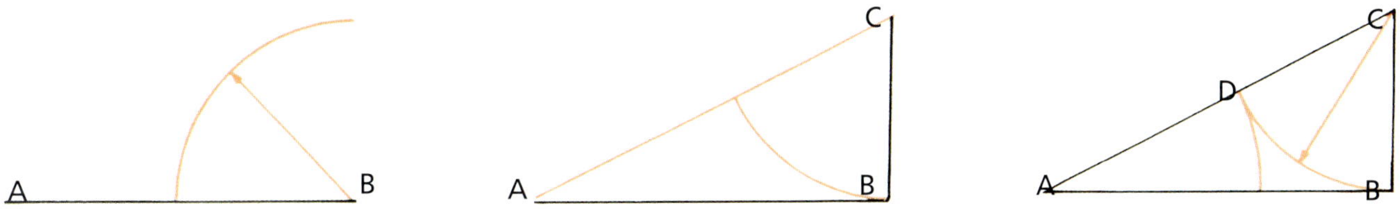

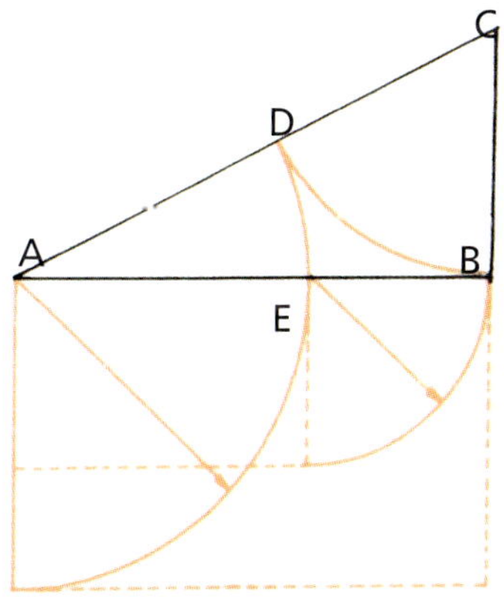

THE GOLDEN SECTION

To divide any rectangle using the proportions of the Golden Section, begin by dividing the line AB into equal parts. Draw an arc from B midway between AB to C at right angles to AB. Then draw in CB and CA. Draw another arc from C with a radius to CB cutting across AC to D. From A draw an arc with a radius AD to divide AB at E. The proportion is such that EB is to AE as AE is to AB. From this a rectangle can be drawn.

MALE AND FEMALE FORM

It is interesting to see how the male and female forms differ in these generalized sketches. Taking only the torso into account and ignoring the legs, the broad shoulders, and thin hips of the idealized male figure form an inverted triangle, while the wide shallow pelvis and narrow sloping shoulders of the female can be seen as a pyramid shape. There is generally more fat in this area of the female, that accentuates the shape of the bone beneath. It would be ridiculous, however, to assume that all female figures conform to a standard shape. The value of diagrams such as these is in prompting an awareness of general shapes that, in turn make it easier to spot the peculiarities of individual figures.

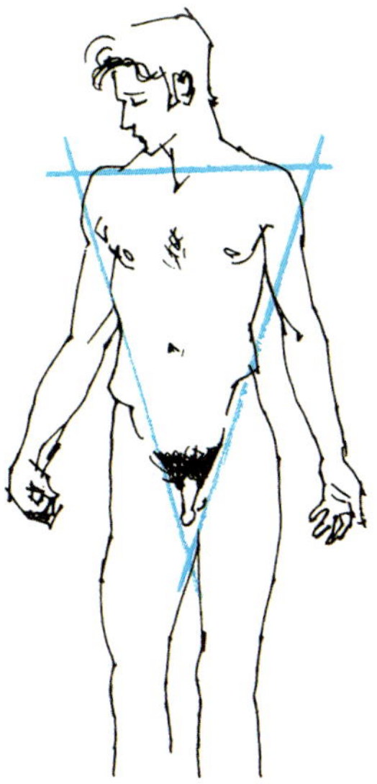

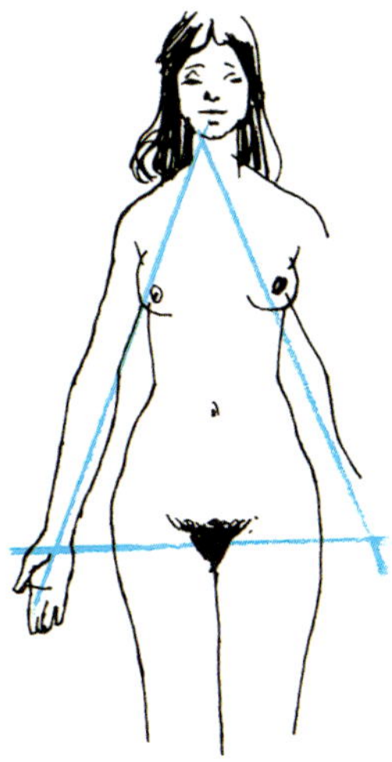

THE RULES AND LAWS OF PROPORTION

The rules and laws governing proportion have occupied artists since earliest times. During the Renaissance, artists such as Leonardo da Vinci and Albrecht Dürer began to apply the principles of proportion to the study of the human body. This development, which was accompanied by the first scientific explorations of human anatomy, perhaps reflects that age's preoccupation with Man. It was found that the body divides into eight equal sections and that these divisions almost exactly reflect the proportions of the Golden Mean. For example, the head, if measured from the chin to the crown, is one eighth of the height of the whole body, and the navel is at five eighths of the height of the whole body from the ground. This way of dividing the body in proportion is an extremely useful guide for all artists, whether beginner or expert.

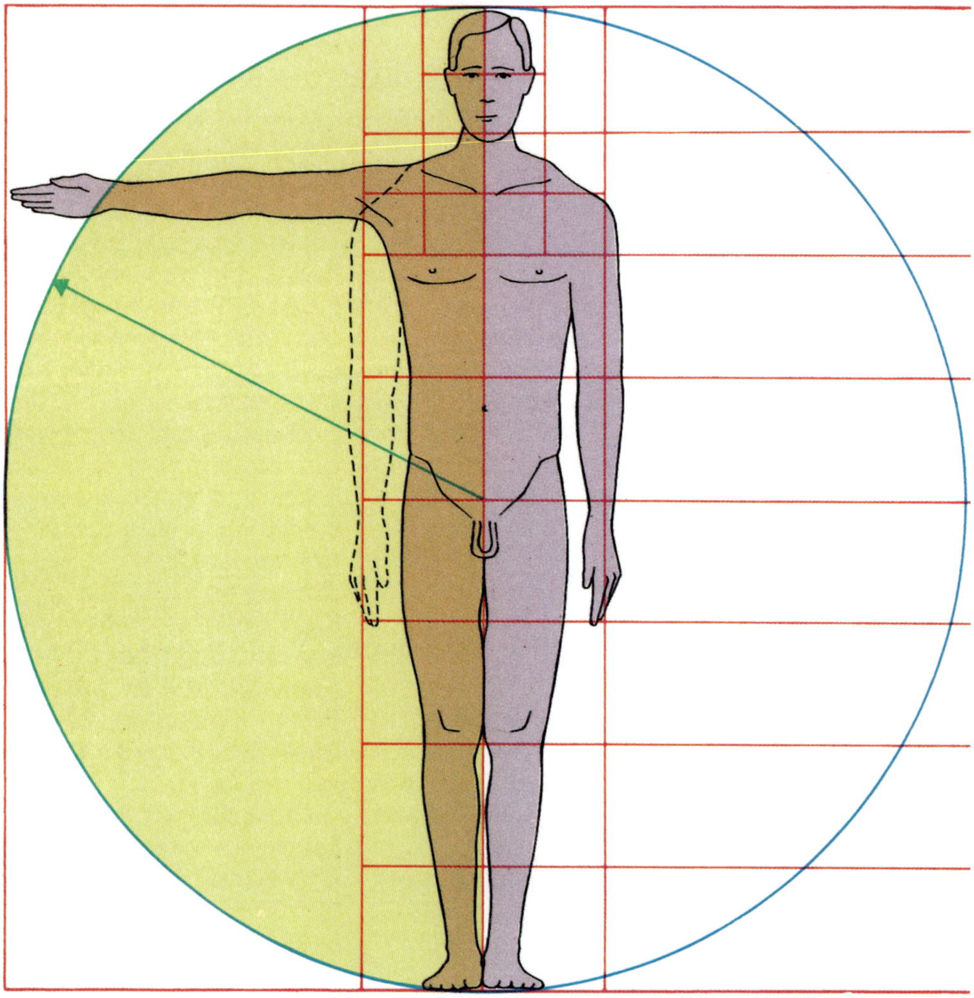

STANDING FIGURES

Drawing the standing figure presents its own particular problems. It is much harder for even an experienced model to stand for a long period of time than it is to sit or recline. The model therefore usually requires more frequent rests and may move considerably while posing. This movement, however slight, is the first problem that needs to be dealt with. Most artists mark the position of the model's feet on the floor (or on a large piece of paper on which the model stands) so that the same basic position can be returned to after resting.

Every figure is slightly different from another, and measuring can be useful in getting one or two main dimensions correct. Students tend to draw the top part of the figure too large, failing to observe that the head is approximately one seventh of the height of the figure and that the legs are one half. The most important problem related to proportion is that of making the figure stand properly in the drawing. The distribution of the figure's weight – on one leg or on both – has to be established, and crucial to this is getting the vertical positioning of the neck, hips, and feet absolutely correct. In order to do so the artist can use any vertical in the background (for example, the corner of a room or the frame of a window) as a reference, but much the most useful device is to use a plumbline to check the precise position of key parts of the figure. Some artists attach the plumbline to a horizontal rod that is secured to the top of the drawing board and position it to mark a single vertical reference line running through the model's neck and the ankle of the foot on which most weight is placed.

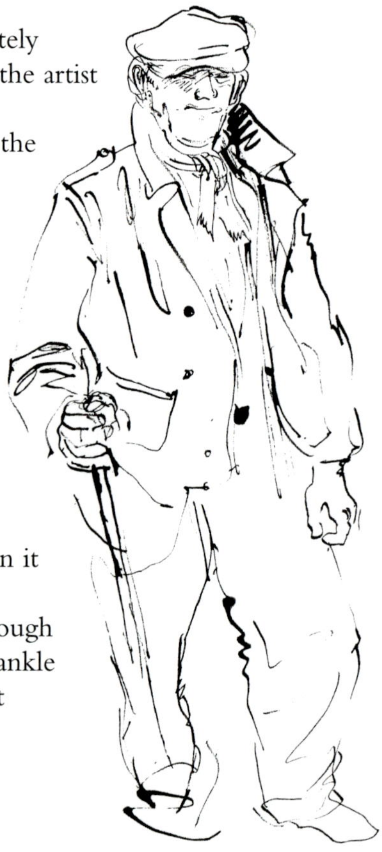

Perspective

Perspective is a system of creating an illusion of three dimensions in objects drawn on a two-dimensional surface. Although an important technique, it should not be allowed to become more important than the subject.

PRINCIPLES

When we look across a valley from a high vantage point, we see all the elements in nature that make up a landscape, arranged at varying distances from each other. Trees in the foreground, middle distance, and far distance are perhaps linked by paths, hedges, and rivers. To draw these things "in perspective" means only that we need to find a way of representing the distance of one object from another – in other words, "fixing" their position in our drawing.

There are certain ground rules that act as a useful guide in doing this, but as with all art theory, there is no real substitute for training the hand and eye to register things directly without recourse to drawing systems.

The picture plane is a kind of imaginary vertical screen, that is transparent and is positioned on the ground at a distance from the artist, depending on where he intends his drawing to begin. The "picture" he conceives lies behind this imaginary screen, although some objects in the immediate foreground would touch it. The precise position of the viewer on his side of the picture plane is critical. This will determine how high the eye is from ground level and whether he is in the center or to one side of the picture. The base of the picture plane is called the ground line. It is from the ground line that one's measurements begin.

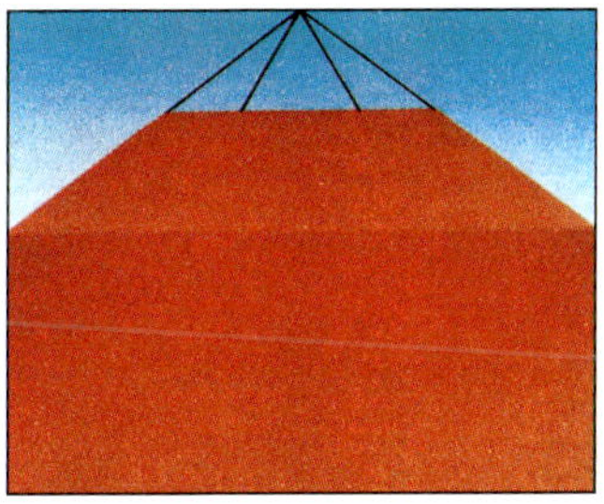

ONE POINT PERSPECTIVE

As the parallel lines recede, they appear to converge at the vanishing point. If only two sides of the cube are visible, it can be drawn in perspective from a single vanishing point.

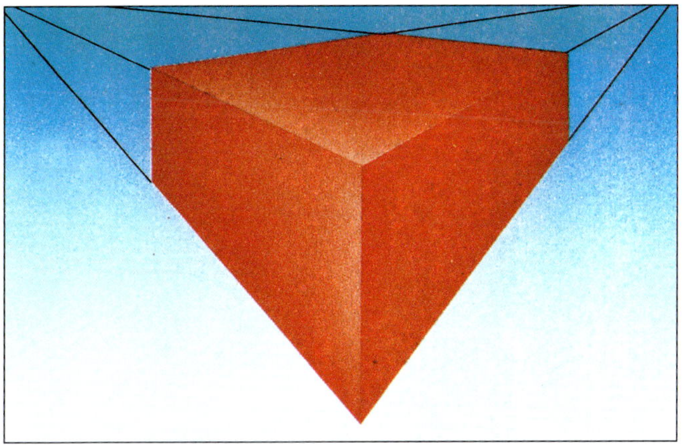

TWO POINT PERSPECTIVE

When three sides of the cube are visible, two sets of parallel lines converge at separate vanishing points.

The artist stands on one side of the picture plane, and on the other side all the things that can be seen are disposed at various points toward the horizon. The horizon line is parallel to the ground line and is the same height as the eye of the viewer. On the horizon line is a point we call the "vanishing" point. This may be in the center, or to one side, depending on the position of the viewer. When the vanishing point has been established on the horizon line, then all vertical lines remain vertical and all lines that are parallel to the ground line remain parallel. Imagine, for instance, that you are standing immediately facing the side of a tall building. Then neither the vertical nor the horizontal lines will converge. For them to do so it is necessary to move backward, or to one side.

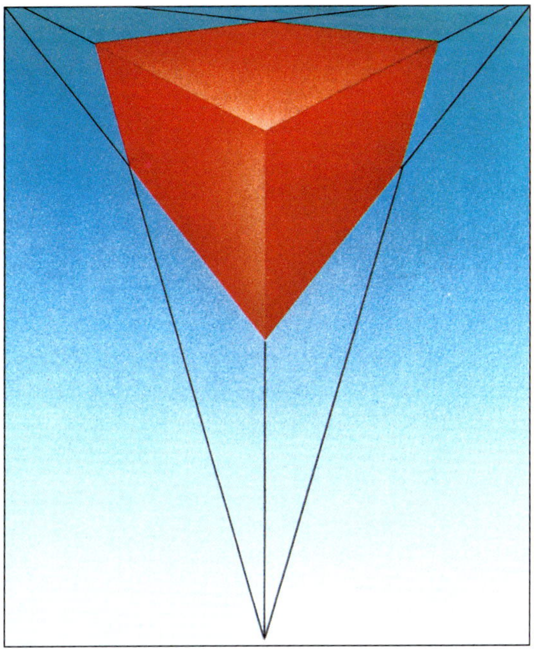

THREE POINT PERSPECTIVE

When the cube appears either above or below the artist's view of the horizon, it is necessary to draw both vertical and horizontal lines converging on three separate vanishing points.

The lines other than those that are vertical or parallel to the ground line are drawn toward the vanishing point. In a landscape, for example, objects of roughly the same size – trees or telephone poles – appear to become smaller as they recede into the distance, and as they get smaller they seem to be nearer the horizon line. Although they diminish in size, there is no distortion in their shapes when seen from the front.

In the diagrams shown here you will notice that the tree in the foreground coincides with the picture plane and the size remains constant. One can therefore find the actual height or width of any object by assessing it in relation to the ground line. On the other hand, the size of an object as it appears in perspective can be determined by taking a line from the ground line to the vanishing point. All the horizontal lines that appear at right angles to the picture plane will converge on the horizon at the vanishing point. If you were drawing a box placed in the center of your line of vision, there would be one vanishing point. If, however, you were to draw two separate boxes several feet distant from each other, there would be two sets of parallel lines, each set with its own vanishing point. Strong diagonal lines that incline steeply upward have their vanishing point above the horizon; conversely, those inclining sharply downward have their vanishing point below the horizon line.

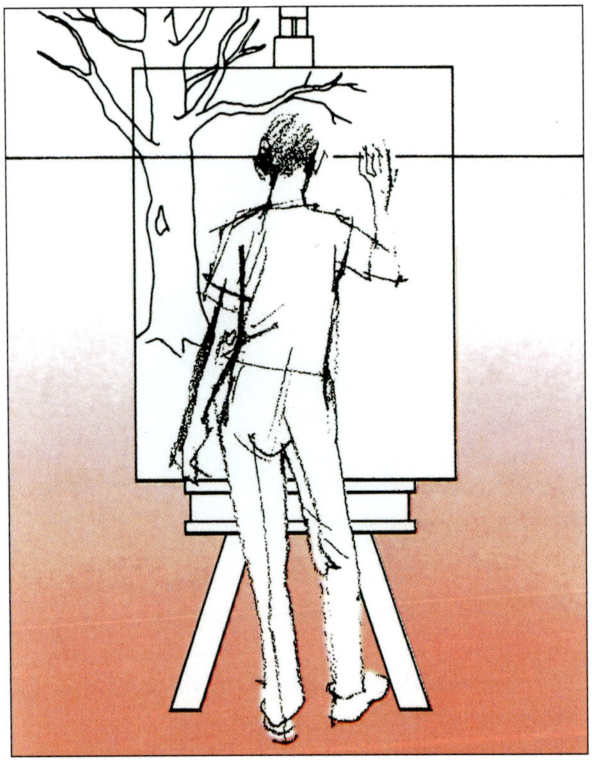

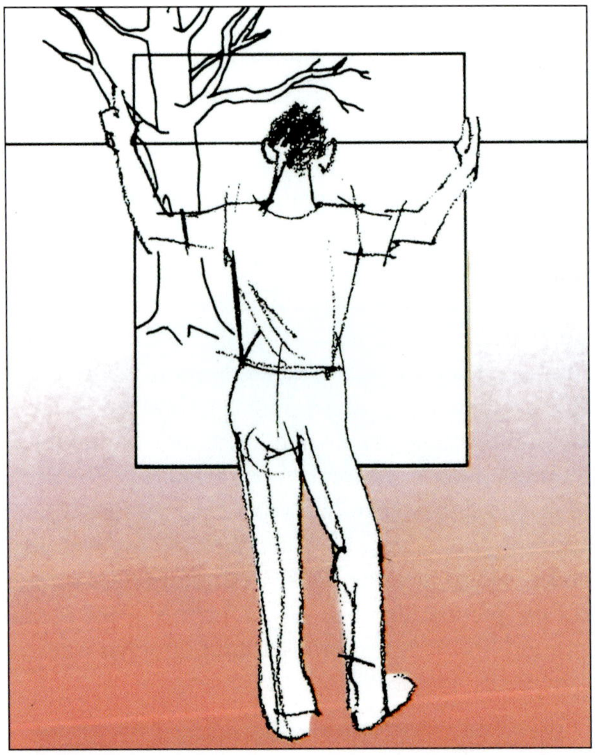

The picture plane is an imaginary transparent screen separating the artist from the subject. The image that you see through this plane is what is transferred to your paper or canvas. When starting to draw, the horizon line should be established first.

AERIAL PERSPECTIVE

This is a way of using color and tone to give a sense of space in a painting, and to indicate recession. It is particularly important in landscape painting. If you look at an expanse of landscape, such as one with fields and trees in the foreground and distant hills or mountains beyond, you will see that the colors become paler and cooler in the distance, with details barely visible. The objects in the foreground will be brighter and have much clearer areas of contrast, or tonal differences, that will become smaller in the middle distance and may disappear altogether in the far distance, so that the hills or mountains appear as pure areas of pale blue. It takes some experience to use aerial perspective successfully; if you accidentally mix a rather warm blue on your palette and try to use it for the distant hills you will find that they seem almost to jump forward to the front of the picture. The same applies if you combine a pale color with a much darker one; there will then be a greater tonal difference than is actually present and the background will begin to vie with the foreground.

Aerial perspective can, of course, be either exploited or ignored. Sometimes, for instance, you might be more interested in creating a flat pattern or you might want simply to use areas of vivid color.

Form and Color

Shapes are recognized by their color as well as their outlines. The stronger the contrasts of color between the object and its surroundings, the easier it is to see the shape.

Although you may see a shape's outline clearly, you must also consider its volume, and this involves assessing the variations of color within each object. As we have seen, the play of light creates areas of light and shade which model form, but the light also effects the colors themselves, sometimes surprising you.

LOCAL COLOR

When you look at anything – a tree, a piece of fruit, a flower, a garment – you will automatically give it a color name, describing it to yourself as green, yellow, red, pink, or whatever. This actual color is known as local color, and it is important to be able to recognize it and decide what kind of green, yellow, red, or pink it is, and whether it is lighter or darker than surrounding colors.

But when you begin to explore the effects of light on an object, you may find that you can't see much of the local color. If you are painting a portrait of a person in a red sweater, the hue in its pure form may only be visible in areas where the light strikes most strongly. Shadows caused by folds and wrinkles and the forms of the body beneath will probably not be red at all, but brownish or purplish depending both on the light and on what kind of red the garment is.

So tonal modeling is not just a matter of making the same color lighter or darker; you will nearly always have to introduce other colors. These must, however, be consistent with the local color, or you will lose the redness or yellowness altogether and end up with a mishmash of unrelated colors. Local color is also effected by the position of an object in space. You will see this most clearly in landscape subjects because the space is greater than in say, a still life.

PAINTING LOCAL COLOR

One of the first painting skills to acquire is that of accurately identifying the colors you see, and learning to mix your paints to match the reality. Painting a still life setup using nothing but local color is an instructive exercise; you will need to analyze each color as well as thinking about the different shapes and how they relate to each other. You will need a good variety of shapes and colors for the group, but avoid anything with a very obvious local color, such as lemons and oranges – these are too easy, and the colors come straight from the tube.

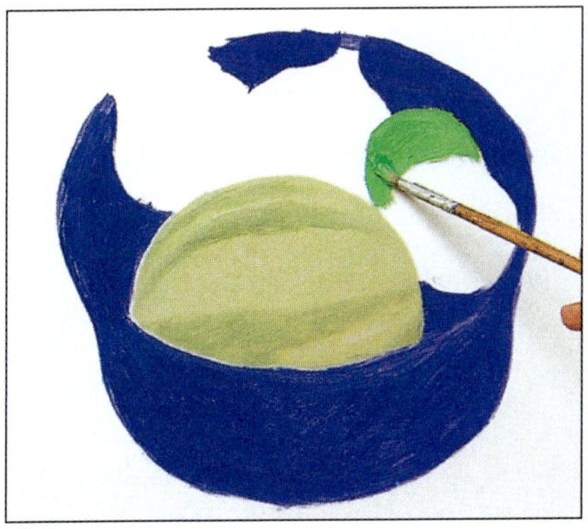

1 The artist is using acrylic, that can be applied flatly with little variation of color and tone. The blue bowl was painted first, as this strong color provided a key against which to judge the subtler local colors of the fruit.

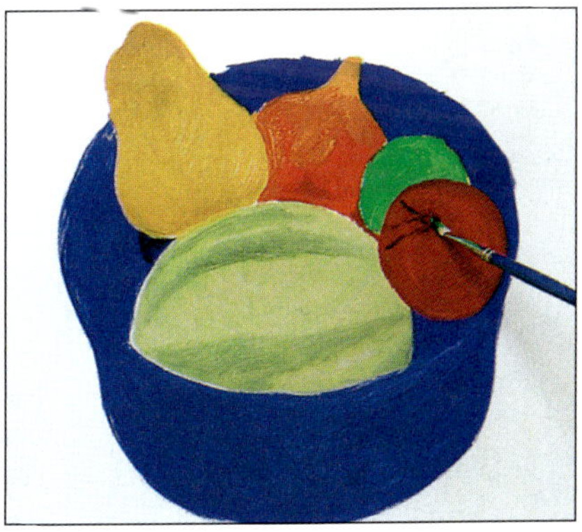

2 When assessing local color, you must consider not only what kind of color it is, but also its relative lightness or darkness. This red is almost the same tone as the bowl, whereas the other fruits are very much lighter.

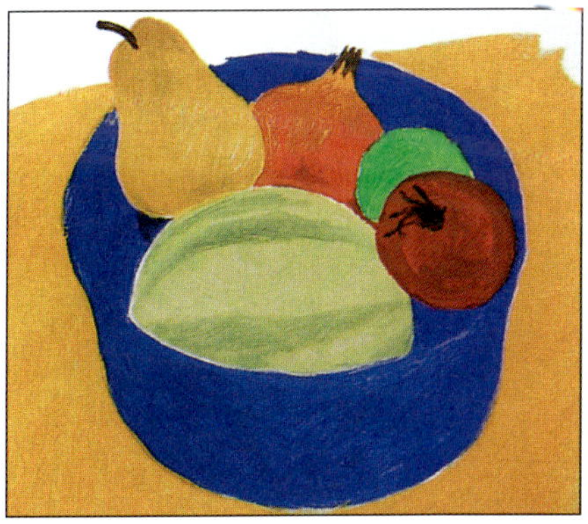

3 Using only local color gives little or no impression of form, but as you can see from this picture, it allows you to exploit the flat-pattern element of painting as well as helping you to learn to identify and mix colors.

FORM AND COLOR

Now try describing both the local color and the variations – painting what you actually see rather than what you know. You can paint the same group as before, but it might be better in this case to choose objects with obvious colors, since the aim is to discover how light effects them. Oranges and lemons, red and green bell peppers, or evenly colored ceramic items would all be suitable. The lighting is important; you will see more of the local color under a flat front light, so avoid this. Instead, light the group from one side (you can use artificial lighting) so that there is a strong pattern of light and dark.

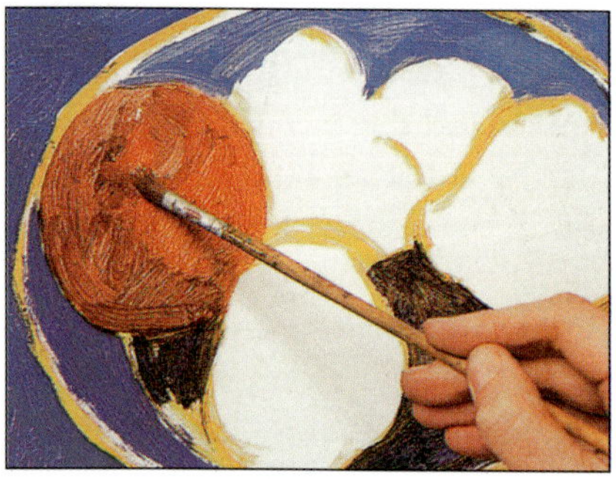

1 As in the previous exercise, the artist has begun with the largest area of color – in this case, the mid-blue tablecloth – so that she can relate the other tones and colors to it. The local color of the orange is quite close in tone to the blue.

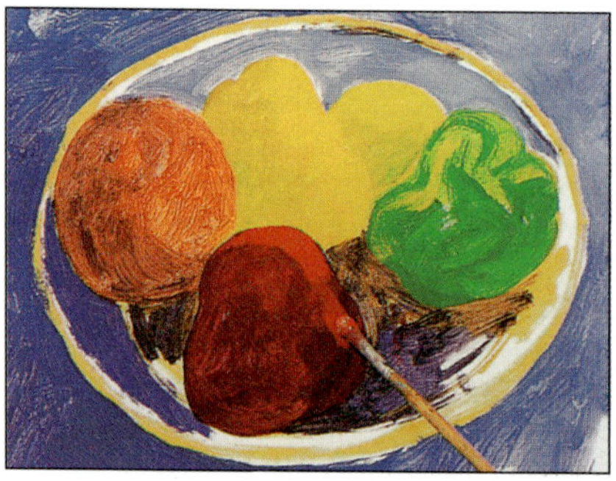

2 Having painted the red bell pepper as a flat color, she now begins to build up the forms by using a lighter, more orange red.

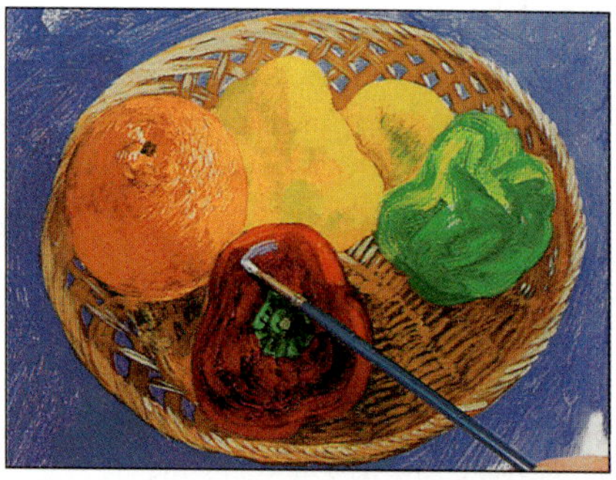

3 The orange has been lightened with yellow and white on one side and darkened with small flecks of reddish brown on the other, and highlights are now added to the bell pepper. These reflect some of the color from the tablecloth, so she uses white mixed with a little blue.

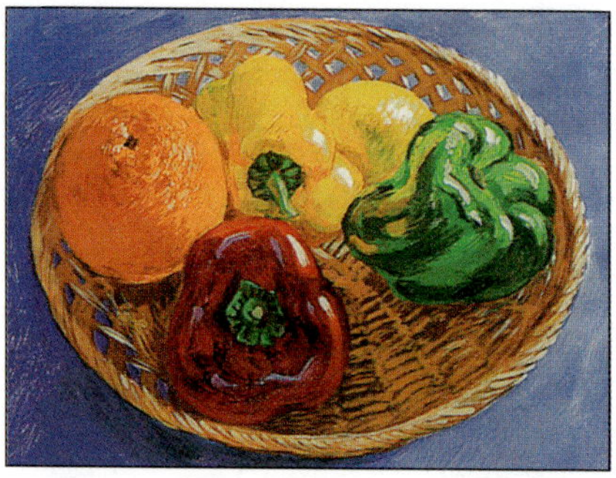

4 Both the local colors and the variations have been faithfully represented. Notice how the colors reflect each other, with touches of green in the yellow bell pepper and lemon, and a band of yellow on the green bell pepper.

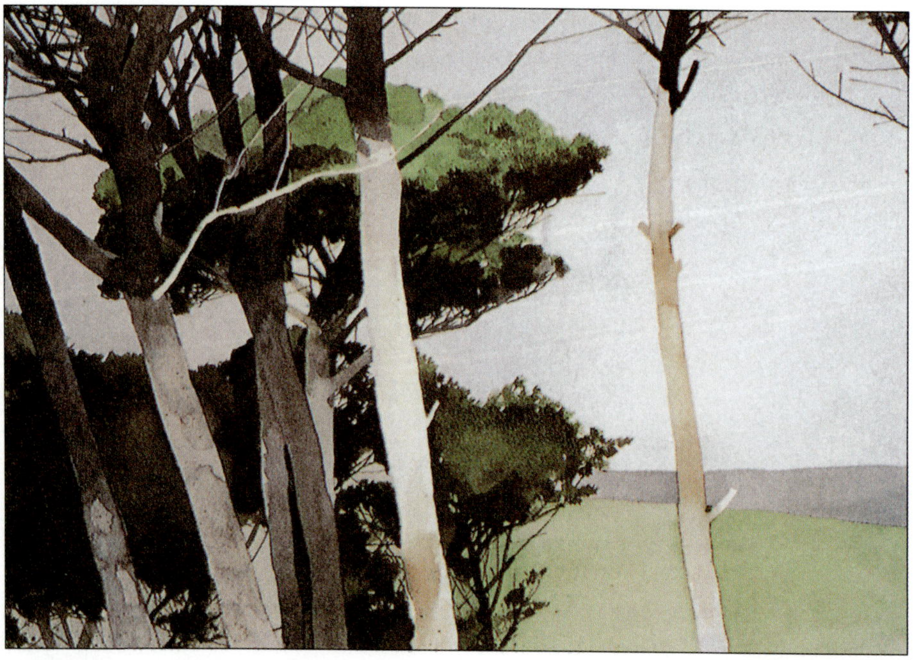

In the painting above the contrast between the dark and light tree trunks has been emphasized by the use of very thin paint. The solid foliage of the evergreen draws attention to the slenderness of the foreground trunks.

DRAWING MEDIA

Practise the basic principles with the drawing mediums of pencil, ink, pen, charcoal, and pastel. Deciding your favorite drawing medium can influence which painting medium you go on to use. As well as appreciating the beauty of these mediums they are an ideal way to finalize the details of your painting before you start.

THE PENCIL

Lead or graphite pencils are a comparatively new medium in the long history of graphic art, for it was not until 1662 that the first graphite pencil was made. Graphite had been discovered in Bavaria in 1400, but its potential for the artist remained unexploited until the first English find of pure graphite in 1504 at Borrowdale in Cumberland. The popular but misleading designation "lead" pencil stems from this discovery, as the deposit was at first thought to be lead. Only later was graphite identified as a separate mineral and even then did not receive its present name until 1789.

From childhood we have used pencils to scribble, make notes, and record our responses to things seen and imagined. Pencils offer the most direct, and the most versatile, means of allowing our thoughts to flow from the mind through the fingertips to a sheet of paper. The artist is concerned with varying degrees of softness to express different qualities in drawing.

Pencil covers a wider range of medium than is commonly thought. The lead pencil is now quite an uncommon medium, although still available. The lead pencil's light, silvery, gray line can produce an effect not dissimilar to that of silverpoint that, before the innovation of the modern graphite pencil, was the main linear drawing instrument, particularly among Renaissance artists, although that too is in less common use today. The silverpoint and lead pencils make their mark by leaving a small metallic deposit on the paper, that in the case of silverpoint can barely be seen when the drawing is first done. The metallic deposit tarnishes, and this increases the richness of tone in the line.

The graphite pencil as we know it today is still often incorrectly called a "lead" pencil. It is a relatively new drawing instrument and has been in common use only for about 200 years. It comes in a variety of grades. The softest grades are denoted by the letter B and range from B to 8B, which is the softest. F, HN and H are in the middle of the range. H pencils are the hard range, from 2H to 8H. There are other grading systems but the H and B system is the most common. If in doubt, always test pencils before you buy them.

A useful alternative to the ordinary pencil, particularly when drawing outdoors, is the propelling clutch pencil, for which the "lead" is purchased separately. This is useful in that no sharpening is required and a fine line can be continuously maintained.

The solid graphite stick, normally graded approximately at 3B, is also very useful for larger, tonal, pencil drawings, and is often used in conjunction with a regular pencil. A number of artists recently have been drawing with raw graphite powder, rubbing it into the paper to make large tonal marks, then bringing out highlights with an eraser and more detailed areas with a regular pencil. This method is suitable for very large works.

A pencil can be used in a variety of ways but is most commonly employed in making a line; the result is a crisp, clear drawing. Shadow can be produced by hatching or crosshatching, which is a set of parallel lines or two opposing sets of parallel lines, respectively. In the detail illustrated, below, note that the lines follow the form, adding to the solidity of the drawing and also giving a considerable amount of information about the surface undulations of the form. This approach has been widely used, and two of its greatest exponents were Raphael and Michelangelo. In addition to crosshatching, darker tonal areas can be shown by a series of regularly spaced dots. The softer variety of pencil can produce very soft areas of tone using the finger or torchon, or by spreading with an eraser. The flexibility of the pencil allows for a great amount of variation and experimentation that can help to decide what is the most suitable approach for a particular subject.

A very large selection of colored pencils and crayons is available, most of which are suitable for use in drawing, although some of the wax crayons have a tendency to fade quickly if exposed to strong light.

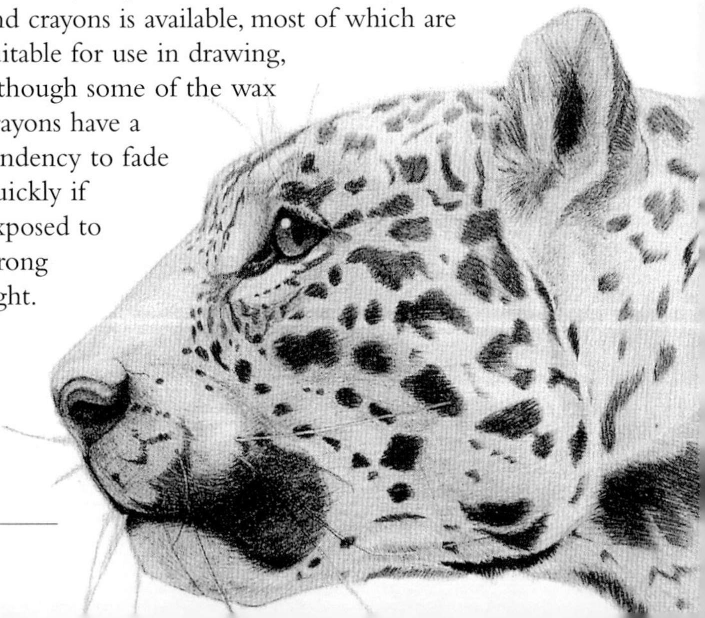

Pencil Equipment

VARIETIES OF PENCIL

Graphite pencils Manufacturers grade graphite or "lead" pencils according to their relative hardness or softness. The commonly accepted scale runs from 8B (the softest) through 7B, 6B, 5B, 4B, 3B, 2B, B, F, HB, H, 2H, 3H, 4H, 5H, 6H, 7H to 8H (the hardest). Another system employs a scale from 1 to 4, with 1 being the softest grade.

Charcoal and carbon pencils Both of these special types of pencil produce a very black line. Like the ordinary graphite pencil, they are available in soft and hard grades, of which even the hardest, unlike graphite, retains a high degree of blackness. Wolff's market a range of carbon pencils, while three of the best-known makes of charcoal pencil are the Royal Sovereign, the General 557, and the Blaisdell.

Standard clutch pencils A variant of the propelling pencil, the clutch pencil is designed to take a range of leads similar to that employed in the ordinary wooden pencil. A special clutch pencil is available that will draw a thin line of constant thickness.

Colored pencils The constituents of colored pencils – filler, binder, lubricant, and coloring – result in a fairly soft lead whose marks can usually be removed only by a blade. An exception is the Venus range of colors that can be erased with an eraser. Derwent, Eagle, Faber, Conté, and Staedtler all market colored pencils in a large range of colors.

SURFACES

Smooth paper, Bristol board, or ivory card provide the best background for soft black leads, although when a special effect is sought other types of paper may prove suitable. Hard leads are more successful on grainy textured papers, such as rough cartridge, watercolor, and Ingres papers, white or tinted. If a tinted paper is needed that is not included in a manufacturer's range, a watercolor wash may be laid on white paper. Pencil drawings on a watercolor background are capable of producing dramatic effects.

SHARPENERS, KNIVES, AND BLADES

Pencil sharpeners are useful but not as easy to control as blades or knives, and have the irritating habit of breaking off the lead just as it is sharpened to a suitable point. There is a special sharpener made for sharpening the leads in clutch pencils.

Scalpels and craft knives are among the most useful adjuncts for the draftsman, although a one-edged safety-razor blade is an efficient, if less safe, substitute. A pencil that has been properly sharpened with a blade will reveal more lead and retain its point longer than one sharpened by a pencil sharpener. Blades can also be used to scratch out pencil marks that are imperious to an eraser – although this should be avoided where possible.

Never sharpen a pencil down to a stub so that you cannot see the point when you draw. Some art supply stores stock metal holders that enable a pencil to be used almost down to the end. For continuing a flowing line, a short pencil (not a stub) can be more useful than a long pencil, but this is a matter of individual technique.

ERASERS

Nearly all hard erasers have some adverse effect, however small, on the surface of the paper. The familiar India rubber is efficient but inclined to become dirty, and can cause bad smudging. Plastic and artgum erasers have the drawback of crumbling so much in use that the paper has to be constantly "swept," with the consequent risk of damage to the drawing. Best of all are kneaded or putty erasers. As well as being cleaner in use than other erasers, they can be molded into shape, including a delicate point to pick out a small error. They can also be used to reveal areas of white paper to pick up highlights.

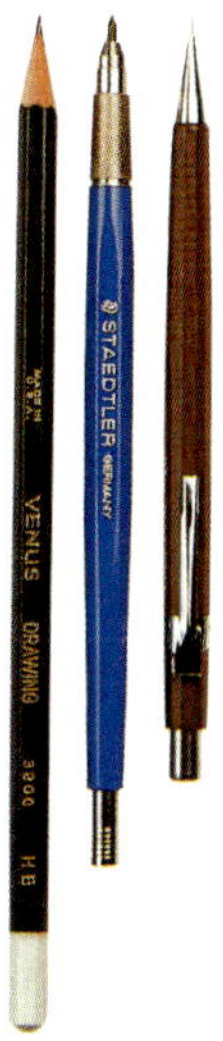

The wide range of pencils available to the artist includes (from left to right): Venus graphite drawing pencil, Staedtler Mars and Pentel clutch pencils, three Derwent color blocks, Stabilotene wax pencil (for writing on film), clutch pencil leads, Grumbacher Midnite sketching pencil, Wolff Carbon pencil, Grumbacher flat sketching pencil, 3 Derwent color pencils, 3 Caran d'Ache Prismato pencils, 3 Carb Othello colored pencils, All-Stabilo, K & E Audiovisual Projection and Staedtler Mars Omnichrom pencils, for film.

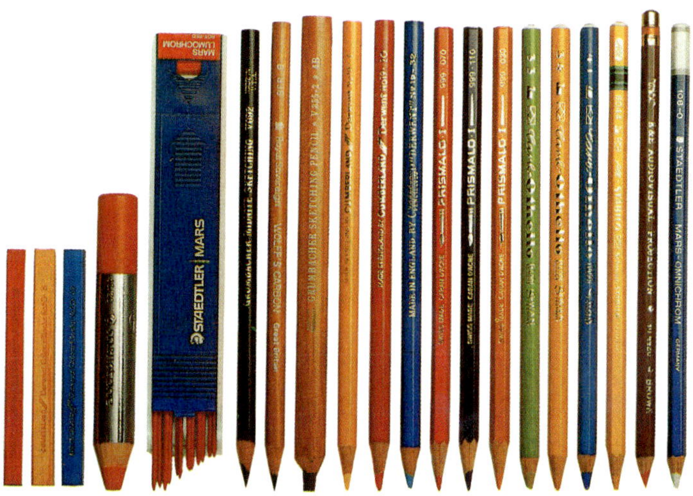

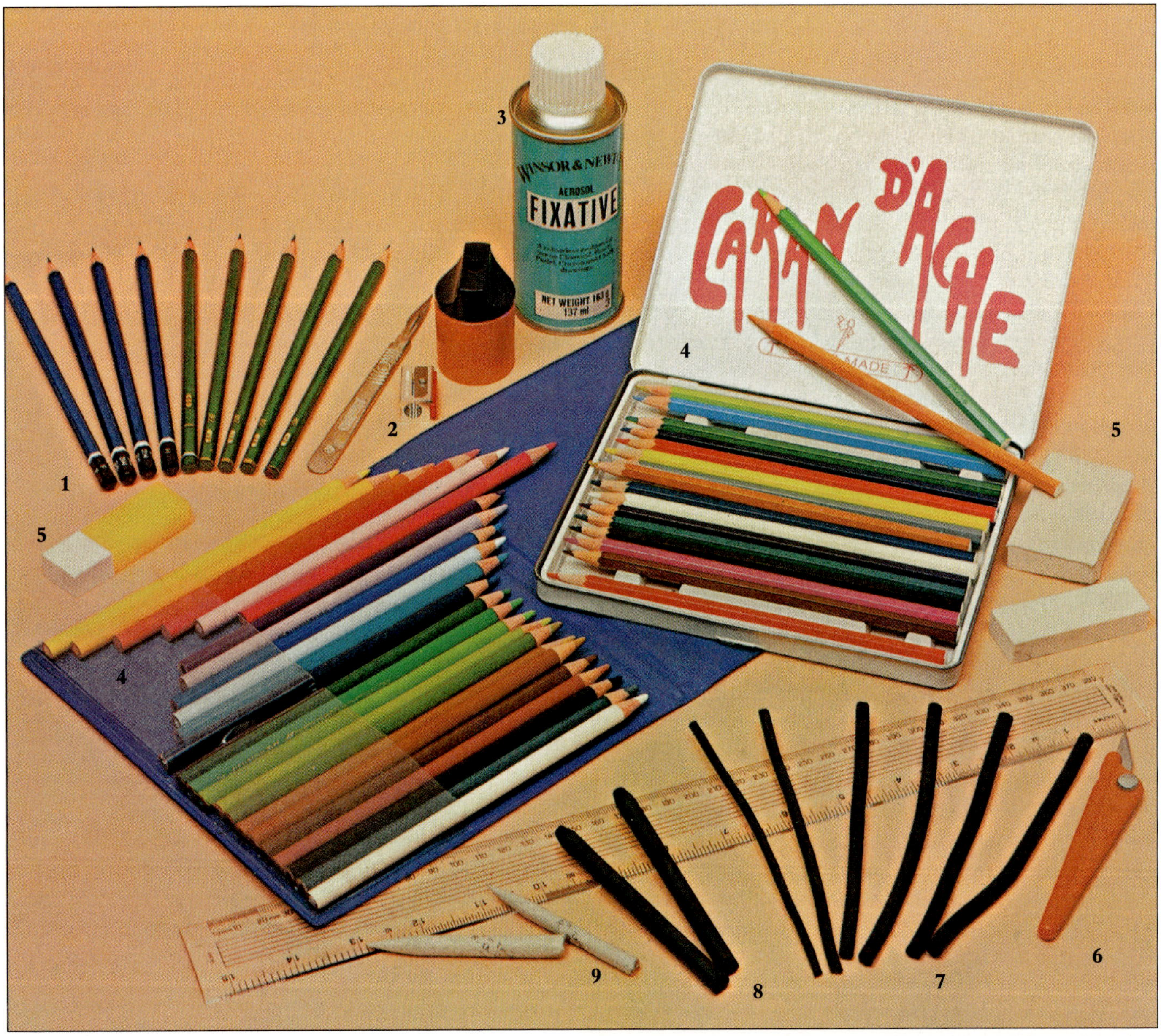

DRAWING MATERIALS

Above is a basic collection of drawing materials: ***1*** *A variety of soft/hard, dark/light grades;* ***2*** *scalpel or sharpener;* ***3*** *fixative;* ***4*** *set of colored pencils;* ***5*** *putty and gum erasers;* ***6*** *knife;* ***7*** *fine and medium willow charcoal;* ***8*** *compressed charcoal;* ***9*** *torchon.*

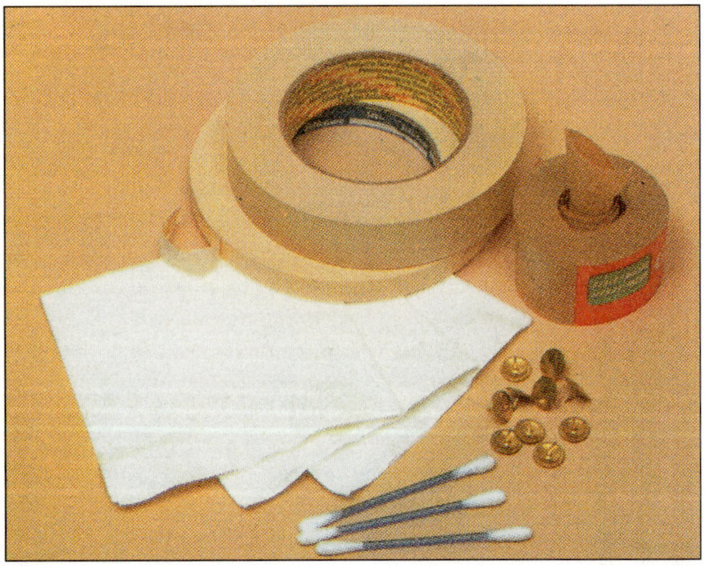

AUXILIARY EQUIPMENT

The more pencil becomes a part of the artist's repertoire, the more he or she will naturally know what equipment is required to facilitate the drawing process. Some of these include masking tape, gummed tape, or drawing pins for mounting paper on board, and cotton swabs and tissues.

Pencil Techniques

Always start with a sharp pencil. This advice applies particularly to the softer grade of pencil, as well as to charcoal and carbon pencils. Unless these are kept well sharpened they will produce coarse, thick lines that will spoil the effect of your drawing. Softer pencils are excellent for quick sketches, requiring less pressure than the harder pencils that demand more accurate control.

Pencil lines vary in appearance according to the speed with which they are drawn, the pressure exerted on the pencil, and the grade of pencil used. Hatching and crosshatching dots, short jabbed lines, marks and lines in random directions, fine lines, thick lines, thick lines trailing into fine, all these can be used to create tonal differences.

Silverpoint artists such as Dürer and Leonardo originated a method of reproducing tone by line that is still used today. They found that by drawing parallel lines close together they could achieve effects of shadow with dark and heavy lines, and of lighter areas with fine light strokes.

Rubbing, either with the finger or an eraser, can also suggest a different tone. Highlights can be reproduced by erasing down to the background, preferably with a putty eraser.

Different textures can be achieved, either on grainy paper or by drawing on paper laid over a textured surface such as wood, stone, or cement – a technique known as "frottage." Try to work as cleanly as possible, and where necessary – in soft, flat areas of "color," or pale gray and fine light line – fix the drawing as you work.

The pencil is very effective when used in combination with other media – both water and oil based – and can be drawn onto canvas and gesso grounds, as well as paper.

PENCIL EFFECTS

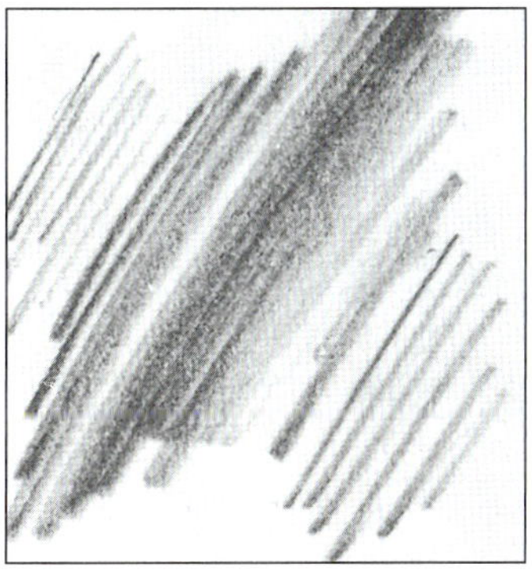

Different combinations of pencil and paper produce a wide range of effects. Here a 2B pencil has been used.

A fairly soft pencil (4B) creates a gradated tone on a moderately smooth paper.

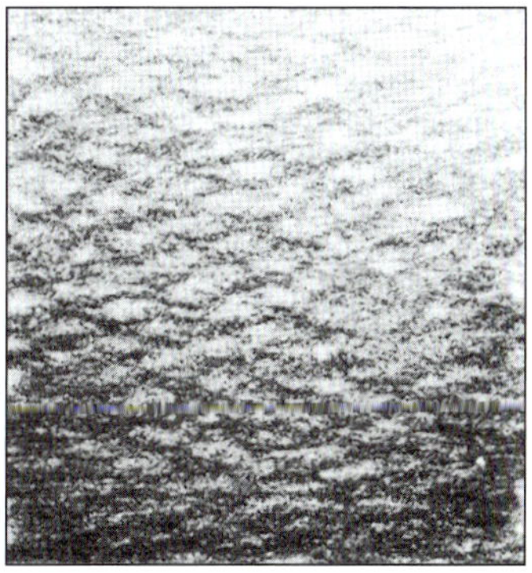

Used on a rough paper, this same 4B pencil gives a much less even result.

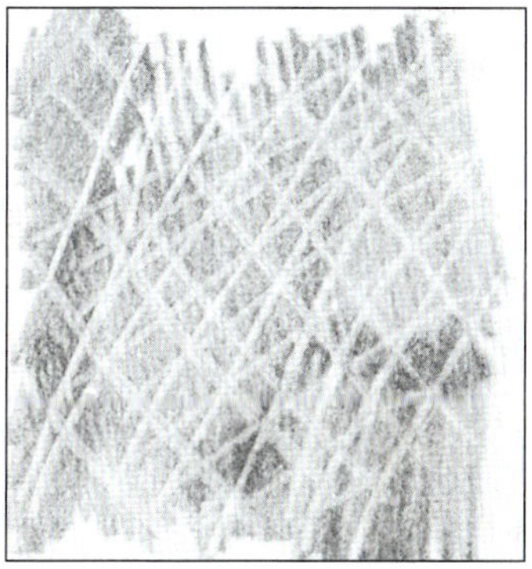

Achieve the above effect by drawing with the reverse end of the pencil to create indentations, then shading.

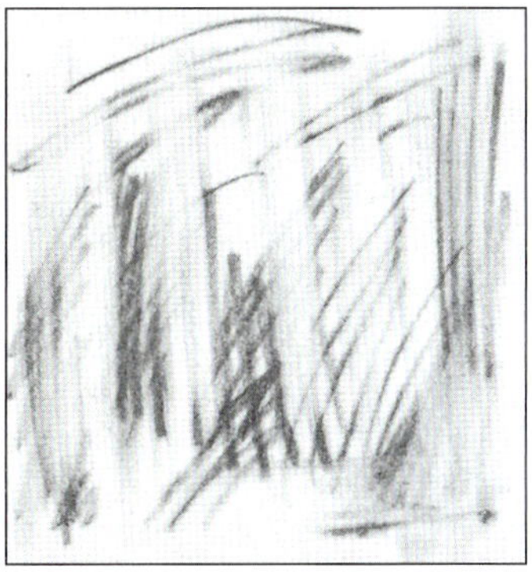

An eraser is a useful adjunct to pencil drawing when specific effects are required. Here 2B lines have been partially erased.

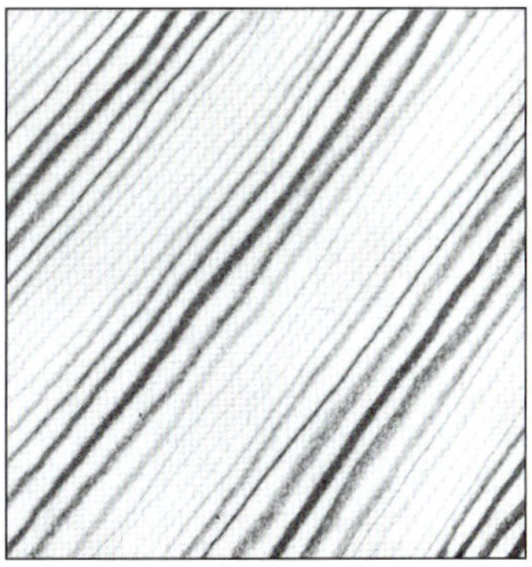

A series of lines drawn with pencils ranging from 6H to 6B shows the differences in the weight that can be achieved.

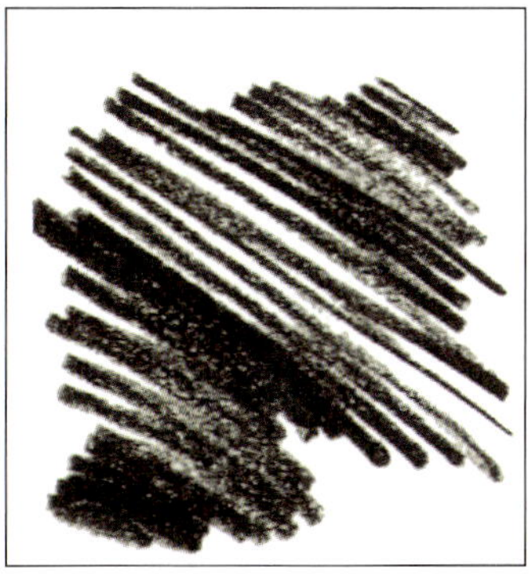

For a very strong, dramatic effect use carbon paper on top of your drawing surface.

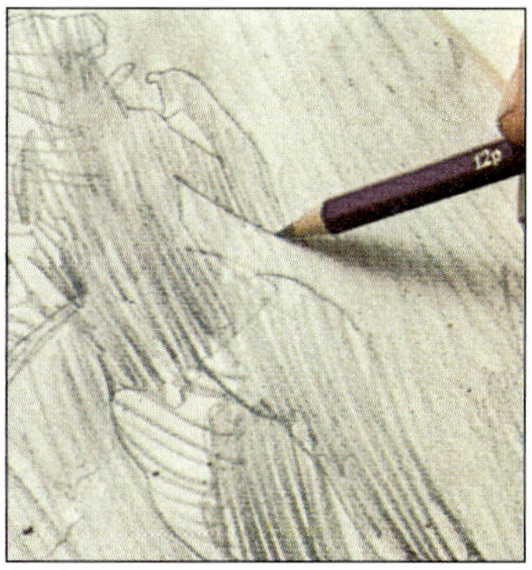

Pencil can be used to produce tone as well as line effects. Here, tone has been blocked in using a 2B pencil.

CROSSHATCHING

This form of shading is a development of hatching and combines two or more sets of parallel lines, one set crossing the other at an angle. It is a technique employed extensively in engraving and etching when tone is produced through linear means as opposed to stipple or aquatint. It is commonly used in pen and ink drawings.

At one time artists were taught to crosshatch their lines at a regulation 45° angle and in black ink only. There is no need now to adhere to such strict practises, which were really conventions related to commercial engraving. It is not only pencils that can be used to crosshatch, all kinds of linear media can be used, including ballpoint pens, felt-tipped pens, and fine brushes. Lines don't have to be straight. For example, try crosshatching curved, zig-zagged, or dotted lines with colored ink or felt pens.

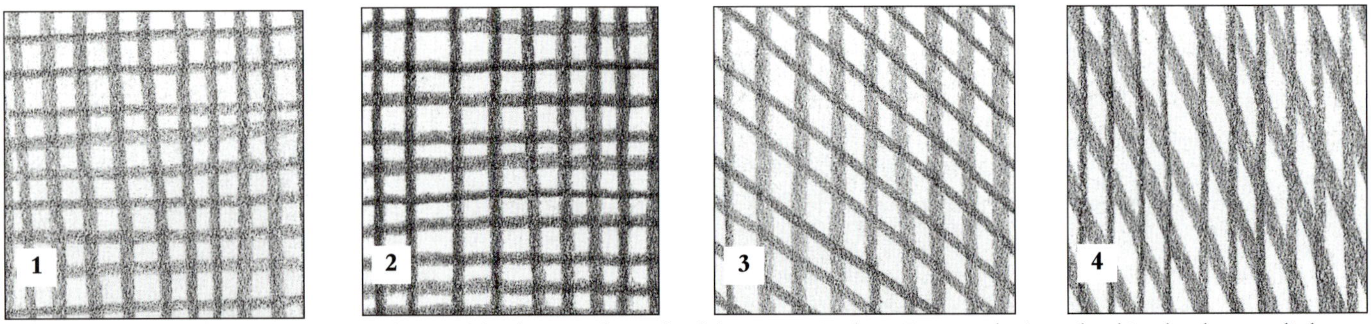

*The effects produced by crosshatching can be varied by changing the angle of the intersecting lines. In example **1** crosshatching has been applied vertically over horizontal hatching. Note the difference in example **2**, where the same effect has been executed with heavier strokes. Example **3** shows crosshatching laid at a 45° angle to vertical hatching. The angle can, of course, be altered, as in example **4** where a more acute angle is used. Examples **5** and **6** demonstrate hatching and crosshatching involving the three primary colors. Apart from creating an intriguing texture, the overlaid strokes produce secondary colors where they mix on intersection.*

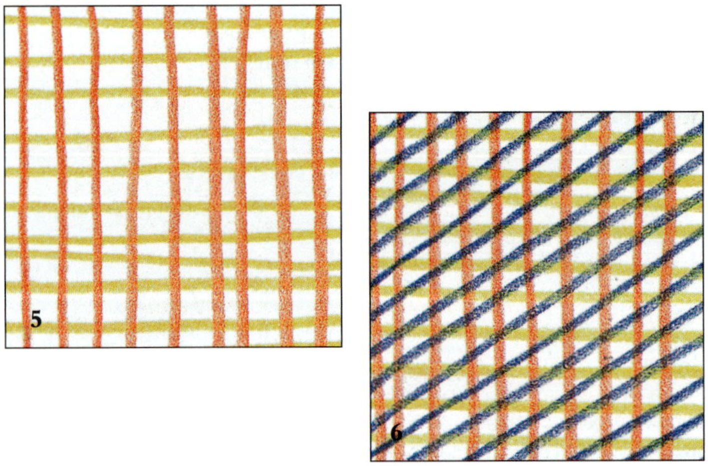

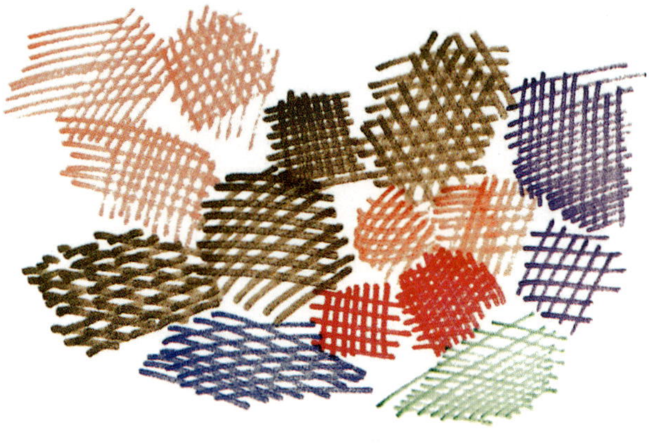

The individual lines of this crosshatching made with colored felt-tipped pens combine to produce an effect of softened color patches.

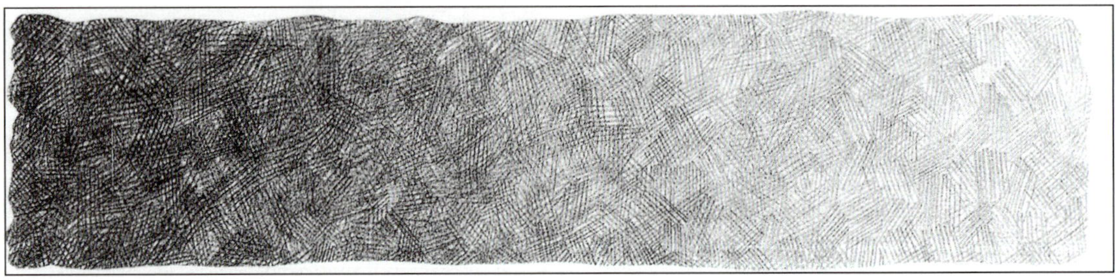

This crosshatched tonal scale indicates the degree of nuance that can be achieved with the technique. The variety and gradations in tone were accomplished by varying the line density and the amount of pressure applied.

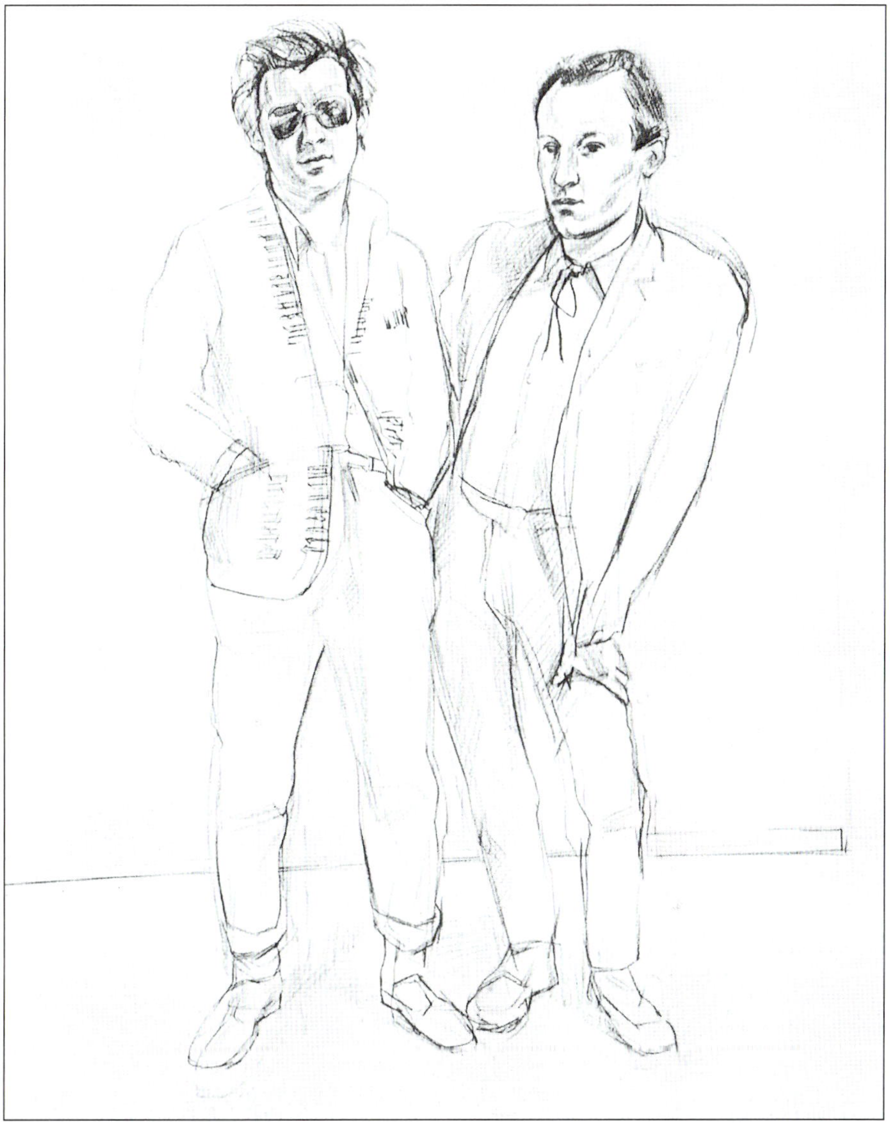

TWO MUSICIANS (pencil on paper)

The hair and facial contours of the first figure are filled in using a 2B pencil; this is suitable for both light and shading and for the darker blocked-in areas of the sunglasses. Hatched shadows across the clothing add detailed volumes to the precise contours, but they are light and sparsely distributed because the contours work well on their own. Textures in the cloth, and small details like collars, a tie, buttons, buckles, and turn-ups are added, while the second figure's hand is given precise form. The pencil is used to create stronger, darker lines overall, to blacken the hair and firm up the whole image. An indication of a wall behind the figures gives them a location in space, although it is left deliberately ambiguous to emphasize the fact that they are acting or posing, and do not belong anywhere specifically.

PALM TEXTURED (colored pencil on paper)

Colored pencils allow the artist to build up layer upon layer of subtle color to create a transparent effect. For instance, crosshatching in different colors – overlaying one area of colored strokes over another color – can create an interesting tone and texture in the picture. Drawing with colored pencil requires patience and thoroughness. The point of the pencil being relatively small, it is difficult to cover large areas with any evenness of tone and stroke. A smooth, hardish paper or board is normally used with pencil work, however, a roughly textured surface can create interesting white "gaps" and grainy effects.

In this picture (right) the artist starts by blocking in areas of dark color as in the windows of the house. To create the texture of a palm tree, the artist overlays thin strokes of color. Working around the shape of the far dome, the artist develops shadows by overlaying a dark green area with light green strokes.

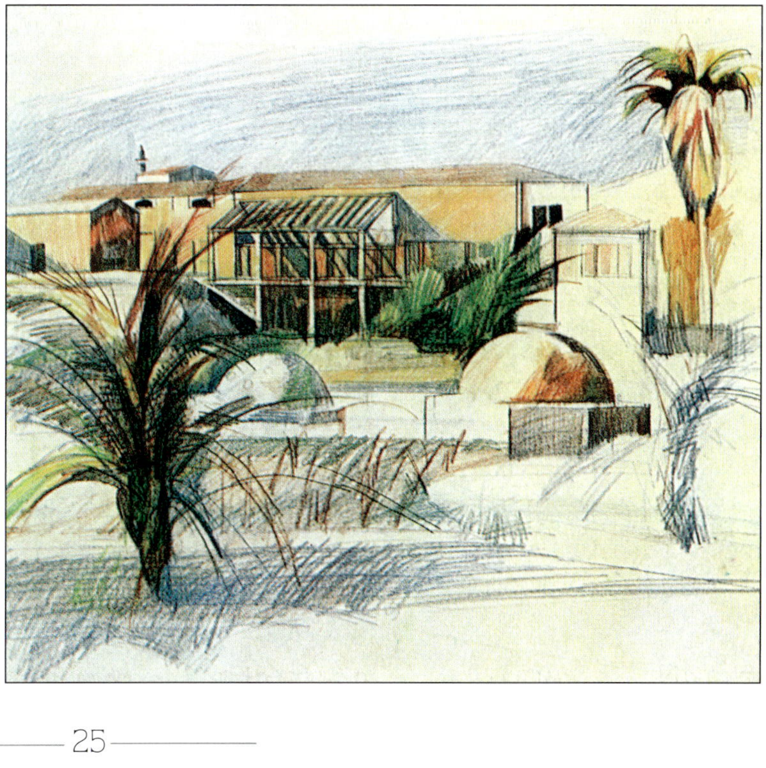

Pen and Ink

Pen and ink has been a tool of artists and illustrators for many centuries. Artists working in pen and ink are on the whole particularly fortunate, since their basic requirements are so modest. He or she needs only a sheet of paper, a pen, and some ink to practise their craft. The medium itself allows an enormous variety of individual expression, whose possibilities can never be exhausted.

Pen and ink has a long tradition as a drawing medium. Leonardo da Vinci (1452–1519) and Michelangelo (1475–1564) both used pen and bistre – a dark brown ink – to make studies. Many of the preparatory drawings for the Battles of Cascina and Angiare, as well as the Sistine Chapel frescoes, are in this medium, with very precise detailed features etched out and strong tonal passages indicated by hatching. This and crosshatching are the terms used to describe the technique.

Pen and ink has also been a favorite with cartoonists over the centuries. Here, the results were often effected by the limitations of the processes available for reproduction. The cartoons and illustrations worked up by such artists as Charles Keane (1823–91), who used pen and diluted ink to hatch and define lively caricatures, were drawn onto woodblocks, later to be engraved by superlative craftsmen.

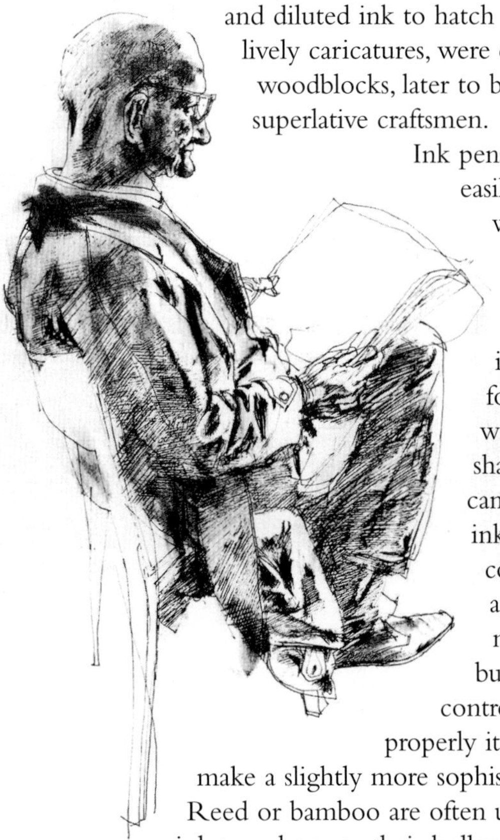

Ink pens can be made easily and cheaply, which accounts for their widespread popularity. In its simplest form, a stick with a slightly sharpened end can be dipped in ink, or any other colored liquid, and used to make a mark, but in order to control this mark properly it is better to make a slightly more sophisticated version. Reed or bamboo are often used to make ink pens because their hollow centers allow for a reservoir of ink to be retained. The ends are usually tapered either to a point or a blunt chisel-like shape. If the ends are also split then the artist can vary the width of the stroke by exerting a greater or a lesser pressure on the pen.

A favorite choice for drawing in ink has always been the quill pen. Any kind of feather can be used, but the best are the long wing feathers of swans or geese. These are sharpened and shaped in the same way as reed or bamboo pens and are springy and pleasant to use. The drawback, however, with quill pens and others of this type is that they wear out quickly so the quality of line can alter a great deal during the course of the drawing. This can be turned to good effect: many of Rembrandt's pen and ink drawings, acknowledged as being among the best of their kind, show evidence of his having used an increasingly worn nib, but with such empathy that the finished result is considered enhanced.

More durable, if slightly less sympathetic, are nibs made from different types of metal that fit into a shaft or holder. The best and most expensive metal nibs are made of gold, but silver, steel, and chromium are all common and perfectly satisfactory. However, a metal-nibbed pen imposes a greater uniformity of drawing technique and many artists prefer the freshness and vitality of the reed or quill.

With such a variety of different drawing pens available it is best to experiment with as many as possible. A pen with a pointed or rounded end will give a line that varies only slightly in width but is excellent for free, expressive drawing. A sharper edge and greater variation in width of stroke can be achieved with a chisel-ended nib, the type designed for calligraphy, particularly italic writing.

LEFT: OLD MAN READING

This careful study has in fact been drawn with an ordinary cartridge pen, with its easy flowing ink a perfect medium for scribbling and hatching.

Pen and Ink Equipment

TYPES OF PEN

There are many types of pen available today: dip pens with a great variety of nibs; fountain pens; reservoir pens; and the more traditional reed pens, bamboo pens, and quills.

Dip pens These are the most versatile and the cheapest available and are particularly good for the beginner. Buy a handful of different nibs (dip pens take a vast number) and try them out to see which are the most suitable. Nibs of different gauges range from fine crow quills to blunt points. The nibs are known commercially as pens, the holders as penholders. Small holders will take small nibs, such as mapping pens or crow quills, that make very fine lines. Dip pens will take any ink in varying amounts, heavy or light, and do not clog unless the paper has a bad surface that breaks up and sticks to the tip. Besides the standard penholders, some holders can be fitted with small brass reservoirs, but they are unsatisfactory in comparison with fountain or reservoir pens, and need to be cleaned fairly regularly after use to avoid clogging. Among the many fine and blunt-tipped nibs for dip pens are italic, script, five-line nib, and copperplate. A "slip" nib has an open oval-shaped barrel; narrow crow quills and mapping pens have tubular barrels.

Fountain pens Except for the Osmiroid, these should only be filled with non-waterproof and writing inks – the Osmiroid takes waterproof drawing ink. Ink is drawn up into a fountain pen by suction through the nib. The nib range is very limited compared to that of the dip pen.

Reservoir pens Special ink in a wide range of colors is made for these pens. The ink is poured into the reservoir, not drawn up by suction as in the fountain pen. Reservoir ink has a great similarity to drawing ink: it has waterproof qualities, but is smoother flowing. The Graphos reservoir pen has a range of 13 nibs that can be changed quickly to produce wide, thick, narrow, or fine lines.

Stylo tip reservoir pens These, too, have a number of interchangeable tips which produce various widths of line. The stylo tip is a narrow metal tubular point that writes or draws with the same consistency in whichever direction the pen is pushed. Commercial illustrators now use them more than the precision draftsmen for whom they were initially designed. Like the airbrush reservoir, the reservoir pen must be emptied and washed out regularly with warm water after use. If ink is left in the reservoir for a short while, the nib should be covered so that the ink does not dry in the channel before use.

Brushes Buy good sable brushes if you are going to brush-draw your ink lines and always wash the ink off your brushes after use. You will need to practise brush drawing with various inks as well as watercolors. Watercolor dilutes better than Indian ink which becomes grainy in a watered wash. Chinese brushes used with a Chinese ink stick can produce very thin, transparent washes. The ink stick is rubbed on a soapstone palette with distilled water until the color is as black or as gray as desired.

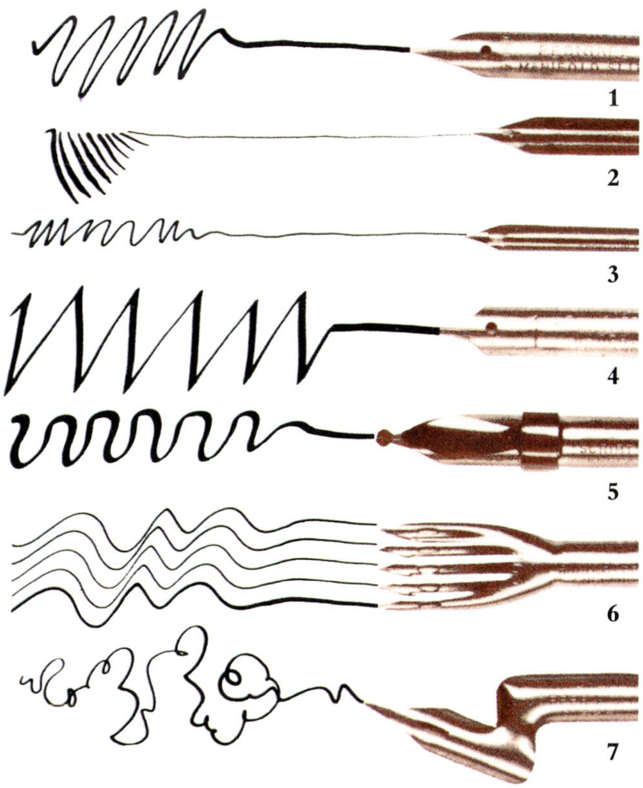

NIBS FOR DIP PENS

*Dip pens can be used with a wide variety of nibs. The slip nib **1** produces a fluid line and the map pen **2** a line of varying width depending on the pressure that the writer applies. The line produced by the crow quill **3** is of constant width because the nib is less flexible. The italic nib **4** writes with alternating thick and thin strokes. The script nib **5** produces a line that, like the italic, is thin on the upstroke and thick on the downstroke, but it is less angular. The five-line nib **6** is particularly useful for crosshatching, as it produces five lines of equal thickness. The copperplate nib **7** is angled to accommodate both vertical and horizontal strokes.*

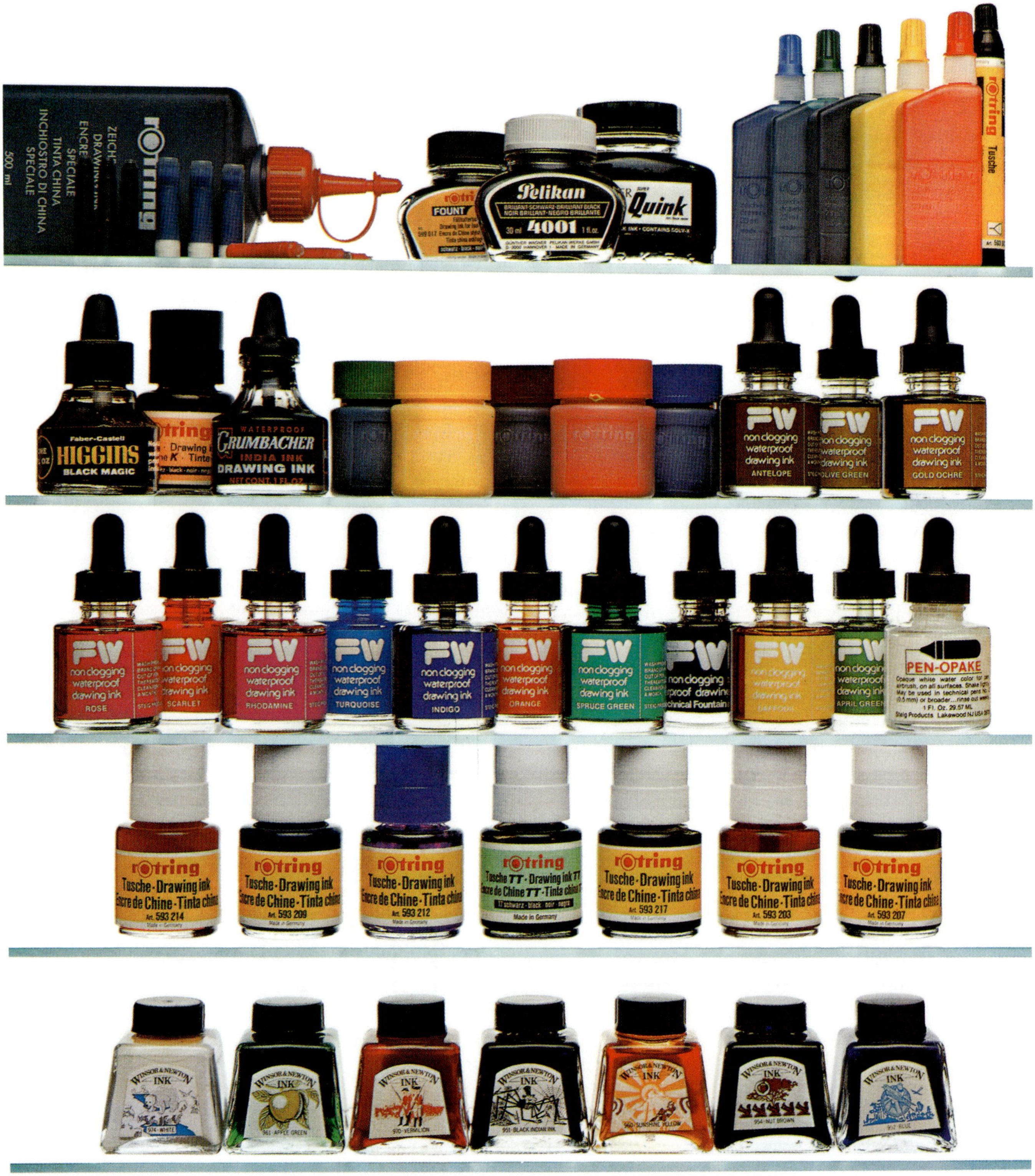

INKS

The range of inks available to the artist includes (from left to right): Rotring special drawing ink in a large container, ink cartridges in different colors, Rotring, Pelikan, and Quink fountain pen ink, smaller bottles of Rotring special drawing ink (top row); Higgins, Rotring, and Grumbacher Indian ink, jars of Rotring special drawing ink in jars, and FW waterproof drawing ink (second row); FW ink and Pen Opake (third row); Rotring drawing inks (fourth row); and Winsor and Newton drawing inks (bottom row). Rotring special drawing inks are for use in stylo tip and reservoir pens. Pen Opake can be used in airbrushes or technical pens.

Pen and Ink Equipment

TYPES OF INK

Artists' drawing inks These are waterproof and dry to a glossy film that can be overlaid. Inks are sold in a range of colors. Grumbacher offer 17, for example, Pelikan make 18, and Winsor and Newton have 22. Reservoir pens have a special range of colored drawing inks. Indian ink is the black drawing ink most commonly used.

Non-waterproof inks There are several non-waterproof inks available in a range of colors. They give the effect of diluted watercolors, drying to a matt finish, and sink into the paper more than other inks. Writing inks can also be used for drawing, but they only have a small color range.

Pigment in ink settles at the bottom of a jar left unused for some time so the jar should be shaken before use. If ink evaporates slightly in summer while uncorked during a day's work, the color becomes deeper and the ink thicker. The addition of just a small amount of distilled water (not a heavy dilution) will thin it again and cause an easier flow.

When choosing an ink you must bear in mind certain of its qualities, for instance, brown and sepia inks tend to fade in time. Some non-waterproof varieties of carbon ink are useful because they dilute easily with water, giving tones that can be blended still further when water is washed over them with a brush.

A wide variety of drawing inks is available at artists' stores. These include colored inks made by Faber Castell, Rotring, Winsor and Newton, and FW. Indian inks include Higgins, Grumbacher, Winsor and Newton, and Chinese ink sticks. Fountain pen inks include Quink, Faber Castell, Rotring, and Pelikan. Rotring make filler bottles of drawing ink for Graphos and stylo-tipped pens, drawing inks for film, and Type K for foliograph or Graphos steel nibbed pens.

PAPERS AND BOARDS

A very thin paper is often insufficiently sized and so the ink will sink in and spread unevenly. For ink drawing it is best to use a heavy cartridge paper, about 60 lb; this will take washes and watercolors and even corrections without harming the paper. Hard calligrapher's paper is as good as expensive hard cartridge, when a sharp precise line is required. Fluffy textured paper is not good as the ink can soak right through and the paper eventually becomes yellow and brittle. It also tears easily and pieces can stick in the nib.

It is best to stretch the paper on a drawing board first (as for watercolor painting) if you are going to apply a heavy wash of ink or watercolor.

Below is the Rotring Graphos reservoir pen, that is an extremely versatile drawing pen.

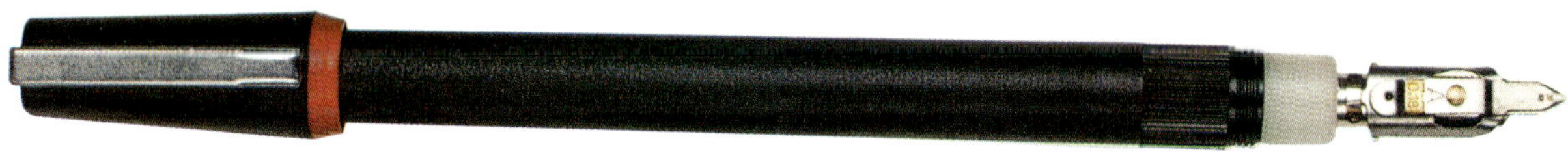

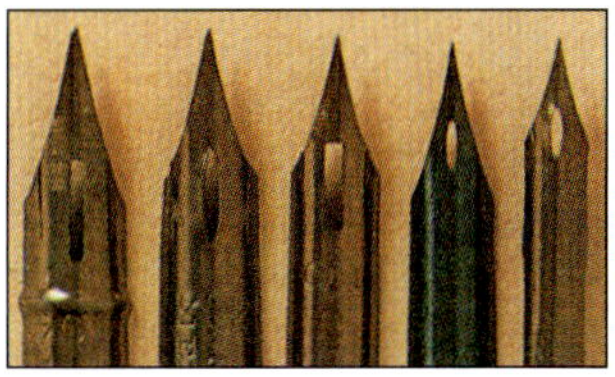

DIP PEN NIBS

There are many types of nibs for dip pens ranging from extremely fine to broad; a range of types are useful to keep on hand. Pen and nibs are fragile and should be carefully cleaned after use.

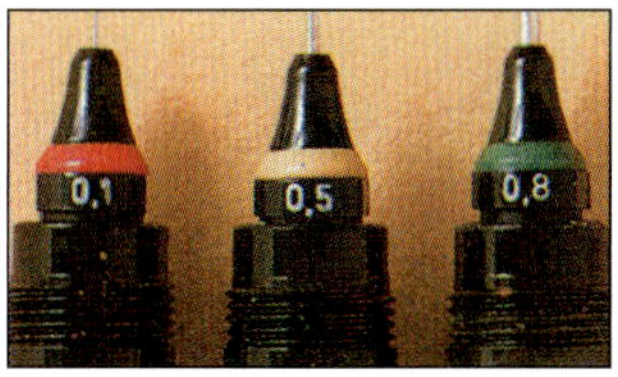

RAPIDOGRAPH NIBS

As with dip pens, there are many types of rapidograph nibs that range from the extremely fine-lined 0.1 nib to the broad, 0.8. The nibs are very sensitive and should be cared for accordingly.

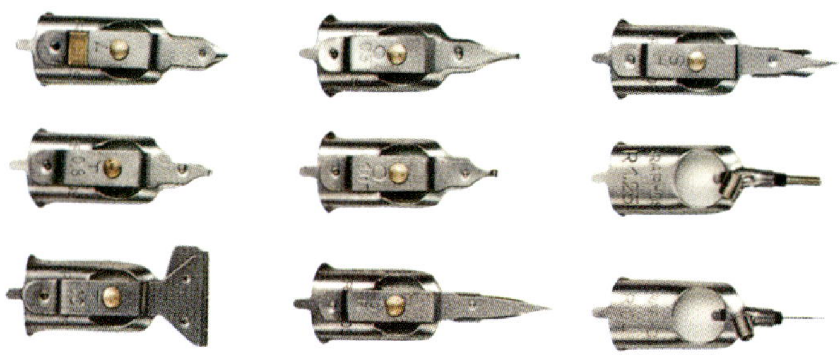

There are almost 70 different interchangeable nibs available with 8 basic nib shapes for the reservoir pen. The ink feed from the reservoir can be adjusted by regulating the ink feed – an invaluable tool for the pen and ink artist.

Pen and Ink Techniques

Technique is a matter of experimenting until one or more methods are discovered that suit your own style or produce certain effects for special purposes. With pen and ink, the basic technique is the use of line and dot. These can produce an infinite number of textures and can also be combined with other media. Like all art, it is always worthwhile to study the good artists in the medium, copying their drawings and techniques in order to learn how to handle the materials yourself.

Do not begin a pen and ink work until you have tried drawing and practicing movement and line with a pen and a brush. Work on a smooth paper and learn to use a minimum of pressure to get an even flow of ink from the nib onto the paper. Try to use exactly the same amount of ink on your nib each time if you are practicing with a dip pen, and learn to judge when the ink will run out, so that you are not in the middle of a long unbroken line or movement when it happens.

It is a great advantage to make a very light preliminary design with a soft pencil if an accurate pen and ink drawing, rather than a quick sketch or note, is wanted. But once the technique of pen and ink drawing becomes more familiar the spontaneity of free-flowing lines and observations translated instantly onto paper often make a far more exciting ink drawing than one that is premeditated and planned.

If a fine designer's brush is going to be used, the flexibility of its tip requires adept handling, and this too should be used a great deal in practise first. Brush, pen, and ink drawing requires wide gestures and movement of the whole forearm, not merely of the hand from the wrist.

TONE

In watercolor, tones come from applications of different washes. These can be used similarly in pen and ink drawing, but, as an ink drawing is basically composed of lines, there are many techniques that may be employed to convey depth of shadow and tonal variations, stippling, hatching, and crosshatching, dots and dashes, toothbrush spattering, scribbling, straight parallel lines graded from thick to fine, for example. A variety of effects are given by overlaying washes of watercolor or diluted inks with all the above techniques. Other effects can be created using the texture of sponges, fabrics (wool and lace), fingerprints, and wood. It is also possible to draw pen lines on turpentine, using ink mixed with white spirit or ink over candle wax or masking fluid, to use blown ink blots, running ink blots, and paper folded over ink blots to make a pattern. But it is the quality of the line that always counts.

An ink drawing must be completely dry before preliminary pencil lines are erased or any watercolor added. Drying time is at least 12 hours, and thick ink on very hard paper will take even longer – about 18 to 24 hours. Ink can be picked up in a watercolor wash if it is applied too soon.

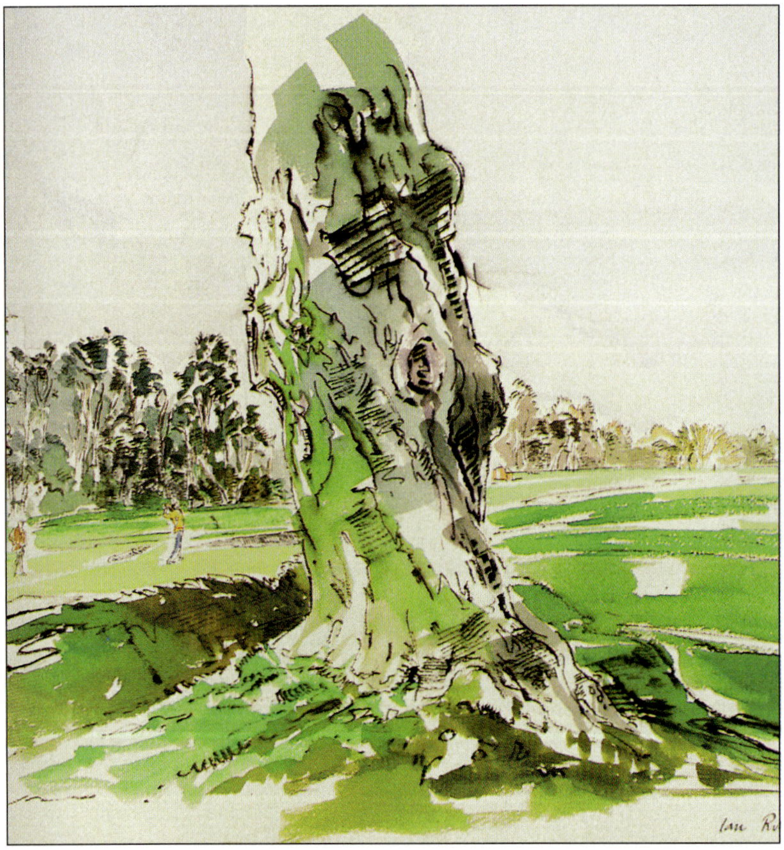

MIXED MEDIA

The flexible qualities of the nib-pen, together with those of the brush, were combined to make this drawing. The foreground tree displays a variety of linear marks – fine outlines, hatching with broad strokes, and calligraphic squiggles. Small dabs of watercolor make up the background foliage, and sweeping brush strokes laid in the greens of the middle distance. The angular washes on the foreground tree were made with a flat (square) brush.

COLORED INKS

As in the case of colored pencils, the range of colored inks is now a part of the artist's repertoire, and a relatively recent phenomena. If used as part of a technique including black and white, these inks are interesting. However, attention should be drawn to the extremely fugitive nature of the color and their tendency to fade with time. For this reason it is preferable to avoid combining colored inks into pictures to be considered otherwise permanent.

MIXED MEDIA

Whether hatching finely or running lines freely over the page, pen and ink will respond in a great many ways. Mixed with other media, a good deal of invention can take place with colored or black ink on colored grounds; or black lines on a carefully rendered watercolor will bring forth fresh results. Combine several types of nib and brush marks. Don't forget the newer types of pen such as the rapidograph and ballpoint pens.

PAINT EFFECTS

Pen and ink is an extremely versatile medium and the small number of effects illustrated here is offered only as a starting point from which to experiment. It is important to try different pens and techniques in order to find those that best suit your style of drawing. Stylo tip pens are particularly useful for drawing straight lines of uniform thickness and for producing a dotted effect (**1–3**). Indian ink, full strength or diluted, and dip pens can be exploited to create a huge range of results (**4–7**).

BRACELET SHADING

This method of shading uses parallel lines like hatching but the lines follow the contours of the form being drawn. To make a line drawing of an object by just copying its silhouette can easily produce a cardboard cut-out effect. To avoid this, it is necessary to use line to describe the volume of the form, that can be done by bracelet shading. The shading is produced by a series of parallel lines that follow the bumps and hollows of the form being drawn. The technique is well suited to pencil, or pen and ink, but is used sometimes with pastels or charcoal.

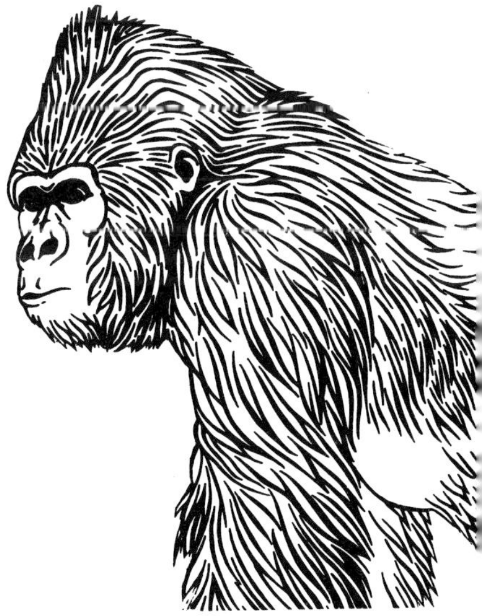

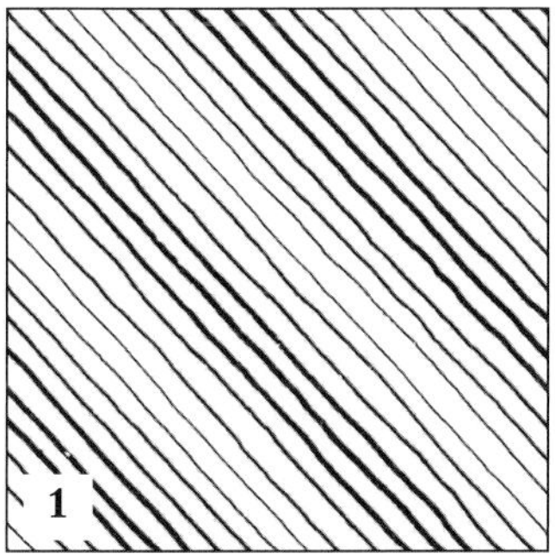

*Using a stylo tip, lines of varying widths are drawn freehand with different nibs. Cross-**hatching can** also create a tartan effect.*

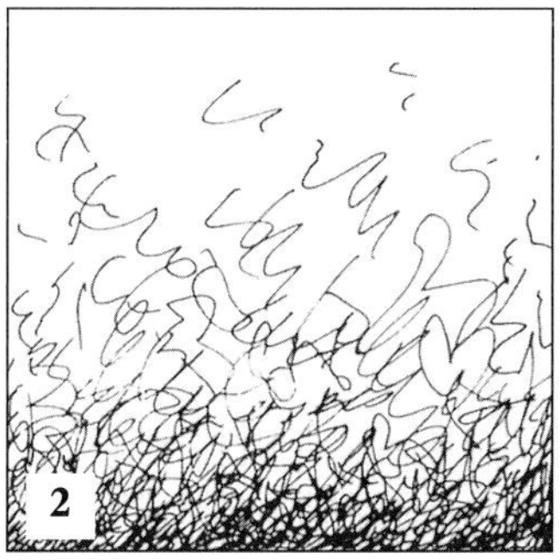

Simple stylo tip scribbles can be profuse and dense or sparse and delicate.

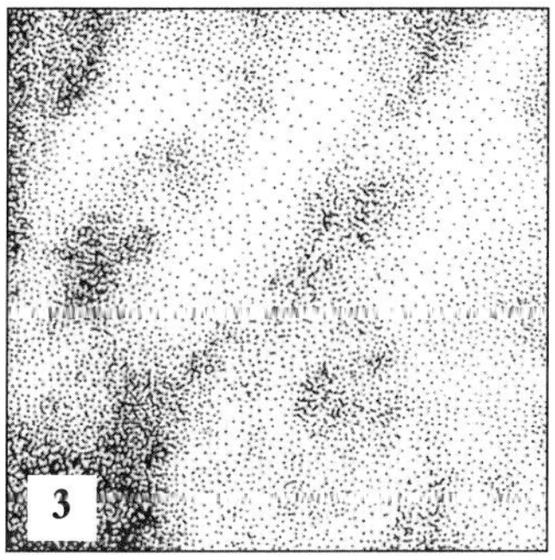

This dotted, or pointillist, pattern has been created by using a fine stylo nib.

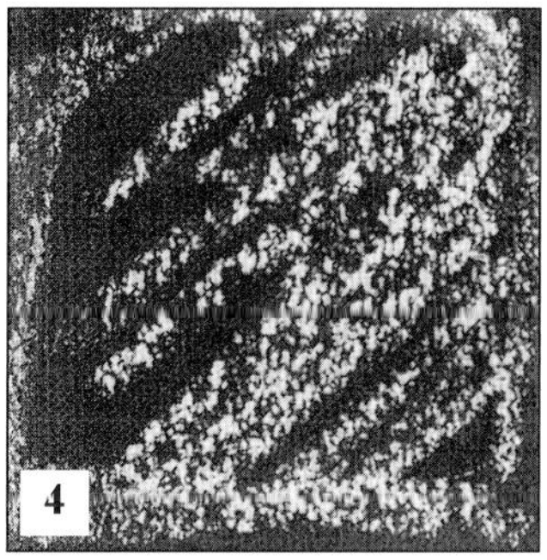

Candle wax repels ink and can be rubbed over the paper to leave highlights or areas untouched by an ink wash.

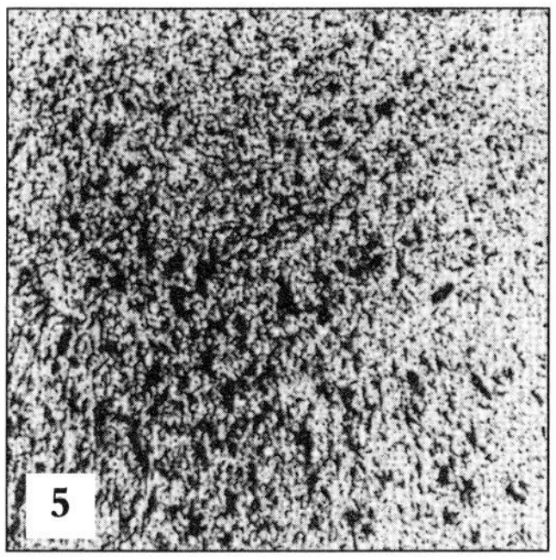

Use an old toothbrush to splatter ink over a surface, blotting it off if a softer effect is required.

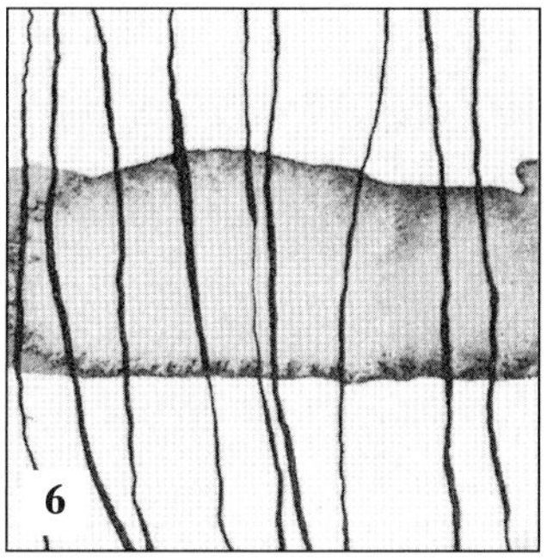

A combination of line and wash requires both brush and pen. Leave the wash to dry before adding the pen lines.

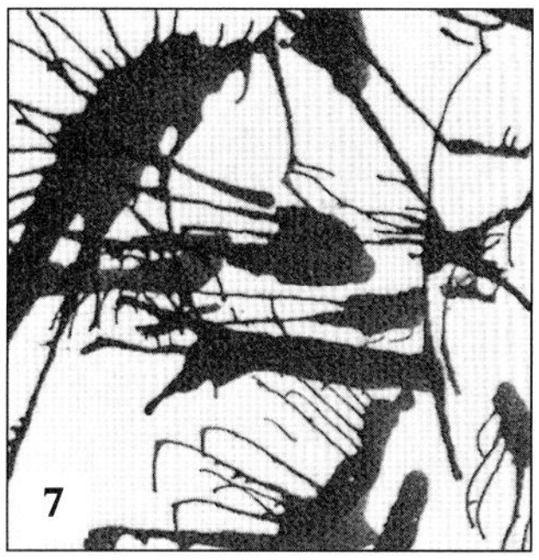

A blob of wet ink can be blown across the support to create random splodges and streaks.

CHARCOAL

Charcoal is the oldest drawing medium. Charred wood from the fire furnished prehistoric man with a tool to draw the outlines of animals on the walls of his cave. The charcoal in use in today's art schools differs little from that used by early man.

In ancient times, bundles of twigs were charred in clay pots with air-tight lids. More recently, the charcoal-burner and his kiln were a familiar sight in our woodlands until well within living memory. Today, charcoal is produced from sticks of wood, often willow, burnt to carbon. Various grades are available, ranging from hard to very soft. Because charcoal particles are inert and not bound to the surface of the paper, it is very easy to smudge and blur, or to shake off and erase. For this reason the particles need to be fixed to the surface of the paper on completion of your drawing. This is normally done by the use of a proprietary brand of fixative.

Recent times have seen developments and changes in charcoal, as in so many other materials. Charcoal pencils, containing compressed powdered charcoal and a binding agent, offer more control and a cleaner instrument with which to work. The density of mark will vary according to the proportions of pulverized charcoal to oil (or wax); a softer pencil contains more binder, a harder one less. In general a toothed paper or board is most suitable for use both with sticks and pencils.

Charcoal was used on frescoes from ancient times until the Renaissance. It was favored, too, by many artists for making preparatory studies from life for oil paintings and for outlining the design on the canvas, as well as being a medium in its own right for drawing.

Honoré Daumier (1808–1879) one of the greatest graphic artists of the French Second Empire, made thousands of drawings in all media. He employed a distinctive curly scribbled line to record the everyday life of the people of Paris. In his vivid rendering of Three Gossiping Women he used pen and ink over charcoal, while his illustration of Don Quixote and Sancho Panza was executed in charcoal washed with Indian ink. His near-contemporary, Jean-François Millet (1814–1875) even succeeded in evoking light and color in his skillful charcoal drawings.

Among the artists to combine charcoal with other media were Edgar Degas (1834–1917), Pierre-Auguste Renoir (1841–1919), and Henri de Toulouse-Lautrec (1864–1901). Lautrec's work covered a wide range and included portraits such as that of the Comtesse Adele de Toulouse-Lautrec, as well as carefully constructed scenes such as The Bar of the Café de la Rue de Rome, which is in charcoal heightened with white chalk. His sketch of the woman jockey La Macarona, was executed in black chalk, oil, and charcoal.

Paul Cézanne (1839–1906), like many other artists, used charcoal for preliminary sketches. His Head of a Painter, Adulle Emperaire displays a firm line, and rapid but even shading. In his study for The Autopsy he relied on heavy line and very black outline shadow.

The advantage of charcoal as a drawing material is that it is soft, gives a sympathetic but positive line, and can be corrected easily if necessary. To exploit charcoal to the full, it should be used on a toned, slightly granular paper. This means that the black areas of tone will be broken up by the untouched cavities in the paper where the charcoal cannot reach; this gives a sparkle and spontaneity to the drawing.

As charcoal can only be used in a negative sense, to show where light is not falling, it is often very effective to use white chalk for highlights or to indicate where light is falling. On toned paper, this combination works particularly well.

Charcoal is at its best when the subject calls for a forceful approach – broad and confident bands of tone with relatively little detail.

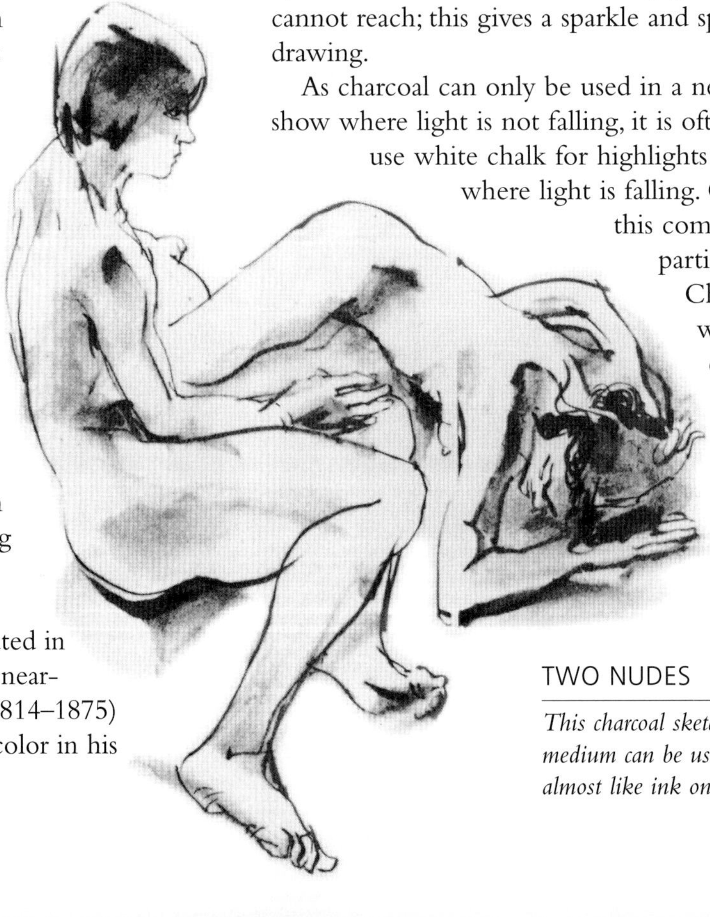

TWO NUDES

This charcoal sketch illustrates how the medium can be used to give an impression almost like ink on very smooth paper.

Charcoal Equipment and Techniques

SURFACES

Charcoal paper has a fairly sharp "tooth," strong enough to withstand rubbing and erasure. Even a fine-textured paper will show its grain through charcoal. Smooth papers are best for compressed charcoal, while colored paper will bring out the intense black of the medium.

TYPES OF CHARCOAL

Stick charcoal Charcoal sticks made of vine or willow are supplied boxed in 6 in. (15 cm) lengths, and in varying thicknesses and degrees of hardness. Thin sticks have to be sharpened with sandpaper, but the thicker ones, that range up to ¼ in. (0.6 cm) in diameter, can be sharpened with a fine blade. The best stick charcoal is made from vine twigs, and, with this type of charcoal, errors can be dusted off the paper.

Compressed charcoal This is made from powdered charcoal and a binder. It is stronger than ordinary stick charcoal but mistakes are harder to dust off. Sometimes known as Siberian charcoal, these compressed sticks are supplied in 3 in. (7.5 cm) and 4 in. (10 cm) lengths and are about ¼ in. (0.6 cm) in diameter.

Charcoal pencils Made from thin sticks of compressed charcoal, encased in wood or rolled paper, charcoal pencils, besides being cleaner to handle than charcoal sticks, have a fine tip that makes them ideal for detailed work or very small drawings. The casing, however, means that they cannot be used for broad side strokes. Like ordinary graphite pencils, charcoal pencils are graded for hardness or softness, ranging from a hard HB through to a medium 2B, a soft HB, and an extra-soft 6B.

Powdered charcoal is used with stumps or torchons. These are made from blotting paper rolled to form a hard pencil with which the grains of charcoal are spread over the paper to obtain varying tonal effects.

Kneaded putty erasers are essential for charcoal work. Besides their property of being able to be shaped to a fine point to pick out detailed errors, they can also be used to blot up mistakes and unwanted lines simply by being pressed against them. However, if the drawing has been loosely executed, it may be better to leave the error and draw a fresh line. At some time, all the Old Masters have made *pentimenti* (repentances) and left them uncorrected.

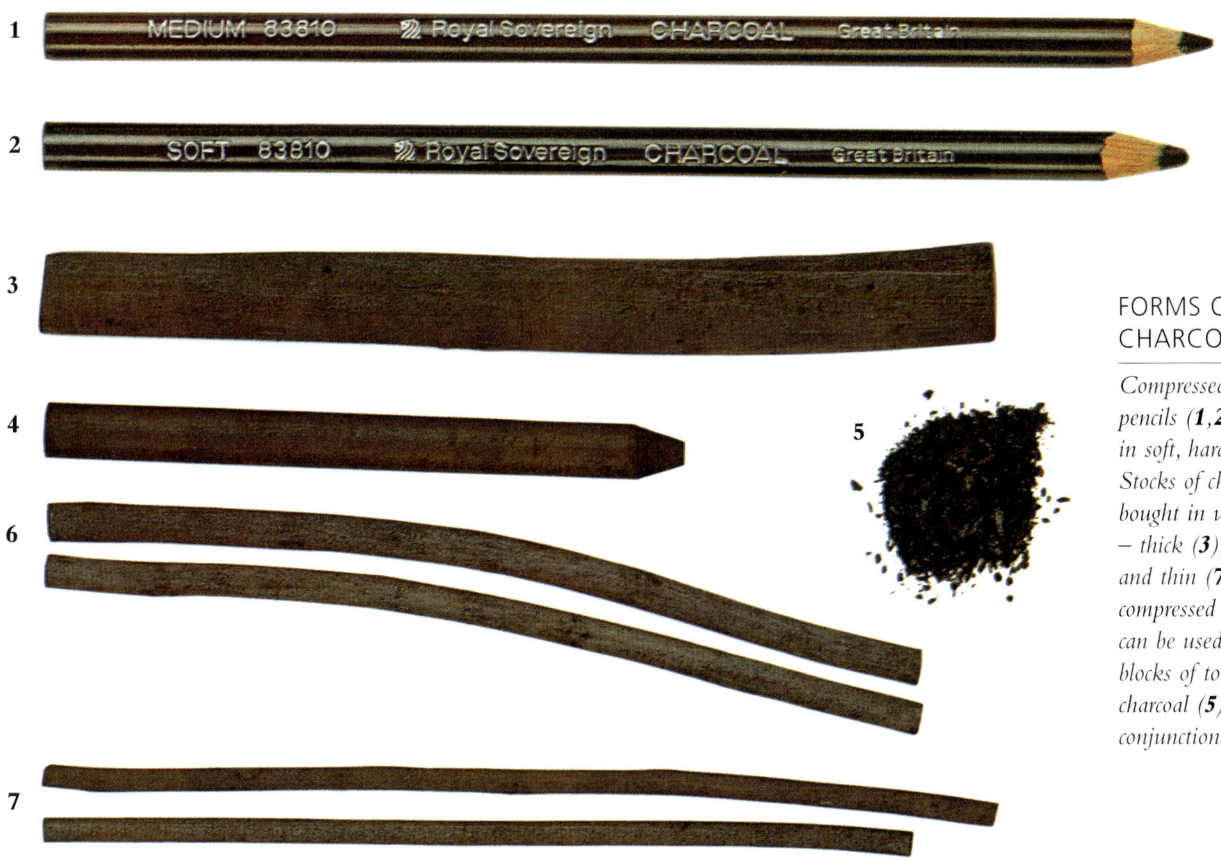

FORMS OF CHARCOAL

*Compressed charcoal pencils (**1**,**2**) are available in soft, hard, and medium. Stocks of charcoal can be bought in varying widths – thick (**3**), medium (**6**), and thin (**7**). Stocks of compressed charcoal (**4**) can be used to make broad blocks of tone. Powdered charcoal (**5**) is used in conjunction with a stump.*

TECHNIQUES

Charcoal has many uses: as a medium for large mural design; for making preliminary sketches for oil and acrylic paintings; or for line and tone drawing in its own right. Among its advantages as a medium are that errors can be easily dusted off with chamois, kneaded putty, or bread, which can also be used to pick out highlights by rubbing away the charcoal to reveal the support. Charcoal can be rubbed with a finger and blended with a stump; it can form part of a pastel picture, or be used for special effects with pencil, wash, gouache, and chalk.

Honoré Daumier (1808–1879) used it as a wash, laying down solid strokes and patches, and working over it, softening the line with a brush dipped in clean water. In this technique, tone can be added by rubbing with a finger, by using lighter pressure or harder sticks, or by spreading powdered charcoal with a torchon or stump. Because charcoal comes off the support so easily, fixative may be added lightly as the work progresses.

LIFTING OUT

Lifting out is a technique for removing areas of tone in a drawing to reveal the white paper underneath. It is often used when drawing with charcoal or conté crayon to introduce a highlight into an area of tone. A pliable rubber eraser is generally the most effective method because particles of charcoal can be lifted cleanly off the paper without too much rubbing. For lifting out small detailed highlights shape the eraser into a point. A tip to remember is that soft bread is useful for "softening" an area of tone that is too dark.

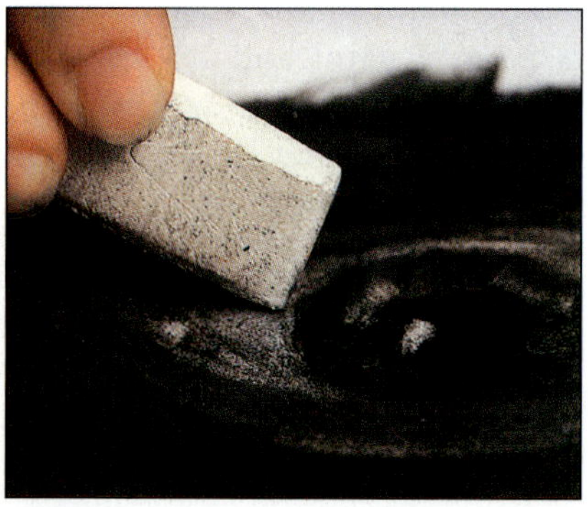

The white of the eye in this drawing is being made by lifting off the particles of charcoal with a kneadable eraser.

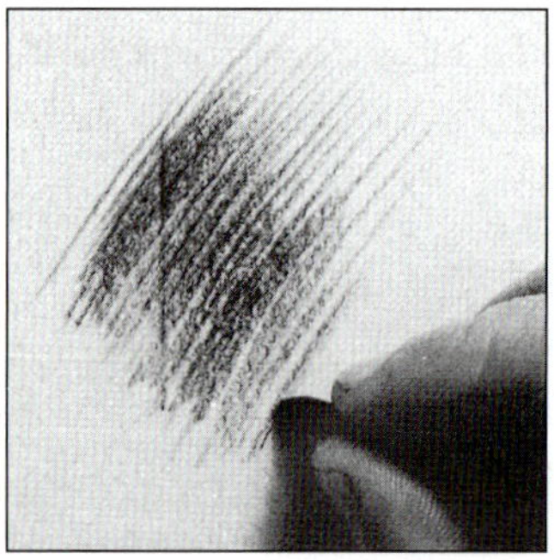

Use fine, hatched lines to build up an area of graded tone, working in one direction and varying the pressure.

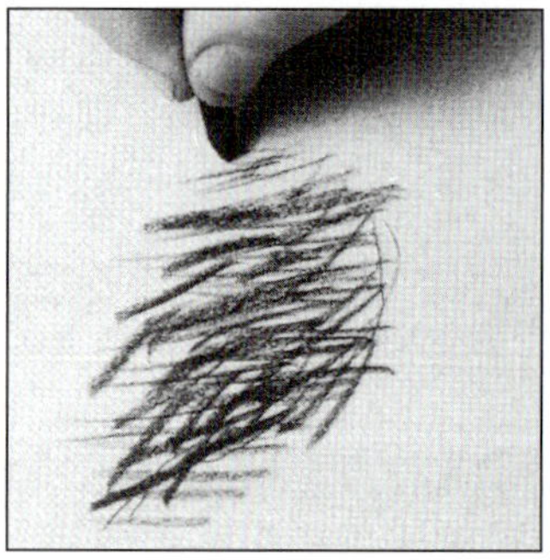

Loose crosshatching is an alternative method of applying texture and building up tonal areas.

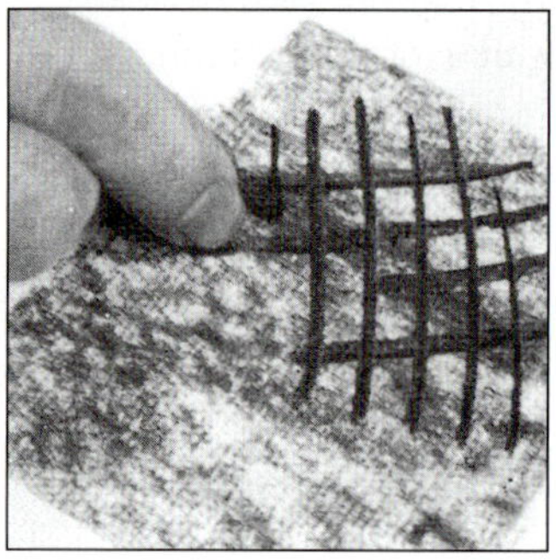

Lay areas of tone with the side of the charcoal stick and crosshatch over the top for a richer texture.

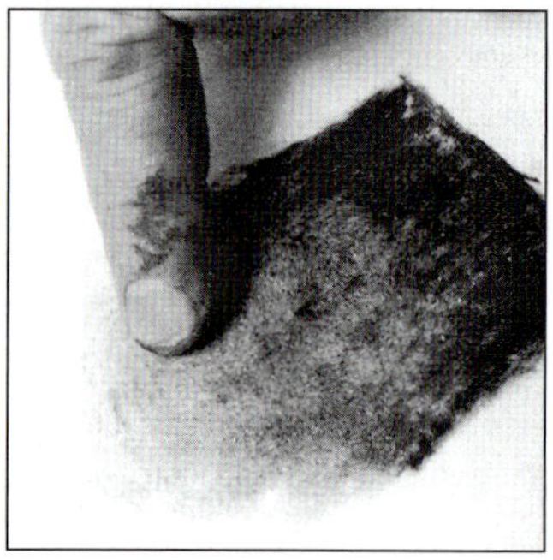

Use a finger to spread charcoal dust evenly over the paper or to vary the tone.

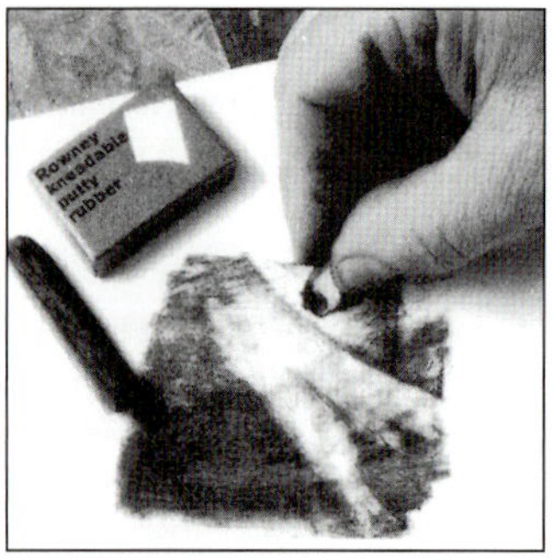

Work lights by using a soft putty rubber. A clean piece will erase charcoal completely.

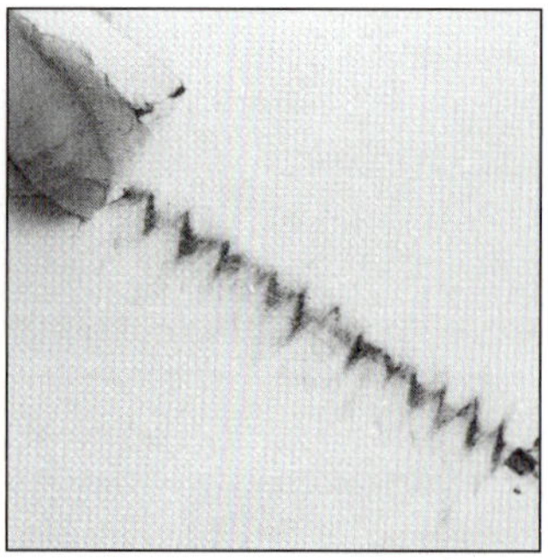

Create areas of pattern and texture by rubbing lines lightly with a putty eraser without erasing them completely.

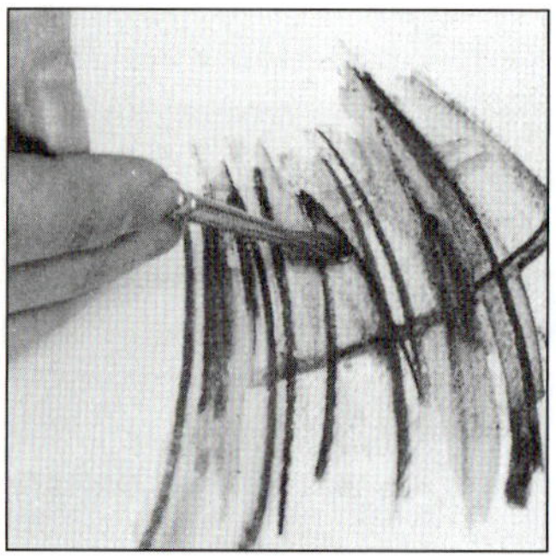

Use a charcoal wash technique to soften and spread the tonal areas. Work gently with a soft brush and clean water.

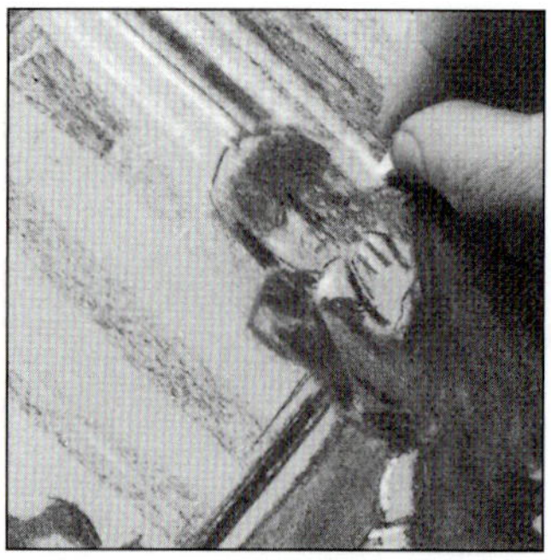

Highlights can be added by using a white chalk or pastel. This is particularly effective on tinted paper.

PASTELS

Chalk and oil pastels as we know them came into use a little more than 200 years ago. In appearance, they are as opaque as watercolor is transparent, and their velvety bloom, softness, and fresh, bright colors make them one of the most attractive of all media. The effect of pastel is immediate from the moment it is applied to paper.

Chalk pastels are bound together with gum and white filler. The crumbling particles are pressed into the surface of a suitable support paper. Unlike watercolor or oil paint, the colors are not mixed before being applied to a support. The color mixing takes place as part of the drawing process itself, by fusing one color into another. This is done with the finger tip or with a paper-felt stump called a torchon. The colors of chalk pastels are neutralized to some extent by the presence of the white filler. Thus we tend to talk of "pastel shades."

Careful examination of a pastel drawing by Degas will reveal his technique of building up color in a web of opposing chalk strokes. Pastel drawings are distinguished from other drawings by the freshness of their color. Degas was much influenced by the pastel drawings of Quentin de la Tour, whose work he collected. But he developed his own techniques and often used a semi-transparent paper to produce progressive states of a composition by laying one drawing on top of another, tracing the contours of the first drawing as a basis for the next. By spraying water onto certain parts of an almost completed pastel drawing, he was able to brush certain passages in the drawing into a paste-like texture. Pastel has often been successfully combined with other media; some painters, for example, first produce an "underpainting," using oil paint or gouache very thinly, and then gradually build up a pastel drawing on top of it. Degas added pastel to his monotype prints, first painting his subject with oil very thinly onto a copper plate. The image on the plate was transferred to a dampened sheet of paper under great pressure through the rollers of an etching press. He then burnished the pastel into the surface of the print with great delicacy, so that the color became a transparent tint over the original drawing.

One should attempt to work in a way that makes use of the particular qualities of pastel – it is no use trying to render fine detail with a stump of chalk. Work broadly and begin on a large scale with a sheet of paper big enough to allow the arm to move freely across the surface. Mistakes in the drawing can usually be brushed away with a hogs'-hair brush. Take care not to destroy the grain of the paper when erasing parts of the drawing. It is the pronounced grain of the paper that anchors the particles of chalk to the surface. The simple, bold statement is usually the most successful; pastels that are overworked lose their "bite" and feeling of spontaneity. Toned or tinted papers make an ideal base for pastel drawings. Watercolor papers can be tinted by using diluted gouache, that can be rubbed into the grain of the paper with a soft pad of cloth.

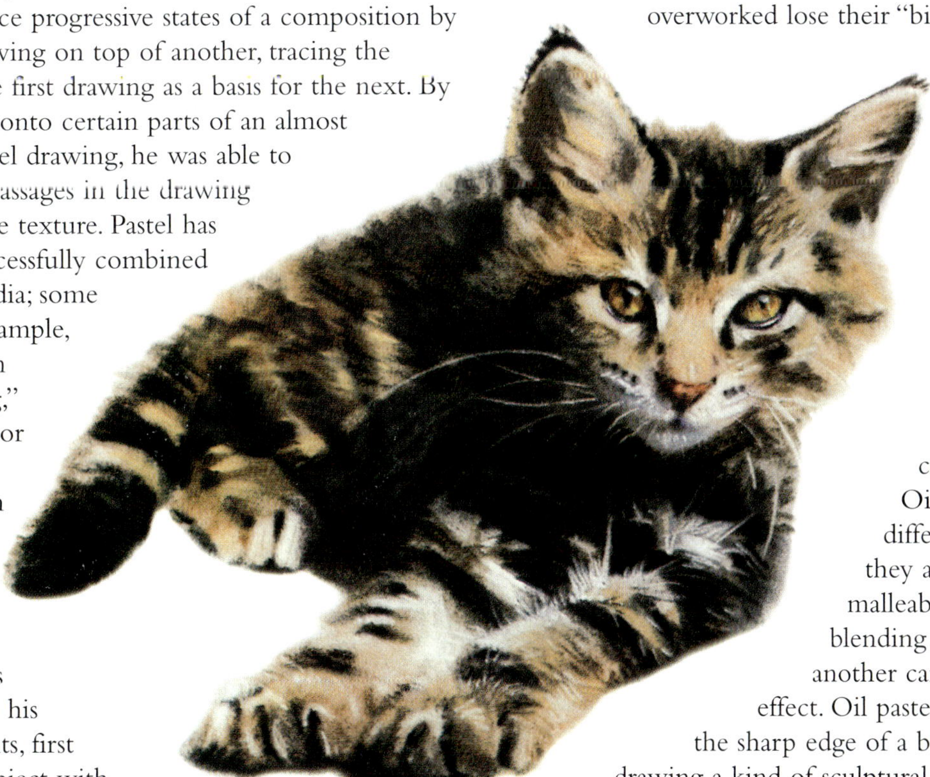

Oil pastels are quite different from chalk pastels; they are softer and more malleable. The resulting blending of one color with another can give a very rich effect. Oil pastels can be scraped with the sharp edge of a blade, that gives the drawing a kind of sculptural quality.

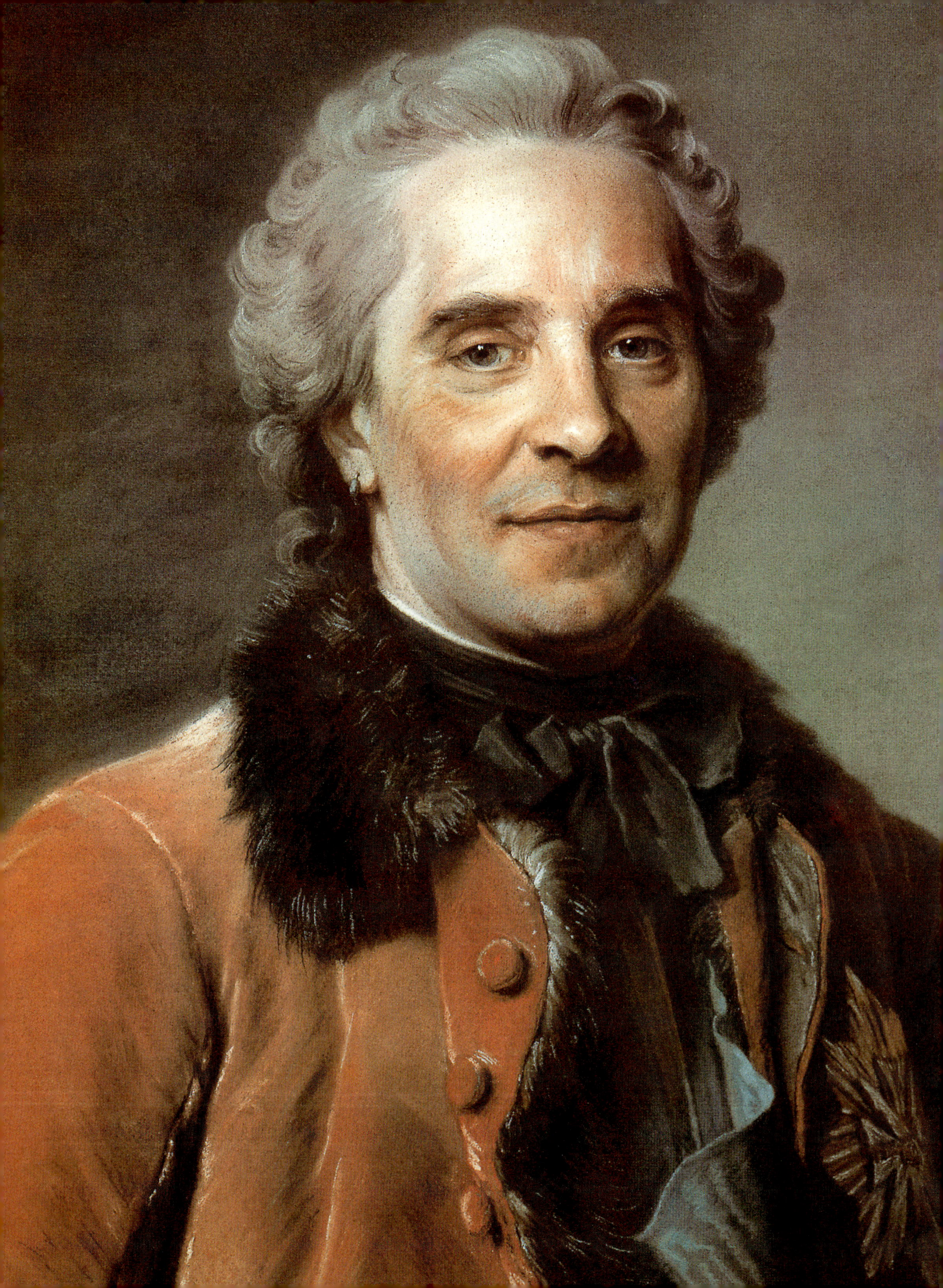

FAR LEFT: HERMANN-MAURICE, MARÉCHAL DE SAXE by Maurice-Quentin de la Tour (1748)

Little is known about the early years of Maurice-Quentin de la Tour (1704–1788), except that he defied his father, who wanted him to be an engineer, and left home to study in Paris when still in his teens. He trained originally as an oil painter, but was converted to the pastel medium by the hugely successful Venetian pastel painter Rosalba Carriera, who visited Paris in 1721–22.

The resistance of the medium makes it most suitable for strong, expressive statements.

Because colors need to be blended on the paper support, rather than on a separate palette, the color range of pastels is vast. Well over 500 tints are manufactured by various artists' colormen. A range of two dozen tints will suffice for most purposes; additional tints can be bought when needed. Graded in soft, medium, and hard, the sticks tend to be used up fairly quickly, especially when working intensely with compacted color. So colors constantly need replacing.

Toned and colored papers, such as Fabriano or Swedish Ingres, make excellent paper supports. One way of understanding color values in pastel is to work on dark-colored paper – brown or even black: all the light areas in your drawing will then have to be imposed on the dark ground with lighter tints of pastel – working from dark to light, that is a reversal of the normal painting process.

It takes some time to adjust to the idea of blending color on the surface of the paper and in your first drawings it is advisable to limit the number of colors to four or five from the same color range such as yellow, ocher, terracotta, burnt umber, and dark brown. Your first drawings will then be essentially monochromatic and it will be easier to understand tonal values.

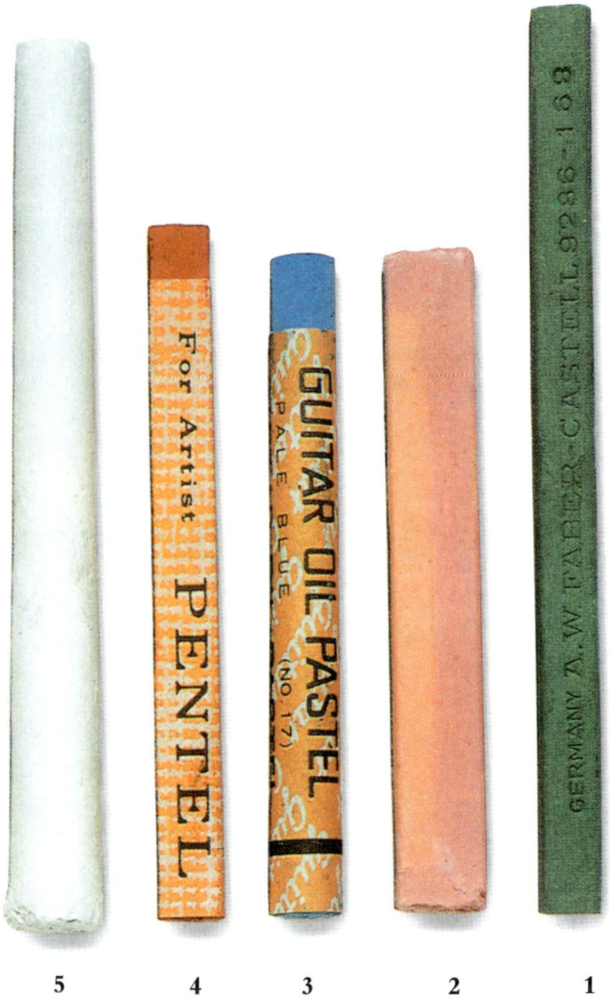

*ABOVE: Types of Chalks and Pastels. Pastels are manufactured in varying degrees of hardness. **1** Castell Polychromos; **2** Inscribe soft pencil; **3** Guitar oil pastel; **4** Pentel oil pastel; **5** Chalk pastel.*

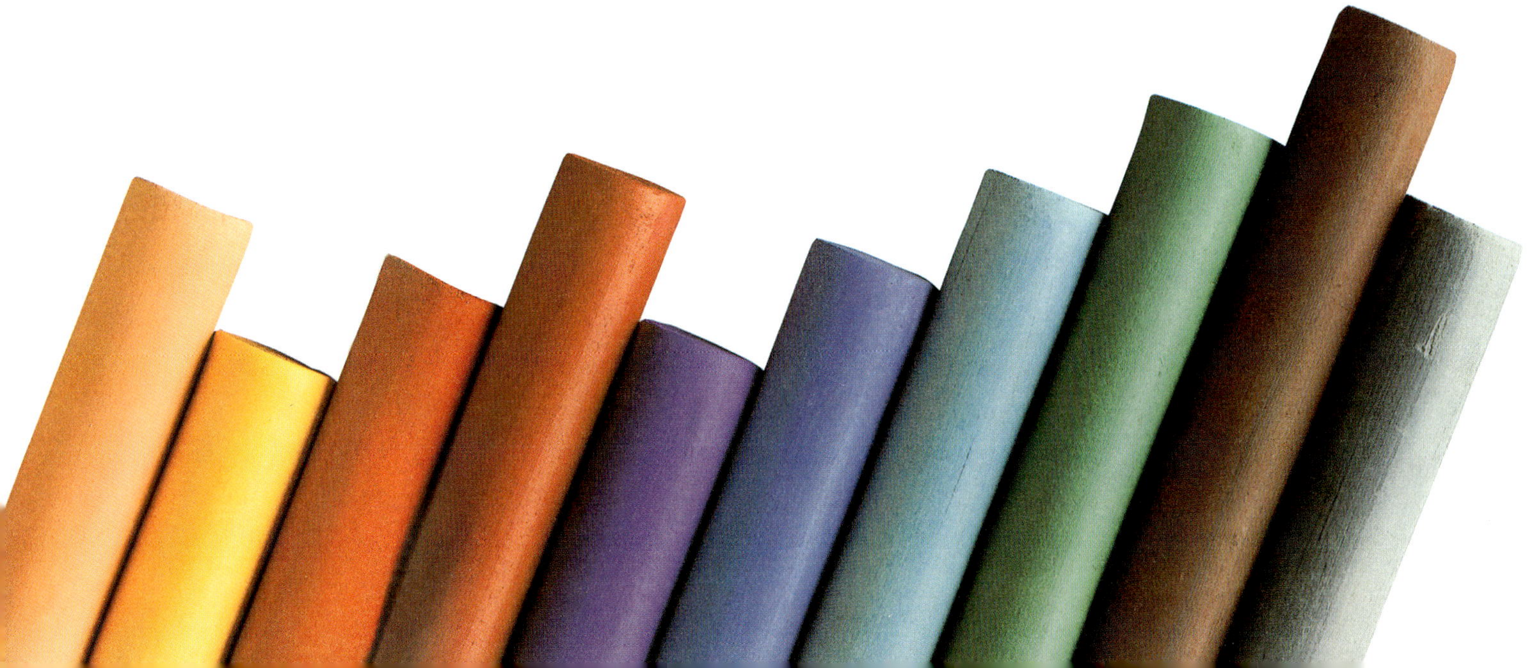

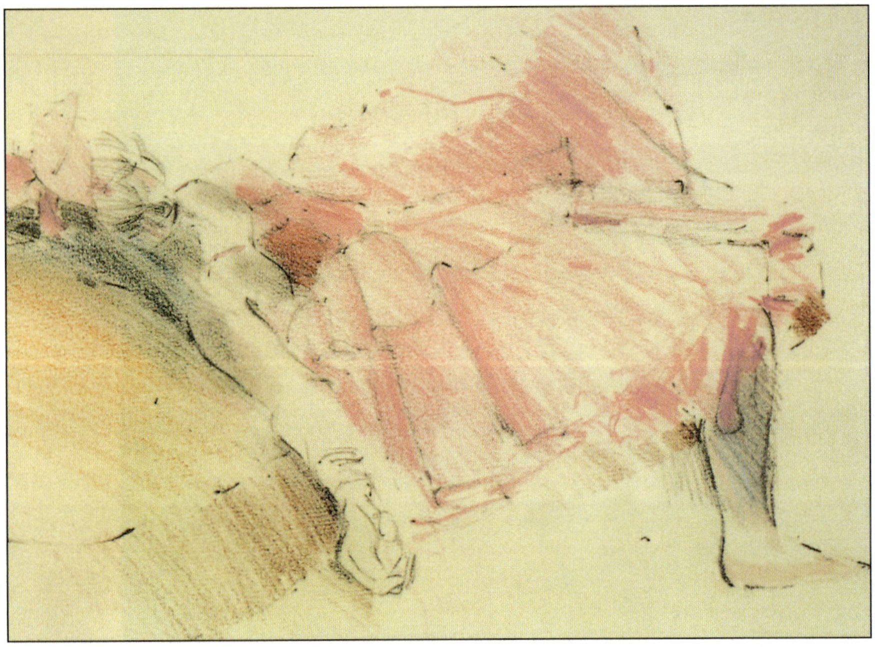

LEFT: DANCER II

Pencil and colored crayon on toned paper. The drawing relies on understatement to lend emphasis to the delicacy of the subject.

BOTTOM LEFT: *Drawing with a paper stoop or "torchon." The tip is used to blend chalk pastels into soft delicate tones, particularly in flesh tints. It can also be dipped into powdered pastel.*

BELOW: *The range of pastel tints available is vast; one light, one medium, and one dark gradation of each color is practicable, and a set of just 12 is probably adequate for sketching outdoors.*

The harder the pigment is pressed into the surface of the paper, the more dense the tone will become. But a great deal of surface manipulation of tones can be achieved by spreading and pushing the pigment over a wider area with a finger or a torchon. A gentle touch is sometimes needed to fuse delicate tones together. Preliminary drawing can be carried out in charcoal.

Fixing is done after various stages, or not until the drawing is completed. Oil pastel is really a species of oil painting and it offers much greater resistance than chalk pastel. Turpentine can be used as a thinning agent or to create washes over the drawing. The color can be scraped away with the edge of a blade and reworked.

For further details about pastel drawing and painting see pages 151–166.

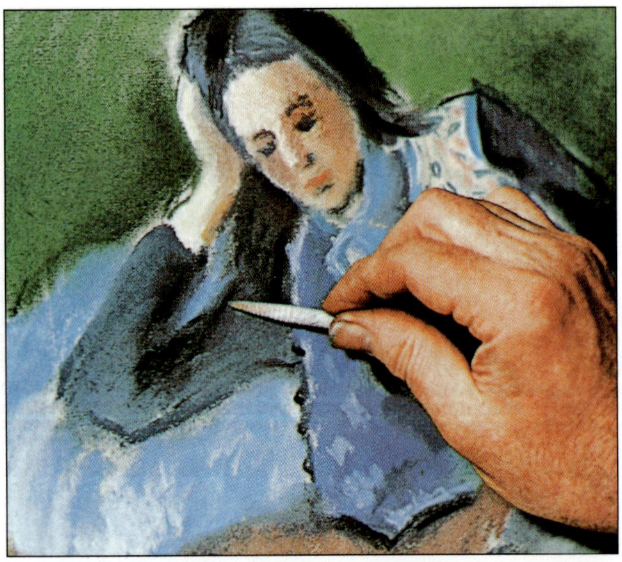

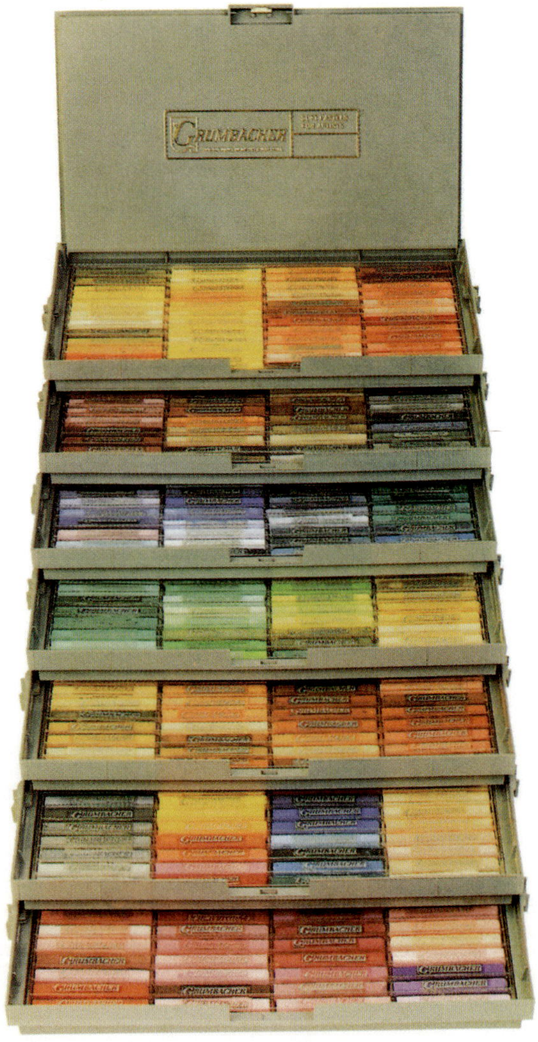

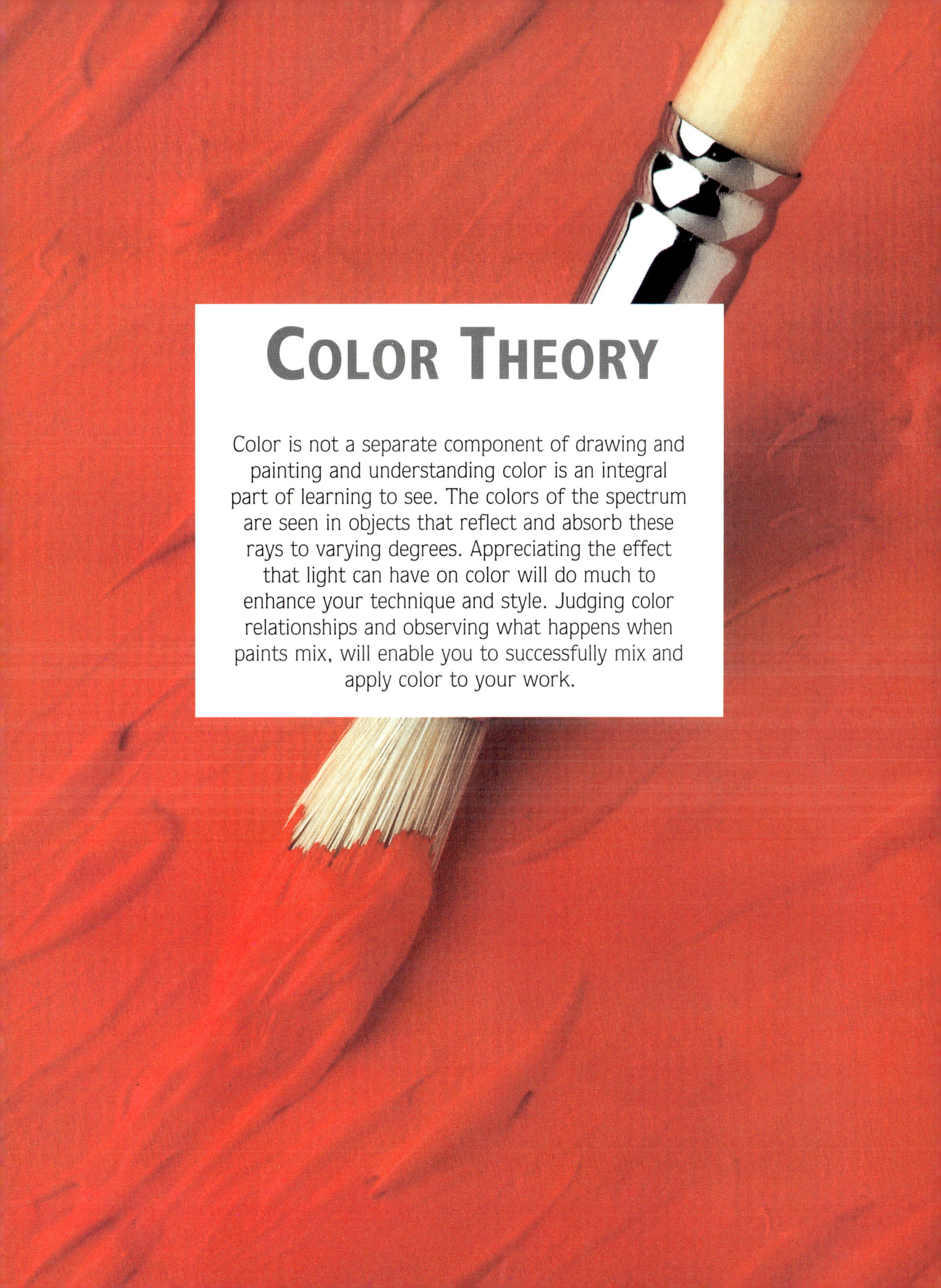

Color Theory

Color is not a separate component of drawing and painting and understanding color is an integral part of learning to see. The colors of the spectrum are seen in objects that reflect and absorb these rays to varying degrees. Appreciating the effect that light can have on color will do much to enhance your technique and style. Judging color relationships and observing what happens when paints mix, will enable you to successfully mix and apply color to your work.

The Color Wheel

This diagrammatic arrangement of colors can be laid out in various different forms, but the color relationships it describes are standard. It is based on the idea of pure color values that derive from three primary colors – red, yellow, and blue. These are defined as the primaries because they are colors that cannot be mixed from combinations of other colors. They are unlike each other, and none contains any element of the other primaries.

It is a mistake to think of color as a separate component of drawing and painting. Understanding color is an integral part of the whole business of learning to see and learning to register what you see. A basic knowledge of color theory is, of course, useful, but time spent observing color in nature is even more rewarding. Cézanne said that painting from direct observation is a way of classifying one's sensations of color. "Drawing and color," he added, "are not separate at all; in so far as you paint you draw. The more the color harmonizes, the more exact the drawing becomes."

Colors can be divided into two categories, warm and cool. An excellent exercise for any painter is to mix a range of grays that are cool (blue-grays) and also a range of warm grays (red-grays). The range should be quite extensive. Then proceed to paint your subject – still life, landscape, or whatever – using this range of colors only. In this way you will learn very effectively how to work without relying on primary colors or strong contrasts.

The three primary colors are red, yellow, and blue and they are located on the wheel at equal distances from one another. Between them fall the secondary colors – orange, green, and purple – that represent mixes of primary pairs. Between the primaries and secondaries are intermediate colors, red-orange, yellow-orange, yellow-green, blue-green, blue-purple and red-purple, each representing a mixture of the adjacent primary and secondary.

Depending on the size of the wheel and the number of subdivisions, these could be split once again into further intermediates. In effect, this would give another, redder red-orange, a yellower yellow-orange, and so on. In theory, you would assume that orange is a perfect middling mixture between red and yellow, red-orange the mid-point between red and orange, the redder red-orange another middling mixture between the two colors directly adjacent.

PAINT COLORS AND THE WHEEL

The color wheel has often been taken as a guide to color mixing, but if you try to create your own wheel, you find immediate practical problems. There are no such colors as "primary" red, yellow, or blue, so you have to choose a

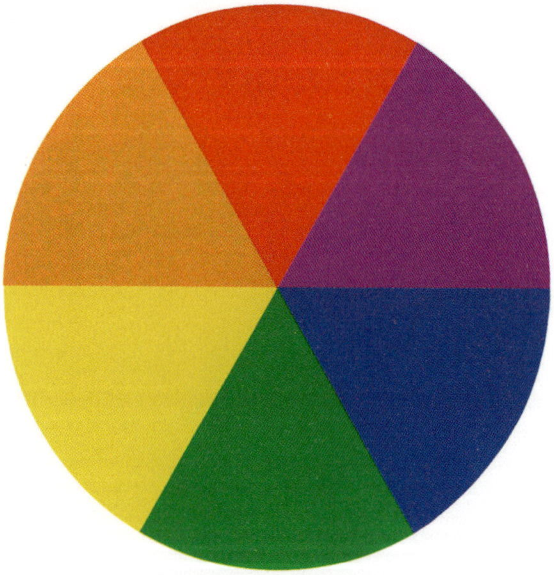

The standard six-color division of the wheel shows only the three primary colors – red, yellow, blue – and the three secondaries – orange, green, purple.

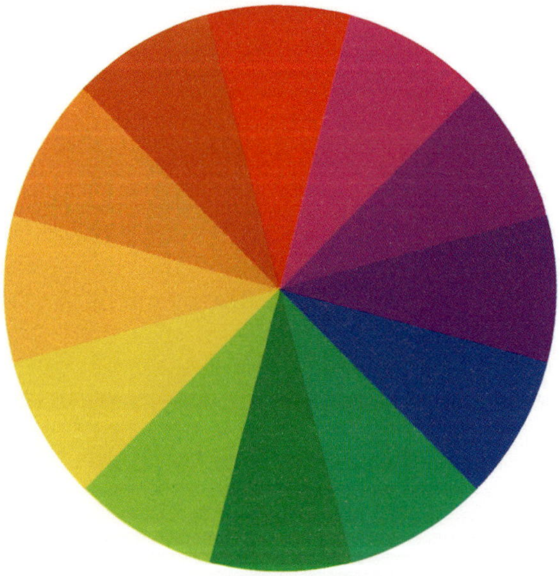

When the wheel is subdivided into twelve sections, you can see the intermediary hues linking the primaries and secondaries, such as blue-purple or yellow-green.

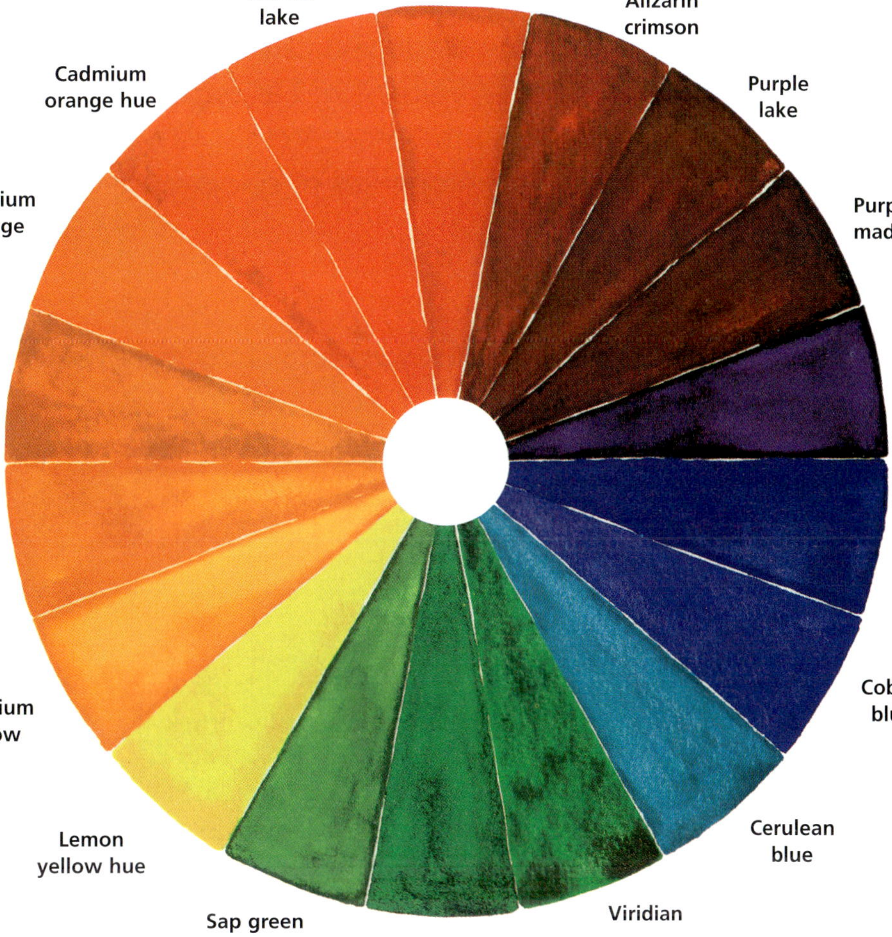

named paint color that seems to you to represent a pure value. You will then find, as you mix them to form the secondaries, that clean mixtures are hard to obtain. Most commonly, you will get a fairly acceptable, or in some cases rather dull orange and green, but the purple will appear brown.

Paint colors generally have a slight bias toward another color and pigments do not all have the same tinting strength. In a 50-50 mixture of cadmium red and cadmium yellow, for example, the red predominates and you obtain a red-orange. You only acquire this kind of knowledge through experience of your paints, but you can learn to predict what kind of mixture you will obtain by considering the character of individual paint colors, and in this respect the color wheel is helpful. You can see, for example, that cadmium red tends toward the red-orange section of the wheel, whereas alizarin crimson is slightly blue and relates to the red-purple section.

Once you begin to look at colors in that way, you can also make use of their relationships as defined by their position on the color wheel. Color blocks running in sequence around the wheel form direct links from one to another – these are related, or analogous colors. Colors that lie exactly or almost opposite each other on the wheel are distinctly unlike – these crosswise relationships are called complementary. Those properties have implications for the ways you juxtapose or oppose particular colors in your painting. We must also realize that color is modified by light. It often happens, for example, that traveling along a country lane, we see a scene that arouses our interest. Returning with a sketchbook and paints a few days later, how disappointing it is to find that same scene transformed, no longer as interesting as it was before. What happens is that our attention is drawn by the way that things appear under certain conditions of light at a particular time of day. We forget that appearances are continually changing.

Tone and Hue

When you lay out a range of colors on your palette you can identify the ways in which they are distinct from each other, both as different colors – red as opposed to blue, say – and, in many cases, that one is lighter or darker than the other. In this way, you are immediately dealing with hue and tone, the fundamental properties of colors.

THE SPECTRUM

An object that reflects all the colored rays of the spectrum appears as white light; an object that absorbs them all appears black. When we talk of light being "absorbed," we are really saying that it is lost. When rays of light are not absorbed, by an object such as a flint wall, for example, they are reflected in the direction from which they came. The term "refracted" light refers to the phenomenon of light passing through a transparent, or partly transparent body: the light is directed, or "refracted."

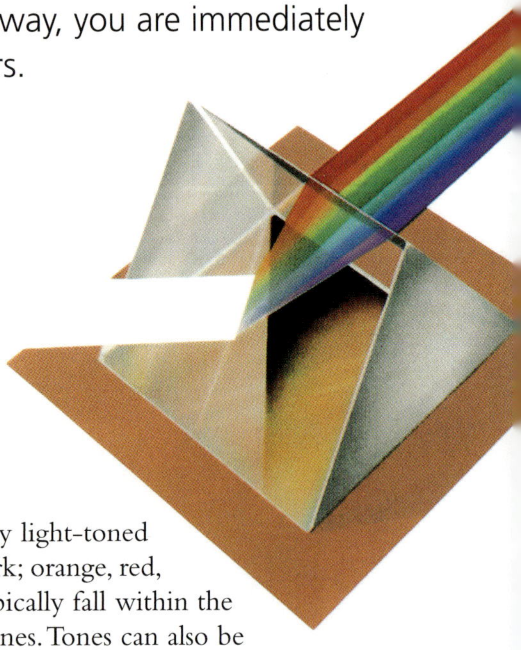

'White light,' or uncolored light, is made up of the seven colors of the spectrum. The colors are separated when filtered through a prism.

TONE AND HUE

The basic form of the color wheel, as shown on page 41, theoretically consists only of pure hues, and their descriptions on the wheel do not exactly correspond to the names of paint colors or to the names we use to describe the colors of materials and objects. Magenta and turquoise, for example, do not appear as such on the color wheel; but they correspond to red-purple and blue-green, that do appear.

Tone refers to their lightness and darkness of colors and it relates to hues in two ways. A hue has inherent tone: yellow is a naturally light-toned color; purple is dark; orange, red, blue, and green typically fall within the range of middle tones. Tones can also be seen as the range of light/dark values that a particular hue can take on, for instance if you mixed blue with variable amounts of white or black you will make a run of blue tones from dark to light. This tonal range does not feature at all on a basic six-color or twelve-color wheel.

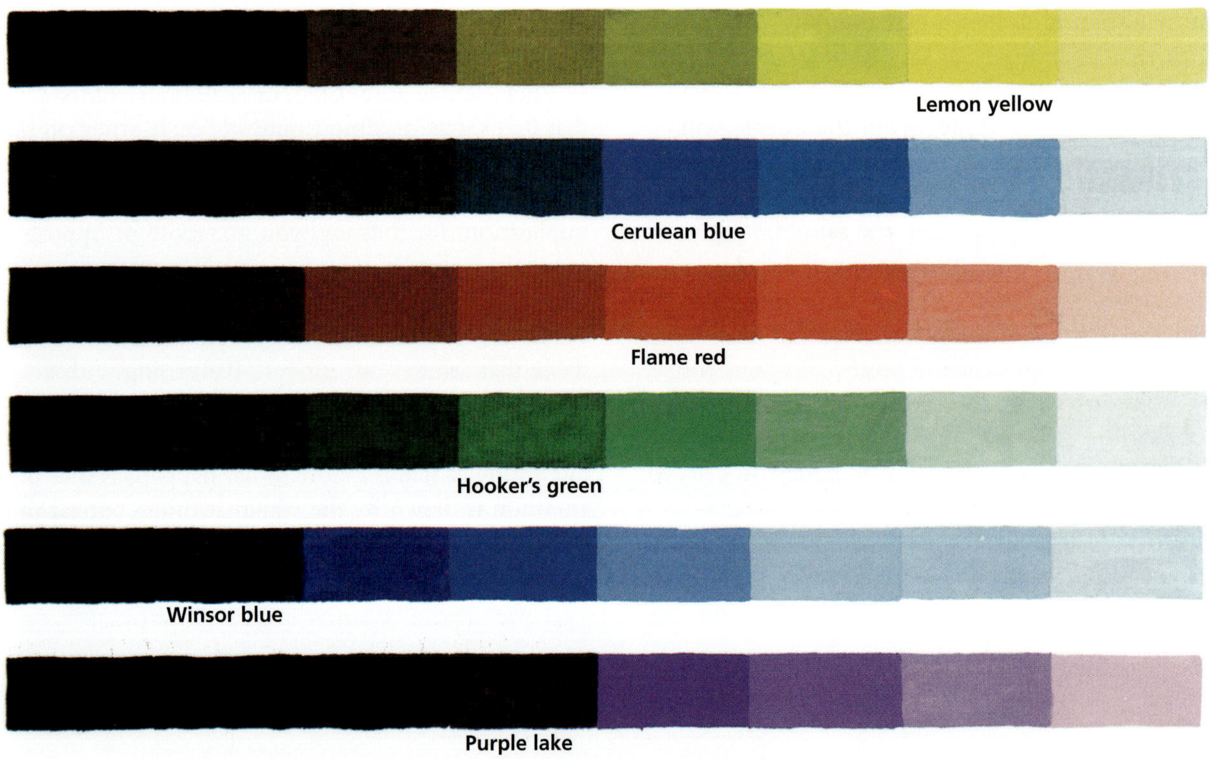

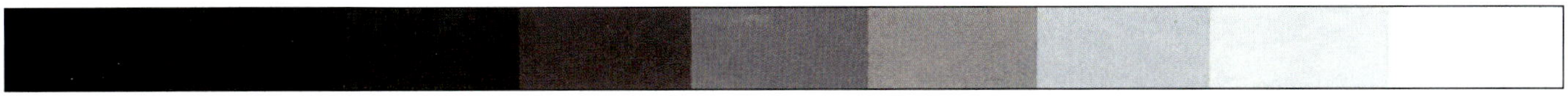

The stepped bands of color, left, show equivalent primary and secondary hues selected from tube colors in a basic tonal range made by mixing the color with black or white. The natural tone of the color means that the pure hue appears at a different position on the scale in each case.

COLOR INTENSITY

The third basic property of colors is described by the terms chroma, saturation, or intensity. All these words mean the same thing, and refer to a color's strength and brilliance, that is, its degree of colorfulness. Mixing colors reduces their intensity; a mixed color rarely appears as intense as either of its components. Intensity is also devalued by mixing with the purely neutral "colors," black, white, and gray. In practical terms, you see this instantly when you mix black with yellow, that turns it into an olivey green, or with brilliant red, when red-brown is the result.

In this context, the word intensity, is used somewhat differently from the way we might apply it to our own sensations of color. You can perceive a vivid pink or pale blue as being very intense in the way it works within a painting in relation to other colors, but technically the hue is reduced in saturation. This is one of the more difficult aspects of color theory to grasp as a principle, but in practise it doesn't really matter; you can make judgements by your visual appreciation of a color's relative intensity and your common sense. You know, for example, that when you mix gray into a bright hue, the color is devalued.

matching tones

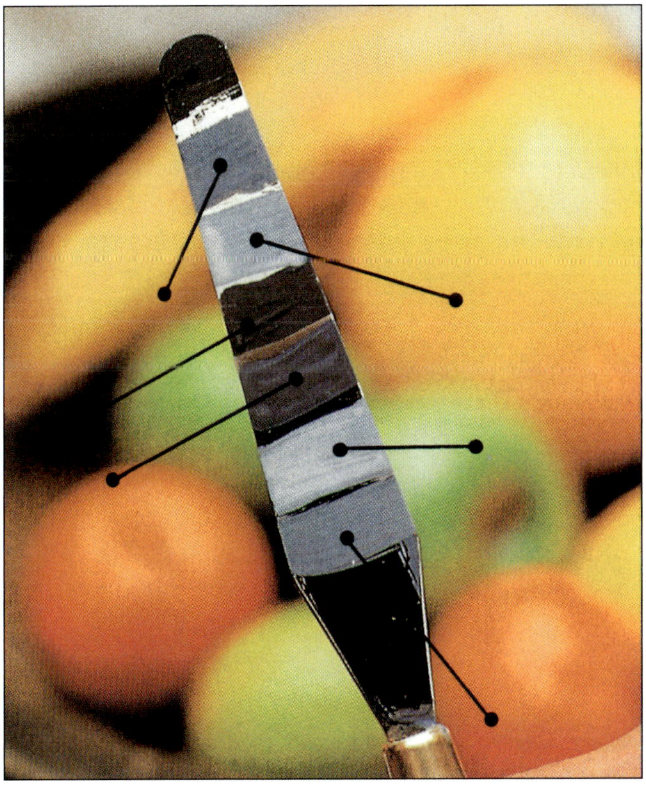

Matched to the gray-scale, seen at the top of the page, you can see how the colors correspond to dark, medium, and light tones. A useful way of estimating tones in your painting is to paint a gray-scale on a palette knife and hold it up to your subject (above).

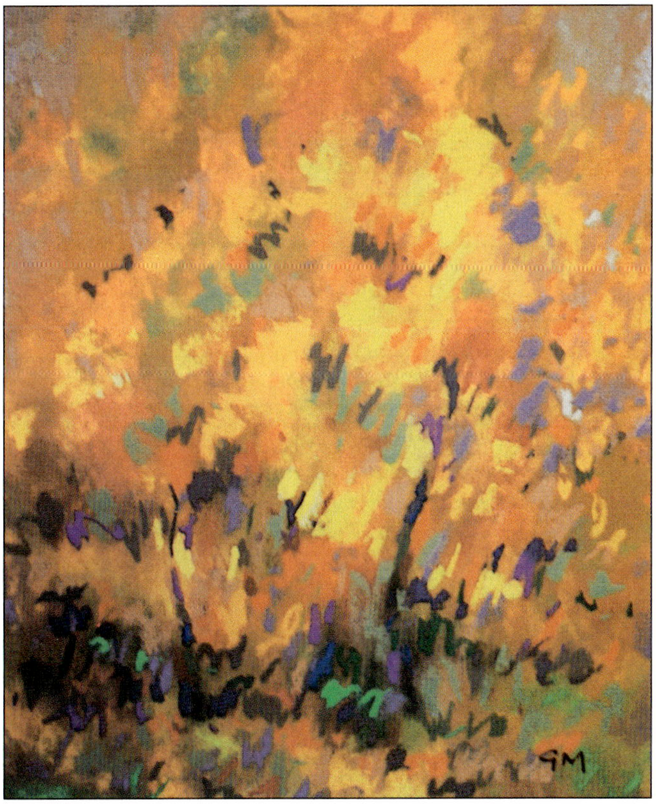

AUTUMN GLOW by Geoff Marsters (pastel)

This very direct, joyous use of color makes the most of pure hues, but there are also delicate variations both in the character of individual hues and the tonal values of the colors. Pastel provides instant, vivid color impact, but also a rich complexity of descriptive marks.

Mixing Primary Colors

To test the principle that you can mix a range of colors from primary hues – red, yellow, and blue – two artists start with a different set of acrylic "primaries." Elisabeth Harden uses acrylic paint in crimson, ultramarine, and lemon yellow. Opposite, Judy Martin works with cadmium red, cadmium yellow, and cobalt blue acrylic.

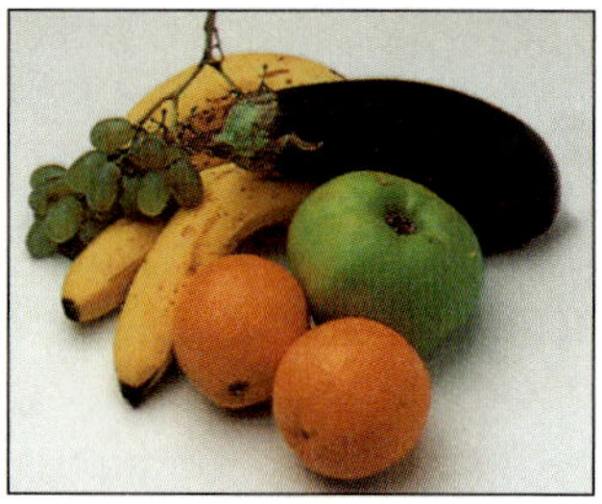

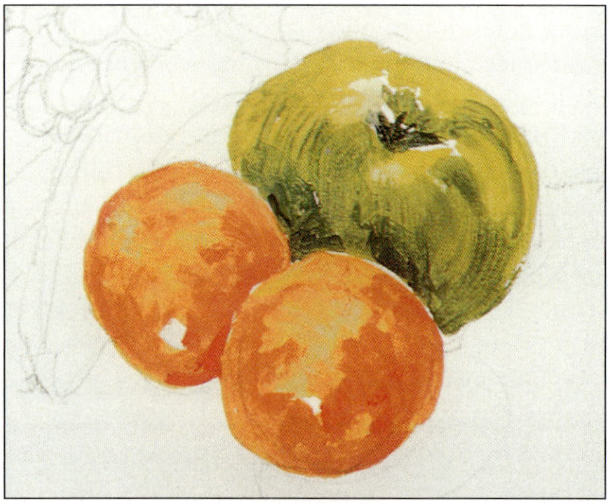

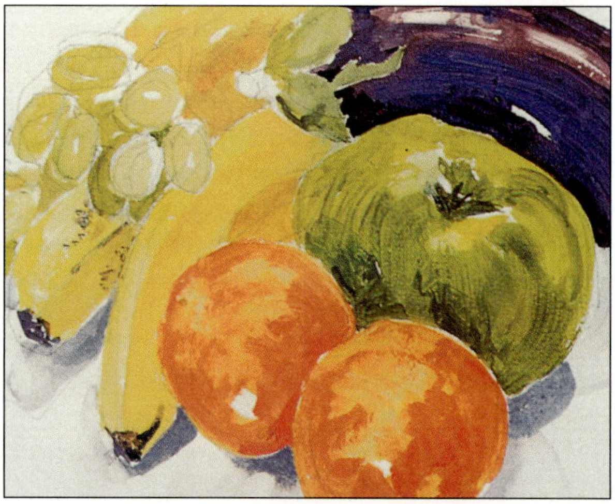

1 & 2 Lemon yellow and ultramarine provide a good, sharp green for the apple, but the oranges mixed from lemon yellow and crimson are soft and lack intensity. Crimson and ultramarine form rich shades of red-purple and blue-purple for the eggplant, and are also used thinly for shadows. The lemon yellow has to be tinted with red to achieve the banana color.

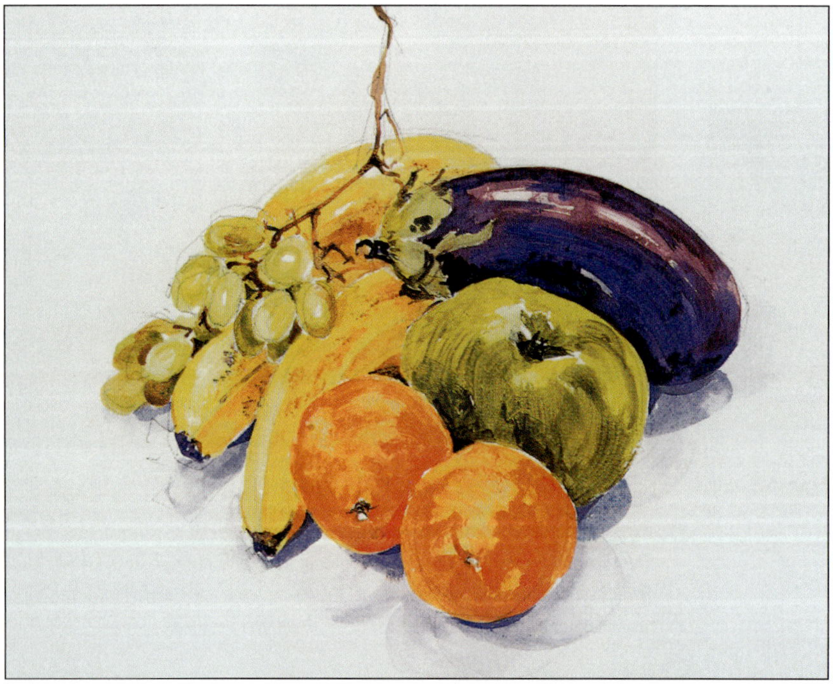

3 With all the local colors in place, the artist works on the mixed colors and tonal variations that enhance the color interactions. She has put a stronger red-orange on the shaded parts of the oranges so they react more strongly against the apple greens. The warm browns representing ripe patches on the banana skin and the grape stems are mixed from all three primaries, with more red and yellow than blue. The ultramarine content is increased to achieve the darker shading. White highlights have been made by leaving bare paper to show through the colors.

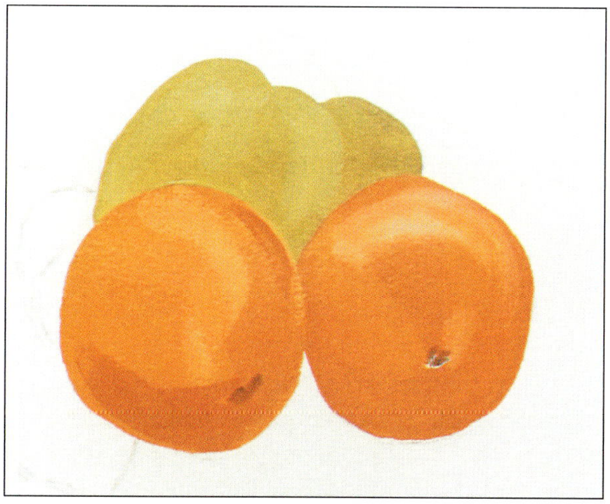

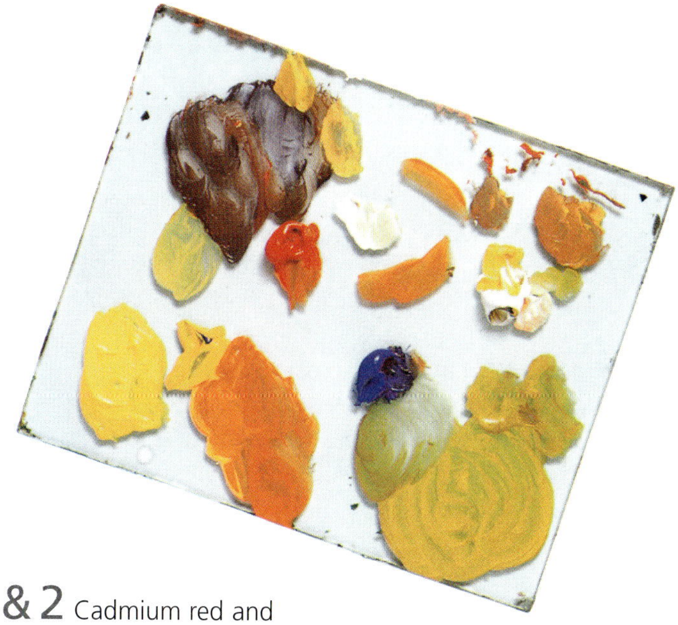

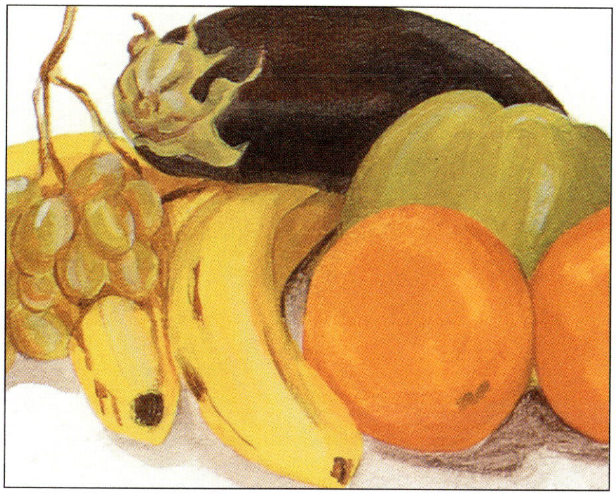

1 & 2 Cadmium red and cadmium yellow are both warm colors that mix strong, "hot" oranges. By comparison, the apple green mixed from cobalt blue and cadmium yellow is relatively dull, because cobalt is cool and neutralizes the yellow. Similarly, the combination of cobalt and cadmium red is muted – the purple mixed for the eggplant is brownish, but the color is useful for the grape stems and patches on the bananas. The banana yellow is almost pure cadmium yellow, just tinged with red.

3 Even by varying the proportions in the mix, it is impossible to produce a "true" purple from cadmium red and cobalt blue. The artist uses a contrast of brown-red and blue-brown to suggest the sheen on the eggplant. The greens remain rather dull, which suits the natural colors of the grapes but is less successful for the apple. Intensifying the red-oranges in the foreground helps to "lift" the greens, and the apple green is given more yellow to brighten it. Because the initial colors were applied solidly with opaque paint, the artist has to introduce white to overlay highlights and pale tones.

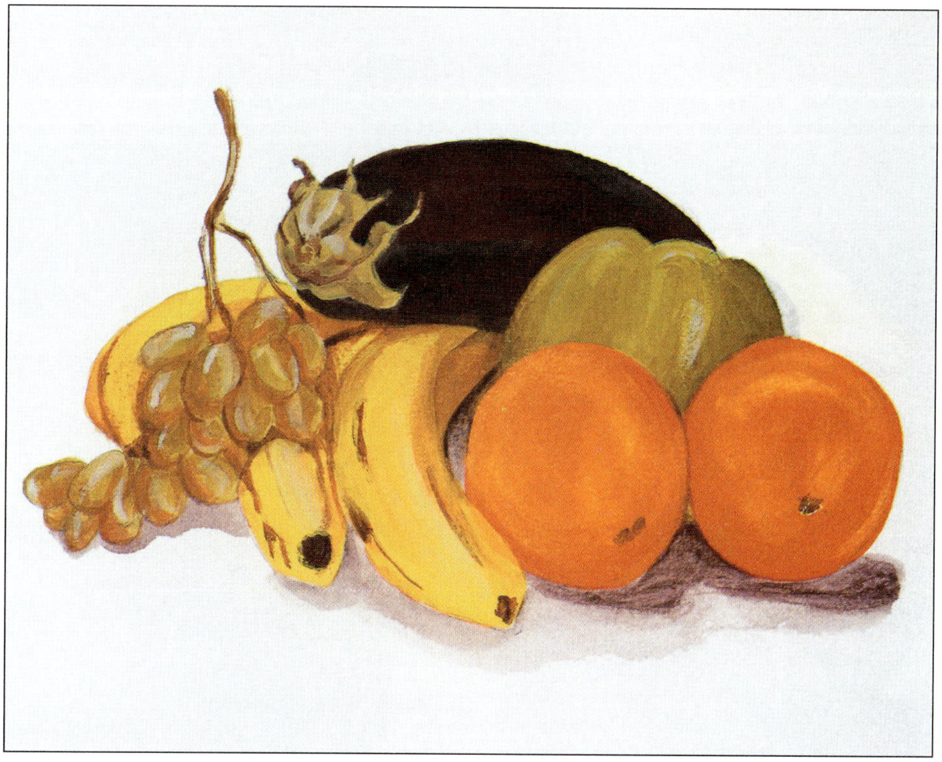

Related Colors

Using the color wheel, you can trace direct relationships between colors and work out how these might correspond to the tube colors and mixes on your palette. There is a basic harmony between related colors due to a shared component.

Colors adjacent to one another on the wheel in any given section form a related sequence. The closest relationships are between a primary color and the secondary that contains that primary, through the intermediary hue (or hues) created by mixing the two – such as blue, blue-green, green. Another kind of related sequence occurs between a primary or secondary and the intermediaries on either side – blue-purple, blue, blue-green; or blue-green, green, yellow-green.

The wheel also demonstrates direct links between primaries – such as in the simple sequence, red, purple, blue; or the more subtly extended range through red, red-purple, purple, blue-purple, blue.

When you employ a scheme of related colors in a painting, it tends to produce a harmonious effect. Although any pair of primaries makes quite a strong contrast because all the three primaries are unlike, once you add the secondary and intermediary links, the contrast between the primaries is softened. The harmony of a primary or secondary and the intermediary colors immediately adjacent is more obvious, since all contain the same hue in varying proportion and intensity.

The underlying harmony survives variations of hue and tone provided the color scheme is broadly integrated. If you select a related color sequence but isolate individual components in different areas of the painting, you may be breaking some of the links so that the different character of the unlike colors becomes more apparent. But it needs only touches of one color in another or a subtle distribution of color accents to form the connections.

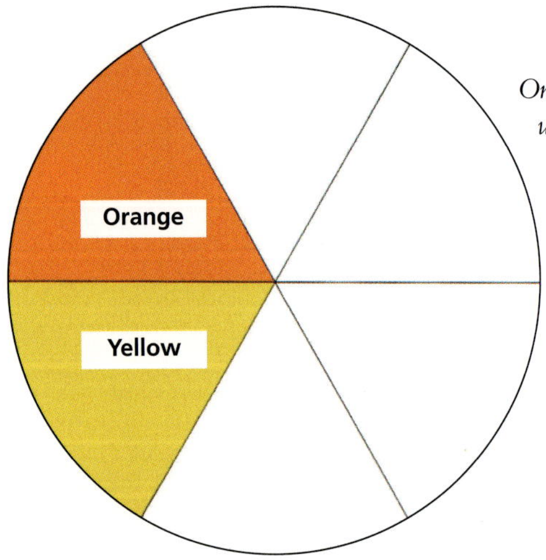

On the six-color wheel, related colors are one primary and the secondary color of which it is a component, such as yellow and orange.

The secondary hues link the unrelated primaries. The red, purple, blue sequence makes a color harmony.

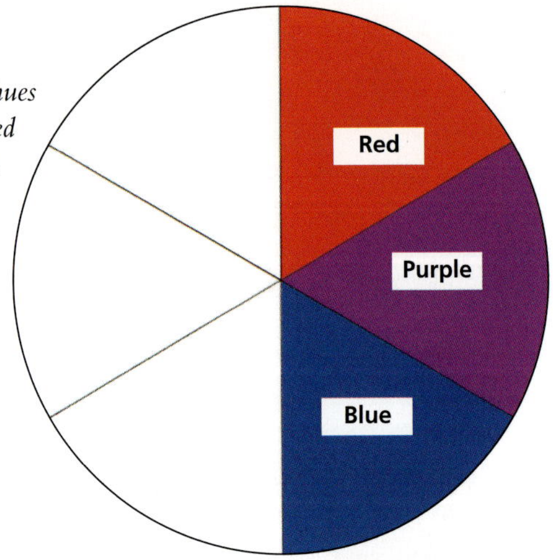

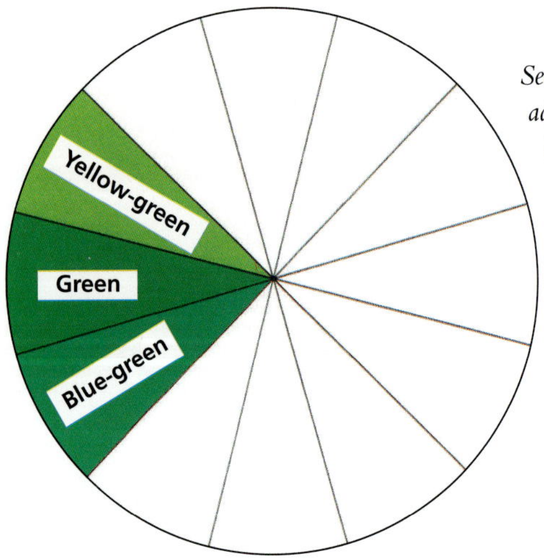

Secondary and adjacent intermediate hues form, in effect, shades of one color, as with green linking yellow-green and blue-green.

A more subtle and complex sequence is obtained by going from one primary to the next through all the intermediate and secondary hues.

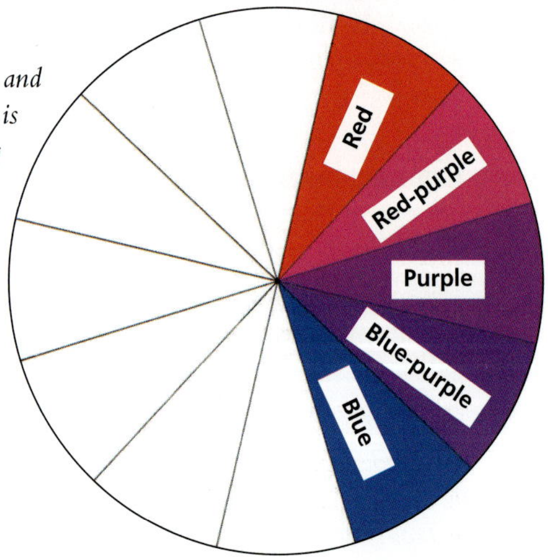

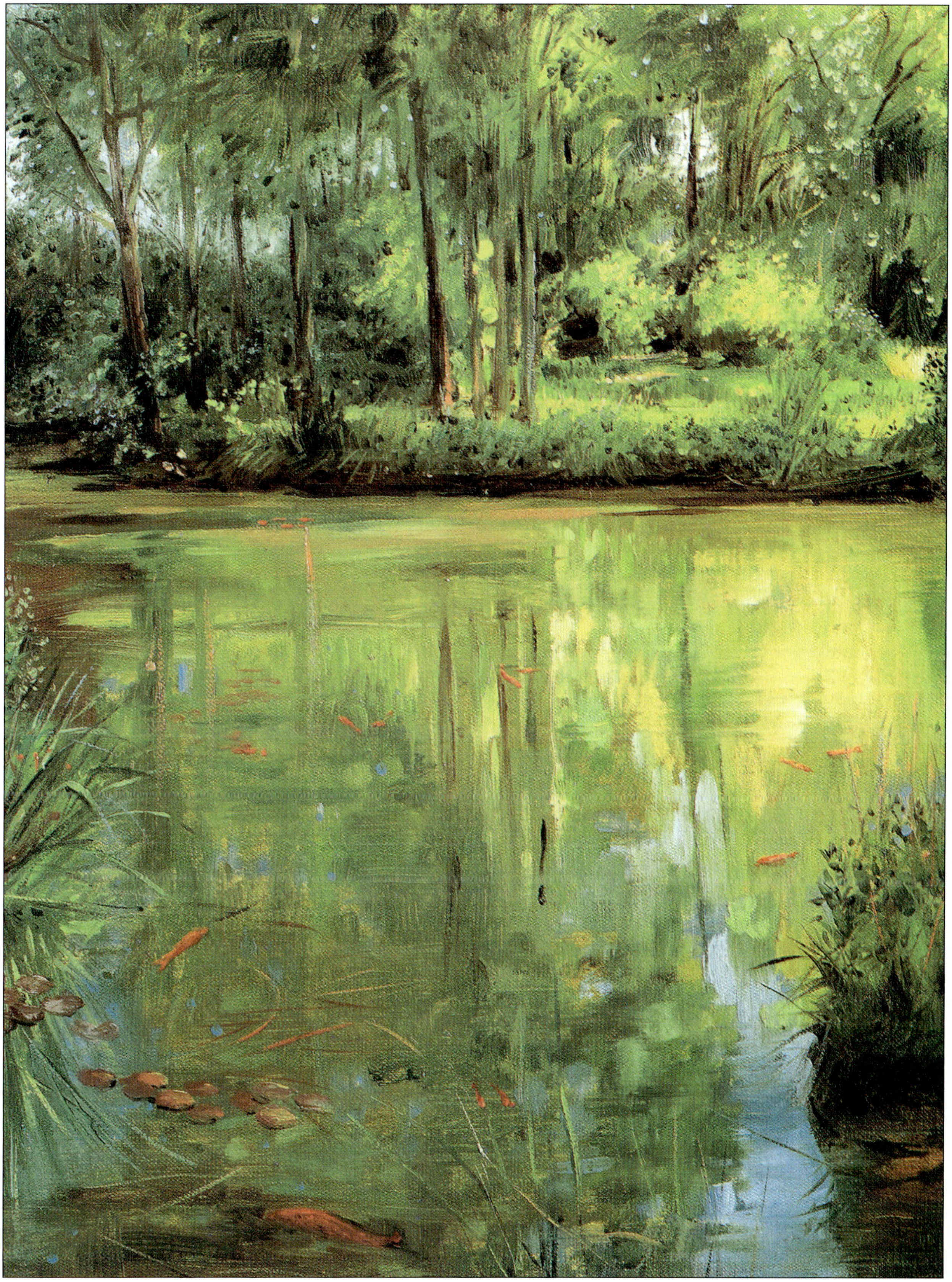

THE FISH POOL by Timothy Easton (oil)

Landscapes almost invariably have a natural harmony, that can often be compared to a sequence of related colors. However, the color nuances in nature are subtle and unpredictable. In this painting the greens are primarily shades of yellow-green, which gives them some contrast with the cold, pale blue, but there is also a unity of tone that anchors the colors in the foreground.

Color and Light

Color can be a very complex subject indeed – whole books have been written on color theory. Such theory is beyond the scope of this book, and in any case would be more likely to be a hindrance than a help to an inexperienced painter, but there are some basic guidelines which will help you to make a picture work, and there are also some terms which you will need to understand.

Color has two main qualities, tone and intensity, the first being the darkness or lightness of a particular color and the second being its brightness. If you take a black-and-white photograph of a landscape composed entirely of greens, you will see that some appear darker than others proving that a single color can have dark tones and light tones. In the same landscape, some of the greens will be brighter and more vibrant than others – in other words, more intense.

Colors that are opposite one another on the color wheel, such as red and green, yellow and violet, are called complementary colors. These can be used in a deliberate way to balance and "spark off" one another; for example, a small area of bright red in a landscape could be used to enhance and intensify a large expanse of green. The Op Art painters of the 1960s used complementary colors in a highly intellectual way: by juxtaposing complementaries of the same hue and tone they created restless, "jumping" effects.

Colors are basically either "warm" or "cool," and the warm ones will tend to "advance," or push themselves to the front of a painting, while the cool ones will recede. In general, the warm colors are the reds, yellows, bright yellow-greens, and oranges, while cool ones are the blues and colors with blue in them, such as blue-green. Some blues, however, are warmer than others, and some reds are cooler than others. You can see this by placing ultramarine and cerulean blue (both quite warm) next to Prussian or Antwerp blue (both cool), and alizarin crimson (cool) next to cadmium red (warm).

There is no color without light, and the direction, quality, and intensity of light constantly changes and modifies colors. This fact became almost an obsession with the Impressionist painter Claude Monet; he painted many studies of the same subject – a group of haystacks – at different times of the day in order to understand and analyze these changes. You can see the effects very easily for yourself if you look at any scene – the view from a window or a corner of the garden

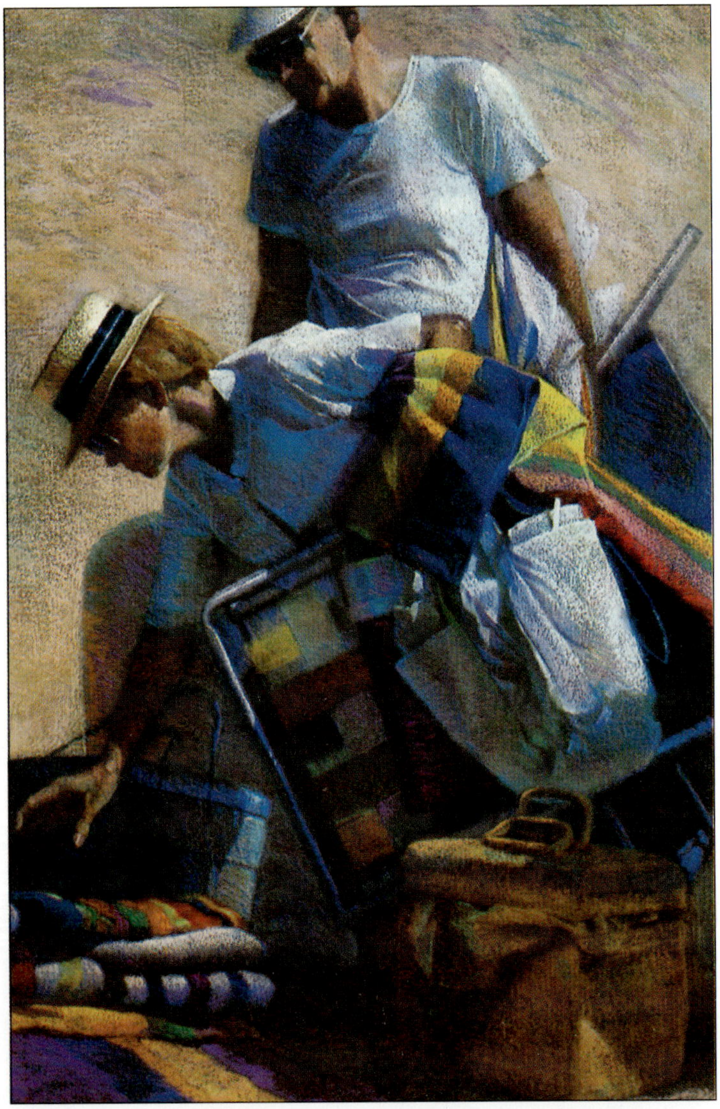

HEADING HOME by Sally Strand (pastel)

Near-complementaries – blues and yellows – are woven throughout this composition, creating a color scheme that is lively yet harmonious. Note how the most intense complementaries are placed near the center of the painting, providing a focal point around which the rest of the composition revolves.

– first on a cloudy morning and then in low evening sunlight. In the evening everything will suddenly become golden and a brick wall that might have appeared a drab brown in the morning may now be a bright hue of orange or pink.

Light is vital to a painting, whether a landscape or a still life or portrait study, and the way it falls defines the shape of objects and determines their color. Both photographers and painters of landscape know that the high midday sun is their enemy, as it creates dense patches of shadow and drains the landscape of color and definition. A portrait or still life can also look flat, dead and colorless if lit directly from above, while a side light can suddenly bring it to life, creating exciting shadow areas of purple or green and vivid, sparkling highlights.

LIGHT AND LOCAL COLOR

Of all the visual influences acting on the way we perceive the colors in any subject, local color is perhaps the element easiest to identify as the reference point from which to begin a color analysis.

Local color is the actual color of any object irrespective of lighting conditions or surrounding colors. It is the basic characteristic that helps to distinguish the components of a subject in simple terms, for example, one object is red, one blue, another green. But more qualification is needed if the description is to be useful, and the words you use to describe a color more exactly may relate to basic attributes of hue and tone – orange-red, brilliant red, dark red; or they may be associative words – tomato red, brick red.

If you could see an object under pure white light, falling evenly from all directions, you would see the object's local color almost completely unmodified. But you would have little sense of three-dimensional form and depth, as these elements are normally modeled by their relationship to the angle and intensity of light. These pictures show how local color becomes gradually less dominant in the simple still life as the quality of the lighting is changed.

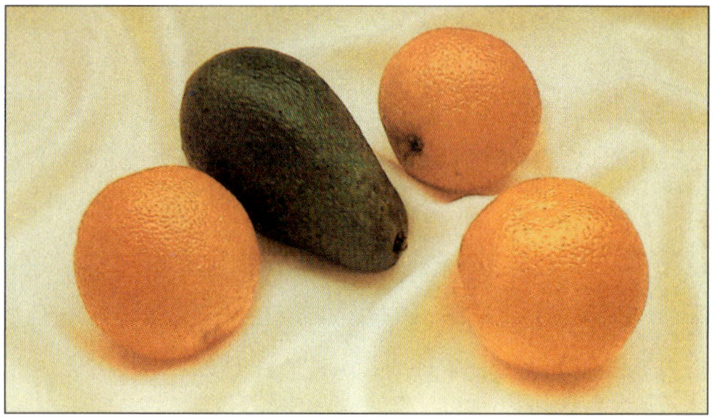

You get the strongest impression of local color under flat, clear lighting that shades forms and surfaces minimally. This picture shows very intensely the individual color qualities of the objects.

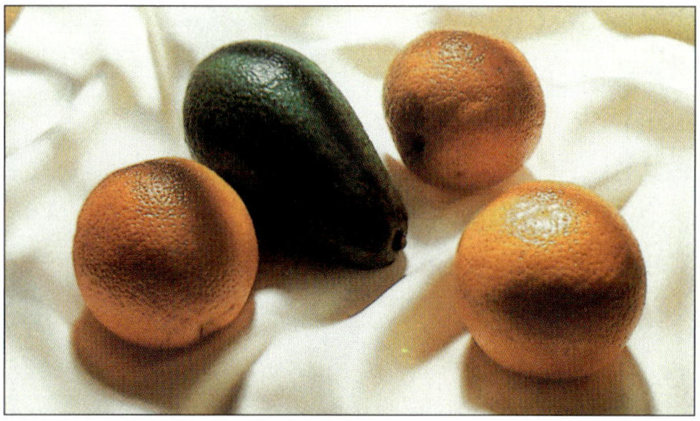

In most settings, indoors or out, the continuity of local color is disrupted by the way light from a particular source models three-dimensional forms, and by reflected colors, as where the orange on the left reflects brightly on the avocado.

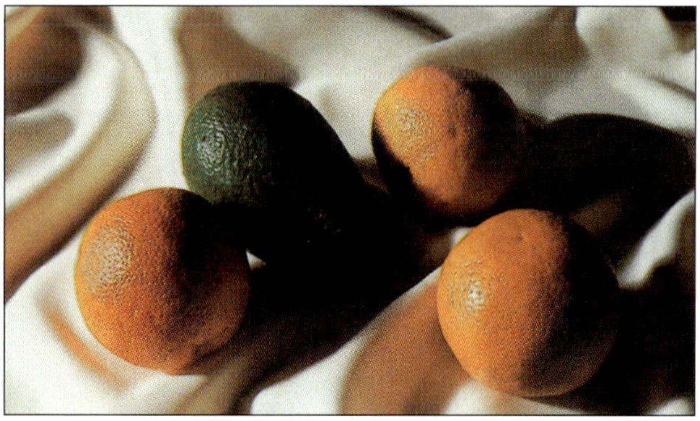

Angled lighting creates a dramatic pattern of shadow that knocks out much of the local color. Each object is heavily shaded and cast shadows also cut across the shapes, darkening and neutralizing the colors.

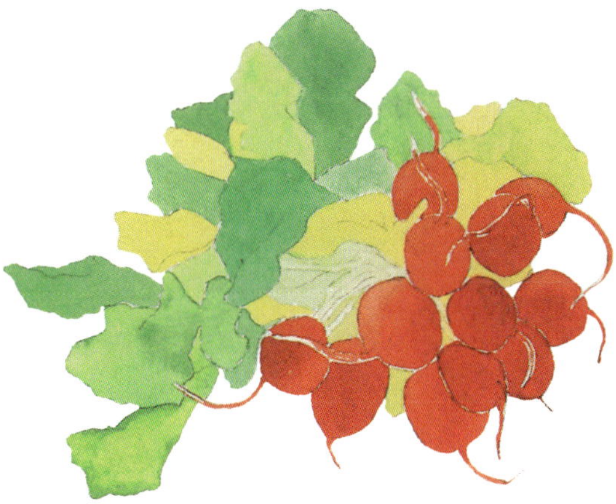

Trying to define exact qualities of local color is a good exercise in sharpening your color perception. It provides, in effect, a basic plan of your subject and also requires you to give some precision to the component shapes, that can suggest space and form even though the color variations are simplified.

Color Harmony

A scale of related colors can be relatively narrow – say, blue and purple only – or it can pass through three adjacent segments on the color wheel. In this flower painting by Elisabeth Harden the blues are offset by greens on one side and blue-purples on the other. Your approach to color mixing will depend on the range of your paint stock. Here the artist selects watercolors in several key hues; this enables her to achieve very subtle variations. Alternatively, you could base your palette on two or three blues, and depend on yellows and crimson, or rose for mixing the related colors.

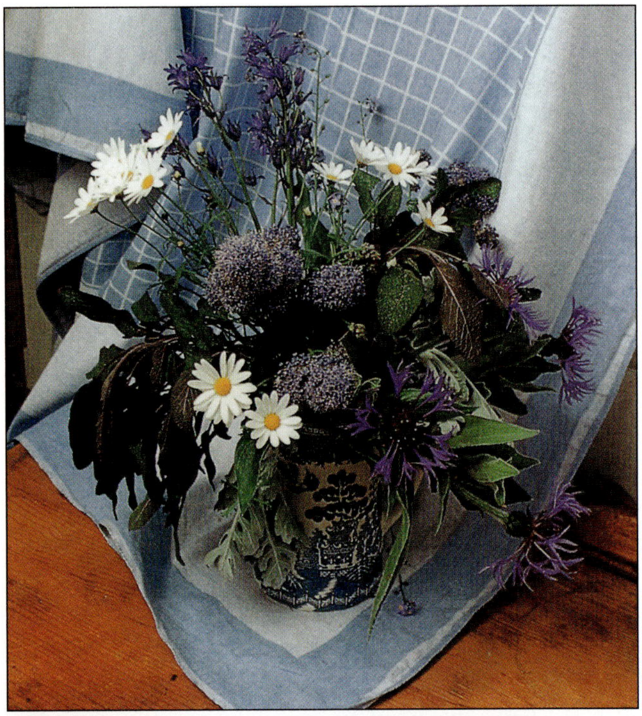

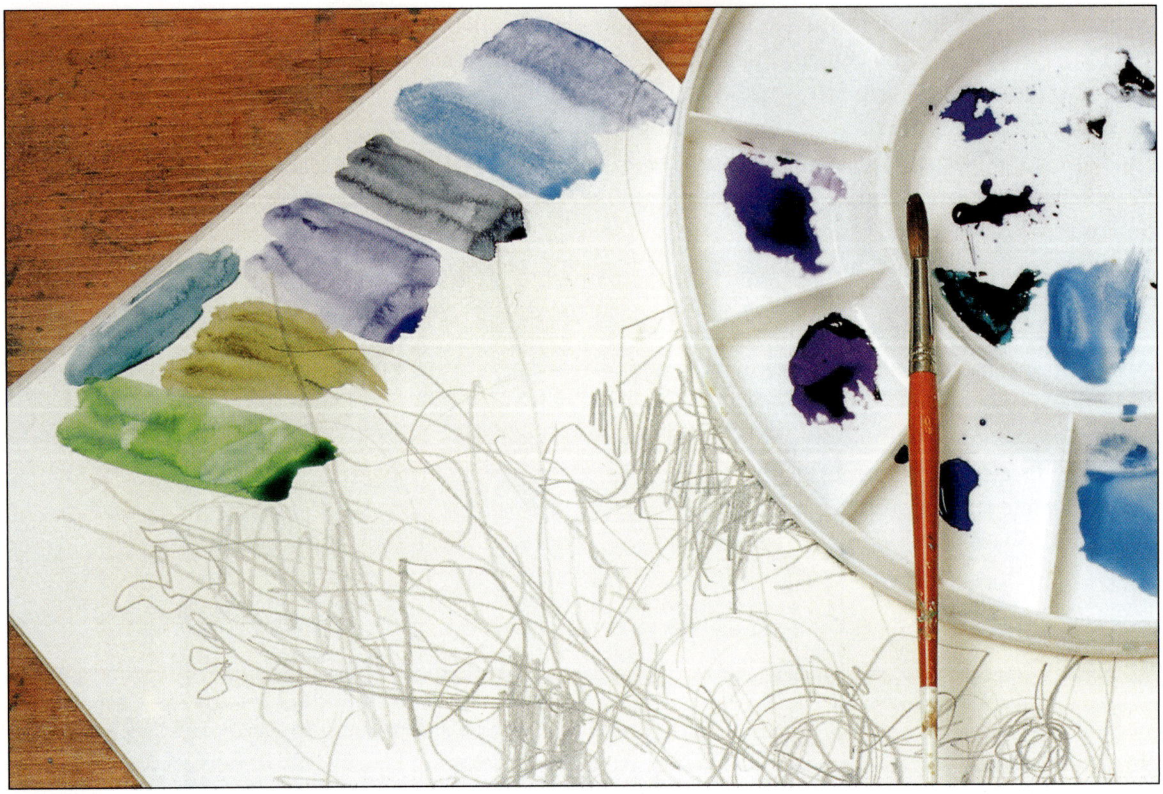

SELECTING THE PALETTE

Building up a watercolor can be a delicate operation, and the artist takes time to study the subject before starting work on the full painting. She makes a rough pencil sketch of the composition (above) and tests the colors she intends to use. Her color range is small but includes different hues from each of her three main color families – ultramarine and cerulean blue; sap green, olive green and Prussian green; alizarin violet and glowing violet.

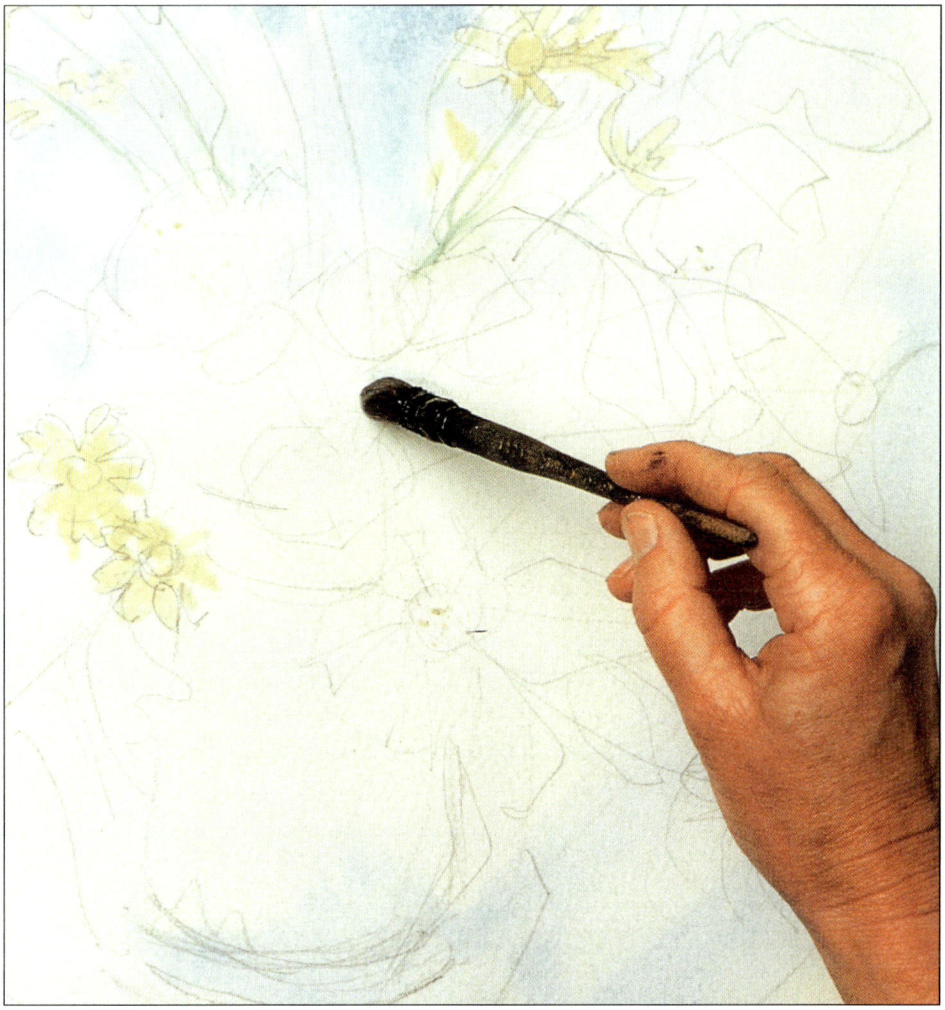

1 The artist begins with a light pencil sketch mapping the main elements of the composition. To "reserve" clean paper in the areas that are to remain white, she applies masking fluid before starting the color work (the dried masking fluid appears yellow in these pictures). This enables her to brush in the color washes very loosely and freely, beginning with a broad patch of cerulean blue.

2 The softly spiky forms of the deep blue flowerheads are suggested by dampening the paper and drawing a fine brush loaded with ultramarine through the dampness so that the color spreads irregularly. This wet-into-wet technique can be controlled by confining the initial damping to small areas of the paper.

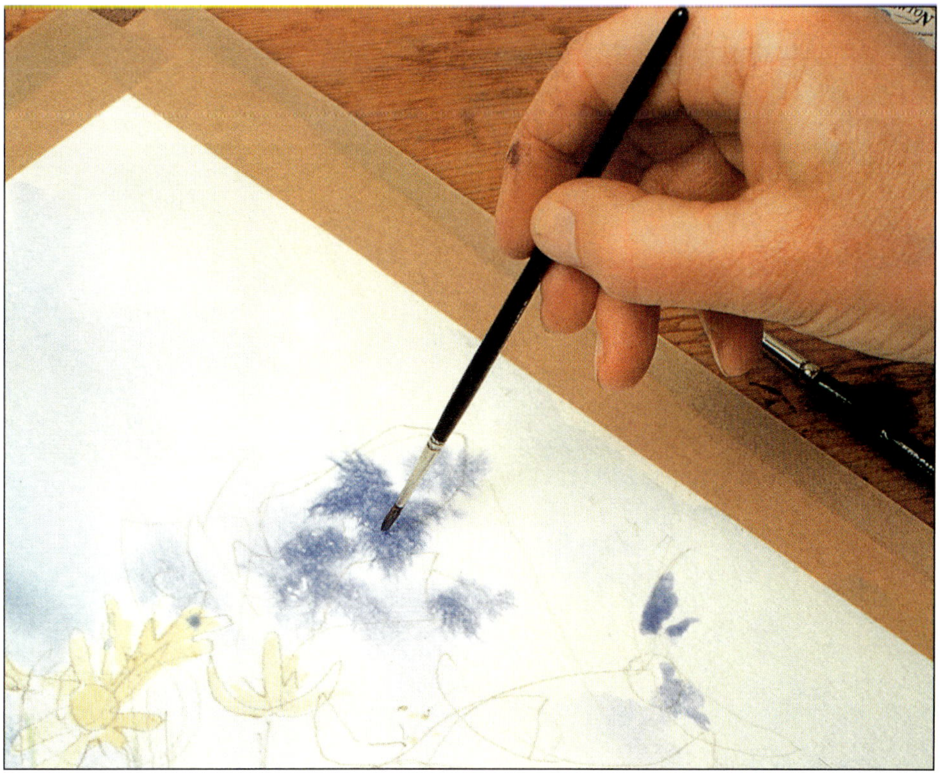

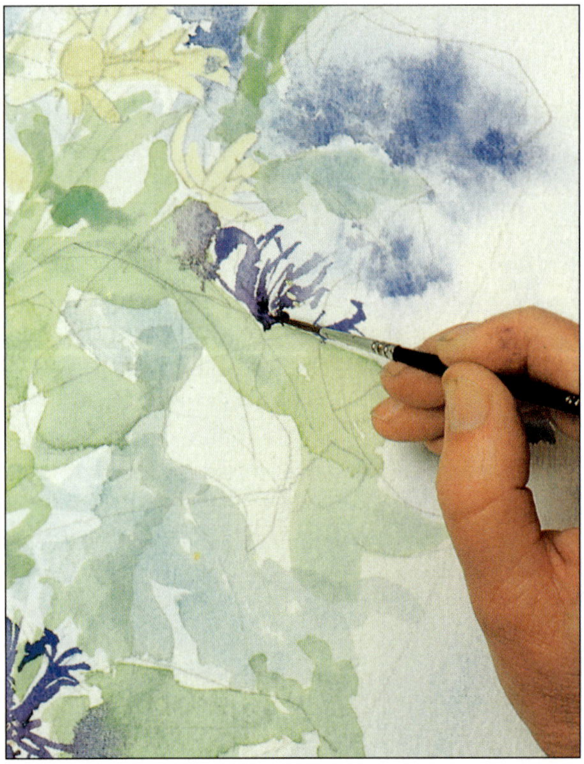

3 All three greens are employed to add patches of color washes representing the leaf shapes. In places a deeper concentration of color settles along the edge of the wash as it dries. Then the artist applies more detailed brush drawing of the flowers in alizarin violet.

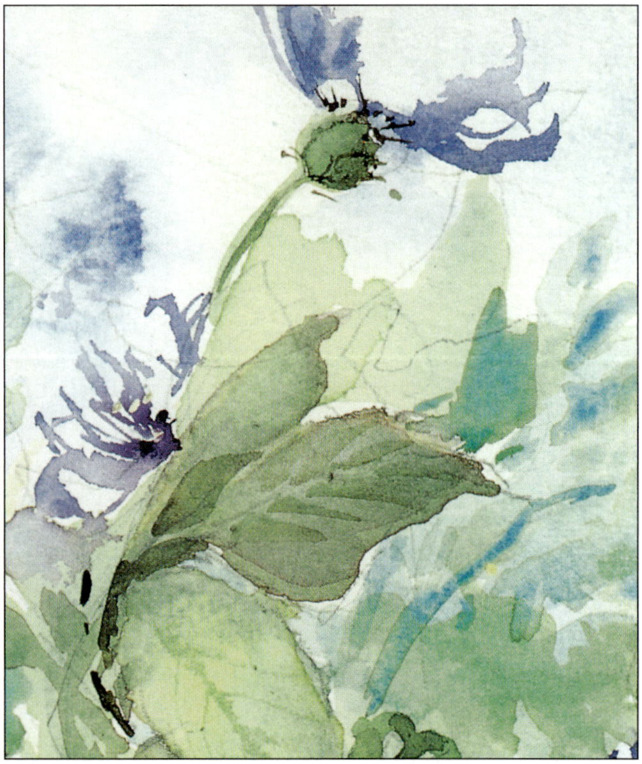

4 The same techniques are combined to build up the strength of the colors and develop the detail of flowers and leaves. By overlaying colors, the artist achieves some subtle mixes, such as the dull greens modified with light washes of violet and ultramarine.

5 The colors are applied at greater intensity to break up the shapes and add depth to the image. Heavy patches of sap green, used straight and neutralized with violet, provide darker tones that model the edges and undersides of the leaves.

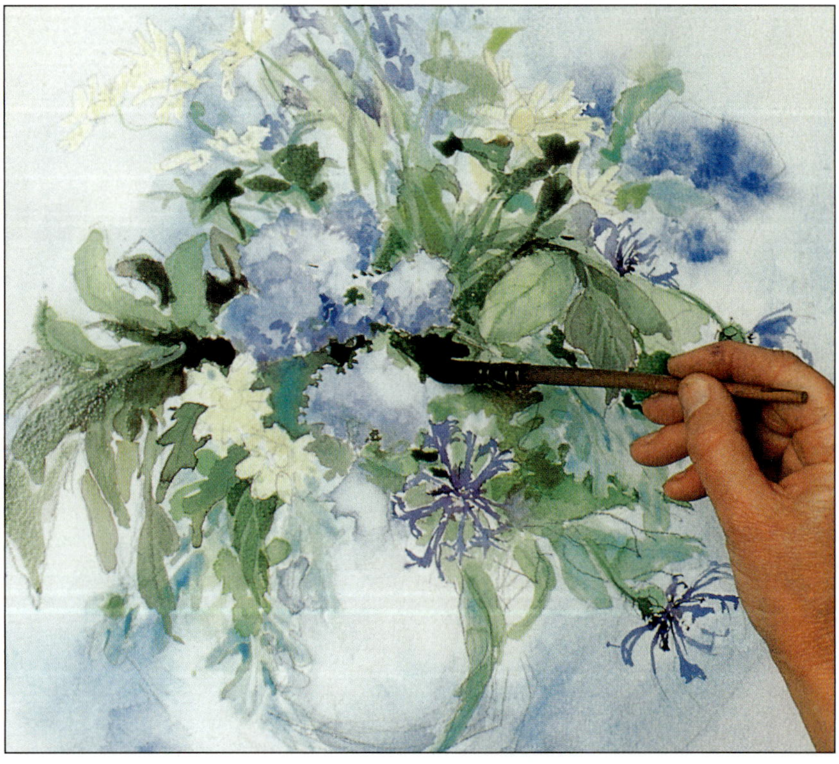

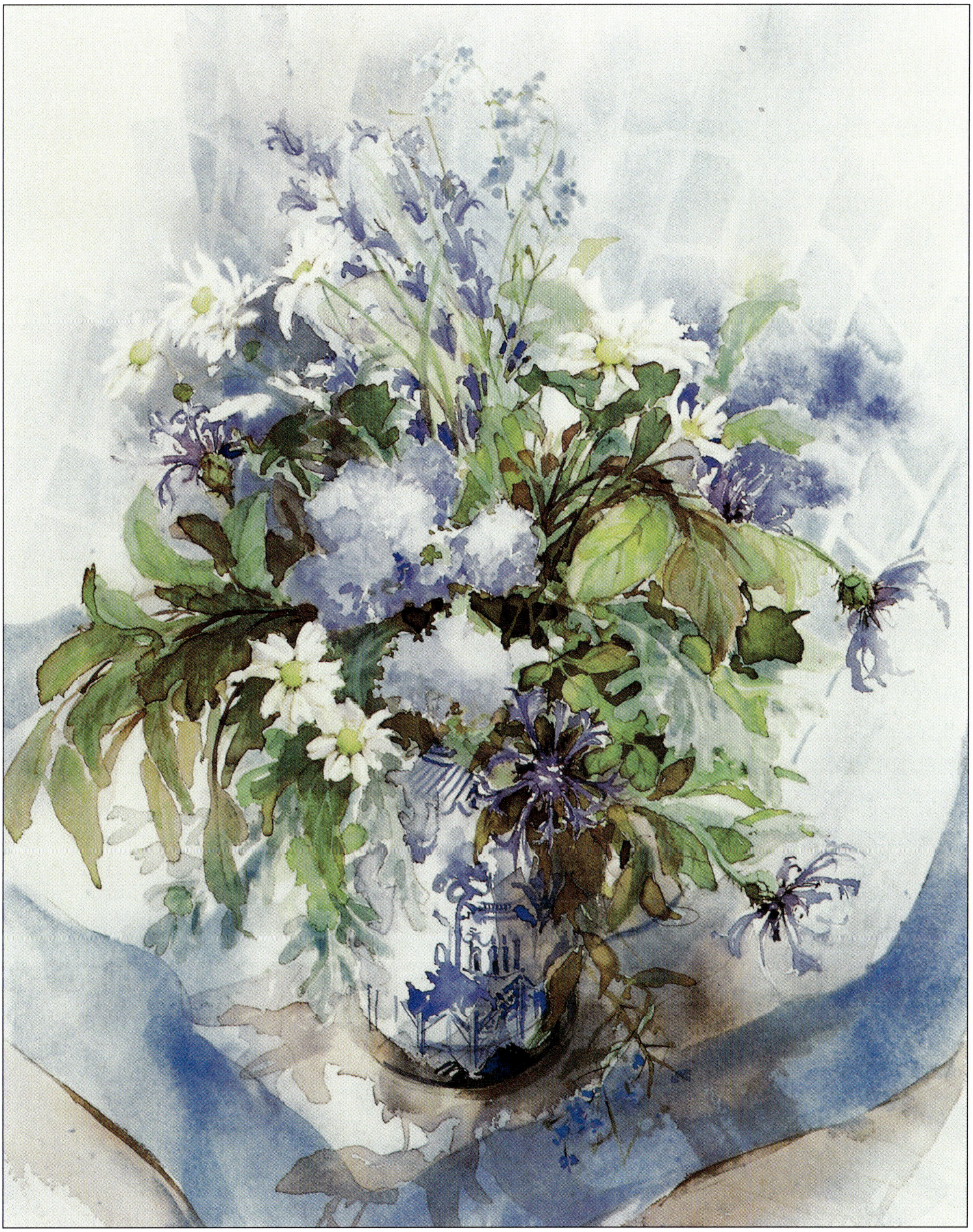

6 Keying the tones from the darker greens, the artist builds up the blues in the same way on the flowers, then adds the detail of the pattern on the jug. The foreground is made much more positive, with the broad band of ultramarine defining the edge of the tablecloth, and the slightly grayed purple cast shadows echoing the irregular flower shapes. With the masking fluid rubbed off, the finishing touch is some light shading on the white petals.

Neutral Colors

There are different degrees of neutrality. Mixed hues can become neutralized, but even grayed and muddied colors are not as purely neutral as the grays formed by black-and-white mixes. Understanding how to manipulate the "colorful" properties of neutrals can help to give your paintings impact.

Black, gray, and white have not yet entered the color spectrum as we have defined it on the color wheel. They have appeared as an "extra" element in terms of the tonal scale relating to the values of pure hues. The idea of using the color wheel as the basis of mixing all colors would theoretically include black and gray: black should derive from a mixture of all three primary colors, gray from a mix of any given complementary pair. In practise, however, you have seen that mixing unlike colors tends to produce a range of greenish or brownish "neutrals" rather than the kind of gray produced by a mixture of black and white.

White slips the net entirely in this theoretical framework. Although in the spectrum, based on the colors of light, a combination of all colors produces white, this obviously cannot occur with any mixture of pigments, that have physical substance.

Where black, white, and gray have no apparent color bias, they provide a pure tonal scale and a foil for the interaction of hues. In painting, neutral grays (black-and-white mixtures), become subject to the principle of simultaneous contrast once integrated with colors in an image, and may take on "color" by the influence of adjacent hues.

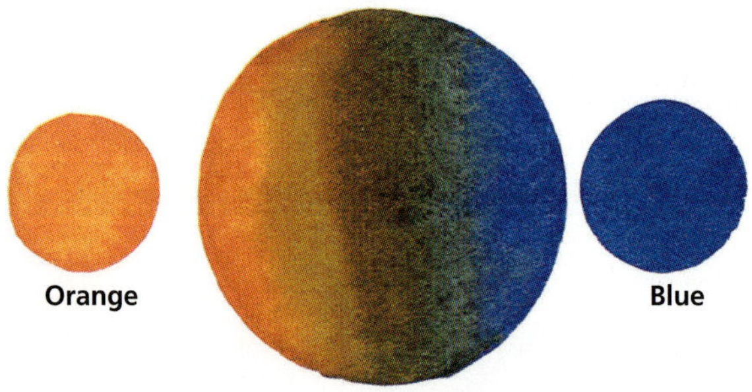

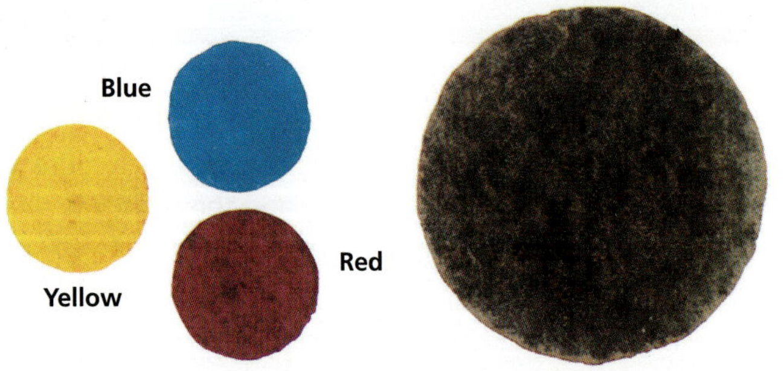

Mixtures of complementary colors produce neutralized hues. In pigments these are rarely pure gray, but the colors are grayish. Mixes of the three primaries naturally do the same, as they form complementary elements.

Common Problems and Solutions

Common problems are put to the experts for practical advice. From tackling difficult subjects to choosing the right method to correct your work, there is a solution to many of the problems that often prevent us from achieving the desired effect in our work.

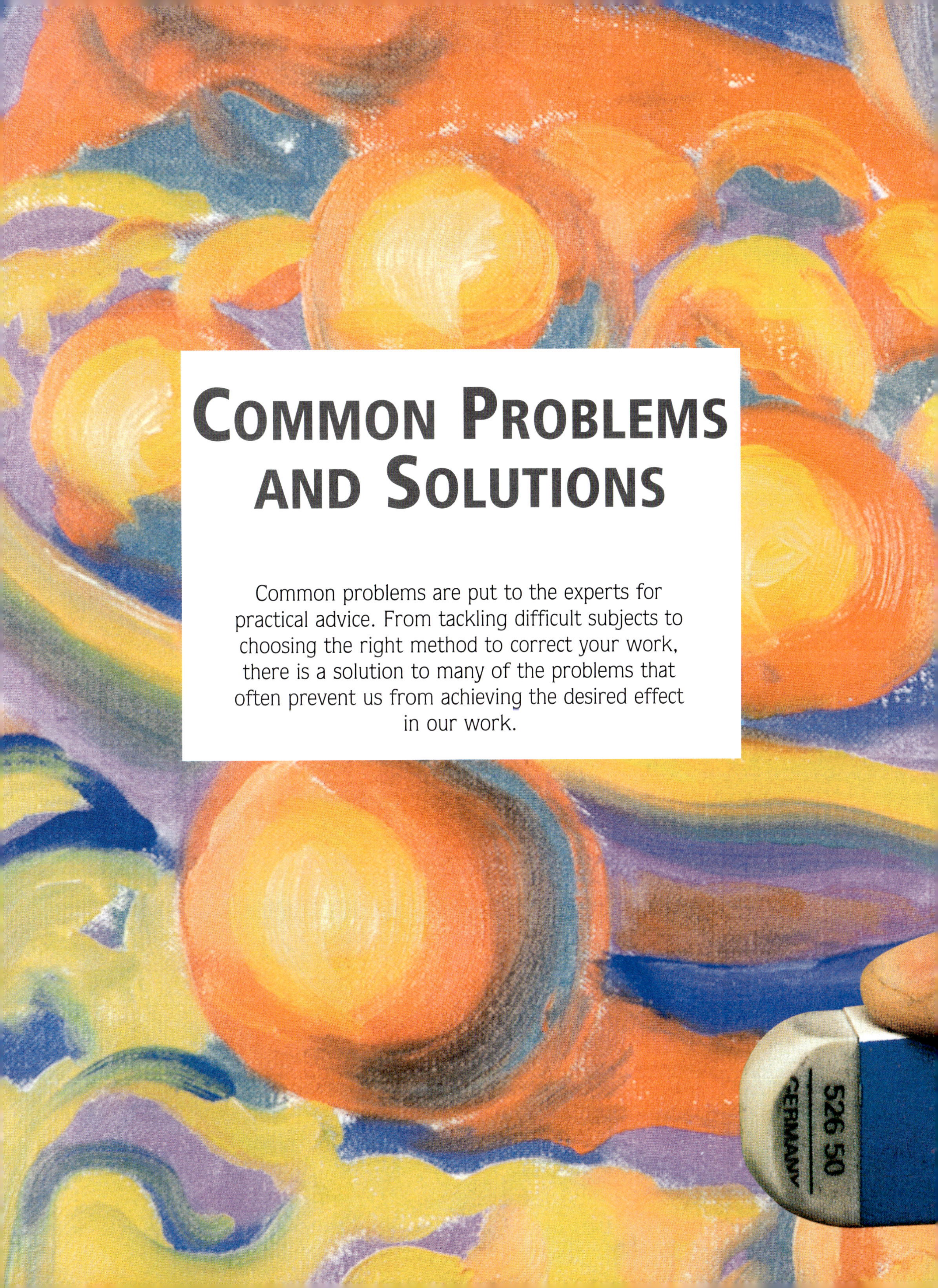

Avoiding Discouragement

If your painting goes wrong at an early stage you are bound to feel depressed and discouraged. Various suggestions are given here that will help you to avoid or overcome the more common problems.

TINTING THE GROUND

Starting to paint on a glaring expanse of white canvas can be quite daunting, but even more important is the fact that a white surface is also "dishonest," as it prevents you from judging the tones and colors correctly. There is very little pure white in nature, as white, like any other color, is always modified by the light or shadow falling on it. Also, no color exists in a particular way except in relation to the colors surrounding it. Thus, if you start a flower painting by putting down a bold brush stroke of pure cadmium red on a white canvas it will almost certainly be wrong, as the red you are seeing is actually given to quality by its relationship to the background, that may be neutral or even dark.

A method often used by artists is to tint the canvas in a neutral color, usually a warm brown or gray, before starting the painting. This can be done either by mixing pigment in with the primer or by putting a wash of oil paint, such as raw umber, heavily diluted with turpentine, over the white ground. Acrylic paint can also be used for this since it dries much faster than oil paint, and you could buy a single tube just for this purpose. But remember that acrylic paint should not be used over an oil ground; oil can be used over acrylic, but acrylic cannot be used over oil.

PREPARATION

Always start with an adequate drawing or underpainting in order to place the main design elements in the way you want them. Even a simple subject such as a bowl of fruit can go very wrong if you fail to judge correctly the size of the fruit in relation to the bowl, or the bowl in relation to the table it is standing on. You may be impatient to start on the real business – the laying on of paint – but it does pay to take your time at this stage, for it will avoid a lot of frustration later.

KEEPING THE PICTURE MOVING

Try to avoid working in detail on one part of the painting at the expense of others. This approach can lead to a disjointed-looking painting, since you are more likely to tire of it halfway through. Generally, it is better to work on all parts of the canvas at once, so that you have a better idea of how one part relates to another in color, tone, and texture.

Some artists, such as the English painter Stanley Spencer (1891–1959), successfully reversed this process by starting with a careful and detailed pencil drawing and then painting area by area. There is theoretically nothing wrong with working in this way, but an inexperienced painter is unlikely to have the very clear vision of the finished painting that is required for such an approach. In general, it is easiest to build up oil paint light over dark, as white is the most opaque color; so keep to dark and middle tones in the early stages, working up gradually to the light and bright tones and colors. Always try to see the background as part of the painting, not just as an unimportant area; even a plain white wall has colors in it, and a totally flat background can be used as a shape, to form part of the composition. Avoid getting bogged down in detail too early; fine lines, such as the stems of flowers or small facial details in a portrait, are best left until last.

BELOW: *A detail from a painting of a French vineyard: the artist decided that the converging lines of the field were too heavily colored. He solved the problem by loosening the color with a soft brush and clean water, before lifting it off with a tissue.*

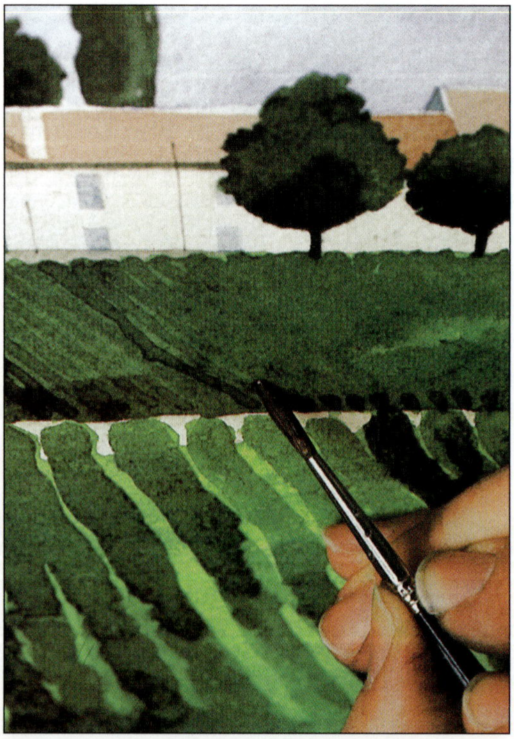

Watercolor

Although watercolors cannot be altered so drastically or so often as paintings in any of the opaque media, changes are possible. It is a mistake to abandon a picture because a first wash has not gone on quite right.

PROBLEM SOLVING

The first thing to remember is that a wash that looks too dark or too vivid on a sheet of otherwise white paper will dry much lighter and may look quite pale when surrounded by other colors. If the first wash looks wrong, let it dry. If you are still quite sure it is not what you intended, sponge it out with a clean sponge and clear water. This may leave a slight stain on the paper, depending on the paper used and the color itself (some colors stain the paper, like a dye, while others do not) but when dry it will be too faint to spoil the new wash. When a wash has flooded, sponge it out immediately without waiting for it to dry; flooding cannot be entirely remedied, though it can sometimes create an interesting effect, even if not originally planned.

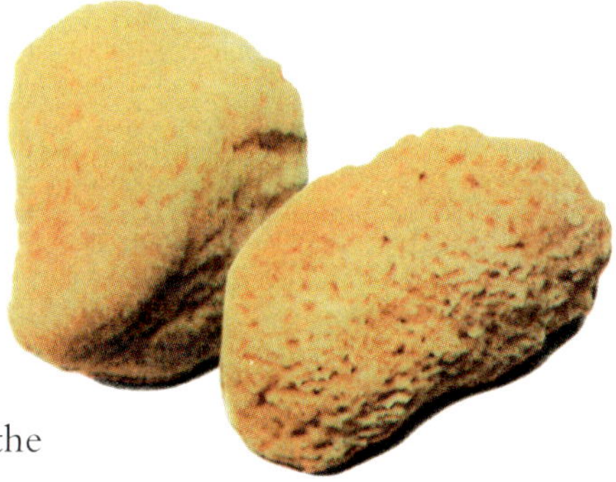

Small natural sponges are an invaluable aid for correcting or modifying areas in a watercolor painting.

One of the most common faults is accidentally to take a wash over the edge of an area to be reserved. There are three ways of dealing with this, depending on the size of the area and the type of edge desired. If the wash is pale and the area to be reserved is a broad and imprecise shape, such as a stone in the foreground of a landscape, you can simply sponge out the excess paint with a small sponge or cotton wool damped in clean water. A soft edge will be left. For a more intricate shape, or one requiring a sharp, clear edge, you may have to scrape the paint away (after it is dry) with a razor blade or scalpel, the former for broad areas, the latter for small ones. Hold the blade flat on the paper so that the corners do not dig in and scrape gently. The same method can be used to lighten an area or to create texture by removing a top layer of paint. The third rescue technique – to apply Chinese white with a fine brush – should be used only when the painting is otherwise complete; if the white is allowed to mix with other colors it will muddy them and spoil the translucency.

The small blots and smudges that often occur when you take a loaded brush over a painting or rest your hand on a still-damp area can also be razored out when dry. If a splash of paint or dirty water falls on the painting, quickly soak up the excess with a twist of tissue or a cotton swab, let it dry and then razor it out gently. If you are intending to apply more paint to the area, rub it down lightly with a soft eraser to smooth the surface, which will have been slightly roughened by using the eraser.

Even professionals, of course, sometimes find that a painting has gone so wrong that small corrections will not suffice, or has become so clogged with paint that further work is impossible. If this happens you can, of course, throw it away. But you can also wash out the whole painting, or large parts of it, by putting the paper under running water and sponging the surface. Leave it on its board if you have stretched it. A slight stain may be left, but this can be an advantage as the faint shadow will serve as a drawing for the next attempt. A whole sky or foreground can be removed in this way, while leaving intact those areas with which you are satisfied.

RIGHT: Small blots are easily removed by scraping with a knife or razor blade. Be careful not to apply too much pressure or you could make holes in the paper.

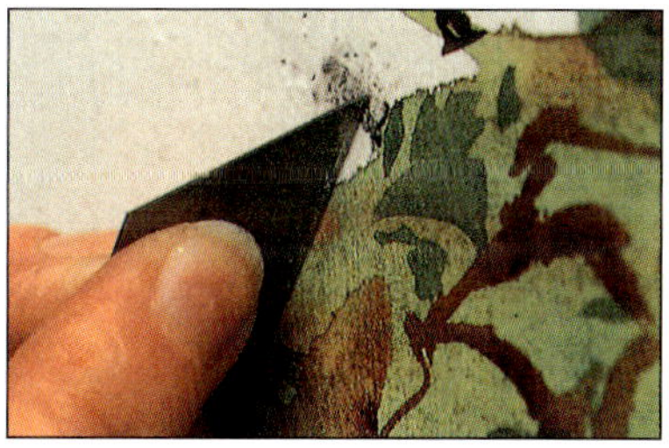

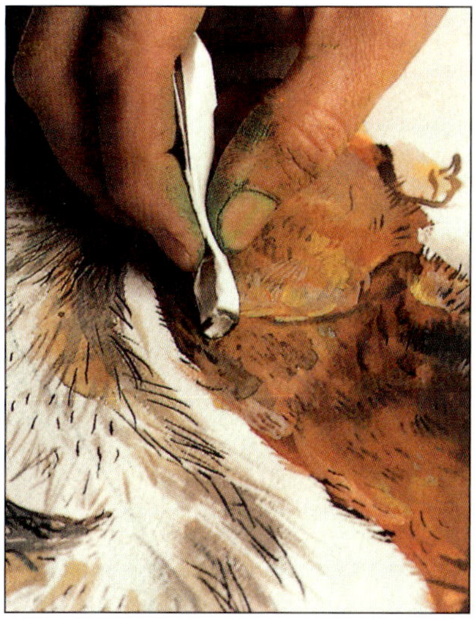

LEFT: If one color floods into another to create an unwanted effect, the excess can be mopped up with a small sponge or piece of blotting paper.

A wash that has "gone wrong" (left) and flooded has been worked in to create a sky effect not originally planned (below).

One of the attractions of watercolor is that new uses of the medium are often supported by "mistakes."

Correcting a Watercolor

Watercolor will allow some degree of alteration, but it is seldom possible to reclaim the pure white of the paper. Keep a tube of opaque white, either Chinese white or white gouache paint, in case you need to make the kind of corrections shown here.

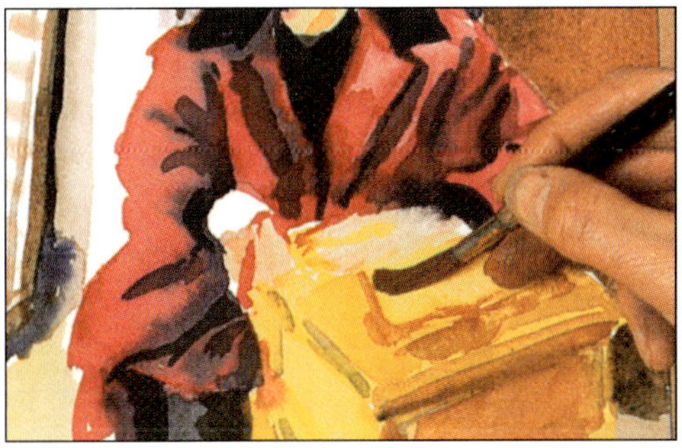

1 The artist has decided that the book on the desktop needs more emphasis. Working carefully within the outline of the shape, she lifts out some of the yellow paint with a wet brush.

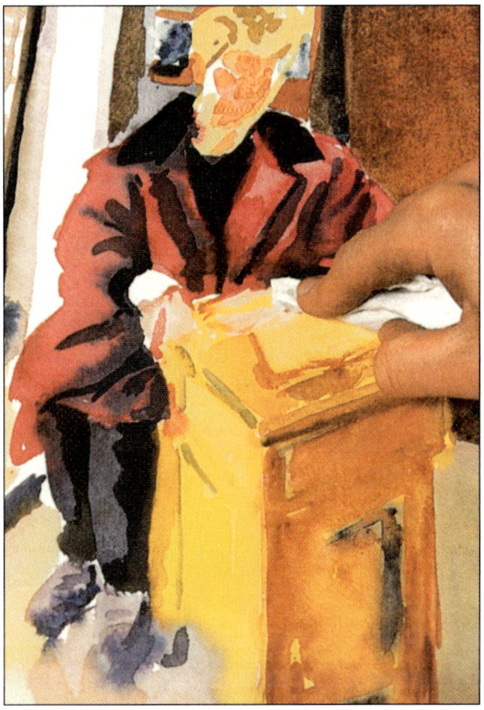

2 The area is now blotted with paper towel, that takes off more of the paint as well as surplus water. The color cannot be removed completely, as it has stained the paper.

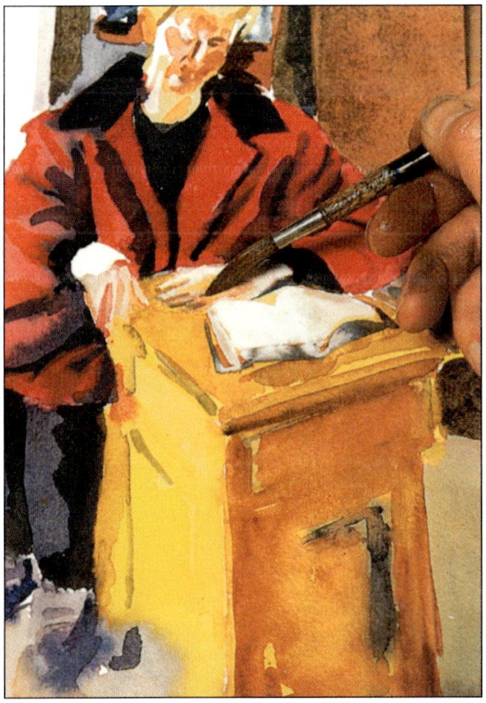

3 The pages of the book have been painted with opaque white, and the darker edges with pure watercolor. Final touches of definition are given to the hand.

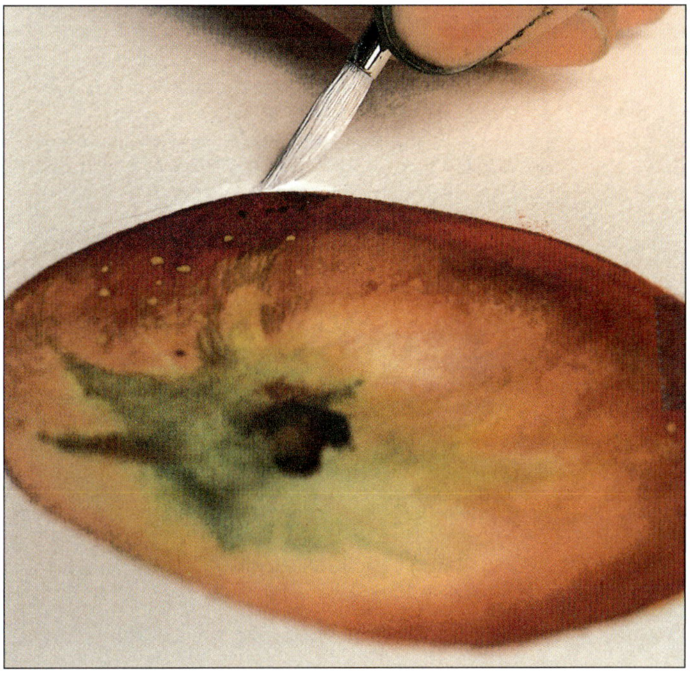

RIGHT: Ragged edges can either be tidied up with a knife, as shown on page 57, or with opaque white gouache paint, as shown here.

Blot-lifting with Tissue and a Sponge

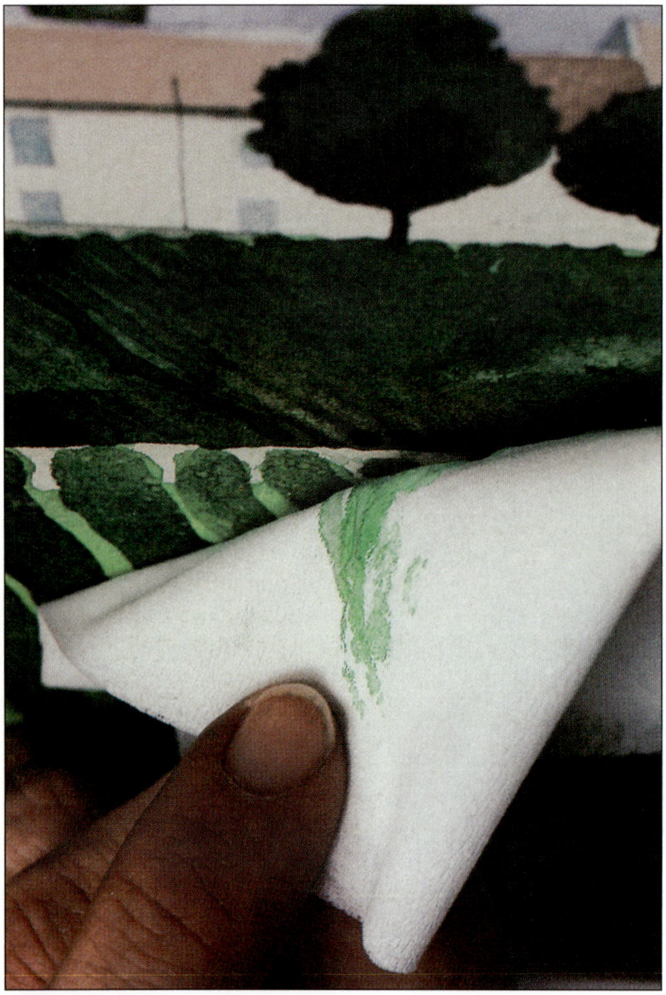

1 The artist considered that the converging lines of the field in the foreground of this painting were too strong in color and needed softening. First he loosens the color by gently stroking the area with a soft brush and clean water. After waiting a few moments for the water to be absorbed, the artist lifts off the color with a piece of tissue.

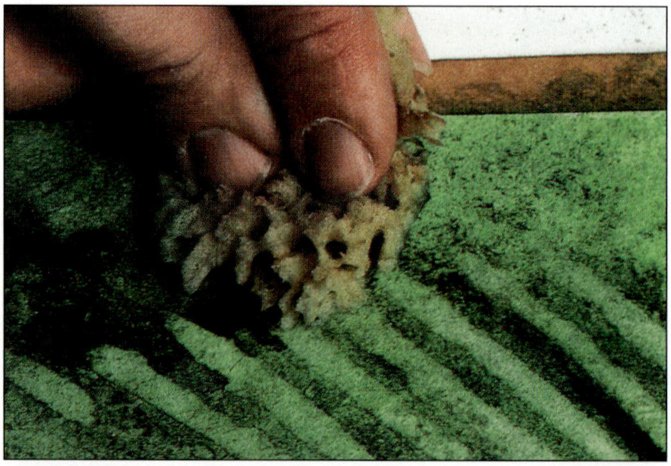

2 In another area of the painting, the artist uses a small natural sponge to soften the color. The sponge is dipped in water and squeezed out so that it is just damp. The paint is then gently massaged with the sponge. This method softens the forms as well as reducing the intensity of color.

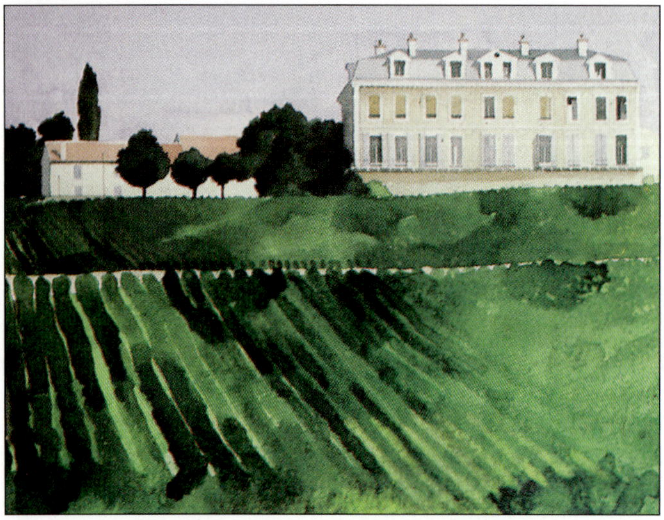

3 The completed picture. By varying the intensity of color in the foreground, the artist has introduced greater textural interest and a sense of light into the painting.

USING A COTTON SWAB

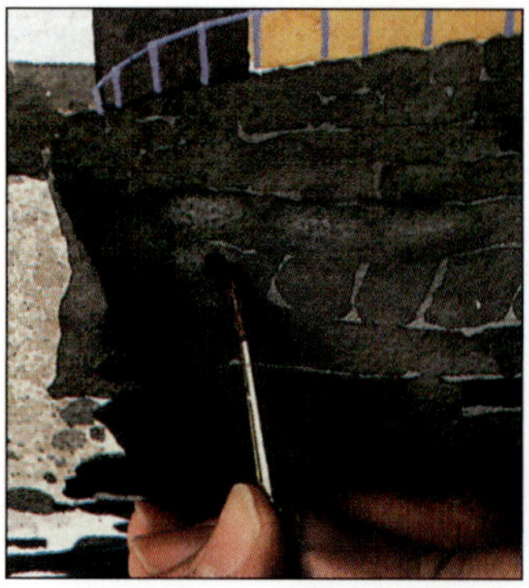

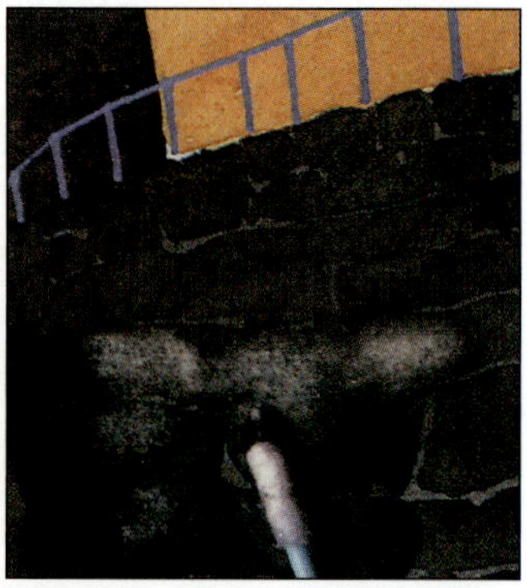

1 & 2 An ordinary cotton swab is an excellent tool for lifting out color in small areas when making corrections. In this painting of a canal-side scene, the artist wishes to add detail and textural interest to the stone wall, that has become too dark and solid-looking. He begins by picking out the shapes of some stones, using a soft brush and clean water. Using a cotton swab, the artist gently massages the area to lift out most of the color.

Correcting Acrylic

Acrylic paint can't be moved once dry, so it is seldom possible to scrape down, but you can make alterations by overpainting. However, unless the new paint is really thick, you can't always completely cover a dark color with a lighter one; the "ghost" of the wrong shape or edge will show through. In such cases, block out the whole area with opaque white, leave it to dry, and then rework.

Although acrylic is an opaque medium, it has less covering power than oil paint, and new colors do not completely hide what is beneath unless the paint is very thick. If you want to make radical changes, overpaint the area in white before applying the new color.

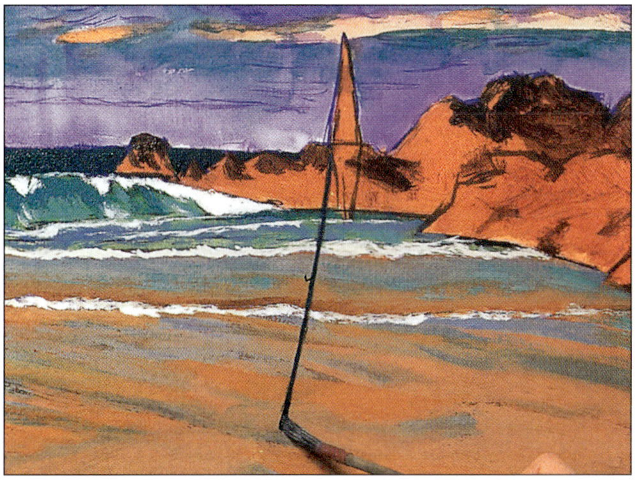

1 Midway through the painting, the artist decided to change the shape of the flag. As the sea went in, it became apparent that it should be flying.

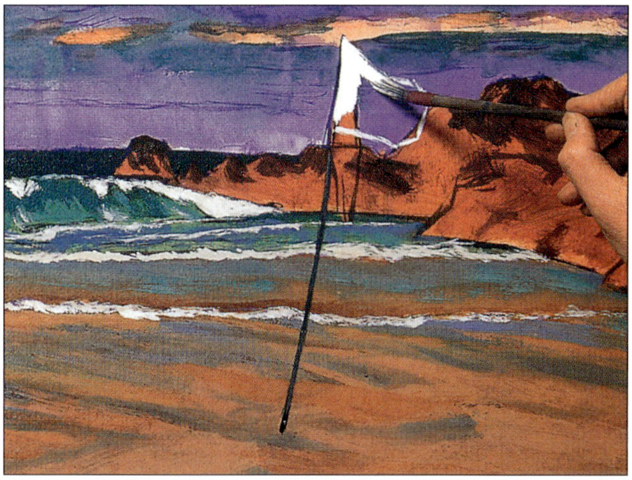

2 He makes a brush outline of the new shape and then fills in the whole of it with thick white.

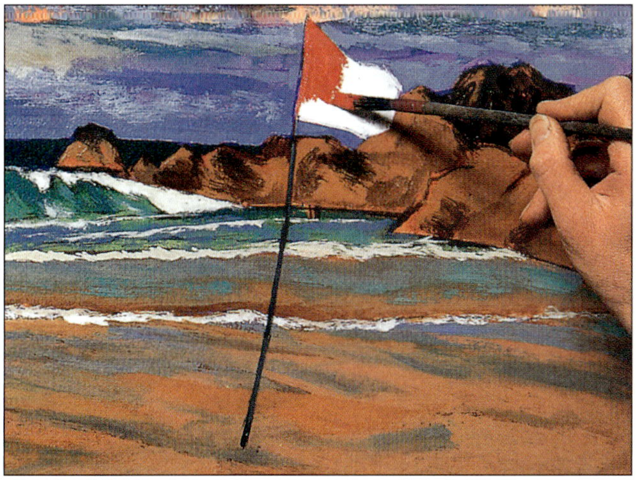

3 Without the layer of white, some of the red now applied would have sunk into the sky color, reducing its intensity.

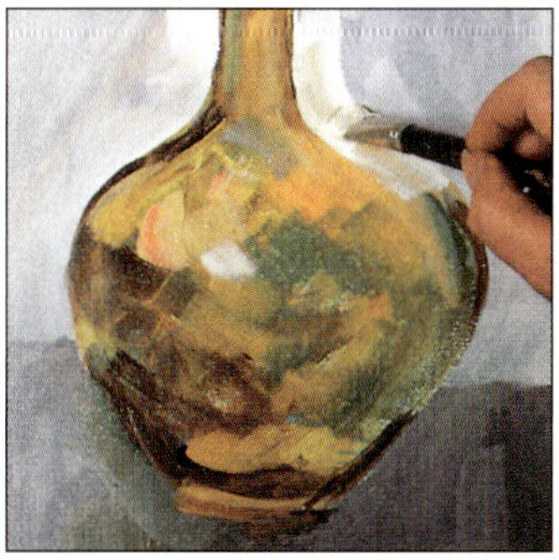

1 Symmetrical shapes often cause problems, and this vase is lopsided. The edge of the vase is redefined by laying the light blue-gray background color firmly around it.

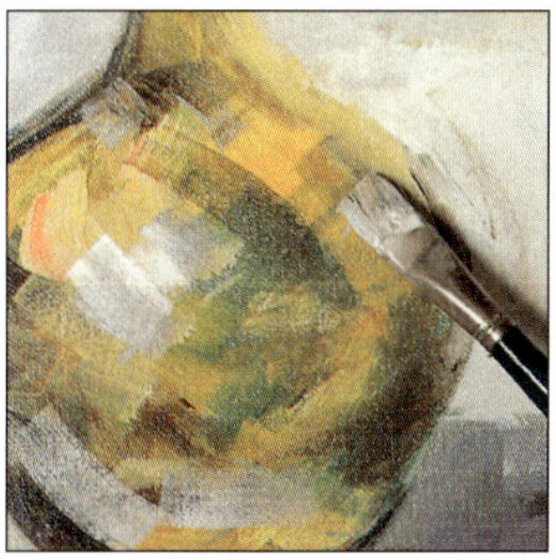

2 The edge was also too hard, failing to give an impression of form, so some light gray is applied to blur the edge and merge it into the background.

Correcting Tempera

Egg tempera dries to the touch in a very short space of time, so it is worthwhile keeping a piece of muslin in your free hand while you paint, to erase any mistakes while the paint is wet. A dry tempera surface can be corrected by rubbing gently with a small piece of sandpaper.

SCRAPING WITH A BLADE

Even though egg tempera dries to the touch within a short time, corrections are actually quite easy to make. Keep a piece of damp, clean muslin handy for wiping out mistakes while the paint is still wet. Once the paint is dry, mistakes can be "erased" by scraping with a scalpel or craft knife. Hold the blade at an angle of almost 90° and scrape very lightly and carefully, taking care not to dig into the gesso. To avoid scraping the area adjoining the correction, mask it off with masking tape.

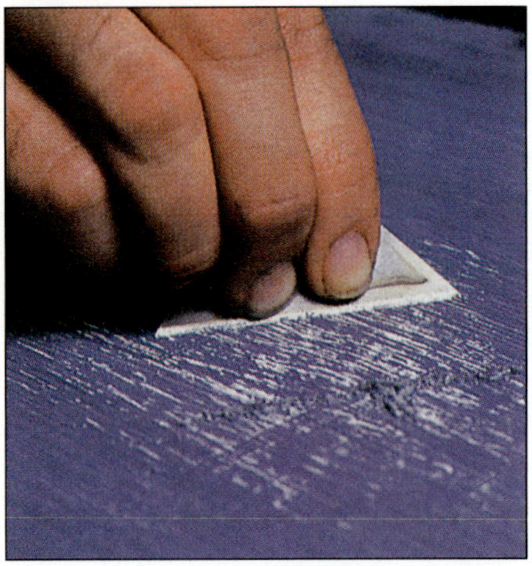

SCRAPING WITH SANDPAPER

Scraping out with a blade leaves the gesso with a very smooth surface. This surface must be roughened up to provide a key for the subsequent layers of paint, so sand the area with a fine grade of sandpaper. Cut up into small pieces, sandpaper is excellent for scraping small or awkwardly shaped areas. Wipe away the dust before repainting over the gesso.

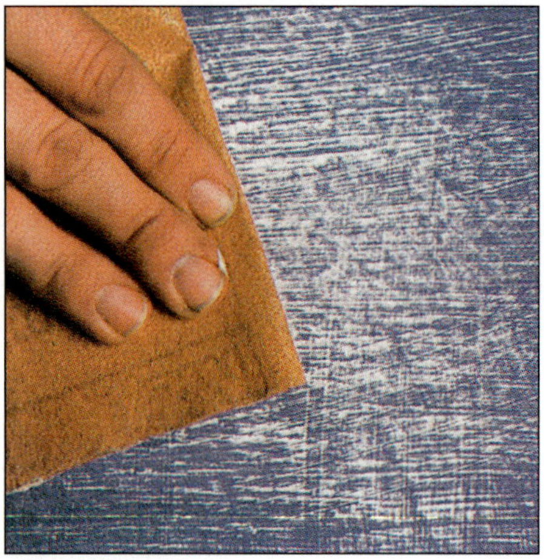

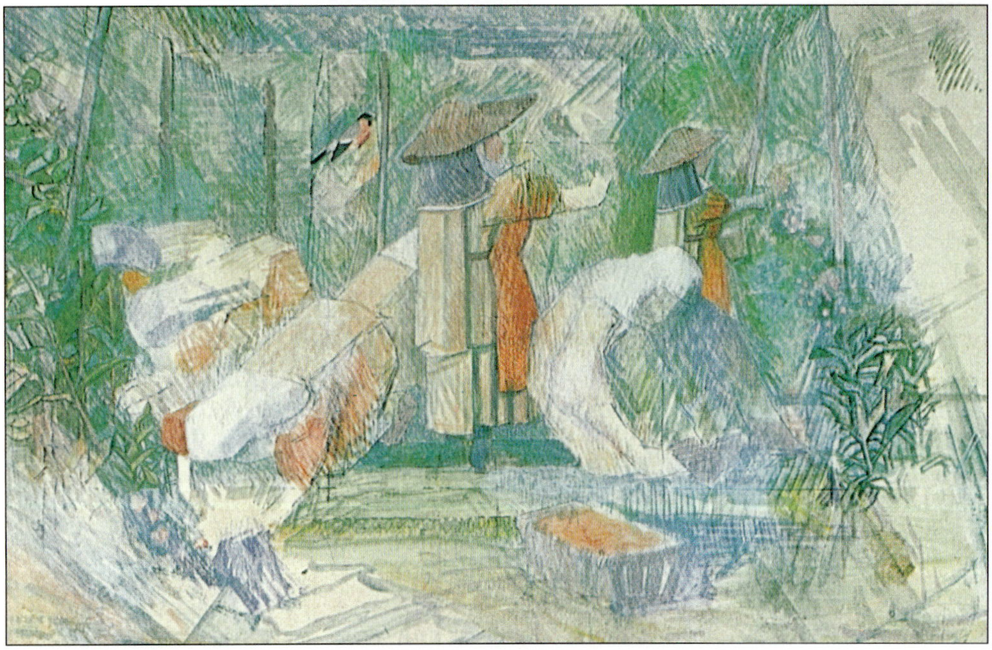

USING WHITE TO CORRECT AND REWORK

At a more advanced stage, white mixed with yolk can be used to tone down previous color areas. White can also be used to correct and rework, but the color laid over this will lose some of its translucence in the process.

Mistakes

All of us, at some time or another, make mistakes, but before crumpling up your work and giving up in despair, you might try some of the following handy tips.

For each medium there are different ways of making corrections. However, often you will not need to make a correction and can adjust your work to include your mistake, or even turn it to your advantage. You can help prevent mistakes by using a clean sheet of scrap paper under your hand to prevent smudging and moisture or grease from spoiling the surface of the paper. Always have a roll of paper towels at hand. Use paper towels as tissue tends to disintegrate too easily. Paper towels can help in a multitude of situations, from mopping up spilt water, to cleaning up edges or removing a too-wet wash.

MOLDING A KNEADED ERASER

A useful tip is to keep a kneaded eraser in your pocket to keep it warm. This way it retains its malleability.

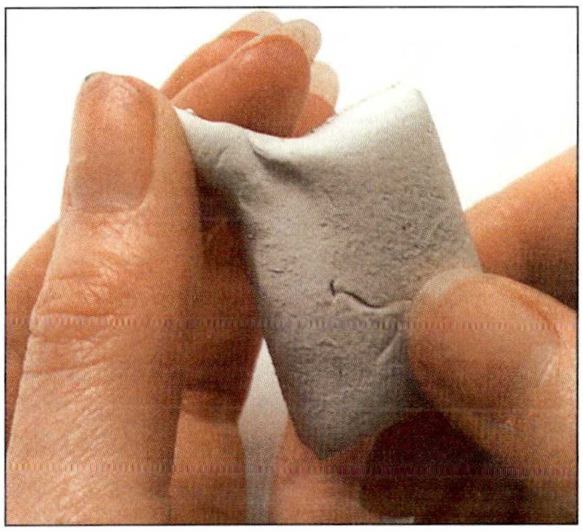

When a kneaded eraser is brand new, it is quite hard. Before you use it, warm it up in your hand and squeeze it between your fingers. After a while it will soften, enabling you to mold it into a fine point, ideal for erasing small, intricate areas. These erasers last a long time if looked after. Try not to drop them on the floor, as they pick up dirt and hair very easily.

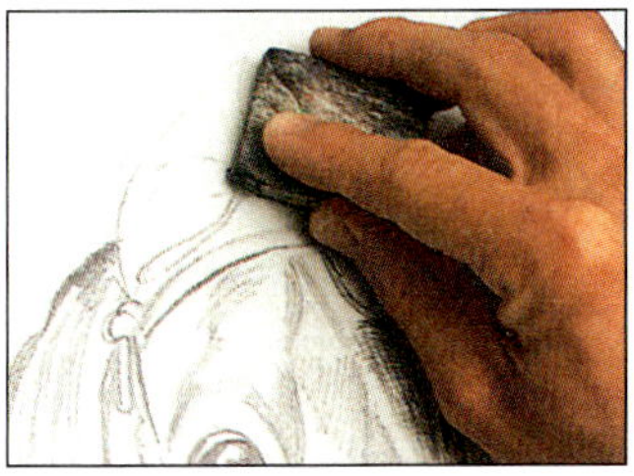

The artist was halfway through this pencil drawing of a horse's head when he decided that one ear was in the wrong position. Using a kneadable eraser, he completely removed that part of the drawing before re-drawing the ear in the correct position.

USING A SCALPEL

A scalpel can be used for corrections in almost any medium. Always make sure that the scalpel blade is clean and sharp. In this demonstration, the illustrator is using a No. 10A blade, that has a pointed end, ideal for removing details. Take care when using this technique on lightweight papers, or you may go right through the paper.

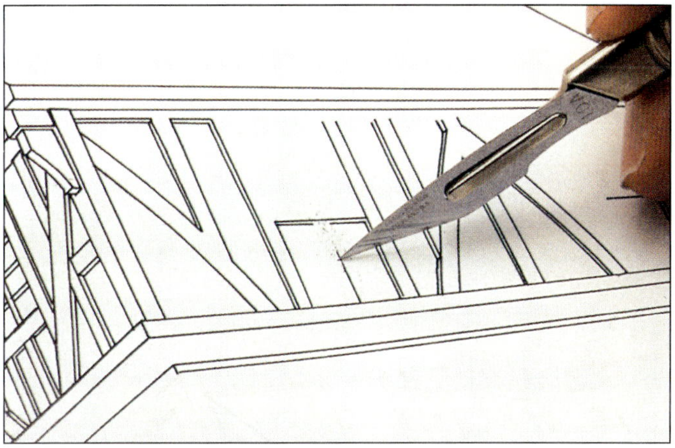

1 A mistake in a technical pen drawing can sometimes be best rectified with a scalpel. Try to scrape the blade in one direction only as this will help prevent the paper surface from roughening.

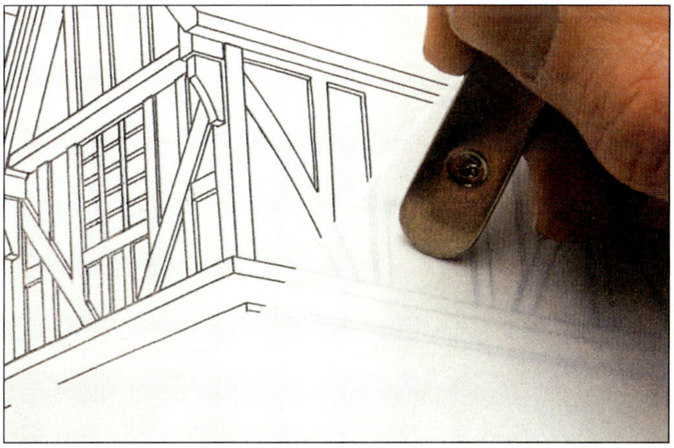

2 If, when the correction is complete, the paper has roughened, the end of the scalpel, your nail or other smooth, hard, rounded surface can be used to gently burnish the paper fibers flat.

WASHING OUT

This correction technique is suitable for water-based media, and is particularly suited to watercolor. For best results, it must be attempted as soon as the mistake has been made, before the paint has had time to dry. Drying times vary depending on atmospheric conditions, and the type of paper used; more heavily sized papers take longer to dry.

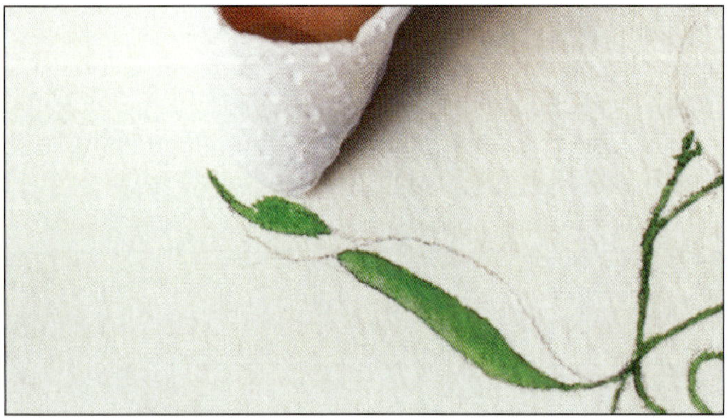

1 As soon as the mistake has happened, dab the area with a clean corner of paper towel to remove a good quantity of the pigment. Take care not to spread the pigment further by pressing too hard, too quickly.

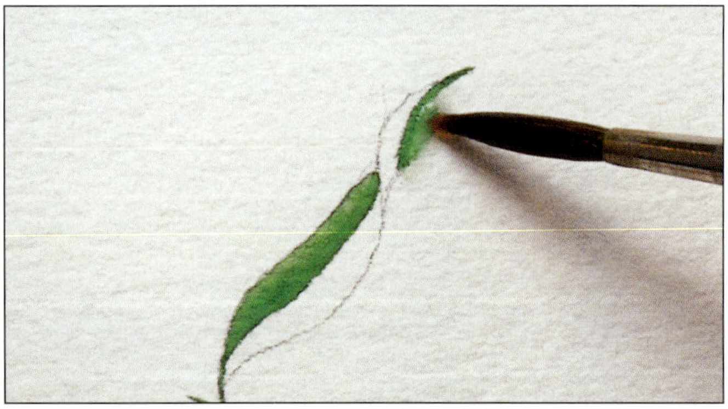

2 Then, using a clean brush and water, loosen the pigment with small circular strokes. Again, dab the area with paper towel. Continue this process until the painted paper returns to white.

PATCHING

Sometimes it is necessary to make fundamental changes to an illustration after it has been completed. At this stage it is often difficult to use some of the easier correction methods, or the surface area may be too large to make them feasible. In these cases, patching is the last resort. It is time-consuming, but you will learn to judge if it is going to save time in the end.

1 In this example the third cherry is to be completely removed. The first step is to map the area to be patched onto tracing paper.

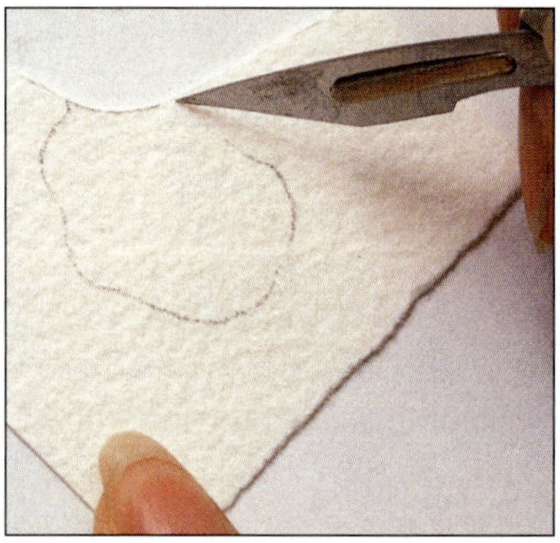

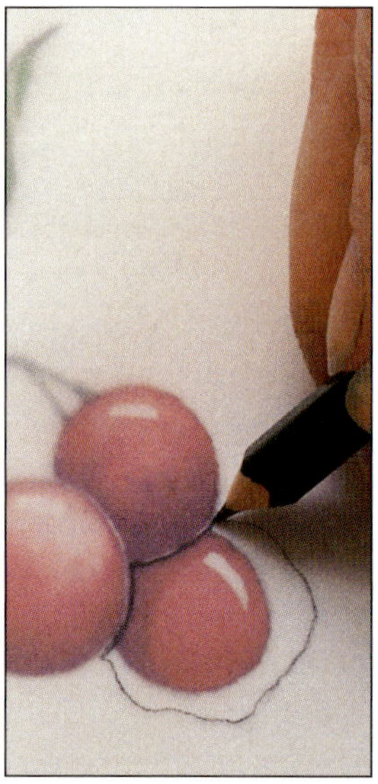

2 The shape is traced onto a piece of watercolor paper identical to the paper used for the illustration. Then, using a new scalpel blade, cut out the patch.

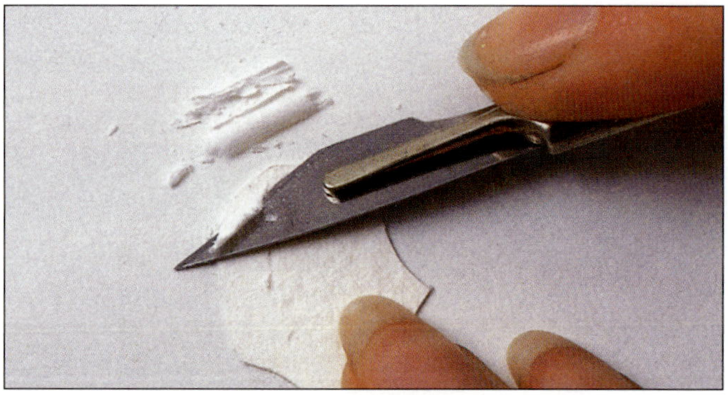

3 If the patch were to be superimposed on the illustration as it is, it would create a shadow. To eliminate this problem, the edges of the patch are shaved down with a scalpel. This is done on the BACK of the patch, shaving from the center to the outside edges.

4 The patch is then stuck to the illustration using a small amount of glue. When the illustration is reproduced, the camera will not pick up the patch and will read the paper as white. With a perfect patch, that takes practise, it is possible to paint over it as if the mistake had never happened.

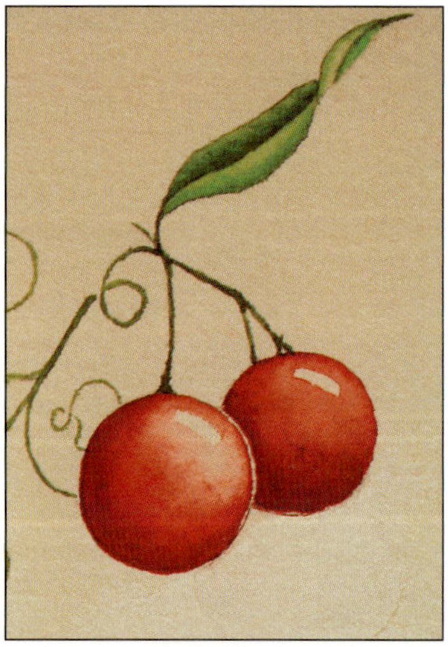

Correcting Oil

One of the advantages of working in oils is that corrections can be made easily either to the whole painting or to small areas. If you suddenly notice that your drawing is incorrect and that you have quite misunderstood a shape or color, the best course is not to try to overpaint, but to scrape off the area with a palette knife and then repaint it. You may even decide to scrape down the whole painting and start more or less from scratch – this is often more satisfactory than trying to alter each individual area only to find that something is still not right.

TONKING

If you find that the surface of the painting has become so overloaded with paint that you are just churning it up by continuing to add layers, there is a useful method, invented by a painting teacher called Henry Tonks and named tonking after him. Tonking is done by laying a sheet of absorbent paper such as newspaper or paper towel over the overloaded area – or the whole painting – gently rubbing with the palm of the hand and then carefully peeling off. This takes off the top layer of paint, and leaves you with a thinned-out version of the original, with softer outlines, that serves as an ideal underpainting over which to continue.

Tonking is particularly useful in portraiture because it eliminates details while leaving the main structure of the head firmly established. It is usually details, particularly within the eyes and mouth which, even if only slightly misplaced, will destroy the likeness in a portrait. These also tend to become heavily loaded with paint, as there is a tendency to put on layer after layer in an attempt to get them right. Sometimes the action of tonking produces an area of the painting that needs little or no further painting.

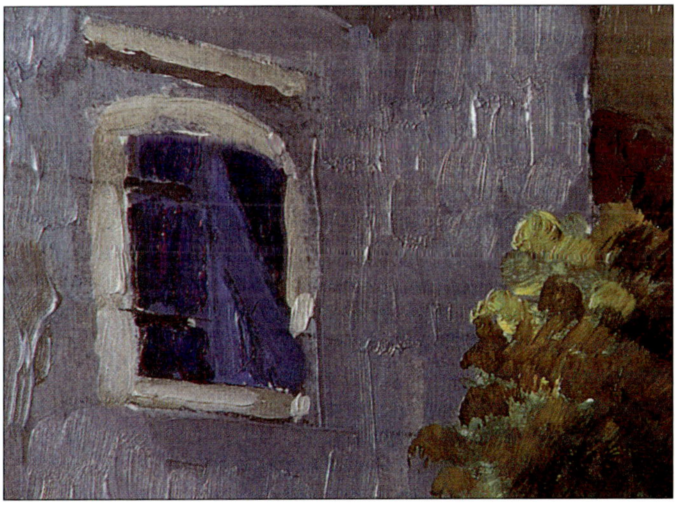

1 A common mistake is to build up the paint too thickly in the early stages. It is virtually impossible to continue working over this thick a layer of impasto.

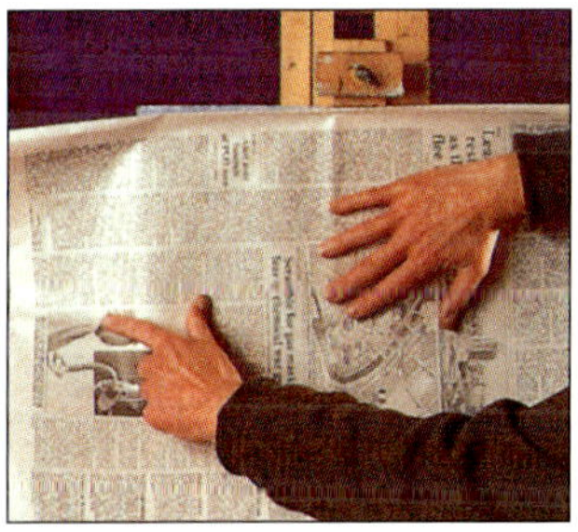

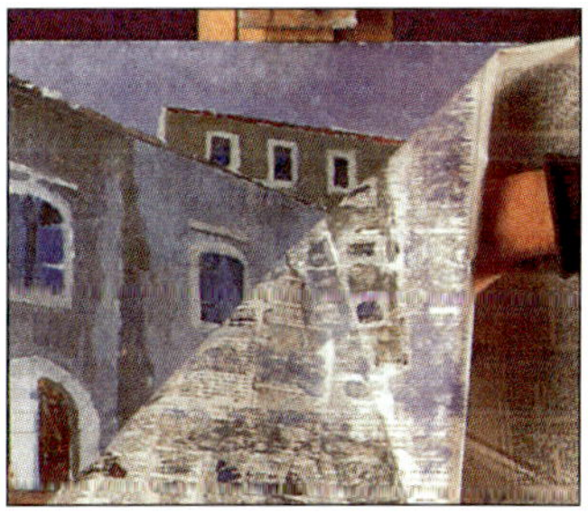

2 Newspaper or any other absorbent paper is carefully laid over the part of the painting to be tonked, and is rubbed firmly with the palm of the hand to make sure that the upper layers of paint adhere to it. The paper is slowly peeled off the painting, bringing the paint with it.

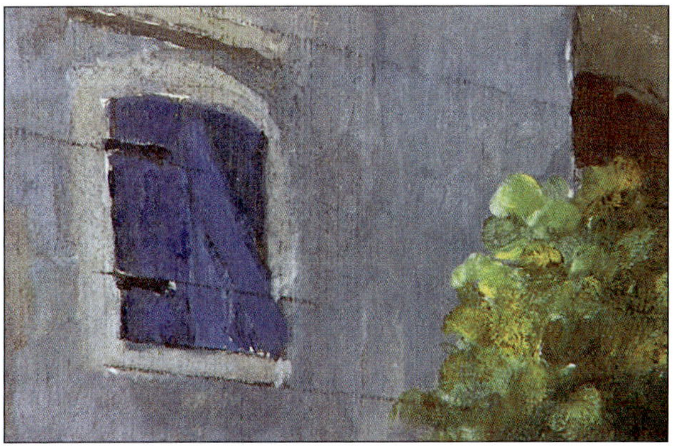

3 After tonking only a thin layer of paint remains, with brushmarks smoothed away and details eliminated. This is an ideal surface for further working. Tonking can be performed as often as you like during the course of a painting.

SCRAPING BACK

When painting alla prima, wet paint can simply be scraped off with a palette knife. This may leave a ghost of the previous image, that can either be retained to act as a guide for the fresh attempt or removed with white spirit on a rag.

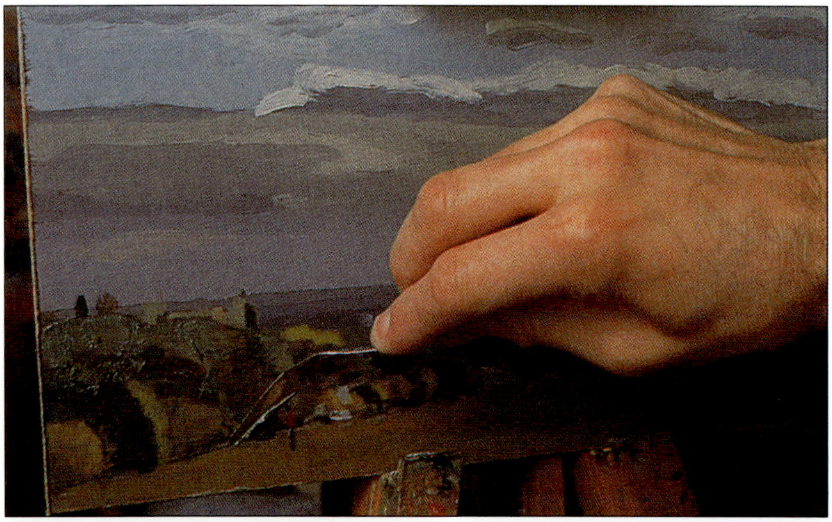

1 Much of the paintwork at the lower left is unsatisfactory and has become thick and unworkable. It is thus removed, initially by scraping off with a small painting knife.

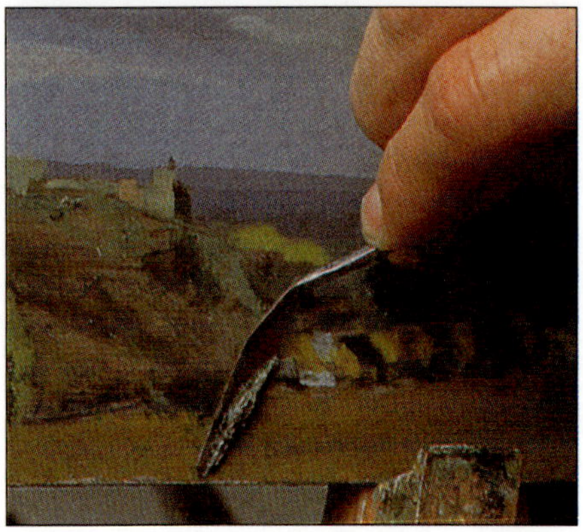

2 Scraping back leaves a ghost of the original image that can often form a helpful base on which to rework.

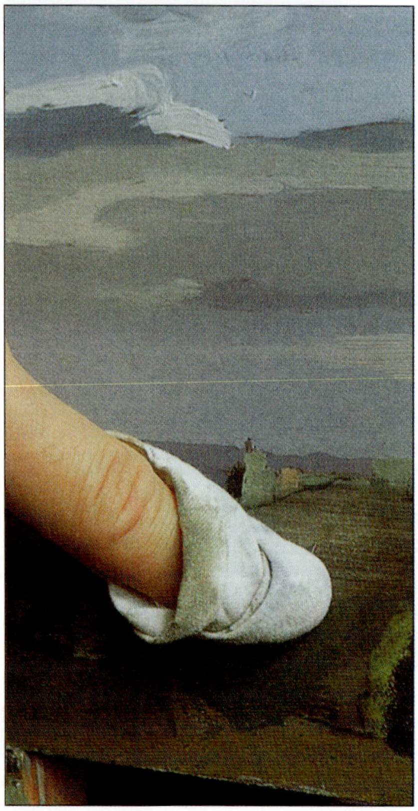

3 In this case, however, scraped-back paint is completely removed with a rag dipped in white spirit.

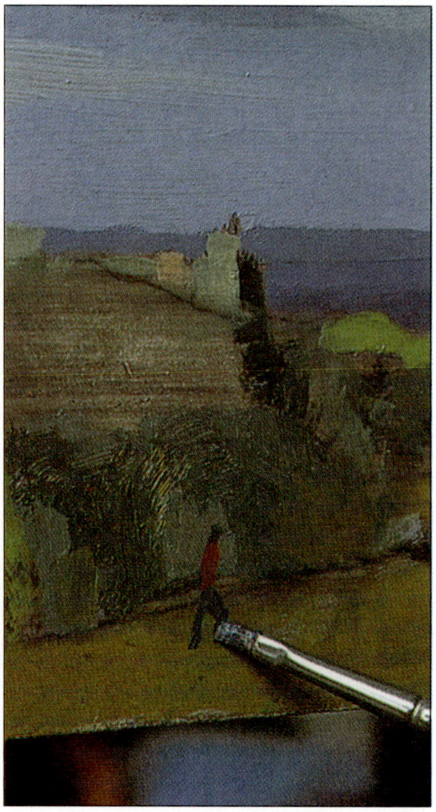

4 The area is now reworked. Corrections such as these are easy to make when the paint is still wet.

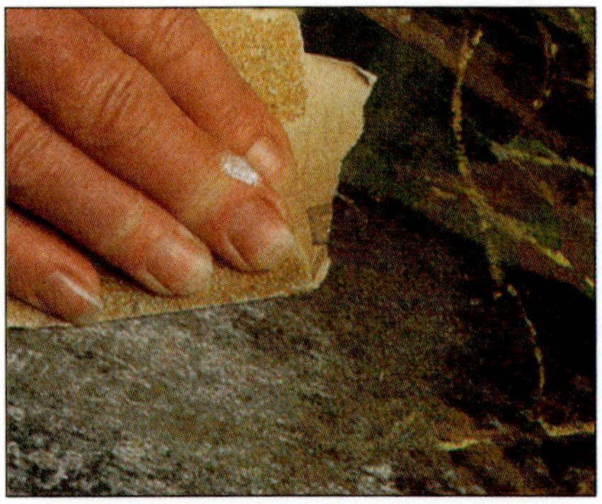

5 Dry paint can be removed with sandpaper as long as it is not too thick.

Correcting Pastels

It becomes progressively more difficult to erase pastel as you build up the color layers. Any method you use for erasure interferes with the natural texture of the pastel strokes and can also spoil the paper surface. In other words, do not count on making major changes in this way beyond the early stages of a pastel drawing.

As long as the pastel has not completely filled the paper grain, in later stages you should still be able to make corrections by overworking the part you want to change.

While the pastel is still thinly applied and fairly loose on the surface, you can use a hog-hair or synthetic bristle brush to flick away the powdery color. The best type of commercially made eraser for pastels is a kneaded eraser – it has a slightly tacky consistency that picks up the loose pastel without the need to rub the surface heavily, that can smear the color or flatten the paper grain. A plastic eraser is useful for cleaning off the color dust that accumulates around individual shapes and at the edges of a composition; carefully manipulated, it can also be used to erase thinly applied color and retrieve highlight areas. Heavy pigment particles can be scraped away with a single-sized razor blade or lightweight, sharp knife blade, and you can then follow up with a kneaded eraser.

Many pastellists recommend fresh bread as the only medium for erasing soft pastel. A small piece gently rolled between the fingers can be used to lift out color delicately and precisely. It is similar in principle to a kneaded eraser, but has a lighter and cleaner touch.

OIL PASTEL

These techniques work with dry pastel types, but the greasy texture of oil pastel is very difficult to erase. Because oil pastel clings to the paper, it is more or less impossible to erase drawn lines, but you can, to some extent, make corrections by overworking, again providing that the paper grain is not fully filled. If this has happened, it is possible to remove earlier layers of color by gently wiping with a rag soaked in white spirit, or for small areas, scrubbing the color off with a brush. You will be left with a stain on the paper, but this does not matter, because it will be covered by the new colors.

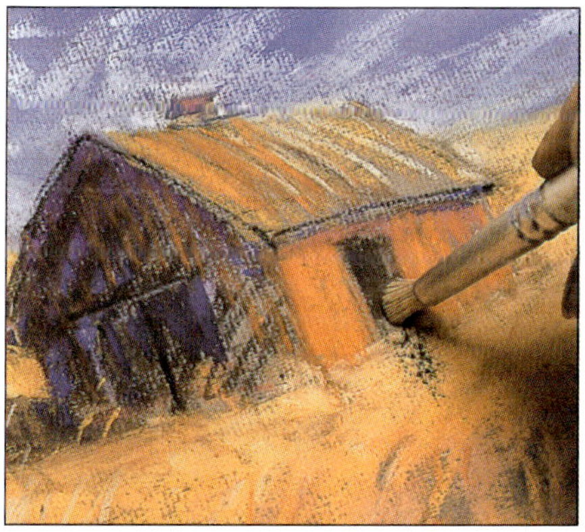

1 The artist has decided that the dark door is too obtrusive, so he flicks off the color with a stiff brush.

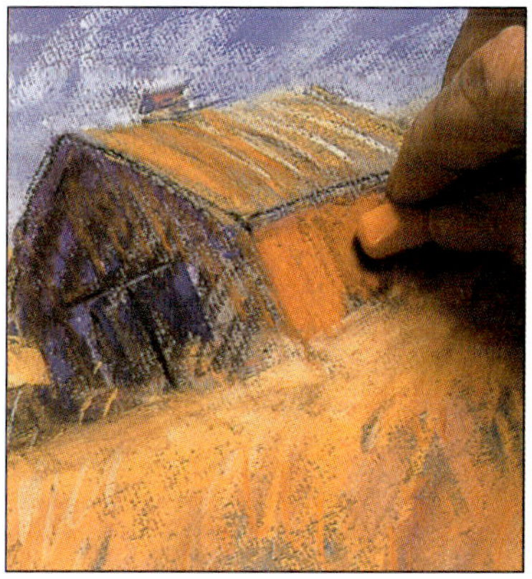

2 He then works new colors firmly over the corrected area. It may be necessary to spray with fixative first if you want to add further layers.

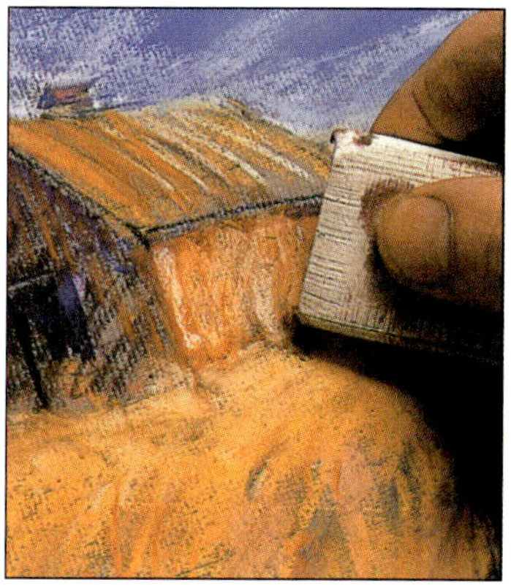

3 He continues to build up the colors. There is now a good deal of pastel on the surface, and dust has collected at the bottom of the strokes, so he picks this up with a kneaded eraser.

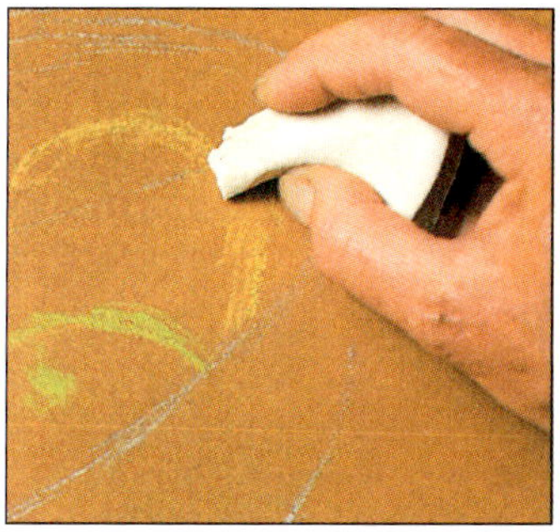

USING A KNEADED ERASER

Shape the eraser to give a firm edge or point, depending on the quality of the mark you wish to erase and the area it covers. Use gentle dabbing motions to lift the loose color. A faint trace of the marks may be left on the paper.

Correcting Techniques for Colored Pencils

Using an eraser to make corrections is a limited process in color pencil drawing. Only lightweight strokes can be eradicated completely; a dense application typically leaves a color "stain" on the paper even after quite vigorous rubbing with an eraser, and heavy linear marks will also leave an impression on the paper surface that may show through subsequent workings.

The efficiency of erasures depends on the type of eraser and the texture of the colored pencils you are using. A plastic eraser used on waxy colored pencil marks may spread the color rather than lift it – you can use this effect positively as a means of blending colors or burnishing the surface.

An eraser may retrieve the surface sufficiently to allow you to rework the area to modify hues and tones. Where you have a thick build-up of waxy color, use the flat edge of a scalpel blade to scrape away the excess before using the eraser. If you have made a serious error in one part of the drawing at a late stage, it may be possible to insert a patch correction (see page 64).

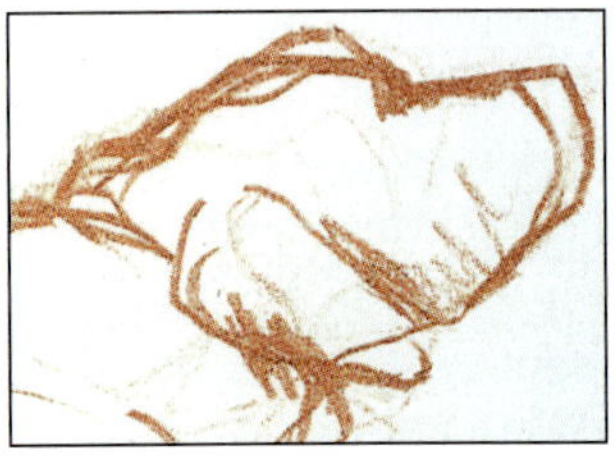

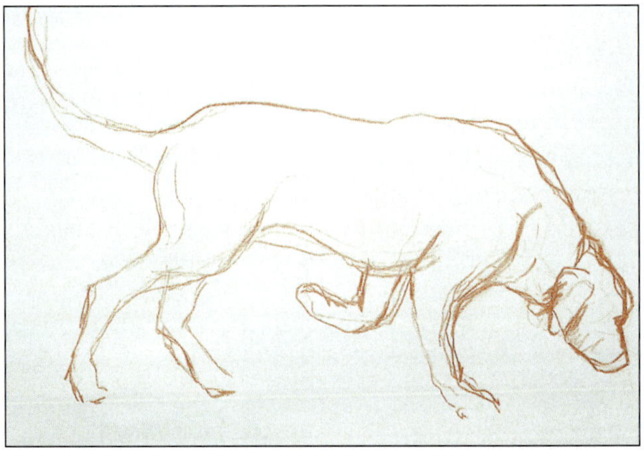

1 Eraser techniques can be used both for correction and as a positive drawing element. The outline of the dog is drawn on smooth paper. The detail (left) shows where corrections have been made to the head.

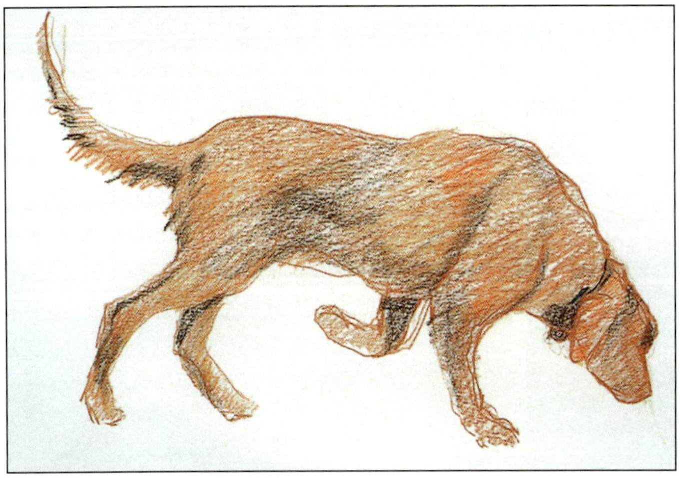

2 The shape of the animal is roughly modeled overall, using light warm brown and dark umber to shade in the basic tones and colors.

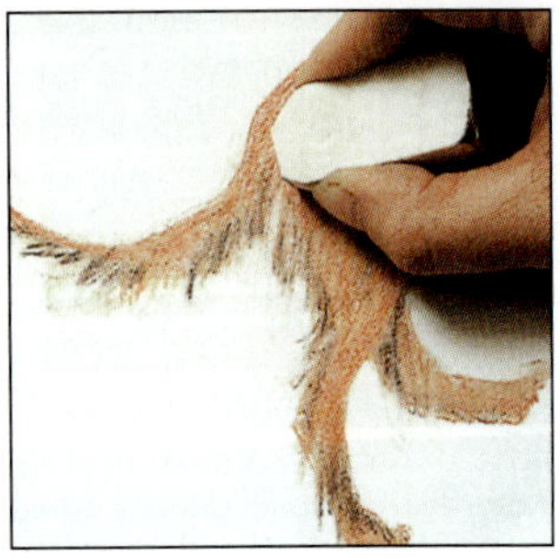

3 A plastic eraser is used at the contours of the animal's tail and underside to drag the color outward, making light, feathered marks corresponding to the texture of the longer fur.

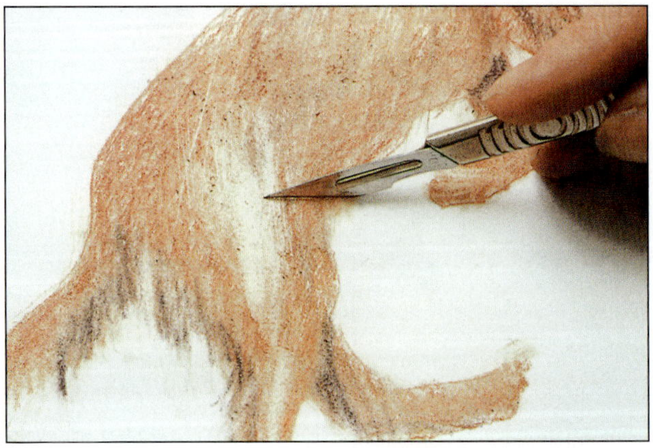

4 To brighten the highlight areas on the flanks and shoulders, the color is scraped back with a scalpel blade. This works best on smooth-surfaced paper, and you must keep the edge of the blade flat to avoid gouging the surface.

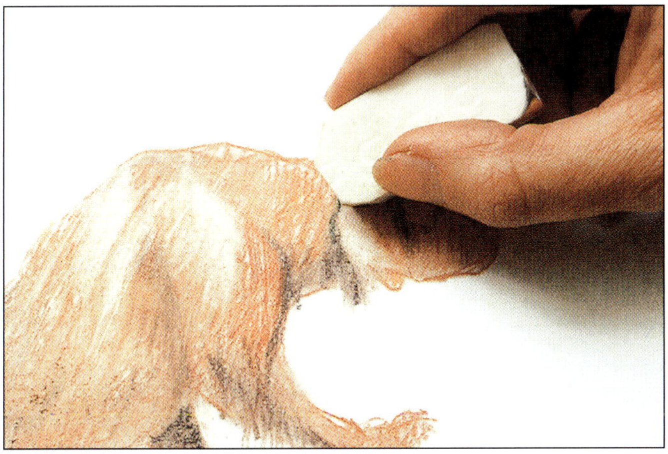

5 The plastic eraser is used again, this time for cleaning up the drawing and burnishing (applying friction or pressure to make a surface smooth or shiny) the highlight areas where the color has already been scraped back.

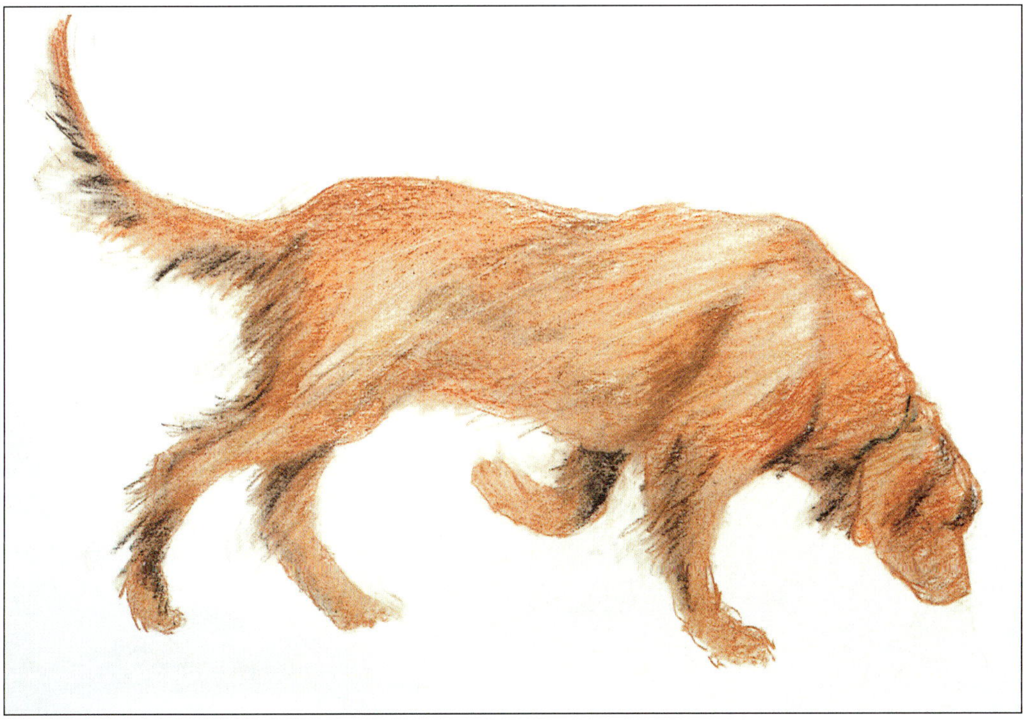

6 Compare the finished image to stage 2: the work with eraser and blade has enhanced the impression of form and texture as well as allowing amendment of incorrect shapes and over-heavy color. A little more loose pencil work has also been applied to roughen up the furry texture.

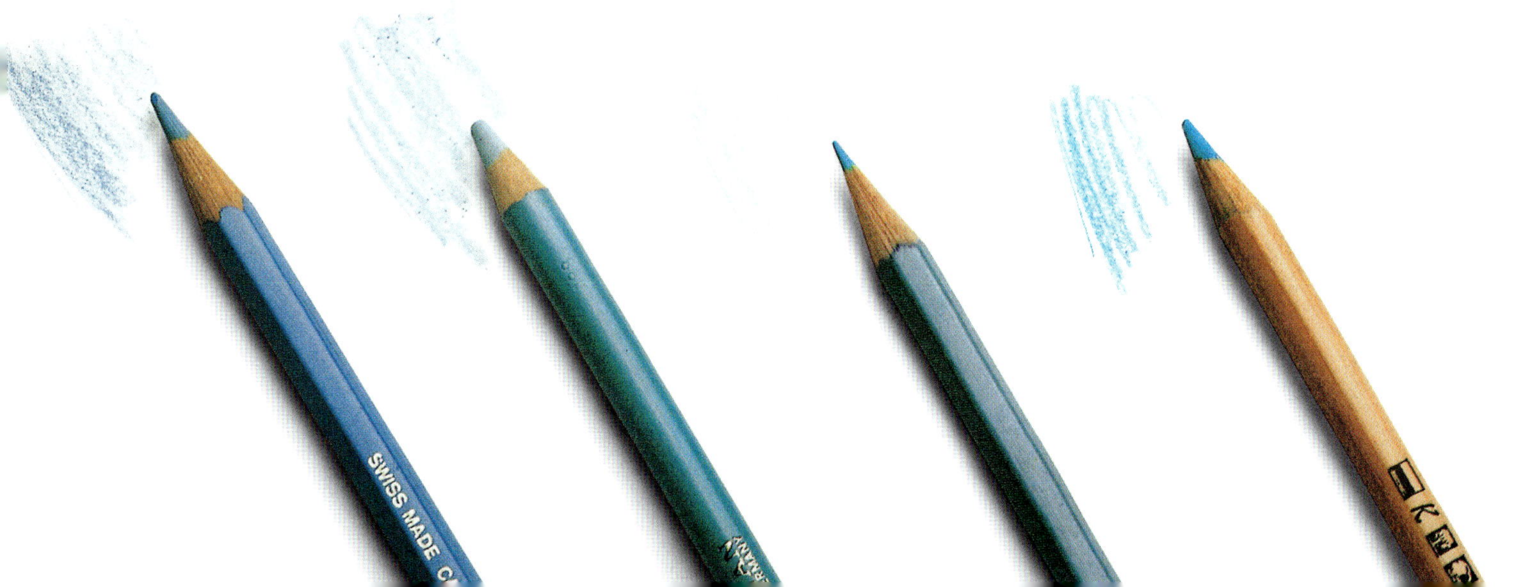

How to Make Clouds Look Realistic

When painting clouds, the chief fault is nearly always being too timid, while overworking runs a close second.

Being too timid results in little, shapeless, "cotton wool" clouds, usually created by dabbing gingerly at the wet sky wash with a piece of tissue to lift out pale shapes – as is the case in the painting on the right. It needs to be emphasized that clouds actually have form, they're not just reversed-out shapes. On the other hand, pushing the paint around and generally overworking the colors tends to result in clouds that look as heavy as lumps of concrete.

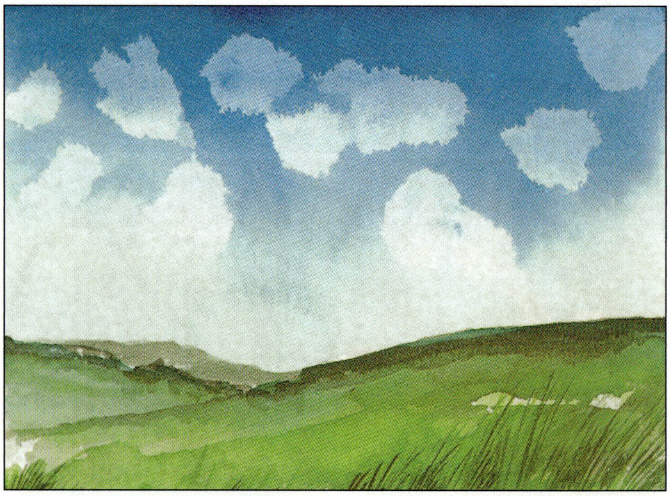

THE SOLUTION

The colors and shapes of clouds can change very quickly, and this often causes the novice painter to panic and make a mess of things. The solution lies in learning to harness the light, fluid qualities of watercolor and working quickly and spontaneously to capture a fleeting impression of clouds instead of trying to create an exact replica.

Resist the temptation to push the paint around too much when you are painting clouds, as this quickly destroys the freshness and translucency that is so vital in a sky painting. Decide which colors you want to use *before* you start painting – don't muddle them around on the paper trying to get them "just right." To retain maximum transparency, keep your color mixes simple: why mix three pigments when one or two will do the job far better?

Apply your colors with as few brush strokes as possible. The more you push and prod, the less cloud-like your clouds will become. If you do need to modify an area, remember that correct timing is vital. If you apply a second wash while the first is still wet, or when it has dried too much, there is a danger of unsightly streaks and marks. The second the shine begins to go off the first wash is generally the optimum time to add a second wash.

Most clouds, particularly heaped cumulus clouds, are three-dimensional and have distinct planes of light and shadow. Pay attention too to the edges of the clouds. Clouds are predominantly soft-edged, although cumulus clouds also have some hard edges, particularly where the lightest part of the cloud is outlined against a deep blue sky.

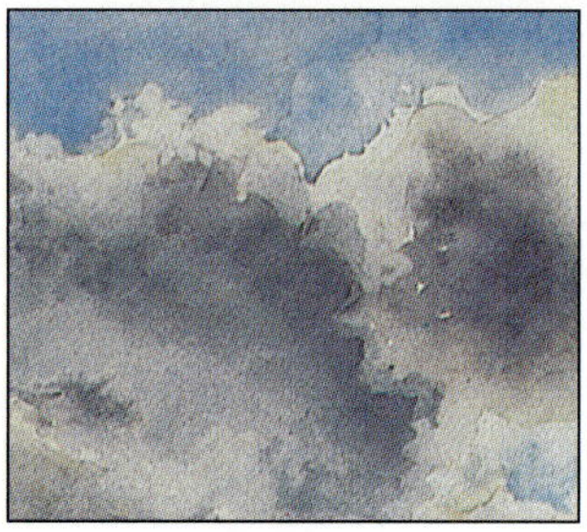

Cloud shadows are modeled with warm and cool grays built up from light to dark. Slivers of bare paper create bright highlights in backlit clouds.

A variety of hard and soft edges gives form to the clouds. Color is scumbled and lifted out to give movement and a vaporous effect.

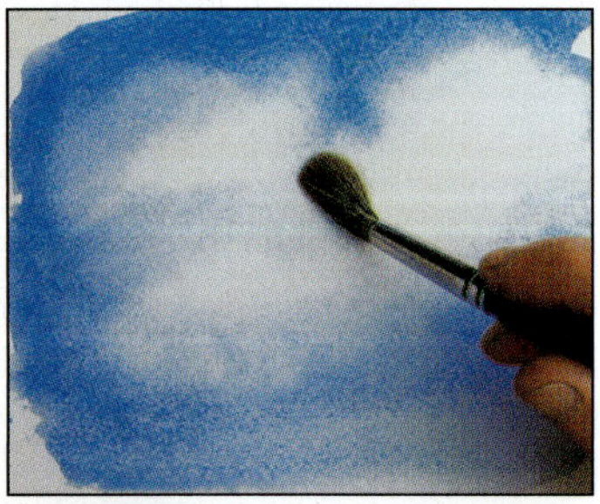

Here the artist uses a clean damp brush to make scumbled strokes at the edges of the clouds to give a soft, vaporous effect.

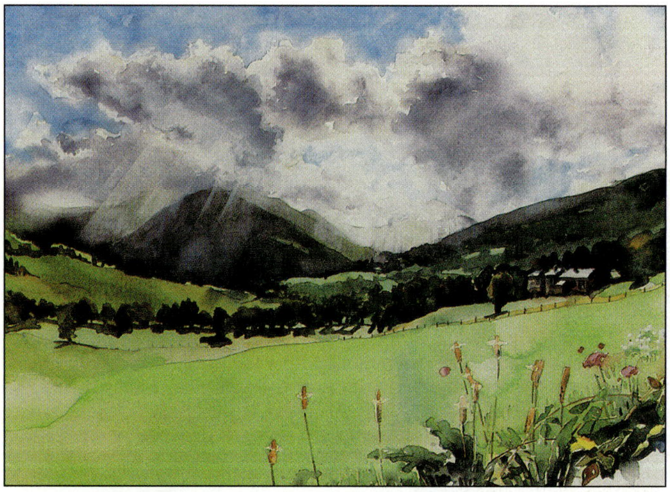

MOUNTAIN RETREAT by Moira Clinch

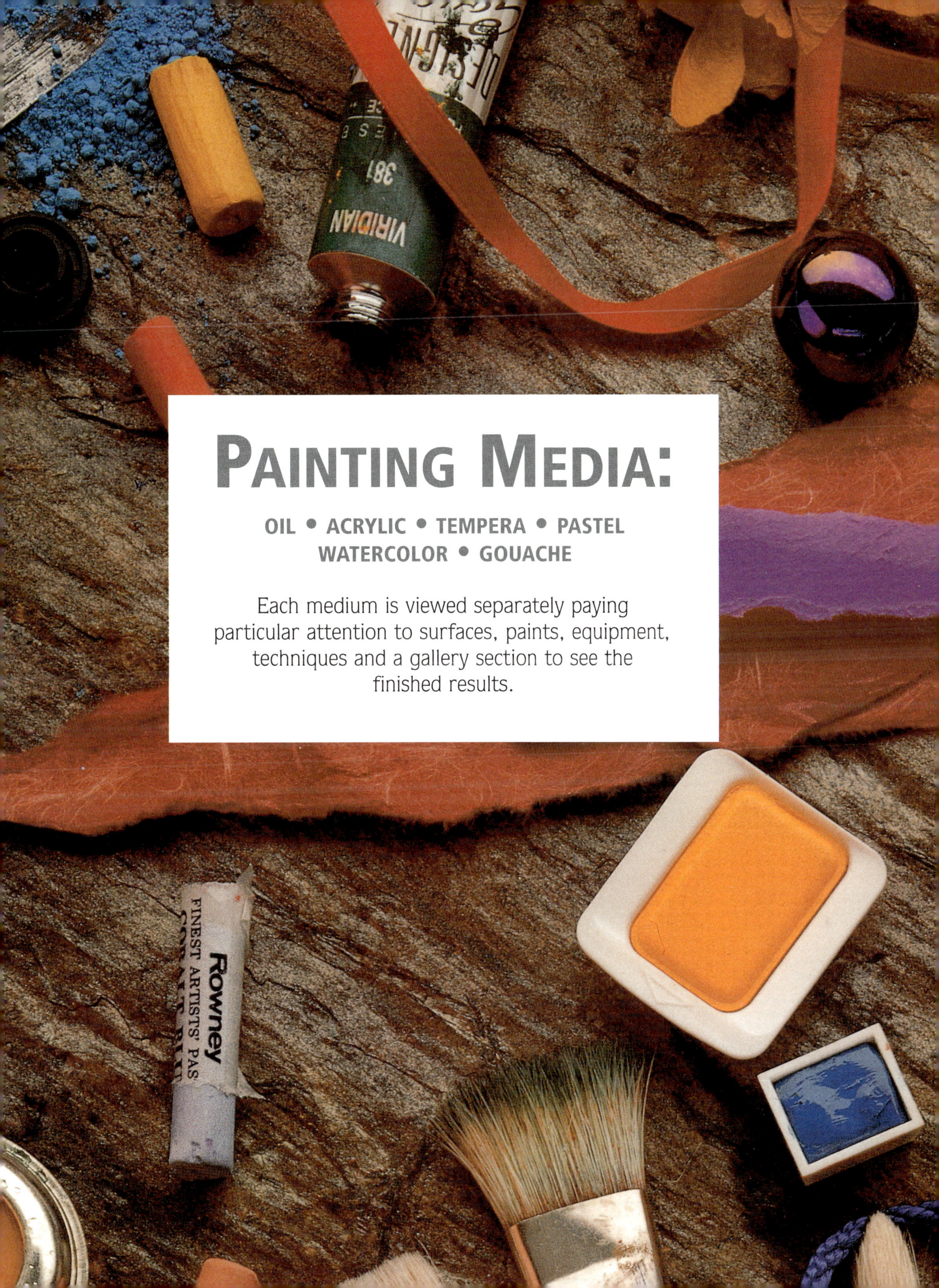

PAINTING MEDIA:

OIL • ACRYLIC • TEMPERA • PASTEL
WATERCOLOR • GOUACHE

Each medium is viewed separately paying particular attention to surfaces, paints, equipment, techniques and a gallery section to see the finished results.

PAINTING MEDIA

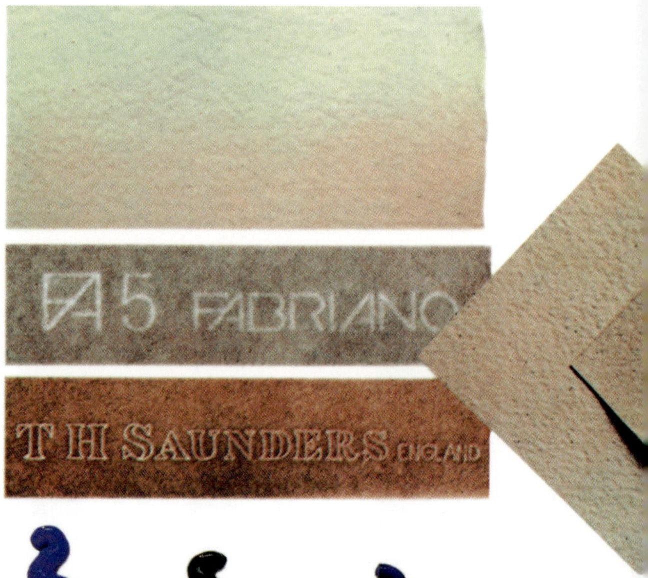

SURFACES

Paints perform differently depending on what they are painted on. The pros and cons of the various surfaces are examined within each paint category, looking at the benefits of materials such as canvas, wood, papers, chipboard, and metal. Priming your surface is of importance if the painting is to last. Different techniques for applying a ground to protect the support is explained for all the mediums.

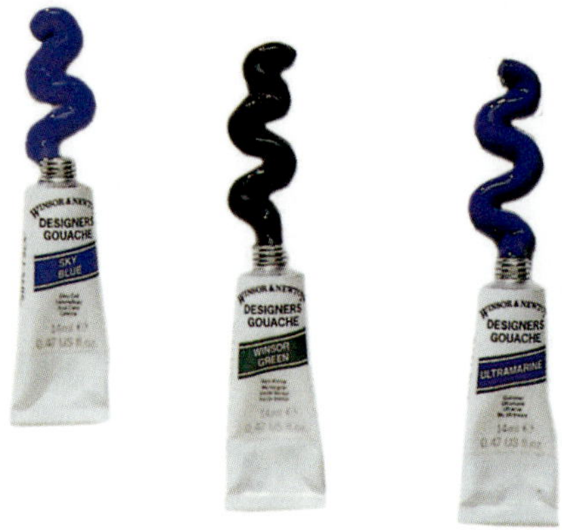

PAINTS

This section looks at paints in detail. From grinding colors and mixing pigments with binders and mediums for extra control to the color strength, quality, and consistency of paints. Learn how to mix powders with pigments and egg to create tempera paints, prepare your palette, and generally how to care for your paints to get the most out of them.

EQUIPMENT

An integral part of painting is the suitability of your equipment and this will be reflected in the finished work. It is very important to have a good selection of brushes and understand the different effects that bristle types can create. Advice is given for choosing, using, and caring for your brushes. Each medium focuses on their specific equipment from knives, easels and palettes to paper, paint boxes, and other essential tools.

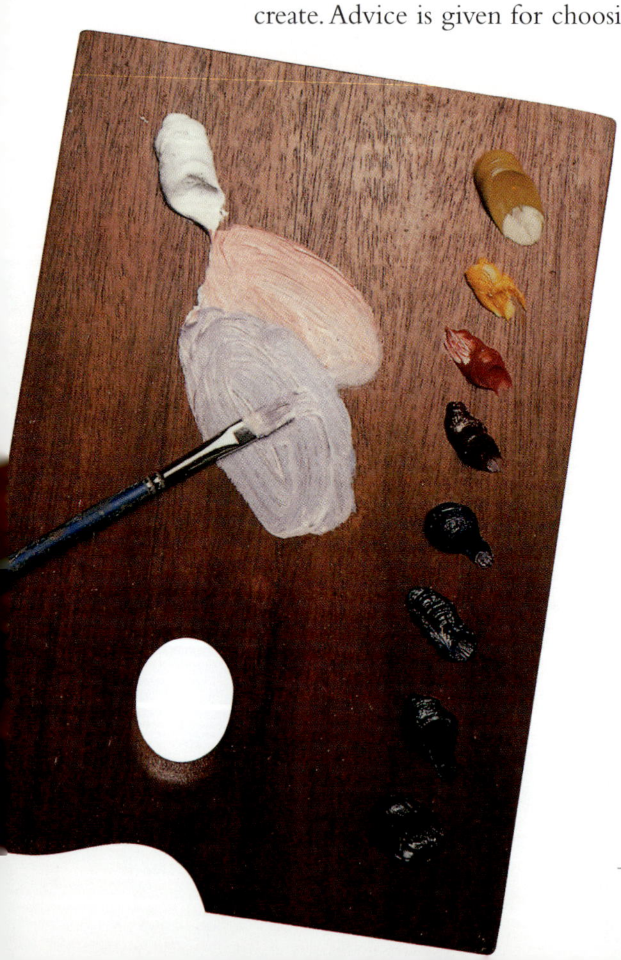

TECHNIQUES

Techniques specific to each medium are described with their advantages and limitations. Whether you are planning and sketching your painting, underpainting or varnishing a finished work the step-by-step instructions will help you to ensure the best result. Some of the techniques described are scumbling, wet-on-wet painting, frottage, impasto, alla prima, using the ground, drawing with line, templates and shields, splashing, stippling, and many more.

GALLERY

A gallery features at the end of this section to draw on the works of a selection of artists. It will illuminate the different approaches you can take to painting and the magnificent results that can be created.

OIL

Surfaces

The choice of surface (or support) is very important, as it effects the way the paint behaves. In general, textured surfaces are nicer to work on as they hold the paint to some extent, whereas on a shiny, non-absorbent one like hardboard it tends to slide about and takes a long time to dry. It is not possible, however, to recommend an "ideal" support; the choice must necessarily involve some trial and error, and will depend on your style of painting, the size of the picture, whether you are painting indoors or outdoors, and, ultimately, what you feel comfortable with.

CANVAS AND CANVAS BOARD

Canvas is the most widely used support for oil paintings. It provides a sympathetic working surface, is light and easy to carry, and can be removed from the stretchers and stored without taking up too much space.

Some of the unique properties of oil paint can only be brought out by the texture of canvas. In areas where paint is applied thinly, the grain is always visible, to become an integral part of the picture and contrast with any impasto work which hides the grain. When dry brush or scumbling techniques are used, the paint will deposit on the top of the weave only, which results in a characteristic grainy paint surface through which the underlying paint layer still shows. The rough texture provides "tooth" to help the paint adhere during application, and the springy flexibility of stretched canvas enables a range of brush strokes which reflect both the shape of the brush and the way it is handled.

Canvases are available ready-stretched and primed, but you can also buy stretchers and "raw" canvas and prepare your own, as shown on page 74. Several different types of canvas are available from the larger art suppliers, but the cheapest, and ideal for the beginner to experiment on, is cotton duck. Linen is superior in that it is less abrasive, keeps its shape better, and tends to have less unpleasant knots in it. For a very coarse grain you can even use sacking or hessian, favored by both Gauguin (1848–1903) and Van Gogh (1853–1890).

Canvas does not have to be stretched; it can simply be glued to a plywood or hardboard panel (with rabbit-skin glue if possible), but this does sacrifice its flexibility. Before painting it must be sealed by priming with acrylic primer, or with a coat of size followed by an oil primer.

A popular alternative to canvas is prepared painting board. This is made in a variety of surface textures, the less expensive being a rather unconvincing imitation canvas texture. This usually has a slightly greasy feel and does not hold the paint well, but some manufacturers produce a canvas board which is actually fabric stuck onto board.

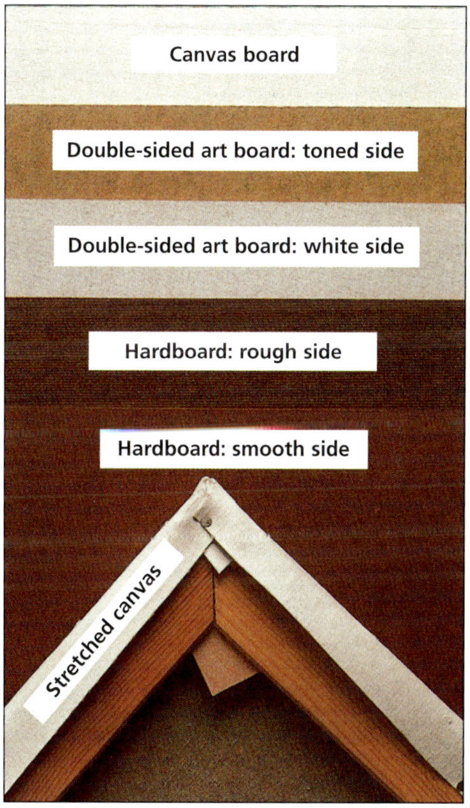

BOARDS AND PLYWOOD

Plywood or the smooth side of hardboard is often used for small paintings, while some artists like to work exclusively on hardboard even for large-scale pictures. It is particularly suitable for those who like to apply paint thinly, with sable brushes, and a practical advantage is that it can be cut easily into any shape, either before or after painting (there are artists who consistently paint on triangular, hexagonal, or completely irregular panels).

The paint will grip better if the surface is rubbed down with sandpaper and then primed with acrylic, which is slightly more absorbent than oil primer. Large sheets of hardboard warp easily, and should be strengthened with a frame of wood battens on the underside.

PAPER AND CARDBOARD

Inexperienced oil painters do not always realize that the choice of painting supports need not be restricted to canvas and painting board. Both paper and cardboard can be used provided they are primed first (see page 76). One of the advantages of painting on paper is its lightness. A selection of stiff papers prepared with different colored grounds can easily be carried for an outdoor work session, and if you also take a knife and steel ruler the paper can be trimmed on the spot to the required size and shape.

If you are merely making sketches as reference for a later painting it does not much matter what paper you use, but if the picture is to last it is best to use rag rather than wood-pulp paper – the heavy, rough watercolor papers are ideal, and will provide a pleasant texture on which to work. It should be sealed with gelatin or casein size, applied to both sides of the paper, or primed with acrylic primer. The final picture can be mounted on canvas or hardboard for protection.

STRETCHING A CANVAS

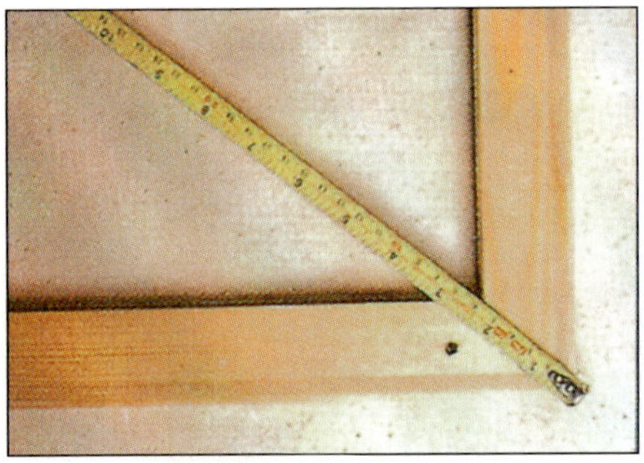

1 First assemble the stretchers, making sure they are correctly joined at the corners. Lay the frame on the canvas and mark off the amount you need, allowing a 2½ in. (5 cm) overlap on each side.

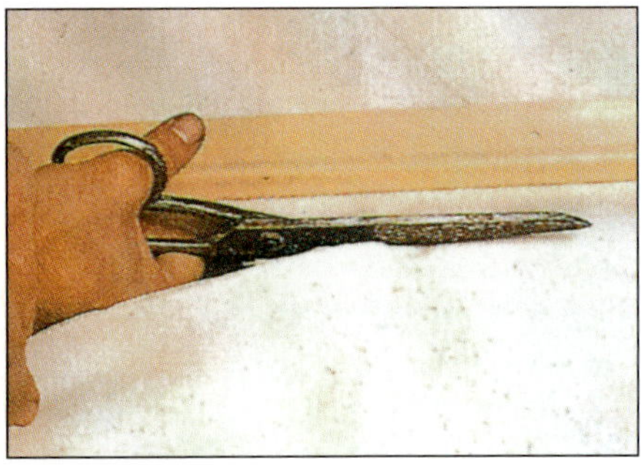

2 Cut the fabric with sharp scissors, taking care not to pull it out of shape; the weave must be parallel. Cut along the weave, using a metal edge as a guide if necessary.

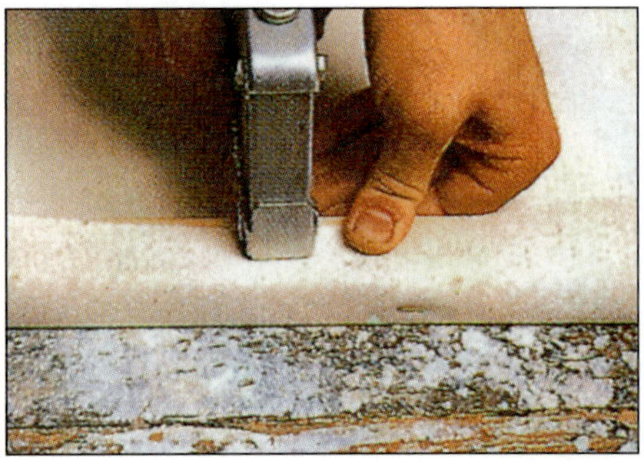

3 Fold the canvas over the stretcher and staple or tack it in the center of first one of the long sides and then the other, pulling the canvas as taut as possible.

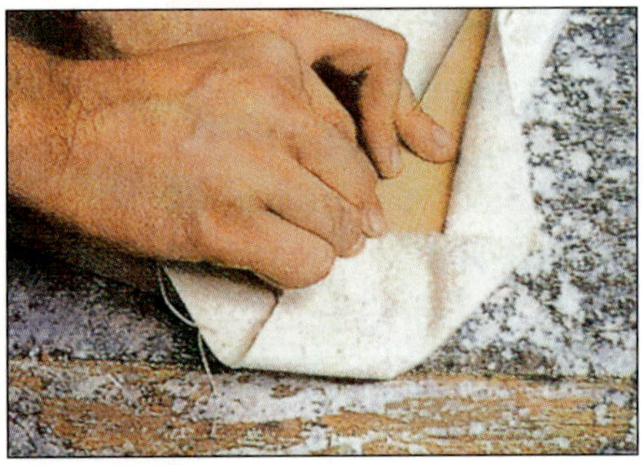

4 Continue in the same way, working outward to each corner, and then fold in the corner flap neatly. The corner must not be too bulky or the canvas will not fit into a frame.

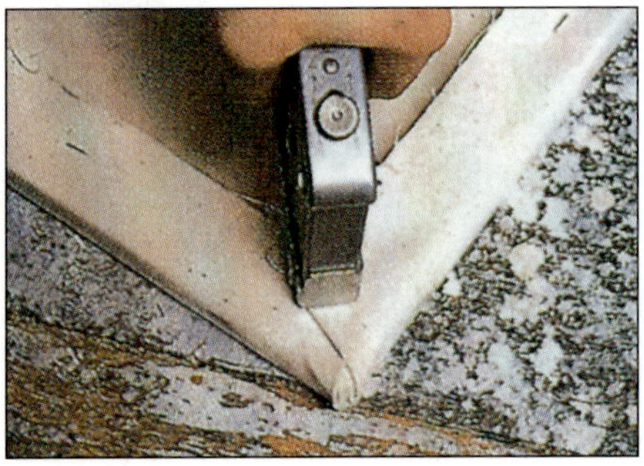

5 Finish the corner by folding it over along the stretcher joint and then staple or tack. Take care not to staple into the joint itself.

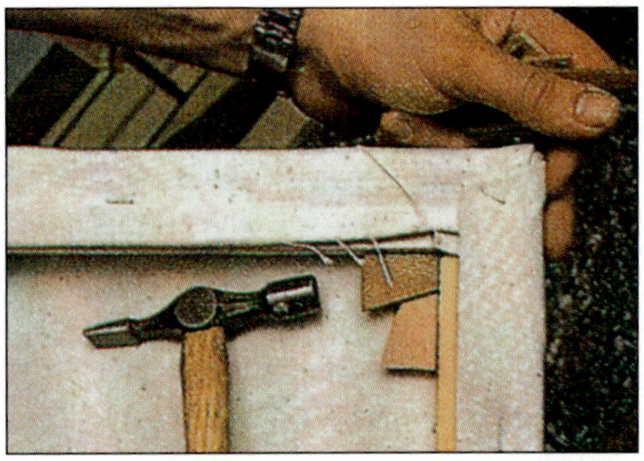

6 Insert the wooden (or sometimes plastic) wedges into the corner slots and hammer them in gently. This pushes the corners apart slightly and enlarges the frame, thus tautening the canvas.

Cardboard is also convenient for painting on, particularly if you like a smooth texture. Heavy mounting board or pasteboard sized or primed as described for paper makes an inexpensive support and is easily trimmed to size. Natural-colored (unprimed) cardboard was favored by both Degas (1834–1917) and Toulouse-Lautrec (1864–1901), both of whom liked the way it absorbed the oil to give a matt, pastel-like effect. Unconventional supports like these are always enjoyable to experiment with, and may suggest a new way of working, but if such a painting is to last it must be glazed.

10 oz cotton duck No. 1

12 oz cotton duck No. 1

15 oz cotton duck No. 1

Unbleached calico

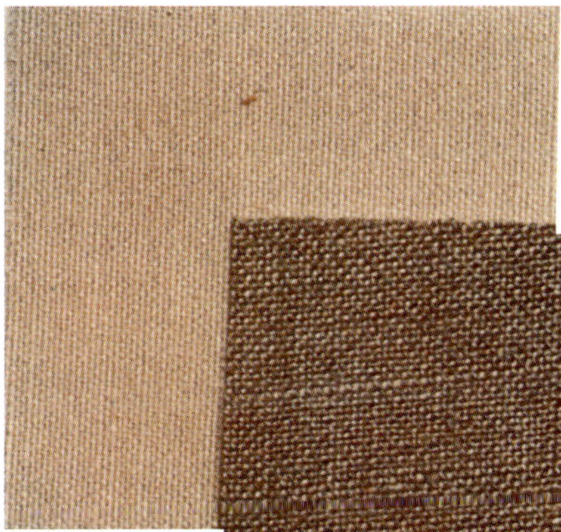

Fine linen (embroidery linen)

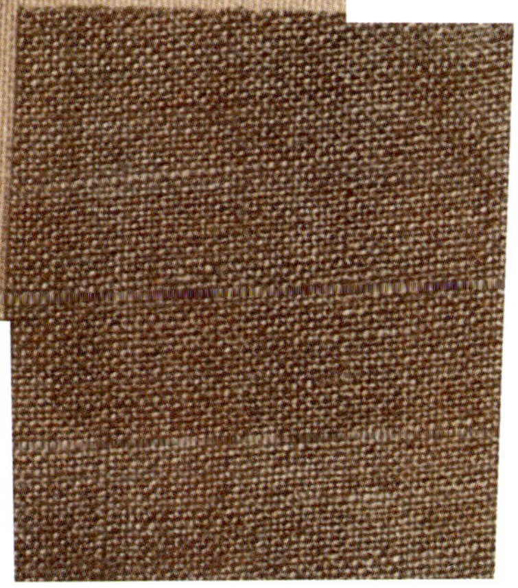

Fine artists' linen

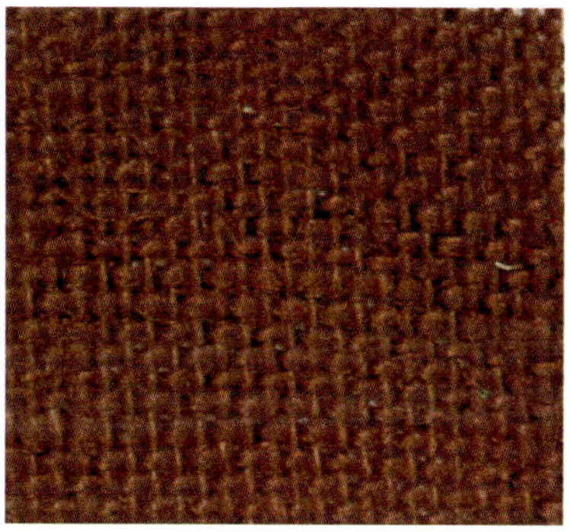

Coarse hessian

Prepared canvas

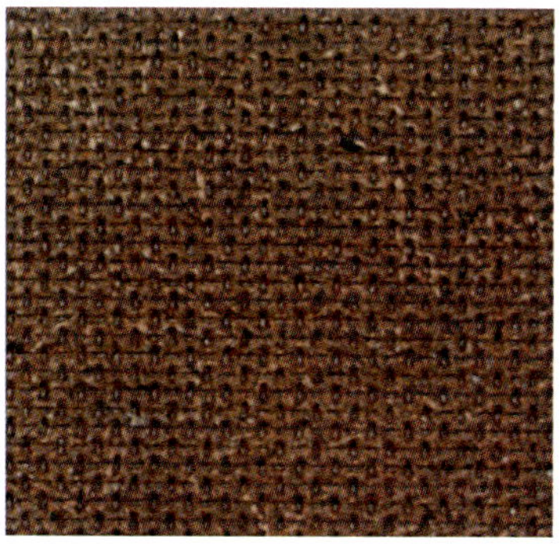

Rough hardboard

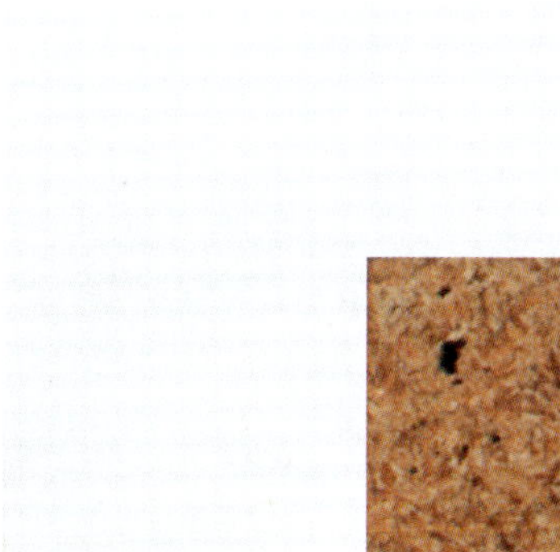

Card

Plywood

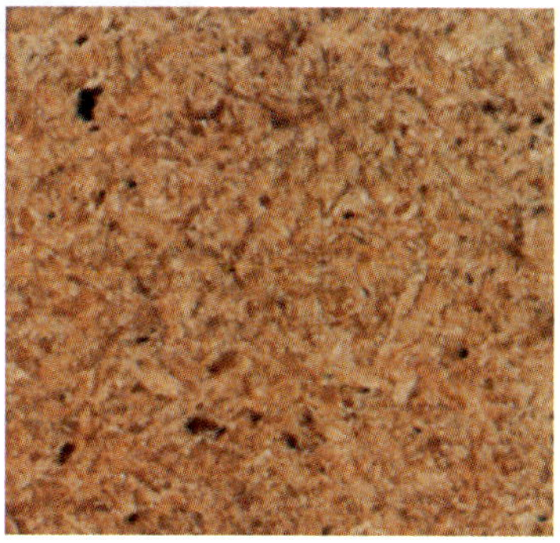

Chipboard

Preparing a Surface

Before any painting can begin, the artist must first select the medium and then prepare the painting surface and the palette. For oil it will be preferable to prepare a canvas or a panel. Different kinds of wood may be used for panels but the cheapest and most convenient is hardboard, and is available in large sizes. These provide expansive work surfaces without needing to join the pieces together. First of all, it is preferable to wipe the hardboard surface free from grease with petrol or denatured alcohol and then, if a gesso ground is required, the panel should be sized on both sides with a preparation of rabbit-skin glue to prevent warping. The glue may be obtained from an artists' suppliers, or an equivalent from household decorators may be used called anti-fungal decorating size. The granules are dissolved in water until soluble and then, with the addition of more water, heated gently in a double pan. Although the size should not be boiled, it should be applied to the panel while it is still hot. The same preparation may be used on canvas.

When the glue is dry a further preparation made from one part glue size solution, one part whiting (made from French chalk or precipitated chalk) and one part zinc oxide powder is applied while it is still warm. On drying, further coats may be applied. It is always preferable to use the smooth side of hardboard that may be roughened slightly with some fine sandpaper to give the primers something to grip to, and several thin coats are preferable to one thick coat.

If a canvas support is required it will be necessary to stretch the canvas over a wooden frame known as a stretcher (see page 74). These may be bought ready-prepared from art shops or alternatively made especially for the purpose. The obvious expense of buying commercially prepared stretchers has resulted in many artists preparing their own. Most art students make them with lengths of 3 x 1 in. (8 x 3 cm) wood; each side of the stretcher is lap-jointed or mitered and then glued and screwed. If the stretcher is to be larger than 3 ft. (1 m) square, it may be necessary to add lap-jointed cross-members for extra support. It must be remembered that once the canvas has been stretched and sized, it will shrink and exert considerable stress on the stretcher, while it is drying. Unless the wood is sufficiently supported or strengthened it will warp, bearing in mind the larger the painting the more cross-members will be required. In a stretcher of moderate size, for example about 5 x 4 ft. (1.5 x 1.2 m), one cross-member will probably suffice.

The quality of different canvases varies considerably. They are usually available in materials such as cotton, linen, hemp, and hessian, and also in different weights. The important thing is that the weave is close and free of knots and flaws. The easiest method of stretching canvas is to use a staple gun. Although tacks were originally used, the ease with which staples may be applied makes this concession to the twentieth century an invaluable time-saver. Roughly staple the canvas in its approximate place with the weave parallel to the sides, using one or two staples at each corner. Continuing from the center of one of the longer sides and on the side directly opposite, apply the staples either to the back of the stretcher or the outside edge. Moving to one of the shorter sides and then to its opposite, add a few more staples. When each side is firmly attached to three or four staples in the center, check that the weave has remained parallel to the sides of the stretcher. Work out from the center of each side by adding half a dozen staples or so and then turning the stretcher around so that each side progresses evenly to the corners. By working in this way a check may be kept on the tautness of the canvas.

SIZE

The most common form of underpriming is that provided by a weak glue size solution. The finest but most expensive is leather waste size from the skins of animals. Bone glue size is the most commonly used.

Sprinkle bone glue into cold water and stir into a smooth paste. For every cup of powdered glue used, add seven cups of cold water, then heat the whole mixture gently until all the size is dissolved. Apply it to the canvas while it is still warm, brushing in every direction so that the size penetrates every part of the weave. When it has dried, apply a second coat.

To make size from casein glue – also known as milk glue – sprinkle the casein powder into cold water, in the proportion of one part of casein to seven of water, and stir until the casein is dissolved. Casein size must be used on the same day it is made. It resists moisture better than glue on gelatin size, but is more brittle.

GROUNDS

A ground forms the layer between the sizing and the paint and provides a suitable surface as well as further protecting the canvas or other support from the oil in the paint. Most grounds are white to lessen the effect of the age-darkening of the paint. Ready-prepared oil-based or acrylic-based primers can be bought for use on sized canvases.

Oil grounds should be used in two coats for the best results. An excellent ground for canvas is made from six parts of turpentine or white spirit and one part of linseed oil stirred into flake white until the mixture is thick and creamy. The second coat should be applied twelve hours or so after the first. If the ground is not dry after four to six weeks and the canvas is needed for painting, it can be given a thin coat of shellac varnish that can be painted on when dry.

Gesso grounds have been used since the Middle Ages for oil and tempera, and are still popular for tempera. Gesso can still be used for oil paintings on hardboard or wood, but it dries rigidly and in time cracks finely. Use one part of whiting to one part of heated glue size. Mix a little of the two constituents separately into a smooth paste, then add the rest of the glue and size slowly and stir until the mixture is creamy in consistency.

Emulsion grounds are a mixture of white pigment suspended in size and oil. Emulsion dries quickly – a canvas coated with it can be used after a week – is more absorbent than an oil ground and more flexible than gesso. It will also take pigment for those who want to work on a tinted ground. Mix one part of whiting with one part of zinc oxide and one part of hot glue size. Use only a portion of the size to make a paste and into this mixture slowly beat a half-part of linseed oil drop by drop until it has completely dispersed. Then add the remainder of the hot size. Keep the ground heated in a double boiler and apply it while it is still warm.

Acrylic grounds are now available for both oils and acrylics and can be applied directly onto the support without size. They have been in use for some twenty years and have not yet shown any major disadvantage.

INGREDIENTS FOR GROUNDS

There are two stages of applying a ground for an oil painting, first the sizing of the raw canvas, then a thick layer of priming, that is applied in two or three thin coats. The following ingredients are used in sizing and for the preparation of various primers: turpentine, linseed oil, Gilder's whiting, flake white, or other white pigment, glue size crystals, zinc oxide. The ground serves to protect the canvas from the oil and provides a smooth, fresh surface for painting. As long as the canvas or other support is properly protected, the thickness and smoothness of the ground are a matter of personal choice. Although it is usual to apply white grounds, it is possible to add colored pigment if a colored ground is required, or to paint a thin layer of color over the dry ground. The powder ingredients in general add body to the mixture and make it opaque. The white pigment adds brilliance to the whiteness of the ground. Powdered ingredients must be kept dry in order to mix smoothly.

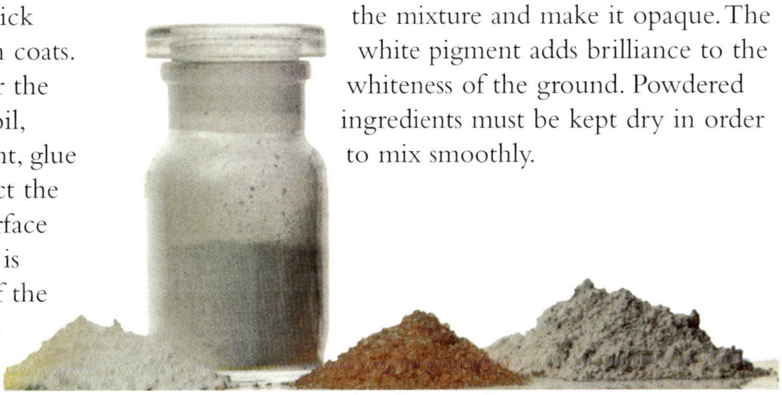

Gilder's whiting — Glue size crystals — Zinc oxide

GLUE SIZE

1 cup glue size crystals
7 cups water

Sprinkle the glue size into the water and stir. Heat the glue in a double boiler, until all the size has dissolved, but do not allow it to boil. Apply the size to the canvas while warm.

OIL GROUND

6 parts turpentine
1 part linseed oil
A quantity of flake white powder

Mix the turpentine and linseed oil together and gradually pour them into the flake white, stirring continuously until the mixture is of a thick, creamy consistency. Apply in two thin coats, allowing the first to dry out before applying the second.

GESSO GROUND

1 part Gilder's whiting
1 part glue size

Heat the glue size gently. Add some of the warm size to the whiting and stir until it forms a thick paste. Gradually add the rest of the size until a smooth, creamy mixture is obtained. Apply gesso carefully in thin layers, or it will crack. To increase the brilliance of the white, add white powdered pigment.

EMULSION GROUND

1 part Gilder's whiting
1 part zinc oxide
1 part glue size
½ part linseed oil

Add part of the glue size to the whiting and zinc oxide and mix it into a paste. Add the linseed oil one drop at a time and beat it into the mixture. Mix in the rest of the glue size and keep the whole mixture warm in a double boiler until used.

Preparing a Size

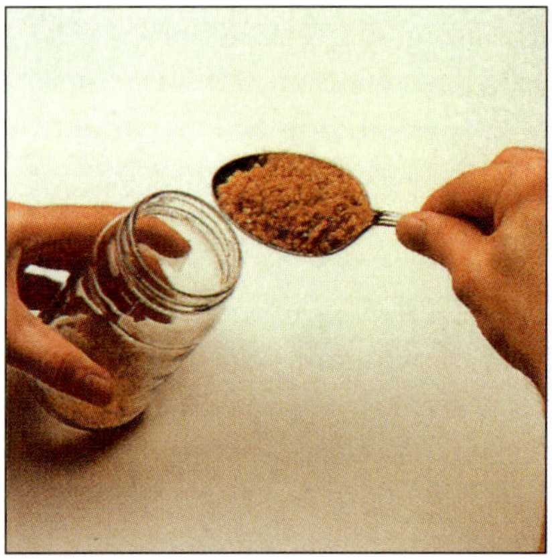

1 Canvases and boards that are to be given an oil ground must be sized first. Use rabbit-skin size (sold in most good art shops) not builders' size, as the latter contains a fungicide that could damage your painting. Put one rounded tablespoon of crystalline or granular skin size into a 450g jam jar.

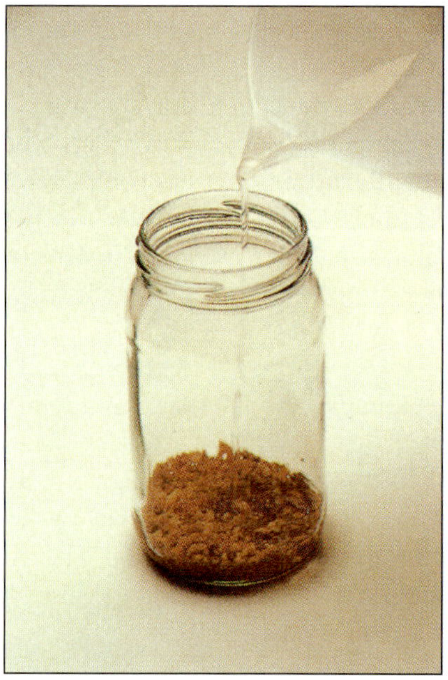

2 Add just enough water to cover the size and allow it to soak for about 20 minutes. It will swell during this time.

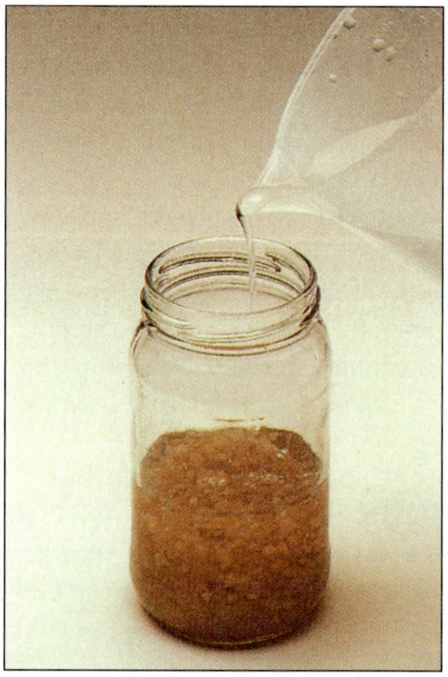

3 Add more water until the jam jar is three-quarters full.

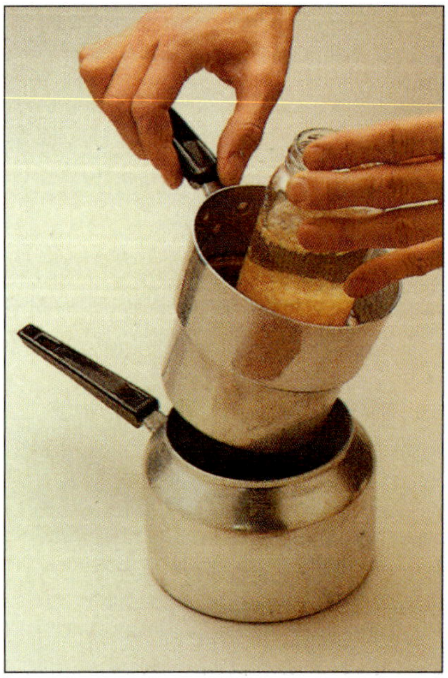

4 The size must now be heated, but not allowed to boil. Place the jam jar in a double saucepan or rest it on a saucer or trivet in an ordinary saucepan.

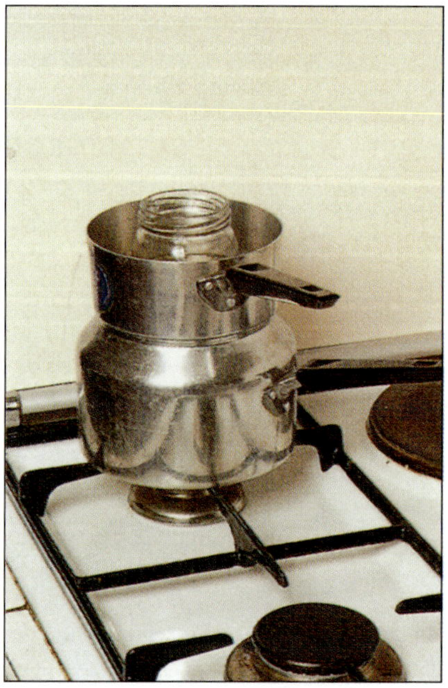

5 Let it warm gently for about half an hour.

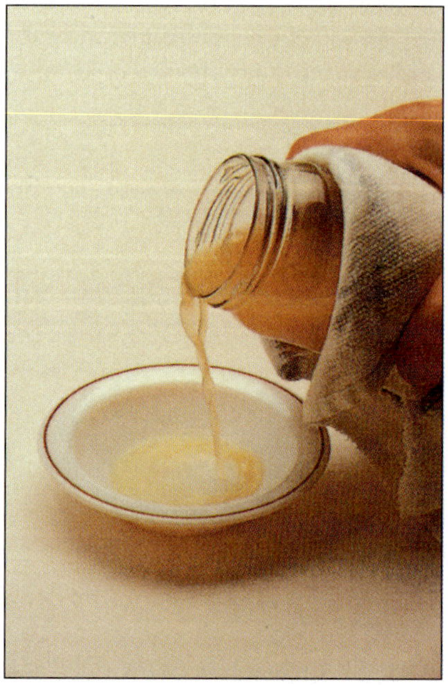

6 To test that the size is of the right consistency, pour a small sample into a saucer and allow it to set.

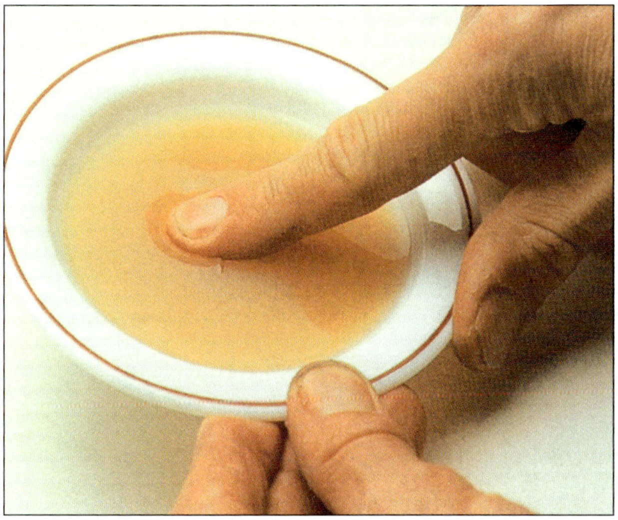

7 It should be rubbery yet soft enough for you to be just able to break it with your finger. If it is too thin reheat with more size; if too solid add more water. The size will take a few hours to set in the jam jar. Freshly prepared size remains usable for two or three days or up to a week in a refrigerator.

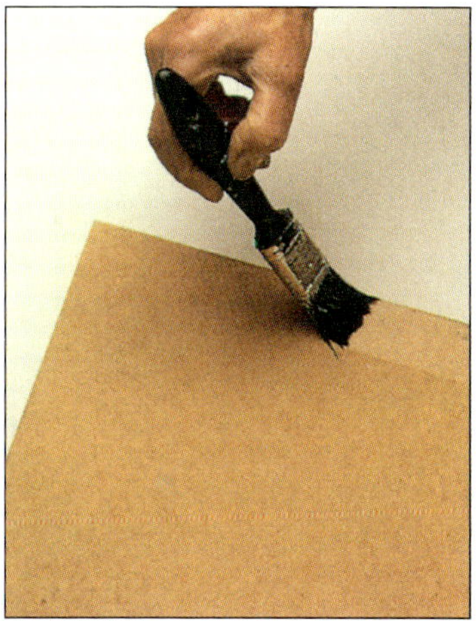

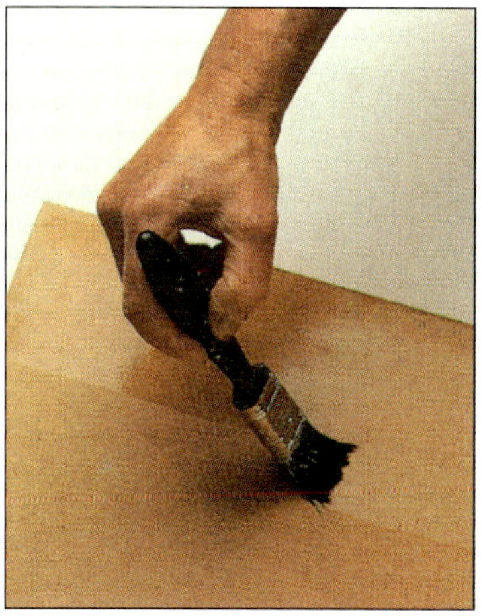

8 Before applying the size to sanded hardboard (as shown here) or canvas, re-dissolve it by warming gently. Use a well-loaded 25mm or 38mm brush and stroke it in one direction only across the surface, starting from one edge. Once dry, repeat in the opposite direction. If using hardboard or cardboard a coat of size on the reverse side prevents warping. Leave to dry thoroughly for 12 hours and then sand lightly. The surface is now ready for priming.

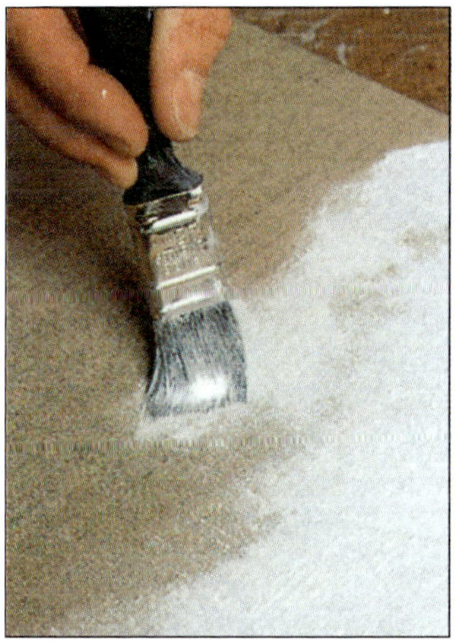

9 If an acrylic primer is used, no sizing is necessary, as these are designed to adhere to untreated surfaces. Using a household brush, apply the primer with a scrubbing motion and work it across the canvas in one direction only.

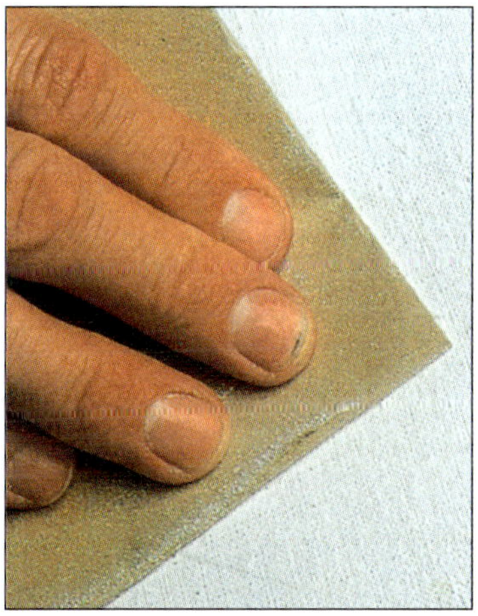

10 Once the first coat of primer is dry, lightly sand it down if the surface is grainy.

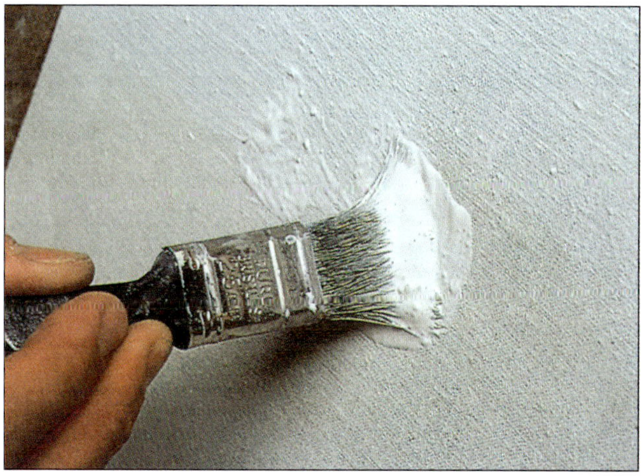

11 If you want to accentuate the brushmarks, apply a second coat of primer in the same direction as before. Alternatively, brush at right angles to give a more even surface. Finally, sand it again very lightly unless you prefer a rougher texture to paint on. If a toned ground is required, acrylic primer can easily be tinted by mixing in acrylic colors (see also colored grounds).

Equipment

PAINTS

Two grades of ready-made oil paints are sold: those labelled "Artists" and a cheaper kind, called "Students," or by some trade name. The cheaper contain lower-quality pigments and may be less permanent.

In general, the same pigments are used in oils as in watercolors, gouache, tempera, and acrylics. Only three pigments are comparatively uneffected by conditions that alter the properties of other pigments: heat, light, moisture, acidity, or alkalinity. These are carbon black, cobalt, and viridian.

Most permanent are the earth colors such as yellow ocher, terre verte, raw and burnt sienna, raw and burnt umber, light red, Indian red, Venetian red, and natural ultramarine. These are natural earths. Artificial mineral pigments include aureolin, the cadmiums, viridian, and cobalt blue. Organic pigments are divided into animal sepia, carmine, Indian yellow; vegetable gamboge, the madders, sap green, indigo; and artificial; Prussian blue. It is vital to use good quality whites, as nearly all colors are mixed with them.

Most pigments are susceptible to chemical interactions and atmospheric conditions. Lead white, for instance, a metal-based pigment, can be discolored by sulphur fumes in the air. Ageing oil yellows can turn chrome yellow into a green. Strong sunlight darkens madder, sepia, and carmine. Metal-based pigments blacken if mixed with sulphides such as the cadmiums; and should not be mixed with certain synthetics, including vermillion and ultramarine.

Many made-up paints contain an excess of oil to increase their shelf life; and although this can be removed by placing the paint on an absorbent surface, many artists prefer to make up at least some of their colors from scratch, adding just as much or as little oil as they need, experimenting with textures and direct blending of pigments.

Raw pigments can be bought at most artists' supply stores, together with the equipment for home mixing: a glass slab or old litho stone, a glass miller or muller and a palette knife or spatula. Pour enough binder on the powdered pigment on the glass to make it flutinous and blend it with the palette knife. Stir the paint with a circular motion until it is of an even consistency, exerting pressure with the glass muller. The paint can be stored in a glass jar, covering it with water if it is to be kept for long.

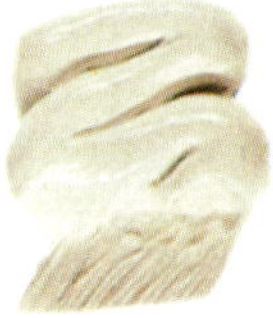
flake white

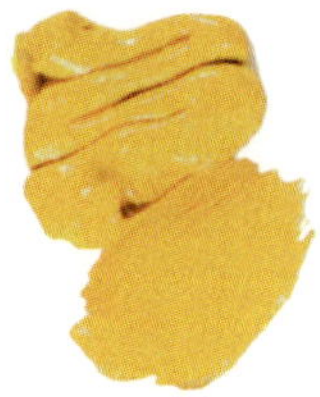
lemon yellow

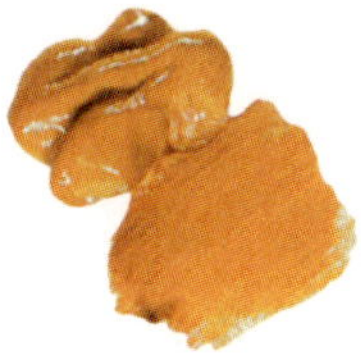
yellow ocher

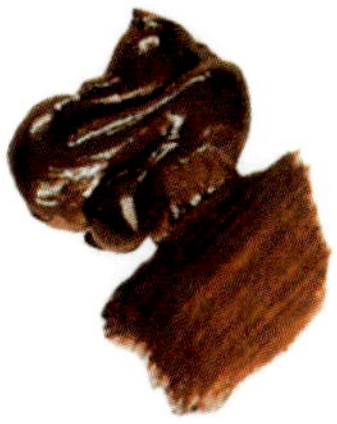
burnt sienna

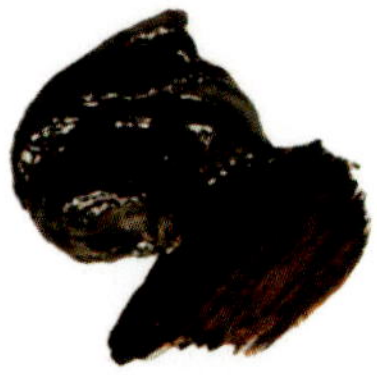
raw umber

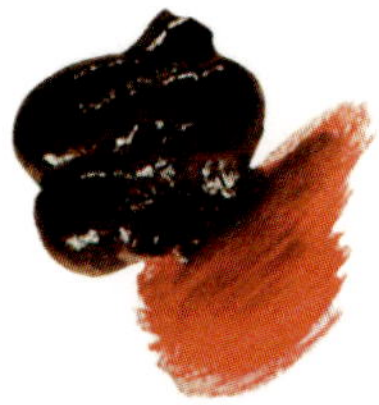
alizarin crimson

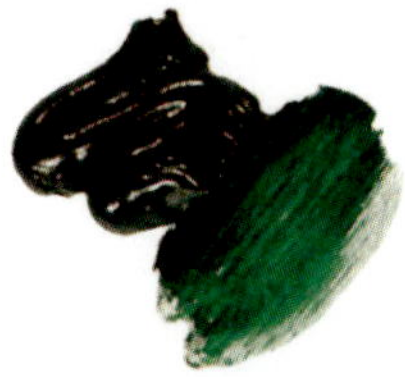
viridian green

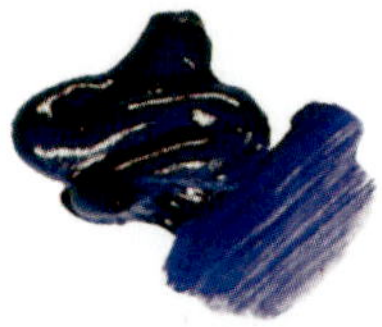
cobalt blue

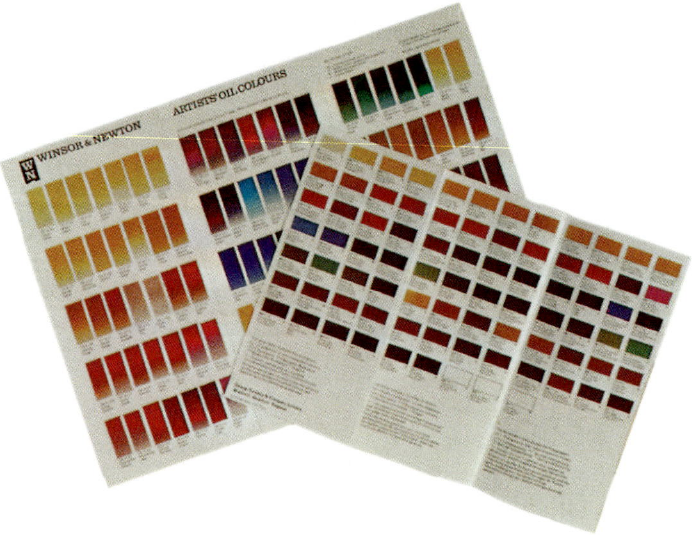

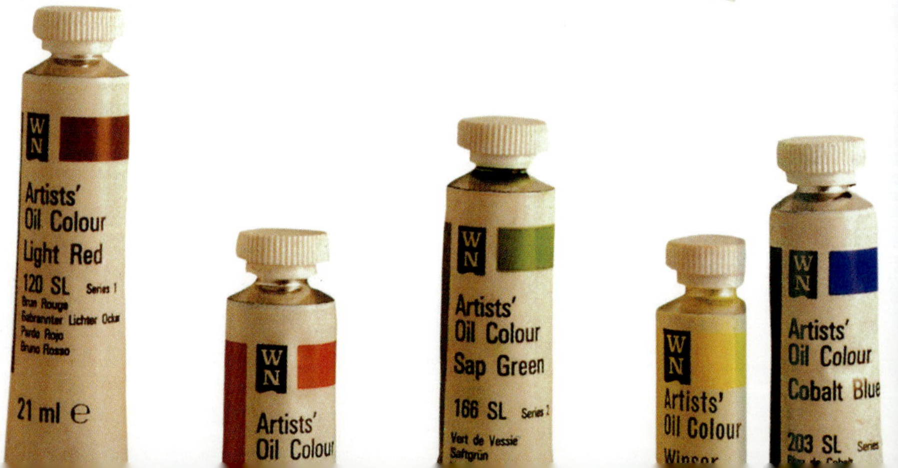

BRUSHES

Oil painting brushes are usually of bleached hogs' hair and red sable hair. The making of good quality brushes, even on a mass production basis, is a skilled craft. A brushmaker will never trim the painting ends of the brushes, but will shuffle and arrange the hairs or bristles and adjust them within the metal grip or ferrule to give the right shape, even utilizing the natural curve of some bristles so that they form a gentle curve toward instead of splaying out.

Hogs' bristle has split ends, which help hold the paint to the brush; and this is reckoned an advantage over sable brushes that, nevertheless, give a smoother stroke and find a place in any good collection of brushes. They are generally thinner and smaller.

The basic brush shapes are bright, round, flat, and filbert. Brights are short-bristled with square ends; grounds are round and round-ended, good for thin paint; flats are similar to brights but with longer bristles, giving a longer stroke; filberts are similar to rounds but wider; "longs" in sable oil brushes are similar to bristle flats; chisel edges, good for painting straight edges, are not often seen today.

Wide, supple badger blenders, made from badger hair, are used to take out brush strokes or blend wet areas into each other. Wipe them often on absorbent cloth when employing this technique. Fan brushes of red sable are used for the same purpose as badger blenders but give a softer effect.

Brushes should be cleaned immediately after each day's use. First rinse them in turpentine or white spirit and wipe them dry, or shake them in warm water with a strong household soap and wash the soap off thoroughly under warm running water.

Brushes that have been caked with paint for a long time can be cleaned with paint stripper, but this shortens their lives. Never leave a brush soaking with the bristles or hairs touching the sides or bottom of the container.

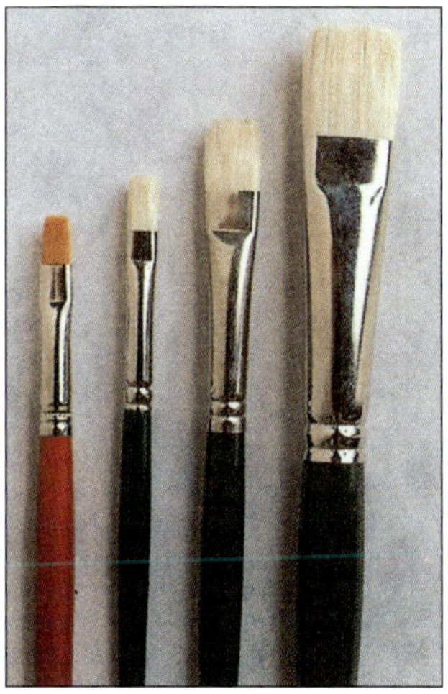

A selection of short flats, one soft-haired (synthetic) and three bristle. Long-haired flats are also available.

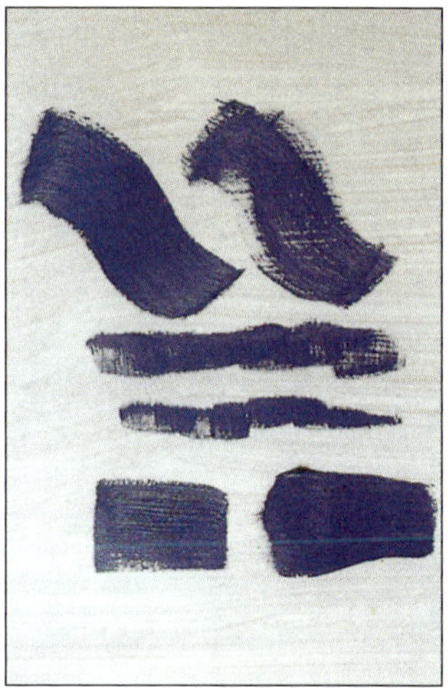

Flats make distinctive square or rectangular marks, much exploited by the Impressionists.

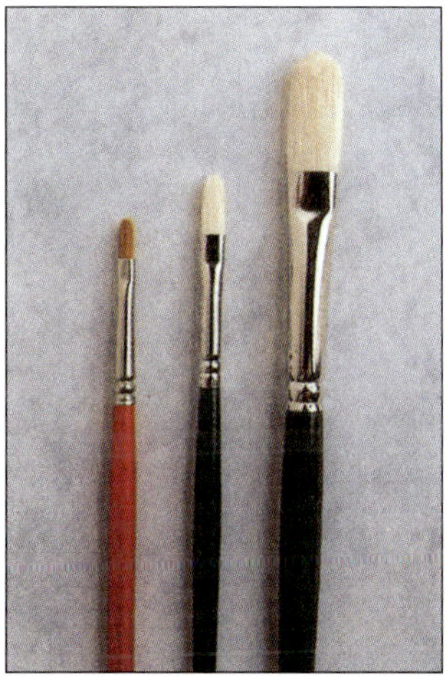

These are filbert brushes, one soft-haired (synthetic) and two bristle. The hairs are quite long, arranged as a flat head and tapered to a rounded tip.

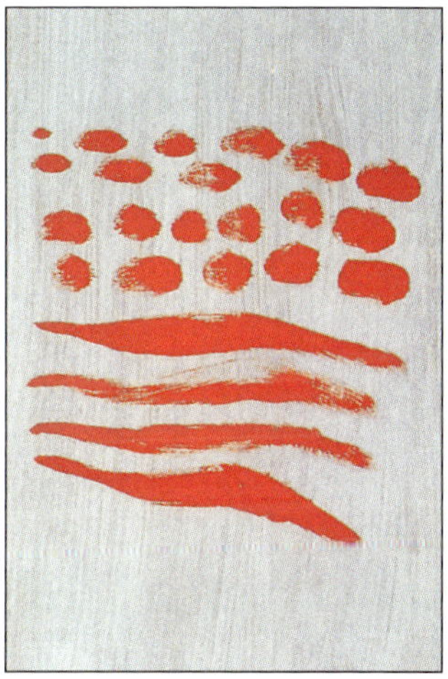

Filberts are extremely versatile brushes. They can leave rounded dabs of paint or be twisted during a stroke to create marks of varying thickness.

Brushes are produced in series, a range of sizes in which the composition of the brush remains the same. As shown here, for instance, a series of round hogs'-hair brushes may be produced in twelve sizes, the smallest numbered 1, and so on up to the largest, 12.

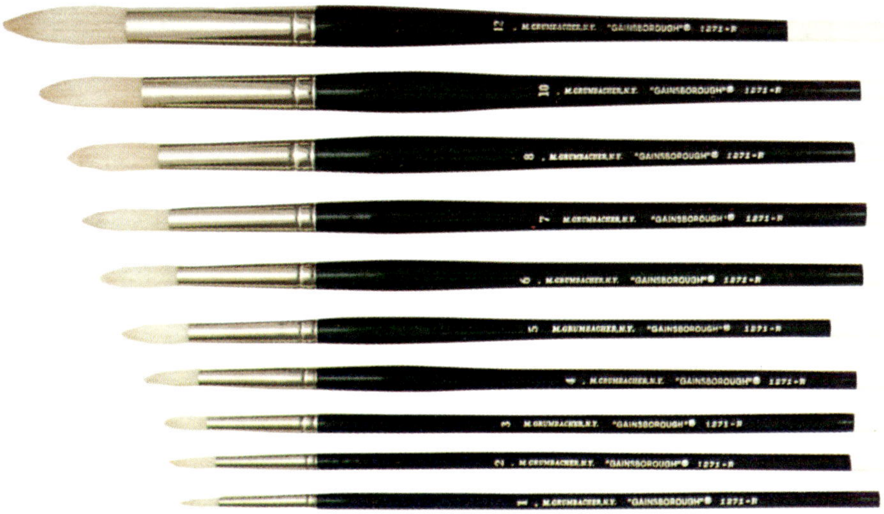

OTHER OIL PAINTING EQUIPMENT

Knives Palette knives, made from smooth flexible steel, come in many shapes and sizes and are used for mixing the paint on the palette; painting knives, with thin, delicate blades and often longer handles, are used to apply paint directly to the canvas.

Palettes Palettes can be oval or rectangular and made of wood, china, or glass. Palettes with thumbholes are made for easel painting; but, in the studio, palettes of almost any non-porous material can be placed handily on a nearby steady surface. Treat new wooden palettes with linseed oil to prevent the wood feeding on the oil in the paint. Disposable paper palettes, with paint-proof peel-off sheets, are now made.

Dippers Dippers are small open-topped cans made to hold oil and turpentine and clip onto the edge of the palette. But in the studio it may be more convenient to use containers resting on a nearby steady surface.

Mahl sticks A mahl stick is traditionally a cane with a chamois tip that rests on the canvas to steady the painting arm. Some are now made of aluminum with a rubber tip and come in 12, 24, and 36 inch sizes. But they are easy to make by tying a bundle of rags to the end of a garden cane.

Easels Easels vary greatly in size and weight. The most comfortable is the traditional artist's donkey, a studio easel at which the artist can work sitting down; but the simplest kind of radial easel is substantial enough for most needs. It has short tripod legs and the upright column can be tilted and fixed by a screw, while the tray and top grip for the stretcher or board slide up and down the column.

1	*Mahl stick*
3,4,5	*Painting knives*
2, 6	*Palette knives*
7	*Plastic palette knife*

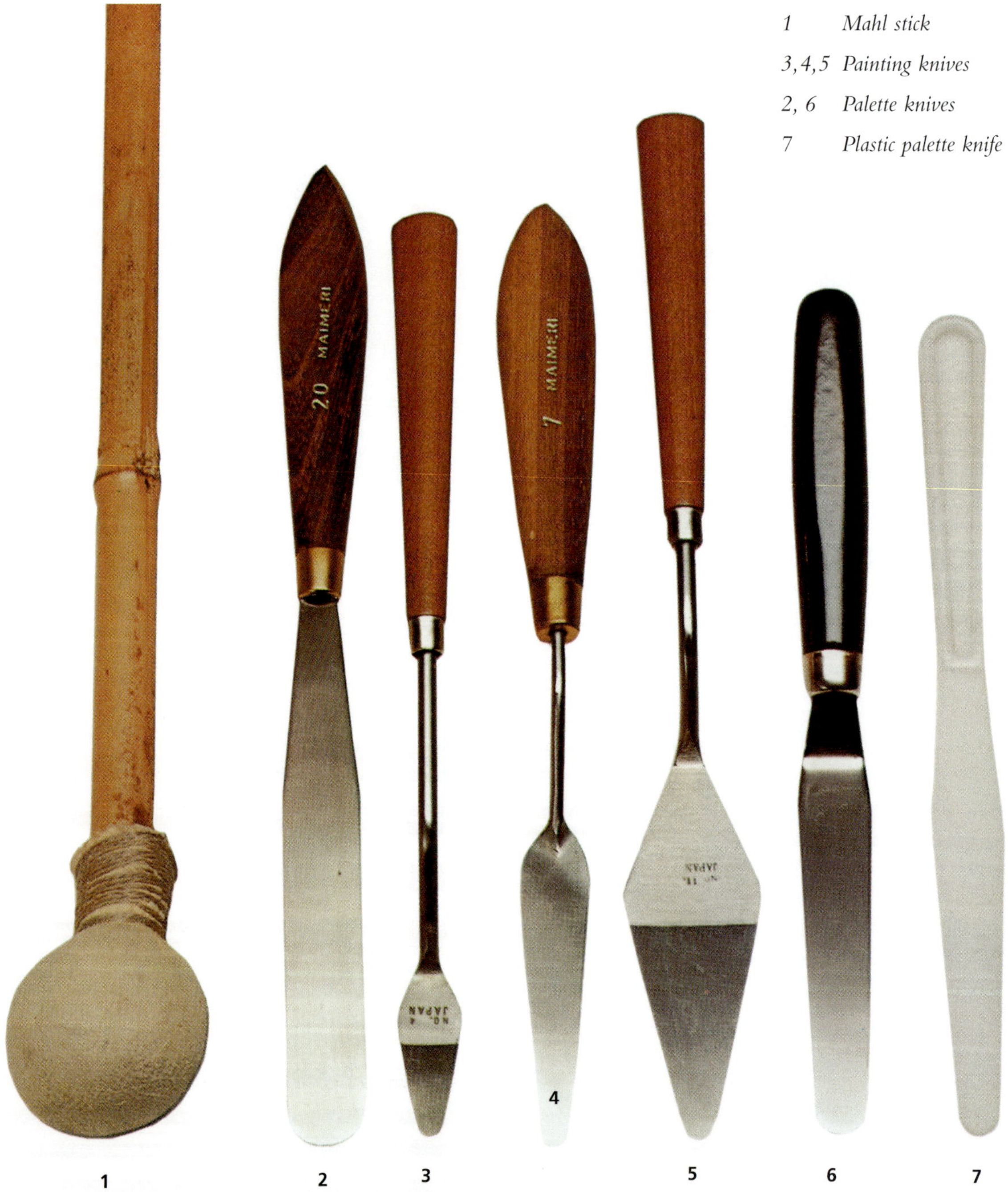

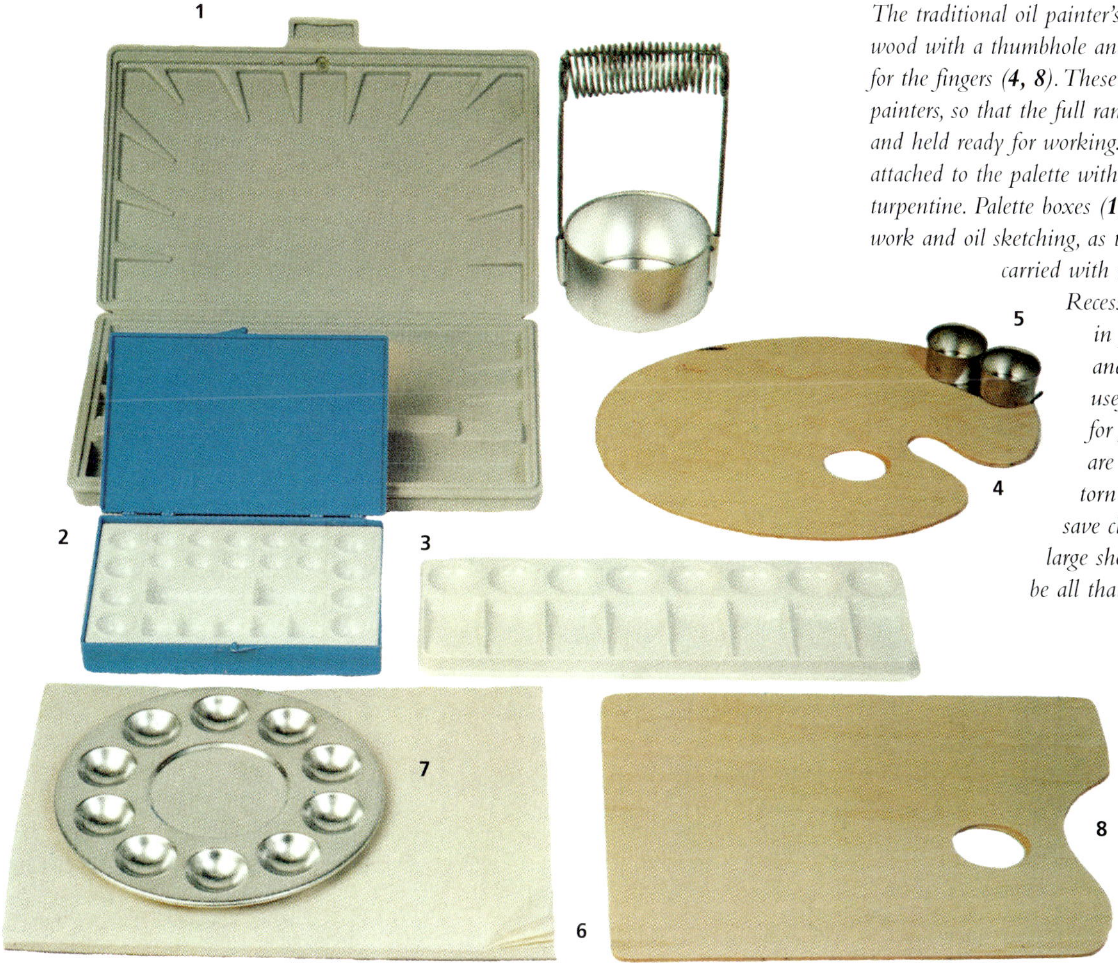

The traditional oil painter's palette is a flat piece of wood with a thumbhole and indentation at one end for the fingers (**4, 8**)*. These are intended for easel painters, so that the full range of color can be laid out and held ready for working. Small dippers* (**5**) *can be attached to the palette with clips to hold oil or turpentine. Palette boxes* (**1, 2**) *are useful for outdoor work and oil sketching, as they can be closed up and carried with the colors still in place. Recessed palettes are available in plastic* (**3**)*, aluminum* (**7**)*, and china, and may be useful for mixing thin paint for glazes. Paper palettes* (**6**) *are disposable and can be torn off as they are used to save cleaning. For studio use, a large sheet of glass or wood may be all that is required.*

PALETTES

Palettes come in a variety of shapes, sizes, and materials, designed to suit your individual requirements. Thumbhole palettes are designed for easel painting. They have a thumbhole and indentation for the fingers, and the palette is supported on the forearm. Before buying a palette, try out different sizes and shapes to see which feels the most comfortable.

New wooden palettes should be treated by rubbing with linseed oil to prevent them absorbing the oil in the paint. You can even improvise your own palette, from any non-absorbent surface, making it any size and color you like.

A sheet of glass with white or neutral-colored paper underneath it would be suitable, or there are disposable palettes made of oil-proof paper – these are a boon for outdoor work, and remove the necessity for cleaning. The nearest object to fulfil all the conditions for the ideal palette is perhaps a large china plate.

A porcelain or glazed pottery surface is easy to keep clean. If paint dries on it, it can be cleaned with hot water. A few minutes' soaking is all that is needed. For more stubborn cases, soak for a longer time in hot water; paint should then scrape off quite easily.

A white plate is an advantage. White allows mixtures to be accurately gauged; a colored surface plays optical tricks and is best avoided.

The lip or edge on a plate is only important if the mixtures are rather liquid. For stiffer mixtures, using thicker paints, a pad of paper palettes has advantages. Mixing is done on the top layer, that can be torn off and discarded. Paper palettes are not very practical for more liquid paint, or washes, as the paper tends to wrinkle and the paint to spill over the edges.

Another possible palette is a sheet of plain white plastic. The advantage here is that it can be bought in any size. Most palettes tend to be small, useful for taking outdoors for sketching trips, but not nearly large enough for working in the studio.

A sheet of firm, white plastic, glued to an old kitchen table, will make not only a good surface for mixing paint on, but can double up as a working desk.

Mediums

This word embraces all the different fluids used both in painting and the manufacture of paint. They fall into four main categories:

Binders are the drying oils that are mixed with pigment particles in the manufacture of paints to form a thick paste. They are usually linseed oil and, for the paler pigments, poppy oil, and they are called drying oils because they dry on exposure to air.

Mediums (a more specific use of the word) are oils or synthetic "oils" used in the course of painting. Their purpose is to change or enhance various properties of paint, such as consistency, drying time, and glossiness. Linseed and poppy oil are also used in this context.

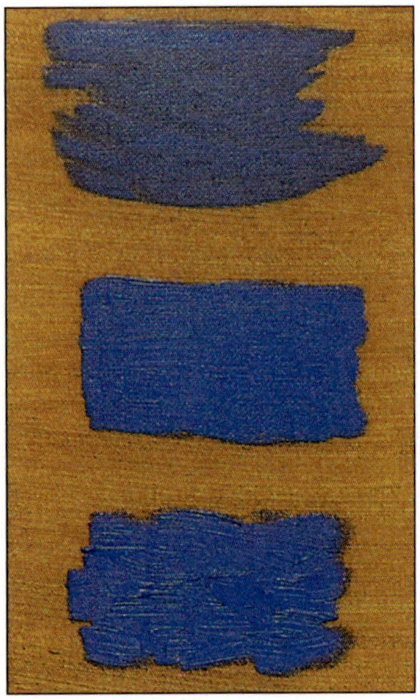

From top to bottom: paint thinned with white spirit; paint mixed with linseed oil; paint mixed with an impasto medium, causing it to retain the marks of the brush.

Diluents are liquids that may or may not act as solvents, used to dilute and thin down paints to aid their application. They evaporate once exposed to the air, leaving paint of the original composition. Turpentine and white spirit are the most-used diluents.

Varnishes are liquids designed to cover a finished painting in order to protect it and to provide the desired matt or glossy finish.

The binders, mediums, and varnishes are all mixtures of one or more of the following: drying oils, resins, waxes, diluents, and siccatives. All of these may either be natural or synthetic. The resins, such as damar, mastic, and copal, contribute toward a hard protective film in varnishes and add gloss to paint mediums. Waxes such as beeswax are used in glazing mediums and also in those designed to improve the impasto effect of paint. Siccatives are drying agents, usually containing lead, manganese, or cobalt, sometimes added to the medium. (Some paints also contain these, and will accordingly be quick driers.) An art shop is usually stocked with a daunting array of bottles, but actually the beginner need purchase nothing more elaborate than one bottle of distilled turpentine with which to thin paints for the initial layers of underpainting, and one bottle of refined linseed oil. The latter, diluted with at least twice its volume of turpentine, gives a fatter, glossier texture to the final layer of paint. You will also need white spirit for washing brushes, but this is usually more cheaply obtained from hardware and DIY stores. It is a cheap mineral turpentine substitute that can also be used as a diluent and is useful for those who are allergic to turpentine.

If in time you find that the basic linseed oil-turpentine mixtures do not suit your needs, the only course is to experiment with other mediums until you find one or more that you are happy with. All manufacturers provide information on their products, so it is wise to consult these before making your choice. You may decide to dispense with a medium altogether; there is no reason why paint should not be applied neat, particularly for impasto areas such as highlights, laid toward the end of a painting.

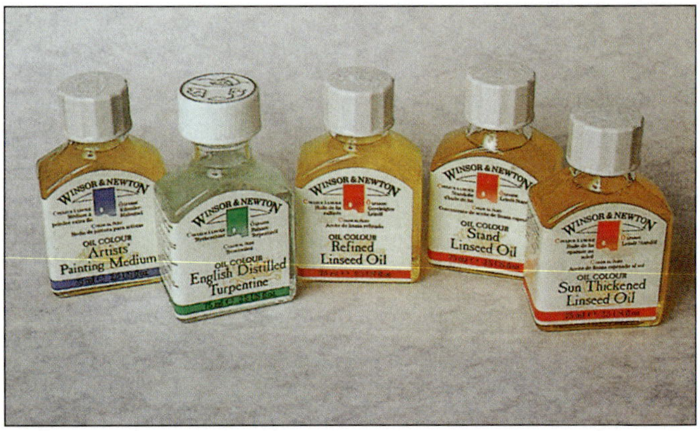

Drying oils and solvents. A large variety of products is available from manufacturers, but most artists start with refined linseed oil and distilled turpentine only, extending their range when specific needs arise.

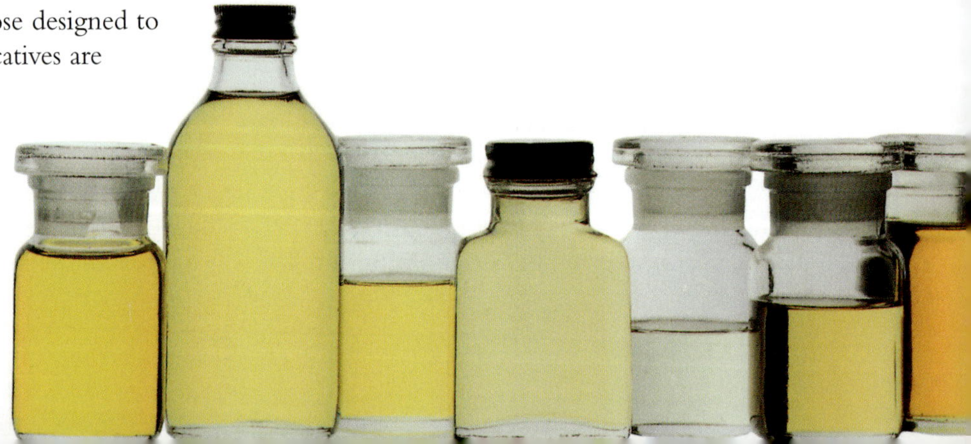

Easels

An easel is a necessity. You may manage to produce one small painting by propping up your canvas on a table or shelf, but you will very soon find out how unsatisfactory this is. Without an easel you cannot adjust the height of your work – essential if you are doing a painting of a reasonable size, as you must be able to reach different areas of it easily and comfortably – and you cannot tilt the work, which you often need to do either to avoid light reflecting on its surface or to catch the best light for working.

There are several different types of easel on the market, from huge, sturdy studio easels to small sketching easels that are light and easily portable. Your choice will be dictated by the space in which you are working, whether you intend to work mostly indoors or outdoors, and by the size of your work and the type of painting you are doing. If you intend to work out of doors frequently you will need a sketching easel (though small sketches can be done by propping the canvas or board against the open lid of a paintbox). If, on the other hand, you know you are unlikely to paint anywhere but indoors, the heavier radial easel could be a good choice, but this cannot easily be dismantled and put away, so you might choose a portable easel for space reasons.

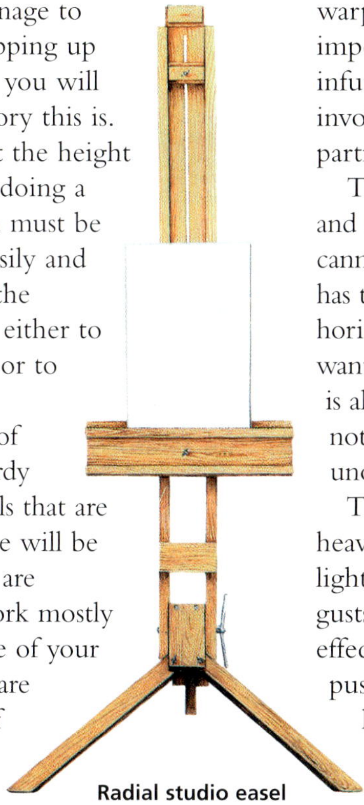

Radial studio easel

There are three main types of sketching easel: the box easel, the wooden sketching easel, and the aluminum sketching easel. The first type combines an easel and a paintbox, and can be folded up into a case for carrying. These were at one time very expensive, and the best ones still are, but cheaper versions are now appearing on the market, and for an outdoor painter they are a good choice, as everything can be carried in one piece of luggage.

Wooden sketching easels are inexpensive, but are not recommended, as the blocks that slide up and down in slots to enable you to adjust the height of the work tend to become warped, so that they either do not slide at all or are impossible to fix in position. There is nothing more infuriating than having to fight your easel, which often involves knocking it over, just when you want to work particularly fast because the light is changing.

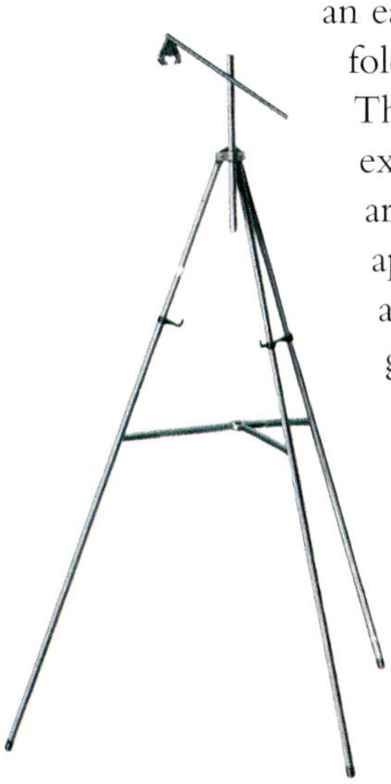

Aluminum sketching easel

The metal sketching easel, on the other hand, is excellent, and suffers from none of these disadvantages because metal cannot warp. It is easy to adjust, holds the work firmly, and has the additional advantage of being adjustable to a horizontal position for watercolors (you may find that you want to experiment with other media from time to time). It is also quite adequate for indoor work, providing you are not working on a vast scale, and can be tucked away unobtrusively in a corner when not in use.

The problem with all sketching easels, except the heavier version of the box type, is that because they are light, and thus easy to carry, they are also vulnerable to gusts of wind, the canvas or board acting as a most effective sail! Some artists manage to anchor their easel by pushing tent pegs into the ground and tying the easel legs to them, or by hanging a heavy stone from the center of the easel.

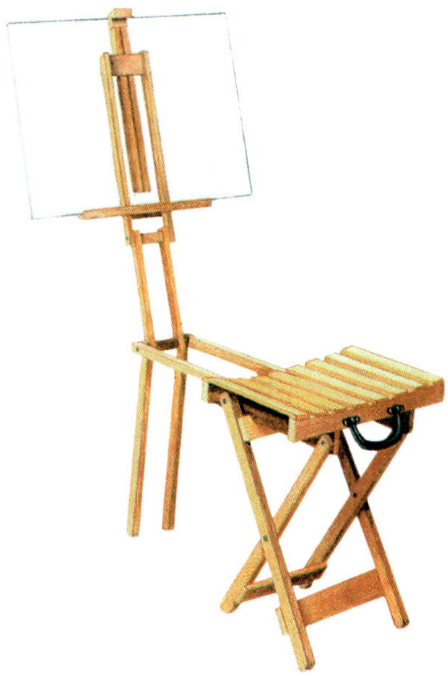

Portable sketching easel with stool

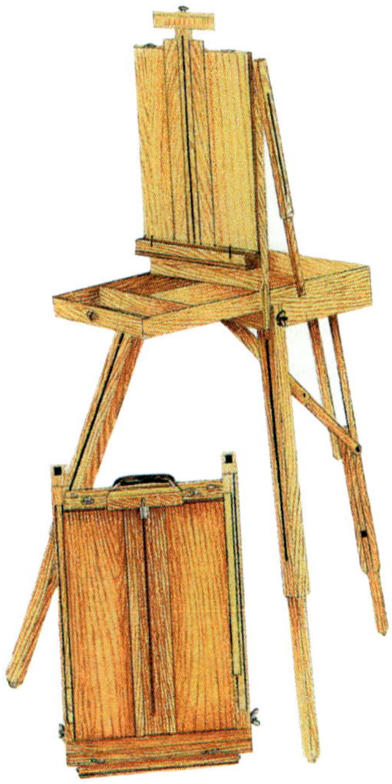

Box easel

Techniques

Although there are really no hard-and-fast rules in oil painting, it is helpful to have an idea of the various ways in which artists go about things so that you can experiment with different techniques, color schemes, and compositions as you evolve your own particular style. Painting involves seeing as well as doing: it is your personal vision that is to be translated into marks on canvas, and the wider your technical range the better.

GENERAL PAINTING TECHNIQUES

If you are painting a very simple subject, such as an empty landscape with a wide expanse of sky, there is often no need for an underdrawing or underpainting, except perhaps a line or two to delineate the horizon. However, for a more complex subject such as a figure study, or perhaps a landscape including people or buildings, a preliminary drawing on the canvas is usually advisable. This enables you to work out the composition and the position of the main elements within it, and to plan the balance of dark colors and light ones. For a portrait or figure painting you will need to establish how you want to place the figure in relation to the background, and you will need to get the proportions of the figure right. If you start an ambitious painting with inadequate drawing you will be forever altering parts of it, that will not only spoil your enjoyment, but will also produce a labored and overworked painting. Careful planning at the start enables you to be more spontaneous later.

Underdrawings can be done either in pencil or charcoal, the latter being preferable, as it is a broad medium and is easier to use freely. To avoid loose charcoal mixing with the paint and muddying it, brush it down lightly with a rag before starting to paint – you will still retain the main lines of the drawing.

Underpainting – another form of drawing but done with a brush – can be made either in monochrome or an understated version of the finished color scheme, in both cases using paint, well-thinned with turpentine. If you find a blank canvas somewhat intimidating, you will find that an underpainting overcomes the problem by providing a "stepping-stone" from which you can build up the succeeding layers of color with confidence.

A monochrome underpainting should concentrate on the main masses of light and shade, a colored one should avoid bright and light colors, as you will want to build up to these as the painting progresses. Nowadays artists often use acrylic paint for underpainting, as this dries much faster than even thinned oil paint, enabling the next stage to proceed immediately.

A good general rule for oil painting – and a very old one – is to work "fat over lean." This simply means that in the initial stages the paint should be used fairly thin (diluted with turpentine only) becoming thicker and oilier as the painting progresses. Working in this way reduces the risk of the paint cracking as it dries out. If, however, "lean" paint is brushed over a layer of "fat" paint (containing a greater proportion of oil) what happens is that the lean layer dries first, and when the fat layer beneath it eventually starts to dry it contracts, causing the dry layer on top to crack.

Not all paintings, however, are done in stages in this way; many are completed at one sitting, with a minimum of drawing or underpainting or even none at all. This is known as *alla prima* painting, and is much used for landscape or quick portrait studies where the painter wants to record his impressions rapidly in a free and spontaneous manner. The paint is used thickly, with each color laid down more or less as it will finally appear. When oil paints are used in this way, the colors blend into each other, particularly when one is laid on top of another. This is a feature of *alla prima* painting, known as working "wet-into-wet," and was much exploited by the Impressionists, particularly Claude Monet (1840–1926) in his outdoor paintings. For anyone who has not used oils before, *alla prima* is a good way of starting, as it will give you an immediate "feel" for the medium and force you to work fast without being over-conscious of each brush stroke.

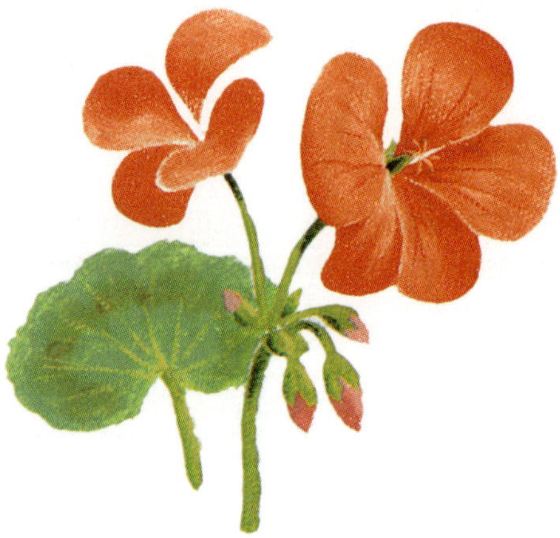

SCUMBLING

Scumbling involves applying an uneven layer of paint over a dry, then, relatively oil-free underpainting so that the first color shows through to some extent. In skillful hands scumbling can create some of the most magical effects in a painting, giving a veil-like impression rather like a filmy fabric placed over a matt one. It is an excellent way of modifying color without sacrificing liveliness, and indeed the scumbled layer itself can be modified by the under-painting so long as this had been planned in advance. For example, you might use a flat, dark red underpainting as a basis for scumbling in lighter red, pink, or even a contrasting color. In addition, the surface texture of the paint is more evocative than flat color, and may well carry the illusion of its subject more effectively.

Dark colors can be scumbled over light ones, but the method is usually more successful with light used over dark. One way to apply a scumble is to load a wide, flat bristle brush with diluted paint, squeeze it to expel as much moisture as possible and then lightly drag it over the surface to produce a very thin film of paint. Thick, undiluted paint is often applied in a circular motion with a well-loaded round bristle brush held perpendicularly. Alternatively a fairly wide flat hog carrying thick paint can be dragged nearly flat to the surface leaving a flecked, broken layer of paint. A round hog or fan dabbed over the surface will create a stippled effect.

Scumbles can also be applied with the fingers, the side of the palm, a rag, a sponge, or a palette knife. The coarser the texture of the canvas the more effective is the scumble because the paint is deposited mainly on the top of the weave. Experimenting with different thicknesses of paint, different surfaces, and different implements held in a variety of ways will give you an idea of the many effects that can be achieved.

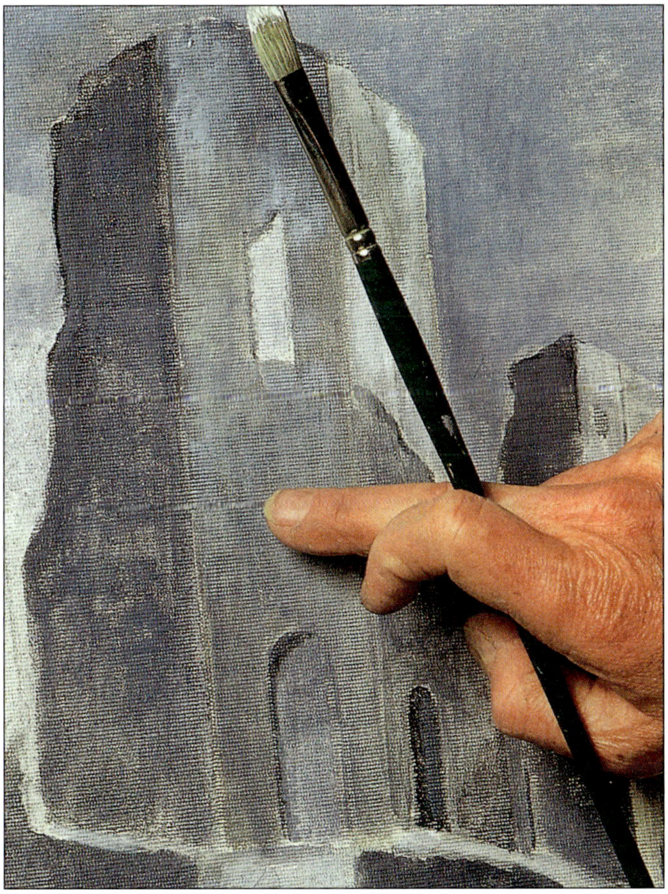

ABOVE: *Generally a light scumble over a dark color produces the best results. The paint should be fairly dry and applied thinly in gradual stages. Here paint is scumbled gently with the finger.*

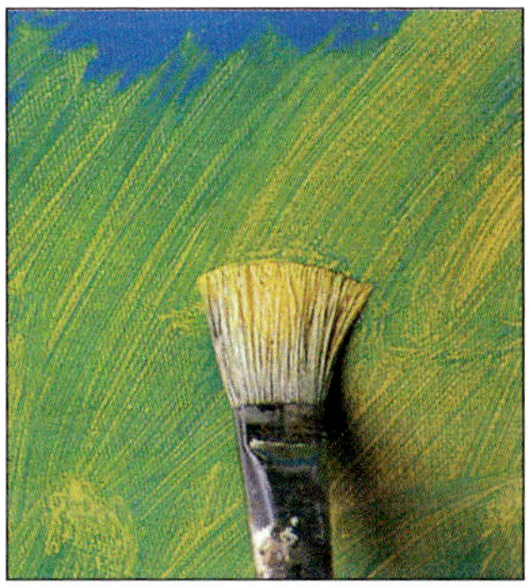

Paint for scumbling should be fairly dry – wipe the brush on blotting paper to remove any excess moisture. Use a bristle brush (a soft brush is less effective) to scrub the paint on with free, vigorous strokes. The paint can be worked with a circular motion, with straight back-and-forth strokes, or in various directions. The idea is not to blend the color but to leave the brushmarks showing.

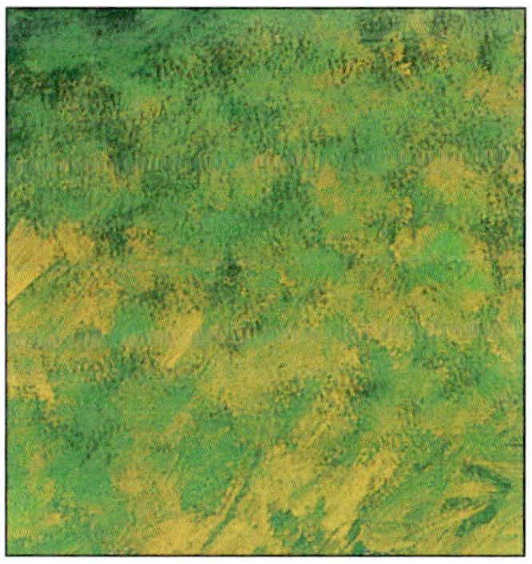

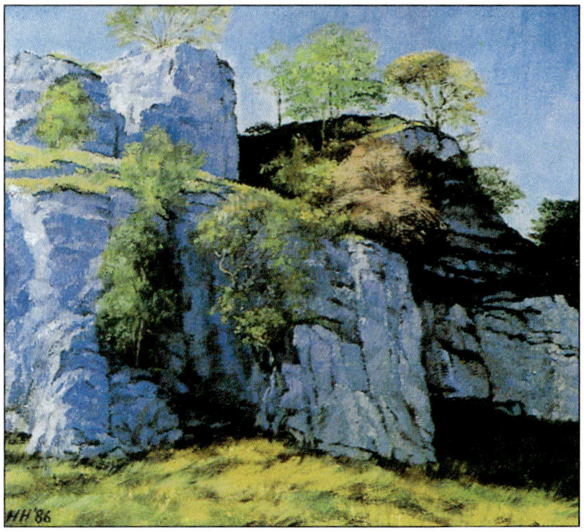

RIGHT: *Here scumbling was used to suggest the texture of the chalk cliffs. The paint was scrubbed on with a brush over dry paint below, and in places was worked in with the fingers. The foreground was put on rather dry.*

ALLA PRIMA

This is an Italian term meaning "at first," and it describes paintings completed in one session. This necessarily involves working wet-into-wet rather than allowing a first layer to dry before others are added. The essential characteristic of *alla prima* is that there is no initial underpainting as such, although artists often make a rapid underdrawing in pencil or charcoal to establish the main lines.

After the introduction of tubed paint in the mid-nineteenth century, artists were able to work out of doors more easily. This *plein air* painting, as it is called, first undertaken by painters such as Constable (1776–1837), Corot (1796–1875), and later the Impressionists, established the rapid and direct *alla prima* approach as an acceptable technique. Artists began to work directly from nature, which inspired a new liveliness and freedom, of brushwork, a sense of light and spontaneity that could never be captured in the studio. Before this oil painting had been largely a studio activity as pigment had to be ground by hand, and paintings were built up slowly in a series of layers.

The direct method creates a lively and free effect that is seldom seen in more deliberate studio paintings. This is certainly true of Constable, whose small landscape sketches done on the spot have much more immediacy and vigour than his larger works such as The Haywain.

Working *alla prima* requires some confidence, as each patch of color is laid down more or less as it will appear in the finished picture. Any modifications must be kept to a minimum so that the fresh effect is not destroyed.

It is a good idea to use a limited palette, as too wide a choice of colors may tempt you to put in too much detail – there is no room for inessentials in *alla prima* painting. It is usually easiest to leave the lightest and darkest passages to the end so that the brush strokes used for these lie undisturbed on top of adjacent colors without mixing and muddying.

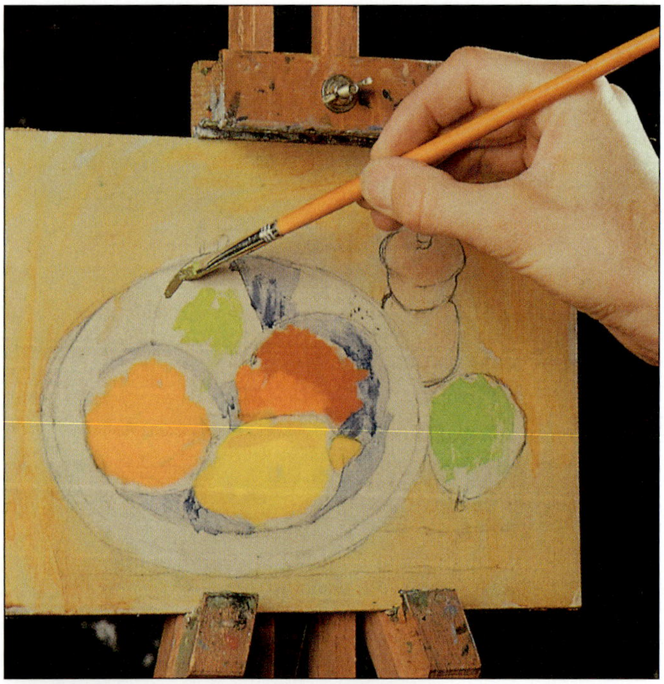

1 Because it is difficult to get ellipses right, these were first drawn with pencil. The next stage was to block in some of the shaded areas with cobalt blue and the tablecloth with ocher, which helped to establish the feel of the composition. This photograph shows some of the basic colors being laid in with rather thicker paint. The colors are those that will appear in the finished painting, though minor modifications can be made as the work progresses.

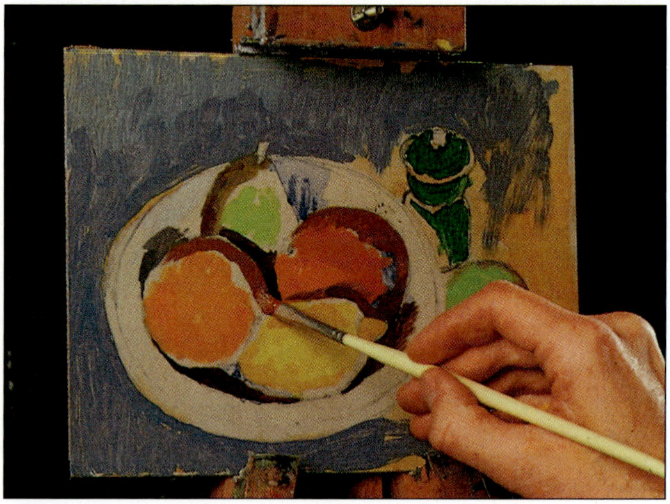

2 The tablecloth has been loosely painted, and now the darker tones of the fruit are developed. The bold brush strokes give a three-dimensional appearance.

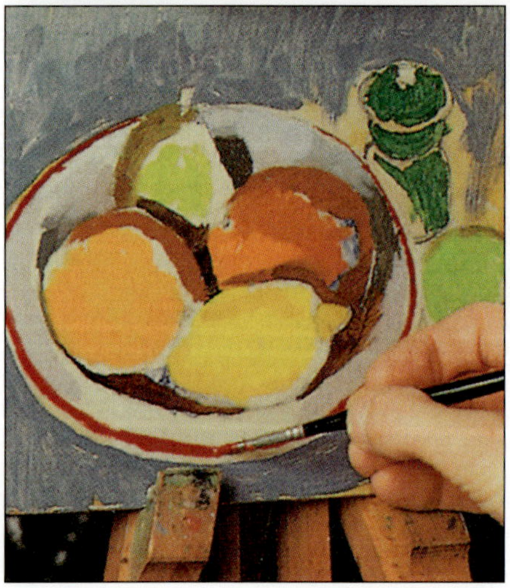

3 The red stripe around the bowl is crucial to the composition, so it is painted next, in a mixture of cadmium red and alizarin crimson. A higher proportion of crimson is used toward the far side.

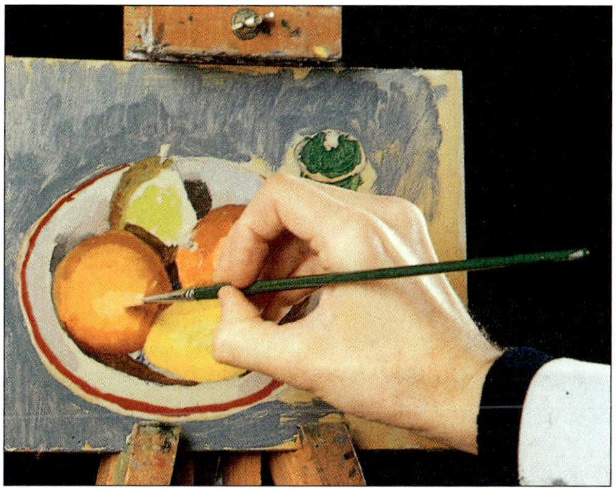

4 On the fruit, intermediate colors have been introduced between the darks and the lights without blending their boundaries. The final highlight has now been scumbled onto the orange, using a round bristle brush. This will not be touched again.

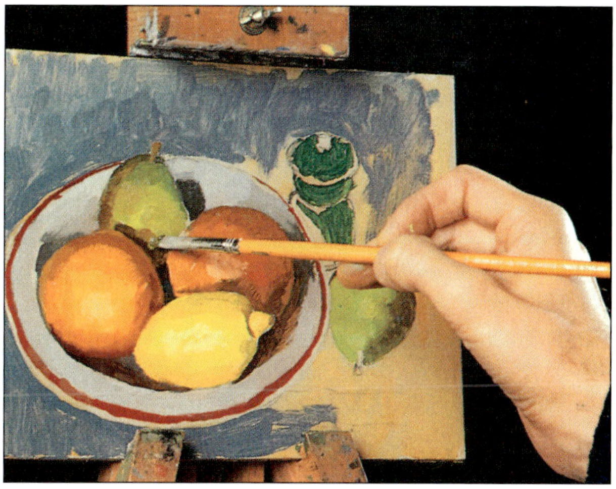

5 The other pieces of fruit are treated in a similar way, taking care that the intermediate colors successfully link the dark with the light areas. Here the addition of a patch of greenish brown contributes to the final brushwork of the pear.

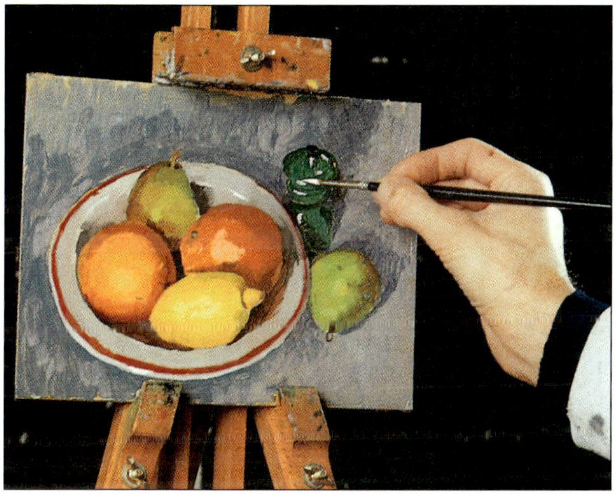

6 The tablecloth has been completed, and the shadows of the bowl, pepperpot, and pear added. A fine sable is used for laying small highlights on the pepperpot in thick, undiluted paint.

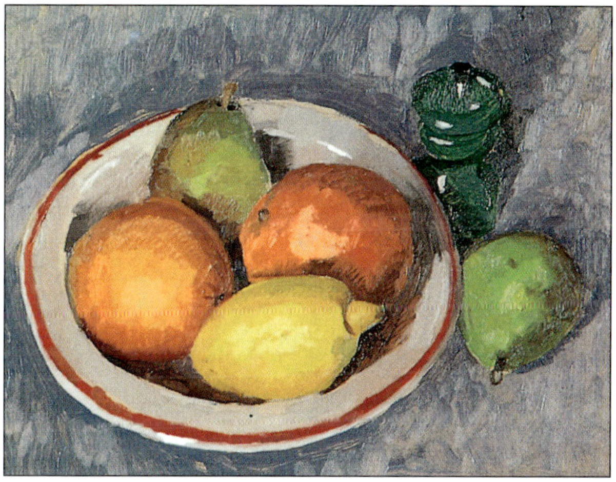

7 After approximately two hours' work, the painting is complete. Although certain areas have been modified by painting wet-into-wet, the majority of the paintwork remains exactly as it was first applied.

WET-INTO-WET

One of the main features of modern *alla prima* painting is the wet-into-wet technique. While the first layer is still wet, the artist paints or scumbles into it, at times making the colors deliberately run into each other. Because each new brush stroke mixes to some extent with those below or adjacent to it, the results are softer, with forms and colors merging into one another without hard boundaries. Painting wet-into-wet requires a sure hand and no hesitation; too much reworking will destroy your brushwork.

WET ON DRY

If you are completing a painting over a series of sessions you will probably find that you are painting wet on dry whether you planned it or not. Some artists, however, take a more methodical approach and deliberately allow each layer to dry before adding the next, perhaps in order to build up by means of glazing or scumbling. It is important to think of each layer as the prelude to the next, and to build up gradually to achieve the contrasts between light and dark areas that will give depth to the painting.

SGRAFFITO

This technique, whose name comes from the Italian *graffiare* – to scratch, involves scoring into the paint after it has been applied to the support. Using any rigid instrument such as a paintbrush handle, a knife, fork, or even a comb, the surface layer of wet paint is scratched into to reveal either the ground color or a layer of dry color beneath. Lines of any thickness can be drawn into the paint, and the separate layers of color chosen to contrast or complement each other. Dark brown paint, for example, could be scored to reveal a pale blue, or a dark green to reveal a brighter, lighter one beneath.

Scoring is often used as an accurate way to depict hair, creases in skin, and marks on flat surfaces such as walls or pavements. Rembrandt (1606–1669) used the technique extensively, scribbling into thick, wet paint with a brush handle to pick out individual hairs in a sitter's moustache or the pattern of lace on a collar. Shaded areas can be developed by hatching with the scorer to reveal dark underpainting. Wavelets on the sea, patches of light sky within foliage, or flashes and sparks in fire can all be suggested in this way.

The quality depends on the thickness of the paint and to what extent it has dried. Even when thoroughly dry, paint can be scratched into as long as a really sharp point is used. In this case the scored lines will be white, as all the layers of paint will be removed, but this can be effective for some subjects. It is best to restrict scratching into dry paint to rigid boards, however, as it might damage canvas.

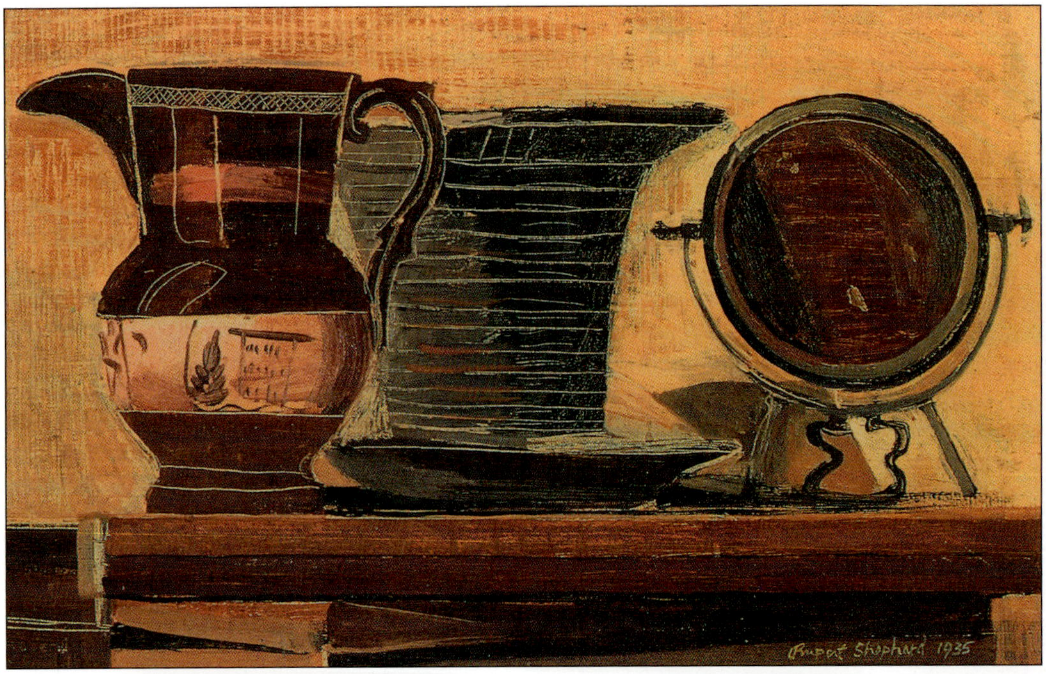

THE LUSTRE JUG by Rupert Shephard

The overall effect of the picture relies heavily on the sgraffito technique, which has been used very skilfully to define contours and describe pattern on both the objects and background. The latter is basically flat, but is enlivened by fine crosshatching. In this case the paint has been scratched back to the white ground, that is best done when the paint is dry or semi-dry.

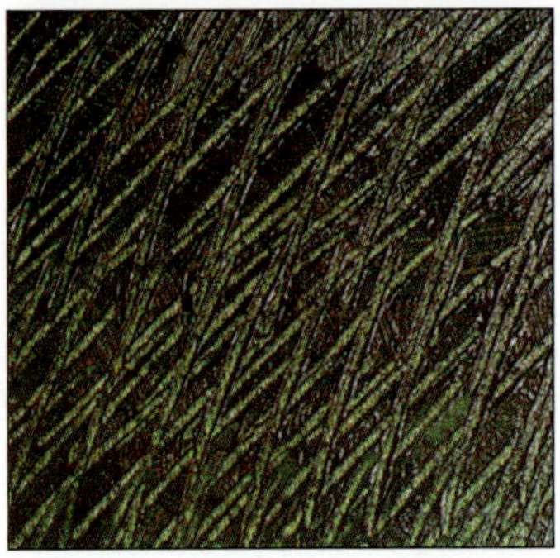

Apply a thick layer of paint, straight from the tube or diluted with just a little medium. While it is still wet, "draw" lines into the paint with the end of the brush hand or the handle of a knife.

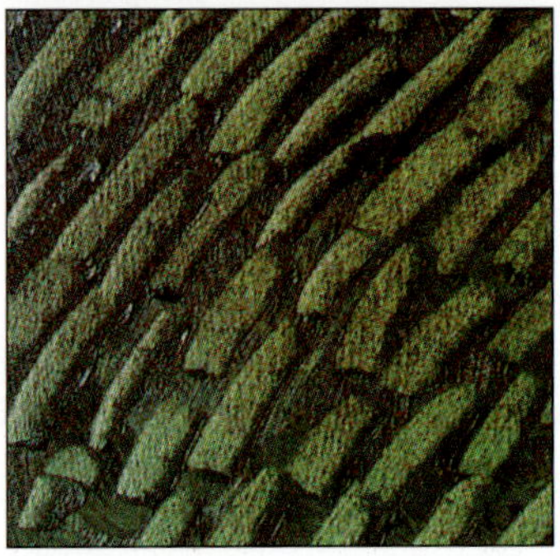

Experiment with different scraping tools to discover the variety of textures and patterns that can be achieved. Here, a trowel-shaped painting knife was used to make broad marks.

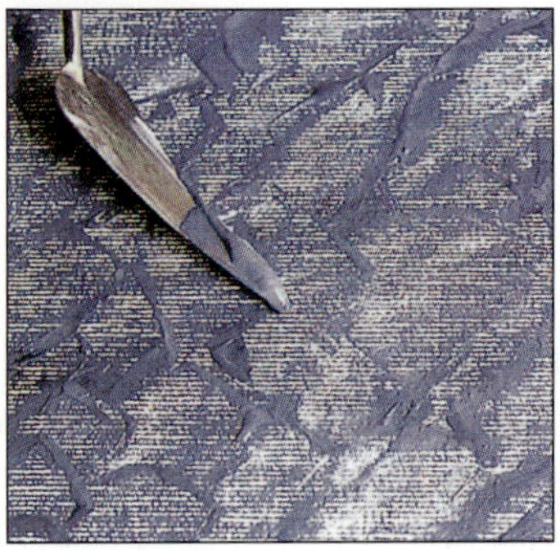

A more delicate texture can be obtained by applying a thin layer of paint and then using the edge of a painting knife to scrape off some of the paint right down to the canvas.

IMPASTO

This term describes paint that has been applied thickly enough to retain the marks and ridges left by the brush or painting knife. The ability to build up oil paint is for many people one of its main attractions. The picture surface can acquire a three-dimensional quality that can be used to model form and even mimic the texture of the subject. Turner (1775–1851) built up layers of paint in the pale areas of his paintings, such as clouds and sun, and some of Rembrandt's portraits are almost like relief sculptures.

Thickly applied paint is often used in conjunction with glazing. A dark glaze over a light-colored impasto will cling to the grooves and pits, emphasizing the brushwork. This can be an effective way of depicting texture; for example, rough stone or wood.

The paint can be applied with a brush or painting knife for impasto work, or it can even be squeezed out straight from the tube. Some makes of paint are particularly oily, in that case excess oil should be absorbed by blotting paper or the brushmarks may become blurred. If the paint is too thick a little linseed oil can be added. There are also mediums specially made for impasto work, that act as extenders, bulking out the paint. For anyone working on large scale these are very helpful, as they can halve your paint costs. They also help the paint to retain the marks of the brush and speed the drying process, that is an important consideration when more layers of paint are to be added.

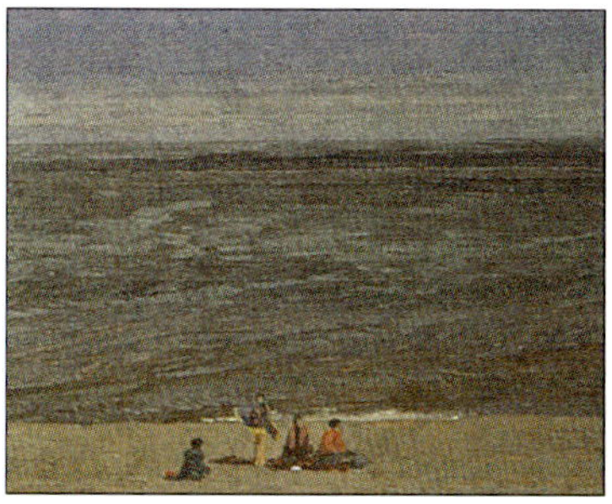

1 So far only fairly thin paint has been used. The brushwork is rather monotonous and the picture lacks vitality, so the artist decides to introduce some eye-catching elements.

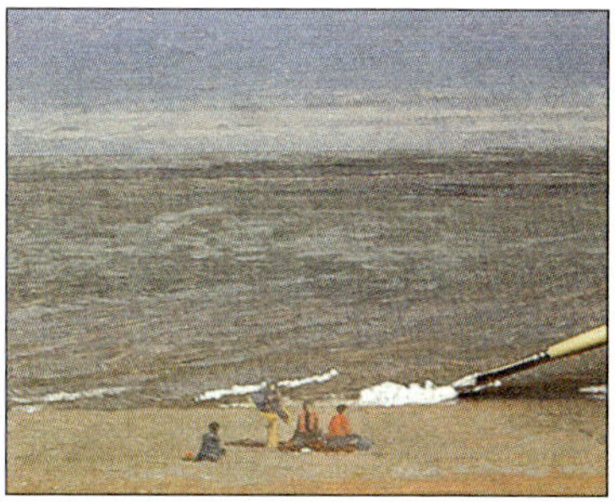

2 Thick, unmixed white paint is dabbed in place to represent foaming breakers.

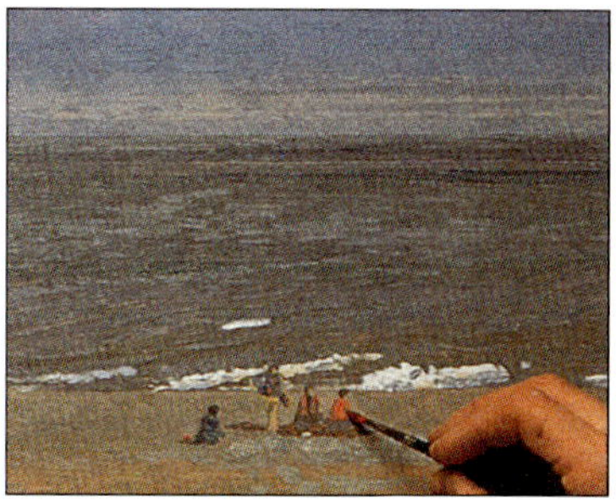

3 Some yellow ocher "pushed" into the white suggests churned-up sand, while the gray provides shadows below the tops of the breakers. Finally a thin sable brush was used to lay cadmium red impasto as a foreground accent.

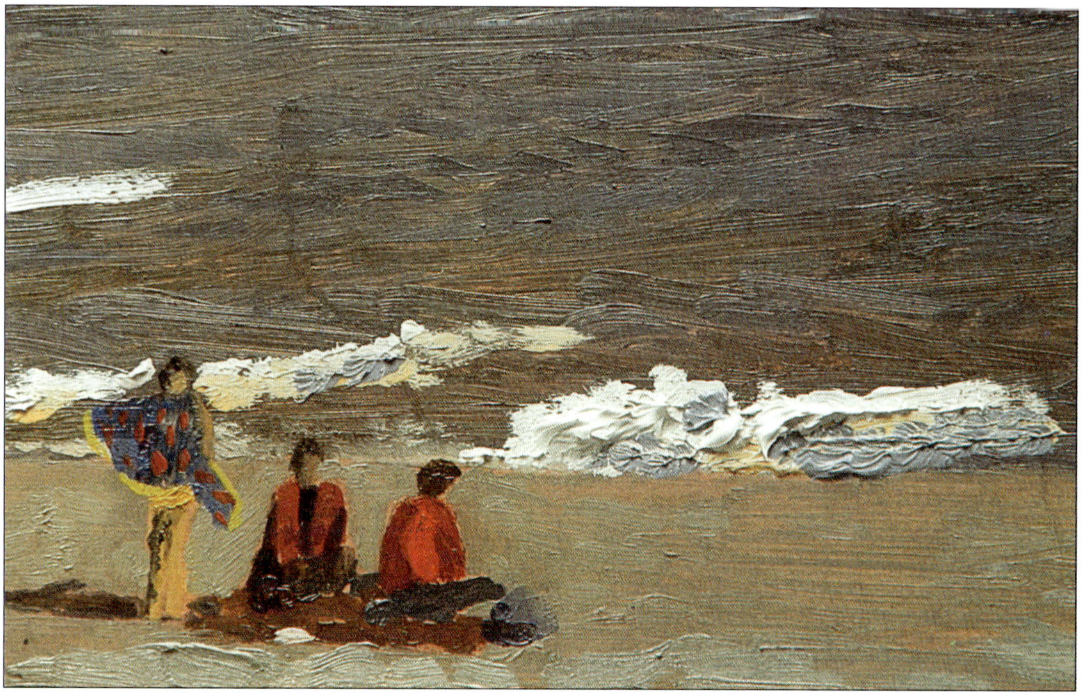

4 The whipped cream quality of the impasto is clearly seen in this picture. It will not change as it dries – one of the unique characteristics of oil paint.

DRY BRUSH

The dry brush technique is a method of applying color lightly so that it only partially covers a dry layer of color below. The minimum of paint should be used on the brush, and the brush strokes should be made quickly and with confidence – overworking destroys the effect. Dry brush is most successful when there is already some existing texture, either that of the canvas or that provided by previous brush strokes.

It is a useful method of suggesting texture, for instance, that of weathered rock or long grass, but like all "special" techniques, should never be overdone or treated as a short cut.

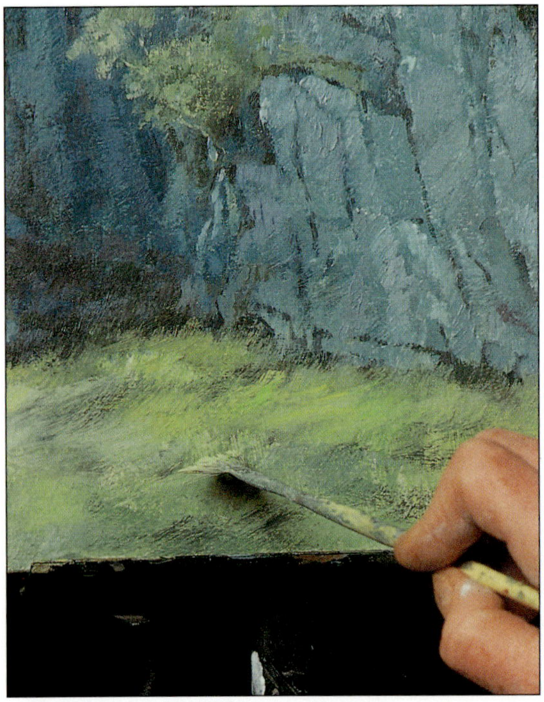

1 The artist uses a fan brush to lay a scant overpainting of thick, undiluted paint. The bristles of this type of brush are well-splayed and deposit paint in a light covering of fine separate lines.

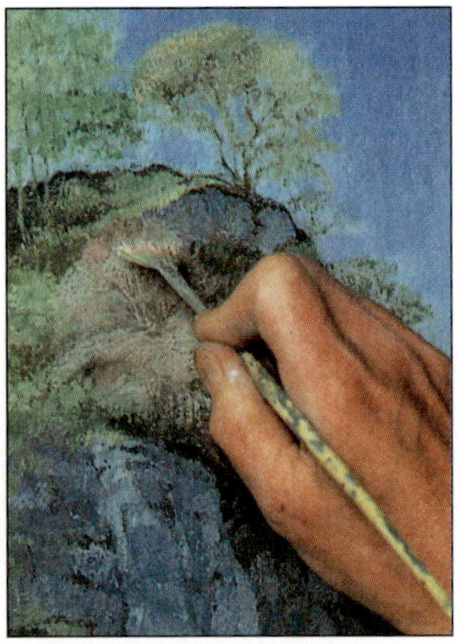

2 The same technique has been used for the intricate pattern made by the branches of the small tree.

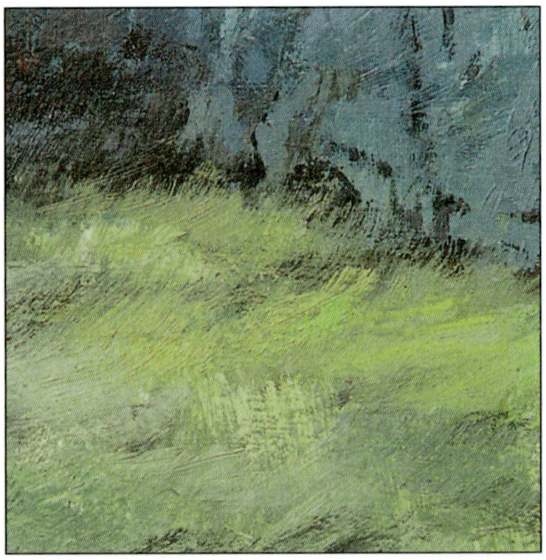

3 Dry brush is most effective when used light over dark. Here you can see how a succession of mostly paler layers are added one over the other.

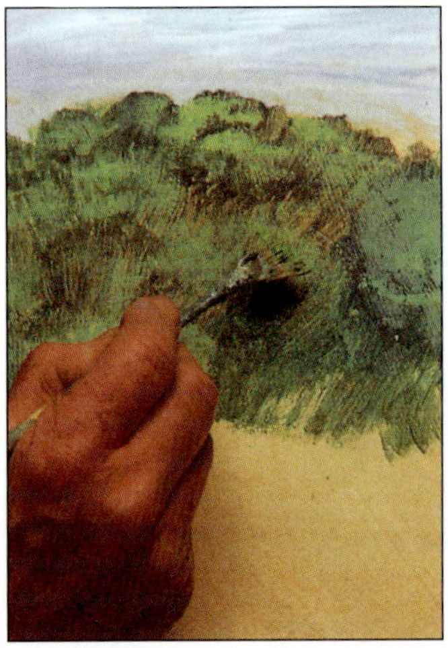

4 Again using a fan brush, these trees are given a soft, feathery appearance, with each thin spray of foliage being represented as one brush stroke.

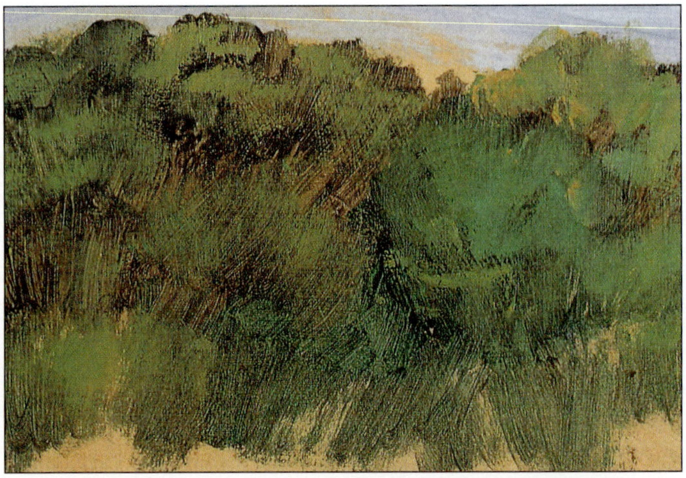

5 Brush strokes must be decisive and not overworked, since the essential character of dry brush is the ability to see between the bristlemarks to the layers below.

POINTILLISM

Pointillism is a method of painting that relies upon small dots of pure color to create shapes, tones, and color effects. These dots are placed close to each other, but not overlapping, so that from a distance they appear to merge.

This same principle can be seen if you look at a color photograph in a magazine through a strong magnifying glass: the image is composed of thousands of tiny dots of color, which the eye forms into recognizable shapes.

Georges Seurat (1859–1891) and Paul Signac (1863–1935) are the two painters chiefly associated with Pointillism (which Seurat preferred to call Divisionism). Seurat was fascinated by color theory, and much influenced by the new scientific discoveries about the properties of light and color made by Chevreul and Rood, who had shown that different colors when lying next to each other will mix in the eye of the viewer. The principle of optical mixing is made use of in both color television and color printing: an entire picture is composed of countless dots of three primary colors.

What Pointillism achieves is not so much a color of greater intensity, but a more luminous color. This is because the incomplete fusion of the dots produces a flickering optical sensation, known as "lustre." As a result, the surface of the picture appears to palpitate with light.

The use of complementary colors adds to this luminous effect, because small areas of complementary color placed next to each other also set up an optical vibration. If you look closely at a painting by Seurat or Signac, you will notice how, among the blue of a shadow for example, touches of contrasting yellow are often added to depict the warmth of reflected light penetrating the shadow.

Using tiny dots of color also allows the artist to note even the most minute gradations of tone and hue, and so register all the subtle halftones, shadows, and glints of reflected light that are experienced in nature. This amplifies still further the feeling of light and luminosity.

Pointillism is regarded by some artists as too exacting a system of painting, at odds with an artist's need for freedom of expression. It is a method worth experimenting with even so, because it can teach you a lot about the behavior of colors and about the infinite gradations that occur within a seemingly flat area of color. Pointillism can be used in any medium, even oil pastel, so long as the pastel stick has a sharp point. It is particularly suited to egg tempera, exploiting to the full the luminous quality of the paint.

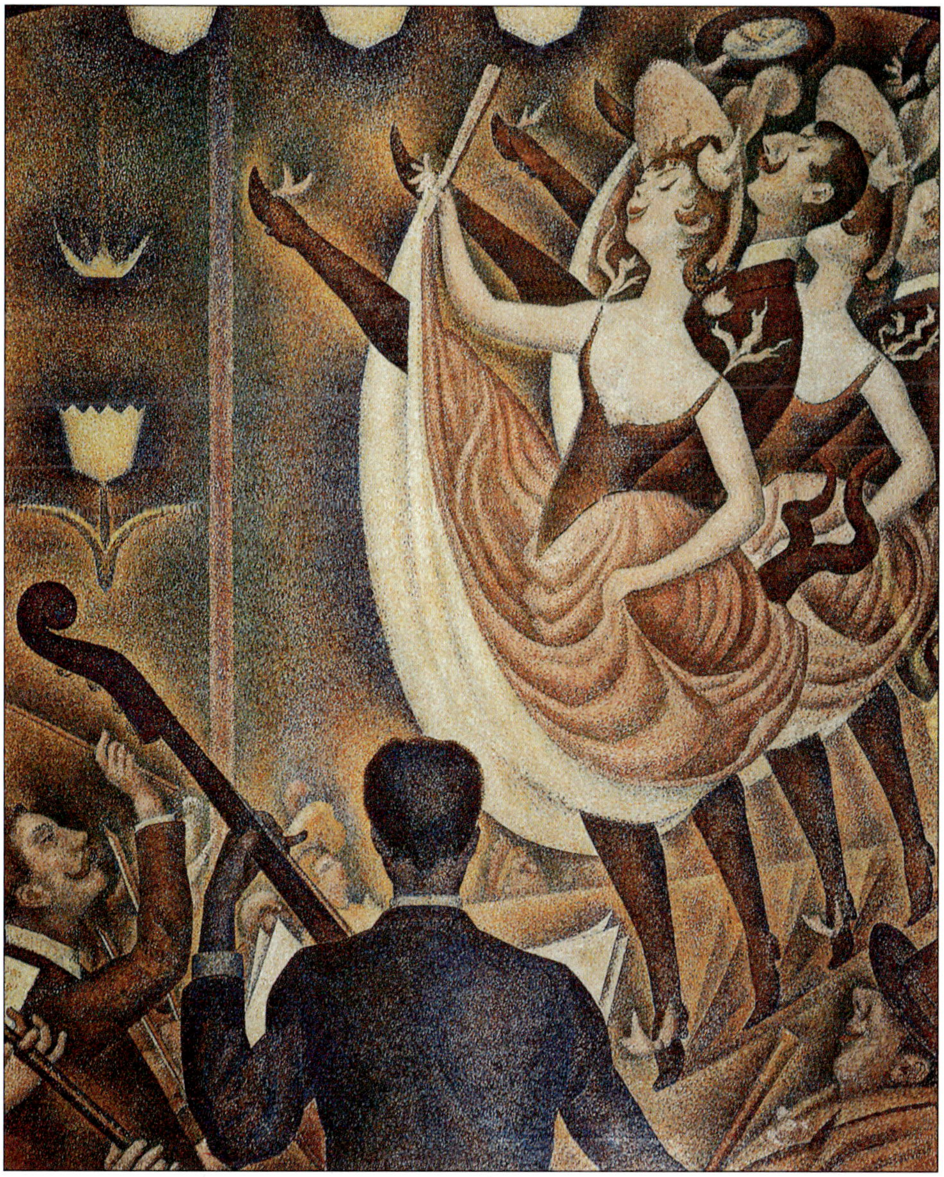

THE CAN-CAN by Georges Seurat

In this painting the separate dots of pure color have resulted in an overall subdued tint. This may be at least in part because of fading; Seurat's contemporaries began to notice a dulling of the colors soon after his pictures were finished. The minute size of each brush stroke gives a good idea of how slow and laborious the method must have been. It is hardly surprising that later artists modified it, but Pointillism has nevertheless been extremely influential.

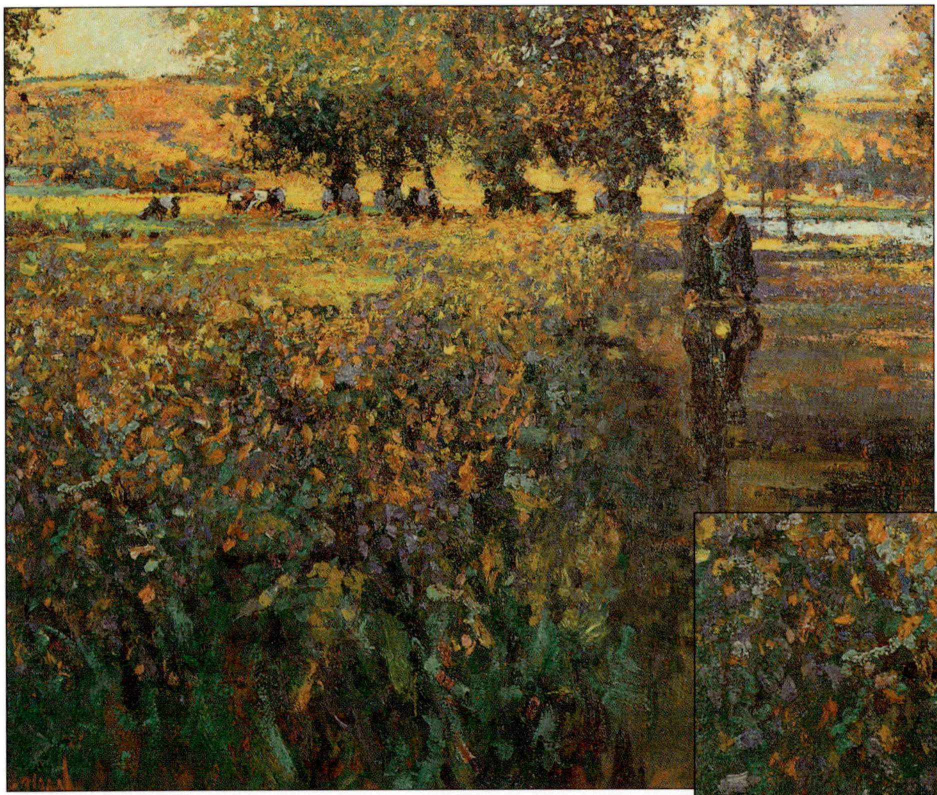

POINT OF SUNSET, DORDOGNE by Arthur Maderson

Fine stippling in the distance varying in size through to rich, slurred gestures in the foreground form the basis of this essentially Impressionist painting. A bright red ground can be seen at intervals between the brushmarks, enhancing the vibrant effect. The artist has consistently avoided any dark browns, grays, or blacks, constructing the shadows from violets, blues, and greens.

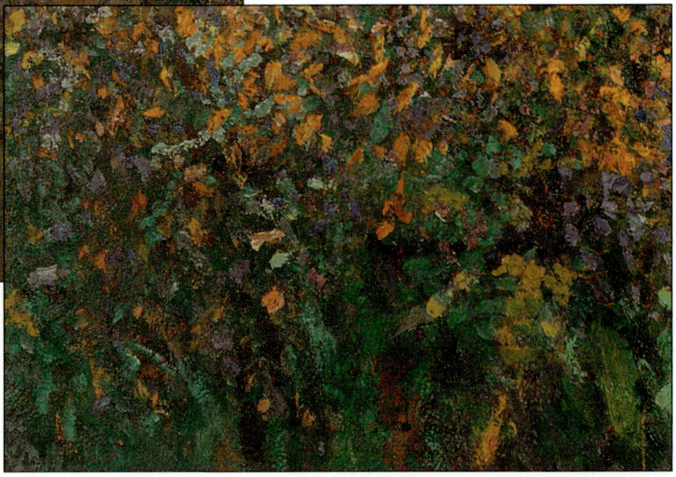

RIGHT: *This detail shows the artist's working method very clearly. Over the red ground there is underpainting consisting of a network of mainly dark greens. On top of this, a multitude of paler dabs of impasto build up a shimmering web of color.*

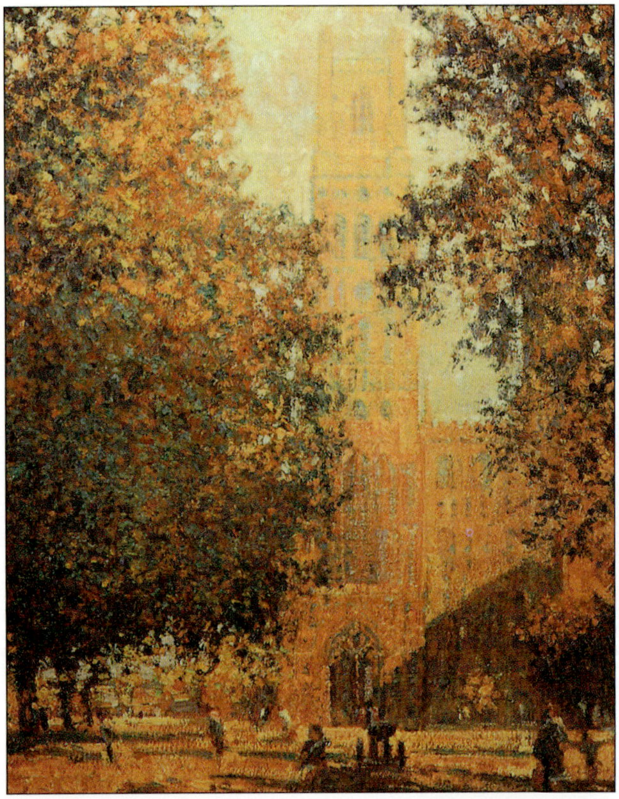

ELY CATHEDRAL by Arthur Maderson

The major part of the overpainting (left) is made up of stabs of relatively dry paint dragged onto the surface, allowing the previous statement to show through. The artist has used fairly pure colors that mix optically when viewed at a distance, and parts of the painting are very close to Seurat's own Pointillism, as can be seen in the detail below.

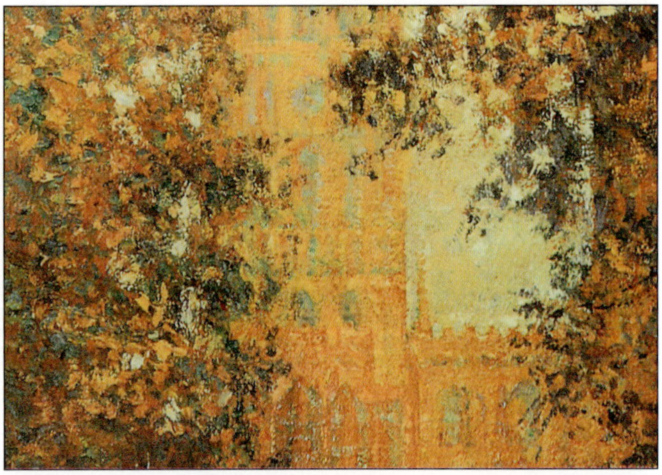

GLAZING

Glazing is a technique most often associated with oil painting, but can also be used with acrylics, egg tempera, watercolor, and inks. A glaze is a thin layer of transparent paint that can be either thick or thin. Since the lower layer is visible through the glaze, the effect is quite different to anything that can be achieved with opaque paint.

The reason for this is that a glaze, being transparent, allows light to pass through it and be reflected back off the underlying color. The colors thus combine optically – in the viewer's eye – and take on a resonance impossible to achieve by mixing them physically on the palette.

Glazing requires an understanding of how different colors react with each other, and it is worthwhile experimenting on pieces of scrap canvas.

Paint for glazing should be thinned with a glazing medium that contains special film-forming ingredients that impart a soft lustre to the paint surface. For best results, use a ready-made medium that contains beeswax – linseed oil is not ideal for glazes because it tends to move about after it has been applied.

Do not dilute the paint with turpentine alone – this makes the color go flat and dull, and sometimes results in a cracked surface. For best results, apply the glaze with a large, flat, soft-haired brush. Position the canvas or board at an angle of about 15° rather than vertically.

The Renaissance painters achieved wonderfully luminous reds and blues by building up successive layers of ever-richer color, using little or no opaque paint, but glazing over impasto is equally effective. Rembrandt (1606–1669) built up the light areas of his portraits with thick flake white modified by a series of glazes, and Turner created his distant luminous skies by the same method. Rembrandt always used transparent paint for shadow areas, that gave the dark passages a rich glow and an effect of insubstantiality – the eye is unable to judge exactly where the light is coming from.

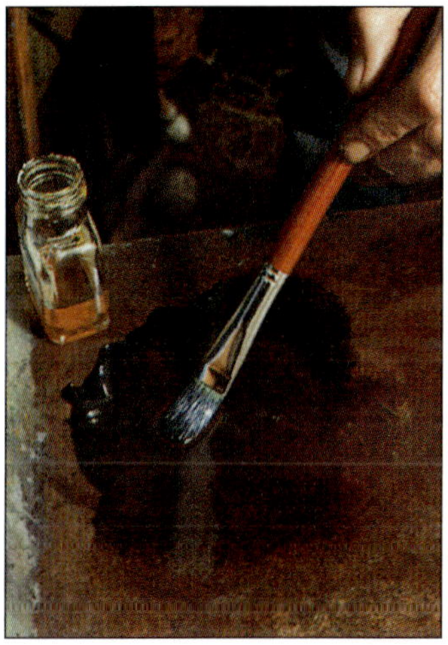

1 Mix the color on your palette, then add an equal quantity of medium. The paint should have a thin but oily consistency. Beware of overthinning!

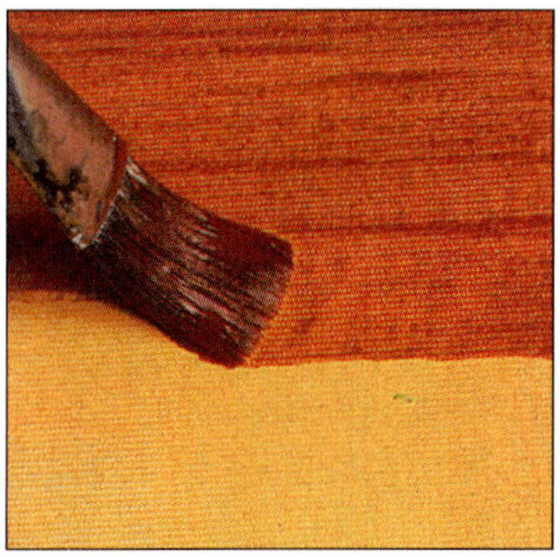

2 Apply the glaze in a thin layer over a light ground. The color appears bright because of light reflecting back off the canvas. Lay the canvas flat to prevent drips and runs.

3 Allow each layer to dry fully before adding more glaze. This example shows how the color underneath glows through the glaze, giving the paint a three-dimensional quality.

GLAZING TO MODIFY TONE

If you are unhappy with a certain color or tone, you can adjust it by glazing over it. A glaze will soften contrast and help to unify disparate tones, although it will not obscure the form beneath it. Shadow areas, in particular, appear more luminous when deepened with a dark glaze.

KNIFE PAINTING

Applying thick paint with knives (see impasto on page 91), gives a quite different effect to applying similarly thick paint with brushes. The knife squeezes the paint onto the surface, leaving a series of flat, smooth planes often bordered by ridges or lines where each stroke ends. It is a versatile and expressive method, although initially somewhat trickier than brush painting. The marks can be varied by the direction of the knife, the amount of paint loaded onto it, the degree of pressure applied, and of course the knives themselves.

Painting knives are not the same as palette knives, that are intended only for mixing paint on the palette and for cleaning up. Unlike the latter, they have cranked handles and extremely flexible blades of forged steel. They are made in a wide variety of shapes and sizes from large straight ones to tiny pear-shapes ideal for flicking paint onto the surface.

Knife painting is ideal for the artist who enjoys the sensuous, "hands-on" aspect of mixing and applying thick, creamy paint. However, care must be taken not to build up the paint too thickly; it may crack if it is more than about half a centimeter thick at its maximum.

Oil paints are perfectly suited to knife painting, because they have a soft, creamy texture and can be handled without trickling or running. This technique works best on stretched canvas, that has a "give" in it that responds well to the springy blade of the knife.

Knife painting demands a bold approach. Set the paint on the surface with a decisive movement, lifting the blade away cleanly at the end of the stroke. Avoid going back over the stroke, because this deadens the color and reduces spontaneity.

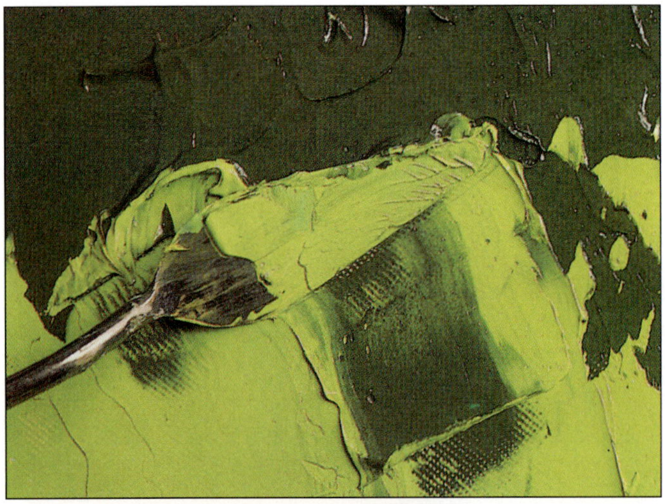

LEFT: Apply the paint thickly to the support and spread it with a trowel-shaped painting knife to achieve a variety of interesting textures. One way of moving the paint is to rest the heel of the knife on the support and move it in an arc, spreading the paint with it.

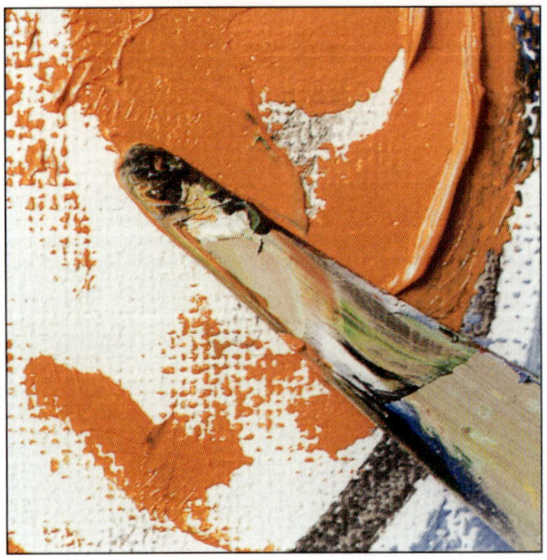

1 Thick paint is smeared onto the surface in a sideways sweep of the knife. Impasto is applied right from the start in this still life.

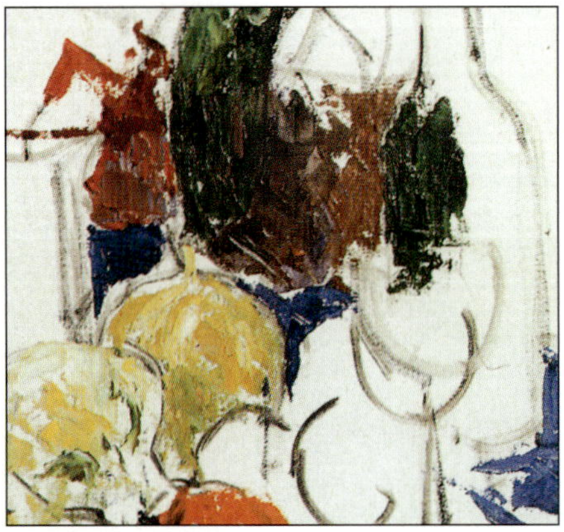

2 The picture is built up over a rapid drawing done in thinned paint, underpainting would be pointless, as it would be completely obscured by the impasto.

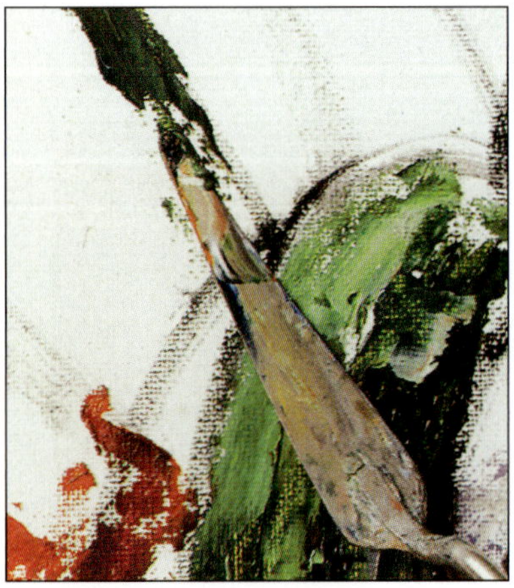

3 A narrow-bladed knife drags paint onto the surface in a long, thin stroke.

4 The side of the knife can be useful to make fine, linear marks. You can also make dabbed marks the exact shape of the blade if desired.

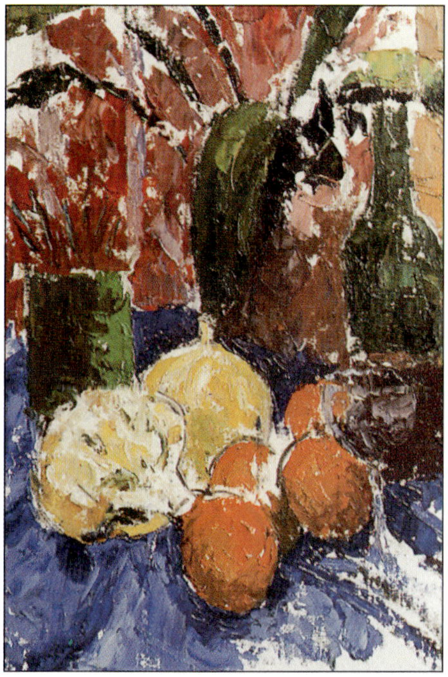

5 The picture is built up gradually, rather in the manner of a jigsaw. Each new color is well-mixed before application.

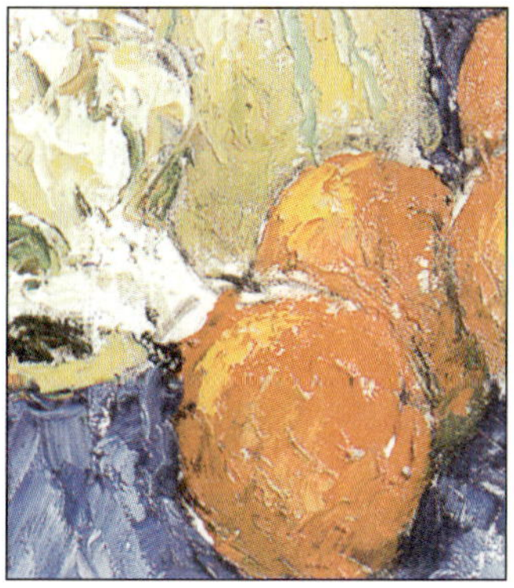

6 The texture of the paint gives a satisfying three-dimensional quality to the fruit.

7 Each separate patch of color joins with its neighbors to form a near-continuous covering of paint. The final texture of smeared and ridged paint has a lively, sparkling quality.

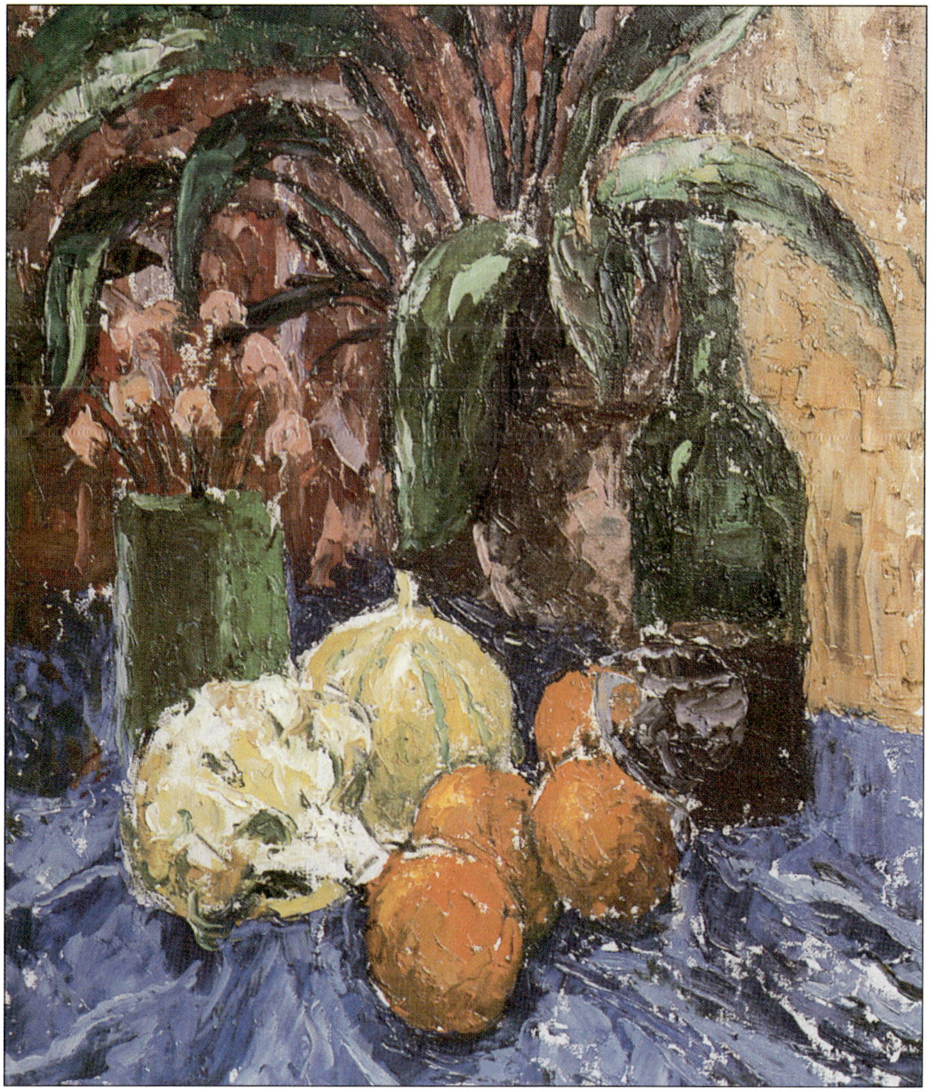

GALLERY

"A MOST BEAUTIFUL INVENTION"

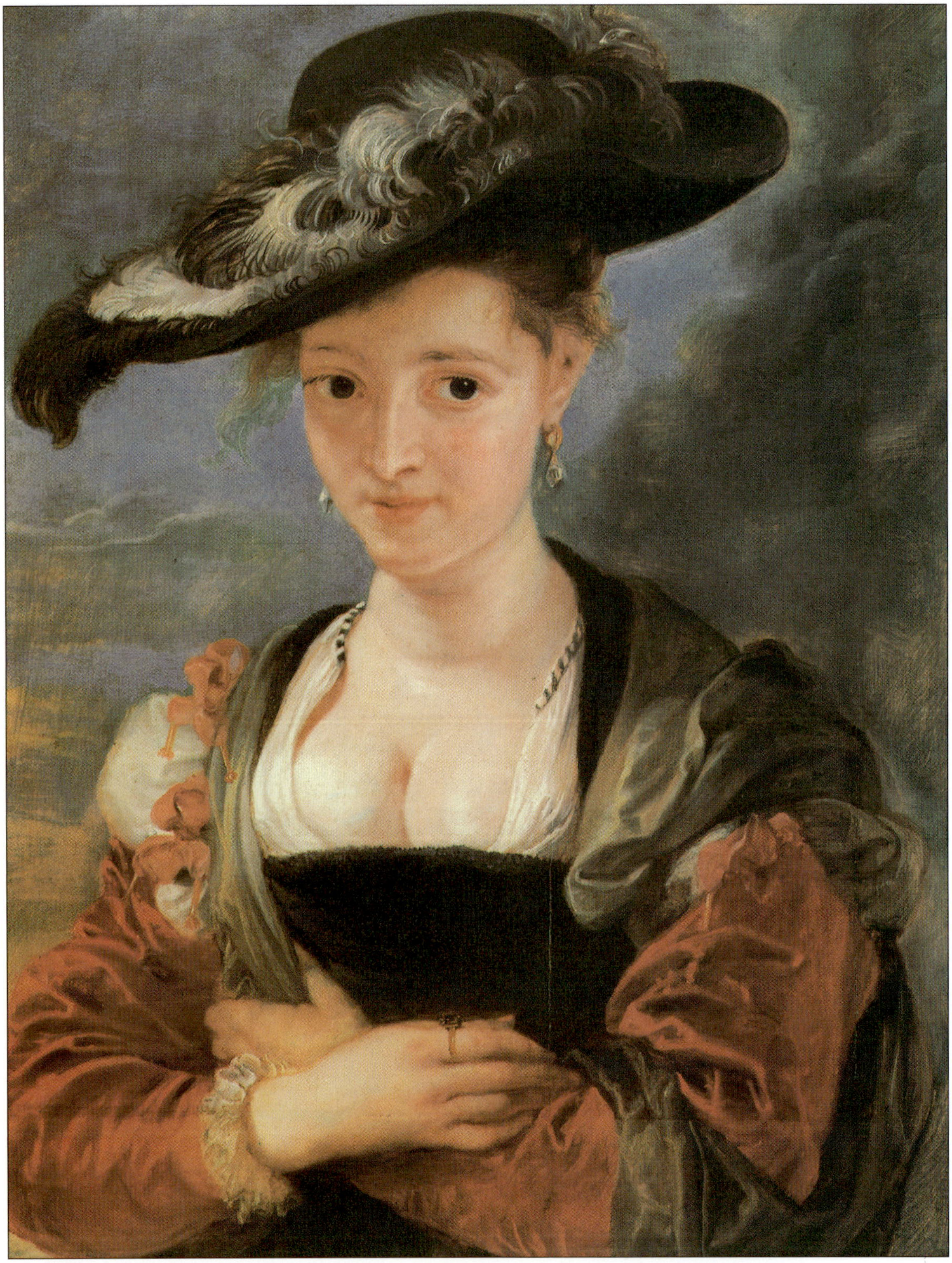

PORTRAIT OF SUSANNA LUNDEN NÉE FOURMENT by Peter Paul Rubens (1577–1640)

Rubens was a skilled exponent of the relatively new technique of oil painting and was admired for the assurance of his drawings and the virtuosity of his brushwork. His work influenced many artists of succeeding generations.

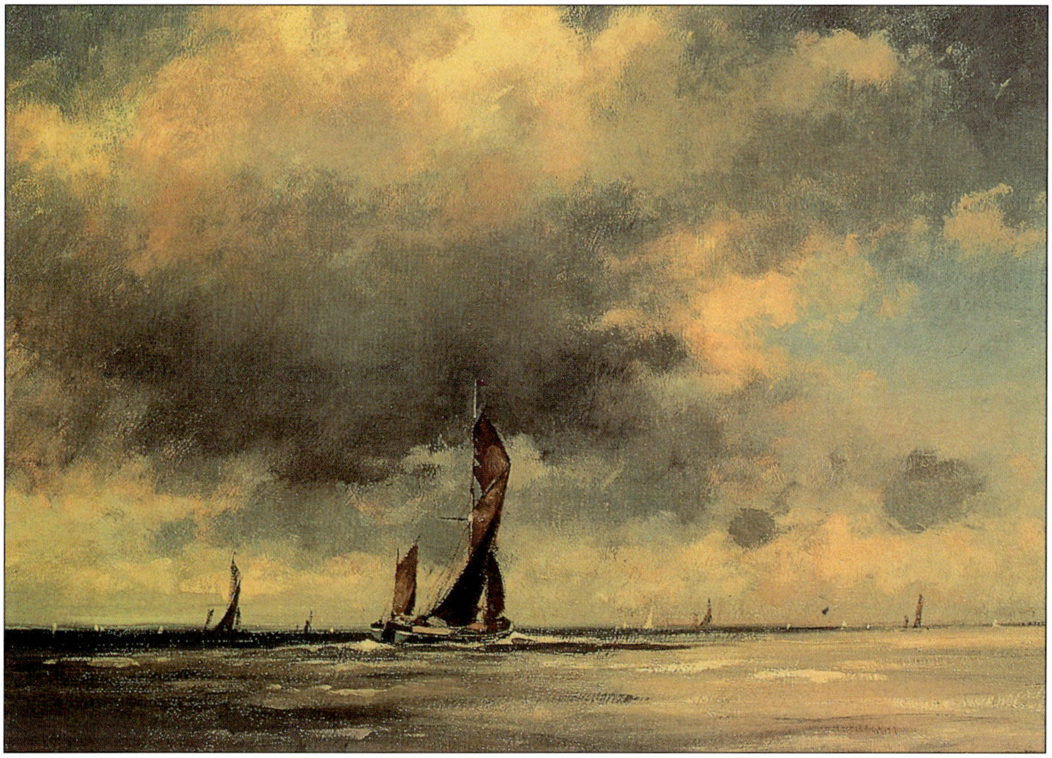

AN EASTERLY BREEZE by Raymond Leech

Here the dramatic cloud formation has been used to reinforce the focal point, the central boat with its brown sail, placed a little left of center. It is no coincidence that the darkest part of the cloud is directly behind the white mast, picking this out and dramatizing the picture very much in the manner of the Dutch seascape painters. The cloud's shadow has been skilfully used to darken the water on the left, throwing the illuminated central area into prominence.

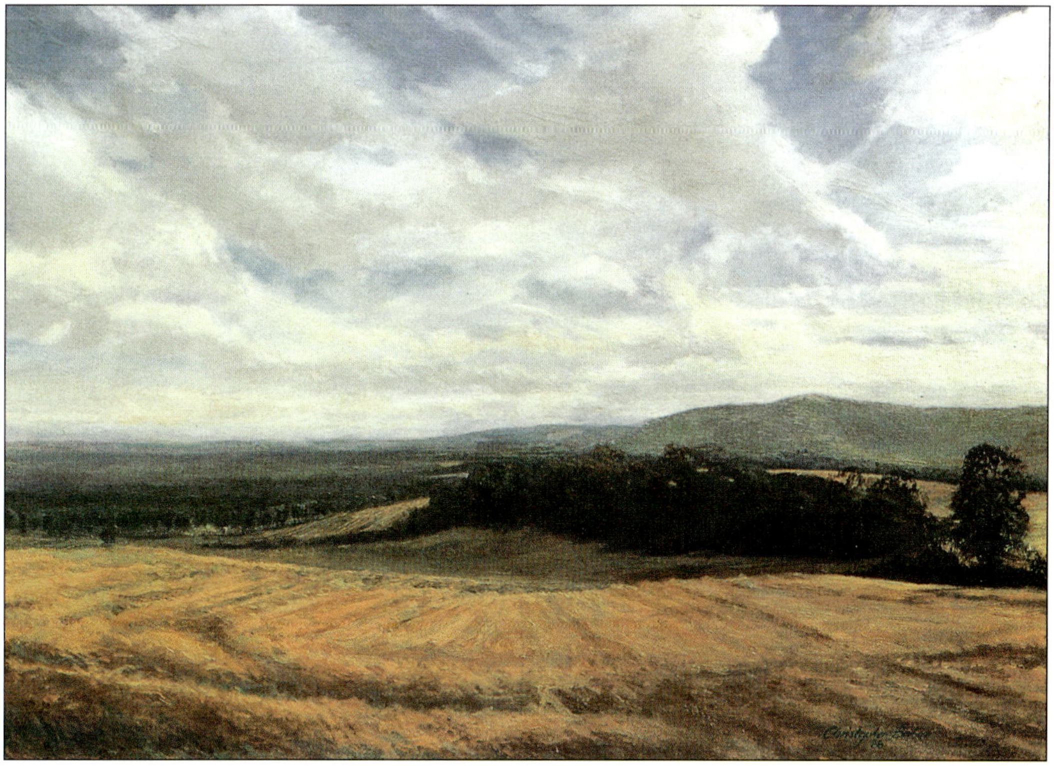

UP ON THE DOWNS by Christopher Baker

Scattered fair-weather cumulus dominate this sky, and the artist has made sure that they are an integral part of the composition. The sizes of the clouds, diminishing the distance, echo the perspective of the fields, woods, and hills, and some of the shapes in the sky almost exactly repeat the sweeps in the contours of the land, giving the effect an overall diagonal striping.

MOVING WATER

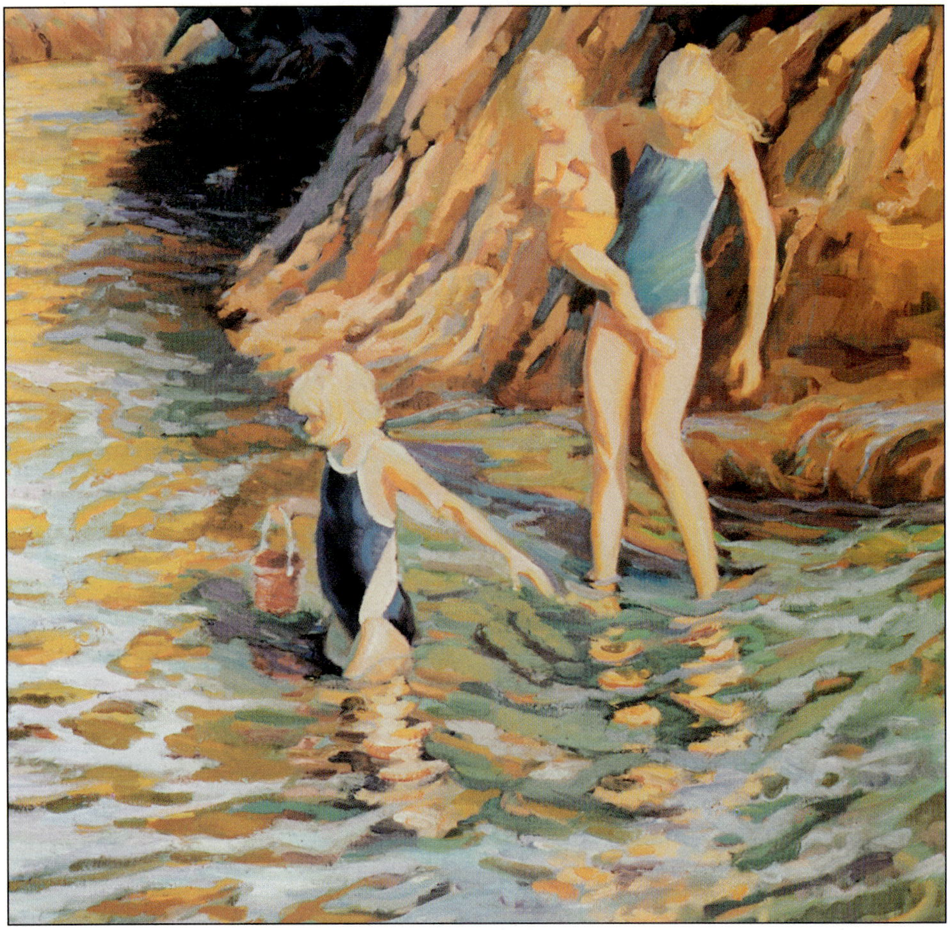

SUNSHINE KIDS by Denise Burns

Reflections of the figures, rocks, and sky are fragmented by the swell, giving little peepholes into the green-blue depths of the water below the surface. The subtleties of color and tone, built up in carefully placed strokes WET-INTO-WET, *are well observed.*

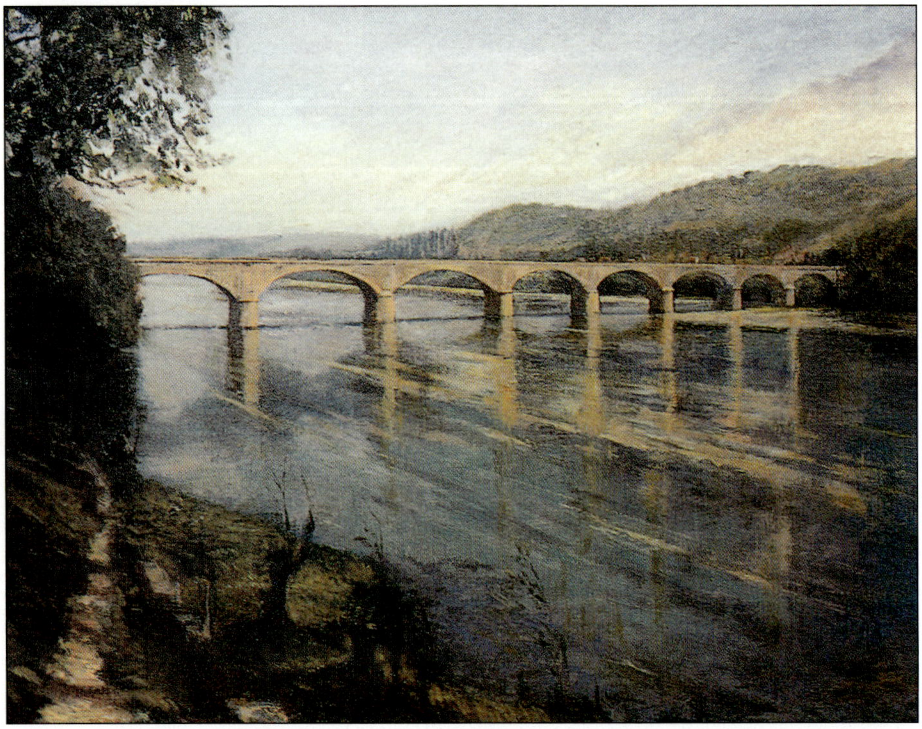

BRIDGE OVER THE RIVER DORDOGNE by Christopher Baker

This picture conveys a powerful impression of a huge mass of water forging its way downward, with pale streaks of vegetation carried by the flow. The artist has used thinned, translucent colors, built up in layers WET ON DRY, *and the brush strokes follow the direction of the rushing water.*

WORKING ON LOCATION

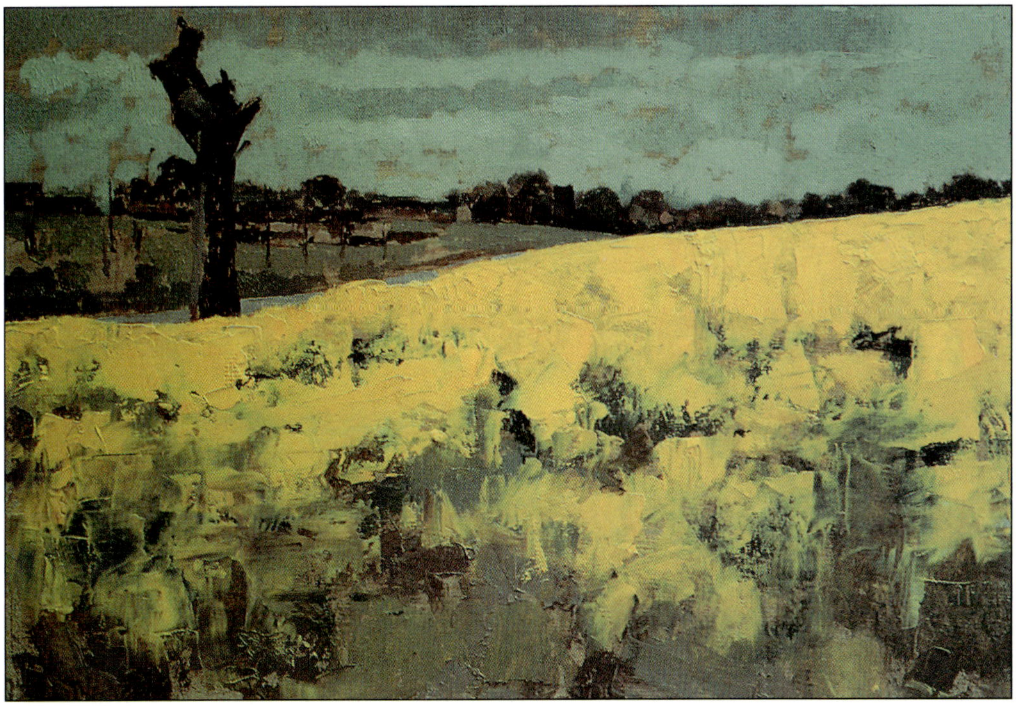

RAPE FIELD by James Horton

The bright yellow flowering rape and the fully foliaged distant trees instantly suggest early summer, albeit on a dull and overcast day. Although the rape field covers two-thirds of the picture surface, the artist has prevented the yellow from becoming overbearing by balancing it with strong green areas in the foreground. The richly textured picture surface has been achieved by KNIFE PAINTING.

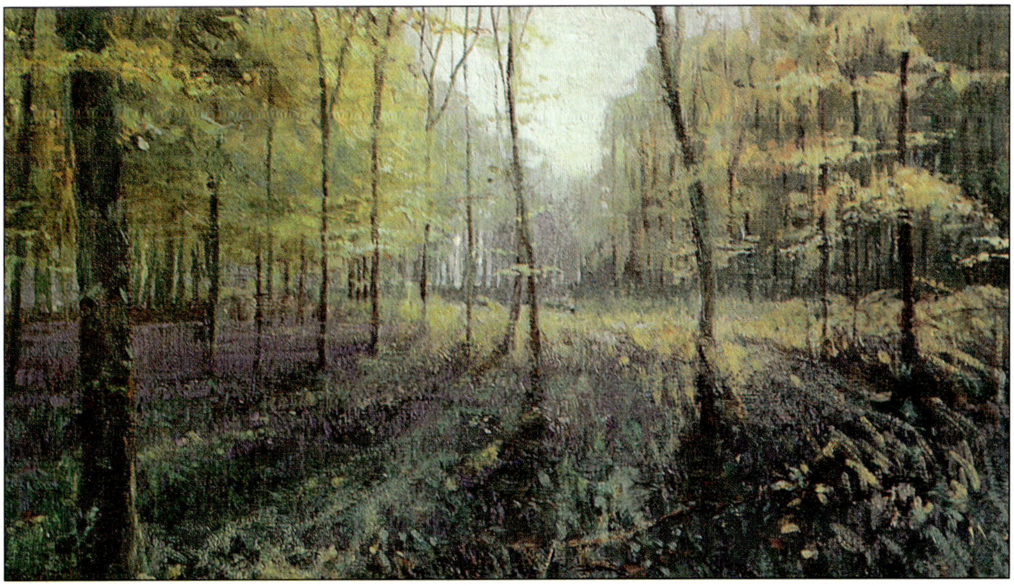

A TURN IN THE WOODS by Christopher Baker

Weak sunlight is beautifully captured in this painting, filtering through the spring foliage down to the carpet of flowers. The converging shadows lead the eye through to the clearing and beyond the pale, distant trees. The more prominent foliage and foreground vegetation has been STIPPLED, SCUMBLED, *and* DRY BRUSHED *in thick paint. Thin underpainting is visible in places over much of the canvas.*

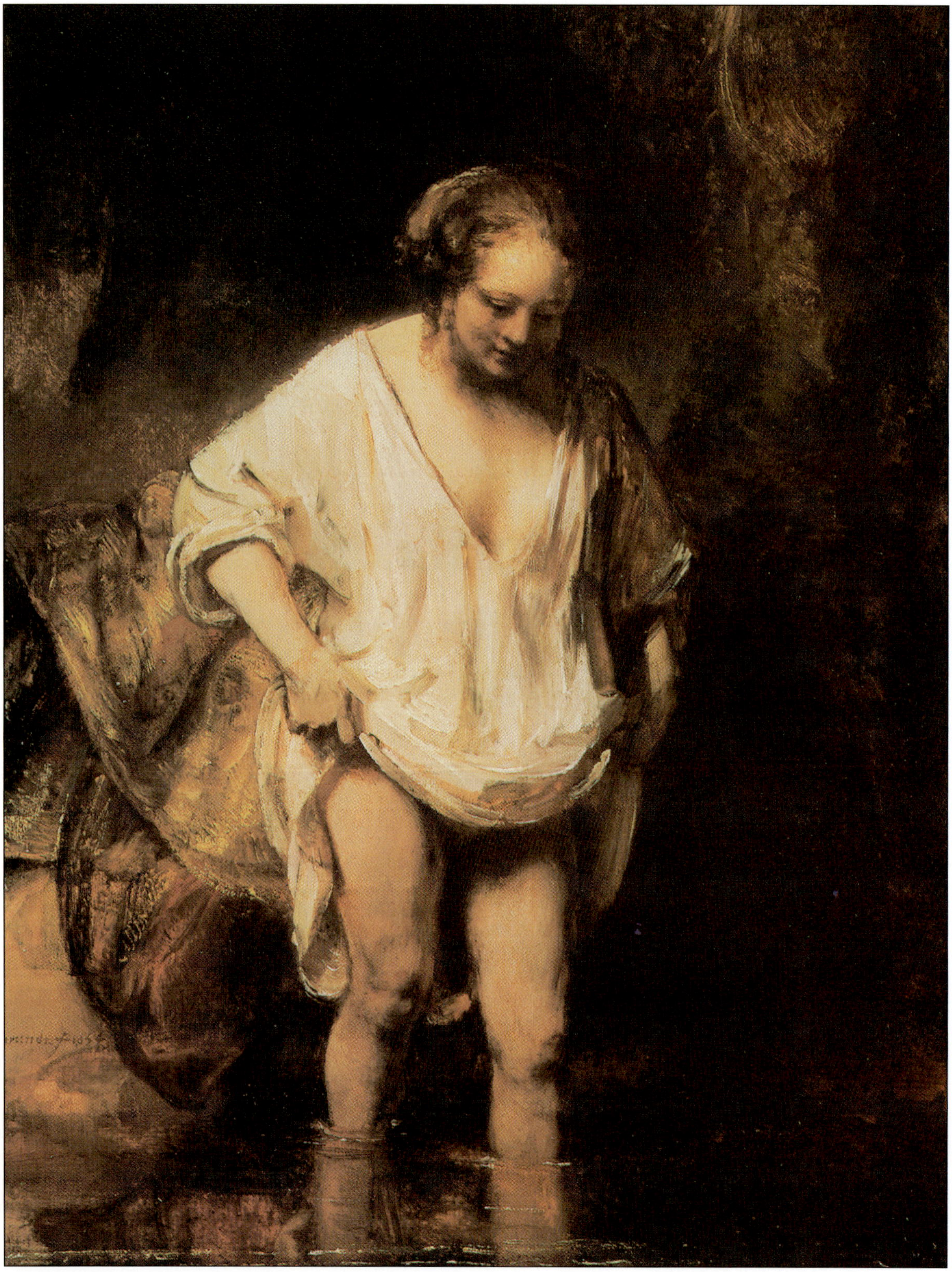

WOMAN BATHING by Rembrandt (1606–1669)

Rembrandt used both GLAZING *and* IMPASTO *in his paintings. In this painting the delicately glazed areas of flesh contrast with the bold brush strokes and thick paint of the garment.*

ACRYLICS

For those who are new to acrylic painting there could be no better medium. You can do virtually anything with acrylics, which is why they are favored by artists who like to experiment.

Acrylics are water-based and odor-free, that is a bonus when you work at home. Some people are discouraged from using oil paints because of the pervasive and lingering smell, and a few are allergic to oil-paint solvents such as turpentine and mineral spirits. Acrylics also dry fast, so you will not encounter the oil painter's difficulty of carrying wet pictures home from an outdoor session.

Paintings in acrylic do not crack, fade, or discolor with age or exposure to sunlight. Used on paper, acrylics are less prone to damage than other paints, because once dry they form a tough skin. But their capacity for diversity is the main reason for the popularity of acrylics. You can change their thick creamy tube consistency by adding water, or thicken it for oil-painterly effects with one of the special mediums mentioned later in this section. You can combine different paint consistencies in the same painting, using thin, transparent glazes over thick or medium-thick applications, and vice versa. You can use different paint surfaces (page 105) or different grounds (pages 117–118). Acrylic is especially suitable for textured effects that can be produced by painting over a pretextured ground or by mixing paint with substances, such as sand, or one of the mediums made for this purpose.

FINDING YOUR OWN WAY

Because of their versatility, acrylics have gained a reputation as an imitative medium. It is true that a painting in acrylics can look very much like one in oils. Oil painters sometimes use acrylics as a substitute when working outdoors because their short drying time makes them more convenient. Acrylics can also mimic the effects of watercolor or gouache (opaque watercolor). But there is little point in trying to make one medium behave like another unless you do so for a specific reason. Acrylics have their own characteristics, and you will enjoy using them more if you learn to understand and exploit these in your individual way. Sympathy with the chosen medium is one of the factors that marks a successful painting, and this book aims to help you achieve it.

If you are not sure what methods to adopt for your first attempts, begin by looking at the pictures shown in this section. If you respond more to some than others, take them as a starting point for developing your own

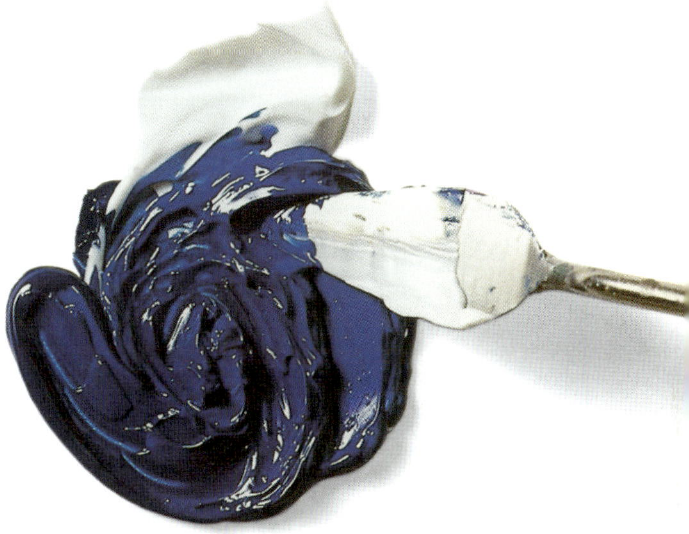

approach. To a large extent, painting is learned by example, and the work of other painters can give you more ideas than weeks spent struggling on your own.

HOW ACRYLICS ARE MADE

Acrylics were originally a by-product of the plastics industry, developed hand-in-hand with the emulsion paints that we use on our walls. Like all paints, they consist of coloring matter, known as pigment, as a binder, which in the case of acrylics is a synthetic resin. It is the nature of this resin adhesive that makes acrylic the most durable and versatile of all artists' paint. The pigments in acrylics are mostly the same as those used for other paints. The majority are chemically synthesized to give stability and permanence of color.

Acrylic paint is made by mixing powdered pigment with acrylic adhesive. The adhesive looks milky when wet but becomes transparent when dry, revealing the true color of the pigment. In factories where the paint is made you can see the enormous vats of this raw, jelly-like substance before the enhancing color is added, being wheeled to and from the mills and mixing machines that eventually produce the finished paint.

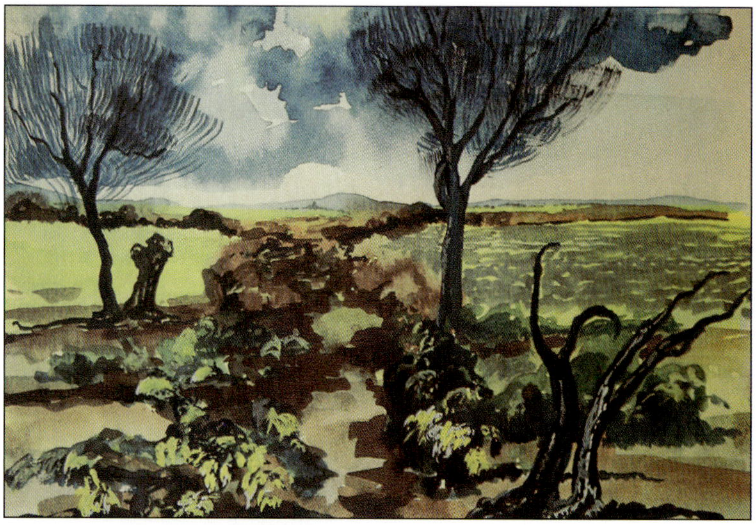

WATERCOLOR EFFECT

LATE AUTUMN, NEAR CLIFF, KENT by Roy Sparkes

This work on paper could be mistaken for a watercolor were it not for the dark tones and colors in the foreground and on the trees. With watercolor, these would need to be built up gradually with overlaid washes. With acrylic, considerable depth of color can be achieved with just one application.

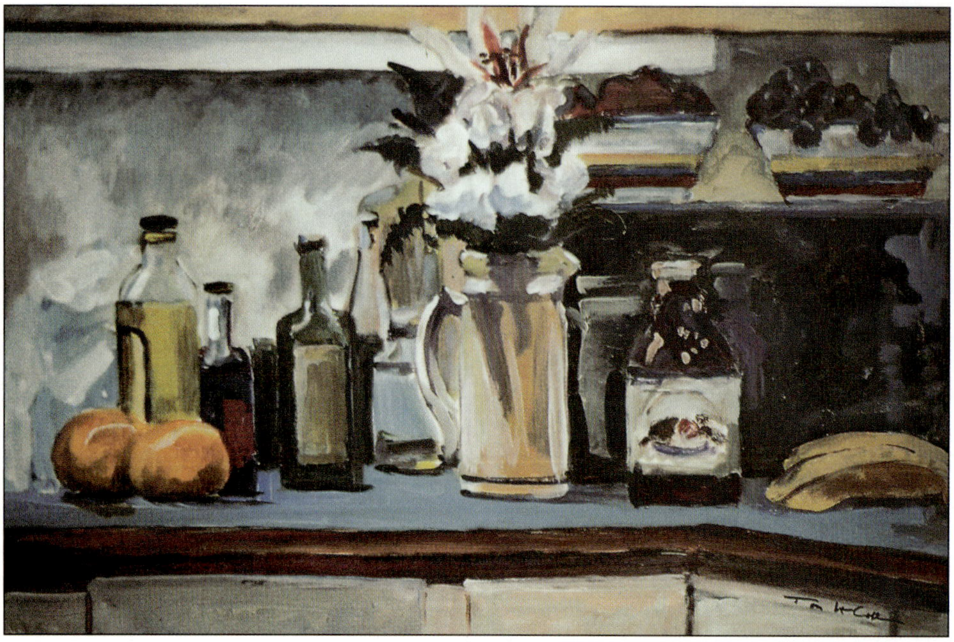

ACRYLIC ON BOARD

GROCERIES by Thomas McCobb

In contrast to the painting above, this resembles a work in oils. The artist worked on board, primed with acrylic gesso to reduce the absorbency, and applied the paint thickly with the traditional oil painter's bristle brushes. Rather than using an acrylic medium to thicken the paint, he gave it extra body by mixing it with the gesso used for the priming.

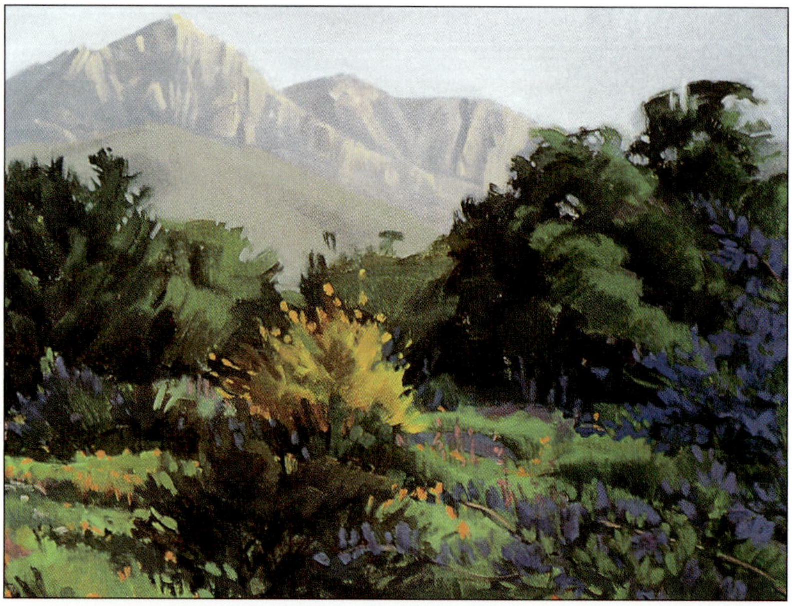

ACRYLIC ON CANVAS

EARLY SPRING ON THE PORTER TRAIL by Marcia Burtt

For this nature study created direct from the subject, the paint was used at tube consistency, applied with bristle brushes on fine-grain canvas. As she worked, the artist made continual adjustments and rearrangements, and built up the stronger tones and colors gradually.

Surfaces

Finding "something to paint on" is not usually a problem when using acrylics because you can work on almost any surface you choose. Canvas, hardboard, and paper are the choices that come immediately to mind, but there is a surprising variety of more unusual supports which are just as suitable. Wood, metal, plastic, and various fabrics have all been used successfully with acrylics, and it is this versatility which has made the paint so popular with so many artists. Nor is acrylic color used exclusively by painters. Many modern sculptors find it compatible with contemporary modeling materials such as fiberglass and polystyrene, and acrylics often provide the final coat of color to a piece of sculpture or mixed media work.

There is one important thing to remember, however, when you are choosing a painting surface – acrylics will not adhere to any surface that contains oil or wax. This fact rules out all canvas and board which has been prepared for oil paint. Of course you can buy special painting surfaces, and these are fine, but if you use acrylic paint on a surface prepared for oils, sooner or later the paint will come off.

Very shiny surfaces can also cause problems. Many artists do use acrylic on metal, plastic, and glass, but the color can sometimes be scratched or peeled off. It is therefore a good idea to roughen the surface before applying the paint. If you have ever cleaned an acrylic palette, for instance, you will know that it is quite possible to peel or scratch dried paint off a smooth, plastic surface, however difficult and time-consuming this may be. A quick "roughening" with sandpaper will provide the support with a "key" for the paint to adhere to, making sure that the color remains intact.

BOUGHT SURFACES

Primed boards, canvases, and cheesecloth-covered supports are available from art shops. Many of these are primed specially for acrylic paints, and care should be taken not to buy those that are prepared for oils only. The linseed oil in these repels acrylic color and the paint will eventually come away from the surface of the support.

Bought surfaces are quick and convenient, especially if you prefer to work on a fairly small scale. But the sizes and shapes of ready-made supports are limited and they are by far the most expensive type of painting surface. A good alternative is to buy acrylic primed canvas off the roll. Art shops sell this by the yard, often in a choice of two thicknesses. The heavier quality is recommended for large-scale works and murals.

ECONOMY SURFACES

A good rule to follow when you start painting in acrylics is never to throw things away. Keep packaging materials, such as brown wrapping paper and cardboard, as these make attractive painting surfaces. Use the matt side of wrapping paper, and treat brown cardboard with acrylic gesso. Paint on inexpensive plain wallpaper sold for walls, and try out your brushwork and color mixes on old newspapers.

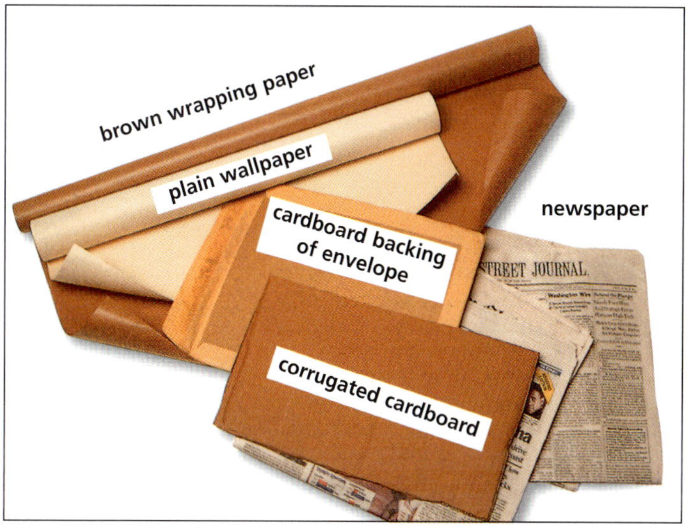

One of the best inexpensive surfaces to use is hardboard. Many professional painters actually prefer this to canvas, and it is certainly worth trying. Most artists paint on the smooth side of the board, but there is no reason why you cannot use the reverse side if you prefer a rough texture. Large pieces of hardboard tend to be unwieldy unless they are battened from behind to stop them from bending. They can be primed with acrylic gesso if you prefer a white support, or you can seal the surface with acrylic medium, thus preserving the natural color.

ACRYLIC SKETCHING PAPER

Pads of acrylic sketching paper contain sheets of specially primed paper with a canvas-like texture. They are useful for outdoor work, because their cardboard backing removes the necessity for a drawing board. They come in several sizes.

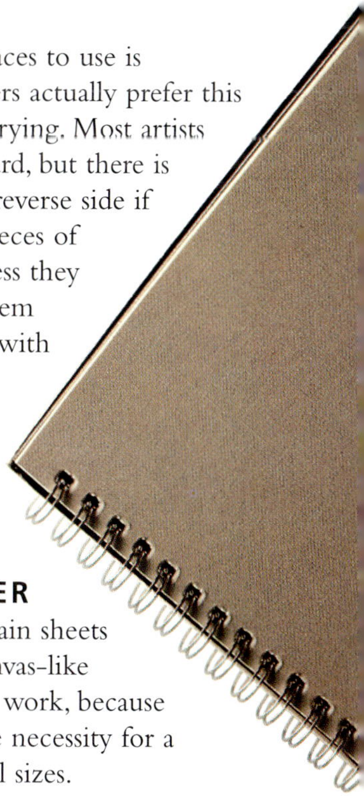

Acrylic Mediums

The word "medium" with regard to acrylics, describes substances that are added to the paint, either during its manufacture or when mixing color on the palette. Because acrylic is water-based, you can thin it by adding more water. This is the only medium you need for early experiments. But there are several mediums made especially for acrylic work that you may find useful later on. They change the nature of the paint in various ways, making it slower to dry, more transparent, or thicker. Based on the polymer emulsion used in the manufacture of the paint, the mediums are white when applied but become transparent when dry.

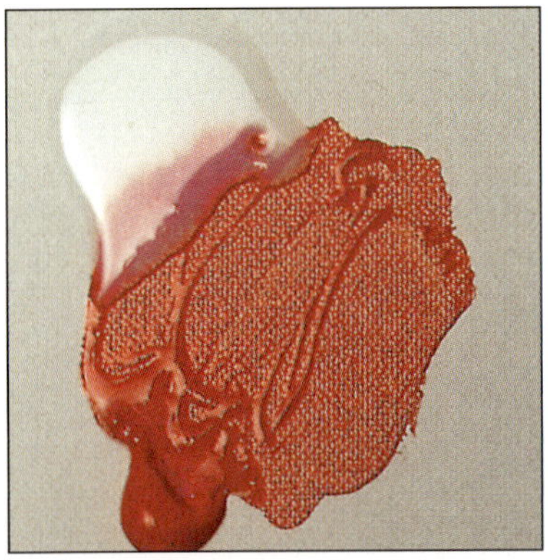

GLOSS MEDIUM

This is mainly used for glazing methods (see page 112). It makes tube colors thinner and more transparent, so that they can be built up in successive layers.

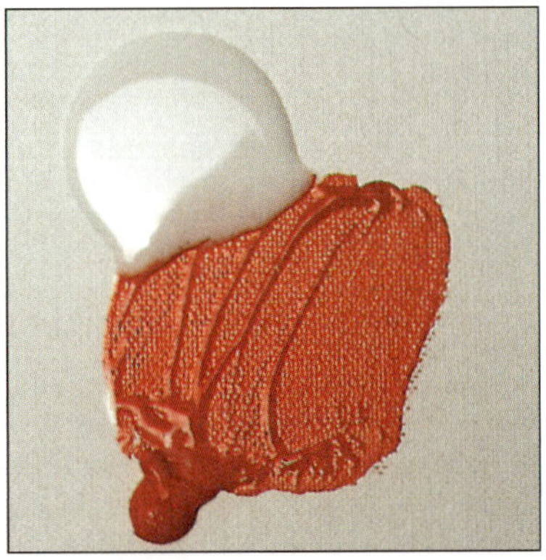

MATT MEDIUM

Similar to gloss medium, but thicker, because it contains a waxy substance to reduce shine. Use it for glazing if you want a matt surface.

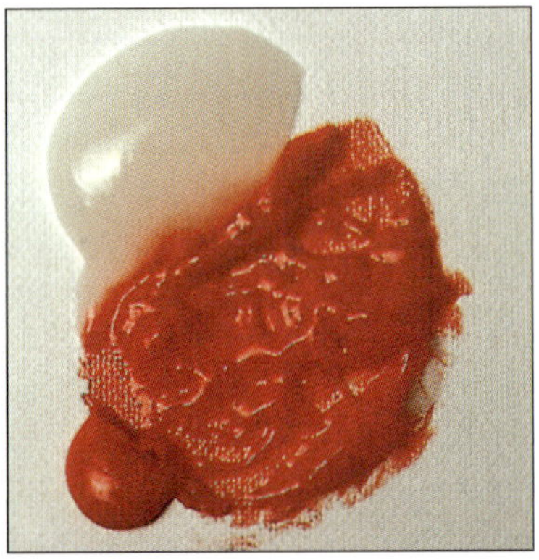

GEL MEDIUM

A jelly-like form of gloss medium, that thickens the paint for impasto effects (see pages 113–114). It does not effect the translucency of the colors.

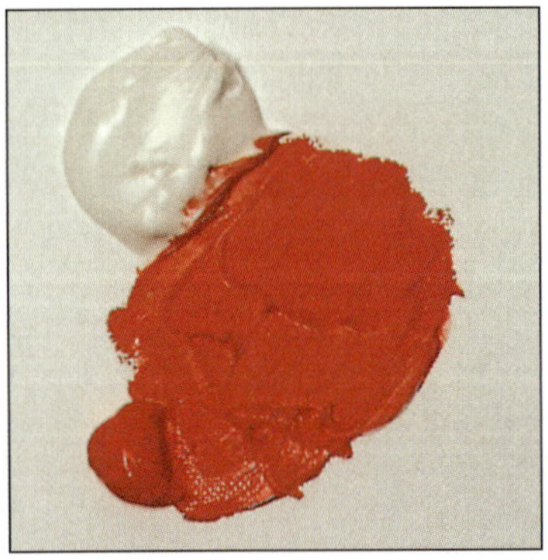

TEXTURE PASTE

Also known as modeling paste. A very thick medium for heavy impastos and special texture effects (see pages 117–118).

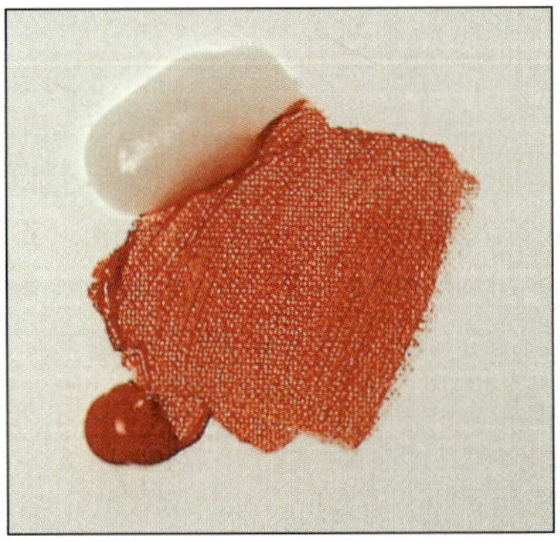

RETARDING MEDIUM

Used by artists who like to achieve oil-painting effects. This slows the drying time so that colors can be blended.

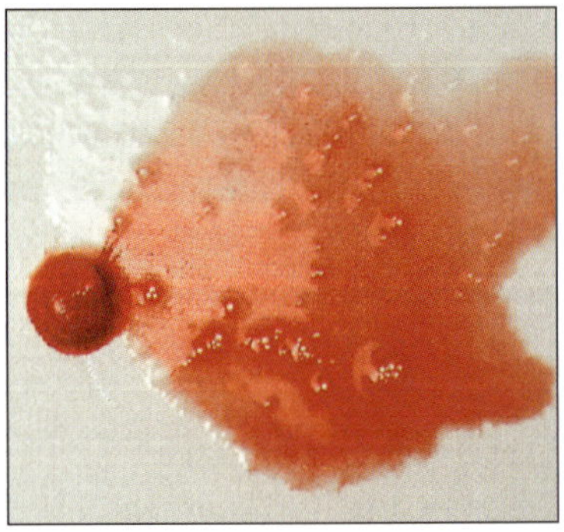

FLOW IMPROVER

Also known as flow enhancer, this is a solution of wetting agents that helps to break down the gel structure of acrylics.

SEALING WITH ACRYLIC MEDIUM

An ideal surface for acrylic paints is one that is slightly porous, absorbent enough to provide a "key" for the paint to adhere to, yet not so porous that it becomes difficult to apply the paint. A support or surface that is too absorbent can normally be given a coat of acrylic medium to seal it. The medium leaves tiny pores that provide sufficient "key" to allow the paint to cling to the sealed surface. Supports can be sealed with a gloss or matt medium depending on the type of surface required.

Acrylic Paints

The ever-increasing popularity of acrylics has multiplied the variety of paints on the market, and the same manufacturers sometimes produce several lines. This can be confusing for the beginner. What do the terms "artist's quality" and "flow-formula" signify, and how do you tell which you need?

PAINT QUALITY

The only difference between "artist's" and "student's" quality paints is that the latter are made from less expensive pigments. In most cases, however, they are vivid and durable. They also cost considerably less than artist's quality paints, so they are a good choice for first attempts. They are seldom denoted as student's quality on the tubes, but the more expensive paints are always marked artist's quality or artist's acrylics. If in doubt, ask for the manufacturer's information sheet.

PAINT CONSISTENCY

Some acrylics are relatively thick and buttery, described as full-bodied, while others are runnier, known as flow-formula. Again these characteristics are not always indicated on the tube, but some brands contain the word "flow" in their name. Artist's quality acrylics are made in both consistencies, but most of the student's quality paints are the flow type.

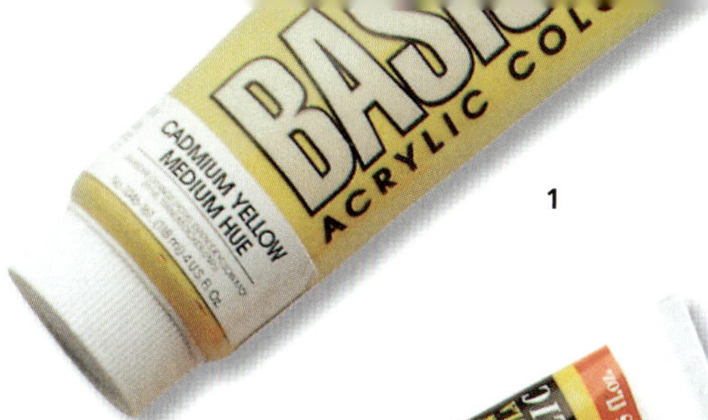

1

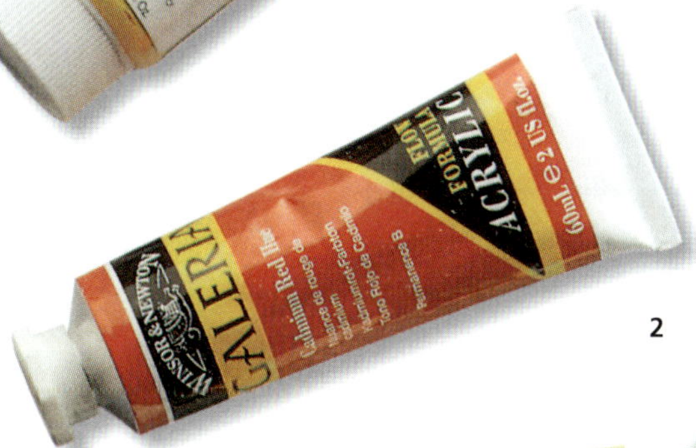

2

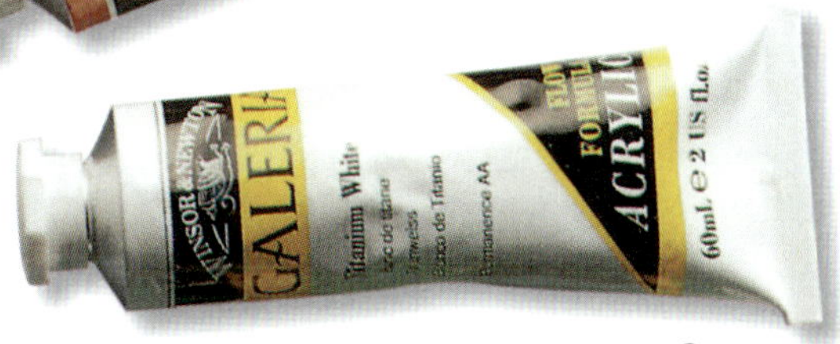

3

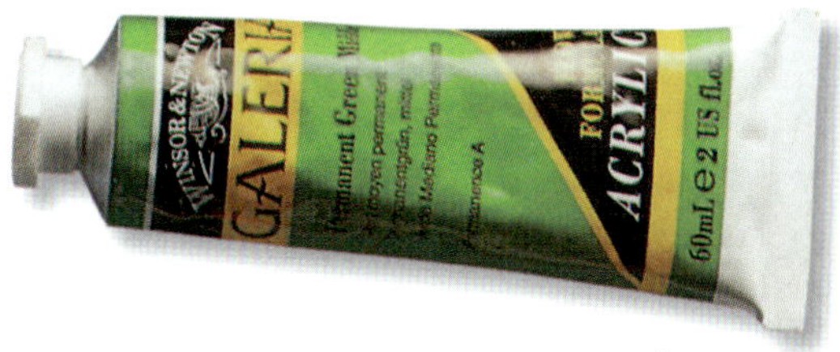

4

STUDENT PAINTS

*A beginner's line (**1**), produced by a well-established manufacturer specializing in acrylics. A line from another well-known company (**2**,**3**,**4**) aimed at the amateur market. The range of colors is smaller than in artist's paints, but the quality is excellent.*

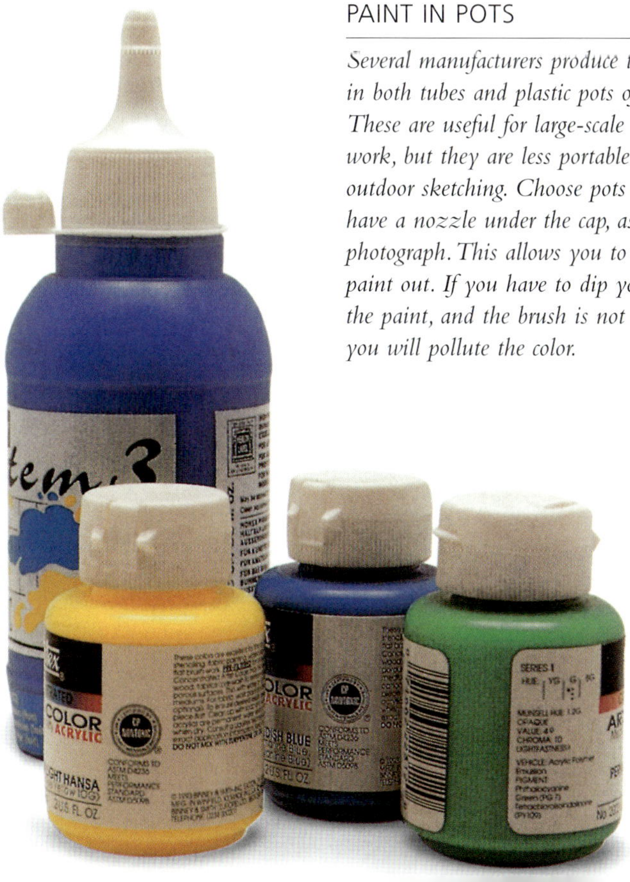

PAINT IN POTS

Several manufacturers produce the same paints in both tubes and plastic pots of various sizes. These are useful for large-scale and indoor work, but they are less portable than tubes for outdoor sketching. Choose pots or jars that have a nozzle under the cap, as shown in the photograph. This allows you to squeeze the paint out. If you have to dip your brush into the paint, and the brush is not perfectly clean, you will pollute the color.

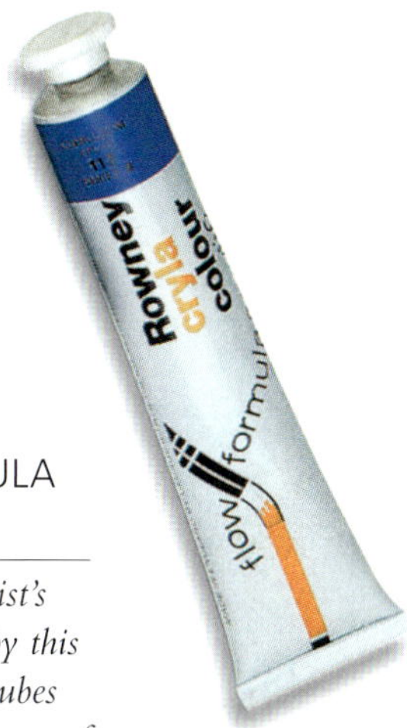

FLOW-FORMULA PAINTS

Flow-formula artist's paints produced by this manufacturer in tubes come in a wide range of colors.

Suggested Starter Palette

This suggested palette contains nine colors, plus white and black, which is more than adequate for most subjects.

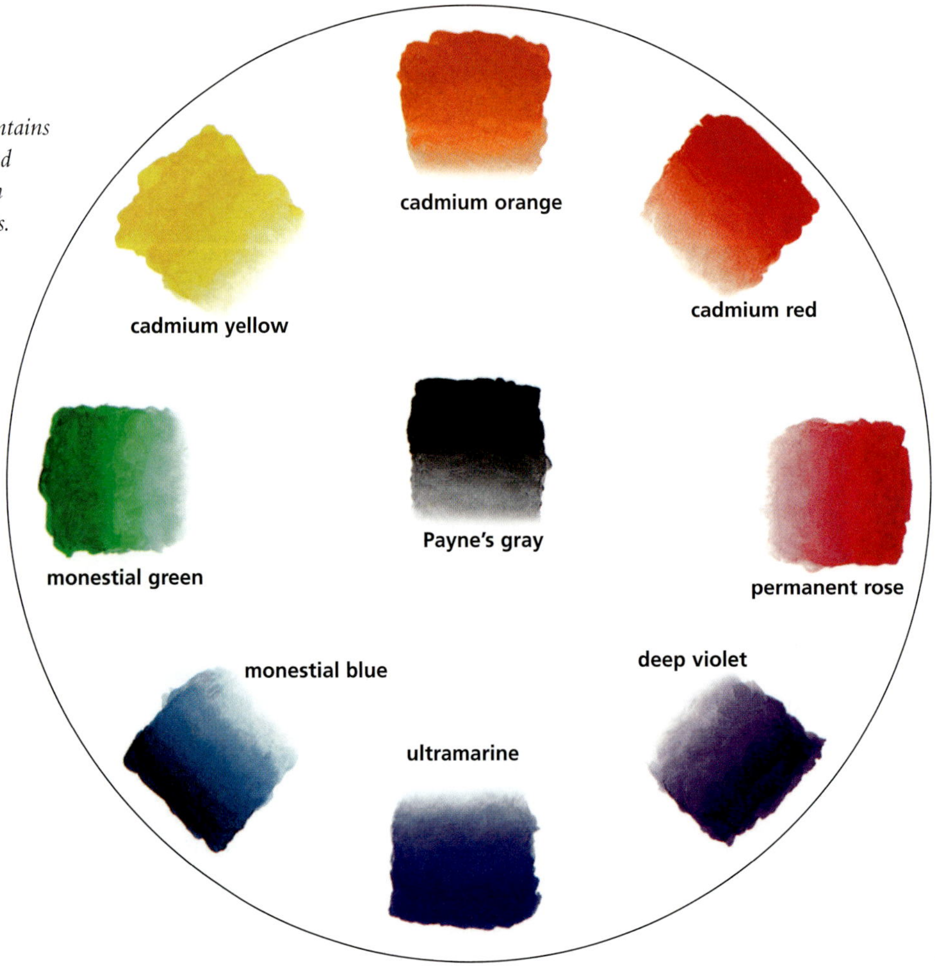

MIXING COLORS

The art of successful color mixing is to be able to create the maximum color range from a minimum number of paints. A manufacturer's range can easily number over 70 colors. Each one will have its own special qualities, but the important thing when selecting your palette is to have a balance – a group of colors that is evenly distributed.

We have used a relatively small number of colors in the exercises in this book, as it is possible to learn far more initially from using a small group of colors extensively. For our purposes we want to begin with the most vivid colors available, because every time you mix colors the result loses some brightness.

Using just the nine colors, plus a black and white, featured in the illustration you can discover much of what you need to know. By the way, despite its name, Payne's gray is really a black and monestial is also known as phthalocyanine.

As your awareness increases and your painting needs become greater you will almost certainly want to expand your palette, and the six additional colors illustrated are suggestions. Please remember they are only suggestions, as everybody will have their own favorites. In this book we have also used a number of other colors.

Remember that you are likely to use white far more than anything else, and finally, do try to avoid mixing more than three colors at a time, because if you do it is very likely you will end up with lifeless colors.

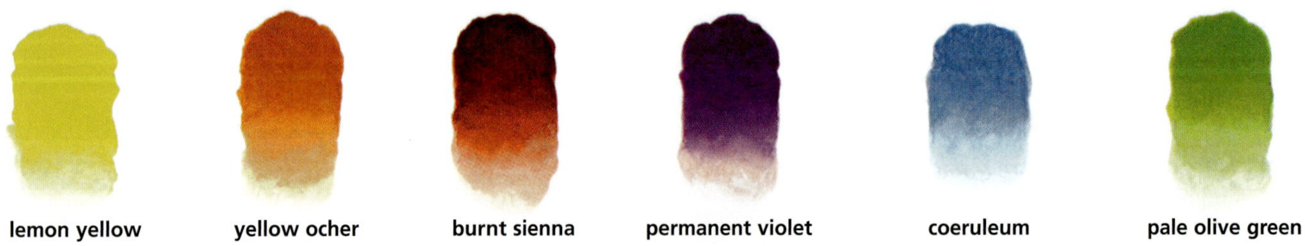

Palettes

Acrylic will not adhere permanently to a non-porous surface, so this is the main requirement for a palette. Do not use the wooden palettes sold for oil painting as you will not be able to remove the paint after use. Some art suppliers carry white plastic palettes for acrylic painting, but you can easily improvise your own mixing surface.

For acrylic used relatively thickly, a sheet of glass is ideal, though only for indoor work. An alternative would be a piece of laminated particle board, such as formica, or you can use old ceramic or enamel plates. These are easy to clean and will not stain, whereas laminated board will retain some of the paint dyes.

Acrylics will dry out quickly on any of these homemade palettes, so use a plant spray or other atomizer to spray the colors with water from time to time – before they begin to acquire the skin that indicates drying. To keep the paints workable while you take a break, cover the palette with plastic wrap.

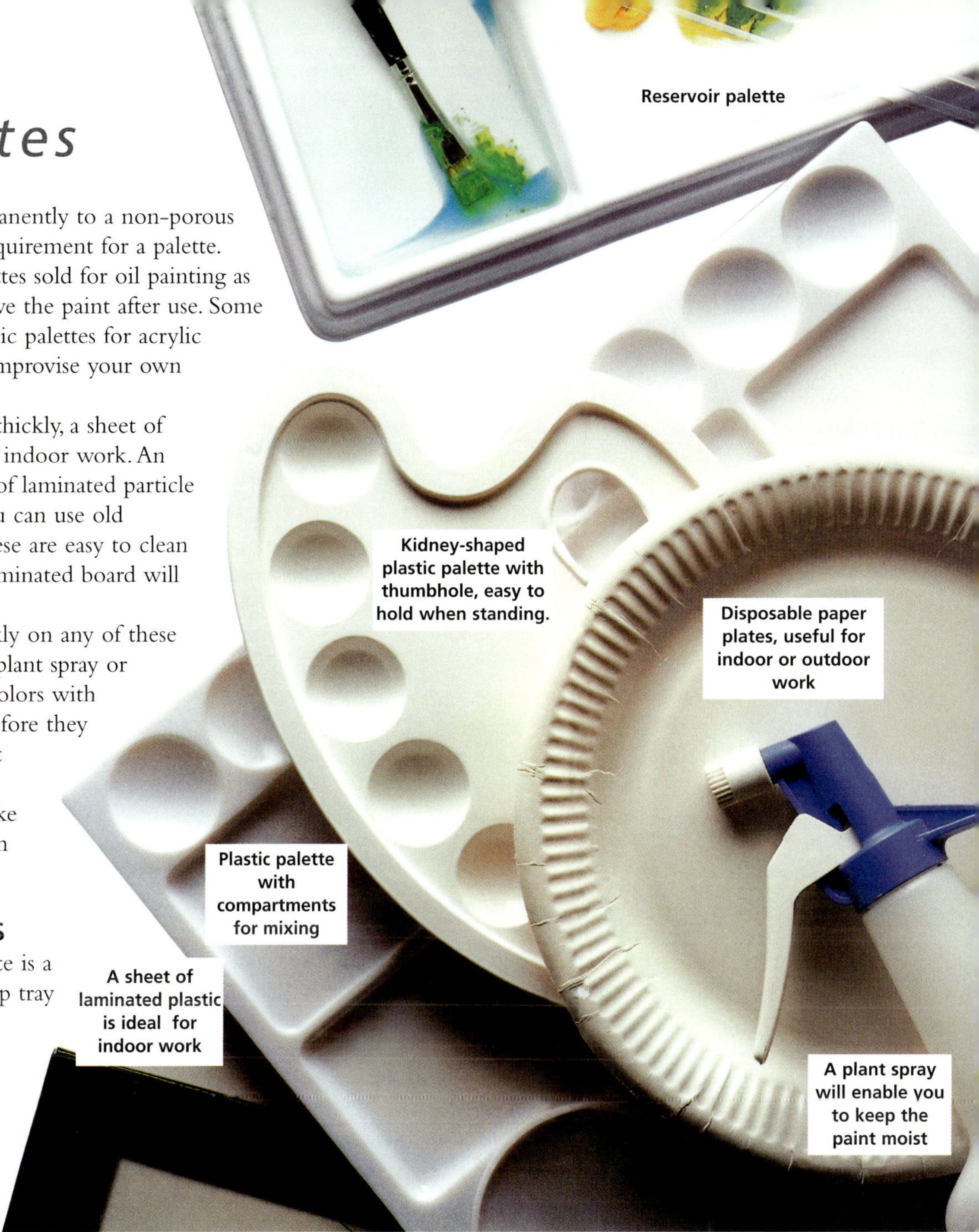

RESERVOIR PALETTES

One useful ready-made palette is a reservoir palette. This is a deep tray with a clear plastic lid that holds water to keep the paint moist. The paints are laid out and mixed on a sheet of special paper, with a piece of dampened absorbent paper underneath. Sufficient water seeps up to keep the paint moist while you work, after which you put on the lid to trap the moisture. The palette incorporates a compartment for laying brushes in water.

MAKING A RESERVOIR PALETTE

At present, reservoir palettes are produced by only one or two manufacturers, so if you have difficulty obtaining one, try making your own. You will need a metal or plastic tray, sheets of blotting paper or capillary matting (sold for gardening purposes), and several pieces of wax paper or thin tracing paper, both cut to the same size as the tray.

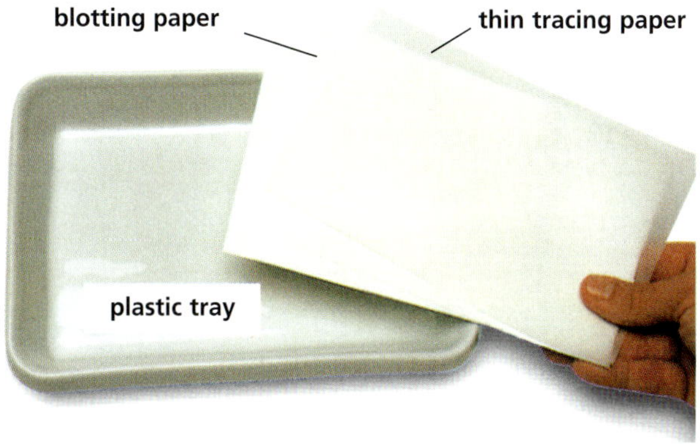

Equipment

BRUSHES

Any brushes used for oil or watercolor are also suitable for acrylic paint. If you already have these brushes, it should not be necessary to go out and buy new ones specifically to use with acrylics. If your brushes were last used with oil paint, however, they must be very carefully cleaned to remove all traces of oil or turpentine from the bristles. These substances will not mix with acrylics and can react adversely with the paint.

If you are intending to invest in new brushes in any case, it is probably worthwhile considering buying nylon ones rather than the traditional bristle and sable. The new synthetic brushes are considered particularly appropriate for the synthetically based acrylic paint, and are generally thought to be stronger and better able to withstand the tough handling and cleaning demanded by acrylics.

THE TRADITIONAL CHOICE

Oil painting brushes are normally made of bristle. The four basic types – round, flat, bright, and filbert – are used with acrylics in exactly the same way as you would use them for painting in oils.

Round brushes are shaped like watercolor brushes, although, being made from bristle, they are stiffer and, like all oil painting brushes, have long handles so that you can stand back and assess your picture as you work on it. The bristles of flat and bright brushes are cut into a square shape, curving slightly at the sides – on flat brushes the bristles are long and flexible making a smooth, regular stroke; bright brushes have short, stiff bristles that are useful for laying areas of thick, textural paint. Filberts are a convenient combination of both round and flat brushes, having long, flexible bristles which are shaped to a gentle point at the end. A filbert has many uses, making marks similar to those made with a flat or watercolor brush, depending on the consistency of the paint.

When used thinly, acrylic is very similar to watercolor or ink wash, and you should choose your brushes accordingly. Real sable has a unique springiness which has made it a favorite with watercolorists for centuries. Oxhair is a slightly "floppier" but less expensive alternative.

THE NEW BRUSHES

All the brush shapes are now available in nylon. Some artists prefer them to the traditional types, even when using oil and watercolor. Others will use only real bristle or sable, even when painting with acrylics. It is largely a matter of preference and there are no hard-and-fast rules, only the vague idea that nylon brushes and acrylic paint should be used together because they are both synthetic.

It is easy to remove acrylic paint from nylon brushes – both during work and when cleaning up afterward – and they are also exceptionally durable when looked after. But, like all paintbrushes, they must be cleaned and stored properly, otherwise they soon become stiff and unusable.

Large nylon brushes, such as those sold in hardware and decorators' stores, can be invaluable for applying large areas of color and blocking in. They come in all sizes from about half an inch wide to six inches and more. They are cheaper than those sold in art stores, and the better quality ones are just as good and often easier to use.

PAINTING WITH A KNIFE

The buttery consistency of acrylics has tempted many artists away from traditional brush strokes, encouraging them to apply the paint in thick, textural wedges, and solid areas of color, put on with a knife.

Both painting knives and palette knives have flexible blades that make it easy to apply and manipulate the

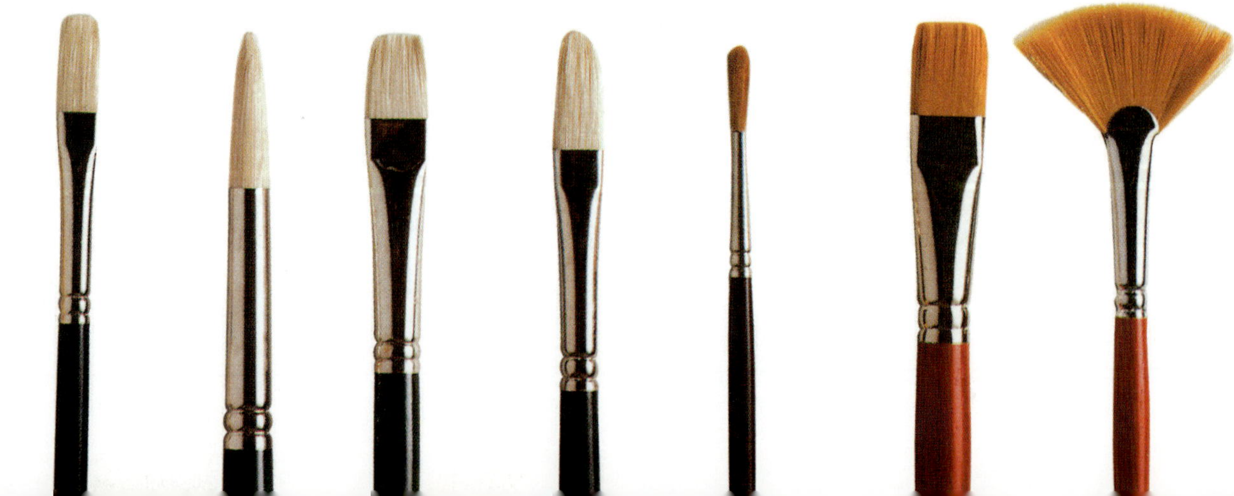

paint. Palette knives have straight blades and are essentially used for mixing colors on the palette (although they are also handy for applying approximate quantities of paint to the support). Painting knives have curved handles, making it easy to control and move the paint around on the picture without the end of the knife damaging the canvas. A "cranked blade" is a cross between a palette knife and a painting knife, and can be used for either purpose.
All the knives are obtainable in a range of sizes. Some painting knives are tiny, which makes them suitable for working in detail and applying relatively small areas of paint.

AIRBRUSHES

Acrylic paint can be used in airbrushes in the same way as oils, gouache, and watercolors. As with oils, acrylics can be airbrushed onto canvas, board, and metal sheets provided that the surface has been prepared. The smallest form of airbrush today is an atomizer. Airbrushes are precision instruments that can produce extremely fine lines and tonal gradations that give an almost photographic effect. Those used for delicate work have a small paint or dye reservoir that is filled with an eye-dropper or paintbrush. Those used for larger works have a bigger nozzle and a paint reservoir into which paint is poured. Sprayguns are used for really large areas: the paint is diluted until it is as thin as milk.

Airbrushes must be cleaned thoroughly and the parts checked regularly to make sure that they have not worked loose. Spitting could mean that the needle is stuck on a coarse particle of pigment or that the paint needs thinning. If the paint comes out irregularly it could be that the needle is out of place or fitted too tightly, the nozzle is worn, or the pigment has dried in the nozzle's fluid passage. The latter requires the nozzle to be soaked for a long time and cleaned. A bent needle or an obstruction in the air cap can cause a lop-sided spray. The nozzle cap can cause the paint to build up; it should be cleaned either by removing it and placing the tip flat on a piece of paper and blowing, or by unscrewing it and cleaning it inside and out with a stiff brush, a damp lint-free cloth, or a toothpick.

CARE OF YOUR BRUSHES

The most important thing to remember about acrylic paint is that it dries rapidly, and it can ruin brushes unless you keep them wet throughout the working process. Do not leave them to stand for long periods in water, because this can bend and splay the bristles. Rinse them well after each application of paint so that they remain damp, or place them flat in a shallow dish. The reservoir palette shown on page 109 has a compartment designed for this purpose.

EASELS

Unless you are using thin washes of acrylic, any one of the many available easels could suit your purpose. The final choice will depend on what size you normally work on, the type of support you paint on, whether you prefer sitting or standing and, of course, whether or not you need an easel that is portable.

If you use a lot of water with the paint, applying it in washes of thin, runny color, then an upright easel is not for you. An adjustable drawing board that tilts to any convenient angle could be the answer. Or, if you prefer something that can be folded up and carried around, an easel that adjusts to a horizontal position to prevent the paint from running off would be more suitable.

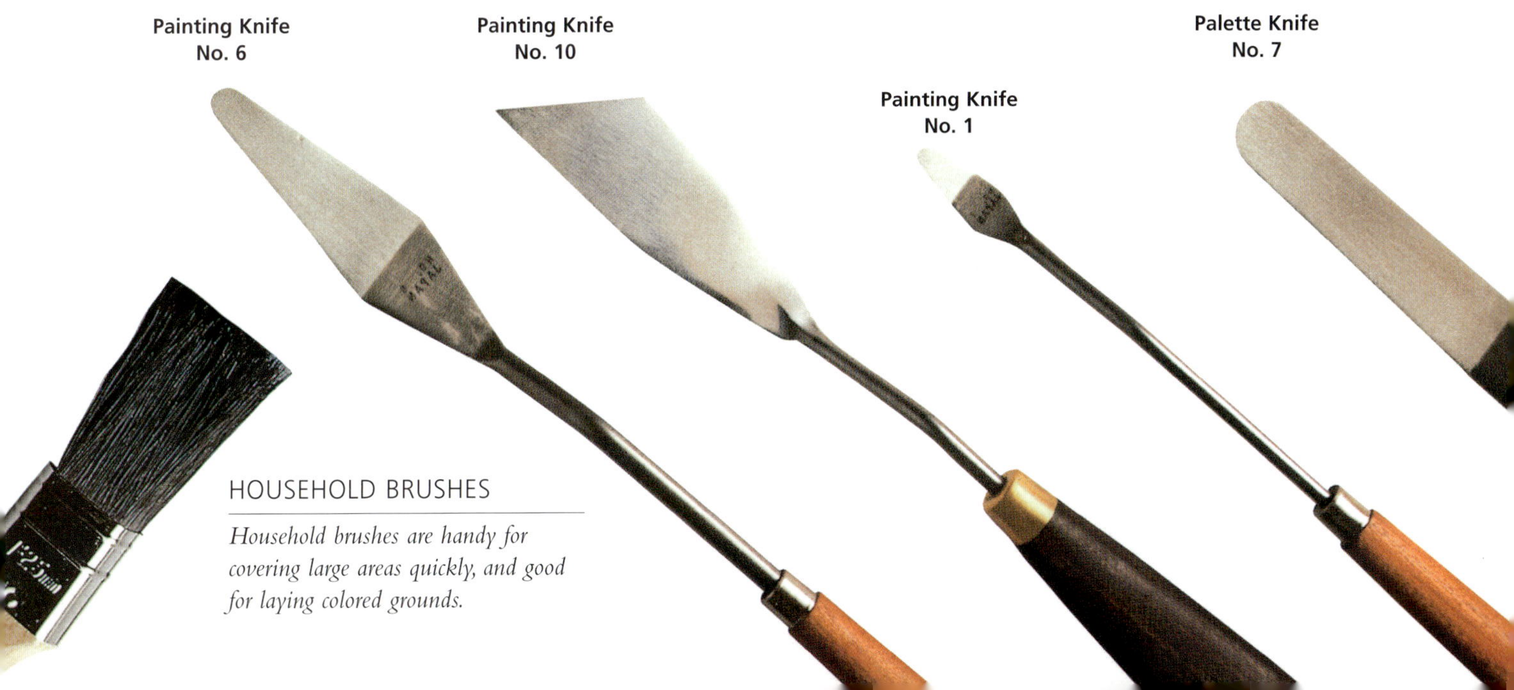

HOUSEHOLD BRUSHES

Household brushes are handy for covering large areas quickly, and good for laying colored grounds.

Techniques

GLAZING

A glaze is a transparent film of paint, usually applied over another color. It can change the underlying color without actually obliterating it, producing a subtle film-like quality instead of a flat opaque finish. If the glaze is to show up clearly, the underlying color must be paler than the glaze itself. Occasionally a light colored glaze is used over a color that is the same tone, or perhaps even darker, but in this case the result is always subtle, adding a barely noticeable sheen to the glazed area rather than actually changing its color.

The strength of a glaze depends partly on the staining capacity of the particular pigment you are working with and partly on how much water or medium you use to dilute the color. Some pigments produce a stronger tint than others. For instance, phthalocyanine green makes a bright glaze which will tend to dominate the color underneath; a color with low tinting strength, such as raw umber, will tone down or modify the underpainting without overpowering it.

If you use water by itself to dilute the color, the glaze dries to a dull, matt finish. When the paint is diluted with acrylic medium, it dries gloss or semi-gloss, depending on how absorbent the underneath surface is. A glaze mixed with medium is usually richer in color than one mixed with water, but the dullest of finishes can be enlivened and the color brought up to its full potential by applying a coat of acrylic varnish, gloss medium, or acrylic fixative.

Multiple glazes can be superimposed to create complex color variations. Always work from light to dark, gradually building up the tone and color until you arrive at the effect you want.

Glazes are often used over thickly impastoed paint and highly textured surfaces. The glazing gives a touch of delicate transparent color to an otherwise heavy finish. If the glaze is gently wiped with tissue or rag while the paint is still wet, the darkest color will remain in the crevices, cracks, and indented marks. This produces an effectively varied surface which – if the glaze color is neutral and subdued enough – can often resemble that of an old oil painting or even a texture from nature. The bark of a tree or a mossy stone wall, for instance, could easily be depicted in this way.

SELECTIVE GLAZING

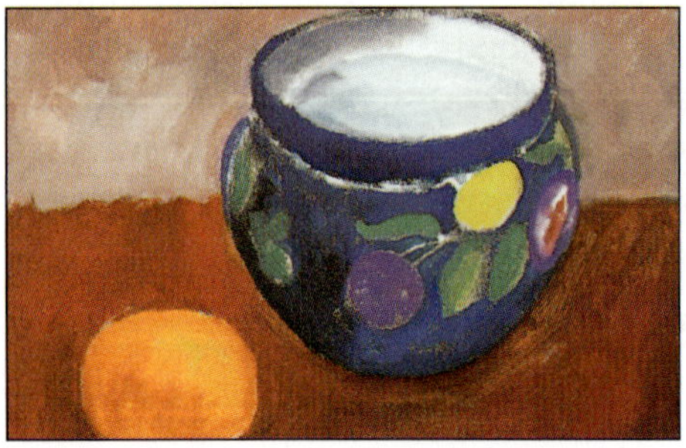

1 Work on canvas or canvas board. Begin by blocking in the complete image – including the pattern on the vase – with opaque paint of medium consistency. You can then enrich the colors and build up the forms with glazes.

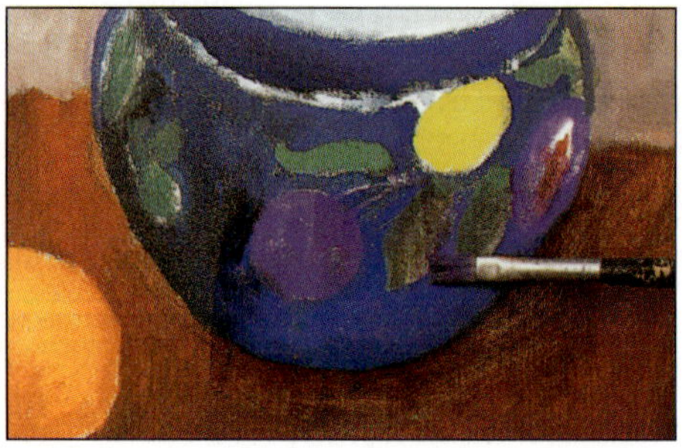

2 To create the shadow at the bottom of the vase, where the form turns away from the light, use a glaze of dioxazine purple thinned with a half-and-half mixture of water and gloss medium. This darkens the tones slightly.

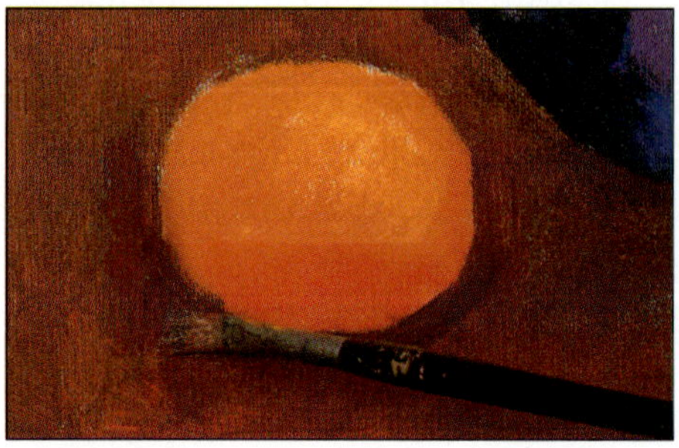

3&4 Build up the form of the orange in the same way, using a glaze of alizarin crimson for the shadowed area. To suggest the shadow on the background as well as that on the fruit, take the brush across both in one broad sweep.

The tone and color gradations on the orange must be refined to make it appear solid. Apply a glaze of cadmium yellow over the entire area to bring out the highlights, then add a touch of transparent green at top right.

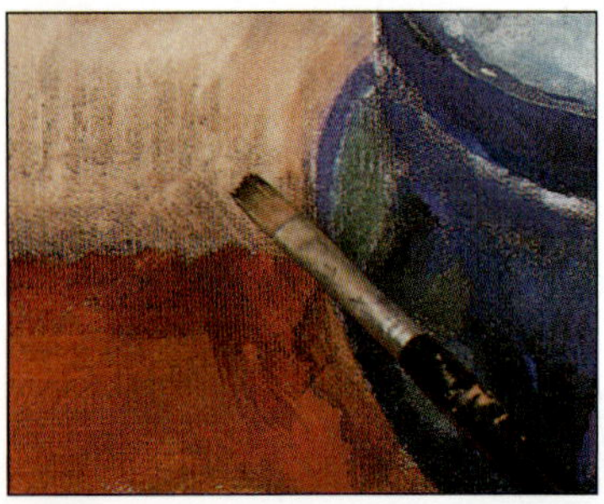

5 Complete the background wall and the back of the red cloth by darkening them slightly with glazes of diluted burnt umber. This helps the vase to stand out, and avoids too much contrast between the opaque paint and the transparent glazes.

IMPASTO

A technique borrowed from oil painting is the use of thick paint that stands out from the picture surface. Impastoed paint can be applied throughout a picture or in a single area. Thick paint, with highly visible brushmarks, has a stronger presence than thin paint, and will always draw the eye, so artists often restrict impasto to areas they want to emphasize. You see this effect in many oil portraits by Rembrandt, where thickly painted highlights on skin, clothes, and jewelry stand out strongly against the thin paint used for backgrounds and dark areas. Adapt this idea to a landscape or still life, painting the background more thinly than the foreground objects to create the illusion of space.

IMPASTO MEDIUM

Most acrylic paints are runnier than oils, so if you want to use heavy impastos for an entire painting you may need to thicken the paint with acrylic gel medium (see page 106). This is also an economy measure, because without it you might need a whole tube of paint for one area. If you are using white, you are unlikely to need the medium. White is the thickest and most opaque of all of the colors.

USING THICK PAINT

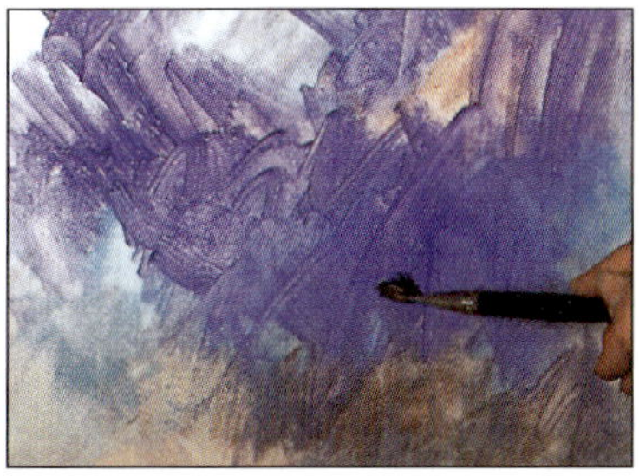

1 You may find yourself in trouble if you use thick paint from the start, because the colors will mix together. Block in the colors first with thinned paint using a scrubbing motion to push them well into the surface.

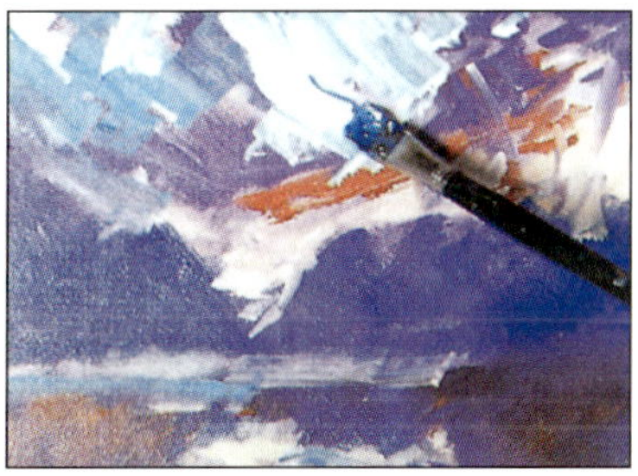

2 Now begin to build up the sky with a thick, juicy mixture of white and phthalo blue. Try mixing the color only partially on the palette, so that each brush stroke consists of streaks of two or more colors of paint.

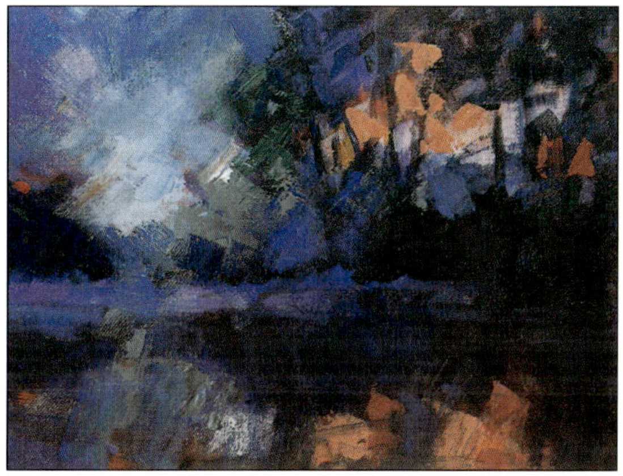

The finished painting.

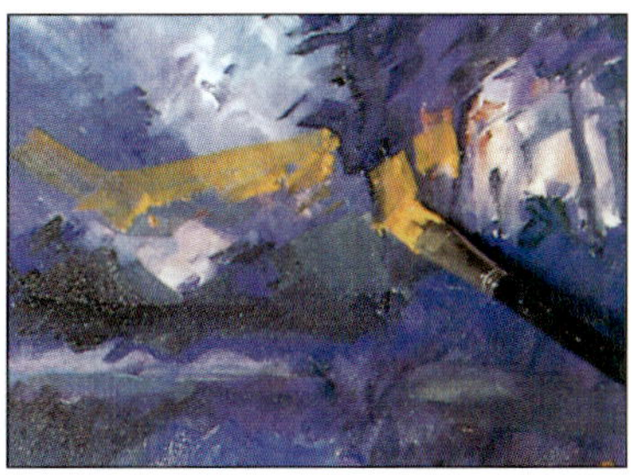

3 Introduce some yellow into the sky and foreground to contrast with the blues. Do not worry if the color looks too bright. Simply paint over it with another color while it is still wet, and the two will mix (see finished painting).

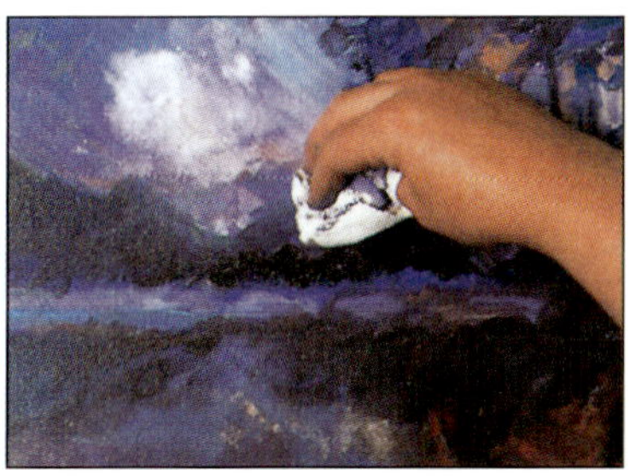

4 The thicker the paint, the longer it takes to dry. If the build-up of paint becomes too heavy for you to add colors without creating muddy mixtures, wipe some of the paint off with a rag before continuing.

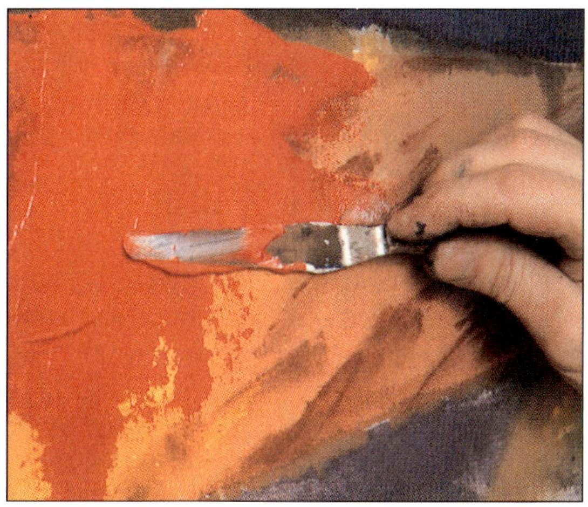

Using a palette or painting knife instead of a brush creates solid wedges of color with a characteristic "ridged" effect.

TONAL UNDERPAINTING

The term "underpainting" refers to the preliminary blocking-in – the first stages of a painting, when the composition and tonal values are worked out before any detail is added. Occasionally some basic color is used, but traditionally the underpainting is in monochrome, its purpose being to establish the correct tones before the problem of color is tackled. It is especially helpful if you plan to use a lot of glazes, because here the tonal design will show through the transparent layers of color to some extent, giving a sense of form and solidity to the painting as a whole.

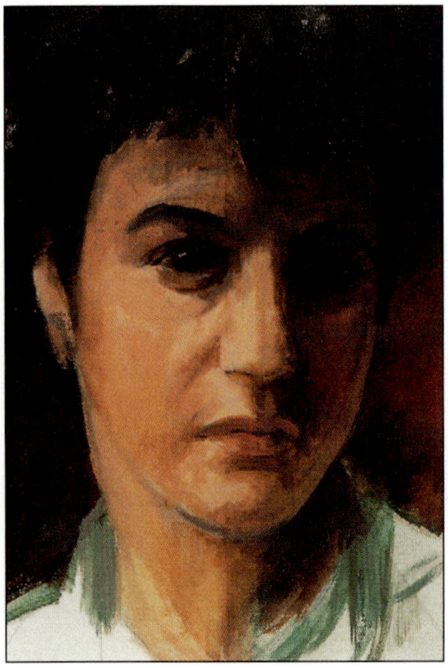

The finished painting.

Until the advent of acrylics, the business of underpainting took a long time. Oil painters were obliged to wait for each stage to dry before they could proceed with the picture, and many of the Old Masters had to put their underpainted canvases aside for several months before the paint was dry enough to enable them to carry on working. These days, with quick-drying acrylics there is no need to wait so long between stages, and the whole process takes hours and days instead of weeks, months, and even years.

Modern oil painters have the best of both worlds. They can use acrylics for the early stages of a picture, often establishing the main color areas as well as the structure and tonal composition, in an acrylic underpainting. The work is then developed in oils, using the slower, traditional oil painting techniques to complete the painting.

Avoid very dark tones and even blacks in your underpainting, since they will deaden the subsequent colors. The darker areas will be intensified as you lay on the colors, so try to make the underpainting a light-toned "ghost" image of your subject, using only middle tones and leaving the palest parts white or near-white.

Warm browns or grays are suitable for underpainting most subjects, but you could try the effect of a contrasting color, leaving parts of it uncovered to set up contrasts. The Renaissance painters favored a green underpainting to counterbalance the warm colors of skin. Like a colored ground, an underpainting can influence the overall color scheme of the picture.

COLOR OVER TONE

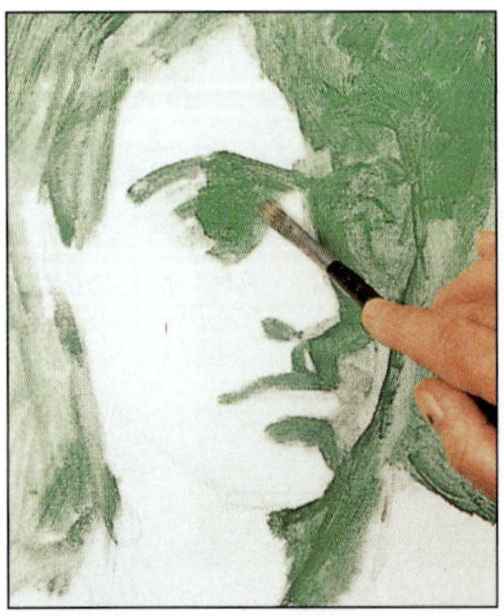

1 Use cobalt green well-diluted with warm water for the underpainting. Block in the head broadly with a bristle brush, paying particular attention to the shadow areas that define the planes of the face and the features.

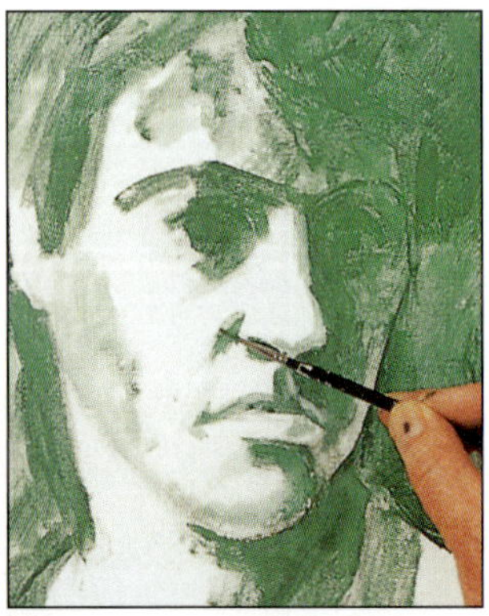

2 Continue to work on the underpainting until you achieve a full tonal "map" of the head and face. Use a small synthetic brush for details such as the shadow at the side of the nose.

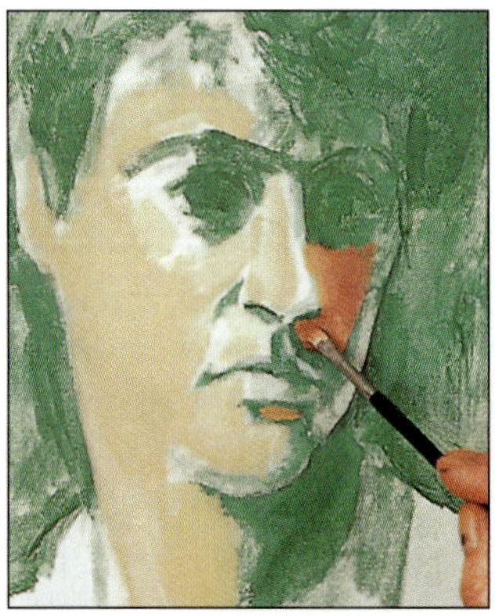

3 Begin to apply color: a mixture of yellow ocher, white, and a touch of cadmium red for the light side; the same but with less white and more red for the shadowed side.

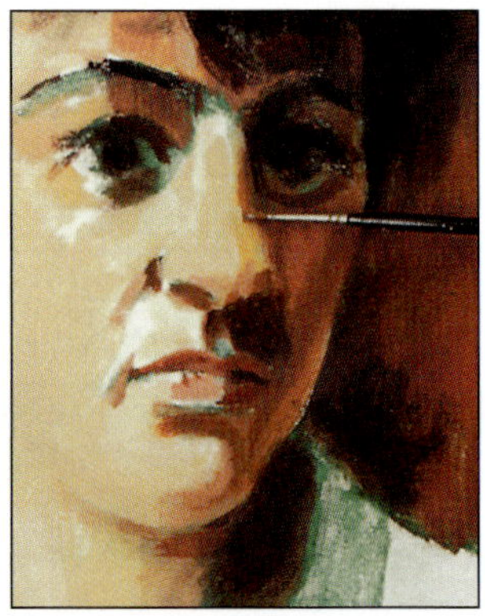

4 Bring some of the warm reddish skin color into the background. Then continue to build up the features, again using a small brush for details. Leave little patches of the green underpainting showing around the eyes.

FURTHER IDEAS

If you intend to work with thin or transparent paint, give thought to the color you choose for the underpainting, because the darker areas of tone will show through. You can deliberately leave areas of underpainting uncovered, as when working on a colored ground.

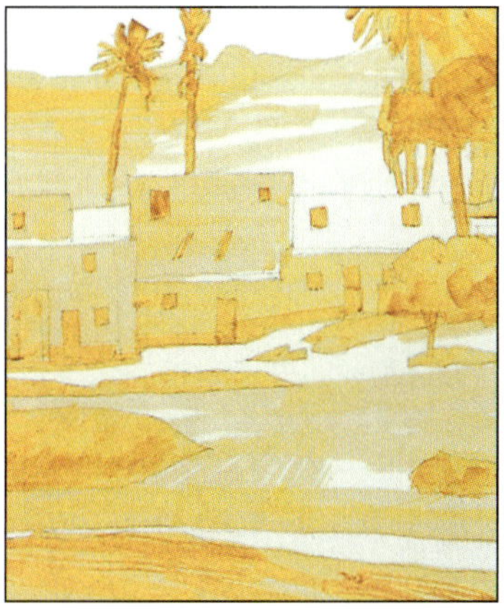

A yellow underpainting is chosen for a picture of yellow and blue.

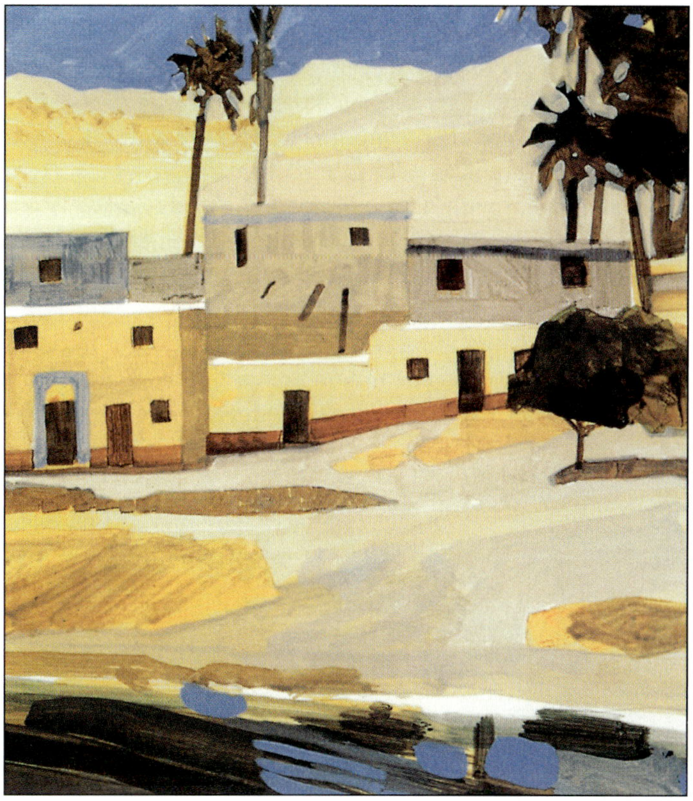

In parts of the foreground, blues are painted over yellows to give greenish hues.

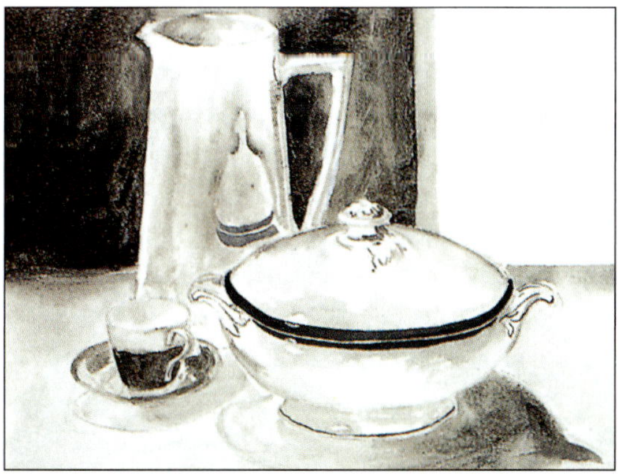

A gray underpainting, made by thinning black paint with varying amounts of water, establishes the tonal structure of the composition.

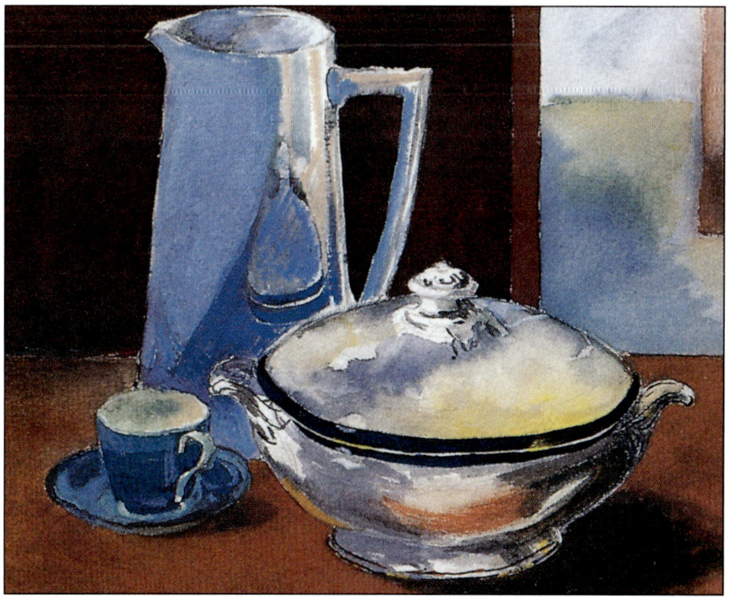

Again, some areas are left white or pale gray to avoid muddying the translucent, watercolor-like washes. The dark gray used for the background gives strength to the red-brown laid on top.

THE OPAQUE TECHNIQUE

Acrylic paint lends itself naturally to an opaque method of working. The consistency of the paint used directly from the tube or jar is thick and creamy, and if you don't mix this with too much water or medium the color dries to a dense, smooth finish. For the inexperienced acrylic artist, this is probably the best way to get acquainted with the medium – especially if you are already accustomed to working with oils or gouache, where a similar technique is used.

If you are familiar with oil paints you will already be aware that some pigments are more transparent than others. Exactly the same is true of acrylics, and some colors have far less covering power. There is no need to avoid these transparent colors when using the opaque technique; but it is sometimes useful to mix them with one of the more opaque pigments to maintain the color density.

Some common colors that have a relatively poor covering power are ultramarine, phthalocyanine blue, phthalocyanine crimson, phthalocyanine green and Hansa yellow. Try mixing any of these with a small amount of one of the more opaque colors. This will, of course, alter the color slightly but you won't necessarily lose the effect entirely. Titanium white, for example, is so opaque that a very small quantity of it can increase the opacity of any color it is added to. Similarly, Mars black and raw umber are both very opaque, although their addition will inevitably have a darkening effect.

Remember that the gel mediums – both the matt and the gloss – will thicken your paint, but they can also turn it transparent if you use too much of the gel, so add these mediums sparingly if you are aiming for an opaque effect.

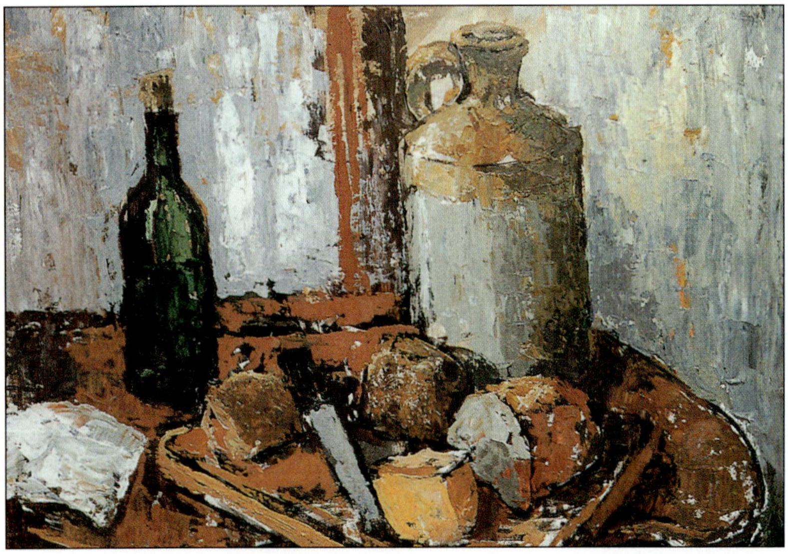

FOOD ON THE FARM by Gordon Bennett (opaque technique)

Most acrylic colors are naturally opaque unless diluted with water or one of the various mediums available. In this painting the artist has taken advantage of this property, applying layer upon layer of color and texture to create a solid, rugged image.

THE TRANSPARENT TECHNIQUE

As mentioned earlier, acrylics can be used like watercolors. One of the great advantages of this is that once the color is dry, acrylic is insoluble and therefore permanent. This means that your picture is protected from damp – the longstanding enemy of watercolor paintings – and is therefore more durable than the traditional medium. This insoluble characteristic also makes it easier to apply successive washes and will give you maximum control when working with transparent overlaid color. If you have worked with watercolor, you will know that when you apply one color over another, the first color can start to dissolve and blend with the second, thus restricting the amount of color which can be added before the paint starts to turn "muddy." With acrylics this is not the case. The colors remain separate, and it is possible to build up intricate layers of wash to create complex yet spontaneous effects.

As mentioned above, with the opaque method of acrylic painting the transparency of some of the pigments can often be a problem. With the transparent technique the opposite is true, and the more you can restrict yourself to these transparent colors the better. You can, of course, use any color you choose, and there is nothing to stop you from trying out diluted opaque colors, but these can sometimes look chalky and dull – no matter how thinly they are applied – and will deaden any colors underneath.

Acrylics have been especially welcomed by those artists who like working in watercolor but feel restricted by the traditional small scale of watercolor materials. With acrylics, the scope is broader – not only does the paint come in larger quantities, but you also have a wider choice of supports. All the traditional watercolor papers are suitable, and acrylic washes can be used directly on fabric – including unprimed canvas – as well as gesso boards and other primed surfaces.

TEXTURES

There are few limitations when making texture with acrylic paint. The worst problem you are likely to encounter is that you get so carried away with the different possibilities that the painting actually takes second place. This initial over-enthusiasm is not necessarily a bad thing, however, and you can take advantage of it to find out as much as possible about the potential of the paint and the different textural effects that can be made with it.

You can apply the paint thickly with a brush, palette knife, painting knife, or any other suitable implement. Acrylics dry quickly enough to enable you to continue building up the layers almost indefinitely. Some acrylic artists work almost in relief, their work taking on such a heavily impastoed surface that it can only be described as a three-dimensional art form.

Once the paint is committed to the support and starts to dry, it cannot easily be moved or changed. Indeed, it is usually a mistake to try to improve on the first effort because this may spoil the characteristic freshness of the paint surface. It is better to think carefully before applying the paint, making absolutely sure that the correct quantity of the right colors goes exactly where you want it to go, than to try to change it once it's on the canvas.

If a heavily impastoed surface is what you want, it is better to build up the paint in layers than put it on as one thick coat. This is because the top surface of the acrylic, which is exposed to the air, dries before the paint underneath and this sometimes causes cracking. Of course, if you don't mind this addition to the texture of the picture, you don't need to worry.

TEXTURE WITH GEL AND MODELING PASTE

The volume and thickness of the paint can be increased by mixing the color with gel medium or modeling paste. In this way the color can be literally troweled onto the picture, especially if you are using the paste, that is thick and gives the paint a cement-like consistency. This can be great fun and a very satisfying way of working, but it is important to stop and think about the effect and whether it is actually what you want. Mediums should be used as a means to an end, not an end in themselves, and it is all too easy to get carried away with texture to the detriment of the picture.

Gel dries transparently and there is a limit to how much you can use without affecting the color. This can be counteracted to some extent by restricting your palette to opaque pigments and using titanium white to give body to the color where necessary. Modeling gel dries with a shiny surface to that of gloss medium – the more you use, the shinier the paint will be. The glossy finish makes acrylics dry like oil paints, so unless you specifically want this to happen, be cautious about using too much thickening gel.

Modeling paste is usually used as a thickener, and as such is mixed with the paint before it is applied. This gives the acrylic a stiff consistency which allows the paint to keep its shape as it dries. Any brush strokes, palette knife marks, and other textures show up clearly, ensuring the crisp, fresh paint surface that is often as important to the acrylic artist as the content and form of the picture.

Modeling paste is sometimes used before the paint is applied. If you are working with opaque color this usually proves unsatisfactory, and the picture surface may seem dull and lifeless as a result. What you are actually doing is painting a thin layer of plastic onto a plastic shape – and that is exactly what it will look like in your picture. The method is more satisfactory if you use thin glazes of color over the hardened paste, when it is possible to achieve subtler effects without causing the surface to look like molded plastic.

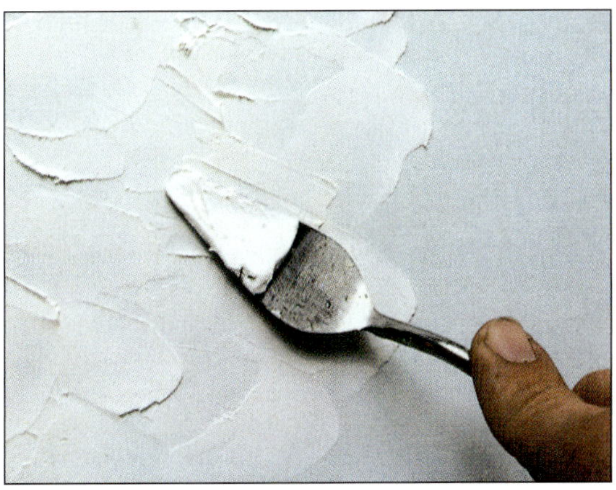

TEXTURE PASTE

The thickest medium made specially for use with acrylic color is texture, or modeling paste. This is applied directly to the support with a painting knife (left) and can be built up in layers to achieve an almost three-dimensional effect. Paint is applied to the textured surface either as a delicate glaze (right) or opaquely to obtain an area of solid, textural color.

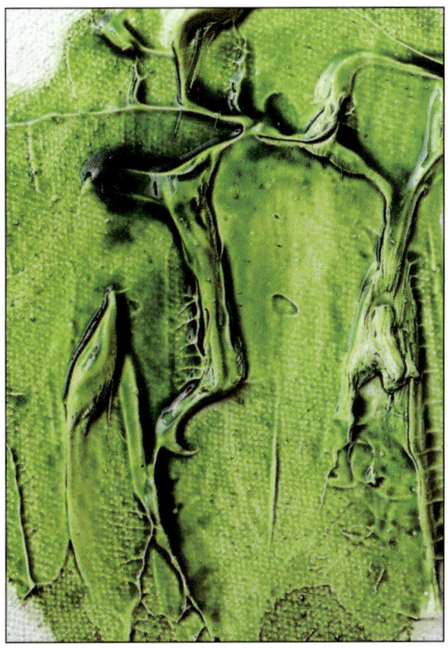

INVENTING YOUR OWN TEXTURES

You are not restricted to the paintbrush and painting knife when it comes to making textures and surface patterns. One of the reasons why acrylic was popular with so many artists when it first became available in the 1950s and 1960s was its entire versatility in this respect.

Because it is so adhesive the acrylic can be mixed with almost any substance and it will take on the texture of that substance. Sand, sawdust, rice, and many other materials have been used successfully to produce a gritty or granular surface. Sometimes the texture is directly relevant to the subject – using sand for a beach or to depict the surface of a rough stone wall would be good examples of this – but more often it is used in a purely creative way to get as much textural contrast as possible into the painting.

Modeling paste is useful for making imprints. A whole range of unexpected patterns and textural effects can be created by taking impressions of various objects and materials and incorporating these into the picture. Here, too, it is usually better to be inventive than literal. If you try to imitate textures that are present in the subject itself, the result is usually decorative rather than realistic, and your picture may take on an unwelcome "naive" quality.

Good overall textures can be made from crumpled paper, tinfoil, a stiff brush, comb, or anything else capable of making an imprinted texture in wet modeling paste. Of course these are only a few of the possibilities. Doubtless you will want to experiment and discover your own techniques, ones that suit your own style and particular way of working.

FURTHER IDEAS

Experimentation is part of learning to paint, and it is always worth trying different methods of creating texture. Make up a series of samples like the ones shown here. If you cannot immediately see a way of incorporating them into a painting, keep them handy for future inspiration. You may find a subject that seems to demand texture, or one that could be enlivened by such an approach.

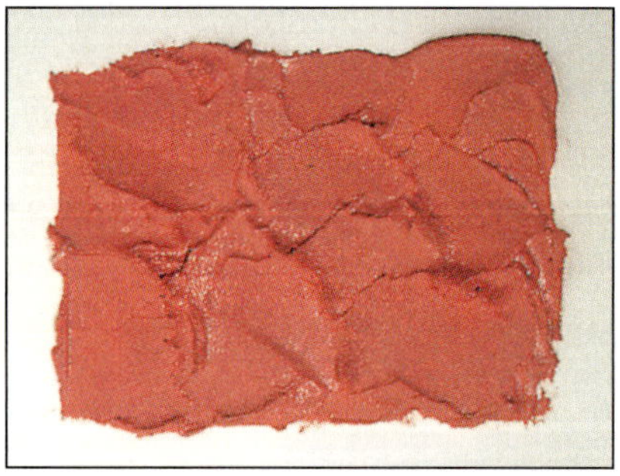

Paint mixed with sand. Using a dull red or gray, this grainy texture could imitate old brick or stonework.

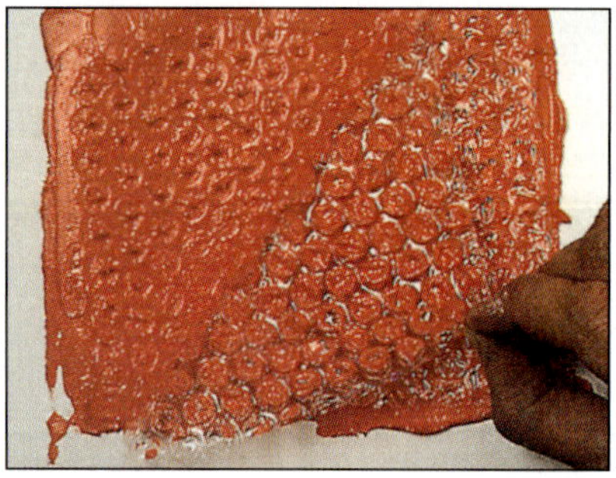

Bubblewrap pressed into paint creates an even texture, that could bring interest into the background of a still life.

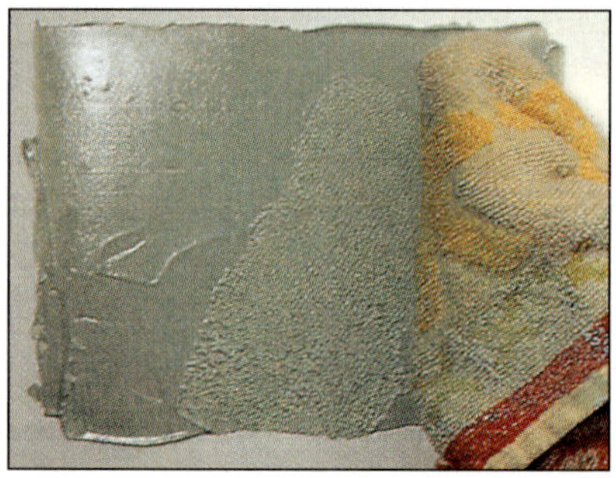

Fabric, such as terrycloth pressed into thick paint, gives a less obtrusive texture. Ideal for actual fabric in a portrait.

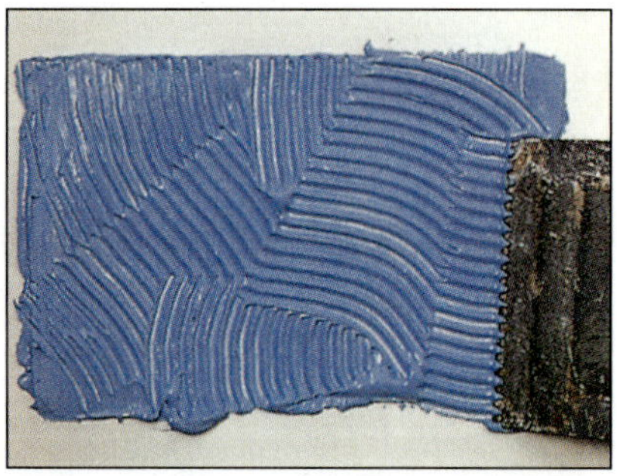

Combing or scratching into paint can create a variety of effects. These could suggest trees or grasses blown in the wind.

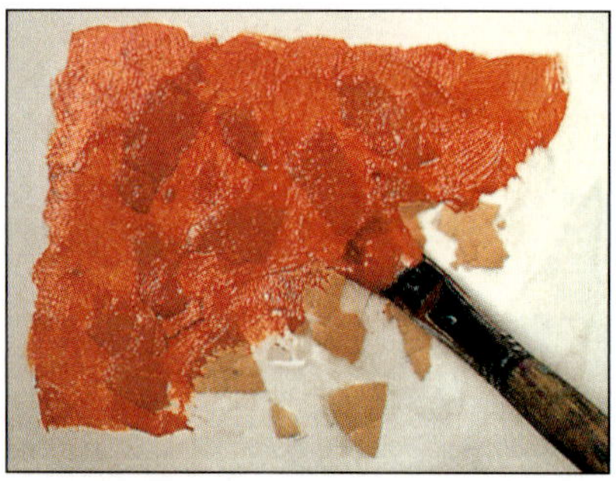

Crushed eggshells stuck down with gloss medium and painted over. Use for the foreground of a stony beach.

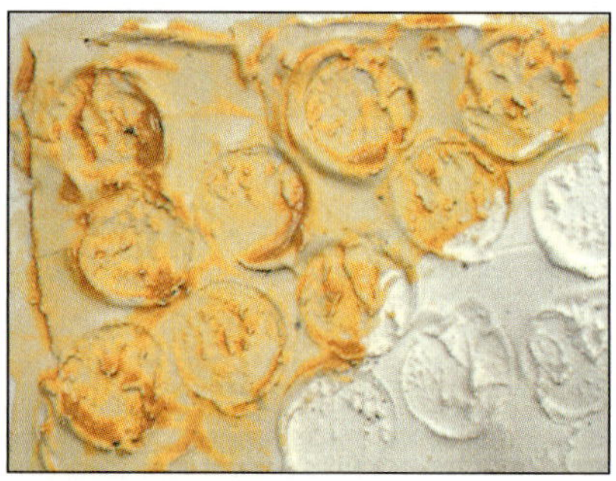

Coins pressed into acrylic modeling paste and painted with transparent paint. Could contrast with flatter paint in a semi-abstract work.

WET-INTO-WET

Oil effects When two or more brush strokes of wet paint overlap, the colors mix, creating soft blends. This is the technique known as wet-into-wet. Unlike oil paint, that remains wet for a long time, acrylic does not, so to imitate this oil technique effectively with acrylics you must adopt one of two stratagems. The first is to wet the working surface before you begin and periodically thereafter with a spray bottle. The second is to mix the colors with a retarding medium (see page 106) before applying them. The medium slows down the drying time for several hours, allowing you to blend colors and move them around on the surface as oil painters do. Do not spray with water if you use retarder, because water affects its performance, and do not dilute the paint for the same reason; use it at tube consistency.

Watercolor effects Wet-into-wet is also a watercolor technique, and this too can be imitated in acrylics. Retarding medium is no use here, since you will be using a lot of water with the paint. All you need to do is to dampen the paper well in advance and keep it damp – again you can use a spray bottle from time to time. The paint will remain wet and workable until the paper dries.

OIL PAINTING METHOD

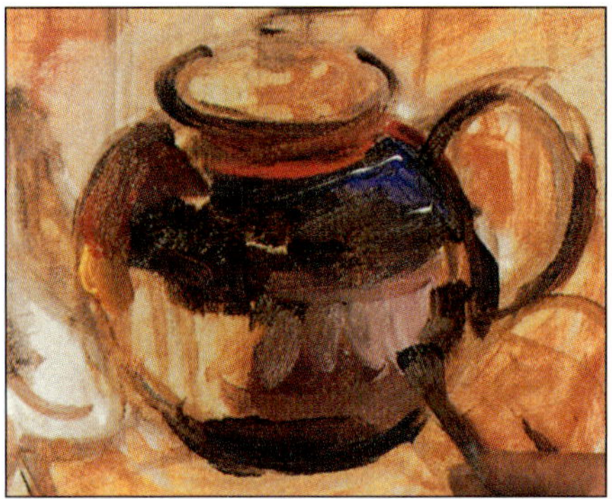

1 Block in the background with thin mixtures of yellow ocher, burnt umber, and a little cadmium red. For the teapot, use dark red-brown, green-brown, and pinkish mixtures of paint, with touches of pure red and blue. Add retarding medium but no water, and encourage the colors to mix.

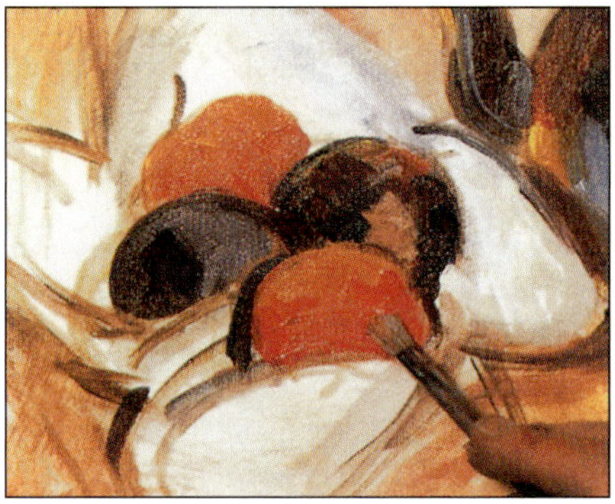

2 Use the same method for the fruit, applying a rich deep red over orange. A bristle brush is best for this method, because it pushes the paint on and helps the colors to blend rather than sit on top of one another.

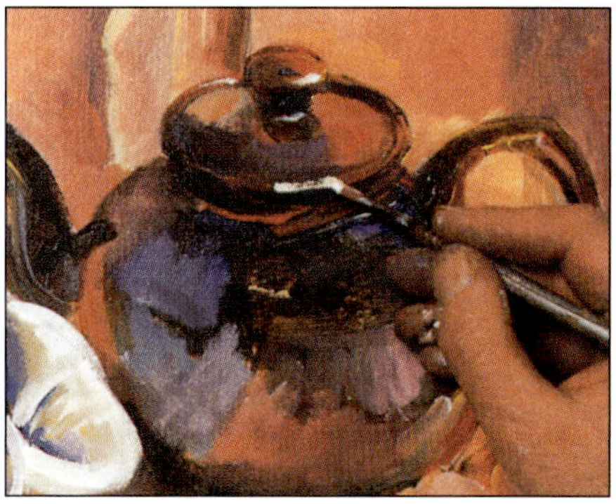

3 For details, such as this highlight, you want a crisp effect, so let the paint beneath dry. Paint mixed with retarding medium remains tacky for half an hour or more, depending on the thickness of the paint, so make sure it is thoroughly dry, or you may scuff it when you add a new color.

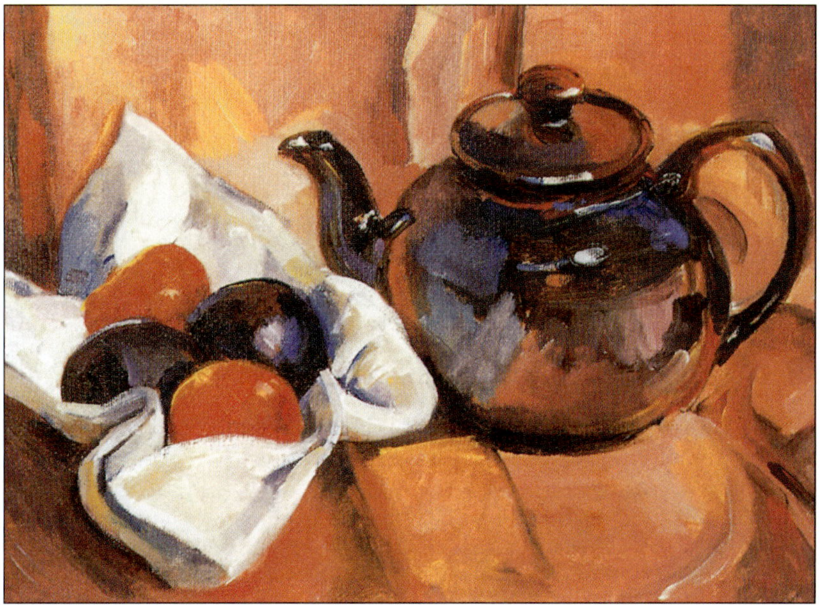

The finished picture.

WATERCOLOR METHOD

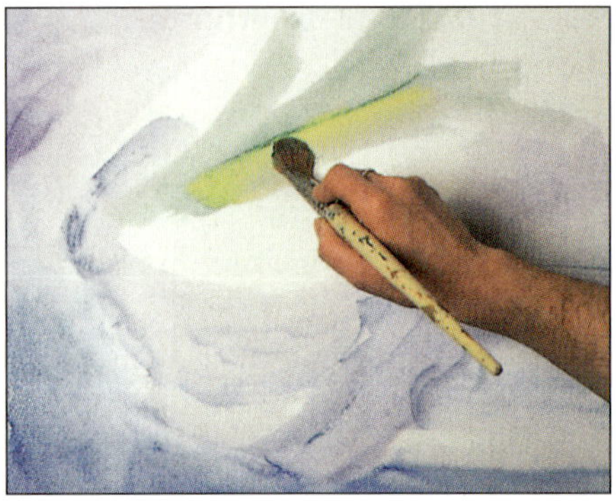

1 Work on a heavy watercolor paper that will not buckle when wet. Dampen it all over and use a large, soft brush to lay on broad washes of pale blue, mauve, green, and yellow-green.

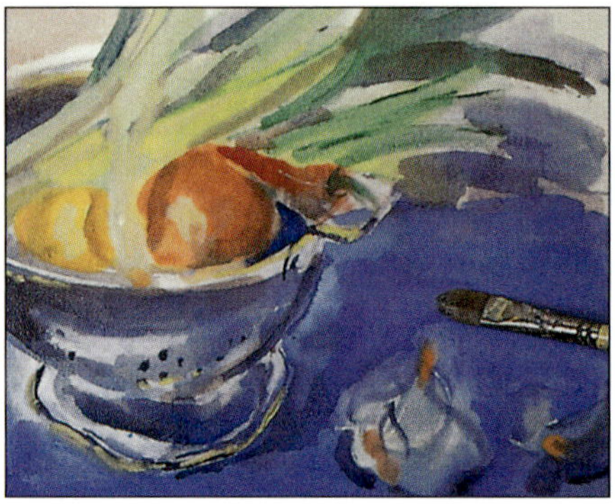

2 While the paper remains damp, the colors will mix slightly without forming hard edges. Continue to build up the image, using well-watered paint and redampening the paper as needed.

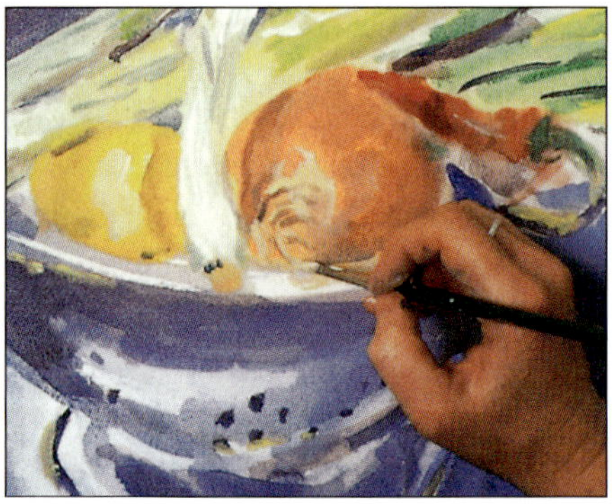

3 A painting done entirely wet-into-wet can look too vague, so let the paper dry before adding crisper touches of detail. If you lose a highlight, use a little opaque paint in the final stages to retrieve it.

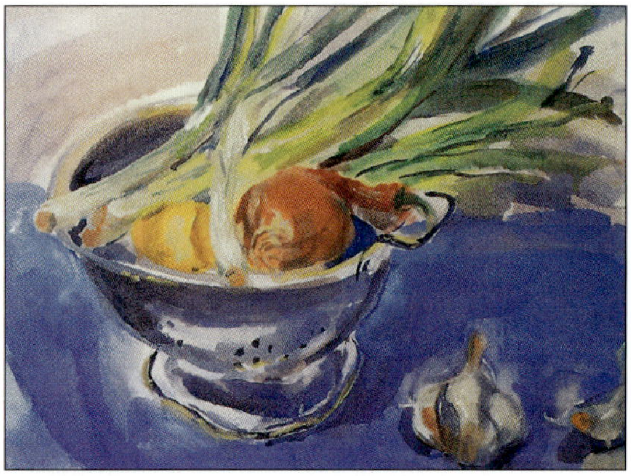

The finished picture.

FURTHER IDEAS

The wet-into-wet method can be applied to any subject, but is especially suitable for landscapes and seascapes, where you will often want to minimize hard edges. You can work in the same way throughout the painting or reserve the soft effects for certain areas.

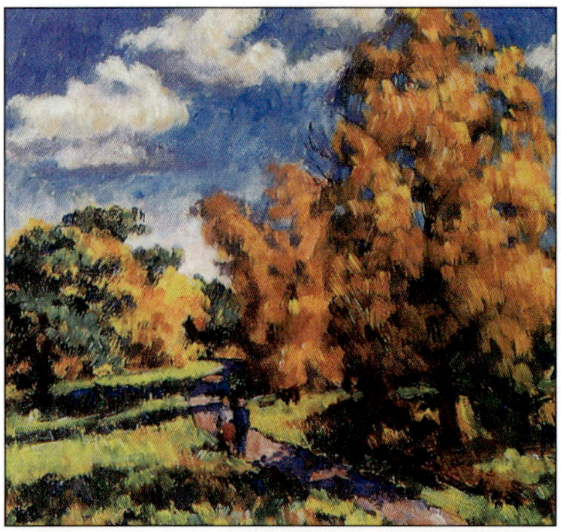

LEFT: *The method was used throughout this picture. The paint was mixed with retarding medium and applied thickly in oil-painting mode.*

RIGHT: *This shows a more selective use of the method. Much of the water was painted wet-into-wet in watercolor mode, contrasting with thicker, drier paint used for the foreground beach.*

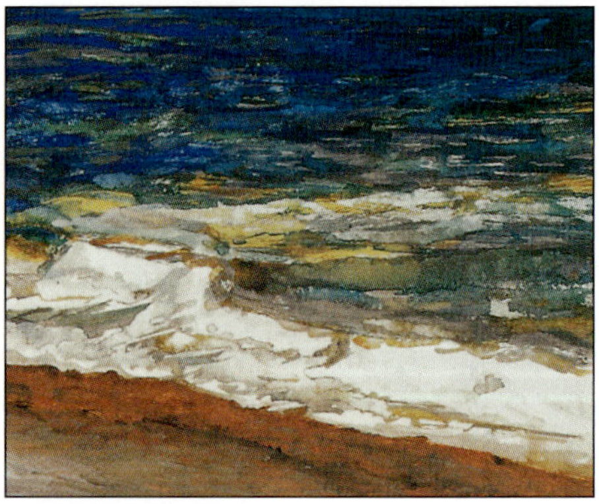

PAINTING ON A COLORED GROUND

Artists often color their canvas or paper before starting a painting, and there are two good reasons for this. The first is purely practical – white can be difficult to work on. In nature you seldom see any pure white because white, more than any other color, is altered and modified by the effects of light. Thus by providing an artificial comparison, a white surface makes it difficult to assess the first colors you lay down.

You will quickly find this out if your subject includes a number of pale tones. The blue of a wintry sky, although substantially paler than shadows or tree branches, is still much darker than pure white, so even a correctly mixed pale blue will look too dark initially. If you work on a middle tone, such as gray or light brown, it is easier to work up to the lights and down to the darks.

LETTING THE GROUND COLOR SHOW

The second reason for coloring the ground is that it will influence the overall color scheme of your picture and can set up exciting contrasts. Artists often choose a color for the ground that is opposite of the dominant color in the painting. For example, a dark yellow will set off the blues in a flower painting, or a red underpainting may contrast well in a green summer landscape. If you use the paint thin or at medium consistency, the ground will show through, creating vibrant passages of color.

If you prefer to work thickly, in oil-painting mode, you can leave small patches of the ground color showing between and around brushmarks, that achieves a lively broken-color effect (see page 123).

COLORING THE GROUND

Laying a ground color is simplicity itself; all you do is paint a color over the entire surface using a broad brush. If you prefer to use the paint in a series of thin layers, either on paper or canvas, a transparent color might be best, using well-diluted paint. You can also use thick paint, vigorously working it into the surface so that it provides a slightly rough texture.

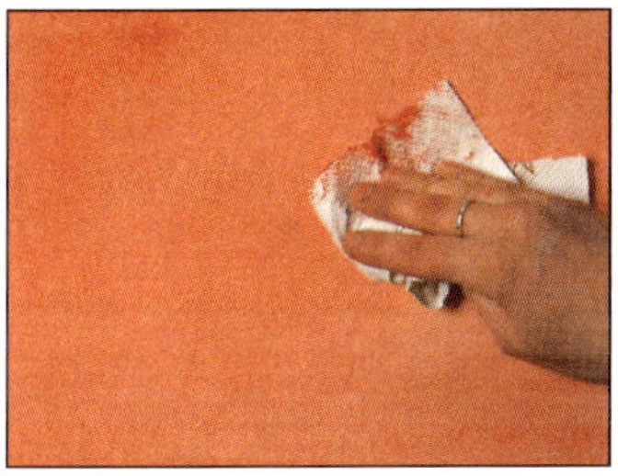

A rag spreads the paint thinly so that a strong color, such as the red used here, becomes paler.

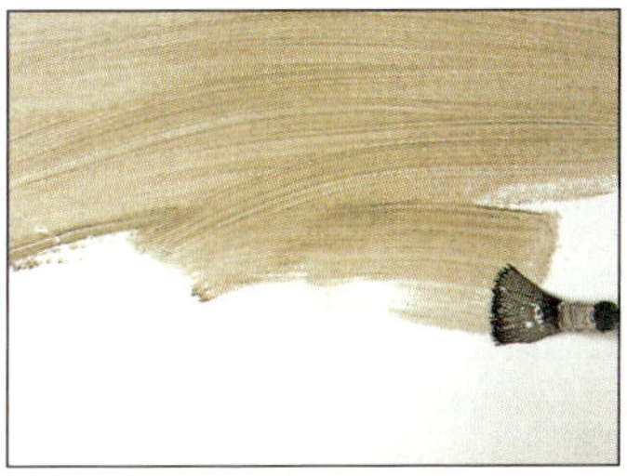

A broad brush, used with medium-consistency paint, makes a series of striated marks that provide added interest to the painting.

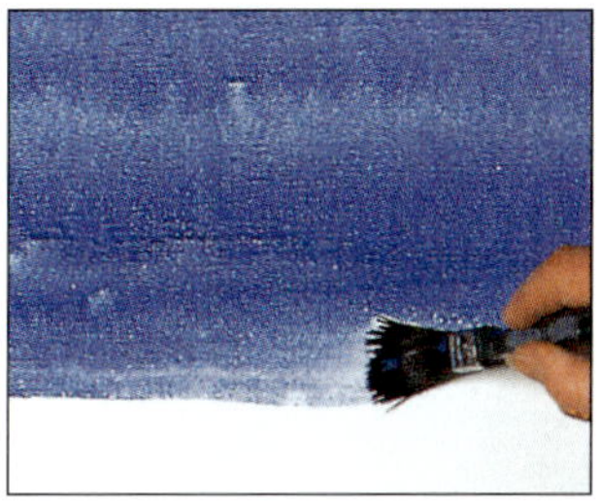

An uneven watercolor-type wash also makes a good ground for many different painting techniques.

PAINTING ON A RED GROUND

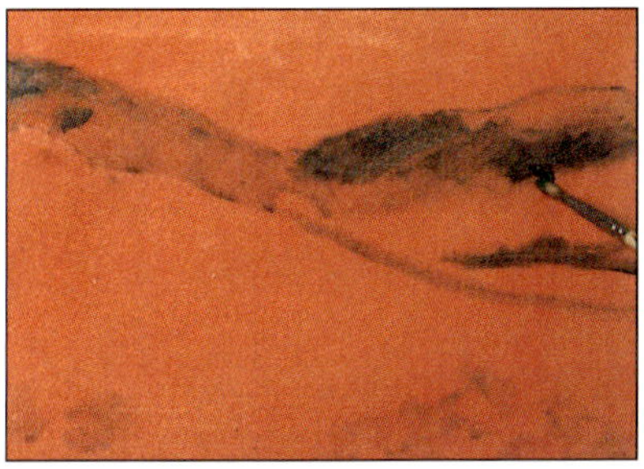

1 Apply a cadmium red ground, as shown above, and leave it to dry. Then paint the dark blue-green of the hills, using the color thinly, so that it does not obliterate the red.

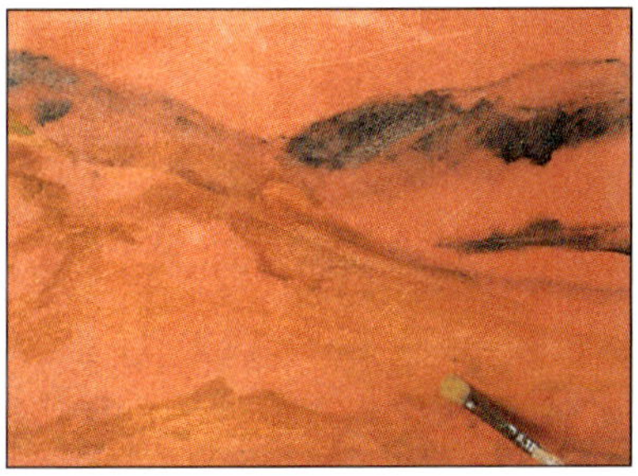

2 The red ground is a middle tone, which helps you to judge both the dark and light tones. Paint some of the yellowish foreground next, so that the extremes of light and dark are established.

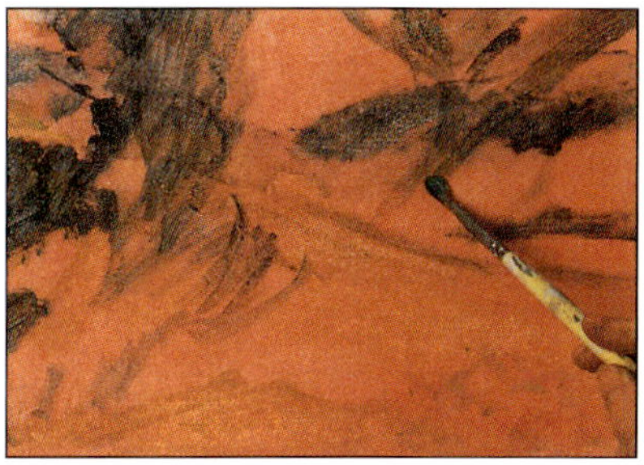

3 Still using the paint thinly, suggest the shapes of the trees and strengthen the blue-gray tones of the distant hills, which will contrast with the more vivid light and dark greens of the trees.

PAINTING ON A RED GROUND (continued)

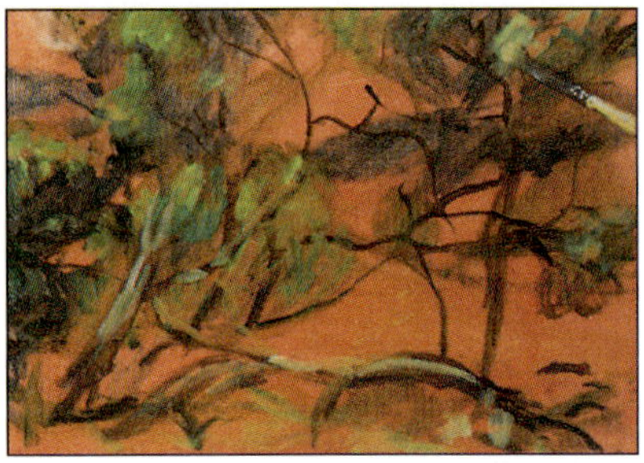

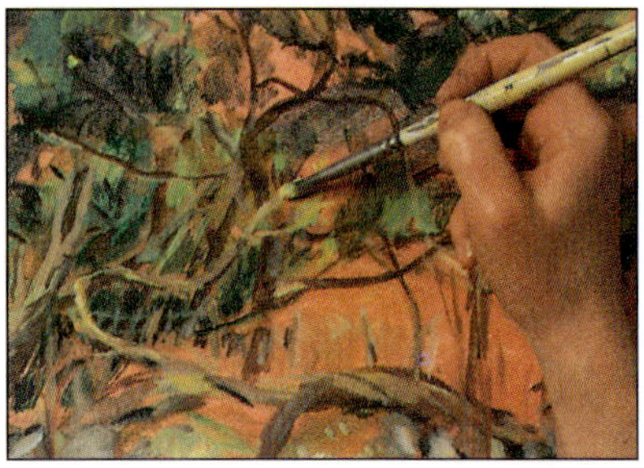

5 The foreground branches need to stand out more strongly than those behind and above, so again use thick paint. Avoid a detailed treatment; use a medium-size round bristle brush and let it "follow" the shapes and direction of the branches.

4 Begin to build up the foliage with a variety of greens, using the paint unthinned. The contrast between the thin and the thick paint creates an impression of space and depth, because the full-bodied paint "advances" to the front of the picture.

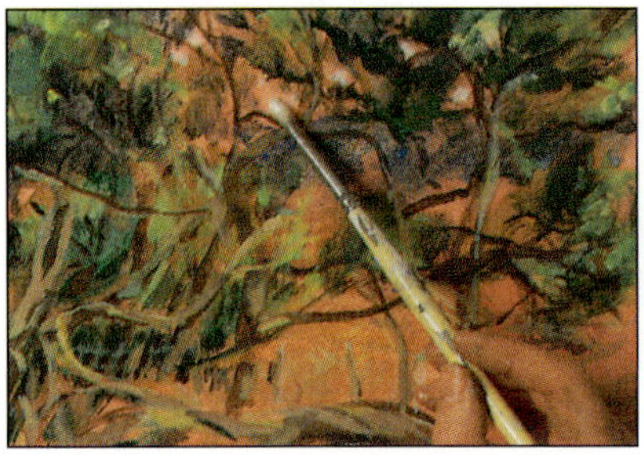

6 Trees are seldom a solid mass of green; there are small gaps where light shows through the foliage. In opaque techniques, you can add these last. Use medium-consistency white paint to make dabs that suggest "sky holes."

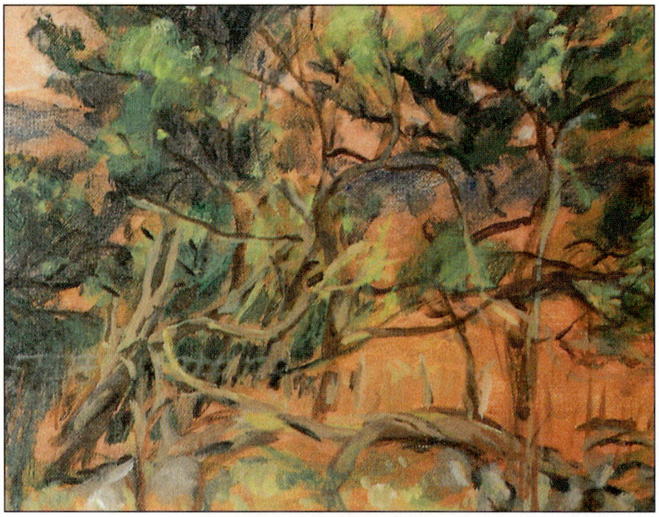

The finished picture.

FURTHER IDEAS

Whatever your subject, you can use a colored ground as a starting point. First decide what the overall color scheme is to be, because the ground will influence the applied colors.

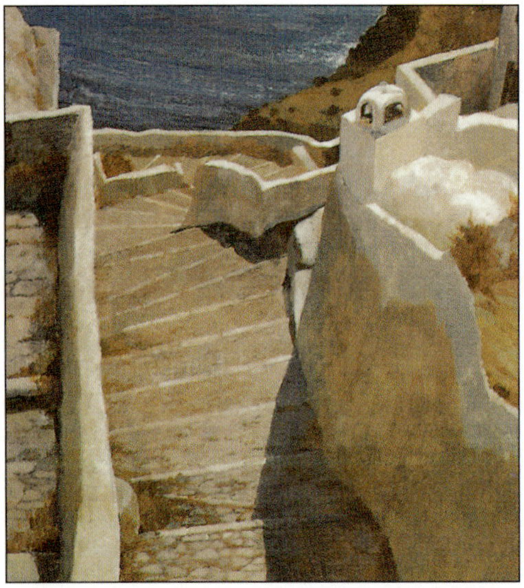

LEFT: A traditional ocher ground helps to warm up the whites, and contrasts well with the blue of the sea.

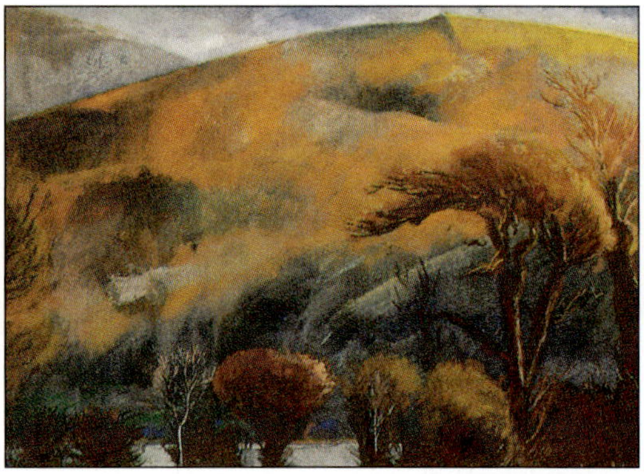

ABOVE: A medium-blue ground, also on watercolor paper, was used for a landscape using harmonies of blue and yellow.

BROKEN COLOR

When a color is built up by juxtaposing brush strokes of different colors, instead of being applied flatly, the result is described as broken color. You might paint a sky, for example, in various blues and mauves, with each patch of color remaining separate, or a tree with a selection of greens, blues, violets, and yellows. When the painting is seen at a distance, the colors will mix in the viewer's eye, an effect known as optical mixing. They read as a single color, but create a more vibrant effect than flatly applied blue or green.

The colors must be close in tone; if you put a dark blue among middle tones in a sky, the colors will fail to cohere and the sky will not be credible as a flat surface.

SCUMBLING

Another way of breaking colors is to lay them in such a way that each new application only partially covers those beneath. Scumbling involves lightly brushing on opaque or semi-opaque paint to create a veil of color through which earlier colors show irregularly. You can scumble light over dark or vice versa, and you can use the technique to build up several layers of color.

A related method is dry brushing, in which you use a fairly stiff brush or synthetic brush to apply a small amount of thick paint. You should use light strokes to avoid covering the surface completely.

SEPARATE BRUSHMARKS

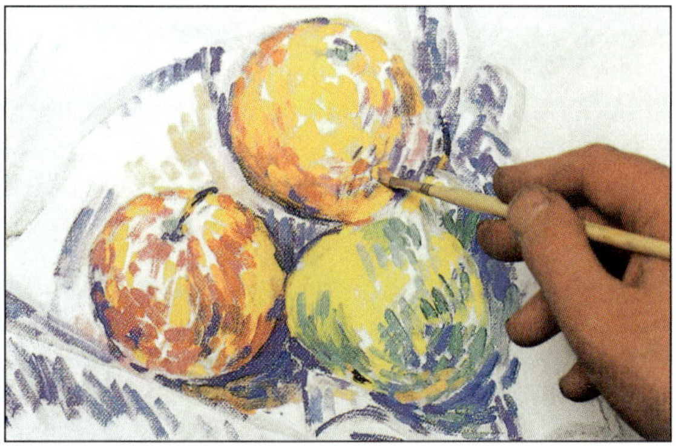

1 Using a square-ended synthetic brush and paint thinned with a minimum of water, apply small brush strokes of different colors, curving them slightly to suggest the rounded forms.

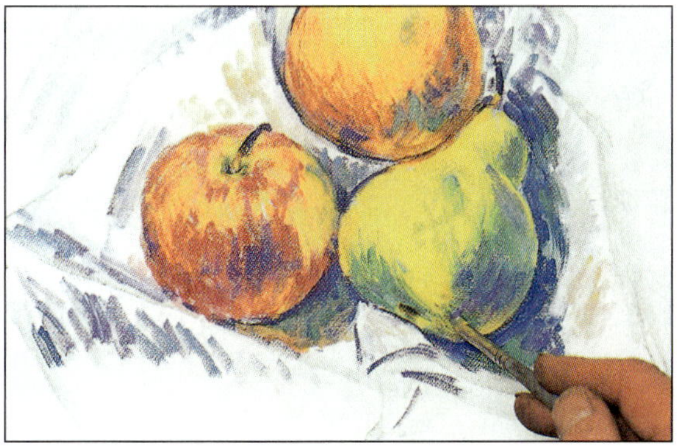

2 Continue to work in the same way, overlapping the brush strokes and laying one color over another. Keep the colors in each shadow area close in tone.

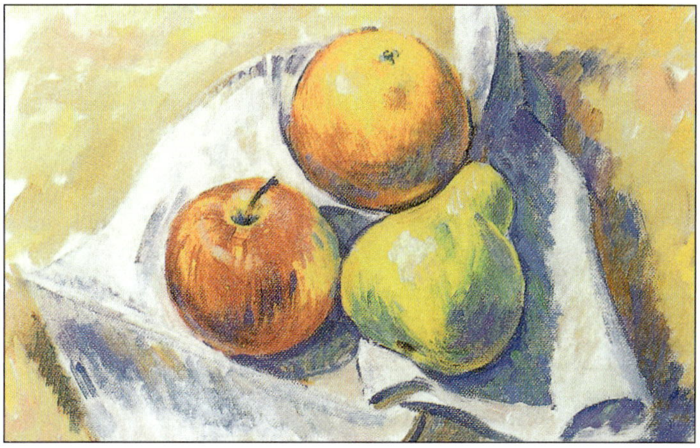

SCUMBLED SKY

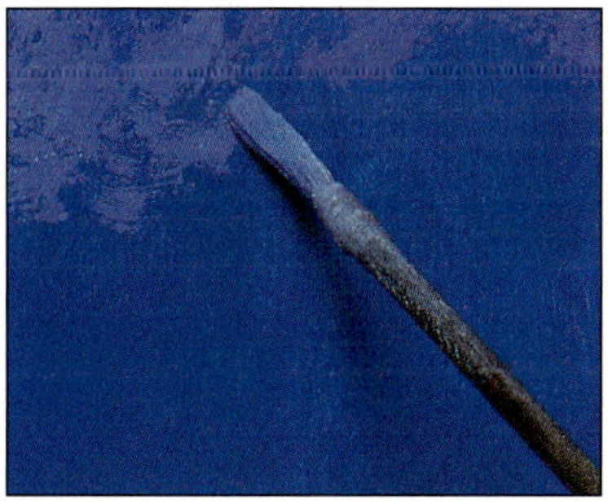

1 Lay a flat base color and allow it to dry. Using unthinned paint and a bristle or synthetic brush, apply a paler mauve-blue lightly over it. Vary the direction of the brush strokes and leave patches of the first color visible between them.

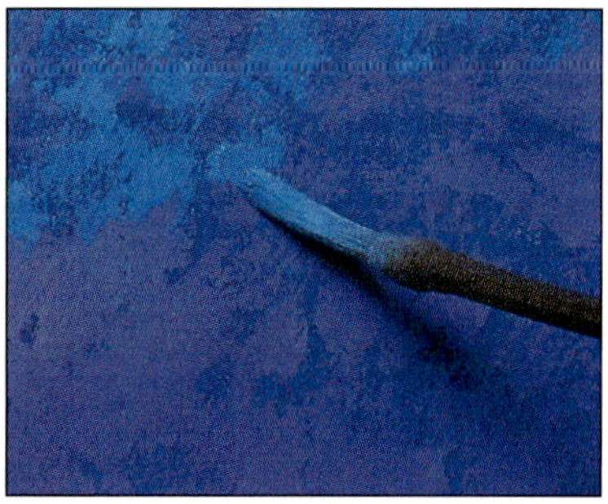

2 When the first scumbled layer is dry, introduce a third color, such as cerulean blue. Take care not to cover the first colors completely; the effect comes from the way one color shows through another color.

DRY BRUSHING

The dry brush technique is also used to apply broken color over another flat undercolor. Here the paint should be fairly stiff, with only a trace of the opaque color picked up on the end of the brush. This is applied lightly across the picture surface and will pick up the texture of the support provided that the paint underneath is thin enough. Because the color is used opaquely, dry brush can be applied as light over dark or dark over light with equally successful results.

Unlike oil paints and watercolor, acrylics cannot easily be blended to get a smooth gradation from one color to another. The gel mediums and retarder can help to some extent, but the result is never perfect. Many artists prefer to make a virtue of necessity and to adopt scumbling or dry brush techniques to merge colors. The lively, prominent brushmarks play an important part in the final effect.

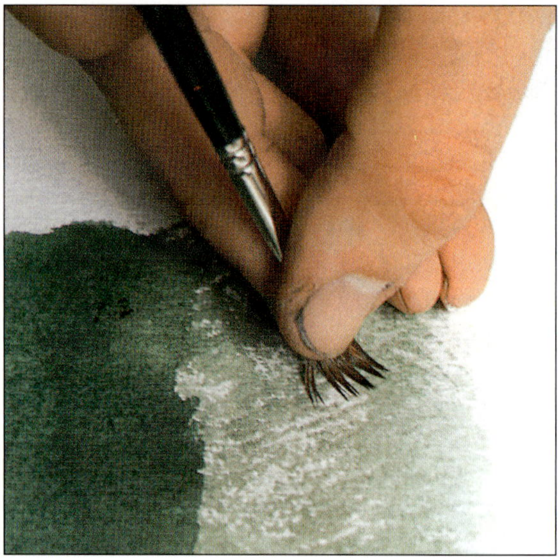

Pick up a trace of color on your brush and move this lightly across the support as shown above. Dry brush is useful for blending or painting areas of finely broken color.

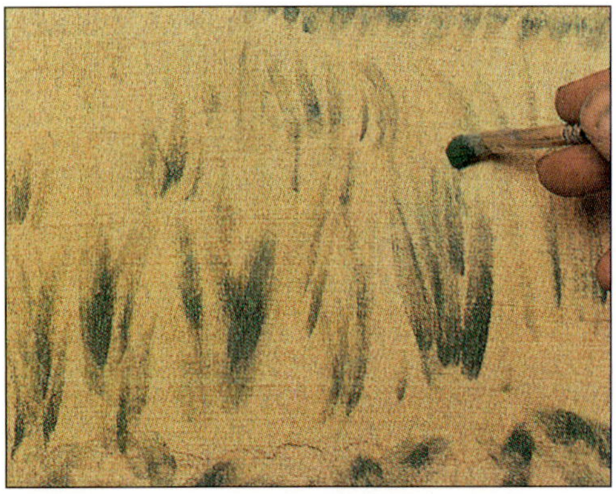

1 Work on a textured surface, such as canvas or canvas board. Make a thick mixture of paint, pick it up with the tip of the brush, and pull the paint lightly over the surface to suggest the upward growth of the grasses.

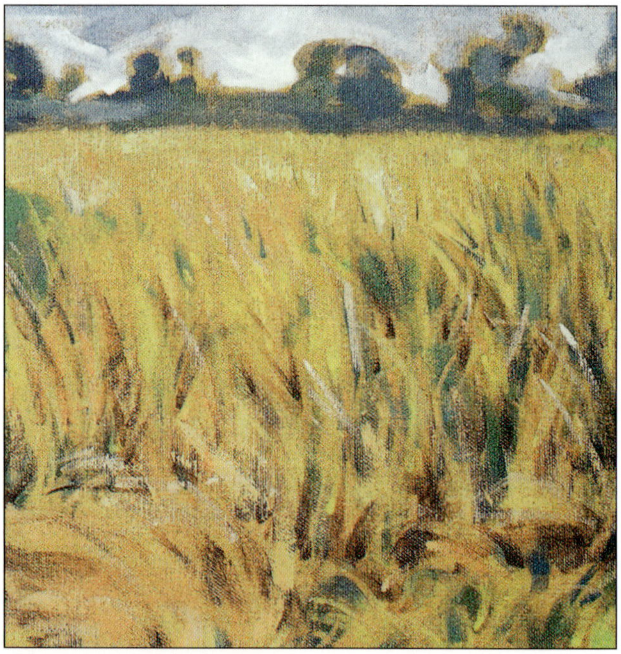

The finished picture.

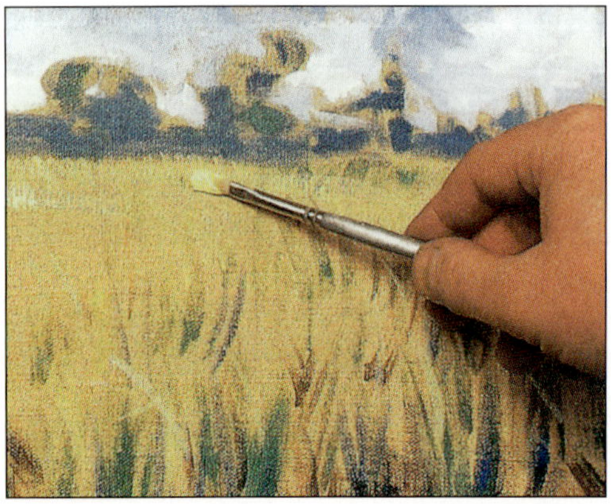

2 Build up the grasses with a variety of colors. Use horizontal strokes for the far end of the field. In the foreground you can see how the paint catches only on the raised grain of the surface.

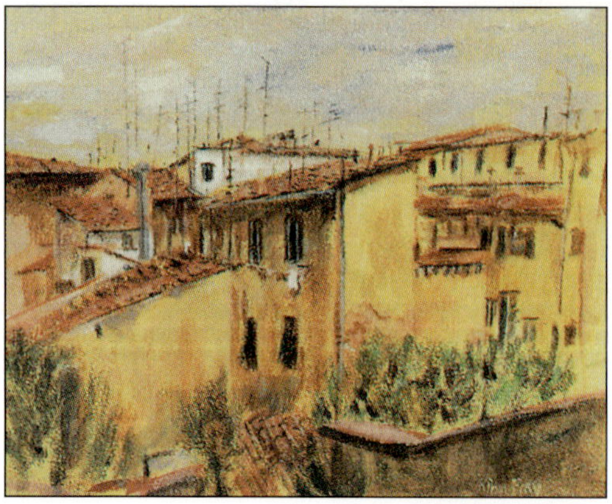

Broken color techniques can be adapted to any subject. The dry brushing methods can be used selectively, for example, to suggest the texture of old stone.

In the picture on the left, dry brushing one color over another color gives a good impression of the crumbly texture of the walls.

KNIFE PAINTING

If you enjoy applying paint thickly, try using a painting knife, a selection of these is shown on page 111. Knife painting is another form of impasto, but the effect is entirely different from that of brush impasto. The flat blade of the painting knife spreads out and squeezes the paint to produce a flat plane with ridges where each stroke ends.

The ridges catch the light and cast tiny lines of shadow that you can utilize to define the edges and shapes in your subject. In a flower painting, for example, make separate, differently shaped knife marks for each petal or leaf and use the side or point of the knife for fine lines such as stalks.

Painting knives are also good for imitating textures. A rough stone wall, for example, could be rendered with a variety of knife strokes and later glazed over with other colors. Impasto methods are often combined with glazing techniques.

A painting done entirely with painting knives has a lively surface effect and can enhance the drama of the subject; this could be the perfect technique for a rocky landscape. But as with brush impasto, knife painting can be confined to selected areas, adding emphasis to foreground grasses or tree trunks, for example.

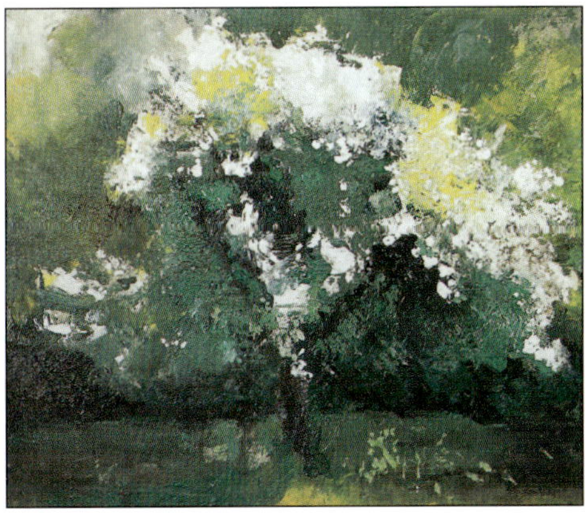

FOLIAGE AND BLOSSOM

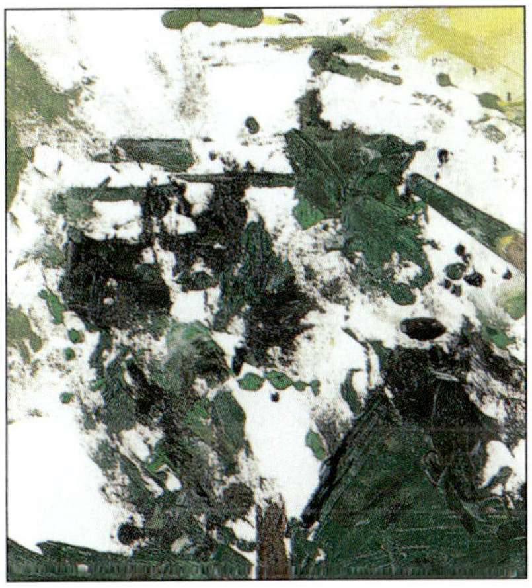

1 Start with a long, straight-blade knife. Lay down some sweeping strokes of yellow-green for the background, then begin to establish the dark areas within the tree, leaving the blossom as white canvas. Use mixtures of green and black and thicken the paint with gel medium.

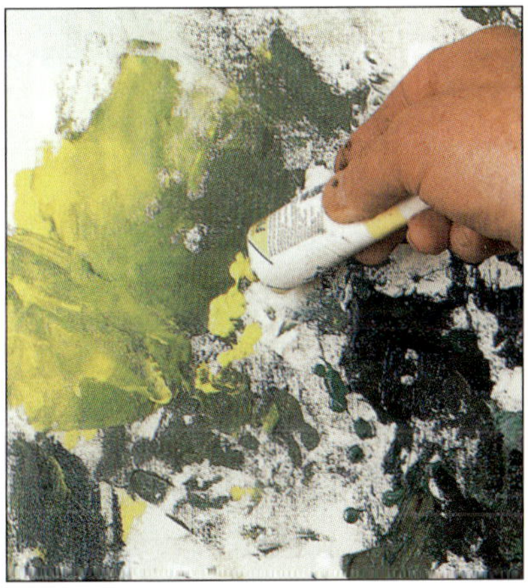

2 Begin to build up the foliage and lighter leaves. Squeeze cadmium lemon straight from the tube onto the surface, so that very thick paint stands out well from the more flatly applied paint on the background tree.

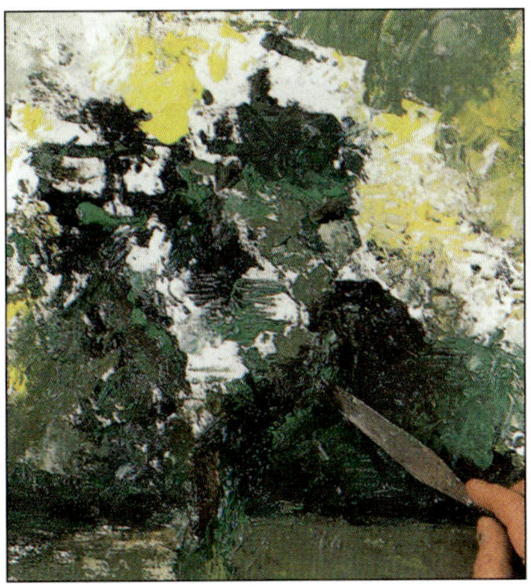

3 For the flurries of blossom on the right of the tree, use a small triangular-blade knife, making short strokes of pure white and yellow that mix slightly on the surface. Then continue to build up the contrasting dark greens with broad strokes of the straight-bladed knife.

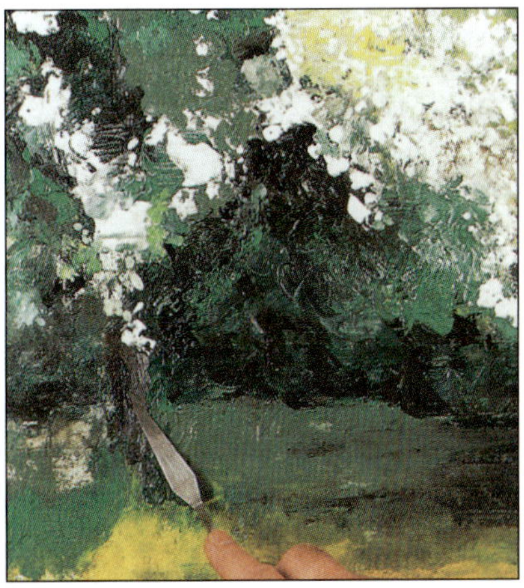

4 When you have completed the blossom, paint the foreground with horizontal strokes of the straight knife. Use the triangular knife again for the tree trunk. Make a raw umber and white mixture, thickened with medium, and pull the paint downward with the point of the knife.

COMPARING METHODS

The preceding pages showed you various ways of handling acrylic paints, and these three pages demonstrate the techniques in the context of a finished picture. You will see two artists in action, both painting the same subject with the same range of colors from the starter palette (page 108) but achieving very different results.

The divergence of technique is apparent from a quick glance at the finished paintings below. The pictures are revealing in other ways, too. No two artists will approach a subject in an identical way, even when the same basic technique is adopted. There will be stylistic differences, as there are here, with artist one applying sweeping strokes and softer blends of color, and artist two using shorter, separate brushmarks. There will also be compositional variations, with each artist choosing a different viewpoint and arrangement of elements on the surface. A comparison of the photograph with the paintings shows how and why the artists made particular choices. On pages 127 and 128 you will see the artists in action.

DIFFERENT PAINTING METHODS

The two pictures below show very different uses of acrylic. In the painting on the left, the artist created an oil-painterly effect, applying thick, opaque paint, with areas of broken color and dry brushing. In contrast, the colors in the painting on the right were built up gradually, through a series of overlaid transparent glazes, using paint mixed with acrylic medium. Both paintings are on canvas and both are rich in color, but the overall tonality is darker in the first painting due to the middle-toned colored ground.

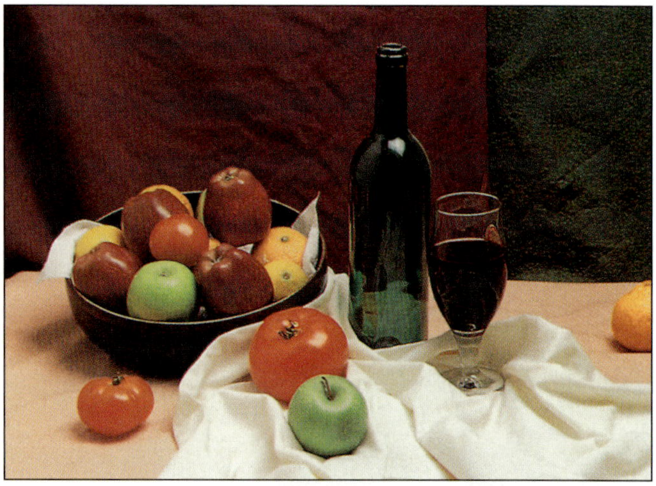

THE ORIGINAL PHOTOGRAPH

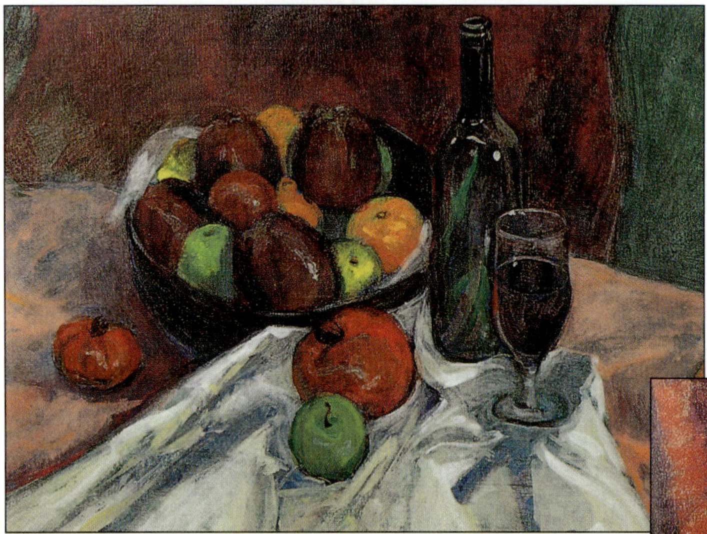

ARTIST ONE

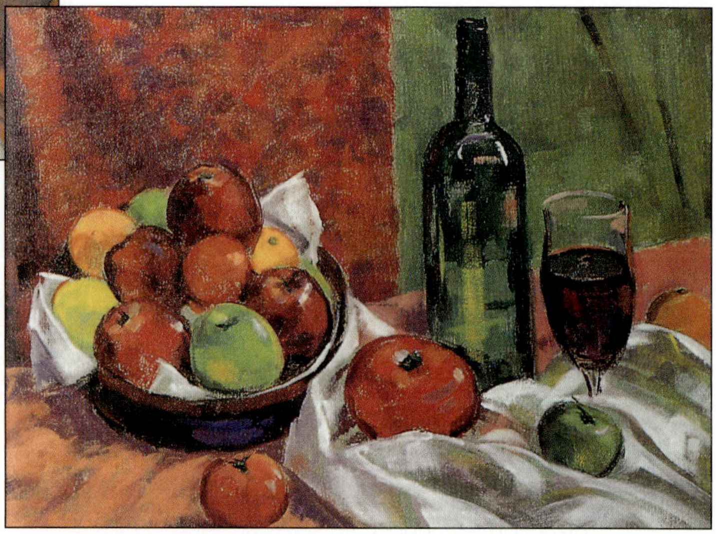

ARTIST TWO

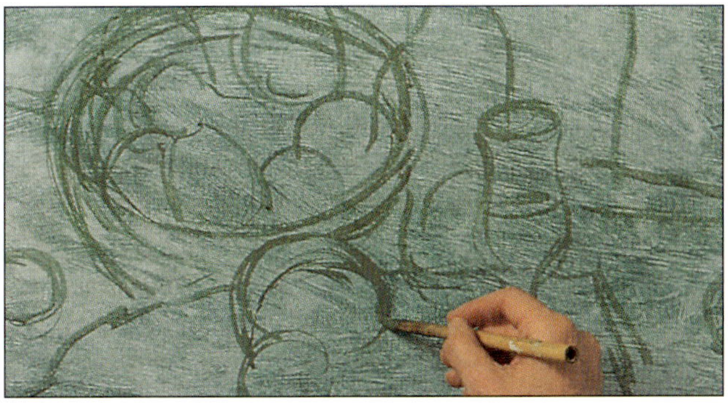

1 The artist chose a darker background color than artist two, of cobalt green mixed with matt medium, achieving a deliberately uneven effect by wiping over the canvas with the palm of her hand. She plans the basic structure of the composition with chromium oxide green and a Chinese brush.

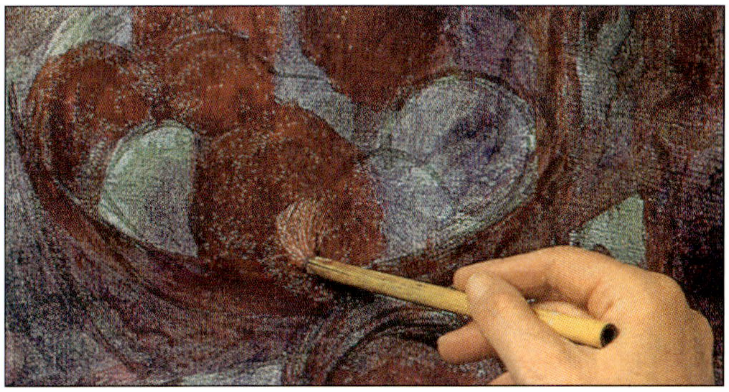

2 Unlike artist two, she likes to begin with the cool colors – the blues and blue-greens – and work up to the warm reds and yellows. After applying a thin purple glaze over the greens in the central areas, she paints a base color of dark red for the apples, using paint mixed with gloss medium.

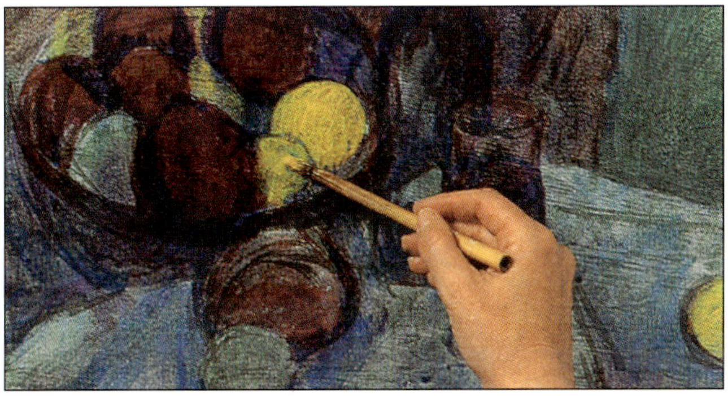

3 The detail shows the effect of the glazing method, with several layers of color mixed with gloss medium laid over one another to build up a scintillating effect. For the lemons, the artist uses pure cadmium yellow which is enriched and subtly modified by the earlier green ground and purple glaze.

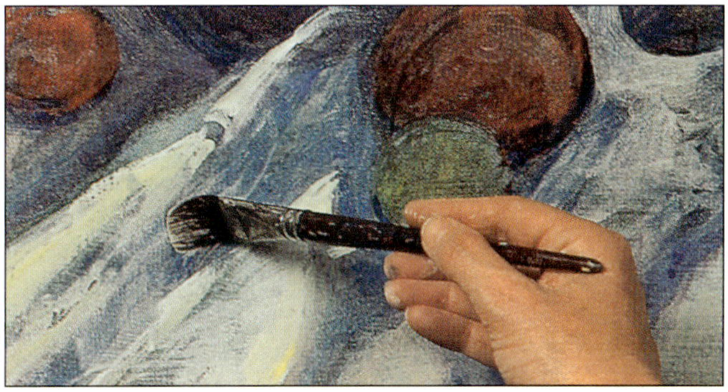

4 With the dark and middle tones established, she begins to work on the lighter areas. The diagonal lines of the cloth are important since they draw the eye in toward the bowl of fruit. For these highlights, she follows the direction of the folds, using long, sweeping strokes made with a soft, square-ended brush.

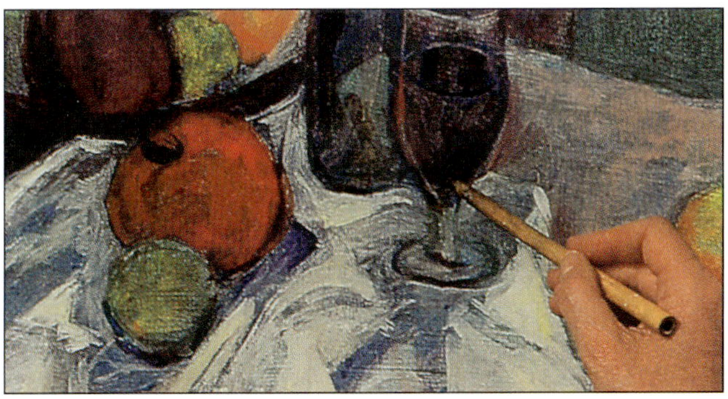

5 She works on the entire picture at the same time. The forms of the tomatoes were built up more strongly with glazes of cadmium red over the purple base color and next she turns her attention to the glass of wine, defining the bottom curve with a deep purple applied with the point of a Chinese brush.

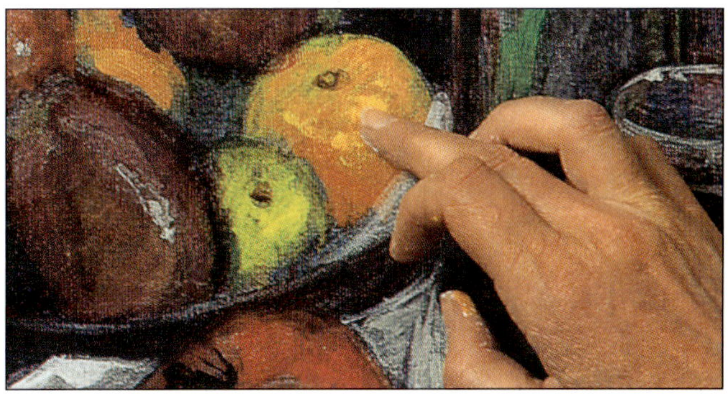

6 Touches of definition, such as the stalk of the tomato and the highlights on fruit and bottle, were left until last. For this final highlight, opaque, unthinned paint is dabbed on very lightly with a finger – a scumbling method that suggests the texture of the tangerine skin.

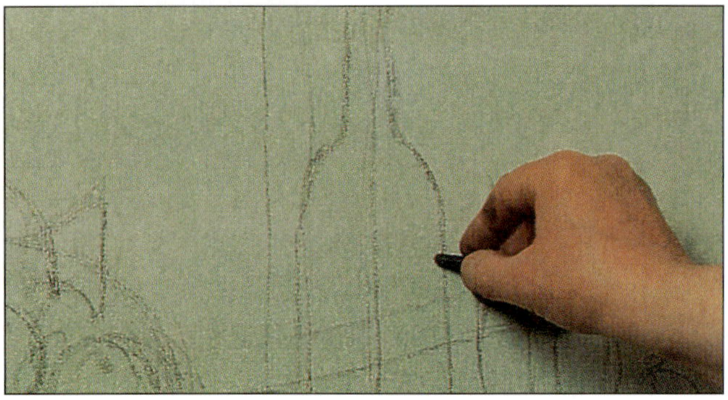

1 To reduce the glare of the white canvas, a pale wash was laid by brushing on color and then rubbing it down with a cloth to even it out. A line drawing is made in charcoal to place the objects. The lines are kept light to avoid the muddying effect of charcoal dust mixing with the paint.

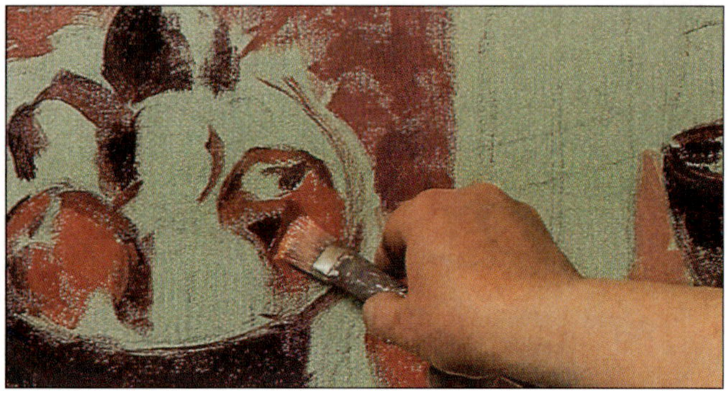

2 Using unthinned paint and a square-ended bristle brush, the artist builds up the colors and tones of the fruit. The same brush was used for the red background, with the brushmarks applied in different directions to create a lively effect.

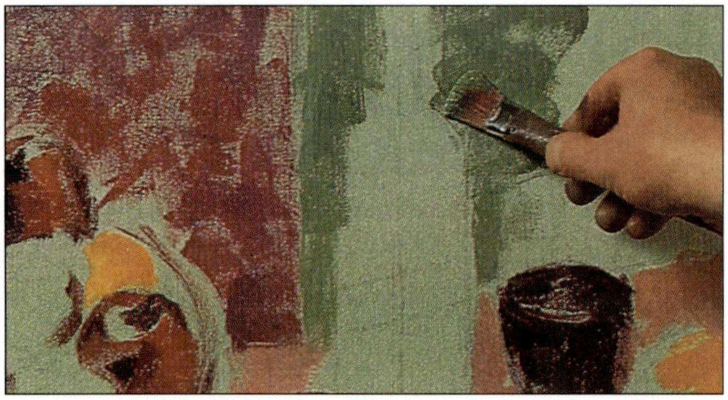

3 Before painting the green background, the artist established the vivid colors and some of the darkest tones, which makes it easier to judge the strength of color needed in this area. The paint is taken around the edges of the bottle, with the brushmarks again following different directions.

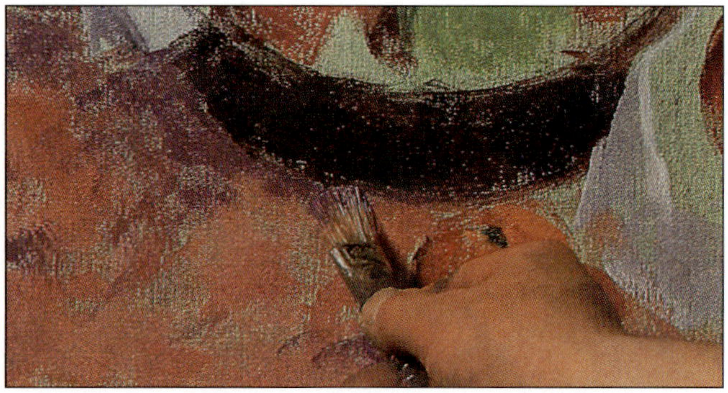

4 To unify the picture, the artist repeats the same or similar colors from one area to another. The mauve he now uses for the shadow beneath the bowl echoes the brush strokes of mauve among the reds in the background. He is still using large bristle brushes because he likes to work broadly until the final stages.

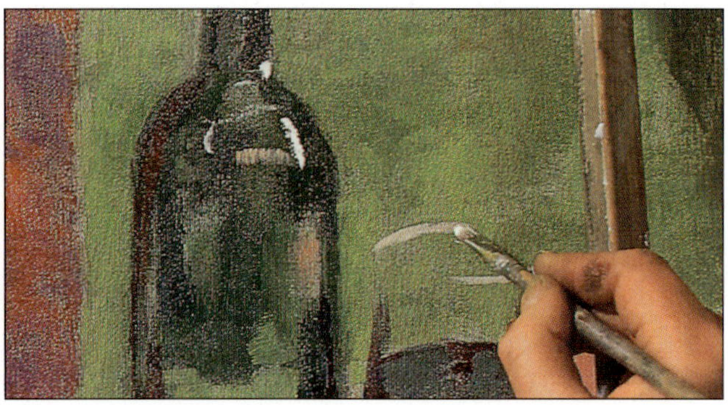

5 The green background can be seen through the clear glass, so all that is needed to describe its shape is the highlight on the top of the rim. Ellipses require careful treatment, so here the artist uses a smaller brush, with an improvised mahlstick resting on the top of the canvas and supporting his hand.

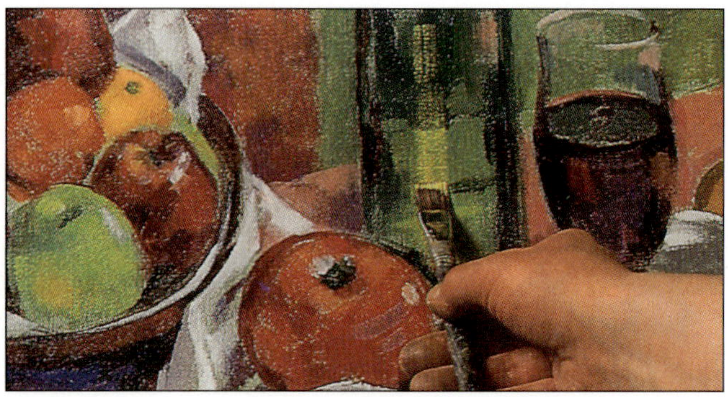

6 The glass was completed with pink highlights reflected from the cloth, and now the bottle is given final definition, with dry yellow paint dragged lightly over the earlier colors. Again repeated colors were used, with the purple in the wine echoing the purples of the background and the bowl.

BLENDING

Blending is a means of achieving soft, melting color gradations by brushing or rubbing the edge where two tones or colors meet. Because acrylic dries so rapidly, you don't have time to brush and rebrush a passage to achieve a subtle transition from light to dark or color to color as you do in oils. However, the addition of a little gel medium to acrylic paint gives it a consistency nearer to that of oil paint, allowing a smoother gradation.

The simplest way to blend two colors is to wet-blend them; while the paint is still wet, quickly draw a moist brush along the edge where the colors meet.

The delicate effects obtained by blending are very attractive, but the temptation is often to overdo it, with the result that all the life is taken out of the colors. When painting an object – say, an apple – it is not necessary to blend the entire area. From the normal viewing distance, the form will look smoothly blended if you blend just that narrow area where light turns into shadow or where one color melts into another.

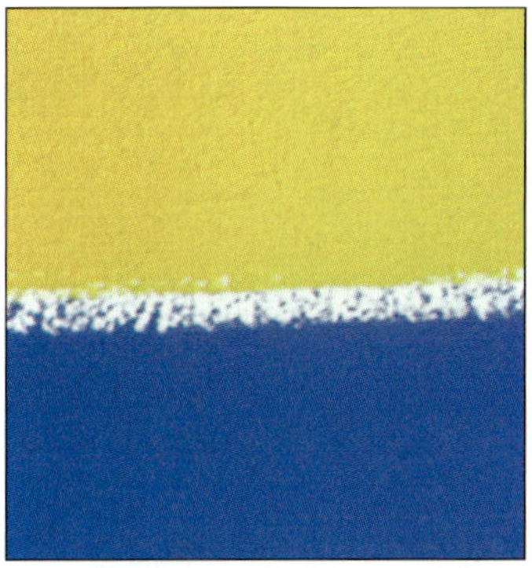

1 Using a No. 7 flat bristle brush, the artist applies cadmium yellow and cobalt blue, side by side but not touching.

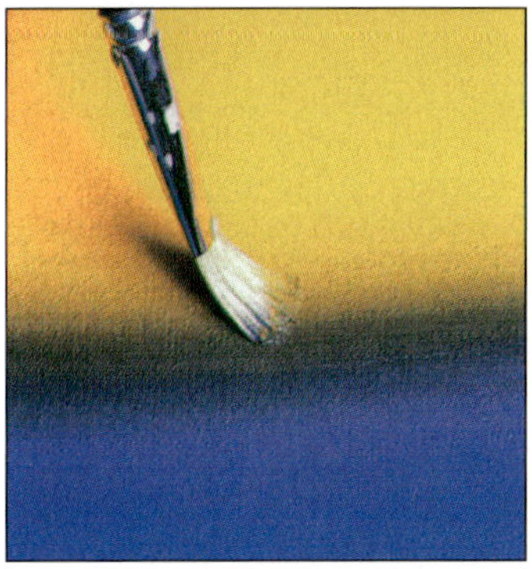

2 Working quickly before the paint dries, he uses a clean, wet brush to blend the two colors together lightly. Do not apply heavy pressure with the brush, because this tends to leave grooves in the paint.

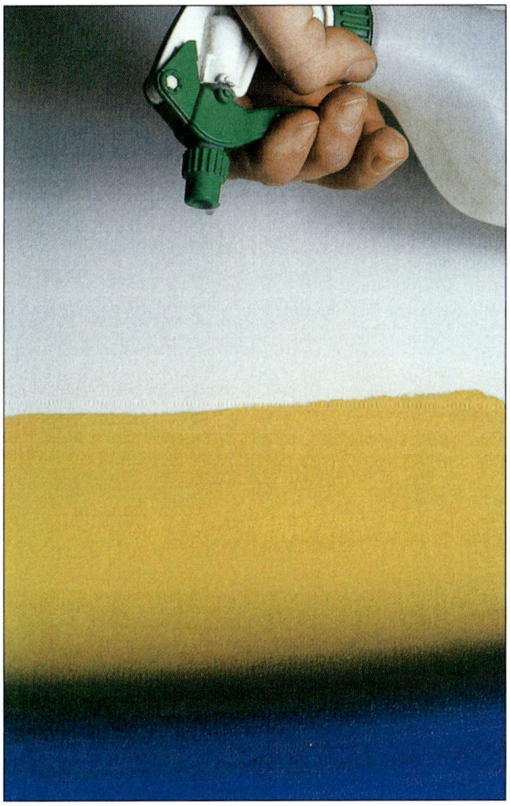

3 When you are working on a large area, if you spray the surface lightly with a spray diffuser this will help to keep the paint moist. Alternatively, add a little gel medium or retarder to the paint on the palette to lengthen the drying time.

4 The finished effect, showing a smooth transition from one tone to the other.

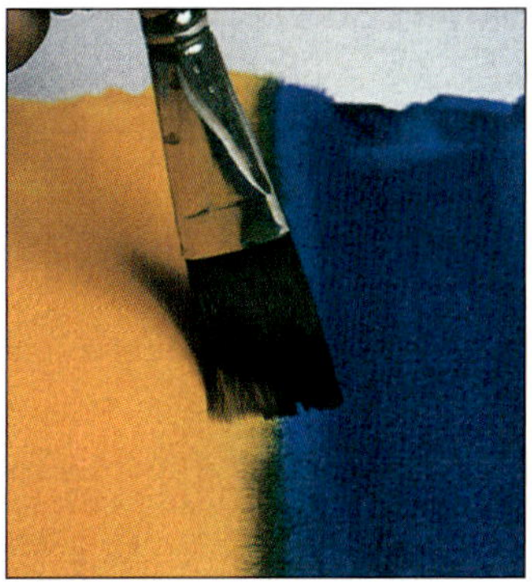

5 Alternatively, tones or colors can be blended rapidly with vertical strokes of a soft, moist brush.

GALLERY

OIL OR ACRYLIC?

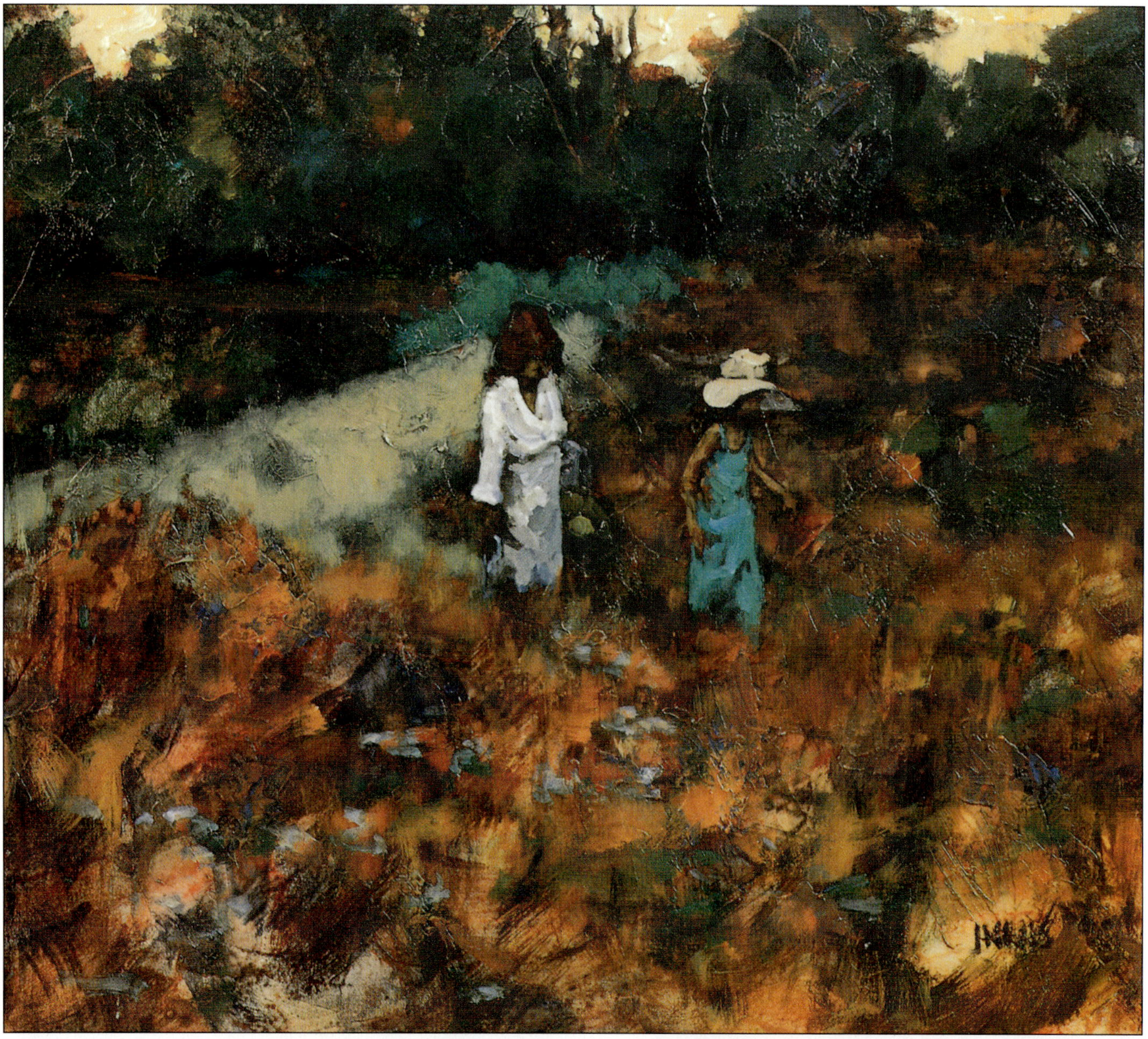

TWO FIGURES, STILL POND by W. Joe Innis

This painting on canvas bears a superficial resemblance to an oil painting, but closer examination reveals effects that are special to acrylics. The artist achieved a lively surface through varied brushwork and contrasting paint consistencies. Also, an extra dimension of texture was created by working over a textured ground made from a combination of acrylic modeling paste and sand applied with a knife. To increase the surface contrast, the texture was restricted to certain areas.

FLOWER STUDIES

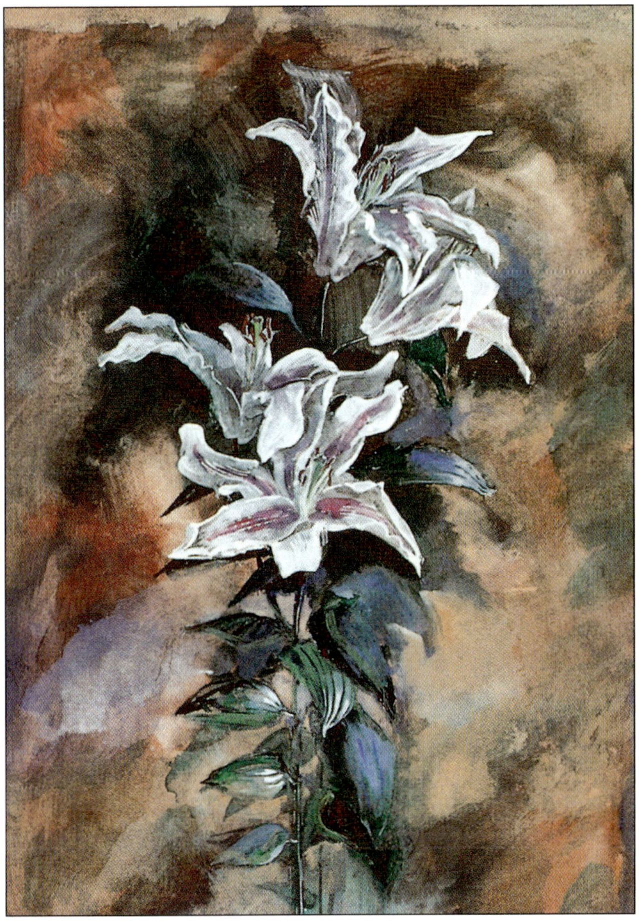

LILIES by Ros Cuthbert

This painting is one of a series of flower studies for which the artist evolved her own method of working. Working on watercolor paper, she began with the background, using broad bristle brushes and laying wet, sloppy paint all over the surface so that the colors blended into one another wet-into-wet (see pages 119–120). The flowers were painted over this ground with a thicker paint applied with a Chinese brush to give crisp, clearly defined edges.

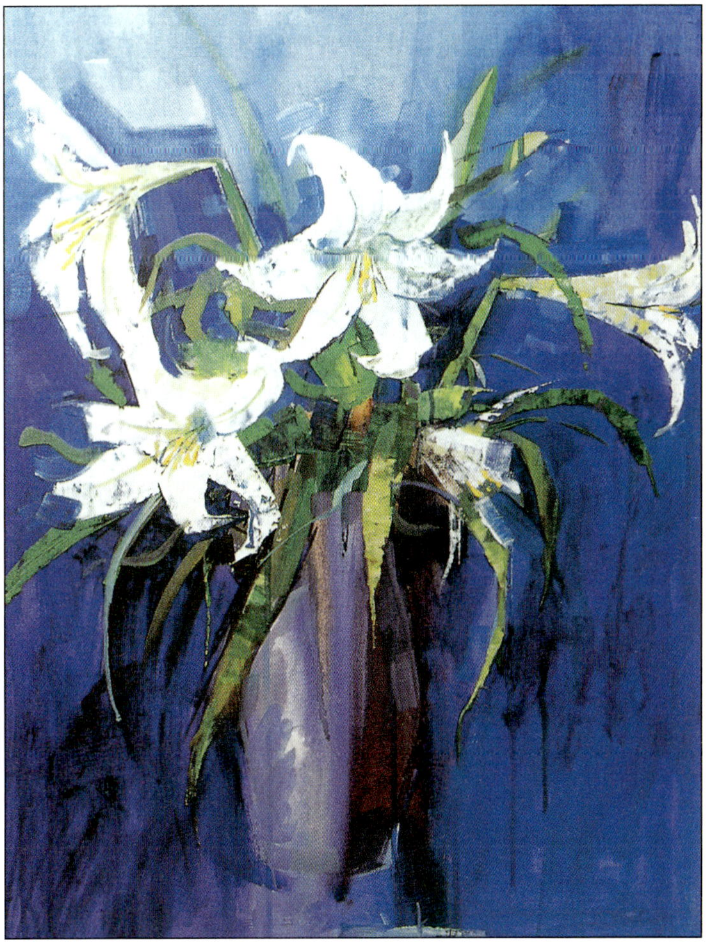

LILIES IN THE BLUE by Mike Bernard

In this painting there is enough detail to carry conviction, but the blooms are treated broadly, and the background and vase even more so. The painting is on canvas board with transparent and opaque techniques combined. Thin watercolor-type washes were used for the background and vase, and thicker paint for the flowers, which helps them advance to the front of the picture plane.

FOCUS ON BUILDINGS

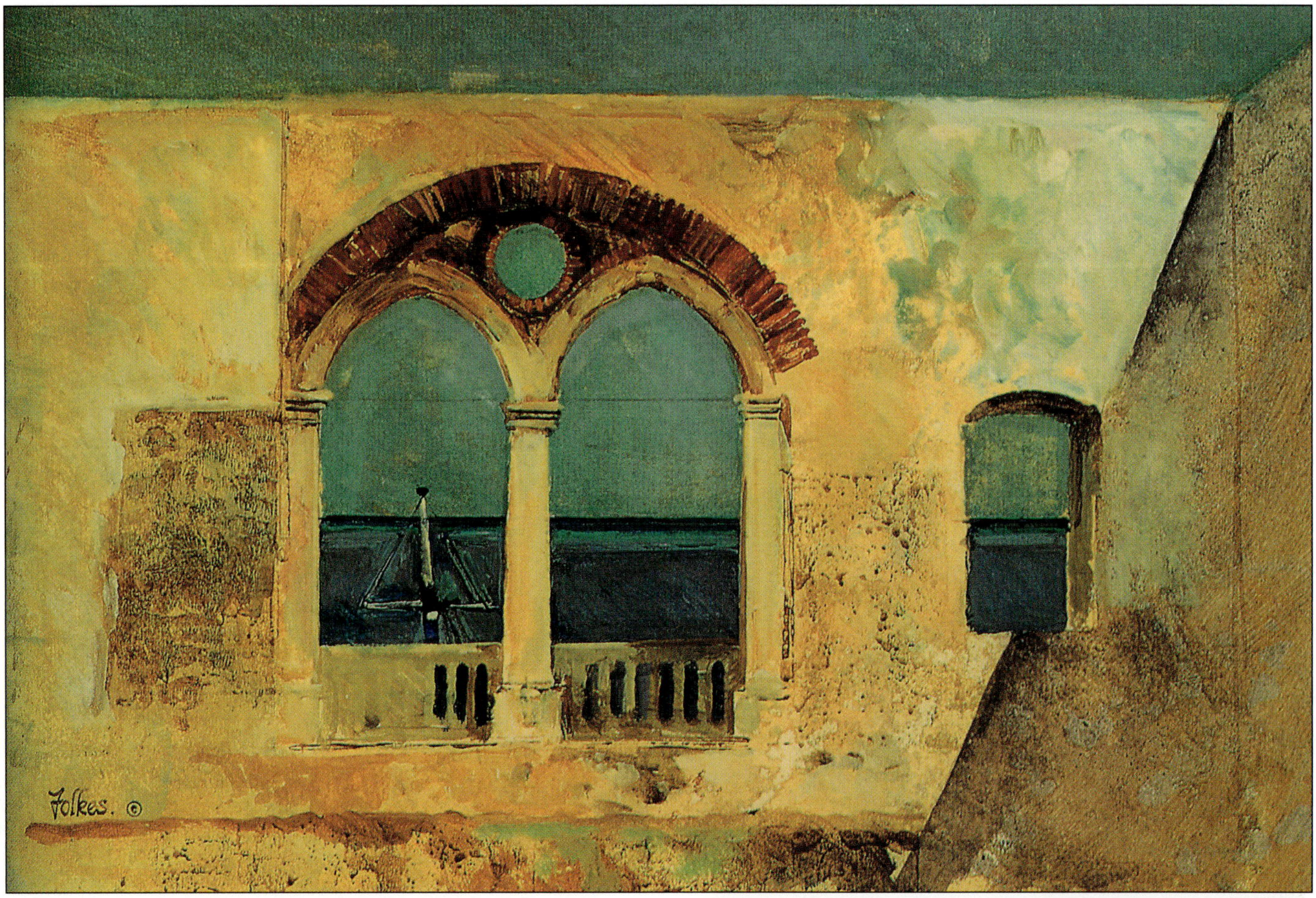

THE VENETIAN WINDOW, CHANIA by Peter Folkes

You need not paint all of a building; separate details, such as windows and doors, often provide exciting possibilities. The artist contrasted the curves of the window with horizontals and verticals to make a balanced and satisfying composition in which lighting also plays a major role. The evening light casts a golden glow over the stonework to contrast with the blues of sea and sky.

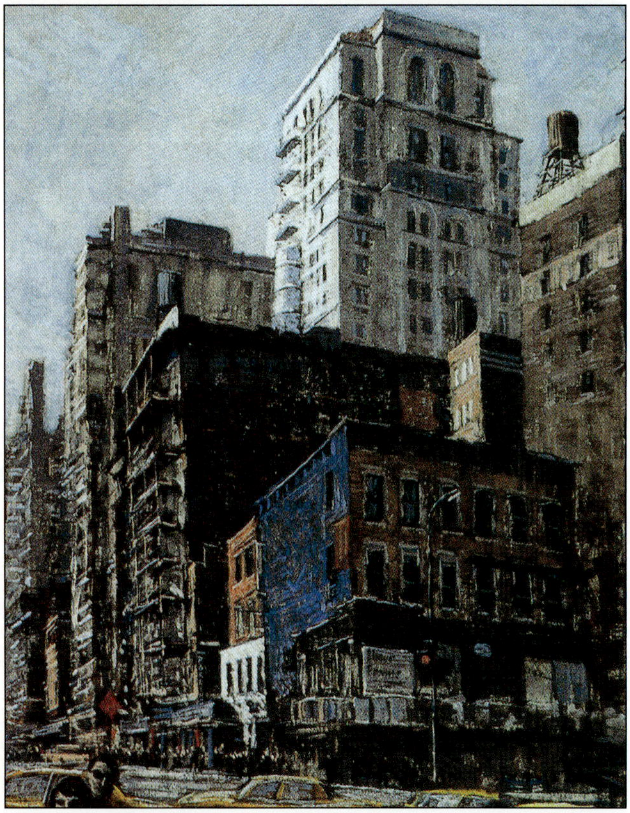

DOWNTOWN MANHATTAN by Gerald Cains

Whether you pitch the overall tones high or low depends on the subject and what you want to say about it. You would probably not choose a low tonal key for a summer landscape, but you might for a portrait of an old person. The low-key approach was well-suited to this cityscape, not only because it allowed the artist to express the atmosphere of this area of the city, but also because dark and middle tones give a sense of stability, anchoring the buildings solidly in space. The effect is enhanced by the careful control of color. Avoiding striking contrasts, the artist chose a range of harmonizing colors, giving additional richness and unity by painting on a red-brown ground. He used an oil-painterly technique, working on cardboard with mainly large brushes.

PAINTING PEOPLE

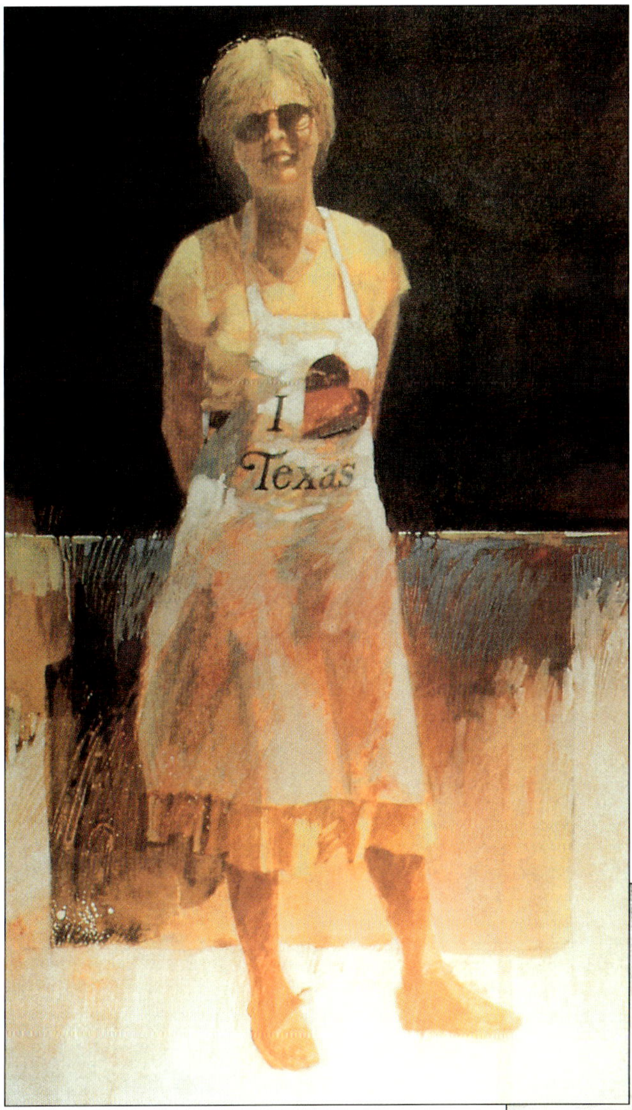

THE YELLOW ROSE OF TEXAS by Al Brouillette

When painting a standing figure, look for the way the weight is distributed, because this affects the whole body. Here the model stands with most of her weight on one foot, so the hip that carries the weight is pushed upward. Painting skin requires more careful observation and practise in mixing colors than any other subject. There is no one color that will guarantee success so you will have to experiment.

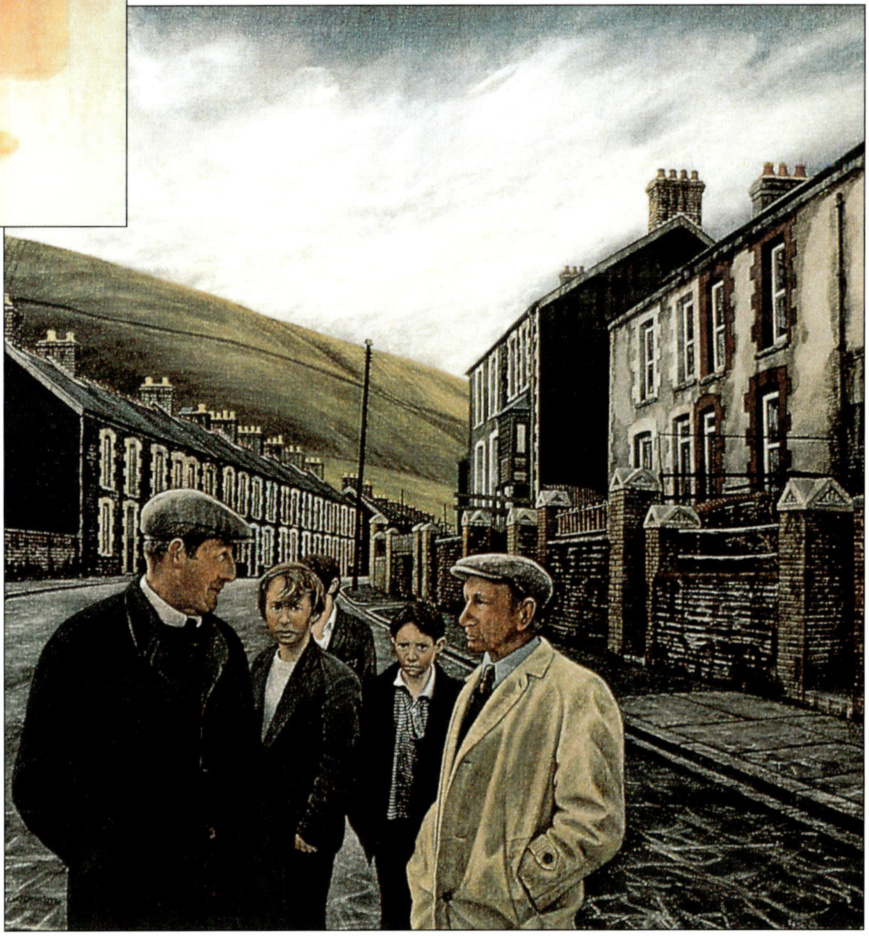

AND FAR AWAY THE SILENCE WAS MINE by David Carpanini

These figures are linked through their shared conversation and environment. But there are pictorial connections also, with the device of overlapping used to bond the group and explain both spatial relationships and the relative sizes of the figures.

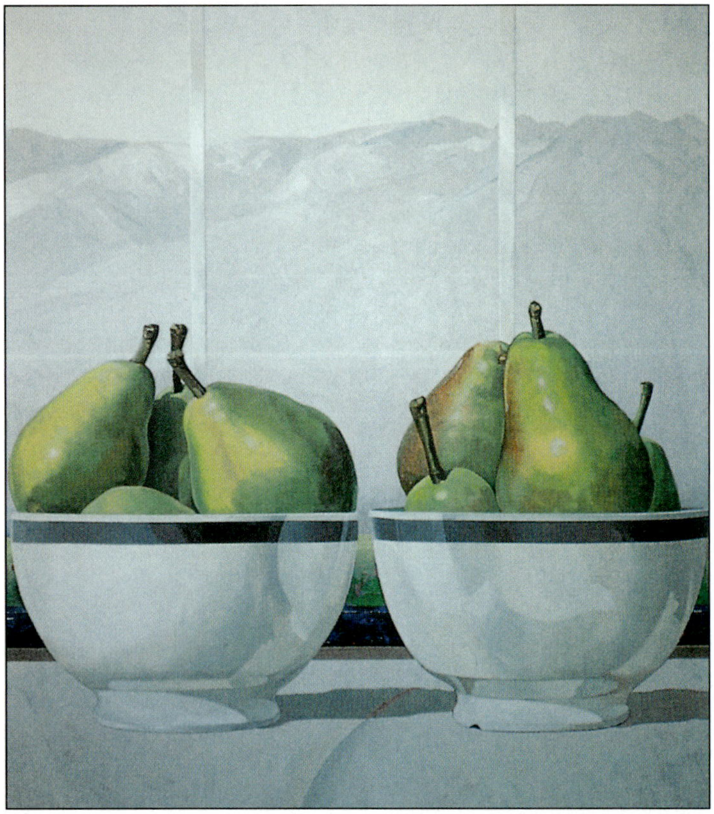

STILL LIFE

MIST ON THE MOUNTAINS by William Roberts

This group comprises the simplest of ingredients, but instead of aiming for the natural look which most still life painters seek, the artist introduced a sense of artificiality through his arrangement. The effect is enhanced by his smooth, yet hard-edged technique, and the controlled use of color and tone. As is often the case in still life paintings, the spaces between objects – known as negative shapes – play an important part, with the small dark areas between and beside the two bowls balancing the shapes of the pears.

DRIFTWOOD WITH HEATHER by Jill Mirza

This painting has a more natural look than the still life above, partly because it features objects you would expect to see outdoors on a seashore. But, in fact, it was arranged with equal care to achieve a balance of colors, tones, and shapes, and an interesting composition. Notice how the dark tones of the metal waste in the center are echoed by those of the branch of heather at the top and the narrow dark shape on the right. The color scheme is based on the blue-yellow contrast, with the yellow of the foreground stone repeated on the shell and driftwood.

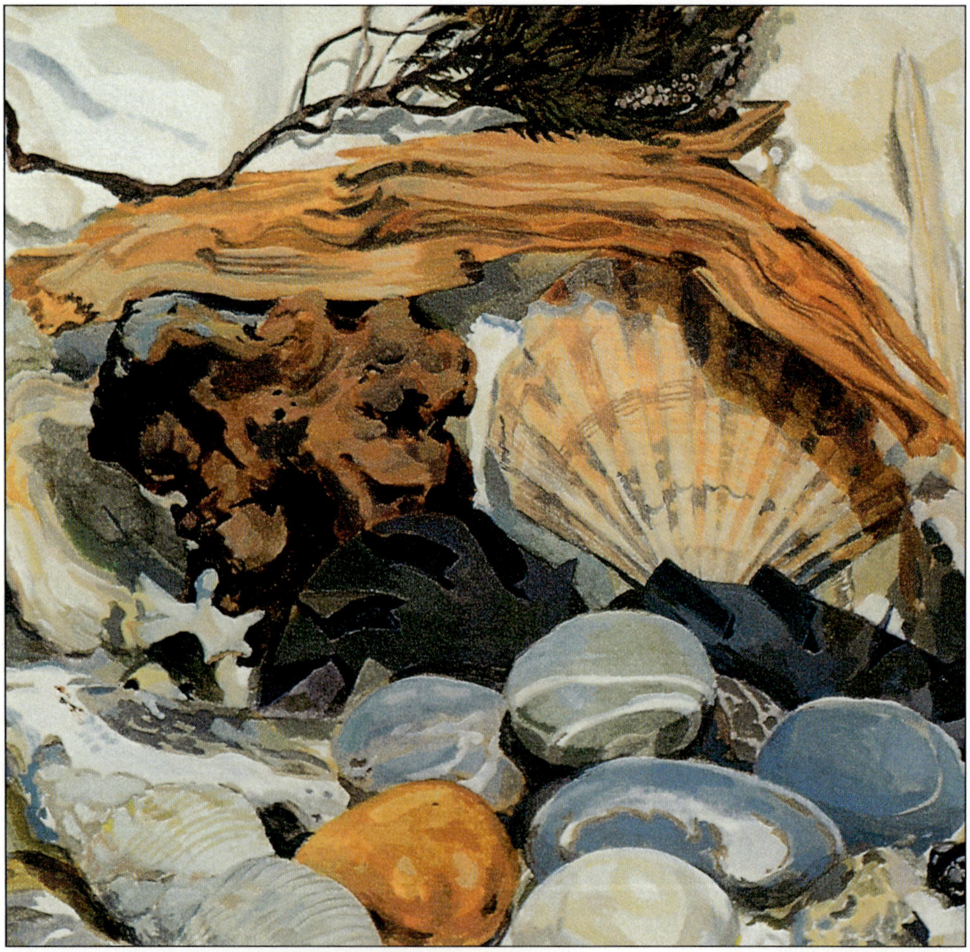

TEMPERA

Painting in the tempera medium has a longer history than fresco painting. The word "tempera" comes from the Latin verb "temperare" which means "to divide or proportion duly; to qualify by mixing; to regulate; to discipline." The literal translation seems appropriate; the mixture of pigment and medium is difficult, needing precision, and the method of applying tempera paint to a ground is itself a discipline.

The method has been widely used both in the Orient and in Europe from the earliest times and was extremely popular through the Middle Ages to the fifteenth century, when it was superseded by oil painting. Occasional revivals of interest in this technique have kept it alive until the present day, although it is no longer widely popular.

The normal ground for tempera painting was a wooden panel which was occasionally covered with canvas. The choice of wood varied according to availability. In Italy, poplar was most commonly used, as recommended by the Italian artist and writer Cennini (born c.1370); in central Europe the choice was pine, while in Flanders and northern Europe it was oak. Other woods, including larch, maple, box, lime, fir, and willow were also used. The wood had to be well-seasoned, planed and, if necessary, jointed. The practise of covering panels with canvas or linen was to prevent joints opening later and spoiling the picture. Next, several layers of gesso ground, the main ingredients of which were size and some form of whitening agent, usually plaster of Paris, were laid over the panel. The gesso was sanded down after it had dried to provide an even, smooth surface on which to work. Sometimes the gesso ground was toned by a coat of resin or size with an added coloring agent, although it was more usual to retain the white surface which reflected light back through the translucent paint, adding brilliance and depth to the color.

A number of different media are favoured by different people as the best vehicle for the pigment in tempera painting. Vasari was firmly of the opinion that the yolk of an egg excelled all others. The following is his description of the way in which the Old Masters prepared tempera paint:

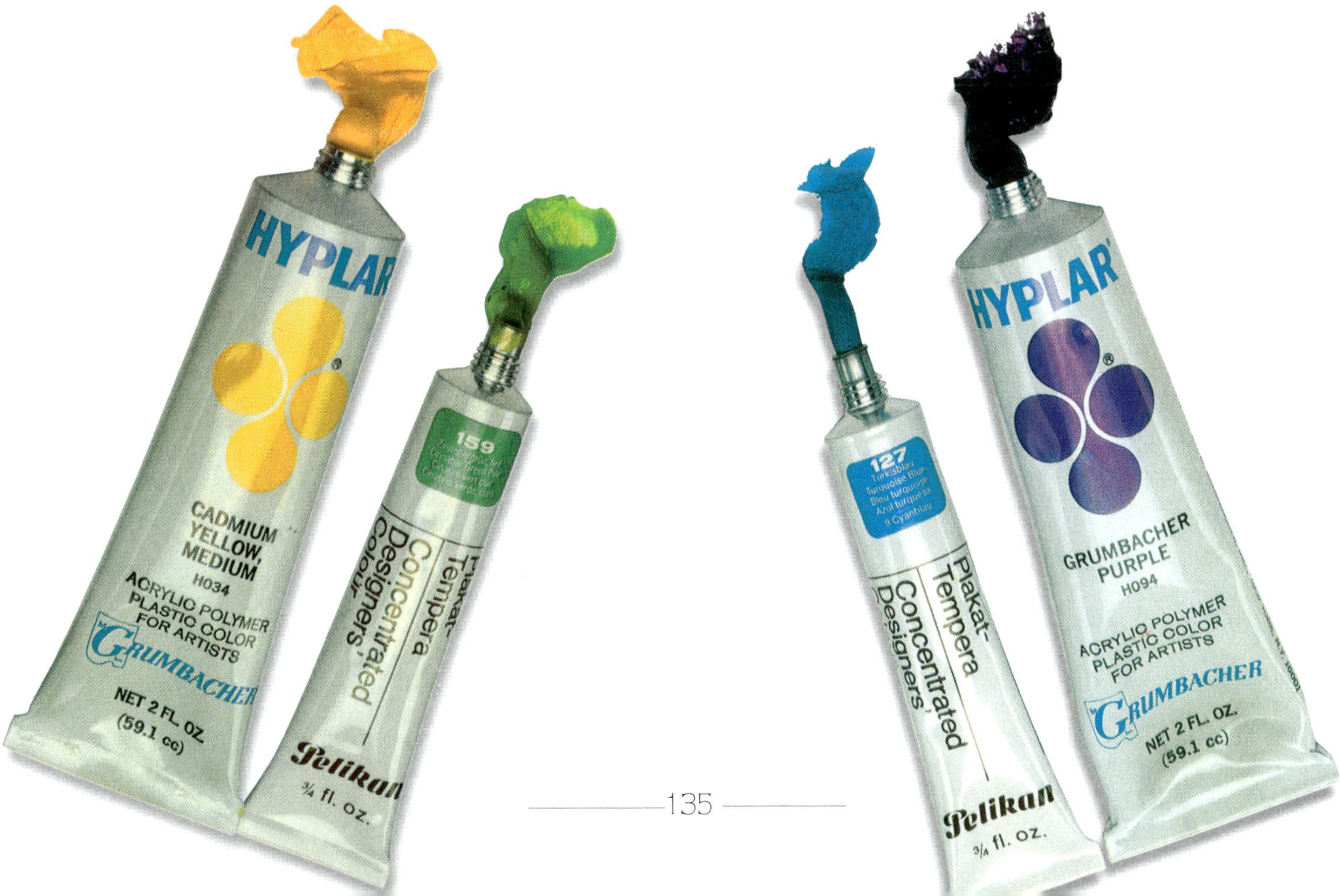

They whisked up an egg and shredded it into a tender branch of a fig tree, in order that the milk of this with the egg should make the tempera of the colors, which are being mixed with this medium were ready for use. They chose for these panels mineral colors of which some are made by the chemists and some found in the mines. And for this kind of work all pigments are good, except the white used for work on walls made with lime, for that is too strong. In this manner their work and their pictures are executed and this they call coloring in tempera. But the blues are mixed with parchment size, because the yellow of the egg would turn them green, whereas size does not affect them, nor does gum.

Tempera paint has a number of advantages over fresco painting and many of the great exponents of the latter worked their smaller pieces in tempera. With its brilliant white gesso ground the paint has a greater luminosity than it was possible to achieve in fresco work, and also a slightly greater depth of tone. Because the paint could be laid on in thicker layers, the light areas could be built up more strongly. It was also the practise of artists to create softer transitions of tone by "scumbling." This is the laying of semi-transparent light paint over darker areas, sometimes in an irregular way, to modify the paint beneath by creating areas of broken color. Being a flexible medium, artists were able to include areas of fine elaboration in tempera paintings.

Medieval artists were beginning to establish a method for painting the human figure. Areas which were to be flesh were given an underpainting, usually of terre verte. This subdued green complemented the pinkish color of the flesh and was allowed to shine through in areas of shadow to provide the half-tones. The green underpainting was sometimes heightened by the addition of white and occasionally greater depth was added by shading areas in transparent brown.

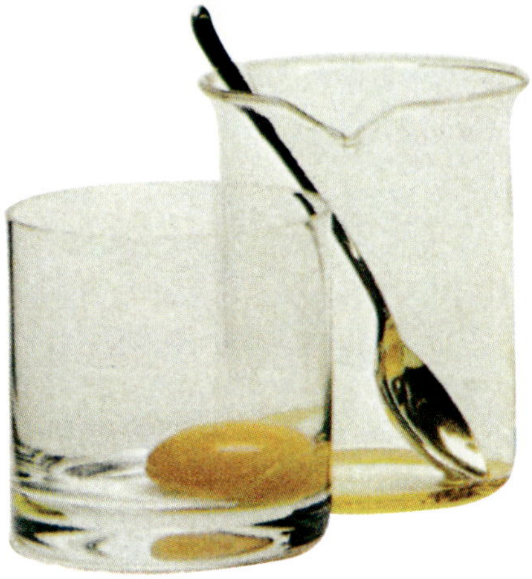

All this preparatory work was extremely important in helping to give tonal depth to the finished painting and was, interestingly, closer to the techniques of the Impressionists than to the practise of adding black to arrive at darker tones, that was more customary at the time.

After the underpainting, the artist mixed enough of each of the colors he intended to use, to avoid running out before completing a painting. As with fresco, tempera changes as it dries and the colors lighten by several shades. The experienced tempera painter would make allowances for this but it was always difficult to match a new batch of color with any that had already dried. The preparatory mixing partly accounts for the continuity of hue that is noticeable with this method of painting. Three main colors were mixed in order to paint the flesh. The artist began by laying in the main area with a mid-tone, then worked over the top with the darker then the lighter tones. Later, a semi-transparent mixture of black and yellow ocher called "verdaccio" provided the deepest shadows.

When painting the clothed figure, the system used by medieval painters was almost the same as for flesh. The colors for the underpainting were carefully chosen to complement whatever colors were chosen to go over the top; red, for example, took a greenish-gray underpaint, and blue usually took a white-gray or occasionally a green. The top color was similarly painted in stages: the mid-tone first, then the darker, and then the lighter areas.

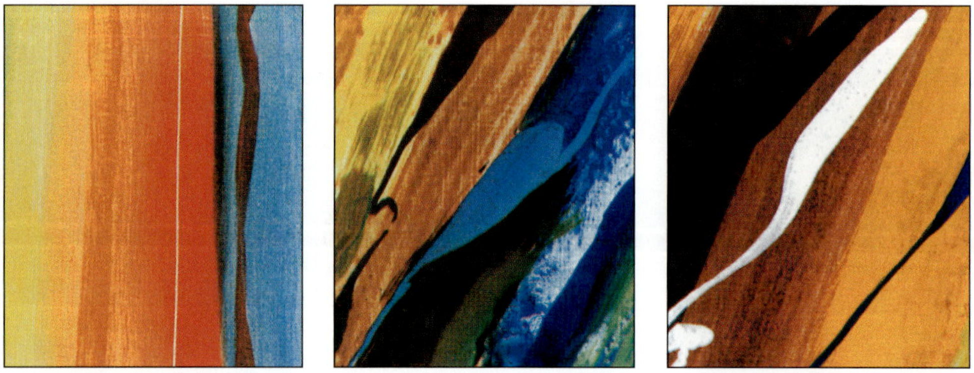

Looking from left to right, different consistencies can be seen. A directly applied and unworked pure egg tempera is similar to thickly laid watercolor. Painted in a similar way, an egg yolk, stand oil emulsion, and damar varnish resemble a mixture of pure tempera and oil paint, resulting in very dense color. A whole egg mixed with damar varnish and oil of cloves emulsion produces a flat, dense color.

Surfaces

Tempera paints were first used to decorate walls and panels and the best results are still obtained on a firm surface. Seasoned wood is ideal, but it is hard to obtain and expensive. Do not use wood that has been seasoned with chemicals; softboard and plywood are unsuitable because they tend to warp.

The best surfaces to use are chipboard, hardboard, and Masonite – all are easy to find and not too expensive. These boards can be rubbed down with fine sand-paper in a backward and forward motion, then coated with methyl alcohol. Buckling can be prevented by sizing the back with glue.

Canvas can be used, stretched as for oils, but it must be the finest quality fine-weave canvas and it is essential to stretch it really taut. Alternatively, the canvas can be stretched and glued to a hardboard backing. Size the back of the hardboard or glue paper to it to prevent buckling.

Use thin board and sand down the top surface. Coat with glue size, then press it down onto the canvas. Turn the whole board over and smooth down the canvas through a sheet of thin paper.

SIZES

Size all painting surfaces with rabbit-skin glue or artists size before laying a ground. Rabbit-skin glue is the best but it is expensive. Mix the size in the proportions 1:10 with water, then brush on.

Stand one part glue or size in ten parts water overnight. Warm to blood heat, then apply with a brush.

A good size can be made by soaking six gelatin leaves in $1^{1}/_{4}$ pints of water for 15 minutes. Heat until the gelatin dissolves, then apply. Leave to dry overnight.

GROUNDS

Apply gesso grounds to board or canvas for all tempera painting. For a board surface, make a gesso from Gilder's whiting mixed into a warm size until it can absorb no more. Stir, scooping off any bubbles with a spoon. Paint onto the board between four and eight coats, allowing 20 minutes drying time between each coat. Leave to dry for several days before sanding and polishing with a moist cloth.

For a canvas surface mix the gesso as above, but adding one part of zinc white to every three of Gilder's whiting. A serving spoonful of linseed oil to every half-pint of gesso will prevent the canvas cracking.

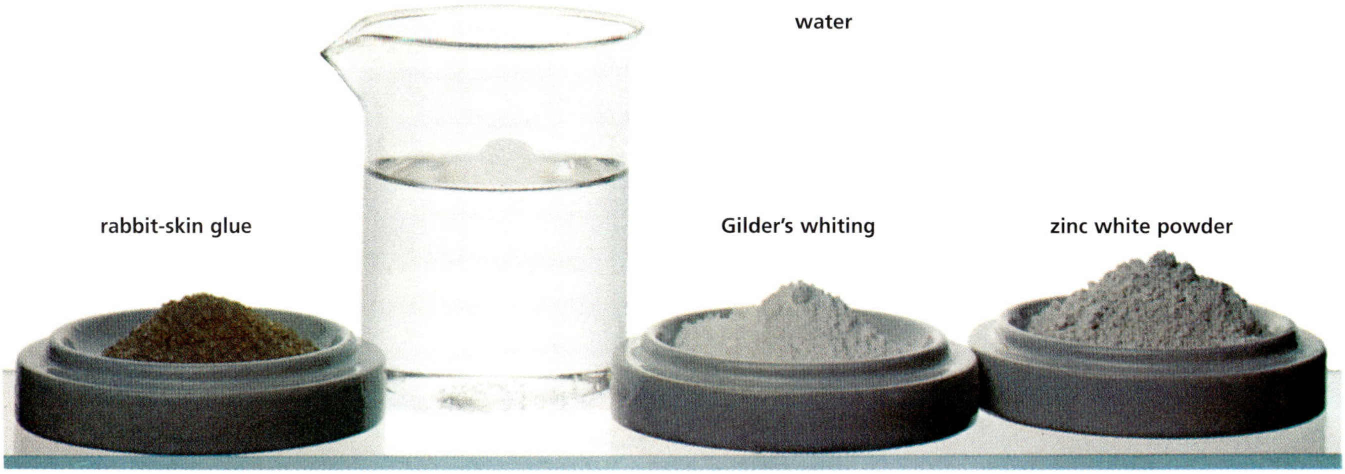

SIZE AND GESSO INGREDIENTS

For making size, mix 1 part rabbit-skin glue with 10 parts water. To make the gesso ground, which is necessary before applying tempera to canvas, Gilder's whiting and zinc white are needed. Add linseed oil to the gesso to prevent the canvas cracking. *See page 138 for instructions on making size and preparing gesso.*

MAKING SIZE

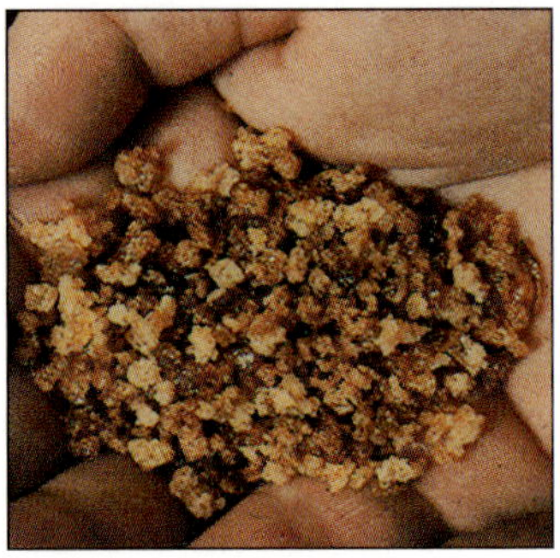

1 Measure out a quantity of size crystals. Soak them overnight in 10 parts of water to 1 part size.

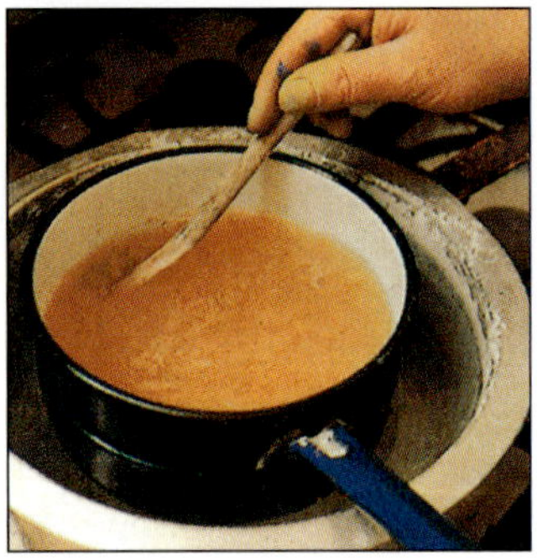

2 Heat the size in a double boiler until the crystals are dissolved. Do not overheat – it should not be allowed to boil.

PREPARING GESSO

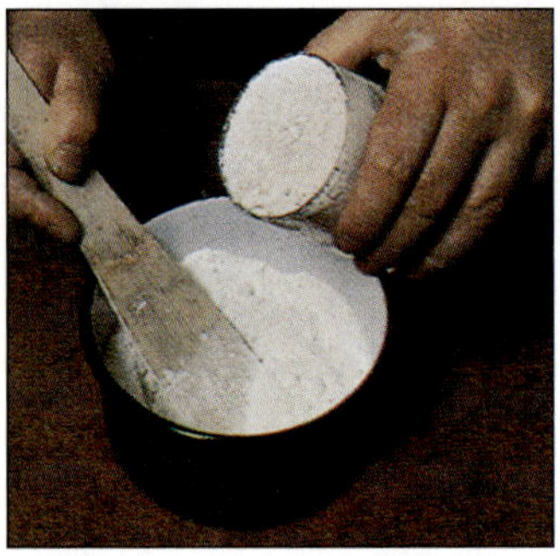

1 Mix 1 part of whiting with 1 part of titanium white. Use an enamel pan and a wooden spoon.

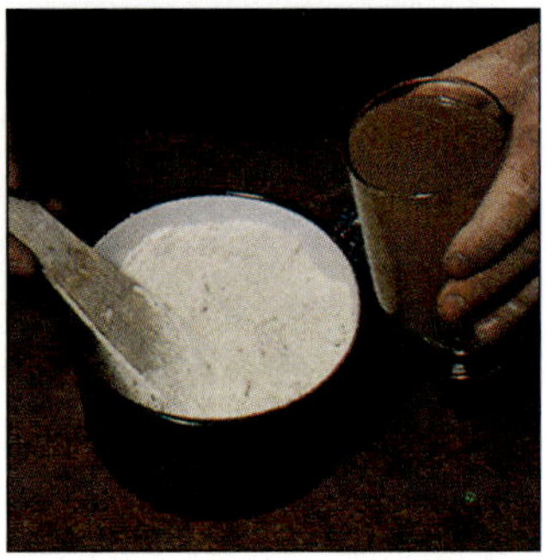

2 When the powders are well mixed together, measure out 1 part of size (the same volume as 1 part of powder).

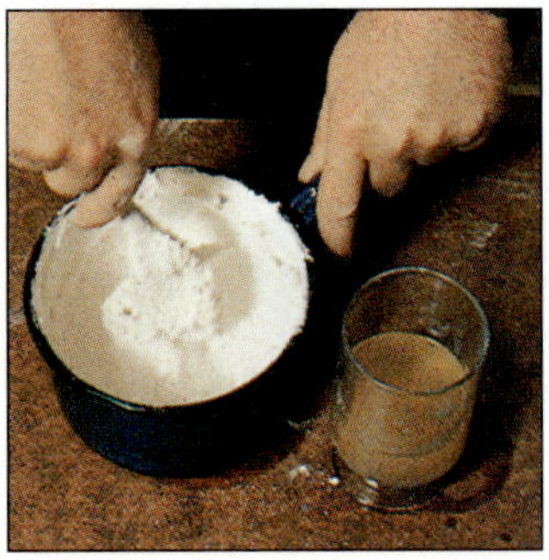

3 Add size to the mixture to form a thick paste. Stir well, but do not allow air bubbles to form in the gesso.

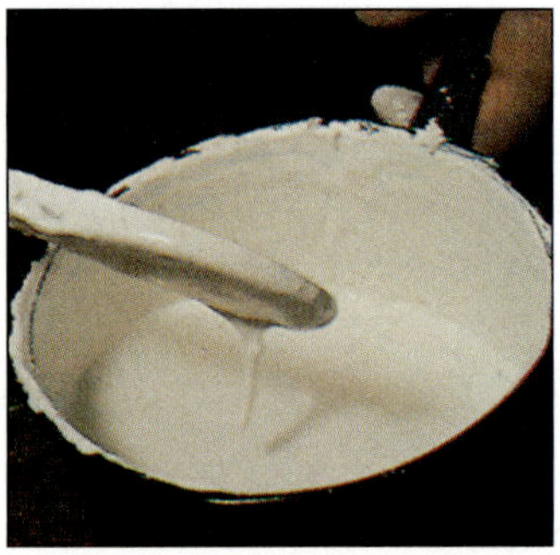

4 Continue adding the size slowly, until the mixture has a liquid, creamy consistency. If it is lumpy, strain it through cheesecloth.

PREPARING A PANEL

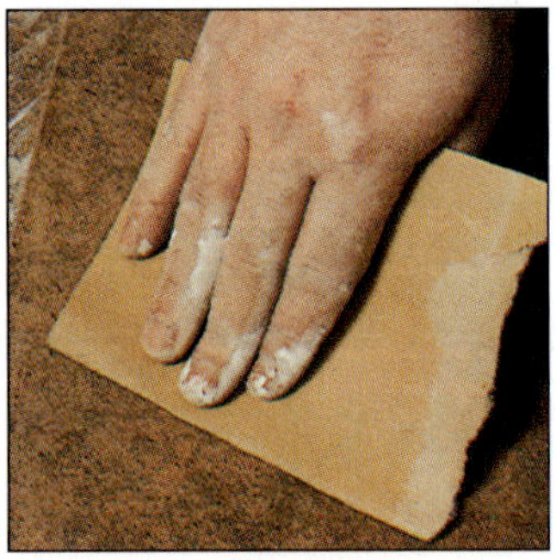

1 Sandpaper the surface of the panel lightly to provide a tooth for the gesso.

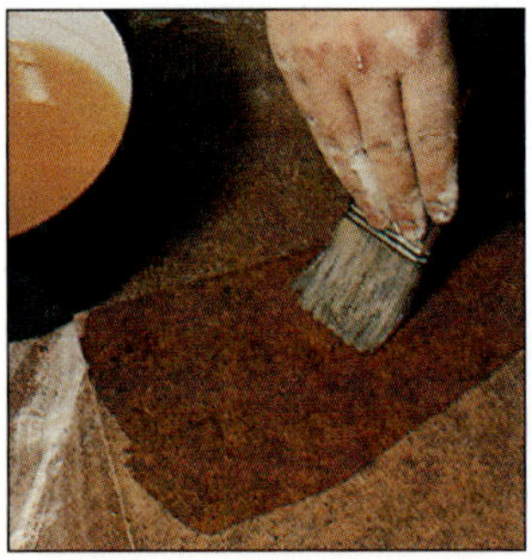

2 Apply size evenly over the whole surface of the panel. Leave it until it is completely dry. Size the back of the panel.

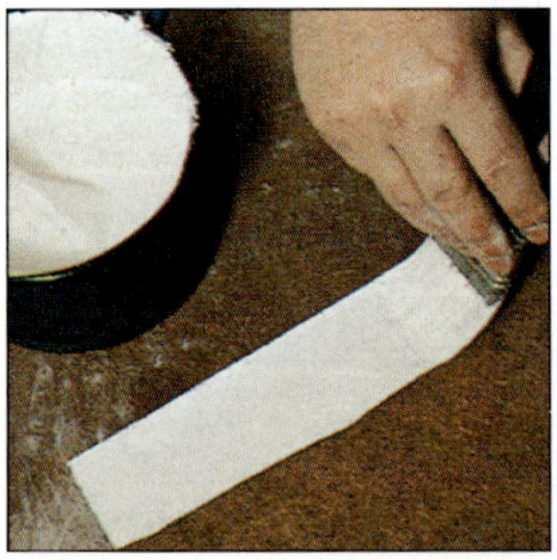

3 Brush gesso on the panel, working evenly and lightly in one direction. When it is dry, apply a second coat across the first. Repeat applications for 6 to 8 coats of gesso. When dry, rub the surface lightly with fine sandpaper. Gesso the back of the panel.

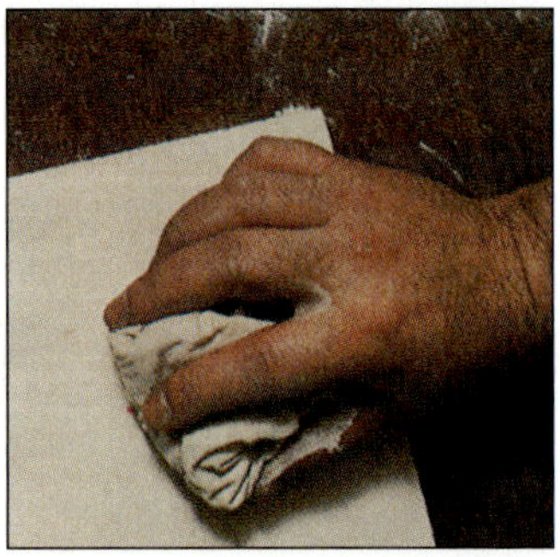

4 Give the surface a final polish with a damp linen rag, so that the gesso is completely smooth and clean, ready for painting.

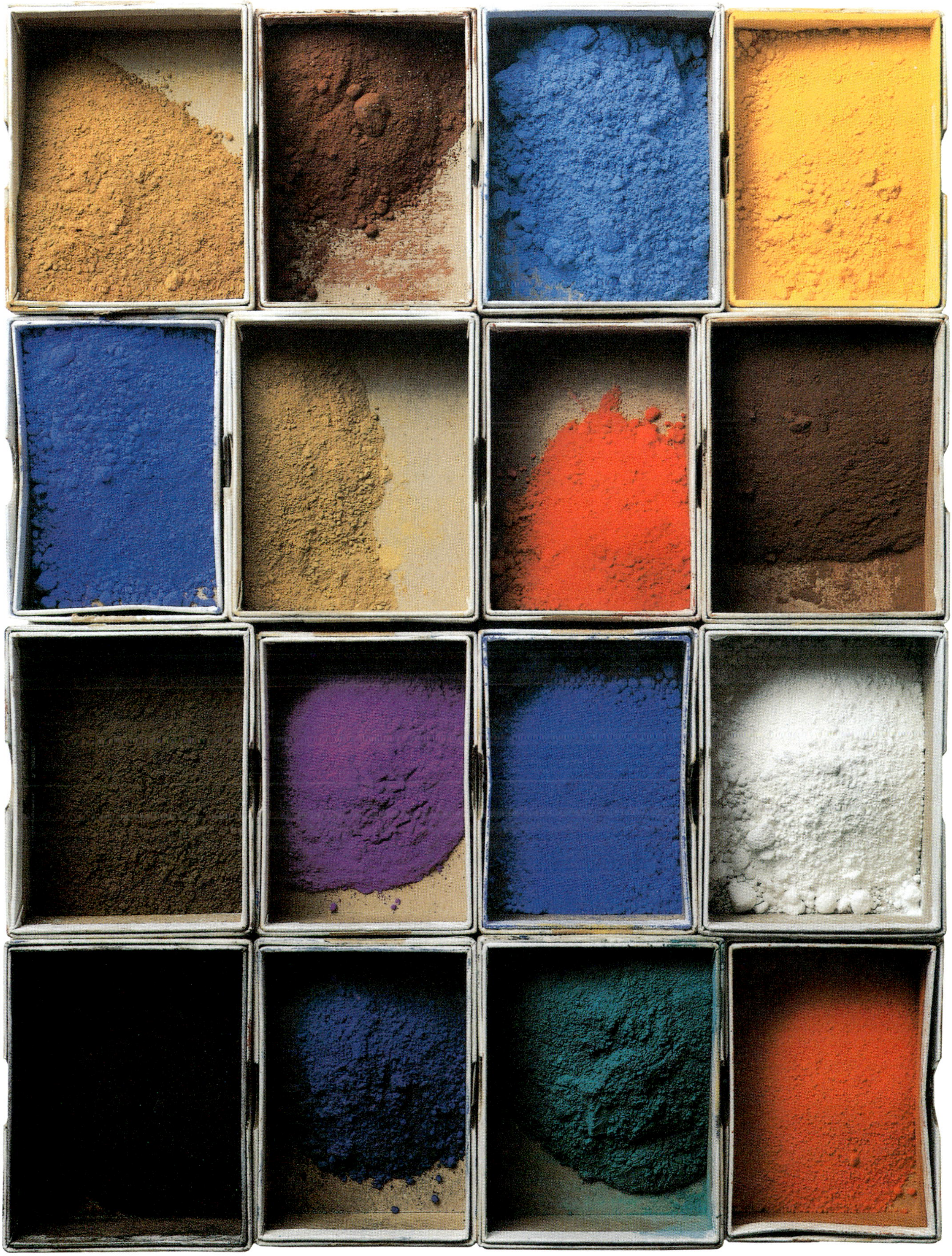

Pigments

Tempera paint is made by mixing powdered pigment with an egg solution. An extremely wide range of pigments can be used to produce tempera (see page 139) in a vivid range of colors. Ready-manufactured tempera is available in a limited selection of colors. For the artist, whether beginner or expert, it is usually best to make up the paint when it is needed – tube tempera colors do not dry as quickly as hand-made paint. The main advantage of hand-made tempera is that it can be made in a wide range of colors to suit the artist's purpose exactly.

Most pigments will combine with egg yolk to give a tempera medium, but there is no need to begin with a vast palette. Pigments are easier to use if mixed first into a thick paste with distilled water and kept in airtight jars. Bear this in mind when choosing your palette, because some pigments, such as French ultramarine, set hard if left as a paste. Whites must always be mixed directly into egg yolk, but avoid flake white, which is poisonous; so are the chrome pigments. If you do choose them, take care. Monestial blue is best left out because it does not combine well with egg. Other colors, such as Prussian blue and alizarin red, will not form a lasting water paste unless a little alcohol is added.

A useful palette to begin with might consist of lamp black, titanium white, burnt umber, Indian red, French ultramarine, and yellow ocher.

You can buy ready-mixed tempera paints, but there is little advantage in doing so – and there are several drawbacks. To start with, it is not difficult to mix tempera mediums and in making your own you can create a wider range of colors than you can buy. The manufactured products tend, also, to dry more slowly and this can lead to the artist lifting an underpaint instead of putting on a new layer.

It is not essential to keep your pigments ready-mixed in little jars. Some painters prefer to mix the pigment, egg, and water in one action on the palette, and this is obviously necessary when mixing the whites or French ultramarine. When covering a large area with one color do not leave it exposed to the air on your palette, or it may harden off before you can finish the job. Keep the paint in little jars, and if you do not want to keep screwing a top on and off, use a moistened rag as a stopper.

EGG YOLK TEMPERA

This is the classic medium for tempera painting. An egg yolk contains albumen, a sticky protein that sets hard when exposed to air, a non-drying oil, and lecithin, a fatty substance that helps liquids to combine in a stable mixture. It makes an ideal painting emulsion when mixed with pigment and distilled water.

Always use fresh hens' eggs – the fresher the egg the longer the emulsion will take to set. Separate the yolk completely from the white, then wipe it dry on a paper towel. Puncture the yolk skin with a scalpel or sharp point and let the yolk flow into your mixing jar. Add the distilled water and stir with a glass rod until it is like thick cream.

Most pigments will mix ideally with egg yolk in equal measure. Examples are: French ultramarine, cadmium yellow, scarlet lake, Indian red, yellow ocher, raw umber, and ivory black.

Use $\frac{3}{4}$ measure of egg to 1 of paste when mixing cerulean blue, cadmium red, viridian, and zinc white. Use $1\frac{1}{4}$ measure of egg to 1 paste when mixing titanium white, Venetian red, burnt umber, burnt and raw sienna.

Never mix more paint than you think you will need – none of it will keep until the next day. Keep everything scrupulously clean. Wipe off all old traces of egg from your mixing jars and do not let egg get into your pigment pastes, or they will be set hard when you next go to use them.

Use an eye dropper when mixing small quantities. Lay pigment paste on a paper palette, then add the mixed yolk and distilled water, stirring with a plastic palette knife.

Once you have mixed your paint, use it as quickly as possible. Test first by painting a thin strip on a sheet of glass. If it peels off in a strip when dry it is ready for use. If it crumbles, add more egg to the mix.

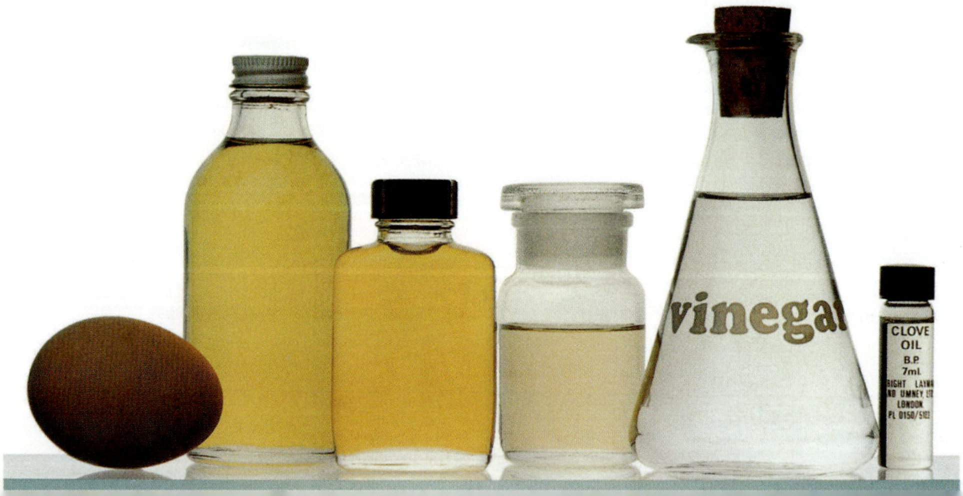

Making Tempera

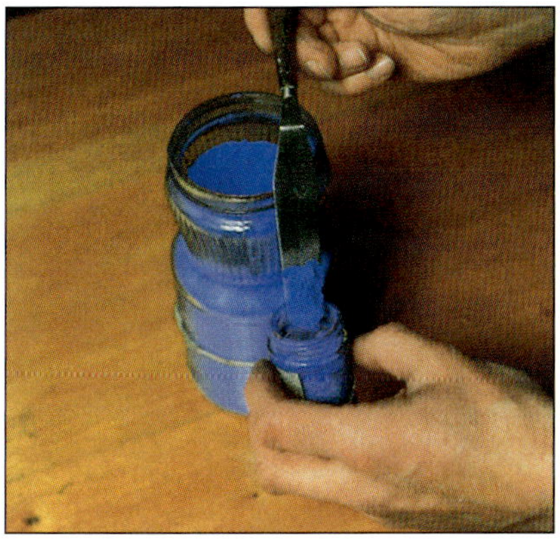

1 Transfer dry powdered pigment to a small jar.

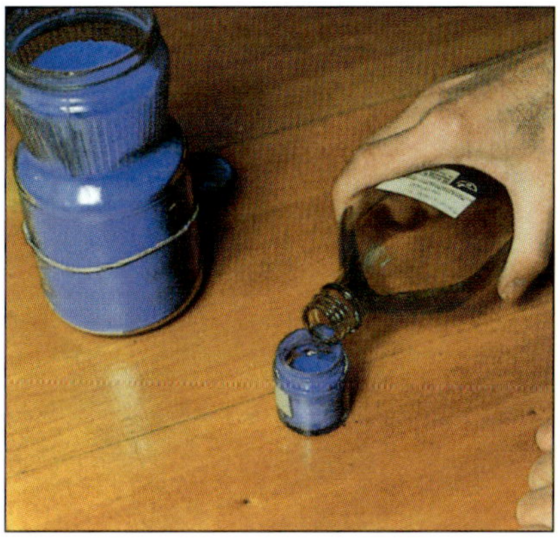

2 Add distilled water sparingly to make a thick paste.

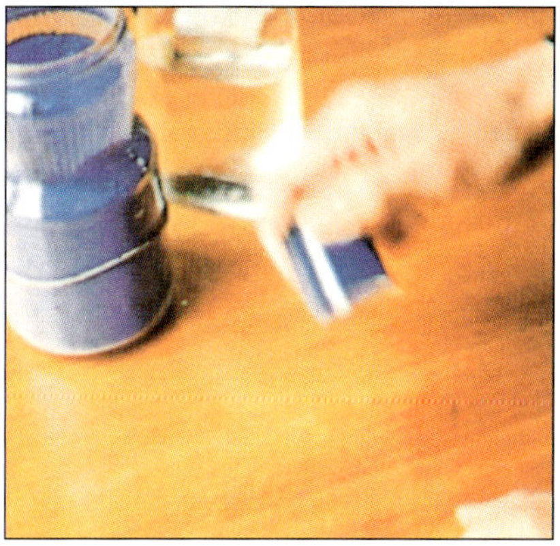

3 Replace the top securely and shake the bottle vigorously.

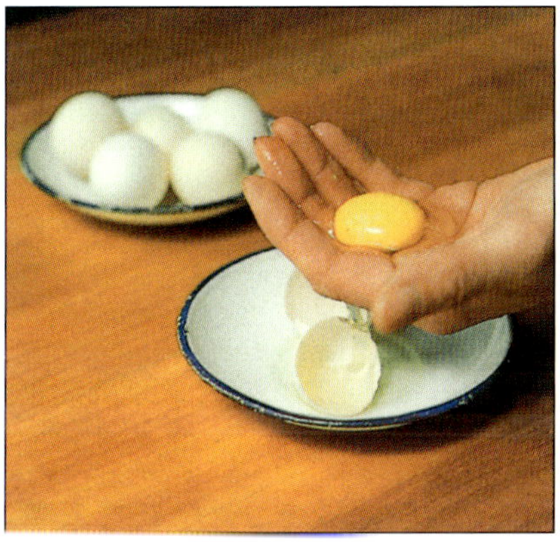

4 Break the egg and separate the yolk by allowing the white to drain through the fingers into a bowl.

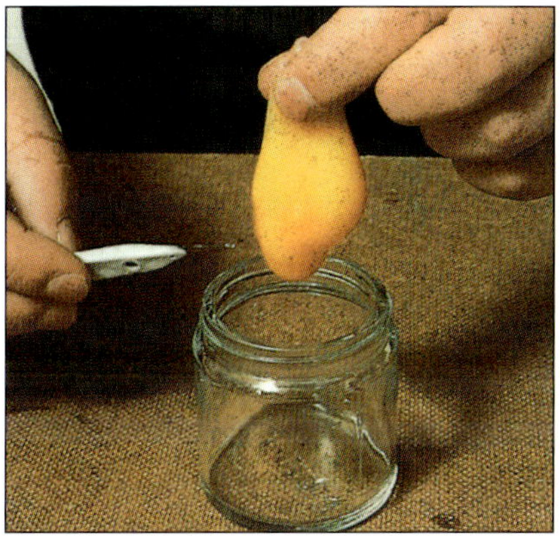

5 Make the yolk dry by passing from one hand to the other. Hold the yolk carefully and make an incision to allow the liquid to run into a glass container.

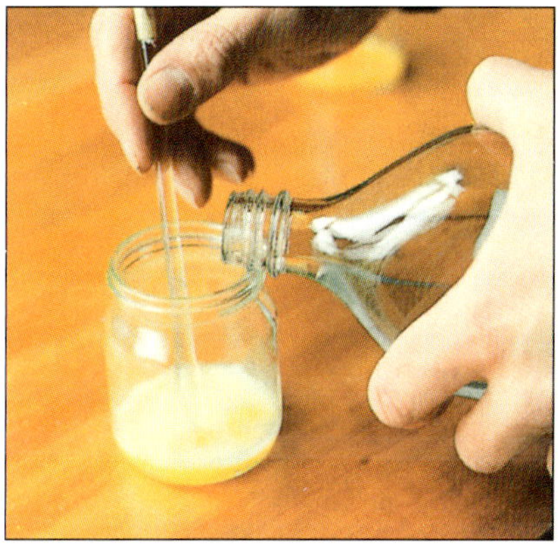

6 Add distilled water and stir until the mixture reaches the consistency of cream.

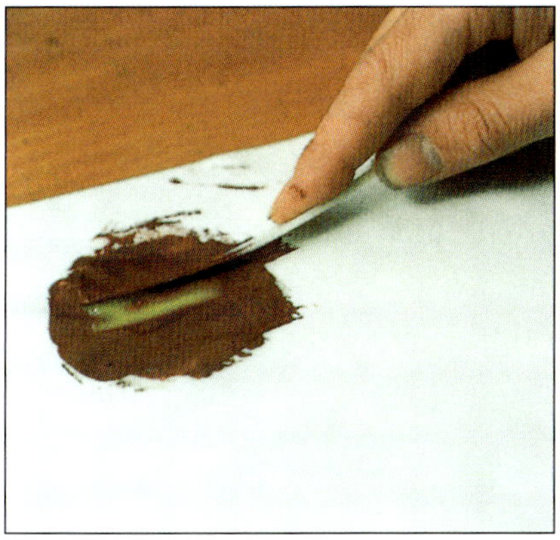

7 The pigment and the egg yolk binder are now blended together with a palette knife.

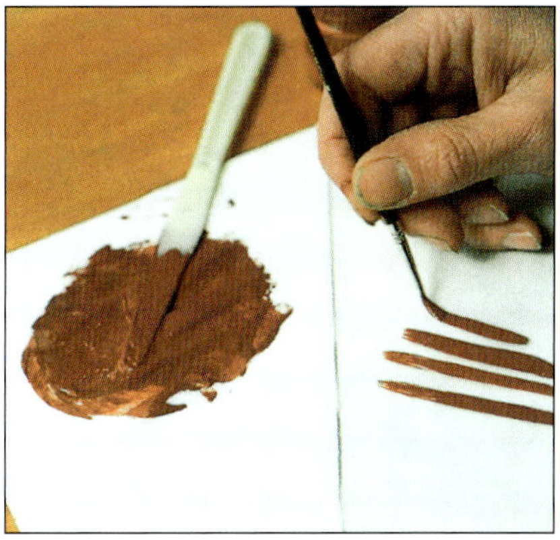

8 Test the paint on a piece of glass.

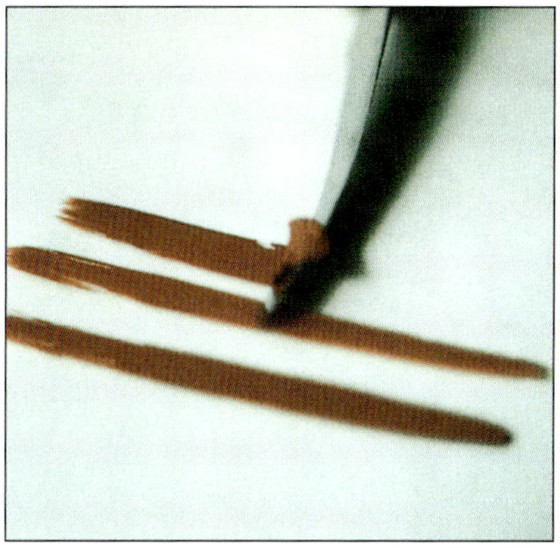

9 When dry the paint can be scraped off and stored for use. If it is too dry, add more egg.

Equipment

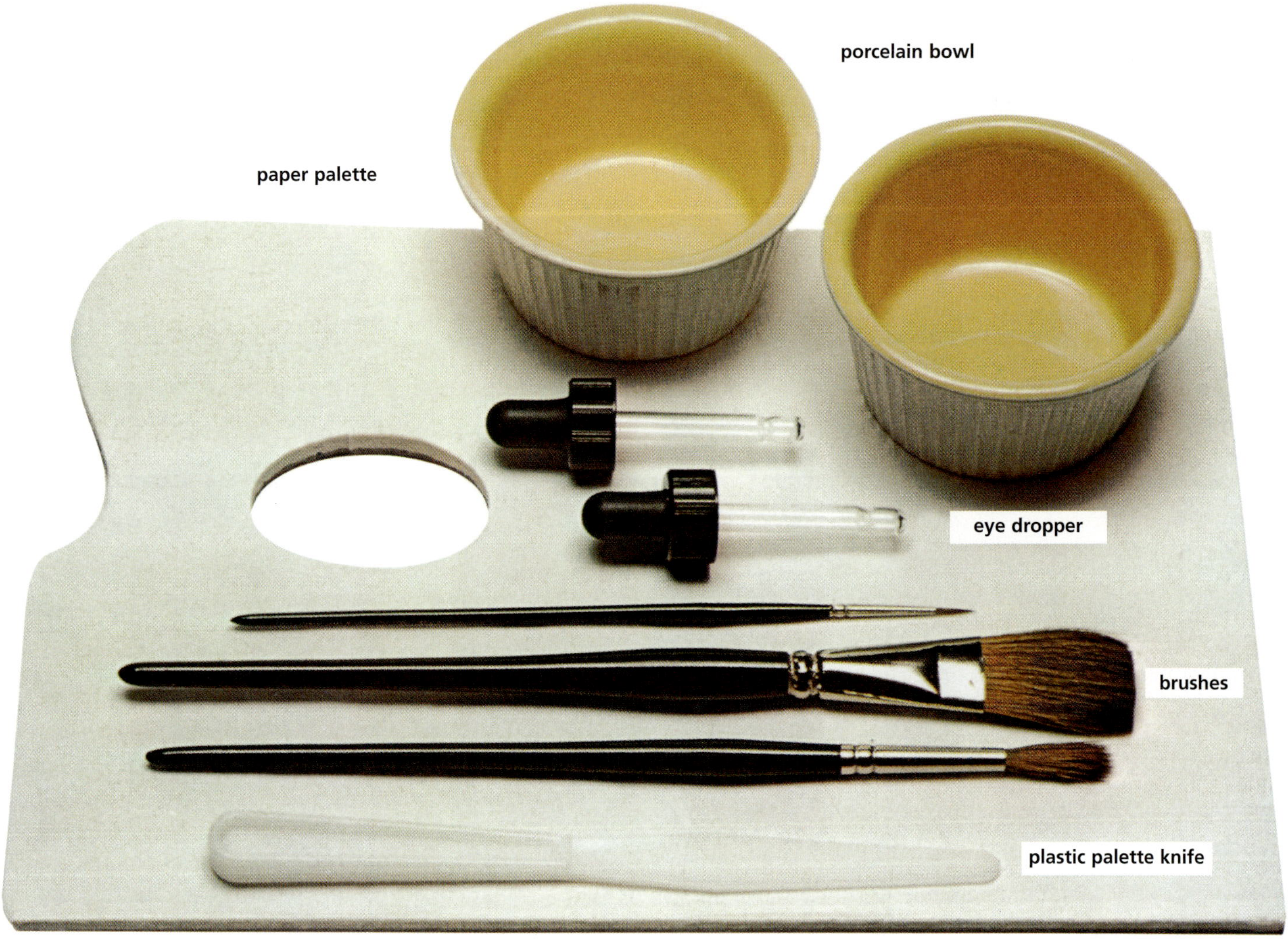

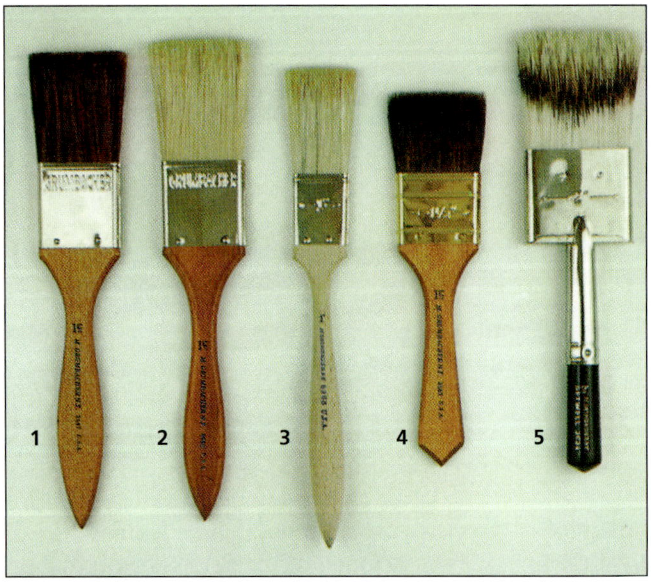

BASIC EQUIPMENT

A paper palette is best for mixing and applying tempera because it is then easy to remove any paint or egg from the surface completely, by tearing off one of the sheets of paper. To mix the paint, use an eye dropper to put the pigment paste and egg on the palette and mix with a plastic palette knife. If large quantities of paint are needed, they can be made and kept in a porcelain bowl. A glass rod can be used to mix the paint, however, a plastic palette knife is more than adequate.

WIDE BRUSHES FOR TEMPERA WORK

*For detail work in tempera, it is best to use brushes that would be suitable for oil or watercolor painting. Wider brushes (left) are useful for painting over large areas, particularly with size or gesso, although large areas of paint can also be applied in this way. However, the brush should not be so harsh that it would scratch any underlying layers. Possible sizes and types of bristle include: ox hair and bristle, $1^1/_2$ in. (**1**), white, unbleached bristle, $1^1/_2$ in. (**2**), white bristle, 1 in. (**3**), camel hair, $1^1/_2$ in. (**4**) and badger hair, 2 in. (**5**).*

Egg Oil Emulsion

Egg tempera in particular, dries quickly, hardly changes color, and is fairly waterproof - sufficiently so not to pick up when over-painted. It has a good surface that wears well, provided it is treated wth care. It is by far the best of the mediums, but requires technical knoweledge and expertize to handle it well.

There are other drawbacks: speed of working is slow, it does not cover large areas well and is therefore better confined to small panels. There is always the difficulty of making flat, even coats of color on a large scale because the emulsion binder cannot accomodate huge amounts of pigment - something that acrylic can do with ease.

Adding oil to the egg medium for tempera paint changes some of the characteristics of the paint. The paint handles more like oil paint – for example, it can be used to create fuller impasto effects than pure tempera. An egg oil emulsion dries to give a glossier finish than pure tempera; and adding more oil it gives a heavier gloss. However, egg oil emulsions must be made up and handled with some care – the ingredients must be pure and the utensils scrupulously clean, as impurities may cause the oil to separate out. When dry, an egg oil emulsion gives a harder finish than that of pure tempera. A recommended way of mixing the different types of emulsion is to place the ingredients in a screw-top jar or bottle, and mix them by shaking thoroughly. Emulsions can be made with both egg yolks and whole eggs. It is important to try out the various emulsions to see which best suits your purposes. Paint a sample out on paper, which may have been coated with gesso. Check carefully on its brushing, binding, and drying qualities, as well as its flexibility, yellowing, and adherence.

RECIPES

EGG YOLK AND LINSEED OIL EMULSION

1 egg yolk
1 teaspoon linseed oil
distilled water

Add the linseed oil to the egg yolk drop by drop. Use the yolk and oil in the proportion 3 : 1 – the amount of oil will be about 1 teaspoonful. Stir with a glass rod. Using an eye dropper, add the same amount of distilled water as egg yolk to the linseed oil and egg mixture. Add the water drop by drop to aid the emulsification.

EGG YOLK, STAND OIL, AND DAMAR VARNISH EMULSION

1 egg yolk
1 teaspoon stand oil
1 teaspoon damar varnish
distilled water

Mix this emulsion in the same way as the egg yolk and linseed oil emulsion. Combine the prepared emulsion with an approximately equal amount of pigment paste. Initially, apply the paint very thinly. This mixture dries to an extremely hard finish which can even be polished with a silk or paper tissue pad to increase the shine of the finish. If applying several layers of paint, add an extra drop or so of oil to each succeeding layer to produce the necessary flexibility. This emulsion does not need to be varnished.

WHOLE EGG AND LINSEED OIL EMULSION

1 egg
1 teaspoon linseed oil
4 drops white vinegar

Mix the yolk and white of the egg. Using an eye dropper, add the linseed oil drop by drop, then mix in the white vinegar. Strain the mixture. Paint made with this type of emulsion is not so clear as pure tempera and it does not polish up like the egg yolk, stand oil, and damar varnish emulsion.

However, it dries to a hard finish. Mix with pigment paste in approximately equal proportions. Use distilled water if necessary to dilute the mixture.

WHOLE EGG, DAMAR VARNISH, AND OIL OF CLOVES EMULSION

1 egg
3/4 teaspoon damar varnish
20 drops oil of cloves
distilled water

Crack a whole egg into a screw-top jar. Mark the level on the jar, replace the lid and shake. Add a further mark above the first equal to 1 1/4 of the height of the original mark. Fill the jar to this level with damar varnish. Add 20 drops of oil of cloves with an eye dropper. Shake the jar thoroughly. Make another mark 12 times the height of the mixture, fill to this level with distilled water. Replace the lid tightly and shake thoroughly. This type of emulsion should be mixed to a paste with dry powder pigment. The paste can only be diluted by adding more of the emulsion.

Techniques

Be methodical when painting in tempera. It is not a spontaneous medium like oils, so plan your picture first by working out the order in which you will mix and use your colors.

It is wise to draw your design onto the ground before you begin painting. Use fine charcoal or silverpoint, or paint the design with a thin wash and a pointed brush. Never use graphite pencil – it will show through your finished work.

Use only fine sable brushes to apply the paint. Keep a container of distilled or cold, boiled water beside you and dip your brush in it frequently. Never overload the brush, this will give a pasty, unattractive finish and in any case, tempera more than $^{1}/_{25}$ in. (1 mm) thick will not stick to the painting surface.

Brush in single strokes in one direction only. Do not paint immediately over the same spot, you will either pick up the first coat or leave a clogged effect.

GLAZING

Egg tempera is ideal for glazing, because like acrylic, it dries quickly and any number of coats can be laid one on top of the other.

In tempera, most glazing is done with egg glair (white of egg) or oil. The glaze is applied in small areas because large areas are difficult to cover evenly with such a fast-drying medium. An entire painting can be glazed, however, if the surface is dampened first by spraying it with water from an atomizer. This delays the drying process, allowing the paint to flow easily and without streaking.

Tempera lends itself well to crosshatching because it can be applied in several layers and dries very quickly. Crosshatching can be done using any number of colors, brushed on in any direction. In this image umber and ocher have been crosshatched with white on a blue tinted support.

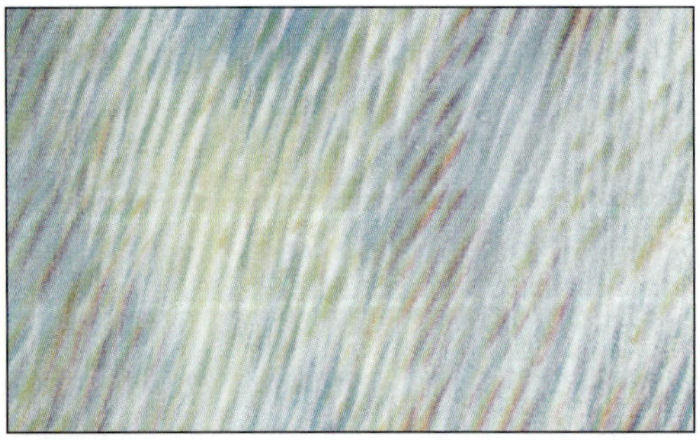

LAYING A WASH

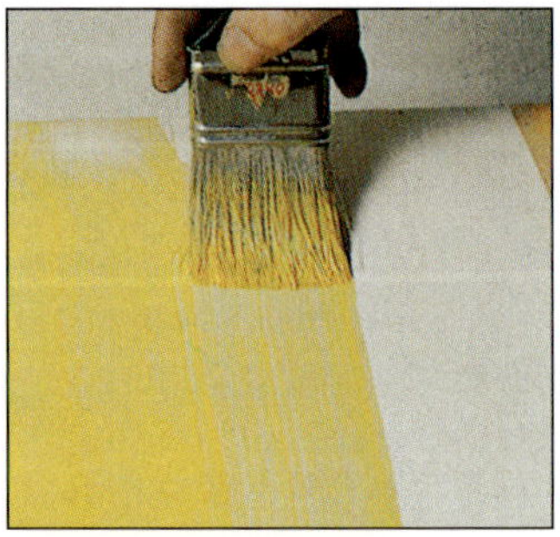

1 Dilute the paint with water and load a large brush. Paint evenly across the panel horizontally.

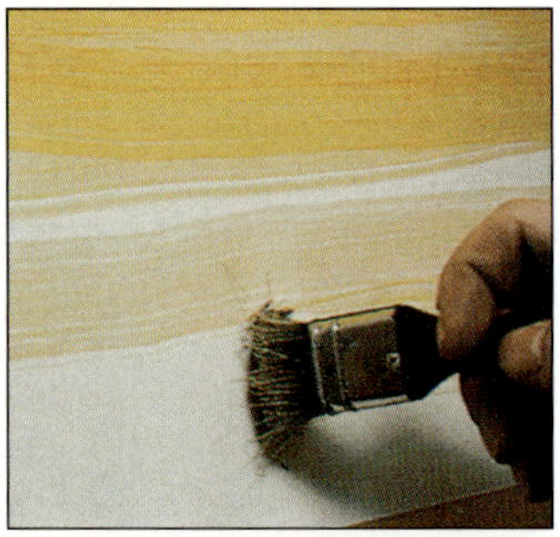

2 Use a bristle brush and drier paint for a streaky, textural wash. The quick-drying paint retains the brushmarks.

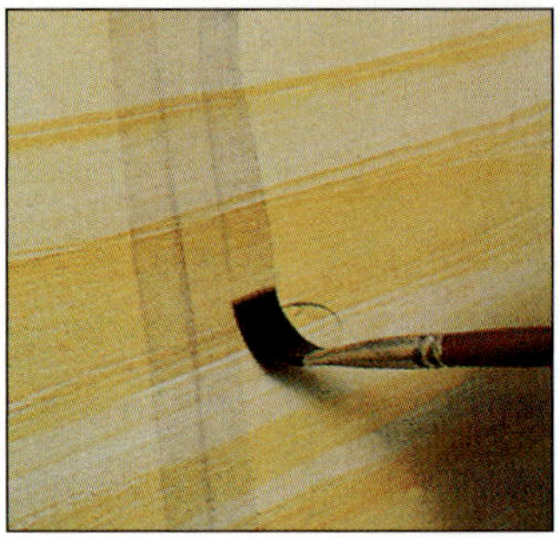

3 Wash over again with another color. The underneath layer shows through. Washes of one color build up a flat color layer.

CROSSHATCHING

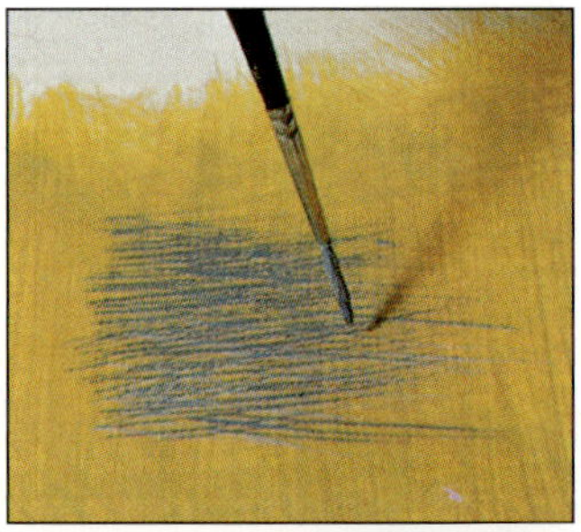

1 Using the tip of a fine brush, paint lines with slightly slanted strokes, working first in one direction and then in another.

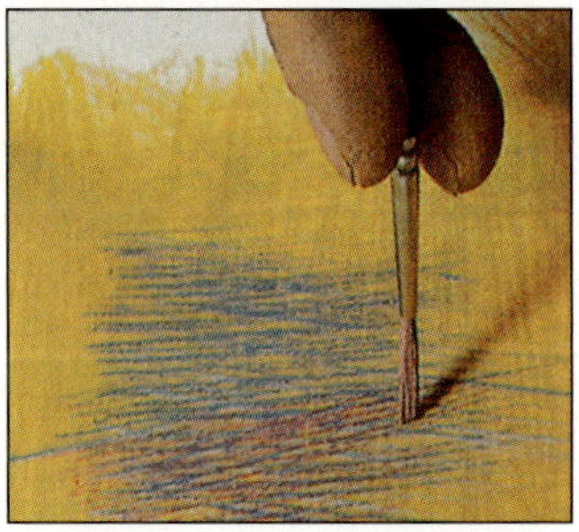

2 Applying a different color, repeat the crosshatched strokes to create a fine mesh of textured color.

SPATTERING

1 Spattering is a popular technique in tempera painting because it produces a stronger, more vibrant surface than a flat wash does. Lay the panel flat on the floor; otherwise the spattered paint may run down the surface. Use newspaper to mask off those parts of the painting that are not to be spattered. This allows you to work with complete freedom within a specific area. The paint should be wet, but not too runny – the consistency of heavy cream. Load your brush well, then draw your finger through the bristles to release a shower of small drops onto the surface. Here the artist is using a 1½ inch decorating brush, held 6 in. (15 cm) above the panel and at a slight angle to it. Leave the panel on the floor until the paint dries.

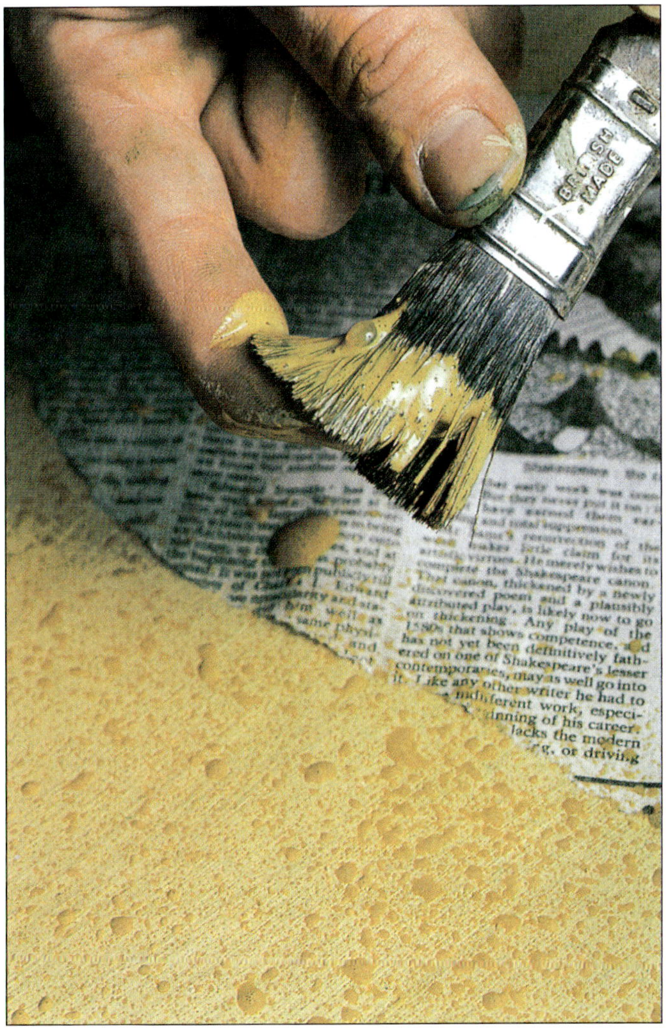

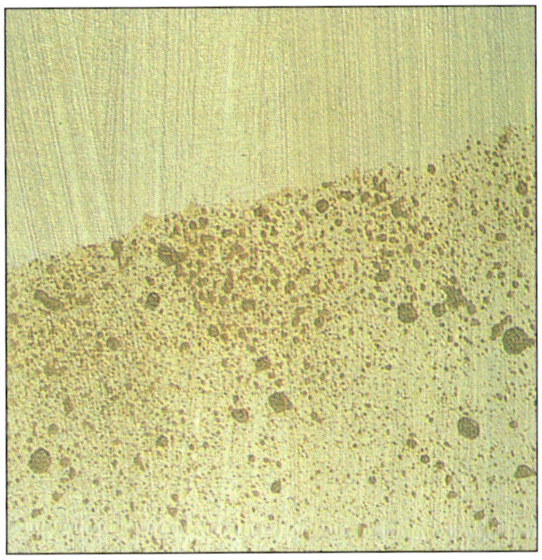

2 When the paint is thoroughly dry, remove the newspaper. Here you can see the edge where the flat wash and the spattered area meet.

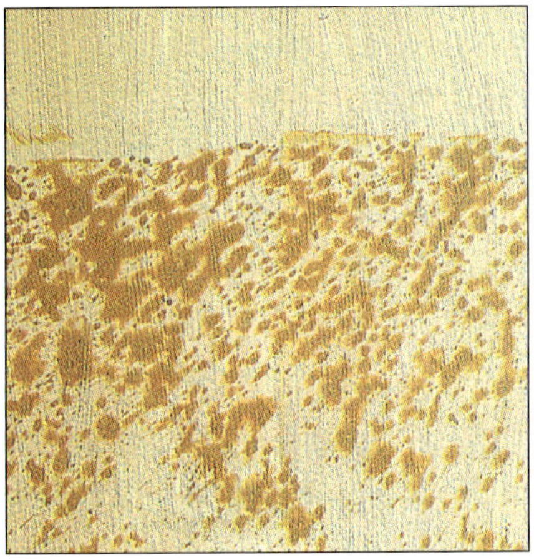

3 Spattering from different directions will give a variety of effects. Here the artist holds the brush closer to the surface and slightly to one side. He then hits the handle of the brush sharply against the palm of his free hand. This method produces oblique marks instead of dots, because the paint hits the surface at an angle.

4 Tempera paint dries very quickly, allowing a densely spattered texture to be built up quickly without the colors running together. The drops of spattered paint should not be so thick that they stand up from the surface; if they do, they may crack off. Correct this problem by reducing the amount of paint on your brush. Avoid spattering tones that are much lighter or darker than the color underneath: subtle shifts in tone help to create the glowing quality characteristic of tempera painting.

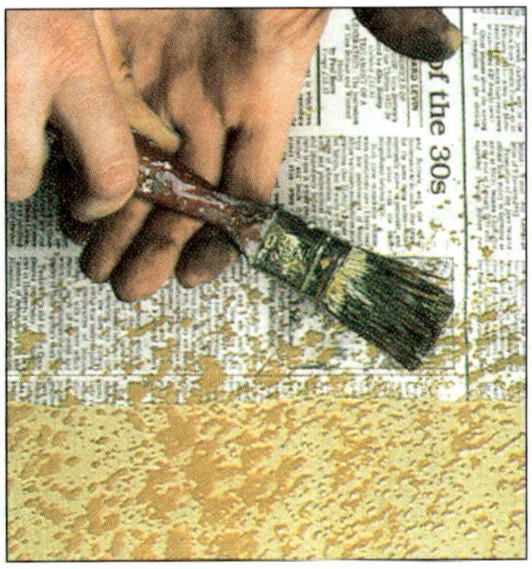

SCRATCHING

1 Paint two even layers of flat, opaque color. Let them dry out thoroughly for at least a day.

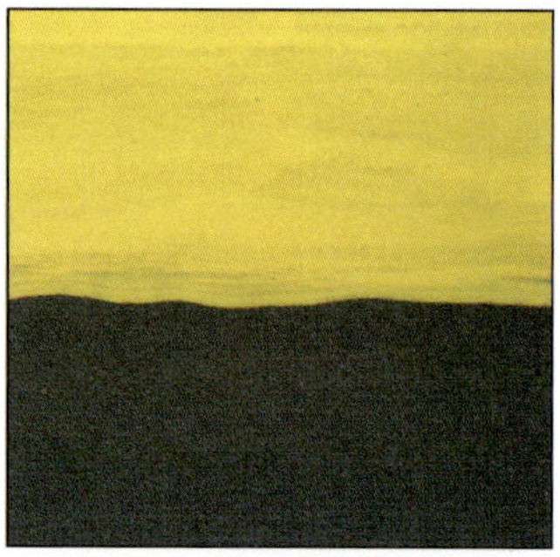

2 Reverse the colors. Paint over each layer with the other color; keep the paint flat and opaque. Let it dry.

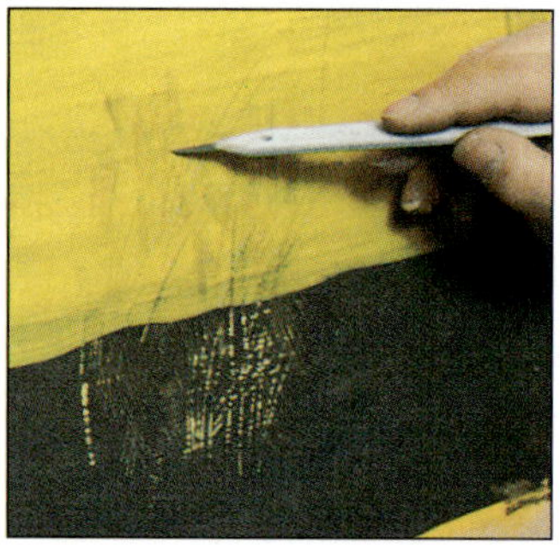

3 To reveal the color underneath, scratch lightly into the top layer of paint with a scalpel or razor blade.

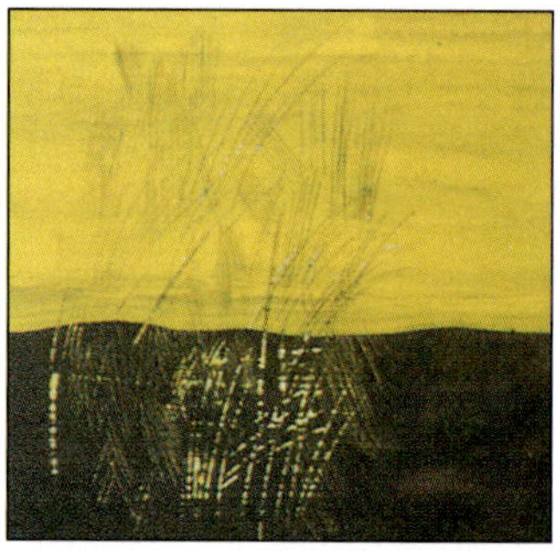

4 To achieve an effect of drawn lines in the different colors, continue scratching into the layers of paint.

SPONGING

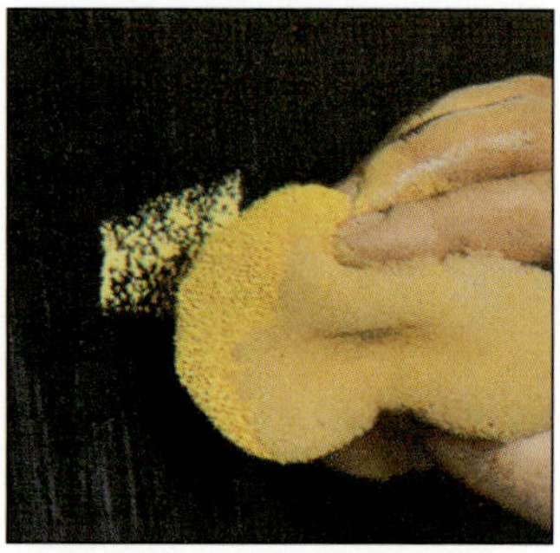

1 Lay an area of plain color. Pick up some paint in a contrasting color on the sponge and dab over the painted area.

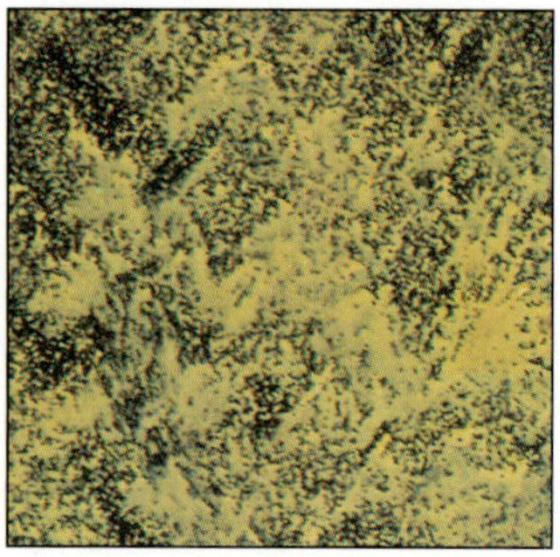

2 In the first layer, the texture of the sponge shows clearly, making a mottled, grainy surface.

3 Repeated sponging can be used to build up an area of flat color, which is modified slightly by the color underneath.

TAPPING

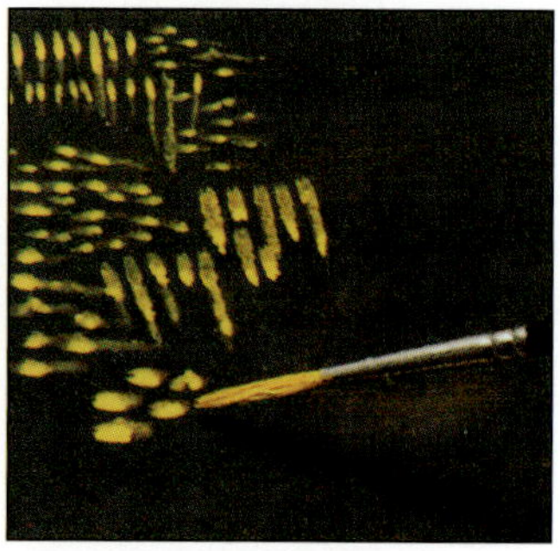

1 Work over the surface dabbing evenly with the side of the brush. Increase pressure for large marks and coarser texture.

SCUMBLING

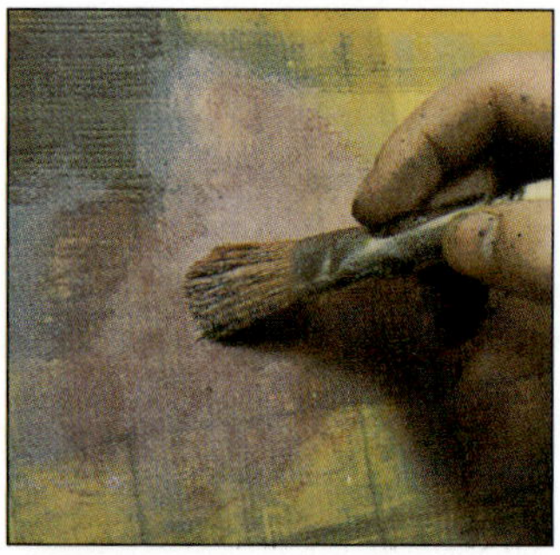

1 Load a brush with paint, wipe off excess. Work over an already painted layer with a circular motion.

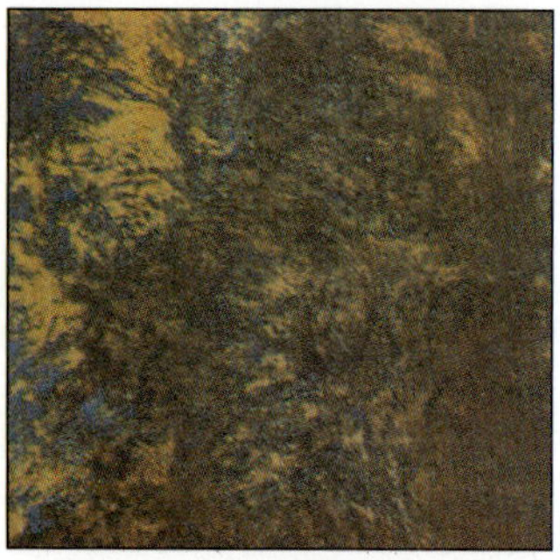

2 A light scumble over a sponged or spattered surface will soften the texture and merge the tones of the color underneath.

DRY BRUSHING

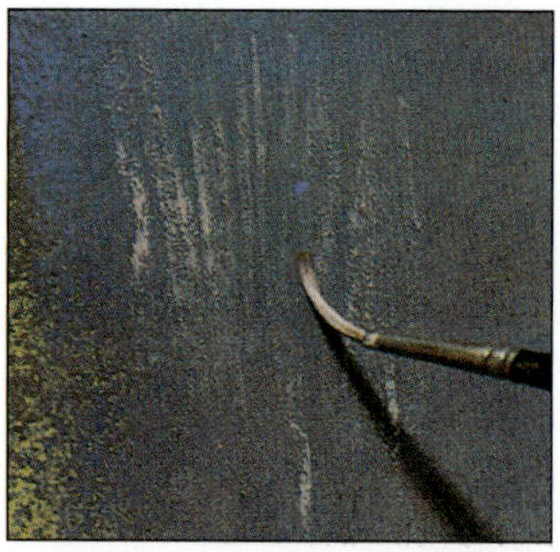

1 Take up paint on the brush, and wipe it to remove moisture. Draw the brush across the panel, leaving broken marks.

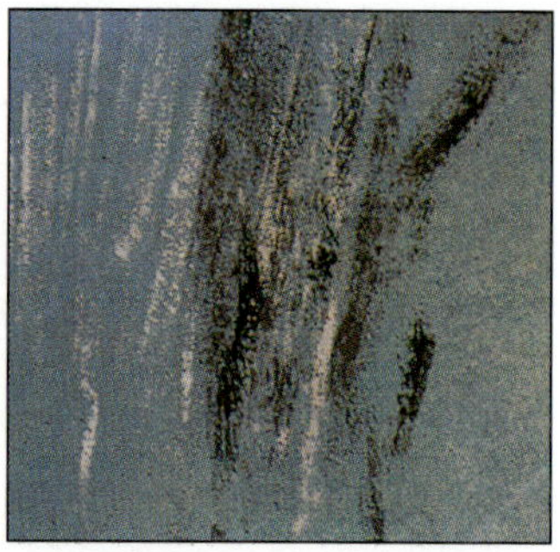

2 Dry brushing makes a light, feathery texture. Add a different color to change the effect. Any number of colors can be applied.

UNDERPAINTING WITH TERRE VERTE – USING WHITE

Tempera is still used by many contemporary painters as a fascinating and challenging alternative to other painting media. When used as an underpainting for an oil painting, tempera will give a glowing, translucent effect. Once the oil paint layer has dried thoroughly, the artist can return to working with tempera if he chooses.

If dry pigments are used, tempera colors will not necessarily dry as they look when applied to the surface; they may dry lighter or darker depending on the type of pigment used. For this reason it is a good idea to rest colors on a separate piece of similar surface before beginning to work. An important point to note is that tempera cannot be easily corrected or overpainted during the painting process, so this process requires careful planning and forethought. Work small areas at a time, allowing each layer to dry thoroughly.

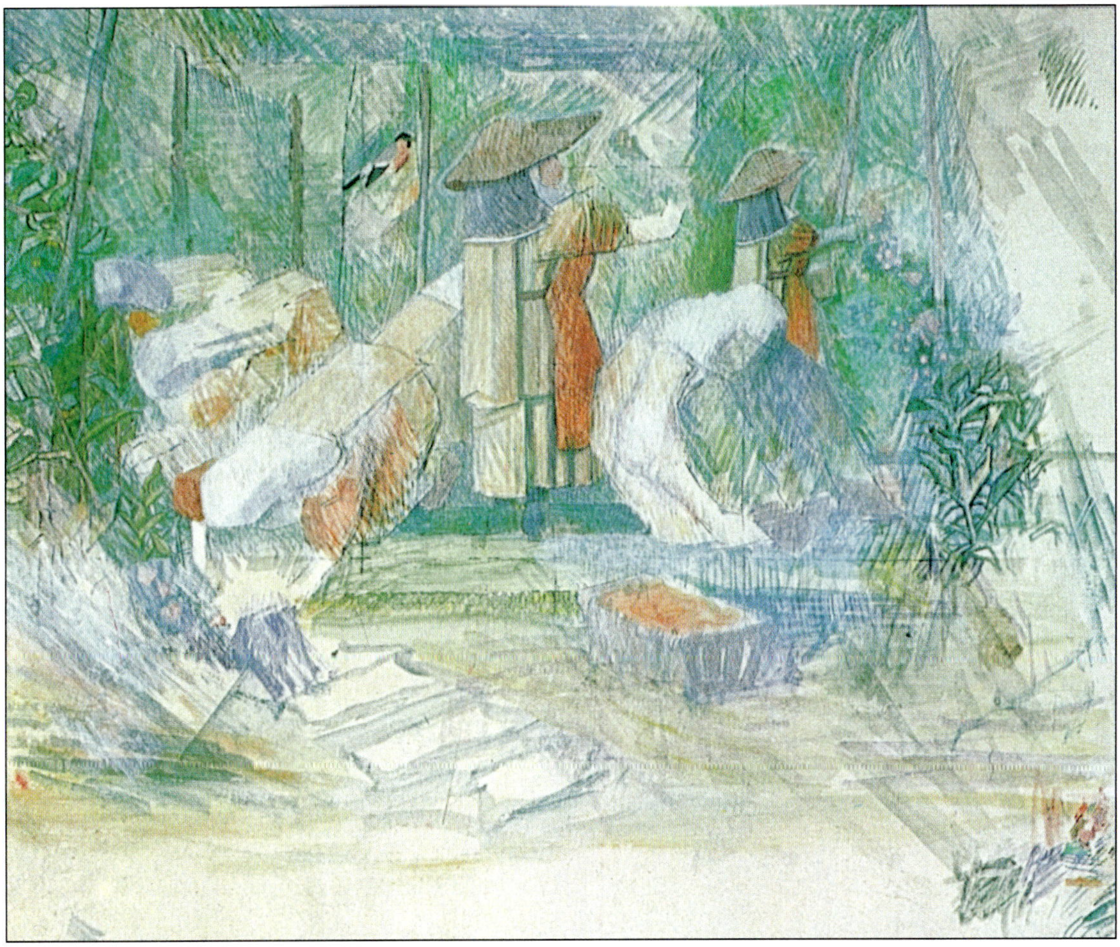

Here the artist is putting in a cool underpainting in terre verte. Note the directional strokes and the light touch required.

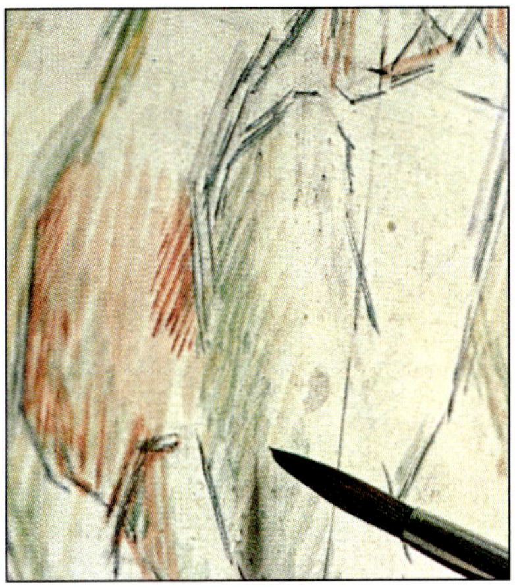

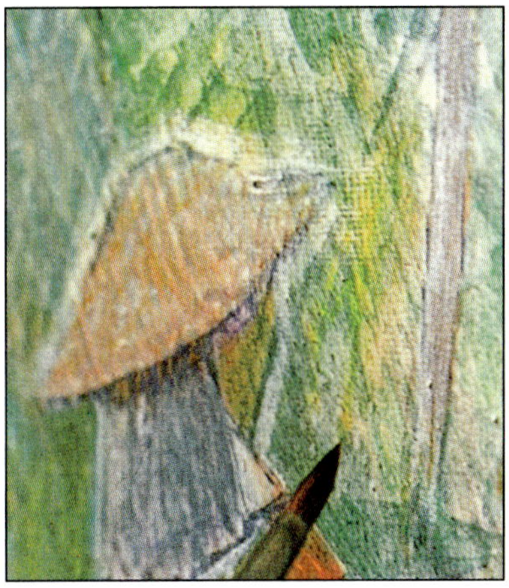

At a more advanced stage, white mixed with yolk can be used to tone down previous color areas. White can also be used to correct and rework, but the color laid over this will lose some of its translucence in the process.

GALLERY

THE BEAUTY OF TEMPERA

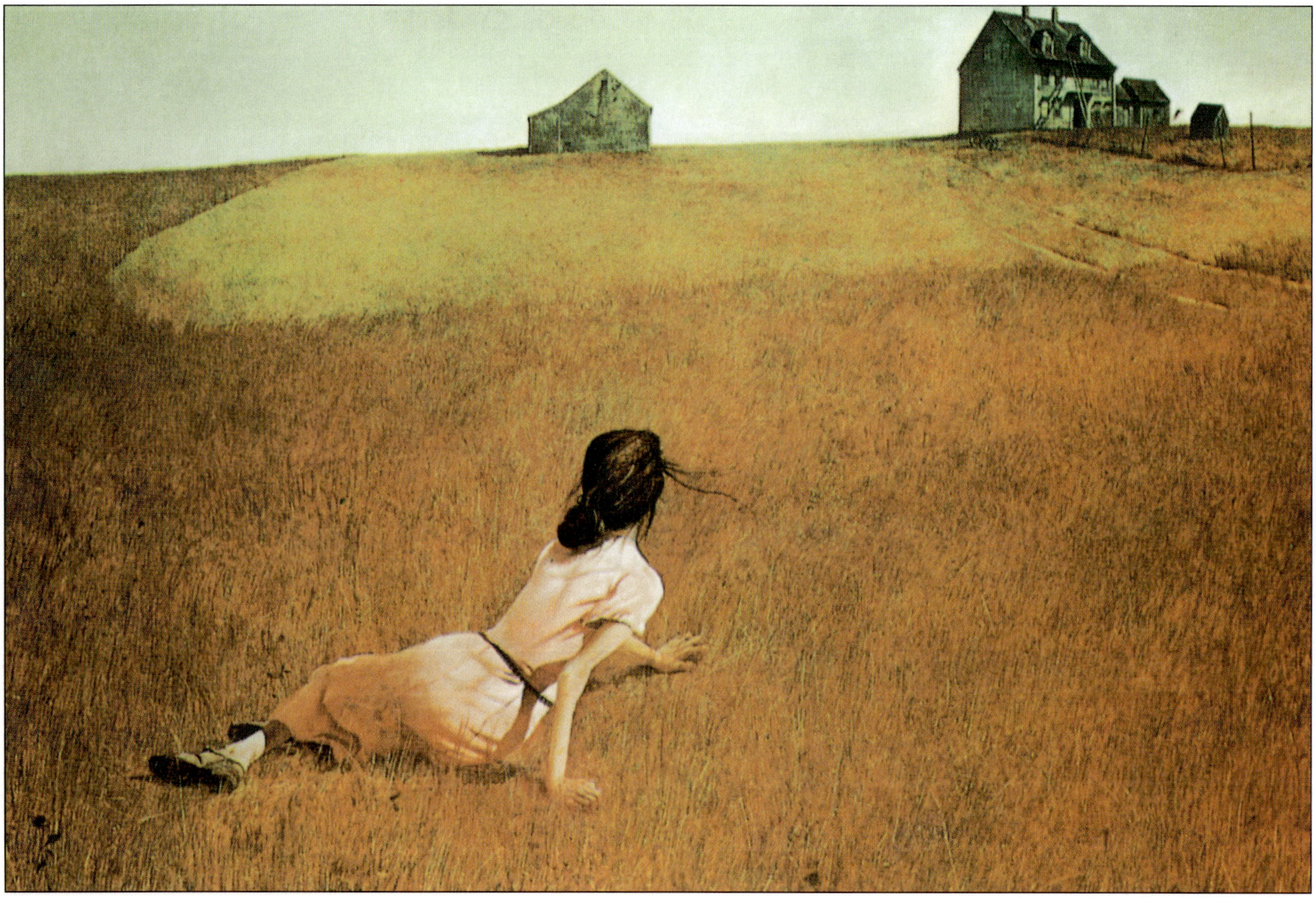

CHRISTINA'S WORLD by Andrew Wyeth

Wyeth is best known for his tempera paintings. The luminosity of the painting and the fine working of the detail is offset by the pale wash of the sky that reveals the gesso ground.

THE OLD AND THE NEW

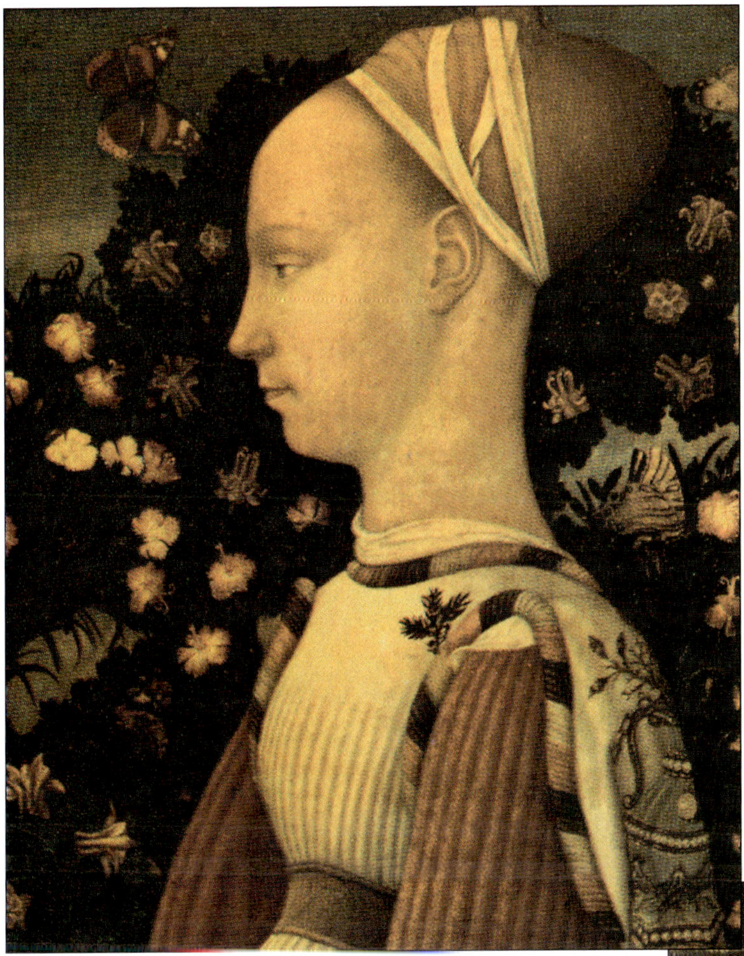

A PRINCESS OF THE HOUSE OF ESTE by Pisanello (c.1395–c.1455)

Also known as Antonio Pisano, the artist was a prime exponent of the international Gothic style that was prevalent in some parts of Europe in the early-fifteenth century. This portrait, painted in tempera in about 1443, is a good example of the style. Intricately noted butterflies and flowers set into the darkness of the bush provide a mysterious but pretty setting.

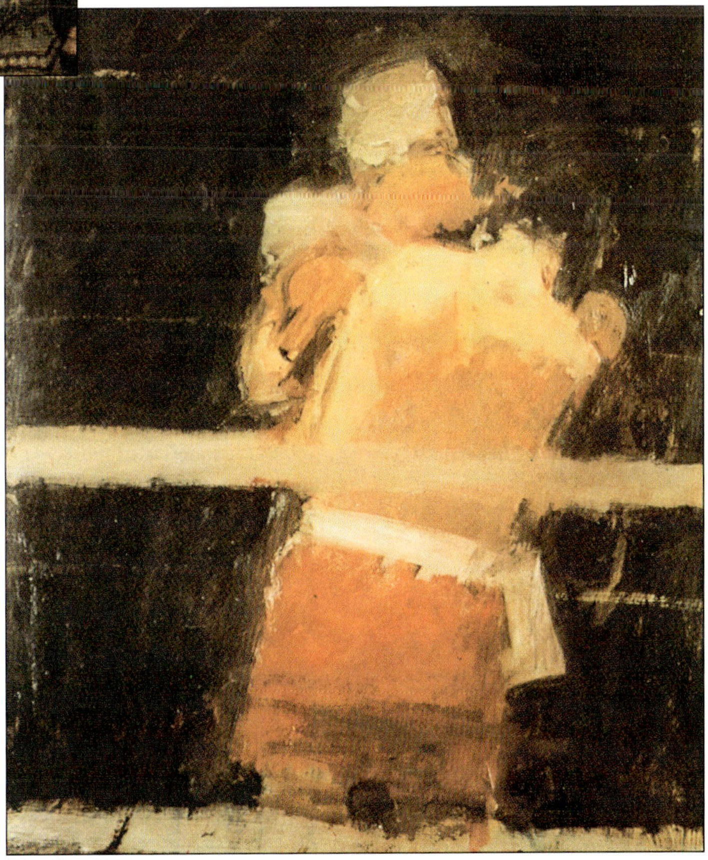

THE BOXERS

This modern painting shows the effectiveness of large blocks of tempera color combined with acrylic.

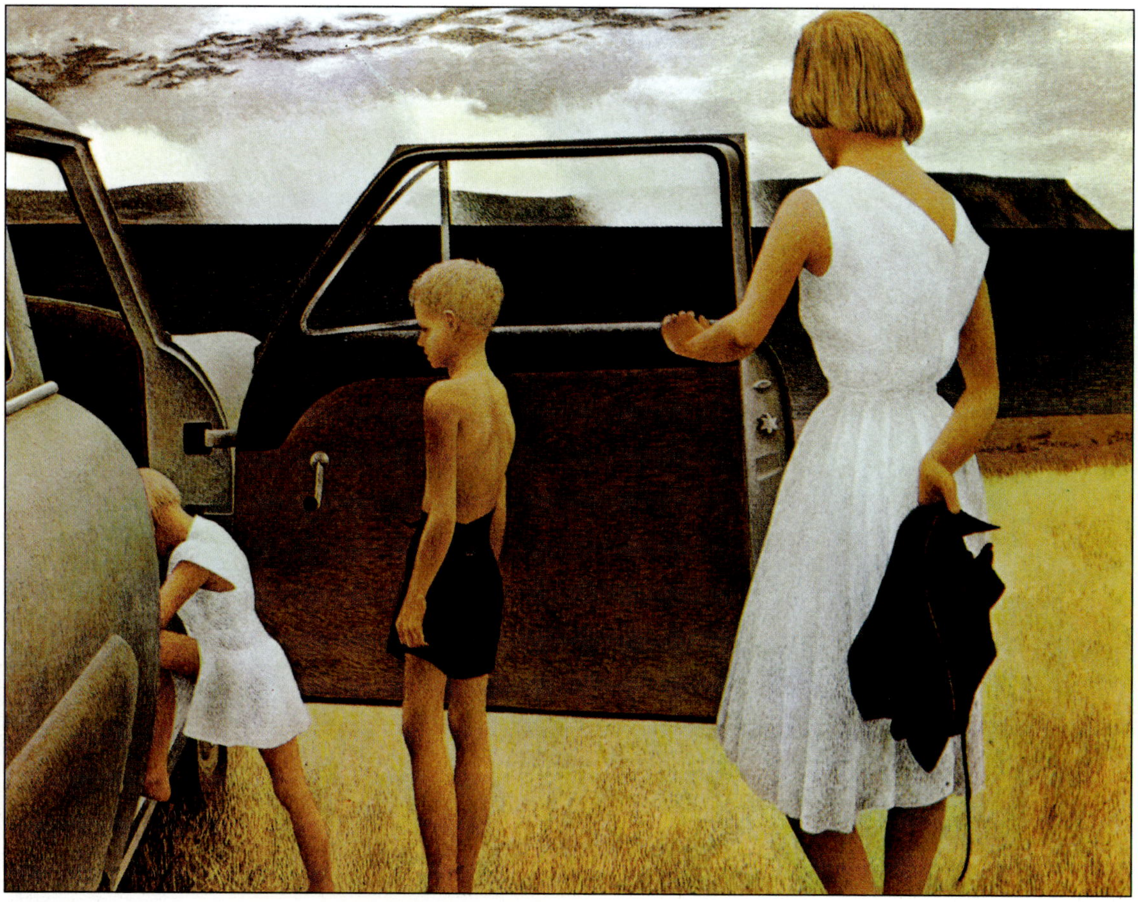

FAMILY AND RAINSTORM by David Alexander Colville (b.1920).

This painting, on a board support and almost photographic in its treatment of the subject, demonstrates the versatility of tempera, one of the earliest types of paint media. The cool colors, gray, yellow, and brown, have a smooth, opaque quality which help to create the sense of stillness and the monumentality of the figures.

PASTELS

There must be a few artists who have not wanted to try their hand at painting with pastels at some time or other – but why? What is the appeal of this increasingly popular medium?

Perhaps one reason is the beauty of the pastels themselves. Unlike paints, that hide their colors in metal tubes, pastels are not shy about displaying their charms. When you open up a fresh box of pastels, your eyes are met by a riot of sumptuous color so that you can hardly wait to begin painting. The allure of pastels not only tempts the eye, it beckons to the hand as well; there is something very attractive about the feel of the pastel stick in one's hands. Unlike paints, but like all drawing media, pastels offer the satisfaction of immediate contact with the paper; the crayon is so easy to manipulate that it feels almost like an extension of your fingers. Perhaps this sense of immediacy touches a deeper instinct, a far older and more primitive urge to create meaningful and lasting marks for others to see. It is the same impulse demonstrated by children when they pick up a piece of chalk to draw on a wall or pavement.

The main differences between pastels and paints is that you cannot premix colors; any mixing is done by laying one color over another on the painting surface. To compensate for this limitation, manufacturers produce large ranges of colors and "tints," i.e. light and dark versions of the same color. Tints are made by adding white to the pure pigment for the pale tones and black for the dark ones.

The colors are given names that usually, but not always, correspond with the pigment name. Certain pigments cannot be used for pastels because they may pose a health risk, so you may find a red labeled "bright red" rather than vermilion or cadmium red. The tints are usually denoted by a number, from 1 to 6 or more. Manufacturers' numbering systems vary, but in most cases the lower numbers are paler tints, with the darker tints at the top of the scale and the pure color in the middle.

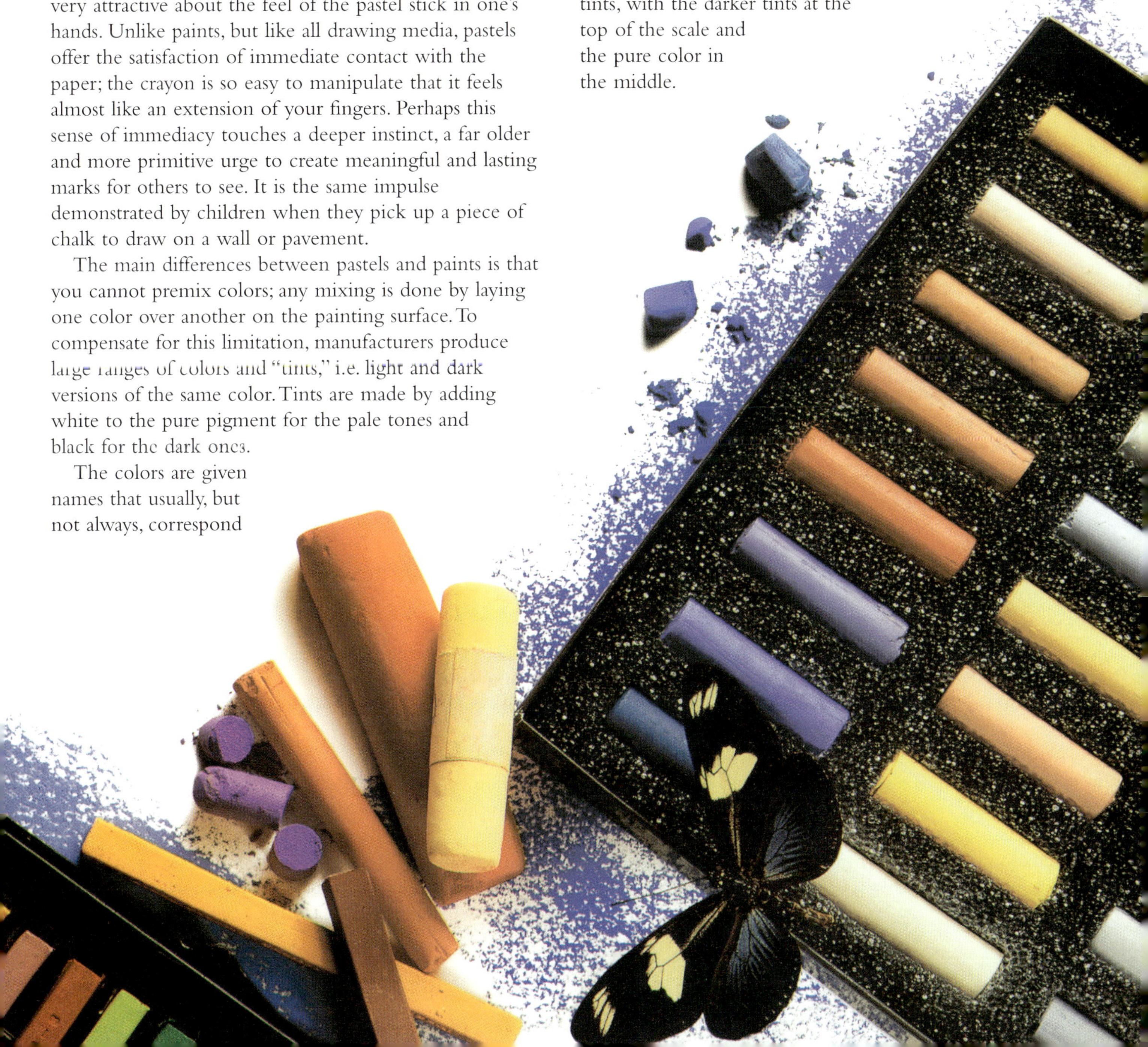

The Pleasure of Pastels

Because pastel is such a rapid and responsive medium, it is ideal for recording the fleeting, transitory effects so often found in nature. Melting mists, scudding clouds, crashing waves – all these can be captured with a few rapid, decisive strokes. There are no colors to be pre-mixed, no drying times to worry about, no brushes to be kept clean – in short, no tiresome procedures to dampen your enthusiasm or dull your response to the subject.

The unique quality of pastels is their versatility; they can be used as both a drawing and a painting medium. Simply by twisting and turning the crayon, using the tip and then the side, you can create several different effects – fine, precise lines; broad, sweeping strokes and solid, dense layers of color – and these can be combined in an almost infinite number of ways. Thus pastel is equally appropriate for highly finished, complex studies and for rapid impressions.

The colors are not only immensely varied, from soft, delicate tints to bright, vibrant hues and rich, deep darks, they are also extremely pure and luminous, due in part to the way in which light reflects off the myriad particles on the surface of the painting. Furthermore, pastel colors remain fresh and lively from the start, and do not change color when applied, unlike watercolor, for example, that appears much paler when dry, or oil paints that sink into the canvas, and can darken or even crack with age.

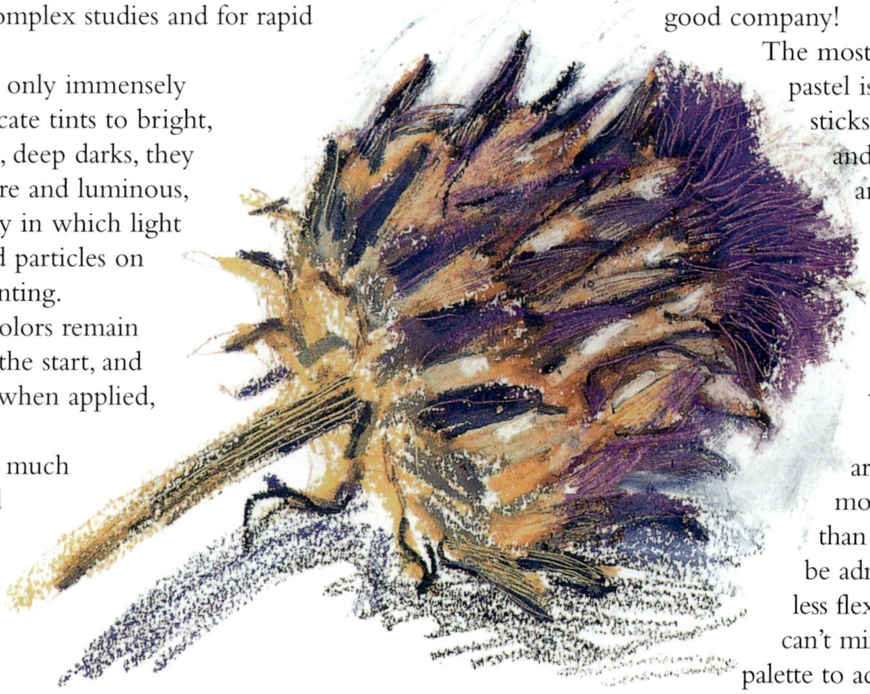

On the purely practical level, pastels are simple and convenient to use. You don't need much in the way of extra equipment such as brushes, knives, and mixing mediums, and no preparation of the painting surface is necessary, as it is for oil and watercolor. Just lay out your pastels and you're ready to start, and when you're finished, all you need to do is put away your pastels – there are no brushes to clean, no palette to scrape, and no need to cover up the pigments to stop them drying out.

Of course, pastel does have its drawbacks, too – what medium doesn't? One of the great masters of pastel painting, Quentin de la Tour (1704–1788) once wrote to a friend: "Pastels, my Lord Marquis, involve a number of further obstacles such as dust, the weakness of some pigments, the fact that the tone is never correct, and that one must blend one's colors on the paper itself and apply a number of strokes with different crayons instead of one, that there is a risk of spoiling the work done and that no one expedient of its spirit is lost." So if you do encounter difficulties with the medium, take heart – you're in good company!

The most obvious drawback to pastel is its fragility. The sticks sometimes crumble and break under pressure, and a pastel painting is vulnerable to accidental smudging and smearing if it is not mounted under glass or protected with fixative.

Also, though pastels are easier to handle and more immediate in use than oil paints are, it has to be admitted that they are less flexible. For example, you can't mix pigments on the palette to achieve just the right color or tone – you must work with a pre-existing range of tints, creating special color effects directly on the paper. Similarly, mistakes are easily rectified in oils and to some extent acrylics, by wiping out with a rag or simply overpainting the offending area, but in pastel they require more careful treatment because the surface can easily become clogged, smeared, or damaged.

Finally, because pastel is both a drawing and a painting medium, the ability of the artist to draw confidently and well is more important than in some other media. Weak drawing can, to a certain extent, be masked in oil painting; but in pastel the marks made by the artist's hand remain visible and unchanging, so you have to get them right first time.

Pastel Types

hard pastels

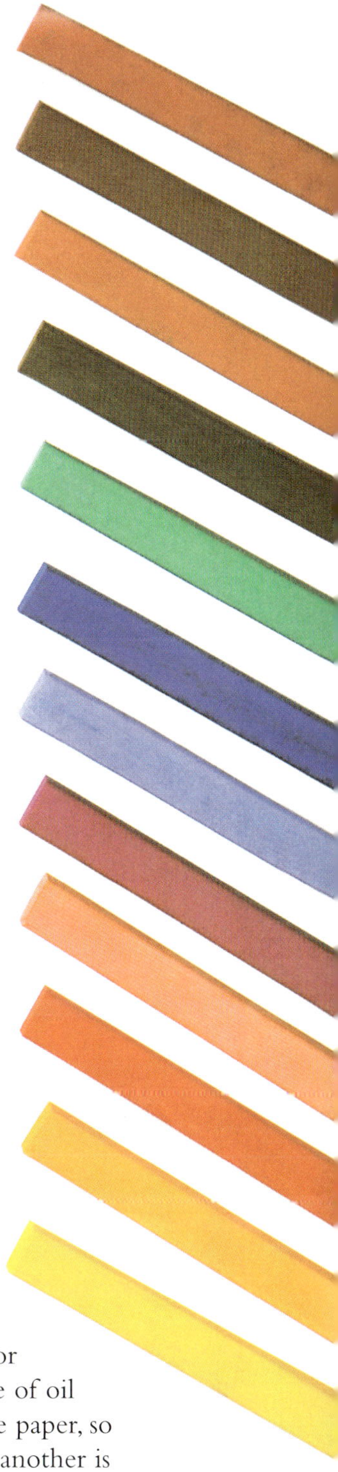

SOFT PASTELS

The basic ingredients of pastels are ground pigments and a binder that holds the pigment particles together. They are mixed to form a stiff paste, which is then compressed into round- or square-sectioned sticks and allowed to dry. Soft pastels have a high proportion of pigment to binder, hence the ease with which they transfer color to the support and the brilliance and rich texture of the colors. Soft pastels may also include white chalk, or a similar filler, which gives luminosity to bright hues and pale tints.

The color ranges vary with the manufacturer, and there is no standard identification of the pigments. Some of the high-quality pastel ranges have literally hundreds of colors, including pure hues together with lighter and darker tones of each individual hue – these may be identified by numerical codes that signify related color values. This abundance of colors acknowledges the directness of pastel as a painting medium – deprived of the ability to mix colors infinitely as you can with paint, you are offered a palette of pastels that would enable you to vary the color of every stroke. Other good brands provide slightly less color variation, but all are likely to meet your requirements more than adequately.

The loose, grainy texture of soft pastels provides great color clarity, but it is also the reason why many people find pastels difficult to use. The powdery color can seem to spread uncontrollably, and it is aggravating when a fragile pastel stick snaps or crumbles in the middle of a stroke. This can lead to a cautious approach, but the best results come from working freely and decisively.

HARD PASTELS

These have a greater proportion of binder to pigment, so they are more stable in use than soft pastels, but do not have such wide potential for varied surface effects. Traditionally, they are used for preliminary sketching out of a composition, and for adding linear detail and "sharpening" touches to soft pastel work – in effect, hard pastels are the drawing medium that complements soft pastels as a painting medium. You can exploit the linear qualities by using the section edge of the stick, or even sharpening it to a point by shaving it with a fine blade, but there are also several techniques you can use to develop effects of massed color, such as shading, hatching, and crosshatching. The color range is quite limited by comparison with soft pastels, with nothing like the degrees of variation in hue or tone.

PASTEL PENCILS

These are thin sticks of pastel encased in wood, and come in a relatively limited color range. The "leads" are typically harder than soft pastels, although they may also be somewhat softer than hard pastels. Their main advantage is that they are clean to use and easy to control. As with hard pastels, you can make use of their linear qualities to add crisp finishing touches to a rendering mainly worked in soft pastels.

OIL PASTELS

This medium is unique among the pastel types, containing an oil binder that makes the texture dense and greasy and the colors slightly less opaque than soft pastels. Typically, the colors are quite strong and the variation of color values is restricted. The moist texture of oil pastel can quickly fill the grain of the paper, so the capacity to work one color over another is somewhat limited, but for painting effects, oil pastel marks can be softened and spread by brushing them with turpentine or white spirit.

soft pastels

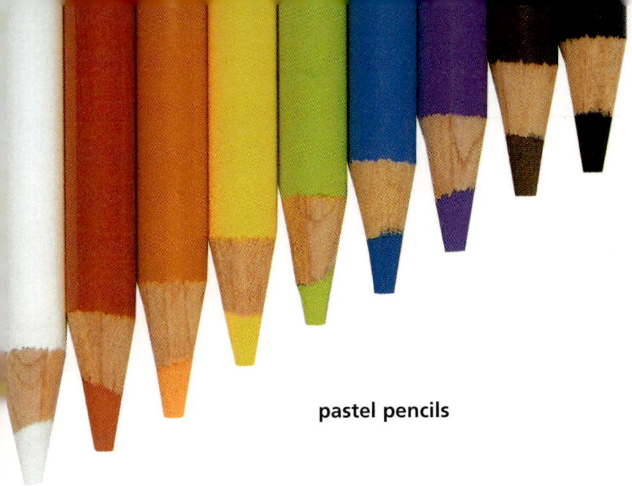

pastel pencils

WATER-SOLUBLE PASTELS

The wax content of these color sticks gives them a slightly moist texture, so that they handle rather like oil pastels when you use them for drawn strokes. But brush over the color with clean water, and it instantly dissolves into an even, semi-transparent wash. The quality of the wet color is like a coarse watercolor wash. You can vary it considerably according to the amount of water that you add – for instance, with a barely wetted brush you can spread the color tint while retaining a strong impression of the linear marks.

The restricted color range is composed of strong, unsubtle hues, but with the potential fluidity of the medium you have more scope for mixing and blending colors on the working surface.

CHOOSING YOUR COLORS

In oil and watercolor painting you need only a dozen or so pigment colors on your palette, from which you can mix a vast range of hues, tints, and shades. With pastels you cannot mix new colors as you work; almost every color, and every tint or shade of that color, requires a separate pastel stick. This explains why there are literally dozens of different colors available in pastels, and each separate color comes in a range of up to eight shades, from light to dark.

From this bewildering array of colors, how do you choose a manageable quantity to suit your needs, without incurring too much expense? My advice is to start by thinking about what sort of subjects you like to paint, and choose your palette of colors accordingly. If your subject is landscapes, obviously you'll need a lot of greens and earth colors; for portraits, a range of flesh tones plus a few extra colors for the sitters' clothing; and if you're a flower painter, you can really go to town on bright, vibrant colors. Even so, you will always need a selection of neutral colors for the shadows and highlights, such as a range of grays and beiges.

Add to these black, white, and a few "workhorse" colors such as yellow ocher, burnt sienna, and caput mortuum, and you'll have a good basic range to start with. But don't forget, whichever colors you select you will need at least three shades of each color (a light, middle, and dark tone). So if you choose a palette of say 20 colors, you will in fact need 40 to 60 sticks of color. Some dedicated pastellists have literally hundreds of pastel sticks at their disposal!

CLEANING YOUR PASTELS

Pastel is not a medium for those who like to keep their hands clean. Maurice Quentin de la Tour complained about the tendency of his "colored dust," as he called it, to spread everywhere, and certainly it would be most unwise to use pastel in a carpeted room. But we can wash our hands and use vacuum cleaners after a working session; a more annoying problem is that the dust from one color gets onto all the others in your pastel box, and soon they are all unrecognizable. You can avoid this to some extent by laying them out on beds of ground rice, that absorb some of the dust, but you may still need to clean them from time to time, again using ground rice, as shown here.

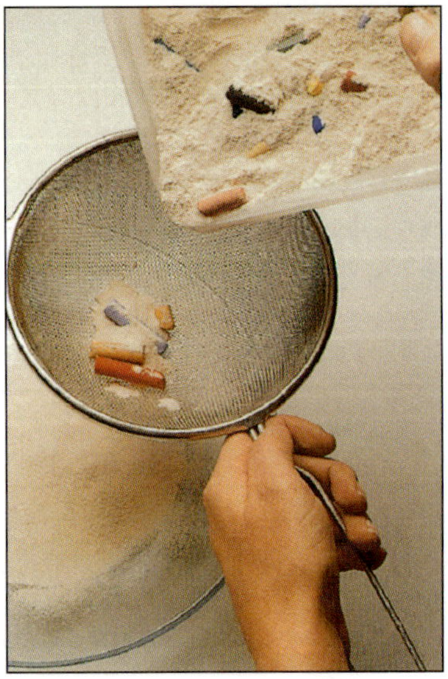

water-soluble pastels

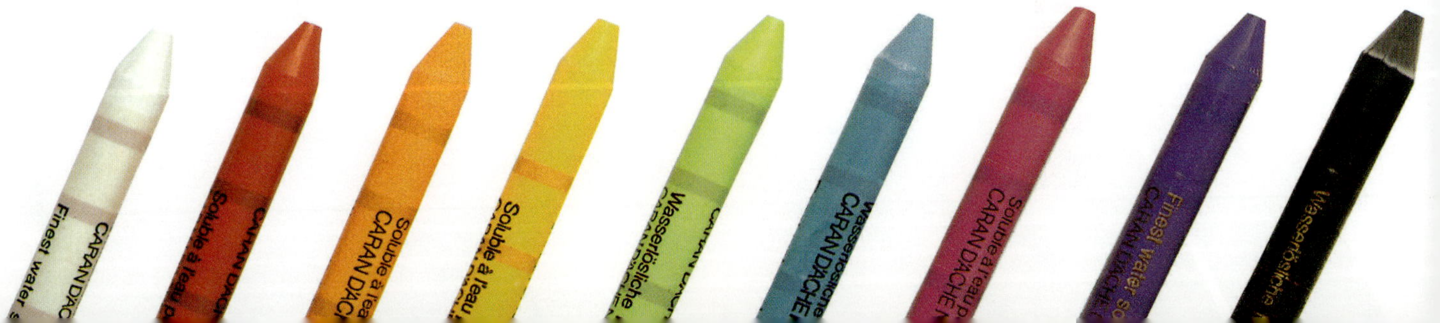

A Recommended Starter Palette

The 26 colors shown here provide a range of values suitable for most subjects, of course you can add more as you need them.

Many beginning artists start with one of the small boxed sets produced especially for newcomers to the medium. If it does not include black, for example, or has only one red, you may need to buy these colors separately.

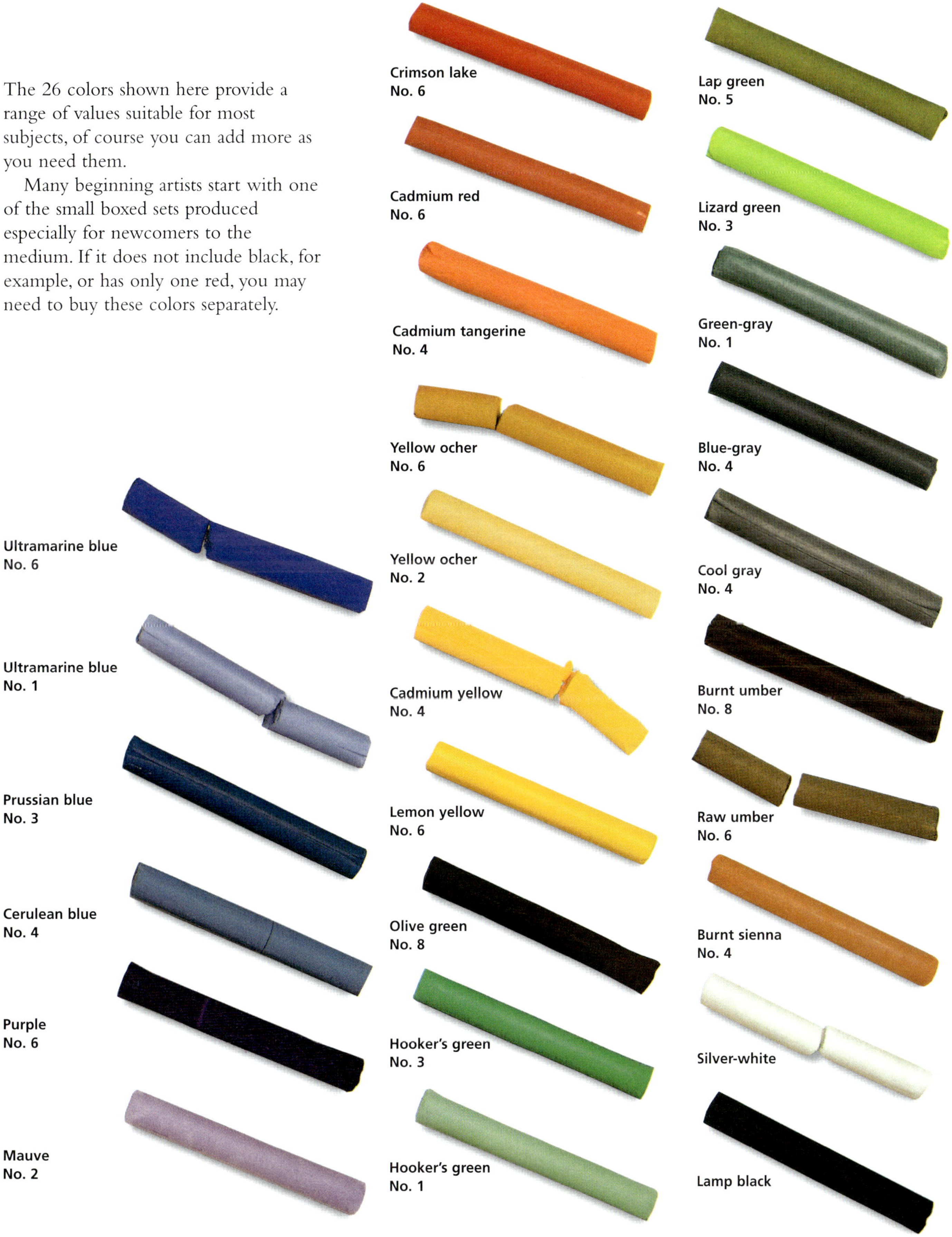

Surfaces

A pastel painting is very much a marriage of pastel and paper. The two work side by side, creating an exciting fusion of texture and color that is unmatched in any other medium. Whatever surface you choose to work on, there are three factors that should always be borne in mind when making that choice. These are: tooth (how rough or smooth the paper's surface is); tone (how light or dark the paper is); and color (whether warm, cool, or neutral).

TOOTH

Whereas an aqueous medium works by actually sinking into the surface of the paper and staining it, pastel more or less sits on the surface. If that surface were as smooth as glass, the pastel pigment would soon start to flake off, since it would have nothing to adhere to. That's why, if you examine a sheet of pastel paper under a strong light, you will see that its surface is pitted rather than smooth. The expression "tooth" refers to these tiny ridges and hollows in the surface, whose purpose is to "bite" the particles of pastel as the crayon is stroked across the paper and then hold them in place.

Rough papers have more tooth than smooth papers do, and the kind you choose depends on the techniques you want to use and the effect you want to obtain. Both types, however, must contain size, and should be fairly thick and of a good quality.

COLOR

Pastel paper is available in a wide range of colors – so wide, in fact, that it can be confusing for a beginner. But it's most important that you make a considered choice, especially if you intend leaving areas of the paper showing through to contribute to the overall color scheme.

On the whole it's best to avoid strongly colored papers since they will fight with the colors in the painting and create a harsh, gaudy effect. If you are in any doubt, remember that you can't go wrong with muted colors such as grays, greens, and browns.

TONE

Having decided on the color of your paper, you now need to consider whether it should be of a light, medium, or dark tone. "Tone" refers to the relative lightness or darkness of the paper, regardless of what its actual color is. For example, the Canson range of papers contains, among other colors, several tones of gray: No. 343 Pearl is light in tone, No. 345 Dark Gray is dark in tone; No. 429 felt Gray is middle in tone. Your choice of tone will depend to a large extent on how light or how dark the subject is. ***Light-toned papers*** are best when you want to emphasize the dark tones and colors in a painting. Pale tones and colors generally don't show up well on a light-toned paper.

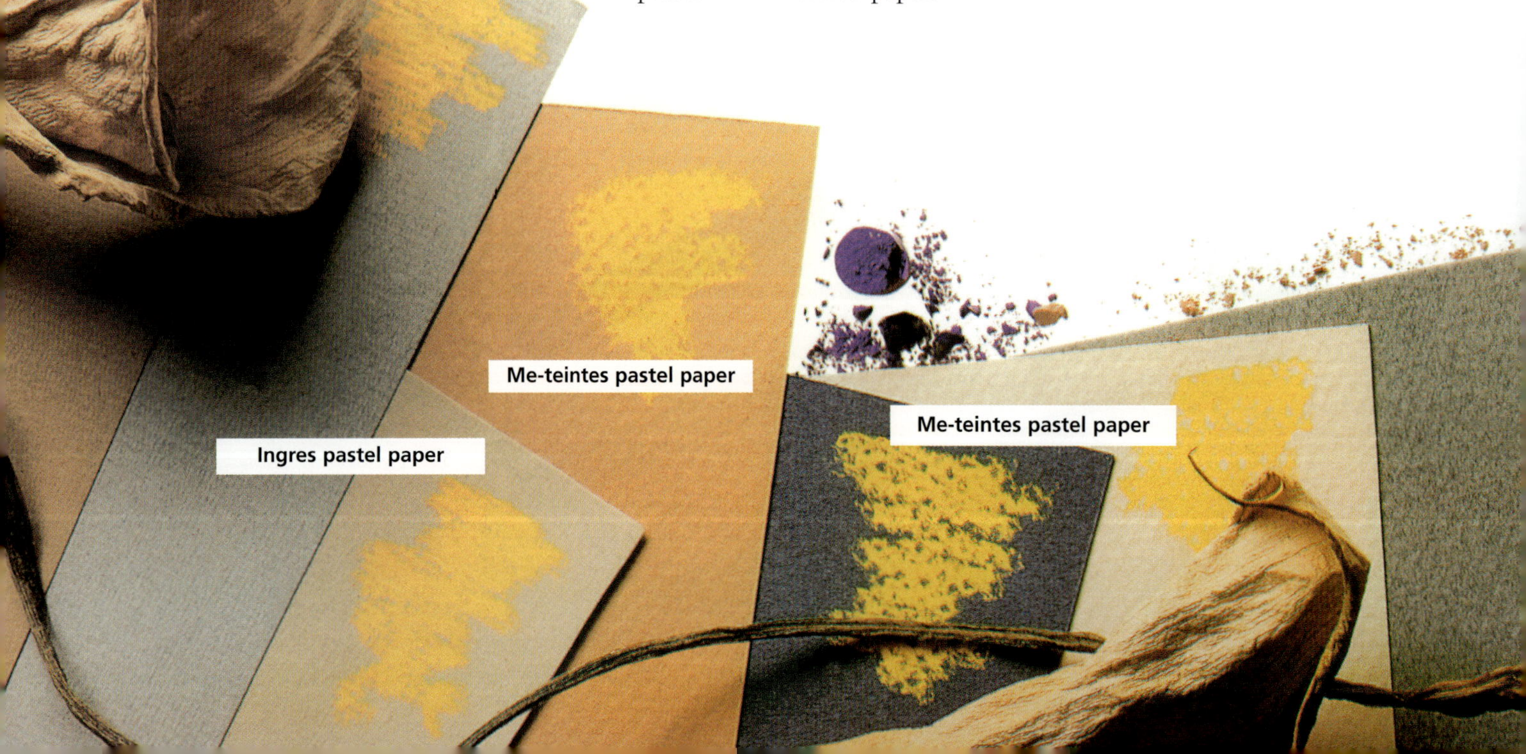

Middle-toned papers are the most popular, particularly with beginners. They allow you to judge both the light and the dark tones in your painting accurately, and they provide a quiet, harmonious backdrop to most colors.

Dark-toned papers are the most difficult to use effectively. They are used when the light areas of the painting are to be emphasized, but in some cases they can make the lights look over-assertive.

OTHER SURFACES

In addition to the papers made specifically for pastel painting, there are a number of other surfaces which are worth experimenting with.

Watercolor paper is suitable for pastel painting, so long as it is a rough-textured one, such as Strathmore papers or Fabriano Swedish Tumba. A smooth, or hot pressed, paper is not suitable because it is too smooth for pastels. It's best to tone watercolor paper before painting. This is because white paper doesn't show the vibrant colors of pastel to their best advantage – it makes them look darker than they actually are. Also, a toned paper makes it easier to judge the tones and intensities of your colors.

Charcoal paper is an inexpensive alternative for rough sketches and experimental work. However, it is rather thin and fragile, and you may find its regular, linear surface texture less than sympathetic.

Fine sandpaper has an interesting grainy texture and provides a very good buff middle tone which is suitable for most subjects. The texture grips the particles of color well, and there is enough resistance to the drawn line to make it very pleasant to work on and give the strokes authority. With its rough surface, sandpaper is well suited to a bold, vigorous approach, though both blending and covering large areas are more difficult.

The disadvantages of sandpaper are that it shaves off the pastel fairly rapidly, making it an expensive surface to work on; mistakes are not easily erased without resorting to a knife or razor blade which could damage the paper's surface; and it can be hard on the knuckles if you hold them too close to the paper!

Pastel boards (pastel paper mounted on board by the manufacturer) are available in a range of sizes and finishes, from soft velour to hard and gritty. Some artists prefer the firm resistance of a board, and boards are certainly less likely to bend and buckle than paper.

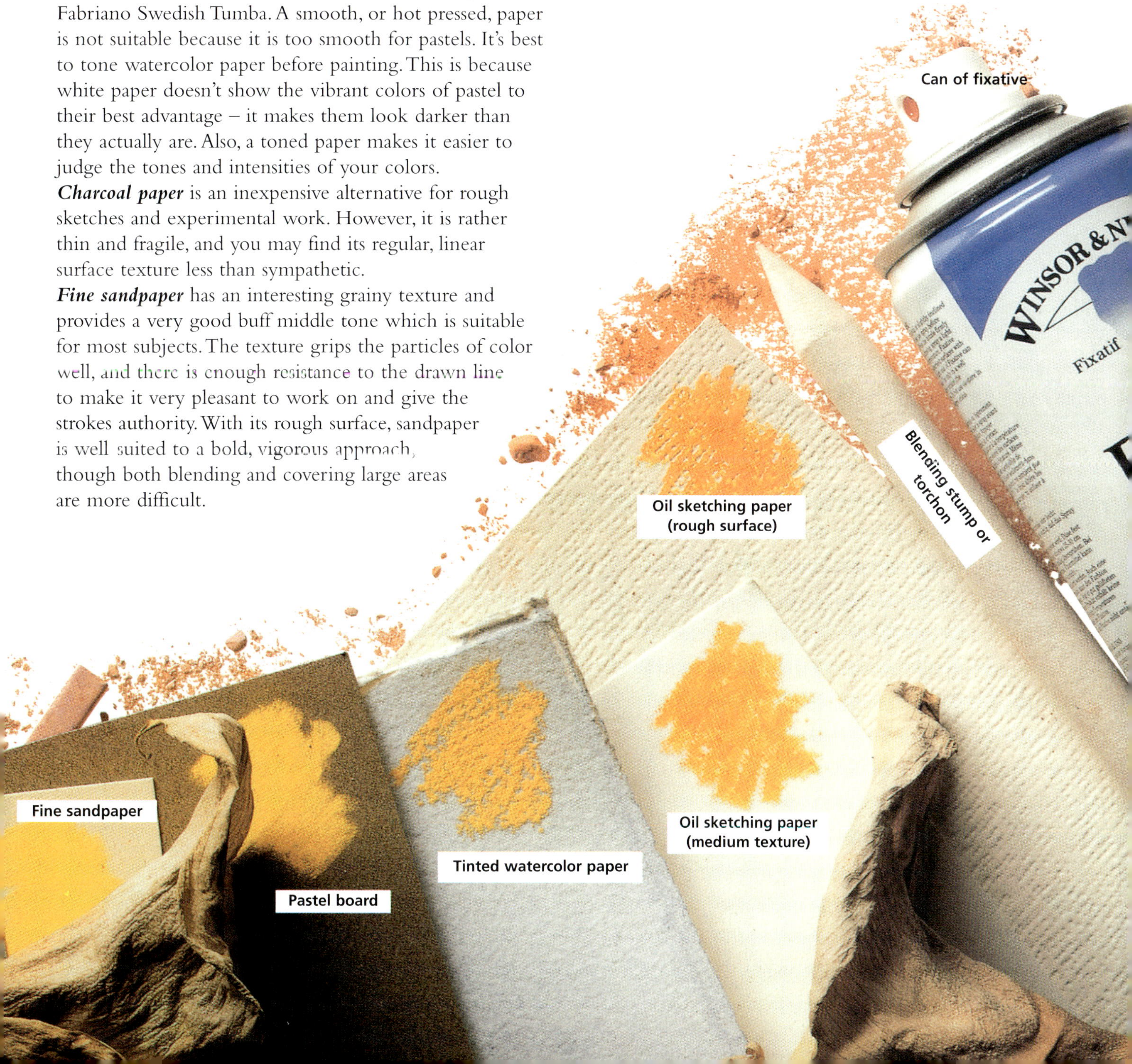

Equipment

One of the many attractions of pastel work is that you don't need much equipment; the basic requirements are pastels and paper. However, there are a few items useful to have on hand before you begin painting.

The first is something to support the paper. You don't have to go to the expense of buying a ready-made drawing board; most of the boards sold as building material are usable – plywood, masonite, or smooth-surfaced particle board.

If you work on a large scale, consider buying an easel. And since you won't want to dirty the floor, you will need some kind of ground cover such as a drop cloth or even an old sheet.

Rags for cleaning your hands periodically are essential – pastel is a messy medium. Rags are also useful for blending. You should have a tortillon and some cotton swabs handy for blending in small areas, and a kneadable eraser for correcting errors. The final item is fixative. There is nothing worse than smudging a completed painting with your hand, and fixative will help to prevent this. Take it on location, and fix your work before carrying it home.

TOOLS FOR ERASING

A pastel painting loses its freshness and looks dead when it is overworked, so if you are going to have second thoughts, you should have them at an early stage when there is not too much pastel on the page. Erasing can also spoil the surface texture of the paper, so should be done with care. After erasing, a light spray of fixative will facilitate further reworking.

Razor blades (the single-edged type) should be used to scrape away pastel particles before finishing off with an eraser. Hold the blade flat against the paper and scrape lightly, no more than two or three times. Razor blades are also used for sharpening pastel crayons.

Kneadable erasers are useful because they can be pinched into a small point for erasing small areas (a small piece of kneaded white bread also works well). Never rub pastel with an eraser – it will make the surface turn slick and greasy. Press the eraser firmly against the offending area and lift the pastel particles away. The eraser should be kept clean by wiping it frequently on scrap paper.

Bristle brushes (the kind used in oil painting) are the kindest way to brush away pastel particles in those areas that haven't been heavily worked. The loose particles should then be lifted off with an eraser.

Torchons (paper stumps) are narrow tubes of rolled blotting paper used for blending colors. You can use your fingertip just as easily, but tortillons are rigid and pointed at the tip, so are good for small, fiddly areas. They also minimize the risk of grease from your skin spoiling the surface of the painting.

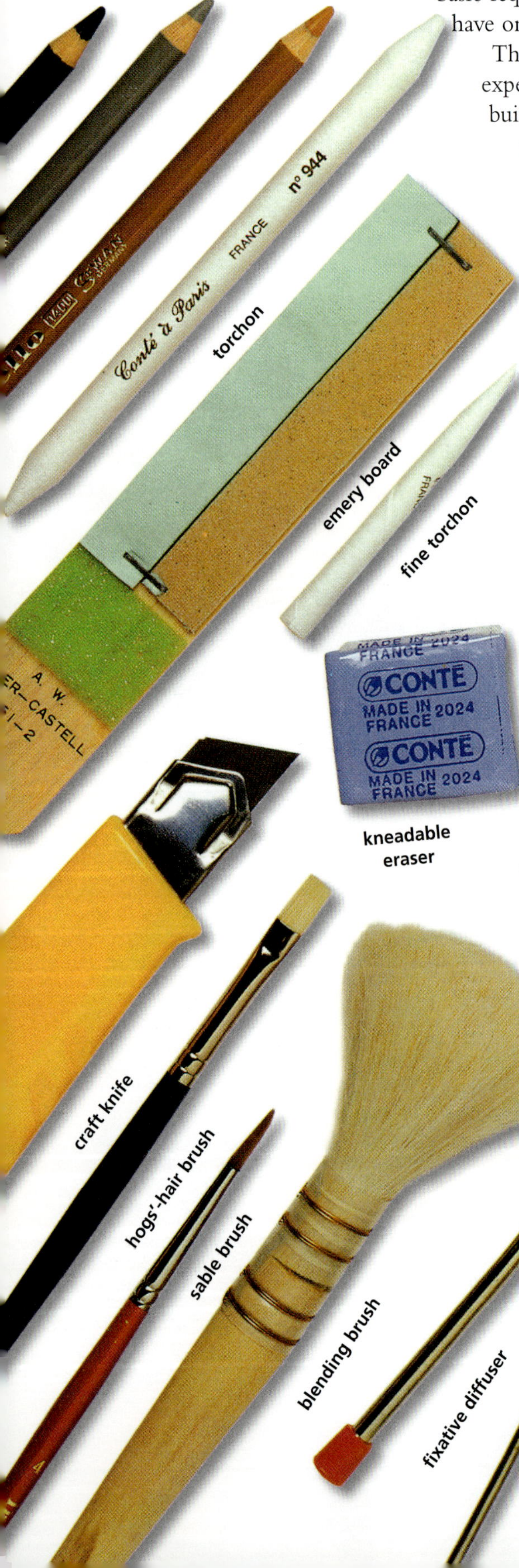

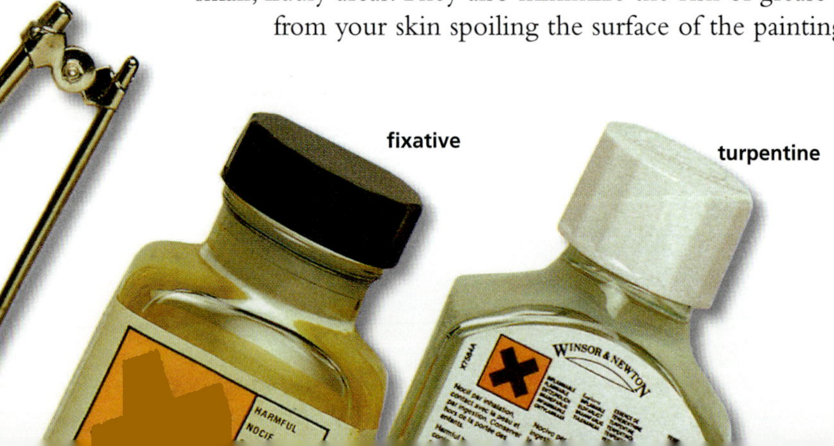

LINEAR STROKES

Much can be learned by experimenting with linear strokes in pastel. You don't have to draw actual objects, though you may like to make gestural strokes which resemble the shapes of leaves, clouds, or waves. Otherwise, you can simply make abstract doodles – anything, in fact, that helps you to get the feel of the medium. The main thing is to keep your mind relaxed and your drawing wrist supple, and just "ride with it," as they say. At first, the marks you make may be tight and stilted, but gradually you'll become less self-conscious and more eager to experiment, and soon you'll begin to recognize the type of strokes that most appeal to you – the ones that express your own personality.

Pastel is a particularly expressive medium to draw with. Use the sharpened point of the crayon, or alternatively snap a hard pastel in two and use the sharp corners to make fine lines. When one corner wears down, simply turn the crayon to find a new one. By twisting and turning the crayon you can create a range of thick and thin lines, and by varying the pressure of the strokes you can create tonal gradations from light to dark. Try making different kinds of lines – precise, patient ones; and sweeping curves. Use both hard and soft pastels, and try them on rough- and smooth-textured papers. A soft pastel on smooth paper glides effortlessly, leaving behind it a satiny trail of vibrant color; the same pastel used on rough paper gives a splattered, irregular line because the tooth of the paper breaks up the color and leaves tiny dots of paper showing.

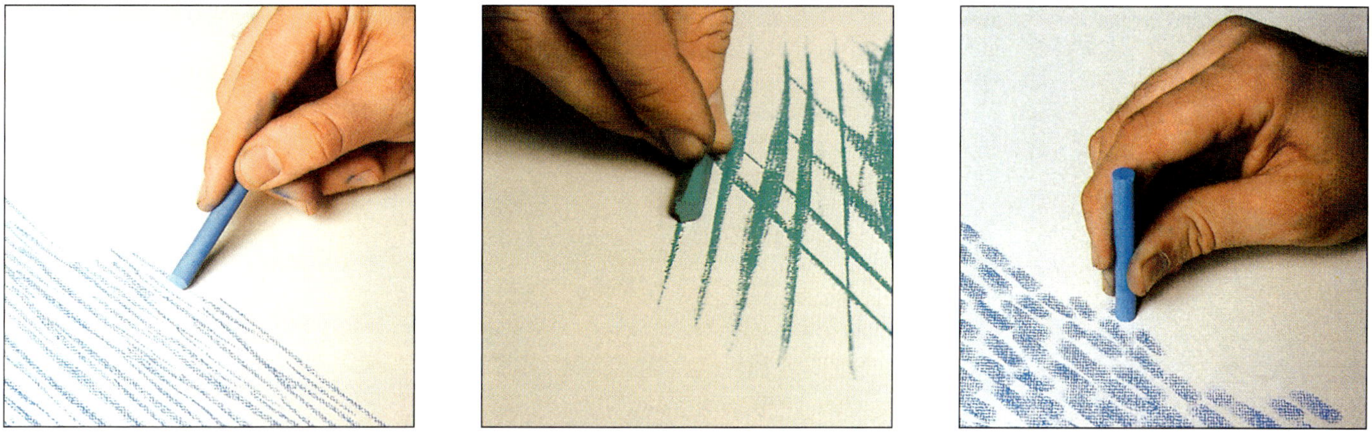

The examples above show the variety of different linear strokes that can be made by holding the pastel stick in different ways. Practise by just doodling, using both hard and soft pastels, until you find the type of stroke that suits you.

SIDE STROKES

Having experimented with the tip of the pastel crayon, you're now ready to try one of the most beautiful and expressive strokes in pastel painting – the side stroke. For this, you'll need a short length of pastel – anywhere between 1/2 in. (1.25 cm) and 2 in. (5 cm) long (so hang onto your broken pieces). Using the entire length of the side of the crayon, press it against the paper and make swift, sweeping strokes across the page.

Numerous effects can be achieved with side strokes by varying the pressure on the crayon and using different movements of the wrist. Heavy pressure forces more pastel particles into the tooth of the paper to create a solid, dense quality. When applied lightly, the tooth of the paper shows through the color, creating a random, broken texture that seems to scintillate with light. As you work, you will soon see the importance of the tooth and the color of the paper, both of which have a direct influence on the finished effect. Try it with hard and soft pastels, and on different grades of paper; work with dark colors on a light ground and vice versa; vary the pressure from hard to soft within a single stroke to see how it creates a gradation in tone from dark to light. Be inquisitive – the knowledge you gain will stand you in good stead when you later come to paint pictures.

Side strokes are excellent for covering large areas in a painting, such as the background in a portrait. When used on rough paper, the grainy effect produced can be used to suggest specific textures, such as tree bark, woven fabric, or perhaps a pebbly beach. However, bear in mind that this technique works best when used judiciously and as a contrast to linear work: the attractiveness of side strokes can lead you to use them too much, resulting in the weak, "cotton candy" sort of image that has unfortunately given pastel painting rather a bad name in the past.

BLENDING

In traditional methods of pastel painting, particularly as applied to portraiture, colors were smoothed and blended together to produce images with a high degree of surface finish comparable to the effects of contemporary oil painting techniques. To the modern eye, much of the medium's impact comes from the grainy, rough textures of pastel and loose networks of individual pastel strokes. But the subtleties of blended colors and smooth gradation of hues and tones are vital elements in rendering specific materials and surface qualities – soft fabrics, for instance, or uniform, reflective surfaces such as metal and glass – and atmospheric impressions. Blended colors also provide visual contrast when integrated with loose pastel strokes and broken color in a composition.

The special tool for blending soft pastels is a torchon – a tight roll of paper that is shaped like a pencil and used in the same way – you "shade" into the pastel strokes with the tip or side of the torchon to spread and blend the powdery color. You obtain a clean point on the torchon by unwinding some of the paper from the tip. A torchon enables you to control the blending quite precisely, and is thus ideal for small areas. Alternatively, you can use your fingers, a cotton swab, tissues or a rag, or a brush (soft-textured fabrics and brushes will lift some of the color).

COLOR GRADATIONS

In nature, you will find a variety of edges, some defined and some gradual. In some, one color or tone will end and another begin as in a dark leaf against a sky, but more often, they merge gradually one into the other. Think of a hazy sunset sky, for example, in which blue fades imperceptibly into yellow, then into shades of pink, orange, and red as it nears the horizon. In a pastel painting, you can achieve this effect by laying in bands of color using side strokes and then blending together the edges where the colors meet.

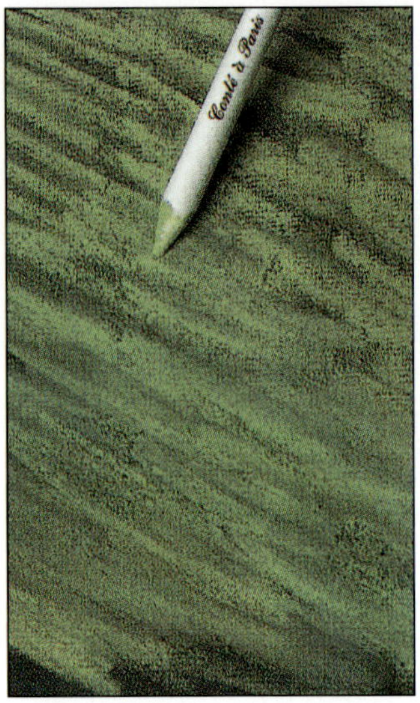

Blending with a torchon
Lay down the pastel color and gently rub the surface with the tip or side of the torchon to soften and blend the colors.

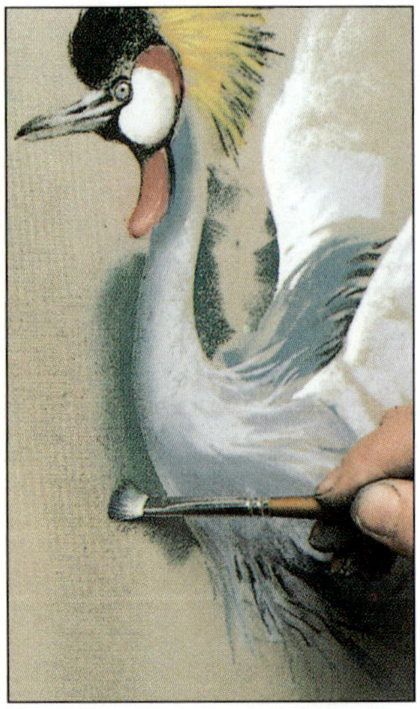

Blending with a brush
Use a short hog-hair or synthetic bristle brush to break down the grain of the pastel particles and spread the color evenly.

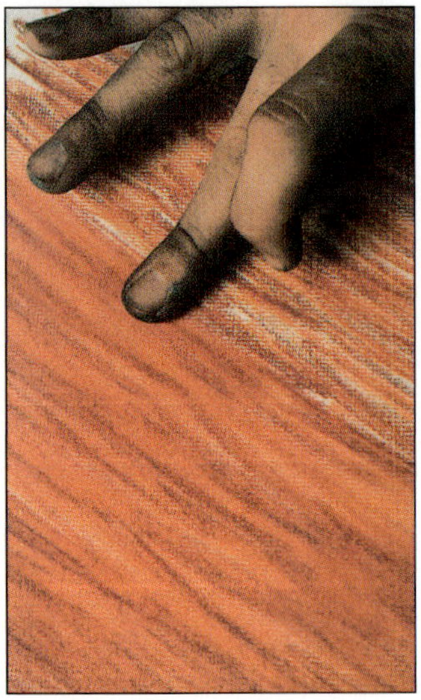

Blending with fingers
Rubbing with your finger merges the colors and presses the pastel dust into the paper grain. It is an effective way of blending linear or side strokes in soft pastel.

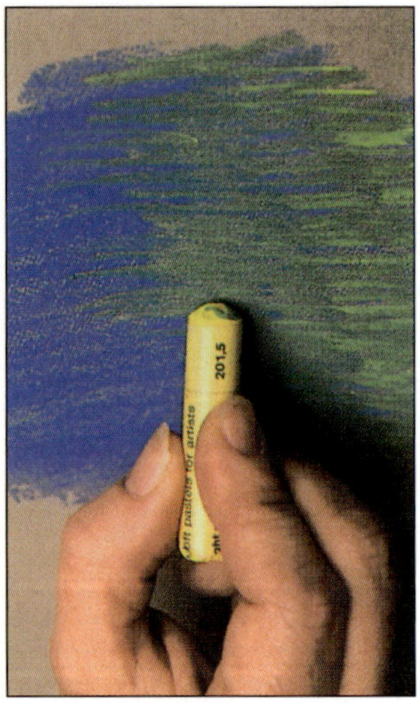

Blended strokes
With oil pastels and hard pastels, which do not spread so smoothly on the surface of the paper, use short strokes to overlay one color on another, varying the pressure so that the integrated marks produce an impression of mixed hues and tones.

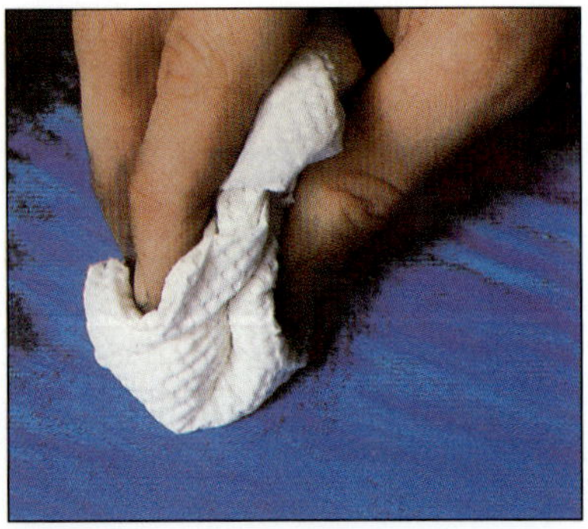

Soft pastels, being powder, can be blended very easily, and using a rag is a good method when you need to cover large areas.

CROSSHATCHING

Crosshatching is the classic drawing technique in which tones are built up with lines criss-crossing each other in opposite directions. Simply by varying the density of the strokes, you can create a wide range of tones; closely spaced lines with a dark pastel on a light-toned paper will create a dark tone, and widely spaced lines a light one, whereas for a light pastel used on a dark paper the opposite applies.

By interweaving different colors you can achieve particularly vibrant color mixtures. Each hue retains its own identity, but blends partially with adjacent colors in the viewer's eye to create a new color which can be much more interesting than a single area of flat color. Also, the lines themselves have life and movement, adding considerably to the surface interest of the painting. For example, when crosshatching is used in a figure painting, it somehow conveys the impression of life more effectively than flat color does.

Being a linear technique, crosshatching has an advantage over blending in that dense, glowing color can be created without prematurely filling up the tooth of the paper, thus retaining a fresh, lively appearance.

Crosshatching works best on a smooth paper, and can be used with all types of pastel, separately or in combination. However, hard pastels and pastel pencils are the most suitable for this technique because they give sharper, crisper lines. For even greater textural variety, the crosshatched lines can be softened partially in places by stroking them lightly with your thumb.

Crosshatching is normally done with diagonal strokes running in opposite directions, but you can also build up a denser web of color by running lines in several different directions – horizontal and vertical, then diagonally in both directions. Practise these techniques, and try different color mixtures on a variety of toned papers to see what effects you can create.

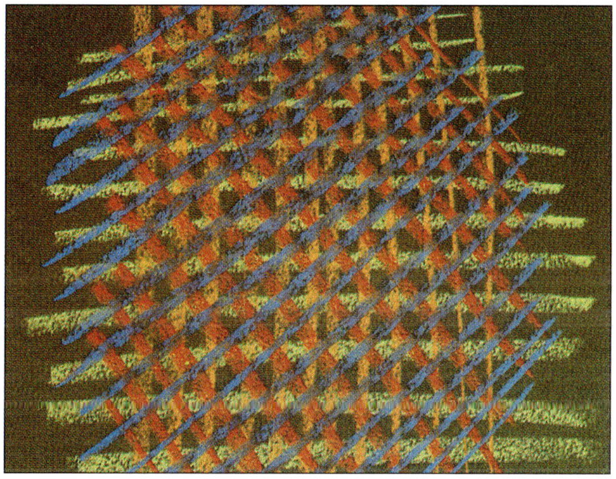

There is almost no end to the effects that can be achieved by altering the space and direction of crosshatched strokes. Here diagonal crosshatching has been used on top of vertical and horizontal strokes.

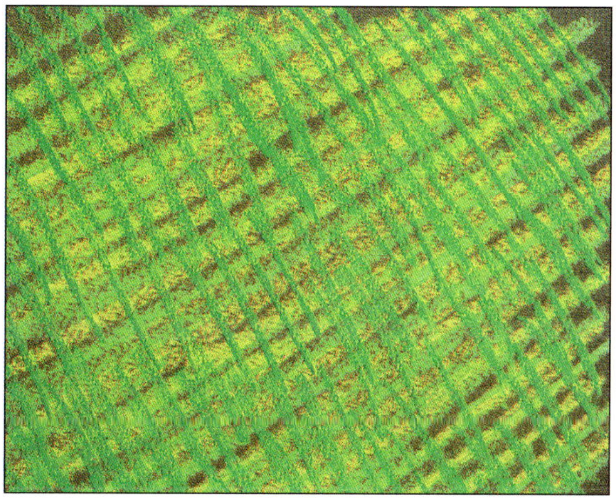

Altering the pressure used so that some strokes are thicker than others gives even further variety.

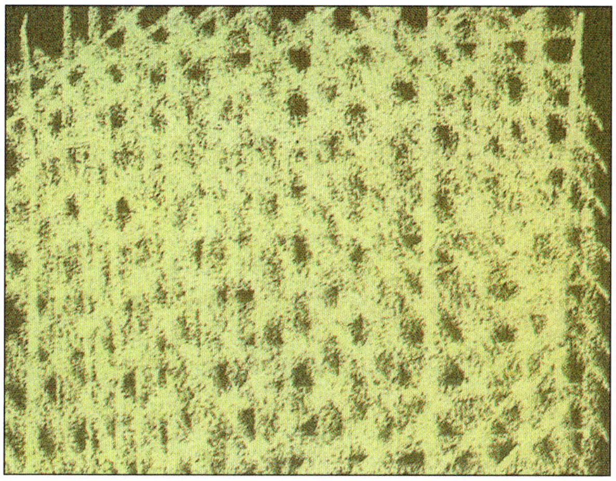

In this example the same strokes have been used, but in four different colors, which vastly extends the possibilities of the technique.

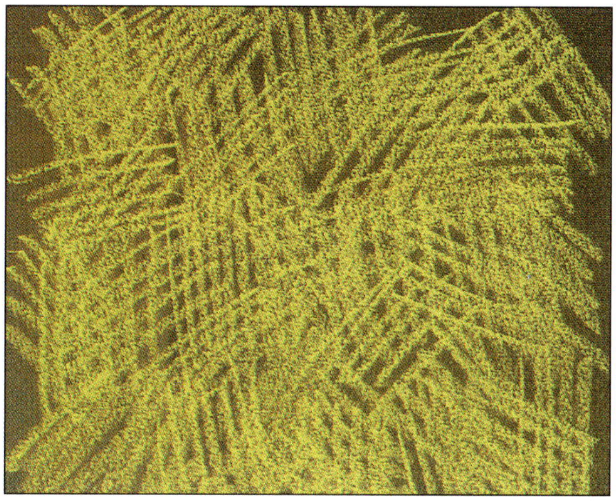

Here an interesting pattern has been formed by making several small groups of crosshatched strokes in different directions.

SCUMBLING

Scumbling is a method of modifying the color of a toned paper or a layer of pastel by applying a thin, opaque layer of another color over it. Scumbling involves using the side of the pastel stick in a loose motion to create a thin veil of color which doesn't entirely obliterate the one underneath. The two colors mix optically and have more resonance than an area of flat, blended color does – the effect is rather like looking at a color through a thin haze of smoke.

Scumbling not only creates subtle color effects, it also gives a very attractive surface texture. Use it to give depth and luminosity to your colors and to soften and unify areas of the painting.

To scumble, use the side of the pastel and make small, circular movements over the area to be covered. Apply only very light pressure, and don't overdo it or the underlayer will be completely covered and the effect will be lost. Soft pastel, in particular, requires a very light touch. This technique works best on a paper with plenty of tooth, which won't become clogged too quickly.

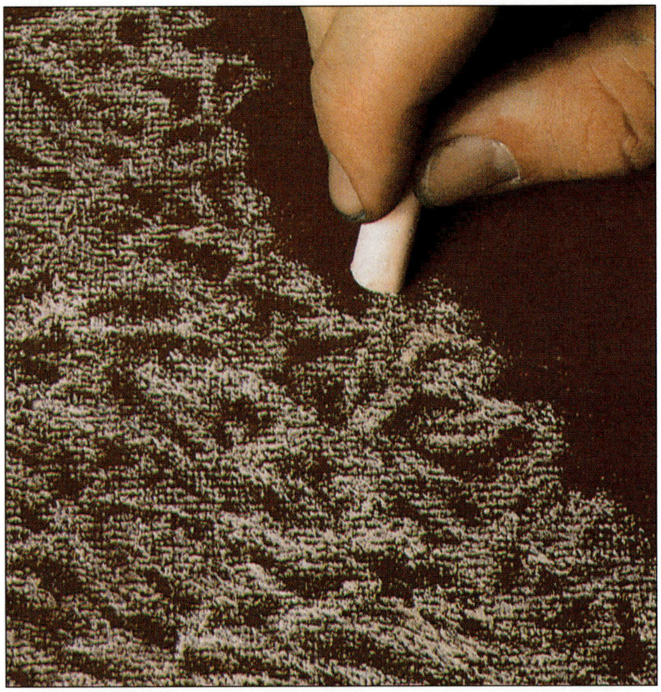

Scumbling creates interesting effects of both color and texture. Here a light pastel is being used on dark paper.

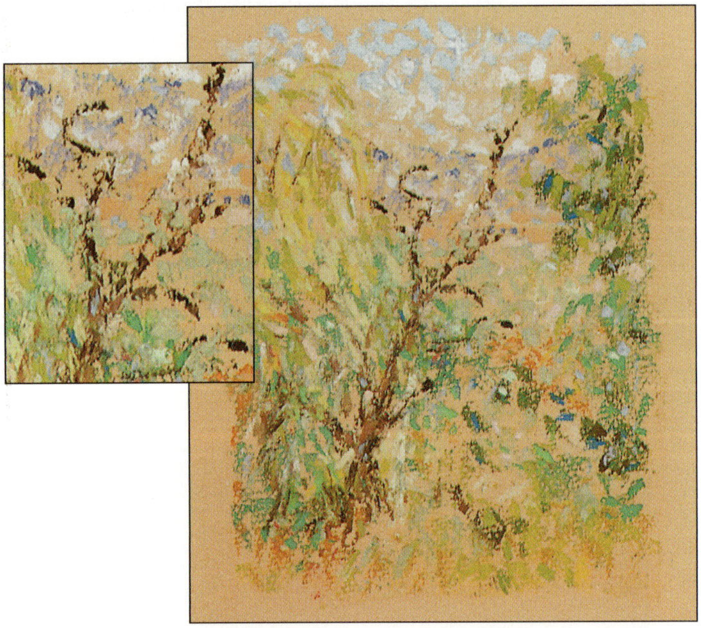

A similar technique has been used here to give a sparkling look to a delicate subject – a distant village seen through trees. The pinky-beige color of the paper, large areas of which have been left uncovered, gives an overall warmth and sunny tone to the picture, and the blobs and dots of pastel have been varied both in tone and in size.

POINTILLISM

The word pointillism is derived from the French word *point*, meaning dot. The technique of pointillism involves building up areas of tone or color with small dots of pure color which are not joined, but leave some of the toned paper showing through. When seen from the normal viewing distance, these dots appear to merge into one mass of color, but the effect is different to that created by a solid area of blended color. What happens is that the incomplete fusion of the dots produces a flickering optical effect on the eye; the colors scintillate and appear more luminous than a flat area of color. If complementary colors are juxtaposed, the effect is even more pronounced. For example, when dots of red and green, or yellow and violet, are intermixed, each color intensifies the other and the effect is strikingly vibrant. However, it is important to note that this vibrancy is only achieved when the colors are of the same tone.

The color of the paper can also contribute to the finished effect, appearing between the dots of color and harmonizing or contrasting with them.

Pastels are particularly suited to the pointillist technique because of their pure, vibrant hues and ease of manipulation. Hard pastels and pastel pencils work best – soft pastels are apt to smudge.

DRY WASH

This technique strictly applies only to soft pastels, as the true effect of a dry wash depends upon the powdery quality of pastels made with a minimum of binding material. To begin with, you reduce the pastel stick to powder by scraping the long edge with a knife blade. Hold it over a palette, dish, or piece of clean paper, to catch the powder as it falls, and try to graze, not chip, the edge of the pastel with the blade, so that the powdered color is quite fine.

When you have a reasonable quantity of powdered color, use a rag, fine sponge, or cotton ball to pick up the powder and spread it on the paper, working evenly across the support to lay down a flat color tint. To produce tonal or color gradations, you can strengthen the color in selected areas, or overlay additional colors.

This is one method of creating a colored ground for pastel work, using colors and textures that will be naturally sympathetic to the pastel strokes you overlay. It is also a good way of developing hazy or atmospheric effects in landscape rendering – representing large areas of sky, land, or water, for example.

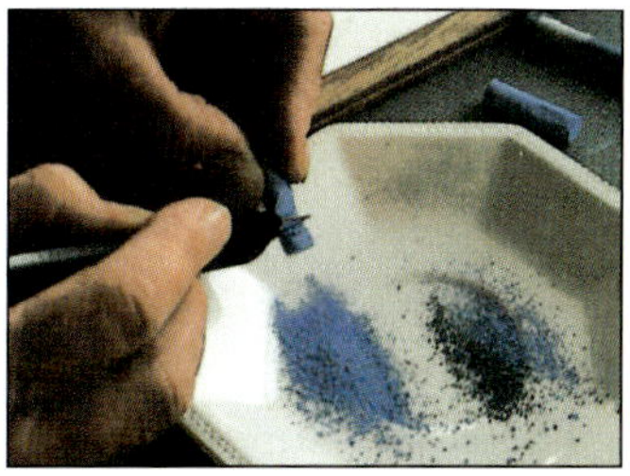

1 Use a craft knife blade or similar tool to scrape the edge of the pastel stick evenly collecting a heap of fine-textured powder color.

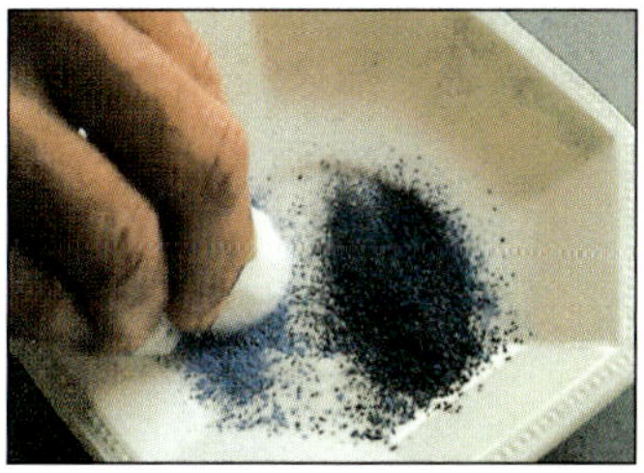

2 If you are using more than one color, these can be mixed and blended on the paper surface. Dab a cotton ball into the first color to pick up some of the powder.

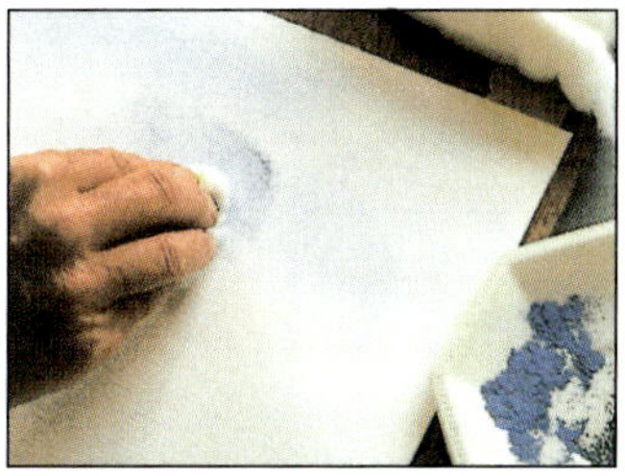

3 Rub the cotton ball across the paper surface, laying down a thin, even color tint. Work it well into the paper grain and increase the tonal depth gradually with successive applications.

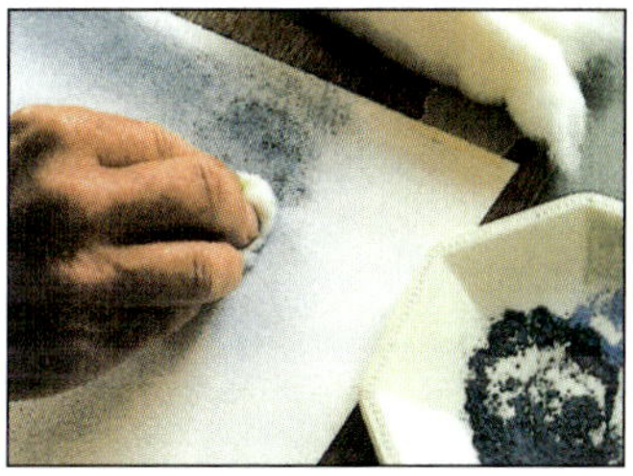

4 Apply the second color in the same way, working it into the required areas of the paper. Varying the pressure you apply to the cotton ball creates subtle differences of tone and texture.

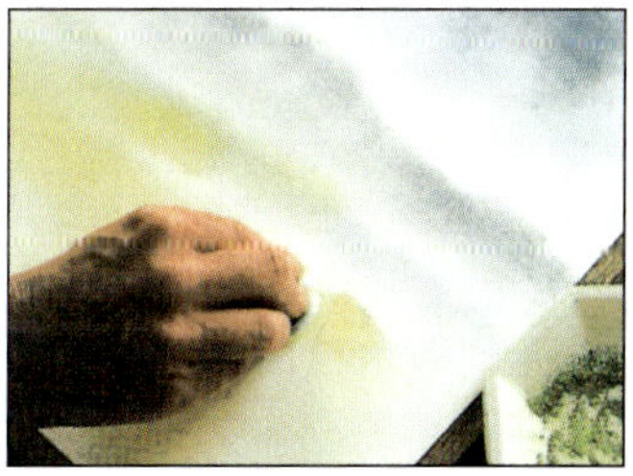

5 To apply a third or subsequent color, simply repeat the process as required. Keep the batches of powder separate to avoid devaluing the colors.

6 As with this example, you can use dry wash technique to block in the basic color areas of a composition, or you can simply use it as a method of tinting the paper to create an overall color key.

SGRAFFITO

This technique, of scratching into one layer of color to reveal another beneath, can to some extent be done with soft pastels, but is much more successful with oil pastels because these adhere more strongly to the paper. It is essential to lay the first color heavily so that it fills the whole grain of the paper, and the second layer thickly enough to cover the first. For the scratching you need a sharp implement, such as a craft knife.

To achieve a good effect, the colors must be worked out in advance so that you have sufficient color and tone contrast to make an impact. You might even use the complementary colors, laying red over green, or using a layer of yellow beneath mauve, and scratching into it to create a linear pattern. This could work well in a still life featuring patterned fabrics or ceramic objects. In a landscape, you might begin with yellow overlaid with dark green, and use the method to reveal the yellow in highlighted areas of foliage or grasses.

Another way of using the method is to paint the first color with acrylic or colored inks, using oil pastel for the second and any subsequent layers – you are not restricted to two-color effects.

USING FIXATIVES

The question of whether or not to use fixatives, and when, causes some controversy among pastellists. The brilliance and fragility of the pigment particles clinging to the working surface are regarded by some artists as essential characteristics of pastel work. Fixatives may be considered to degrade both the color and texture of soft pastels. However, careful fixing need not spoil the surface qualities, and you may feel that any disadvantages are offset by the protection that fixative gives to your work, both during its stages of development and when it is finished.

The key to successful fixing is to use the fixative sparingly. Overwetting the surface can cause the pigment particles to merge, muddying the texture; it can encourage strong colors to "bleed" through overlying tints; and it does tend to darken colors slightly. But if you apply a light layer of fixative at successive stages of the drawing, it enables you to overwork colors freely and keep the hues, tones, and individual marks distinct and clean. Fixing again when the work is finished prevents accidental smudging, powdering, or flaking.

If you are working on a light or medium-weight support, you can spray the fixative on the back of the paper. It will penetrate enough to gently dampen the pastel and make it more secure. If you definitely prefer to do without fixative, try "fixing" the surface of a finished work by laying a sheet of tissue over it and applying even pressure to push the pastel particles a little more firmly into the paper grain.

Aerosol cans of fixative are convenient and are usually now environment-friendly. Some artists still prefer using a mouth diffuser spray to apply fixative from a bottle, but you do get a more reliably even spray from an aerosol.

Do not use fixative in a heated room with the windows closed, as the fumes are unpleasant. A kindlier alternative to fixative is odorless hairspray, which has the same effect but with less smell.

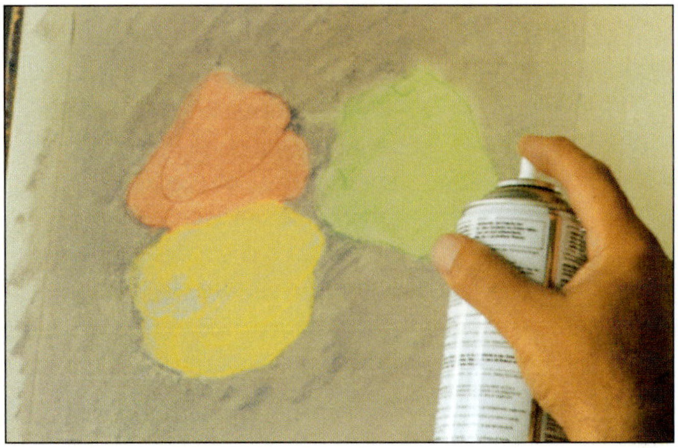

Fixing in stages
Some artists like to use a light fixative spray at intervals throughout the work, even in the early stages, to seal the surface before application of further color layers.

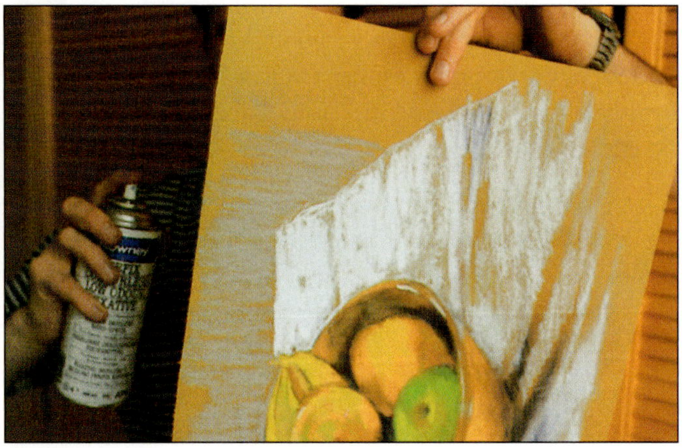

Spraying from the back
Use this method only in light and medium-weight papers. Apply the spray evenly and sparingly as described above, covering the whole of the back of the paper.

CARING FOR YOUR WORK

Unless you take steps to protect your finished work, it can easily become smeared, and the paper damaged. The best protection is provided by a frame and glass, but framing all your pictures would be expensive. A surface such as pastel board or sandpaper, which grips the pastel firmly, needs no fixing, but spray other work with fixative and let it dry thoroughly before putting it away. Pastels must be stored flat, not upright, to avoid damaging the edges of the paper. You can stack a good many paintings on top of one another, but they must be separated by tracing paper to prevent color transfer. Tracing paper is preferable to tissue paper, because it is heavier. The protective sheet should be fixed to the pastel paper with masking tape, so that it does not move when you are looking through your work.

Pastels must be framed under glass to guard against accidental smearing and to protect them from damp and dust. The painting must never touch the glass, however, because moisture caused by condensation will make blotches on the picture surface. If you are having your work mounted professionally, ask the framer to insert a thick mat or small pieces of wood, known as lips, between the painting and the glass.

Keeping your pastels in a portfolio also protects them from dampness and dust. The best type opens out flat, making it easier to look through your work periodically. Do not store the portfolio upright, as this could damage the edges of your work and cause pastel dust to drift downward.

GALLERY

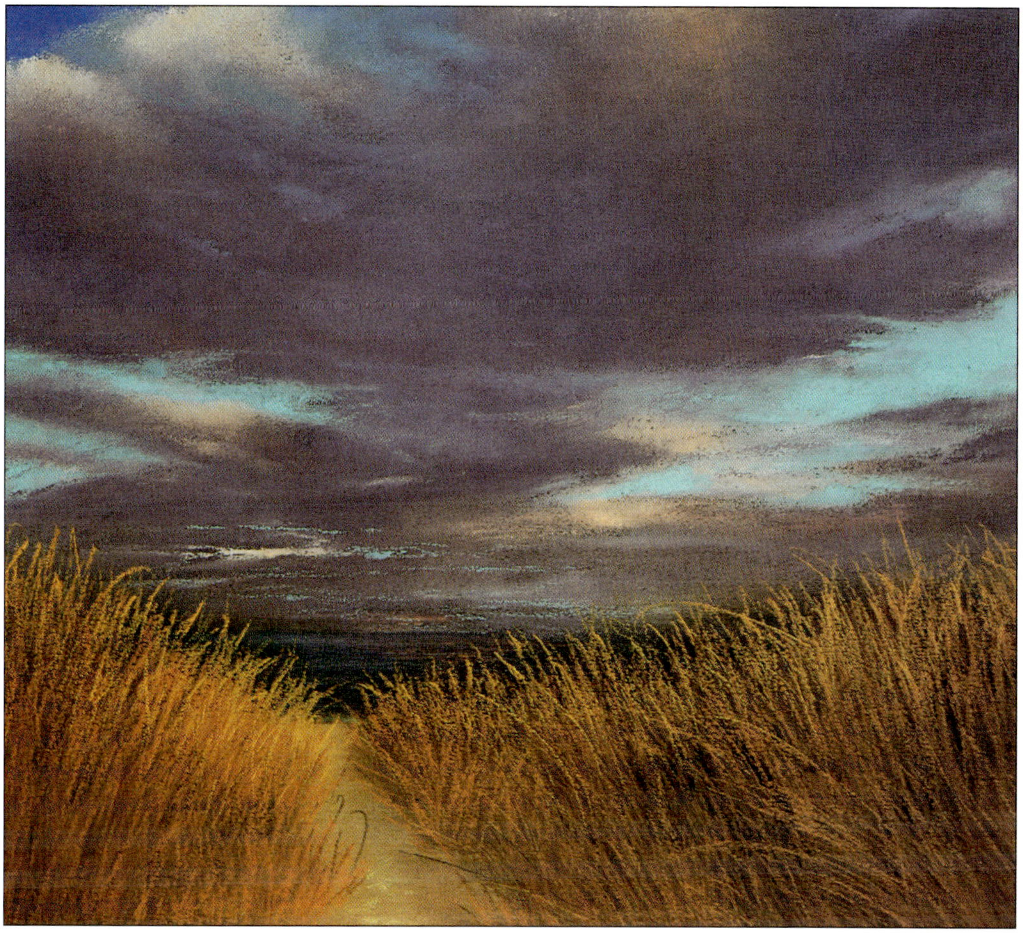

BEACH GRASSES by Lois Gold

The rich colors of this sky were achieved by applying one color over another and then blending them with sweeping motions of the hand. Smaller areas were blended with the fingertips, and for the grasses shown in the detail, the artist used hard pastels over a layer of yellow-brown, blending them with a tortillon.

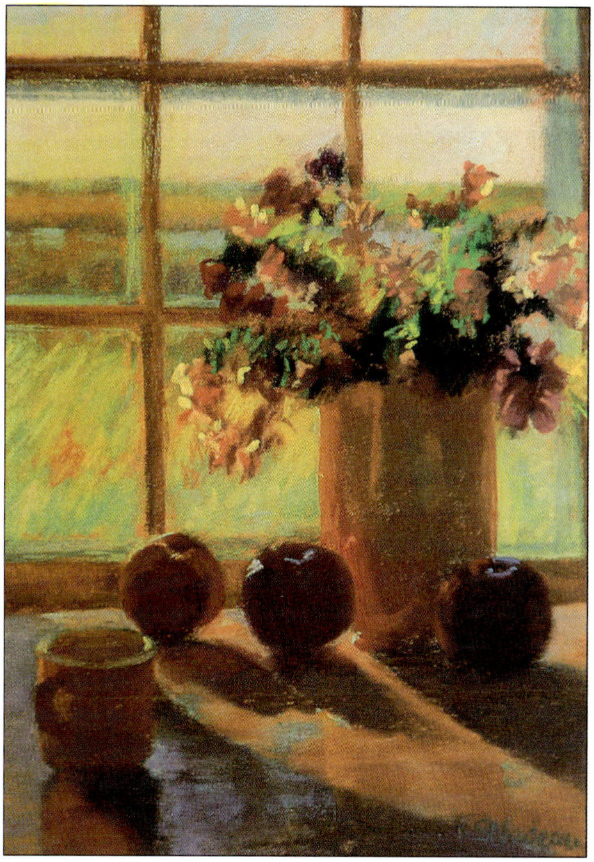

FIESTA BOUQUET by Rosalie Nadeau

In this painting, blended effects were achieved by applying successive layers of color with the sides of the pastel sticks. This is an excellent method for the dark, rich colors of the apples and shadows, shown in the detail. Overlaying colors does not remove pigment: instead, each new color holds the earlier ones in place.

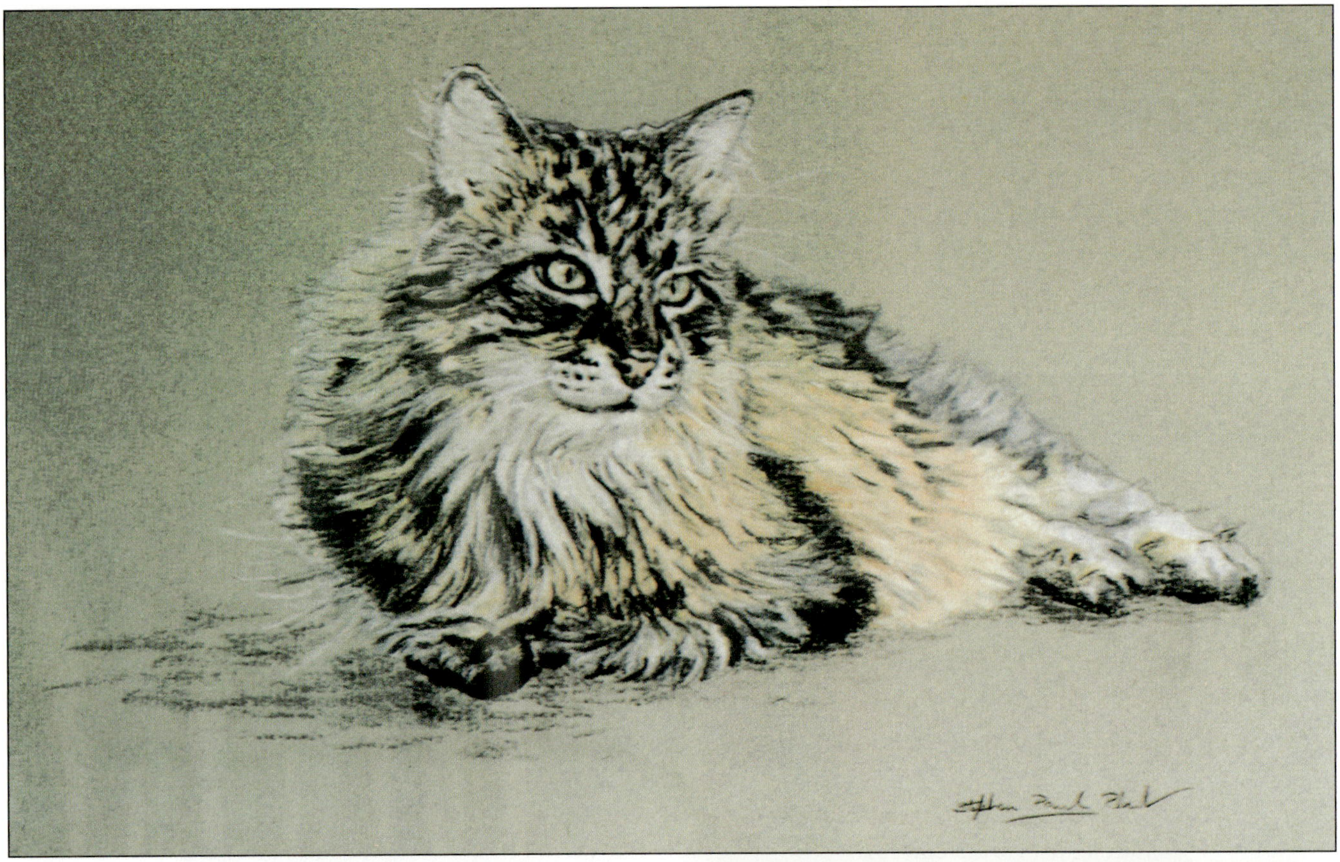

MAINE COON CAT by Stephen Paul Plant

The soft gray of the colored ground provides a mid-tone from which to key in the brindled markings. The face and features are first drawn in detail, then the fur texture is developed. A little charcoal is applied as a base for the strong blacks and in finishing touches.

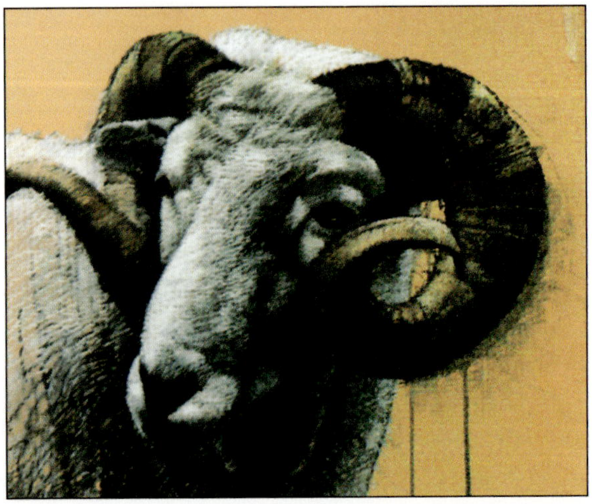

RAM HEAD by Keith Bowen

In this gouache and pastel rendering, fine hatching and crosshatching are used to convey the varying textures of the ram's smooth head, the hard, ridged horns, and the looser hairs on the body. Complex tonal gradations are built up by this method, both directly on the board and over thin gouache washes.

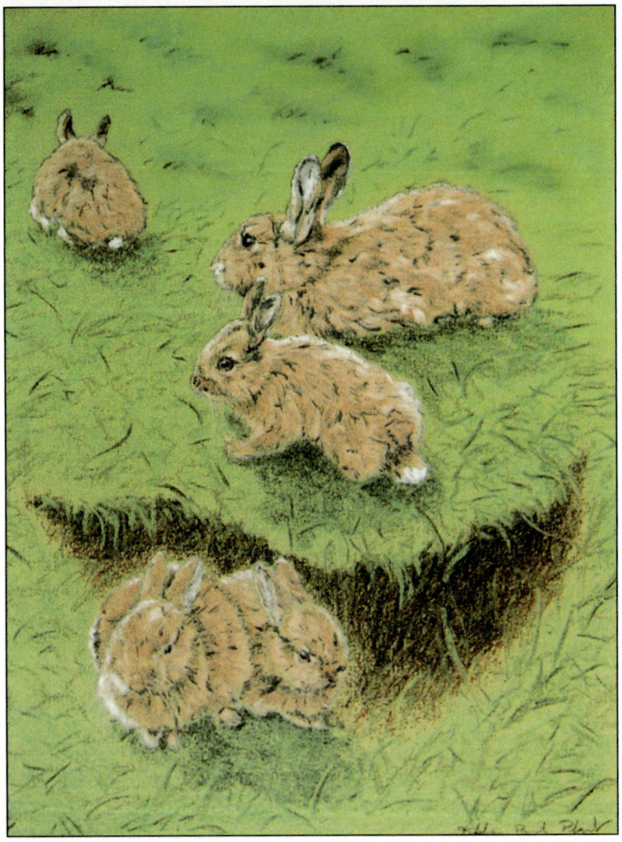

DOE RABBIT AND HER KITTENS by Stephen Paul Plant

The technique of building texture with linear marks over flat color is consistently applied to both the rabbits and their grassy surround.

WATERCOLOR

Of all the painting media, watercolor is perhaps the most idiosyncratic. With watercolor, what is done is done: once applied to paper, a watercolor wash must stay there. But the very unpredictable nature of watercolor painting also brings special satisfaction to the artist.

There is a keen pleasure involved in working with watercolor and adapting to it, rather than determining from the outset what the result will be. The art of watercolor painting has a history that stretches back over 40,000 years. The first known examples were cave paintings, using thick applications of opaque water-based paint. Early Chinese artists, however, used soft-haired brushes and worked on silk and rice paper, whose absorbent surfaces encouraged the use of delicate, transparent washes. With just a few fine strokes, these artists captured a mood of atmospheric space in their landscapes, anticipating by several centuries the work of Western watercolor artists such as Turner and Girtin. This is the strength of watercolor: its ability to let the texture and tone of the paper mingle with the vivacity of the paint, creating that illusion of light and depth for which many artists strive. True, watercolor may have a mind of its own, but that is all part of the excitement of this intriguing medium.

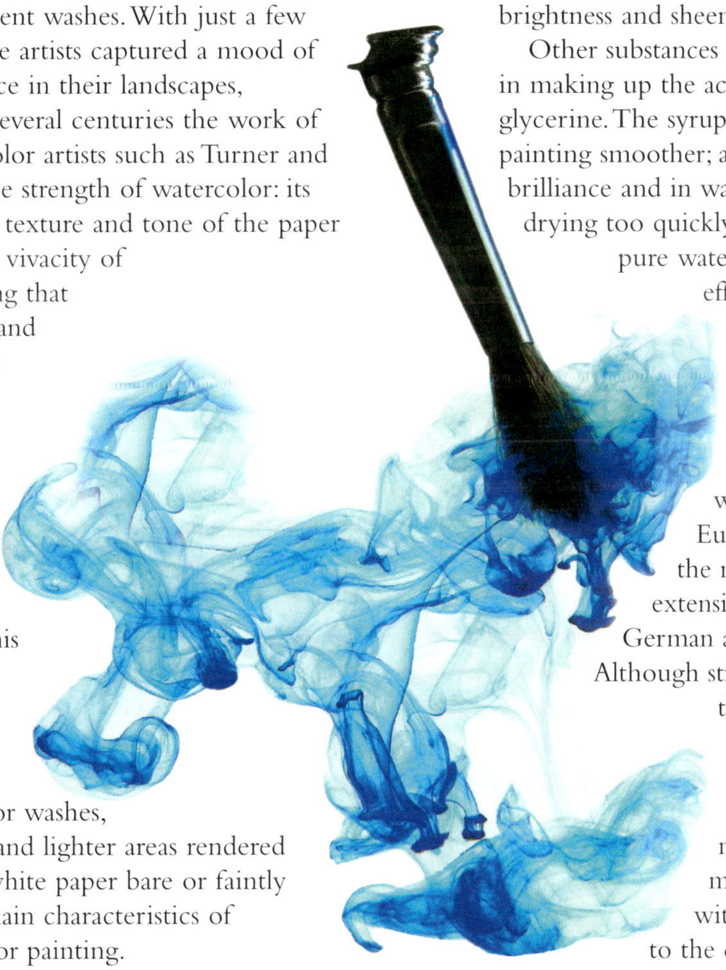

Transparency and the soft harmony of color washes, with highlights and lighter areas rendered by leaving the white paper bare or faintly toned, are the main characteristics of "pure" watercolor painting.

The color cannot be worked on its ground to the same extent as with oils or other opaque media – errors cannot be merely painted over, for instance – so that a higher initial standard of technique may be involved to produce a satisfactory watercolor painting. But the freshness and brilliance of a good watercolor is ample compensation for the time spent in acquiring sound technique.

Since the time of the ancient Egyptians, water has been used as a diluent in many types of paint, including size paint, distemper, fresco, tempera, and gouache. True watercolor, however, consists solely of very finely ground pigment with gum arabic as the binder. The water-soluble gum acts as a light varnish, giving the colors a greater brightness and sheen.

Other substances may occasionally be added to the water in making up the actual paint, including sugar syrup and glycerine. The syrup acts as a plasticizer, making the painting smoother; and the glycerine is said to lend extra brilliance and in warm weather prevents the paint from drying too quickly. White pigment is never used in a pure watercolor palette. Its addition creates, in effect, a different medium – gouache.

Although many medieval illustrators used pure – that is transparent – watercolor in small works and on manuscripts, others added opaque or body color to make a background on which gold leaf was laid. The first European fully to recognize the value of the medium in larger works, using it extensively in landscape paintings, was the German artist Albrecht Dürer (1471–1528). Although strong lines and opaque passages played their part, the unique transparency of watercolor washes was a major feature of these works.

One of the earliest English artists to make full and effective use of the medium was John White, a draftsman with Sir Walter Raleigh's 1585 expedition to the coast of North America. White's use of the full range of watercolor in clean washes when making drawings for the record of the life and scenery of the North Carolina coast have caused some historians to claim him as the "father" of the English watercolor school.

Indeed, on the Continent, watercolor became known as

"the English art;" but it was not until nearly two centuries later, in the latter part of the eighteenth century, that the art blossomed into its full pride and distinction in the hands of such painters as Paul Sandby (1725–1809), William Blake (1757–1827), Thomas Girtin (1755–1802), J. M. W. Turner (1755–1851), John Crome (1763–1821),

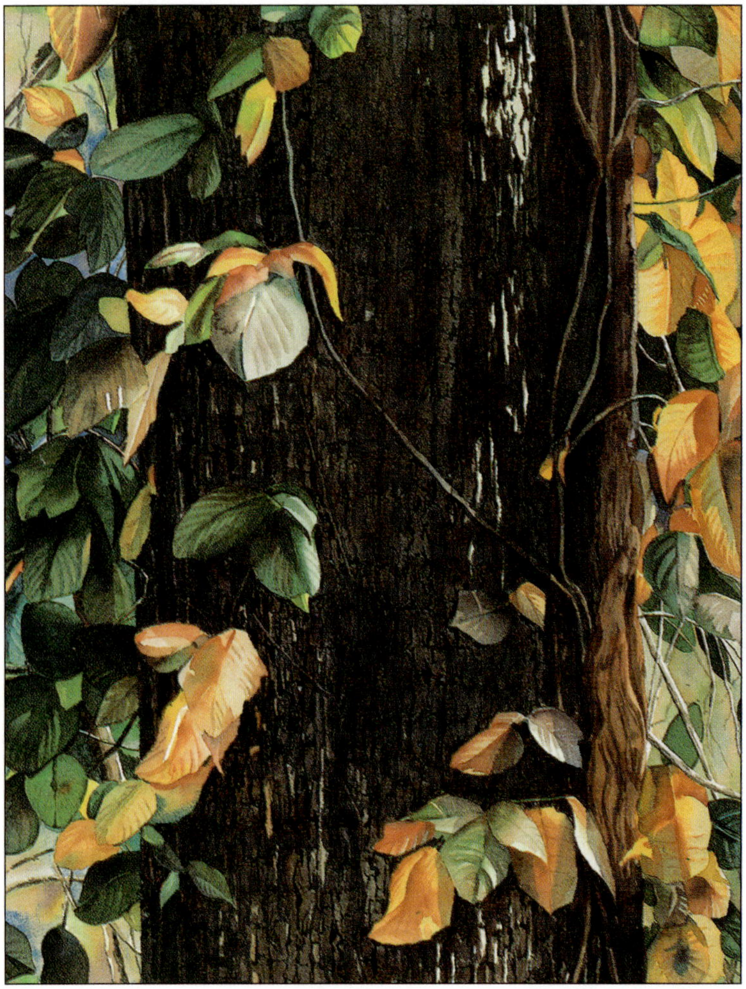

CHANGING SCENE by Joel Smith

John Sell Cotman (1782–1842), John Varley (1778–1842), David Cox (1783–1859), and Peter de Wint (1784–1849).

Only those who have mastered a basic technique and recognized the limitations of a medium can afford to depart from the rules and, in doing so, evolve new styles. Thomas Girtin, for instance, regarded the limitations of watercolor as a challenge and, in effect, increased the challenge by deliberately restricting the range of his palette. He used only five basic colors: yellow ocher, burnt sienna, light red, monestial blue, and ivory black. He applied the paint in thin washes, allowing each wash to dry before applying the next, building up deep tonal gradations and contrasts. Like most of the "English school" he left areas of white paper untouched to provide highlights; but occasionally, and effectively, broke a "rule" by using gouache for the odd highlight.

William Blake devised something akin to offset printing to apply his first layers of color, painting on an impervious surface such as glass, porcelain, or a glazed card or paper, and pressing this over his painting paper. When the "print" was dry, he worked over it in opaque or body color to elaborate and enliven it.

J. M. W. Turner virtually forced the paint to obey his rules, shifting it while wet, scumbling and scratching it on heavy paper until gleaming and glowing effects were produced – unrecognizable at first as true watercolor. He mixed techniques and made them compatible. In Tintern Abbey he built up strong tonal contrasts with flat and broken washes. Heavy wet-into-wet methods, scumbles, and dry brush strokes were all combined in the harmonies of Kilgarran Castle, while Venice from the Ciudecca is alive with thin, wet washes, and delicate touches of opaque paint.

The Victorian age saw a rise in the general popularity of watercolor painting, particularly in Britain; and some Victorian artists, including John Everett Millais (1829–1896), found a ready sale for watercolor copies of their larger oil paintings. Watercolor had already been used for the opposite process –making quick color sketches for later rendering as larger works in oil – by such masters as van Dyck (1599–1641), Gainsborough (1727–1788), and Constable (1776–1837).

They discovered that quick-drying watercolor enabled them to experiment with color contrasts and make swift notes of passing atmospheric effects, such as mists, rainbows, changing reflections, and fast-altering cloud formations.

The distinction between fine art and the art of the illustrator, always blurred, became more so in the nineteenth century with the invention of half-tone reproduction. Overlaying of red, yellow, and blue inks, broken down by screens to produce many tones, made possible the reproduction of illustrations in full color. Watercolor was found to be an ideal medium to submit to the process, which enabled books containing full-color illustrations to be produced comparatively cheaply for the mass market. Among the many fine artists who used watercolor for their illustration originals are Rackham (1867–1939) and Edmund Dulac (1882–1953). Dulac outlined and pointed up many of his drawings with Indian ink. In printing – although the black itself could not be reproduced by the three-color process – this tended to soften and enhance the watercolor washes lying within his outlines.

Why Watercolor?

Watercolor is the most popular painting medium today. Once regarded as the "poor relation" of oils, it has become the first choice of many modern artists.

A good watercolor has a compelling vitality and immediacy. Watercolorists are drawn by the medium's magical if sometimes elusive qualities, its unexpected effects – which can be exasperating but also exciting – and by its capacity to adapt to the visual responses of the individual artist. They like the way watercolor can capture a particular light or mood. And they like its practical advantages for working either indoors or on location.

The fluidity and transparency of watercolor is unique, but these are the very qualities that have given the medium a reputation of being "difficult." Because the paint is transparent, you can't correct mistakes by overpainting, as you can with opaque paints. In fact, watercolor is no more difficult than any other medium; but like all painting, it takes practice and a willingness to experiment.

The fresh and spontaneous appearance of successful watercolors depends upon planning, technique, and a knowledge of the medium – all of which can be achieved in time.

Acquiring watercolor techniques is both a challenge and a delight. Using them successfully will not only be a source of great satisfaction but will free you to find and use your own artistic vision.

The bonus is that you can enjoy yourself while you learn. The most important task is to become familiar with the medium through "hands on" experience. There are few more agreeable ways of spending your time than letting the brush glide over the paper as you lay washes, or observing the way colors merge as you work "wet on wet." By direct involvement with the materials, you will get to know their characteristics and learn how to make the most of both planned and unpredictable effects.

The second task – which may take longer and entail more trial and error – is learning to recognize your own pictorial interests and knowing what you want to "say" in paint. Watercolor is such a versatile mode of expression that once you have learned to use it, you'll find there is little it cannot convey. If you are interested in atmospheric landscape you can make rapid sketches, catching impressions with just a few broad washes and brush strokes. If you like detail, you can build up intricate effects with a small brush; you can paint flowers in delicate colors, still lifes in vivid hues, or portraits in somber shades. Discovering what you enjoy painting is the first step toward developing your personal style, and it is the ability to instill something of yourself in your paintings that makes you an artist.

You will find that no two approaches are the same, even when the subject is similar, because each artist has a different way of looking at the world. If you attend watercolor exhibitions, you will find that you respond to some paintings more than others. This will help you decide how and what to paint. Whatever their approach, the experience and experiments of other watercolorists can help to inspire and enhance your own artistic development. One of the best ways of learning is from other people, even when they don't know they are teaching you.

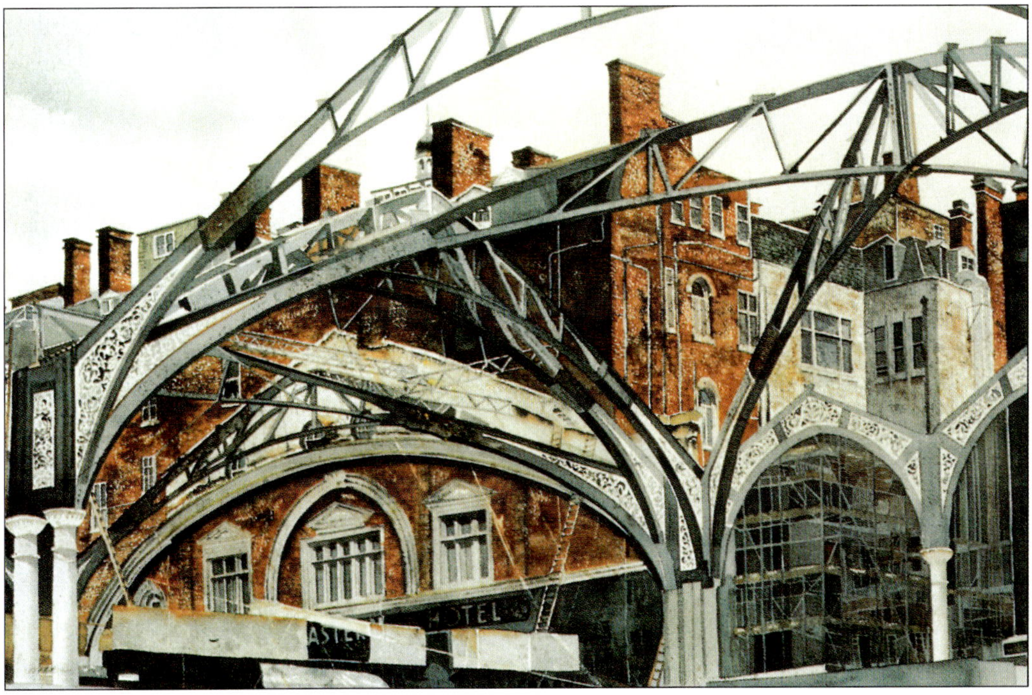

LIVERPOOL STREET STATION
by Sandra Walker

Watercolor is equally suited to detailed work, and is the chosen medium of many artists who specialize in elaborate botanical, zoological, and architectural subjects. Urban architecture is this artist's particular interest. She managed to paint each door, window, and chimney pot as well as every inch of decorative detail without the paint becoming overworked.

SHEET PAPER

From top to bottom:
1 *watercolor board*
2 *cold-pressed paper*
3 *rough paper*
4 *hot-pressed paper*
5 *and* ***6*** *two different hand-made papers*

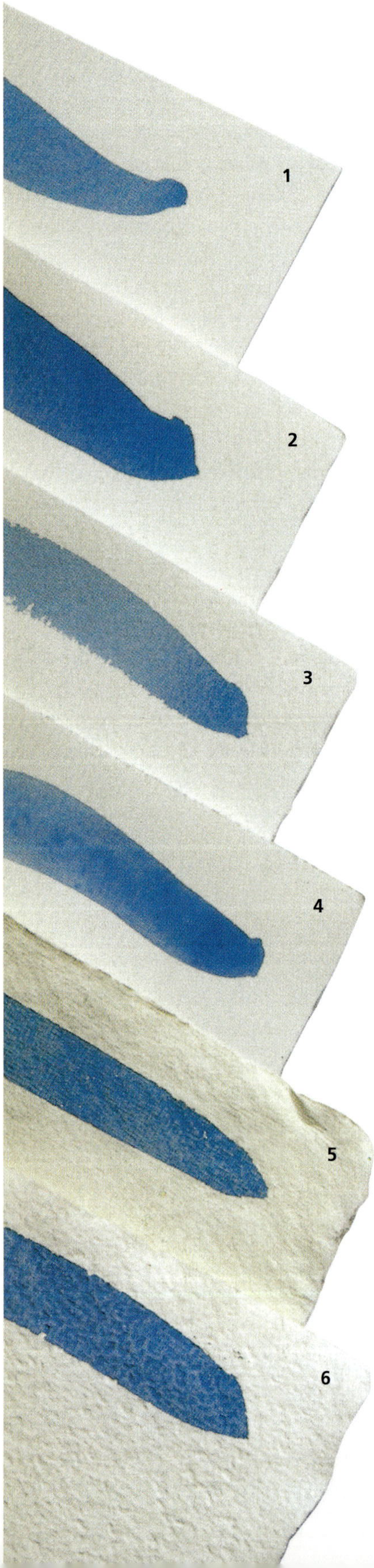

Surfaces

Paper is available in a wide variety of weights, sizes, qualities, and colors. With the exception of the paler shades, toned papers are seldom suited to transparent watercolor whereas gouache covers the paper completely so that the tone of the paper need not be taken into consideration unless areas are to be left untouched in any way. More exotic types of paper include rice papers, of which Kozo, Mutsumata, and Gambi are the most popular. The surfaces are delicate, fragile, and highly absorbent and experimentation will produce a technique which will make full use of these characteristics.

HAND- OR MACHINE-MADE

The best paper for watercolor work is hand-made from pure linen rag. Because of the skill involved in making it and the cost of the raw material it is expensive, but the price of such paper is reflected in the quality. The very best is made from 100% rag; all impurities are filtered out and the paper is sized according to the needs of the watercolorist. These papers are easily recognized by the watermark which can be read by holding the paper up to light. Great care must be taken to use the right side of the paper; this can be detected by the surface texture which in hand-made paper is more irregular than the mechanical surface of a mold-made paper which will show itself to have a strong diagonal pattern under close inspection.

Mold- or machine-made paper is cheaper and paper mills often sell off seconds which are quite satisfactory for most purposes. It comes in three different finishes, hot-pressed, cold-pressed, or rough. Hot-pressed paper has a smooth surface which is more suitable for the drawing than for watercolor as the surface will not take the paint readily.

Cold-pressed paper is usually known as not (in other words, not hot-pressed) and this together with rough paper is the most favored of surfaces for watercolor painting. It is a textured semi-rough paper which is good both for large, smooth washes and for fine detailing.

Rough paper, as its name suggests, has a much less smooth surface than not. When a wash is laid over its surface this rough texture causes some of the crevices in the paper to remain unfilled, presenting a speckled effect. While the aesthetic qualities of such a wash are pleasing and satisfying, the handling of such a surface is fairly daunting for an inexperienced artist as it is difficult to control. However practice and experimentation will reap rich rewards.

GRADES AND SIZES

The grading of paper is by weight of the ream (usually 500 sheets). This varies from 40–44 lb (16.5–17 kg) for a lightweight paper to 400 lb (165 kg) for the heaviest paper. The weight is of great importance; the heavier the paper the more ready it is to accept water, and the lighter papers are in need of stretching before they will present a surface on which to paint. Heavier grades of paper say upward of 140 lb (65 kg) can be worked on without stretching, but if the surface is to be awash with water at any time stretching might still be a wise precaution.

Cheaper papers such as cartridge are classified by the international A sizes; for the better quality hand-made and mold-made papers traditional sizes, listed below, are still used:

Antiquarian	31 x 53 in. (787 x 1346 mm)
Double Elephant	27 x 40 in. (686 x 1016 mm)
Elephant	23 x 28 in. (584 x 711 mm)
Imperial	30 x 22 in. (762 x 559 mm)
Half Imperial	15 x 22 in. (381 x 559 mm)
Royal	19 1/2 x 24 in. (490 x 610 mm)

A good selection of hand- and mold-made papers is readily available from good art stores or direct from the manufacturers.

Apart from these conventional papers, a variety of prepared boards are available as supports. These are simply ordinary watercolor papers mounted firmly onto stout card. Their advantages are mainly convenience, not only for transportation but also in that they dispense with the need for stretching paper. You can easily prepare your own boards by gluing paper onto a pasteboard, but be sure it sticks securely; if not, your paper will lift off the board as soon as it becomes damp.

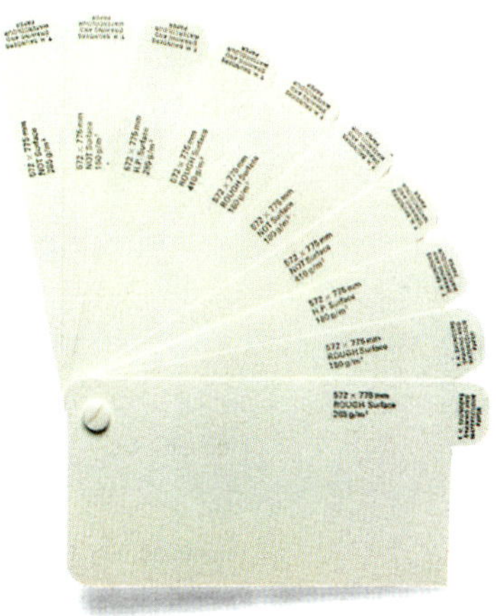

LEFT: *Manufacturers often produce small swatches of paper samples, which enable the artist to compare the different weights and textures of the various types. As the quality papers are quite expensive, there may be a charge for a sample swatch, but it is very useful reference material for artists working mainly in watercolor.*

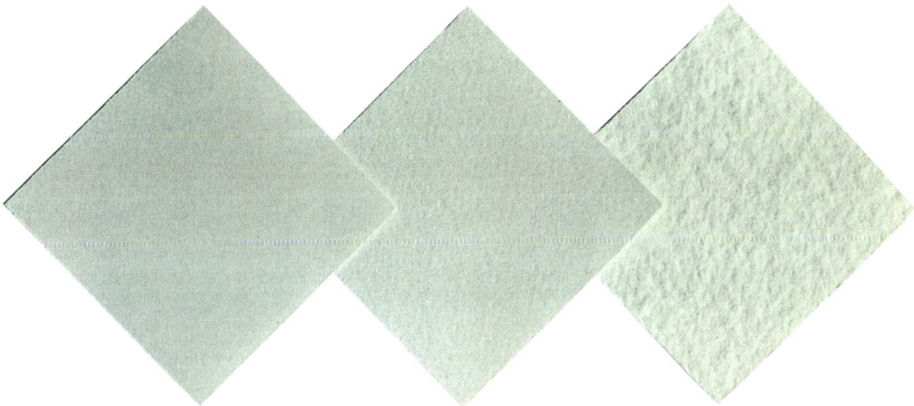

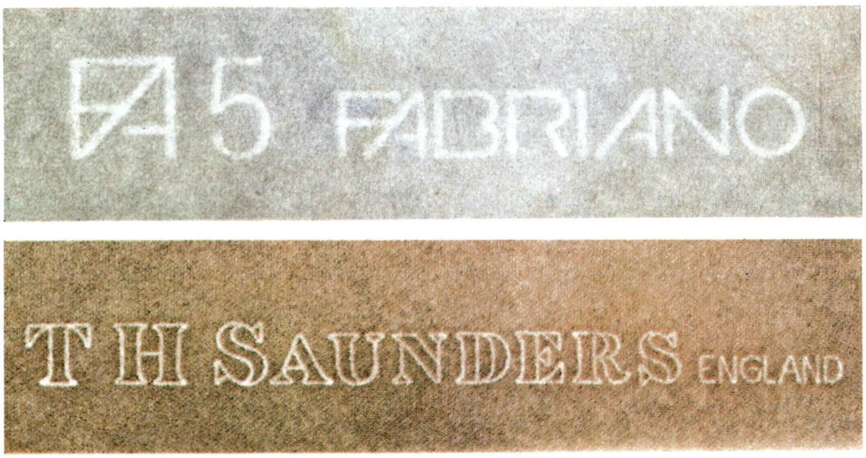

LEFT: *Texture is one of the main characteristics which will concern an artist when choosing paper for watercolor painting. Three types are available: hot-pressed, cold-pressed or "not", and rough. Hot-pressed is the smoothest surface and is possibly more useful for drawing than for watercolor, though it does suit some approaches. It takes washes of paint very easily so might be useful for quick work, and it is also suitable for a style which requires fine detail. It can, however, quickly become flooded with paint, so the transparency of the watercolor is lost. Cold-pressed paper is probably the most popular surface. Rough paper has a definite tooth to it and when a wash is laid over, some of the deep cavities are left unfilled, giving a sparkle to the paint, with clear white paper showing through. It is not perhaps the ideal surface for a beginner. Good quality papers have a right and a wrong side; the right side is coated with a size which is extremely receptive to watercolor. A simple way of determining the correct side of the paper is to look for the watermark (bottom left) which is visible if the paper is held up to the light.*

Stretching Paper

Light- or medium-weight papers tend to buckle when wet paint is applied, but they won't do this if they are stretched. Stretching paper may seem a chore, but there are two excellent reasons for doing it. One is that you can save a good deal of money, because light papers are considerably less expensive than heavy ones, and the other is that stretched paper is more pleasant to work on – it is frustrating to paint over ridges caused by buckling. Stretching isn't difficult, but you'll need to do it well in advance of painting. The paper has to be soaked and will take at least two hours to dry thoroughly.

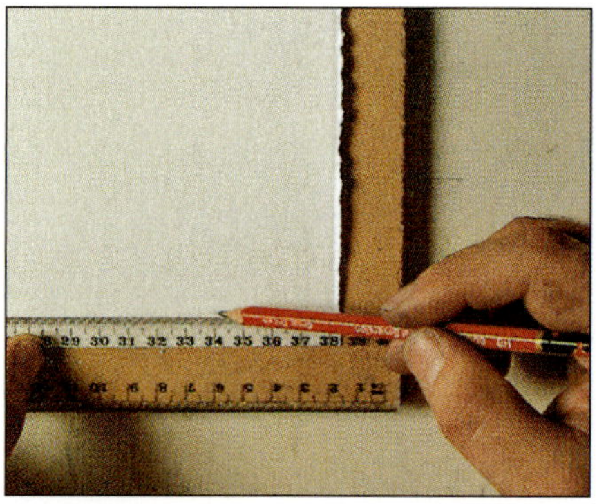

1 Rule light pencil lines about half an inch from the edges of the paper to help you put the tape on straight.

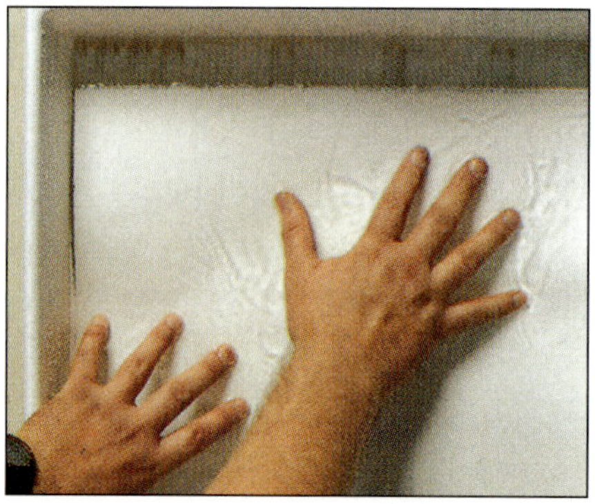

2 Immerse the paper briefly in water, turning it over once to make sure both sides are evenly wetted. You can do this in a bathtub, sink, or plastic tray.

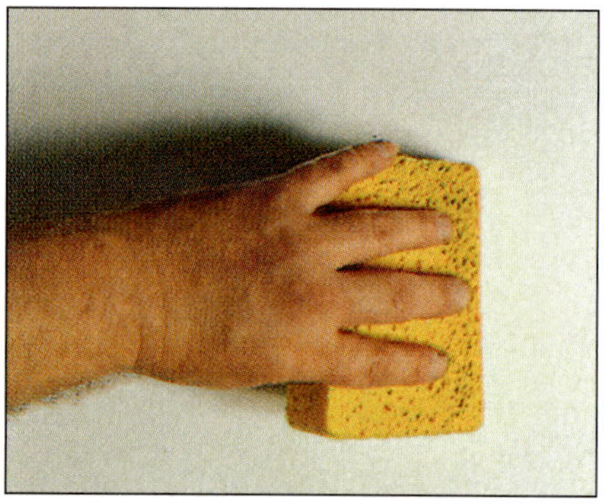

3 Place the paper on the board and smooth it with a damp sponge to remove any creases or air bubbles.

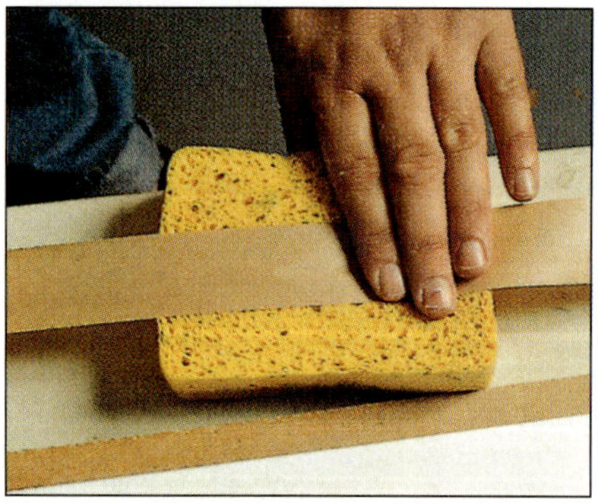

4 Cut four pieces of gummed tape roughly to length and dampen each one just before use by running it over the sponge. Don't make it too wet or it may stretch and tear.

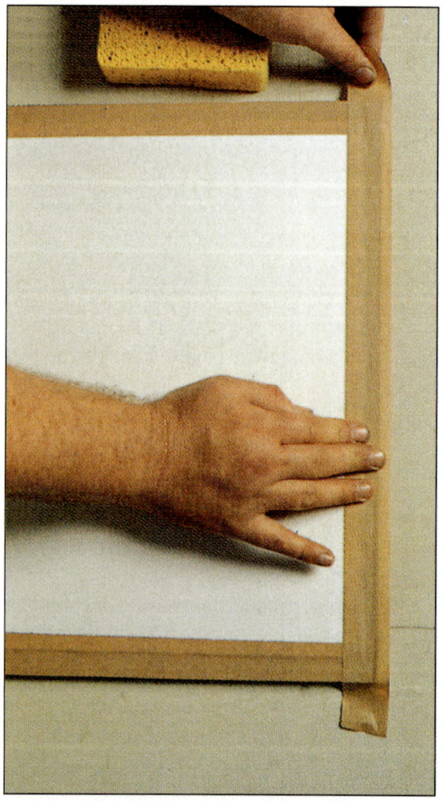

5 Place the strip around all four edges, smoothing it with your hand as you go. Trim the corners with the scissors or a sharp knife, and stand the board upright until the paper is completely dry.

SKETCHING PADS

The major manufacturers produce their paper in large sheet and sketchpad form. The pads usually contain 10 or 12 sheets, and are available in a variety of sizes.

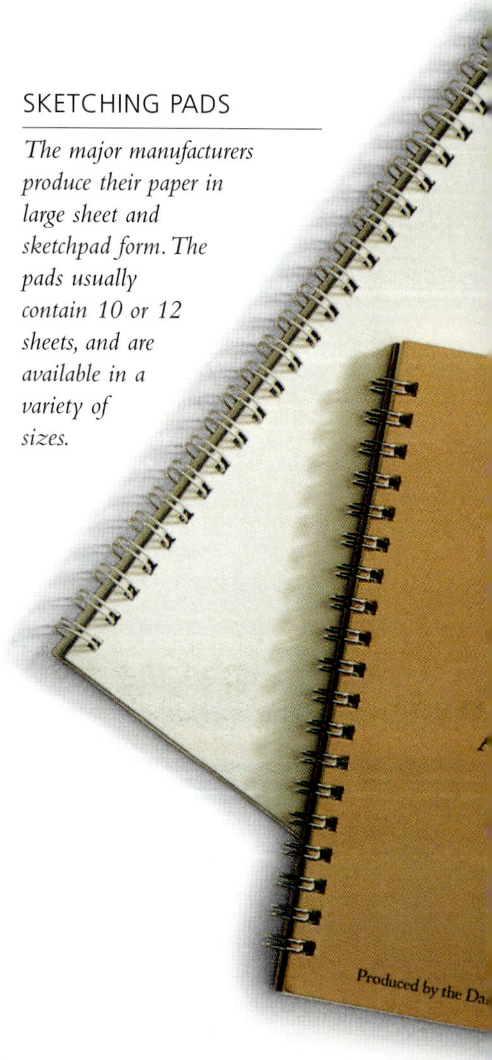

Paints

Watercolors are available in sets as well as in individual pans or tubes. Half pans (back, center, and center left) can be purchased both individually and in sets. The boxes (left and right) can easily double as palettes. Bottled, concentrated watercolors (center) usually have an eye dropper applicator. Tube colors (front, back) just need to be squeezed onto the palette before being used.

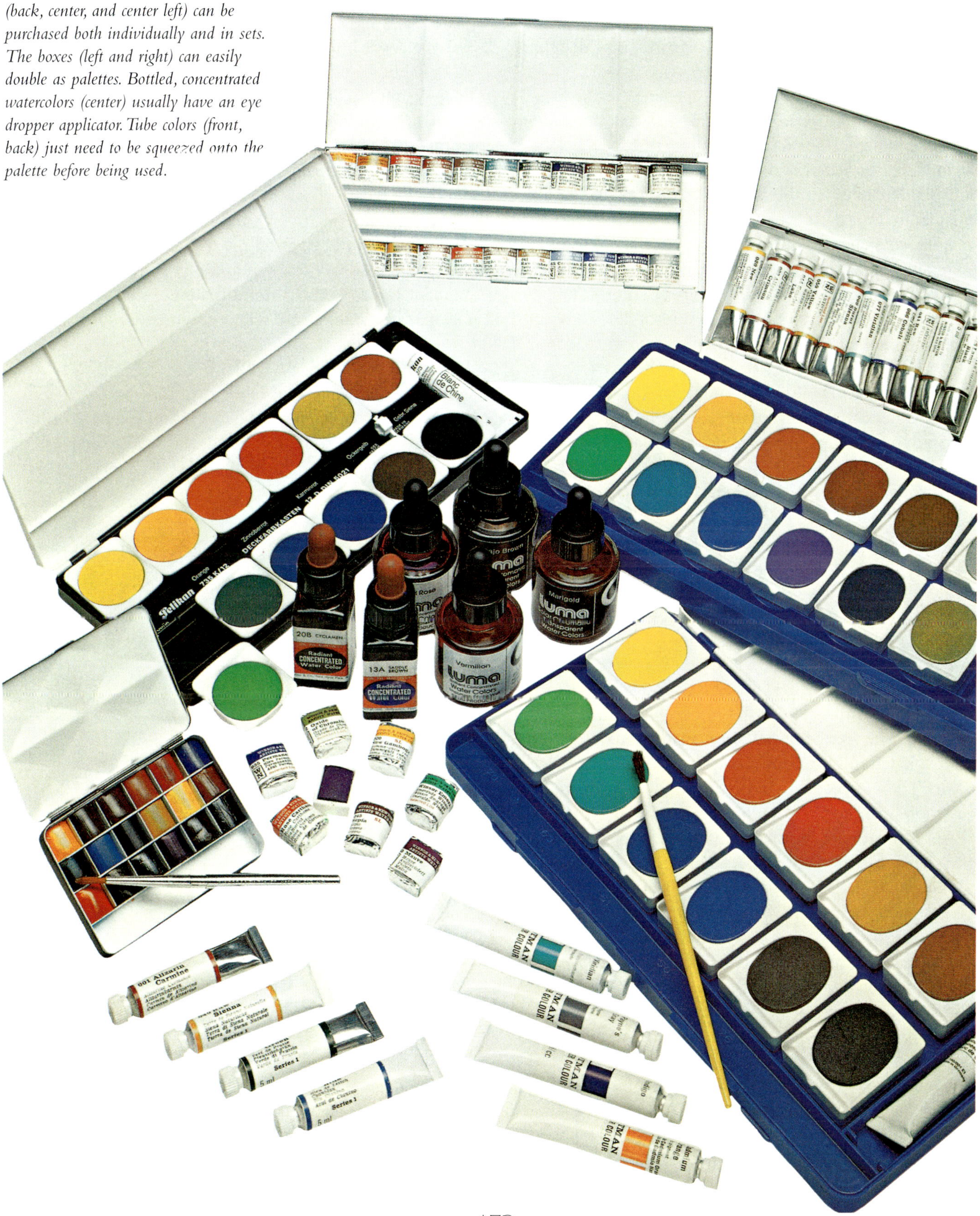

Paints

In buying watercolors, price more accurately reflects the quality than in any other medium. Large, cheap multi-hued boxes of so-called watercolor, muddy, impermanent, and consisting more of filler than pigment, may delight the eye of a child but are useless for serious work. "Students' Colors," usually put in smaller boxes or in tube-color sets, are good for practice especially if made by a reputable firm. But only those paints labelled "Artists' Colors" can be relied upon to give the transparency, glow, and permanency that the keen artist, professional, or amateur, requires.

In this expensive, highest-quality range, there is no essential difference – except in terms of portability and convenience – between "solid" and tube colors. The quality names to keep in mind are Winsor and Newton, Rowney, Reeves, and Grumbacher.

Dry cakes and semi-moist pans are little-used nowadays; half-pans, also semi-moist, are the best-known form. The best-quality half-pans can be bought singly in their tiny white boxes, and are often sold as sets in small flattish tins which double as palettes.

Semi-liquid tubes of watercolor are preferred by artists who wish to apply large washes. Fully liquid watercolor can be bought in bottles, with an eye dropper provided to transfer paint to palette. Good ranges include Luma and Dr. Martin's. It is obviously quicker to use these, or the watered-down "liquid" tube color, than to lift color from a half-pan with a wet brush to make up a wash.

Few watercolor artists, even the most expert, would claim to use more than 11 to 12 colors, from which the whole range could be mixed. But early English watercolorists, like Thomas Girtin, painted masterpieces using a palette of no more than five basic, permanent colors. There is certainly no need for any artist to keep any more than 10 or 11 colors.

An adequate modern palette is: ivory black, Payne's gray (optional), burnt umber, cadmium red, yellow ocher, cadmium yellow, Hooker's green, viridian, monestial blue, French ultramarine, and Alizarin crimson.

Professional artists may argue about the "best" basic palette, but few would disagree that a beginner or early student is best advised to stick to a restricted palette, which not only forces him or her to consider the basics of color mixing but imposes a pleasing harmony and consistency on the finished work.

Some pigments with a chemical dye base will stain paper rather than create a transparent wash on the surface. The "stainers," which might be quite useful for certain purposes, can be quite easily discovered: blob the color on paper and let it dry. Then rinse under running water. "Stain" pigments will remain.

Purists – and experimenters – can make their own watercolors at home or in the studio – a time-consuming process, but some may find it worthwhile. They will need finely-ground pigments of the finest quality, a plate glass slab, a grinding miller or muller, a plastic palette knife or spatula, and gum arabic, glycerine, distilled water, ox gall, sugar solution, and carbolic acid solution.

Pour one part of mixed sugar and glycerine solution plus two or three parts of gum arabic and a few drops of ox gall into a little pool on the glass. Then, with the palette knife, slowly draw in and mix the little heap of pigment placed beside it until there is a stiff paste. Grind this with the muller, and scrape the mixture into a pan.

THE GOUACHE PALETTE

Gouache is available in tube or cake form in an enormous range of colors. The selection illustrated below contains some of the most useful, and would form the basis of a palette when starting to paint.

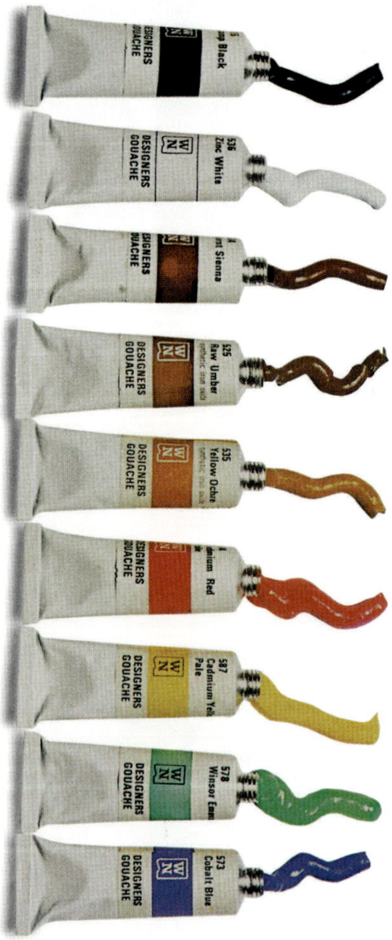

Lamp black

Zinc white

Burnt sienna

Raw umber

Yellow ocher

Cadmium red (pale)

Cadmium yellow (pale)

Winsor emerald

Cobalt blue

Brushes

Soft brushes are normally used for watercolor. The best ones are sable, made from the tips of the tail hairs of a small rodent found chiefly in Siberia. Sable brushes are extremely expensive, but if looked after properly they should last a lifetime. Watercolor brushes are also made from squirrel hair (known as "camel hair" for some reason) and ox hair. These are good substitutes for sable, but have less spring. There is now a wide range of synthetic brushes, usually made of nylon or a mixture of nylon and sable, and although they do not hold the paint as well as sable, they are excellent for finer details and are very much cheaper.

Only by experiment will an individual discover which shapes and sizes suit them. It is not necessary to have a great many brushes for watercolor work; for most purposes three or four will be adequate, and many artists use only two. A practical range would be one large chisel-end for laying washes and two or three rounds in different sizes. Some watercolorists use ordinary household brushes for washes, but care must be taken to prevent hairs from falling out as you work.

If you want your brushes to last, it is essential to look after them well. Wash them thoroughly in running water after use – if they are still stained use a little soap. Never leave brushes pointing downward in a glass of water, as this will bend the hairs out of shape, possibly permanently. If they need to be stored for a length of time in a box or tin make sure that they are absolutely dry; otherwise mildew may form. Store them upright.

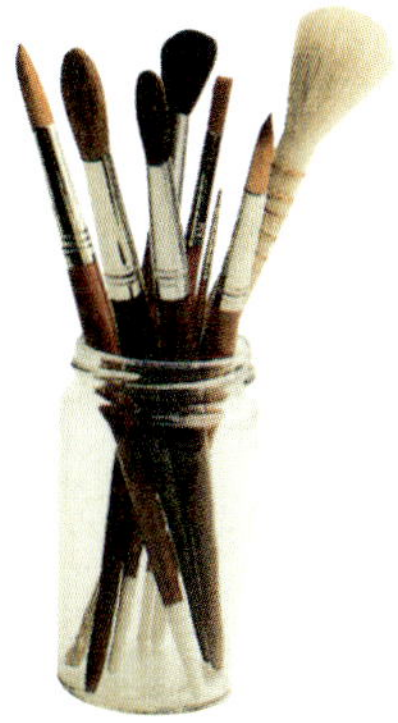

BELOW: *This selection of size 5 brushes from different series indicates the variations. The brushes are (from left to right): Proarte Series 1 and 3, LP Series 38, Winsor and Newton Series 7, LP Series 1A, Winsor and Newton Series 3A, 16, and 33. The Winsor and Newton Series 7 is the highest quality red sable brush available.*

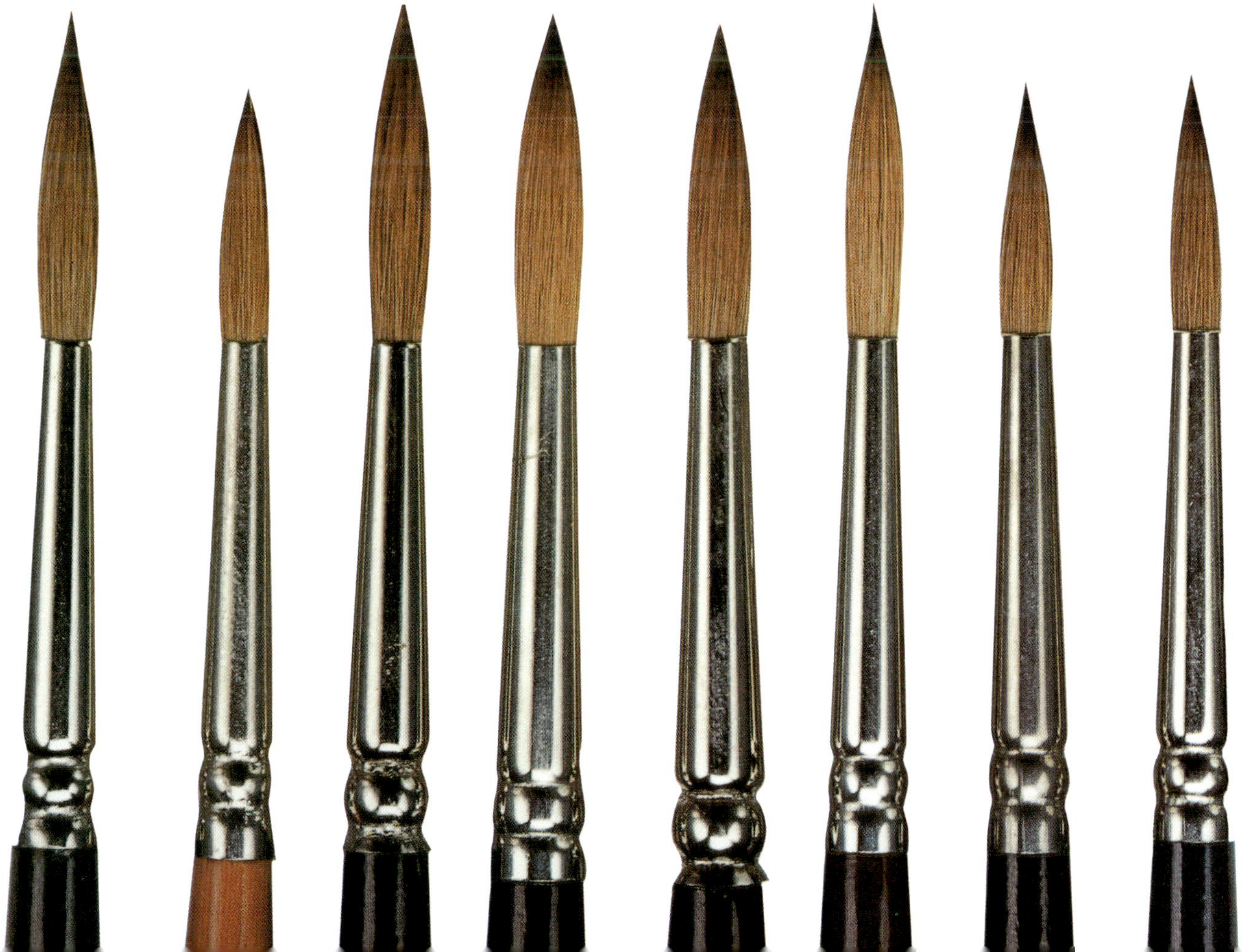

Boards, Palettes, and Other Equipment

You will need a drawing board, or possibly two boards of different sizes, to support the paper and stretch it where necessary. A piece of plywood or blockboard is perfectly adequate provided the surface is smooth and the wood soft enough to take drawing pins. For outdoor work a piece of hardboard can be used, with the paper clipped to it, though the paper must be heavy enough not to require stretching.

If you buy paints in paintbox form you will already have a palette; if not, you will need one with compartments for mixing paint. Watercolor palettes are made in plastic, metal, or ceramic, in a variety of sizes, and some have a thumbhole so that they can be held in the non-painting hand when working out of doors. Water containers are another necessity for outdoor work; there is nothing worse than arriving at your chosen spot to find that you have forgotten the water. Special containers can be bought, but plastic soft-drink bottles can be used to carry the water and any light (unbreakable) container such as a yogurt pot will suffice to put the water in when you reach your destination.

Various other items, though not strictly essential, can be useful and inexpensive aids for watercolor work. Small sponges can be used instead of brushes to apply washes, to sponge out areas and to create soft, smudgy cloud effects; kitchen roll, blotting paper, and cotton wool can be used in much the same way. Toothbrushes are useful for spattering paint to create textured effects: to suggest sand or pebbles on a beach, for example. A scalpel, or a razor blade, is often used to scrape away small areas of paint in a highlight area. And both masking tape and masking fluid can serve to block out areas while a wash is laid over the top, leaving a hard-edged area of white paper when removed.

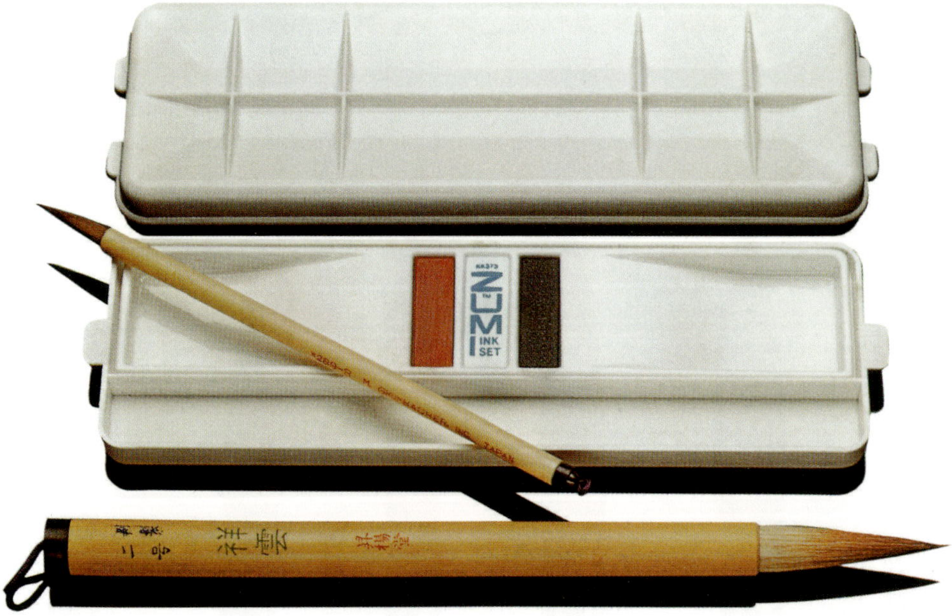

JAPANESE INKS AND BRUSHES

Watercolor painting techniques are traditionally associated with ink drawing and wash. To some extent, painting with stick inks combines the two types of work. Soft brushes are used, set in bamboo handles, which can be splayed out for broad sweeps of color, or drawn up to a very fine point for line work. This small ink set (left), produced by Grumbacher, gives one colored ink and black, and a fine bamboo brush. Several sizes of brush are available. The materials may be used in the manner of ink or watercolor, or combined with ordinary water-based paints.

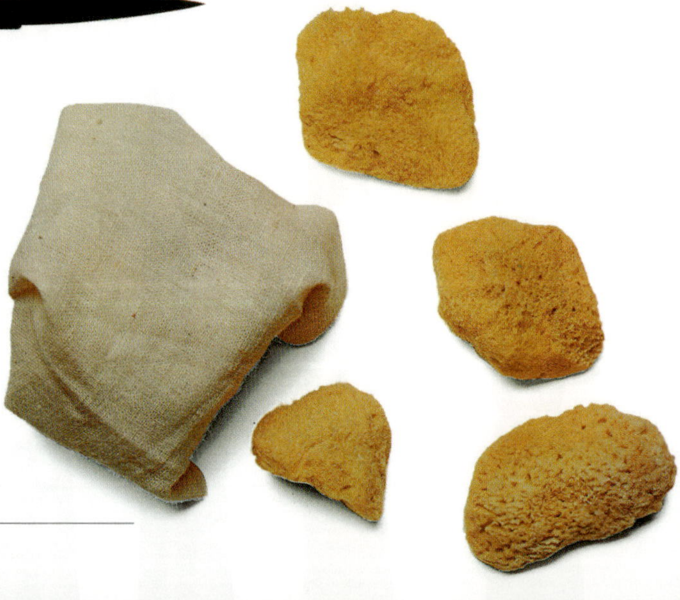

RAGS AND SPONGES

As the characteristic feature of watercolor painting is the extreme liquidity of the paint, rags and sponges are very useful both as painting utensils and to control or mop up the paint if it runs too much. Paint dabbed on with a sponge has a rich, rough texture.

Easels

Watercolors, unlike oils, are best done at close quarters, with the support held nearly horizontal, so that an easel is not really necessary for indoor work. However, an easel can be helpful. It allows you to tilt the work at different angles (many artists prefer to do preliminary drawings with the board held vertical) and to move it around to the best light, which is more difficult with a table. The most important aspects to consider – apart, of course, from price – are stability and the facility for holding the work firmly in a horizontal position.

For outdoor work, the combined seat and easel, which folds and is carried by a handle, is particularly useful. For indoor work, the combination easel, which can be used both as a drawing table and a studio easel, is more convenient. Both are adjustable to any angle from vertical to horizontal. Good easels are not cheap, however, so that it is wise to do without one until you are sure of your requirements; many professional watercolorists work at an ordinary table with their board supported by a book or brick.

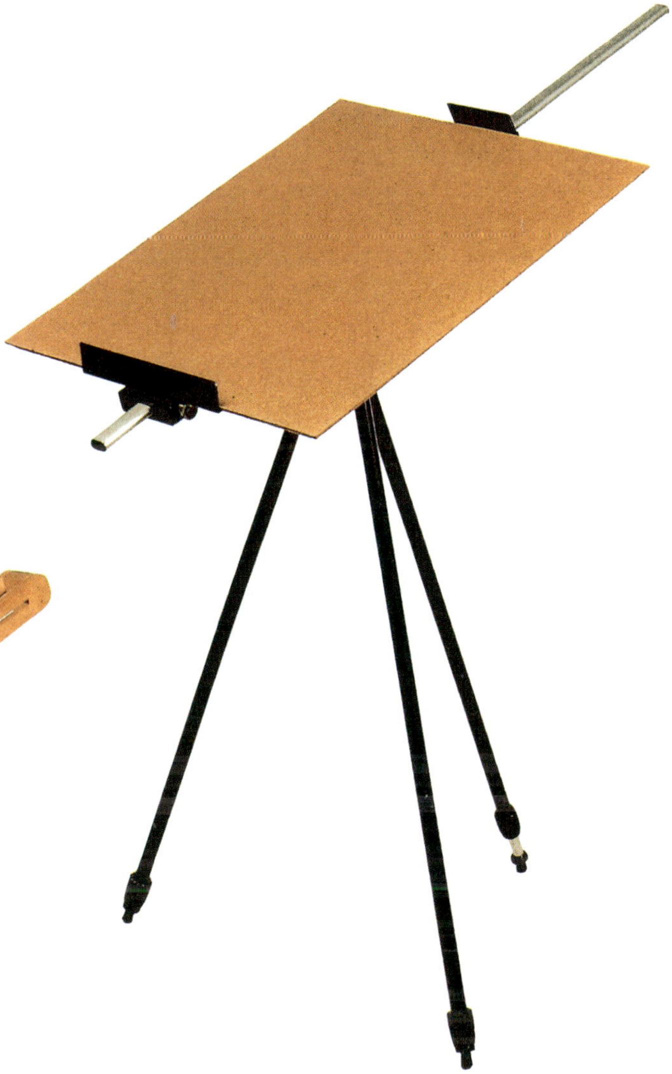

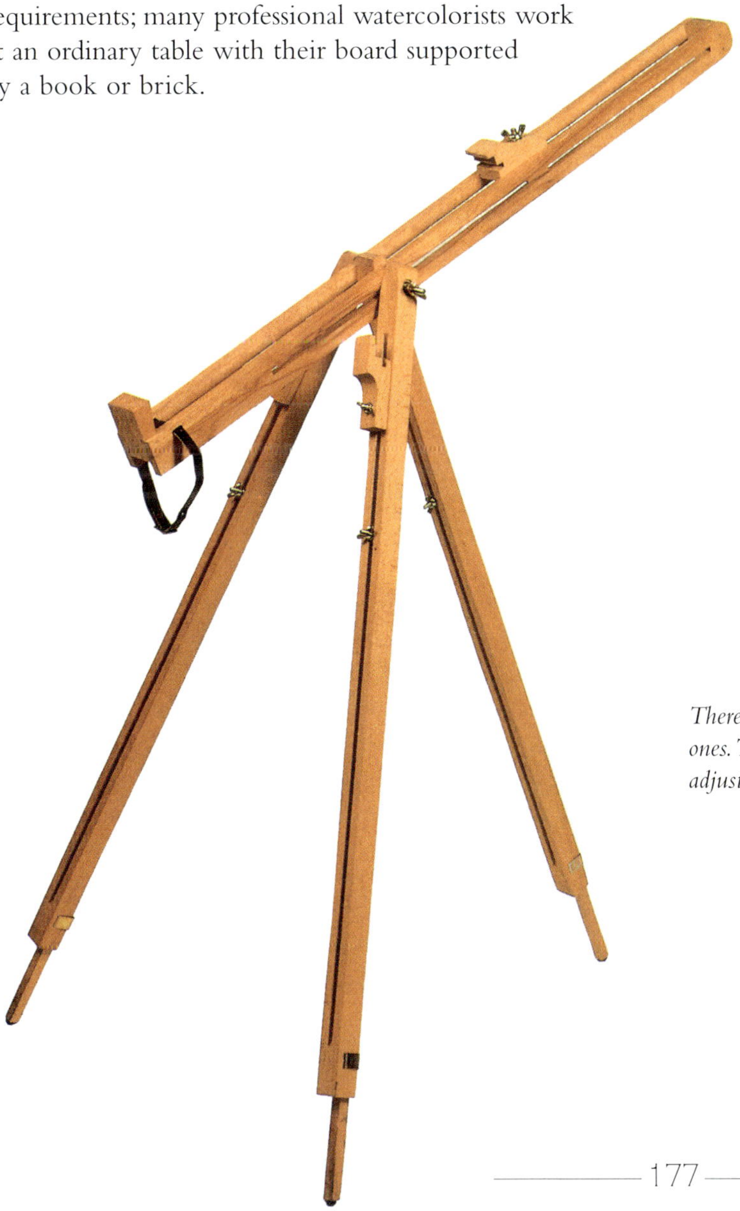

There are two main types of sketching easel – wooden ones and metal ones. They both weigh about the same, and the height and angle can be adjusted.

The Colors You Will Need

The three primary colors – red, yellow, and blue – can be mixed to produce all the other colors, so obviously these must be included in our basic palette. But if we ask in our local art shop for red, yellow, and blue paint, we will be asked "Which one?" because there are so many different reds, yellows, and blues to choose from. The first ones to buy must be of the brightest, most intense hues because mixing always results in loss of color intensity.

Sometimes you will need colors that are not obtainable by mixing the three primaries, so you will need to extend your palette to include these colors. As an example you might need violet, magenta, and different versions of the primary colors – alizarin crimson, cadmium yellow, and cobalt blue – browns (raw umber, burnt umber), yellow ocher, and black.

BLUE PAINTS

If you want to buy only one blue, French ultramarine is a strong, rich paint. Other artists might recommend the greener and slightly paler cobalt blue, but ultramarine is that bit brighter and more versatile even though a little less permanent. It also mixes better than cobalt blue and can form a greater range of colors when combined with other paints.

Whichever one you choose at first, make yourself thoroughly familiar with it and then try the other. Later on you could buy a tube of cerulean blue. This is particularly suitable for some skies, but although a lovely rich hue, it has low coloring power. Prussian blue, a very strong greenish blue, is favored by some painters, as is phthalocyanine blue (or more simply phthalo), similar to Prussian blue, but even more intense and with a higher permanency rating. Proprietary names for it include monestial blue (Rowney) and Winsor blue (Winsor & Newton). Both these blues have high coloring strength and can be mixed with yellows to form very rich greens.

YELLOW AND BROWN PAINTS

There are two bright yellows which should be included in any palette – cadmium yellow and lemon yellow. Cadmium yellow is the warmer color, with a hint of orange in it. It mixes with the blues to form warm yellowish greens. Lemon yellow is cooler and paler, and forms blueish greens when mixed with the blues.

Yellow ocher also has a place on most artists' palettes. It is a dark yellow verging on the brown. It has great strength and mixes well when added in small amounts. A similar color is raw sienna, which is slightly redder than yellow ocher and less powerful, making fine adjustments easier when mixing.

Also available are cadmium yellow pale and cadmium yellow deep, but neither are really necessary, as both can be made, in the first case by mixing cadmium yellow with a little white, and in the second by adding a little ocher. Naples yellow, on the other hand, is a useful color for obtaining skin tones, although it can be imitated by mixing yellow ocher with white and a tiny proportion of cadmium yellow. Other yellows include aureolin, chrome yellow and chrome lemon. These are less permanent and generally can achieve nothing which cadmium yellow or lemon yellow cannot do.

There are only two browns which you really need when you start painting. The first is raw umber, a versatile, slightly greenish brown ideal for dulling the blues, yellows, and greens; it has a fairly low strength so is easy to mix. The second is burnt sienna, a rich reddish brown which has such coloring power that even tiny quantities added to a mixture can alter it drastically. Burnt sienna mixed with white forms a warm pink. I often use it to modify blue and white mixtures to obtain sky tones. Another useful, though not essential, brown is burnt umber, which I think of as being the "brownest" of the browns.

RED PAINTS

The essential reds are cadmium red, a dense, opaque color and alizarin crimson, a deep, powerful, transparent one. Cadmium red is very brilliant, identical in color to poppies, but it loses its identity quickly on mixing with other colors. Mixed with white, it forms a warm pink, and mixed with blue, a very muddy purple. It is at its best when used straight from the tube, or either darkened with alizarin crimson or lightened with yellow ocher. Mixing it with cadmium yellow gives a brilliant orange, identical to cadmium orange, so it is unnecessary to buy an orange paint. Alizarin crimson is most useful in mixtures – with white to make a cool pink; with blues to counteract their brilliance when painting sky and sea; and combined with yellows and browns to achieve skin tones. (Alizarin is one of the slowest paints to dry on your palette and areas of painting where it has been used will remain tacky for a long time.)

GREEN PAINTS

A range of greens, including most of those occurring in a natural landscape, can be mixed from yellows with either blues or black, so you may not need to buy any greens initially. However, you will soon find you want some of the brighter greens to cope with the man-made colors of clothing or paintwork and also vegetation in unusual lighting conditions such as sunlit foliage, sparkling in a dark forest. Viridian is perhaps the most useful. It is dark and transparent, cool and blueish. When mixed with white, it retains its hue, giving pale, cool greens which cannot be matched by mixing yellow and blue. The opaque counterpart of viridian is called opaque oxide of chromium. Many painters use it a great deal for landscape.

Brighter than these two are colors like chrome green and cadmium green, both pale, yellowish greens which can be good on occasion for foliage. Another useful green is terre verte, a dull green of low coloring power. Straight from the tube, it is often identical to the dark foliage in a landscape. It can also be used in mixtures to modify the colors of sky, sea, foliage, flowers, skin – in fact almost anything. However, it is not essential, since an identical green can be mixed from cadmium yellow, lamp black and a little ultramarine. Emerald green in the Winsor & Newton range is an artificial-looking, pale color which does not mix well, but in some ranges it is an excellent and reliable alternative for viridian.

PURPLE AND VIOLET PAINTS

Purple, like greens, can be mixed, but only in a low intensity. The brightest violets or purples will have to be taken straight from the tube or mixed together to yield exactly the color you want. Cobalt violet is excellent, but I find the most useful is Winsor violet which, when mixed with rose madder, alizarin crimson or magenta, together with white, will give almost any violet or purple. It is also extremely useful for modifying the blues of the sky or sea, and for making grays with yellows, browns, and greens.

BLACK AND GRAY PAINTS

Black is useful for mixing with yellow to make greens, and for this purpose lamp black is the best, because it is slightly bluer than ivory black. Black will also darken any green, but only small amounts should be used, and it destroys the vitality of other colors, so should be treated with caution. Sometimes, of course, these dark tones can be just what one needs, as when painting the very darkest shadows. In such cases, ivory black is the best one to use as it is more neutral and a little more transparent. Payne's gray is basically a kind of dilute black which, having relatively less strength, is very useful for modifying blues, browns, and greens.

Color Mixing

The next stage is to practice making new colors from mixtures of your "basic palette." The colors on the chart on page 180 are all two-color mixes; you can make an even wider range by using three. It is not advisable to mix more than three, or all you will achieve is characterless mud.

Charts like these are useful for reference, but you will learn more if you do your own experiments on the same lines. First, though, here's a brief look at some of the properties of colors and the terms used to describe them.

Primary colors are the ones you can't produce by mixing other colors. They are blue, yellow, and red. Secondary colors are made by mixing two primaries, such as blue and yellow, which make green. Tertiary colors are mixtures of one primary color and one secondary, or three primaries.

You can buy both secondary and tertiary colors ready-made. (You already have three of them in your palette: viridian, raw umber, and Payne's gray.) However, you can achieve more variety of color through mixing – and it is much more fun.

MIXING INTENSE SECONDARIES

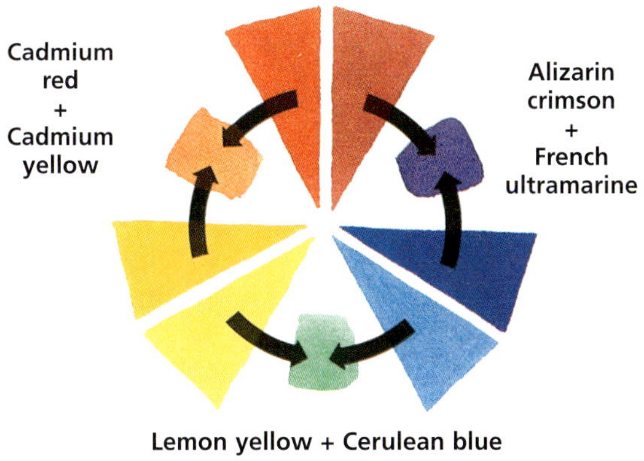

MIXING MUTED SECONDARIES

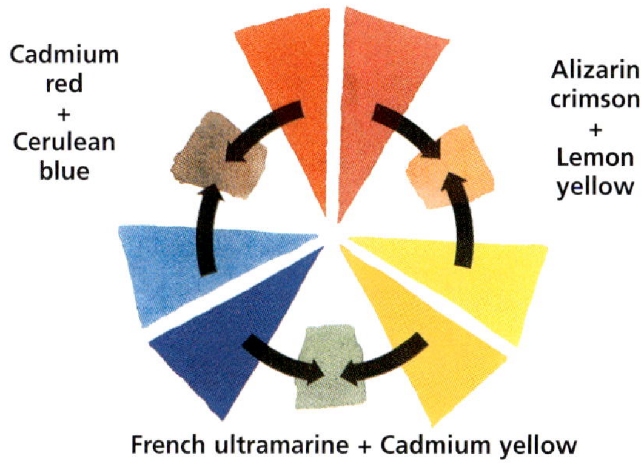

TWO-COLOR MIXES

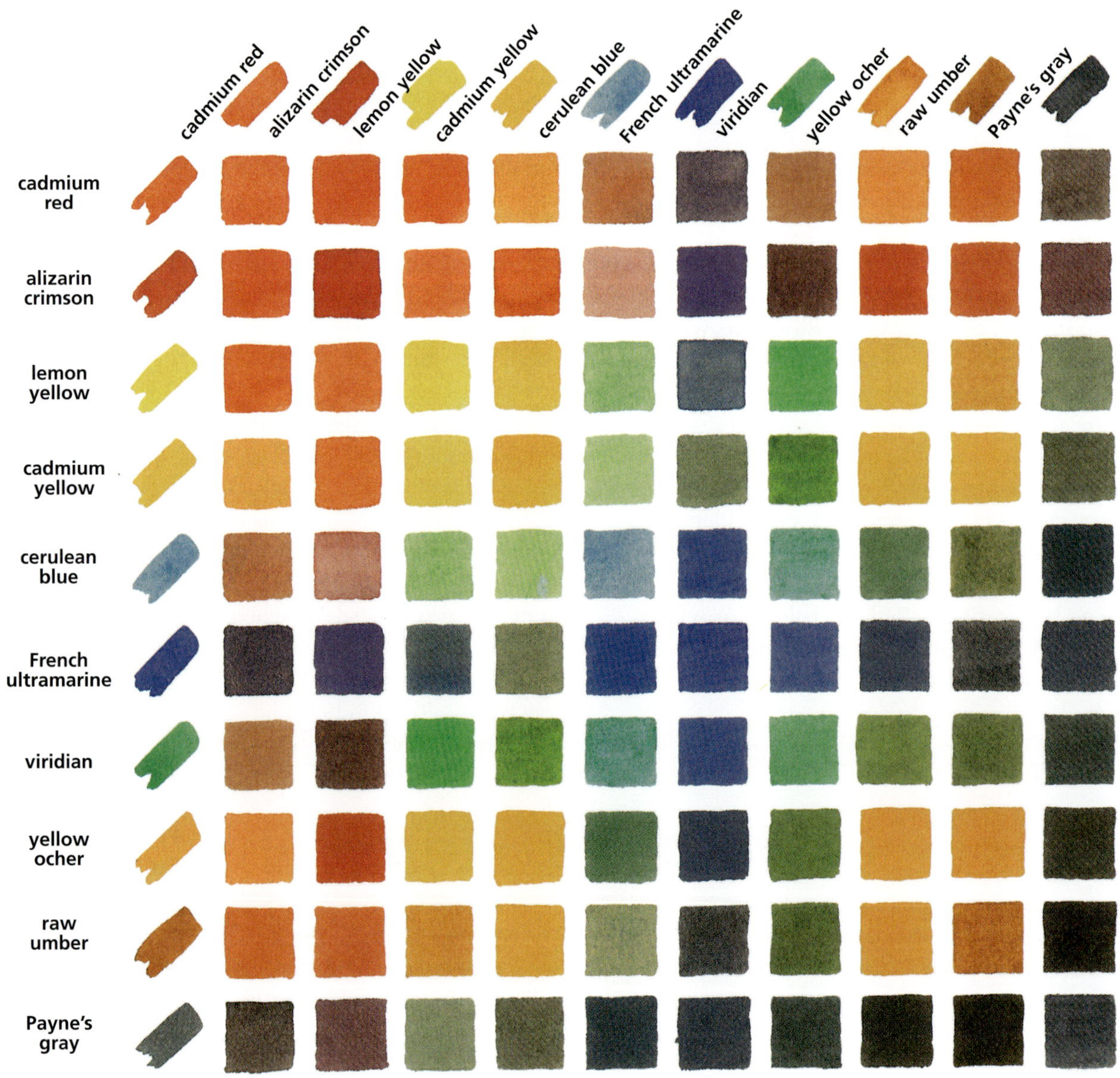

THREE-COLOR MIXES

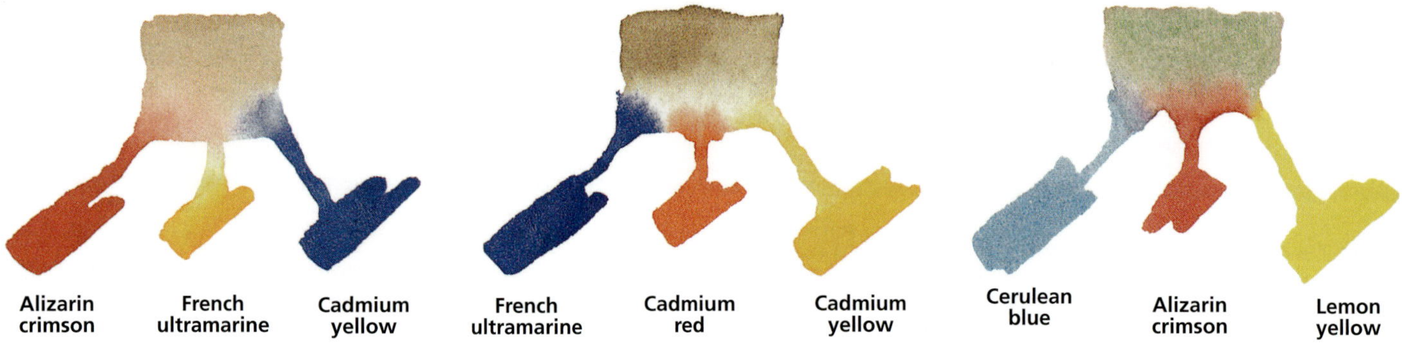

Although the primary colors are bright on their own or when mixed with another primary, a mixture of all three makes a neutral color, and often a more interesting one than a mixture of two secondary colors. Here, a small quantity of a third primary color (shown in the middle) was added to a mixture of two other primaries.

Techniques

LAYING A FLAT WASH

The term "wash" is a rather confusing one, as it implies a relatively broad area of paint applied flatly, but it is also sometimes used by watercolor painters to describe each brush stroke of fluid paint, however small it may be. Here it refers only to paint laid over an area too large to be covered by one brush stroke.

A flat wash in watercolor, thinned gouache or acrylic can be laid either with a large brush or a sponge. The paper is usually dampened to allow the paint to spread more easily, though this is not essential. Washes must be applied fast with no dithering, so mix up plenty of paint before beginning – you always need more than you think. Tilt the board slightly so that the brush strokes flow into each other but do not dribble down the paper. Load the brush with paint, sweep it horizontally across the paper, starting at the top of the area, and immediately lay another line below it, working in the opposite direction. Keep the brush loaded for each stroke and continue working in alternate directions until the area is covered.

Sometimes it is necessary to lay a wash around an intricate shape, such as a skyline of roofs or chimneys. In this case the wash must start at the bottom, not at the top, to allow you to paint carefully around the shapes, so you will have to turn the board upside down. If you are dampening the paper first, dampen only up to the edge, as the paint will flow into any wet part of the paper.

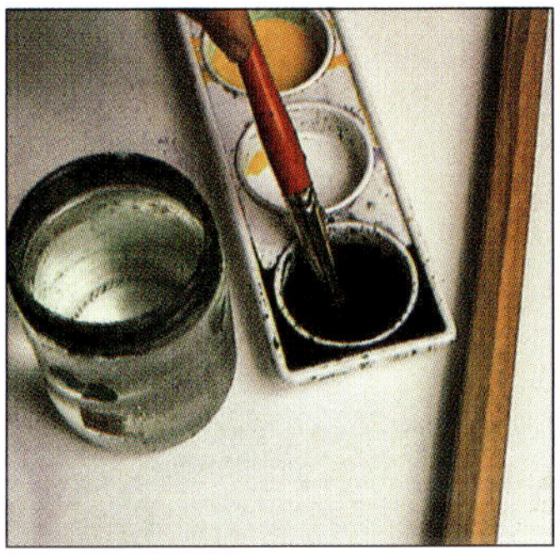

1 Mix up a wash of color in a saucer or jar, making sure that there is more than enough paint, so you won't run out.

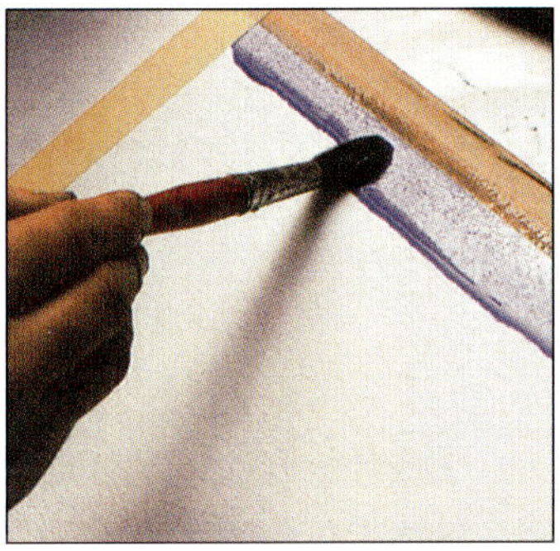

2 The first step in laying in a flat wash is to dampen the entire paper to enable the paint to flow more easily. The color should be fluid, but quite strong, to compensate for the fact that it will dry much lighter on the paper. The drawing board should now be tilted to an angle of 10 to 15°. This allows the wash to flow downward but at the same time prevents drips. To lay the flat wash, load a large brush (round or flat) and draw a slow, steady stroke across the top of the area. Due to the angle of the board, a narrow rill of paint will form along the bottom edge of the stroke.

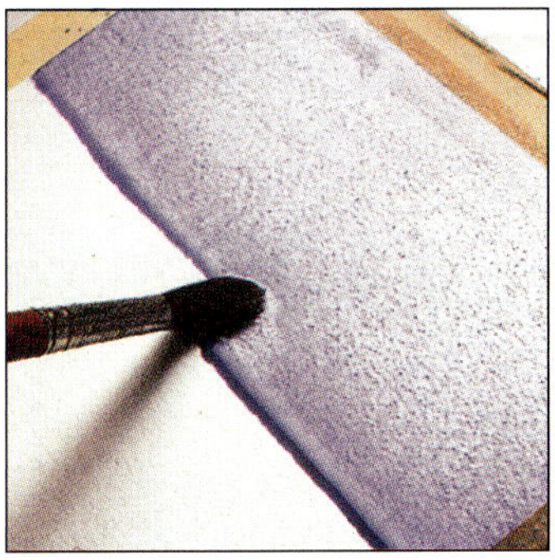

3 Load the brush again and paint a second stroke beneath the first, slightly overlapping it and picking up the rill of paint. The excess paint now rolls down across the second stroke and reforms along the new bottom edge.

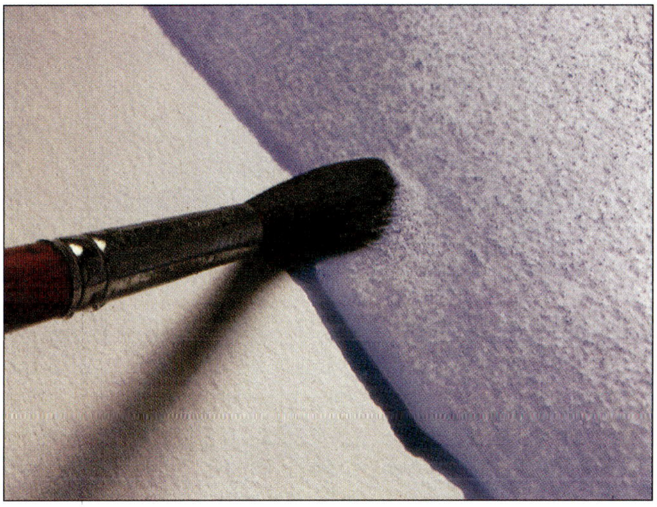

4 Repeat these overlapping strokes all the way down the area to be covered, each time picking up the paint from the previous stroke. To encourage a smooth, even flow, work quickly and apply a light pressure only to the brush.

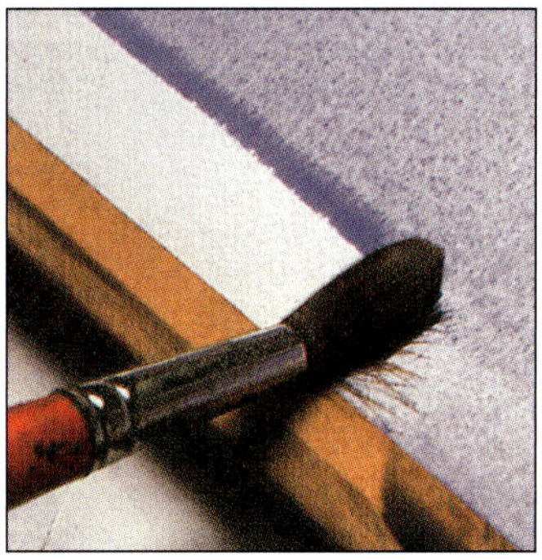

5 At the end of the wash, squeeze the brush until semi-dry and blot up the excess pool of color that forms at the bottom. The wash should then be allowed to dry in the same tilted position; if left to dry flat, there is a danger of the paint flowing back and causing blotches and "tide marks" in the wash.

GRADATED AND VARIEGATED WASHES

Colors in nature are seldom perfectly flat and uniform, and it is often necessary to lay a wash that shifts in tone from dark to light or one that contains two or more different colors.

A gradated wash shades from dark to light, and is laid in the same way as a flat wash, the only difference being that more water is added to the pigment for each successive line of paint. It is a little tricky to achieve a really even gradation, as too much water in one line or not enough in another will result in a striped effect. Keep the paint as fluid as possible so that each brush stroke flows into the one below, and never be tempted to work back into the wash if it does not come out as you wished. You may find that a sponge gives better results than a brush, as it is easier to control the amount of water you use.

Variegated washes are those using more than one color and are much less predictable than flat or gradated ones. However, you can achieve very exciting, if totally unexpected, results by allowing the colors to bleed into one another.

If you intend to paint a sky at sunset, blending from blue at the top to yellows, oranges, and reds at the bottom, mix up three or four suitable colors in your palette and then lay them in strips one under the other on dampened paper so that they blend gently into one another.

ABOVE AND BELOW: *Variegated washes need to be applied quickly and with no hesitation. These washes were worked on well-dampened paper with the board at a slight angle. For the sunset she turned the board upside down to allow her to lay the yellow, red, and blue from light to dark, turning it again to add the streaks of gray over the blue. Once the colors had blended together to create the desired effect, the wash was left to dry flat.*

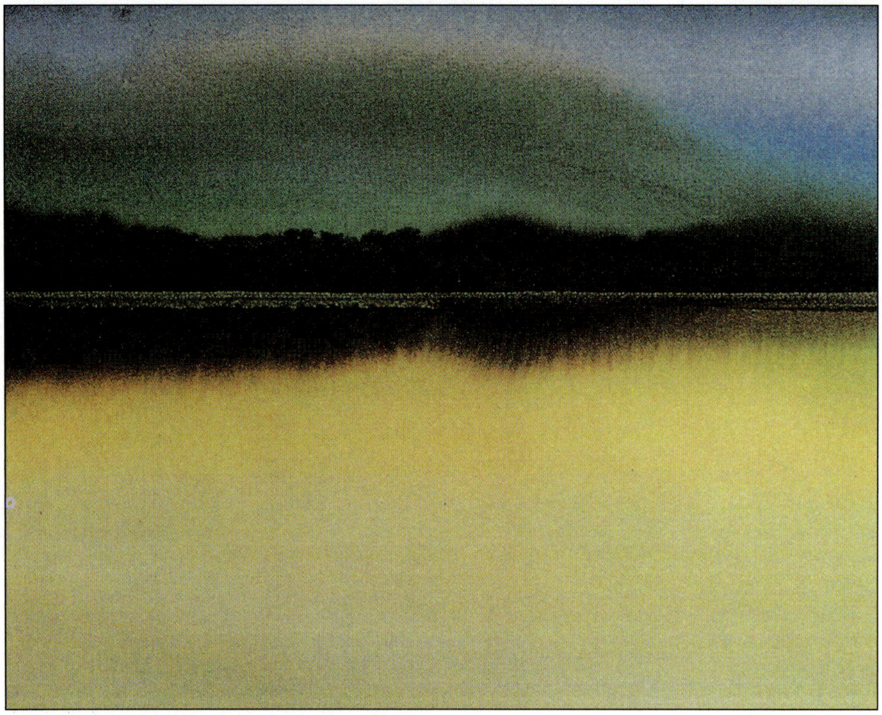

RESERVOIR REFLECTIONS by Robert Tilling

This lovely painting relies for its effect on the way each color blends into its neighbor with no hard edges. The artist works with large brushes and very wet paint, tilting his board so that the colors flow down the paper, but controlling them very carefully.

WORKING WET ON WET

Painting wet on dry means allowing each wash to dry before putting on another color. In the wet on wet method new colors are added to damp washes so that they bleed into one another, creating soft edges and a variety of exciting effects.

The two techniques are not entirely separate, and it is difficult to avoid painting wet on wet altogether. The variegated wash (page 182) is a step toward wet on wet and so is blending. Even a heavy paper is liable to buckle. You'll also have to work fast, because the paper must remain wet, or at least damp, all the time. This doesn't mean that you have to dash off a picture in ten minutes, or even half-an-hour, because well-dampened paper takes a while to dry. Apart from these two cautions, there are no firm rules: one of the great attractions of working wet on wet is that it is never predictable.

Controlling the paint The effects vary according to how wet or dry the paper is. However, you can exert some control. Placing a loaded brush of wet paint into a sopping-wet wash is similar to dropping a stone into water: the weight of the water in the new brush stroke causes the first color to draw away, so that the two don't mix, although they may bleed into each other. If the paper is just damp, the colors will blend more subtly.

Artists who work in this way learn to judge exactly how wet the paper must be, something that only practice can teach. Another way of controlling the paint is by altering the angle of the board. If the board is flat the colors will stay more or less where you put them, but by tilting it you can make the paint flow downward, upward, or even sideways. This can be a useful method for subjects such as rainy skies, or flowers, where drips of paint can suggest leaves or petals.

1 Working on stretched and well-dampened paper, the artist begins by dropping dark gray paint into light to create the effect of heavy clouds.

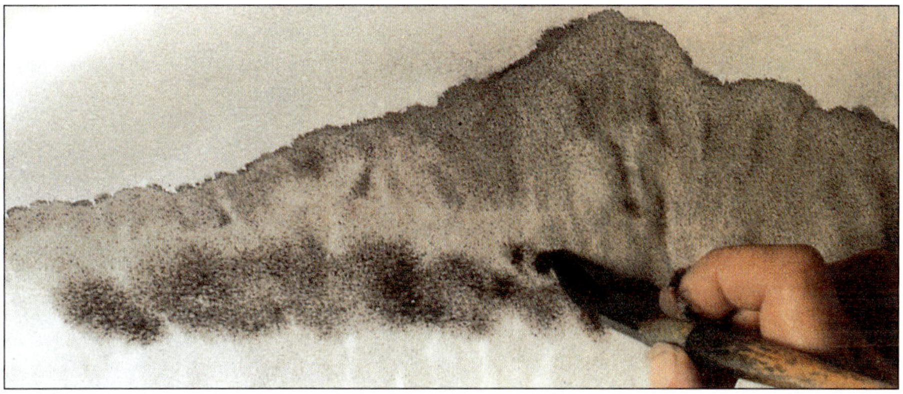

3 The mountain was created by allowing the paper to dry slightly, laying a rough band of gray and tilting the board upside down until the paint flowed into a suitable shape. The board was then laid flat.

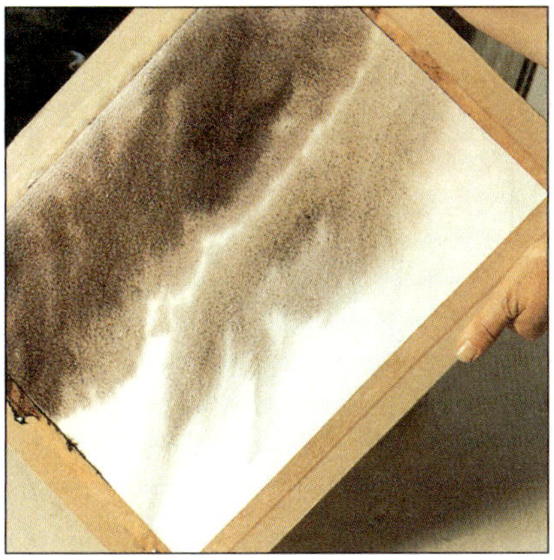

2 Holding the board sideways at a sharp angle makes the paint flow toward the bottom corner. You can exert control by varying the angle of the board; if the paint flows too far in one direction, simply reverse the angle.

4 The paint will continue moving until it has dried. Be prepared to lose an effect you liked. The detail added in Step 3 became a series of blurred, rounded shapes.

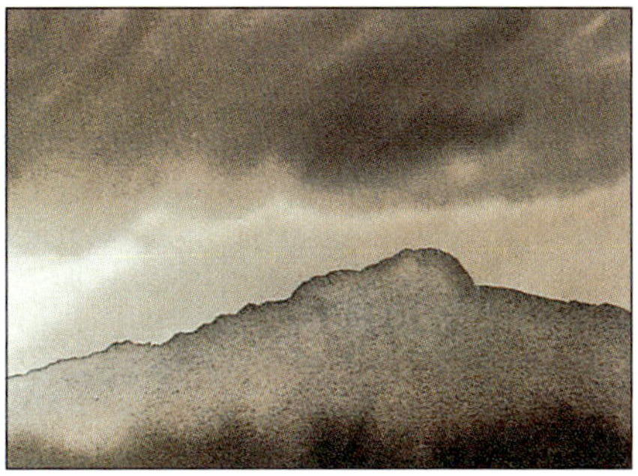

5 The color flowed upward and downward, creating a jagged edge at the top of the mountains, and giving a realistic impression of a dark forest below.

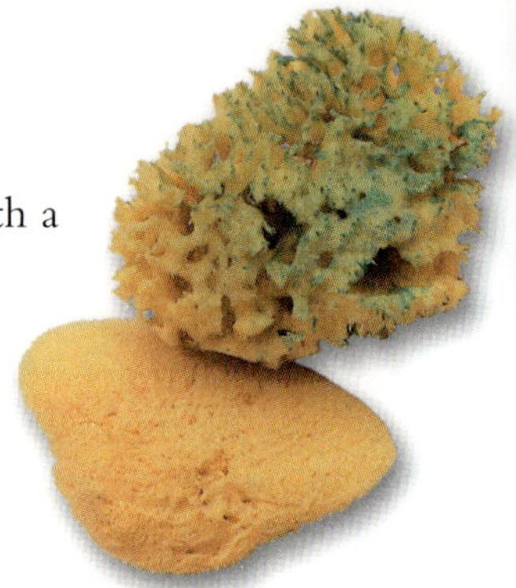

SPONGE PAINTING

The sponge is a highly versatile painting tool, capable of producing a broad range of effects in any painting medium. Most artists keep two sponges in their painting kit: a synthetic one for laying a flat, even layer of color in large areas, and a natural sponge for creating patterns and textures. Natural sponges are more expensive than synthetic ones, but they have the advantage of being smoother and more pliable to work with, and their irregular texture produces more interesting patterns in the paint. For example, a mottled pattern is produced by pressing a moistened sponge into fairly thick paint and then dabbing it onto the paper. You can dab one color over another, or produce a graded tone by dabbing more heavily in one area than another. This technique is successful in rendering foliage on trees, or the pitted surface of weathered stone.

Also, by twisting or stroking with a paint-soaked sponge, you can achieve subtle gradations of tone when painting soft, rounded forms such as clouds, fruit, or perhaps misty hills in the distance.

Natural sponges Painting with a sponge gives textural effects that are often impossible to render with a brush. The mottled patterns produced by dabbing color on with a sponge are perfect for simulating the textures of weathered rock and crumbling stone, pebbles and sand on a beach, sea spray and tree foliage. In addition, you can create lively broken color effects by sponging different colors over each other.

FOLIAGE TEXTURE

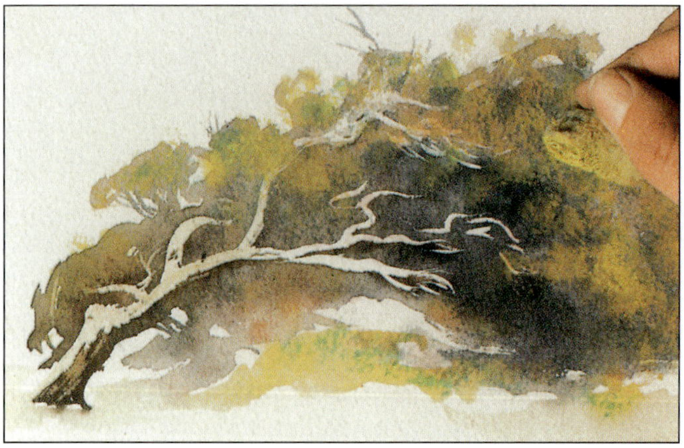

1 For this study of a tree, the artist begins by painting the trunk and branches with masking fluid. Having laid in dark green for the mass of the foliage, allowed it to dry, and removed the masking fluid, she now dabs a thick solution of lemon yellow onto the lighter areas of the trees.

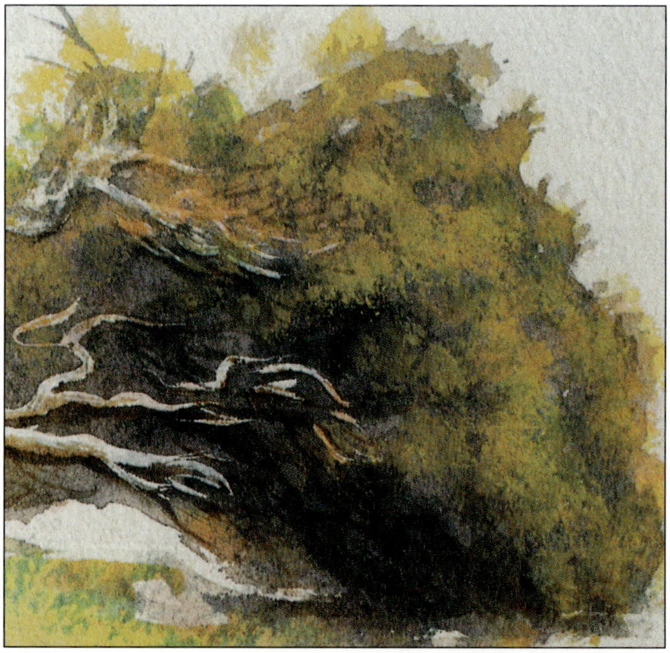

2 The effect is attractive and realistic – an ideal method for this "fluffy-looking" Mediterranean pine.

ROCK TEXTURE

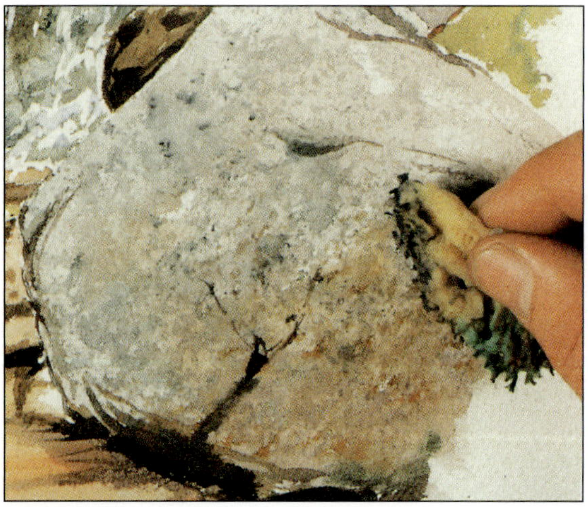

LEFT: Several layers of sponging, using a pale gray-brown mixture with touches of yellow, create an accurate impression of the weathered, mottled surface of the rock. The dark crevices of the rock and the shadows below form fine lines which could not be achieved with a sponge. A small pointed brush was used for these essential descriptive touches.

BACKRUNS

One of the charms of watercolor is its unpredictability, but sometimes the unexpected result is more exciting than the planned one. Backruns are a good example. If you have tried to correct a wash before it has dried you may have noticed how the new paint seeps into the old, creating irregular blotches with jagged edges. Backruns are sometimes called "cauliflowers" because of their appearance.

They can be alarming when you are doing your best to lay a perfect flat wash, and even more so when you've started a painting and have to abandon it. Backruns are one of the "happy accidents" that can become a technique in their own right, and many artists induce them deliberately. You can't control their shape very precisely, so they are best for suggesting a shape rather than delineating it. But, they can be perfect for cloud effects, foliage, or the petals of a flower. You might also like to try the method for reflections in water, working new paint or clean water into a still-damp wash so that it spreads outward, giving an area of soft color with the crisp but irregular edges characteristic of reflections.

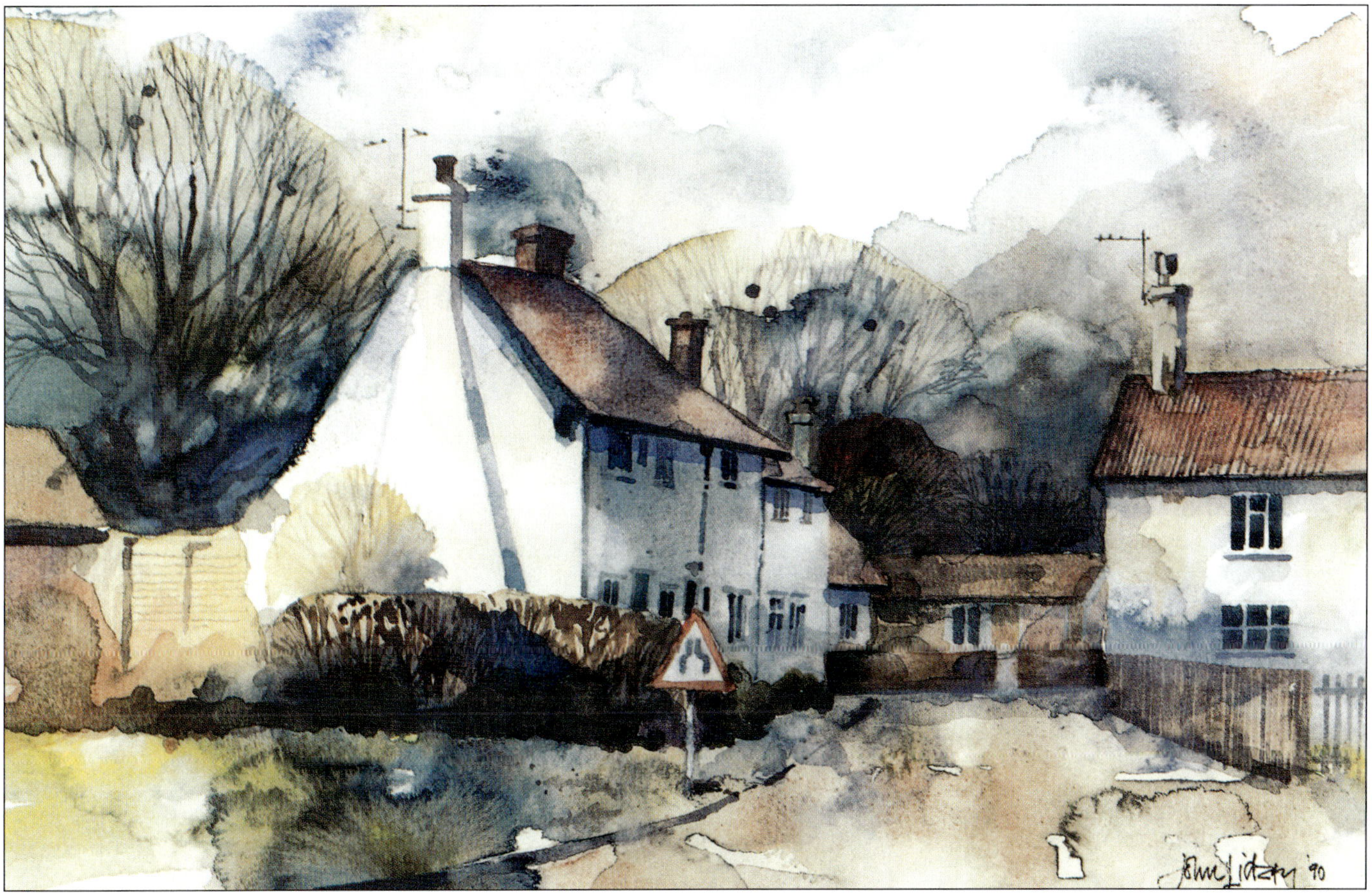

VILLAGE ROAD by John Lidzey

This artist loves to exploit the characteristic of "accidents" in watercolor work. On the left-hand side of the foreground he allowed three backruns to form, one behind the other, providing irregular jagged edges and intriguing shapes that balance those of the trees behind. It is not necessary to ask what these shapes are; they just work in the context of the painting.

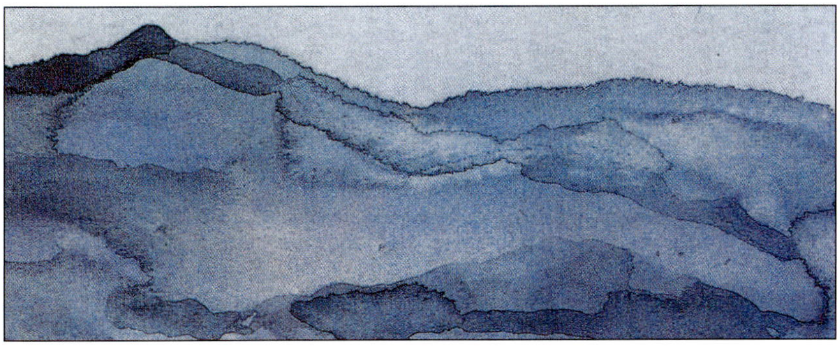

LEFT: *Here backruns have been deliberately induced and then blown with a hairdryer so that they form definite patterns. Techniques such as this are particularly useful for amorphous shapes such as clouds, reflections, or distant hills.*

LINE AND WASH

The line and wash technique is as old as watercolor itself. Historically, it was mainly used to put flat tints over drawings, usually done in pen and ink. This type of line and wash drawing can still be seen mainly in illustration work. But many watercolorists now use the technique in a bolder and freer way, integrating the line and color to avoid the appearance of "coloring book" drawings.

There aren't any rules about line and wash. You can do the drawing first, or start with color and add drawn details, or develop both at the same time. There is no prescription for the materials either. You can use a dip pen, a fountain pen, or a pencil; but pencil lines, being lighter, are best if your colors are pale. If you decide on pen, you will probably have to try out several types before you find one that suits you. The important criteria is that it feels comfortable and provides the kind of line you like. First, go to an art store where you can test pens before buying. Be wary of felt-tips; although they are inexpensive and easy to draw with, the colors tend to fade quickly.

Traditional line and wash drawings were done with waterproof ink, which didn't run when the washes were laid on top. Some contemporary artists like the effect of runs and therefore prefer water-soluble ink. This is another decision you'll only be able to make after experimenting.

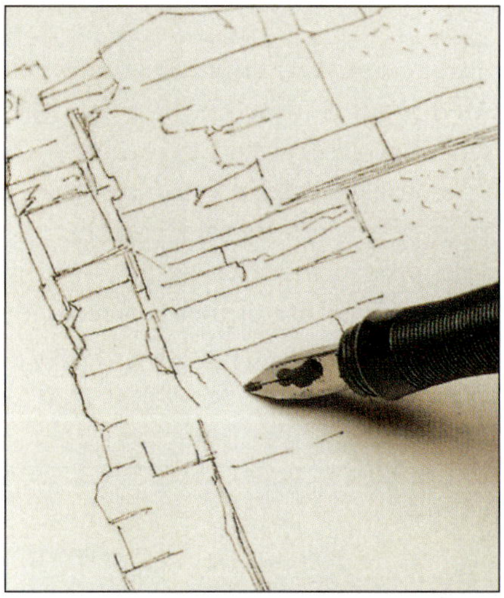

1 The artist chooses a pale color scheme, keeping the initial pen drawing light. She selects a fine nib pen and water-soluble ink, because she wants the ink and paint to run together in places.

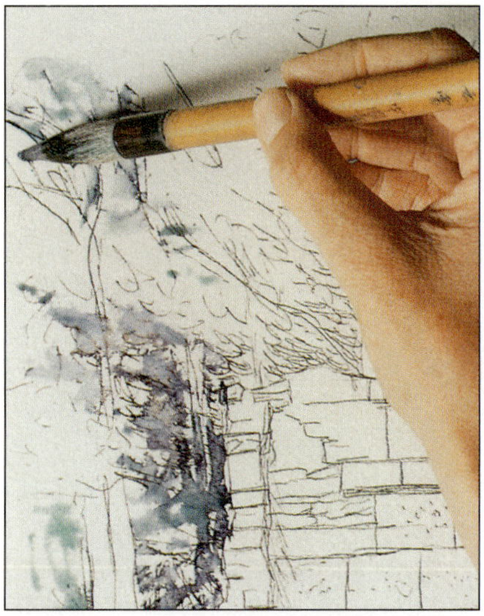

2 She uses a Chinese brush to make a series of loose, varied brushmarks that complement the drawing.

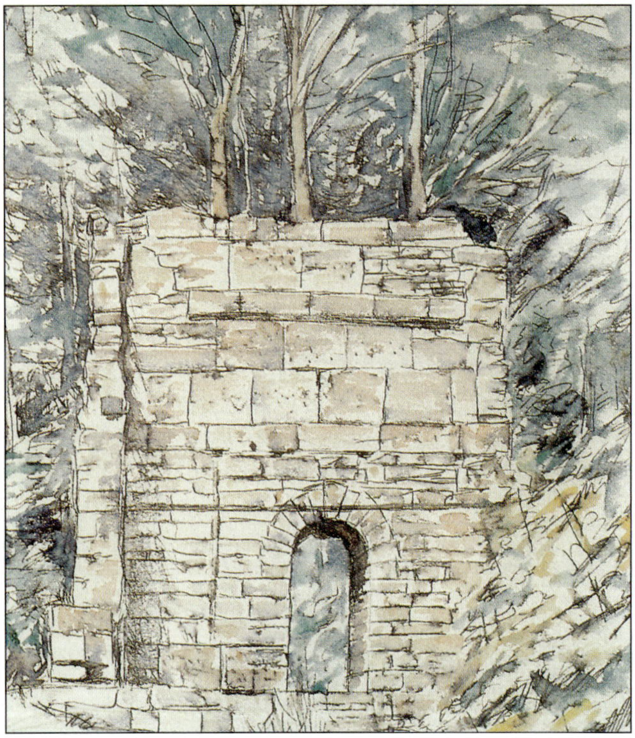

3 On the stone structure, the drawing is still clearly visible. Where the ink has run into the paint the lines soften to suggest the small shadows seen on old stonework.

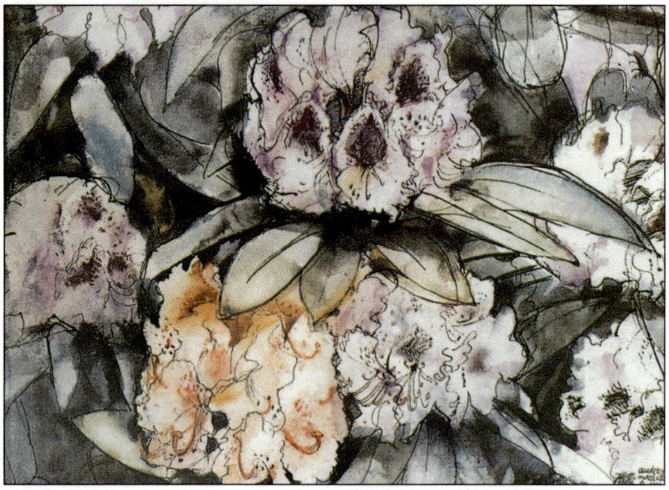

RHODODENDRONS by Audrey Macleod

This artist likes to exploit the contrast between the crispness of pen lines and the delicacy of watercolor. She uses the line and wash technique extensively in her studies of flowers. To enhance this contrast, she sponges the paint in places to soften the color, an effect seen on the leaves. She never overworks the paint, and on the blooms, touches the color in lightly to the edges of the shapes.

DRY BRUSH

In the dry brush technique, a small amount of thick color is picked up on a brush which is skimmed lightly over a dry painting surface. The paint catches on the raised "tooth" of the paper or canvas and leaves tiny speckles of the ground, or the underlying color, showing through. The ragged, broken quality of a dry brush stroke is very expressive, and there are many subjects that lend themselves to dry brush treatment. The technique can be used to portray the coarse texture of the weathered surfaces of rock, stone, and wood for example. Loose dry brush strokes convey a sense of movement when painting delicate subjects such as grass, hair, or the foam of a breaking wave.

Dry brush allows you to suggest detail and texture with minimal brushwork; in waterscapes, for example, a deft stroke of dry color that leaves the white ground showing through can convey the sparkle of sunlight on water with the utmost economy.

Never labor dry brush strokes: use quick, confident movements. This technique works best on a rough-textured ground which helps to break up the paint.

You can build complex color effects by working one layer of dry brush over another, splaying out the bristles to make a series of little parallel lines.

The best way to ensure that you don't put on too much paint is to dip the tip of the brush into the paint mixture and then dab it lightly on a paper towel. It takes practice, so experiment on a spare piece of paper before working on a painting. A word of warning though, once you've got the hang of the technique you'll find it so easy that you may over-use it, and too much dry brush work in one painting can look monotonous.

LANDSCAPE TECHNIQUE

1 Depending upon the effect you want, you can work on white paper or on top of light washes (which must be dry), as shown here. To outline individual grasses, a pointed brush with very little paint on it is dragged lightly over the paper. The color catches only on the raised grain. The effect is a broken line, similar to that made by charcoal on rough paper.

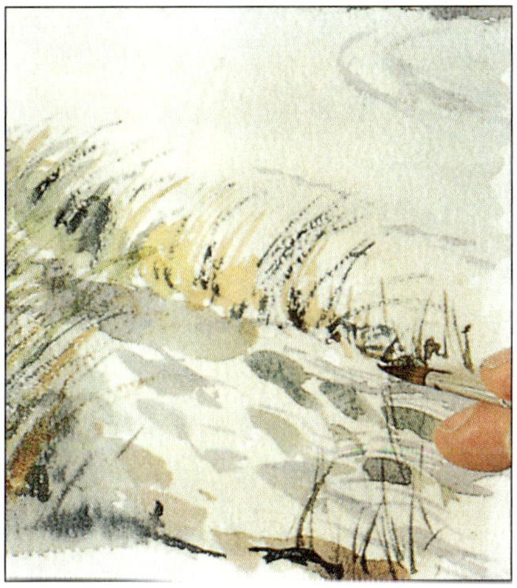

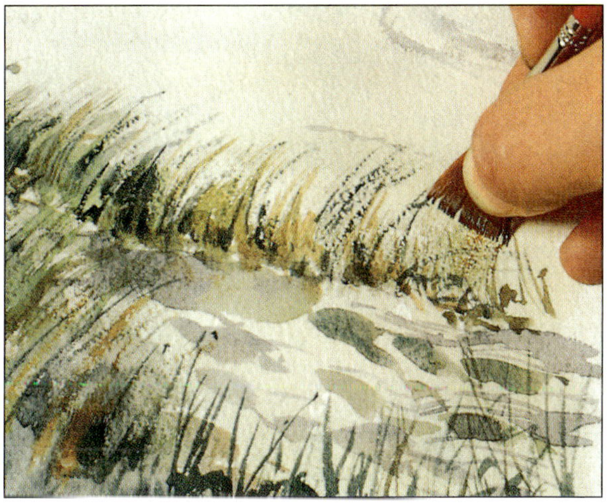

2 The artist uses a square-ended brush for the large clumps of grass. The hairs of the brush are splayed between thumb and forefinger and pushed gently over the paper.

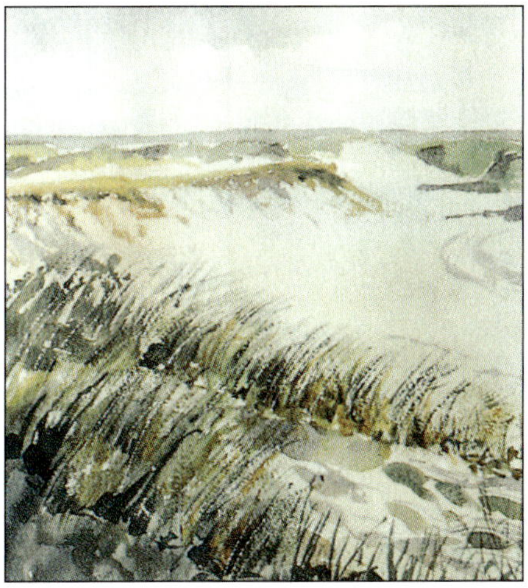

3 Dry brush work creates a realistic impression of the windblown marram grass, and a nice contrast with the larger, "wet brush" strokes used for the immediate foreground. The fine white lines, where the sun catches a few of the grasses in the foreground, are made by scratching into dry paint with the point of a knife.

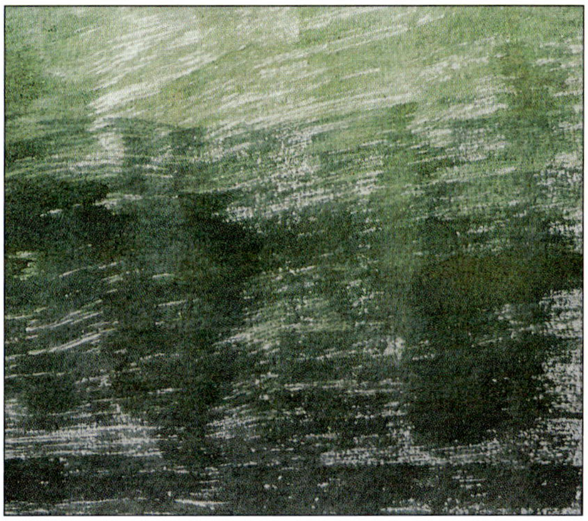

RIGHT: *Dry brushing with more than one color or tone can create highly expressive effects, particularly when used in conjunction with washes; the underlying hue breaks through the dry brush to produce a fascinating optical mixture. Always work quickly – dry brush is a technique that looks best when handled freely and loosely.*

DRY BRUSH: ANIMAL TEXTURE

1 As before, dry brush work is applied over washes. The main colors of the horse's head are lightly painted and allowed to dry before shadows are added.

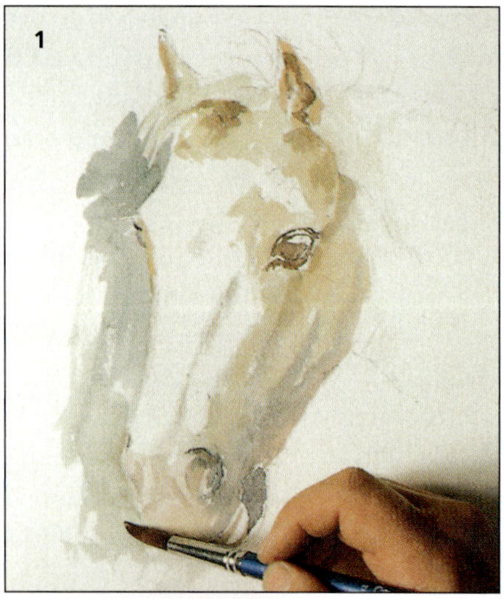

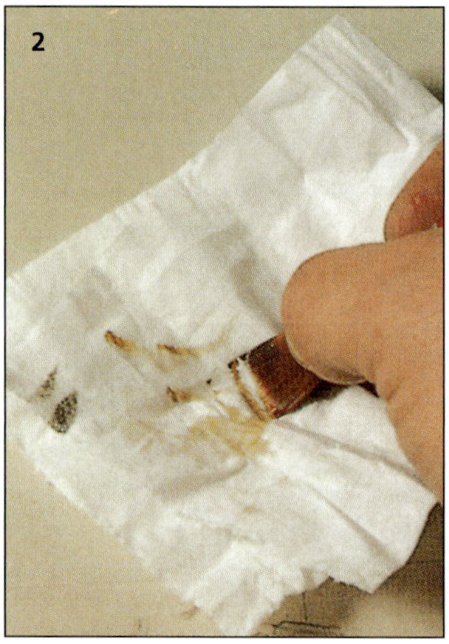

2 A square-ended brush is dipped into paint and partially dried. Make sure that there is not too much paint on the brush by experimenting on a spare piece of paper before painting.

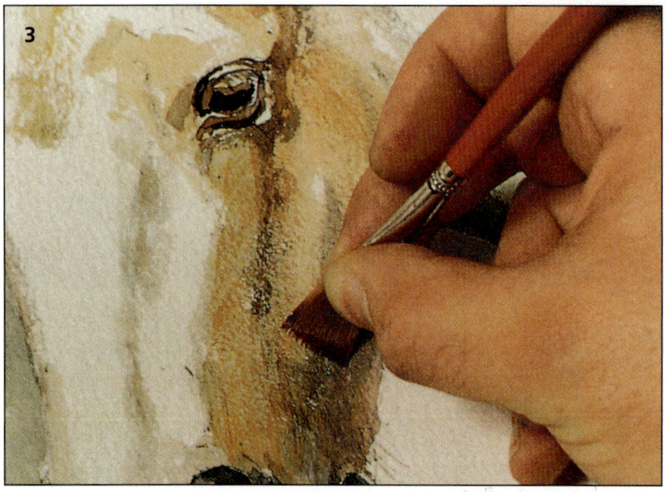

3 Because he wants to give just a hint of the hair texture, the artist uses a color that is only very slightly darker than the wash beneath, and makes quick, light brush strokes.

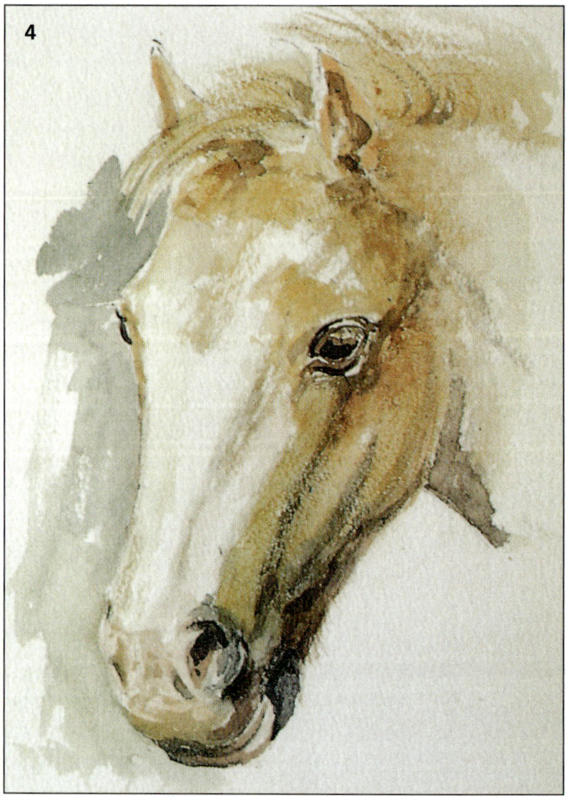

4 By means of successive light applications of dry brush, the artist models the forms accurately, suggesting the different textures of the horse's head and mane.

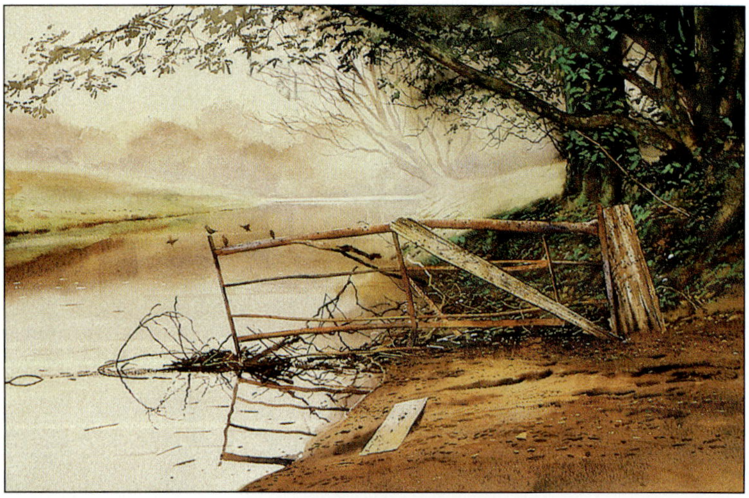

THE RUSTY FENCE by Richard Bolton

The texture on the gatepost is achieved with a combination of wax resist and dry brush strokes. Details, tones, and colors are much stronger in the foreground than in the background.

GLAZING

The glazing technique is used to great effect in watercolor, particularly when conveying the illusion of atmosphere, space, and light in landscapes.

Some watercolor pigments are more opaque than others – the earth colors and cadmiums, for example – and these do not work well in glazes. Stick to the truly transparent colors which allow the light to reflect up off the white paper through the colors.

Do not apply more than two or three layers when glazing in watercolor – any more and the delicate, transparent nature of the medium is lessened.

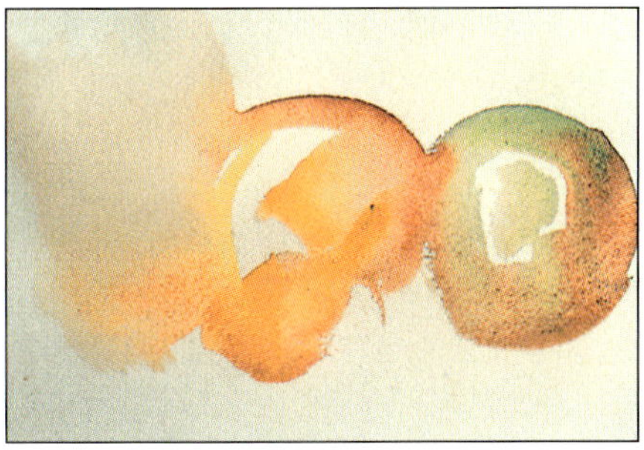

1 Working in acrylic on watercolor paper, the artist starts with the paint heavily diluted with water. Acrylic used in this way is virtually indistinguishable from watercolor, but it cannot be removed once dry, a considerable advantage in the glazing technique.

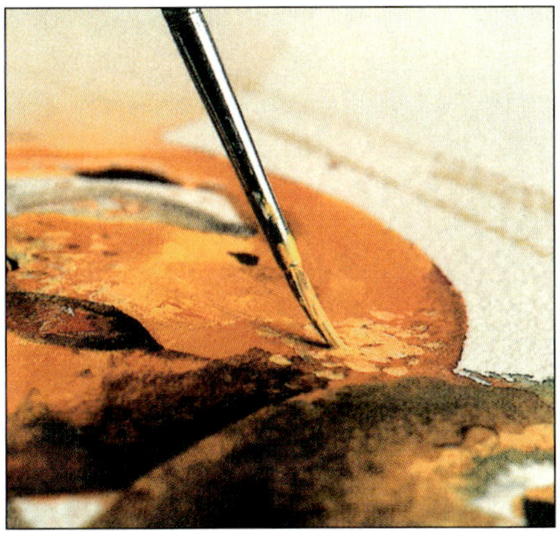

2 A layer of darker color mixed with special glazing medium has been laid over the orange, and the artist now builds up the highlights with opaque paint.

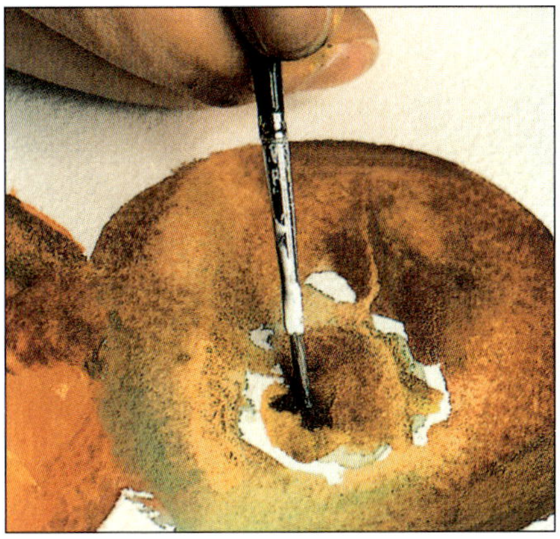

3 Deep-toned glazes are now laid on the apple. The way earlier layers of color reflect back through subsequent glazes gives a rich, glowing effect.

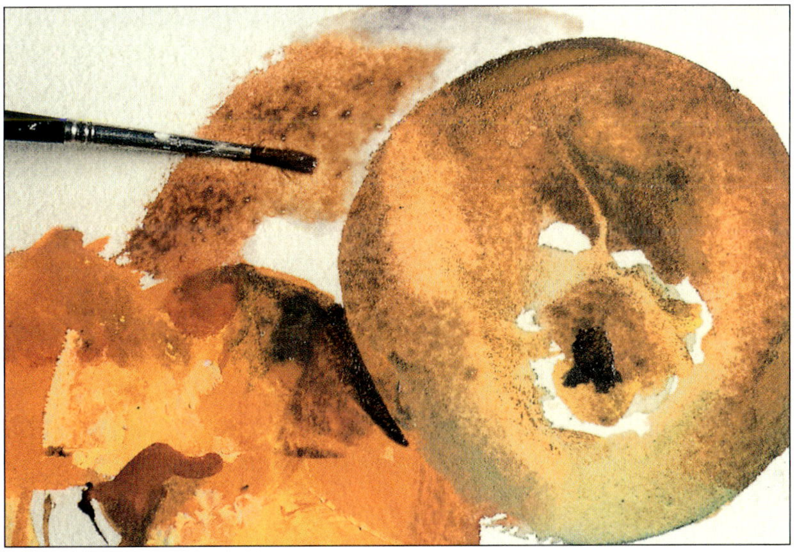

4 Here the transparent, slightly gluey quality of the paint can be seen. Either water or the special medium can be used for acrylic glazes, but it takes a little practice to achieve the right consistency.

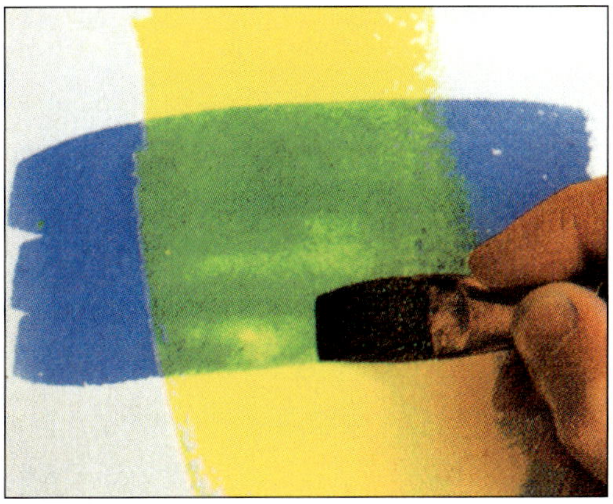

RIGHT: *Thin, transparent glazes allow light to reflect off the paper and up through the colors, giving them greater clarity and vibrance.*

LIFTING OUT

Removing paint from the paper is not only a correction method, it is a watercolor technique in its own right and can be used to great effect to soften edges, diffuse and modify color, and create those highlights that cannot be reserved. For instance, the effect of streaked wind clouds in a blue sky is quickly and easily created by laying a blue wash and wiping a dry sponge, paintbrush, or paper tissue across it while it is still wet. The white tops of cumulus clouds can be suggested by dabbing the wet paint with a sponge or blotting paper.

Paint can also be lifted out when dry by using a dampened sponge or other such tools, but the success of the method depends both on the color to be lifted and the type of paper used. Certain colors, such as sap green and phthalocyanine blue, act rather like dyes, staining the paper, and can never be removed completely, while some papers absorb the paint, making it hard to move it around. Bockingford, Saunders, and Cotman papers are all excellent for lifting out in this way, so if you become addicted to the technique, choose your paper accordingly. Another useful aid to lifting out is gum arabic. Add it in small quantities to the color you intend to partially remove.

Large areas of dry paint can be lifted with a dampened sponge, but for smaller ones the most useful tool is a cotton swab. Never apply too much pressure when using a cotton swab, as the plastic may poke through the cotton tip, scratching the surface of the paper.

As seen from the examples shown here, you can produce beautiful and surprisingly complex effects by laying one wash over another and lifting out to the color below. The technique need not be restricted to skies, however, it is equally valuable for other landscape features, such as the gentle highlights on massed foliage or color variations in fields and hillsides. Use it wherever you want soft-edged effects.

CIRRUS CLOUDS

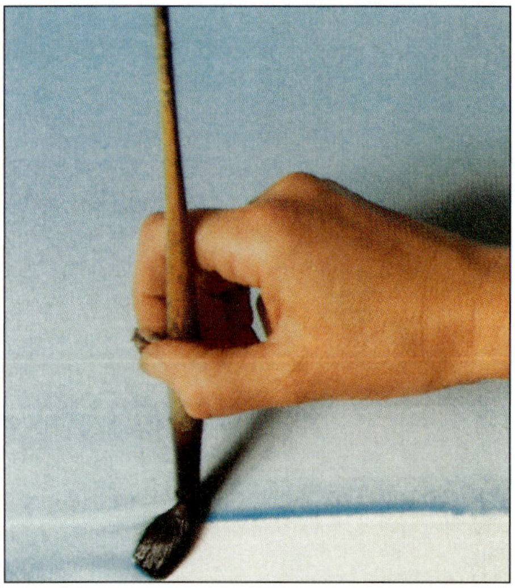

1 To create the effect of clouds in a blue sky, first lay a gradated wash. Don't worry if it is not perfect, since you will be removing much of the paint.

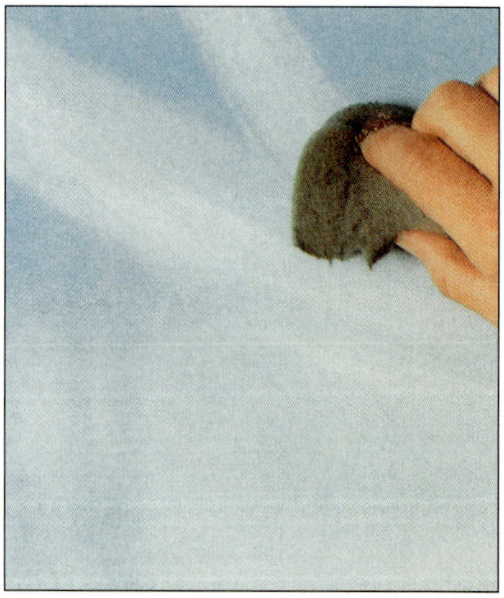

2 Use a slightly damp sponge or a piece of absorbent cotton. Sweep it over the wet wash in the desired direction.

3 An effect like this would be virtually impossible to achieve by any other method. Lifting out is one of the easiest and most useful watercolor techniques.

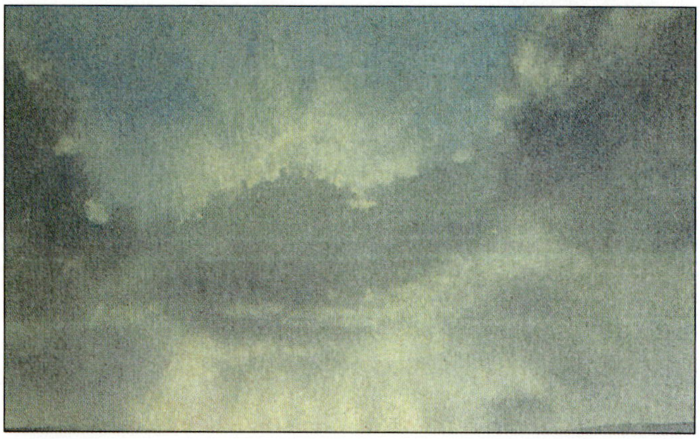

RIGHT: *Here a gradated wash of blue was laid over the whole sky and gray added when still wet. The lighter areas of the clouds and the sun's rays were lifted out with tissue rolled into a point.*

DIFFERENT CLOUD EFFECTS USING THE LIFTING OUT METHOD

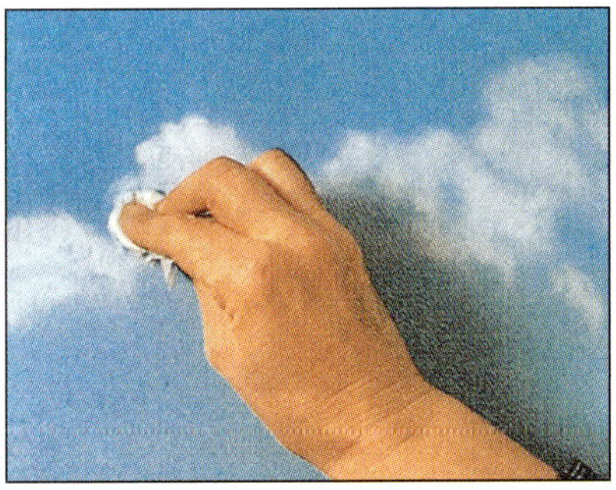

1 With the blue wash still wet, areas are lifted out with a piece of crumpled tissue to give a deliberately uneven effect.

2 Less pressure was used toward the bottom of the sky; clouds are always smaller and less distinct above the horizon.

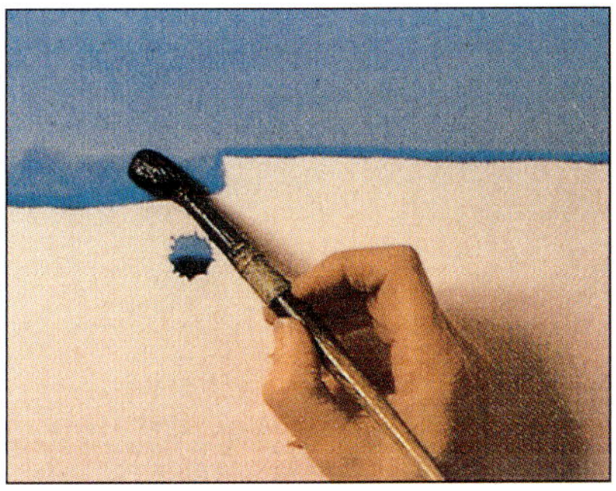

1 In this case two washes have been laid, and the blue is to be lifted out to reveal the dried pink wash below.

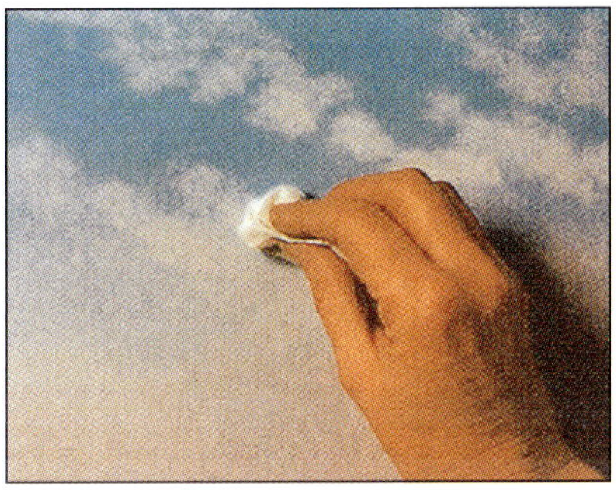

2 Again, a small piece of tissue is used to dab into the paint. For broader effects you might try using a sponge, rag or, large piece of cotton wool.

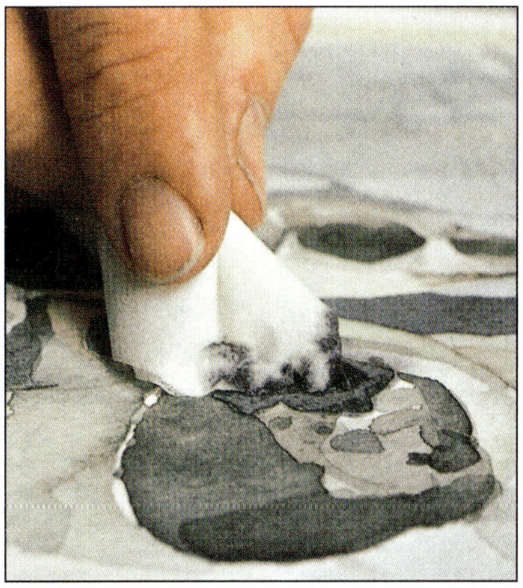

TISSUE

When working with lots of wet washes, tissue is useful for wiping areas that have become too wet, and for controlling the flow of paint. Use a blot-and-lift motion with the tissue – rubbing may damage the surface of the paper. Tissue can be used to lift out amorphous shapes in a wet wash – when painting clouds, for example. Use this technique judiciously, however; when overdone it looks unconvincing.

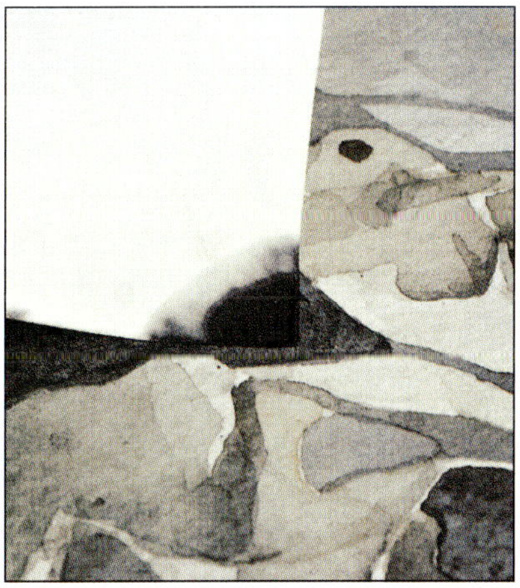

BLOTTING PAPER

Blotting paper is thicker and more absorbent than tissue and, once dry, it can be re-used. If you wish to lift out a small, precise area, hold the corner of the blotting paper against the surface until the excess paint is absorbed.

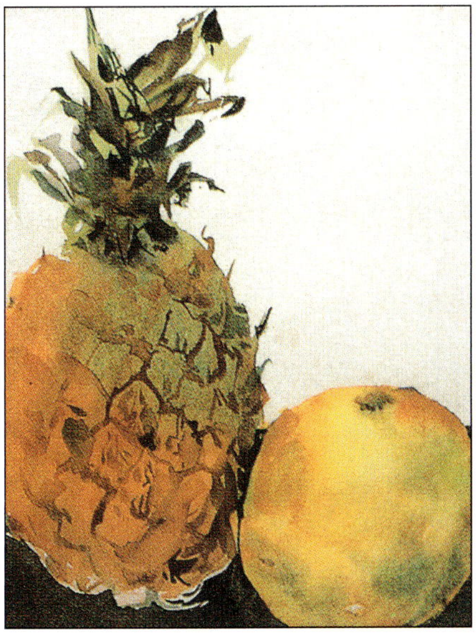

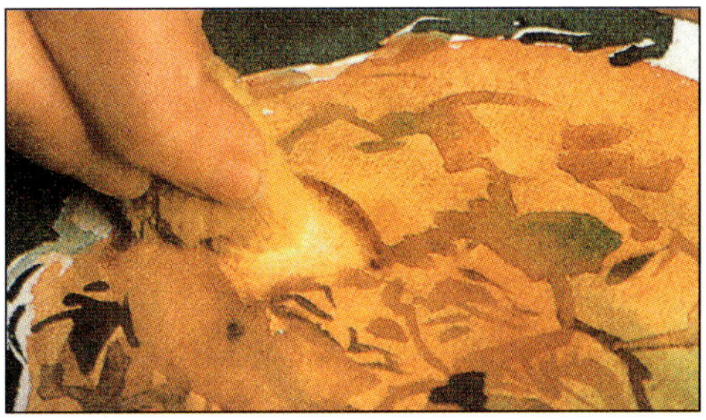

With this fruit group nearly complete, the artist has decided to lighten certain areas, using a dampened sponge to coax the paint off the paper. The success of lifting out dry paint depends very much on the paper used (this is Bockingford), but highlights created in this way can be very effective, as they are softer and less obtrusive than reserved areas of white paper.

SPATTERING

If you're interested in landscape or architectural subjects, you'll find that one of the problems you face is showing texture. How, for example, do you set about painting a sandy or pebbled beach, or the lightly pitted surface of old stone or brickwork?

There are several tricks to use. Dry brush (see page 187) is one of them, and sponge painting (see page 184) is another. You can even abandon the traditional brush and wash method and spatter paint onto the surface with an old toothbrush.

Spattering can create exciting effects provided you don't overdo it. It works best when it doesn't look too obvious, so keep the color and tone of the spattered paint close to that of the wash below. You can use the same paint for both wash and spatter – the spatter will be slightly darker because you'll have added an extra layer of paint. You'll find that paint flicked on in this way sometimes travels too freely. To avoid spoiling other parts of the painting, use a rough mask cut from paper.

A variation on the method is water spatter, where you flick droplets of clean water into a wash. You can do this either when the wash is very wet or just damp – water spatter is often used in conjunction with wet on wet (see page 183). It isn't as good for texture as paint spatter, but it has other possibilities.

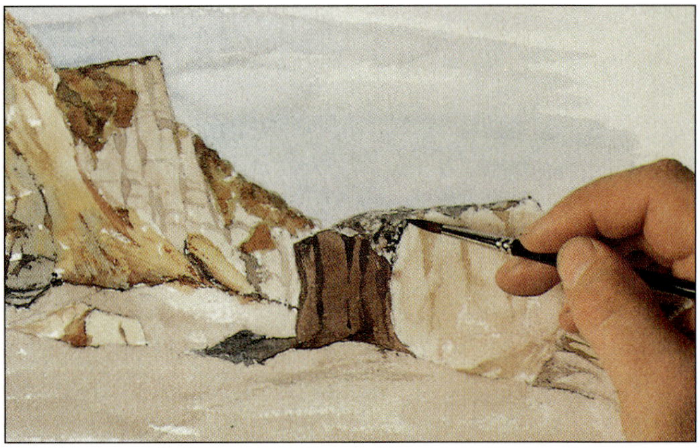

1 Spattering is one of the final stages in a painting. Here the artist has completed the cliffs and rock. The foreground, however, looks fairly flat and lifeless.

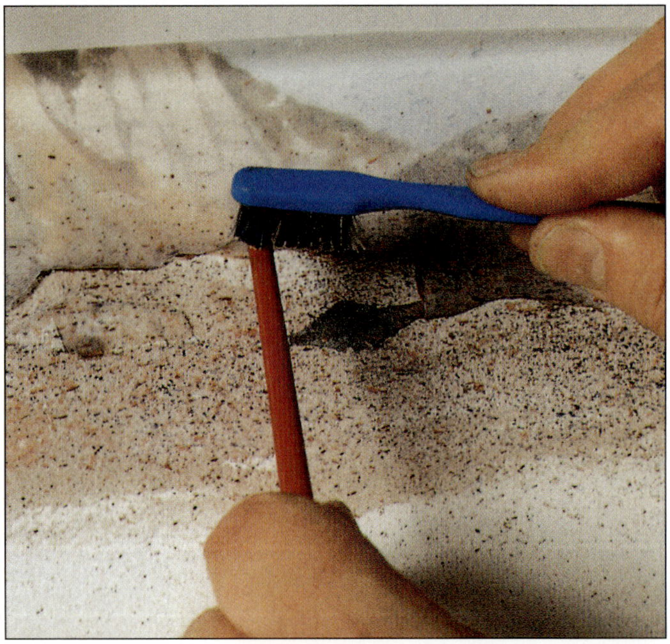

2 Because he wants to prevent the spattered paint from going over the finished areas of the picture, the artist masks these with tracing paper. He now spatters two layers of paint over the light brown foreground wash.

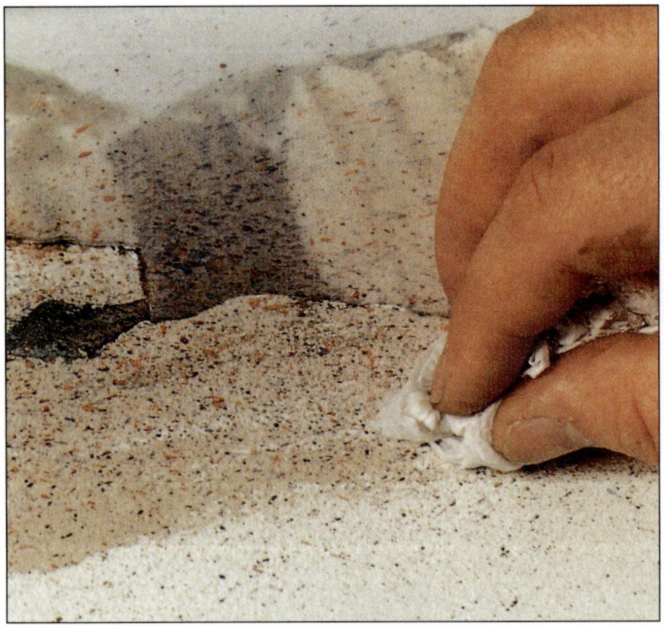

3 Any over-large or over-dark blobs can be removed with a cotton ball or sponge while the paint is still wet.

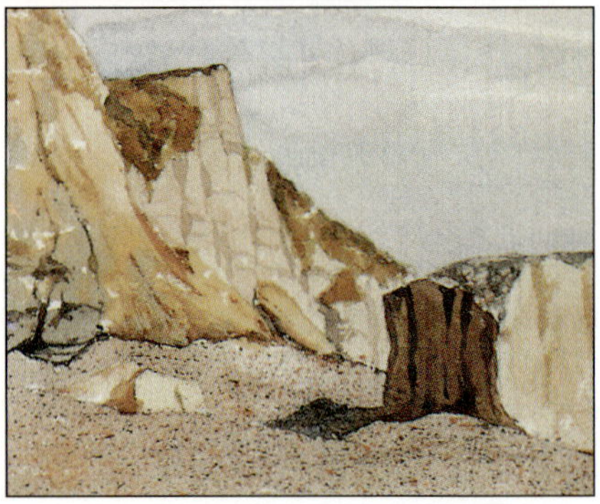

4 The spattered paint gives a realistic impression of the rough-sand and pebble beach. The dark line formed by the paint collecting at the edge of the mask helps to suggest the shadow where the beach meets the cliff.

EXPERIMENT WITH SPATTER

WITH WATER

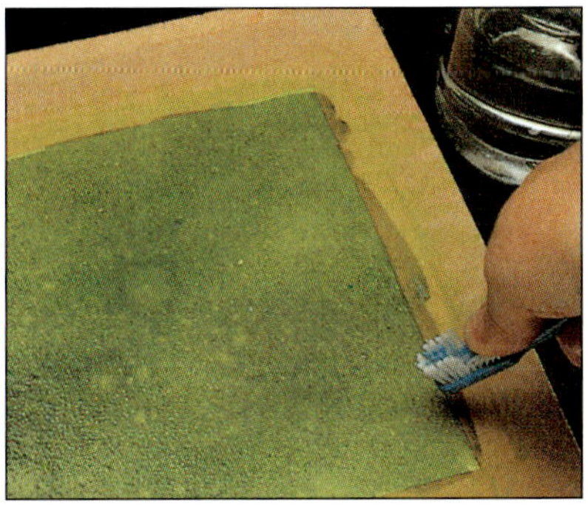

Spatter water with the brush held upward and draw your thumb across it.

Water flicked onto damp or wet paint will produce irregularly shaped drops and blobs.

WITH MOUTH DIFFUSER

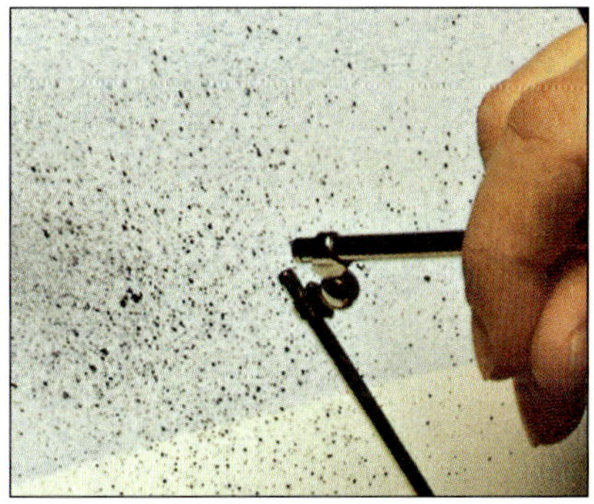

These devices produce a finer spray than the standard toothbrush and paint method shown on page 192.

WITH MASKING FLUID

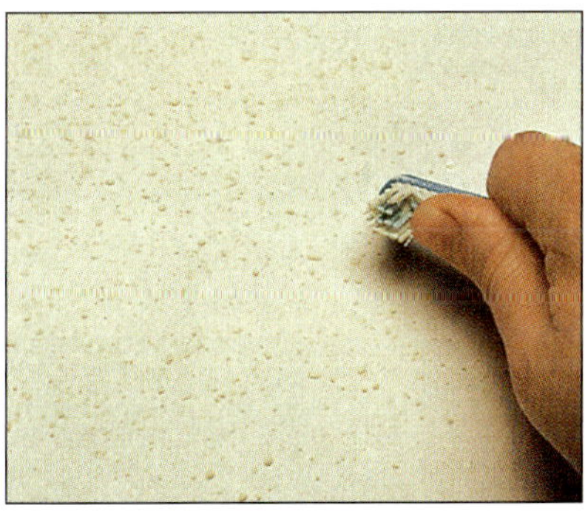

Masking fluid is tricky to spatter, so you will have to experiment to find the best position.

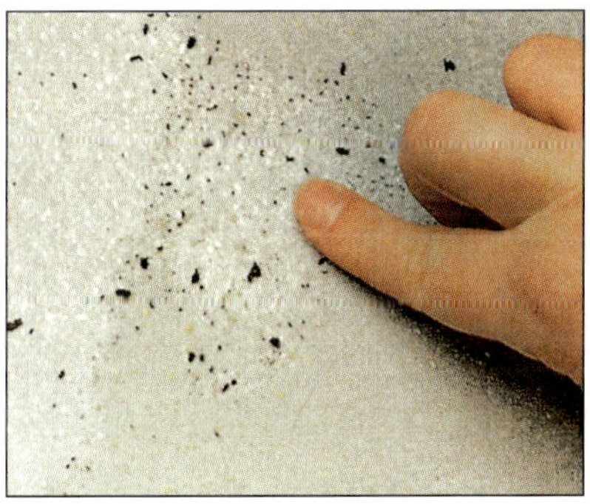

When the wash has dried, remove the fluid by gently rubbing with a fingertip.

This could be the perfect method for winter-weather effects; the pattern of tiny white spots is reminiscent of a snowstorm. Make sure you lay down plenty of newspaper for masking fluid spatter, as it can travel a long way, and is hard to remove.

MASKING OUT

Because of the transparency of watercolor, it is impossible to paint a light color over a dark one; the artist must plan where the light or white areas are to be and paint around them, which can be a fiddly problem.

The two main purposes of masking are to create highlights by reserving certain areas of a painting and to protect one part of a picture while you work on another. If you have planned a painting that relies for its effect on a series of small, intricate highlights, such as a woodland scene with a pattern of leaves and twigs catching the sunlight, or a seascape where the light creates tiny bright points on choppy water, masking fluid can be an effective solution.

This liquid, rubbery solution is applied with a brush, just like paint, and dries within a few seconds to form a water-resistant film which can be painted over without affecting the paper underneath. When the painting is completely dry, the rubbery mask is easily removed by rubbing with the finger.

The advantage of masking fluid is that it can be applied in any shape you desire. It forms a firm, waterproof resist, and doesn't have to be held in place manually on the support. The one disadvantage is that areas treated with masking fluid always have a hard edge, which may not be compatible with the rest of the painting.

Always use an old brush to apply masking fluid, and wash it in warm, soapy water immediately after use to prevent the rubber solution from drying hard and clogging up the bristles.

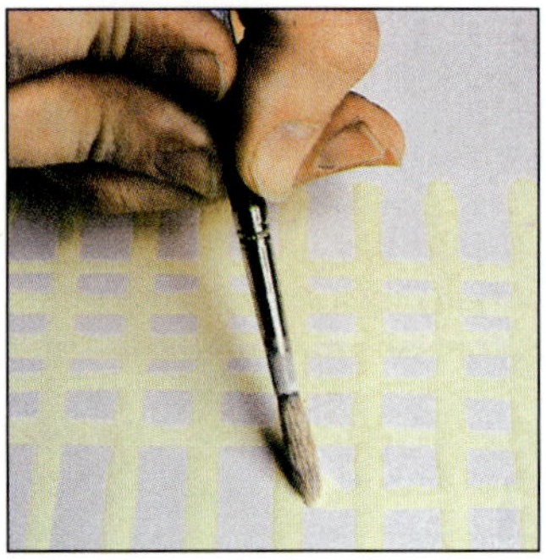

1 Using a soft brush, paint in the area you intend to leave white and allow it to dry hard. The fluid must be fresh or it will yellow the paper. Wash the brush out immediately to prevent the fluid from drying on the bristles.

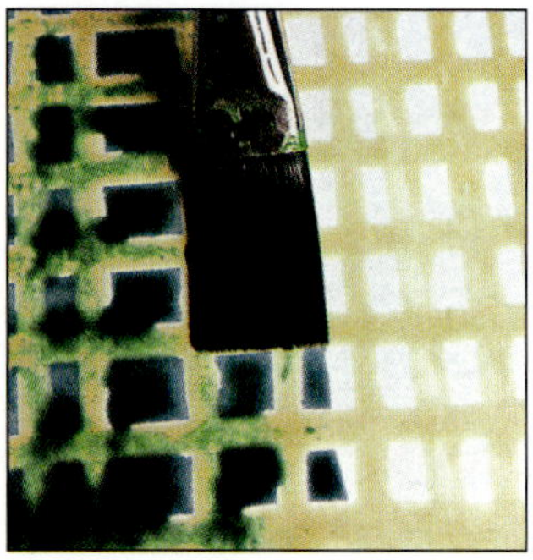

2 When the fluid is dry, you can brush washes freely over the surrounding area without having to be careful to avoid the white shapes.

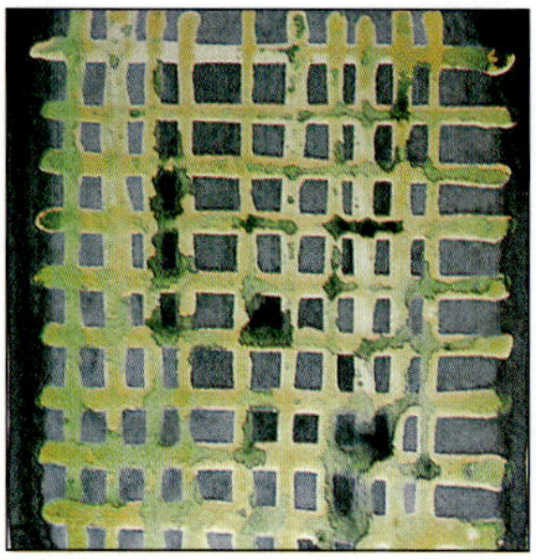

3 It is essential to let the watercolor dry before continuing.

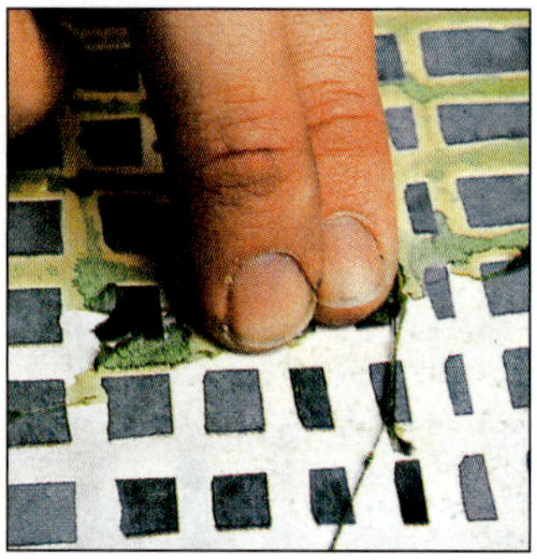

4 Remove the dried masking fluid by gently rubbing with your fingers or a soft kneadable eraser and peeling it away. If the paint is not dry the color will smudge.

TREE TRUNKS USING MASKING FLUID

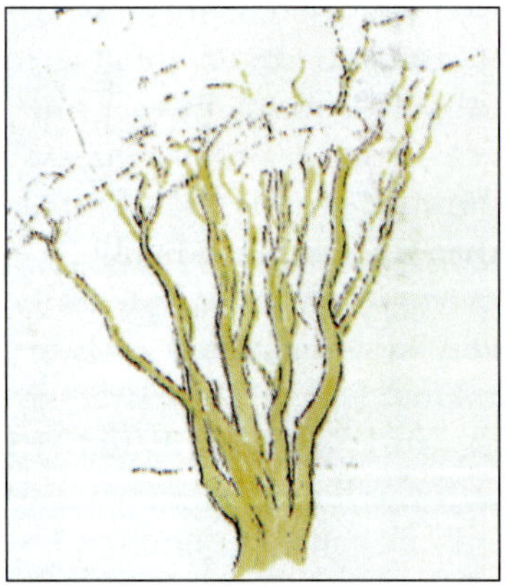

1 The tree trunks are carefully drawn, masking fluid is applied, and then left to dry before any further work is done. The artist is working on Bockingford paper with a "not" surface, from which the rubbery fluid is easily removed; it is not suitable for use on rough papers as it sinks into the "troughs" and cannot be peeled off.

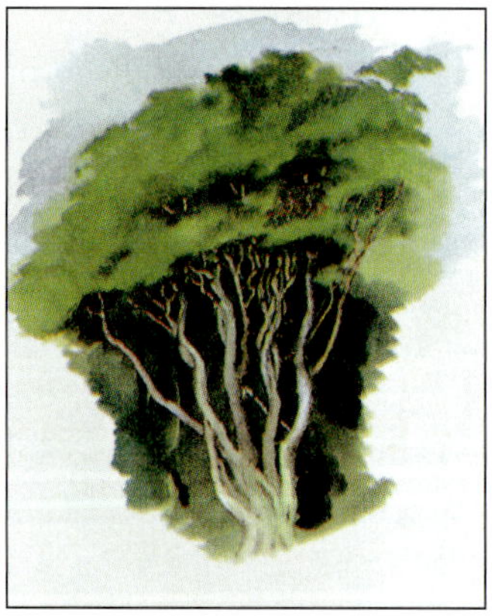

2 With the fluid protecting the intricate shapes of the trunks and branches, dark washes are built up behind and above without fear of paint splashing onto the pale areas. When the washes are dry, the fluid is removed by rubbing with a finger. The trunks and branches are then modeled with darker paint in places and touches of white gouache define the highlights.

WAX RESIST

This technique is also based on blocking the paint, but it yields a different and more subtle effect from that created by masking fluid. The principle is simple: wax repels water. If you draw on paper with a wax crayon – or an ordinary household candle – and lay a watercolor wash on top, the paint will slide off.

The method was pioneered by British sculptor and painter Henry Moore (1898–1986), who used it for a series of drawings of people sleeping in the London Underground during World War II. Try to find a book of reproductions in your local library and have a look at these marvelous drawings.

The effects of wax resist are always exciting, and you can vary them according to how much pressure you put on the crayon (or candle) and the kind of paper you use. If you were to push the wax into smooth paper it would block the paint completely, but watercolor paper is not smooth, so the wax settles only on the "peaks," allowing paint to seep into the "troughs" and create a slight speckling.

Wax resist is yet another way of imitating textures, such as rocks, cliffs, tree-trunks, and old buildings, and is also much used for clouds and the broken effect of light on water. It is an excellent way of creating pattern in a painting, too. With inexpensive colored wax crayons you can create all kinds of different effects, building up layers of wax, then paint, and more wax.

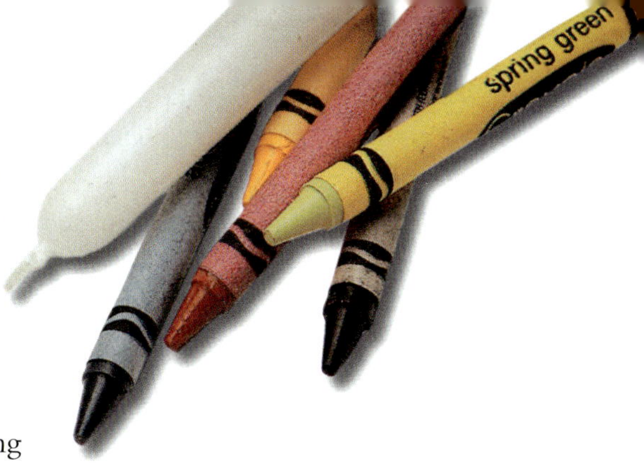

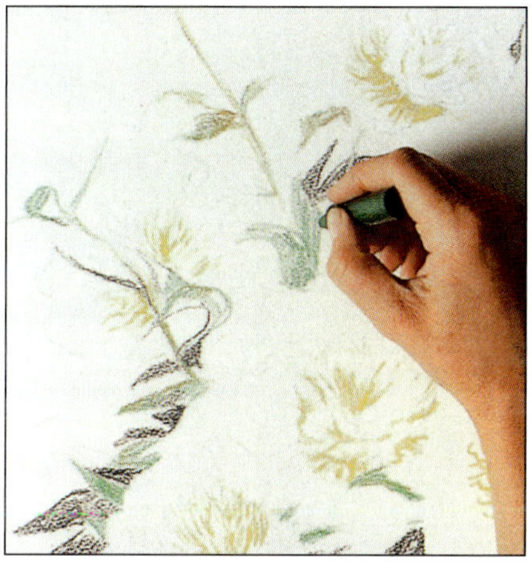

1 The stamens are drawn with the tip of a yellow wax crayon. Black and green are used for the leaves. Pressure is kept light so that the wax does not repel too much of the paint.

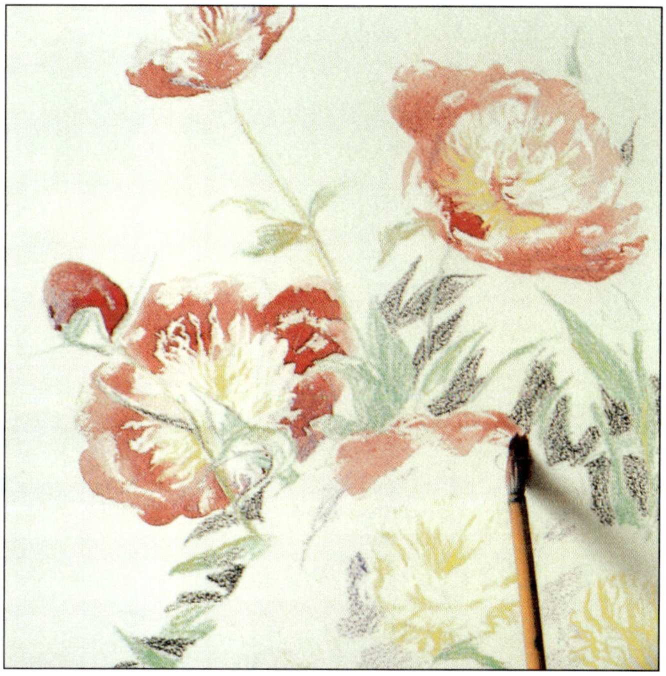

2 A fairly strong solution of alizarin crimson is applied over the wax drawing with a Chinese brush. These brushes are excellent for flower painting, as they are capable of a wide range of strokes as well as fine definition.

3 Green paint – a mixture of viridian and cadmium yellow – is laid over the black wax crayon. The green is most visible where the pressure of the crayon was lightest.

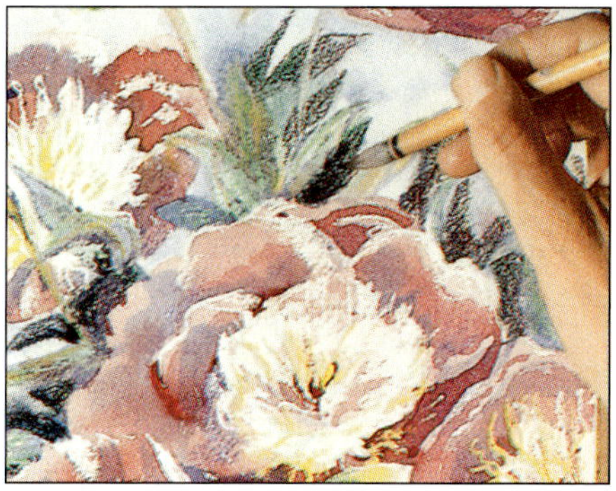

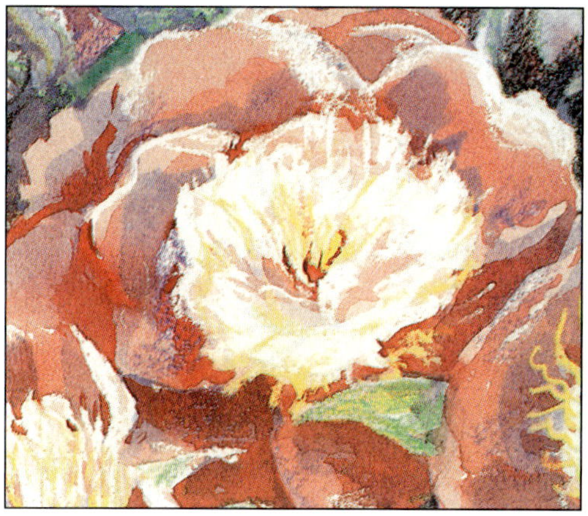

4 This detail of the flower heads clearly shows the effect of the resist method. Notice the way the paint has slipped off the waxed areas, leaving the yellow stamens outlined against the deep pink of the petals.

GALLERY

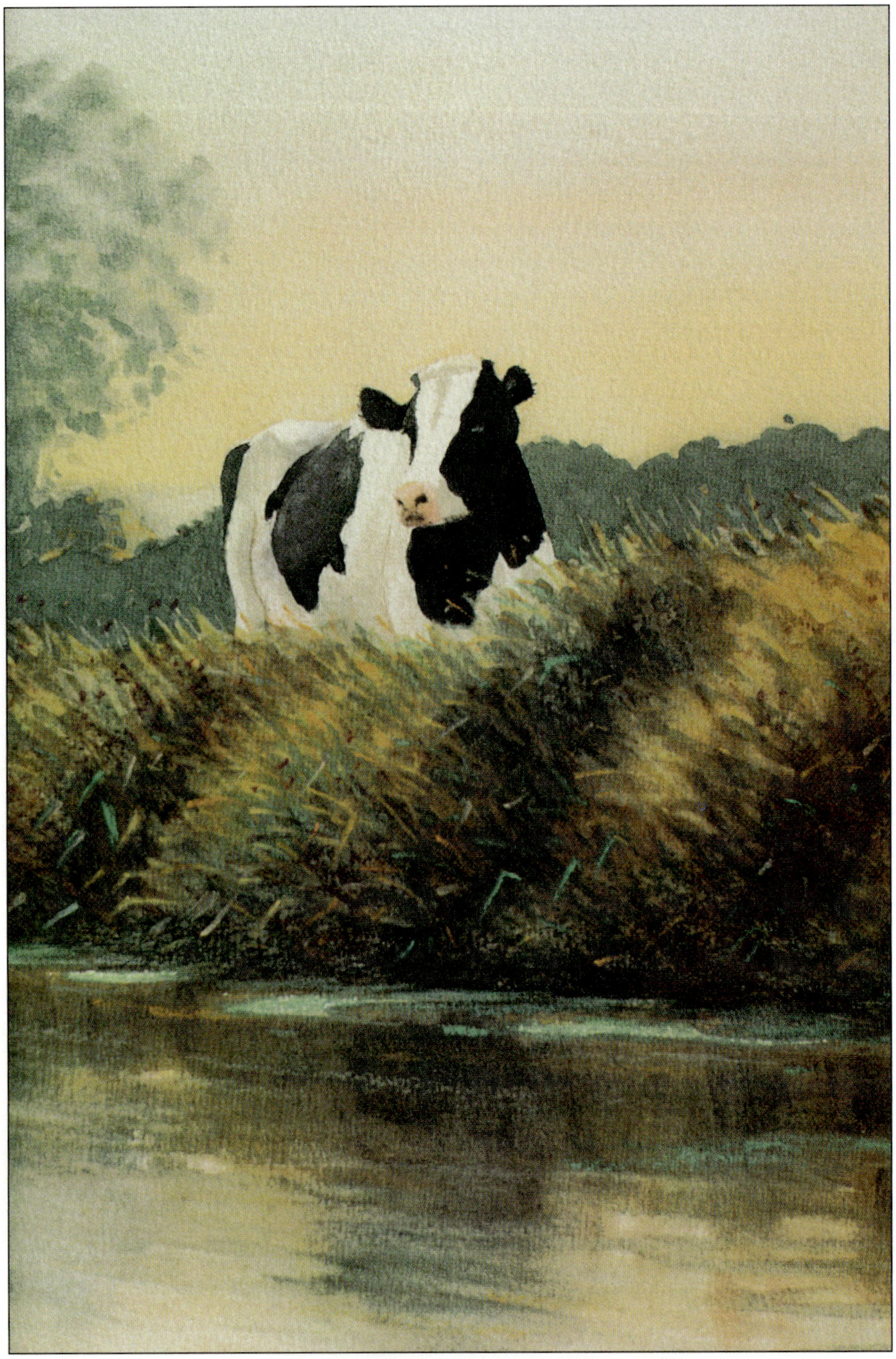

REFLECTIVE MOOD by Bart O'Farrell

With dull light and broken water, the reflection of the cow is just suggested. Soft dry brush techniques capture the calm water surface.

DIFFERENT APPROACHES

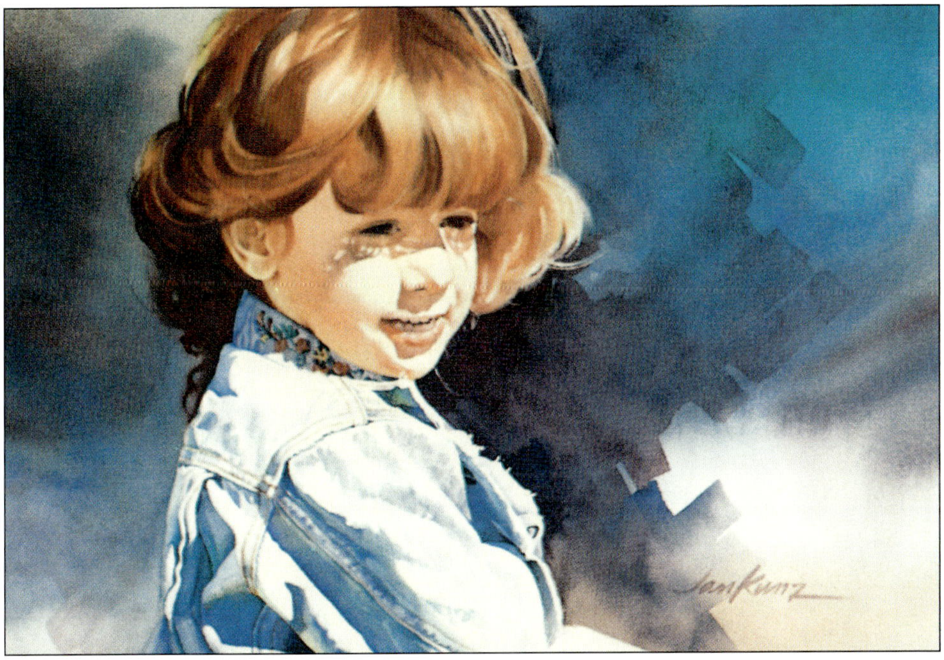

YOUNG GIRL by Jan Kunz

There is plenty of detail in this striking portrait, but nowhere was the paint overworked. The bright light allowed the artist to leave large areas of the face and body almost pure white. The shadows and details of the features were touched in with a sure hand, and the thick, waving hair was simplified into a series of clumps.

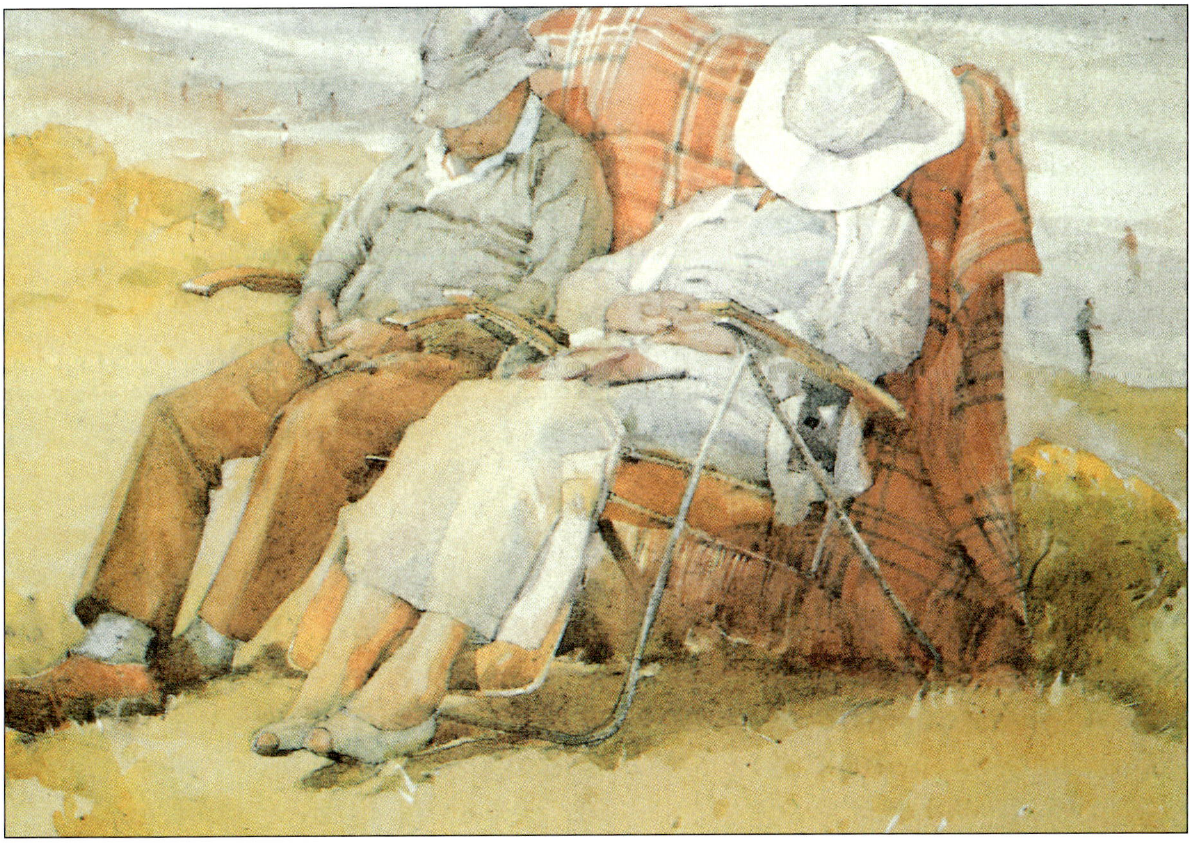

FRED AND EDNA by David Curtis

This delightful study, although not a portrait in the usual sense of the word, is a likeness. We can see only a tiny part of the man's face, and none of the woman's, but the shapes of the bodies and the way the couple are sitting are peculiar to them, and so are their clothes. If you find yourself on the beach with some time to spare, make some sketches – beachgoers will often obligingly sleep or lie reading for long periods without moving.

BEAUTIFUL BIRDS

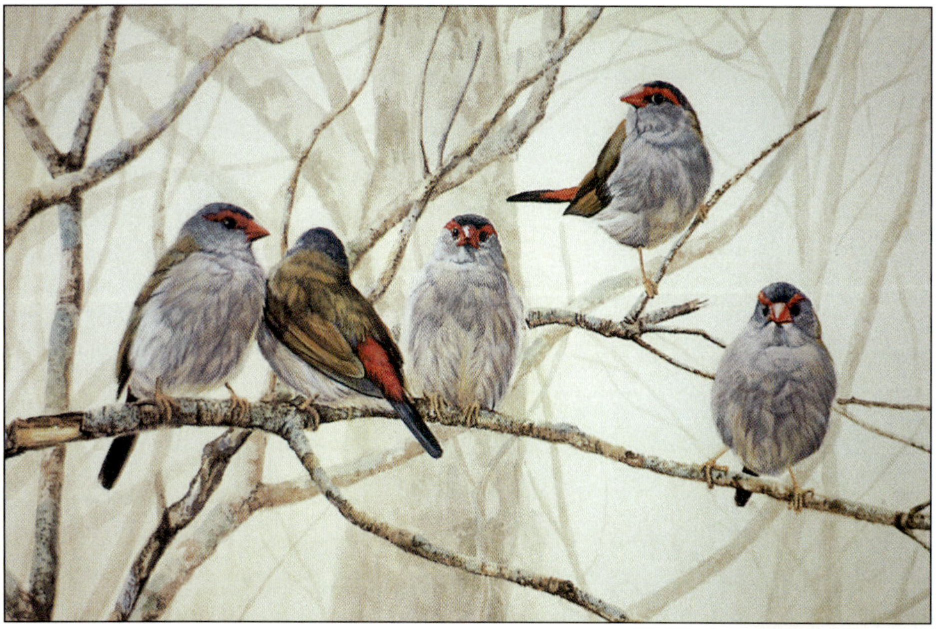

RED-BROWED FIRETAILS by James Luck

Opaque paint was also used in this painting, but more precisely. The plumage is built with a series of tiny strokes using a small brush. The misty background is beautifully captured, and provides the ideal setting for the birds.

MICHAELMAS by Ronald Jesty

Geese are a popular subject; their heavy white bodies and long, twisting necks make beautiful shapes and patterns. A farmyard, which offers all sorts of fascinating subjects as well as animals, can be an excellent painting location, provided you have the farmer's permission.

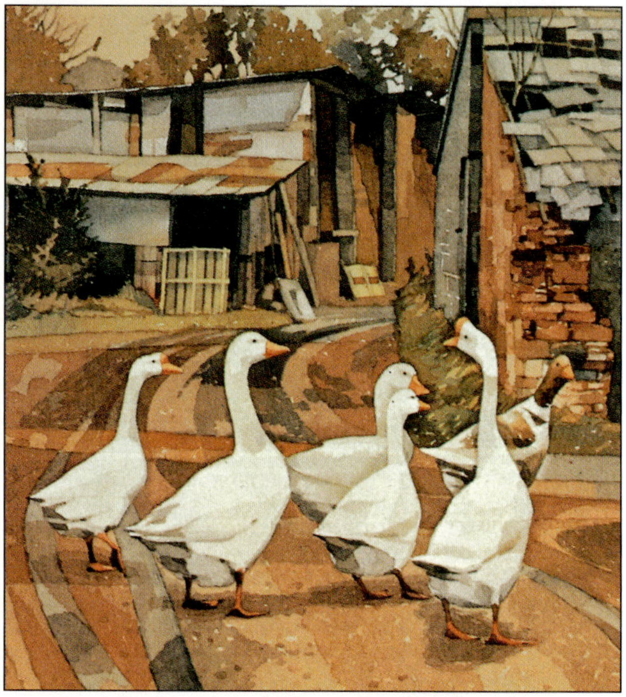

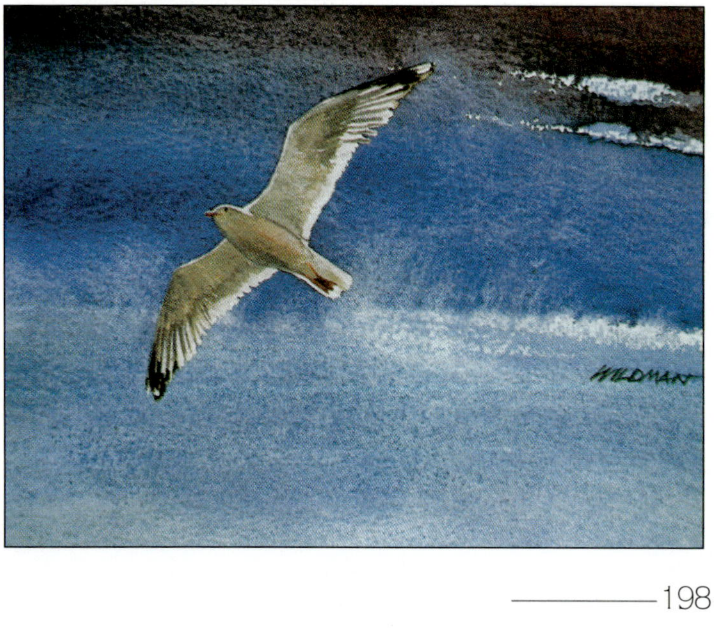

THE SEAGULL by Phil Widman

Seagulls may move fast, but they don't fly high as they wheel above cliffs, beaches, and rivers. If you spend a day or so making quick sketches, you should gather enough material for a painting. This is a lovely evocation of flight, with the bird, just risen from the sea, outlined against the dark water.

GOUACHE

Gouache, or body color, is included within the broad definition of watercolor. It is a water-based paint, usually made of coarsely ground pigments, but instead of having the distinctively transparent quality of pure watercolor, it is opaque.

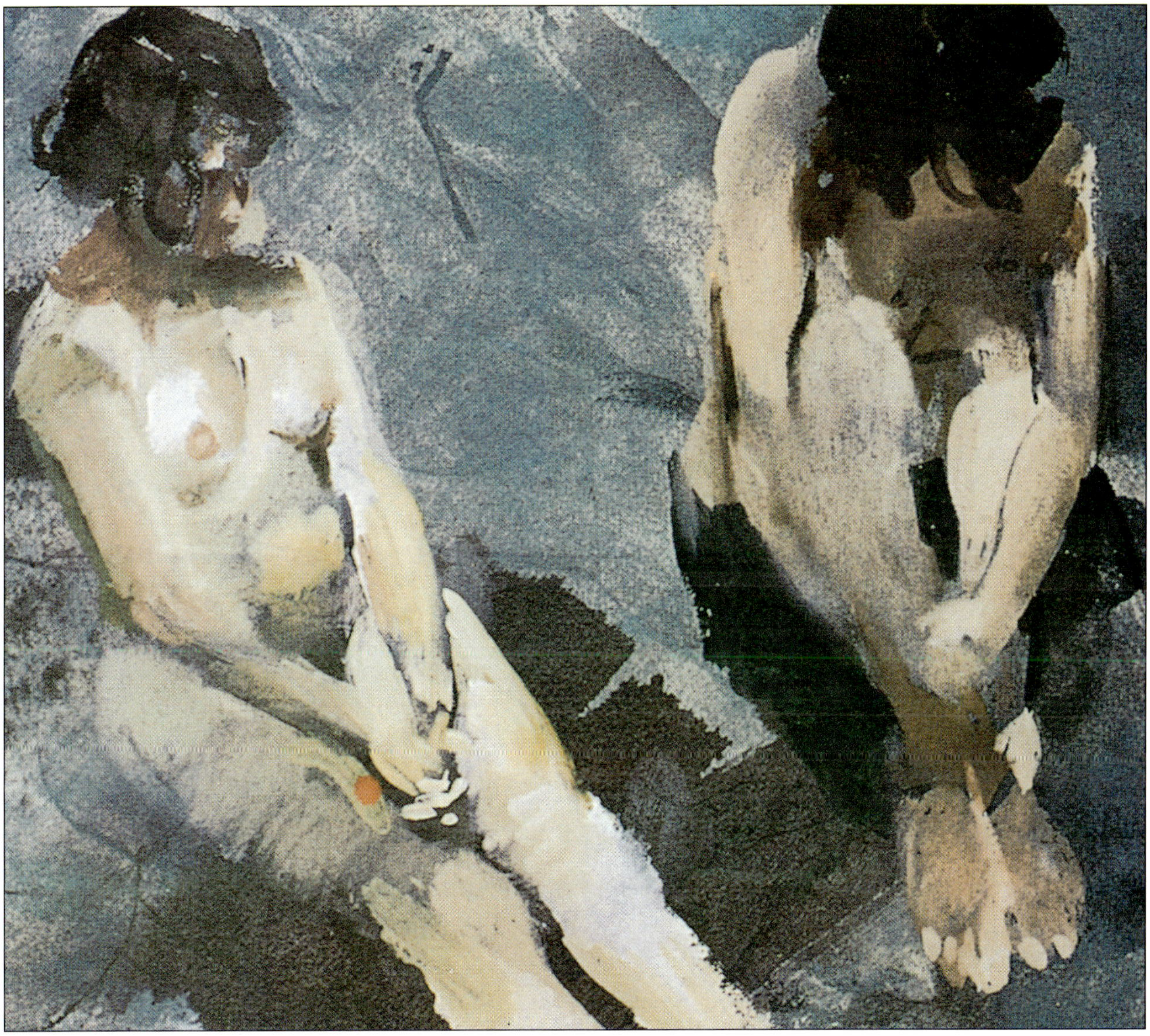

THE HISTORY OF GOUACHE

Somewhere in Europe toward the end of the fourteenth century, a monk found that, by adding Chinese or zinc white to the usual transparent watercolors when he was illustrating manuscripts, the resulting opaque effect set off his gold decoration even more brilliantly.

Gouache had thus been "discovered" as a medium in itself, although it was – and remains – only one of a family of water-slaked paints, including fresco and distemper, the use of which was already known in pre-Christian times.

Definitions of the word, in terms of the actual composition of the medium, differ among artists. Only one definition is universally agreed, because it is broad enough to include all other definitions – gouache is simply opaque watercolor.

Its opacity and covering power make it a quite separate and distinct medium from pure, transparent watercolor.

The effects it produces are not unlike those of matt oils, and brush techniques similar to those used in oil painting are often employed. However, gouache dries far more quickly than oils and lends itself well to a rapid, *alla prima* style of painting.

In all painting, rules are made to be broken by those artists who have mastered basic techniques. Gouache has, perhaps, fewer rules governing its use than any other single painting medium. So long as the main coverage is with opaque watercolor, a picture containing other kinds of media may legitimately be described as "a gouache." Individual artists have achieved technically excellent results using combinations of gouache colors, pure watercolor, India ink, charcoal, pastels, and even pencil in the same picture.

Although patches of transparent watercolor may be surprisingly effective in a painting that is predominantly gouache, the opposite application – gouache passages in a transparent watercolor – is generally far less acceptable. But even this "rule" has been broken by many good French artists.

Unlike both watercolor and tempera, which can glow from the light, reflective grounds on which they are laid, the brightness of gouache comes solely from the reflecting power of the pigments in the paint surface itself. Since the flat, contrasting colors are essentially as the eye sees them, gouache is especially suitable for color reproduction work.

There have been no "grand" periods in gouache; no national schools of painting in the medium, or even special times of heightened popularity, as with pure watercolor in late-eighteenth century England. Nor are there any great, single masterpieces in gouache to compare with those in other media; but it has been, and continues to be, used by fine artists for its own special qualities.

Albrecht Dürer (1471–1526), the masterly German Renaissance painter, used gouache for his studies of landscape and animals. There are gouache works by Rubens (1577–1640) and his Flemish compatriot van Dyck (1599–1641). Other seventeenth and eighteenth century Europeans who were exponents of the medium include Gaspard Poussin (1615–1675) and van Hysum (1682–1749).

The French painter Joseph Goupy (1689–1783) is credited with bringing gouache to London, where he made his home. Marco Ricci (1679–1729) of Venice and Zuccarelli of Florence (1702–1788), both notable gouache artists, also spent periods in the English capital; and Zuccarelli in particular is said greatly to have influenced Paul Sandby (1725–1809), sometimes dubbed the "father" of English watercolor. Sandby certainly used gouache well and often, but his reputation rests mainly on his examples of the pure watercolors which marked the eighteenth-century English school. Gouache and mixed gouache-watercolor never became as popular in England as in France.

It might be said that, in general gouache, while never highly fashionable, has never been out of fashion either. There are many modern exponents, including Picasso (1881–1973), Henry Moore (b. 1898), Graham Sutherland (1903–1980), and America's Ben Shahn (1898–1969).

Picasso employed large flat patches of red in his costume design gouache Pulcinella (1917), a picture that contained many elements recognizable in his later abstract designs.

Social realist Ben Shahn used gouache for a large mural, Women's Christian Temperance Union Parade (1934), now in the Museum of the City of New York in Vacant Lot (1939) he mixed transparent washes with gouache, using the opaque paint to highlight stones and rubble.

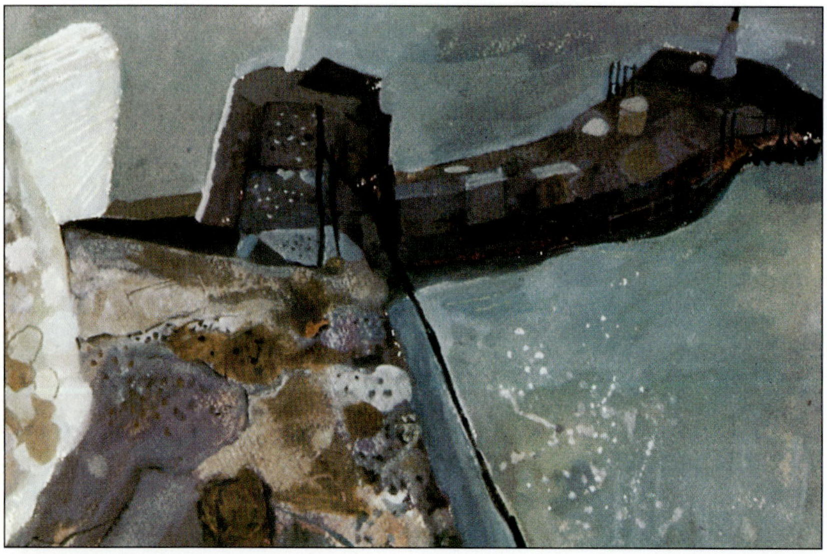

QUAY

This gouache explores the qualities of the medium with a great variety of grays. These have been enriched by areas of underpainting, made with transparent and semi-transparent washes of warm color. In places these warm colors have been allowed to show through. The decorative qualities of the stones have been fully exploited.

Materials

A greater variety of supports and grounds can be used for gouache than for almost any other medium. So long as the surface is free from oil and grease it will take gouache. Cardboard, composition board, wood, and even cloth, properly stretched and sized, are usable.

As with watercolor, paper is the main support for gouache works. For fine art work it should of course be of good, lasting quality. Any watercolor paper can be used for gouache, including lightweight, stretched, and tinted papers. Prepared boards can be bought.

The texture of the surface is largely a matter of preference. Some artists believe that a grainy surface, which drags at the brush, is technically more satisfactory, as it "pulls" paint from the bristles; but good work is done by others on quite smooth, virtually unabsorbent surfaces.

All sizes and shapes of brushes recommended for watercolor can be used for gouache, with hogs' hair or bristle brushes added for certain broad or textural effects, and the easels and boards used for watercolor are also adequate for gouache.

"True" gouache colors come in tubes, jars and, in recent years, pans similar to those in which pure watercolor paint is made up. There is a great range of choice; but the artist should be guided by the names of colormen – paint manufacturers – familiar in other painting fields, or he or she may find the pigment rapidly fading or changing.

Gouache colors can be made up more easily and inexpensively at home or in the studio than either oils or watercolors. A flat glass plate can be used for grinding, with a muller; but since more medium is used than in watercolor a pestle and mortar is more convenient to handle the liquid or semi-liquid color, which should be stored in screw-top jars.

Precipitated chalk, obtainable from colormen, is the main way of achieving the desired opacity in gouache. It should be ground with the pigment, and with a solution of gum arabic and distilled water, to a smooth and syrupy consistency.

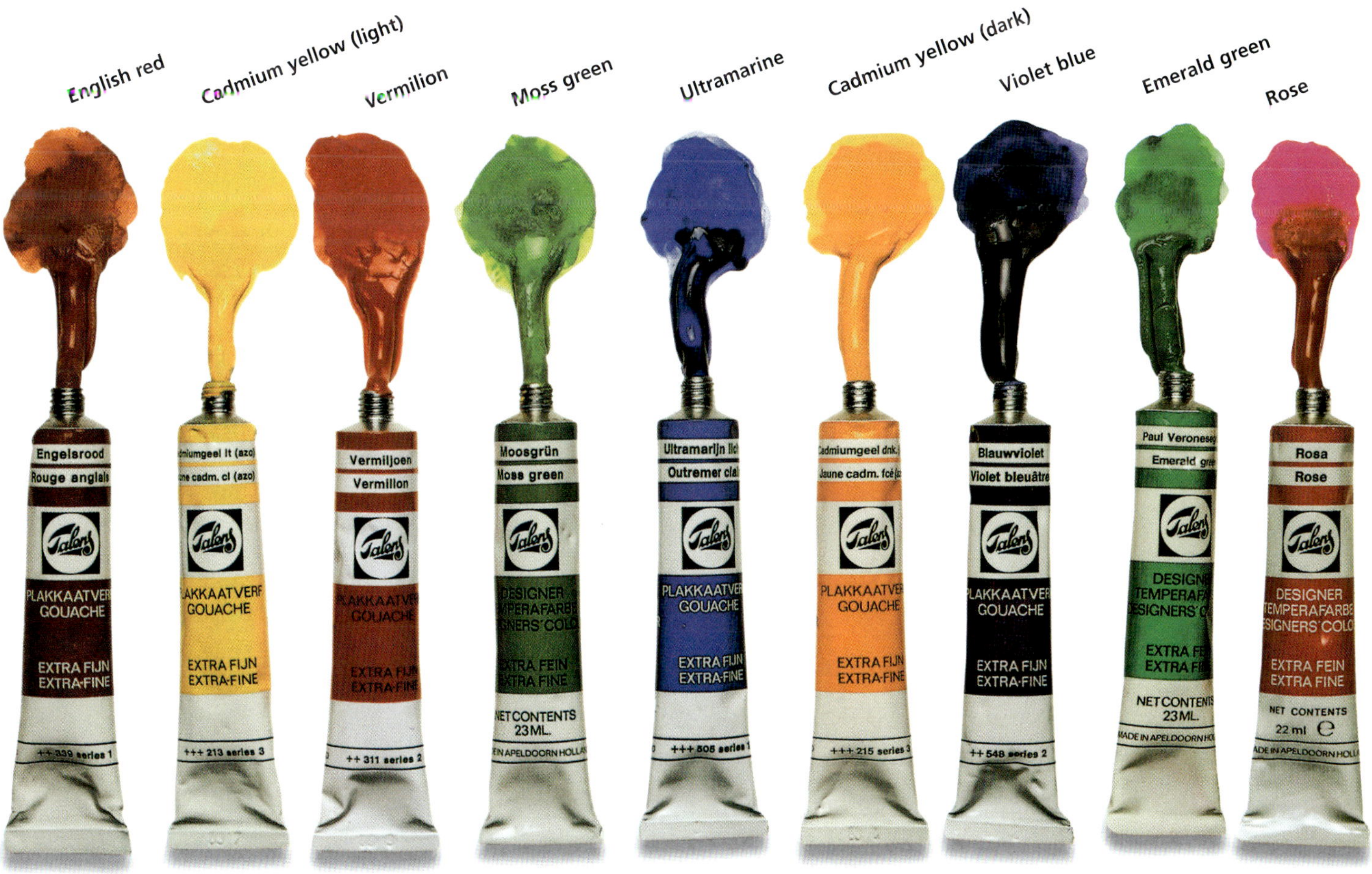

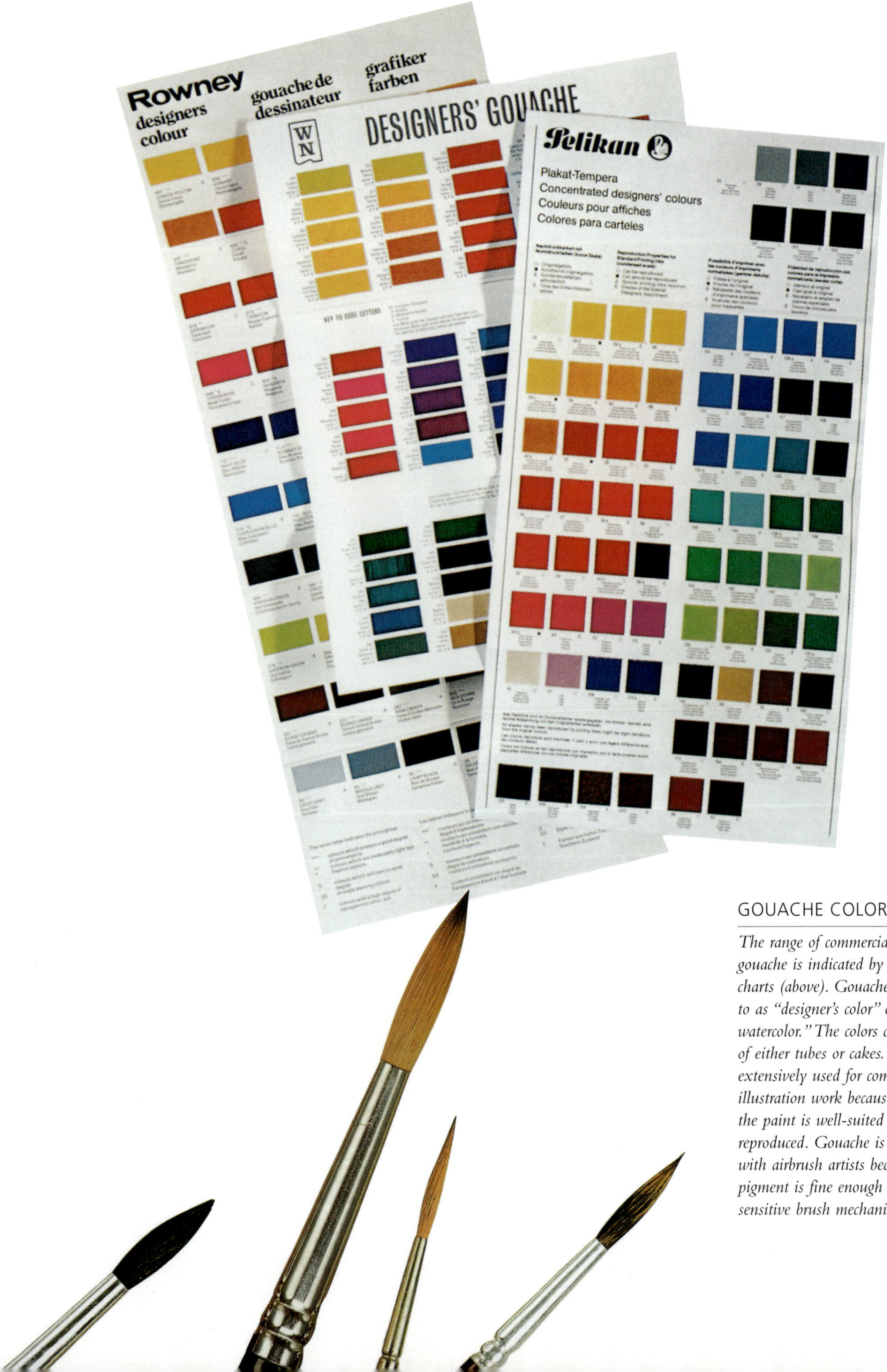

GOUACHE COLORS

The range of commercially available gouache is indicated by these color charts (above). Gouache is also referred to as "designer's color" or "opaque watercolor." The colors come in the form of either tubes or cakes. Gouache is extensively used for commercial illustration work because the opacity of the paint is well-suited to being reproduced. Gouache is also popular with airbrush artists because the pigment is fine enough not to clog the sensitive brush mechanism.

Equipment

For gouache painting, use the same type of brush as you would for watercolor. For applying the paint thickly, round bristle brushes are particularly useful. The range of sizes of brush can be used as for watercolor work, as can the different varieties of brush shown below. However, because gouache does not handle in exactly the same way as watercolor, it is important to experiment to see exactly which type and size of brush suits your purposes best. Palettes for gouache can be made from either plastic or porcelain. They are available in many different shapes. The round palettes are specially useful for mixing colors. The palette should not be absorbent, so wood is not a suitable surface.

Remember, when using gouache it is important to work on a flat surface because the paint is so liquid.

A ruler can be a very useful tool when working with gouache. To draw a fine line with a brush, hold the ruler firmly against the paper bunching your fingers underneath it, so that it is not touching the surface of the paper. To make the line, place the ferrule of the brush against the edge of the ruler and draw the brush gently along. This technique can be used with watercolor as well, but it is especially useful with gouache, for example when adding highlights.

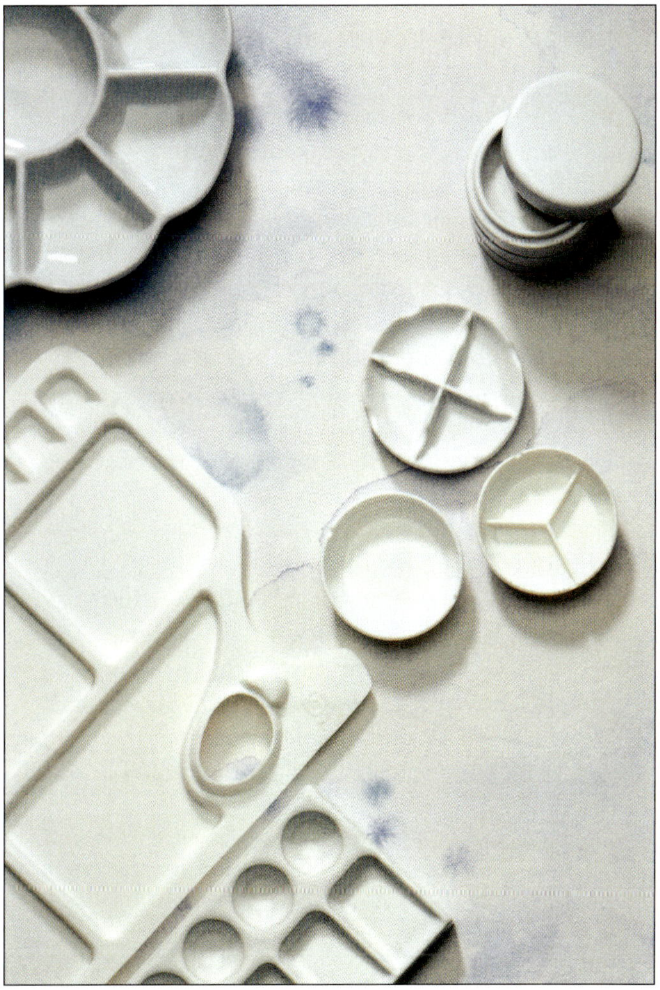

FROM LEFT TO RIGHT: *blender, fine synthetic roundhair, broad synthetic roundhair, mixed fibers round, ox hair round, squirrel hair round, sable fan bright, sable square-ended, sable round, fine sable round.*

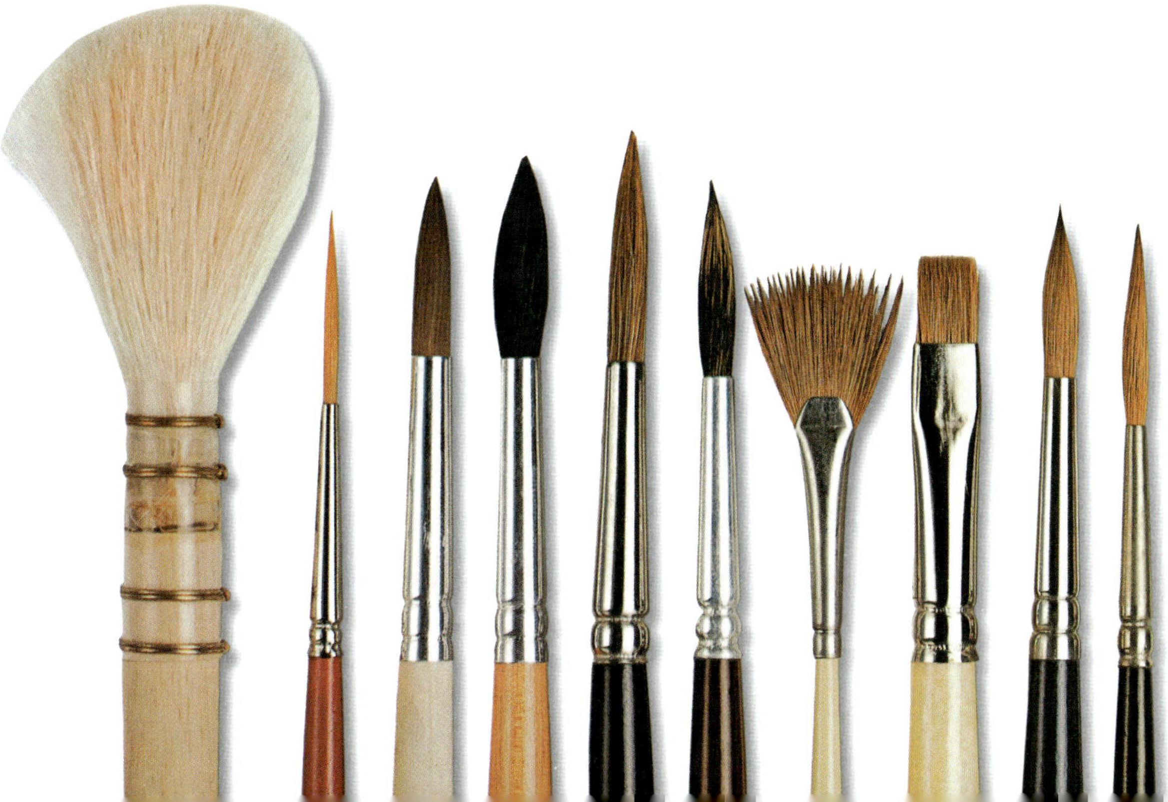

Getting Started

Gouache offers the illustrator enormous flexibility as it combines the solubility and translucency of watercolor with the opaque qualities of heavier paints.

Gouache is considered easier for the beginner to master than watercolor. It can be worked, rather like watercolor, in thin washes, or superimposed in opaque layers, from dark to light, similar to acrylics or oils. To darken colors, superimpose further layers of the same color with less water, and to achieve pale areas, use the white of the paper, as in watercolor, to shine through thin washes, or add white to your mix and superimpose it over dark.

Gouache remains more soluble than watercolor when it is dry, making it easier to manipulate and blend when superimposing new layers. It is possible to overlay opaque layers over transparent and vice versa.

DIFFERENT EFFECTS

Depending on the type of paper used, the results achievable with gouache paint can vary quite dramatically. Gouache paint can be used either neat from the tube or in watered-down washes. The more water that is added to a wash the more translucent the pigment becomes and the thinner the paint; the thinner the wash the more paper texture shows through.

OPAQUE COLOR

This method of using gouache is possibly the simplest and takes advantage of its individual properties. The amount of water added to the pigment affects the opacity of the paint; the more water you add, the more transparent it becomes.

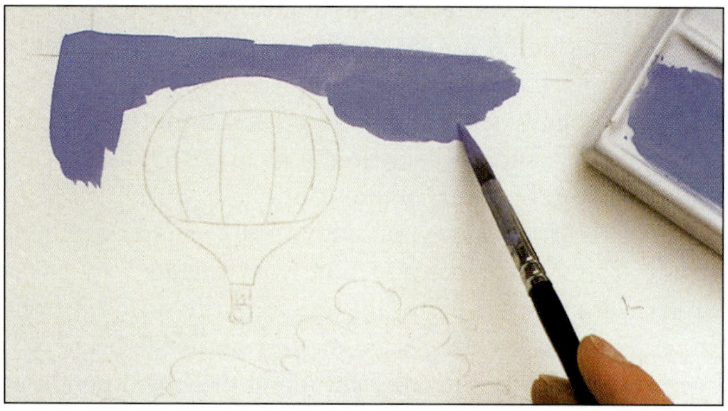

1 First draw the outline of the design lightly in pencil using a 140 lb/300 gsm "not" surface paper and a No. 3 sable brush. The gouache paint is mixed with water until it is the consistency of single cream.

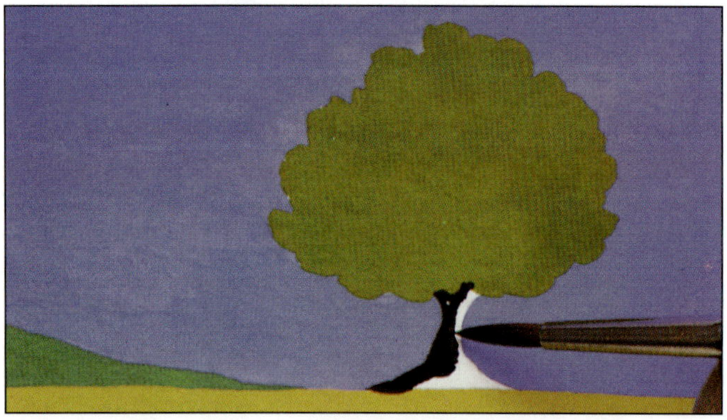

2 Starting at the top and working down, fill each area with a flat wash. If when dry you find the wash is patchy, you will have added too much water. Don't worry; mix the same color with a little less water and go over the same area again.

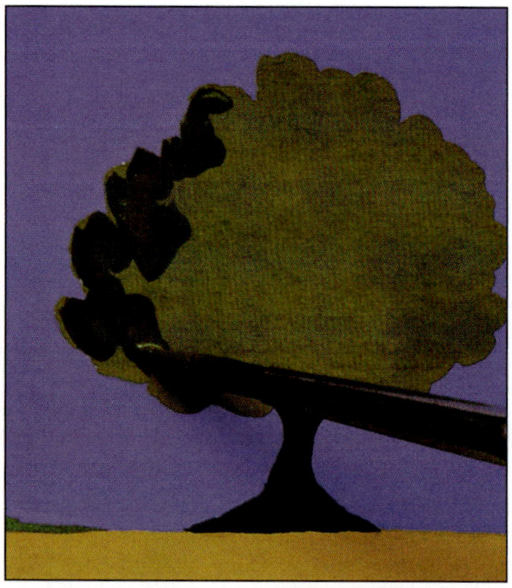

3 When the first wash is completely dry, the shadow colors can be added. Apply the paint with confidence; if you are too fiddly, you may disturb the first wash so that the two colors mix.

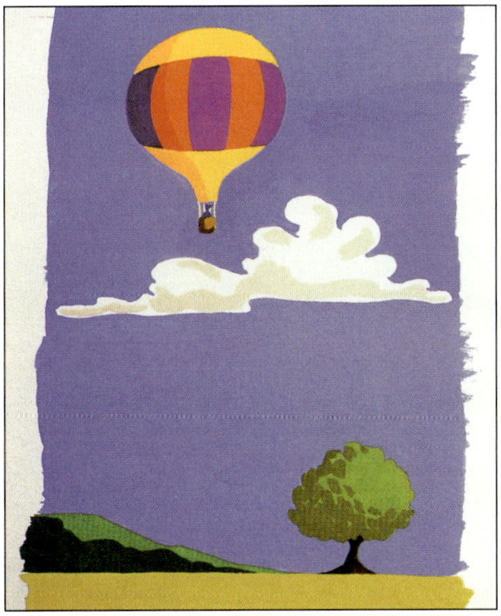

4 The finished illustration shows the solidity of color possible with gouache. It reproduces successfully and is particularly suited to stylized work.

OPAQUE AND TRANSLUCENT WASHES

Gouache can be combined in thick, opaque washes superimposed into thinner, translucent layers. For this picture use 140 lb/300 gsm "not" watercolor paper and sable brushes.

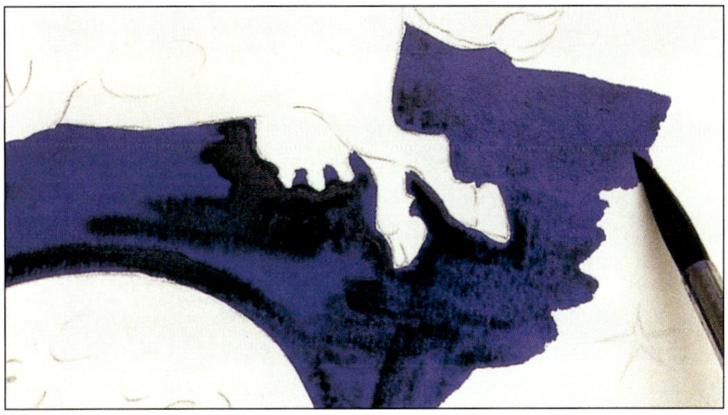

1 After the outline has been completed in pencil, an opaque wash is applied. Try to work quickly so that the wash is worked very wet. It will then dry to an even surface.

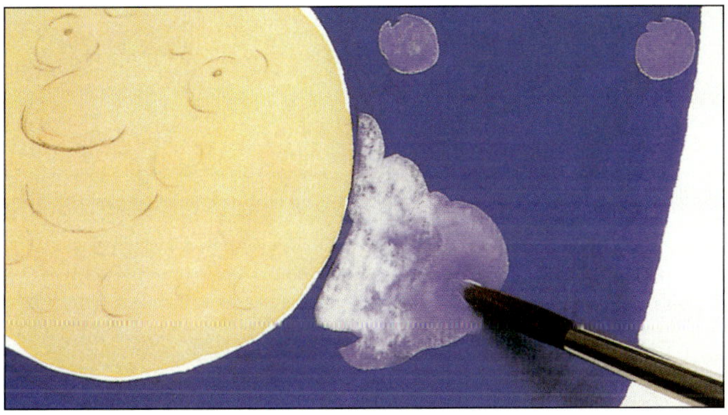

2 Once the opaque wash has dried, the thinner translucent washes can be applied on top. The paint is mixed until it is quite runny; this mixing can be done on the illustration itself. Work quickly so as not to disturb the opaque wash beneath. Some mixing is desirable.

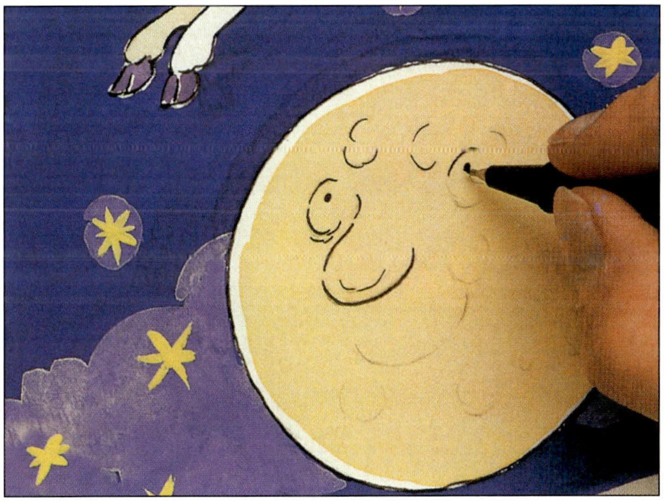

3 Fine detail can be added after the washes with a fine felt-tip pen. Do not use a dip pen and ink, as the ink will bleed into the paint.

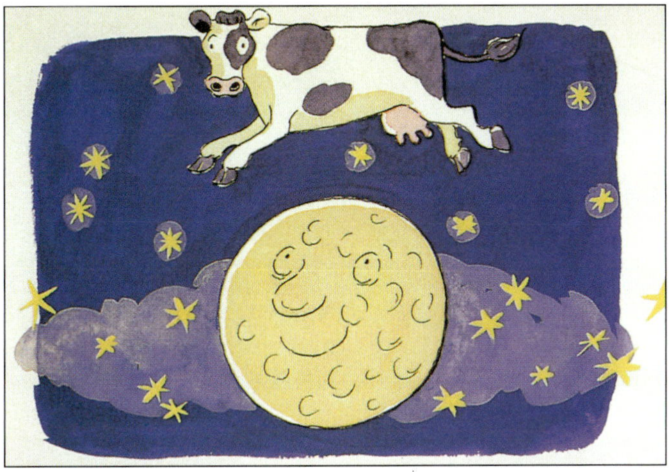

4 When all the washes are dry, other detail can be added with thick gouache, as can be seen in the stars in this illustration. Modeling and shadows are rendered in thin washes, such as the creamy shadow on the cow.

Techniques

WASH-OFF

Ink and gouache wash-off is an exciting technique that produces a textural effect not unlike that of a woodcut or lino print. The process, though quite a lengthy one, is highly satisfying and the results can be spectacular. The secret of success lies in a patient, methodical approach: each stage must be allowed to dry completely before the next stage can be started.

The basic method is as follows: a design is painted onto paper with white gouache and allowed to dry. The whole paper is then covered with a layer of waterproof black ink. When this is dry the painting is held under running water. The gouache, being soluble, dissolves and is washed off. This causes those areas of dried ink that were covering the gouache to wash-off at the same time. Meanwhile, the areas of black ink that covered parts of the design not painted with gouache remain intact. The result is a negative image of your original design.

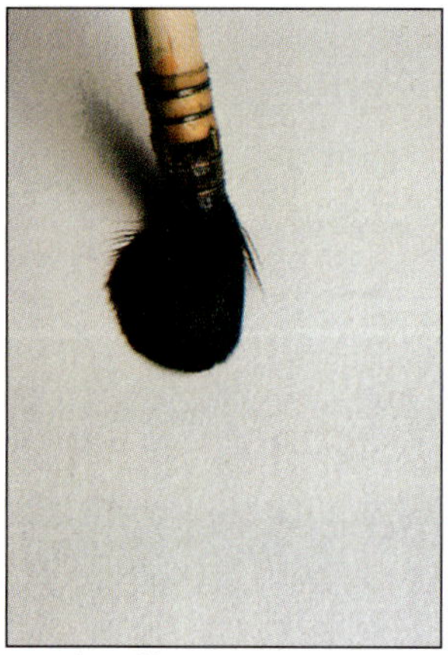

1 Ink wash-off must be done on a good-quality white paper, strong enough to withstand thorough wetting without tearing. The paper should be pre-stretched and taped firmly to the board to prevent it from wrinkling. If it does buckle a little when wet, don't worry – leave it to dry naturally and it will correct itself. The first stage in the wash-off process is to cover the entire paper with a flat wash of watercolor. This makes it easier to distinguish the white gouache design when you come to paint it. Here the artist is laying a diluted wash of raw umber, applied with a large mop brush.

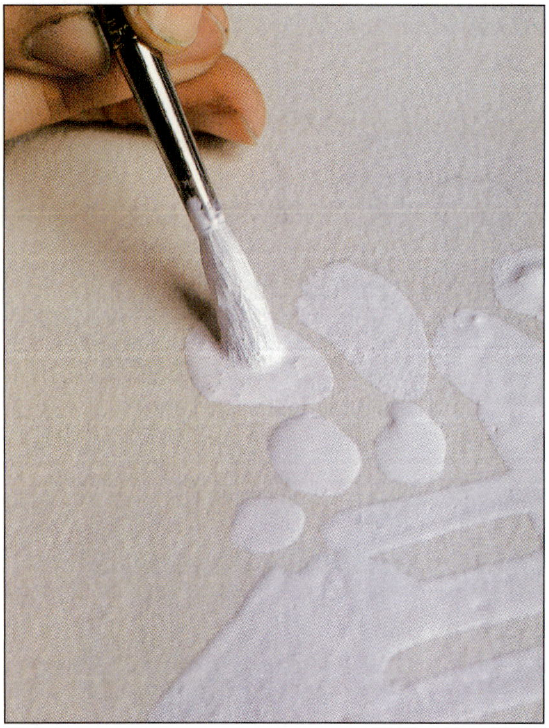

2 When the watercolor wash is completely dry, paint your chosen design in white gouache. If the image is to be an intricate one, you may prefer to make an outline sketch of it on the paper before applying the watercolor wash. The gouache will eventually be washed off, leaving negative shapes on a black background.

3 Allow the gouache to dry thoroughly, then cover the entire painting with black waterproof ink. This is the trickiest part of the process – the effect can be ruined if it is not done properly. Check that you have enough ink to cover the whole paper and shake it well before starting. Always use a large flat brush to apply the ink – here a No. 16 sable is used. Starting from the top, apply the ink in broad horizontal strokes. Make sure your brush is well-loaded, because you can only go over each area once – otherwise the white gouache starts to come off and mix with the ink. Leave the ink to dry naturally until it is bone hard.

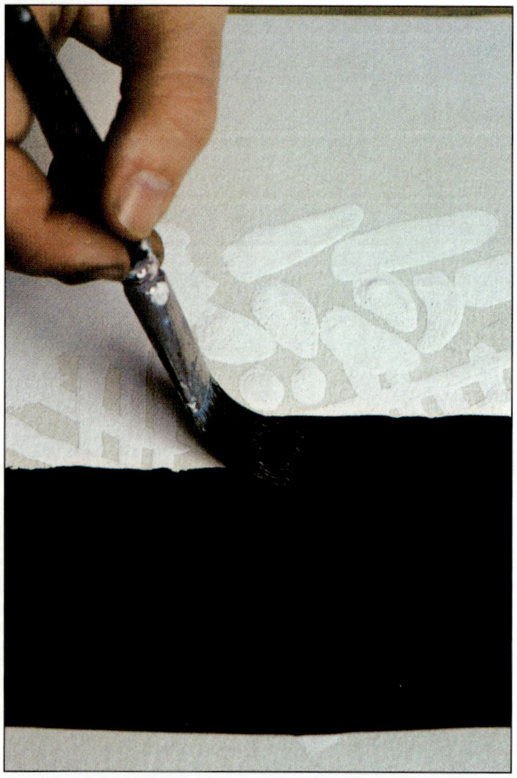

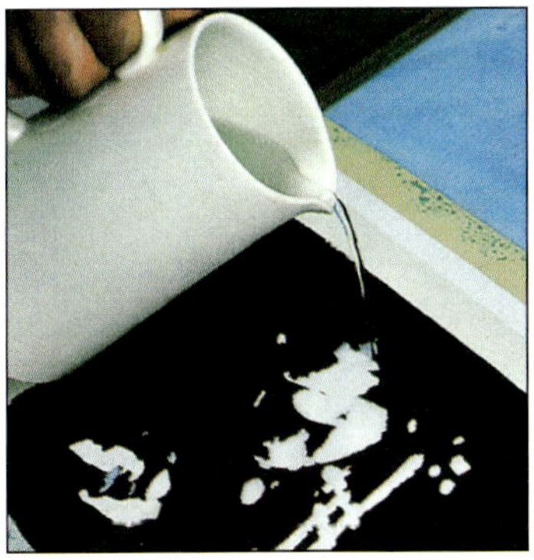

4 Now the wash-off part begins. Hold the board in a tilted position and pour large quantities of cold water over the paper (or hold the board under a running tap). Eventually the white gouache starts to dissolve and the ink that covers it also breaks up and is washed away. It may take several washings before all the removable ink comes off the board.

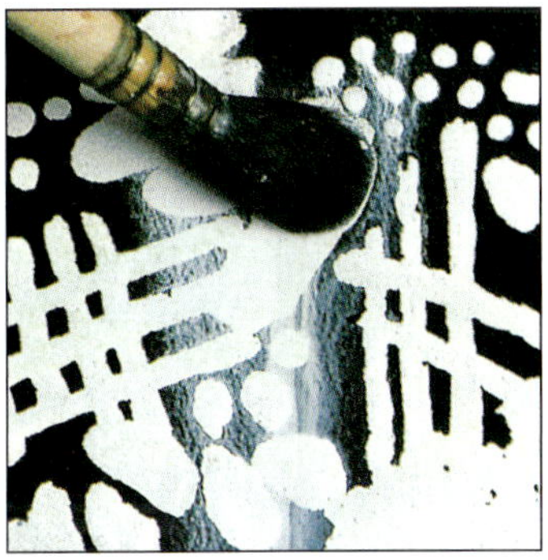

5 Use a soft brush to remove any excess gouache. The waterproof black ink which was not painted over gouache stays firmly in place, despite repeated washings.

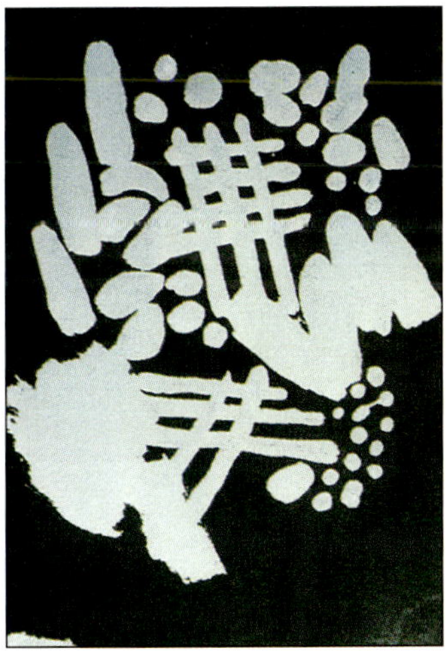

6 The finished effect is a silhouetted image. This can be left as it is, or it can be developed by adding color to the white parts of the design. For demonstration purposes, the design shown here has deliberately been kept simple. However, the technique is best-suited to a more intricate or textural design such as that used for leaves and flowers. Animals, with their fur texture and markings, are another suitable subject.

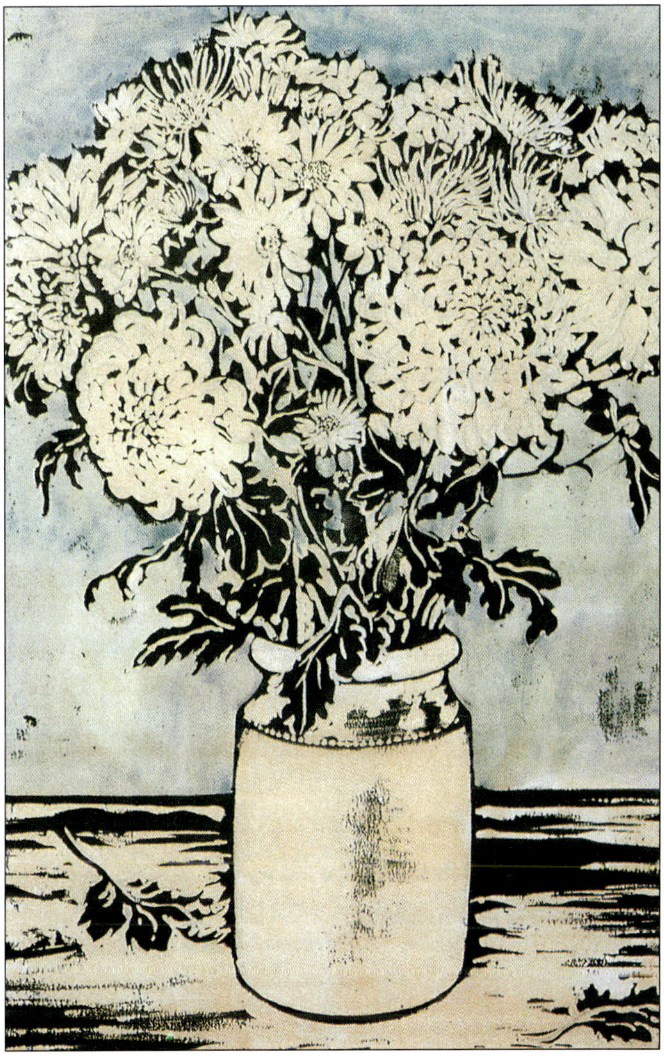

WASH-OFF

In this example, a wash of burnt sienna was laid over a pencil drawing and, when dry, the shapes of the flowers, the vase, and the table were painted over it with white gouache. When the gouache had dried the whole image was covered with waterproof India ink. Once this was dry cold water was poured over the paper and within several minutes the ink on the gouache came away, with the gouache. Excess gouache was removed with a paintbrush, still leaving the waterproof black areas on the paper. A thin background wash of Prussian blue was then applied to lift this decorative image out of the purely monochrome.

GOUACHE SPATTER

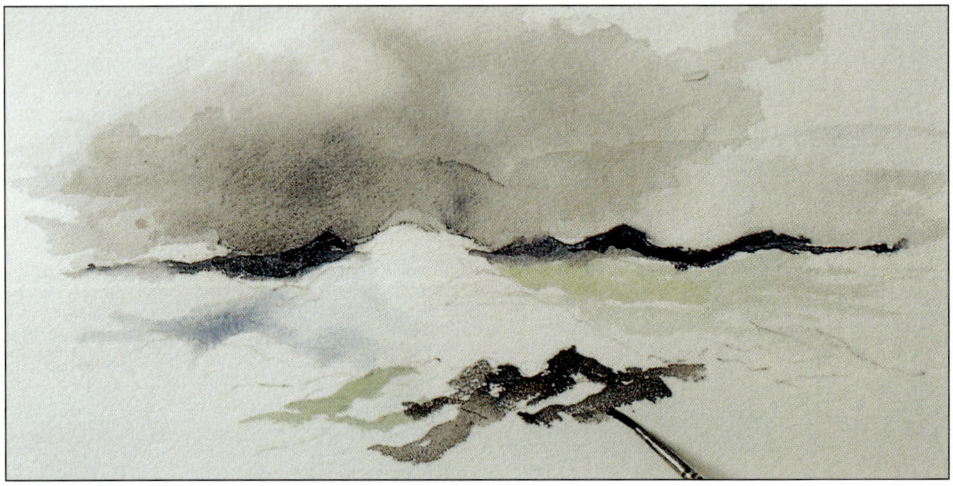

1 Occasionally you will encounter an effect, such as the fine spray of windblown foam above a breaking wave, which is difficult to render in transparent watercolor. In this case, opaque white gouache spattered over dry watercolor provides the answer.

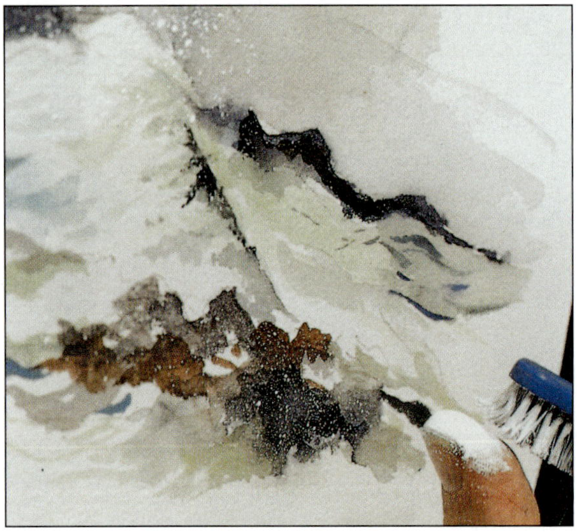

2 White gouache spatter should be the final stage of a painting. Working over it will stir up the paint, sacrificing the effect. The paint needs to be mixed fairly thickly – too thin and it will sink into the watercolor washes. Always try the mixture first. If it goes wrong, you can remove the gouache, but this involves washing the entire area and beginning again.

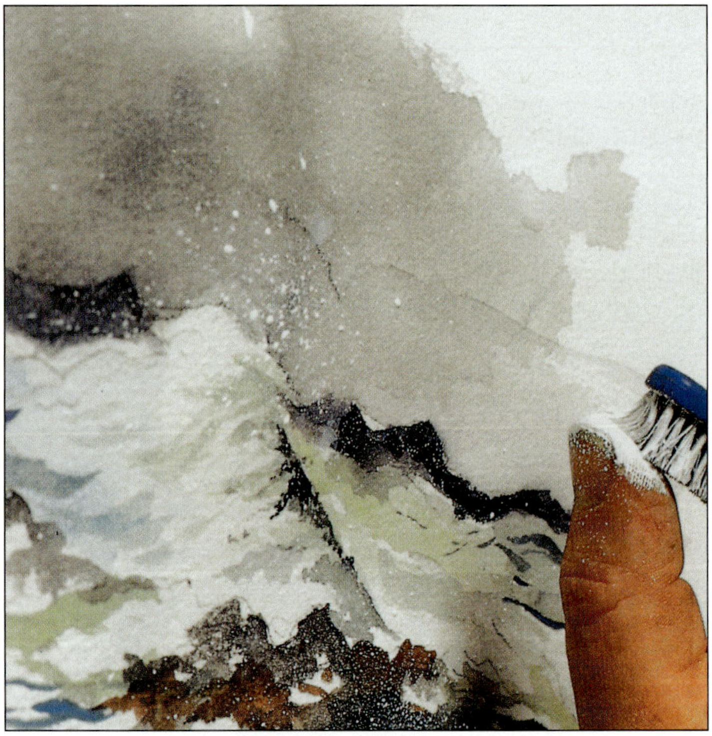

3 Gouache, being thicker than watercolor, is easier to control, and you can place the spattered paint precisely. Hold the toothbrush a few inches from the paper, and run your thumb (or the handle of a paintbrush) quickly along the bristles.

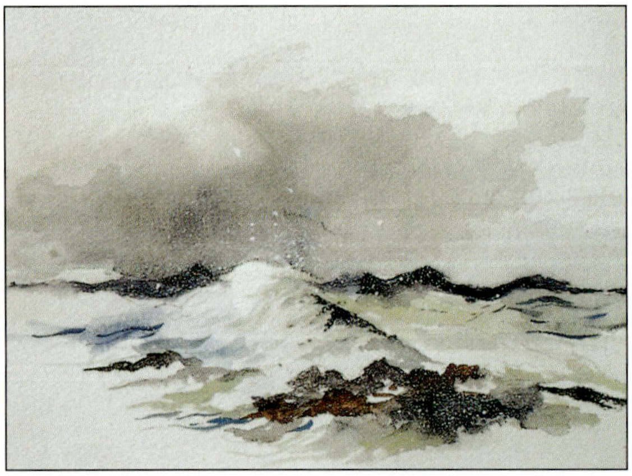

4 Don't overdo the spatter; it is most effective when kept light, as in this example.

IMPASTO

This technique is probably more effective if you are working with acrylic paint, but using gouache can also be successful. The paint is used as it comes out of the tube. Do not add extra water as the consistency will be lighter, which will detract from the impasto effect.

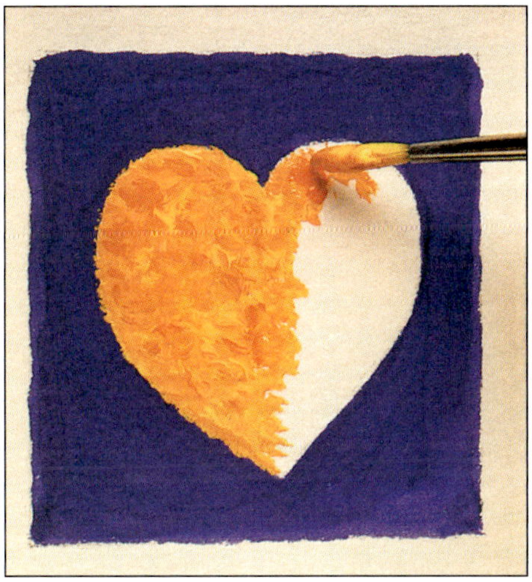

1 Here the background area has been applied first in flat gouache to enhance the impasto effect. The orange paint is then applied as thickly as possible. Try to create as much surface texture as you can with the brush.

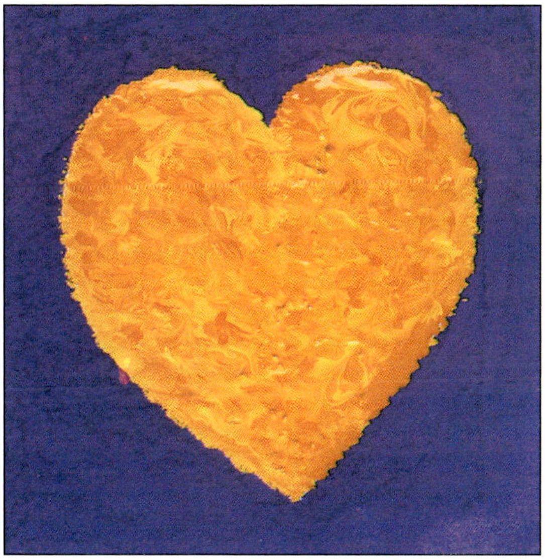

2 In this example two colors – red and yellow – were mixed on the paper, which strengthens the impasto effect.

OPAQUE GLAZE

With a 2 in. (5 cm) flat brush, lay a glaze of semi-transparent white gouache over a dry painting. Mix plenty of paint to create an even, milky consistency.

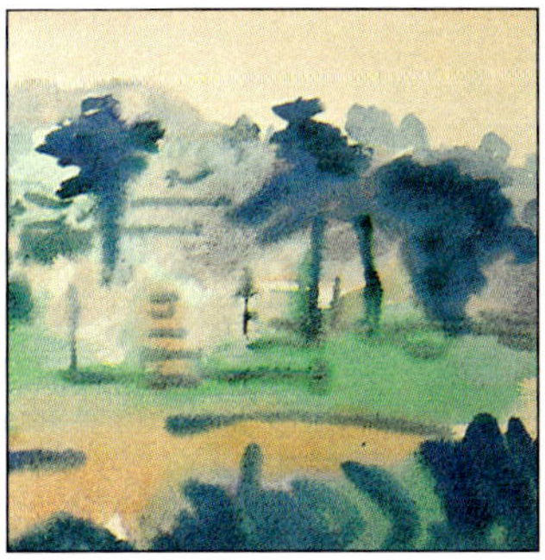

1 Paint the landscape wet in wet, with bold playful strokes, letting the colors spread softly.

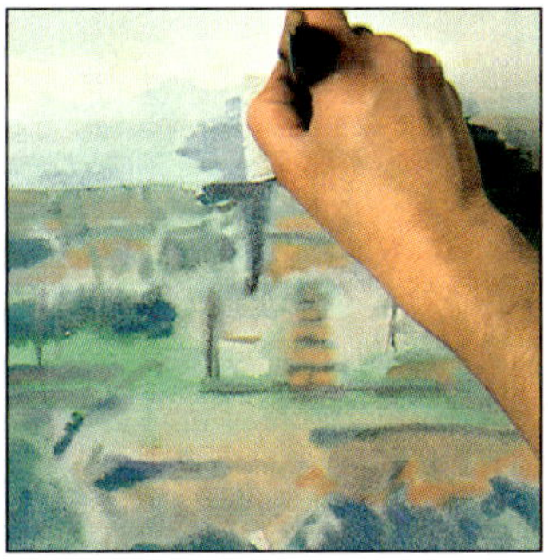

2 Overglaze with white gouache laid in horizontal stripes, allowing them to merge of their own accord. Lift out any area that picks up too much white with a tissue.

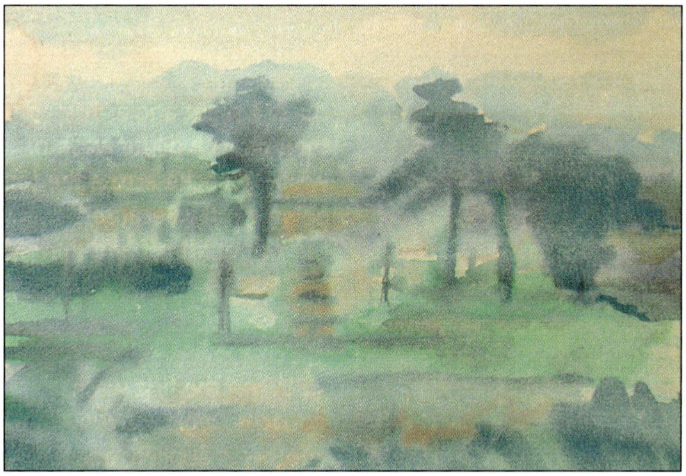

3 Blot the darker trees before the white dries so that they appear to loom out of the mist. Avoid going over the painting too much or you will lift out the color.

MIXED MEDIA

One of the most exciting aspects of modern painting is that artists are free to break as many artistic conventions as they like. By mixing techniques and combining different media in the same painting, it is possible to broaden the range and expressiveness of your work beyond anything you thought possible.

GOUACHE AND CHARCOAL

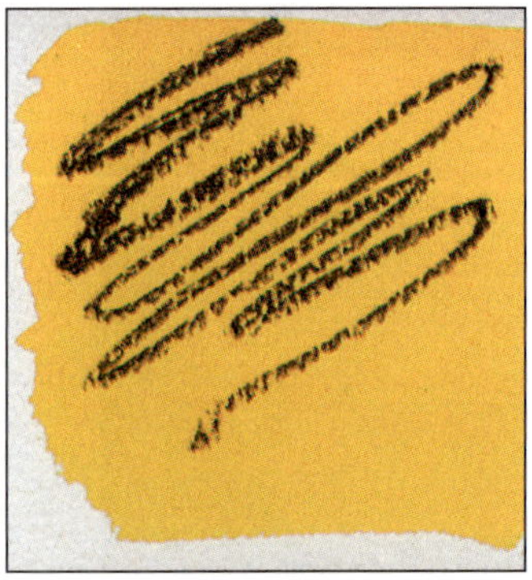

1 The artist first applies a thick layer of yellow gouache. When this is completely dry he draws a design onto it with charcoal. Note that if the paint is still wet, the charcoal will not take.

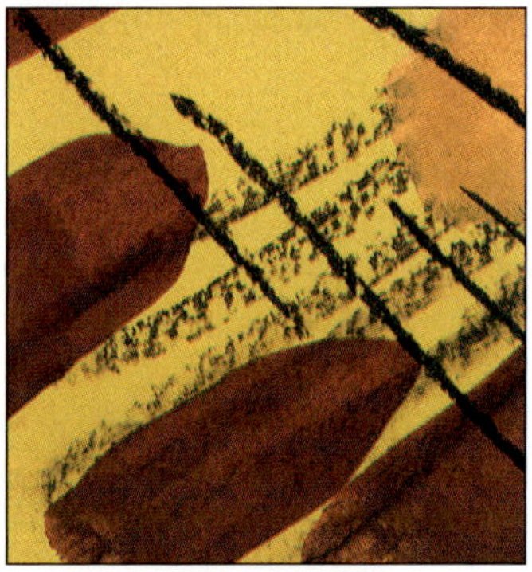

2 Using a No. 4 bristle brush, the artist works into the charcoal drawing with further gouache colors. Interesting variations of tone are achieved by allowing the charcoal to dissolve into the color in places.

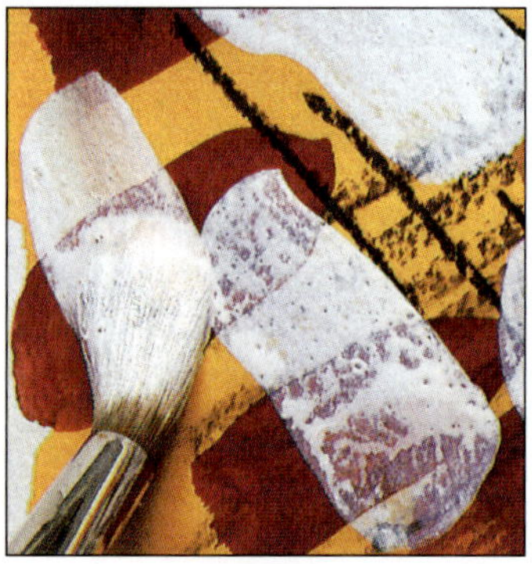

3 When the paint dries, the process can be repeated, adding further charcoal marks and color washes.

ACRYLIC AND GOUACHE

Acrylic and gouache paints work well together because of their versatility. Acrylic can be used for transparent washes or heavy impasto; it dries quickly and won't lift off, so that further washes of transparent color can be applied, producing effects of great depth. Gouache, too, can be used thickly or diluted with water to create semi-transparent washes. Here the artist combines the covering power of acrylic with the smooth-flowing, translucent quality of gouache to create an intriguing effect that could be used for painting a stormy sky or a night scene.

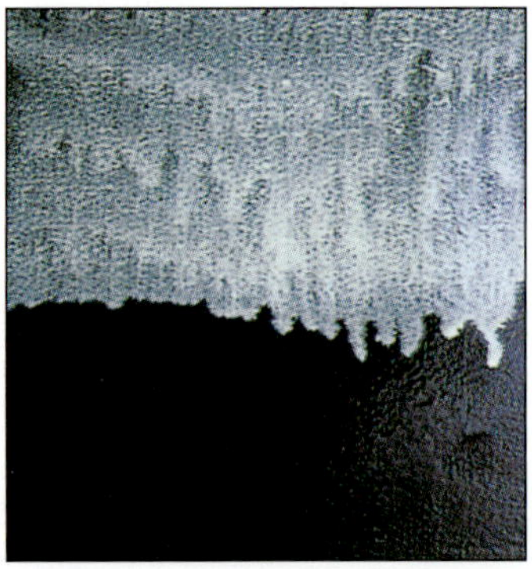

1 Working on a sheet of 200 lb cold-pressed watercolor paper, the artist applies a flat wash of acrylic in a dark color and allows it to dry. The surface is then rewetted with water, and the upper edge of the board is tilted up at a slight angle. The artist then floats a dilute wash of white gouache across the top of the paper and allows it to flow down gently. Because the acrylic underlayer has dried insoluble, it does not lift off and muddy any succeeding washes.

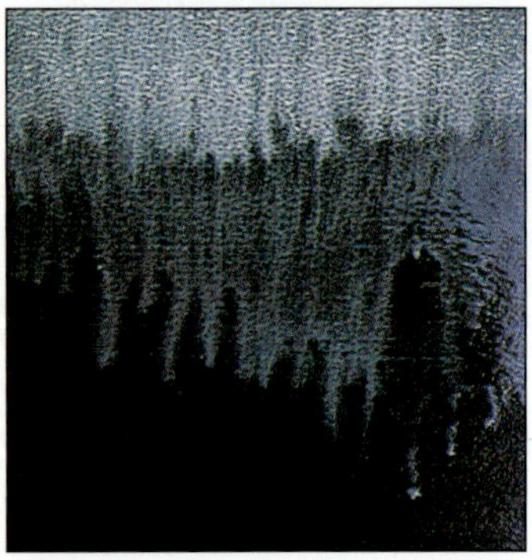

2 When the first wash of gouache begins to run out, another is applied, again across the top of the paper. As this wash travels downward, it merges with the first wash. The painting is then allowed to dry.

3 The dark wash of acrylic glows through the translucent wash of white gouache. The finished result is very subtle, and evocative of a rainy sky.

UNDERPAINTING WITH INK

This painting demonstrates an innovative and imaginative method of combining gouache with another water-based medium – ink – to create an individual and expressive seascape. There is nothing innovative in the use of an underpainting in itself, but it is not generally used with water-based media such as watercolor or gouache due to the inherent transparency of these media. In this instance, the artist has first executed an underpainting in bold, primary colors, which serves to unify the painting and help eliminate the inevitable chalkiness of gouache.

Since the more traditional method of underpainting requires time-consuming layering of color upon color, the use of these bold colors for the underpainting expedites the painting process. In this method, the artist can jump directly from the underpainting to developing the basic structure of the painting without having to wait for previous coats to dry.

While opaque and flat, gouache retains many of the qualities of all water-based paints and can be worked wet-into-wet, spattered, or dry brushed. Here the artist has used a combination of all these techniques which, when combined with a subtle mixture of color and tone – all of which are enhanced by the initial underpainting – results in an evocative and atmospheric painting.

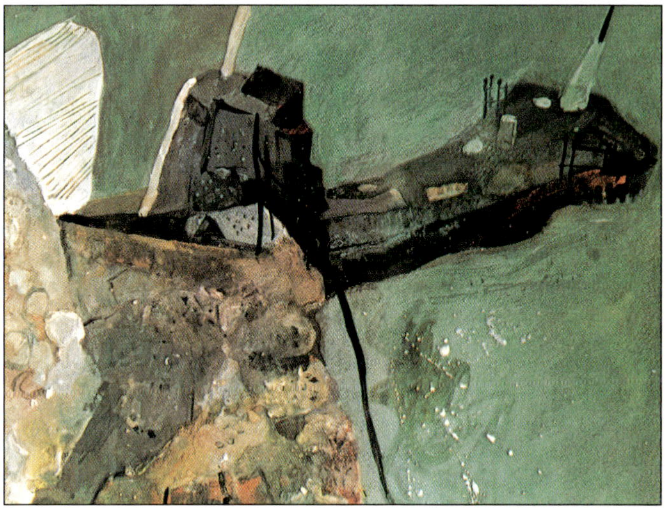

The very bold colors of an underpainting done in colored inks will later be modified by opaque gouache. Here, in the first step, the inks are bleeding into one another.

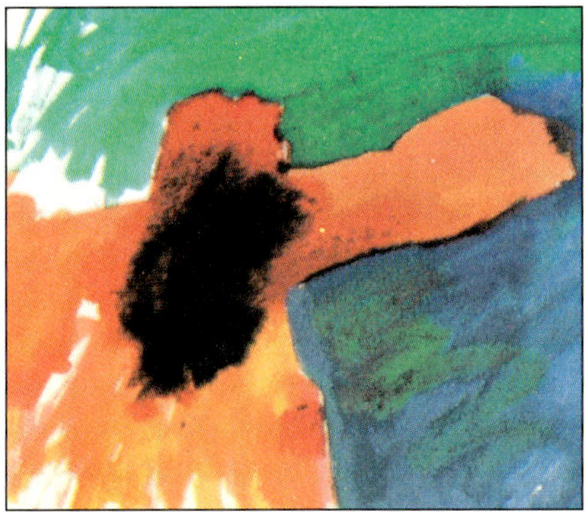

1 With a No. 10 brush, lay down broad areas of red, orange, blue, and green ink corresponding to the shapes and color tones of the subject.

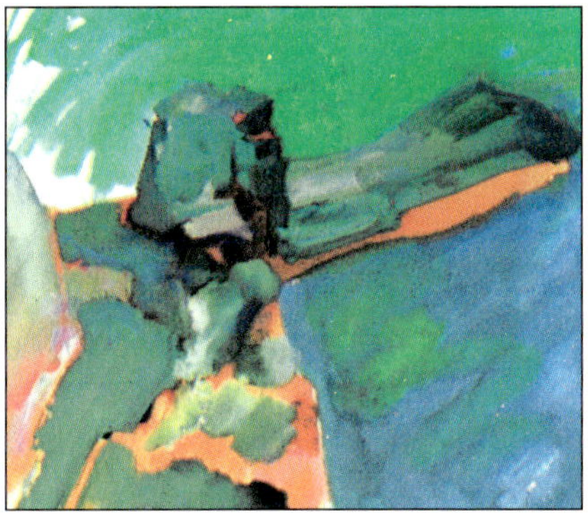

2 While still wet, mix a variety of gray tones from white, olive green, and Payne's gray gouache. Very loosely rough in the pier allowing the ink and gouache to bleed.

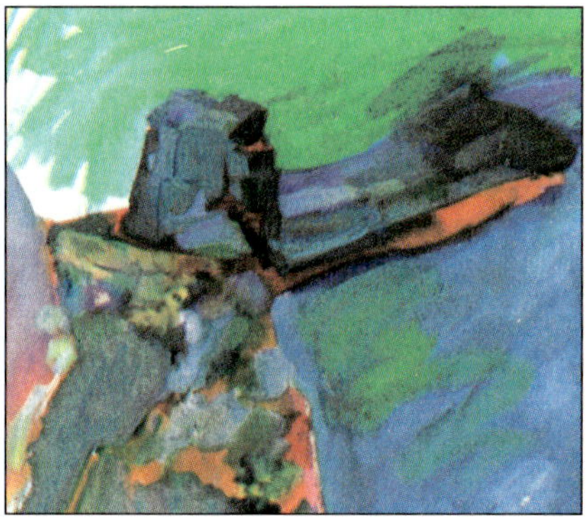

3 With a No. 4 brush, begin to dot in lighter tones of gray and white, once again allowing the colors to bleed together.

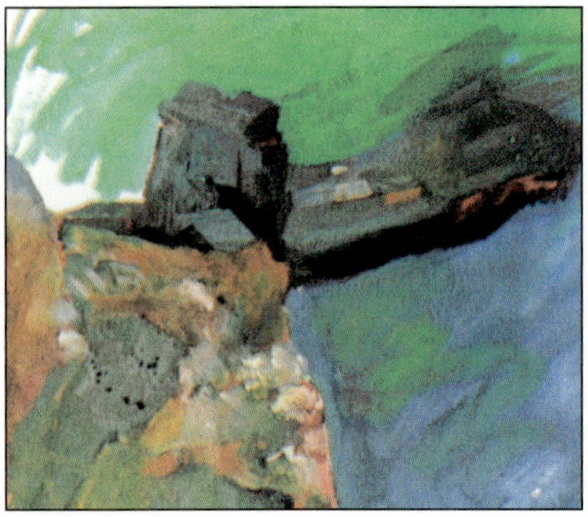

4 Cover the orangeish underpainting in the foreground with a thin wash of burnt umber.

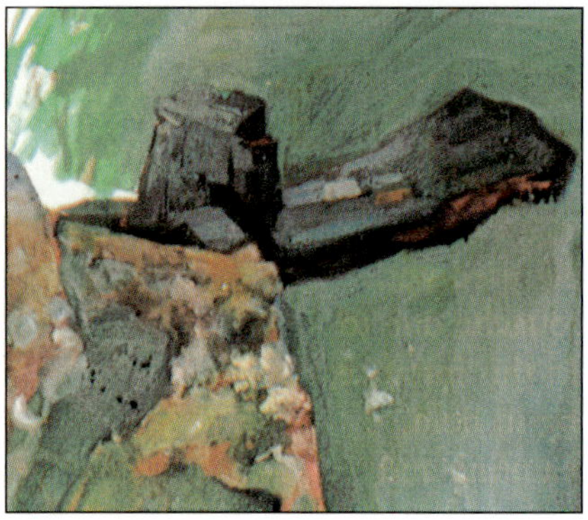

5 Add a touch of olive green to the white, Payne's gray, and green mixture, and with the No. 10 brush cover the sky and sea area with broad, loose strokes.

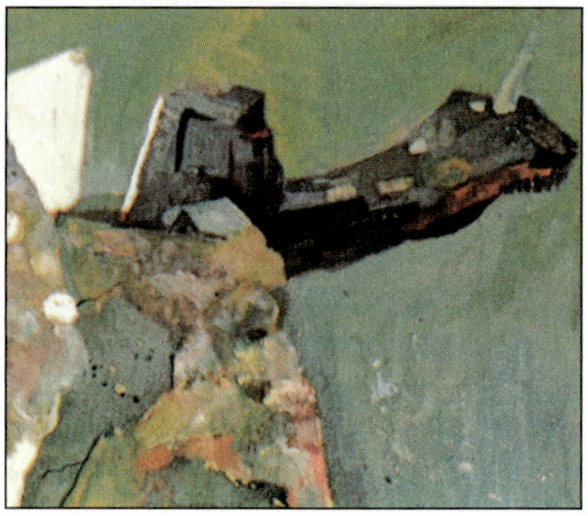

6 Cover the remaining sky area in this same color and let dry. Using pure white gouache, block in white shape to left and small touches of white in the foreground.

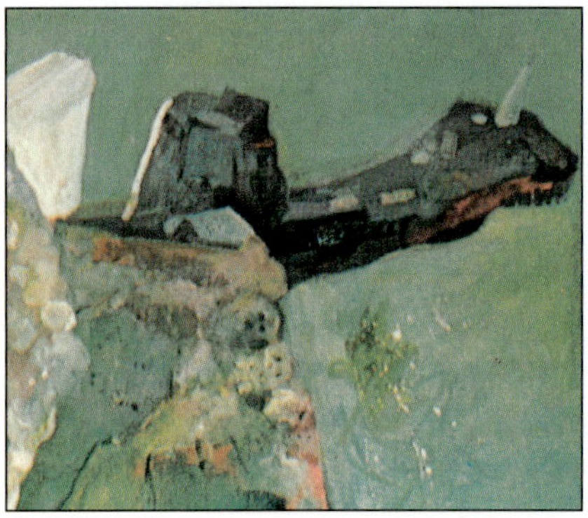

7 Add more olive green to the mixture and loosely put in strokes in sea and foreground rocks. Put pure white on a No. 4 brush and spatter.

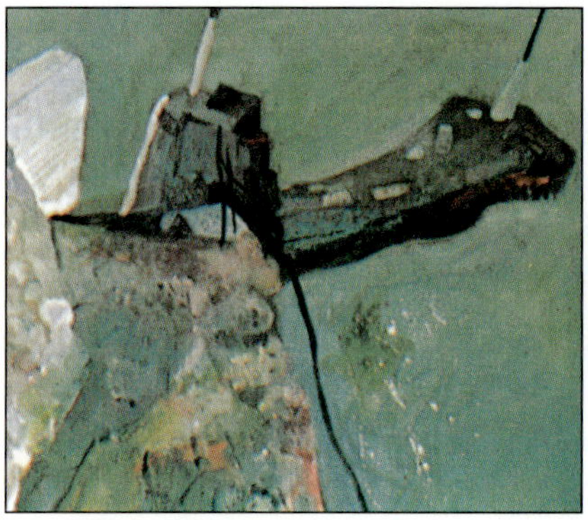

8 With a No. 4 brush and black gouache, put in the fine details of the picture.

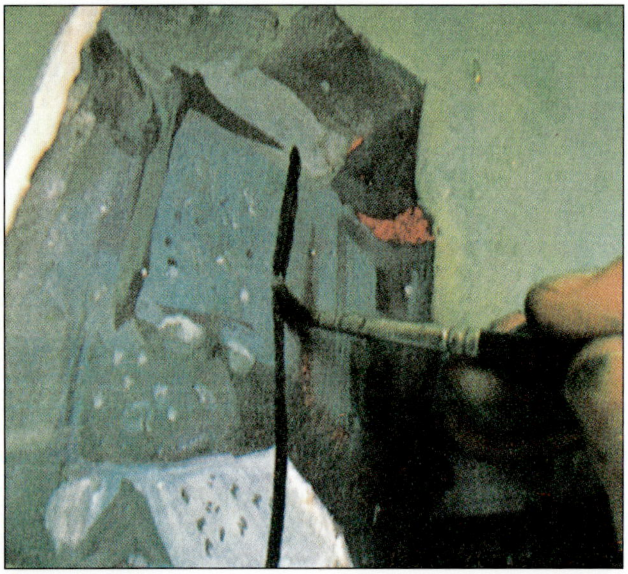

In the final steps, the artist puts in small details of pure black gouache with a small sable brush.

BUILDING UP LAYERS

Gouache is especially well-suited for building up opaque layers of paint. Due to its excellent covering powers, the artist is free to alter the image as much as he chooses. Here the artist is building up highlights over a darker paint layer.

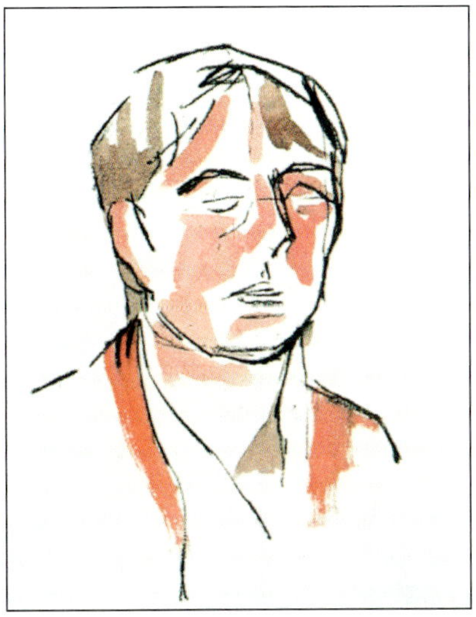

1 Draw the outline of head and shoulders with charcoal, indicating eyes, nose, and mouth. Lay thin washes of red and brown to indicate shadows with a No. 6 brush.

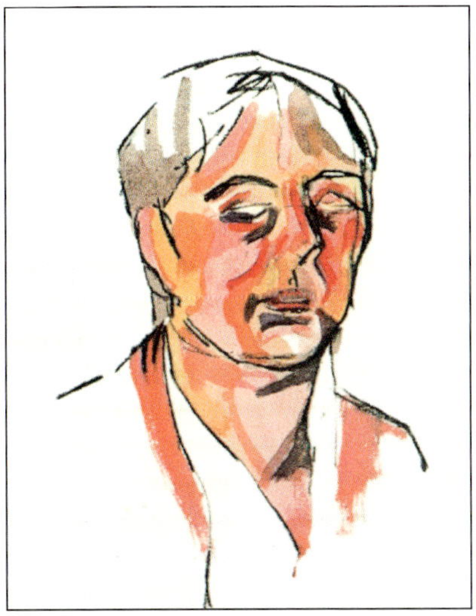

2 Identify basic colors in the face and neck. Draw out contrasts by exaggerating the tones slightly, overlaying patches of each color to build up the form.

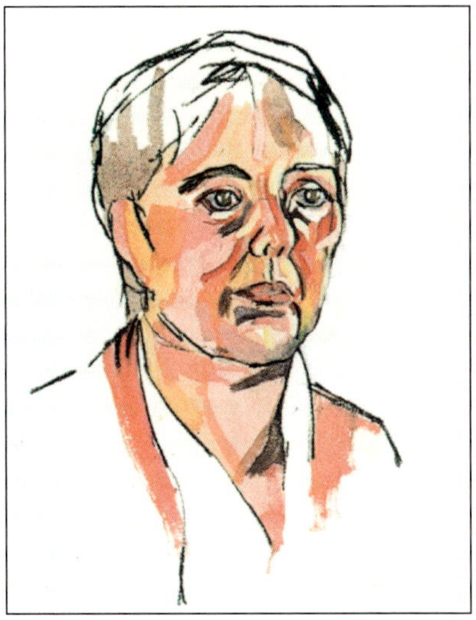

3 Draw into face with charcoal, and paint in linear details with the point of a No. 3 brush in dark brown. Work up the color in and around the features.

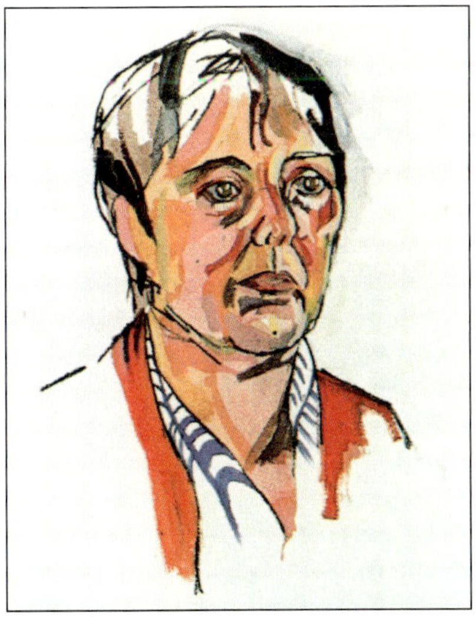

4 Alter the shape of the head and lay in dark tones of the hair. Paint the stripe pattern on the scarf in cobalt blue and strengthen the red of the jacket.

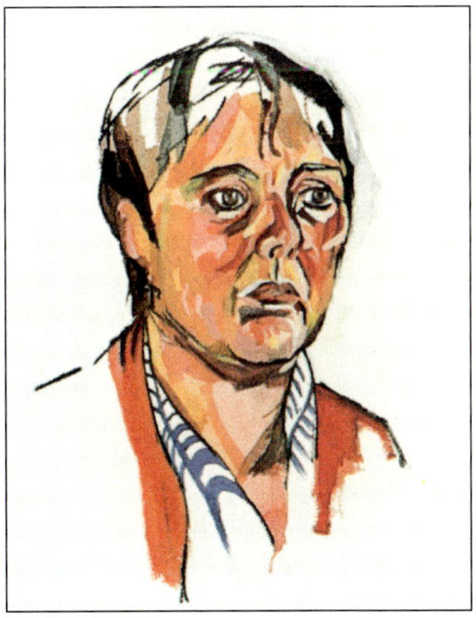

5 Develop the structure and color of the face, drawing into the features with the No. 3 brush and adding thick white and pink highlights with brown shadows in the flesh.

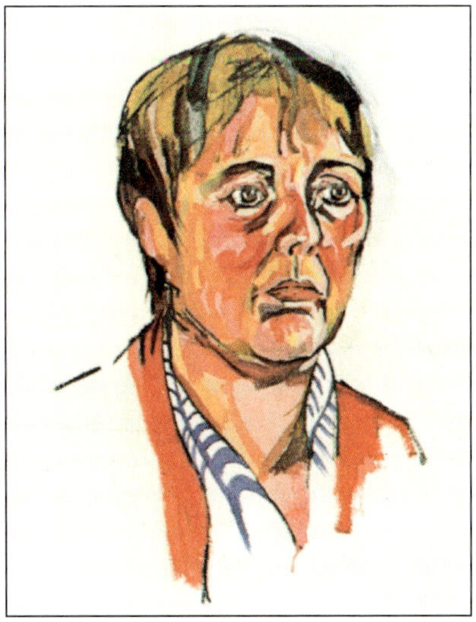

6 Block in the hair with a thin wash of yellow ocher and delineate separate strands with burnt umber. Reinforce the shapes of eyes and mouth with small color details.

GOUACHE IN LANDSCAPE PAINTING

Gouache is an ideal medium for recording the changing conditions of light in landscape painting. It dries quite rapidly and with a limited palette one can continually modify tones in such a way that the right balance is achieved. The opacity of the color makes it possible to rework certain passages of the painting in a way that is not possible in watercolor.

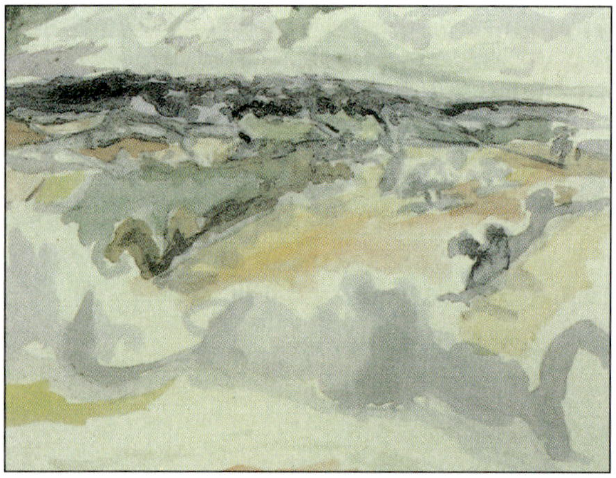

1 The color is diluted almost to the consistency of watercolor to register the main forms in the landscape view.

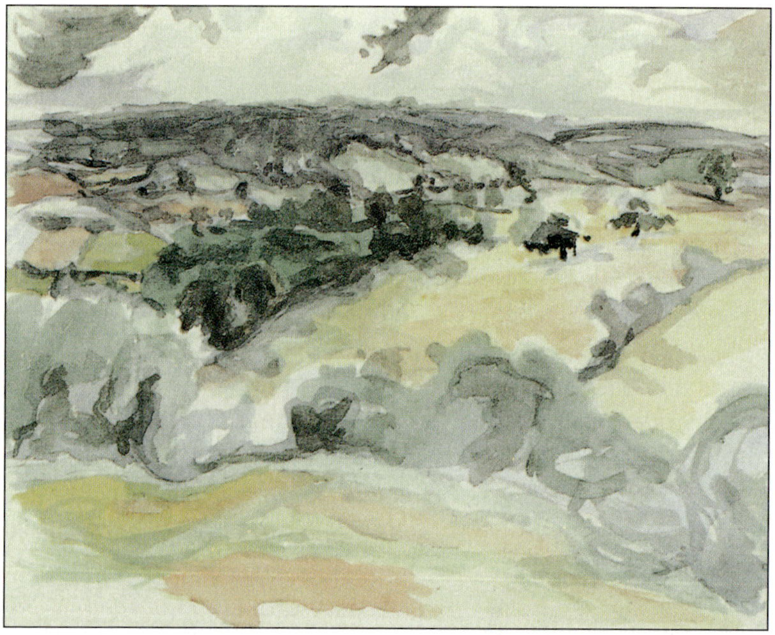

2 The colors in the middle distance are intensified to concentrate attention on that part of the composition.

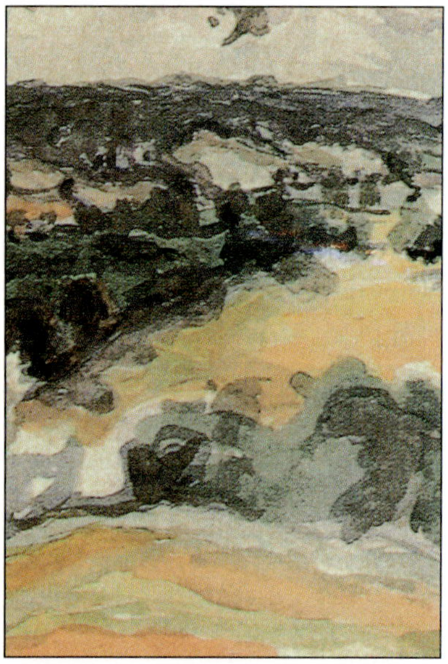

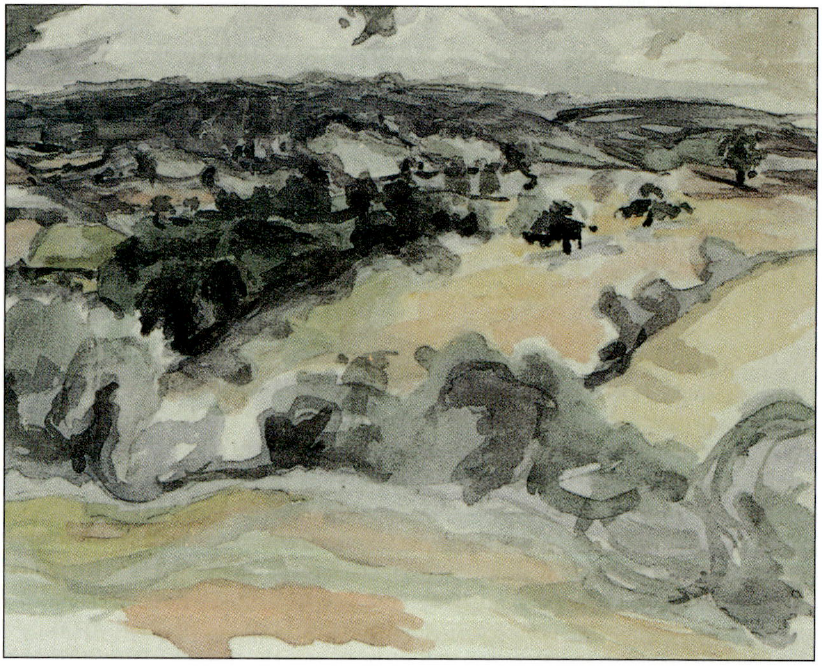

3&4 The various parts of the painting begin to work together. The detail in the foreground is understated in order to focus on the valley and hills.

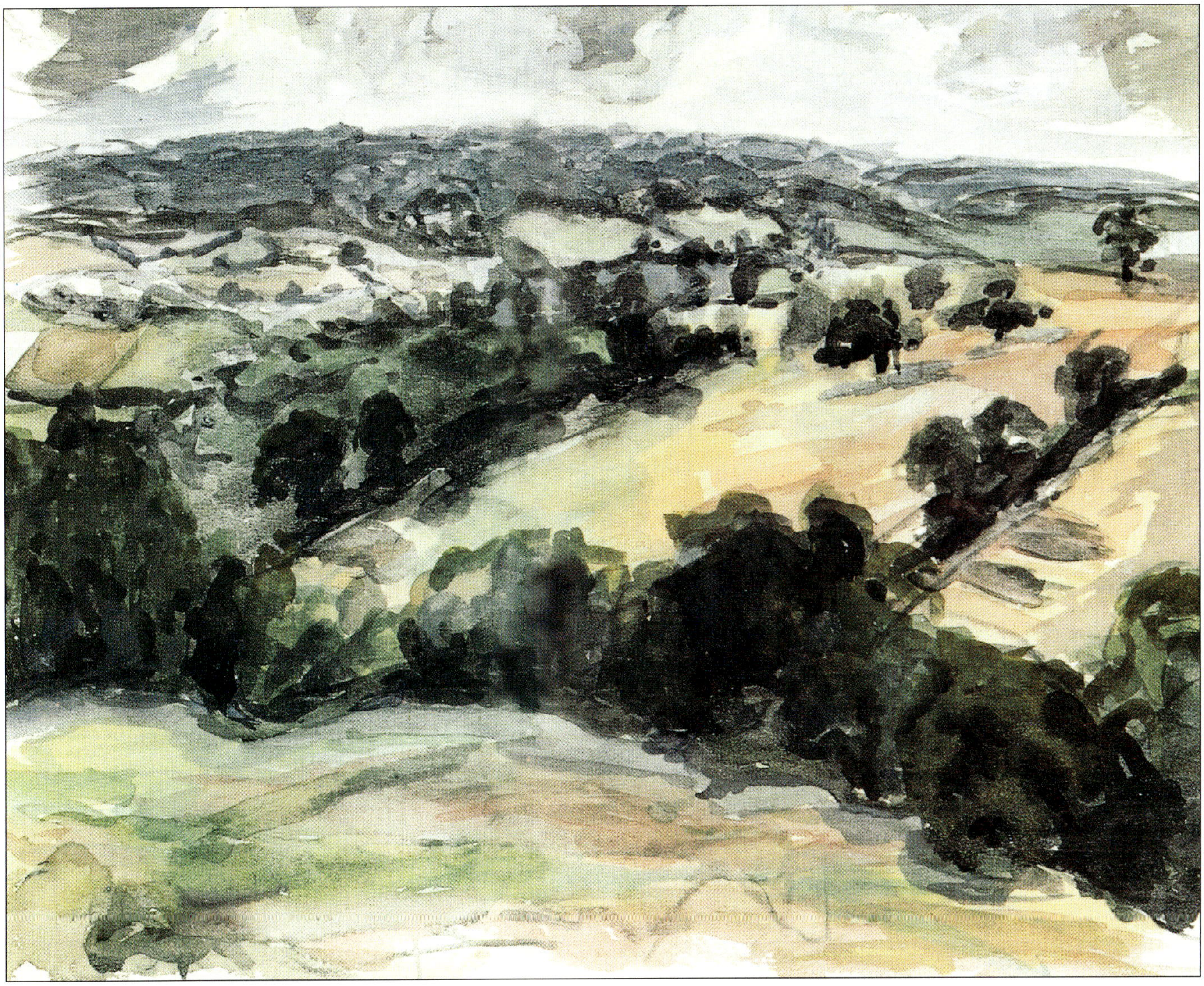

In the finished picture above, the darker tones of the trees provide a visual link from the foreground to the distance.

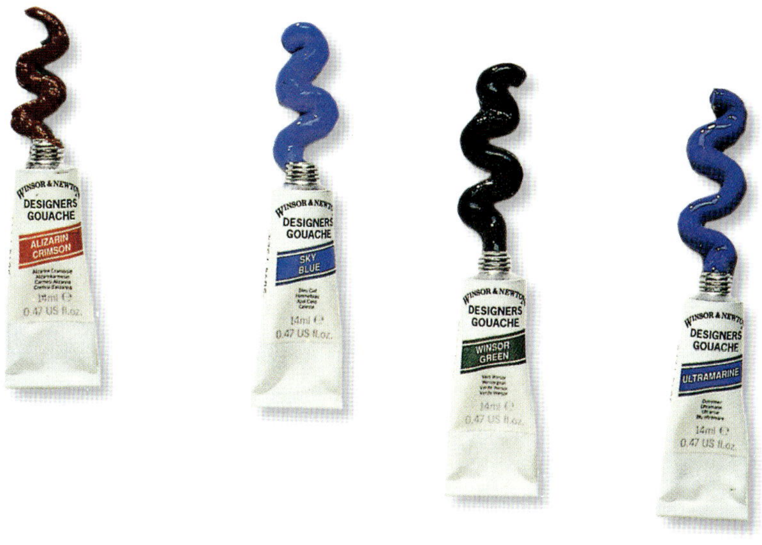

SNOW IN GOUACHE AND WATERCOLOR

In the painting on this page, the artist tackles the problem of rendering an impression of falling snow so that it looks natural and uncontrived. One of the best ways of doing this is with the technique of spattering; the tiny droplets of paint fall onto the paper in a random fashion which perfectly captures the effect of swirling snowflakes.

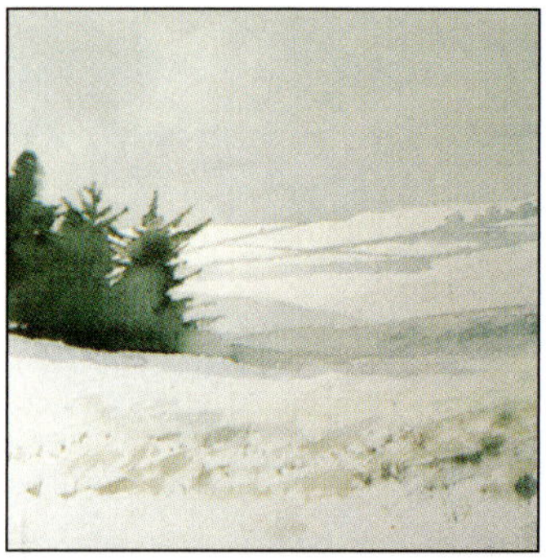

1 Working on a stretched sheet of 200 lb Bockingford paper, the artist begins by painting the sky with a pale tone of Payne's gray. Saving the white of the paper for the brightest areas of the snow, he indicates the shapes of the distant trees and hedgerows with faint gray lines. The spruce trees on the left are then painted with a dark wash of Hooker's green and Payne's gray. In the foreground quick dry brush strokes of burnt umber indicate clumps of grass and earth uncovered by the partially melted snow. This addition of a warmer tone in the foreground accentuates the sense of depth in the painting.

2 The painting is left to dry naturally. Meanwhile, a thick but fluid wash of white gouache is mixed on the palette, ready for spattering to begin. This is the tricky part of the painting – the droplets of paint must be of the correct size and density, otherwise the effect could be ruined. Always do a "test run" on a piece of scrap paper before applying the technique to an actual painting. This way you will learn to gauge the fluidity of paint required and also the best distance between the brush and the paper (generally this should be at least 6 in. (15 cm)). Here the artist is using a $^1/_2$ in. (1 cm) decorator's brush, running his finger through the bristles to create a fine spatter.

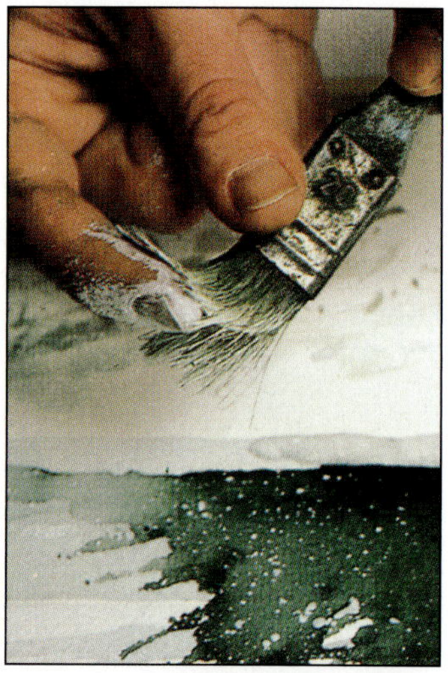

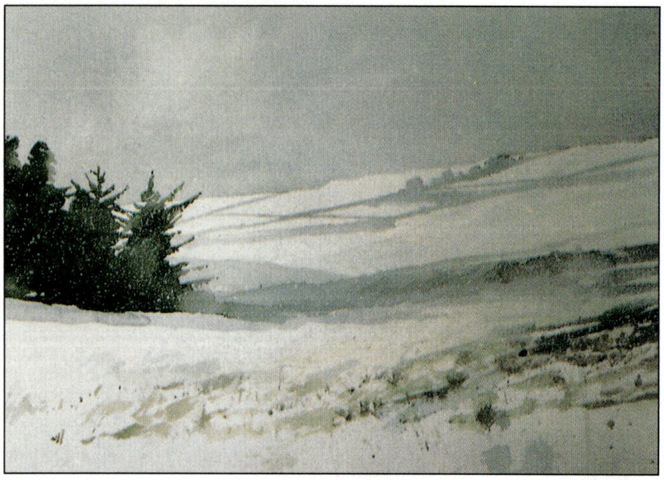

3 In the finished painting, notice how subtly the spatter has been applied to give a naturalistic effect. It is important not to overdo the spatter – too little is better than too much, unless you deliberately want to create the effect of a snowstorm. The "veil" of semi-opaque gouache also softens the forms and colors underneath, just as real snowflakes partially obscure the landscape as they fall.

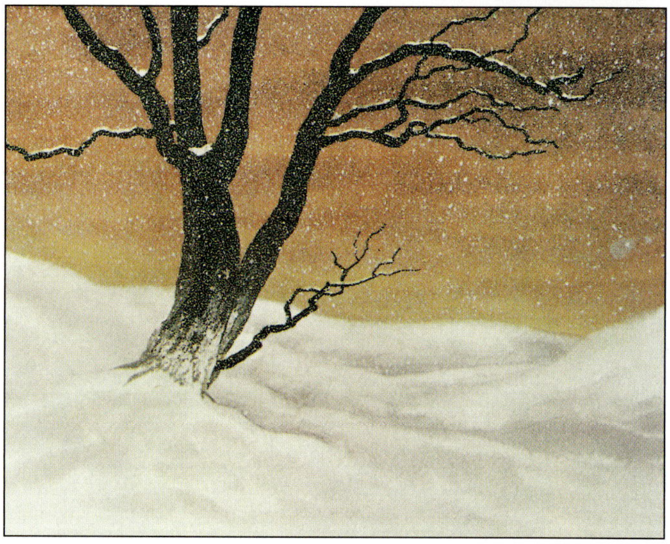

In the painting above the snow was created by dipping a toothbrush in white gouache and releasing speckles of paint by drawing a finger swiftly back across the bristles.

FLOWER TECHNIQUES

Crown imperial

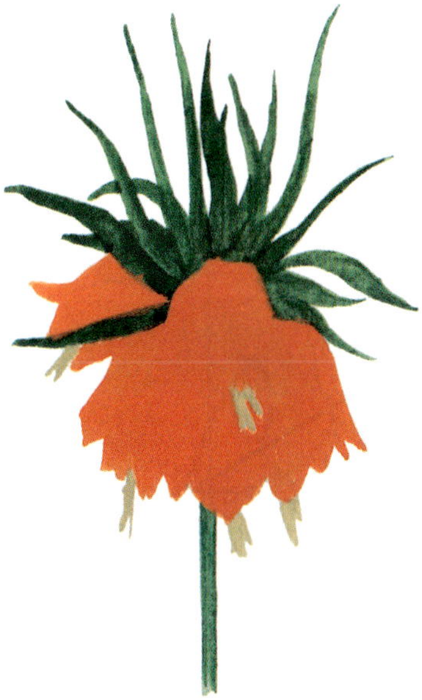

1 Gouache is an excellent medium for laying areas of flat color, with little or no blending and sharp divisions between tones. Start with a pencil drawing and then lay down the middle tone for both flowers and leaves.

2 Next, paint the lighter tones on top, still using the paint thick and opaque. It will sink into the underpainting slightly, but can be lightened further if necessary by adding another layer.

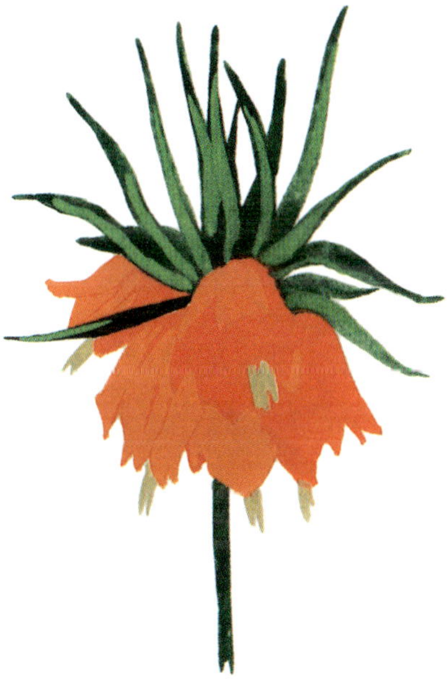

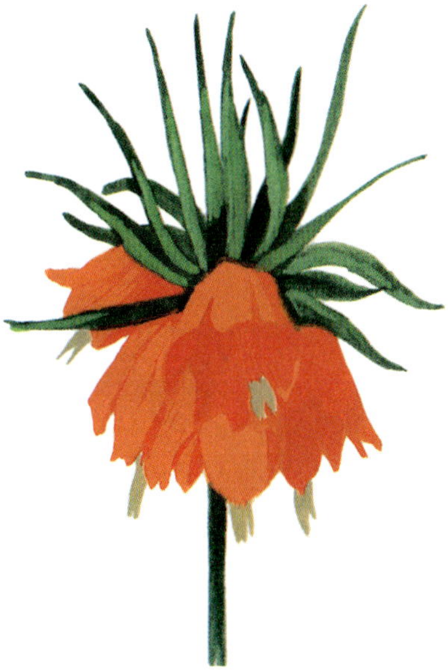

3 Finally, paint in the darker areas of the flowers, taking the new color carefully around the edges of the petals to make a strong line that describes the flowing, curving shapes.

Day lily

1 Like acrylic, gouache can be used in a layering technique, but avoid too many layers or the colors may become muddy. Gouache is water-soluble even when dry, and new applications can melt and mix with earlier ones. Begin with the background, laying a deep solution of Prussian blue. When this has dried, make an outline drawing with a yellow crayon or pastel pencil.

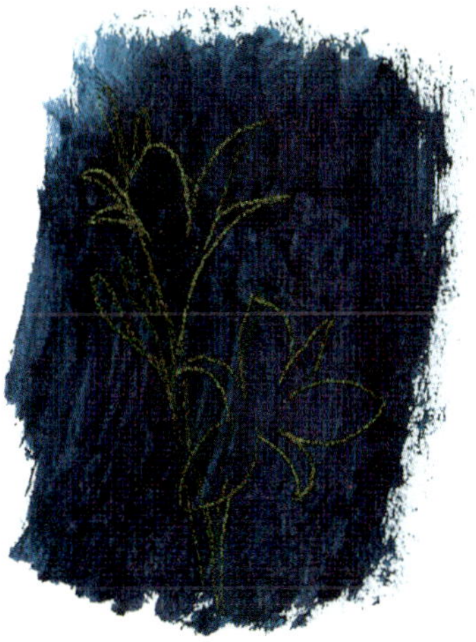

2 Paint in the flowers with lemon yellow diluted with a little water so that it is semi-transparent. Let the brush follow the direction of the petals, allowing some of the blue to show through between each brush stroke to create shadow areas.

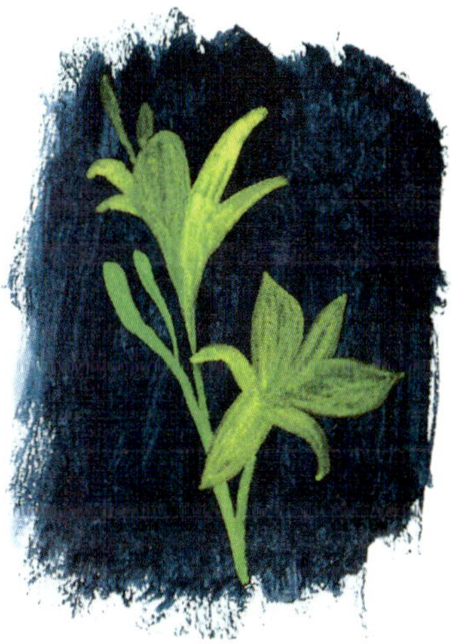

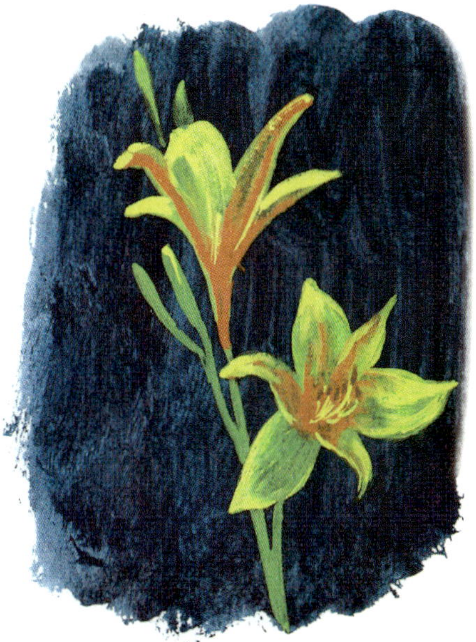

3 Now use the paint more thickly and dryly to build up the highlights, blending with a wet brush where necessary. Paint the stamens and the top underside of the top flower with a light reddish brown the same tone as the greenish yellow.

Solandra

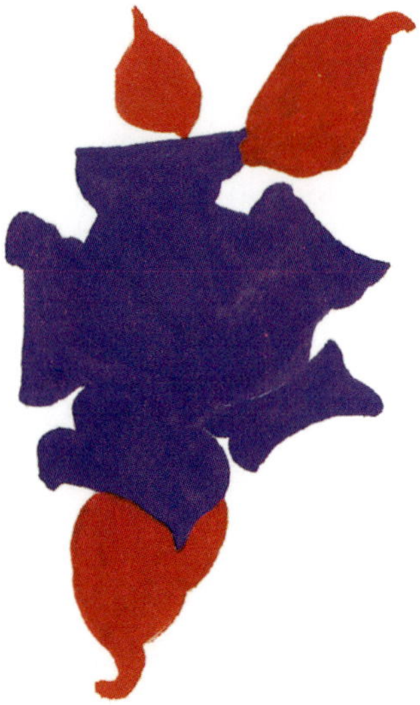

1 Gouache can be used in a variety of ways. If you enjoy this medium, try working semi-transparent paint over an underpainting of colors that are complementary to those in the subject. You can adapt the method of acrylics if you prefer.

2 Mix up a green (the complementary of red) from lemon yellow and viridian and overpaint the leaves. Overpaint the flower with lemon yellow (the complementary of purple). Use just a little water and no white, so that the paint is semi-transparent, and the first colors will show through the second to create an intriguing effect.

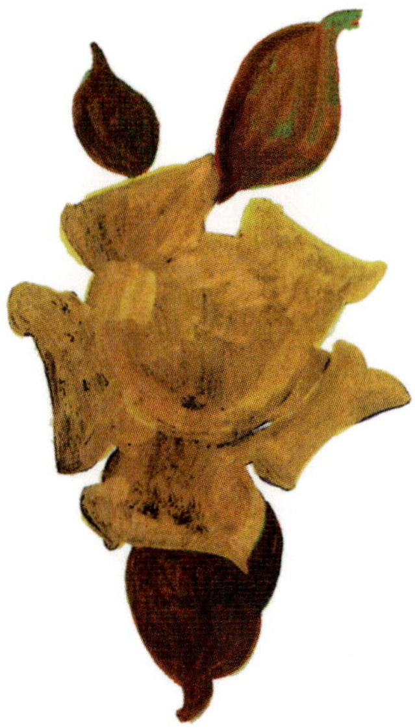

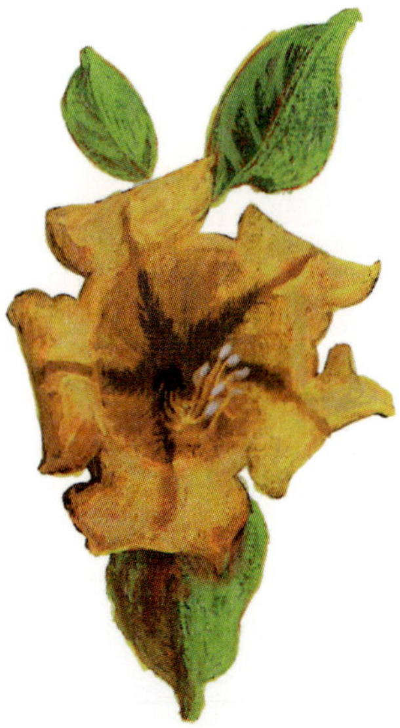

3 Finally, using a thicker version of the yellow and green, build up the lightest areas by scumbling the paint on. This involves using a dry bristle brush with very little paint on it so that the new color sits on top of the earlier ones without melting into them.

Forget-me-not

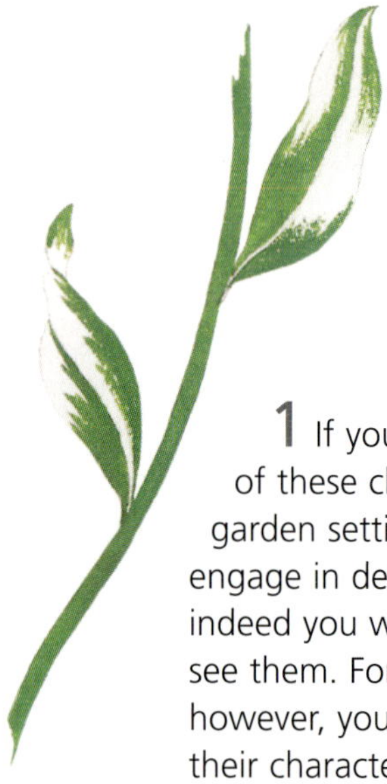

1 If you were painting a group of these charming flowers in a garden setting you would not need to engage in detail with the stems, indeed you would probably not even see them. For a close-up study, however, you would want to show their characteristic slight ribbing and the sparse hairs. Working on smooth paper with thinned gouache, paint the stem as a flat color.

2 Let the first wash dry and then paint darker lines right down the stem for the ribbing. You will need a very small brush (No. 1) for the hairs, and take care not to overload it with paint, as this could make blobs. For a larger plant the hairs could be drawn in with pencil or colored pencil, but in this case painting them with the small brush is preferable, as it gives much finer lines.

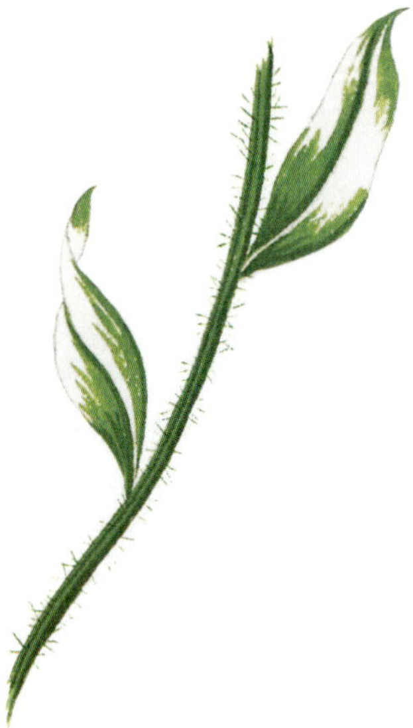

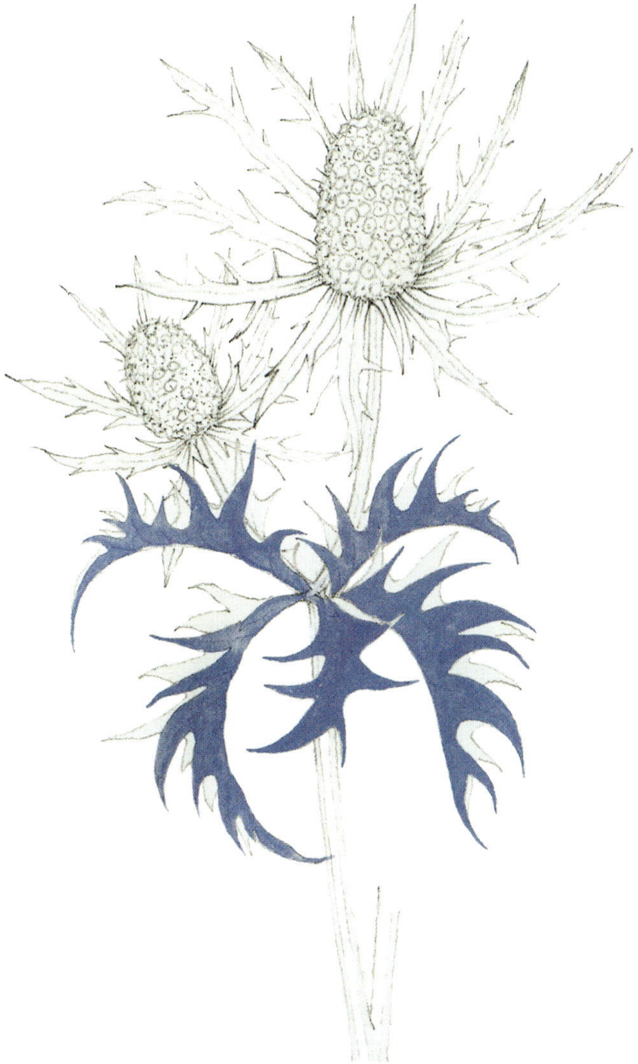

Eryngium

1 These leaves seem to demand a hard-edged treatment, which will make the most of the spiky, spiny, almost thorn-like qualities. Gouache is an excellent medium for this, as you can lay areas of flat color, overlaid with unblended darker colors. Begin with a careful drawing, and then lay flat color over the fronts of the leaves, leaving the back edges as white paper.

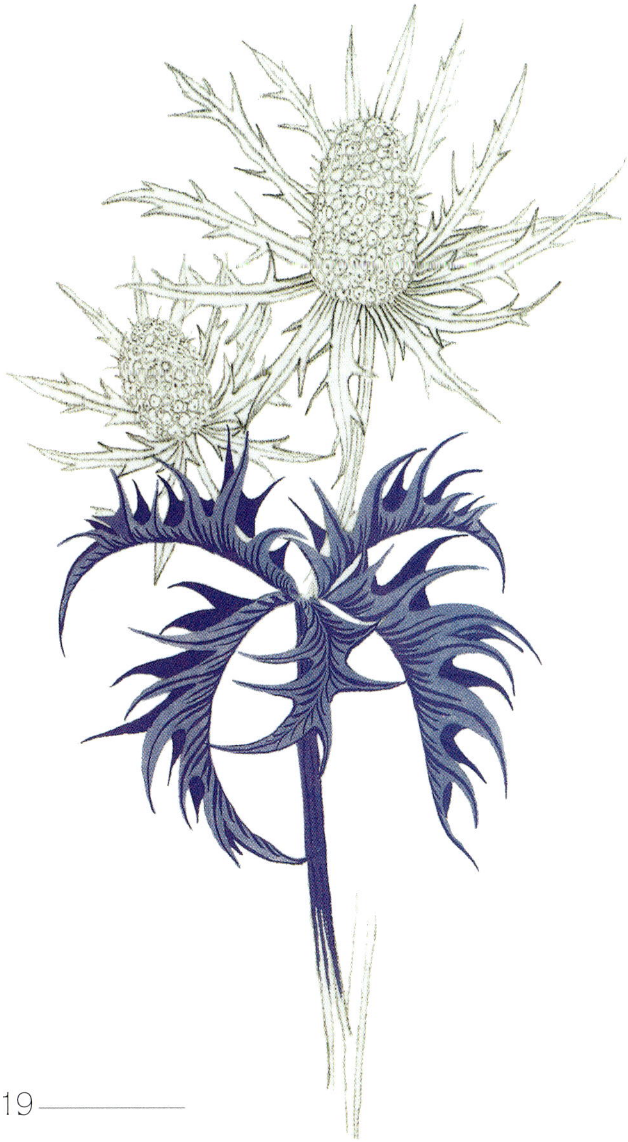

2 Now mix up a darker color and carefully paint the back edges. For the pattern of veining, paint the same color over the initial wash, using a small, pointed brush. Gouache is normally worked from light to dark, because although it is opaque, it is less so than oil paints, and light colors will not always completely cover dark ones.

FEATHERS

In most birds, the wing and tail feathers are quite smooth and precise in shape, while those on the neck and throat have a downy quality. Begin by painting the bird with a pale underwash in watercolor. Then use a small soft brush to delineate the marks of the main feathers, working wet over dry to achieve a precise pattern. The soft, downy feathers should be added last, using light, scumbled strokes.

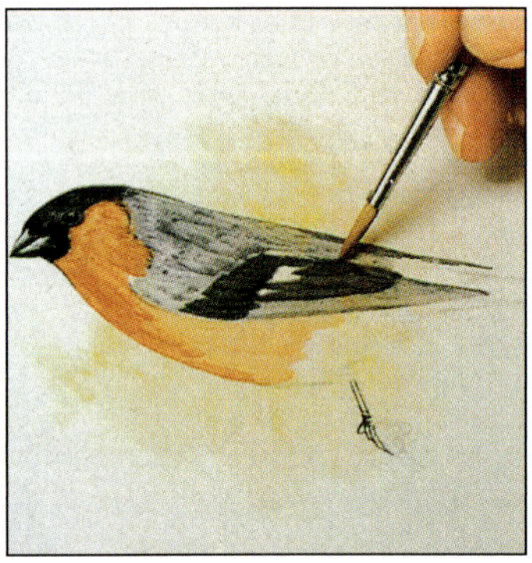

1 Once the washes of base color have dried, you can start adding details to the plumage, gradually building up the color and texture. The artist here has used a very dry brush with the occasional touch of liquid paint to emphasize the changes in tone, and to bring vitality to the image.

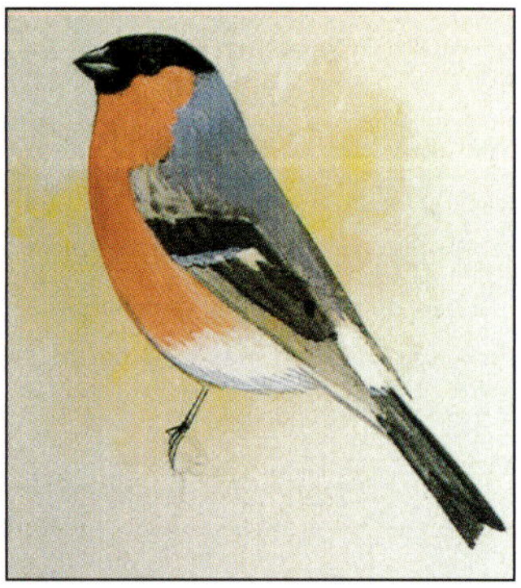

2 The vivid colors of the breast feathers are added in crimson and cadmium red. The texture of the feathers on the back is built up in tones of gray, using a fine sable brush.

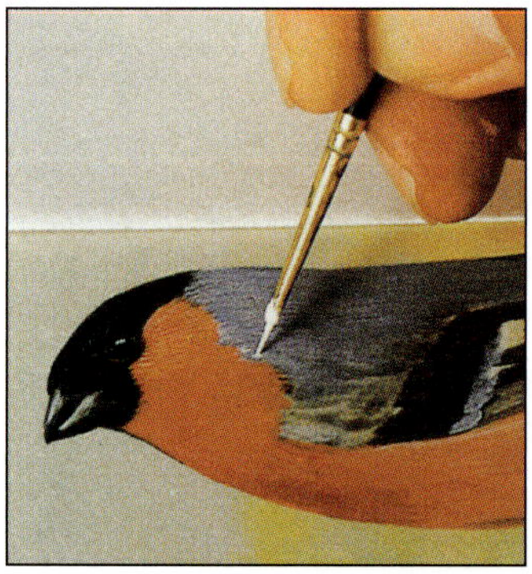

3 Stroke by stroke the artist creates the fine texture of the back feathers. Highlights have been added using white paint, and here he is adding darker tones using a No. 0 sable brush.

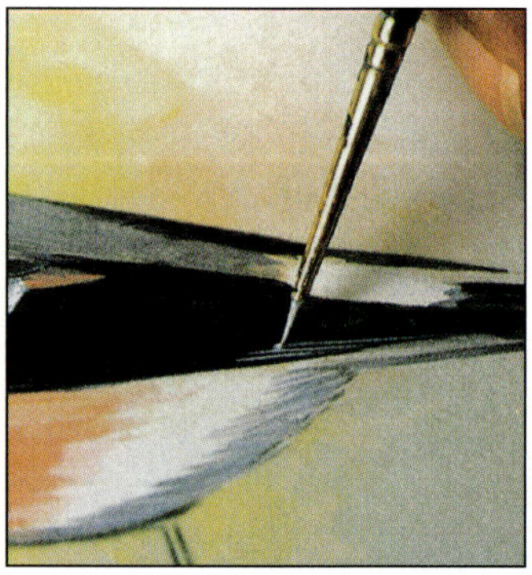

4 Using a very small sable brush the artist paints fine, parallel strokes in dry, undiluted paint to add the final touches to the plumage. This hatching technique is particularly good for conveying the texture of feathers.

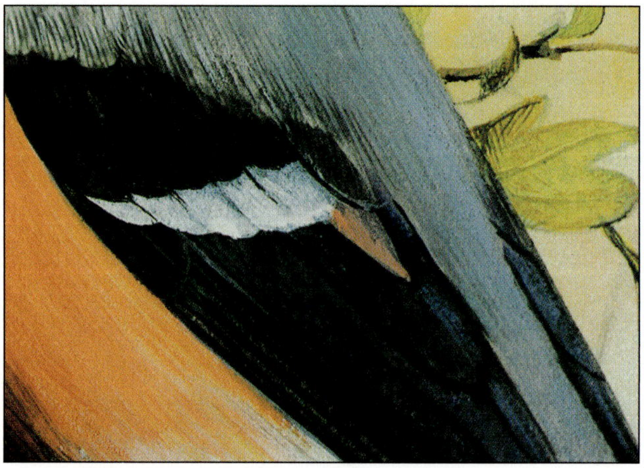

5 In this detail, you can see the wide range of tones used, and the careful hatching and crosshatching of the strokes.

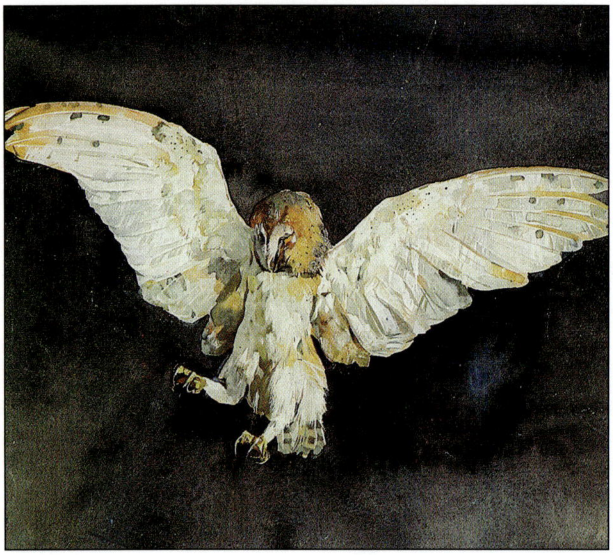

ABOVE LEFT: This detailed study of an owl was made from a dead owl which the artist had found, so it was possible to elaborate arrangement of the feathers quite closely. The rich texture and clear colors of gouache enabled the artist to build up a complex representation of the bird but at the same time he paid careful attention to qualities of the painting itself, achieving a dramatic image with the clear, light shape of the owl against the heavy, dark background. The warm brown and beige tones in the feathers are contrasted with cool tones. The detail of the feathery texture is created by fine lines of opaque paint applied over dried washes and areas of flat color.

STILL LIFE

Gouache is a water-based paint but thicker and more opaque than watercolor. The colors are clear and bright; mixed with white they create sparkling pastel tints. Use thick paint straight from the tube to overlay strong colors, or thin it with water to flood in light washes.

At first glance this painting may appear to be carefully detailed and realistic, but as the steps show, the technique is fluid and informal. The first step, for example, is not a meticulous drawing but a mass of vivid, liquid pools of color suggesting basic forms. As the paint is laid on in layers of loose streaks and patches, the impression of solidity and texture gradually emerges. Each object is described by carefully studying the subject colors and translating these into the painting.

In general, the technique used for this painting was to thicken the paint slightly with each application; but thin washes are laid in the final stage to indicate textures and shadows. The combination of thin washes with flat, opaque patches of color is most effective in capturing the reflective surface of the bottle and glass.

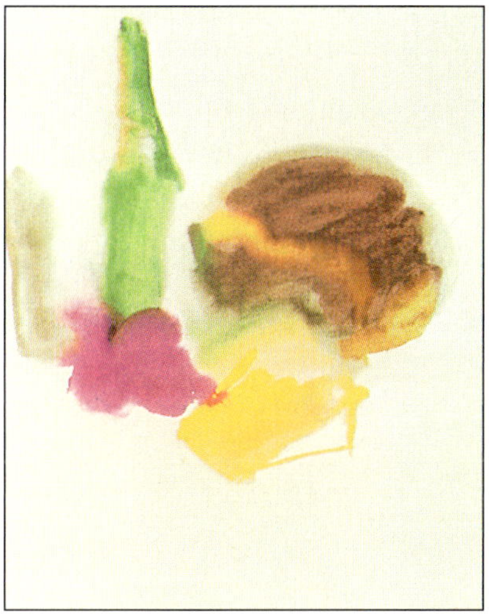

1 With a No. 8 sable brush lay in the basic shapes of the objects with thin, wet paint. Use burnt umber, sap green, magenta, and yellow and let the colors flow together.

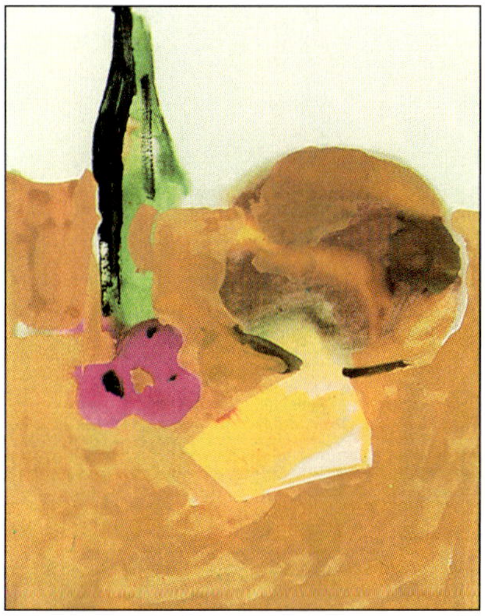

2 With a No. 5 brush, put in yellow ocher around the shapes and into the foreground. Work over the bottle and loaf of bread, painting in shadow details.

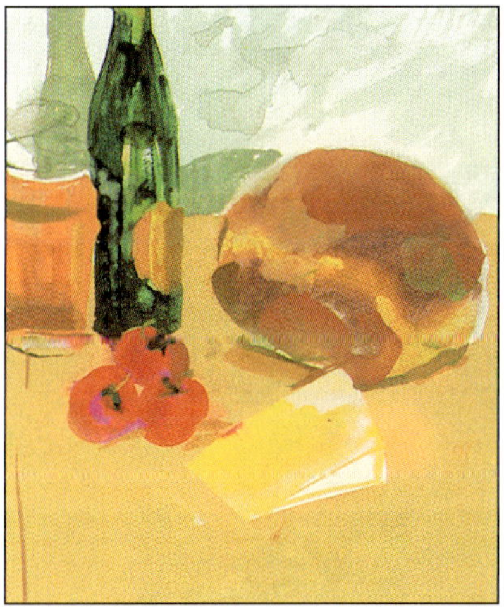

3 Indicate shadows in the background with a thin layer of green. Apply small patches of solid color to show form and surface texture in each object.

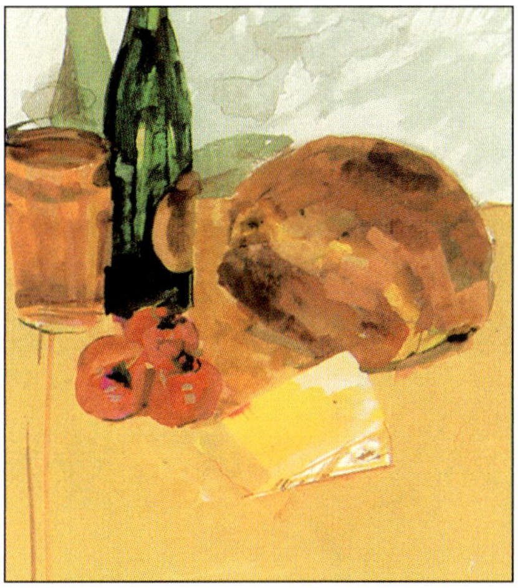

4 With a No. 12 brush, block in small dabs and streaks of color, developing the tones and textures.

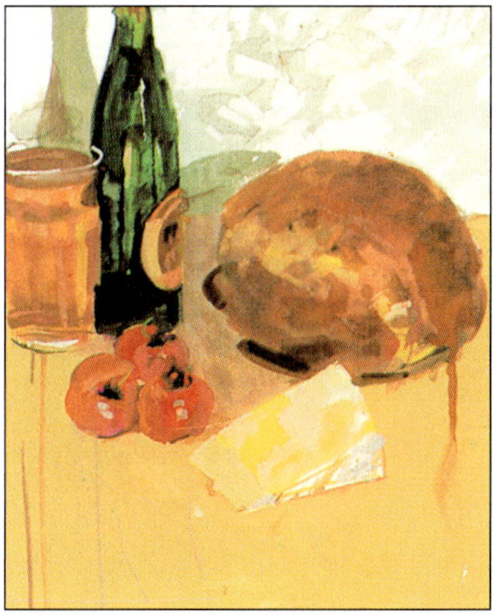

5 Intensify the contrast of light and dark with white highlights and brown shadows with the No. 5 brush. Work into the background with white.

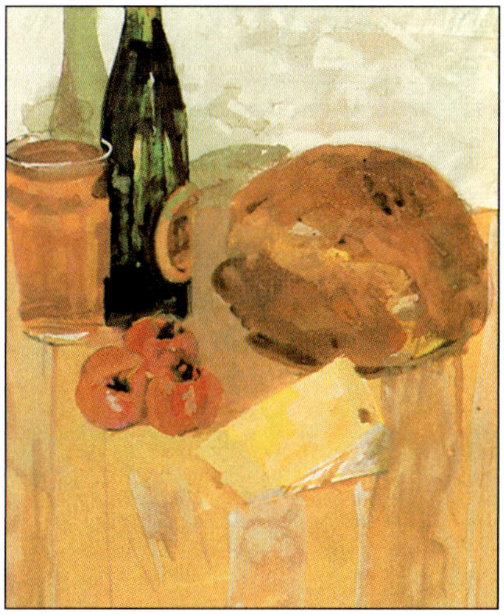

6 Work over the foreground and background with light tones of pink and yellow, keeping the paint thin. Spatter brown and black over the loaf.

PORTRAIT IN GOUACHE

The fluidity of water-based paints such as gouache means that they are ideally suited for making either color studies, in preparation for larger oil paintings, or quick, complete pictures when time is limited. This type of paint is usually regarded, however, as better suited to landscape subjects than faces and some experimentation will be necessary when attempting to render the solidity of the human figure and the precise values of skin tones.

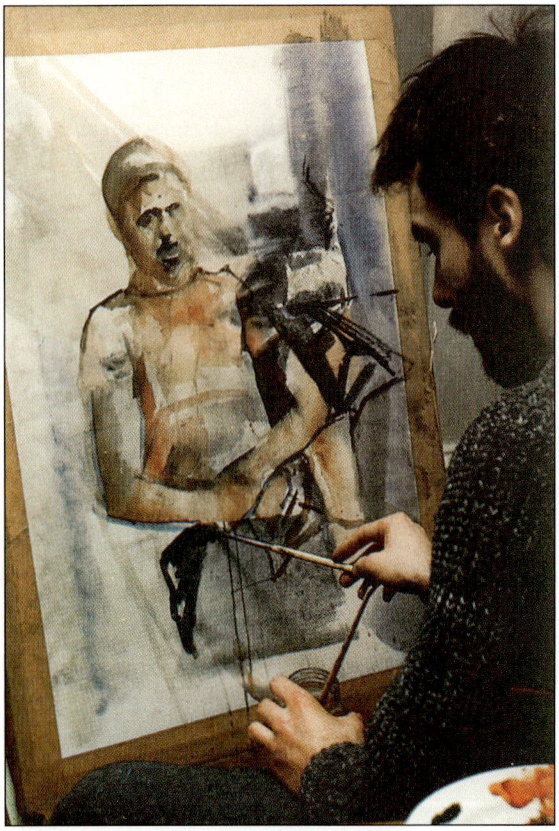

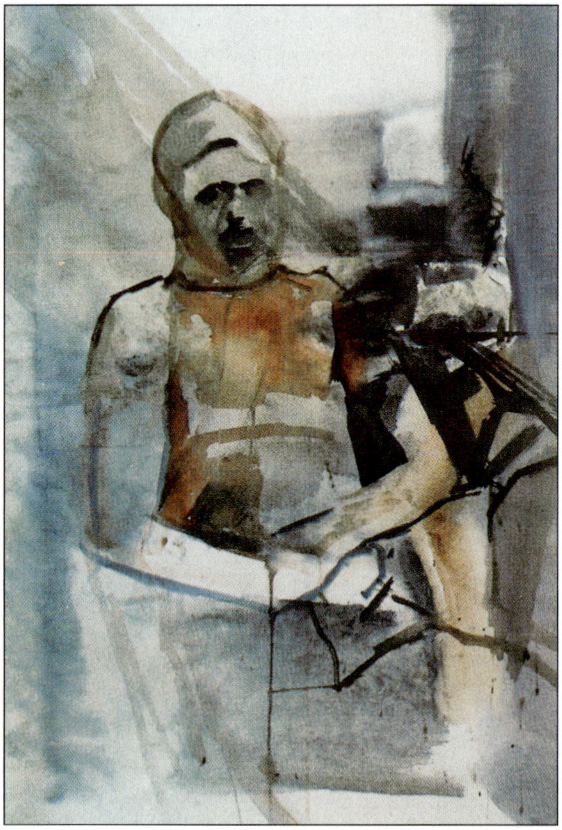

1&2 The artist begins by drawing with the brush rather than making a preliminary pencil sketch.

3 This method allows more freedom to convey the effects of light, especially on the face.

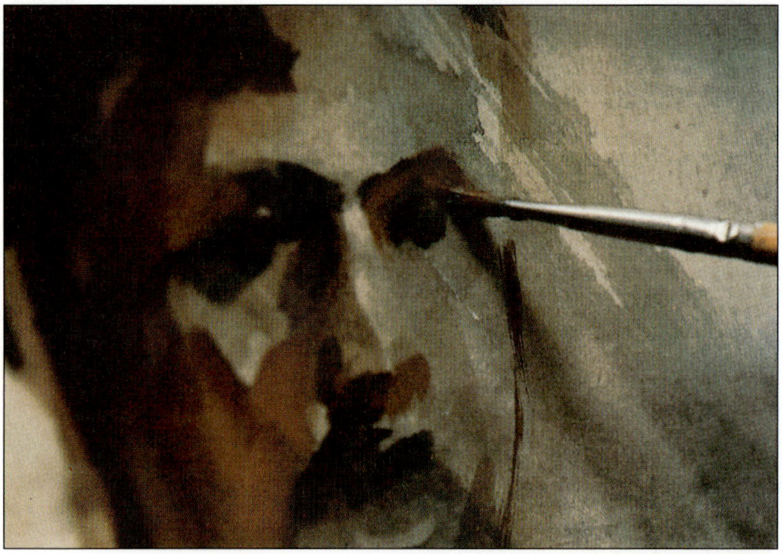

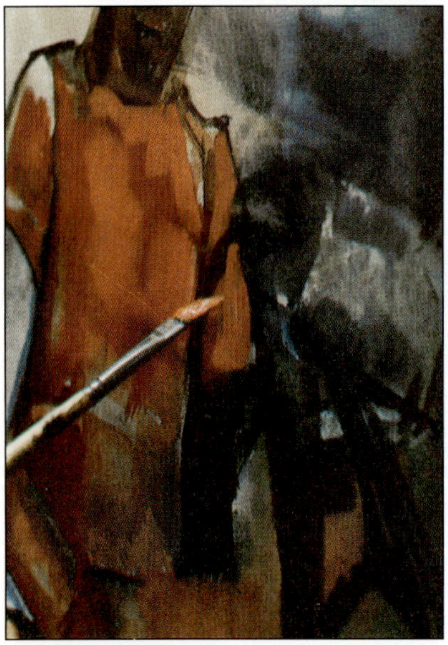

4 The painting grows out of the drawing rather than being considered as a separate activity from the initial statement. The paint is kept as fluid as possible.

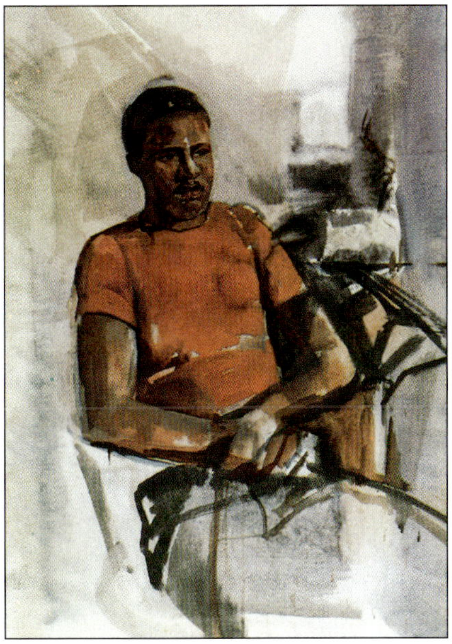

5 Gouache always remains water-soluble, unlike acrylic paint which is also water-based. The application of wet paint over dry may disturb and mix with the preceding color. This need not be a disadvantage, if a fluid result is required. Here the area surrounding the figure is conveyed by overlapping washes of color.

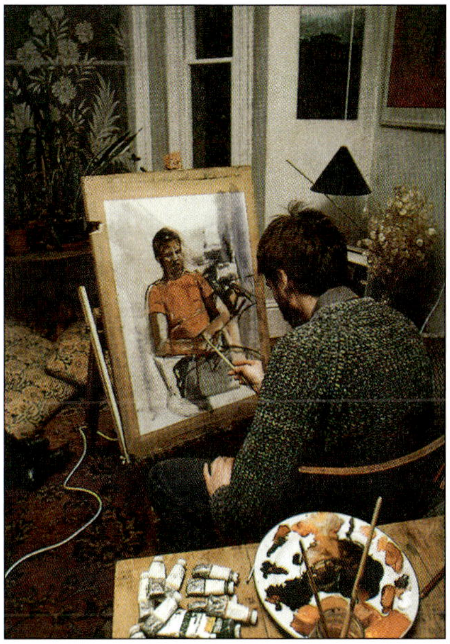

6 The bulk of the figure is indicated in a broad painterly treatment. The positions of areas of paint are considered with respect to their abstract qualities within the rectangle of the surface as well as their more obvious representational associations.

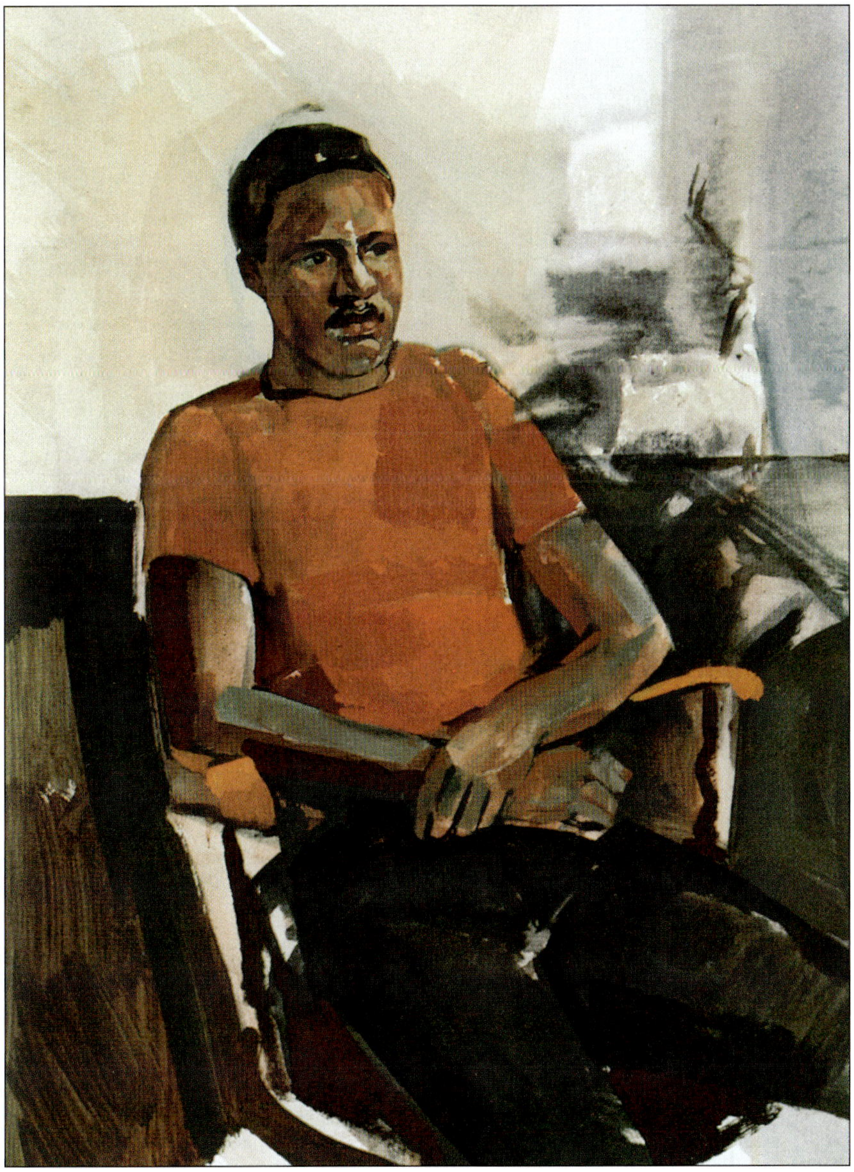

7 The structure of the head is continually assessed and reassessed during the course of the work. By the final stage, the earlier, more approximate statement has been subtly altered. More time is spent painting the face – the focus of interest for the portraitist – than any other part of the picture.

PURE GOUACHE

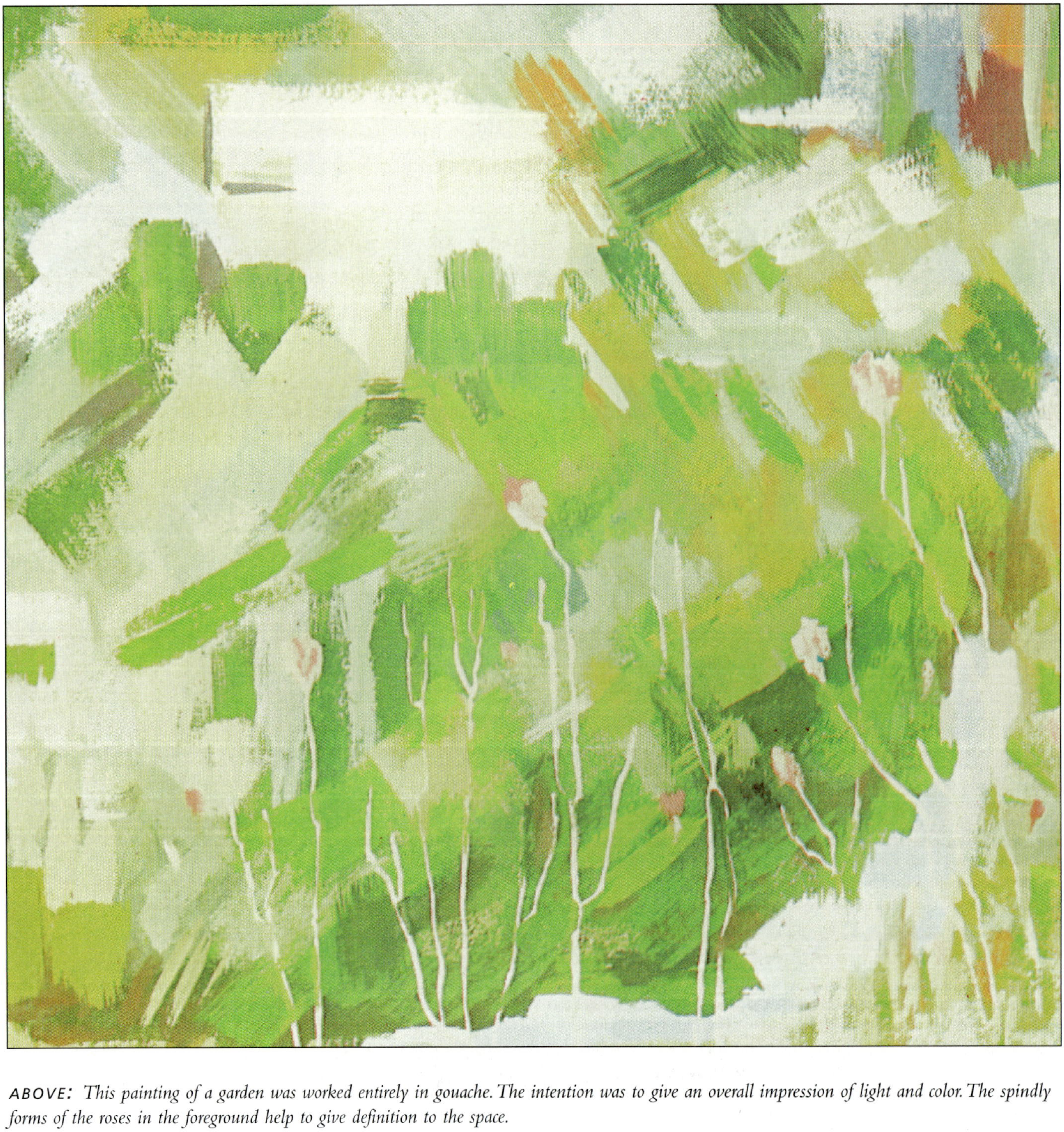

ABOVE: This painting of a garden was worked entirely in gouache. The intention was to give an overall impression of light and color. The spindly forms of the roses in the foreground help to give definition to the space.

GALLERY

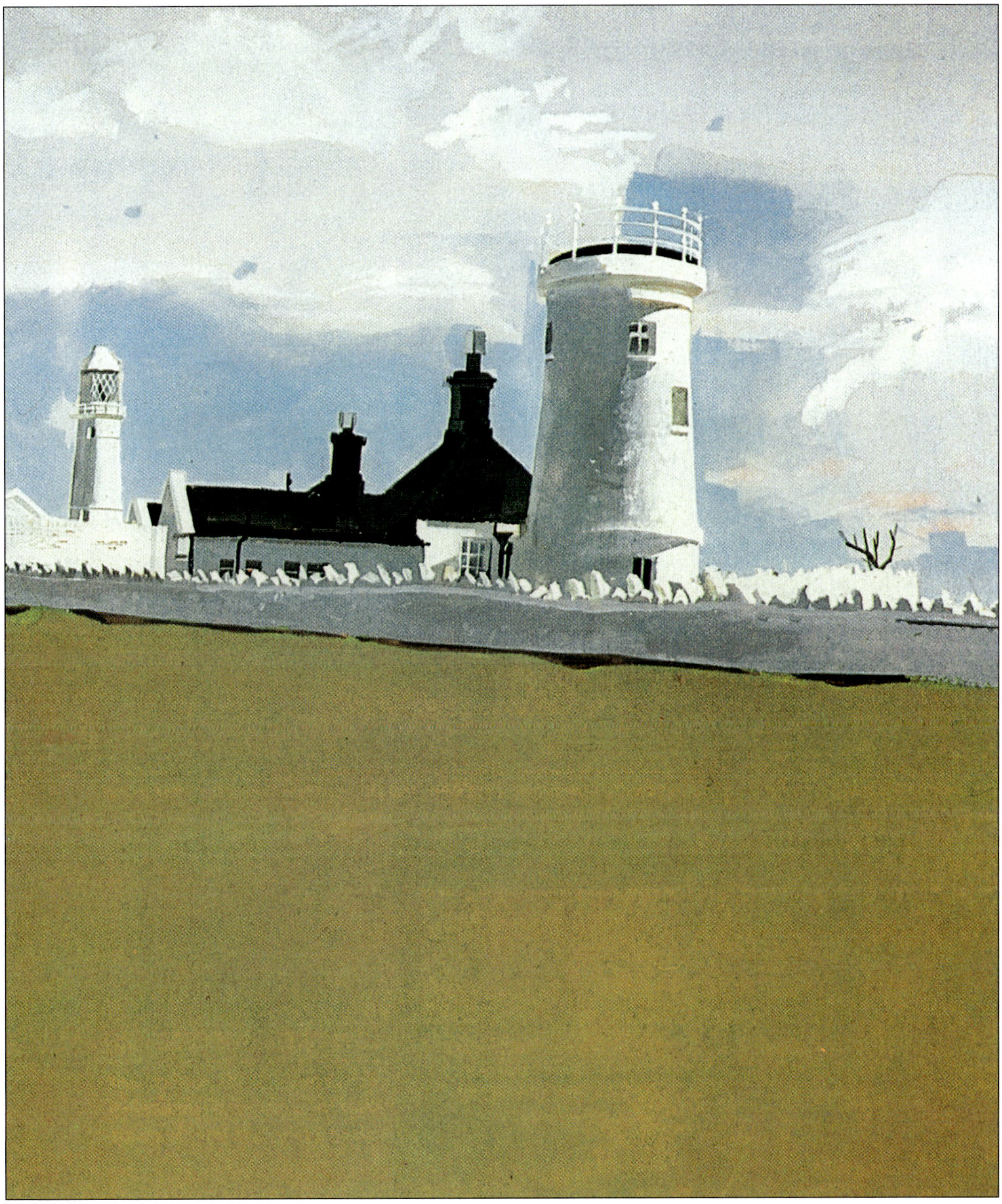

THE LIGHTHOUSE

This painting is on tinted paper and the light blue and white washes of gouache across the area of sky are qualified by the tone underneath. This enhances the brilliant white of the buildings, which gain strength and solidity from the use of pure, opaque white gouache. A hint of pink on the horizon line suggests evening, as do the long, deep shadows on the buildings. The simplest possible statement of the broad expanse of green clifftop grass in the foreground is an obvious foil to the detail and clarity of color in the forms above.

WATER EFFECTS

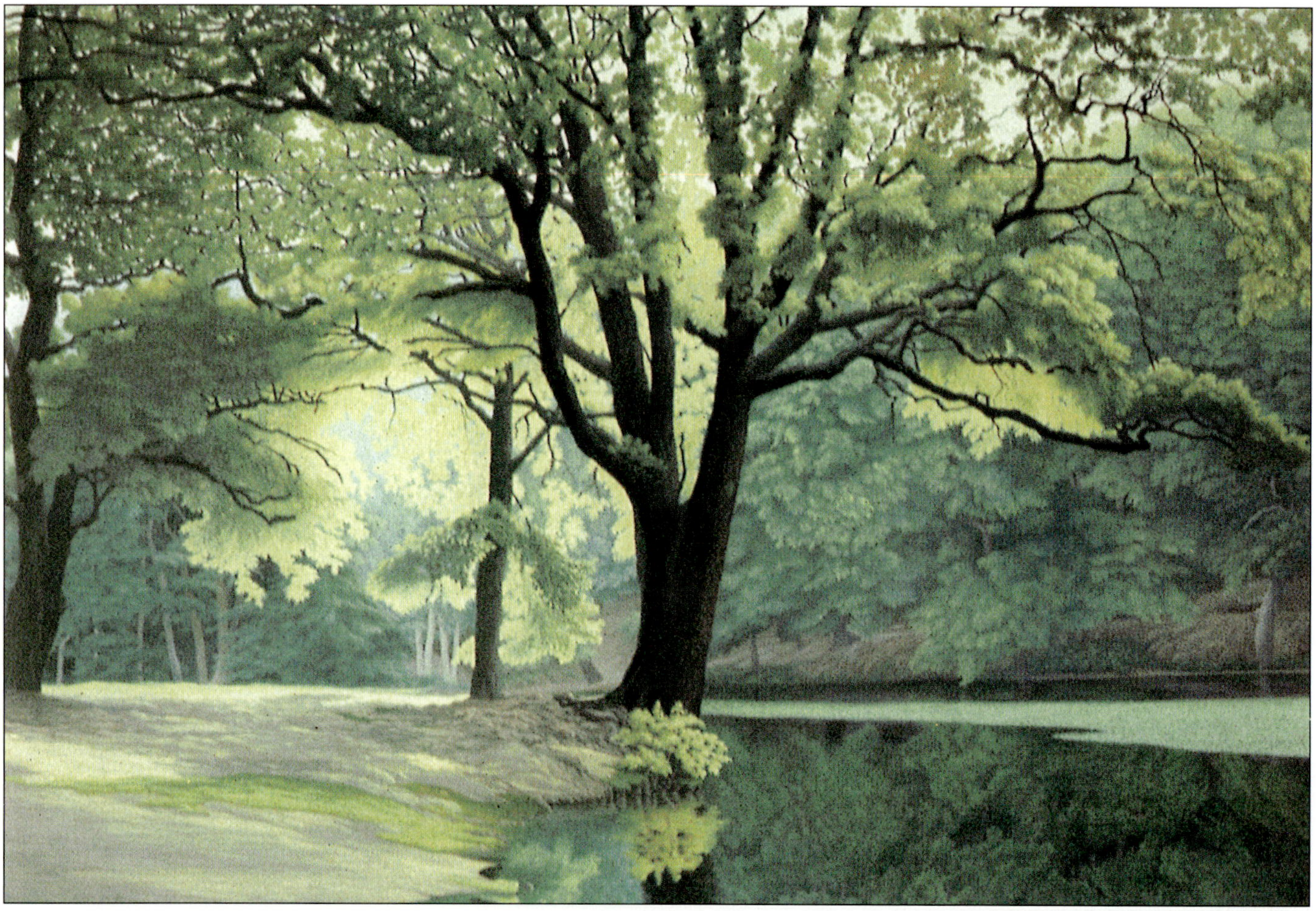

WAGGONERS' WELLS by Jean Canter

In the water area dark washes have been applied wet on dry over lighter green ones, and the reflections have been lifted out with absorbent paper wrapped around the end of a brush.

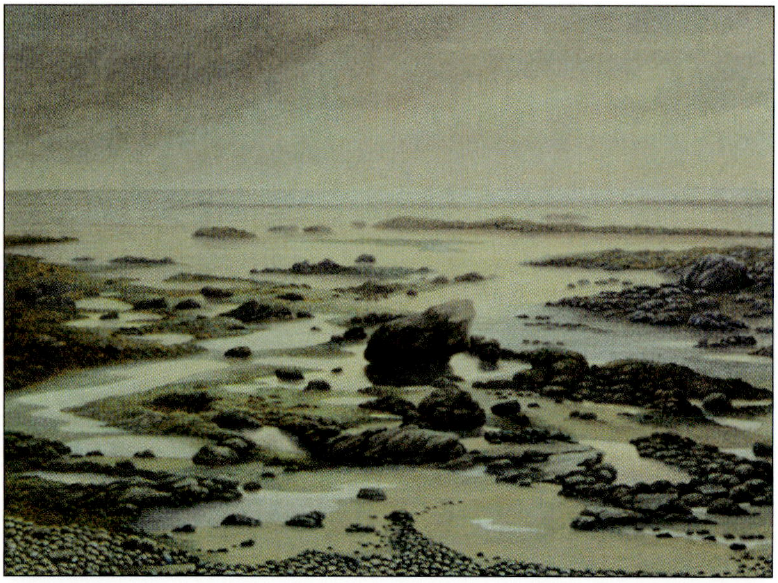

LOW TIDE, LYME REGIS II by Jean Canter

The natural lie of the seashore creates a grid of intersecting diagonals. These are emphasized by the light on the water, taking the eye deep into the picture space.

LANDSCAPES

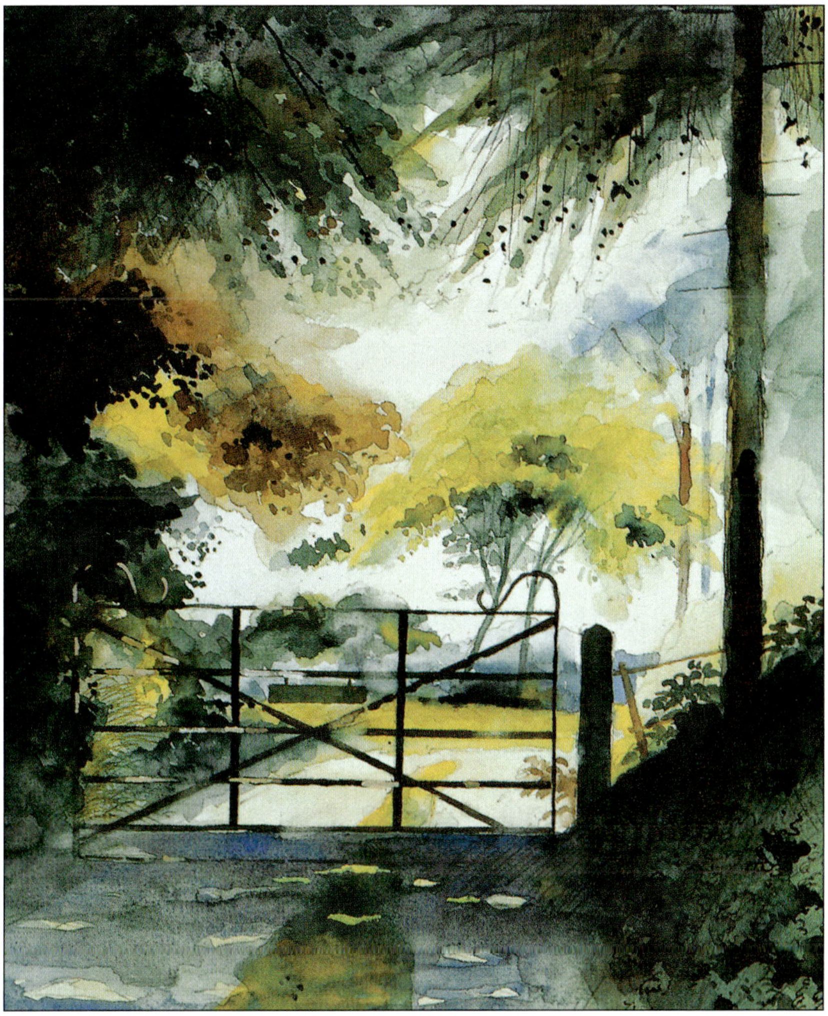

LANDSCAPE WITH LARCH TREE
by John Lidzey

In the final stages of this painting, pen drawing was added to the trees and foreground. The area at the top left was darkened, first by a fresh application of paint, and then by scratching over the dry wash with a soft pencil. Small touches of gouache were added to the gate, and the patch of light on the path, which was accidentally painted over, was also touched in with gouache. Notice how the trees have been simplified. Having treated the foliage initially as broad masses of color and tone, the artist put in just enough detail to make it look convincing.

AMBERLEY AND KITHURST HILL, SUSSEX by Robert Dodd

Dodd has given drama to his quiet subject by the use of bold tonal contrasts and inventive exploitation of texture. He has used his gouache quite thickly, building up areas such as the ploughed field in the foreground by masking and sponging. The more flatly applied paint used for the background and sky allows the textures to stand out strongly by contrast.

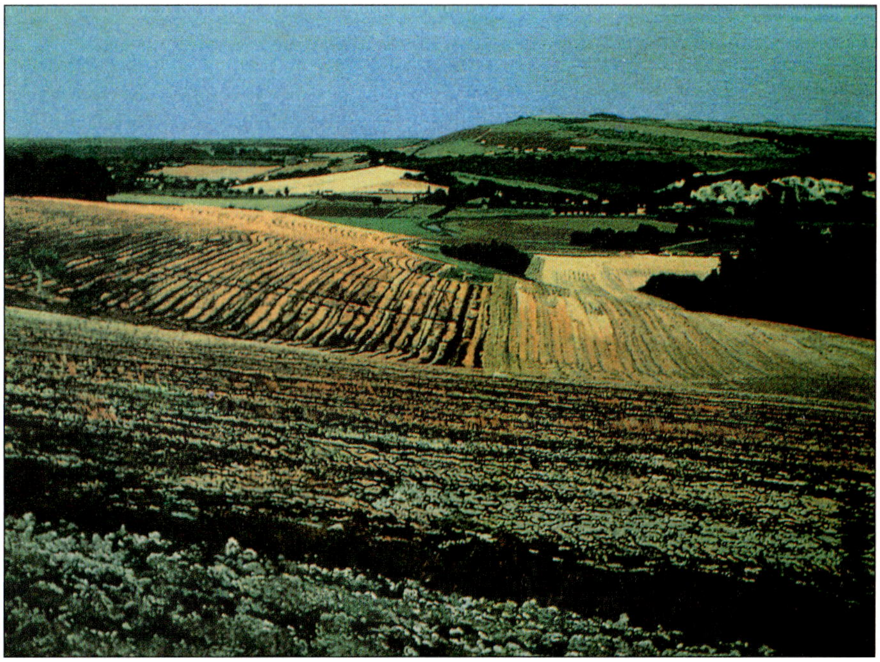

NATURE

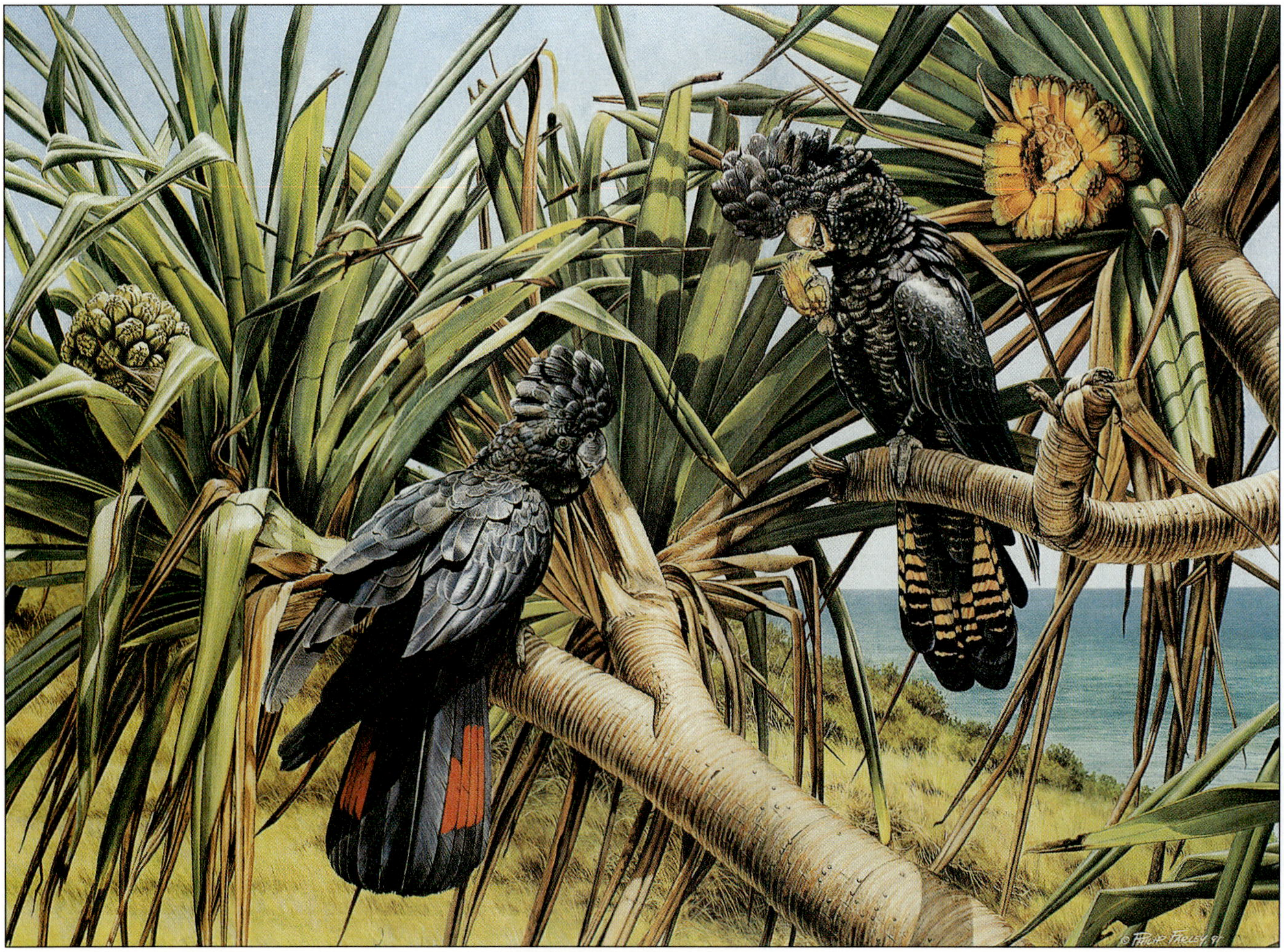

PANDANUS PARTY by Philip Farley

At first sight it is hard to believe that this marvelous painting, with its rich colors and wealth of detail, is a watercolor. But long before watercolor was used in a loose, free manner it was valued by natural-history artists for its capacity to create precise detail. Farley works out his composition with tracings and sketches, moving the elements around until he is satisfied. Then he slowly builds up colors, mainly with dry brush over washes. He uses gouache paint for small highlights, and sometimes covers areas with masking fluid so he can work freely on others.

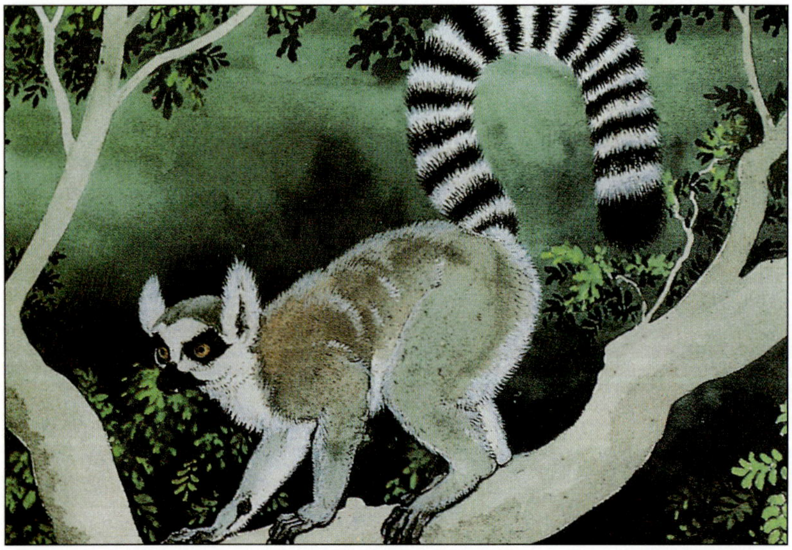

RING-TAILED LEMUR by Sally Michel

Michel trained as an illustrator, but began to exhibit paintings when her book illustration work decreased. She became a wildlife artist more or less by accident and is also well-known as a painter of dog and cat portraits. She works in pastel and watercolor and always from life, although she sometimes takes photographs to record a particular pose. Here the detail of the lemur's tail and coat are highlighted in gouache.

BUILDINGS

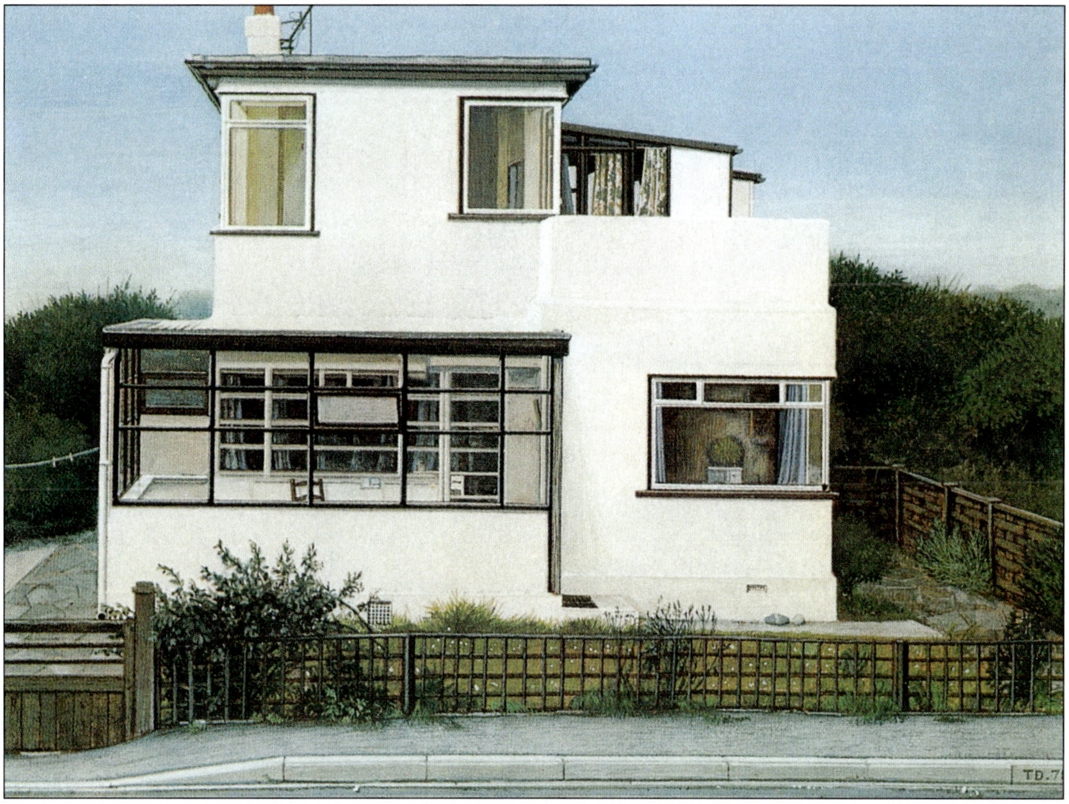

UNTITLED by Terence Dalley

This painting by Terence Dalley exploits the opacity of gouache in a detailed analysis of the scene.

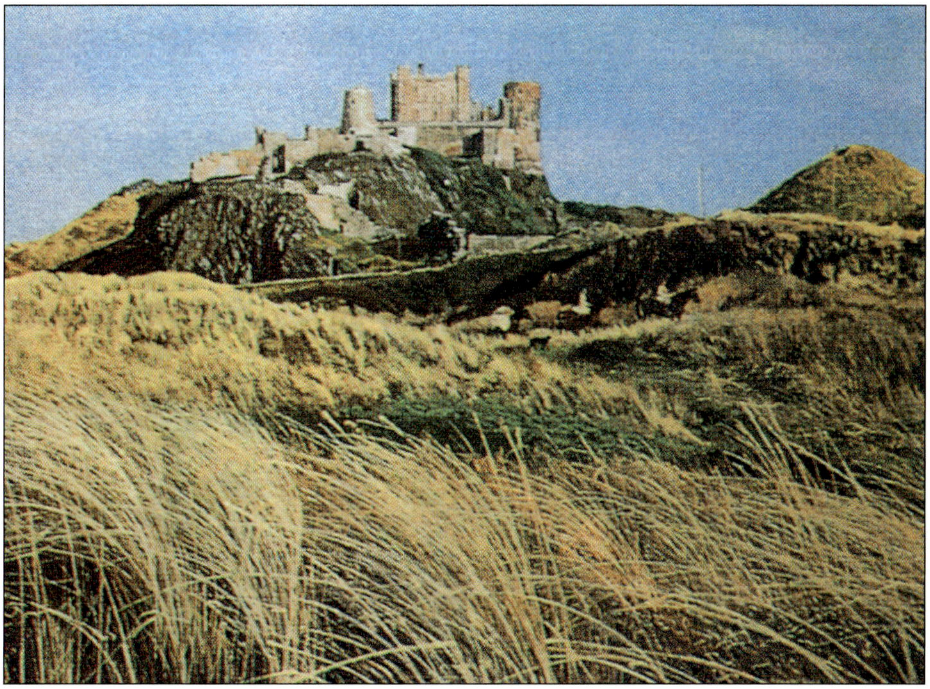

BAMBURGH CASTLE by Robert Dodd

This painting is entirely in gouache, used quite thickly, particularly in the foreground. One of the problems with gouache is that the paint becomes dead and muddy-looking if too many layers are built up. Dodd brings up the colors by varnishing them, so that his paint has rather the appearance of acrylic.

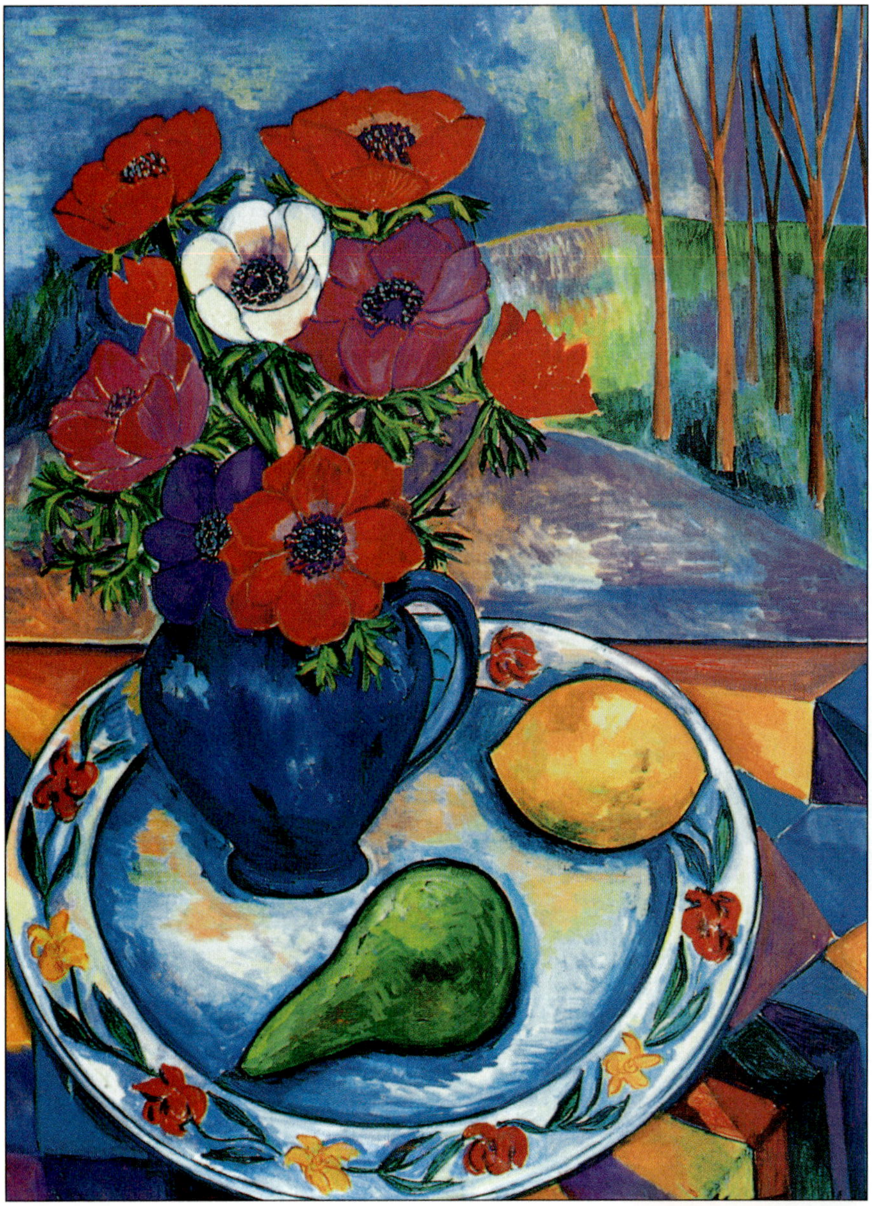

ANEMONES by Mary Tempest

This bold, highly-patterned composition, with the emphasis on carefully distributed areas of bright color, is somewhat reminiscent of Henri Matisse. Although the painting is predominantly two-dimensional, there is a considerable degree of modeling in the fruit, jug, and flowers, which ensures their place as the focal point of the painting. Tempest uses gouache almost like oil paint and for this painting she has mixed it with an impasto medium (Aquapasto) in order to build it up thickly.

STUDIO MANTELPIECE by Geraldine Girvan

Girvan has used a combination of diagonals and verticals to lead the eye into and around the picture. Our eye follows the line of the mantelpiece, but instead of going out of the frame on the left it is led upward by the side of the picture frame and then downward through the tall flowers to the flowing heart of the picture – the daffodils. She has avoided isolating this area of bright yellow by using a slightly muted version of it in the reflection behind and has further unified the composition by repeating the reds from one area to another.

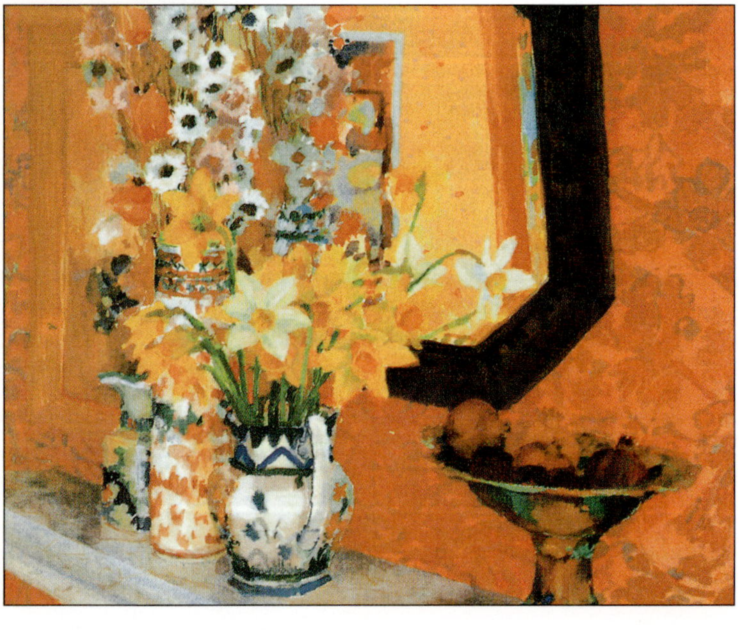

How to Paint

Now you are familiar with the preparation and have mastered the techniques, experiment with different subject matters in this "How to Paint" section.

Learning to see the subject is as important as painting it successfully. Each one presents its own challenges and this section concentrates on overcoming them. Each subject has its own characteristics and preferred starting point from which to develop your skills. For example appreciating the basic structure of the face will ensure a well-drawn face, and understanding how to paint a sky is the basis for all good landscape painting.

Of great importance is the effect of light and shade on your subject and thinking carefully about setting, pose, the time of day, and what you want to paint before you pick up a brush.

Step-by-step instructions, useful tips and specific information relating to each topic are explained in this section.

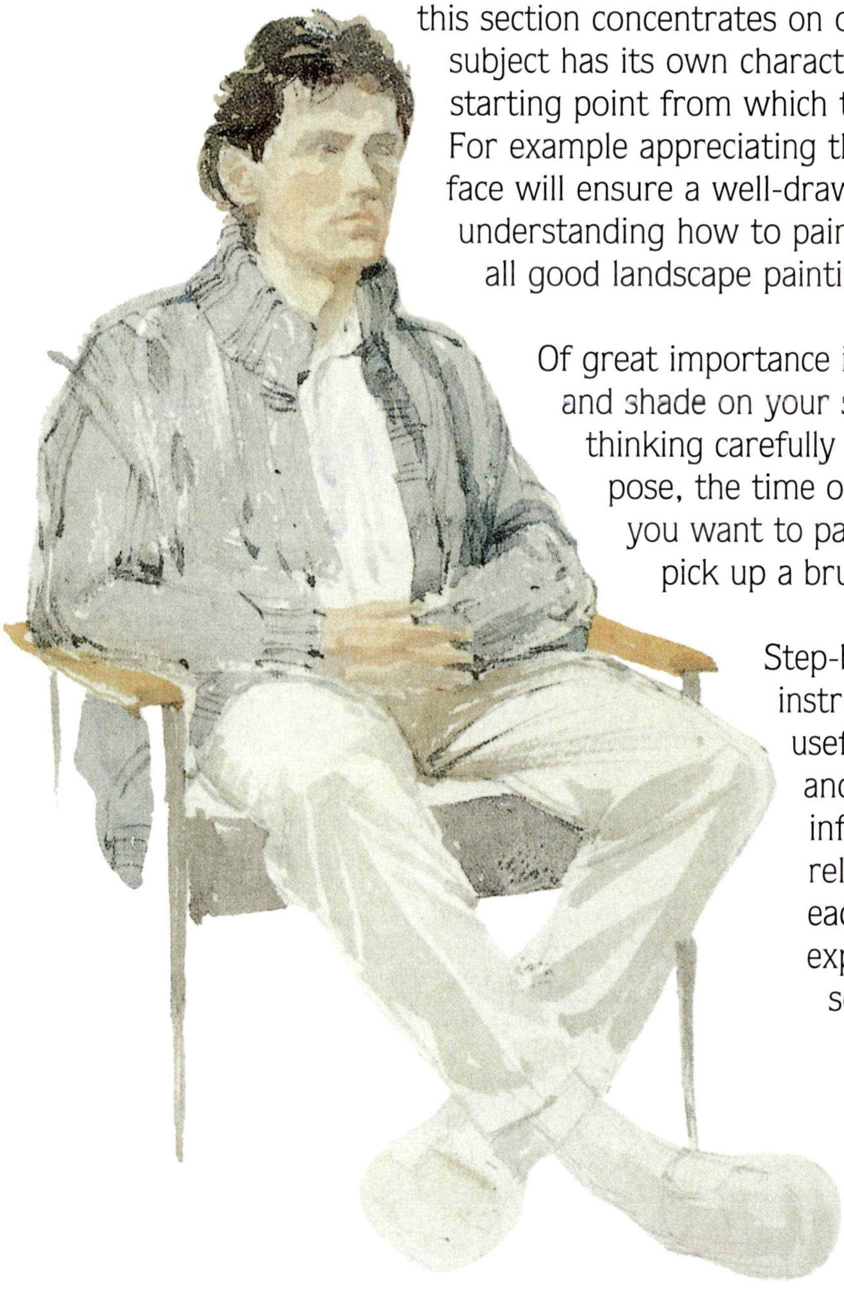

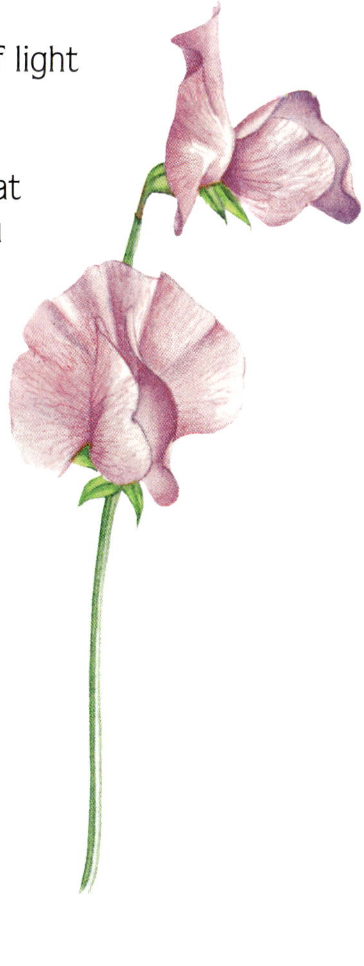

How to Paint: Portraits

Of all the subjects which an artist is likely to tackle, the human face is without doubt the most challenging. Even experienced painters feel a twinge of anxiety every time they begin a new portrait, because each one is unique and presents a fresh set of problems.

The main difficulty faced by the artist is in creating a portrait which not only looks lifelike, but is also recognizable as the person who is the subject of the painting. You must capture the essential characteristics and features of the subject, while at the same time injecting life into the features and conveying the idea of a living, breathing person.

Before attempting your first portrait, you will find it helpful to make sketches of faces at every opportunity. Sitting on a train or bus, you can sketch faces and individual features such as eyes and mouths. Studying your own face in the mirror is also a good idea; this gives you the chance to study features and try out various expressions at leisure, without the pressures of producing a flattering likeness which comes when painting friends or relatives.

Another way to develop your confidence is to start by painting a portrait from a photograph – this is less inhibiting than painting a real person who is capable of criticizing your efforts. However, once you have gained some experience, it is best to avoid painting from photographs. It is difficult to create a convincing three-dimensional image from a two-dimensional source, and your painting may well end up looking somewhat lifeless and tightly rendered. In addition, the delicate nuances of tone and color in skin and hair are invariably lost in a photograph.

Probably the best way to practise portrait painting is to start by asking friends and relatives to pose for you and, because you are familiar with their personality traits, you will find it easy to put these across in your painting.

Assuming that you have found a model and are ready to begin painting his or her portrait, there are quite a few preliminary steps to consider before you actually put brush to canvas. The most important step of all is establishing a rapport with your sitters and helping them to relax. Even a sitter you know well may suddenly be overcome with nerves and self-consciousness, so treat the whole thing in a relaxed, informal way. Engage your sitters in conversation as you paint, and provide some background music if you like. Make sure they are comfortable, with plenty of support for their back, if they are seated, and allow them to move and stretch if they feel the need.

THE POSE

The most important thing to remember is that the pose should look natural, as well as feeling comfortable to the sitter: if he or she feels ill at ease, their tense expression will come through in the painting. The simplest poses are best, so don't fuss about the pose and ask your sitters to move an arm to the left, or to incline their head this way

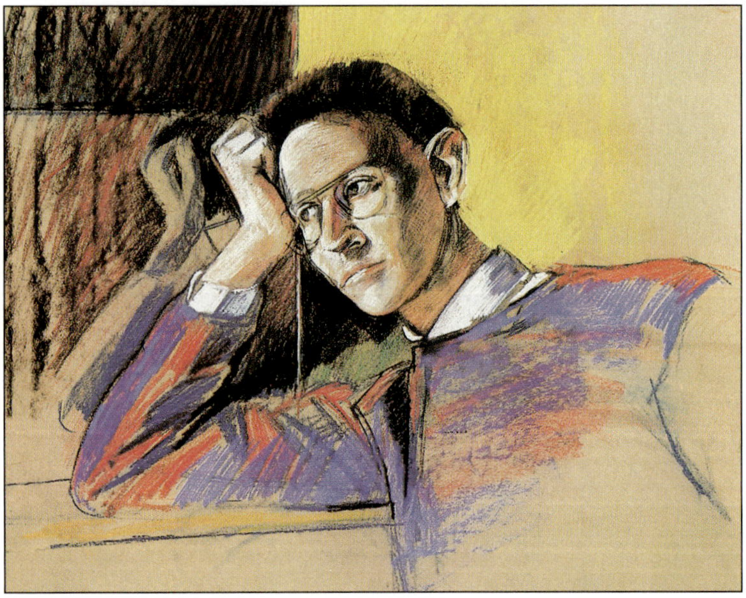

or that. Simply ask them to relax, and they will instinctively take up a pose that is both comfortable and perhaps indicative of their character and personality.

In general, a sitting pose is better than a standing pose, because it allows the model to relax and hold the pose indefinitely. A standing pose tends to look formal, and is much more demanding of the model's stamina. Whether the pose is standing or seated, though, it is important to allow your model frequent breaks.

BACKGROUND

Backgrounds play a secondary role in most portraits, but they do nevertheless require a good deal of thought and

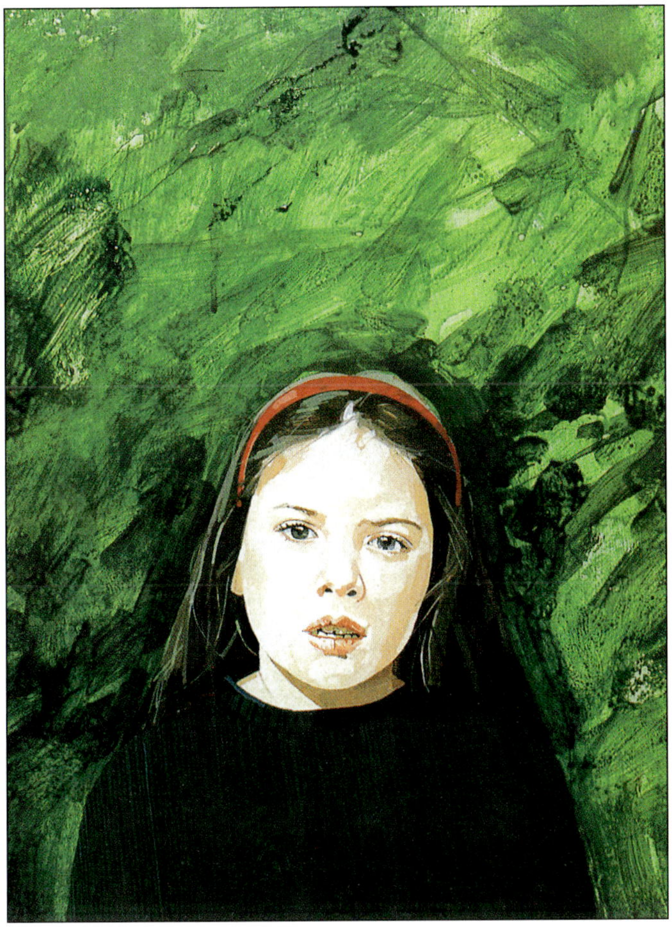

attention. You may choose to paint the interior scene in which the sitter is placed, or to treat the background as a simple color area with no detail. In either case, try to choose colors that provide pleasing contrasts with the face or figure. The cool tone of a green wall or drape will heighten the warmth of the model's skin; a dark background tone will accentuate strong light falling on the model, whereas a pale background provides a good contrast for a model wearing dark clothing.

Keep the background more subdued than the figure, both in color and in the overall treatment. Cool, neutral colors accentuate the warmth and luminosity of the model's skin, whereas bright colors detract from it. Similarly, avoid any distracting details or patterns that might divert attention from the subject. If these are present in the background, subdue them by painting them loosely and broadly.

Having sorted out all the preliminaries and made some rough sketches, you are now ready to embark on the painting. The approach you adopt should be exactly the same as that used in painting a landscape or still life: begin by resolving everything down to basic shapes and tones, and build up gradually from there. Don't make the mistake of drawing a detailed outline of the face and then filling it in with color. By all means indicate the overall shape with loose strokes as a rough guideline, but a hard, rigid outline inhibits and stultifies the painting process. You should always be free to alter the painting as it progresses.

So, begin by using large brushes to indicate the main masses, lights, and shadows with broad washes of color. Having established the three-dimensionality of the form, proceed in a natural sequence from broad, sweeping strokes to smaller, more precise ones, indicating the angles, curves, and contours of the face. Even at this stage, don't become too involved with details such as the eyes and mouth – the form of the face as a whole is what's important. Getting a good likeness is not simply a matter of accurately painting the eyes, mouth, and nose. The shapes, sizes, and relative proportions of the face differ from one individual to another. Observe these surface shapes closely, because these are what give your sitter his or her particular identity.

At this stage it is a good time to take a break from the painting for 20 minutes or so. When you come back to it, any faults will be more readily apparent and can be corrected before it is too late.

When painting the features, work from the inside to the outside of the face. Some artists like to start with the eyes; others prefer to start with the nose and work up to the eyes and down to the mouth. Whichever method you choose, always work from one feature to another, keeping the paint wet, rather than treating each feature as a separate entity. Then, when the painting is almost finished, take another break from it. After making any necessary adjustments, you can add the final highlights, and the portrait is complete.

CLOTHING

The clothes which your sitter is to wear in the portrait must be selected with care. They should reflect the personality of the sitter and be in tune with the overall mood of the painting. Generally, quiet colors and restrained patterns are best, and if the clothing is darker than the face, all the better. Remember, the subject of the painting is the face; bright colors and patterns will divert attention from the face and reduce the impact of the portrait. Some kinds of cloth are more clinging than others. The qualities of silk and satin are, for instance, not at all the same as those of wool or linen. The former are flimsy lightweight materials which serve to cover the flesh while revealing the form, whereas the latter are thicker and retain much of their own character being less affected by the shape of the body underneath. The more tactile silks and satins are a popular choice when the female body is being represented as an object of desire.

Media

The boundaries of portraiture are almost indefinable, and the methods and techniques by which they may be created can no longer be defined in the rigorous terms of previous centuries. The fact that oil paint dominates the history of portraiture does not preclude the use of other, more immediate methods of painting.

EXPERIMENTS IN WATERCOLORS AND GOUACHE

Watercolor and water-based gouache paints are suitable for quick color studies and the limitations of such techniques in portraiture are compensated by their advantages. The importance attached to oil paint is mostly due to its imitative abilities. It is not possible to paint skin with such accuracy in watercolors but their transparency is suited to experiment, and to coming to terms with paint generally. An awareness of the fluid nature of handling watercolors will prepare the artist for the more daunting prospect of painting in oils or acrylics. The opaque quality of gouache, which has white added, is useful for practicing working up to the lights, with pure watercolor used for shadows and mid-tones.

Another advantage to experimenting with water-based paints is the relatively inexpensive support that is required for the purpose. Although watercolor paper is preferable, any fairly substantial paper will suffice and this may be pinned to a board or soaked in water and attached to the board with lengths of gum strip around each edge. Once the paper is glued to the board in this way it will shrink when dry and be stretched taut enough to absorb the wet pigment without the surface wrinkling.

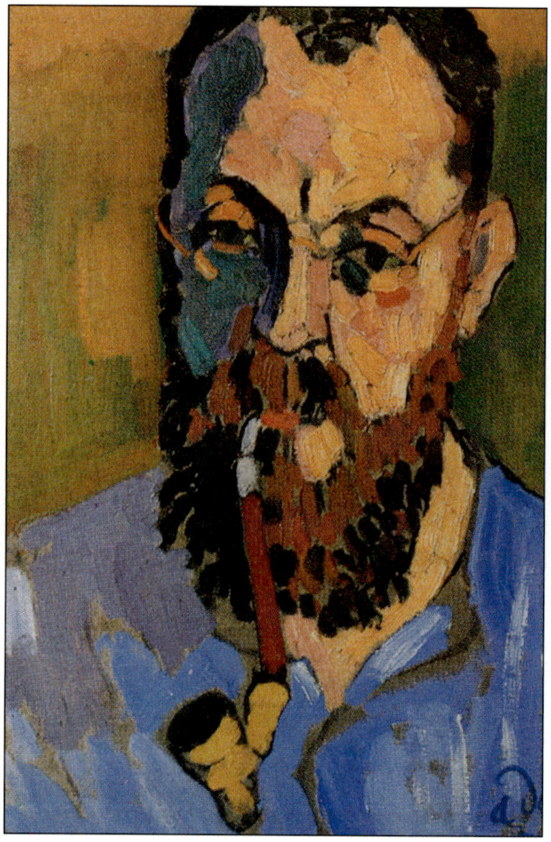

PORTRAIT OF MATISSE by André Derain (1880–1954)

Derain was a member of the Fauve group of artists which included Matisse, Roualt (1871–1958), and Vlaminck (1876–1958). They were all interested in the use of pure color to express emotion; sometimes they used it arbitrarily or for decorative effects, but otherwise to create volume, as Cézanne and van Gogh had done before. Here, Derain exploited intense colors to mold the shape of Matisse's face seen in a strong light.

USING ACRYLICS

The most significant development in recent pictorial techniques is the invention of acrylic paint. The properties of this versatile medium are often underestimated and they possess many of the characteristics of both oil and watercolor. Unlike both, acrylic paint dries in distinct layers and is therefore well-suited for glazing. With watercolor, the subsequent additions of paint to the same area of paper dissolve and mix with the preceding ones, except at the edges of dry areas. The problem in oil painting is that the length of time necessary for an area to dry conditions any further applications of paint to the same area. Acrylic paint's most distinctive advantage is its ability to dry quickly and permanently. This allows the artist considerable freedom and allows constant changes to occur throughout the procedure. Acrylics may be used on paper, cardboard, hardboard, and canvas with equal success. When used on paper the properties of acrylic are similar to those of other water-based paints; when they are used on canvas their properties are not dissimilar to those of oil paints.

One of the most interesting and useful qualities of acrylic paint is that it can be employed in conjunction with, or instead of, oils. Rather than working directly into a white ground with oil paint, the initial stages of the work may be indicated with washes of acrylics. Because of their quick-drying qualities, they are suitable for spontaneously and creatively establishing the main forms of a portrait.

Often the most daunting yet enjoyable aspect of painting involves coming to terms with the untouched surface of the canvas. For the painting to progress, it is necessary to cover the areas of white primer. By using acrylic paint the whole surface may be covered with a thin wash of color, or alternatively different colored washes for different parts of the painting. This may be particularly helpful when the subject is situated against a light-colored surface such as an interior wall. If the artist attempts to paint something of light tonality onto a white ground, the color may appear to be lifeless. By first painting the area in a mid-tone or a neutral gray, the final color will appear to have more body. By using acrylic paint for this purpose the painting may involve several layers of quickly applied color which, if they were in oil paint, would take a considerable time to dry. It should be remembered that it is not possible to paint with acrylics over oils.

The choice of technique is obviously a personal matter and may depend on the time available or the size of the painting in question. Using acrylic the portrait painter will be able to paint the initial washes of transparent color in the same sitting as the oil paint. This kind of technique is considered by many to be indispensable when approaching the difficulties of painting human skin. Although some painters since the time of the Impressionists have favored the technique involving the direct application of opaque paint onto a white surface, this is not suited to conveying the subtlety of human skin. Prior to the nineteenth century, painters realized that fair skin often changes in color depending on reflected light and the color of the surrounding objects. It was also realized that the tone of the skin appears to be cooler in some parts of the body, especially where the bone structure is more visible. By using a cool underpainting of blues and greens, thinly applied flesh tones will give this impression; the skin at certain points on the forehead, for instance, can be made to look thinner than the skin of other parts of the body.

OILS

If the artist chooses to use oil paints, any preparatory application of paint, unless left to dry, will mix physically with the subsequent paint applications. Oil paint is a remarkably versatile and flexible medium, and many artists have capitalized on its slow-drying quality by moving the paint about on the surface for the duration of the painting. The technique of *alla prima*, or painting the complete picture in full color in one session, has gained popularity since the nineteenth century. This usually involves working directly onto a ground with wet paint and adding color without gaps for drying. The spontaneity of such an approach can be more immediately creative, and painters who prefer this method rarely resort to any preparatory stages on the canvas itself. However, the activity of painting wet-into-wet can sometimes lead to an uncomfortable build-up of paint which, because of its opacity, renders the ground color or priming useless. The physical thickness of the paint itself can clog the surface to such a degree that further application is hindered, and in this situation it is sometimes as well to scrape off the excess paint.

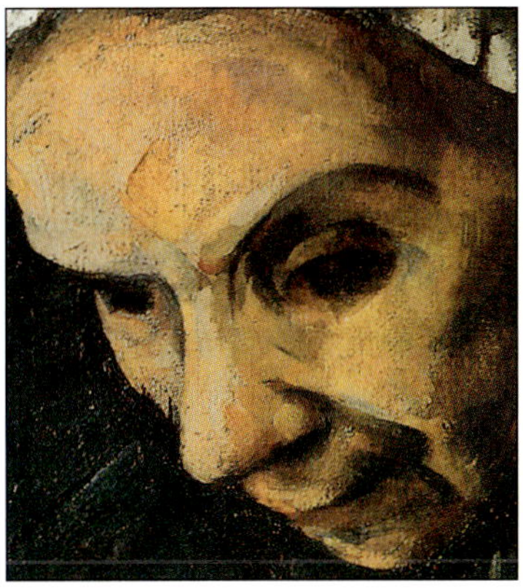

WOMAN WITH ROSARY by Paul Cézanne

Using strong brush strokes to delineate contours, Cézanne involved a mass of different colors and tones in thinner paint to achieve the look of flesh.

Occasionally, however, this kind of necessity provides interesting results that could not otherwise have been anticipated. A close examination of some of Degas' paintings reveals that he used this kind of accidental effect to advantage. His creative nature was often not satisfied by the results of orthodox painting procedures and sometimes while painting a figure he would feel that the head was being overpainted. He would then wipe away the excess paint and in the course of so doing reveal a more interesting paint quality closer to his intentions. Rather than wiping out the image completely, Degas would keep the remaining thin paint or stain which suggested a particular quality or mood that the more logical paint application hindered. Although he was interested in traditional methods of oil painting, his personal technique did not rely on such means of describing visual appearance. Even a cursory glimpse at his paintings reveals quite different techniques varying from thin transparent washes to thick opaque paint. Sometimes he applied the paint in short strokes or hatchings, sometimes in carefully modulated areas. In some parts of the painting the grain or tooth of the canvas would be evident and yet an adjoining area would reveal a history of color changes.

Lighting

In most cases, portraits are painted indoors, which gives you a choice of using natural or artificial light. There is no doubt that natural daylight is preferable, especially when it comes from a fixed source such as a window or skylight. If you are working with artificial lighting, choose "warm white" fluorescent tubes, which are the best substitute for natural daylight.

Whether working with natural or artificial light, it is best to illuminate the subject from a single source only. Soft, diffused light coming from one side of the head is flattering to the model and brings out the form of the model's features. Light falling just in front and to one side of the model – referred to as "three-quarter lighting" – is probably the easiest to paint. The light illuminates one side of the face and part of the front, throwing the other side into shadow. This makes the lights, half-tones, and shadows readily distinguishable and helps to solidify the form. If you notice that the shadows on the figure look too dense, this can be remedied by placing a reflective white board on the shadow side to provide some fill-in light.

If you are painting a portrait outdoors, bear in mind the same guidelines. Position your model so that the sun strikes him or her from one side and slightly to the front. Early morning and middle to late afternoon will give the best results.

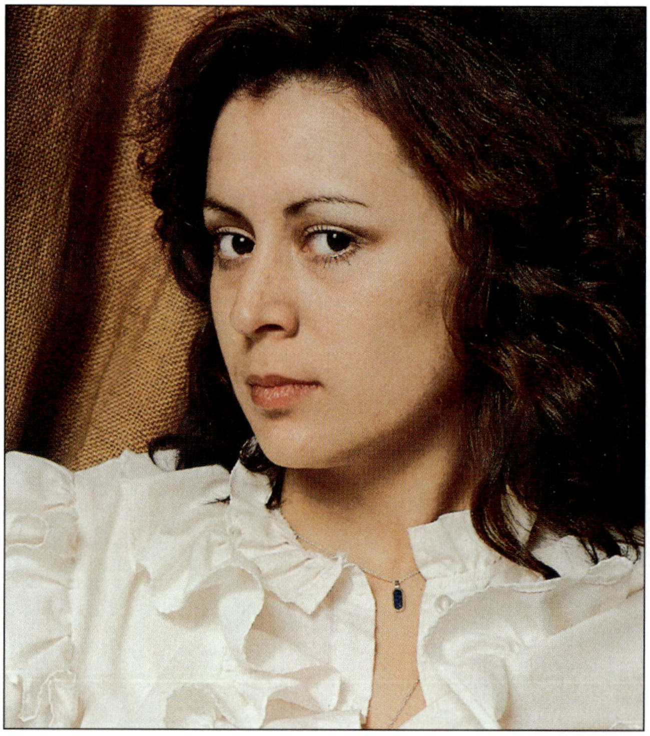

ABOVE: Natural light from a skylight produces soft contours and shadows. However, natural light changes constantly, and many artists find it necessary to make color sketches or take a photograph, enabling them to continue work after the light has changed or dimmed.

THE IMPORTANCE OF LIGHT

Light and shade are the portrait painter's most valuable tools when painting the human face. The complex anatomy of the head and face – the bone and muscles and the skin which covers them – are only seen by means of a constant source of light.

Traditionally artists have depicted the light source as above, and slightly to one side of the sitter. This is because it was realized that a painting looked more natural if the light source imitated the position of the sun. Leonardo da Vinci held this view and in nearly all his portraits the light source is made to look like sunlight. He used this constant light source to help indicate the changes in direction of the planes on the forms. Painters after Leonardo adopted the same device, and it became common practise to indicate the shadows of the nose and brow to explain the volume and shape of the head. In a similar way the chin would cast a shadow across the neck, and the cheekbone furthest from the source of light would be bathed in shadow.

Leonardo's advice about lighting was connected with his realization that the emotional content of the picture would be, to some extent, the result of it. If the lighting were directed from below the face, the effect would be quite

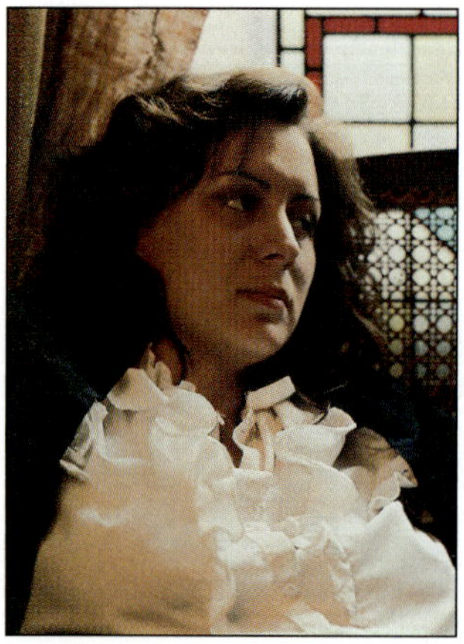

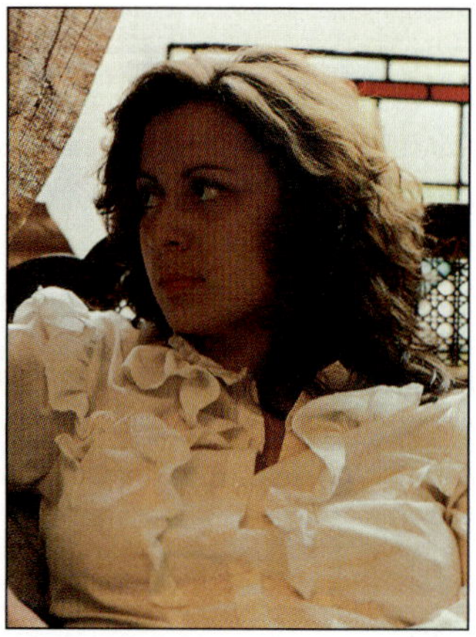

Turned towards the window, the form of the face and features is clearly defined by the daylight (left). When the model turns her face the other way, the features are lost and the face flattened into a dim shadowy shape (right).

different – some artists have used this quality to their advantage, creating unusual theatrical or dream-like effects which automatically distance the spectator.

Edgar Degas was fascinated by the effect of artificial lighting and sometimes transferred the elements of theatricality into a portrait set in a domestic interior. He realized that by not revealing the source of light he could take more liberties with its effects.

CREATING MOOD WITH LIGHTING

Painting a portrait involves much more than simply achieving a likeness. Your painting should also say something about the character and personality of the sitter, an emotional quality that the viewer can empathize with. In this respect, the amount, quality, and direction of the light will have an influence on the impression you wish to convey. As in a landscape, lighting affects the values and colors in the subject, which in turn convey a particular atmosphere and sense of place and time. For example, bright sunlight creates strong contrasts that convey energy and light-heartedness, whereas low lighting creates dark, somber values that convey an air of mystery and introspection.

You can also play two sources of light on the subject: the cool, weak daylight coming in from a window and the stronger, warmer light of a lamp. This creates a range of warm and cool colors that give a special luminosity and atmosphere to the portrait.

So before you start painting a portrait, first decide what kind of mood you wish to convey and arrange the lighting accordingly. Even if you don't have a proper studio, this shouldn't be too difficult; all you need is enough space to work in and a couple of lights with adjustable stands. The portrait paintings that follow demonstrate how to use specific lighting arrangements to create a range of very different moods.

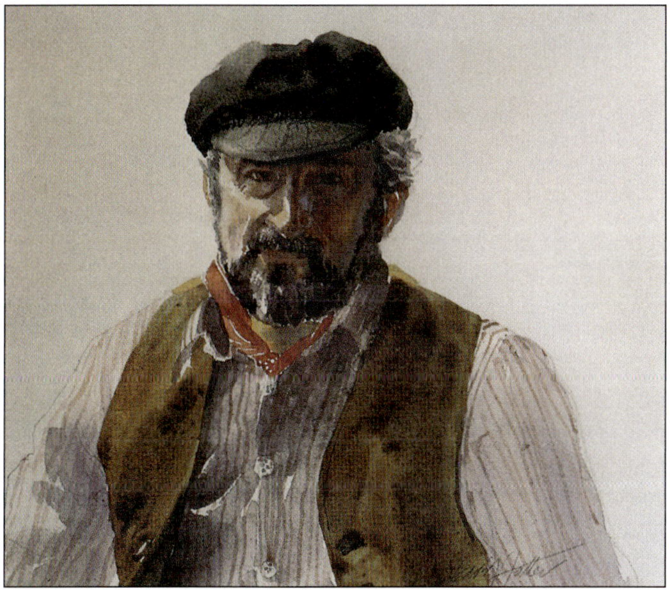

Three-quarter lighting *is so called because it falls on about three-quarters of the face. This is the most popular type of lighting for most subjects, but is especially good for portraits, since not only does it give a strong impression of volume and surface texture, it also creates a satisfying range of tonal variations that give life and vitality to a portrait. If your sitter has strong features or a dynamic personality, use three-quarter lighting to emphasize these qualities.*

In planning the portrait, consider whether you want to view the sitter from the shadow side or the light side. Facing the sitter's shadow side is best for expressing strong character; facing the light side creates a softer, more subtle effect. It's also worth experimenting with the angle and height of the lamp to see how this affects the shadows and highlights. Watch particularly for the shadow cast by the nose – a strong shadow reaching right down to the mouth can create a rather unattractive effect.

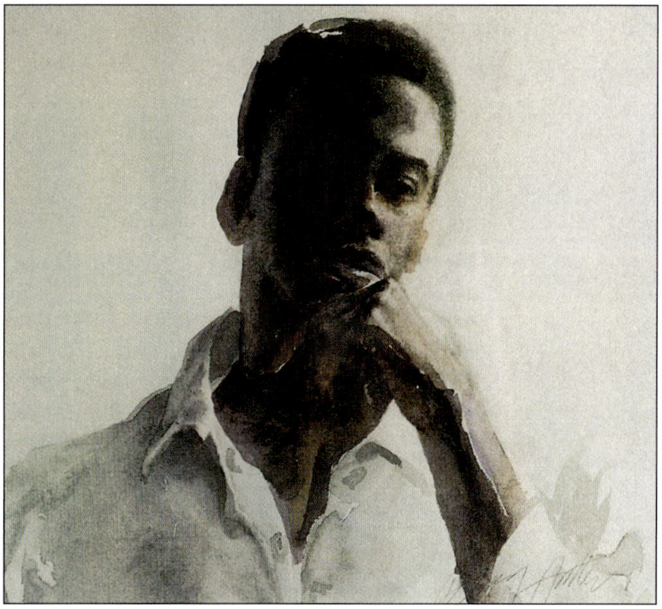

Side lighting *is another type of lighting popular with portrait painters. This time the face is lit directly from one side, leaving the other side in shadow. The strong contrast between light and shadow creates a sense of drama and tension in a low-key portrait, but care must be taken that the effect is not too theatrical. To soften the values slightly on the shadow side, use a white or reflective board to create "fill-in" light in the shadow area. This also creates subtle reflected lights in the hair that prevent it from looking "dead."*

Experiment with the colors, perhaps using cool ones on the shadow side and warm ones on the lit side to emphasize the contrast, and add carefully placed highlights on the brow, nose, and chin.

THE ILLUSION OF DEPTH

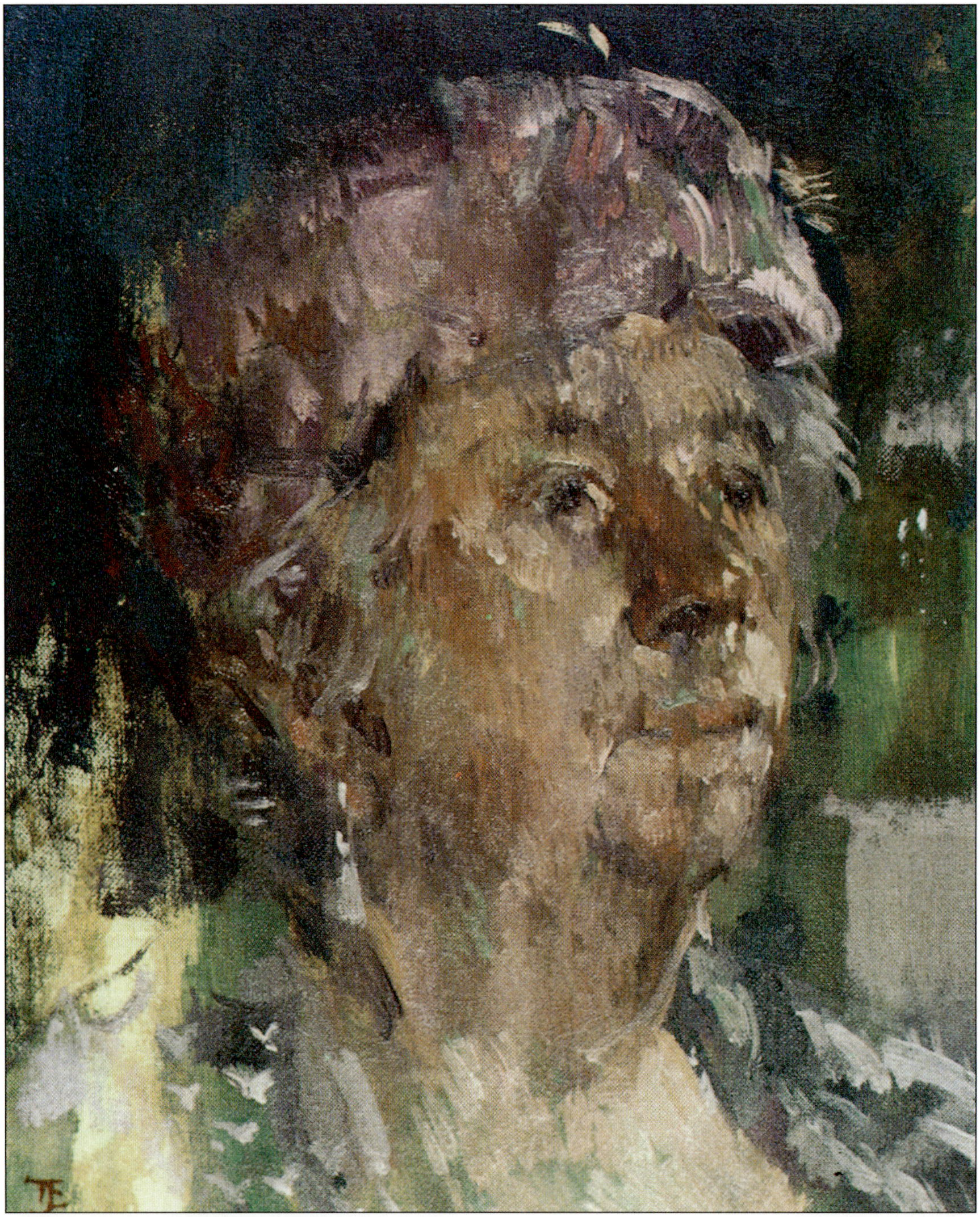

MISS JULIE by Tom Coates (oil on canvas)

This painting demonstrates how to achieve that all-important sense of atmosphere in portraits. The colors in the woman's face are closely related to those in the background, so that sitter and background are tied together. Notice also how the edges, particularly those near the back of the head, have been intentionally softened. There is a vibrant, broken quality to the paint that is more suggestive of light and air than an area of flat color.

Composition

The word "composition" has a slightly alarming ring to it – it sounds as though it might be an intellectual exercise quite beyond the capabilities of the ordinary person. This really is not so: composing a painting is mainly a question of selecting, arranging, and rearranging, just as you might do when deciding on the decor for a room or when taking a photograph.

When you are painting a single figure, the main decisions you will have to make are where to place the figure on the paper and how much of it to show. People in paintings automatically draw the eye and become the center of interest, simply because the viewer identifies with a fellow human. This means that your figure need not occupy a great deal of the picture space; in a garden-lover's portrait, for example, you could give equal space to the flowers, trees, and shrubs and still make a successful portrait study.

Often, however, you'll want to focus on a figure, particularly if a friend or member of the family has offered to pose for you. In this case, you might paint the face alone, or perhaps half of the figure down to the hands. If you are going to "crop," you'll need to do some planning, because cropping needs to be handled carefully. The head and neck form a unit, so for a head-and-shoulders portrait you can usually crop below the hands, but don't let them slip out of the picture so that only the wrists are visible – this creates an awkward and ugly effect.

Don't allow too much space above the head either, because this will "push" the figure down, making it appear to slide out of the bottom of the picture. And whatever you do, avoid placing the head bang in the middle and painting from directly in front, since this rarely makes an interesting composition. The majority of portraits (though by no means all) are three-quarters views, which show up the features and the shape of the head well and avoid a still and over-symmetrical look.

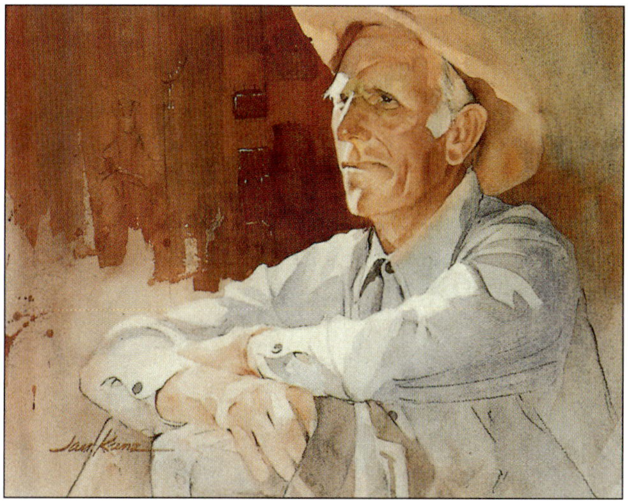

HUMAN PROPORTIONS

Poor drawing is the most common fault in figure painting and portraiture, but this is usually the result of lack of observation rather than insufficient skill. You will certainly improve with practise, but initially it will help you to memorize a few simple rules about the proportions of the face and body.

Artists use the head as a convenient unit of measurement when they are painting a complete figure. The body of an adult is approximately seven and a half heads high, and the foot is about one head in length. We tend to think of the waist as the mid-point of the body, but it is considerably higher, as the legs are relatively long.

Of course, few bodies conform to the "standard model." Heads can be smaller or larger, legs shorter or longer, shoulders wide or narrow, square or sloping. But you'll find that once you get into the habit of using the head as a measuring device you'll make fewer mistakes. Try holding your pencil vertically at arm's length and moving your thumb up and down it to find the size of the head, and then see how many times this measurement fits into a leg, arm, or the width of the shoulders.

When drawing and painting the head, as in a head-and-shoulders portrait, it is important to remember that the features occupy a relatively small part of the head. The bottom of the eye socket is the mid-point. Beginners often make the features too large, with the eyes placed too high. Although faces vary widely (and the first step to successful portraiture is being able to pick out individual differences in proportions) you will find it useful to remember the basic rules.

SEATED MAN by Jan Kunz

This painting is carefully composed. Including more of the legs might have stolen attention from the face, which is always the center of interest in a portrait. Similarly, the artist treated the hands in a sketchier way than the face, and only put in background details where she wanted a strong, dark color to contrast with the light side of the head.

Structure of the Head and Face

The skull determines the basic shape of a person's head, but it is the muscles and movement of the head and face which give life to that head, and which makes one person different from another. These muscles, which are used to make facial expressions, are found under the skin of the face, scalp, and neck. They are directly related to the features of the face and, while it is not necessary to remember the Latin names which identify these muscles, it is extremely useful to understand where they are to know what they do.

Muscle movements are responsible for the way the lips move. The muscle surrounding the mouth, the *orbicularis oris*, is made up of a number of muscles which enter the lips from above and below. Other muscles pass into the mouth horizontally, while the *buccinator* muscle passes from the side of the mouth to the cheek. Each eye cavity is surrounded by the *orbicularis oculi* muscle, which allows each eyelid to close tightly or gently. Knowledge of these basic facial muscles helps artists to describe individual characteristics in detail.

When painting or drawing the head it is important to think how the neck is attached to the head, and how the movement of the neck affects the position of the head. The most important muscle in the neck passes from behind the ear to the inside of the clavicle. It is called the *sternocleidomastoid*. This muscle allows the head and neck to bend forward, the head to turn from one side to another, and the chin to tilt upward. Although it is always tempting to start a drawing of the head with the lips or the eyes, it is wise to bear in mind the main structural parts of the cranium and face.

THE HEAD FROM AN ANGLE

One of the most difficult things when drawing a head is to apply the "rules" of proportion if the head is seen in semi-profile, or is tipped back or forward. From these angles, the eyes, nose, and mouth may appear compressed together or distorted, because they are seen from a foreshortened viewpoint. Because our mind finds it difficult to accept these distortions, and therefore tries to recreate the head-on measurements, the proportions of the head and the positioning of the features have a tendency to go awry.

Drawing the head from an angle involves careful observation and some precise measuring. As you draw, use your pencil as a tool to measure the distance between, say, the nose and the back of the ear and then compare that with the distance from, say, eyebrow to chin. By constantly measuring and comparing in this way you should arrive at an accurate result.

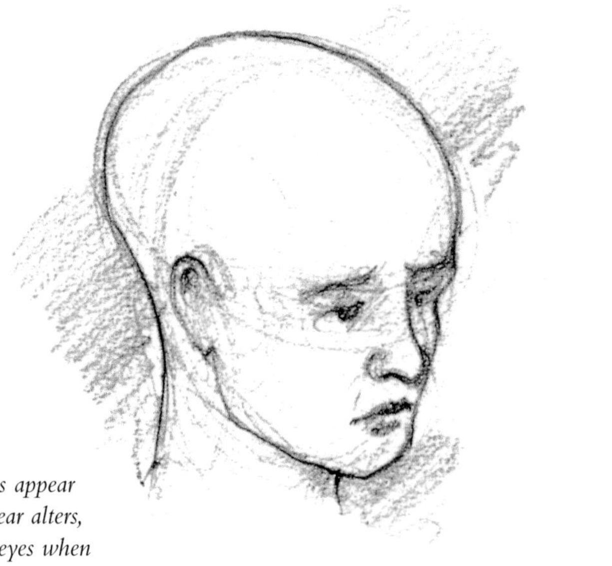

BELOW AND RIGHT: *When the head is cast downward or tilted back the features appear compressed toward the top or bottom of the face. Note also how the position of the ear alters, appearing higher than the eyes when the head is tipped down, and lower than the eyes when the head is tipped back.*

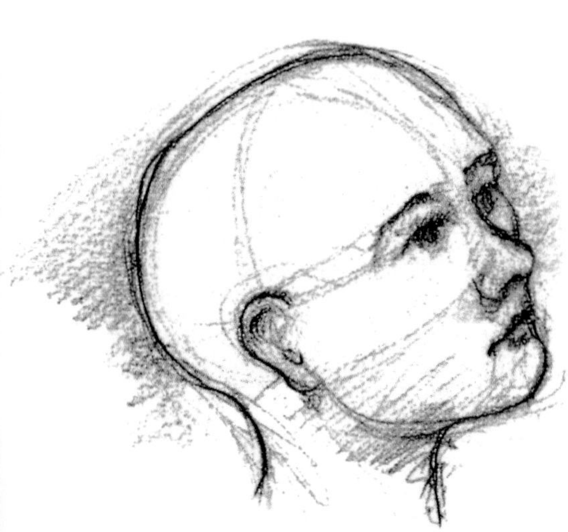

RIGHT: *Seen from the front, the head is longer than it is wide, but as it is turned to the side, more of the back of the head is revealed. Whereas from the front, the eyes are normally about one eye-width apart, from a three-quarter view that distance may vary, and the eyes are noticeably different from each other in size and shape. As you draw, make sure that the slope of the eyes and mouth is consistent with the tilt of the head; a common mistake is to place the eyes level with each other when the head itself is tilted upward or downward.*

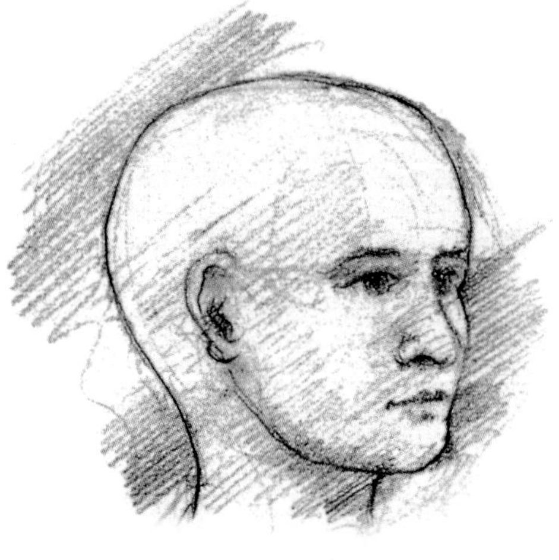

Eyes

The eyes are often referred to as "the windows of the soul," because they convey so much about a person's character and mood. As such, they are a vital element of any portrait, and it is important to get them right. Below is a step-by-step guide of how to paint eyes in watercolor.

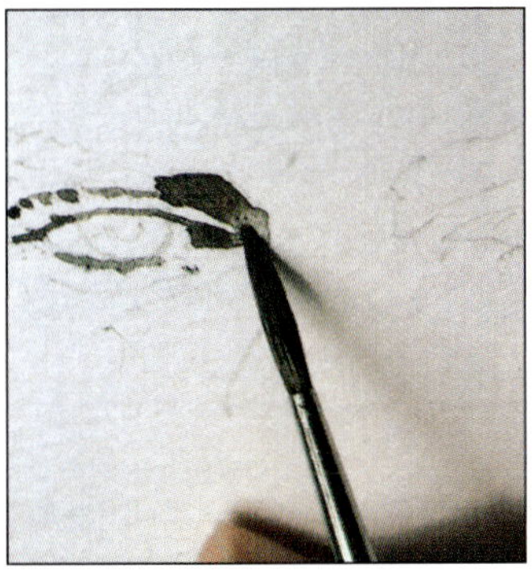

1 After making an outline sketch of the eyes in pencil, the artist defines the shape of the eye rim and the shadow on the inside corner of the eye with a mixture of ivory black and brown madder alizarin and a No. 2 sable brush.

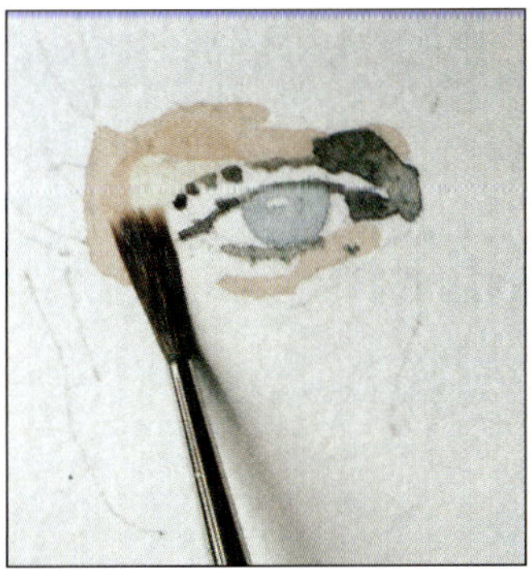

2 When the first wash is completely dry a thin, transparent wash of burnt sienna is used to block in the middle tones around the eye. Then, with a delicate wash of cobalt blue and Payne's gray, he paints in the iris, leaving a tiny dot of untouched white paper for the main highlight.

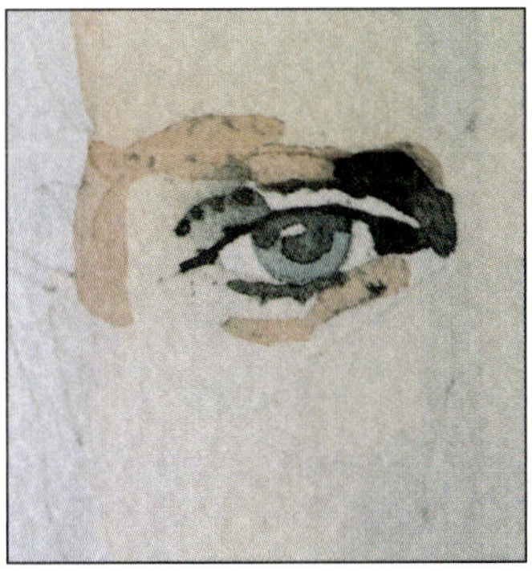

3 The artist now applies a thin wash of Payne's gray to the eye: in one stroke he delineates the pupil and the shadow cast by the upper lid, being careful to work around the white shape of the highlight. With a clean, damp brush, he then carries a little of this color up toward the outer corner of the eye to create a subtle shadow which emphasizes the curve of the eyeball. Checking first that the flesh tones around the eye are dry, the artist now paints the lightest tones of the face with a heavily diluted wash of burnt sienna.

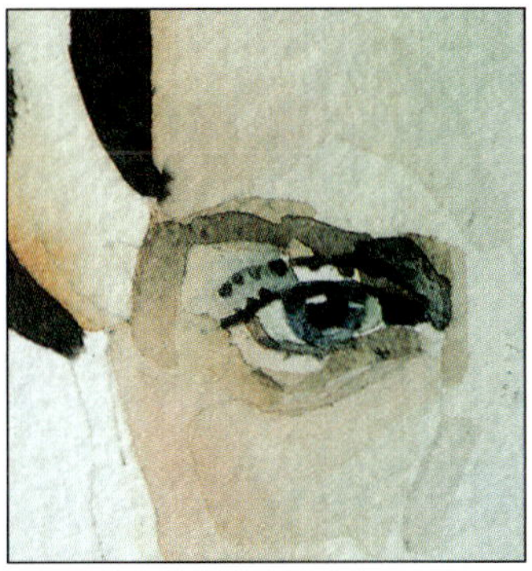

4 When this wash is dry, the flesh tones are now strengthened with further washes, mixed from cadmium orange, brown madder alizarin, and burnt sienna, and the artist begins to paint the various tones of the hair with burnt umber and cadmium orange. The shape of the eyebrow is then strengthened with a mixture of burnt sienna and cobalt blue. When these washes are dry, the color of the iris is developed further with strokes of cobalt blue, leaving some subtle highlights of paler blue. Then the pupil is darkened with a wash of ivory black. Notice how the two colors bleed into each other very slightly where they meet, creating a soft, "watery" feel which is much more lifelike than a hard, unsympathetic edge. Next the "white" of the eyeball is toned down with a very pale mix of yellow ocher and Payne's gray, which is slightly darker in the inner corner where there is more shadow.

It is important to work continually back-and-forth between the eye and the surrounding features, so that the eye becomes an integral part of the face.

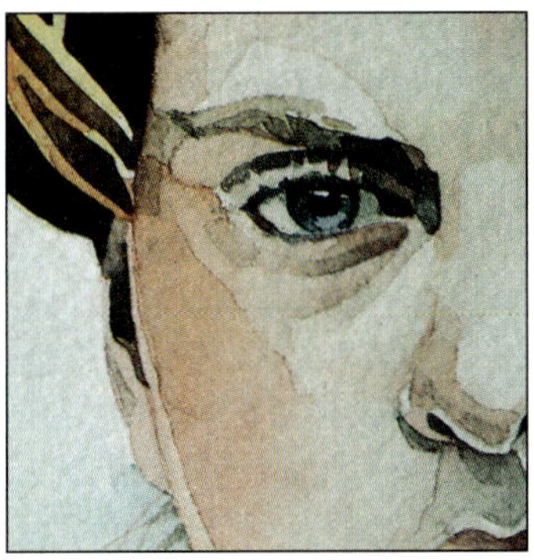

5 With the basic tones and shapes now established, all that remains to be done is to sharpen up the details in the eye to strengthen the "glassy" appearance. Finally, tiny upward strokes of paint are lifted out just above the eyelid. Viewed from a distance these pale shapes give an impression of blond eyelashes.

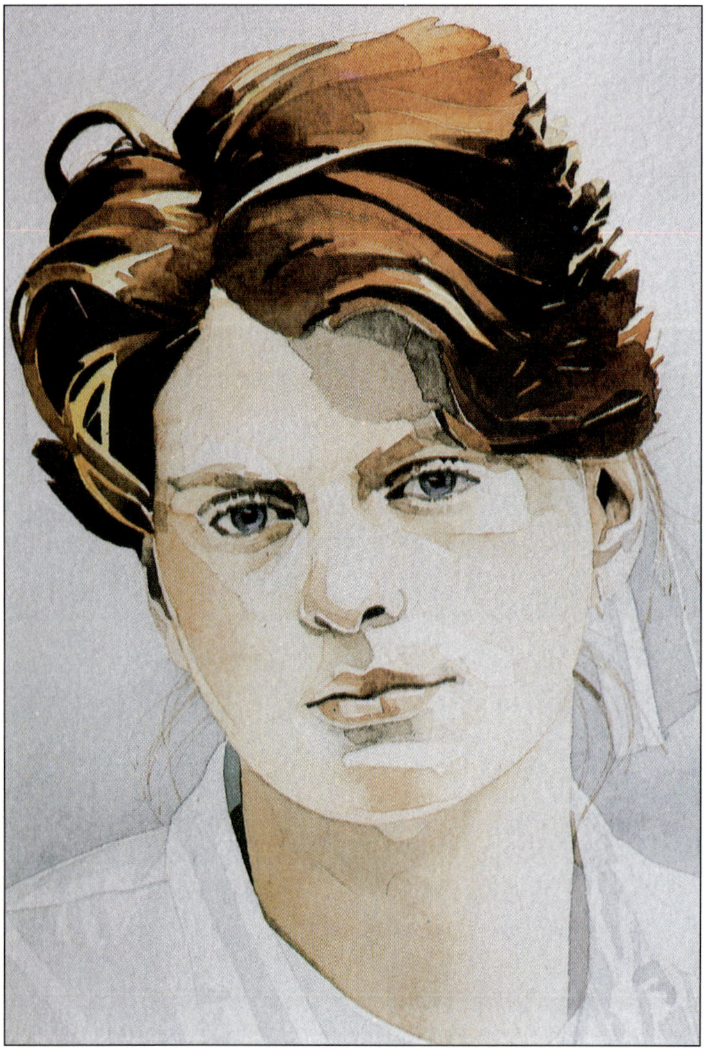

6 The completed painting. Delicate washes and glazes have been used throughout, to create a subtle and lifelike portrait of a young girl.

CLOSED EYES

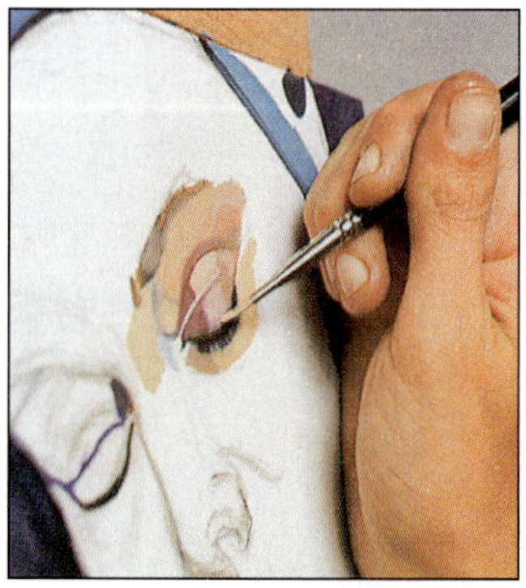

1 Having sketched in the head and the features of the face, the artist works on the eyes.

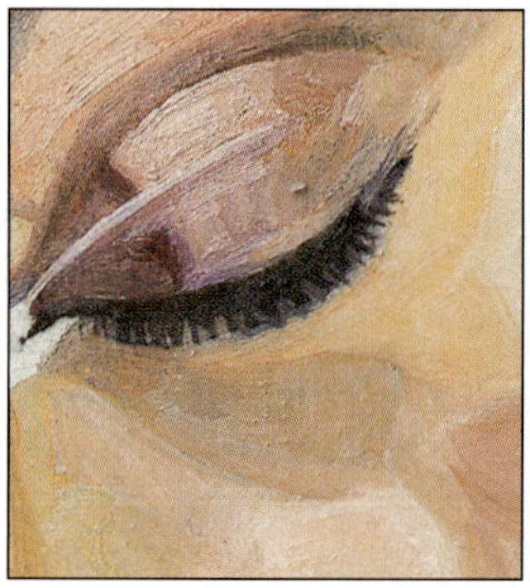

2 In this detail you can see the various skin tones – the lightest areas are made up of yellows, pinks, and oranges, whereas the shadows contain tinges of blue, green, and purple.

3 In the final picture, the various tones merge together. The tones of the eyelids are purple in comparison with the colors of the cheeks.

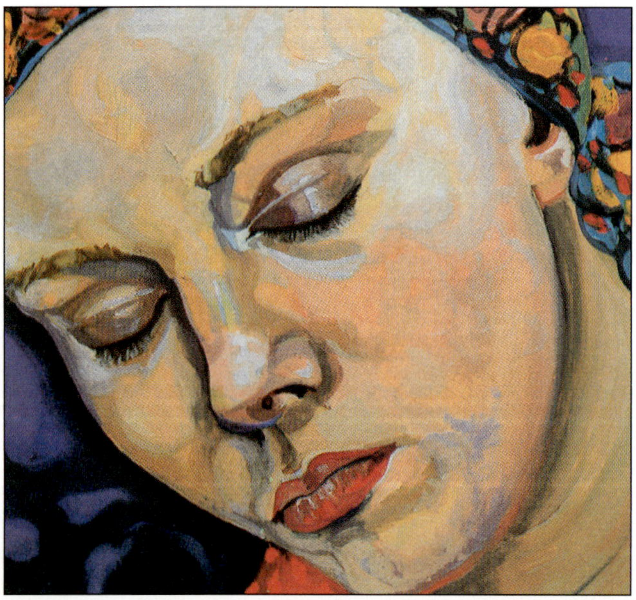

In shape, size, and character, eyes may differ enormously from one person to another, but the basic anatomical structure remains the same. The eye is a convex form in a concave socket, but all too often it is rendered in a schematic way, as an almond shape with a circle in it. The upper and lower lids are never the same shape – the lower lid is much flatter. In addition, the upper lid covers a third to half of the iris, depending on the individual, and the iris "sits" inside the lower lid – not on its edge.

Generally, the eyes should have a soft, "melting" appearance, and this is achieved by avoiding too many crisp hard edges, painting wet-into-wet. Even the blackness of the pupil should be softened at the edges where it meets the iris, to avoid an unnatural, staring look.

Finally, never paint individual eyelashes – nothing looks more amateurish. Use a curving irregular dark line to give an impression of the eyelashes.

Mouths

The mouth is the most mobile part of the face, and capable of many expressions (Leonardo's Mona Lisa is the most eloquent example of the subtlety of expression which the mouth can lend to a portrait).

The most common mistake when painting mouths is to draw the final outline first and then fill it in with color. This linear approach is inappropriate for a painting and gives the mouth a flat, pasted-on appearance. The correct technique is to model the mouth in a sculptural way, in terms of light and dark tones and hard and soft edges.

Assuming that we are looking at a closed mouth, in repose, there are various points to be noted. Firstly, the mouth is not flat, but stretches around the sphere of the head, swelling out toward the middle of the face and narrowing again toward the corners. The upper and lower lips have distinct features: the upper lip may be thin, well-defined, and dark in tone compared to the lower lip, which is usually fuller and softer, and lighter in tone because, being more prominent, it catches more light.

To emphasize the curvature of the lips, begin at the corners and work inward. Put in the darkest tones first – the underside of the upper lip, and the shadow beneath the lower lip. Then apply the middle tones, blending them softly into the darks. Finally, add the highlights.

So that the mouth appears integrated with the surrounding skin, introduce a variety of hard areas and soft areas into it. The top line of the upper lip, for example, may be much crisper than that of the soft, lower lip.

Finally, don't make the mistake of painting the lips too red. Use the same color mixtures as you would for the skin, with the addition of just a touch more red.

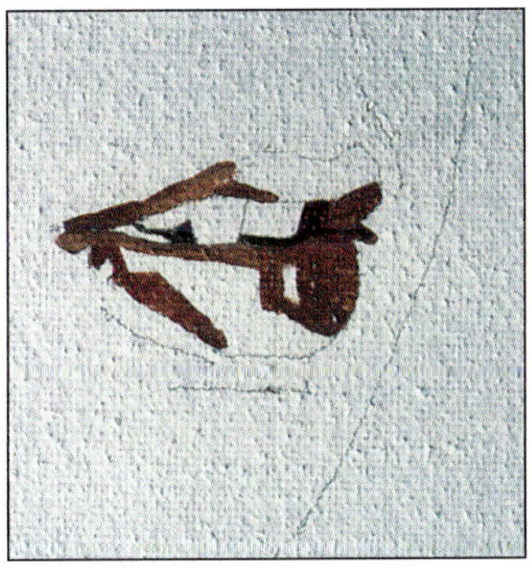

1 The artist begins with a brief sketch to outline the shape of the mouth, and then blocks in the darkest tones with burnt and raw sienna, and a No. 4 sable brush.

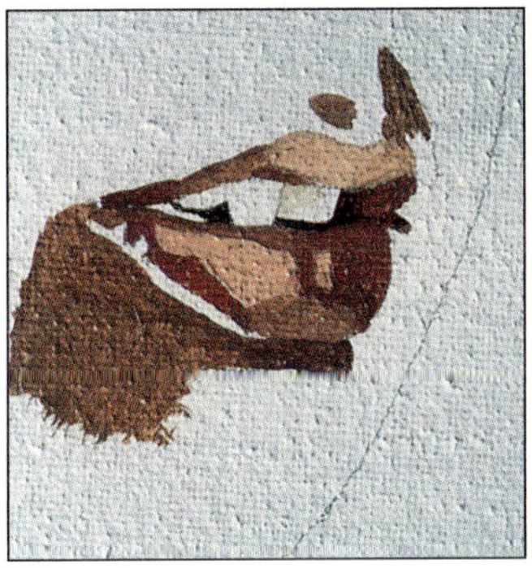

2 Here the lighter tones have been blocked with cadmium red, burnt sienna, and titanium white. A mixture of burnt umber and white is used to define the darkest shadows around the mouth.

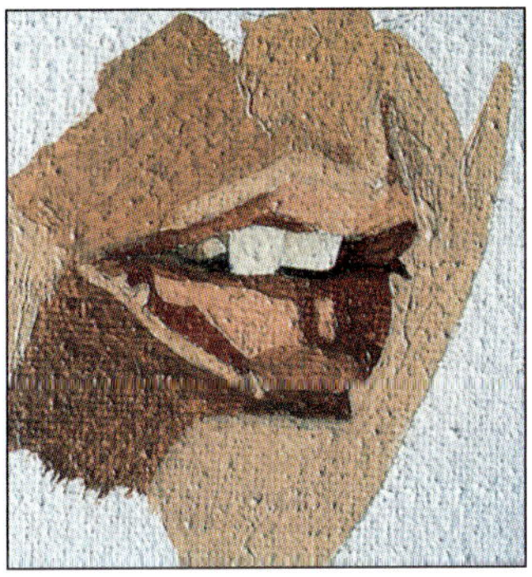

3 The artist now blocks in the lights and middle tones around the mouth, blending them smoothly together. With a touch of cadmium yellow and ivory black, the tones of the teeth are darkened very slightly.

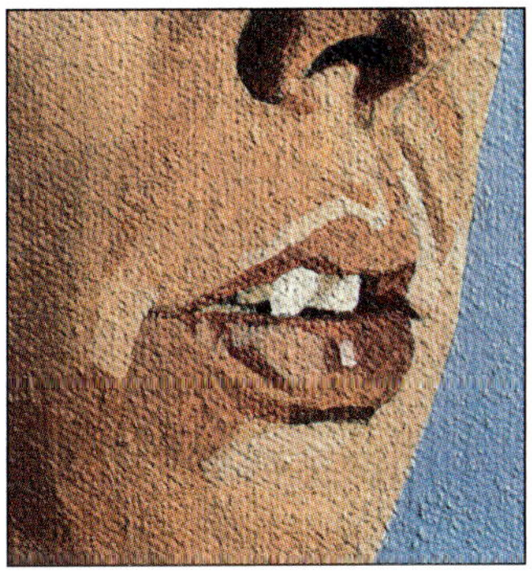

4 Using a very limited palette, the artist has succeeded in rendering a bold, direct impression of the mouth.

A smiling mouth is more difficult to paint than a mouth in repose, since any undue exaggeration of the smile results in a caricature rather than a portrait. The essential thing to remember is that we smile not only with our mouths but with our entire faces. Cover up the mouth in this portrait and you will see that the girl is still smiling. This is valuable proof that all the features of the head are interlinked and supportive of one another. Obviously it would be difficult for a sitter to hold a smiling pose for a long period without the smile becoming somewhat "fixed." In this case, it might be helpful to take snapshots of your sitter and use these as reference during the painting of the portrait.

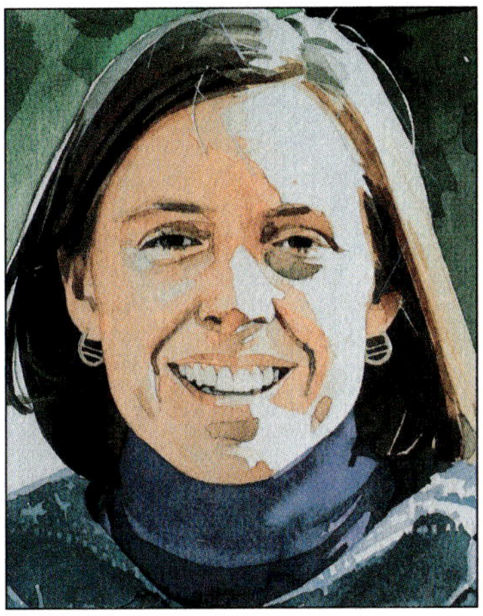

Flesh Tones

There is no single, all-embracing formula for painting skin tones, because they vary enormously, even within the same sex and racial group – and even between one part of the body and another.

Commercially available flesh tint colors are very useful – for painting clouds at evening. Do not rely on them for painting skin, though, because they are dull, dull, dull! With suitable mixing, you can create hues that are infinitely changeable, enabling you to capture all the warmth and subtlety of human flesh. For example, a suitable mixture for "white" skin might comprise roughly equal quantities of white, alizarin crimson, and yellow ocher, with a touch of cadmium red. Mixing these colors in different proportions gives you a good base from which to start. Red, umbers, and siennas can be added to warm up the prominent, light-struck areas, while blues, violets, and greens can be added in the shadow areas and receding places.

The colors that you choose to mix will, of course, depend on the particular skin type of your sitter. Decide first whether it is generally a warm ivory color, pale and sallow, ruddy or olive. Mix a mid-tone accordingly and apply it, well-diluted, as a base color. Paint quickly and freely, wet-into-wet. Working from this base color, start to place the lightest and darkest tones, and then work on the mid-tones – those transitional areas between light and shadow. Remember that the colors in the sitter's clothing and the background will affect the colors of the flesh tones, so develop these along with the face. As you work, it helps to step back from the painting from time to time to check that the combination of colors and tones is creating the desired effect.

Gamboge + a touch of madder lake

Yellow ocher + madder lake

Yellow ocher + madder lake + a touch of cobalt blue

There is no set formula for mixing flesh tones: your best plan is to experiment with different combinations of color and see which ones work best. Some suggestions are offered here.

Viridian + gamboge + burnt sienna

Yellow ocher + madder lake, very diluted

Gamboge + burnt sienna + a touch of viridian

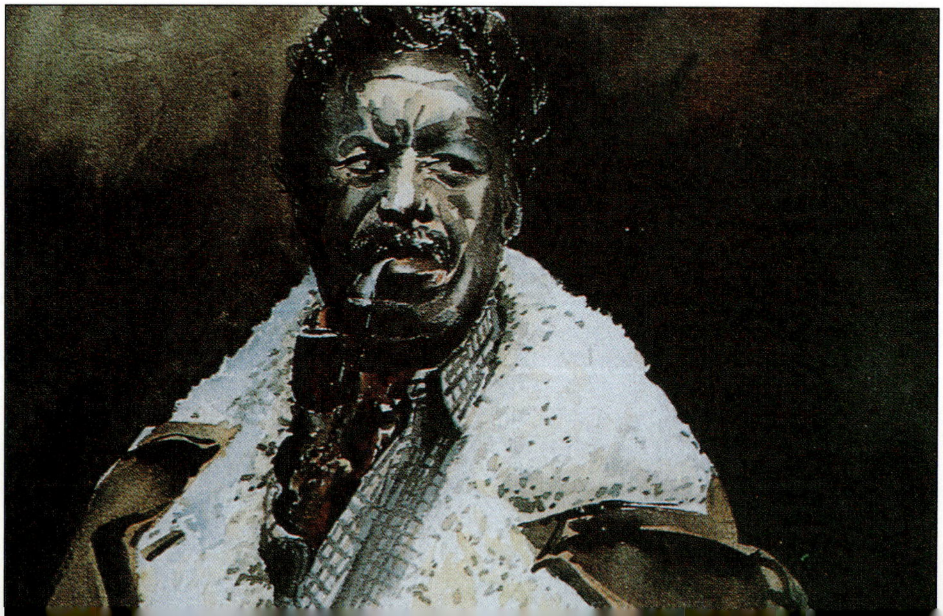

PORTRAIT OF GORDON PARKS by Douglas Lew (watercolor)

Dark skins generally have more of a sheen than Caucasian skins, and thus the contrast between the highlights and the darker areas surrounding them can appear quite strong.

Hair

The average head contains around 100,000 separate hairs, but, as far as the artist is concerned, hair should be rendered as one solid form, with planes of light and shadow.

The volume of the head is defined by the hair, so it is important to begin by defining the hair in terms of shape and mass before thinking about texture. Search out those areas that catch the light and those that are in shadow, and indicate them with broad washes of color. Having established the underlying form, indicate the direction of the hair growth: long, flowing strokes for long hair, short, scumbled strokes for curly hair. Again, think in terms of mass – don't paint individual strands that seem unconnected to the rest of the hair.

To portray the essentially soft, pliant nature of hair, it is best to work wet-into-wet, so that the edges between the hair and the face, and the hair and the background flow into one another. One of the most common errors made by beginners is to make the hairline too hard. The hair and face should flow together as one entity; this is achieved by running some of the skin color into the hairline to soften the division between hair and face. Similarly, the outer edge of the hair should melt into the background color: soft edges here will give an impression of air and atmosphere around the sitter.

The color of hair should also look soft and natural, and should not attract attention away from the face. Even if your sitter has raven black hair, do not paint it black. Hair picks up reflected color from its surroundings; look for subtle hints of blue and brown in black hair, blonde and red in brown hair and brown, gold, and gray in blonde hair.

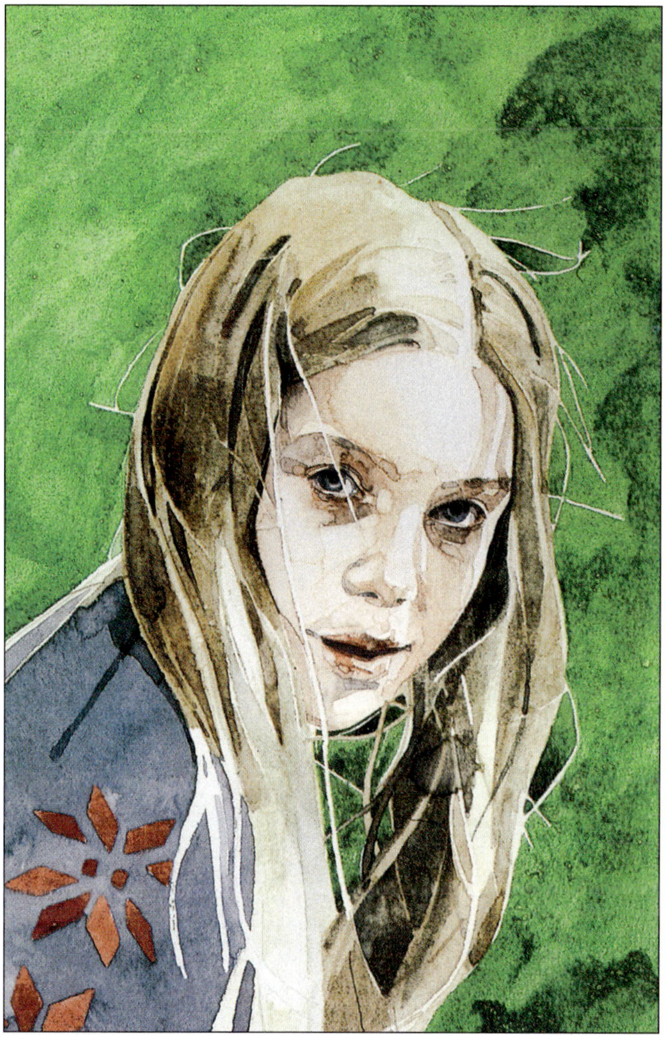

HAIR (watercolor)

In this outdoor portrait, the artist achieves a lively impression of light and movement in the girl's hair. The essence of this technique is to keep the tonal masses strong and simple, allowing a few telling highlights to describe the movement in the hair.

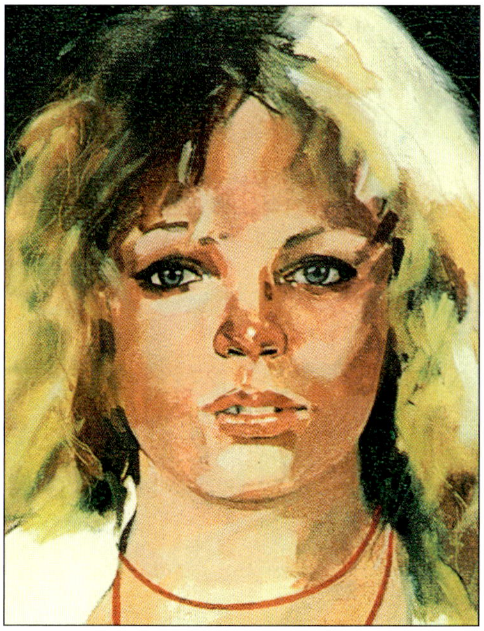

HAIR (acrylic and oil)

The artist began the painting in acrylic and then progressed to oils using several different methods to apply the paint, such as with a painting knife and straight from the tube. In the final picture, the bright colors of the subject contrast with the bland background, and the highlights in the hair are strengthened by the yellow of the dress.

Portrait in Oil

In art historical terms, the technique of working on a stark, white canvas is a recent development made popular by the Impressionists of the nineteenth century.

Before that time it was customary to work on a colored ground, made either by mixing pigment into the priming coat or laying a thin wash of color over a white base. The purpose of this was to establish a middle tone over which to work with light and dark colors and to give the image a warm or cool cast.

The red priming used in this painting is a powerful color which radically affects the whole character of the painting. The forms are constructed with a variety of grays; those which tend toward blue or green are emphasized on the strong red ground, and pink and yellow tones pick up the warm glow of red which breaks through. Although the palette is limited, the relationship of the colors are vibrant and active. You will need to pay close attention to both the subject and the painting to achieve a lively but controlled result.

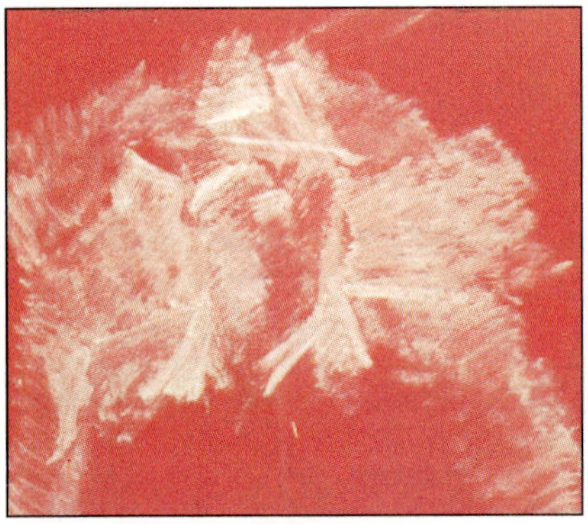

1 Use a No. 6 bristle brush to block in the basic shape of the figure in white. With a No. 3 brush, sketch in the outline and lay areas of light tone.

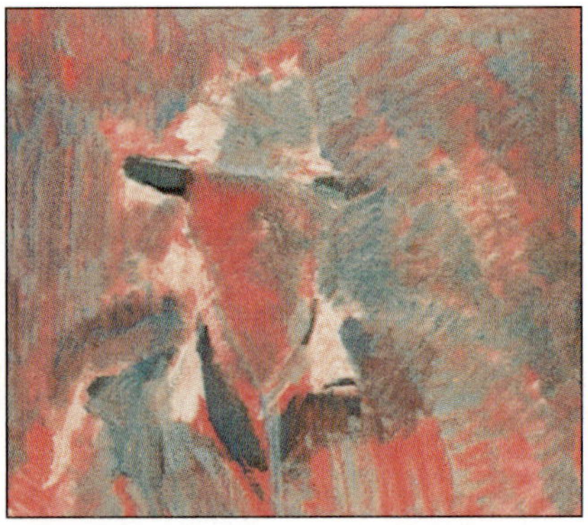

2 Mix two tones of gray from cobalt blue, black, and white. Work over the whole canvas in thin patches of color.

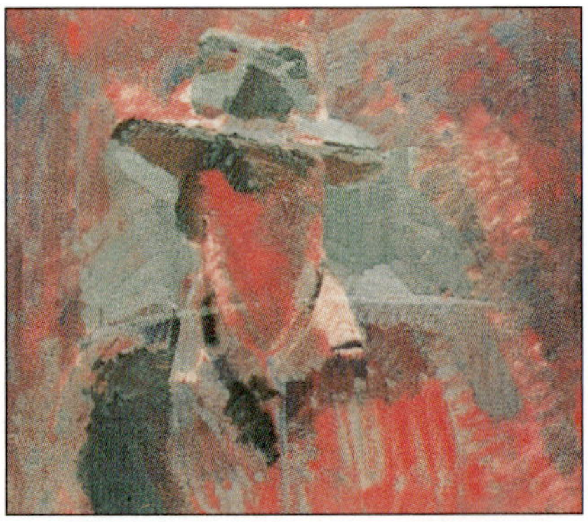

3 Develop the dark tones around the hat, shoulders, and neck. Add a little yellow to the grays and block in the tones behind the head and in the hat.

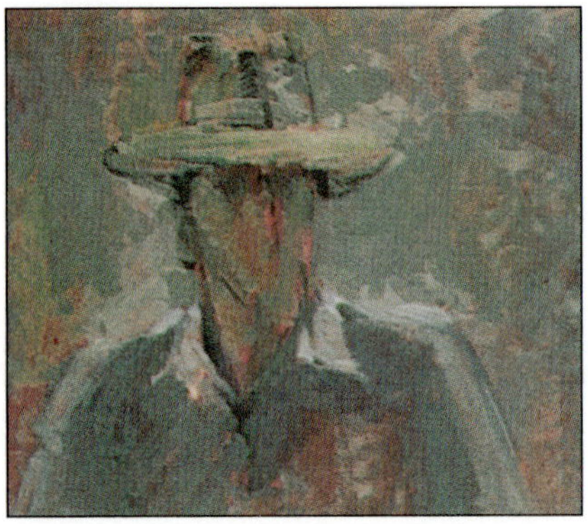

4 Work into the face and neck with a light greenish-gray, roughly mapping out the features. Build up the structure of the image, with detail in the hat and collar.

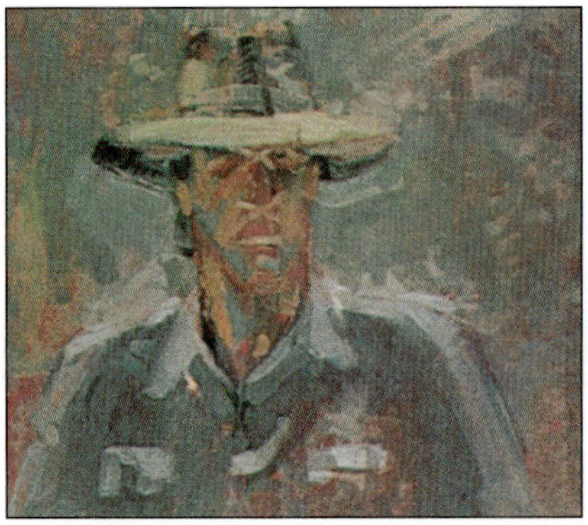

5 Develop the color in the face using cool blue-gray contrasted with a warm flesh tone mixed from yellow, rose, and white. Indicate features with light marks.

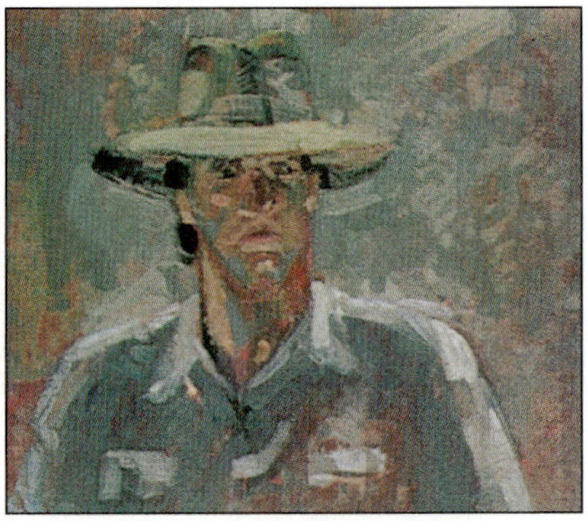

6 Draw into the features with dark red, black, and white. Block in light tones on the shirt with solid gray and white.

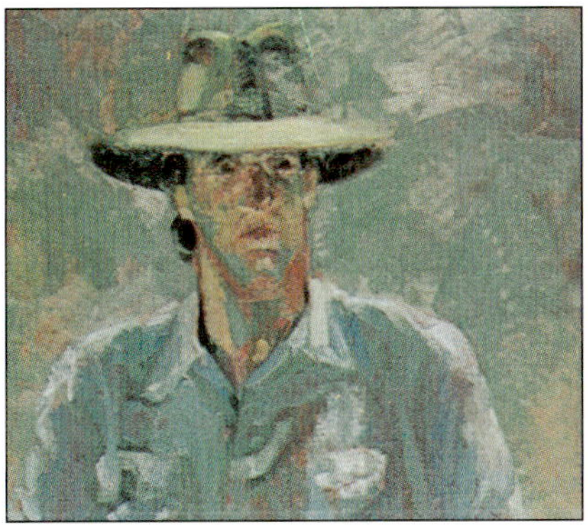

7 Work over the whole image with thick paint developing the tonal structure with warm grays in the foreground and light gray-green in the background.

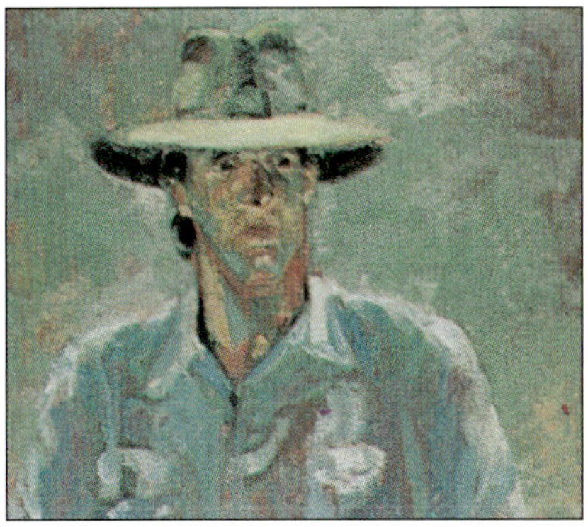

8 Work over the figure with a No. 3 brush, dabbing in color to refine details and add definition to the features.

The finished portrait

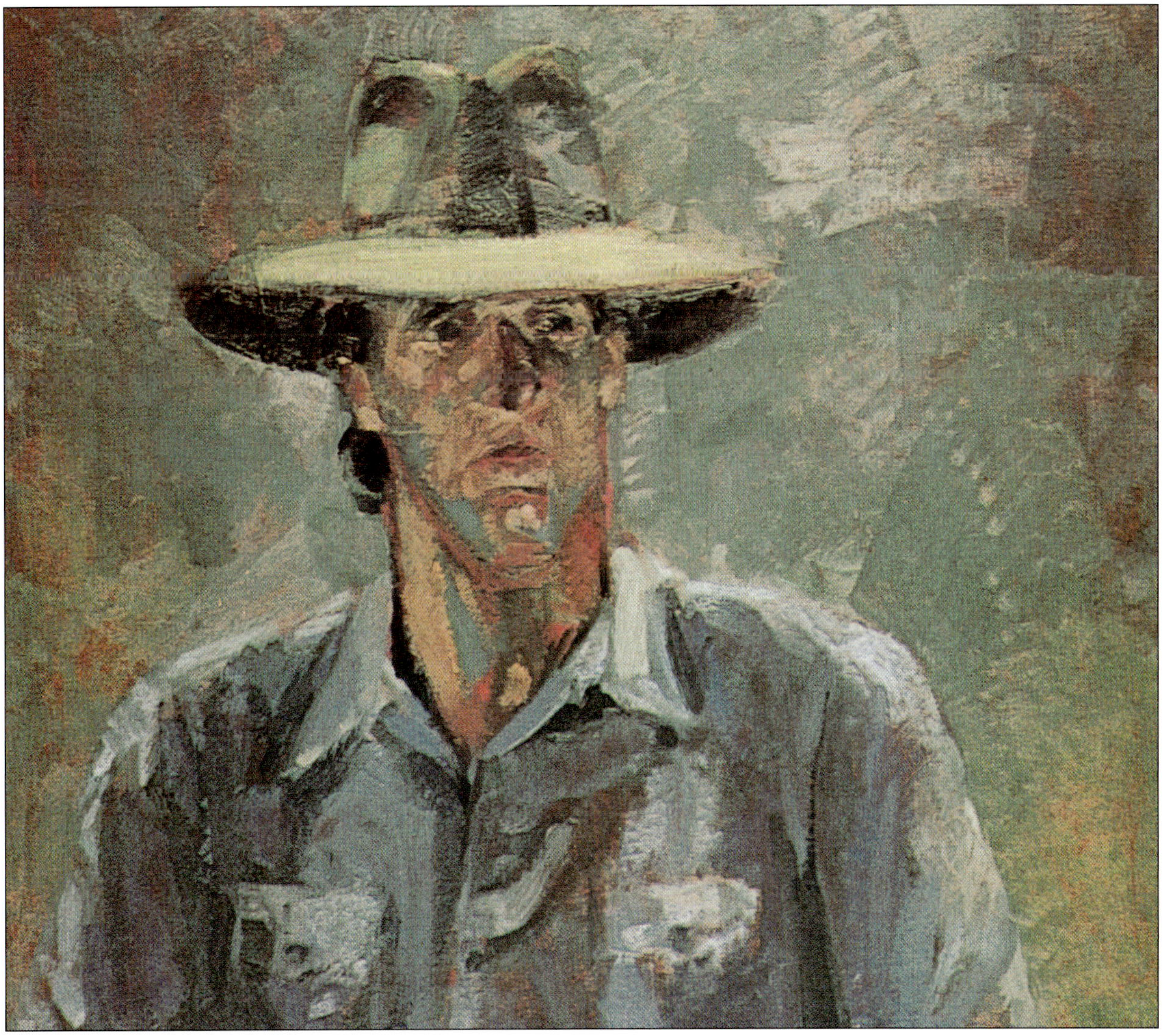

Portrait in Acrylic

Painting a portrait makes demands on the power of visual observation above and beyond those used in everyday contact. In creating a likeness, observation must be disciplined and critical. Every feature of the head and face must be carefully analyzed in terms of color, shape, and tone in order to understand the relationships existing between them.

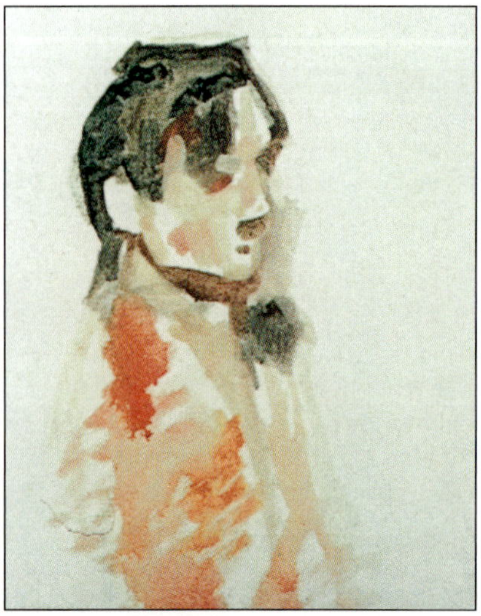

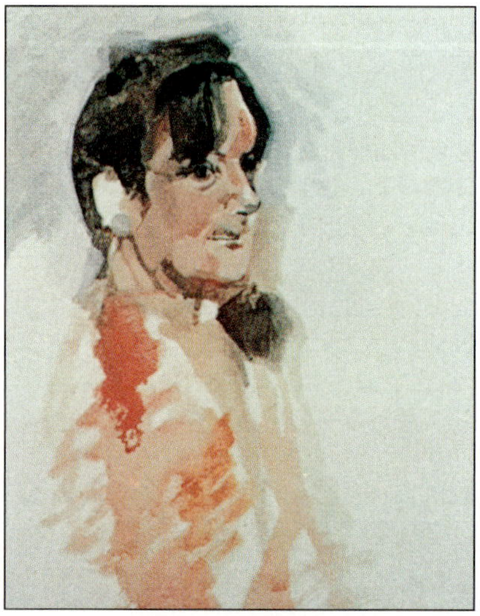

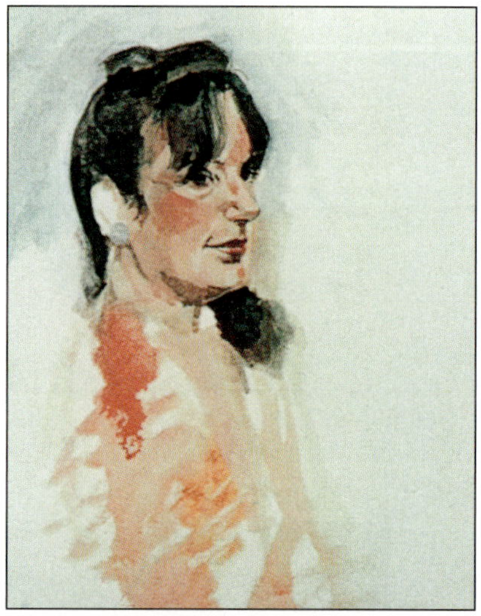

1 Working with black, white, vermilion, and burnt sienna and a No. 6 brush, block in an overall impression of the figure.

2 Lay in the light flesh tones of the face. Put a blue cast into the shadows with cobalt and gray, drawing small, precise shapes with the brush.

3 Add touches of vivid color to the face by using rich reds and browns to define the mouth and lighten flesh tones with pale pinks and yellows.

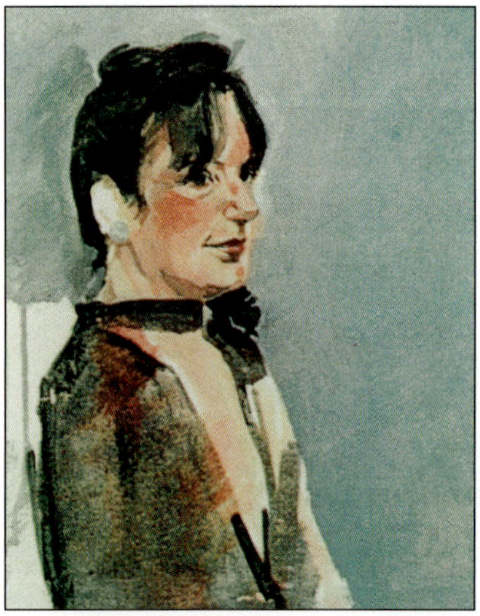

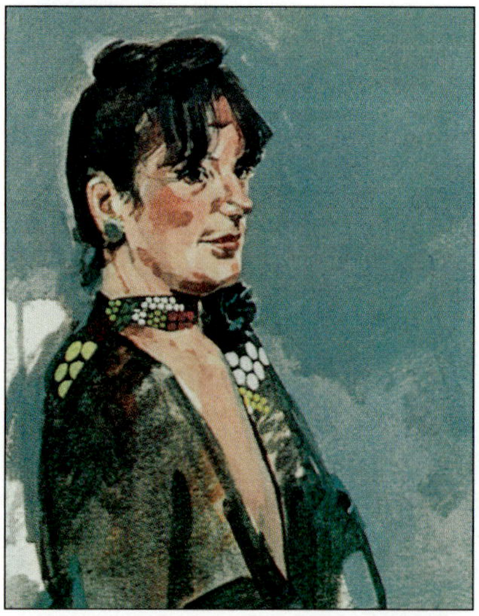

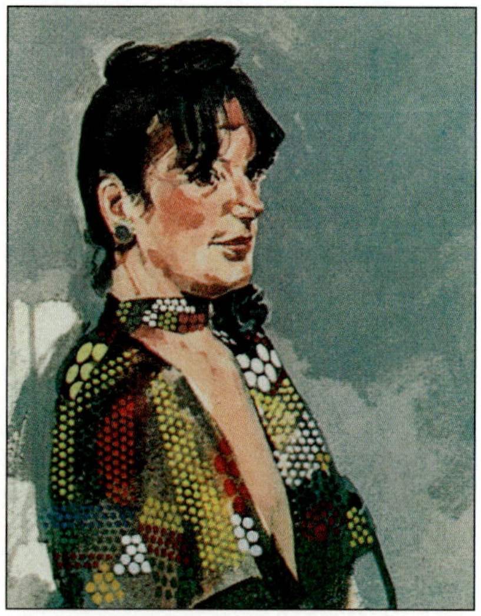

4 Lay in the background color with a No. 6 brush and apply a thin wash of black. Adjust the contours of the figure with a smaller brush.

5 Start to paint the pattern details on the dress using vivid colors. Draw the tiny shapes with the point of a brush, keeping the color thick and opaque.

6 Use a stencil to apply small pattern areas. Angle the dots to describe the directions of the form. Combine this with larger shapes painted by hand.

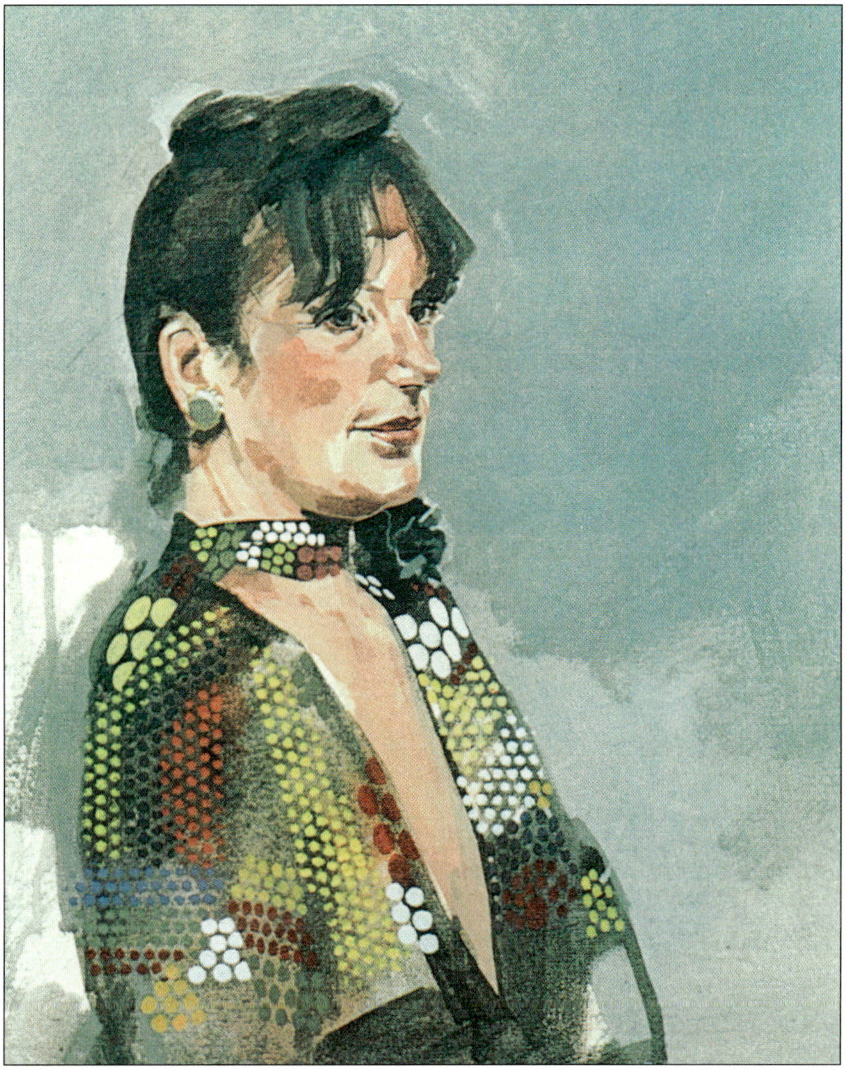

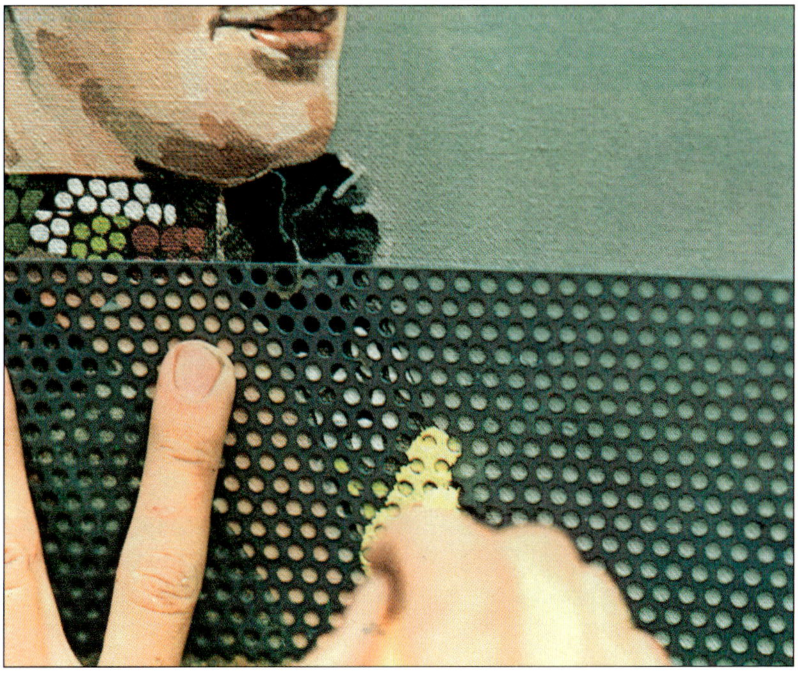

Using a stencil, the artist blocks in dots of yellow over the dry paint surface. These dots are then modified by further applications of color to vary their shape and size.

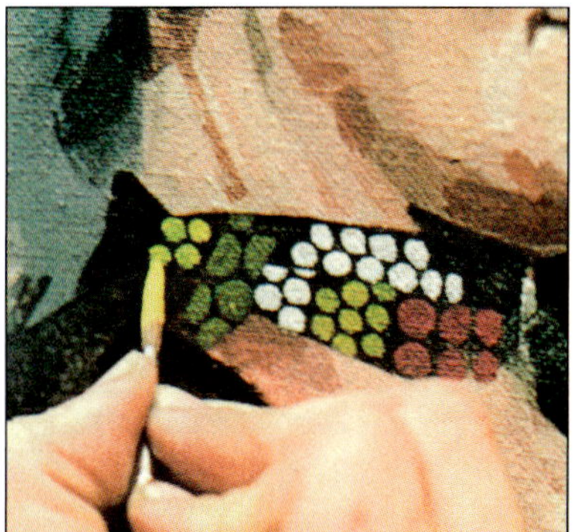

Portrait in Pastel

There is a long history of pastel portrait drawing and some of these drawings, with their finished surface of subtly blended color, are nearly indistinguishable from an oil painting. In fact, the term "pastel painting" has become as common as "pastel drawing."

While the early pastellists most likely spent as much time on their work as a painter would on an elaborate portrait, contemporary artists have developed techniques of drawing which are flexible and less time-consuming than these early drawing methods.

The basic structure of this drawing is built upon woven lines and hatched blocks of tone using a limited range of color. Once the fundamental shapes and tones are established, the subject is rendered with layers of bright color.

Pastel is powdery and difficult to work with if the surface becomes too intensely covered. Therefore it is worthwhile to spray the drawing with fixative frequently to keep the color fresh and stable.

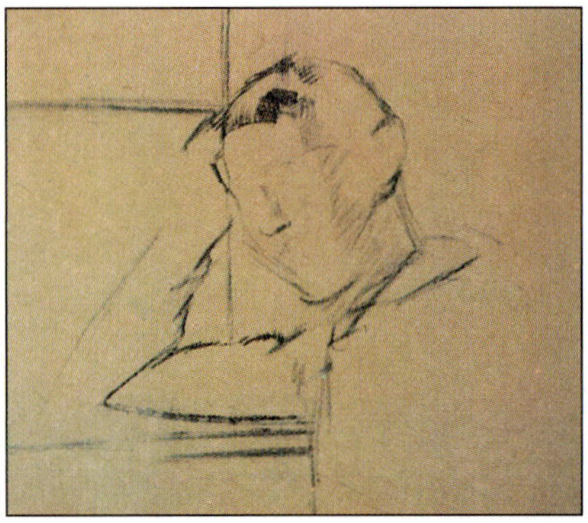

1 Draw up the basic shapes of the image in Prussian blue, sketching in rough outlines and a brief indication of tones.

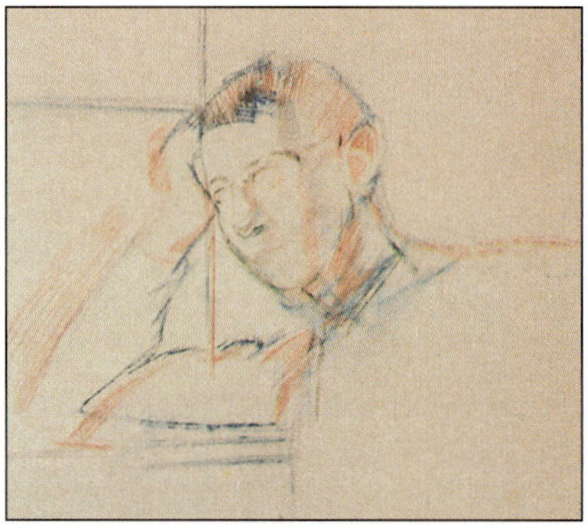

2 Build up the linear and tonal structure with Venetian red, developing the loose modeling of the forms. Strengthen the drawing with fine black lines.

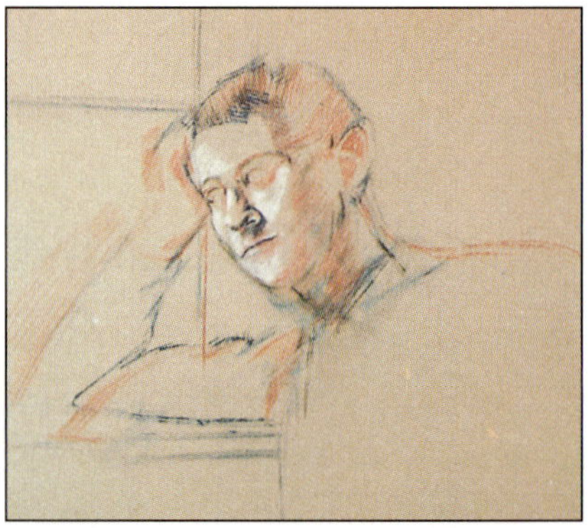

3 Refine details of the features with strong lines of dark blue and flesh out the face with solid blocks of white and red.

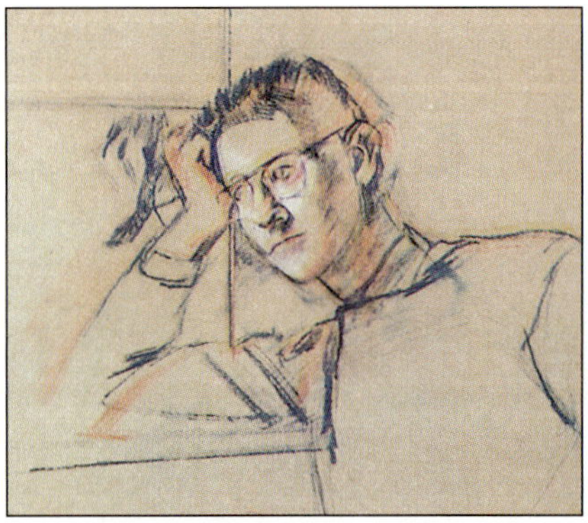

4 Spray the work with fixative and let it dry. Draw into the figure with blue and black correcting the outlines and adding extra details in line and tone.

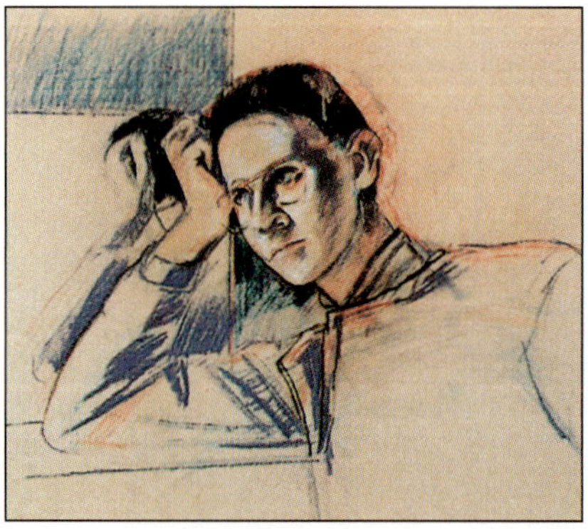

5 Block in light tones in the face with pink and pale blue. Lay in broad areas of dark tone with black and Prussian blue, working out from the figure.

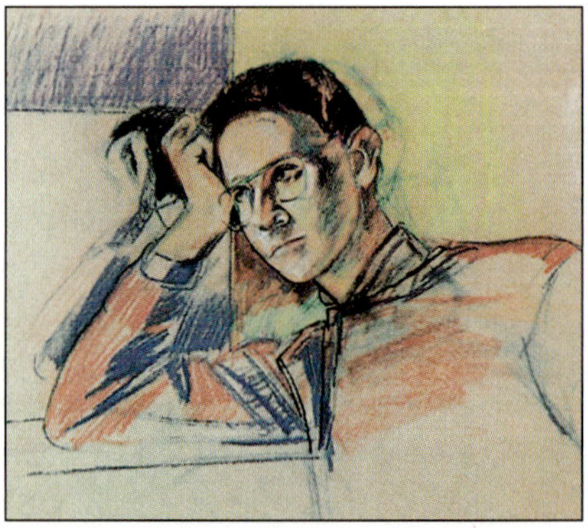

6 Develop the intensity of color, using strong, bright hues to lift the overall tone. Link vivid yellow highlights on the face with the same color in the background.

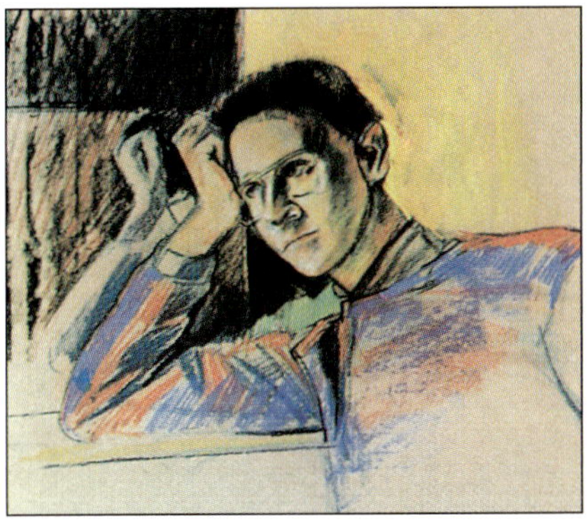

7 Lay in dark background tones to emphasize the form of the figure. Overlay and blend the colors to mix the tones, working over the whole image.

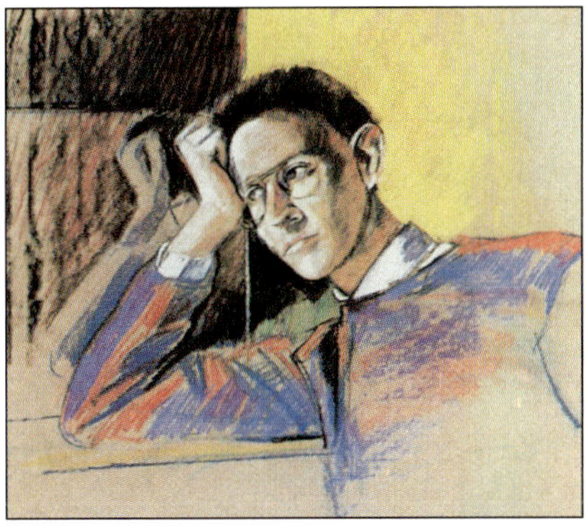

8 Bring out the form with strong white highlights. Apply the pastel thickly and blend the color softly with a dry brush. Strengthen light tones in the background.

The finished portrait

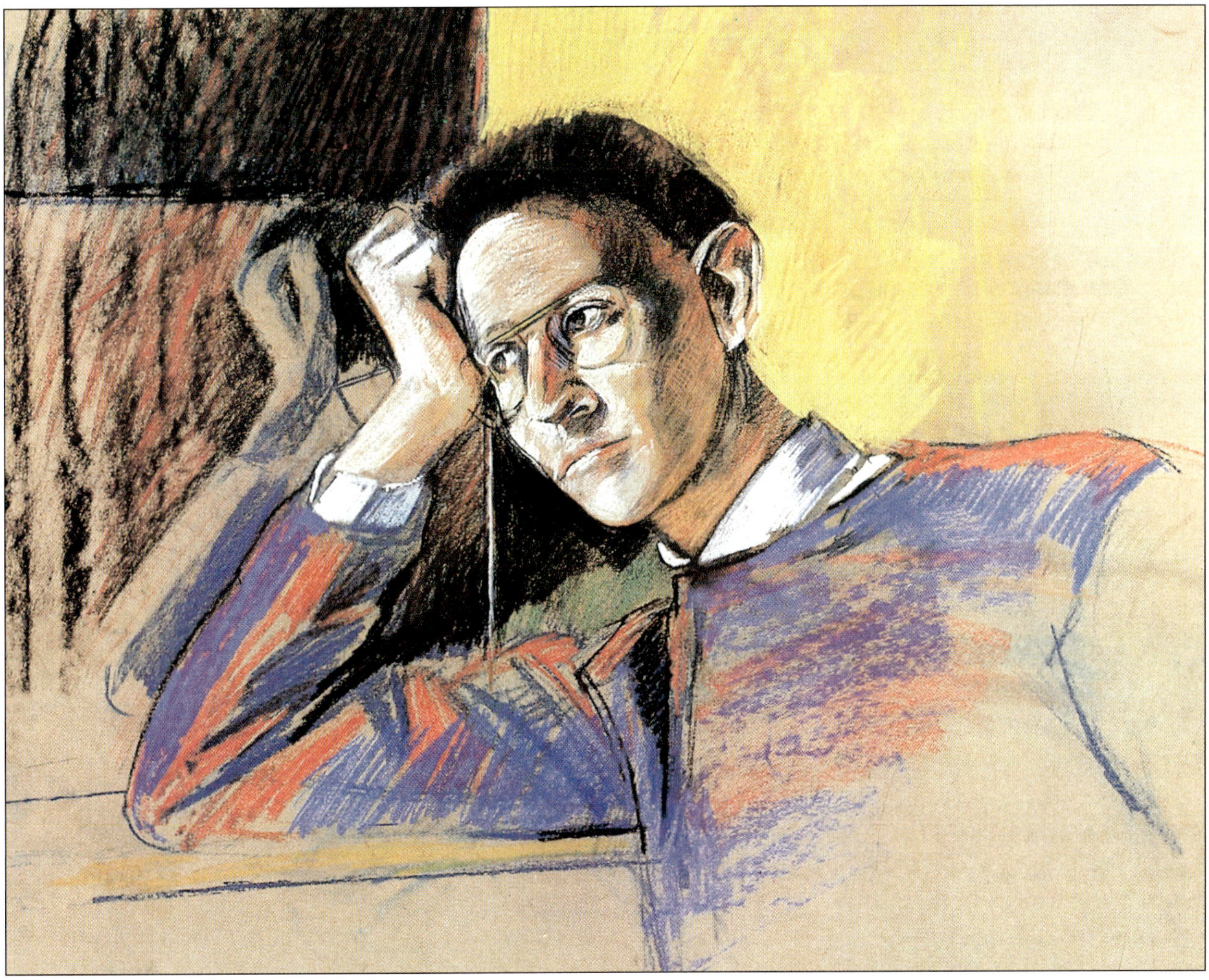

Portrait in Watercolor

In this painting, thin, transparent layers of watercolor have been laid one on top of another giving the flesh a truly "flesh-like" feeling and texture. Few other painting media are capable of this effect.

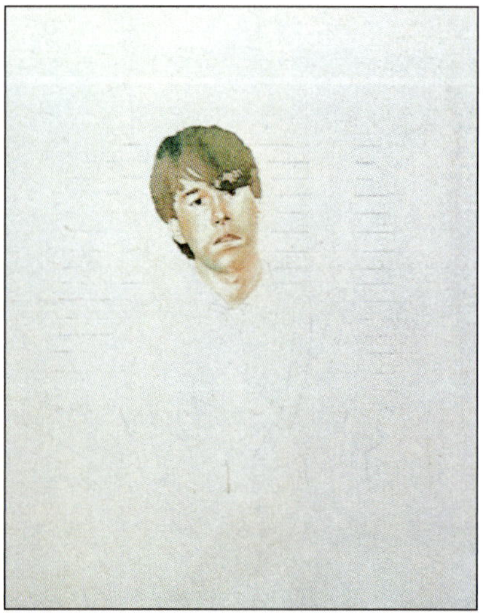

1 Begin by putting in the mid and shadow tones with a thin wash of burnt sienna and green. With a small sable brush and pure umber, add eye details.

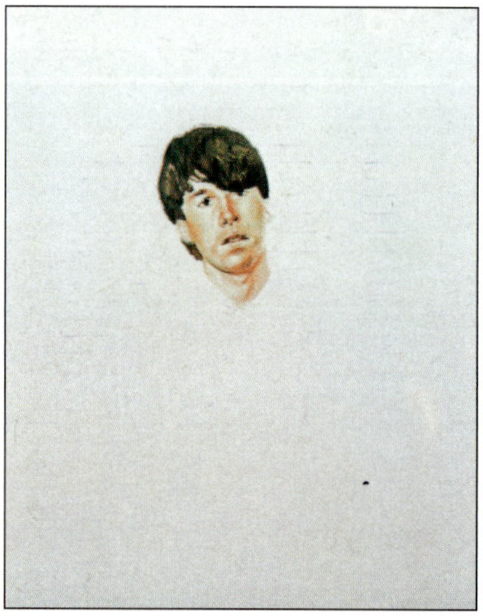

2 Continue with dark details of the eyes, nose, and mouth. If the paint becomes too wet, blot with a tissue and then rework.

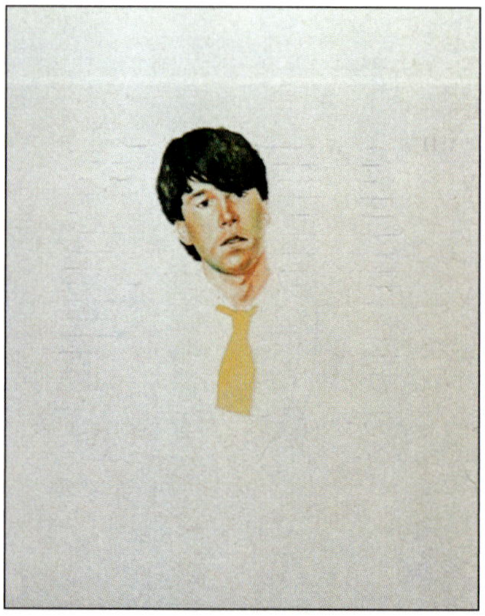

3 Apply a thin wash of yellow ocher over the face and work wet-into-wet with a light wash of green in the shadow area.

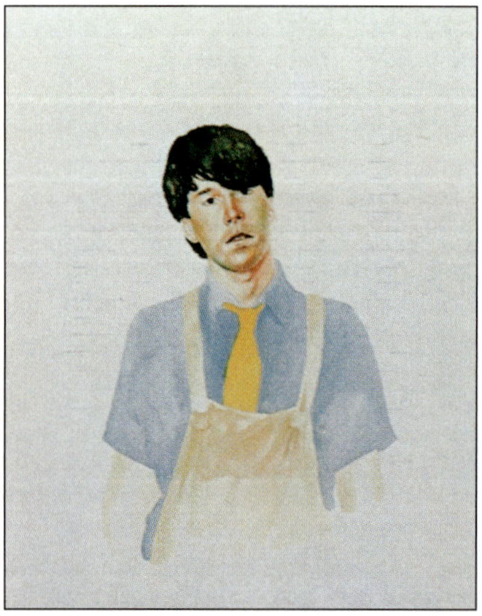

4 Block in the shirt with a thin wash of ultramarine blue. Carry yellow ocher tone into pants leaving white of paper for highlight areas.

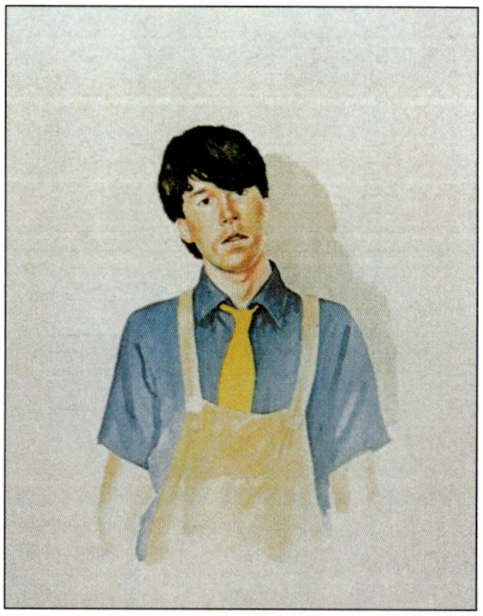

5 Darken hair color with burnt umber and a fine brush.

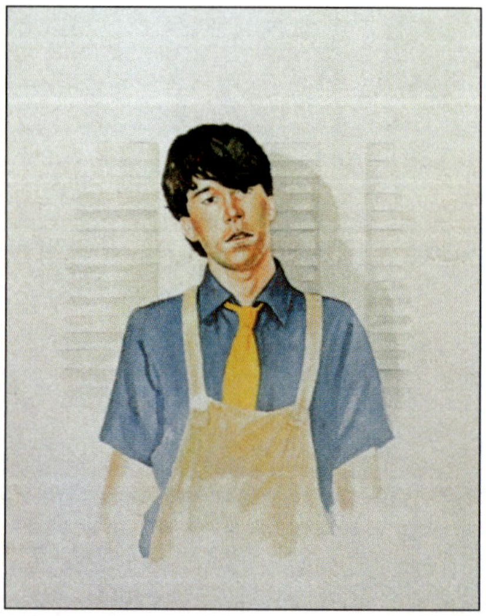

6 With red pencil, work into the face with very light, diagonal strokes, heightening warm areas. With a gray pencil, strengthen horizontal lines of door.

Just as there are countless possible styles and approaches in watercolor, there is no limit on subject matter. The medium is perhaps most frequently used for landscape and flowers. But, as this painting shows, it also can be wonderfully expressive for portraits and figure work. Here the artist has surrounded the figure with almost empty space to draw the observer's eye into the figure.

The only criterion for portraiture is that the painting looks like the person. You don't have to pose someone carefully and paint every detail of their face to achieve a likeness – you can often depict a person very accurately without painting their face at all. When you see someone you know from too far away to pick our facial features, you will still recognize that person – you register the overall shape of the face and body, and perhaps a particular way of walking. These characteristics are just as important as eyes, noses, and mouths.

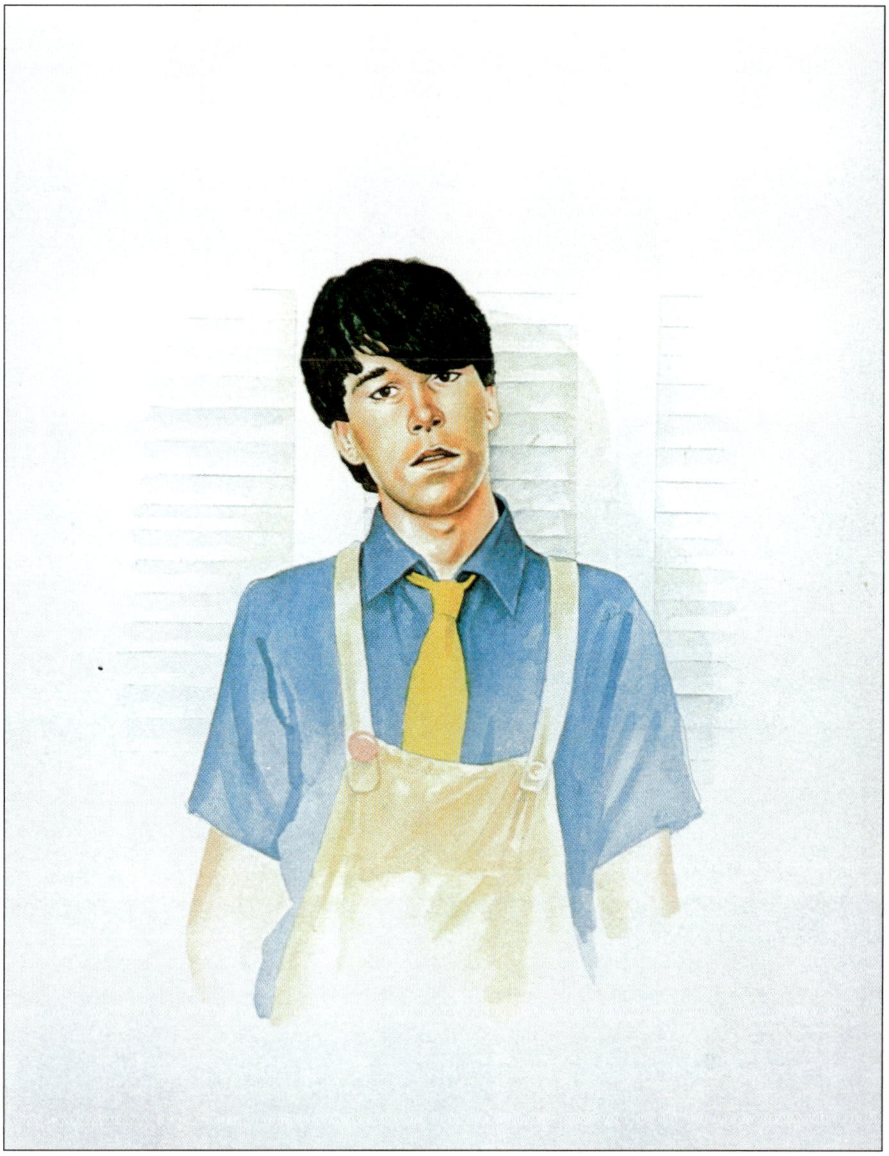

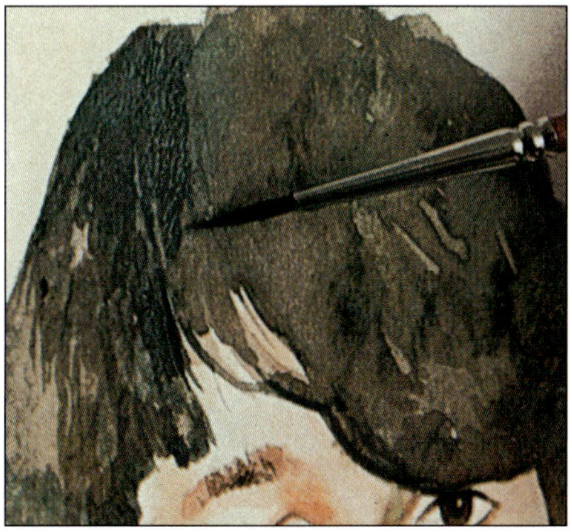

The entire painting progresses from light to dark. Here the artist is putting another wash of color over the hair to create a darker tone.

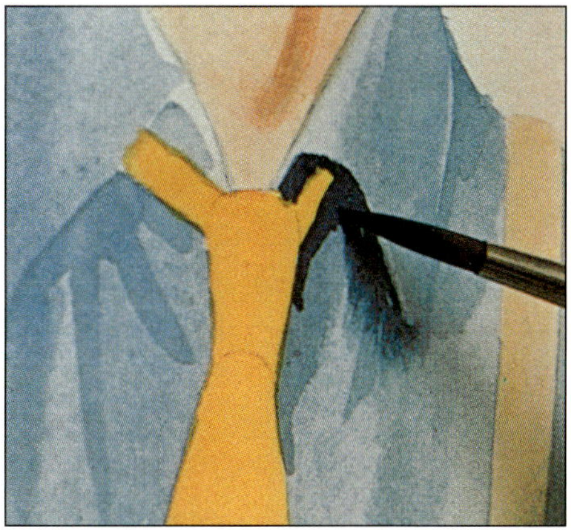

Using a strong blue and small sable brush, shadow areas are created in the shirt. Notice how the paint naturally bleeds into the damp surface, creating a gradated tone.

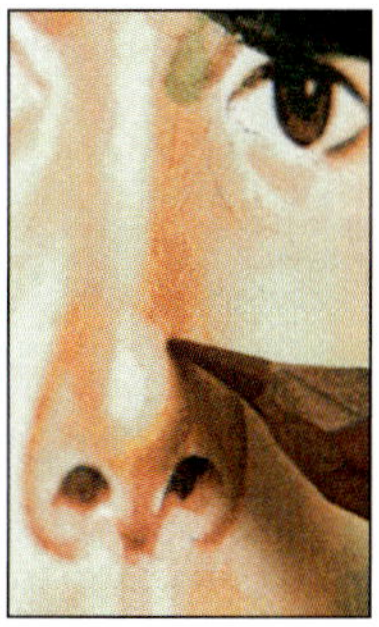

Once the paint surface is thoroughly dry, the artist works back into the face and detail areas with colored pencil, strengthening outlines and shadow areas with light hatching strokes.

Portrait in Pencil

This picture is a good example of the effective use of colored pencils in portraiture, especially when combined with the color of the clean white surface.

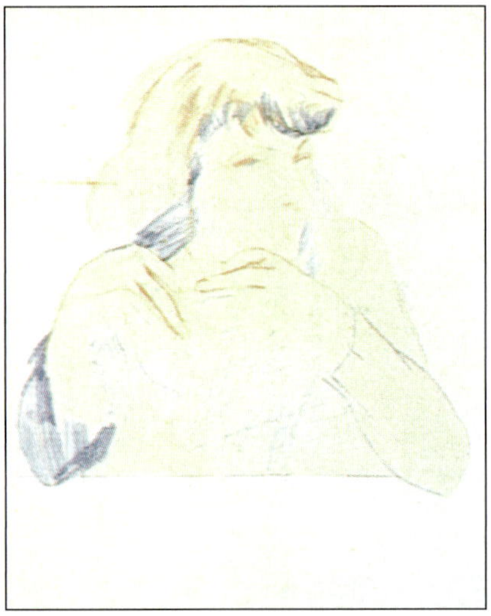

1 Sketch in the outline of the face in raw umber. Use ultramarine blue for shadows and hair and very light strokes of the same color in the blouse.

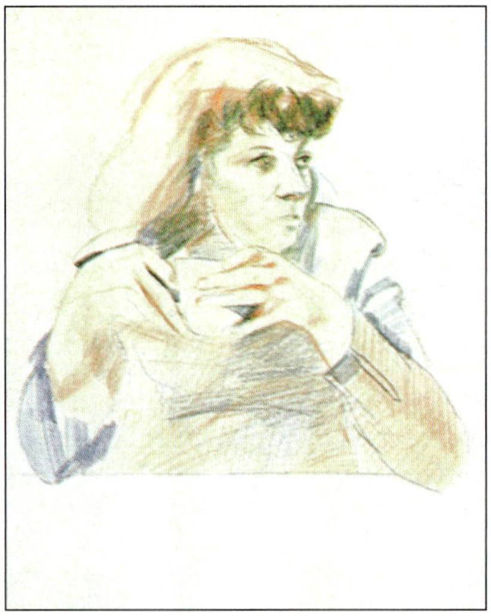

2 With pale green, begin to define shadow areas of the face with very light hatching and crosshatching. With dark blue, put in the eye details.

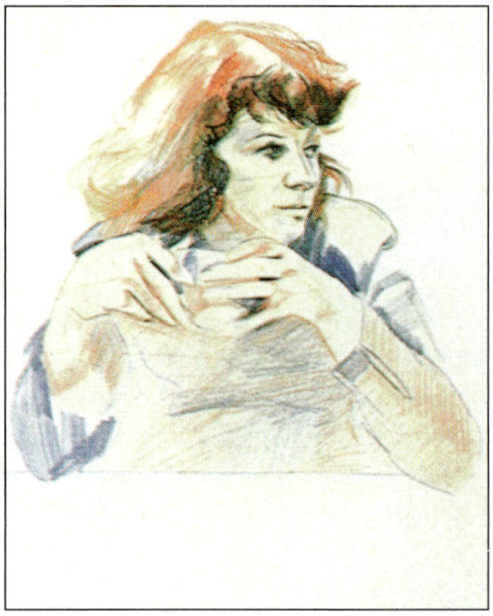

3 With red and yellow, put in loose strokes to define hair tone. Strengthen outlines of face with ultramarine blue. Put in dark shadow area to the right of the face.

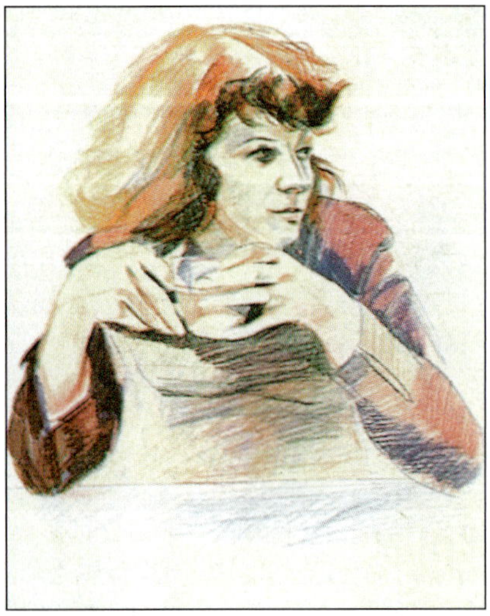

4 Work into the hair with directional strokes of red. Overlay light strokes of blue and red in the blouse with loose, scratching strokes.

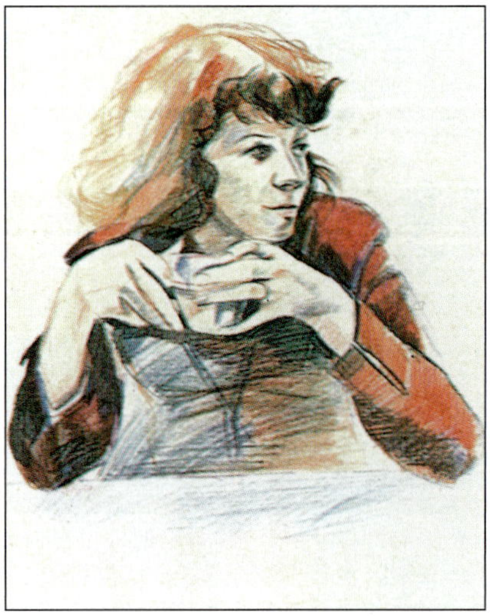

5 Overlay magenta area with red. Create stronger shadow areas with ultramarine blue.

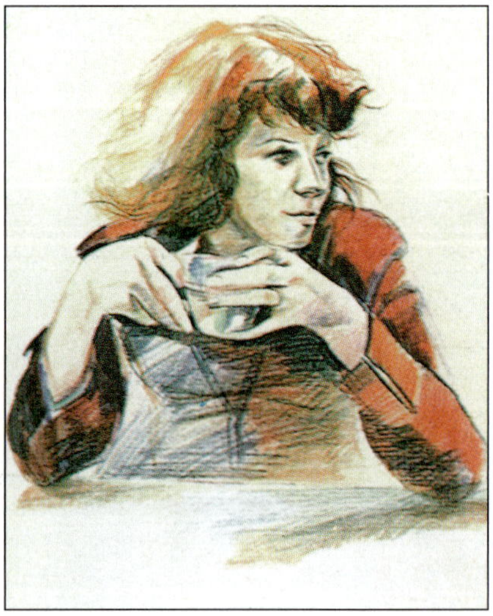

6 Work back into hair with burnt umber. Use pale green to put in highlights in the cup.

RIGHT: This lively portrait has been drawn in brown ink with a fine brush before some touches of watercolor were added. The artist has seized on what he considered important – the wild hair, the well-shaped nose, the glasses, and ears – and recorded these rapidly. The head is hatched in with a few almost vertical strokes in a similar treatment to that used for the hair. In a few free lines, the striped shirt, waistcoat, and suit were indicated and touches of watercolor wash incorporated into the drawing to give color to the features and emphasize the nose.

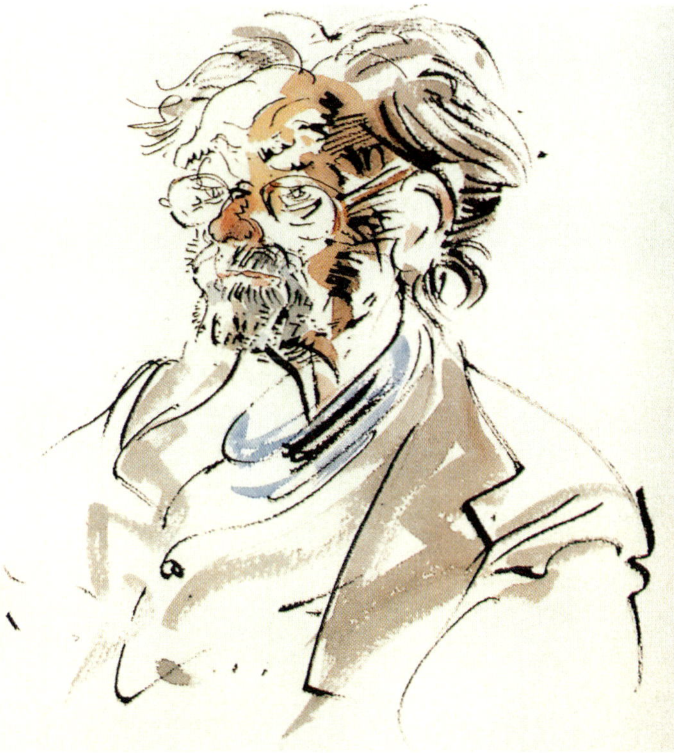

BELOW: A sense of liveliness was imported to this transfer by the use of colored pencil to add light shading and to accentuate the eyes, nose, and mouth. The transfer was made by applying cellulose thinners over a photograph in a color magazine to soften the printing ink. The photograph was then placed face down on a piece of paper and the back rubbed hard with a finger, transferring the image. The result is a softer version of the original magazine picture and gives gently blended tones.

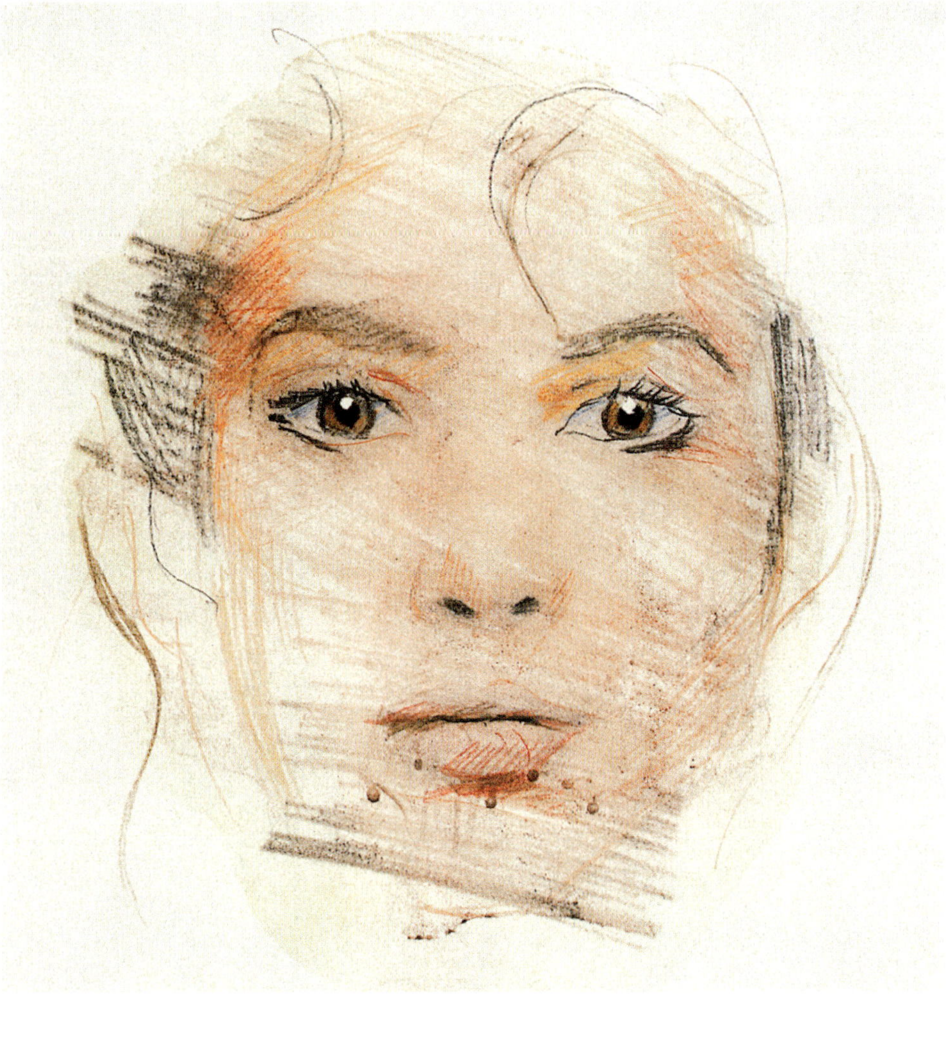

CHARACTER STUDIES

A descriptive sense of character in a portrait is conveyed in the way you select and handle specific details. This does not mean that the style of your drawing has to be detailed and realistic – you can capture the essence of a person with a very simple contour, if it is precisely seen and sensitively drawn. The character of the subject is expressed not only in the face but in particular poses or gestures, and you may choose to feature such aspects in your drawing. You can also use clothing and props that explain something about the person's lifestyle or occupation.

The subject's age is an important aspect of a character study, and there are various physical elements you can identify that suggest different stages of life, such as the angle of head and shoulders, the structure of the face and positioning of the features, and the colors and textures of skin and hair.

Expressive Portraits

Ideally, a portrait expresses something about the sitter as well as making a visual record of the individual.

There are various ways of endowing a portrait with expressive character, deriving from both the composition of the drawing and the techniques you apply.

In selecting a pose, you need to decide on the angle of view – showing a person full-face tends to create a confrontational aspect, while a slightly turned pose can seem mysterious or mischievous. You can focus on face and head only, or include part or all of the body, so that the subject's physical shape and posture contribute to the mood of the image.

Different approaches to tone and color can vary the expressive qualities of the rendering. A tonal study gives emphasis to the modeling of form and features. Colors need not be strictly realistic; to enhance the impact of the portrait you can play up faint nuances, such as warm lights and cool shadows in skin tones, or exaggerate the contrasts of hue and tone to construct a more colorful interpretation.

The kind of marks you make also contribute to an individualist portrait; soft shading and subtle gradations can be organized in ways that create a photographically realistic effect; or you can use more vigorous techniques such as hatching and linear marks to emphasize both structural and surface characteristics.

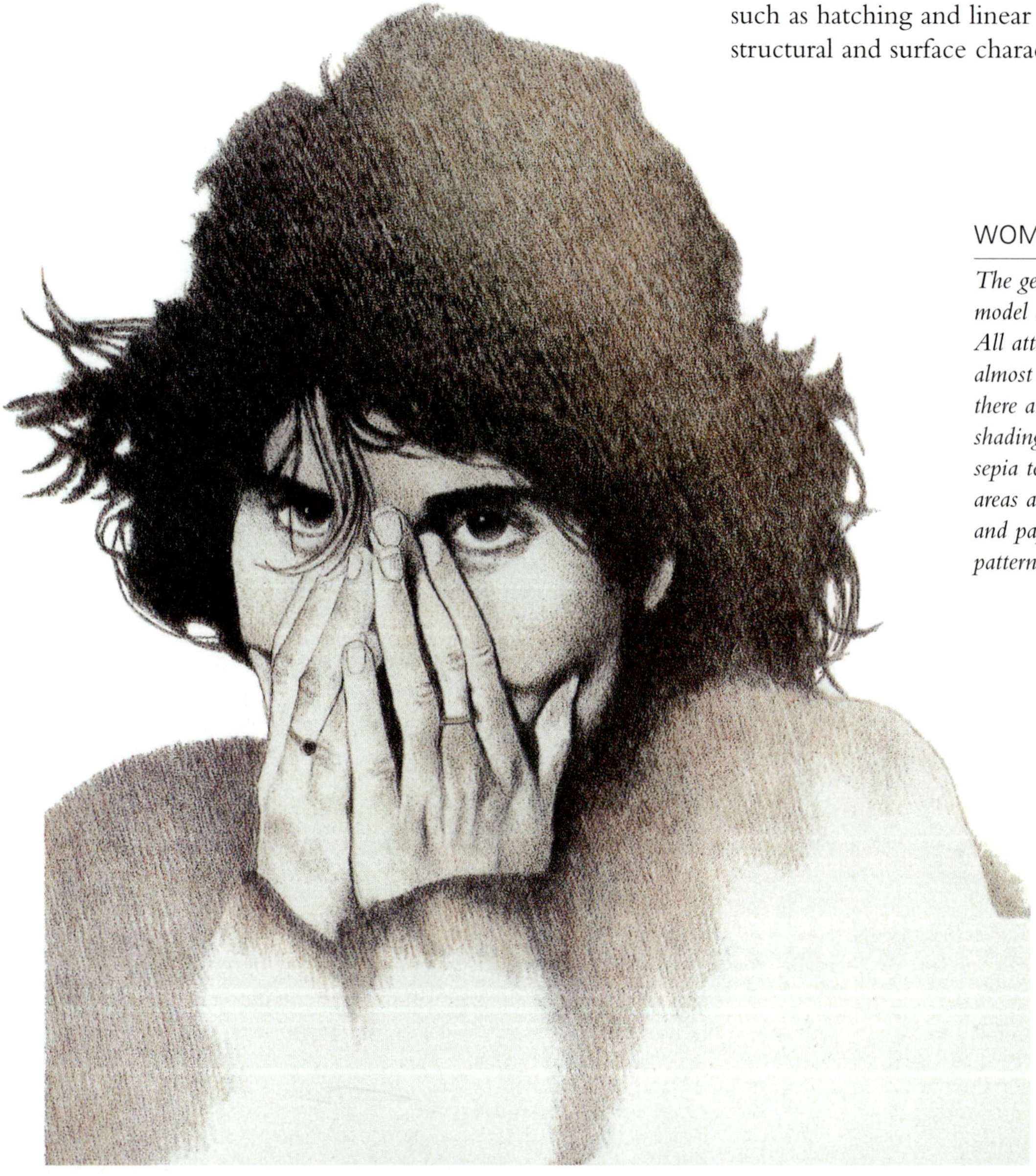

WOMAN by David Melling

The gesture and facial expression of the model are the true subjects of this portrait. All attention is drawn to them by the almost monochromatic tonal treatment, but there are subtle hints of color in the blended shading, which ranges from a dark, neutral sepia to warm red-brown. Although the color areas are cohesive, the direction of strokes and paper texture give a distinct grain pattern to the shading.

SOLDIER by Linda Kitson

Both the colors and the surface qualities of the drawing contribute to a good-natured portrait, capturing the particular shapes of the face and individual features in an expressive manner. The grainy lines of soft waxy pencils are contrasted with solid areas of chalky color and brief patches of watercolor wash.

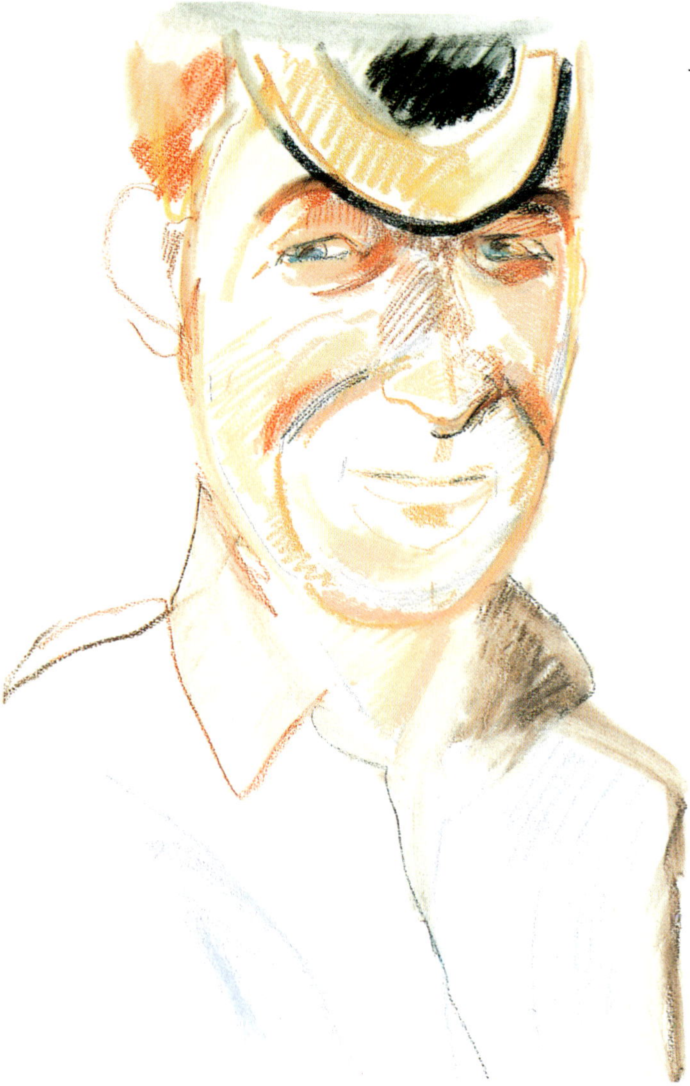

VETERINARIAN by John Townsend

The character of this study is deliberately lighthearted, each element of the composition selected to identify the subject and his vocation. The vet's mischievous, knowing look is played off against the cat's apprehensive pose and the joke is underlined by the way the artist's technique gives an illustrative, naturalistic finish to the rendering. The commentary is all conveyed through the image.

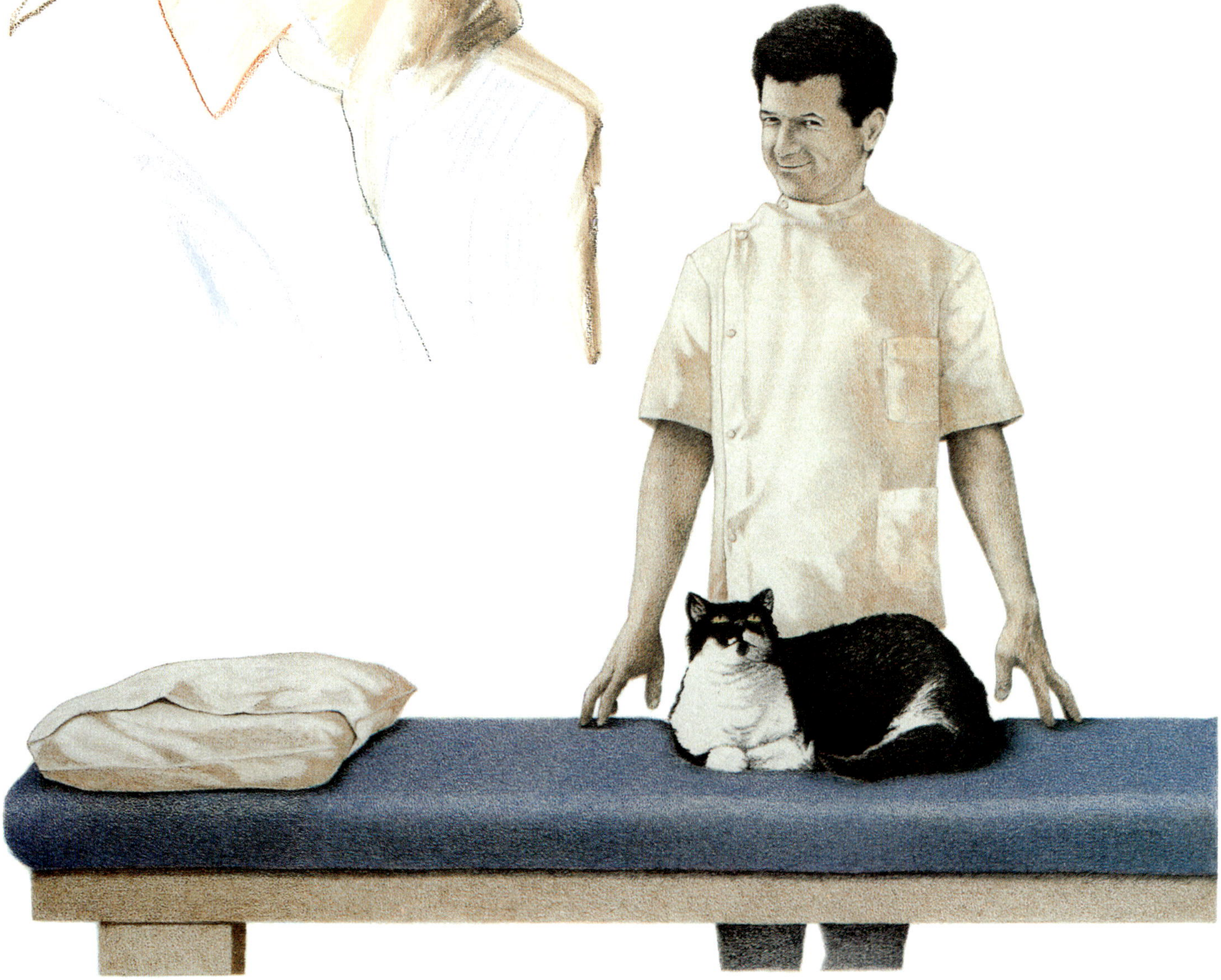

Self-Portraits

If you are looking for a convenient model for a portrait painting – someone who is inexpensive, reliable, and available at times that suit you – then there is no better subject than yourself. Painting a self-portrait has the added advantage that you don't have to worry about flattering your sitter!

Acrylic paints are an especially suitable medium for self-portraits. Their consistency can be varied to suit a whole range of styles, from loose and impressionistic to tight and realistic, depending on the mood you wish to convey.

Strangely, it is usually difficult to "see" ourselves properly. You may think you know your own face extremely well, but when it comes to painting a portrait it is essential to study your features as if for the very first time. If necessary, make a series of sketches before you begin the actual painting.

When posing for a photograph, many of us tend to look awkward and self-conscious. The same thing can happen with a self-portrait, so try to relax in front of the mirror and select a comfortable pose. It is a good idea to mark the position of the easel, the mirror, and your feet so that when you come back to the painting you will be able to take up the position again.

For this self-portrait the artist chose an unusual but effective composition in which his own image is cropped off at the corner.

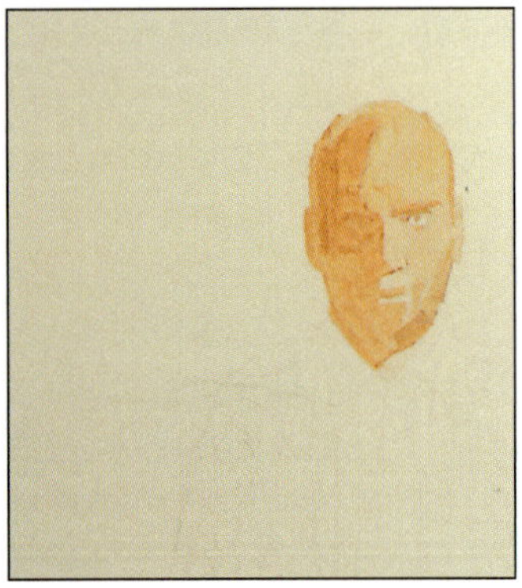

1 The artist begins by making an outline drawing of himself on the canvas, using a B pencil. He then blocks in the main light and shadow areas on the face with broad strokes of burnt sienna, diluted with water for light areas.

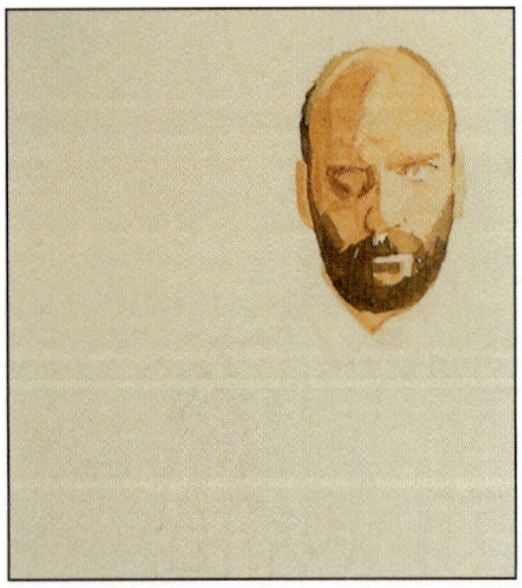

2 Now the dark tones of the hair, beard, and mustache are put in with burnt sienna darkened with cobalt blue.

3 This close-up reveals how the artist is building up the broad masses and planes of the face with thin washes of color which indicate the light, medium, and dark tones.

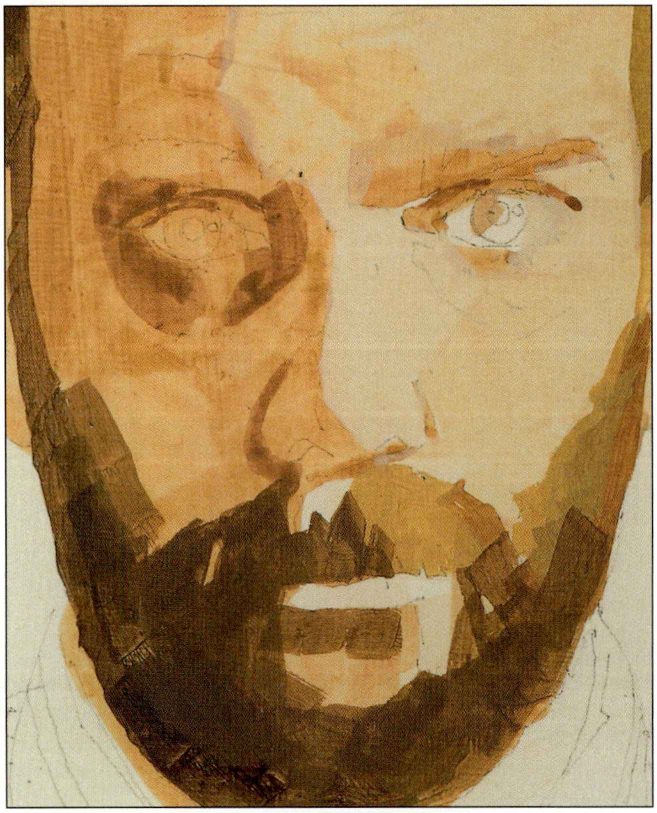

4 The artist continues to model the face using various tones of earth colors such as burnt sienna, burnt umber, Turner's yellow, brilliant orange, and raw sienna. The eyes are painted with Payne's gray and black, and the mouth with red ocher.

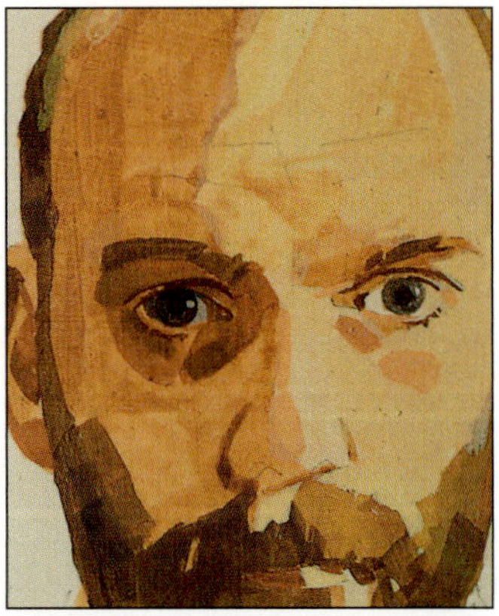

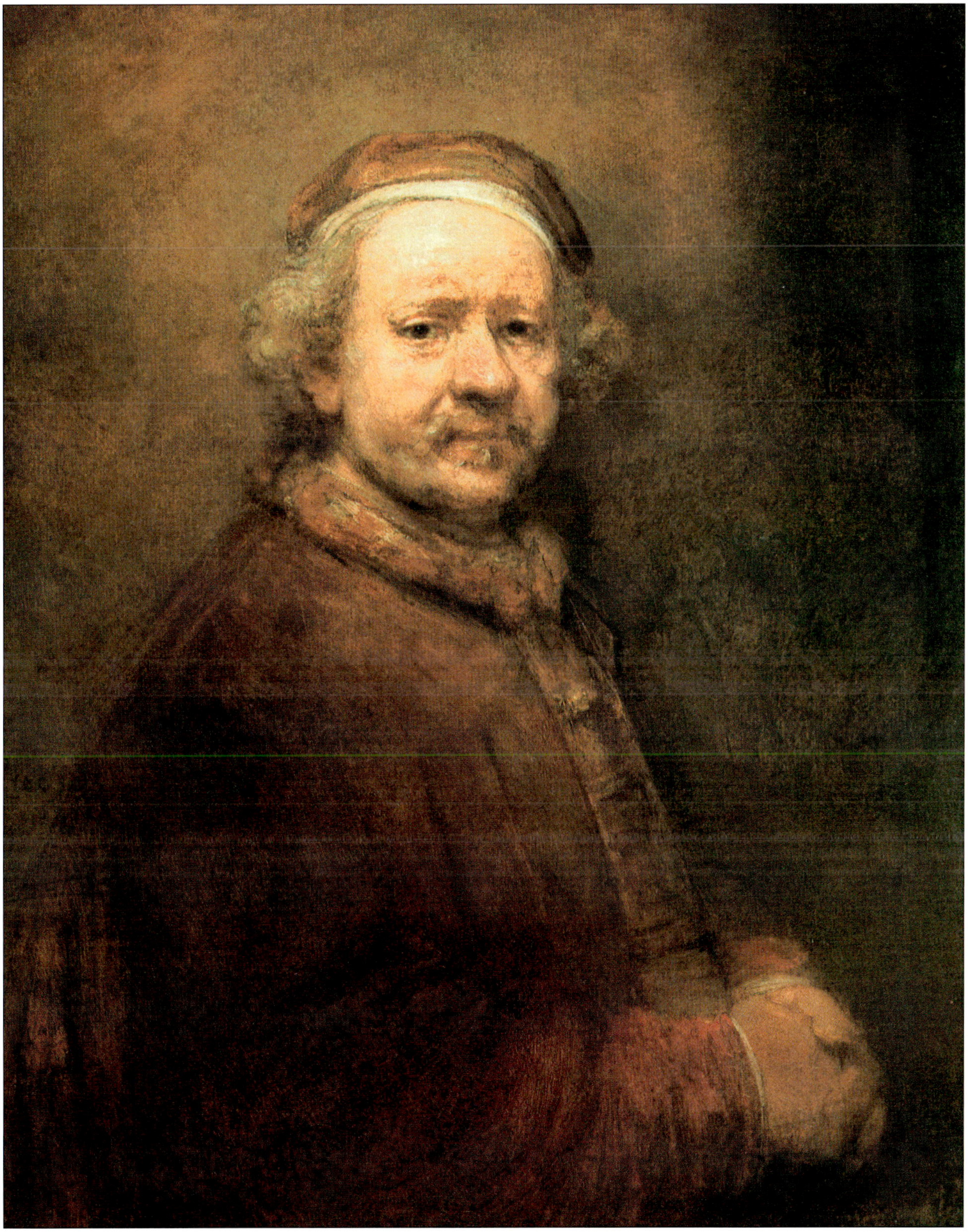

SELF-PORTRAIT by Rembrandt van Rijn

Rembrandt's series of self-portraits are renowned for their technical skill and ability to depict a somber and intensive atmosphere.

Working from a Photo

Photographs should be used with caution, and treated as aids to painting rather than models to copy. Straight copies of photographs can look very dull, missing the character of the person.

Photographs are generally used as a backup, with the initial stages of the painting done from life. The photographs can then be used for details, such as hands and clothing, with perhaps another live sitting for the final stage.

The great advantage of photographs is that they can capture fleeting moments and impressions. The disadvantage is that they do not actually tell the truth: the camera distorts perspective, flattens color, and fudges detail. When you want a clear visual description of some small, but vital part of the subject, you find only a vague blur. A sketch, even a less than brilliant one, would probably have been more useful, because you would have been forced to look hard at the subject and thus have gained more understanding of it.

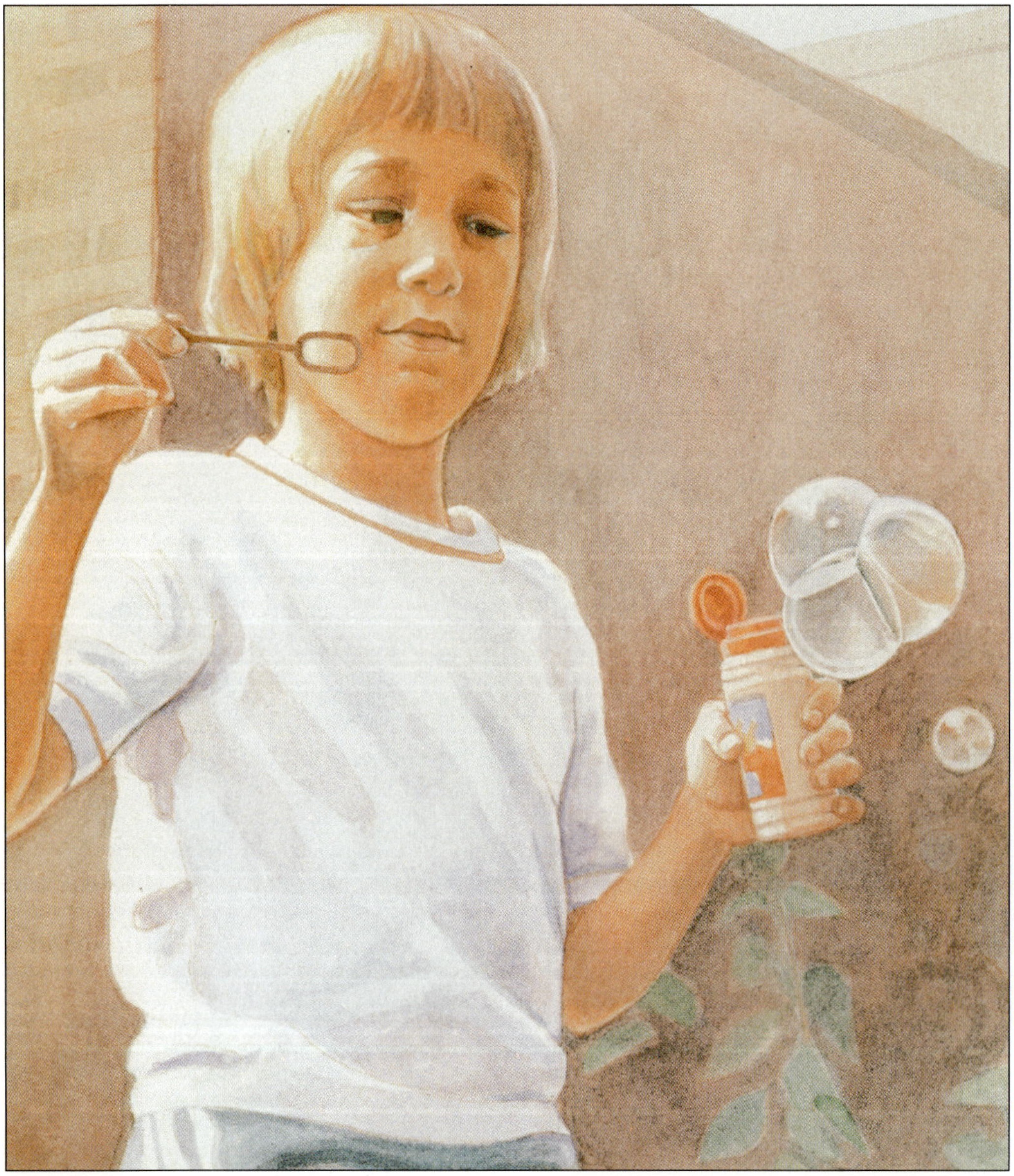

BLOWING BUBBLES
by Elaine Mills

The artist wished to capture the child in movement, not in a stiff, artificial-looking pose. A scaled-up drawing made from the photograph was transferred to the painting surface by means of iron-oxide paper. The painting itself was built up in a series of thin washes, the colors kept light and clean throughout.

A color photograph rather than a live subject was used for this painting, but the information supplied was used only for the groundwork of the painting and the end result is not a straightforward copy. As detailed before, photographs tend to flatten subtleties of tone and color, so it is necessary to add to the image by strengthening or even exaggerating certain elements.

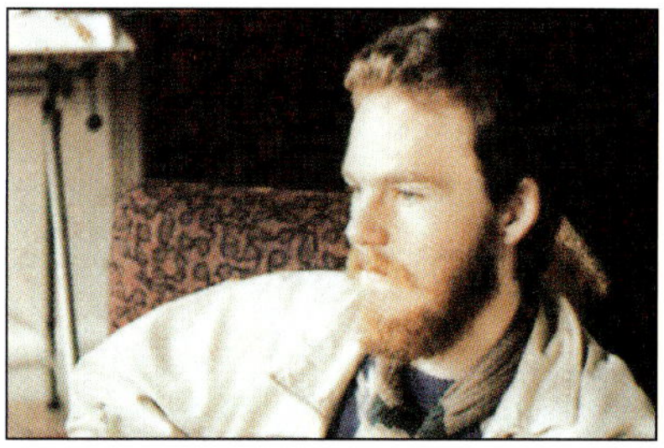

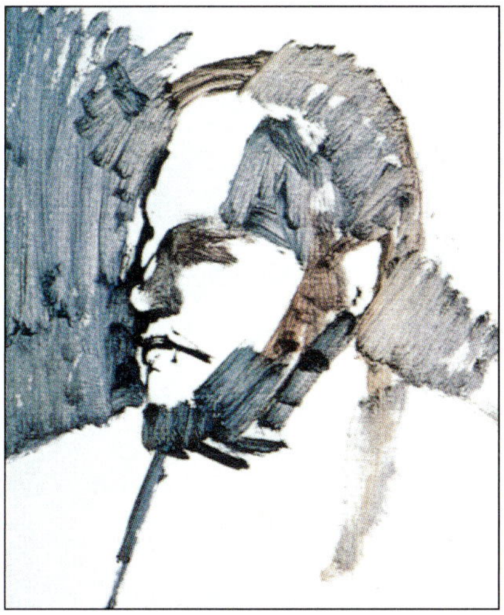

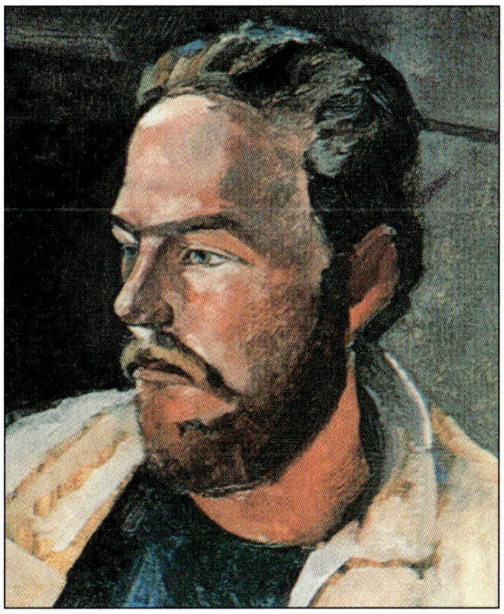

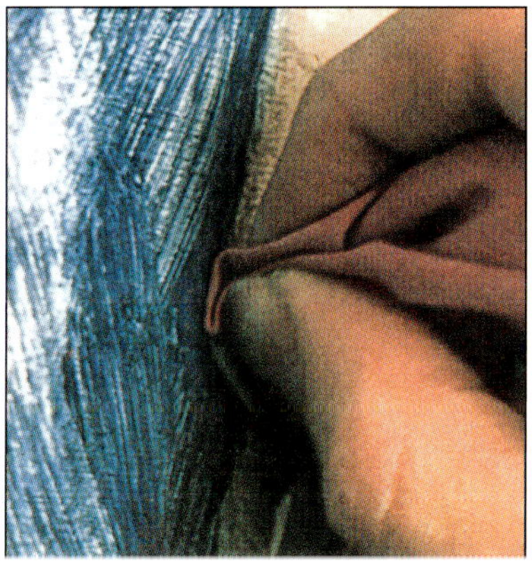

While the paint is still wet, the artist cleans up the facial area where background color has run over with a small piece of rag and turpentine.

RIGHT: *If the paint surfaces becomes too wet to work on, a piece of newspaper or absorbent toweling can be laid over it, lightly pressed and lifted off. Be sure not to press too hard or to move the paper on the surface.*

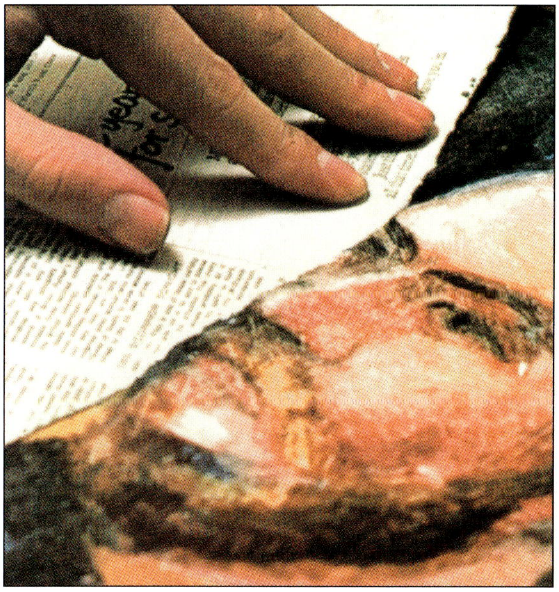

PRACTICAL HINTS

Photographs provide a very useful source of reference for portraiture, particularly if the subject is in motion. Blowing Bubbles is an example of a painting done almost entirely from a photograph. It is advisable, even so, to work from life wherever possible, and since a watercolor study is not likely to take as long as an oil, it should not be difficult to persuade people to sit.

Good drawing is essential for human subjects, since a misplaced eye or an ill-drawn hand or foot can completely destroy the harmony of the painting. Never start a painting until you are sure that the drawing is correct; and as you draw, check proportions and measurements constantly.

Before you even begin to draw, compose the picture carefully and give thought to both the background and the lighting. The light will define the head by casting shadows in a certain way, and lighting can also be used to create atmosphere. A head seen against a window will appear almost in silhouette, the colors deep and merging into one another; a front light will give a hard, flat look, while a strong side light, or one from above, will give drama to the subject by producing strong tonal contrasts.

Full-length Portraits

In a full-length portrait the subject's body and clothing provide certain kinds of descriptive detail that reduce the emphasis on facial characteristics as a means of creating a likeness. Typically, the head and face remain the most closely focused element of the image, whereas in other kinds of figure studies the model may be portrayed in an impersonal and anonymous way.

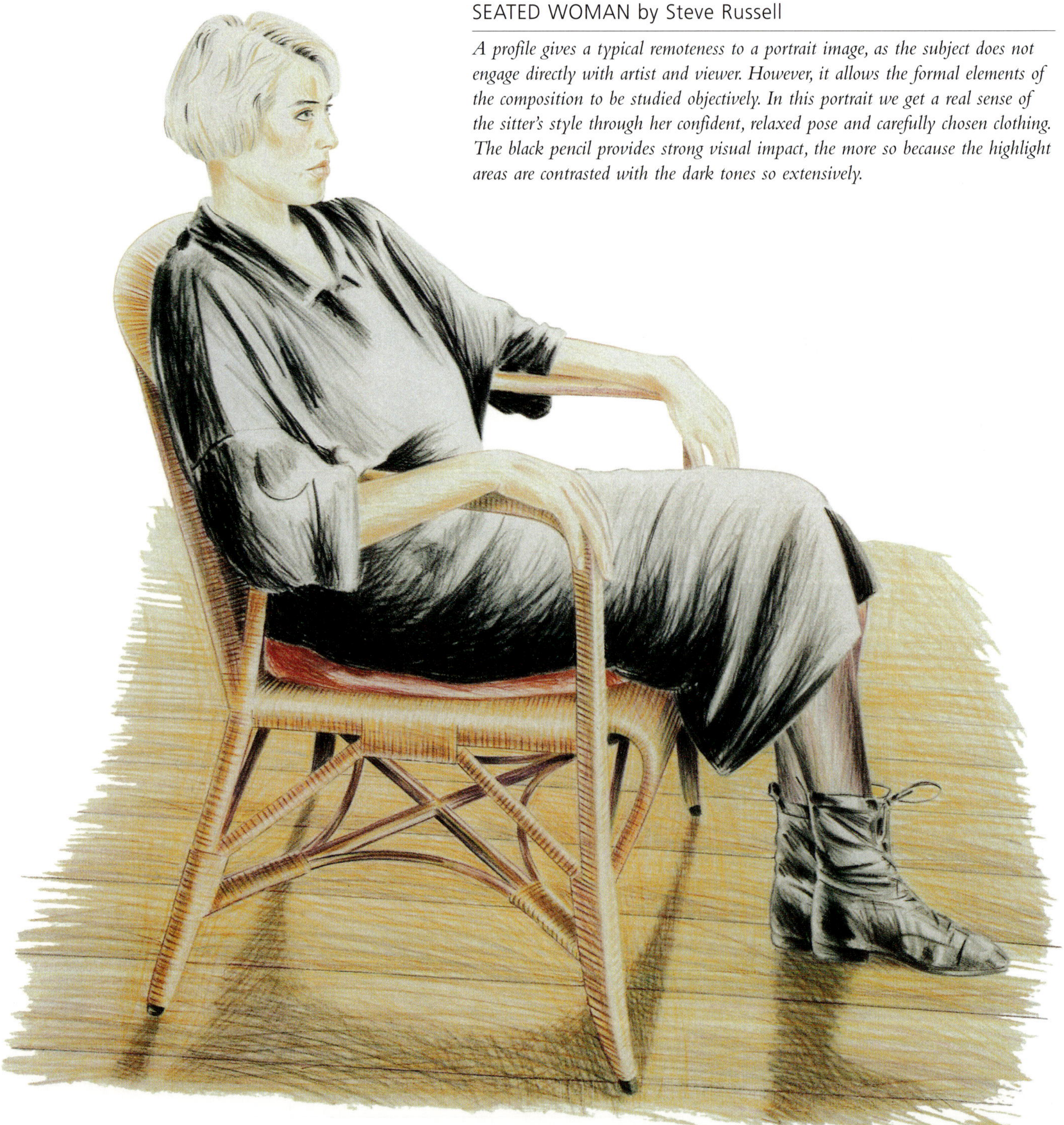

SEATED WOMAN by Steve Russell

A profile gives a typical remoteness to a portrait image, as the subject does not engage directly with artist and viewer. However, it allows the formal elements of the composition to be studied objectively. In this portrait we get a real sense of the sitter's style through her confident, relaxed pose and carefully chosen clothing. The black pencil provides strong visual impact, the more so because the highlight areas are contrasted with the dark tones so extensively.

How to Paint: Landscapes

Whatever the medium used, landscape is among the most popular of all painting subjects. One of the reasons for this is the common belief that it is easier than other subjects. Many who would never attempt a figure painting or flower study turn with relief to country scenes, feeling them to be less exacting and thus more enjoyable. However, a painting will certainly be marred by poor composition or mishandled colors – these things always matter, whatever the subject. The best landscapes are painted by artists who have chosen to paint the land because they love it, and use the full range of their skills to express their responses to it, not by those who choose it as an easy option.

DIRECT OBSERVATION

Another factor that separates the really good from the just-adequate is knowledge, not of painting methods – though this is necessary, too – but the subject itself. This is why most landscape painters work outdoors whenever they can. Sometimes they only make preliminary sketches, but often they will complete whole paintings on-the-spot. Even if you only jot down some rapid color impressions, it is still the best way to get the feel of a landscape.

If you use photographs as a starting point – and many professional artists do take photos as a backup to sketches – restrict yourself to a part of the countryside you know well and have perhaps walked through at different times of the year so that you have absorbed its atmosphere. Nature's effects are transient and cannot be captured by the camera.

COMPOSITION

Nor should you attempt to copy nature itself: painting is about finding pictorial equivalents for the real world. This means that you have to make choices and decide how much to put in or leave out and think about whether you might exaggerate a certain feature in the interest of art. For instance you might emphasize the feeling of space in a wide expanse of countryside by putting in some small figures in the middle distance, or convey the impression of misty light by suppressing detail and treating the whole scene in broad washes.

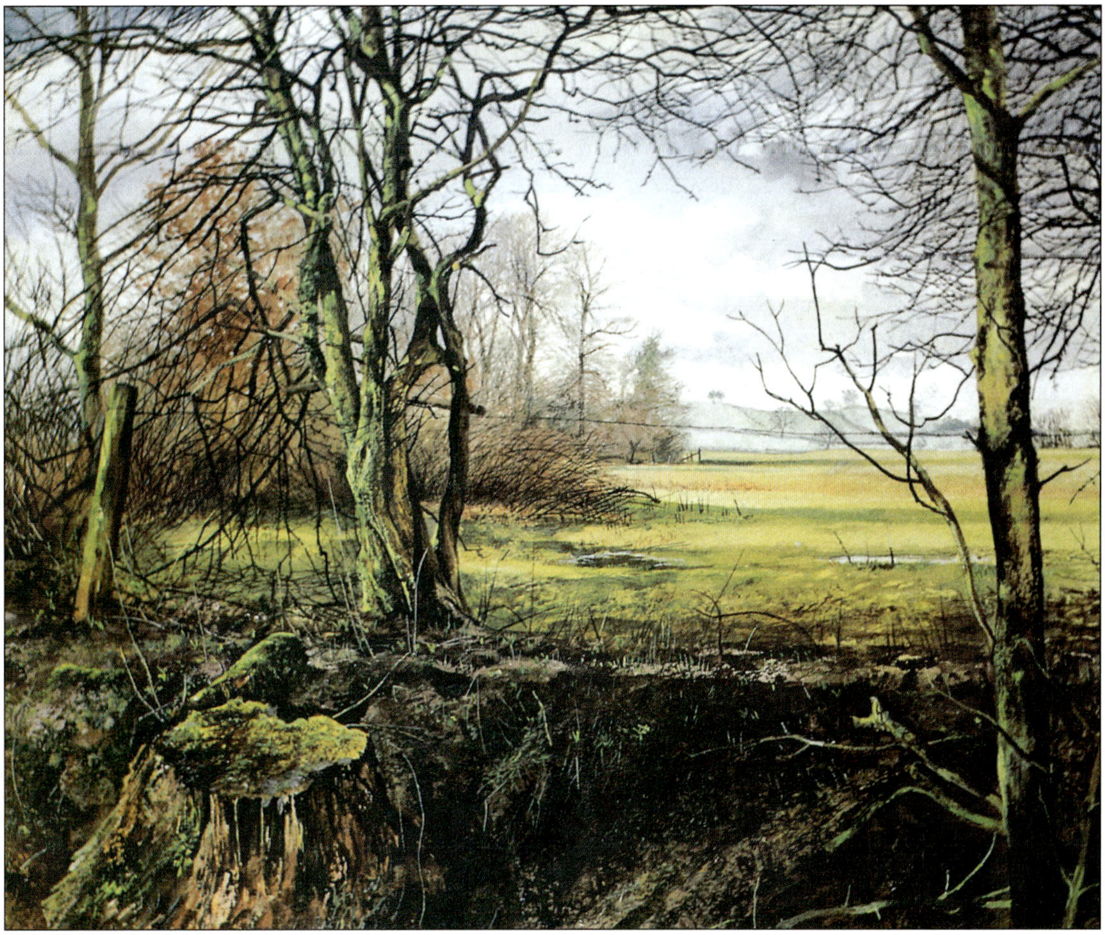

INTRODUCTION

Surprisingly, the landscape *per se* was never taken seriously as a painting subject until the seventeenth century; yet since then it has acquired a wider appeal than any other form of painting, for artists and for people who simply enjoy looking at paintings.

As a source of visual stimulation, the landscape is inexhaustible – and ironically, this is what presents the landscape painter with the first problem: faced with the enormous complexity of shapes, colors, and textures present in nature, it is difficult to decide what to paint. Very often, the solution lies in asking yourself what aspect of nature moves you more than any other. Is it the sky, the rugged texture of coastal or mountain scenery? Or are you fascinated by the play of light on the landscape? Once you've found a subject that elicits an emotional response in you, it will be easier to communicate that response to the viewer.

Ideally, landscapes should be painted on location rather than in the studio or from photographs. The benefits of on-the-spot painting are obvious: standing in the middle of a field or on a riverbank, you are acutely aware of the colors, forms, and textures around you. There is a sense of immediacy, and you are sensitive to the fleeting, often dramatic effects of the light. All this sensory stimulus is important in helping you to produce a painting that is fresh and alive.

Having chosen the scene you wish to paint, the next step is to sit down and calmly analyze it in terms of pictorial design. Nature is bountiful, but a scene that looks breathtaking in reality does not necessarily make a good painting. Trees, rocks, or buildings might be scattered over too wide an area, or might perhaps be too uniform in shape; the sky may be full of small clouds which would compete for attention with the complex shapes on the ground which are the real subject of your painting. Experienced artists know how to spot the potential of such a scene and rearrange the elements within it to suit their compositional requirements. Never feel duty-bound to represent a scene exactly as it is – a camera can do this far more easily. Your aim is to capture a mood, and to present a balanced and harmonious picture. In so doing, you may have to bend reality a little, grouping trees together to form a strong focal point, or eliminating clouds if they threaten to overcrowd your composition.

Similarly the arrangement of lights, darks, and middle tones within the scene is of vital importance. Try to envision the landscape as if it were a black-and-white photograph: does it contain a strong and cohesive pattern of lights and darks, or are the tones scattered and dotted throughout? Once again, you are free to "orchestrate" the tones in order to create a stronger image. For example, if your center of interest is a farmhouse in the middle distance, make sure there is a strong contrast of light and dark at that point: if the building is light in tone, darken the surrounding trees or sky, and vice versa.

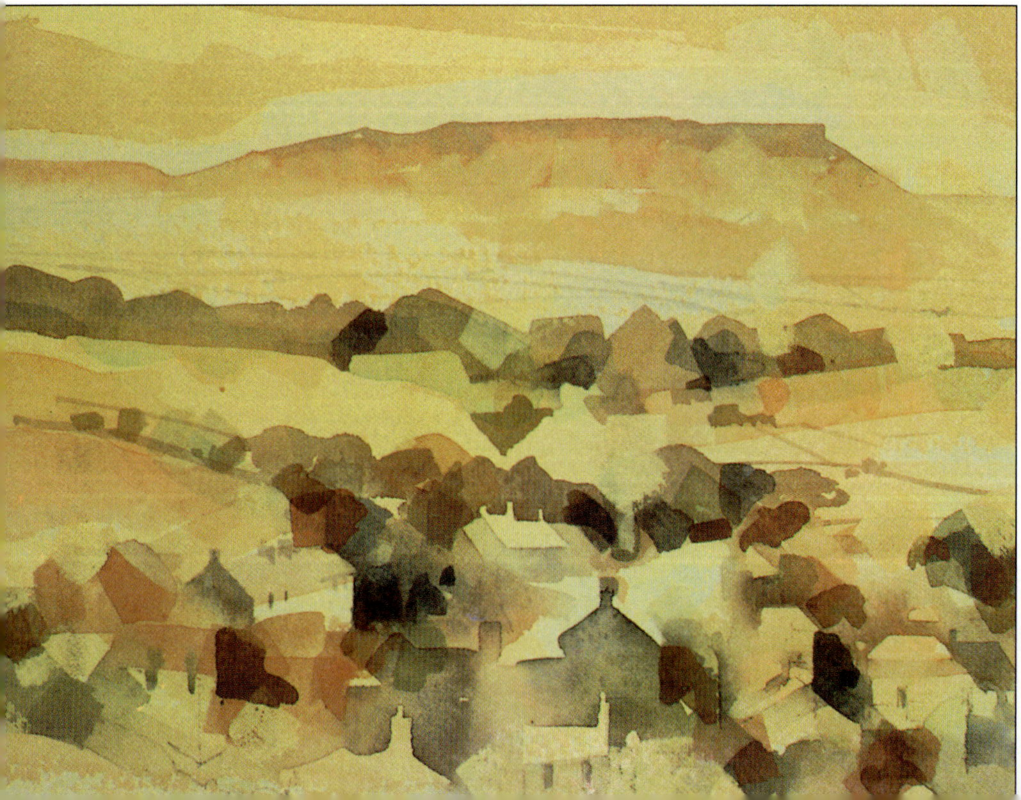

ASKRIGG by Bill Taylor

Patches of color are laid with a flat brush to create this painting of a village nestling in the hills.
A pleasing combination of translucent earth colors overlay each other in an abstracted pattern of almost geometric brushmarks to hint at, rather than describe, the shapes of the houses, roofs, and trees. This is an excellent example of showing how little need be actually painted to suggest much more.

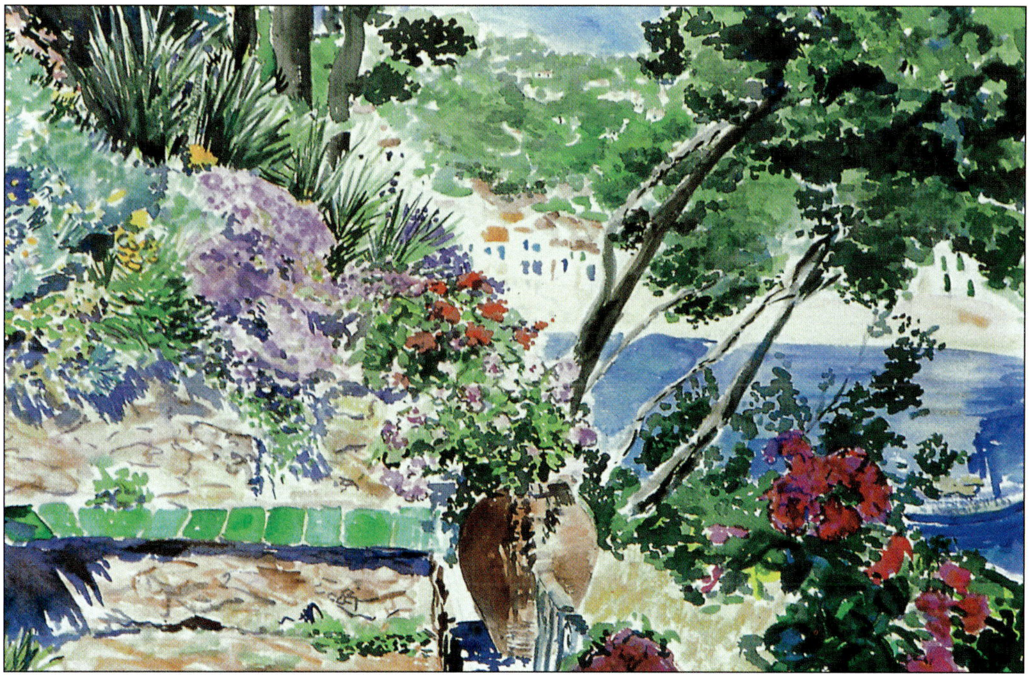

PATH TO THE SEA by Charles Penny

Small dabbed brushmarks combined to create this lively, cheerful corner of the Mediterranean. Three-dimensionality is achieved in this mosaic of color by pushing dark tones in under the light colors of the foliage. The composition appears free and spontaneous, but the opposing diagonals of the flower bank and tree trunks created a V-shaped window through which the distant houses are viewed, making a very strong composition.

As you can see, the success of your landscape painting depends on careful preparation before you begin painting. You must know what you are aiming for and be aware of such aspects as color, composition, light, and tones. As far as composition is concerned, there should always be a center of interest – a part of the picture to which the eye is drawn and which forms the theme of the painting. If there are two large trees in the scene, either group them together or diminish the size of one of them. Never put two objects of equal importance in the same painting.

In addition, try to compose the secondary elements – fences, hedges, paths, rivers, even the cloud patterns in the sky – so that they lead the viewer's eye pleasurably through the composition and to the focal point.

Be on the lookout for interesting contrasts, too. A landscape that is overwhelmingly horizontal in format will benefit from the addition of a vertical accent such as a tree, a building, even a figure, to avoid monotony. Shapes and forms that "echo" each other provide a pleasing harmony, which is accentuated by the addition of a contrasting shape. The geometric form of a building, for example, provides a foil for the curving shapes of hills, trees, and clouds.

Try to include busy areas and restful areas in the same painting, to provide a change of pace; if the sky is the subject of your painting because of its lovely cloud formations, then keep the landscape fairly simple and open. Finally, exploit to the full the contrasting textures of clouds, foliage, rocks, and water.

The most important consideration in any landscape painting is creating a sense of depth and space; so that viewers feel that they could actually "step into the picture." The most common way of achieving this sense is to create the illusion of the landscape receding toward the horizon, and there are several ways of doing this. The most obvious is that of linear perspective – making objects appear to diminish in size from the foreground to the background, but linear perspective alone is not enough. The most important means of establishing a sense of space and atmosphere in your painting is through aerial perspective. As your eye travels from the foreground to the horizon, you will notice certain changes in the appearance of the various landscape elements: those objects that are nearest to you look darkest in tone; in the middle distance they appear somewhat lighter; and objects on the horizon seem the lightest of all. Colors also change, from warm and bright in the foreground to a cool, subdued blue on the horizon. Finally, contrast and detail diminish with distance. All these changes occur because of the water vapor and tiny particles of dust present in the air which partly obscure colors and forms in the distance (this effect is not so apparent in countries near the equator, where the light is much brighter).

Apart from linear and aerial perspective, there are other, subtle ways of creating a sense of depth: overlapping the shapes of hills and trees, for example; or depicting the S-shaped curves of roads and rivers winding into the distance; if there is a fence or hedge in the foreground, either eliminate it altogether or "invent" an open gate in it. Always lead the viewer into the painting – never put up a barrier in the foreground.

Color and Perspective

These can be very complex subjects indeed – whole books have been written on theories. Such is beyond the scope of this book, and in any case would be more likely to be a hindrance than a help to an inexperienced painter, but there are some basic guidelines which will help you to make a picture work, and there are also some terms which you will need to understand.

Additive mixture

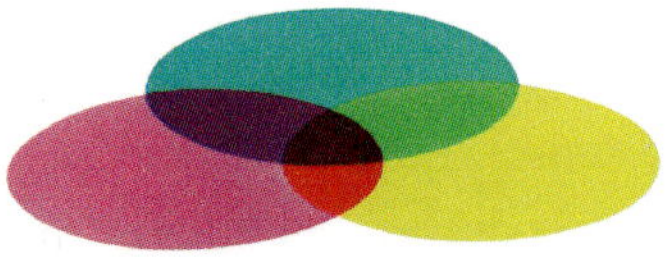

Subtractive mixture

COLOR

It is necessary to study some of the basic theories of picture making and this includes perhaps the most basic, but not necessarily the simplest of all: color. No matter what other features paintings have, the common factor in all is color. Indeed, in the normally sighted human being, what is actually seen is the many and varied sensations of color. The retina of the eye receives sensations from objects which causes a reaction in the appropriate cones. As a result, trees appear green because the cones that have green as their dominant assert themselves and overcome the cones that have other colors. Similarly, the blue of the sky, is caused by the receiving of "blue" pulses into the retina which immediately triggers a reaction to the blue-stressed cones. In color blindness these cones go wrong and often colors are reversed.

Since the complex act of seeing happens only within the brain, it is correct to deduce that nothing has color in its own right but that color is dependent upon light. In darkened conditions, colors are more difficult to see and define, and in total darkness there can be no color at all. An interesting experiment is that of creating an after-image in the retina demonstrating that it is through the brain that color is seen. Stare at a red patch, then shut your eyes and "look" at the after-image. The same shape is seen, but in green – the complementary color of the red patch.

Complementary colors are those at opposite sides of the color wheel. One of these colors, in this case red, reacts through the red cones and the other through the green. Taking complementary colors, we can see that a knowledge of this aspect of color theory is of value when we consider landscape painting.

In an average landscape painting, most areas are of greens of one sort or another. Brilliant, dull, acid; sage, spring, olive, or sea, man has created descriptions for various conditions and types of green. If our painting comprises fields, shrubs, trees, and bushes all made up of these various greens, how better to make the harmony complete than by contrasting a small amount of the opposite, or complementary color, being, in this instance, red. The red will serve to enhance the values of the main body of color – the range of subtly mixed greens. To expand this, since we know that green is a secondary color created from two primary colors (blue and yellow), we can begin to see how this can aid us as well. A similar effect to placing small areas of red beside the green will be created by using blue and yellow in a like manner. By using brilliant Prussian blue and raw umber or raw sienna instead of yellow, an unsuspected green tint will result. Further experimentation will reveal all manner of exciting relationships, not merely of color values – that is "blueness" or "redness" – but also of qualities and tones.

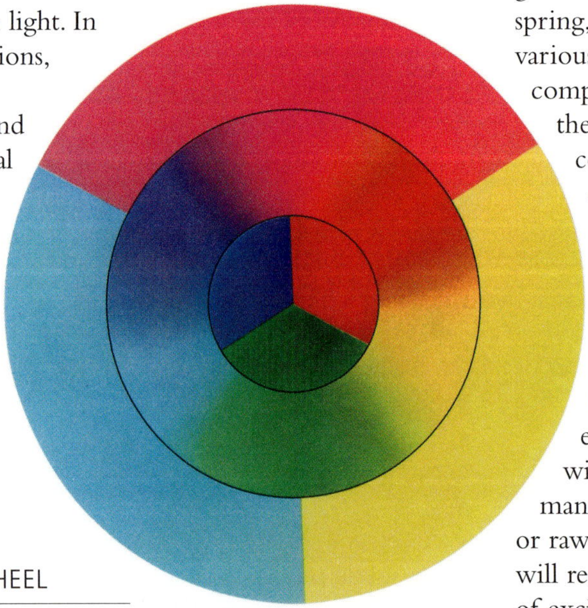

THE COLOR WHEEL

Color has been the subject of study for many hundreds of years ranging from the simple act of observation to highly complex psychological theories. In terms of painting and drawing, some of the most important terms include hue, tone, and warm and cool colors. Hue is the range seen in the color wheel. The tone refers to the brightness of a color. Warm and cool colors describe the orange and blue sections of the color wheel respectively.

TONE AND HUE

Color has two basic definable qualities: tone and hue. Hue is the "greenness" of green paint, and tone is its darkness or lightness. Squinting is indispensable in assessing color tones when beginning to work and throughout the painting's development. Expressionistic color as used by twentieth century artists such as Matisse and Derain, or the more traditional use as seen in Velazquez (seventeenth century) are worthy of close study. In studying paintings, try always to detach the color element from the whole painting in order to examine it better.

There is little point in simply copying "color as seen" without attempting to first organize a scheme. Whether the artist's intention is to shock or to create a mood strictly with a number of tertiary colors, forethought is essential. One method of studying color is to use sheets of specially colored papers, cut-out and placed in various shapes and combinations to see what happens when tones are too close or too distant.

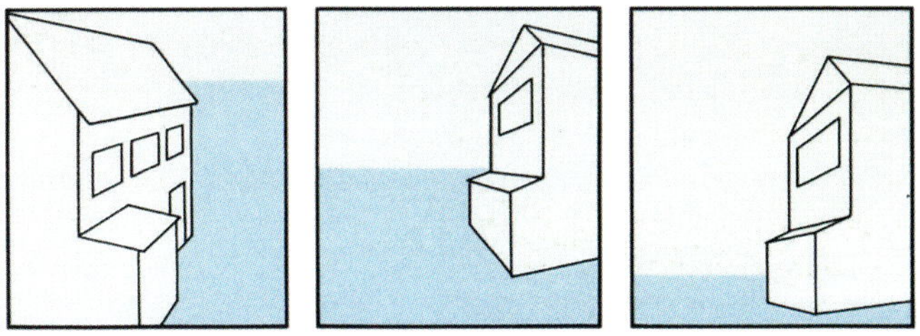

The horizon line is always at eye level. No matter what the size or dimensions of objects, their diagonal lines will all converge on the horizon line.

PERSPECTIVE

What is a good picture? There is no simple answer; perhaps one that excites or disturbs, not one necessarily pleasing to the eye, but containing a great deal of visual interest. Not only should the artist be facile in his knowledge and use of the materials, but he or she should be conversant with these other important ingredients of visual communication and, through the fusion of these various elements, achieve his or her ambitions.

In picture making, the elements every artist needs to understand in order to best exploit them include color, composition, and perspective. The fusion of these components with a good basic drawing ability and sound technique give the artist an opportunity to express his or her personal vision.

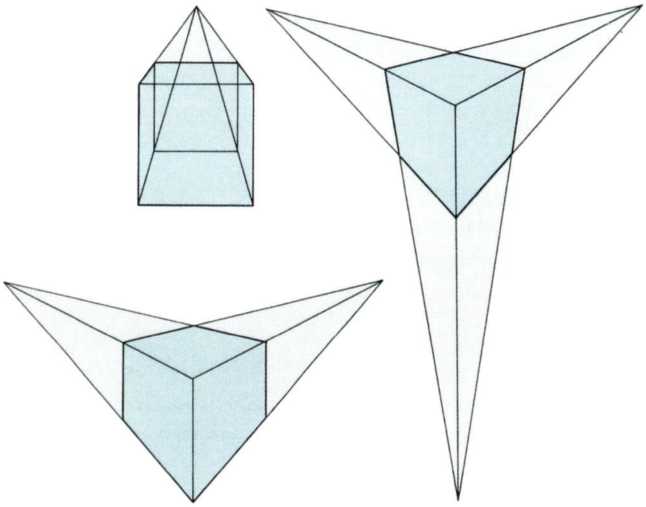

One, two, and three point perspective. When two planes are visible, the parallel lines converge at a single vanishing point. When three planes are visible, two points are required. If a cube is seen above or below the horizon line, three points are used.

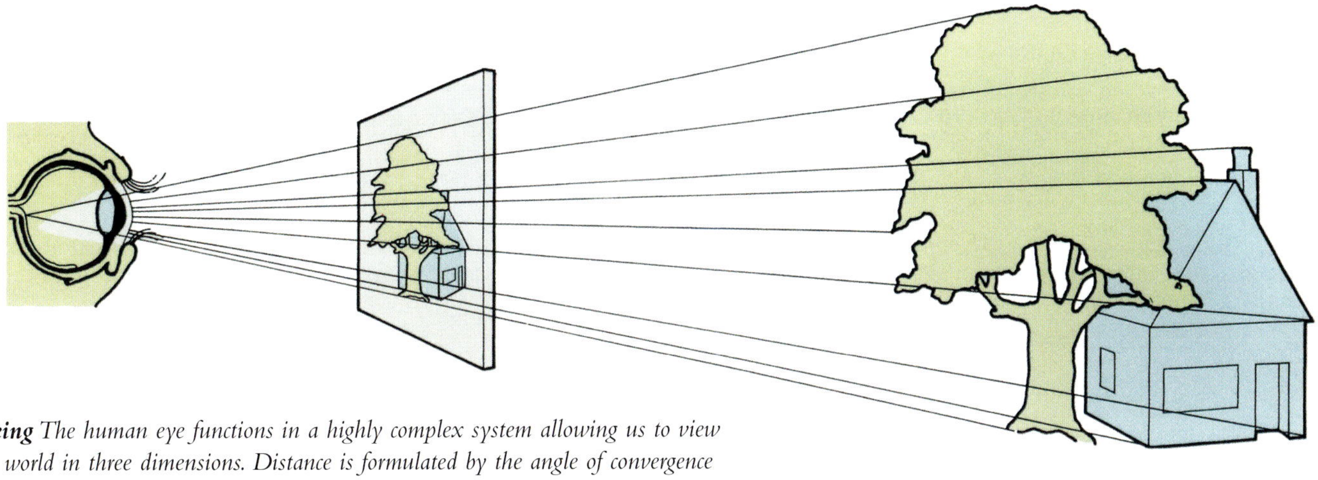

Seeing *The human eye functions in a highly complex system allowing us to view the world in three dimensions. Distance is formulated by the angle of convergence of the image on the retina. When many objects are viewed, sophisticated computations take place in the brain.*

Composing a Picture

Whether you are painting outdoors or indoors, whether your chosen subject is a landscape, a group of buildings, a portrait or a single flower in a vase, you need to have a clear idea of what the main elements are and of how you will place them on the paper before you begin to paint.

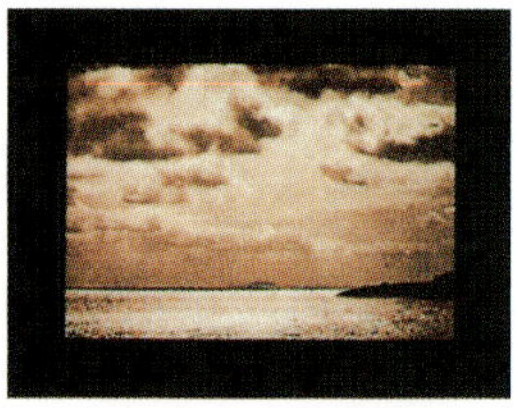

A large, complex painting with numerous people and objects in it does, of course, need some thought; otherwise there may be too much activity in one part of the picture and not enough in another. But even here, it is less a matter of following a prescribed set of rules than of working out the balance of the various shapes, as in the case of planning a room – no one would put all the furniture crowded together on one side and leave the rest empty.

A "good composition" is one in which there is no jarring note, the colors and shapes are well-balanced, and the picture as a whole seems to sit easily within its frame or outer borders. If you are painting a landscape you may think composition is not involved, that you are just painting what you see, but you will have chosen a particular view, just as you would when taking a photograph, and in choosing it you will have gone at least some way toward composing it. You may then find that you want to exaggerate or rearrange some feature in the foreground, such as a rock or a tree to provide extra interest, or alter the bend of a path to lead the eye into the picture.

There are some basic errors which should be avoided if possible. In general it is not a good idea to divide a landscape horizontally into two equal halves – the land and the sky – as the result will usually be monotonous. A line, such as a path or fence, should not lead directly out of the picture unless balanced by another line which leads the eye back into it.

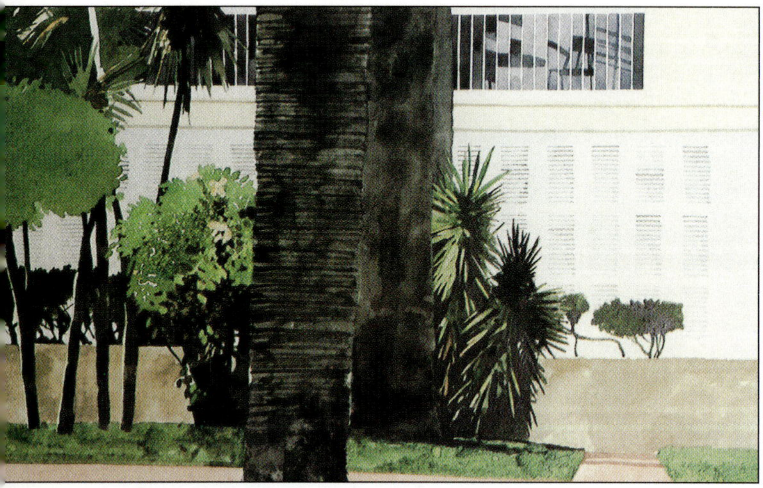

The natural inclination when painting subjects like trees is to try and get everything in, but in this painting the artist has allowed the foreground trees to "bust" out of the frame, giving a stronger and more exciting effect.

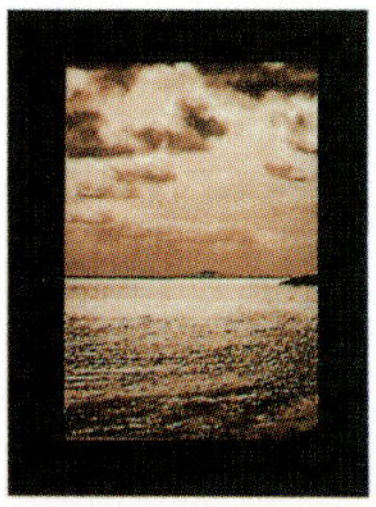

In landscape painting the sky is a vital part of the composition, and should always be given as much care and thought as the rest of the painting. Even if you are working quickly, it is often helpful to make some drawings, known as thumbnail sketches (though they need not be small) before you start on the painting. These may consist of just a few roughly-drawn lines to establish how the main shapes can be placed, or they may help you to work out the tonal pattern of the composition.

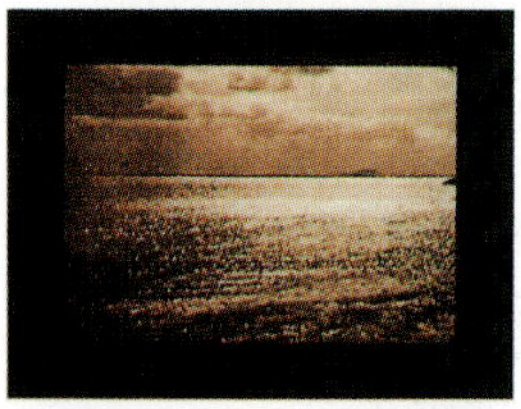

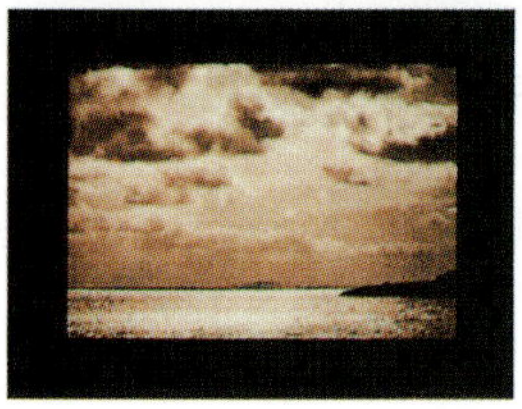

A viewing frame is equally useful, particularly for landscapes painted on-the-spot. When faced with a large expanse of land and sky the problem is always how much of it to paint, where to start and finish, and how much of what you see will actually fit on the canvas. Anyone who takes photographs will be familiar with this problem: you raise your camera at a splendid view only to find that the small section of it you can see through the viewfinder is quite dull and featureless. A viewing frame is simply a rectangular aperture cut in a piece of card – a good size is about $4^1/_2$ x 6 in. (11.5 x 15.25 cm) – which you hold up in front of you to frame and isolate the subject. Once you have chosen the particular area of landscape that interests you, you can then decide how you want to treat it and how much rearranging is needed to make an interesting composition.

When planning a landscape composition, remember that you don't have to slavishly copy everything you see just because it's there. In this demonstration, artist Raymond Leech takes a less-than-inspiring landscape scene and, by rearranging things a little, turns it into an attractive painting.

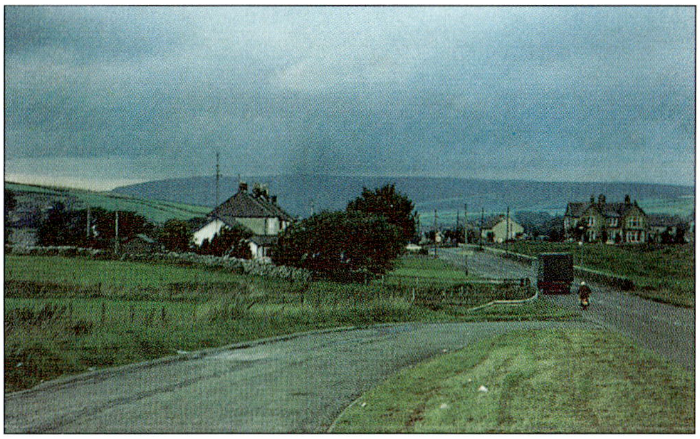

1 The actual view has potential – I like the way the houses on the left are nestled among the trees, and the gathering rain clouds add a note of drama. The problems include a general lack of value contrast, too much busy detail, and a rather clumsy shape in the foreground right, where the two roads intersect.

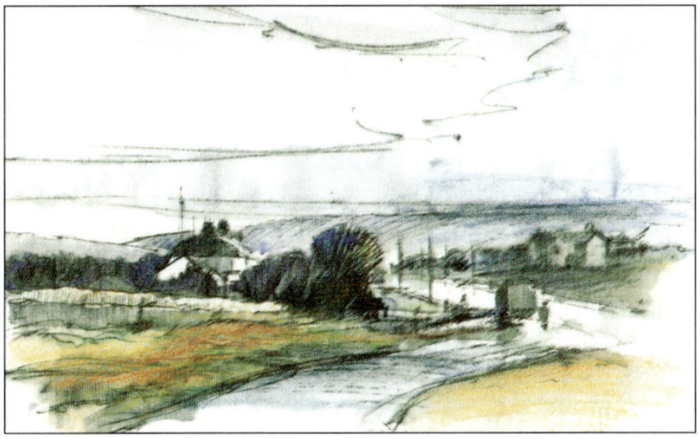

2 My first step is to make a value sketch of the scene in which I iron out these problems and establish a stronger, more coherent image. I alter the shape of the road so that it creates a pleasant S-curve that leads the eye through to the focal point of the picture – the group of houses and trees over on the left. Also, I simplify distracting details such as telegraph poles and architectural features, and I introduce more tonal contrast between the sky and the land.

3 My support is a hardboard panel, which I prime with a textured emulsion paint. It plays havoc with my brushes, but I find the finished effect well worth it because, when dry, the rough-textured finish lends a subtle sense of movement and helps break up the color. When the priming is dry I apply a transparent toned ground all over the support, to establish the color key. For this I use a dilute solution of raw sienna mixed with plenty of turpentine and rubbed onto the panel with a rag. With a soft hair brush and a thin mixture of cobalt blue and burnt sienna, I outline the main shapes and contours in the composition.

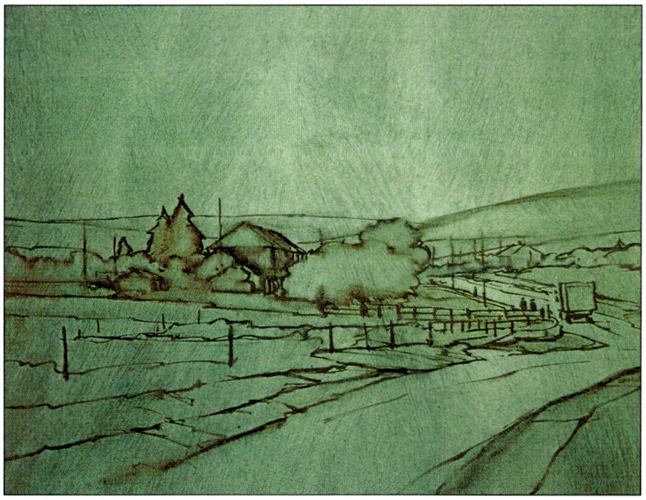

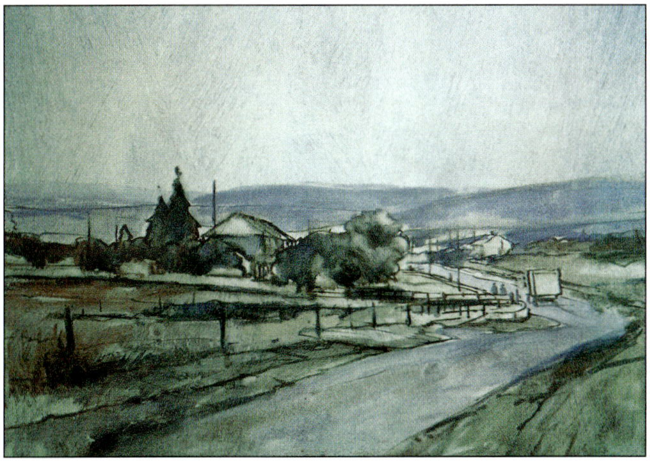

4 Using thin washes of cobalt blue and burnt sienna, I make a rough underpainting to establish the main masses of light, middle, and dark value, and of warm and cool color. This stage is important, because it gives me a firm foundation from which I can build up the succeeding colors.

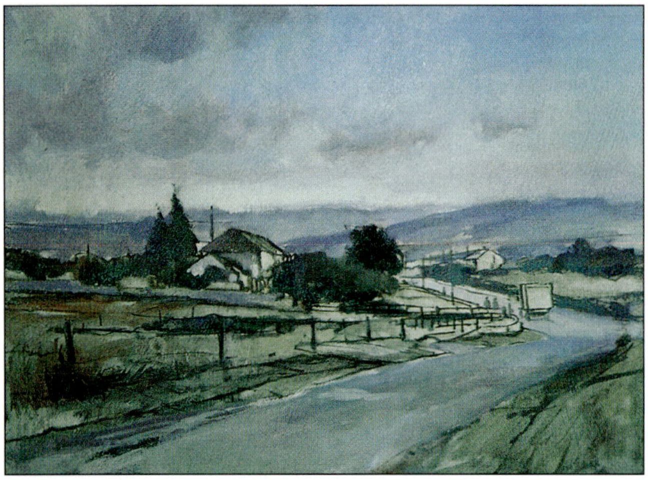

5 I paint the sky and distant hills using mixtures of cobalt blue, cobalt violet, and titanium white. The road is wet and reflects some of the sky color, introducing a pleasing note of harmony to the scheme.

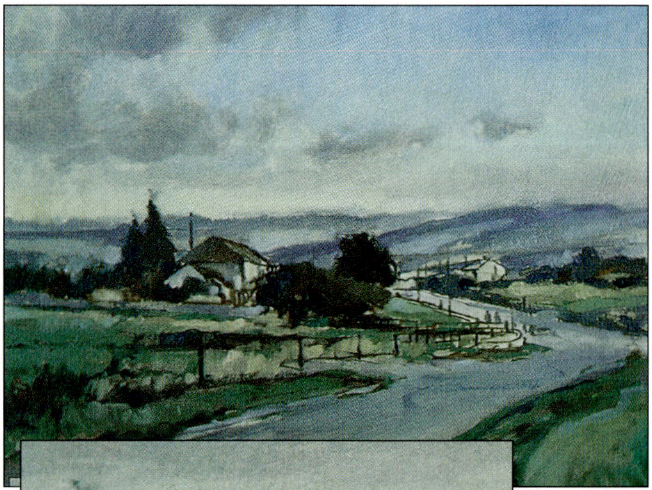

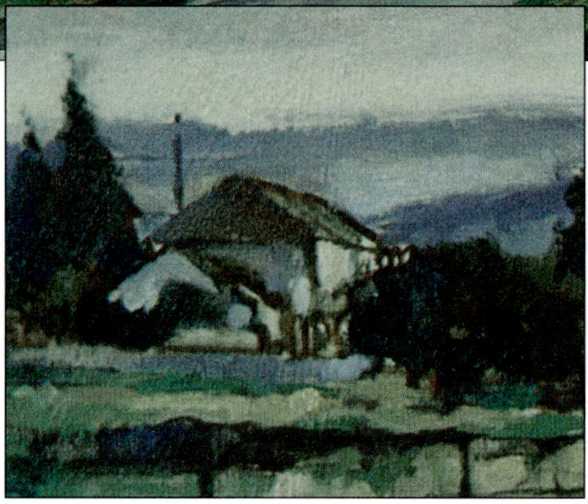

6 Throughout the painting process I am constantly stepping back from my canvas to observe both the painting and the scene itself through half-closed eyes. This way I can check that the balance of light and dark masses is shaping up OK. At this stage I decide to take out the truck on the bend in the road. It is too obtrusive, and prevents the eye from moving freely forward into the picture. Now I begin to thicken the impasto of my paint and to strengthen the darks in the trees and buildings, using the sky colors darkened with raw sienna. This deeper value has an immediate effect of pushing the blue hills way back into the distance, thus strengthening the illusion of depth and space. For the grassy fields I use a loose mixture of yellow ocher and raw sienna applied with broken brush strokes to give variety to the greens. The detail shows how the main focal point of the picture is established by juxtaposing the light value of the building with the dark values of the surrounding trees.

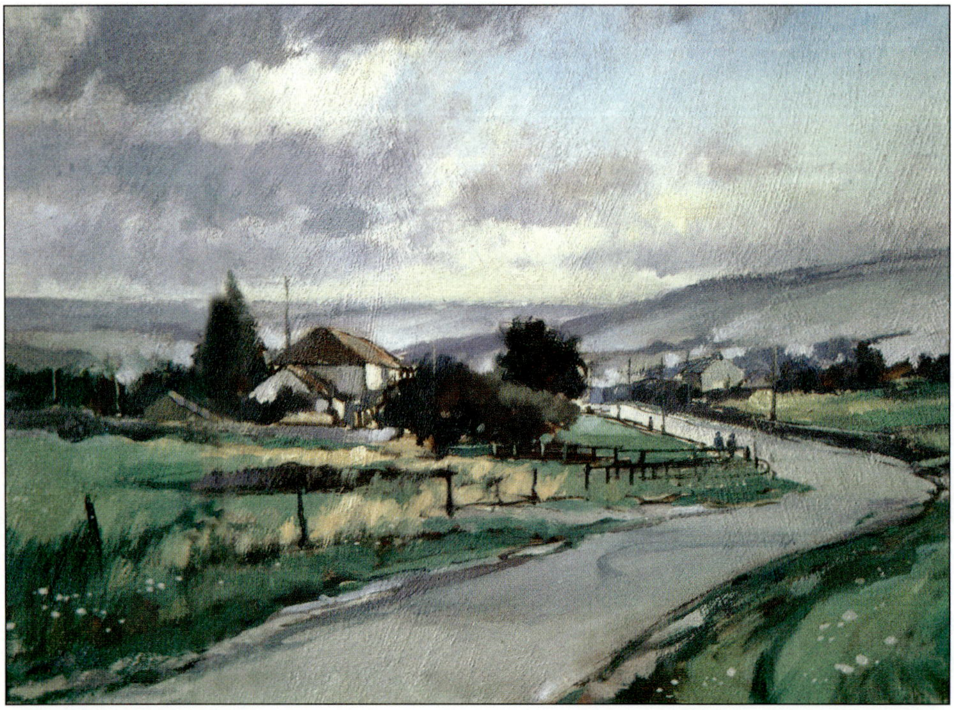

7 In the final stage I strengthen the light values to brighten the scene a little.
I introduce touches of yellow ocher mixed with white into the sky and fields, and finish off by flicking in a few white daisies to enliven the foreground.

Aerial Perspective

The term "aerial perspective" describes an optical illusion caused by the presence of water vapor and tiny particles of dust in the atmosphere, which act almost like a series of invisible veils strung across the landscape. The farther into the distance we can see, the more "veils" we have to look through, which is why colors and forms appear more hazy and indistinct the closer they are to the horizon.

CREATING DEPTH AND SPACE

The effects of aerial perspective are most apparent when there are well-defined planes within the subject, such as a mountain range or a series of cliffs jutting out along a shoreline. They can also be seen clearly when dusk approaches, reducing the forms of the land to almost silhouetted shapes that become lighter in value toward the horizon. This makes it easier to see the changes that occur between the foreground, middle distance, and far distance. Let's say, for example, that you're standing on a hill, surveying an undulating landscape of tree-covered fields and hills. As your eye travels from the foreground to the horizon, these are the changes you will notice:

Values become altered – Those objects that are nearest to you are relatively unaffected by atmospheric haze, so you see their values at full strength. In the middle distance, however, some of the strength of the values is lost, due to the intervening atmosphere, and they appear lighter. Way back on the horizon, they are weakest of all, seeming to melt into the pale value of the sky. You will also notice, however, that white objects in the distance become darker, not lighter, in value because they are grayed by the atmosphere.

Colors become cooler – Atmospheric haze has the same effect on color as it has on value. In the foreground, colors appear bright and warm because they are seen at their fullest intensity. In the middle distance, they lose some of their intensity, become cooler, and take on a blue cast. Compare a foreground tree, for instance, with a tree 500 yards away, and notice how the color of the foliage changes from a warm yellow-green to a cooler blue-green. Farther back still, a tree may not look green at all, but a subdued blue-gray.

Detail and contrast are diminished – Tonal contrasts – say between a light-colored building and the dark shadow it casts – are sharpest and clearest in the foreground. In the middle distance the intervening haze narrows the range of values and causes contrasts to be less marked, while on the horizon there is often no contrast at all – everything is blurred into one pale value. Similarly, texture and detail become less and less defined the farther you get from the foreground.

So, in order to create the illusion of infinite space and depth in our paintings, all we have to do is to reproduce the effects described above. Strong values and warm colors appear to come forward, whereas weak values and cool colors appear to recede into the distance – and it is the contrast between these values and colors that gives the illusion of distance.

It seems simple, but inexperienced painters often ignore what they see in front of them and put too much color, detail, and clarity into their backgrounds. This is because they have fallen into the familiar trap of painting what they know, instead of what they see: they "know" a tree is supposed to be green, so they paint it green, even though it is miles away on the horizon and actually appears blue. The result is always the same – a flat, unconvincing painting with none of the subtle atmospheric qualities that attracted the artist to the subject in the first place.

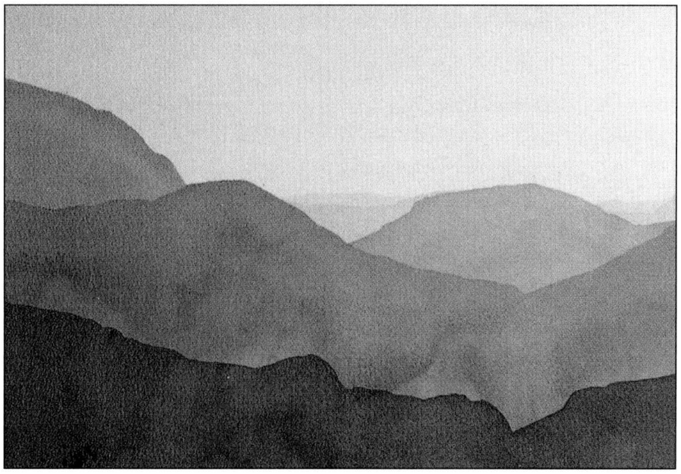

One of the basic rules of landscape painting is that cool, pale tones appear to recede into the distance, whereas darker or warmer tones appear to come forward. Always remember this principle when painting distant landscapes – it is your best means of creating the illusion of three-dimensional space on a flat piece of paper or canvas.

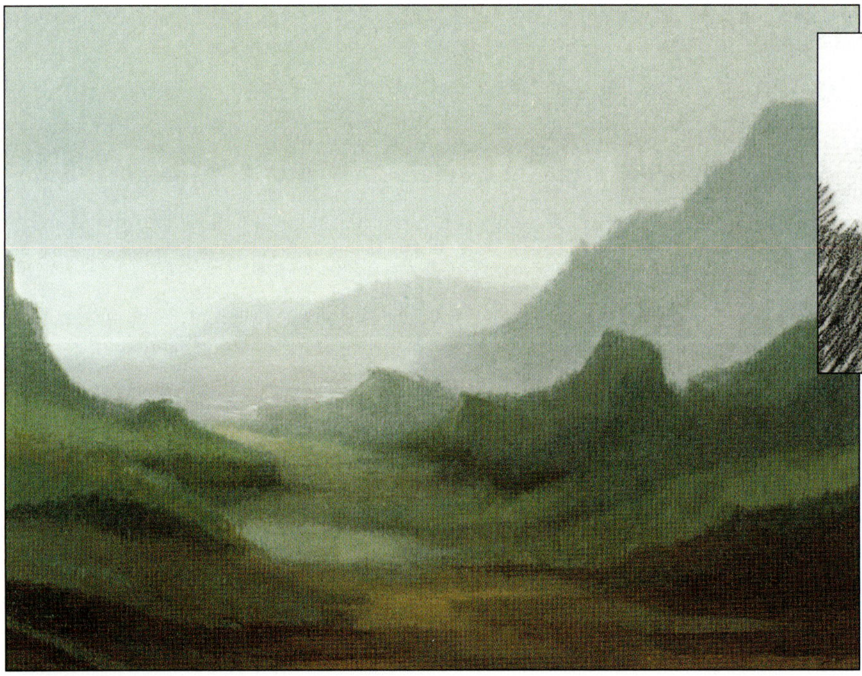

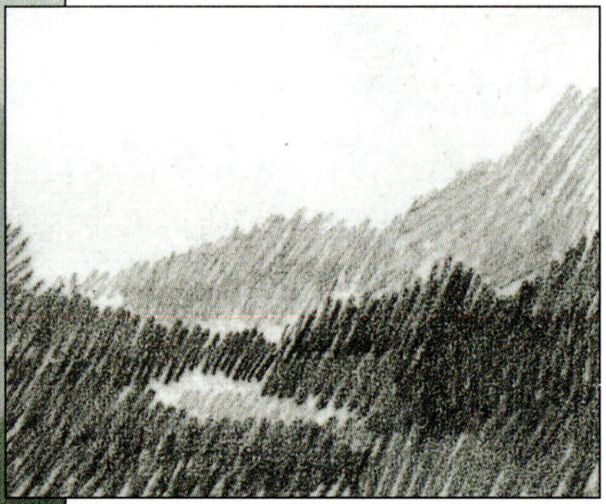

SEA MIST by Clemente Gerez (oil on canvas)

Here we see the classic effects of aerial perspective. Values and colors fade gradually toward the horizon, and forms become less definite. The diagram above shows clearly a receding arrangement of overlapping values, which creates a feeling of depth.

WINTER SUNSET, LLWYNHIR by Diana Armfield (oil on canvas below)

This landscape conveys a strong impression of space and atmosphere. Notice how the hot colors of the setting sun don't jump forward, but are kept in their place by the stronger value of the large cloud. The diagram below left shows how the subtle use of overlapping values draws the eye irresistibly toward the horizon.

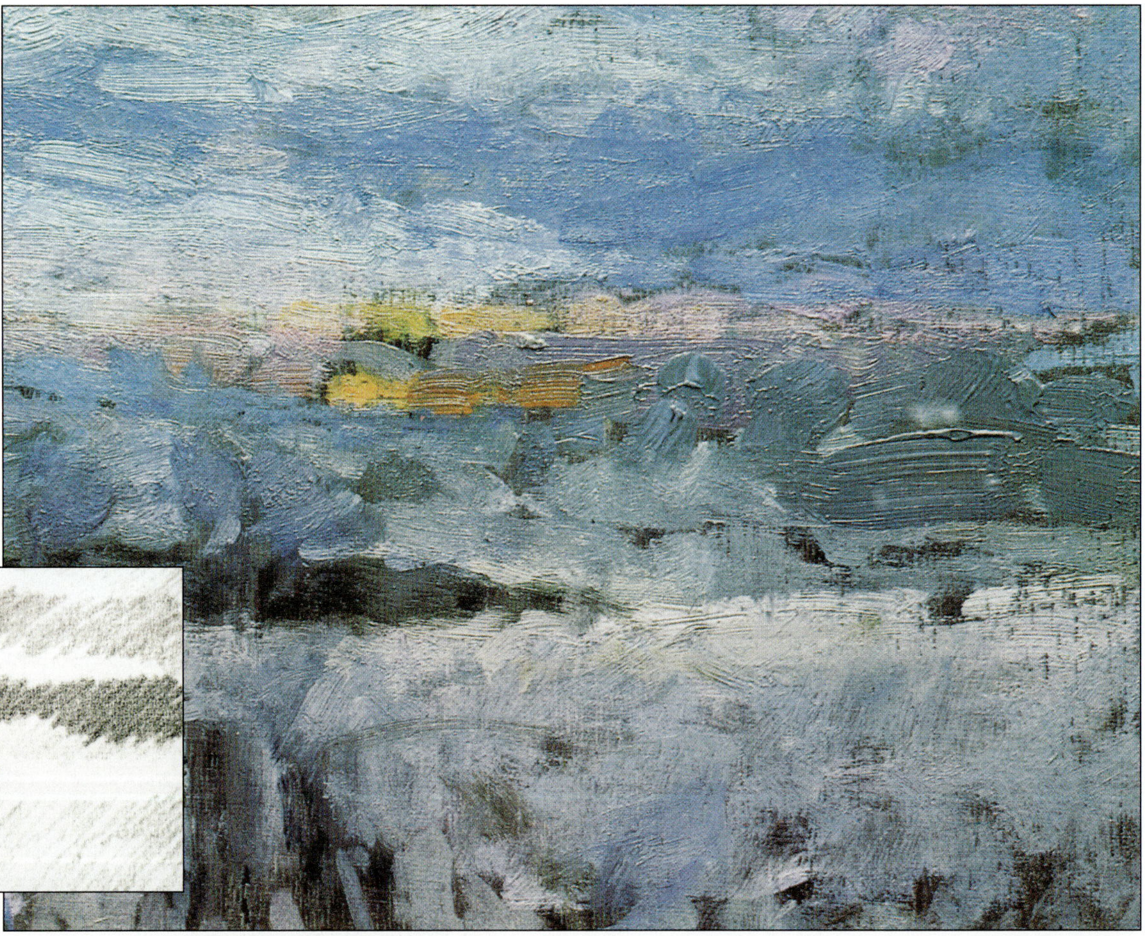

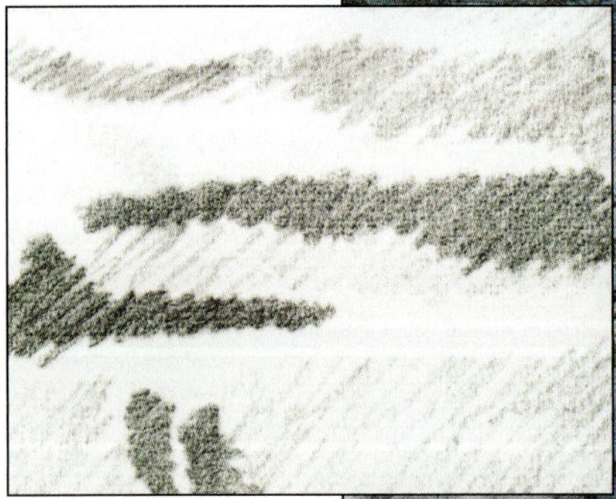

Fields and Grass

It is hard to pinpoint the fascination of fields. Perhaps they appeal because they are the man-made face of landscape. Or perhaps the attraction is the rich array of shapes and colors – patchwork patterns retreating up a hillside; parallel strips of freshly ploughed earth; swaying expanses of poppy-strewn golden corn.

WET-INTO-WET

Vary your technique also, using touches of wet-into-wet for soft distant features, and for hedgerows bounding the fields. In the latter case, dampen the paper above the edge of the field and run a broken line of color along it. The color will spread upward into the damp paper in irregular shapes like the growth of a hedgerow. Strengthen some areas with more color while the paint is still damp.

OVERLAPPING WASHES

The pattern of fields in the middle distance can be built up with overlapping washes of transparent color – ochers, mauves, greens, yellows, browns. Don't let them become monotonous – use broken color in places to suggest texture, and bring in shadows made by clouds, trees, and hedgerows to break up solid color.

For furrowed fields, use just three tones – one pale one over the whole area, a second to delineate the furrows with fairly thick lines, and lastly a dark tone for the thin deep shadows along each furrow.

MASKING

Field paintings often need some foreground interest. Use masking fluid to pick out some vertical stalks of corn, either *en masse* at the edge of a pathway, or as individual stalks against fence posts or at the front of a cornfield. You can treat a few flowerheads among many in the same way. Create an immediate sense of perspective by painting large ears of corn – or poppies, for example – in the foreground, dwindling in size as they recede until they become a mass of color.

THREE TONES FOR THE FURROWED FIELD

The three tones chosen to paint the furrows of the field must be fairly close in color and sufficiently varied in tone. The overall underwash is your lightest tone.

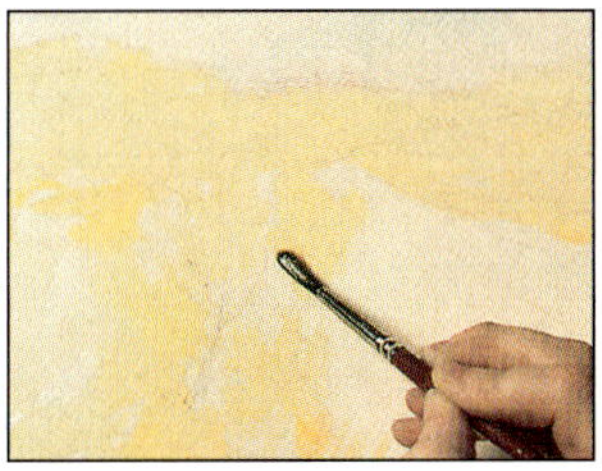

1 Tone 1. Paint a light wash of cadmium yellow, leaving a few scattered areas of white paper peeping through.

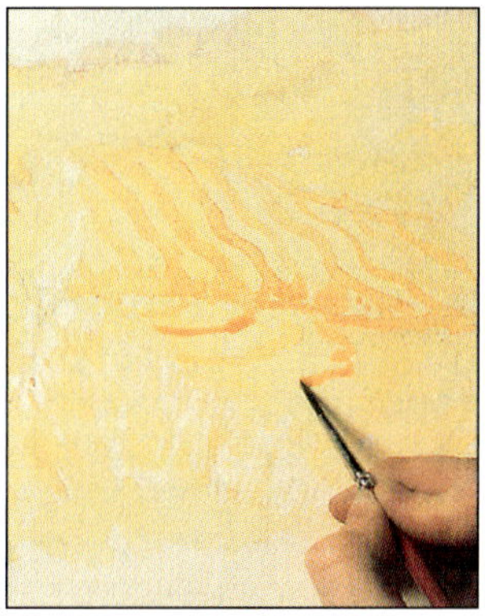

2 Tone 2. With a mixture of cadmium yellow and burnt sienna, draw lines to mark the field's furrows. Use the same color, mixed with green, for the distant hedgerows and foreground tree.

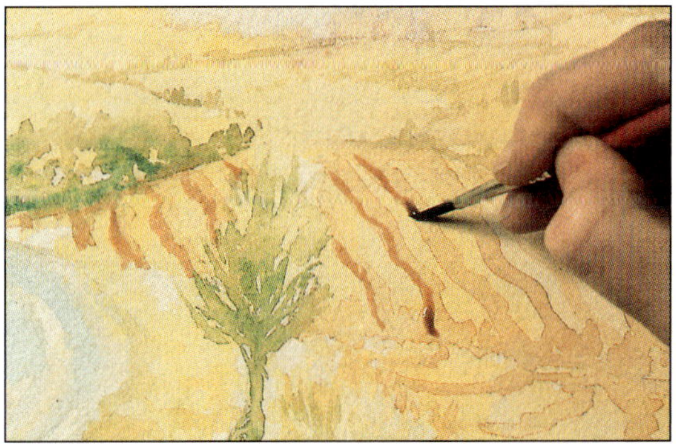

3 Tone 3. Mix a darker tone of cadmium yellow and burnt sienna. Create a deep shadow by drawing it along one side of the furrow. Use the same color for the hedgerow.

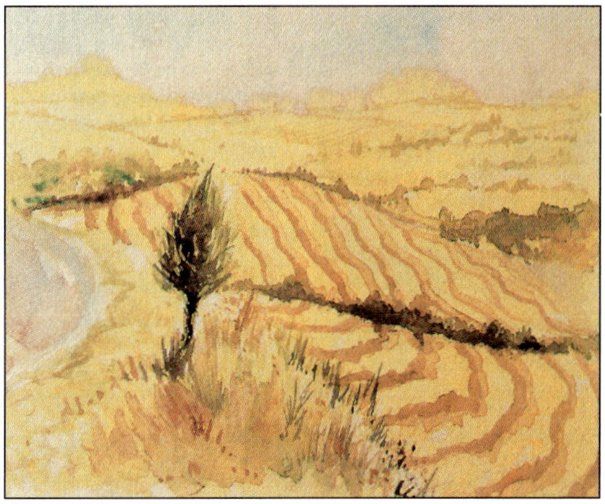

4 Tighten up the division between the fields with touches of dark violet, and strengthen the tree and grasses with the same complementary color.

OVERLAPPING WASHES

Mix a variety of bright translucent colors in the palette or work straight from pans. The variety of colors increases as each overlaps the other in a lively mosaic, suggesting the shimmering movement of grasses.

1 Lay out your poppies in scarlet lake and vermilion. With short, lively brush strokes paint the distant fields and trees in a variety of overlapping colors.

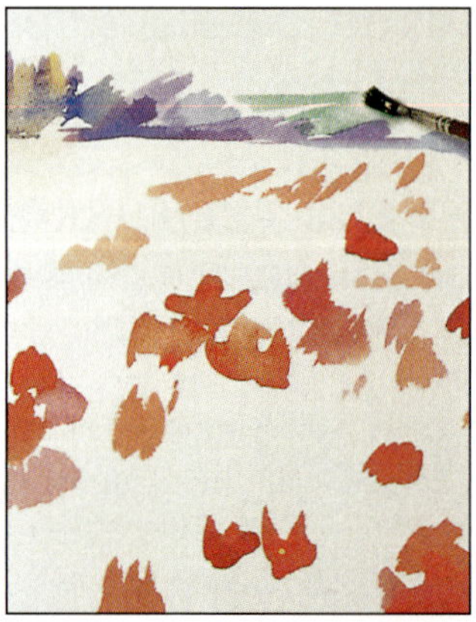

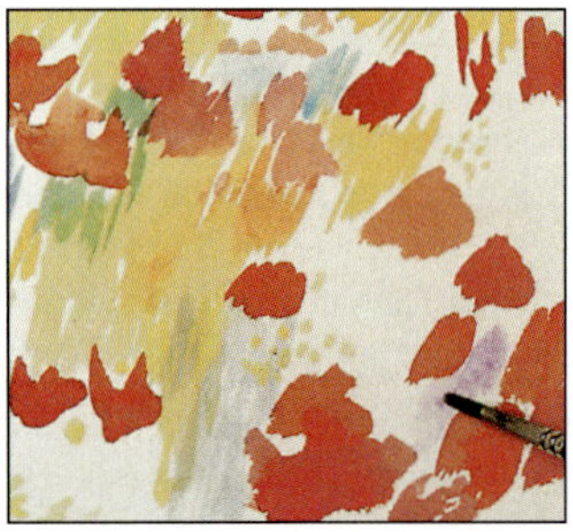

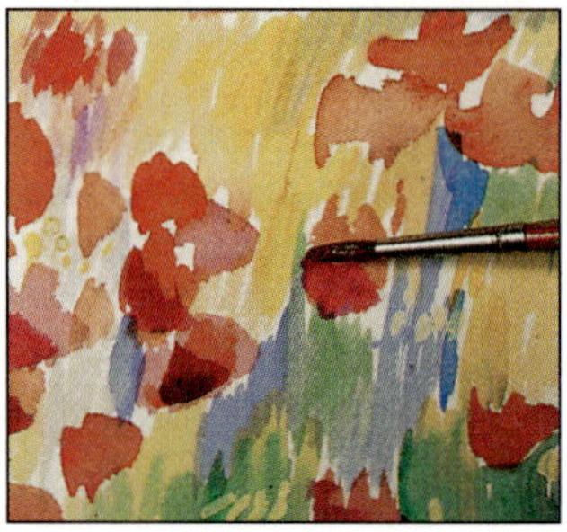

2 Mask out a few daisy heads in the foreground. With a No. 4 brush, lay diagonal strokes of color between the poppies; yellow ocher, cerulean green, and lilac.

3 Continue overlapping diagonal brushmarks until you have built up a lively pattern of color. Describe the petalled heads of the poppies with small, dark red brushmarks.

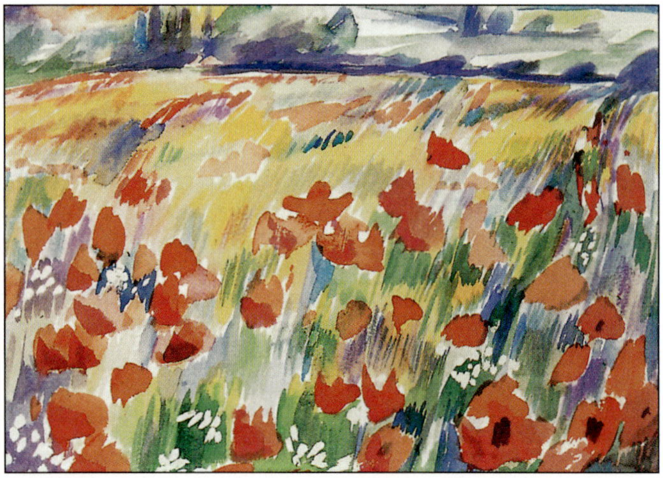

4 Wash the same colors into the background to marry with the foreground colors, and push shadow under the poppies to bring them out. Rub off the masking for the daisies.

MASKING

Paint the masking fluid straight from the pot with an old brush. Alternatively, you can protect a good brush with vaseline by coating the hairs with it. Remove the masking only when the painting is completely dry.

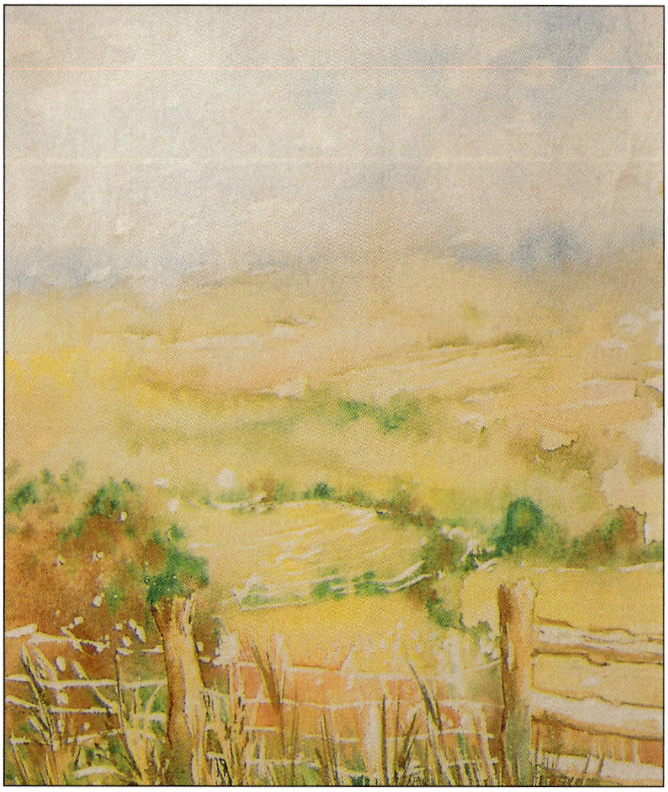

GRASS

This is a detail from an oil painting of a summer meadow, which shows the variety of subtle greens, yellows, grays, and earth colors that go to make up "green" grass. The artist began by covering the canvas with soft umbers and ochers, scumbled together wet-into-wet to suggest areas of light and shadow. Then, with a small pointed brush and lighter colors, he worked back into the wet color to suggest individual stems and blades of grass.

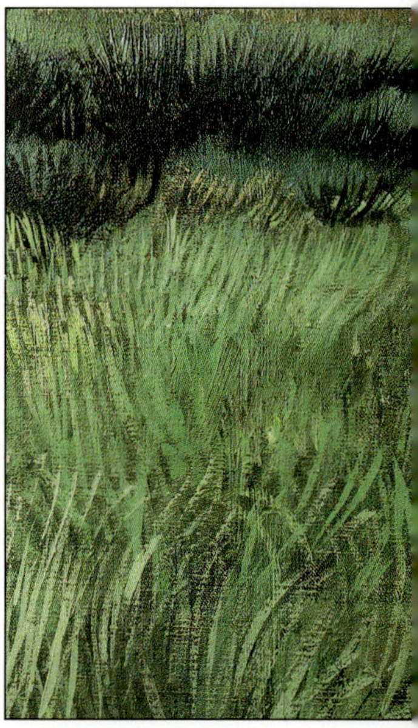

The underpainting provides a soft focus background for the precise strokes of grass in the foreground and helps to give a sense of depth and volume. Notice also how the curving, rhythmical strokes of the grass lead the eye back into the picture plane, where the tones become cooler and bluer – thus creating a sense of receding space.

Hills

Hills have a strong emotive appeal, inviting you to explore what lies beyond, as well as creating a series of lovely and intriguing shapes.

Choose the time of day carefully, as the direction of the light changes the appearance of the hills. When the sun is overhead or directly in front, they will be flattened, with their forms hard to decipher. Oblique sunlight will cast shadows that describe the forms, while low sun, setting behind the hills, will silhouette them, allowing you to see them as simple shapes.

WET-INTO-WET

Softly rounded forms can be painted wet-into-wet. Drop darker color into the valleys before the wash has dried. If the paper is dry, dampen it beyond where you want the paint to run to ensure soft edges. Create the structure of the hills by modeling from dark to light. Lighten the top of a rise and darken the dip beyond if you want the hill to stand out more.

To suggest an upward slope, dampen the paper above an imaginary line that represents the angle of the hill. Drop color into this along the slope line and let it extend softly upward into the damp paper. Clumps of grass and changes in surface created in this way will then also describe the lie of the land.

Be aware how damp your paper is as you lay each brush stroke into the preceding wet wash. Test it with the brush tip to see how far the paint spreads and wait if it spreads too far.

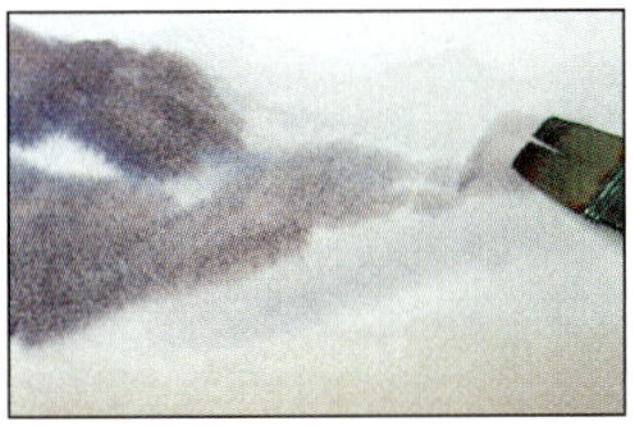

1 Paint a pale pinky wash over all the paper, and darken at the bottom. While wet, brush in the hills.

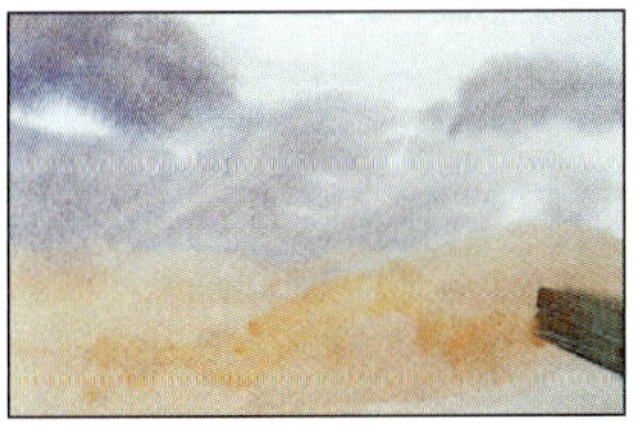

2 Use a warm, strong color in the foreground, letting it spread softly into the drying wash above.

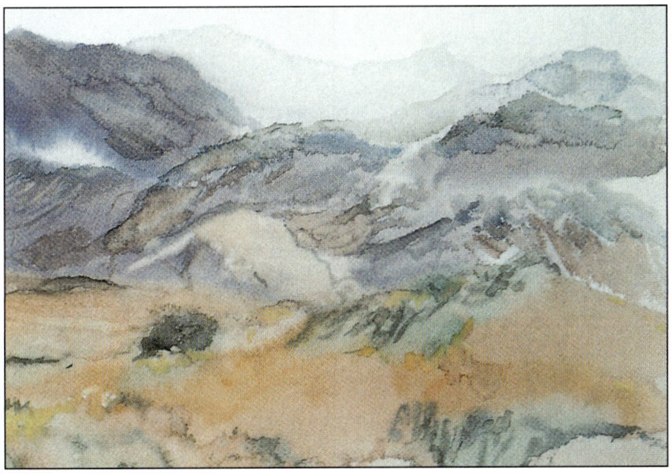

3 Use small washes to describe the hill forms, working into them while they are wet, contrasting light against dark to separate the masses. With a small brush, draw directional lines into the hills while the paper is damp.

GLAZES

We recognize hills mainly by their contours. Draw the shapes carefully, either using a pencil first or going straight in with color, using the tip and edge of your brush as you lay the washes. Successive transparent washes (glazes) are an effective way of building up layers of overlapping hills.

Glazes are thin transparent washes laid one over another. Leave the top of the previous wash exposed each time to create the advancing hills. The color of the top wash will be the sum of all the previous washes underneath.

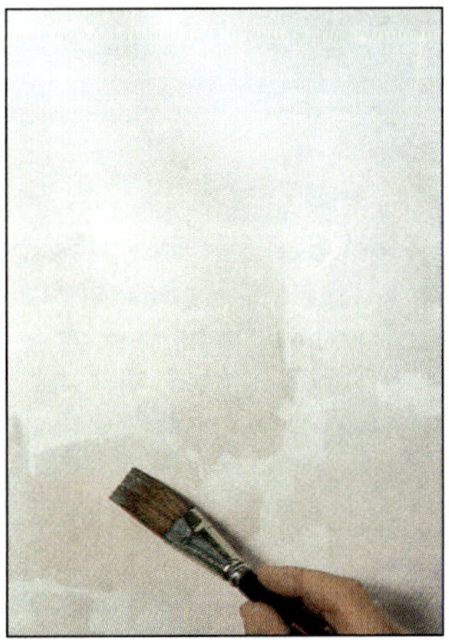

1 With a large flat ⅝ in. (1.2 cm) brush, lay an underwash of pale pink to provide a warm tone under the greens.

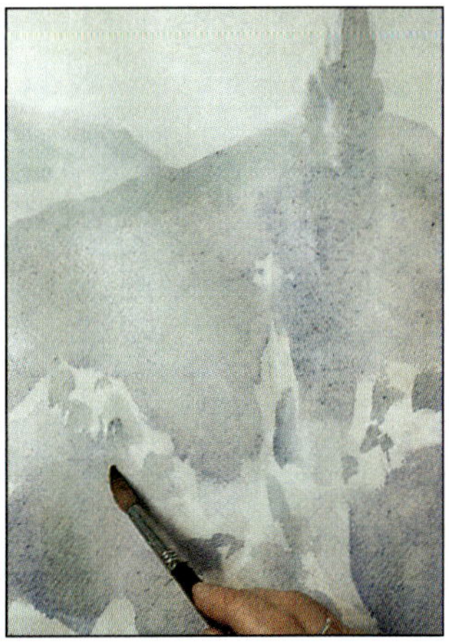

2 Lay the background hill wash over this followed by another slightly darker wash of Hooker's green mixed with red.

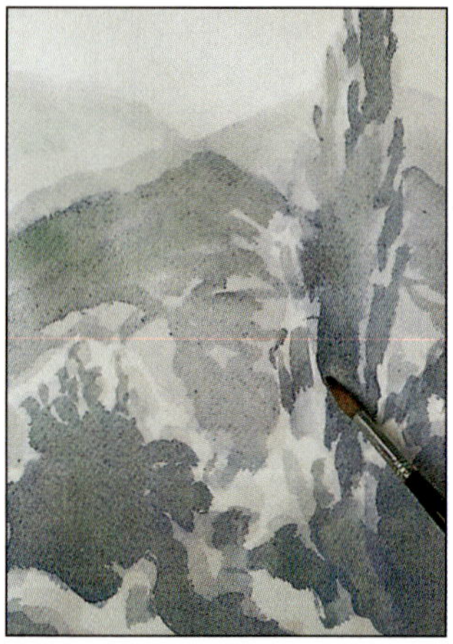

3 Lay further glazes, making the middle-distance hills and foreground trees darker. For soft, crinkly edges, lay the next glaze just before the previous one dries.

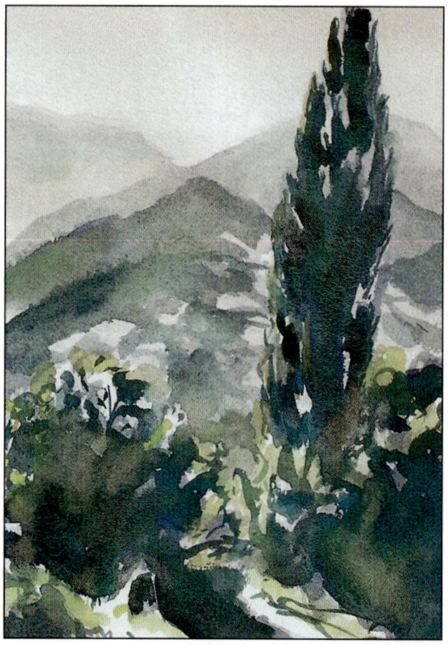

4 Paint a dabbing wash of monestial green to describe the tree and shrubs, and with a lemon yellow wash, lay a final glaze over the sunlit leaves.

WATERCOLOR

Watercolor is an exciting medium to use for landscape painting because it is so flexible and adaptable. You can use all sorts of unorthodox techniques with watercolor and it responds by producing wonderfully descriptive textures.

In this detail below from a hilly landscape in Italy, for example, the artist has created a subtle range of textures to suggest foliage and vegetation. He has added gum arabic to the paint to make the color denser and give it a slight sheen. He has then spattered clear water onto dry areas of paint and lifted off the color to create light patches that suggest the play of sunlight on the leaves.

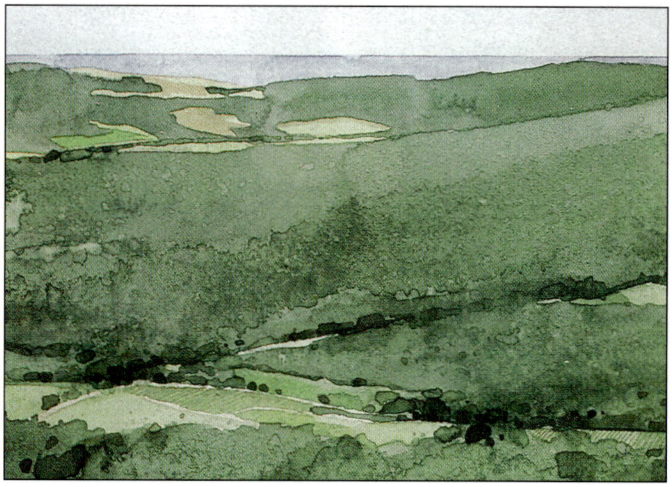

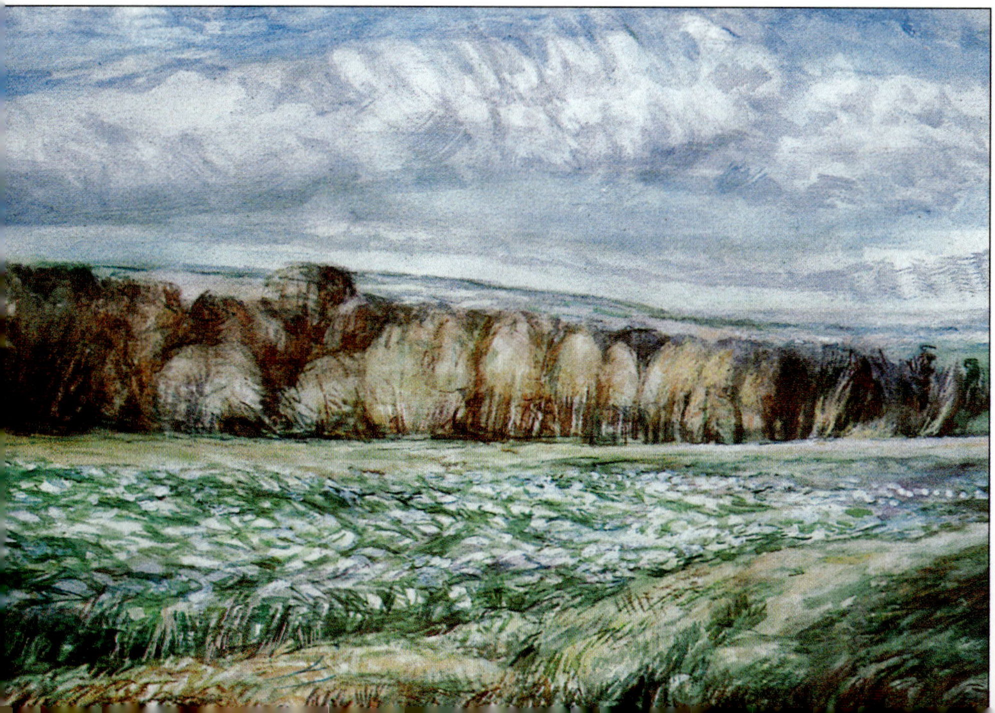

FROSTY AUTUMN MORNING
by Donald Pass

Pass has an unusual watercolor style, using his paints almost like a drawing medium. He makes no preparatory drawing, and begins by laying broad washes of light color. He then builds up each areas with a succession of separate, directional or linear brushmarks. It is easy to imagine how this subject might have become dull, but the brushwork, as well as being effective in terms of pure description, creates a marvelous sense of movement: we can almost feel the light wind bending the grass and sending the clouds scudding across the sky.

Mountains

Few people can fail to be moved by the awesome majesty of mountain landscapes, and for the artist they provide a challenge and a thrill that no other subject can match. Unless the mountains are flattened by mist or distance it is important to establish their solidity. The low angle of the winter sun enhances their splendor by casting dramatic shadows, which also make it easier for the artist to paint convincingly three-dimensional forms.

After sketching in the mountain shapes, suggest their volume by means of cast shadows and shaded crevices. You can either begin with broad washes in a neutral tone, or go straight in with your shadow colors, keying the rest of the painting to them.

You will also want to suggest their size, and you can give a sense of scale by including some familiar feature such as a person, climber's hut, or a group of houses nestling beneath the mountains.

HARD AND SOFT EDGES

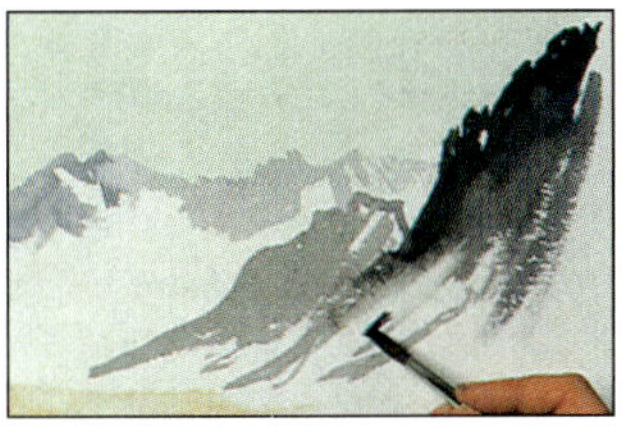

1 Paint the distant mountains over a damp, greenish sky wash. As the mountains come forward, lay linear brush strokes over soft, dried washes.

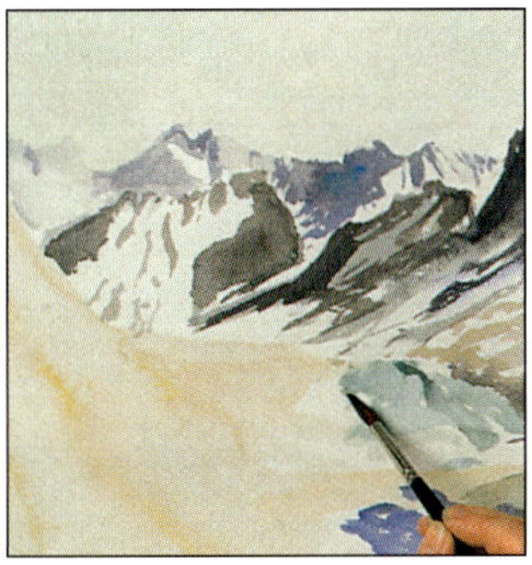

2 Build the outline of the crags with single brush strokes, describing the rocky slopes of the mountain. Paint a very wet wash of ocher for the foreground scree slope.

The combination of hard and soft edges created by painting an area dampened in some parts only is very pleasing for a wild landscape. Evergreen trees merging into each other at the bases but carefully drawn at the top look more interesting than starkly painted individual trees one against the other. Paint ledges and rocks with crisp edges, but let their bases merge into the mountainside wet-into-wet. Interesting textures for trodden snow can be created by scumbling.

Mix washes without too much water to enable you to work quickly on dried paint so that the brush strokes remain hard-edged. Use clear water to soften hard-edged areas.

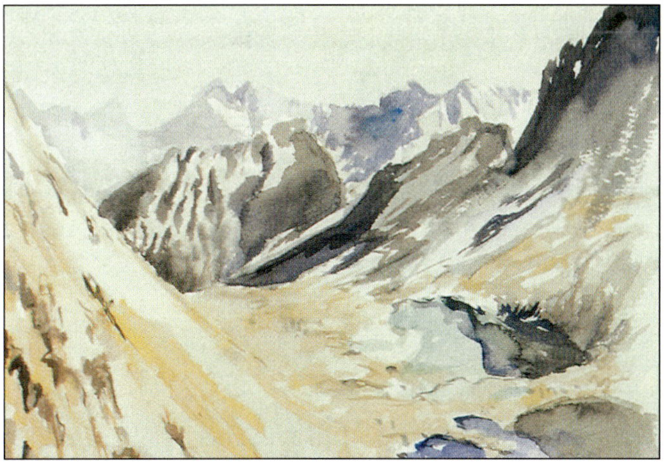

3 Scribble loose detail into the scree surface with the tip of the brush while the wash is wet. Dampen the base of the central mountain with clear water to make the colors spread softly.

RESERVING WHITE PAPER

The beauty of snow scenes is that you don't have to do much painting to create an interesting image – a welcome relief when your hands are cold. Reserving white paper is the best way to "paint" white, with angular blue shadows describing the forms. For crisp white peaks, draw the shapes by taking the sky wash around them, using a large round brush with a good tip.

It will help you to lay more confident shadow shapes if you sketch the mountain scene lightly to begin with. The untouched white paper is the strength and the freshness of the painting. Do not fiddle, and be certain of where the mountain shadows fall.

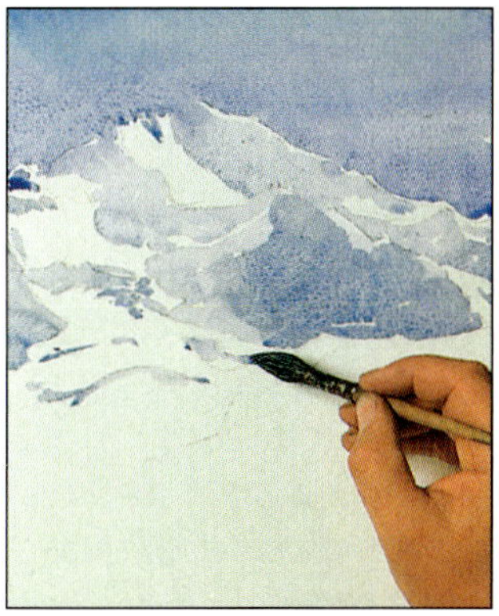

1 Paint a cobalt-blue sky, following the mountain ridge. While drying, use the same wash plus a little Payne's gray to paint in the shadow shapes of the mountain.

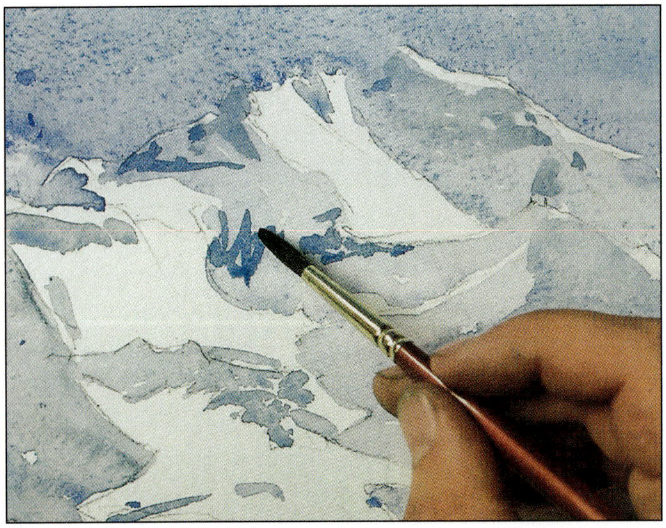

2 When dry, use light strokes of the same color, plus more Payne's gray, to create the surface variations, peaks, and ridges.

3 Into the pale wet wash on the mountain slope, drop small pools of cobalt blue and Payne's gray to show lumps of snow and ice. Dampen the paper slightly before drawing in the fir trees with downward strokes. Let them bleed softly.

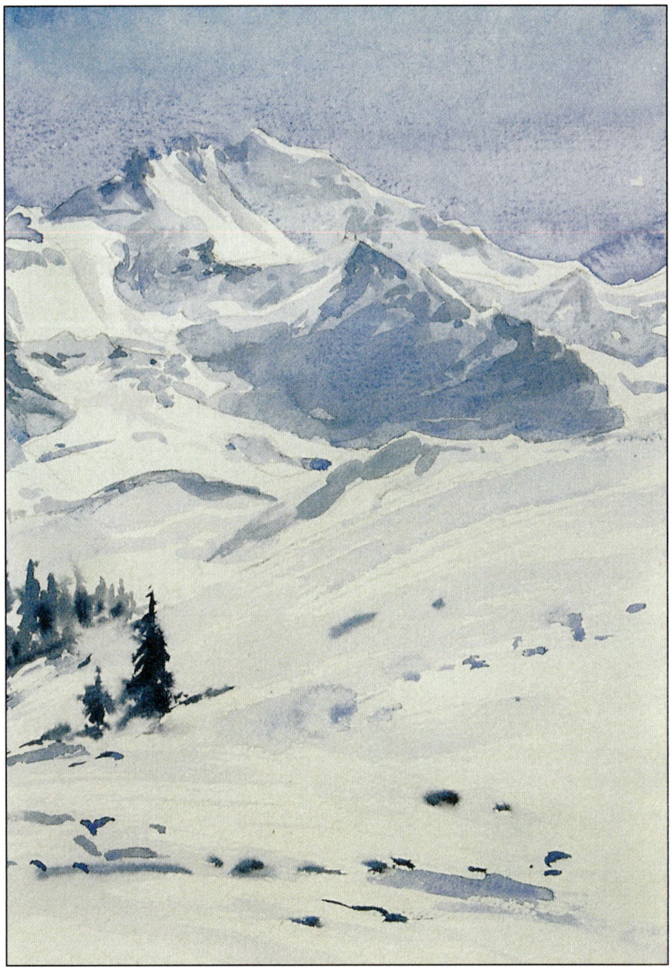

SCUMBLING AND MASKING

To scumble paint onto a surface you should mix up dry paint, load the brush, and with a twisting, dabbing motion of the brush head "grind" the paint onto the paper. Repeat the process for a delightfully varied texture.

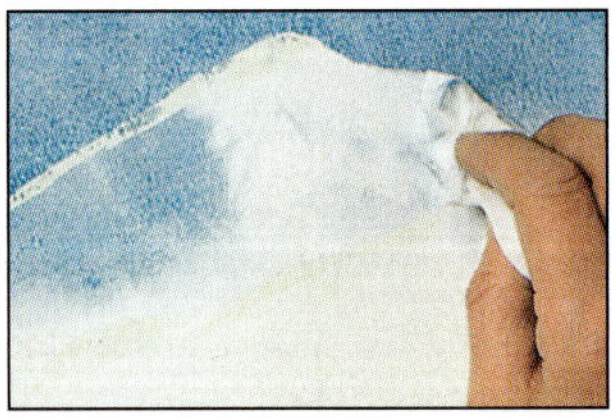

1 Mask out the sharp edge of the mountain against the sky. Wet the paper, and lay a wash of Antwerp blue and Payne's gray. Lift out the color with tissue where it floods over the mountain top.

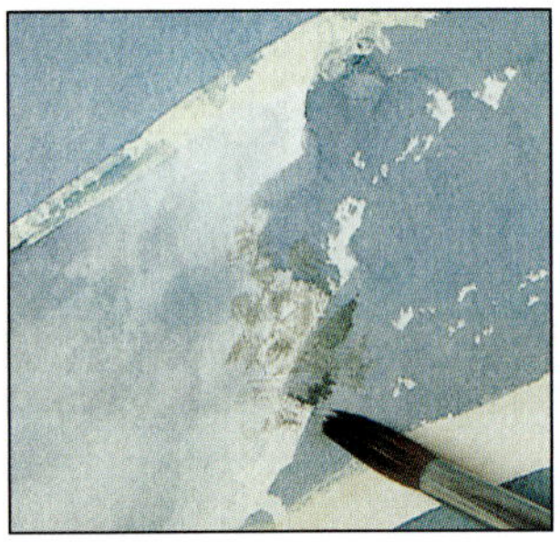

2 Paint the mountain shadows with the same two colors. Scumble dry sepia, with twisting movements, onto the rocks and peppered snow in the center.

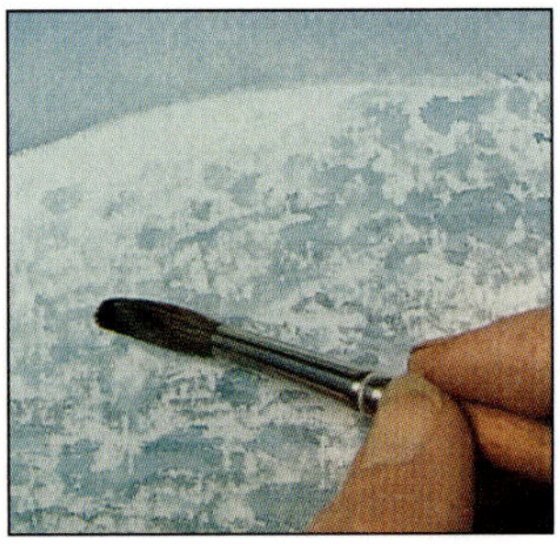

3 With a dilute but dry mixture of Antwerp blue and Payne's gray, scumble the area of trampled snow in the foreground. Repeat the process, patting and twisting the brush head.

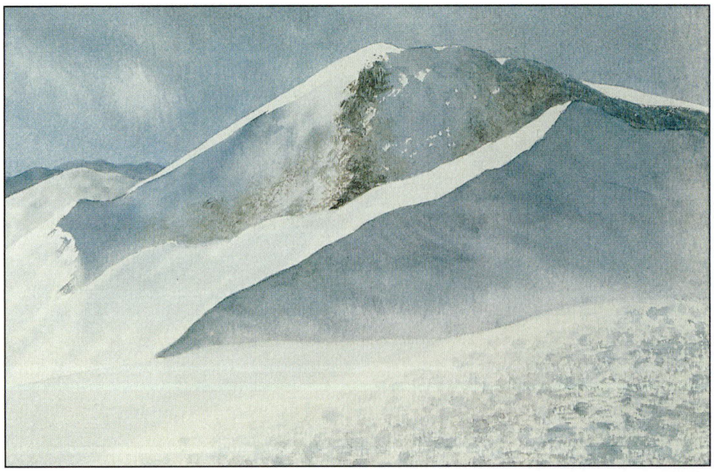

4 Remove the masking with the fingers. Wet the white area and drop in Antwerp blue for soft shadows in the undulating snow.

Rocks

The varied shapes, forms, and textures of rocks offer a wealth of possibilities. Once you have established the structures you can have fun experimenting with texture.

Brush in the main dark areas with a neutral tone, looking carefully at the shapes they make, as these describe the three-dimensional forms. If the rocks are gently rounded, further washes can be applied wet-into-wet, but for angular forms you need crisp, hard edges, so wait until each wash is dry and build up the forms in successive planes. Keep it simple initially: select three tones from pale to dark and build the structure of the rocks with these. If the rocks have an overall pinkish tinge this color could be used for the first wash.

WET-INTO-WET

Working wet in wet on individual rocks and boulders will create exciting textures. Once you have achieved an effect you like, wait for the area to dry before adding more color; if you disturb the surface too much while still damp, your painting will lose its freshness.

TEXTURE METHODS

Crystals of sea salt sprinkled into wet paint make a fascinating patina that imitates lichen-covered rocks.

Painting over wax – candle or white wax crayon – creates another texture suitable for weathered rock, and you can make the paint behave in interesting ways by laying other water-repellent substances, such as turpentine or oil on the paper under a wash.

Sponging paint onto the paper is a quick and easy way to liven up the surface and suggest texture, and for more random effects, blobs of color can be flicked on; this is a useful way to introduce other colors in an irregular way.

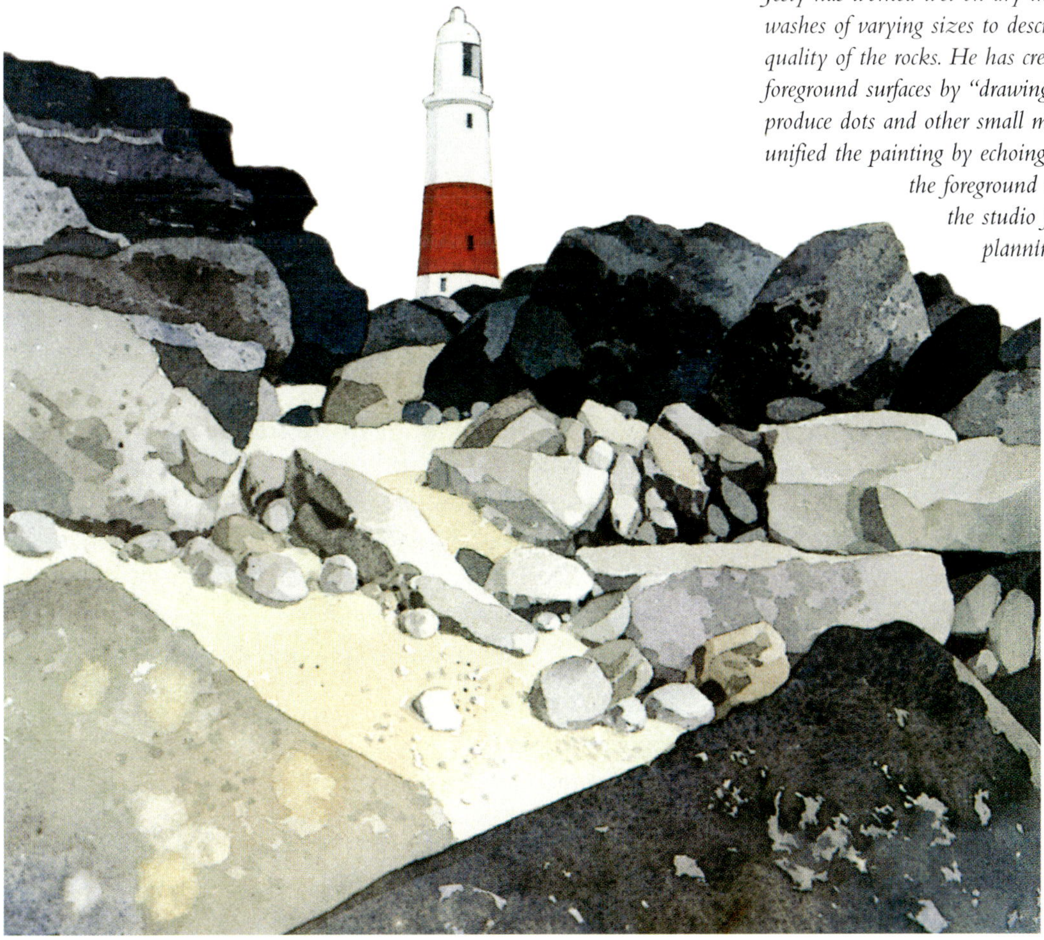

PORTLAND LIGHTHOUSE
by Ronald Jesty RBA

Jesty has worked wet on dry in this picture, using flat washes of varying sizes to describe the crisp, hard-edged quality of the rocks. He has created texture on some of the foreground surfaces by "drawing" with an upright brush to produce dots and other small marks, and has cleverly unified the painting by echoing the small cloud shapes on the foreground rock. This was painted in the studio from a pen sketch. Advance planning is a prerequisite for Jesty's very deliberate way of painting, and he works out his compositions and the distribution of lights and darks carefully.

VARIEGATED WASH

Merge colors, wet-into-wet, to create an underpainting. While the variegated wash is wet, color can be dropped in. The structure of the rocks is drawn on top and the rocks take on individual colors in a total harmony.

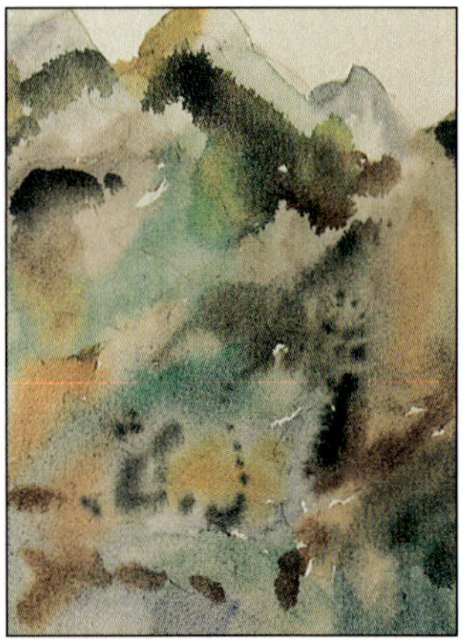

1 Sketch the rocks and lay a washy mixture of viridian, mauve, Indian red, and ultramarine. Drop and flick more color into the wet wash.

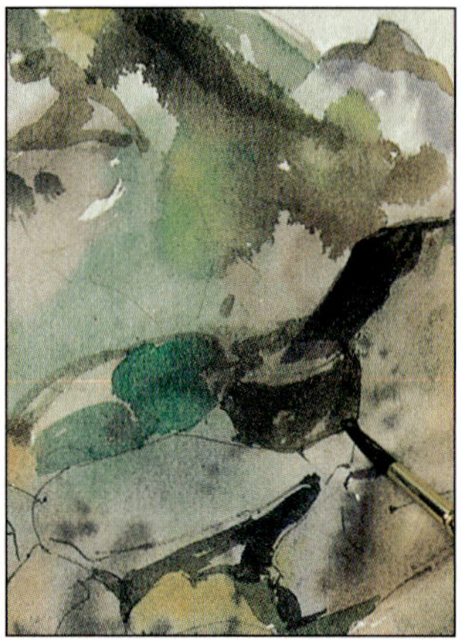

2 With the line and small washes of indigo, itemize the individual rocks and the gaps between them.

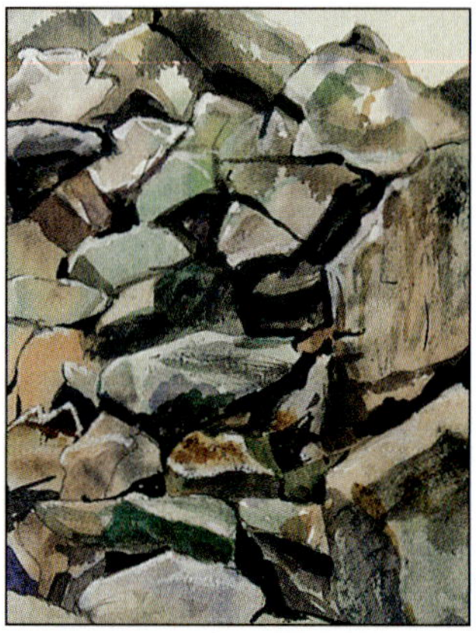

3 Use brush strokes of white gouache to pick out light ridges and faces on the angular rocks. The rocks tumble together as a whole, but appear to have been painted in different colors.

WET-INTO-WET/SPONGING/SPATTER

Create rotund forms by dropping color into the shaded sides of wet washes on the rocks. Once the structure is realized, surface textures can be overlaid by applying dry paint with a sponge and spattering paint from a loaded toothbrush.

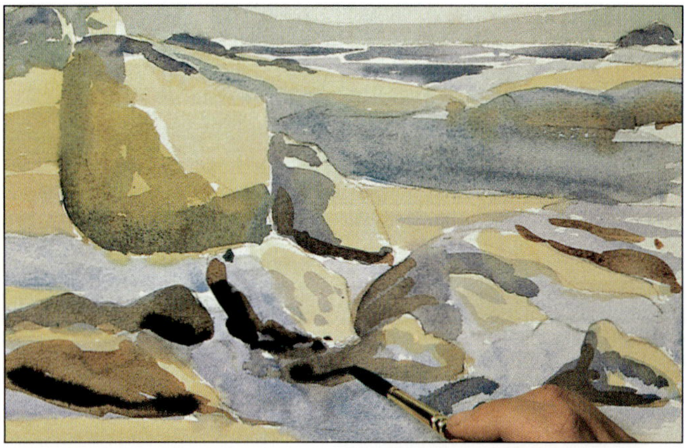

1 Sketch out the landscape. Lay your washes to build up the tonal structure of the composition. Drop indigo into the wet, shaded sides of rocks, allowing it to spread.

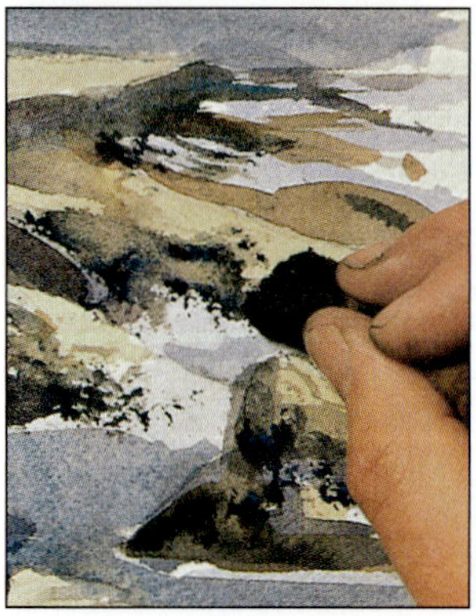

2 Having established the lights and darks of the rocks, sponge indigo across the edges of light as if the grainy surface were turning away from the light and casting small shadows.

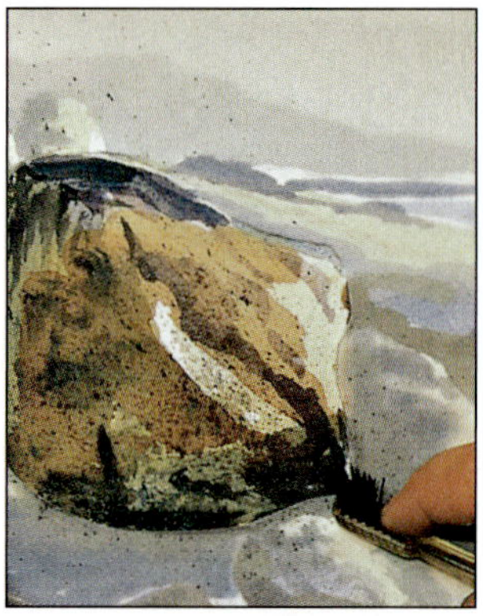

3 Cut the boulder shape out of tracing paper. Load a toothbrush with dark paint and spatter the paint from it across the rock surface from one corner.

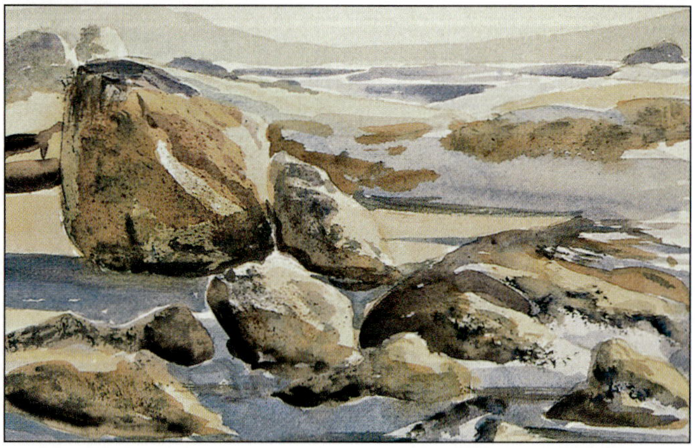

4 Apply paint with a sponge to the dark foreground rocks and, with wetter paint, pat it onto the middle-distance rocks for a softer effect.

Beaches and Sand

Beach landscapes conjure up many things – holidays, chosen loneliness, freedom, romance, the elements. Decide what you wish to convey in your painting. Choose warm, bright colors for a holiday atmosphere, or seek out the earth colors for wild isolation. Before you begin, assess the overall colors.

COLOR AND COMPOSITION

Sand, for example, is unlikely to be yellow; it may be a diluted yellow ocher or raw sienna, slightly pinkish, gray, or nearly white. Wet sand is usually darker than dry sand, and creates intriguing reflections, which you can use to enhance the wetness.

Composition is important. Find a foreground feature to help throw the background into the distance. Sand dunes, rocks, or driftwood give you an opportunity to use some stronger color and tone in the foreground, which will help paler colors in the distance recede.

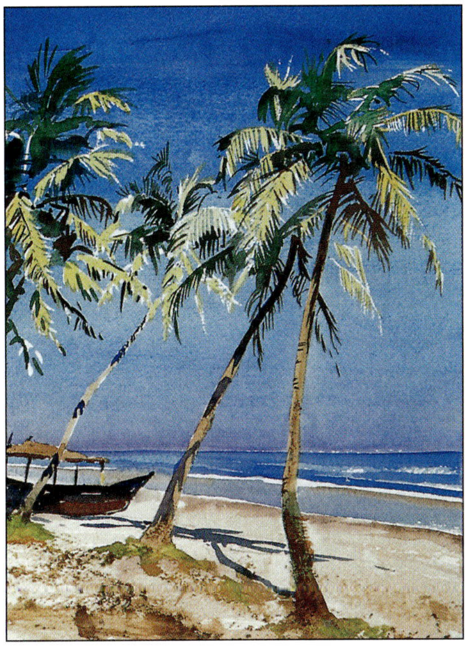

GRADUATED WASHES

The horizontal format of sea and sand, with sky above, lend themselves well to graduated washes. Only dampen the paper down to the crests of waves – or work on dry paper – and do not touch the wash while it is drying. Alternatively, try working on a rough-textured paper – the speckles of white paper left untouched by the pigment create natural highlights. For soft shadows in undulating sand, work wet-into-wet, brushing in the shadow color while the first wash is still damp.

TEXTURE

Sand textures can be conveyed by flicking and spattering, even by using real textures, such as sugar scattered into a wash, or sand mixed with gum arabic.

FLICKING

The grainy nature of sand dunes is enhanced by loading a brush with plenty of strong pigment and literally flicking it across the paper in a chosen direction by holding the brush toward the end of the handle.

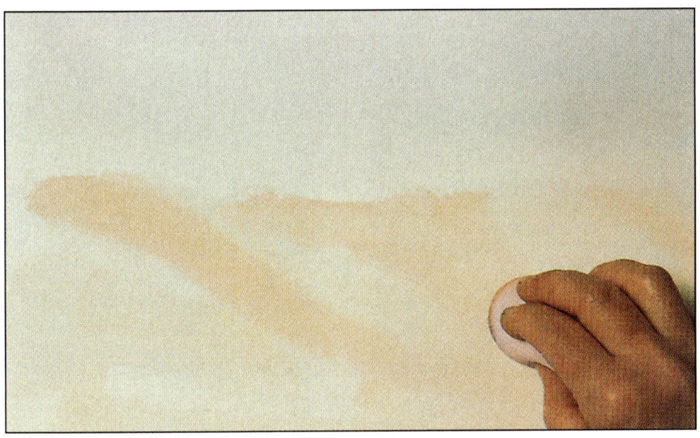

1 First lay a wash for the sky and sand dunes, dropping darker color into the wet dunes to create undulations in the sand.

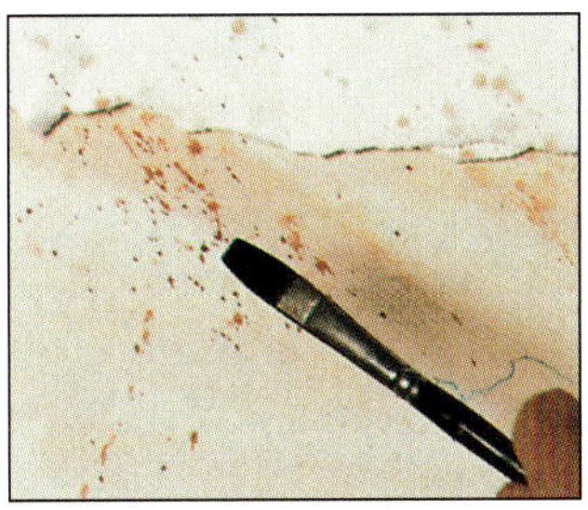

2 Protect the sky with a mask of paper, torn to correspond with the line of the dunes. Load the brush with a strong solution of paint and flick the brush diagonally across the paper.

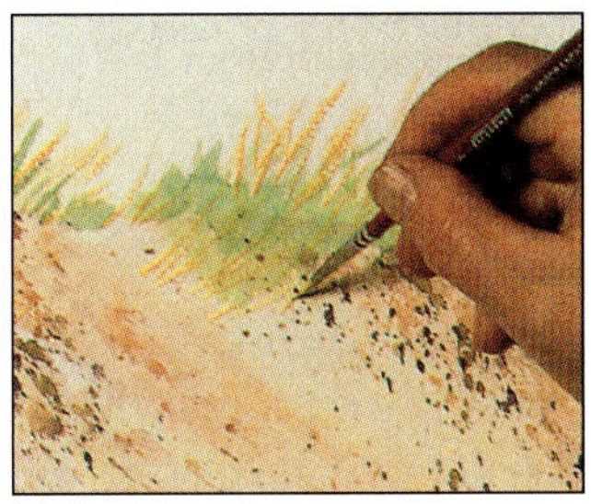

3 After flicking several different colors, remove the paper mask and touch in the grasses with quick, upward brush strokes.

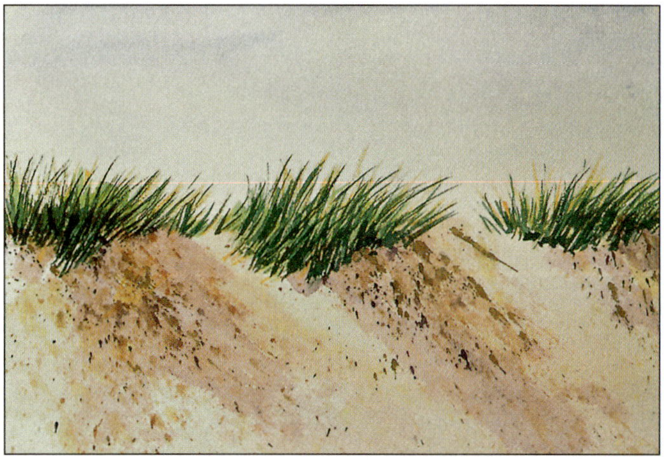

4 Thicken the grasses with stronger color and cast a warm mauve shadow down the face of the dune. Paint this with single strokes of a wide, flat brush so as not to disturb the flicked texture.

GRADUATED WASHES

A delicate underpainting of graduated washes is a good base for quickly creating the subtle variations of wet and dry sand bordering the sea. Prepare plenty of well-diluted paint before you begin. A few subsequent washes and small details complete the picture.

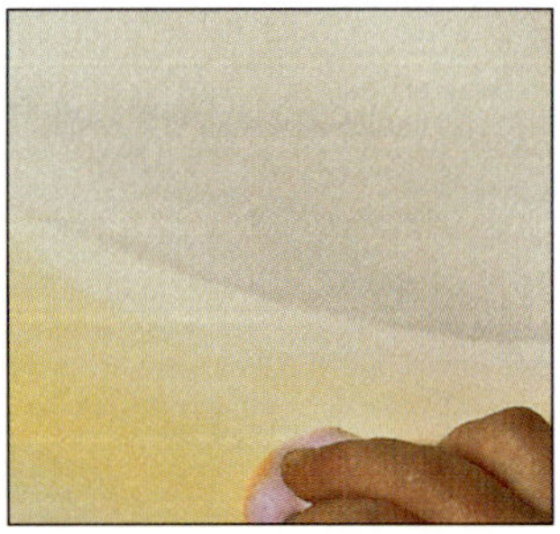

1 Separate the sky wash from the beach by leaving dry white paper between them. Use a flat make-up sponge to lay gently graduating washes, increasing the density of color over the sea and below the area of wet sand.

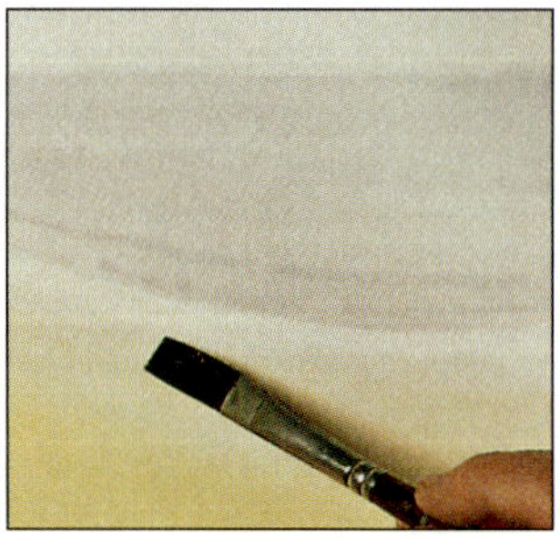

2 Darken the sea with cerulean and Payne's gray. Just before the beach wash dries, brush in a diluted wash of Payne's gray along the wet sand, letting it spread slightly.

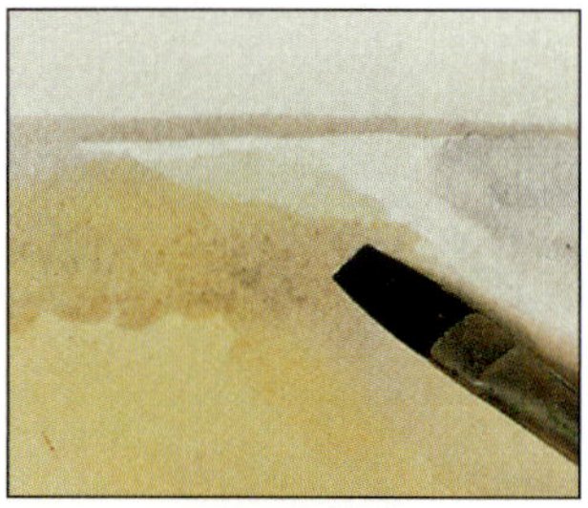

3 Brush in the rock forms while the wash is still wet and allow the color to run into the wet sand. Darken the rocks with burnt umber.

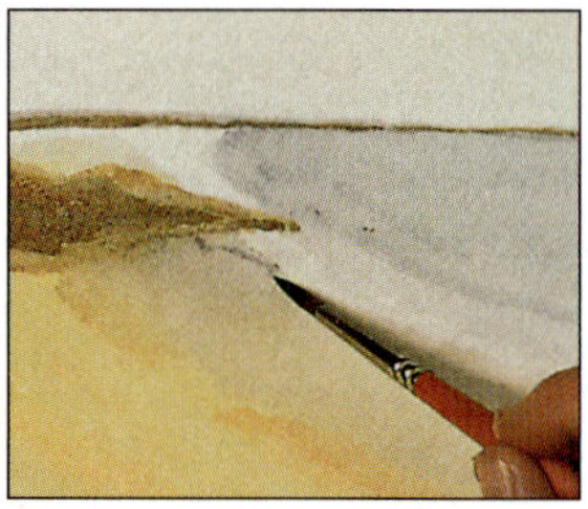

4 When the paint is dry, pick out the shadows under the wavelets with fine broken brush strokes running along the lines of reserved white paper.

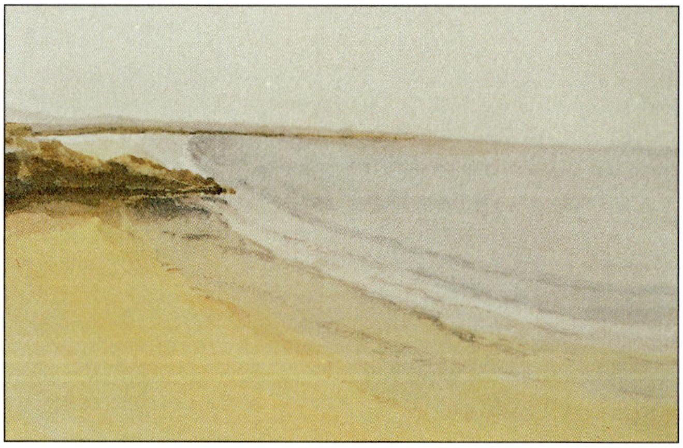

5 Paint a few more brush strokes along the wave lines in the sea and some dry brushmarks across the wet sand and beneath the rocks to emphasize the reflections of wet sand.

Trees and Foliage

Trees are an important theme of many landscapes, and the serious artist should study them as closely as a portrait painter studies the human face and figure. Observation is the key to painting trees convincingly; not only does each species have a particular shape and growth pattern, but each tree within this species has a unique character. It will help your painting enormously if you take the trouble to go out and sketch trees, in all seasons, and learn to look at them analytically.

Deciduous trees lose their leaves in winter, which is a good time to study their characteristic "skeletons" without the distraction of their leaves. Compare the height of the tree to the spread of its branches and try to get the proportions right; note how some of the branches grow almost horizontally, whereas others are almost vertical; try to define the silhouette and "gesture" of various tree species and compare their differences. An oak tree, for example, has a squat, rounded silhouette, with a heavy trunk and gnarled branches. The elm, on the other hand, has a tall, slender, graceful silhouette.

When it comes to actually painting trees, don't allow yourself to become overwhelmed by the apparent complexity of branches, twigs, and leaves. Trying to paint every leaf is not only frustrating, it also makes the tree look stilted, like a paper cut-out. But, making do with a generalized version of a tree – a shapeless mass of green punctuated with a few dark branches – is equally undesirable.

The best approach is to look for the large shapes and masses which characterize that particular tree and which give it volume, and to paint them as broadly and directly as possible. Begin by reducing the outline or silhouette of the tree to its simplest form and blocking in the shape as a solid mass of tone (remembering to leave gaps between the branches, particularly around the outer edges). Next, indicate the main foliage masses within this overall shape. Notice how each mass is modeled by light and shade, and that each casts its own shadow on nearby masses of foliage. Finally, use a smaller brush to add the most important branches and twigs, and a suggestion of foliage.

This procedure is, of course, a very simplified one, to give you the general idea of how to work from the general to the particular. At the same time, there are certain points that you should look out for as you are painting. For example, a poorly painted tree often looks as if it has been stuck to the ground instead of growing up and out of the soil. Avoid this by indicating the roots that spread out at the base of the tree and stabilize it. Also, by darkening the tone of the tree trunk as it nears the ground and by softening the edges of the trunk near its base, you will give it the appearance of being linked naturally to the ground.

Pay attention to the limbs of the tree also. A common mistake is to make all the branches grow sideways, ignoring the fact that some will extend toward and away from you. Notice also how the limbs taper gradually from thick to thin as they reach outward and become lighter in tone near the top of the tree, where they receive more light.

One very important factor which is often overlooked is the gaps between the branches. Even when a tree is in full foliage, there are plenty of "sky holes," particularly around the outer edges of the branches. By introducing them you will make the tree look natural and graceful; ignore them, and it will look solid and heavy.

Trees and foliage give you an ideal opportunity to experiment with brush stroke techniques. In oil and acrylic, the gnarled branches of an old apple tree might be best treated with strokes of thick impasto. In watercolor, a few delicate dry brush strokes will render the papery bark of a birch tree; a whole mass of foliage can be represented by short dabs of broken color, whereas long, graceful strokes of this color can suggest the wispy growth of a willow tree. The most important point, however, is to express the idea of the tree as a living thing. To achieve atmosphere and a sense of the tree moving in the breeze, keep the edges of the foliage soft and feathery by merging them into the sky color, wet-into-wet.

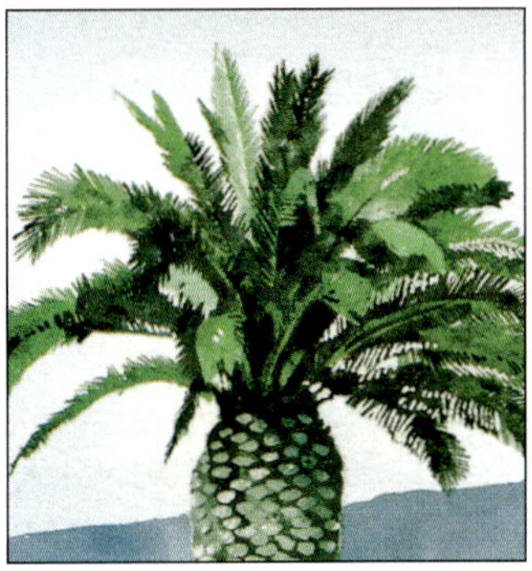

This picture shows a species of palm tree, with softer, more feathery foliage. These forms are very complex, especially since the nearest fronds are foreshortened as they curve toward us. The secret is to capture the essential characteristics of the foliage without overworking the painting. Sap green and Payne's gray are used here to create a few simple tones, laid down in overlapping washes and blotted with a tissue to create texture. Form and volume are preserved by concentrating darker washes in the "inner core" of the foliage, while the lightest tones are found at the outer edges, painted with feathery dry brush strokes.

PEN AND INK

Use a dip pen and waterproof Indian ink. The definition achieved with the pen is used to draw the composition with gestural lines in order to describe the tree shapes and foliage masses. Thin glazes of color are used to build up the color in the painting.

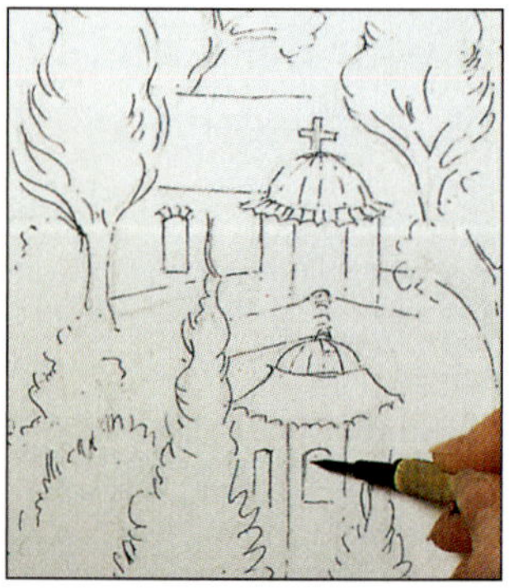

1 Sketch out the painting with the dip pen, lightly at first, and then go over it with a thicker nib. Flick some ink on the foreground bushes.

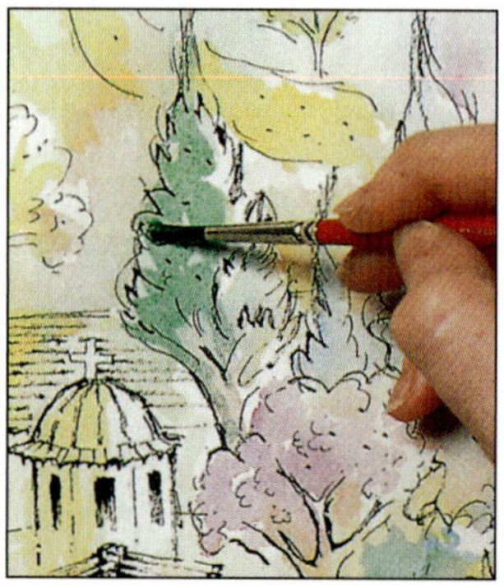

2 Paint a series of different washes over the dried ink and let them blend, slightly wet-into-wet. The colors will overlap the drawing and are not confined by it.

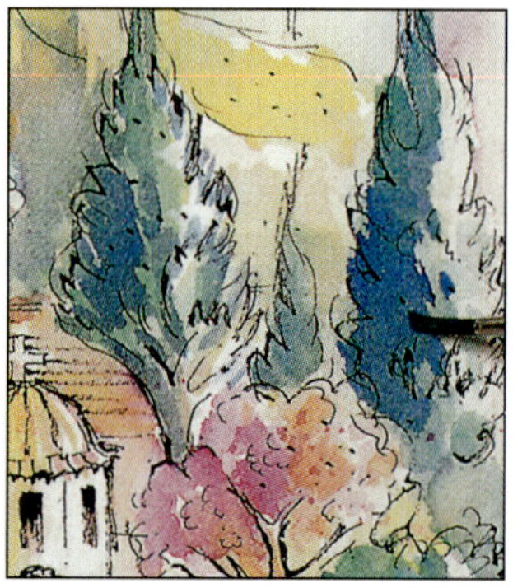

3 Wash a glaze of viridian onto the dark side of the trees, again ignoring the edges.

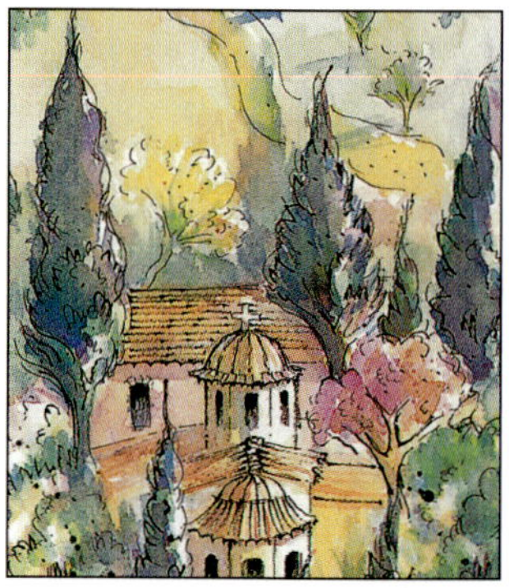

4 Take down the greenness of the trees with a loose wash of rose and Winsor blue, touching it across some of the white areas as you go.

SPONGING

Mix up a pool of color in the palette and dip a slightly damp natural sponge into the paint. Dab it gently over the tree, repeating the process when the previous layer has dried.

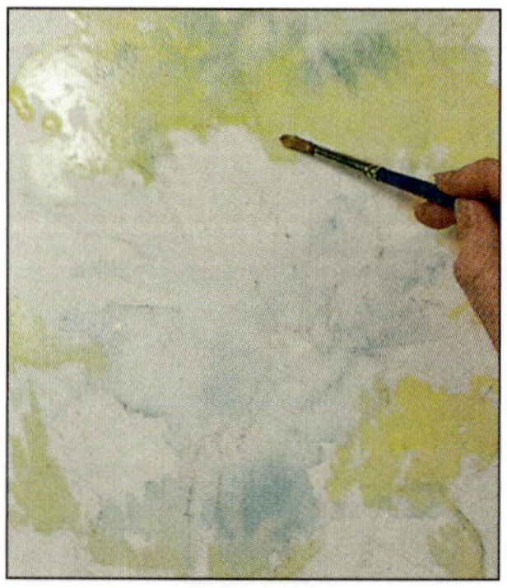

1 Lay a wash of cadmium yellow, pale and cerulean blue over the painting.

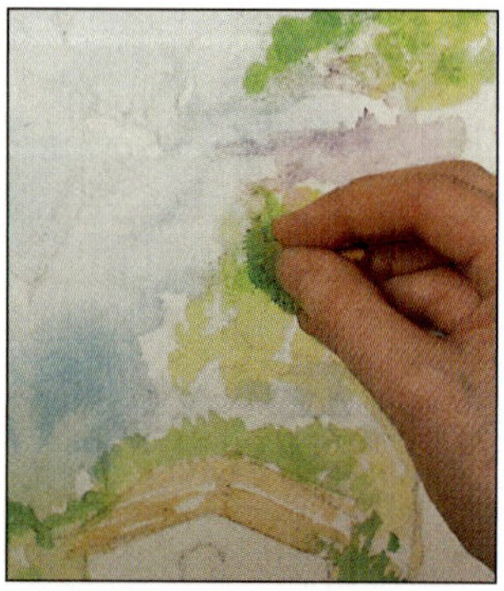

2 Apply a mixture of viridian and yellow with a damp sponge to build up the general shape of the foliage.

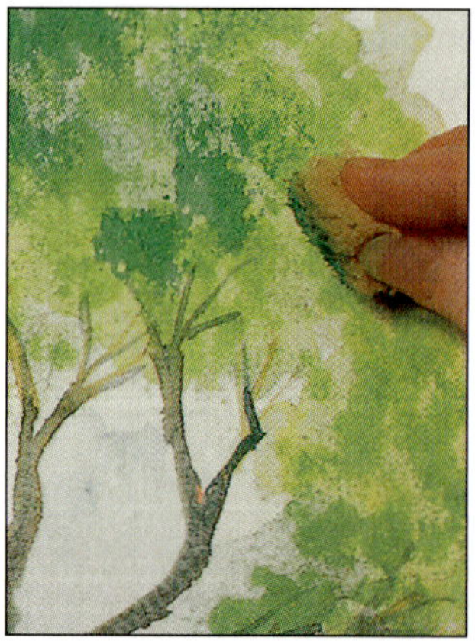

3 Add cerulean to yellow-green and pat over the dark and mid-tone areas of the trees. Sketch in branches.

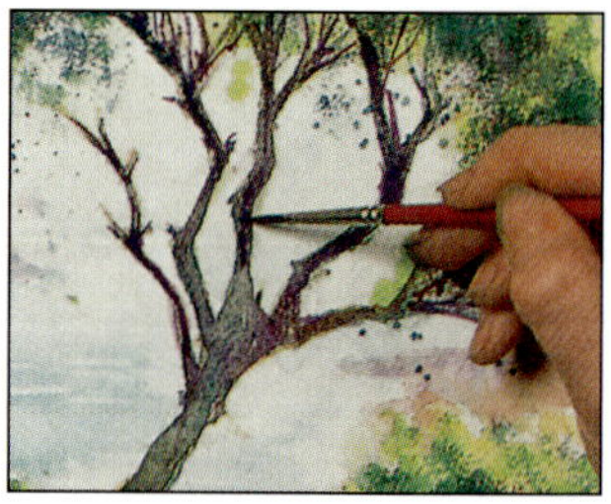

4 Sponge an even darker tone into the dark shadows and draw down the branches while still wet. Darken the trunk with colors that key into the foliage.

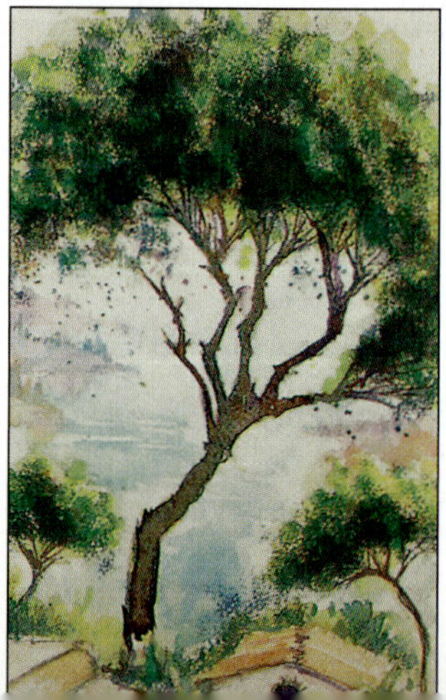

5 Lastly, sponge some yellow ocher on top of the dark foliage to add patches of opacity.

People

The question of whether or not to include figures and animals in a landscape depends on the mood you are trying to convey. If you wish to project a feeling of peace and seclusion, the addition of figures may be inappropriate. But in many cases an element of active involvement in the scene helps to bring it to life.

A group of cows in a distant field, a fisherman by a riverbank, or an old man strolling down a country lane all provide a narrative element, as well as giving life, movement, and scale to the scene. A tiny figure on the shore helps to convey the vastness of the sea; a grand doorway becomes even more imposing with a small figure standing before it.

Having said all this, it is most important that figures be included in the scene for a purpose, and not just to fill up a space. Generally, they should be placed in the middle or far distance, acting as a supporting feature of the landscape; if a figure is placed too centrally, the picture is in danger of becoming a portrait with a landscape in the background.

It is also essential that animals and people be rendered in correct proportion to their surroundings; otherwise a perfectly good painting may be ruined. One way to overcome this problem is to draw the figure on a small piece of tracing paper and lay it on the painting (so long as it is dry). This way you can check that the relative scale of the figure is correct, and you can try the figure out in different positions in the composition. If the result is successful you can go ahead and paint the figure.

Many amateur artists exclude figures from their landscapes because they feel that they are not competent enough at figure painting. But for the purposes of a landscape painting, a detailed figure study is less important than the attitude and activity of the figure. In fact, the less detail you include the better, because it allows the figure to blend naturally with the surroundings. For tiny figures in the distance, a well-placed stroke for the body and a dot for the head may be all that is required. For figures in the middle distance, the best technique is to start with a silhouette of the figures and gradually introduce lights and shadows into them to lend weight and solidity to the forms. The most important thing is to get an interesting shape and a sense of movement. Make sure the figure is engaged in some sort of activity and not just hanging around aimlessly!

The best way to practice figures in landscapes is to make rapid sketches in soft pencil each time you go out on a sketching or painting trip. Keep the sketches small, and aim to capture the gesture and silhouette of the figure or animal. These sketches will be an invaluable source of reference to you when painting landscapes in the studio.

FIGURE SILHOUETTES

With very quick, dryish brush strokes believable figures can be swiftly painted in action. Lively, imprecise lines look more alive than rigid, carefully drawn people. Gesture is important; look for shape. Your people don't have to be accurate to be effective.

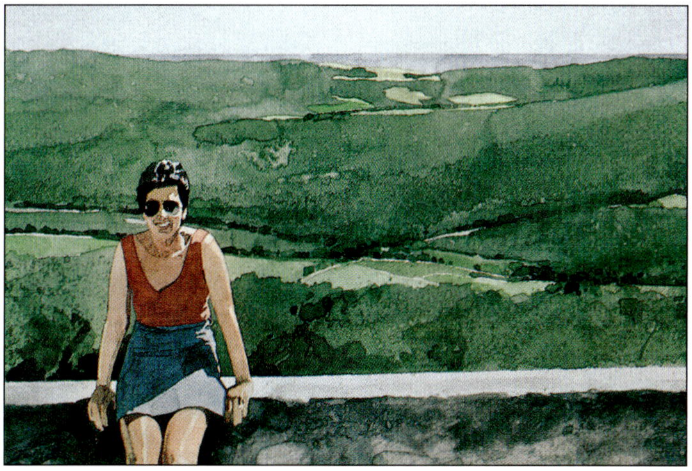

FIGURES IN THE LANDSCAPE

The inclusion of a figure or figures can provide a focal point in a landscape and give an indication of the scale of the other features. In this painting, the figure of the girl in the foreground accentuates the vastness of the mountainous landscape behind her.

The inclusion of a figure or figures can provide a focal point in a landscape and give an indication of the scale of the other features. In this painting, the figure of the girl in the foreground accentuates the vastness of the mountainous landscape behind her. Think carefully about the positioning of figures in your landscapes – they should be an integral part of the overall design. For example, they can be used to stress the importance of the center of interest, or to lead the eye into the picture.

FIGURES IN A LANDSCAPE

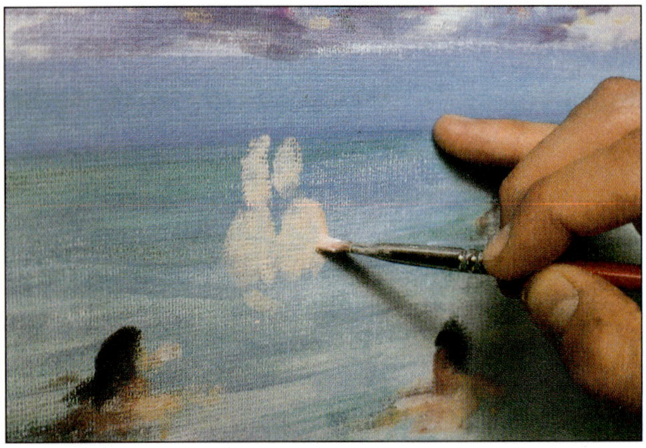

1 In painting the figures in the landscape the artist has decided that they are too small to be painted in detail. With simple broad brush strokes he applies the basic skin tones, laid on top of the background color.

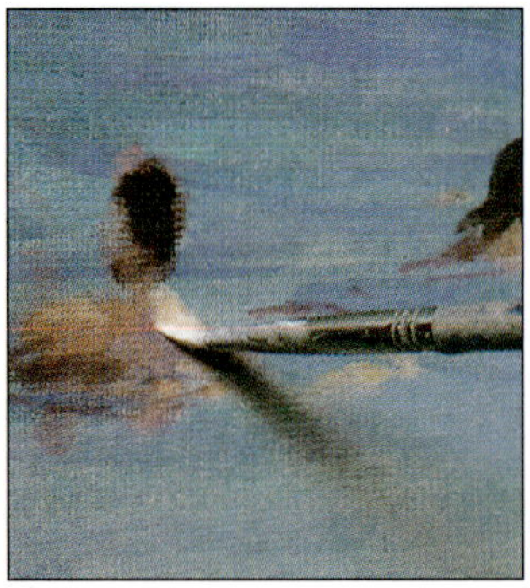

2 Then he adds the darker tones for the hair and the modeling of the figures.

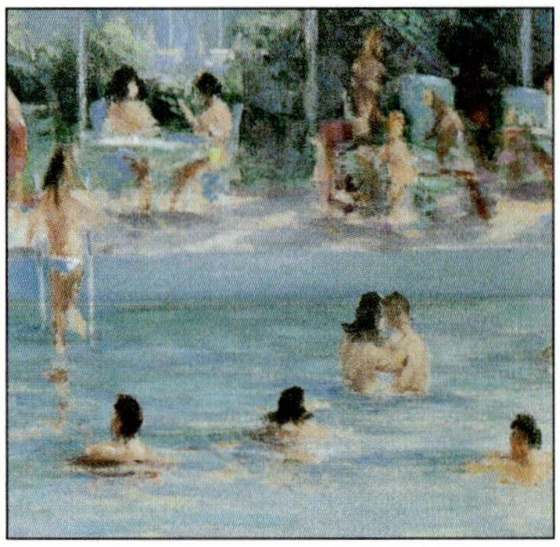

3 In the final picture everything falls into place. The figures, which looked like blobs of paint close up, now look very lifelike.

FIGURE SILHOUETTES

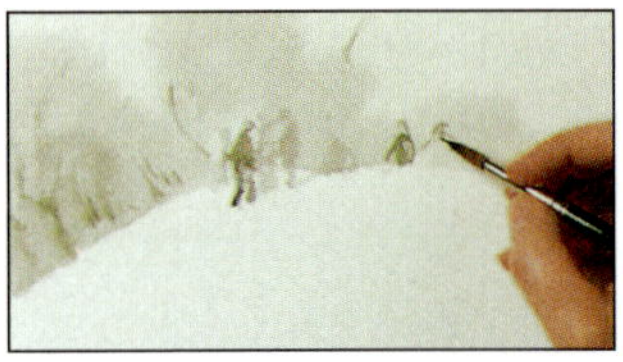

1 Lay a pale wash for the sky and wash in the trees while wet. Leave the snowy hill as white paper. Sketch the figures in lightly with a brush in gray, and emphasize movement with the brushmark.

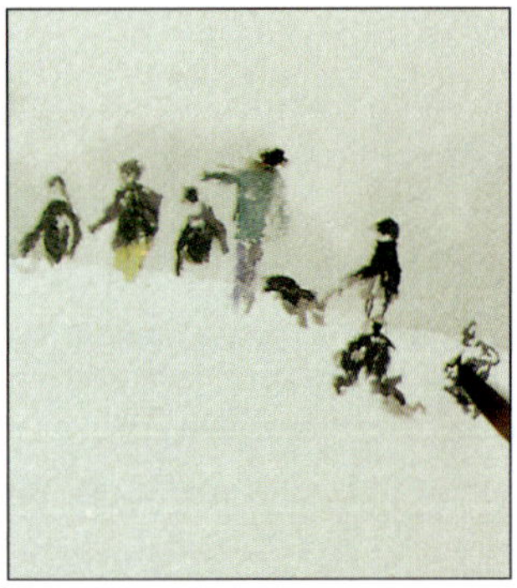

2 As the color dries, paint a dash of color into a couple of figures for variation. Now go over them with a darker color, but leave some of the undertone peeping through.

3 Strengthen the background trees slightly against the figures, and brush in the foreground tree. The figures are lively and descriptive with very little painting.

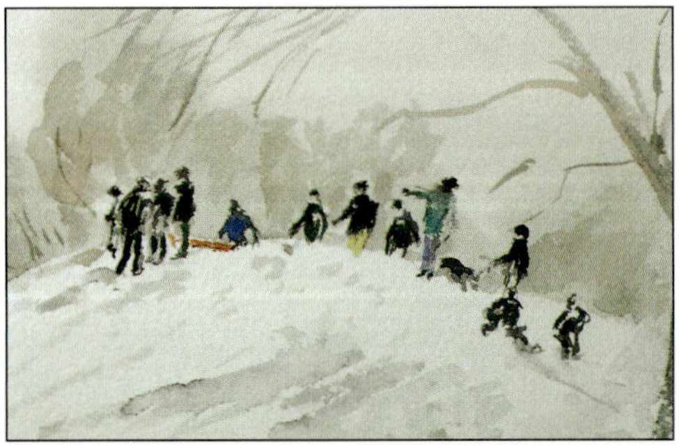

ONE-TOUCH BRUSH STROKES

In this example use a quick touch of white gouache to indicate the body of the man walking his dogs. For the white to stand out, a dark background is necessary. The head and legs are, likewise, quick strokes of the brush.

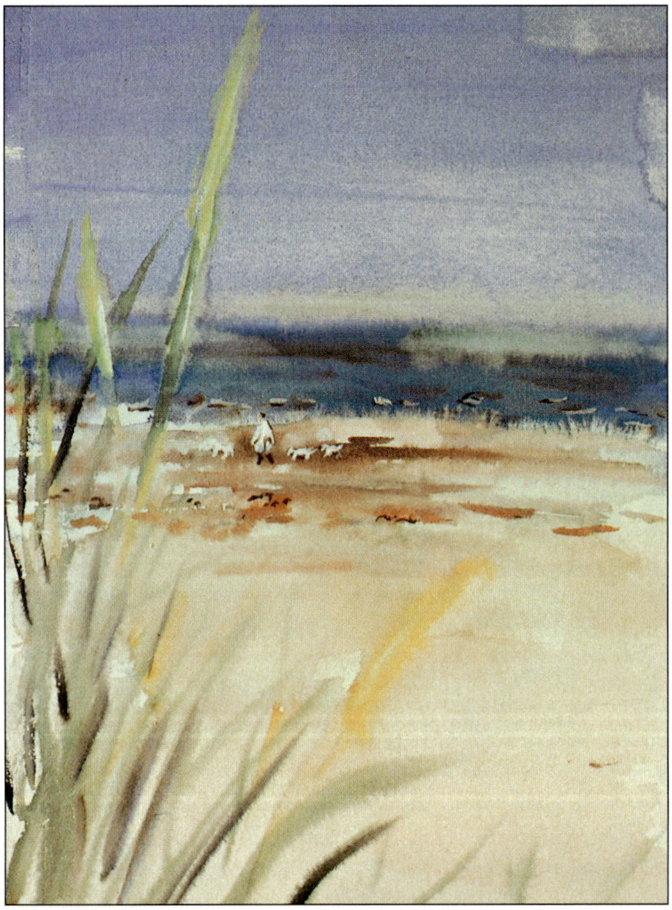

Buildings in Landscapes

Buildings in landscapes tell a story. A small dwelling set beneath hills or mountains may hint at an isolated life and an ancient ruin tells of past splendor.

Buildings can also create a focal point, a foreground feature or even just a splash of color or a regular shape contrasting with natural forms. If the building is in the foreground, the texture of its walls will be an important part of the painting. There are various useful tricks for rendering texture in watercolor.

RESERVING WHITE PAPER

White buildings such as those adorning Mediterranean landscapes are best reserved as white paper. Define their shapes by using the colors of the landscape around them, so that they shine out like jewels against the dark terrain, then pick out details with small brush strokes.

WINDOWS

Windows in buildings are like eyes in a face; they add character. Touch them in with wet one-touch strokes of strong varied color, tilting the paper so that more pigment settles either at the top or bottom. This helps to suggest the reflective nature of the glass.

SHADOWS

Follow the same tilting procedure for any shadows under the lintel and to one side of the window, to create depth.

Settle your buildings well-into the ground. Soften the landscape edge with a damp brush, blur it with grasses or obscure it with foliage. Use the shadow cast by the building to link it to the earth.

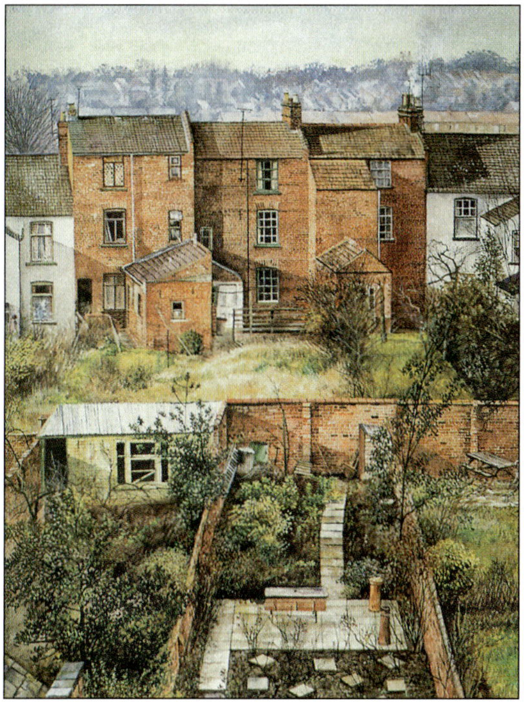

UP THE GARDEN PATH
by Martin Taylor

Taylor loves detail and includes every brick, tile, flagstone, and blade of grass in his paintings. He paints slowly, working on one area of the picture at a time and achieves depth and variety of color by considerable overlaying of brush strokes and washes.

GRANULATED WASH

Some pigments are "heavier" than others, and tend to separate out in a mixture, giving a mottled effect that can be enhanced by working on rough paper. Cerulean, manganese, and ultramarine blues mixed with burnt sienna, alizarin crimson, or yellow ocher make marvelous grainy shadows. The wash must be allowed to dry undisturbed to let the pigment settle.

WAX RESIST

Another way to achieve textures such as stonework or old paintwork is to rub candle wax over the area. The subsequent washes settle only on the unwaxed paper to give a broken-color effect.

Reserving white paper – A light sketch will give you confidence to guide your brush boldly around the shapes of the white buildings. Mix up plenty of pigment and use a size 5, or larger, round brush with a good tip.

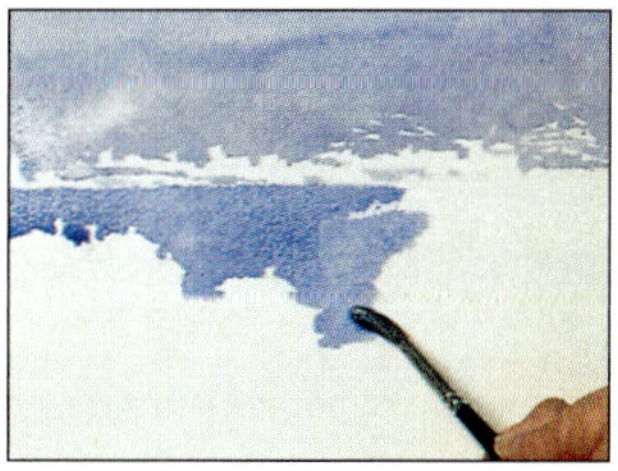

1 Outline the buildings with your brushwork, carrying your wash across the page before it dries around the houses.

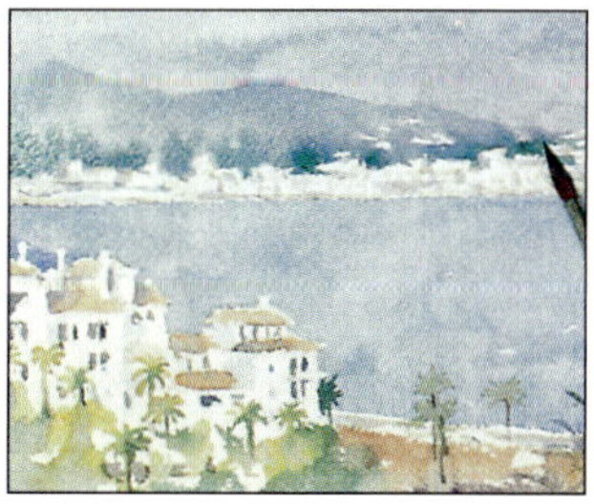

2 Lightly paint the roofs of the distant houses to create a soft mosaic of color. Indicate the windows in the foreground to give confidence to later darker detail. Paint the distant hills with a pale mauve glaze running almost down to the houses.

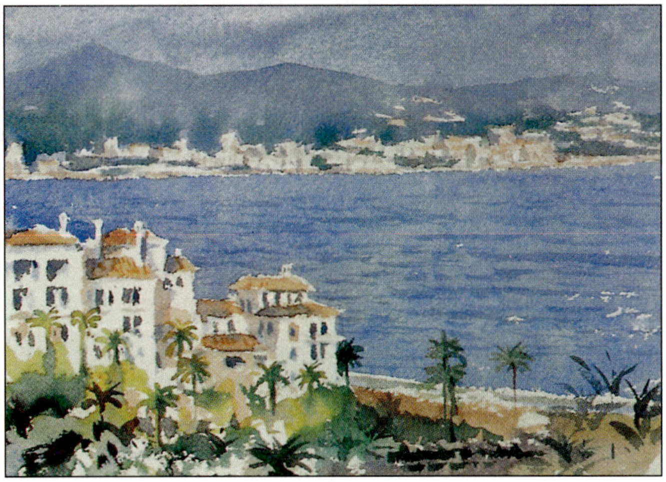

3 Finish the foreground details and glaze over the distant houses with the palest of pinks to set them back from the stark whites of the foreground.

CITYSCAPE

Your choice of viewpoint is an important element in creating a sense of space. The great nineteenth-century French landscape painter Corot always preferred a distant view of his subject, with no immediate foreground, because it allowed him to simplify forms. This artist followed the same practise. He depicts the city from a hill above, with a clear view over the dome and minarets to the farther side of the valley. He works in gouache, an attractive medium, which can be used both thinly and opaquely. The surface is cardboard.

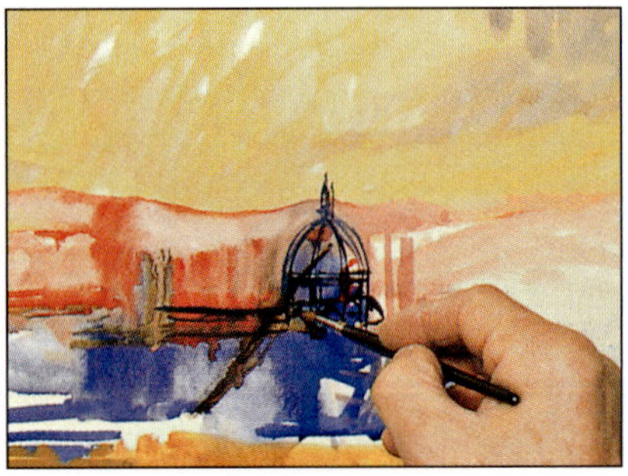

1 The best way to use gouache is to begin with thinned paint. The artist lays loose washes and draws into them with a pointed sable brush.

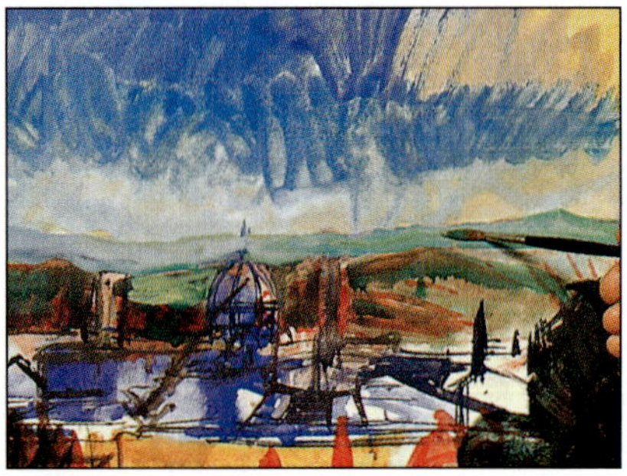

2 He has now introduced sufficient color into the foreground to judge what he needs for the distant hills – a cool gray-green.

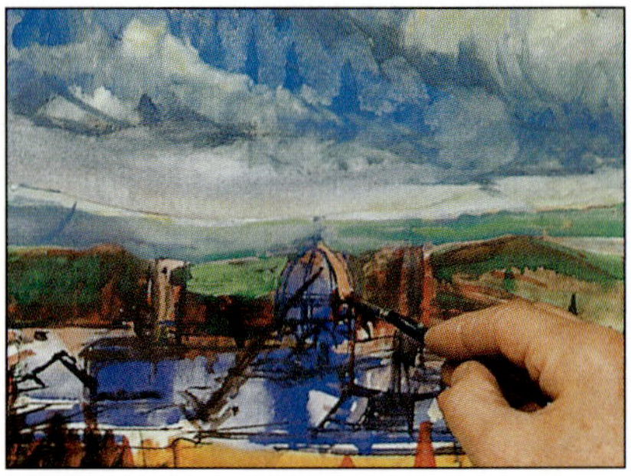

3 Slightly thicker paint, mixed with white to make it more opaque, is used for the sunlit side of the dome, which is lighter in tone than the hills.

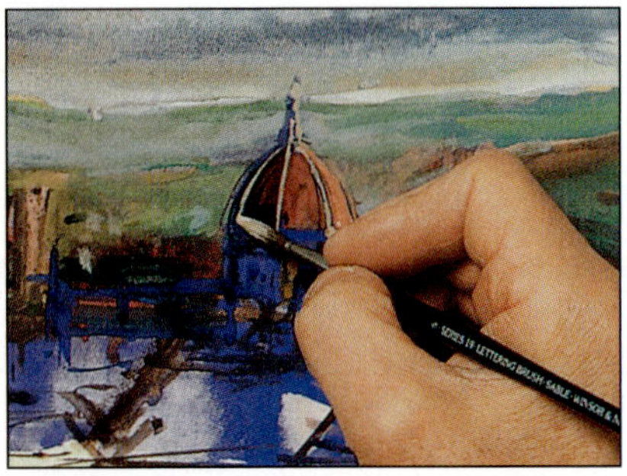

4 The strong light picks out the ribs clearly. This area needs firm definition to make it stand out.

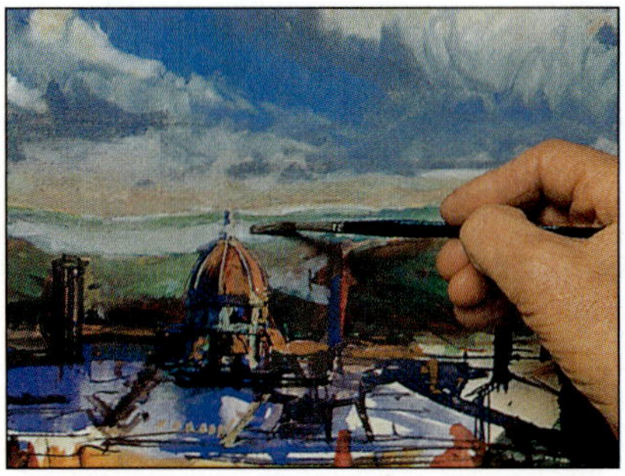

5 A pale wash of blue-white is applied to suggest the layered effect of distant hills. Unlike watercolor, gouache can be worked light over dark.

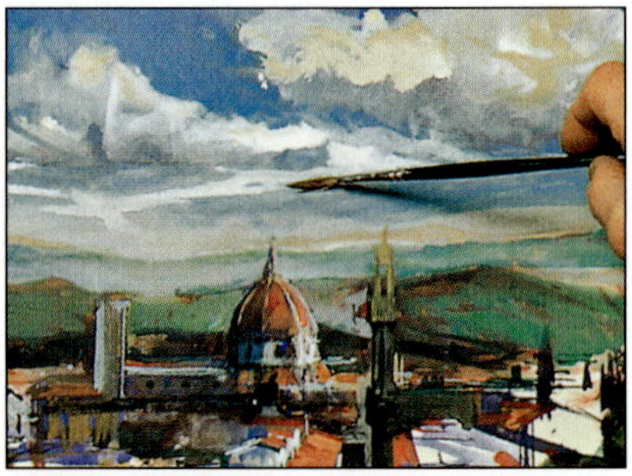

6 White, yellows, and rich blues were used at the top of the sky. On the horizon the tone and color contrasts are less marked, calling for quieter grays.

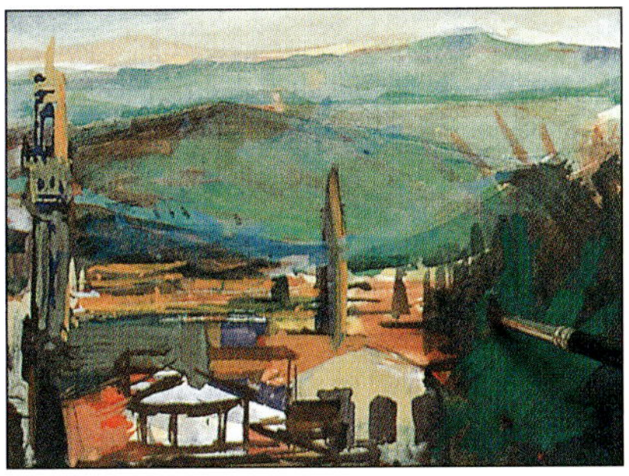

7 Moving to the front of the painting, the artist blocks in the dark tree in the foreground. In Step 10 you will see how he later amends this.

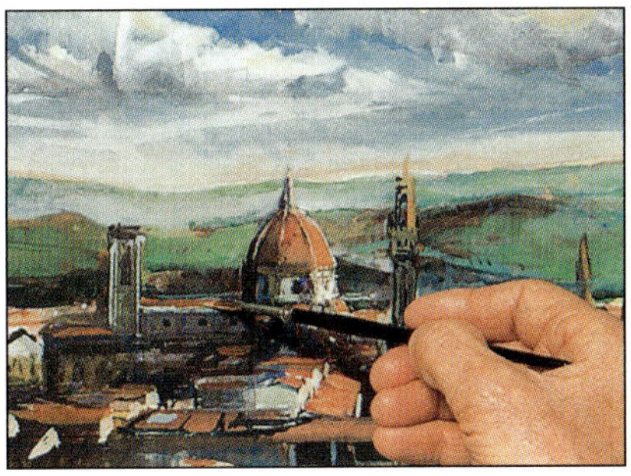

8 Unless used very thickly, gouache tends to sink into earlier colors. The line of the roof became lost and needed strengthening.

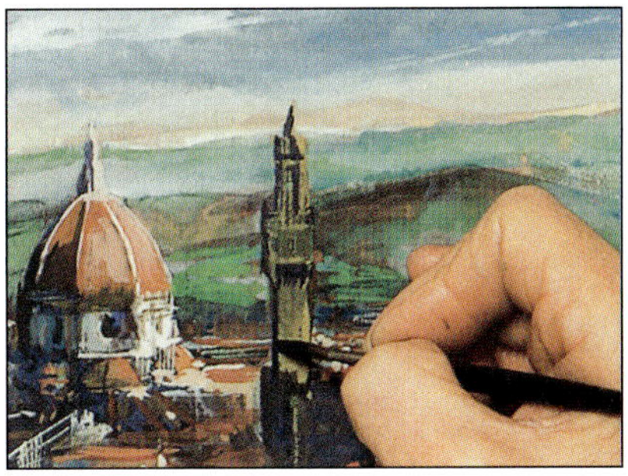

9 A little light-colored paint slipped over onto the shadows side of the minaret to spoil the crisp edge, so this is rectified.

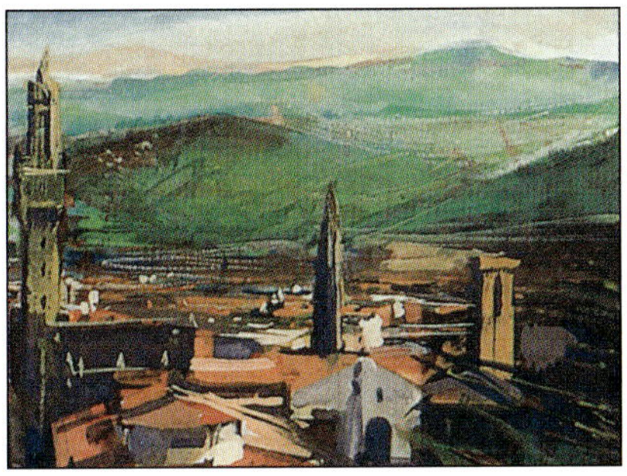

10 The artist now sees that the foreground tree was too obtrusive, so he overpaints with diagonal strokes that lead the eye inward.

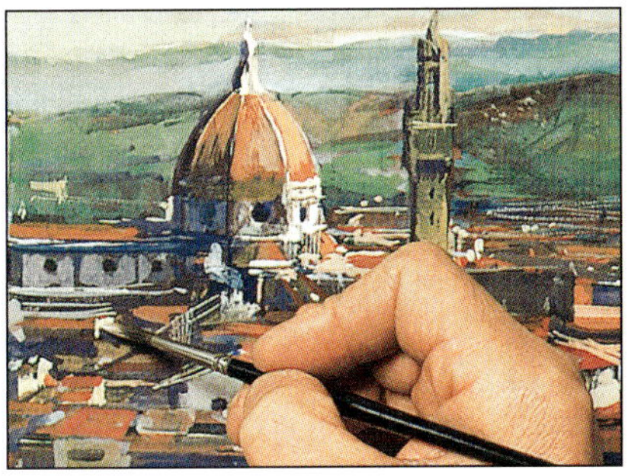

11 The small white shapes formed by the sides of buildings catching the light are also important to the composition, because they lead in toward the dome.

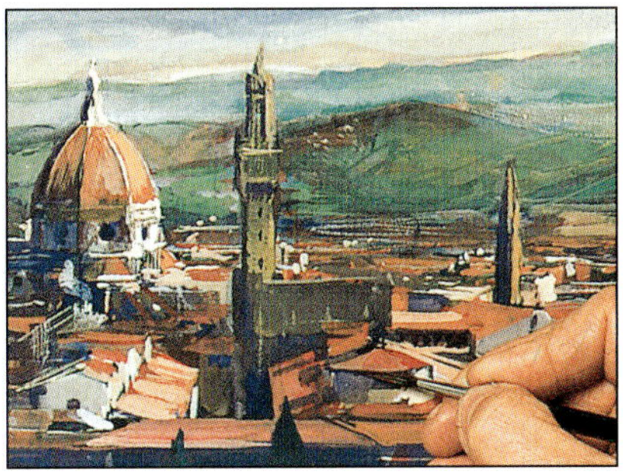

12 A fine pointed brush, held at the ferrule for maximum control, is used for the slender lines of shadow.

THE DUOMO, FLORENCE by David Carr (gouache on cardboard)

The painting derives much of its strength from the deliberate suppression of all unnecessary detail. David Carr has reserved the crispest definition for the central area of the picture around the dome, which is the obvious focal point. On the right and left the buildings are more lightly suggested, and buildings behind the dome are merely hinted at. The warm reds of the buildings, the large area of sky, and the cool colors used for the far hills all combine to create a wonderfully spacious impression.

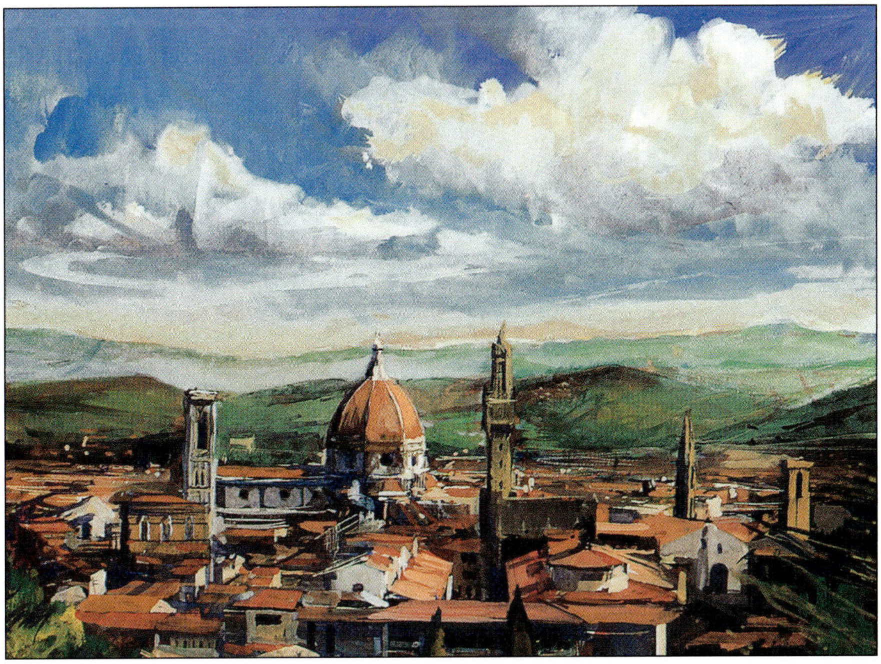

Mood in Landscapes

In a landscape subject, one of the most important elements to consider is light, because light affects both the values and colors of a picture, and both have a significant effect on mood. Claude Monet put it beautifully when he said: "For me, a landscape does not exist in its own right, since its appearance changes at every moment; but the surrounding atmosphere brings it to life – the air and the light, which vary continually."

HOW LIGHT AFFECTS MOOD

Monet became so fascinated by the effects of light and color that he would happily return again and again to the same scene, painting it at different times of the day and in all seasons. Making a series of paintings of the same subject over a period of time is certainly an exercise worth trying, because it demonstrates how even quite small changes in the lighting can alter the balance of values in a picture, and therefore alter the mood it conveys. For example, a seascape viewed at midday might look flat and uninteresting because the light is very even and there is little contrast in values. But a few hours later, as the sun is going down, the luminous values of the evening sky contrast with the cool blue values of the sea and the land, creating a subtle and evocative image.

The seasons, too, offer splendid opportunities to explore the magic of light on the landscape. In winter bleakness, silence and isolation can provide strong mood-themes, as when the branches of bare trees create dramatic patterns of light and dark against the sky. Then again, the same scene is transformed by the sparkling light of a bright frosty morning; this time you might choose a limited range of light values with which to capture the bright high-key mood. A snow-covered landscape on a dull day creates bold patterns of light and dark, and there's also an interesting reversal of values as the sky, for once, appears darker than the land, creating a bleak, wintry feeling.

Viewpoint and composition are important elements in creating mood. The brooding atmosphere of an approaching storm is made more dramatic by placing the horizon line very low so as to place emphasis on the sky. On a sunny day you could try positioning your easel so that much of the view is in shadow except for one telling, sunlit spot. This will create a more dramatic and unusual picture than if the subject were evenly lit.

USING LIMITED TONES

To capture a fleeting mood successfully, it is best to restrict yourself to a limited range of values. Light, by its very nature, is elusive and ever-changing, and often there just isn't time to worry about the finer points – you have to sacrifice details and concentrate on capturing the essentials. With a particularly complex lighting effect, I often make a few simple monochrome sketches in watercolor, using only five values, and these give me enough information about the mood of the scene to be able to create a full-scale painting when I get back to the studio.

This method has much to recommend it, in fact, because it forces you to work from memory when recording the details of form and color. Memory is selective – it "edits out" most of the superfluous details, leaving you with a clear recollection of the elements that most impressed you at first sight. This process of distillation is vital to the success of a picture, because your aim, after all, is to communicate to the viewer the same thrill that you felt – the thrill of the first impression, uncluttered by distracting details.

Even when I make a full-scale based on my sketches, I still try to keep to a limited range of values, because the fewer the values, the more forceful the statement. Remember that as an artist you are in control – you're free to use the subject as a starting point, and to try to express your ideas and feelings about it, rather than slavishly copying everything that's in front of you.

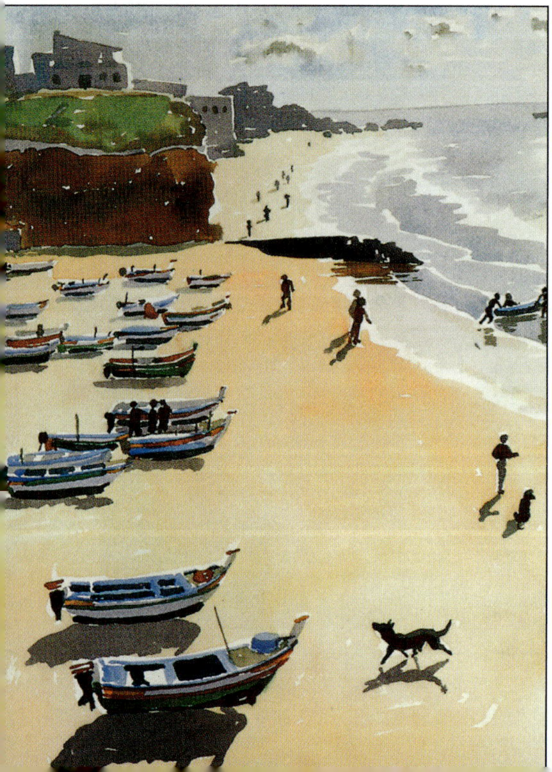

BEACH BOATS by Lucy Willis (watercolor)

This painting emanates a bracing, seaside atmosphere. A sprinkling of dark values helps to accentuate the crisp, bright light that fills the scene.

Landscape in Oil

There are various ways of undertaking the preparatory stages of an oil painting. Here, the composition is roughly outlined using a soft pencil; this method requires a light touch as heavy pressure may dent the canvas and cause the stretched surface to sag.

The composition is divided roughly in half, but the artist has taken care to avoid making a completely symmetrical division of the picture plane, as this would interfere with the spatial illusion.

The low wall and brightly lit garden urn on the left of the painting underline the horizontal emphasis but, more importantly, provide a focal point which contrasts with the large expanse of green. The result is to create an overall sense of harmony. The shades of green are varied by the addition of blue, white, yellow, and red.

The texture of the surface was enlivened by spattering wet paint from the end of the brush and constantly altering the direction of the brush strokes. The best way to apply the paint is to vary the techniques; for instance, lay thin glazes over patches of solid color, scrub the paint into the weave of the canvas, and feather the brush strokes into textured trails.

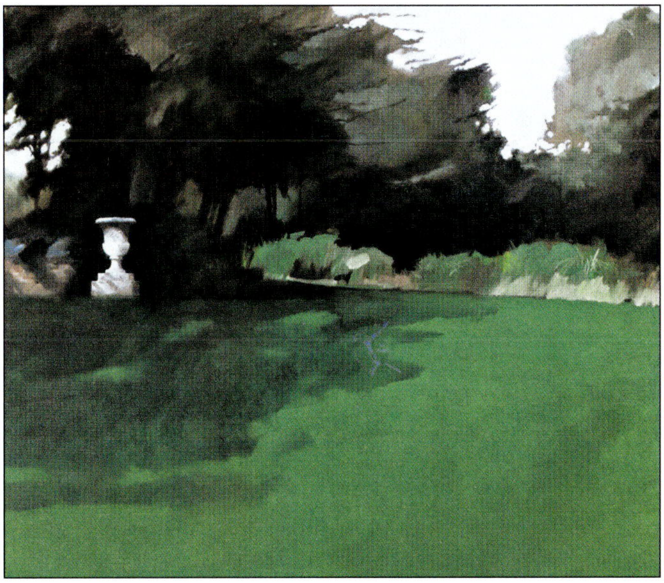

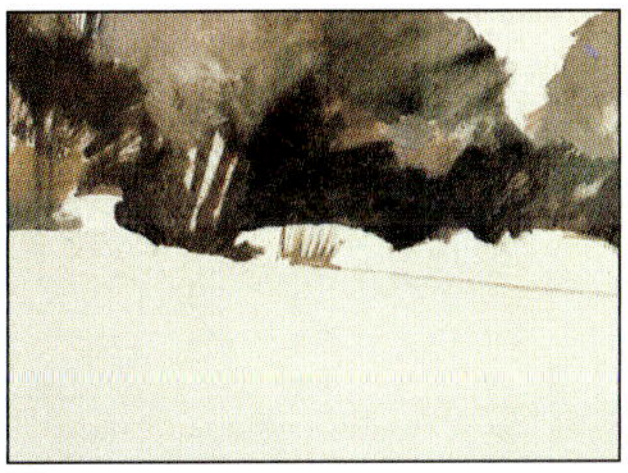

1 Draw up the composition lightly in pencil. Block in a loose impression of the background shapes with thin paint. Use greens with blue, yellow, and red.

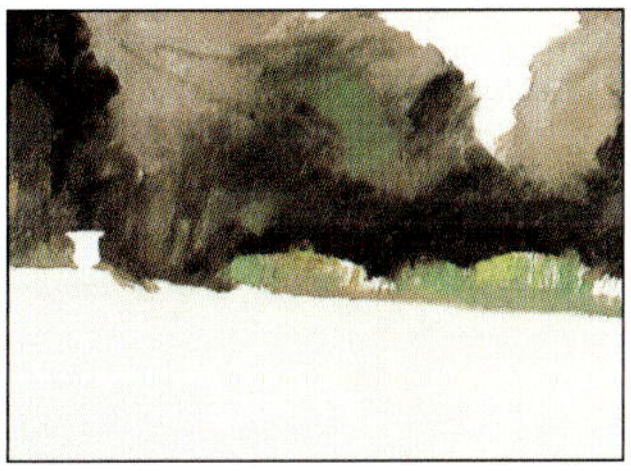

2 Continue to develop the shapes, varying the tonal contrasts and breaking up the color masses with linear brushmarks and small patches of different hues.

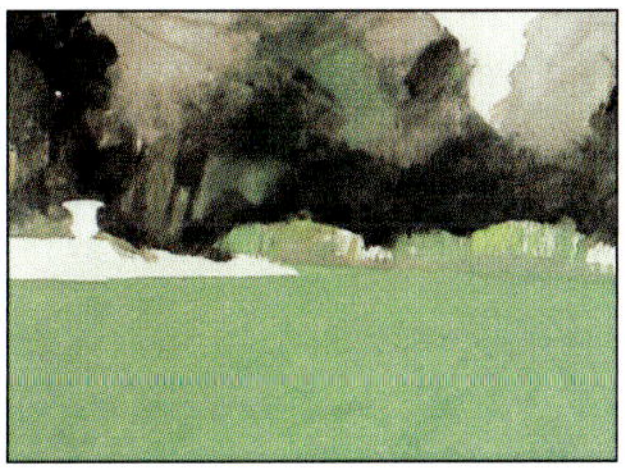

3 Lay in a solid expanse of chrome green across the whole of the foreground, using a 1 in. (2.5 cm) decorator's brush.

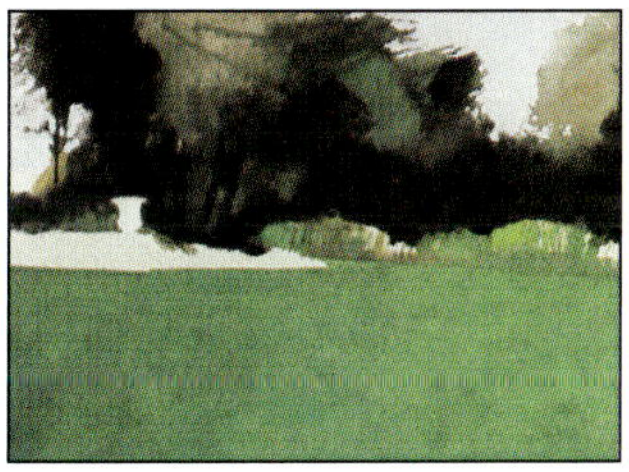

4 Work over the sky and around the forms of the trees with a thick layer of light blue. Draw back into the green shapes with the brush to make the outline more intricate.

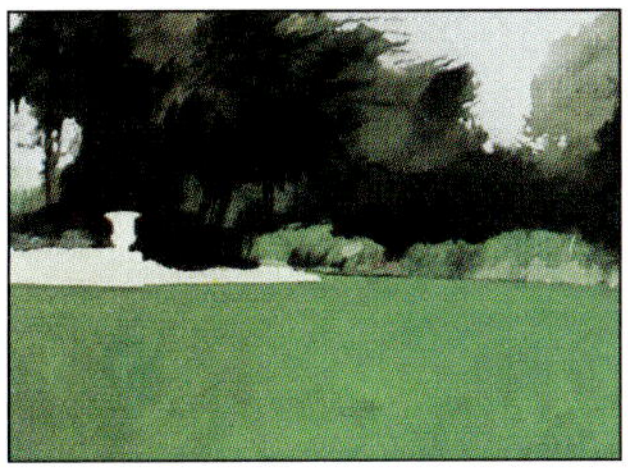

5 Work over the colors with fine linear brushmarks and thin layers of dribbled and spattered paint to increase the variety of tone and texture.

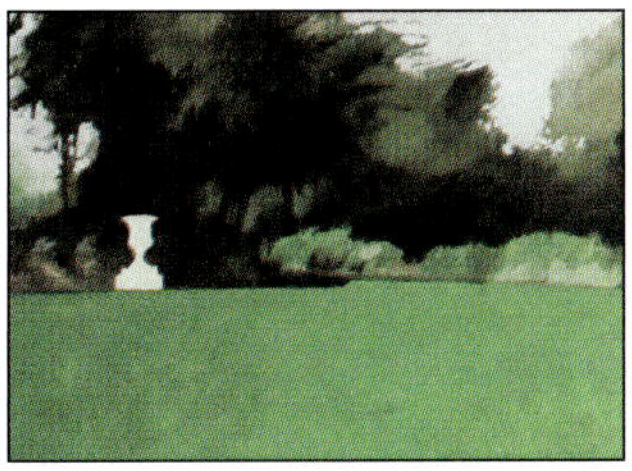

6 Define the shape of the wall with small dabs of brown, red, and pink laid against strong black shadows. Blend and soften the color with a dry brush.

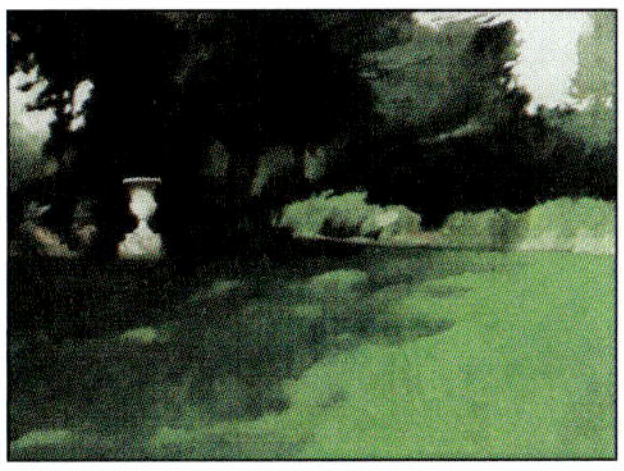

7 Work over the whole image making slight adjustments to the shapes and colors. Bring up the light tones and darken shadows.

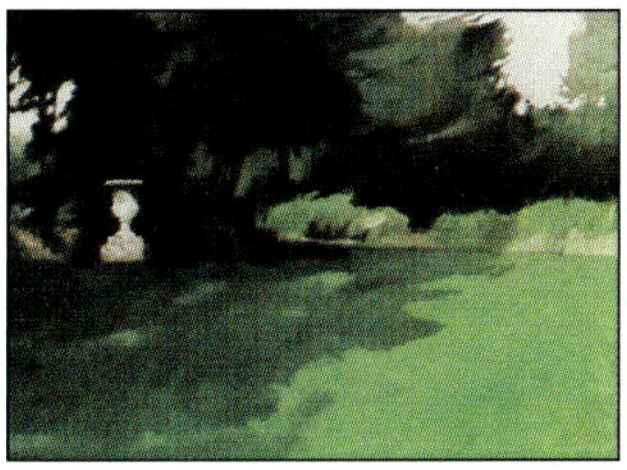

8 Brush in a thick layer of bright green over the right of the foreground, working into the dark shadow area to bring out the illusion of light and shade.

Landscape in Acrylic

Although acrylics are a relatively new phenomena in the painting world, their use has spread quickly, since they are flexible enough for use in most traditional types of landscape painting. Their fast drying time and ability to be thinned to a watercolor-type consistency makes them ideal for the classical technique of overlaying thin areas of color one upon the other.

In the time of the Old Masters, almost all painting was done in this way. It is interesting to note that many of the Masters spent a great deal of their painting time developing the underpainting, and then working quickly through the final stages. Thus what is seen by the viewer in a Velazquez or Rubens are simply the last steps the artist took to complete the picture – with an elaborate underpainting lying just beneath the surface.

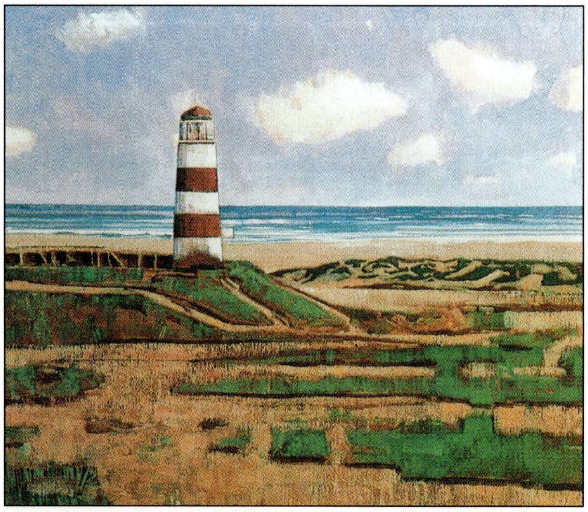

In this painting, the artist decided upon the mood of the picture before laying in the underpainting. As he wanted the painting to have a peaceful mood of a seascape dusk, he chose a reddish underpainting, which would work well with the other colors used and give the entire picture a warmish tone. He has also used the traditional method of working from dark to light – slowly building up highlights from a dark base – and from the general to the specific.

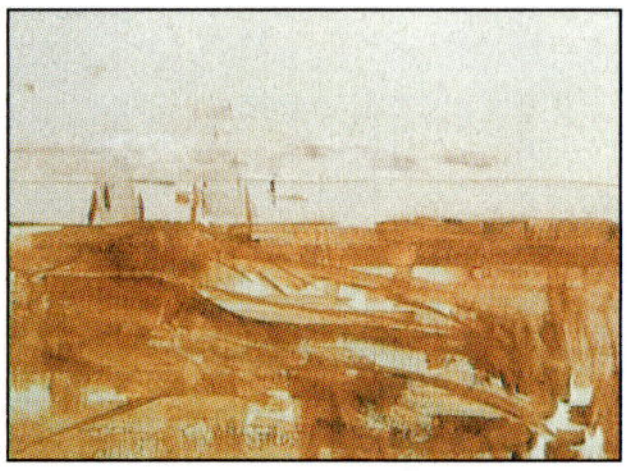

1 Mix a fair amount of burnt sienna and water and apply quickly and loosely with a broad brush. In the foreground, use a drier mixture applied with short strokes.

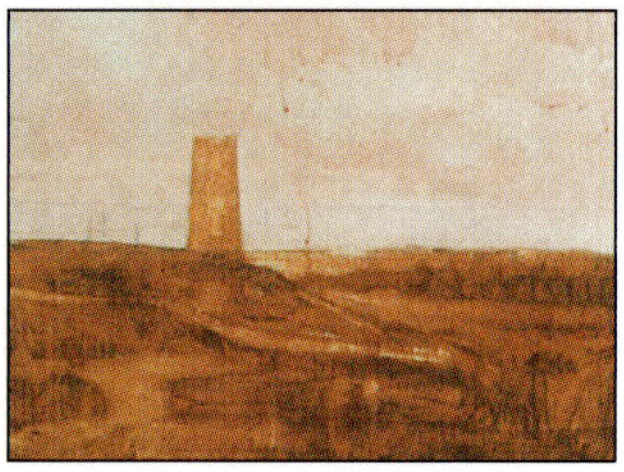

2 Put in the lighthouse in a thin wash of the same burnt sienna. Cover the ground with a more opaque, darker tone. Mix alizarin crimson and brush in sky tone.

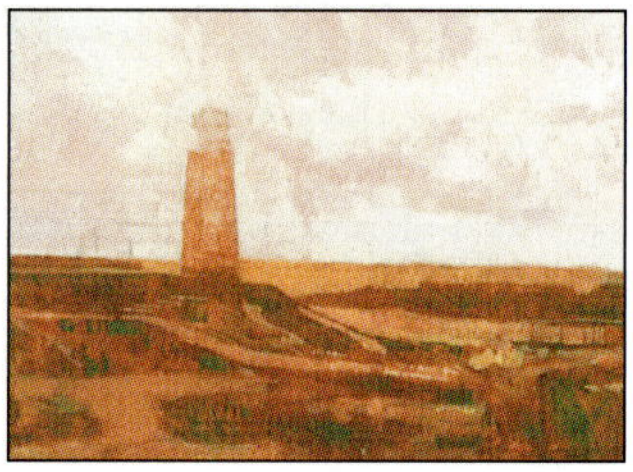

3 Draw in verticals and horizontals of lighthouse and horizon with pencil. Mix chrome green and cadmium yellow medium and lay in small patches of grass.

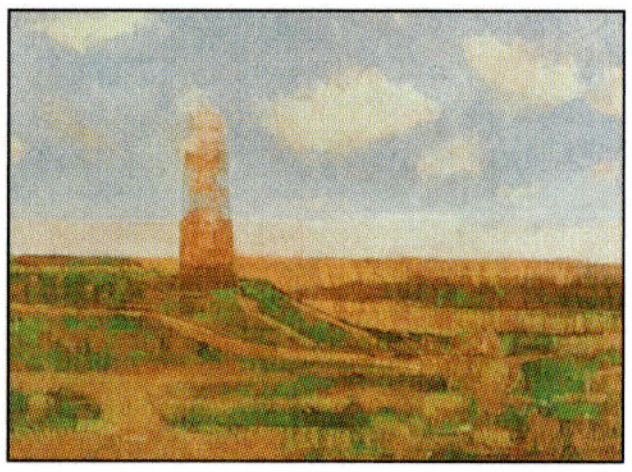

4 Mix thin wash of ultramarine and lay in the sky color. Letting previous layer dry, build up light foreground area with yellow ocher and white in a vertical direction.

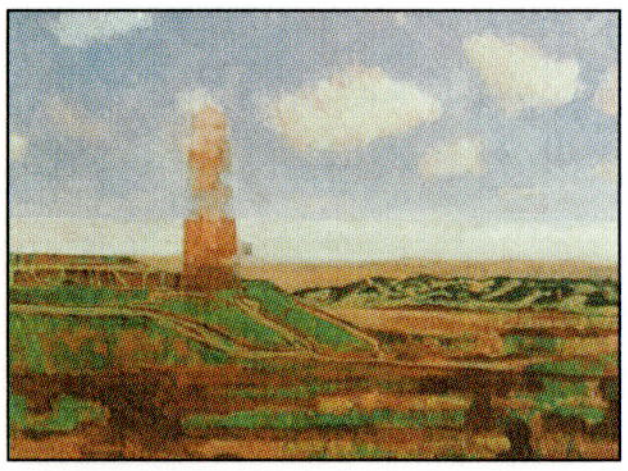

5 Apply a darker wash of blue over the sky. Mix a light tone of white and ocher and put in the sea. Put in strong darks in burnt umber and details in foreground.

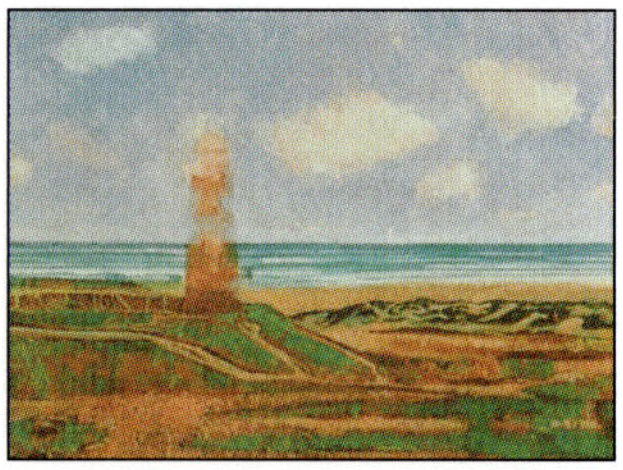

6 Apply a very thin wash of pthalo blue for the sea. Overpaint burnt umber areas in chrome green and redefine highlights with yellow ocher and white.

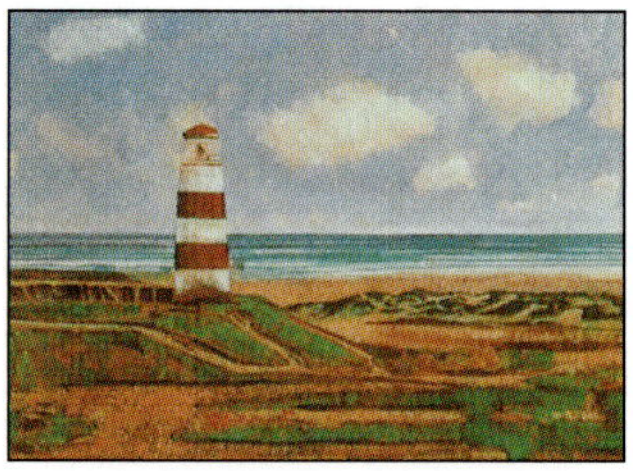

7 Mix alizarin crimson and burnt sienna and carefully put in the lighthouse stripes with a small brush.

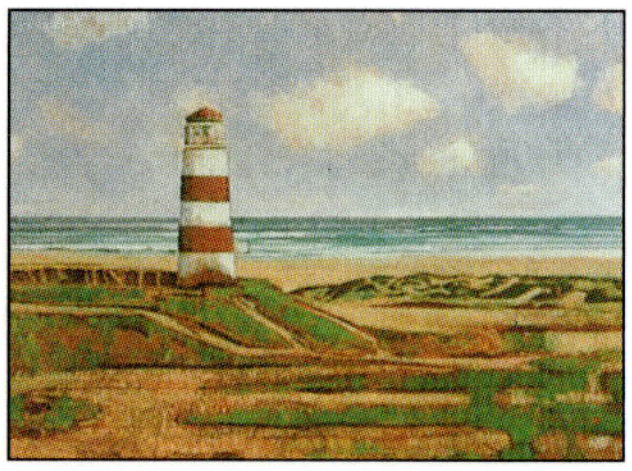

8 Put in white highlights in the sea with a small sable brush and pure, undiluted white.

Landscape in Watercolor

The painting shown here captures a sense of distance by showing how the land recedes gradually from the foreground toward the horizon, using the two trees as a central focus.

This is achieved by carefully varying color tones – placing strong, warm hues in the foreground and colors which are cooler and less intense in the distance. The impression of receding space is enhanced by the sky gradually lightening and finally rising into a thin strip of white where the paper is left bare.

To keep an overall coherence to the picture, the colors in each area are subtly linked together. For example, the same blue has been used for the linear details in the middle distance as in the shadow areas of the trees.

A harmonious balance of warm and cool tones has been applied as seen in the contrast between the warm brown of the foreground, the colder yellow across the center of the painting, and the reddish-brown and blue tones in the trees which deepen the intensity of the green washes.

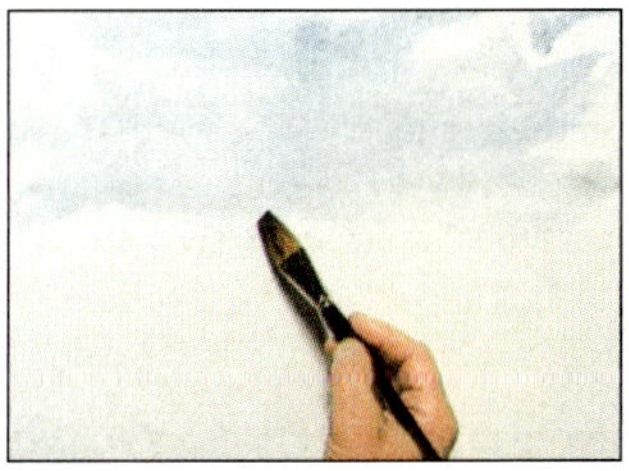

1 First wet the paper using a large No. 8 brush dipped in water. Lay in a thin wash of Prussian blue with a No. 8 sable brush, working down from the top of the paper.

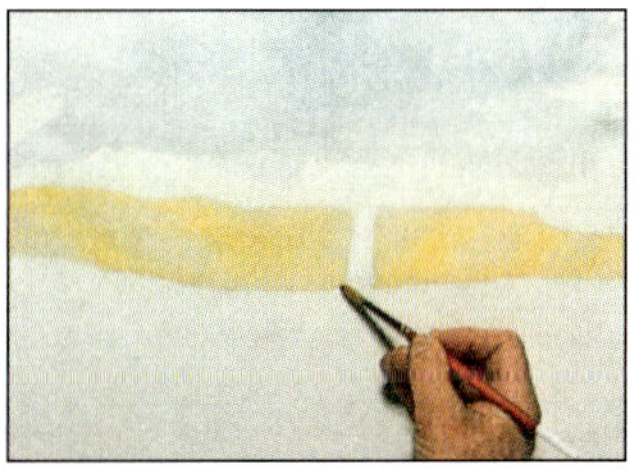

2 Brush in a yellow ocher wash across the center of the paper, leaving white space along the horizon line and in areas where the main forms will be placed.

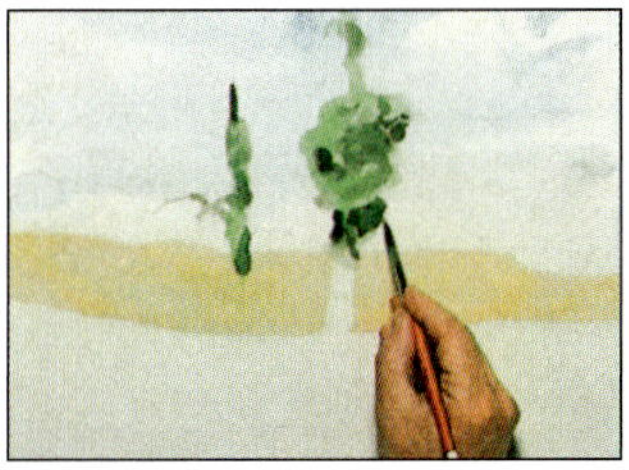

3 Use viridian, emerald green, and burnt umber to apply the basic forms of the trees, indicating areas of light and shade.

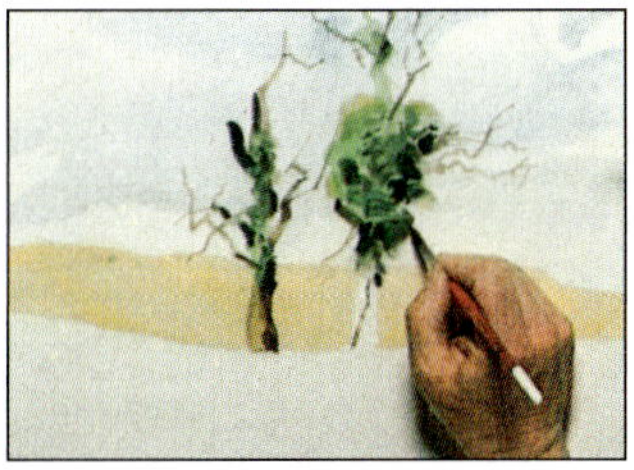

4 Draw into the shapes of the trees in more detail with the point of a No. 6 brush. Darken the burnt umber with a little blue and mix yellow into the greens.

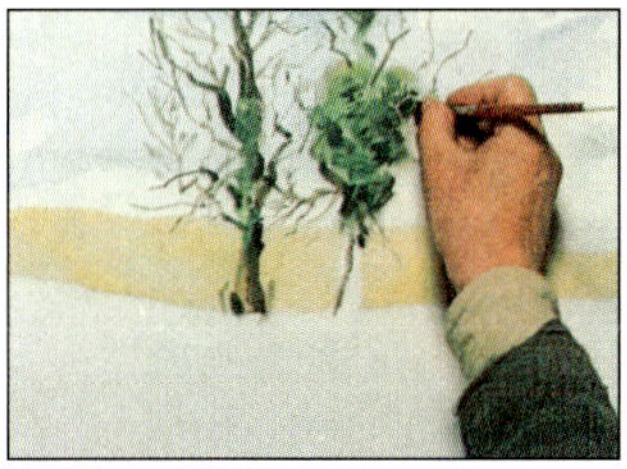

5 Continue to extend the forms and intensify the colors. Fan out the bristles of a No. 8 brush between thumb and forefinger to draw feathery texture.

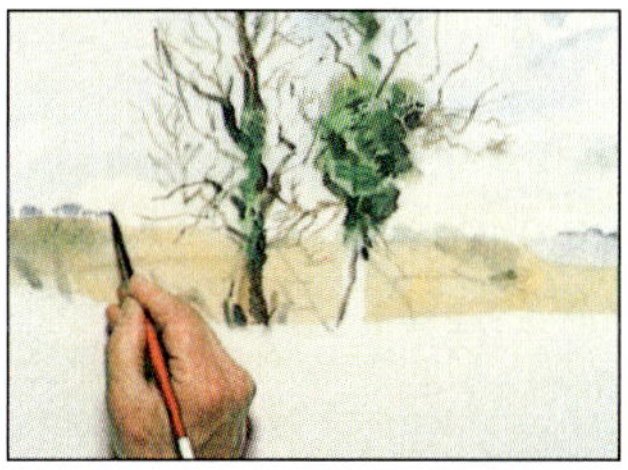

6 Dampen the yellow ocher wash with clean water and draw into it with a mixture of Payne's gray and blue.

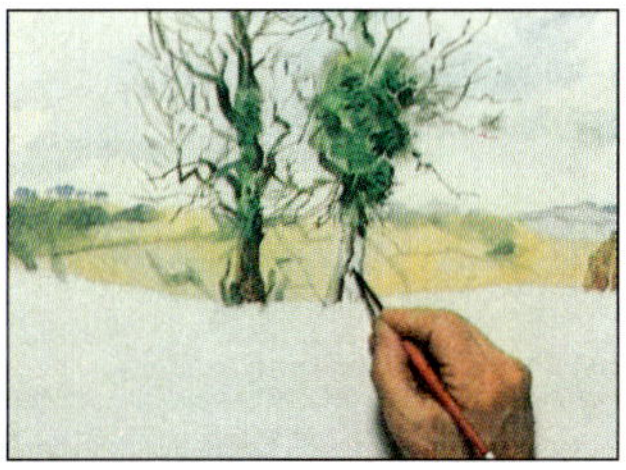

7 Add detail into the gray area with ultramarine, keeping the paint thin and wet. Use the same blue in foliage shadows and contrast with a warm reddish brown.

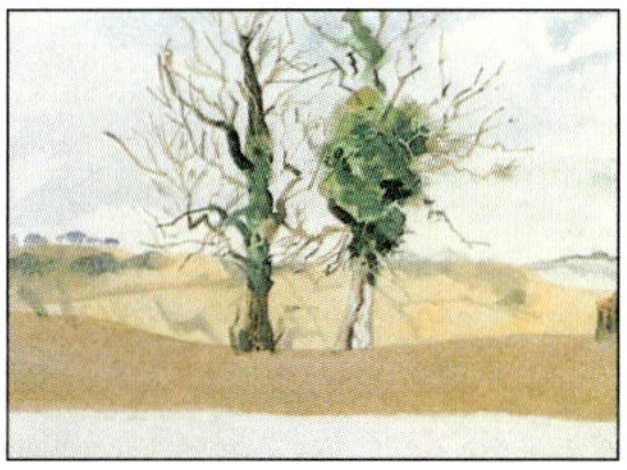

8 Mix up Payne's gray with a burnt umber and lay a broad streak of color across the foreground with a No. 8 sable brush, working directly onto the dry paper.

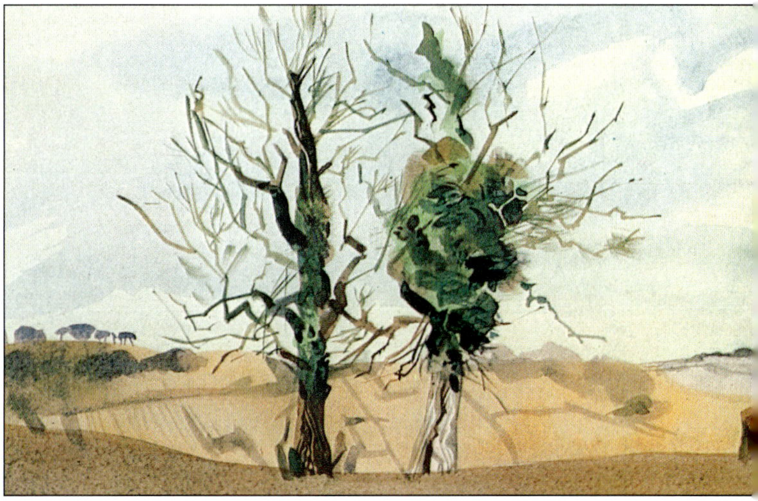

Landscape in Gouache

No one media can completely capture the diverse and subtle range of colors to be found in nature; the total effect is created by the relationships of all the colors together and the influence of light. Even if a landscape is predominantly green, there are a multitude of tones and hues within the one color to be identified and translated onto the painting surface.

A low-key green, for example, may be caused by a subtle cast of blue or red and the painting will be livelier if these contrasts are exploited or exaggerated.

As a general rule, remember that colors in the foreground are the most intense and fade toward the horizon. Within this range there are shifts between warm and cool tones; these help to establish form and position in the overall scheme of the painting. Only one brush and a limited color range have been used for this painting; the variety of hues and tones is due to careful, observant color mixing. As gouache is thick and opaque, be careful not to overmix the colors. The paint can be laid in thin washes of color or thickly daubed depending on how much water is added.

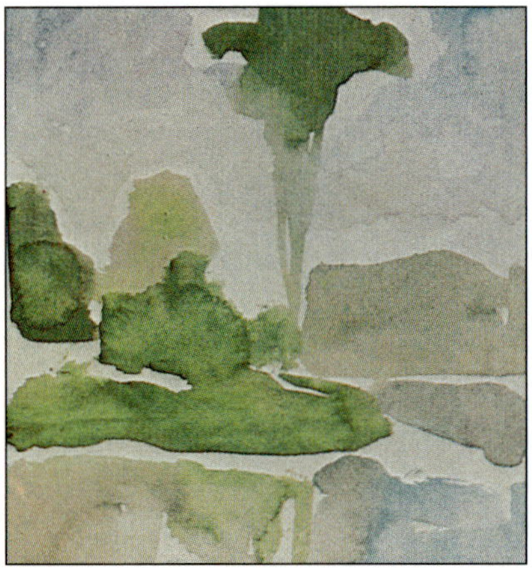

1 Paint in soft shapes to show trees, sky, and water using thin washes of blue and green adding white to vary the tone.

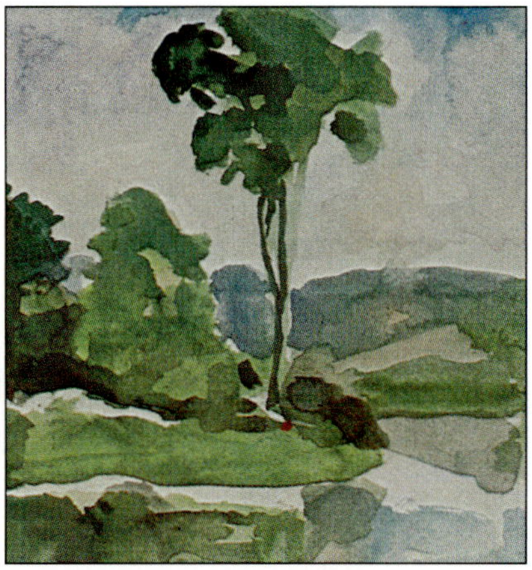

2 Work into these colors with darker tones to establish the basic forms and give the impression of distance.

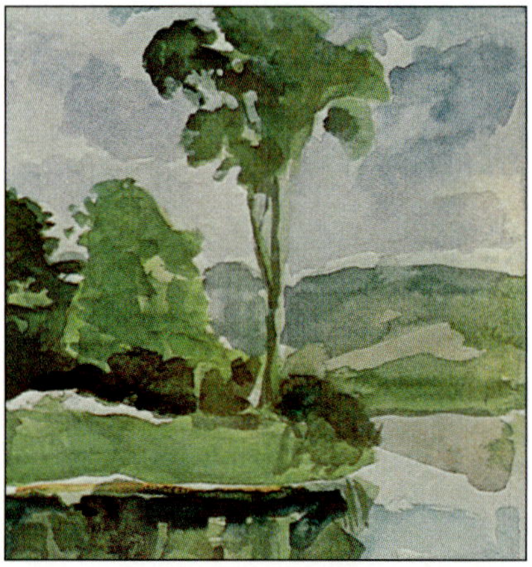

3 With undiluted paint, overpaint the forms in detail, varying the green hues by adding touches of yellow or red. Intensify the colors in the reflections on the water.

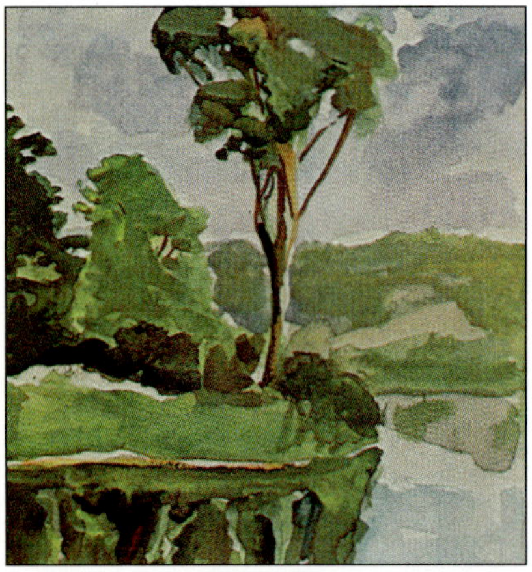

4 Mix brown from scarlet and black and draw up the trunk and branches of the tree. Extend the shape of the tree working with small dabs of red, green, and orange.

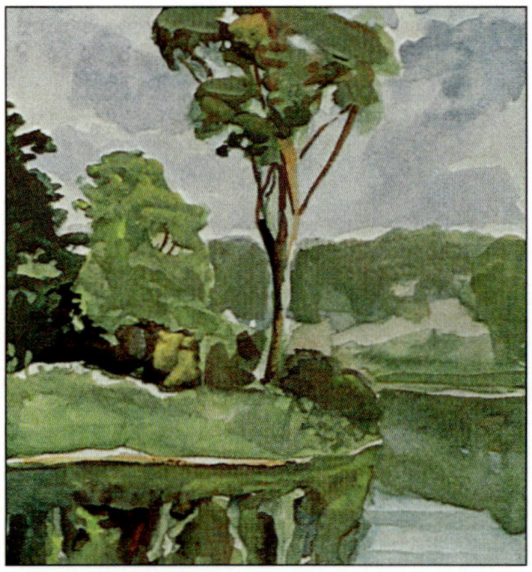

5 Increase the contrast in the light and dark colors over the whole image. Work into the foreground with horizontal and vertical stripes of blended color.

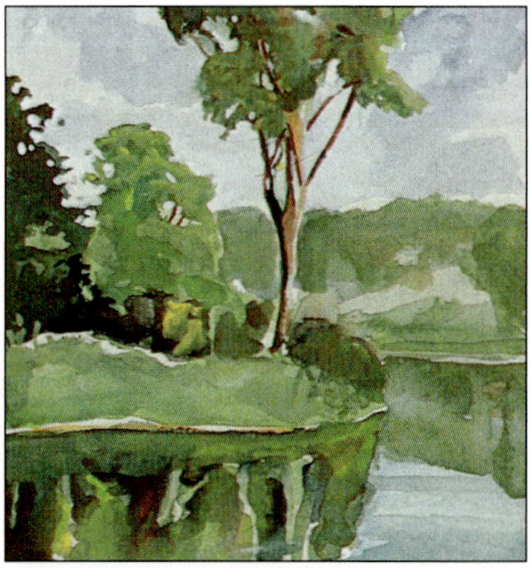

6 Heighten the tones with small patches of thin paint over the sky and trees, mixing white into the colors.

How to Paint: Still Life

The term still life comes from the Dutch *still-leven*, which came to be used in the seventeenth century, and simply describes any painting of inanimate objects such as fruit, flowers, kitchen utensils, or any other non-moving objects.

The French term *nature morte* means exactly the same, but was coined in the eighteenth century, probably in a spirit of disparagement since the French art establishment regarded it as an inferior branch of painting. Still life thus encompasses flower painting, but there is another branch of flower painting that has little to do with still life and springs from a different tradition, namely botanical illustration.

A careful drawing or painting of a flower or plant whose purpose is to record each minute detail of its structure and shape is not a still life, it is an object seen in isolation, independent of environment: a drawing or painting of a single bloom placed in a vase and seen in the context of an interior is, however detailed and precise a still life.

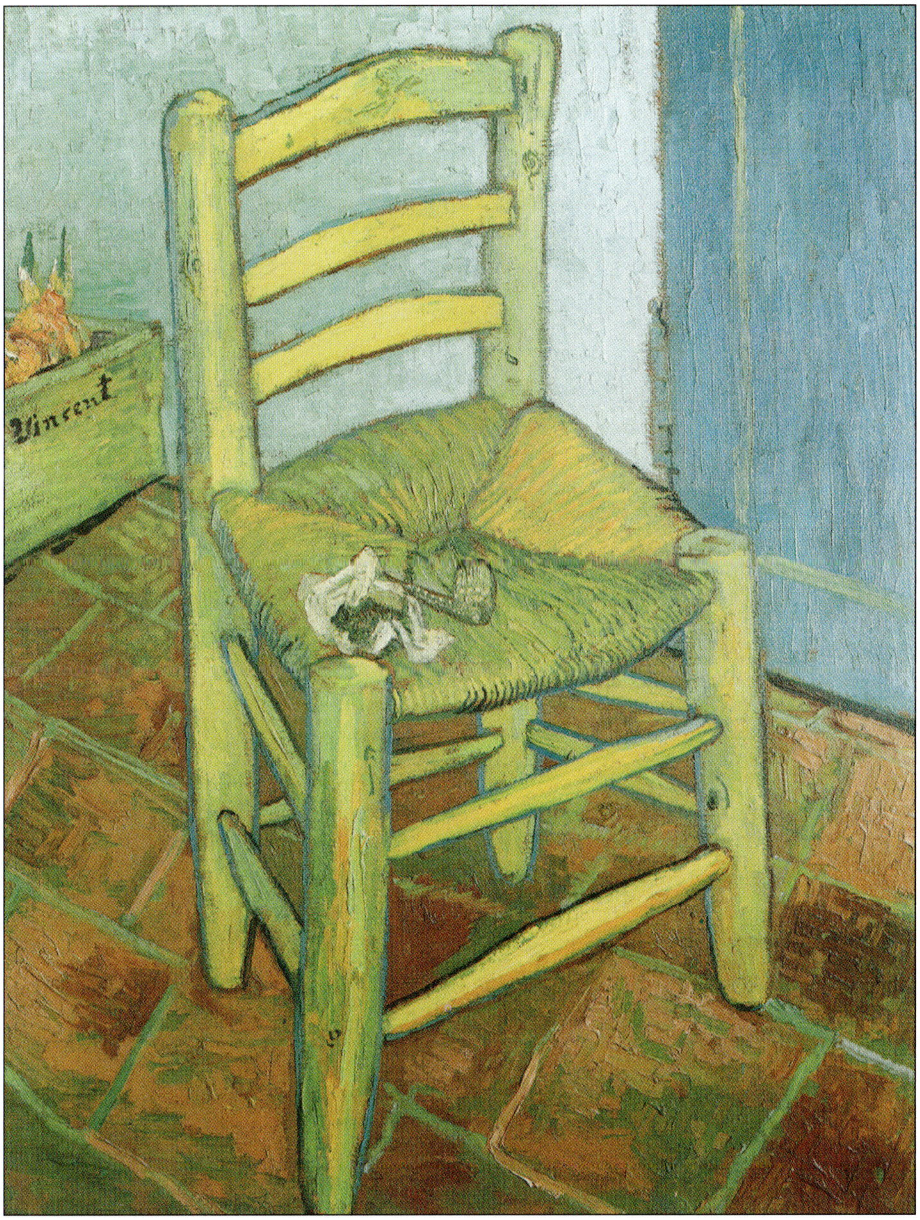

CHAIR AND PIPE by Vincent Van Gogh

The still life need not include only traditional elements such as fruit, flowers, or dishes. Simple, everyday objects can be the subjects for a strong and interesting picture.

MASTERS OF THE STILL LIFE

The brilliant use of still life objects in the early paintings of the seventeenth century artist Velazquez are as strong in form and structure as they are in the faithful rendering of color and texture. A glazed pot shimmers in the sunlight as the figure holding it almost breathes the air about him.

Chardin, an eighteenth century French artist, painted intimate interiors reflecting daily events of little consequence in themselves, but lovingly depicted.

The demands for both a rural element and the picturesque no doubt were factors in persuading these artists to cherish and cultivate such skills.

INTRODUCTION

Still life paintings often present a fascinating commentary on our lifestyles and can be a sort of capsule social history. The Dutch Masters of the seventeenth century, for example, were commissioned by merchants and other members of a growing middle class made rich by trade from the Dutch colonies.

This contact with the East, and the consequent material wealth, is reflected in the magnificent still lifes painted at this time, which are crammed with exotic fruits and flowers, gorgeously embroidered cloths, and shimmering silver and glass, all rendered in faultless detail.

Still life is an ideal subject for painting, because it contains myriads of possibilities for personal expression and interpretation. The objects we choose to paint reflect something about us, as does the way in which we arrange them and render them in paint: the artist may choose to focus on elements such as shape, texture, and color; or he or she may prefer to tell a story through a still life arrangement – for example, an open book or the remnants of a meal left on a table lend an air of mystery, as if someone has just left the scene for an instant.

Unlike landscape and figure painting, still life allows the artist to be in complete control. You have a virtually limitless choice of subject matter to begin with, and, provided you can set up your group where it won't be disturbed, you can spend as much time as you like on composing the arrangement and getting the lighting right. Working under these controlled conditions, you can study at leisure the effects of light and shade on objects, which will be of great value to you in other aspects of your painting.

When setting up a still life group, don't be tempted to include too much. A simple, carefully organized group will have far more impact than a motley assortment of objects in ill-matched colors. Choose just a few objects that you find visually pleasing and that have something in common; a collection of kitchen crockery with some vegetables, fruit, and bread, for example. Above all, look for a variety of shapes, forms, colors, and textures.

Your choice of background is important, too. Generally, a fairly neutral color is best because this helps to throw the subject forward in the picture plane. But if the overall tone of the group is light, then use a contrasting dark color for the background.

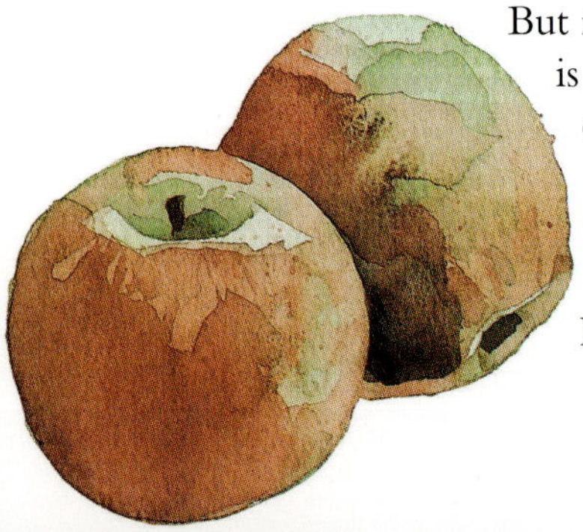

Having chosen your subject arrange the objects in a pleasing and harmonious way. It is worthwhile taking the trouble to rearrange the elements several times, until you are satisfied with the composition of shapes and the overall balance of colors. Try to place objects so that some of them overlap, forming connections that lead the eye naturally into and around the whole composition. Move around the subject in order to find the angle that is visually the most exciting. You could also make a frame from stiff cardboard, cut to the same proportions as those of your support, and hold it in front of the group so that at a glance you can see within it any pitfalls in the composition; make sure that no two objects in the group are of the same height, for instance. Look for a pleasing, flowing pattern of light and dark tones. Decide which object or area is to be the focal point of the piece, and make sure that it contains more light, color, or texture than the other areas. Normally, the most visually satisfying spot for the center of interest is just right of center, because the human eye instinctively reads a picture from left to right.

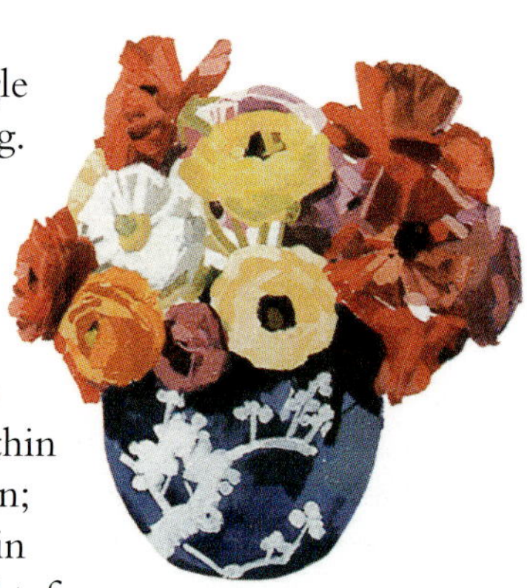

Another aspect that should be carefully considered is lighting. The way in which light moves through the picture helps to give it a feeling of depth and three-dimensional space. Choose a single source of light, preferably coming from the side, because this creates a clear pattern of lights and darks that help to explain forms. In addition, it casts shadows, the shapes of which serve to link up and unify the elements in the group.

Whether you choose natural daylight or artificial light is a matter of preference. Daylight will give you more realistic colors than artificial light, but it is not constant. Artificial light gives you the advantage of being able to alter its position or make it hard or soft, depending on your requirements. It is, of course, constant, but it does tend to affect the colors of objects, giving them a slightly yellow cast.

Unless you are painting *alla prima*, the best way to begin the painting is by covering the support with a toned ground in order to lose the stark whiteness of the support, which can be so intimidating. You can choose to use a neutral gray or earth color, a color close to the dominant hue of the group, or its complement. For example, a warm orange undertone beneath a painting that is predominantly blue creates a shimmering effect when the undertone is allowed to shine through in places. This can then be followed by a monochrome underpainting, which establishes the tonal pattern of the arrangement and gives you a strong base from which to work when adding color.

As you paint, you should constantly compare tone with tone, color with color, and be aware of spatial relationships between objects. Try not to paint objects in isolation: work back and forth between the background and the still life elements, bringing the entire painting along at once. Work from the general to the particular, leaving highlights and details till last. In this way, your finished painting will have harmony and unity, and a sense of space and air.

FLOWERS

When painting flowers in a still life arrangement, do not go for photographic realism, but try to capture the essential characteristics of the various blooms; the rich, velvety texture of roses; the simple, classical grace of tulips; the intense colors of anemones. Because flowers are so lovely to look at, it is hard to restrain the urge to paint every detail lovingly. This is a dangerous trap to fall into, because the resultant painting begins to look like a botanical study. Your concern, as an artist, is to create a living picture, to convey an impression of depth, mystery, and transience, emphasizing the subtle effects of light on the subject.

Detailed over-emphasis of every leaf, bud, and blossom leads to confusion, making the flowers look hard and brittle instead of soft and graceful. In addition, the three-dimensional appearance of the image is lost.

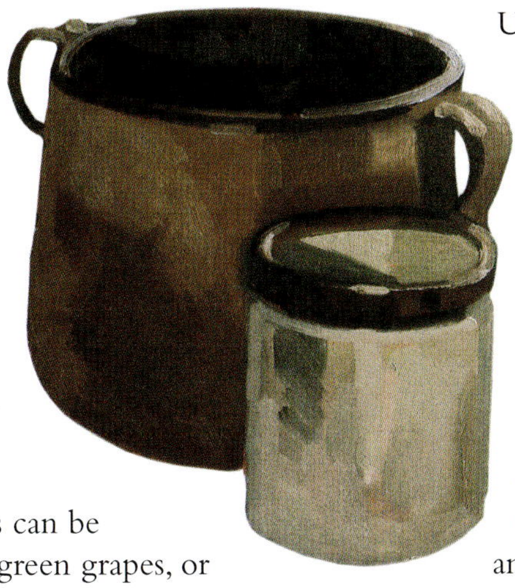

FRUIT AND VEGETABLES

Fruit and vegetables are always popular in still life arrangements. Not only do they have fascinating surface textures, but their colors and shapes can be all-important in lending balance to the composition. For example, a painting that is light in tone overall can be given just the right amount of contrast by the addition of a bunch of black grapes; alternatively dramatic chiaroscuro effects can be achieved by introducing pale, luminous green grapes, or pieces of lemon into a dark painting.

As with flowers, fruits and vegetables look best when they are not forced into a rigid arrangement. Try to place them so that they appear to have just spilled out of a basket, and introduce variety by including pieces of cut fruit or vegetables such as onions and cabbages, chopped in half to reveal their inner patterns.

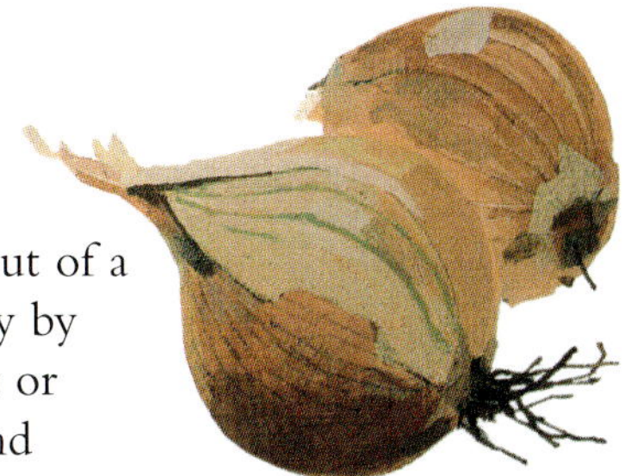

GLASS OBJECTS

When painting glass, take time to observe the subtle tonal variations between the highlights, middle tones, and shadows, their colors and their shapes, which follow the form of the glass object, then record them faithfully, but not too mechanically. Painting clear glass is much like painting water – less detail says more.

Clear glass takes on the colors of objects surrounding it. When painting glass vases, bottles, or other reflective objects in a still life, always indicate the background colors first, being careful to record any distortions of shape reflected into the object. The glass object can then be painted over the background.

SHINY METAL OBJECTS

The attractive shine of metal containers – everything from copper kettles to aluminum saucepans – makes them a favorite still life subject, but they are quite a challenge to paint. The secret lies in close observation of tone, color, and shape, and in not overworking the subject.

EARTHENWARE

Earthenware bowls, jugs, and vases often come in delightful shapes and lend grace to any still life painting. As with glass, painting glazed earthenware is a matter of recording tonal variations and knowing how to render discreet highlights.

Unglazed earthenware pots are equally attractive, their warm terracotta color blending harmoniously with any plants and flowers included in the still life.

CLOTH

Contrary to what some beginner painters think, folded drapery is not an obligatory element of every still life. Nevertheless, a softly draped piece of cloth does serve many useful purposes. It offers an interesting textural contrast to the other objects included in the group, and the lines and folds can be an important compositional element, creating visual direction within the picture.

Arranging the Still Life

The first consideration when making a still life picture is, of course, the group to be painted or drawn. Care should always be taken to make the arrangement as telling as possible.

This does not necessarily mean that it must be full of objects and rhythmic interest, as it may be that an astringent, simple, carefully organized group will possibly hold your interest the better.

Taking the trouble to rearrange the elements several times always repays the painter; taking a different viewpoint or altering the color balance is better done before committing paint to surface, rather than abandoning a half-finished picture.

A few diagrams to demonstrate alternative compositions should be undertaken, and, if one chooses, make a painting of a casual arrangement, such as a table top littered with assorted objects. Edit the final choice by cutting a rectangle to the same proportion to your support in a sheet of stiff white paper and frame the group with it.

By holding the frame close to the eye a completely different composition can be seen than that viewed by holding it at arm's length. Experiment with this so that the dialogue between yourself and the subject is allowed full rein. This may enable you to discover a better alternative and also allows for unsuspected interpretations by cropping objects or putting things into the foreground or lowering eye levels. When the final decision has been taken on the design, color, and other components of the group, and the various alternatives have been fully considered, then painting can commence.

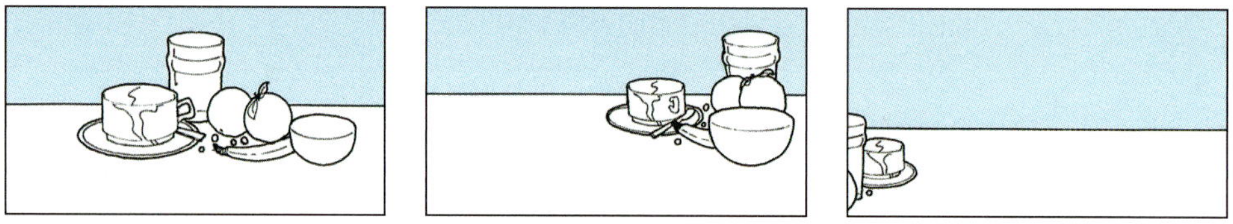

Placement

The placement of objects in the picture plane is determined by the emphasis desired by the artist. Left: Objects are centered to allow the artist to explore their unique and individual qualities. Center: When objects are moved away from the center, interest is created by surrounding the objects with empty space which tends to emphasize, rather than diminish their importance Right: If too much or too little of the object is shown, the picture can become uninteresting.

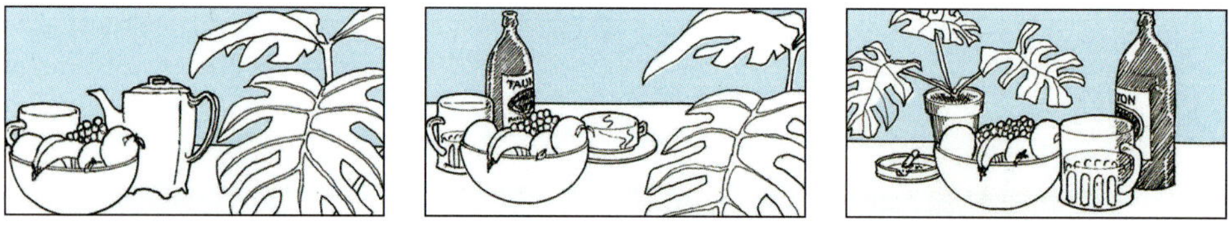

Arranging objects

The still life can be conveniently altered and rearranged to suit the needs of the artist. Left: Objects have been chosen for their contrasting shapes and the plant in the foreground adds visual interest. Center: A bottle replaces the teapot adding a strong vertical element. The plant is moved further right and downward to allow for the eye to focus on the objects. Right: The plant is included in the group of objects to add contrast in shape and texture.

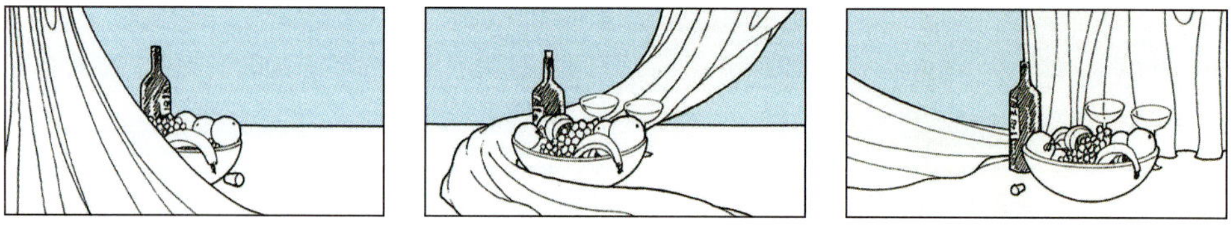

Drapery

Fabrics and drapery are often included in the still life because they offer an interesting textural contrast to the other objects included. For example, a piece of rough sacking is a good counterpoint to either the smooth surface of glass or pottery. Left: Drapery can be used to partially obscure the still life group. Center: The fabric here has been arranged to create a visual direction in the picture; the observer's eye moves from the top, down, and around the objects. Right: Placing the fabric in the background can emphasize the still life group.

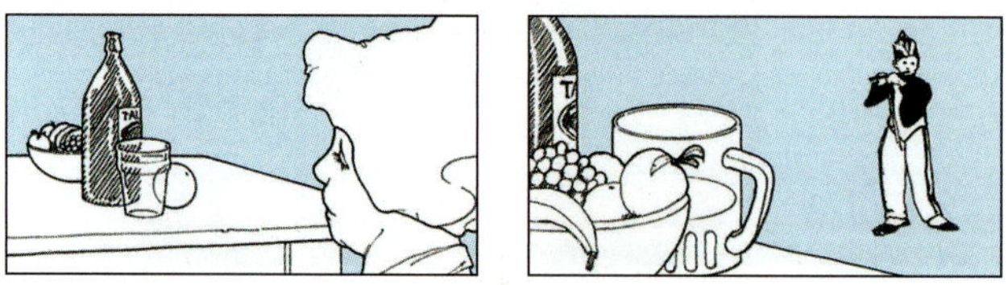

The figure in still life

Left: A picture can contain any number of elements, related or unrelated, and need not be restricted to the traditional still life, portrait, or figure themes. Combining the still life with either a figure or portrait can be extremely interesting and was often used by the Masters as a means of demonstrating their skill in all types of subject matter.

BLACK GRAPES AND WINE by Shirley Trevena

Trevena is a painter who works straight from her arranged group, with no sketching, and composes as she paints. She likes to vary the texture of her paint, using thin watercolor washes in places and thickly built up layers of gouache in others. The lace is the original white paper left untouched. Her work has a lyrical quality: the objects are all recognizable, but we are drawn to the painting by the fluid shapes and colors.

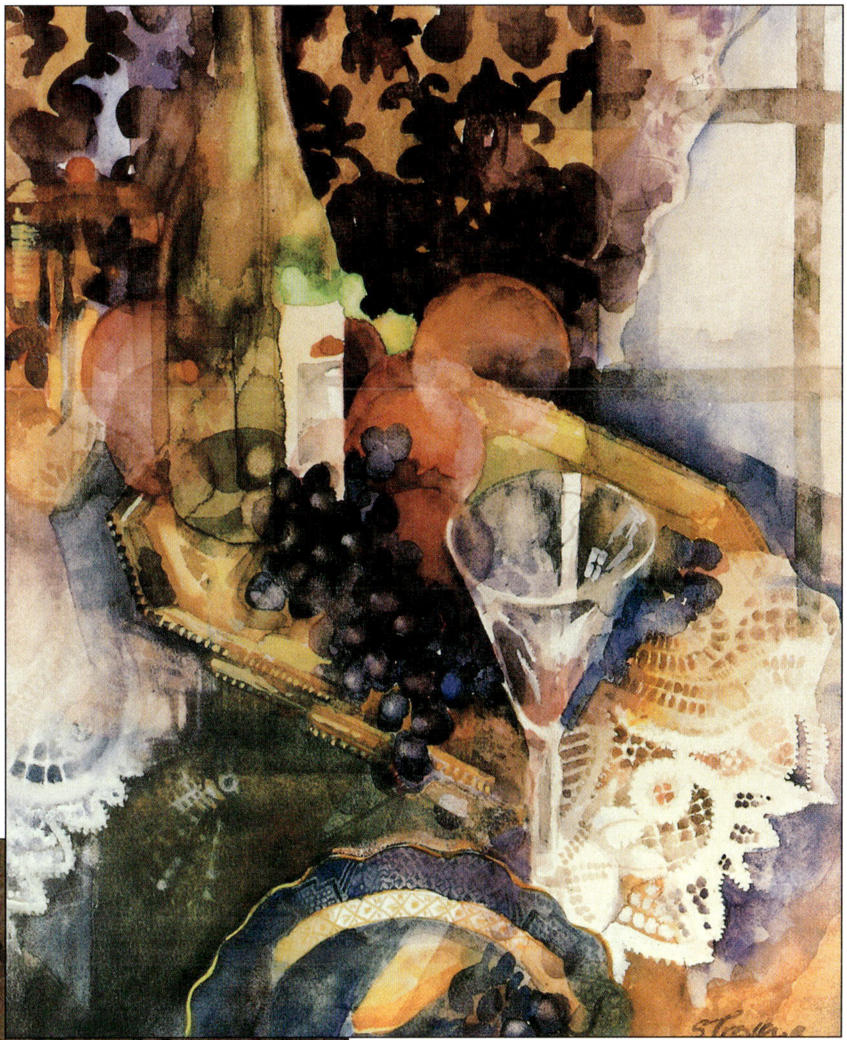

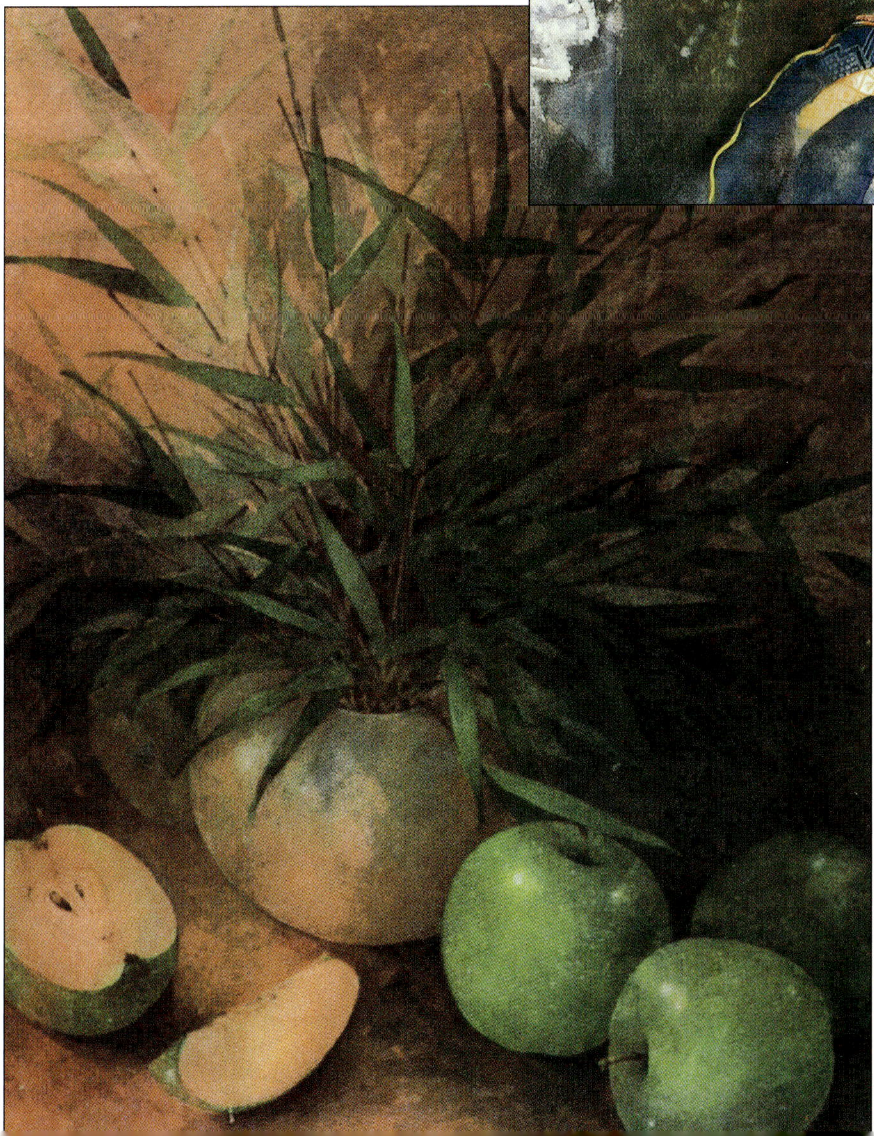

STILL LIFE WITH APPLES by Shirley Felts

For this painting, the artist has chosen a plain brown background that picks up the color of the table top. But she has not painted it flat: there are several different colors and tones in the "brown," including a deep blue, and she has given movement and drama to it by use of brush strokes that follow the direction of the spiky leaves.

Basic Principles

Still life as its name implies, simply means a composition of objects which are not moving and which are incapable of doing so, they are usually arranged on a table or could be a collection of furniture objects; the French call it "dead life" (*nature morte*).

The subjects can be whatever you like, but traditionally the objects in a still life group are in some way associated with each other – a vase of flowers with fruit, a selection of vegetables, with cooking vessels or implements, and sometimes a dead fish, game, or fowl with a goblet of wine, perhaps, or a bunch of parsley. (Culinary still lifes are less popular nowadays, possibly because they run the risk of looking like the cover of a cookery book.) Good paintings can be made from quite homely subjects. Vincent Van Gogh (1853–1890) made a wonderful and moving still life from nothing but a pile of books on a table.

Most artists have painted still lifes at one time or another, and several, notably Jan Vermeer (1632–1675), included them in their figure paintings. In the seventeenth century a group of Dutch artists became obsessed with still life to the exclusion of all other subjects, and vied with one another to produce ever more lavish portrayals of table tops gleaming with edible produce, rare porcelain, and golden goblets. In many of these, tiny insects are visible among the foliage, blood drips from the mouths of freshly killed hares or rabbits, and bunches of grapes shine with tiny droplets of moisture, every object painted with breathtaking skill.

PLUMS by William Henry Hunt

Hunt produced charming portraits as well as genre subjects, using his paint rather dry to depict colors and textures with great accuracy. Plums is an unusual approach to still life, as it has an outdoor setting but it was almost certainly done in the studio from sketches.

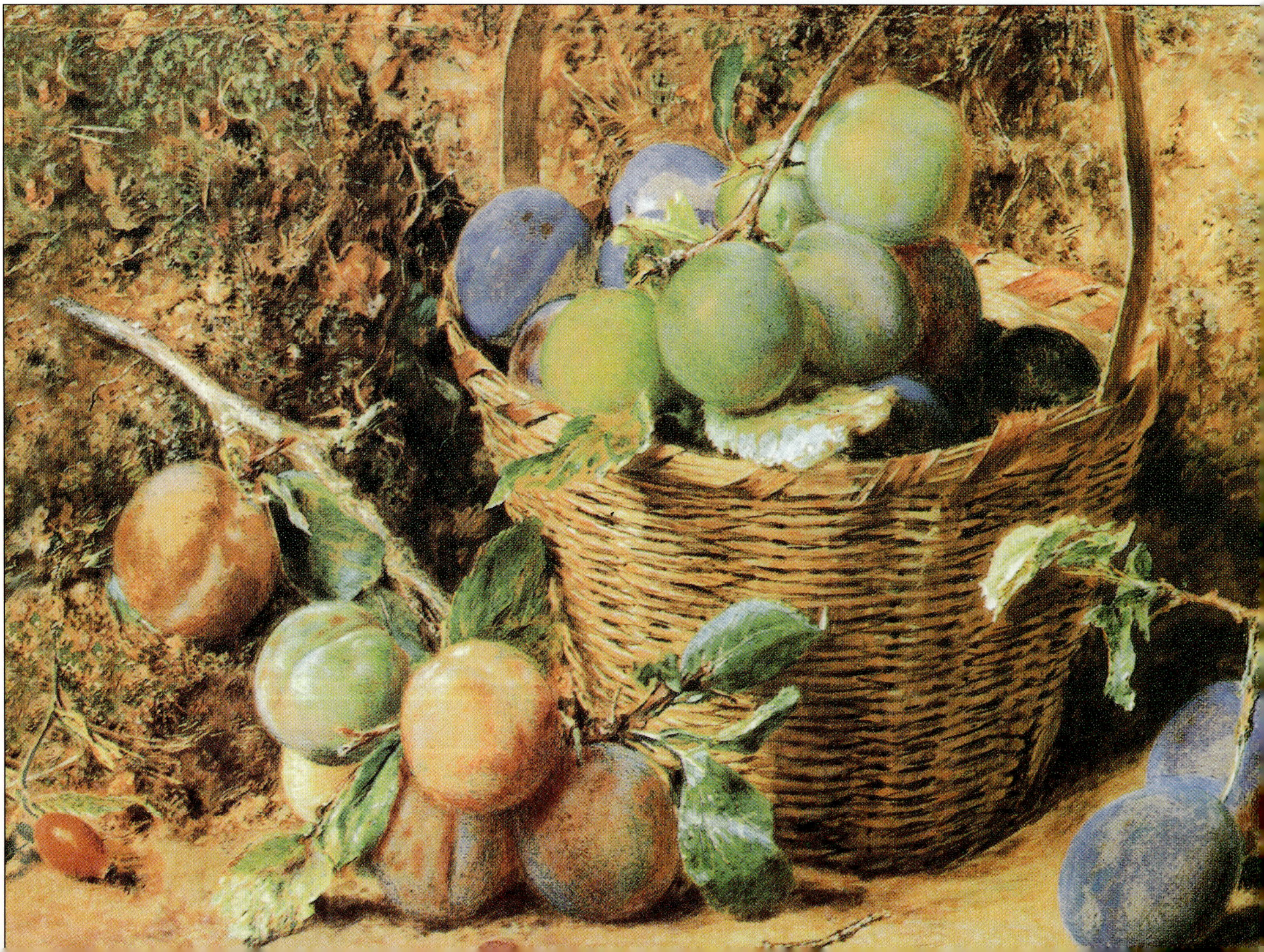

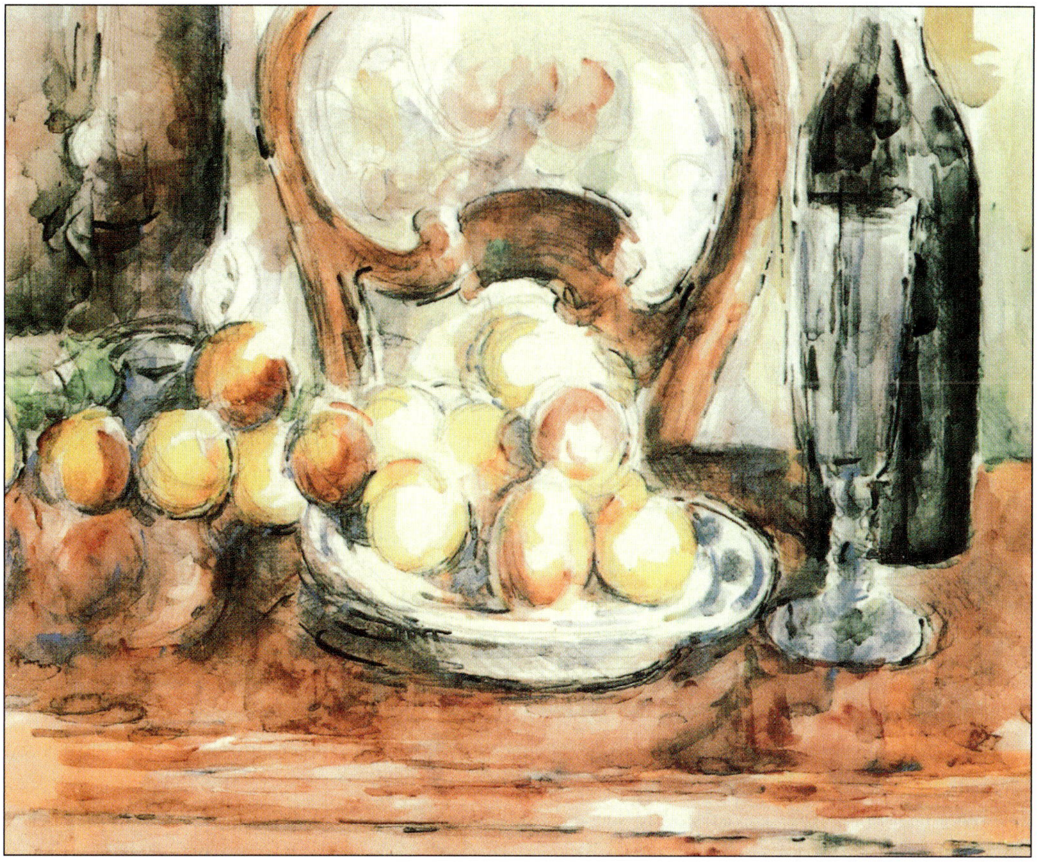

STILL LIFE WITH CHAIR, BOTTLES, AND APPLES
by Paul Cézanne

Cézanne used still life to explore the relationships of forms and their interaction on various spatial planes. He usually worked in oils, but this picture shows his understanding of watercolor.

Because the subject of a still life painting can be entirely controlled by the artist, as can its arrangement and lighting, still lifes present an unusual opportunity for exploring ideas and experimenting with color and composition, the greatest master of the still life, Paul Cézanne (1839–1906), found that the form allowed him to concentrate on such fundamental problems as form and space and the paradox of transferring the three-dimensional world to a two-dimensional surface.

The ability to control the subject of a still life means that you can take as much time as you like to work out the composition and complete the preliminary drawing, and you can practice painting techniques at leisure, trying out new ones as you feel inspired. Oddly, watercolor was seldom used in the past for still lifes other than flower paintings, but it is now becoming extremely popular.

BACKGROUNDS

Backgrounds are a very important element in still life groups, as are shadows, and should always be given careful consideration. In the painting by Giorgio Morandi (see right), the background forms its own geometric shapes, which are balanced by the shadows. This drawing, although very simple, is a good example of a deliberate and careful arrangement, with the background and foreground divided into unequal horizontal rectangles by the line of the table top, leading the eye into the center of the picture.

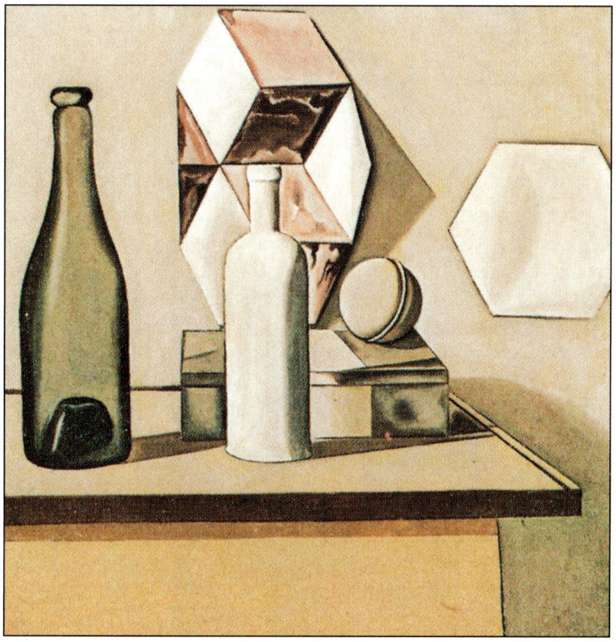

STILL LIFE OF 1918 by Giorgio Morandi

The background in this still life is more prominent than in any of his other pictures. In all still life painting, it is important to work out what kind of balance you wish to achieve between the subject and its setting.

Setting up a Still Life

The great beauty of still life painting is that you can choose the objects that interest you and arrange them in any way you want, which allows you to express your ideas quite freely and in an individual manner, unlike portrait painting, in which you are much more tied to a specific subject.

You can also arrange the lighting so that it shows the group to its best advantage. But first it is necessary to find a suitable place for the set-up, where it can remain undisturbed for the duration of the painting. The corner of a room can be a good choice, as this enables you to control the background by using either plain walls or drapes and to arrange an artificial lighting system that will not change as you work. If you opt for natural light, with the group placed near a window or on a window sill, bear in mind that you will only be able to work for a limited period each day because the tonal values and the shadows will alter drastically from one part of the day to another.

Once you have gathered together the objects you intend to paint, the next step is to set them up in an arrangement, and it is worth taking some time over this. Always try to think of your intentions toward the painting, of how you want it to look and what you are trying to express. If color is your main theme make sure that you have achieved a good balance in the set-up, with a pattern of lights and darks, and colors which enhance one another.

If form is your primary concern pay particular attention to the lighting so that you have a clear transition of tones on each object, defining their shapes. Arrange the objects in several different ways until you are quite sure the composition is one that will make a good painting; it is much easier to change the set-up than to change the painting.

It is often helpful to make a few quick thumbnail sketches of different groupings, and to look at the arrangement through a viewfinder (see previous chapter) made of a piece of cardboard with a rectangular aperture cut in it. This acts as a frame for the group, isolating it from any distracting background and giving you an idea of how the objects relate to one another and how they will fit within the painting surface.

It is only too easy to set up a group which leaves either too little or too much background, or to place one large object in such a way that it diminishes or devalues any smaller ones. Beware too, of over-cluttering a still life group, as too many objects in different colors or textures will create an over-busy, restless impression. Still life should aim at creating harmony, not discord.

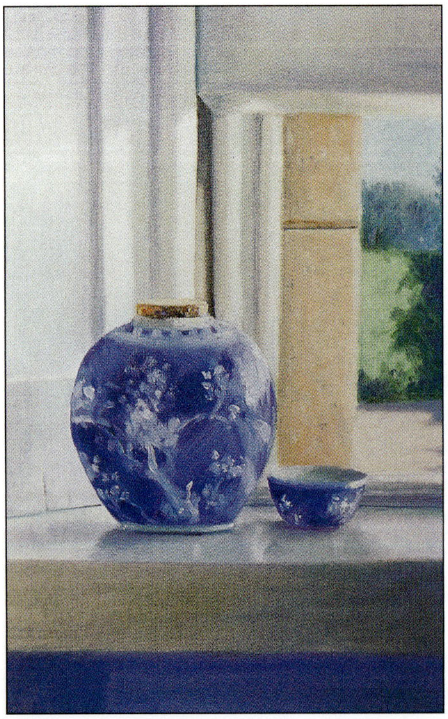

STILL LIFE WITH TEACADDY by Lincoln Seligman

The mood of tranquility set by the color scheme of cool blues with touches of warmer pinkish-beige is enhanced by the repeated vertical and horizontal lines, which form a framework for the curves of the teacaddy and bowl.

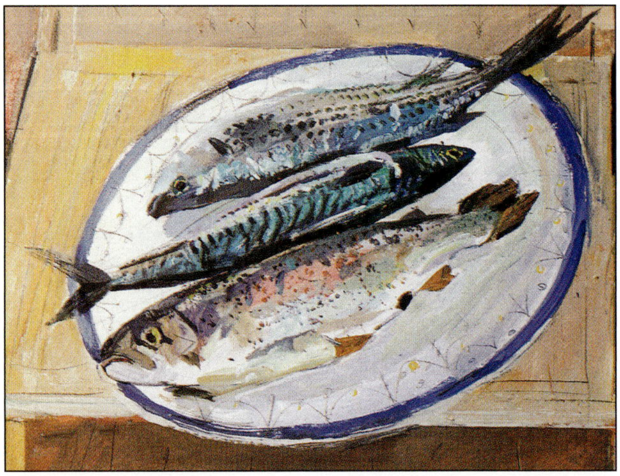

THREE FISH ON AN OVAL PLATE by Stan Smith

Here the artist has been fascinated, not only by the rich colors of the fish themselves, but the geometric possibilities of the composition. He has chosen a high viewpoint, which has given him a simple composition of three diagonals intersecting an oval, all enclosed within the rectangle formed by the table top.

Surface Texture

Surface quality provides vital clues about an object. By paying attention to form and texture, you can make a convincing rendering without using color.

We know that light describes form by creating areas of light and dark, but the kind of tonal contrasts you see depend on an object's texture as well as its shape. A hard, shiny surface reflects more light than a matt one, causing clear highlights and well-defined areas of tone. Highlights on a matt surface may be almost imperceptible, represented by a slight lightening of the local color, and there will be no distinct edges between light, dark, and middle tones.

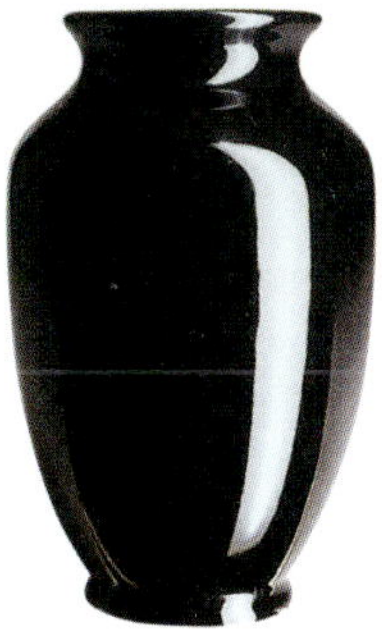

Outlines and internal edges are soft and fuzzy, reflecting the texture.

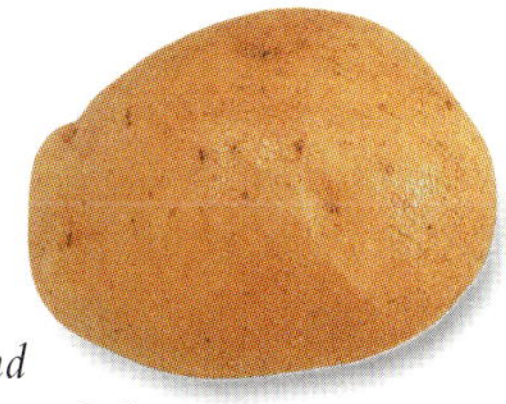

On matt surfaces, highlights are soft and diffused, tonal contrasts slight.

LINE AND TEXTURE

Texture also affects outlines, edges, and contour lines. Drape a piece of heavy fabric over a table, and the hard line of the table front will become a soft one. The outline of a ball of fluffy wool yarn or a child's soft stuffed toy won't be hard and clear; it will be broken by the surface texture, becoming a series of tiny marks or dots rather than a continuous line.

In landscape you will seldom see hard outlines, edges or contour lines. As we noted in the previous chapter, shadows will be fragmented by clumps of grass or other irregularities in the ground. The outline of a tree will comprise different edges, lost in places and found in others. Most of these edges won't be perceived in terms of line, but as areas of darker or lighter tone, varying in size and thickness.

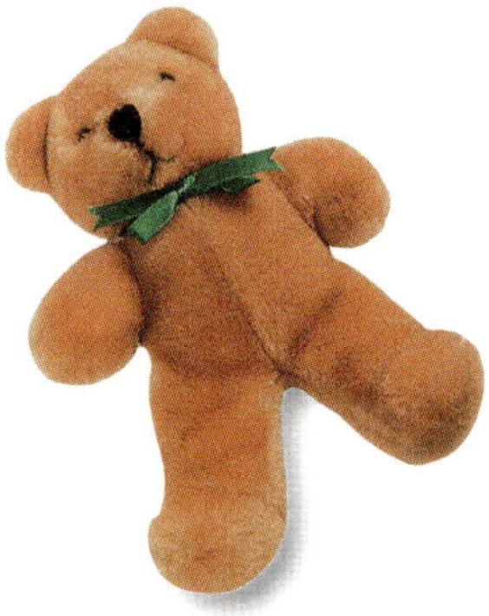

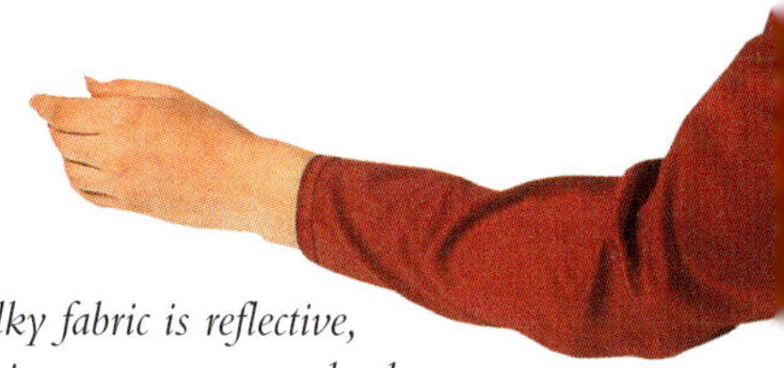

Silky fabric is reflective, giving strong tone and color contrasts.

Shiny surface produces sharp-edged highlights and strong tonal contrasts.

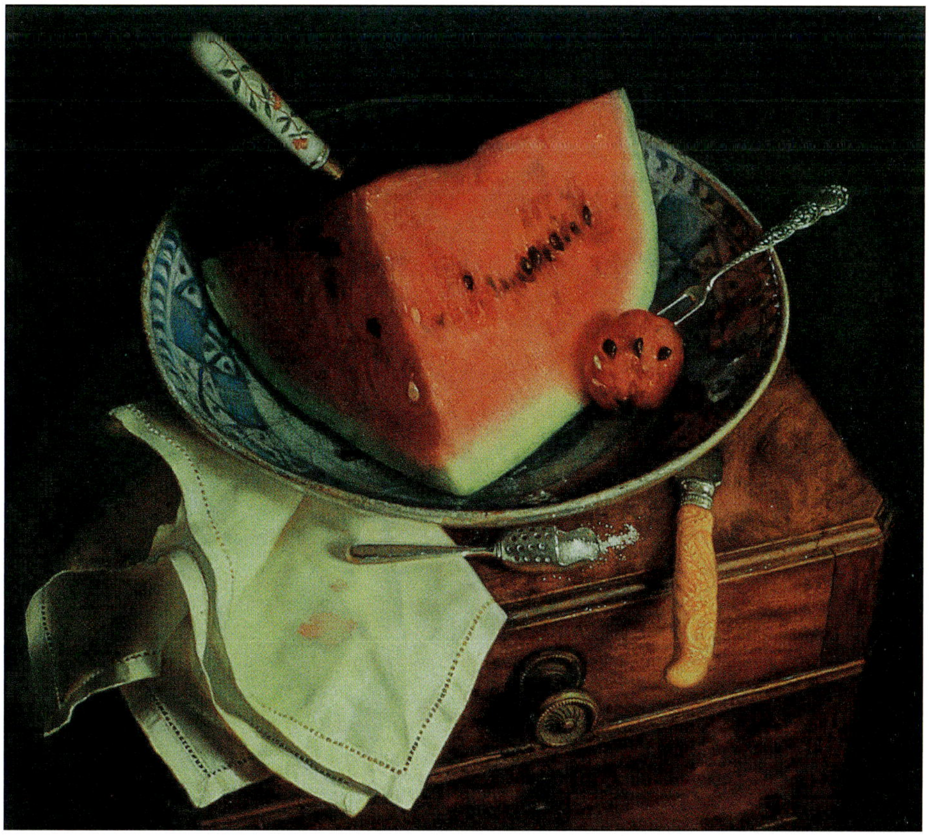

WATERMELON IN BLUE RUSSIAN DISH by Deborah Deichler

Minute attention to texture was one of the features of the Dutch school of still life painting in the seventeenth and eighteenth centuries, and this artist shares their interest. Her technique, with no visible brushmarks, is also influenced more by past than present oil-painting methods. Working on an aluminum panel faced with fine linen, she has achieved an amazing degree of detail as well as exciting contrasts.

Composing a Picture

Many people seem to feel that, just as there are "proper" ways of going about a painting, there are also "proper" subjects. This is quite untrue; as we have seen, there is no way of applying oil paint that is more correct than another, nor is there any one subject that makes a better painting than another.

Still lifes, like nudes, flowers, and landscapes are all types of paintings hallowed by long tradition, but many artists have made fine paintings of just the corner of a room, a wall with a few flowers against it, or a single tree. Vincent Van Gogh made deeply moving and expressive still lifes from such subjects as a pair of peasant's boots.

Still life did not exist as a painting subject until the Dutch artists of the seventeenth century "invented" it. Nor was landscape, except as a background to a figure or group of figures, acceptable until the late eighteenth and early nineteenth centuries. In the past, the subject of a painting was largely dictated by the demands of patrons, but we have no such restrictions.

It should be said, however, that some subjects are more difficult than others, and it can be discouraging to find you have set yourself a task, which your experience is not equal to. Still lifes, like flowers and landscapes, provide good starting points, depending on your particular interest. Subjects for still lifes can be found in most people's homes or the nearest vegetable or flower shop, and you can choose your own arrangement, light it in any way you want and take your time over it.

BALANCE AND RHYTHM

When an artist produces a painting from visual notes (sketchbook studies made from direct observation) he is putting together, or "composing" a pictorial statement. It is this act of putting things together, satisfactorily, that makes a well-composed painting.

Every time an artist produces a drawing or painting, he is consciously, or unconsciously, composing. There are painters whose work follows very closely the classical rules of composition, and others who work more intuitively. One is more conscious of formal composition in a Degas pastel, say, than in an oil painting by Bonnard.

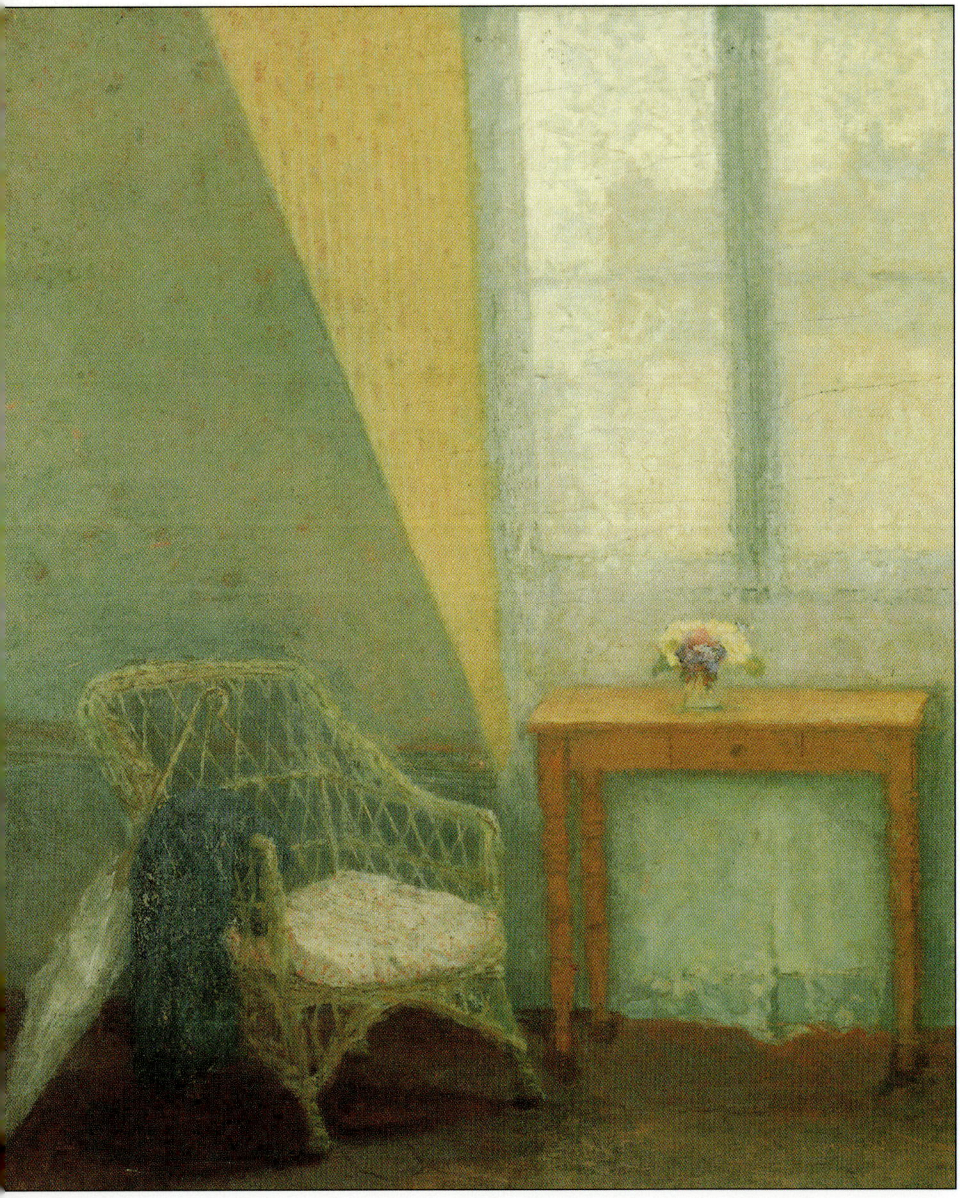

A CORNER OF THE ARTIST'S ROOM IN PARIS by Gwen John

Domestic interiors have been a favorite subject with artists since the Dutch seventeenth century Masters. This picture gives a strong feeling of serenity, just as the Dutch paintings did.

The Role of Light

The way light falls on an object defines both its form and its color, so it goes without saying that lighting is vital to a still life. As any portrait photographer knows, lighting can be a complex subject, but for painting the wisest course is to keep it as simple as possible.

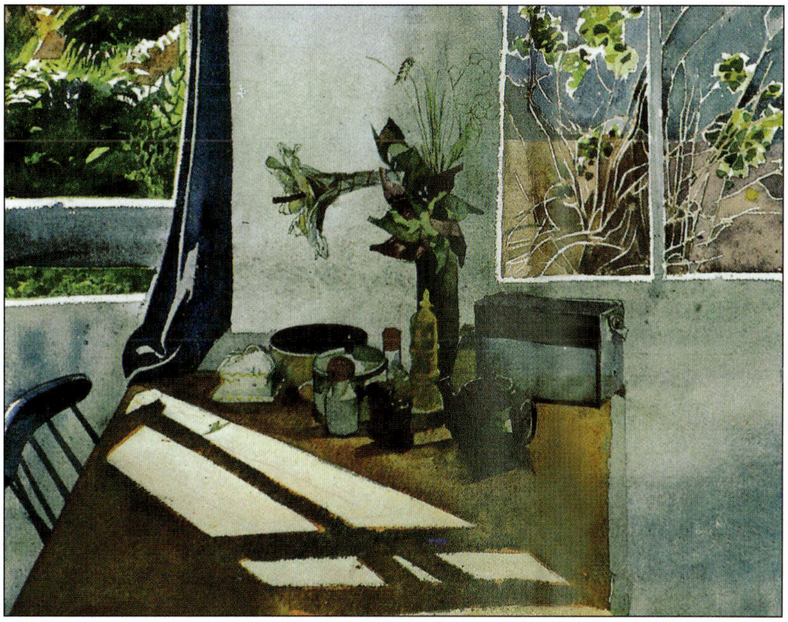

If you are using natural light, try to restrict it to one main source, and overcome the problem of moving shadows by deciding where you want them at the outset. In the painting of the interior (right), the light coming in through the window is the key to the whole painting, its shape underlining the arrangement of various objects as well as taking the eye into the picture. Obviously this pattern would not remain unchanged for long, so the artist blocked it in quickly at the start of the painting, leaving the more detailed work until a later stage.

When using artificial light, be careful not to set yourself impossible problems by, for example, training a strong light on highly polished or reflective surfaces. Reflections and highlights are very appealing, and if used in moderation they can give life and sparkle to a painting, but too many can create a fragmented pattern, which may both destroy the form of the objects and make it difficult to unify the picture. Experiment with indirect lighting, either by placing a screen between the light source and the set-up or by bouncing the light off a reflector, such as a piece of white cardboard or a mirror.

Lighting is particularly important for flower paintings, as patches of light and shade can throw the shape of a stem, leaf, or petal into relief, thus defining the form and character. In general, three-quarter lighting – that is, using a light source between the side and the front of the subject – is the best. This gives good, clear shadows, which describe the shapes well, while direct frontal lighting tends to flatten everything out, just as midday sun does in a landscape.

LIGHT AND MOOD

Whether you choose to illuminate your still life with natural daylight or artificial light is a matter of preference. The main thing is to arrange the lighting to full advantage, that is, to use it as a tool, not only to express form through the contrast of light and shade, but also to establish a particular mood. Remember, you are not simply painting a group of objects: you are painting a group of objects suffused with light.

One way to quickly familiarize yourself with lighting effects and the moods they convey is to set up a simple still life group and paint it under a range of different lighting conditions. Place the objects on a tray, which will enable you to move your still life from one part of the room to another, should you wish to, without disturbing the relationship of the objects. Study the same group under both natural and artificial light, and a combination of both. Observe the effects of bright sunlight, diffuse light, three-quarter light, back light, side light, and so on. You will soon become aware of the different moods and effects created by altering the strength and direction of the light, and how the impression of three-dimensional form is either heightened or lessened. Here are just a few of the options available.

BACK LIGHT

Place your tray of objects on a table directly in front of a window. Position yourself so that you face the window with the tray in front of you. This arrangement, in which the subject is placed between you and the source of light, is sometimes known by the French term *contre jour* ("against the light"). Lit from behind, the objects are seen in near-silhouette, and the overall effects of soft tones and muted colors creates a soft, romantic mood.

SIDE LIGHT

Place a desk lamp to one side of your still life group and shine it onto the objects from a low angle, say a foot above the table. You will see that each object is clearly divided into a bright side and a shadow side and there will be long, sharply defined cast shadows. The modeling of the forms is now much stronger. Because the light falls from a single, isolated source, everything that lies outside the beam of light is cast into shadow. This heightens the sense of drama and intensifies the mood – an effect known as "chiaroscuro."

COMBINED LIGHT SOURCES

For this third experiment in lighting, pick up your tray and move it through 45° so that the still life is lit by daylight coming through the window from one side. Switch on your desk lamp and shine it onto the still life from the other side. The combination of warm electric light and cool daylight will have a magical effect on the colors of the shadows, with warm oranges and yellows combining with cool blues and violets. As the two sources of light interact, a complex pattern of hard and soft shadows is created. This painting will be the most colorful and light-filled of the three and will convey a corresponding bright and cheerful mood.

TONAL CONTRASTS

One thing to watch out for when portraying a particular lighting condition is the degree of tonal contrast between the lit areas and the shadow areas. In bright sunlight, for example, the tonal contrast between the light and shadow areas on any given object will be quite marked; in diffuse or overcast light, the tones will be much closer because of the weaker illumination. Try to keep the degree of tonal contrast consistent throughout your painting, otherwise the impression of light will be lost.

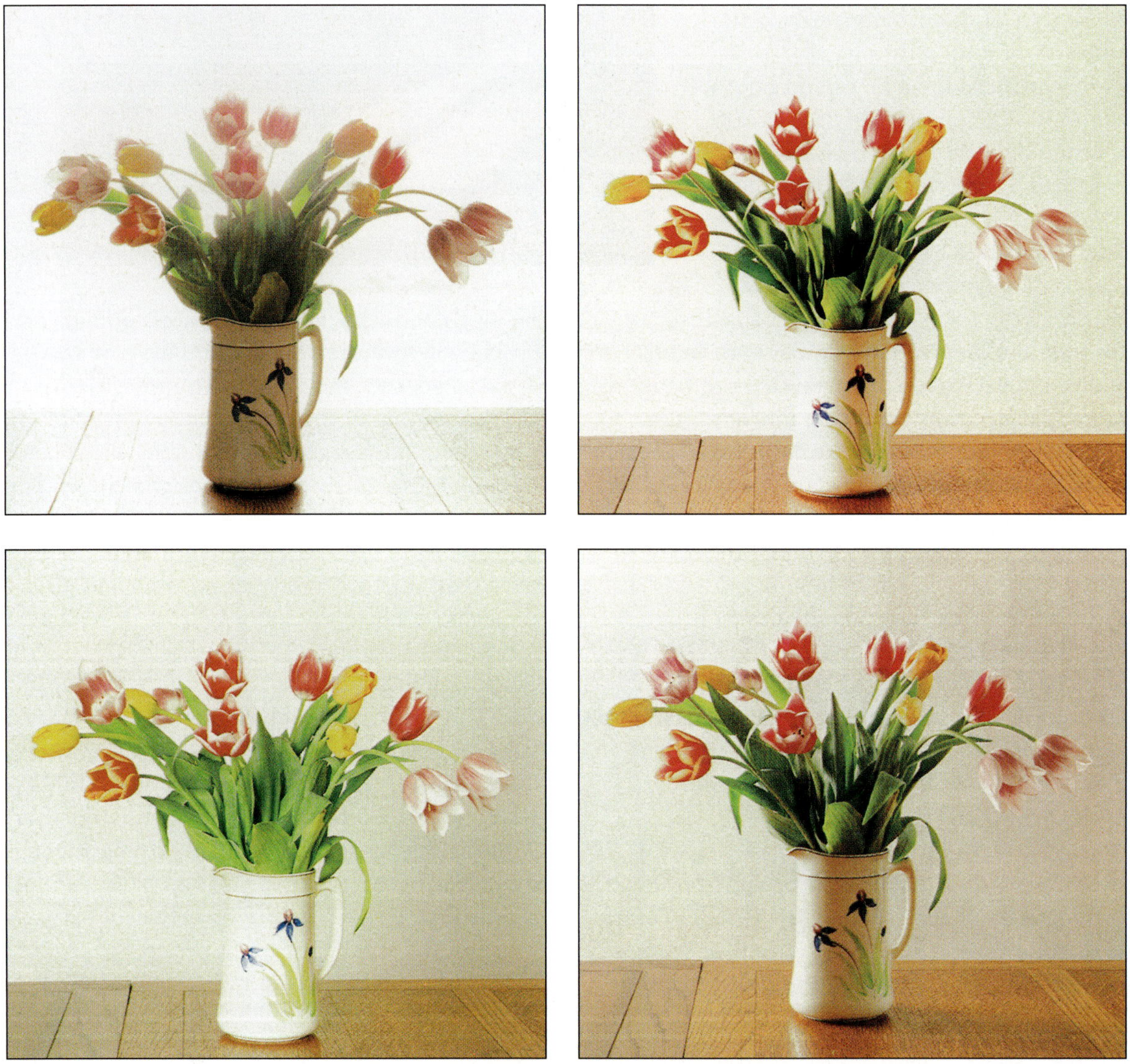

Lighting plays a vital part in the arrangement of a still life, and a subject can change quite dramatically according to the way it is lit. Back lighting (top left) can be very effective for flowers, as the light will shine through the petals in places, giving a brilliant sparkle, with the front foliage and vase appearing very dark. Front light (above left) tends to make any subject seem flat and dull, while side or diagonal lighting (top and above right) will define the forms more clearly.

BEDROOM INTERIOR WITH WHITE LILAC by Jacqueline Rizvi

A still life group does not have to be formally arranged; sometimes a corner of a room, catching the light in a certain way, will provide the impetus for an unusual composition.

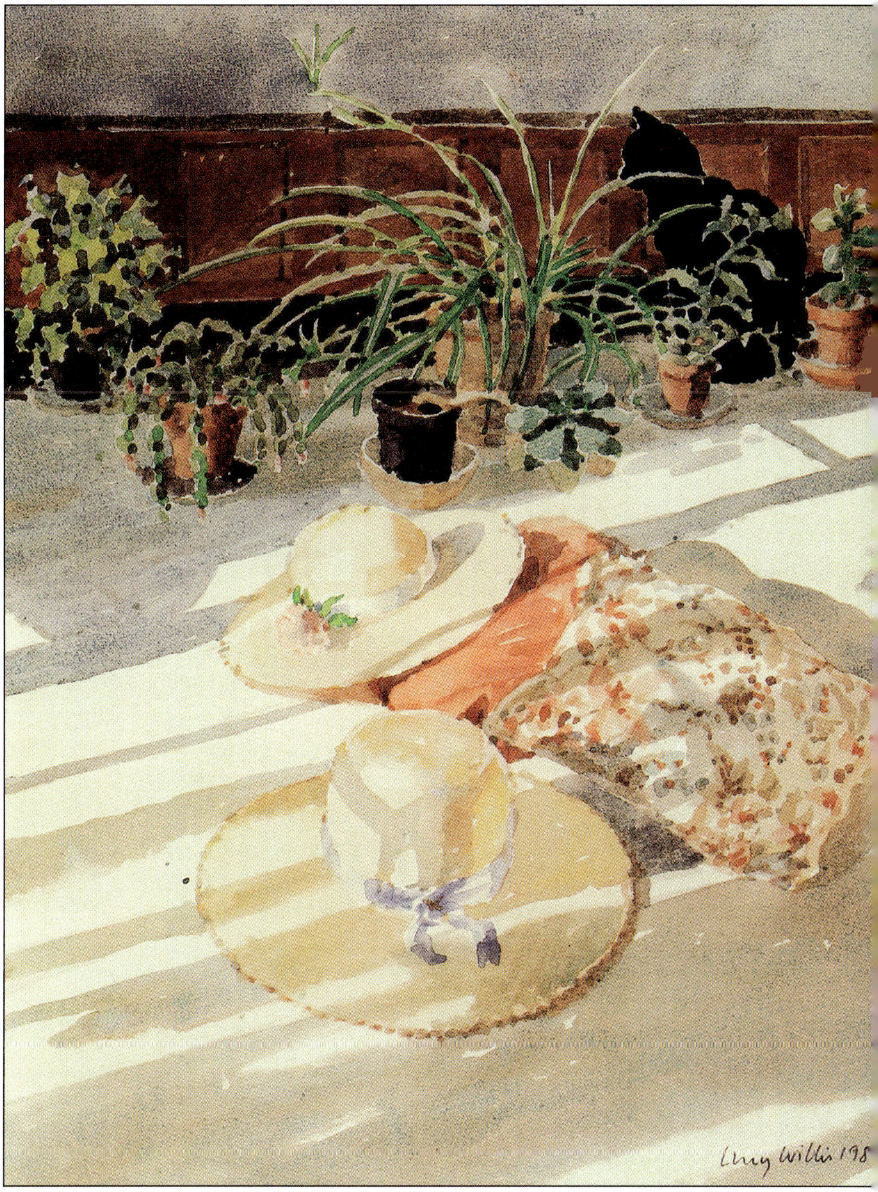

STRAW HATS by Lucy Willis

In this composition, I was interested in the way the long, slanting patterns of light and shadow passed across the floor and over the hats and cushions. There is an interested duality between the solid forms of the objects and the abstract patterns of light that play upon them.

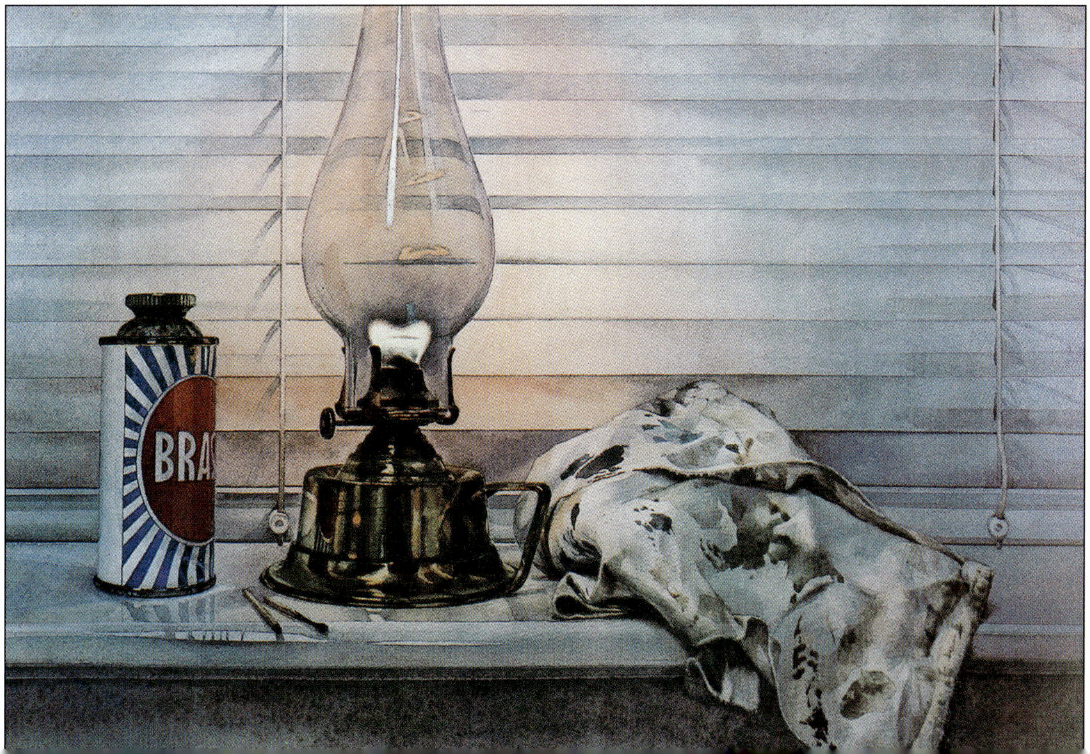

STILL LIFE WITH OIL LAMP by Ronald Jesty

This unusual study has been painted under bright artificial light. The shadows created by the gentle, rosy light from the oil lamp are subtle and delicate.

Pictorial Possibilities

A two-dimensional drawing or painting is made up of flat patterns. These patterns can be caused by the shapes of the objects as well as their color. Now to express their shape we know that we can use a line.

To give an indication of color, all you can do in drawing is to indicate the lightness or darkness of the color, rendering your drawing as a series of flat tonal shapes. Actual shadow and cast shadow in this instance are seen as a variation of color on the object.

All this information in one drawing has a tendency to flatten out the three-dimensional quality of the objects being seen. To express this quality and create an illusion of depth, it is often an advantage to ignore variations in color, and to restrict your drawing merely to showing the light and dark areas caused by actual and cast shadows, because it is the shadow on an object – and the shadows it casts – that make for the realization in a viewer that the object is round or flat. If this is done successfully, the viewer's mind can "assume" the missing tonal values of color.

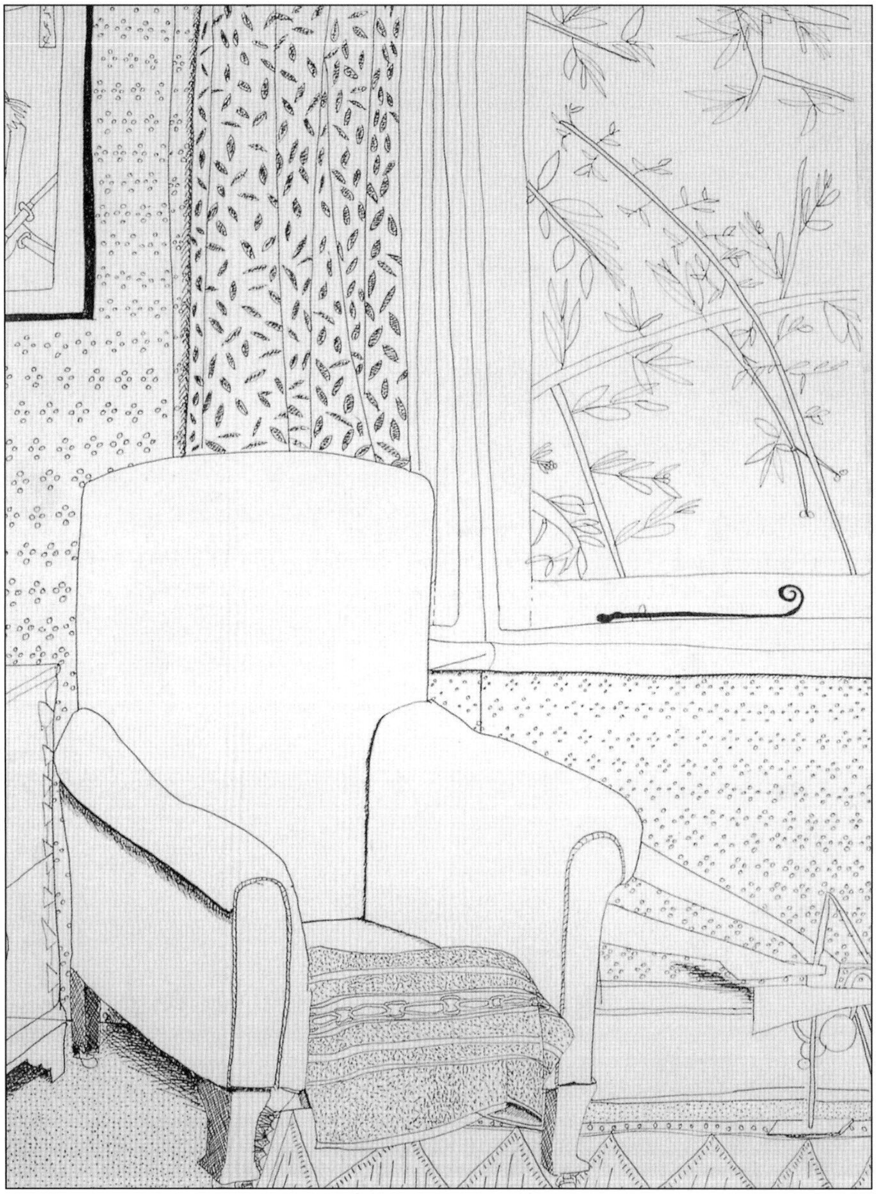

The beginner often finds it difficult to recognize potential subject matter, particularly in surroundings which are completely familiar. This pen and ink study of an armchair by a window must be typical of thousands of homes; such a subject can be treated in a variety of ways. Here, the artist has chosen to concentrate on all the different patterns to create a very two-dimensional image.

Choosing Still Life Subjects

If you have never painted at all, or if you have not used a particular medium before, the idea of making a start can be quite daunting. If you are intending to go to a painting class, it is less alarming, as you will be painting what is put in front of you to paint, and a teacher will be on hand to advise, but if you are working at home there will be a great many decisions to make.

For instance, what will you paint, what size will your work be, and how will you actually begin? This section provides some suggestions and guidelines to help build up your confidence and so increase your enjoyment of still life painting.

CHOOSING A SHAPE AND SIZE

This may seem trivial, but in fact both shape and size have an important part to play in the composition and treatment of a painting. A still life with a lot of objects in it could suggest a rather square horizontal line.

Size is a very personal matter: some artists work on vast canvases too big to fit in most living-rooms, while others produce tiny, detailed work on supports no larger than the average photograph. If you are working at home you are unlikely to want to work on a very large scale, and it is not usually a good idea to start very small. A good starting size is about 20 x 16 in. (51 x 40.6 cm), a standard one in which you can buy both boards and canvases.

Painting is rather like handwriting – people with large writing feel constricted if for any reason they are forced to write small, and if your "natural size" for painting is much larger than the support you have chosen you will soon find out, as your painting will seem to spread of its own volition beyond the edges. Until you have established a size which suits you, it is wise to use an inexpensive support, such as a piece of primed paper or cardboard, oil sketching paper or "canvas board." Hardboard is not recommended for early attempts as it has a slippery surface, which can give a messy and unmanageable paint surface.

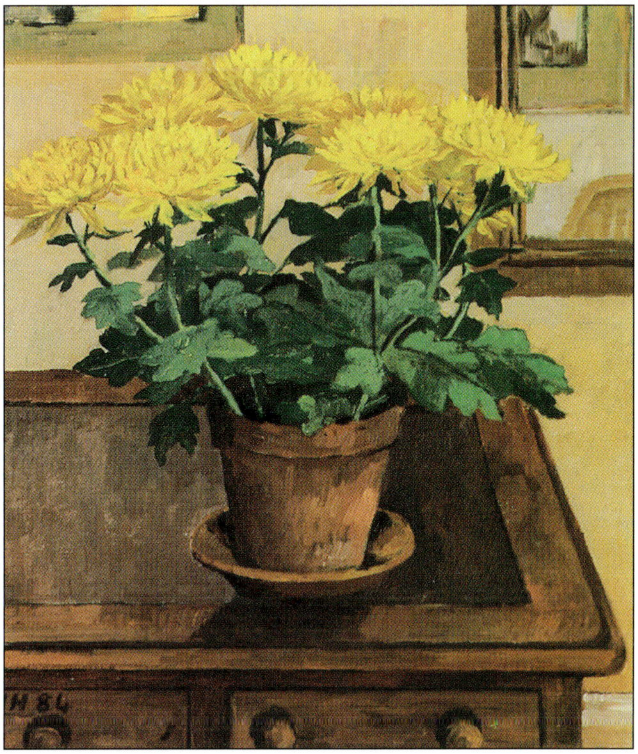

Although still life and flower arrangements need not be elaborate, some thought is needed in the initial setting up if the foreground and background are not to become dull and featureless. Thumbnail sketches and polaroid photographs are useful aids in setting up an arrangement.

AVOIDING DISCOURAGEMENT

If your painting goes wrong at an early stage you are bound to feel depressed and discouraged. Various suggestions are given here, which will help you to avoid or overcome the more common problems.

TINTING THE GROUND

Starting to paint on a glaring expanse of white canvas can be quite daunting, but even more important is the fact that a white surface is also "dishonest," as it prevents you from judging the tones and colors correctly. There is very little pure white in nature, as white, like any other color, is always modified by the light or shadow falling on it. Also, no color exists in a particular way except in relation to the colors surrounding it. Thus, if you start a flower painting by putting down a bold brush stroke of pure cadmium red on a white canvas it will almost certainly be

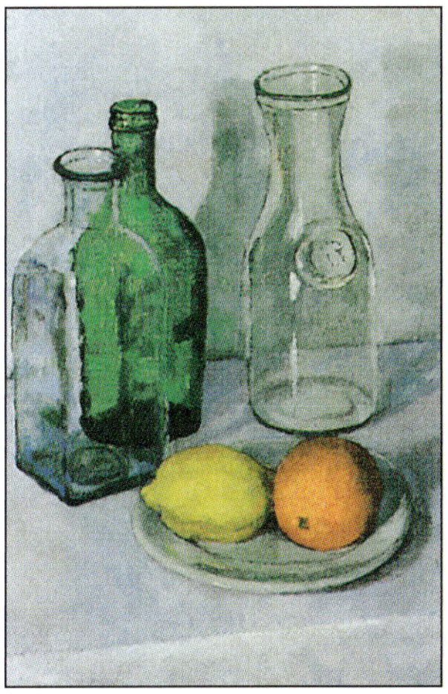

The subject of this simple still life was the artist's collection of assorted bottles, with the fruit used as a balance to the colors and texture of the glass. The lighting was entirely natural, simply the side light coming in through a window, but the objects were set up with care so that the shadows fell pleasingly.

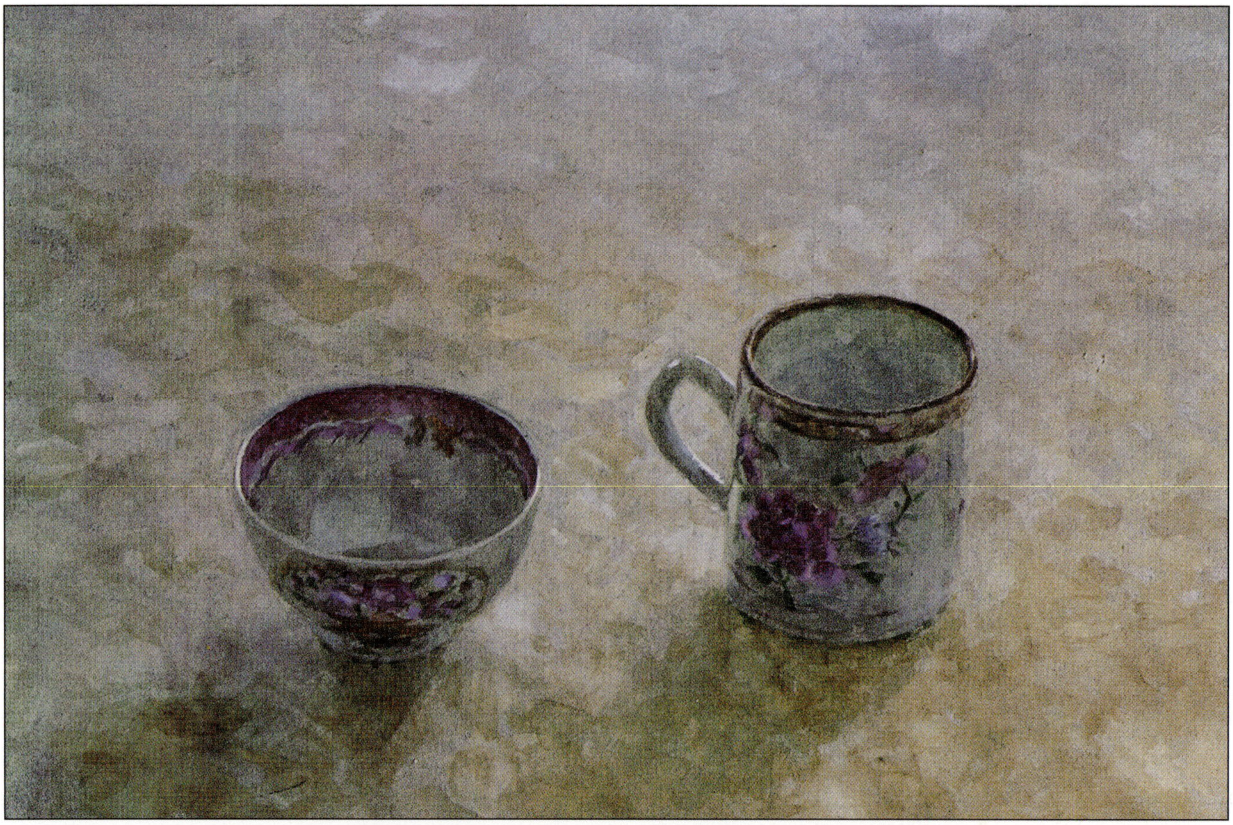

CHINESE CUP AND COFFEE CAN by Jacqueline Rizvi

Pale values and high-key colors give this exquisite still life a delicate, airy feel, in keeping with the nature of the subject.

wrong, as the red you are seeing is actually given its quality by its relationship to the background, which may be neutral or even dark.

A method often used by artists is to tint the canvas in a neutral color, usually a warm brown or gray, before starting the painting. This can be done either by mixing pigment in with the primer, or by putting a wash of oil paint, such as a raw umber, heavily diluted with turpentine, over the white ground. Acrylic paint can also be used for this since it dries much faster than oil paint, and you could buy a single tube just for this purpose, but remember that acrylic paint should not be used over an oil ground; oil can be used over acrylic, but acrylic cannot be used over oil.

PREPARATION

Always start with an adequate drawing or underpainting in order to place the main design elements in the way you want them. Even a simple subject such as bowl of fruit can go very wrong if you fail to judge correctly the size of the fruit in relation to the bowl, or the bowl in relation to the table it is standing on. You may be impatient to start on the real business – the laying on of paint – but it does pay to take your time at this stage, for it will avoid a lot of frustration later.

KEEPING THE PICTURE MOVING

Try to avoid working in detail on one part of the painting at the expense of another. This approach can lead to a disjointed-looking painting, since you are more likely to tire of it halfway through. Generally, it is better to work on all parts of the canvas at once, so that you have a better idea of how one part relates to another in color, tone, and texture.

Some artists, such as the English painter Stanley Spencer (1891—1959), successfully reversed this process by starting with a careful and detailed pencil drawing and then painting area by area. There is theoretically nothing wrong with working in this way, but an inexperienced painter is unlikely to have a very clear vision of the finished painting, which is required for such an approach.

In general, it is easier to build up oil paint light over dark, as white is the most opaque color; so keep to dark and middle tones in the early stages, working up gradually to the light and bright tones and colors. Always try to see the background as part of the painting, not just as an unimportant area (as mentioned before); even a plain white wall has colors in it, and a totally flat background can be used as a shape, to form part of the composition. Avoid getting bogged down in detail too early; fine lines, such as the stems of flowers or small details, are best left until last.

PROBLEM SOLVING

Even paintings by professionals go wrong, but the beauty of oil paint is that they can so easily be altered. If you suddenly notice that your drawing is incorrect and that you have quite misunderstood a shape or color, the best course is not to try to overpaint, but to scrape off the area with a palette knife and then re-paint it.

You may even decide to scrape down the whole painting and start more or less from scratch – this is often more satisfactory than trying to alter each individual area only to find that something is still not right.

If you find that the surface of the painting has become so overloaded with paint that you are just churning it up by continuing to add layers, there is a useful method, invented by a painting teacher called Henry Tonks and named "tonking" after him. This is done by laying a sheet of absorbent paper, such as newspaper, over the painting, rubbing it gently and removing it; this takes off the top layer of paint, and leaves you with something similar to a colored underpainting.

CREATING MOOD

It is important that your subject is suited to a low-key approach. A still life of inanimate objects does not necessarily suggest a particular mood; it's up to you to create one. Try placing your still life against a dark background, lit by a small light source placed to one side of the group. This will create intriguing highlights and shadows, lending a subtle atmosphere and a mood of intimacy.

STILL LIFE WITH TEAPOT by Paul Cézanne

Cézanne used the still life as a means of experimenting with and expressing his innovative concepts of space and depth. The still life has often been used in such a way since objects are easily arranged to suit the artists needs.

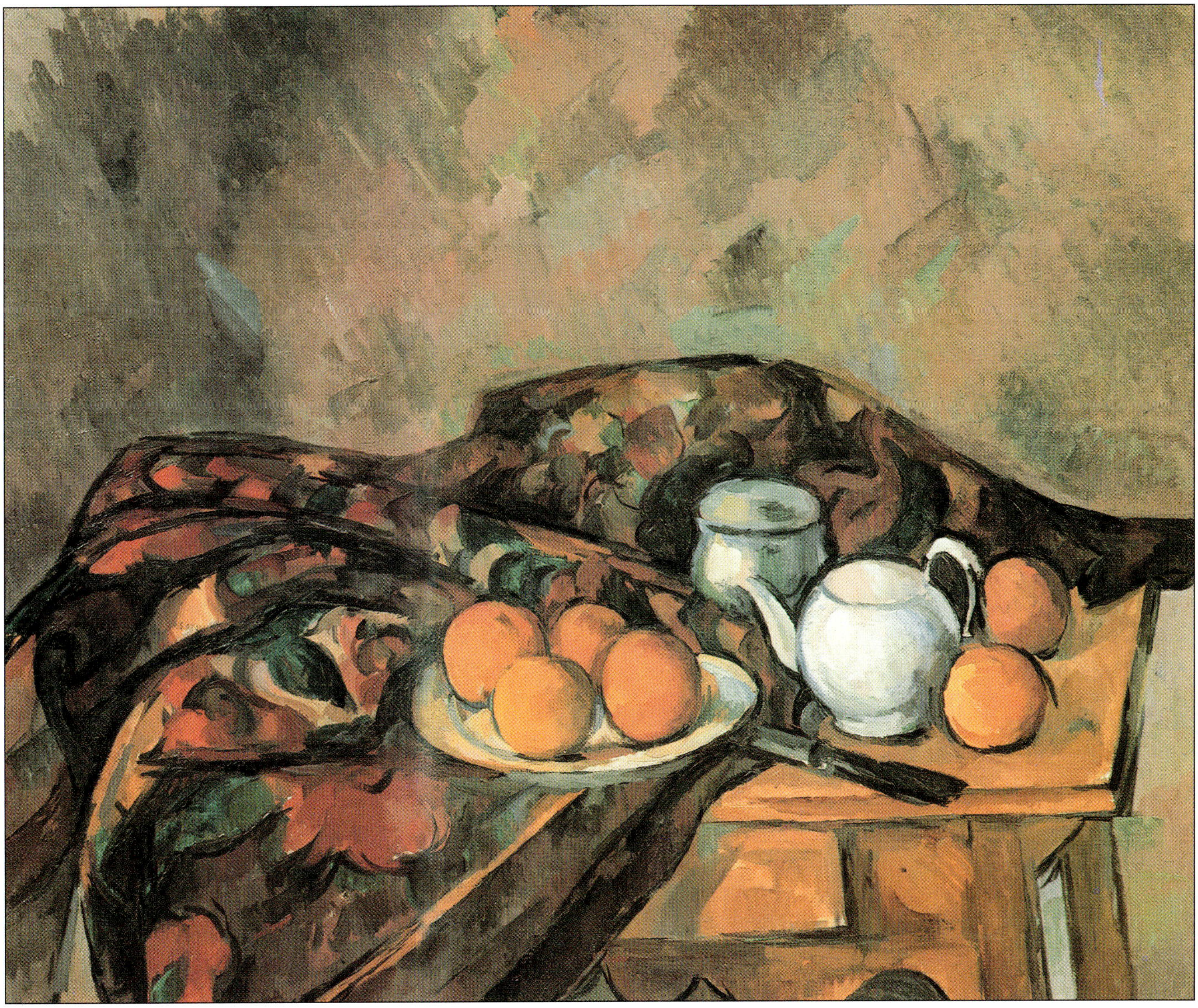

Shadows and Mood

As an exercise, collect together four or five household objects that are no longer required for everyday use. Give them a coating of white emulsion paint so that they all appear to be made of plaster.

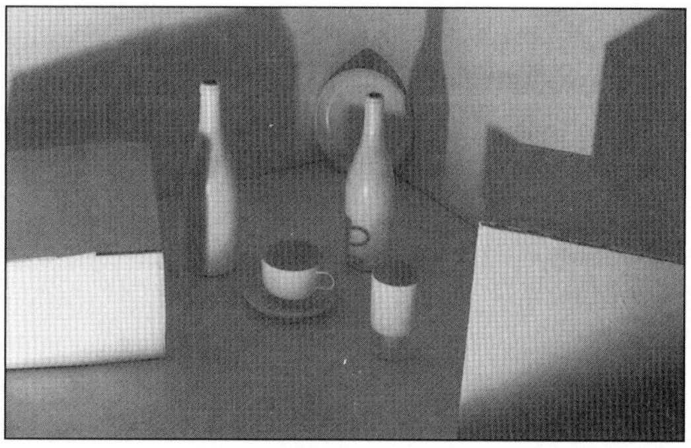

The whiteness of the objects will help you to see the effect light has in causing shadows. Set up your still life in a convenient corner, and with the aid of an adjustable lamp, direct light from one specific direction onto these now white but familiar shapes. Keep your drawing board as upright as conveniently possible and, remembering the picture plane concept, outline the pattern of the objects in front of you. Then draw around the shadows.

Notice that there are two distinct types of shadow. One is the shadow that is present on the side of objects away from the light source. This is called "actual" shadow and is more difficult to see, particularly on a cylindrical or round object, as the dark side gets progressively darker, and the exact line where the grayness begins is sometimes difficult to see. Because the objects are painted white, however, this should be easier to recognize. A simple way for the beginner to draw the actual shadow is to decide where the darkest part is and shade this as dark as possible. Then decide where the lightest gray is. Divide the area between the lightest shadow and the darkest shade into four, and graduate the shading accordingly.

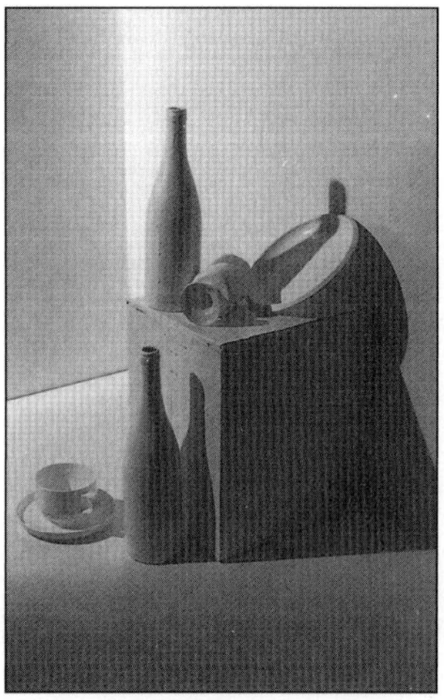

The other types of shadow are "cast" or "projected" shadows. A cast shadow is that area that light cannot get to because there is an object in the way. Because light travels in a straight line, a cast shadow's shape is a version - perhaps a distorted version – of the shape of the object that is casting the shadow. Draw round the cast shadows on your still life and you will notice that there is no variation in the darkness of cast shadow. If there is, this variation is caused by light reflected off an adjacent object and shining into the shadowed area.

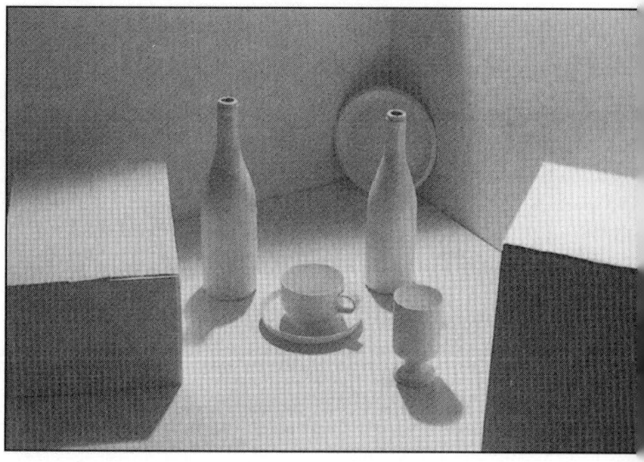

Reflected light can be a very useful decider and is much used by painters.

Without altering the still life arrangement, change the position of the light, and draw the same subject matter again in the same way. Notice that all the patterns and shapes in your second drawing are very different from those in your first, although you have not moved the objects or altered the position from which you are drawing them. Make further experiments by changing the position of the light source.

Now have another look round your home and find a potential subject that is lit by a table lamp or a single light source. Set yourself up to make a drawing of it. The first thing to notice is that because all the objects in view are not white but their rightful colors it is much harder to see the shadows – although even on a black telephone the lights and darks are still there. The part of the telephone turned away from the light is a blacker black than that part of the telephone turned into the light.

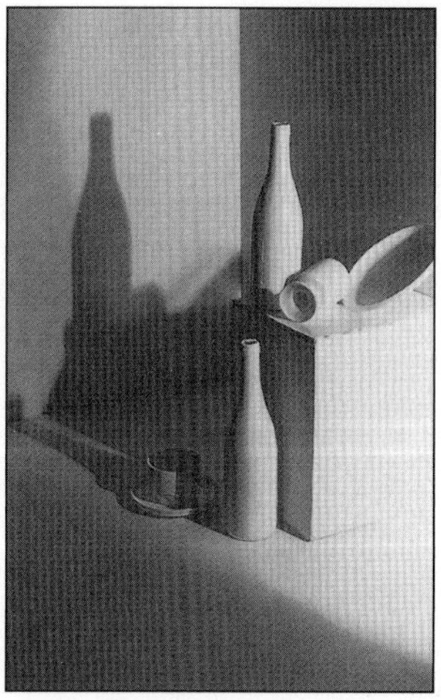

In each of the four photographs the single source of light has been moved, giving each photograph a different two-dimensional pattern of lights and darks. The relative positions of the objects to the camera has not been altered.

USE OF SHADOWS TO CREATE MOOD

The aim of the project illustrated below is to demonstrate the effect that the prevailing light has on shadows, and how this is turn can affect the mood of your painting.

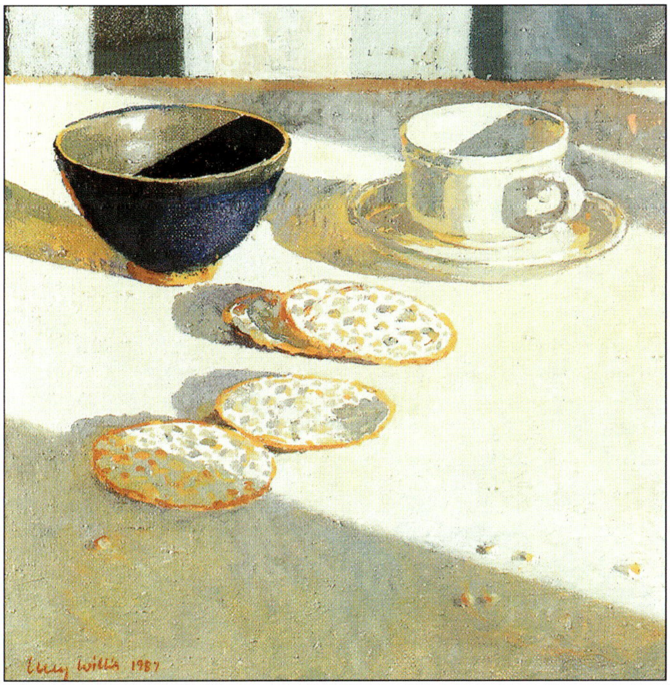

MORNING BREAK I
by Lucy Willis

Strong, clear shadows cast by direct sunlight become important factors in the composition.

Set up a very simple still life in front of a window which receives a fair amount of light – preferably in a place where you can leave the group undisturbed for a few days if necessary, because you are going to paint two versions of it.

Paint the first version of your still life on a bright, sunny day (choose any medium you like). Paint the second version in the late afternoon or early evening, when the light is softer and more diffuse. When both paintings are completed, compare the results and notice how the atmosphere and the composition has been affected by the different kind of lighting.

STRONG LIGHT

Bright, crisp sunlight shining directly through the window casts sharply defined areas of light and shadow, which are as important a part of the composition as the objects themselves. Shadows cast by nearby objects tend to have sharper edges than those cast by objects further away; note here how the shadows cast by the objects on the table have sharper edges than those cast by the window.

DIFFUSE LIGHT

In the second painting the mood is much quieter and more restrained. The same objects are lit this time by a warm, soft evening light, which bounces off the color of the back wall and creates two sets of subtle shadows: those blue-gray ones, which come toward us and orange-tinted ones that fall to the left. Because the light is diffuse the tonal contrasts throughout the composition are much less marked, and all the shadows are soft-edged. To achieve this effect, blend the wet oil paint into the surrounding areas with your finger or a dryish hog's-hair brush.

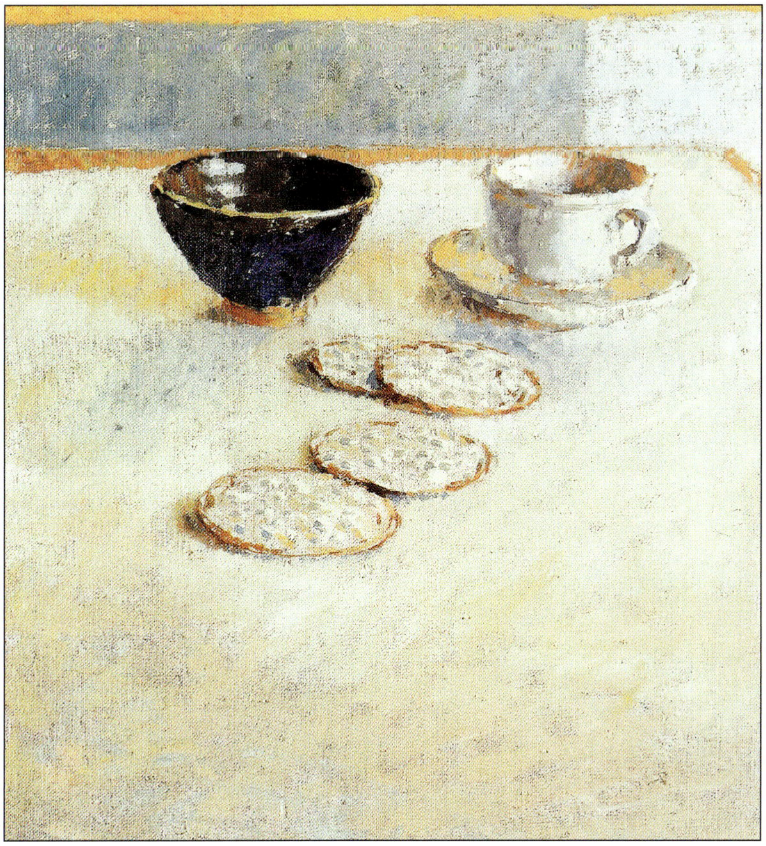

MORNING BREAK II
by Lucy Willis

In contrast, the shadows here are soft and unobtrusive, gently modeling the forms and absorbing reflected light.

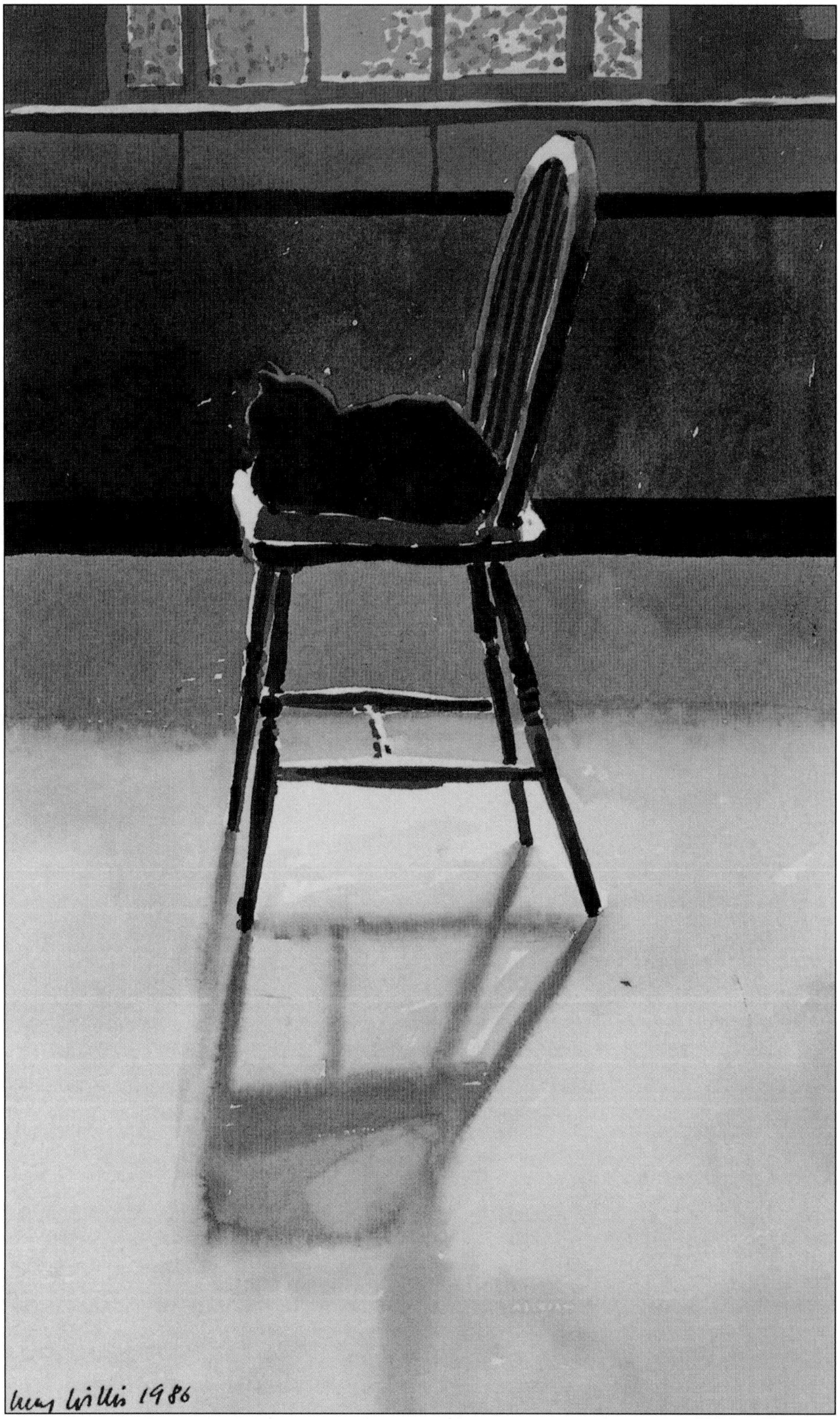

CAT ON A CHAIR by Lucy Willis

An example of a low-key painting, which does not have to be somber. In this charming study of a cat on a chair, back lighting throws the subject into near-silhouette and creates interesting positive and negative shapes.

Still Life in Oil

It is interesting to note in this painting that although the subject is a "portrait" of bell peppers and a crab, the theme of the painting is predominantly non-objective. In fact, it is not so much the crab and bell peppers which determine the strength of the picture, but their surroundings, which, through the use of color, shape and texture, draws the viewer's attention into the center of the painting.

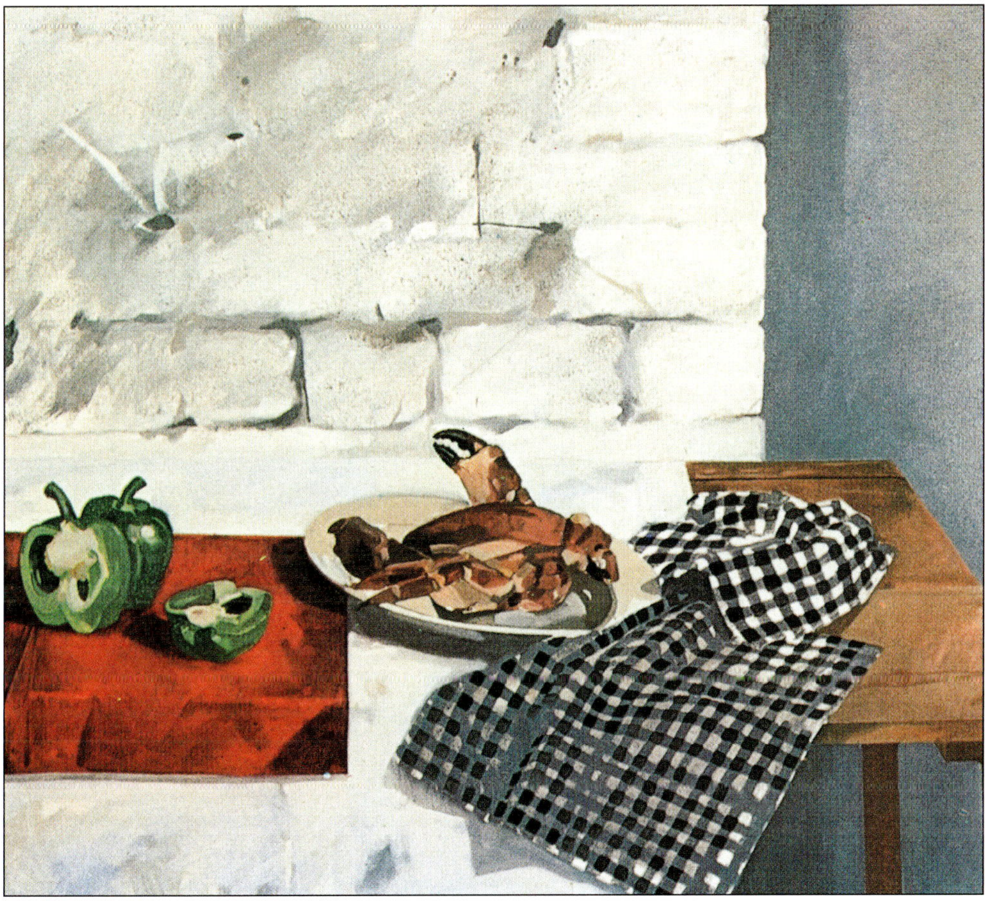

The environment is made up of flat shapes and planes described in neutral and earth tones, which contrast with the roundness of the peppers and crab. Within the wall there are soft, blended tones and strokes, which heighten the distinct lines and tones of the subject. The busyness of the checks in the cloth create a visual interest and, again, draw the viewer's eye into the center of the painting while the red cloth creates tension and contrast with the bell peppers and the stark white background.

Note that the red used in the cloth is of a value purposely chosen to avoid overwhelming the rest of the picture with its "redness" or contrasting too sharply with the green of the bell peppers.

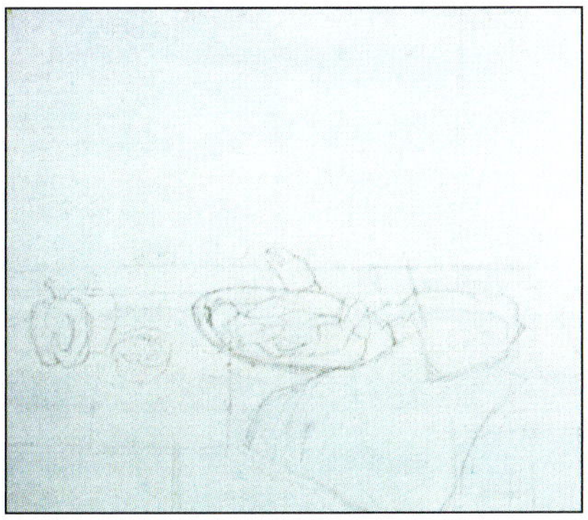

1 With a 2B pencil, lightly put in the shapes and general composition of the painting.

2 Mix white and black, and with a No. 6 brush block in flat areas of color. With a No. 4 brush and more white, rough in outlines and shadows in the brick wall.

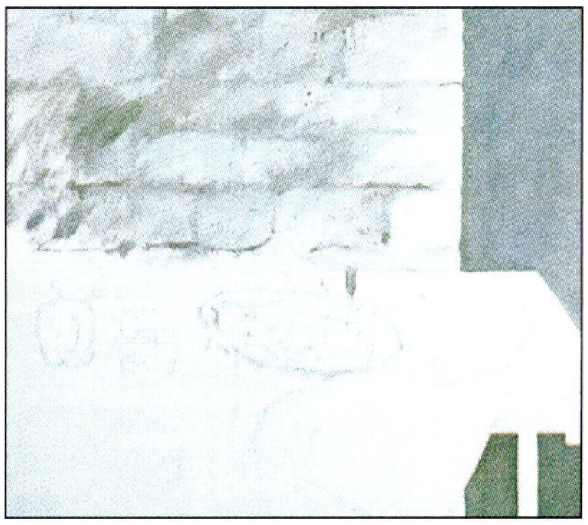

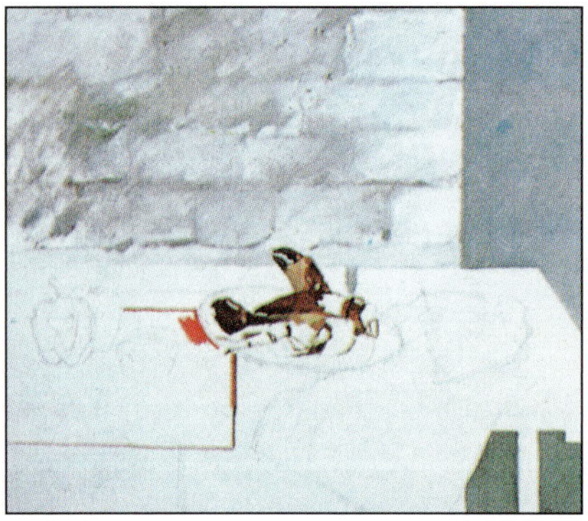

3 With a No. 2 brush and burnt sienna begin to develop the crab. In cadmium red, begin to define the red cloth.

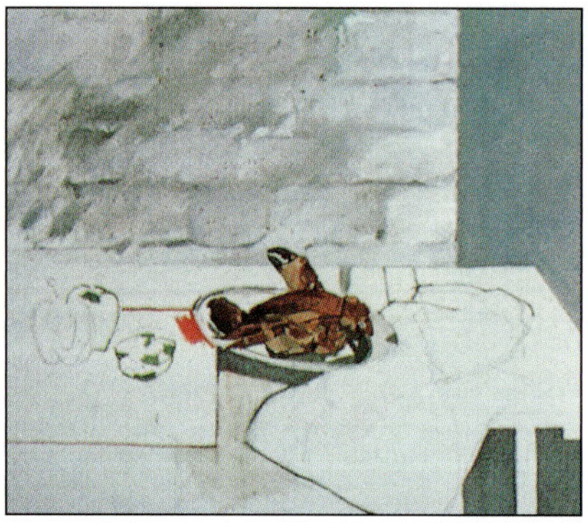

4 Mix chrome green and yellow, and with the No. 2 brush outline the bell peppers and put in light areas of color.

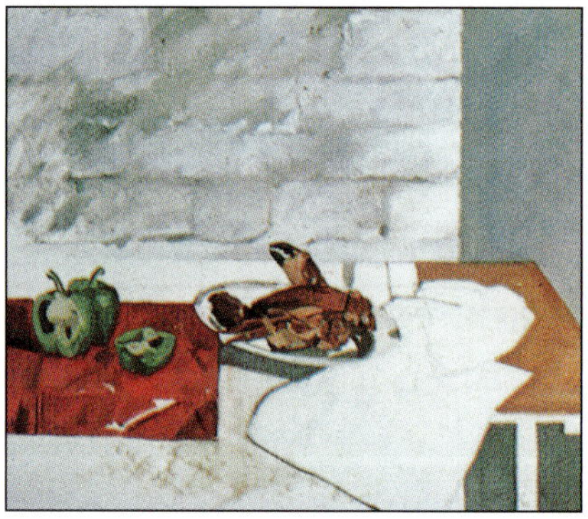

5 Mix umber, ocher, and white, and block in the table with a No. 6 brush. Add a touch of black to cadmium red and develop cloth shadows.

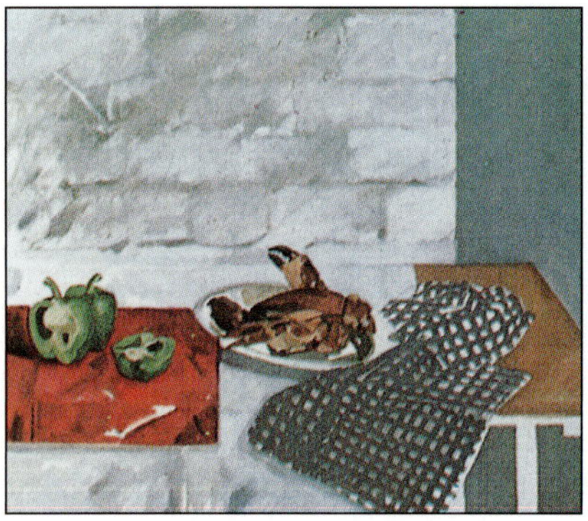

6 With black and white, mix shades of gray. Using the No. 2 sable brush, paint in squares of cloth using the white of the canvas for white squares and light gray for shadow.

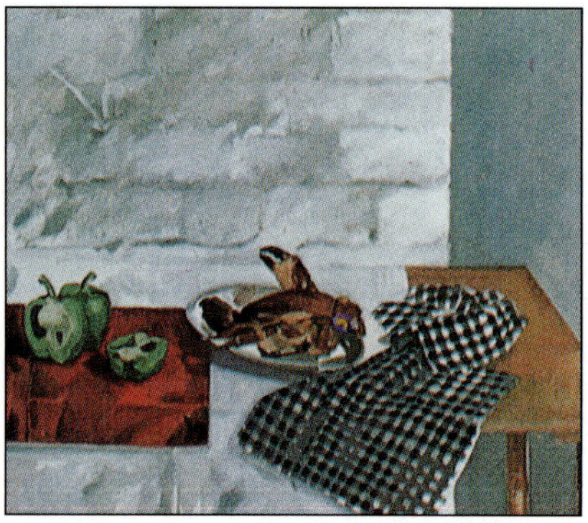

7 Work back into the checked cloth with a darker gray and black to strengthen light and dark contrasts.

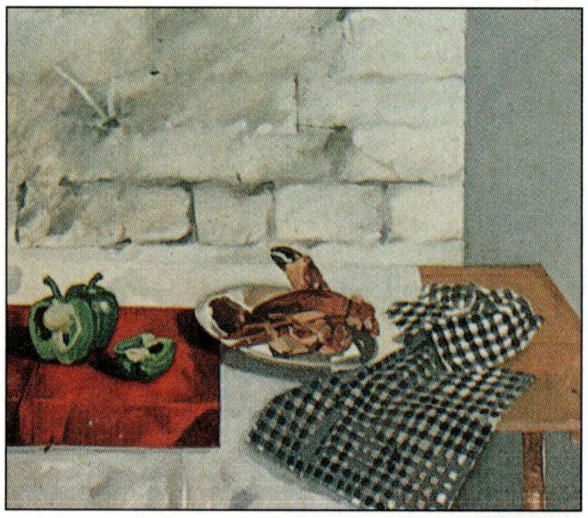

8 Mix white and ocher, and lighten background bricks. Use the same gray tone as in the cloth to redefine brick outlines and shadows

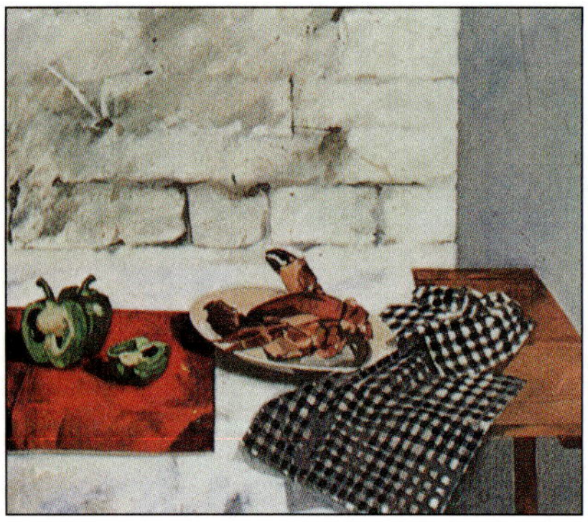

9 Mask the edge of the red cloth with tape and paint over this to create a clean, distinct edge.

10 With the No. 2 sable brush and burnt umber, put in horizontal lines in the table and strengthen the shadow area in the table leg.

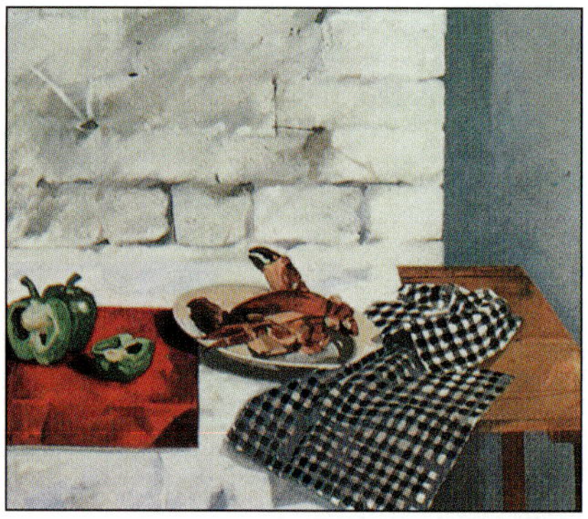

Still Life in Acrylic

Of the many media and mixed media available to the artist, a prime factor should be which media will most successfully capture the subject. If the painting illustrated were executed in watercolor or pastel, rather than acrylic, the final effect would be much different.

In this case, acrylics were chosen because of the bold color scheme of the subject. Unlike other painting media, acrylics have an inherent brilliance and brightness, which makes them particularly well-suited for describing subjects which demand a bold use of color.

In this painting, the aim of the artist was to create a composition using the classic triangle, with the wine bottle as a focal point. One of the demands of the still life is that the various objects be arranged in such a way as to avoid flatness in the painting. A mixture of different sizes, shapes, and textures ensures that the finished painting (on page 318) will successfully avoid this problem.

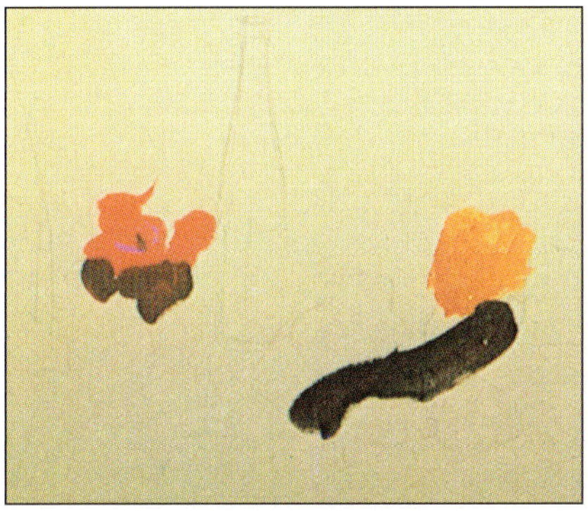

1 With raw and burnt sienna, orange, and red, block in shapes in pure color using a No. 6 bristle brush.

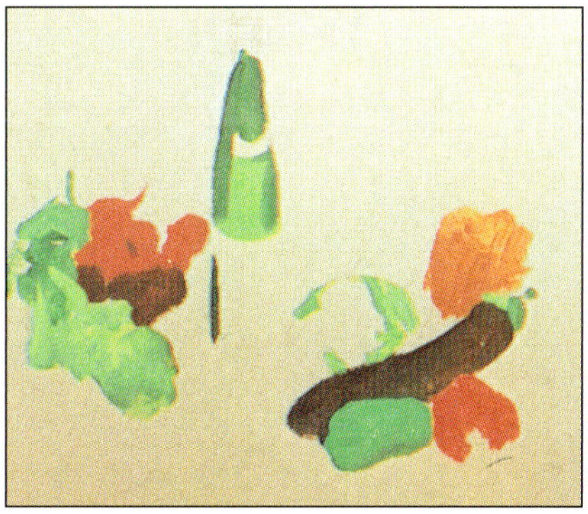

2 Describe green shapes with Hooker's and pthalo green with a No. 6 watercolor brush. Vary tones by adding white.

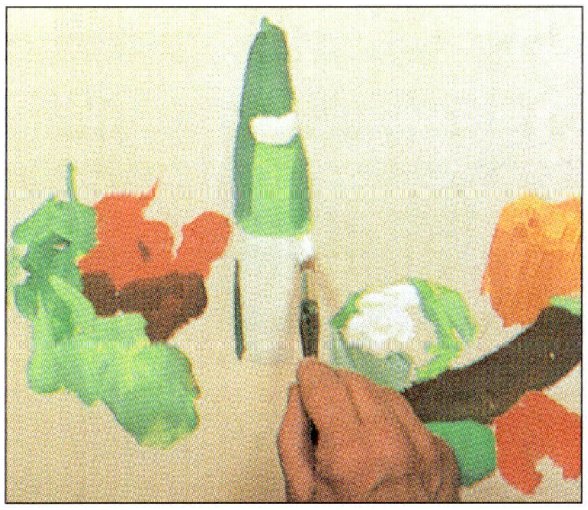

3 Using the same brush and pure white paint, block in the pure white highlight areas of the bottle and cauliflower.

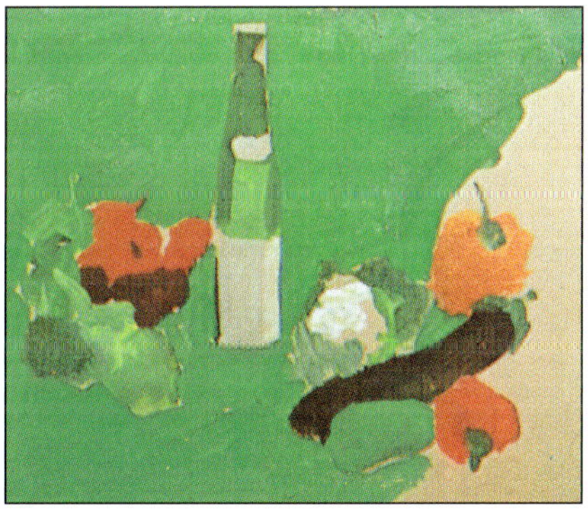

4 Mix a large amount of pthalo green and white and using the No. 6 bristle brush, block in the entire background with consistent strokes.

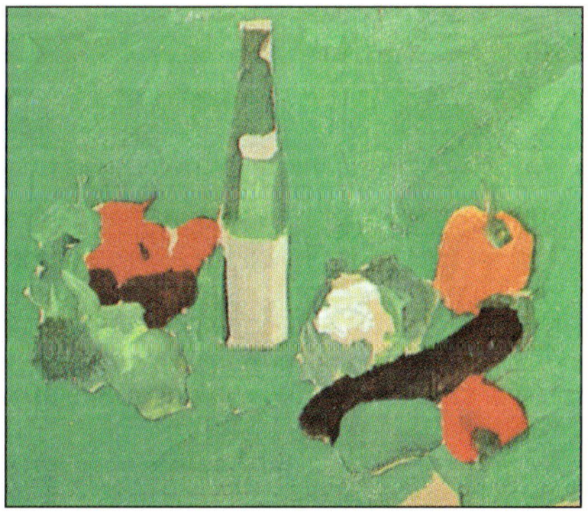

5 Continue across the paper putting in the background. Add a small amount of yellow to the mixture to vary the tone of the green.

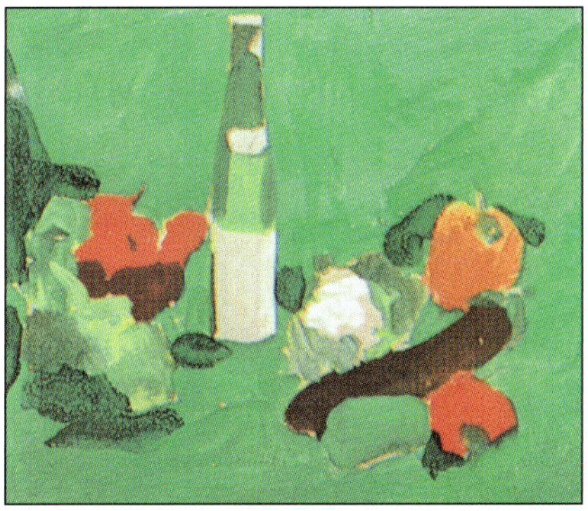

6 Using Hooker's green and a No. 4 brush, block in the dark green shadow areas of the background, keeping the paint fairly wet.

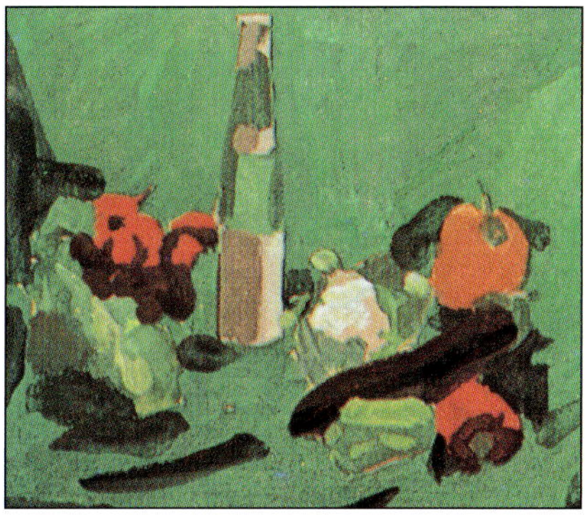

7 Add a small amount of burnt sienna to the Hooker's green, and put in shadow areas of foreground.

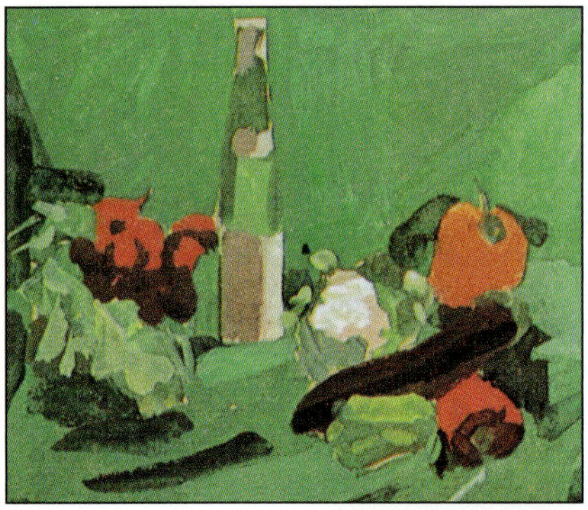

8 Mix pthalo green and white, and with the No. 4 brush, describe light areas of the foreground cloth.

9 Carry this same light green tone into the background area.

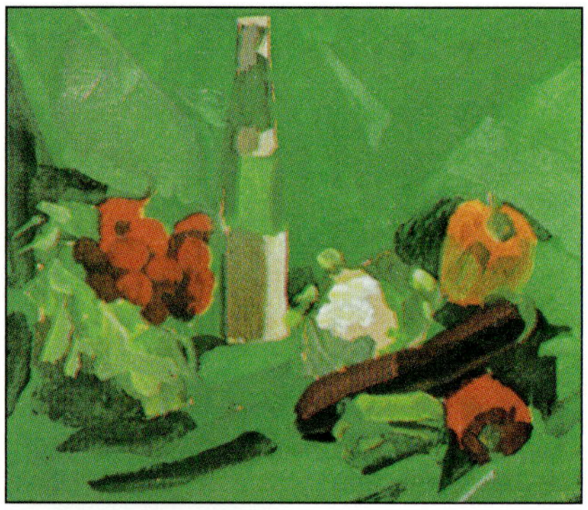

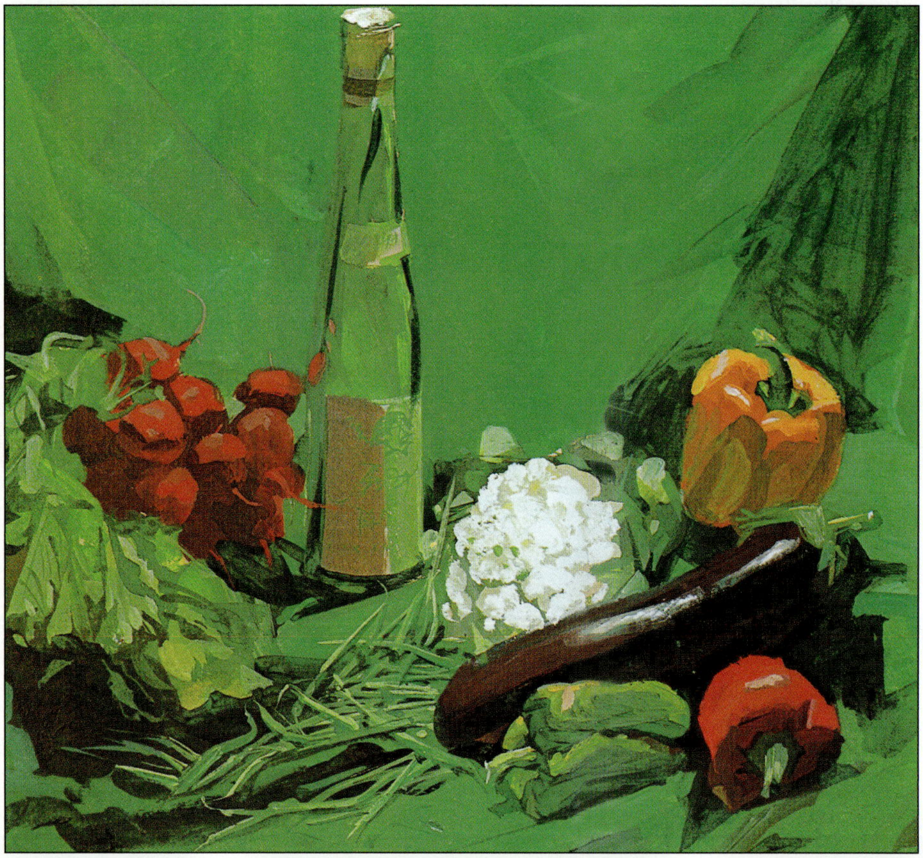

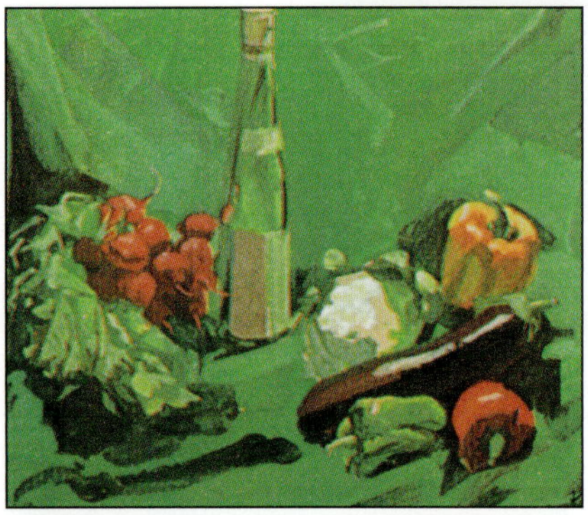

10 With a No. 2 brush and Hooker's green, put in the dark shadow areas of the green vegetables. With the same brush and pure white, put in highlights.

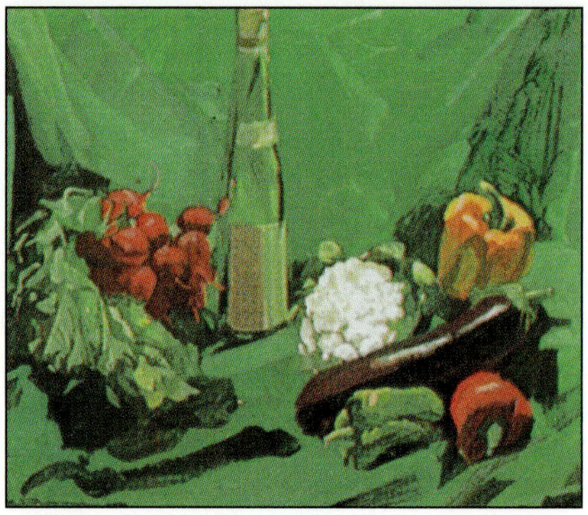

11 With pure white and the No. 2 brush, block in cauliflower. Put in strong highlights in white in the bottle.

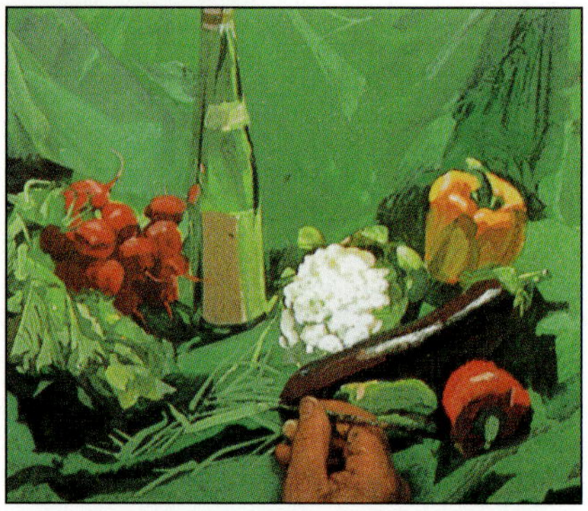

12 Mix pthalo green and white, and with the same brush, put in the beans with fluid, even strokes.

Still Life in Watercolor

The freshness of watercolor depends upon the gradual building up from light to dark, and any attempt to create highlights or pale tones in the final stages of the painting will alter the entire character of the medium. Accuracy is thus all-important in the initial structuring of the composition.

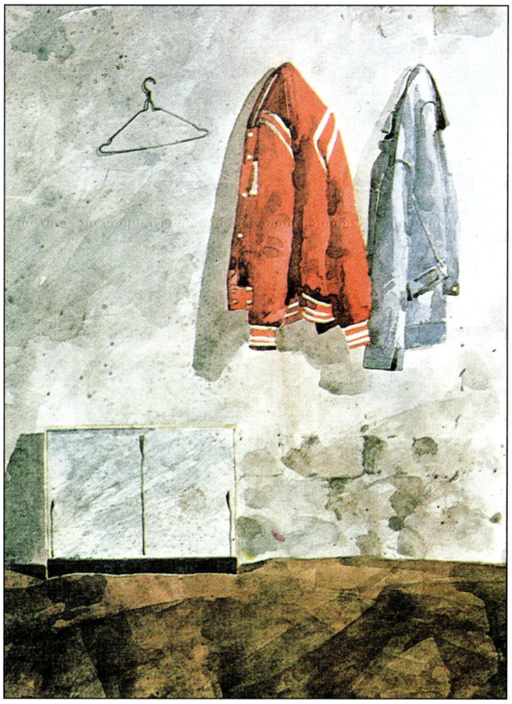

White shapes must be precise and clean, created "negatively" by careful drawing of surrounding color areas.

A light pencil sketch will help to establish the correct proportions, but complex shapes are outlined directly with a fine sable brush. Block in solid colors quickly or a hard line will appear around the edges of the shapes. Use large brushes to work into the foreground and background and lightly spatter paint dripped from the end of a large brush to create a mottle texture.

A limited range of color was used, mixing in black to create dark tones and varying grays with small touches of red and blue. Dry the painting frequently so that colors remain separate and the full range of tone and texture emerges through overlaid washes.

1 Draw the basic shapes of the objects in outline with a pencil. Mix a very thin wash of Payne's gray and block in the whole of the background.

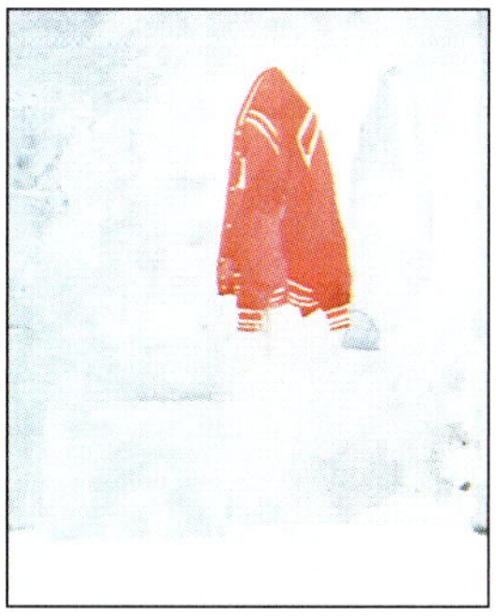

2 Paint in the local colors of the objects building up the paint in thin layers and leaving white space to show highlights and small details. Keep each color separate.

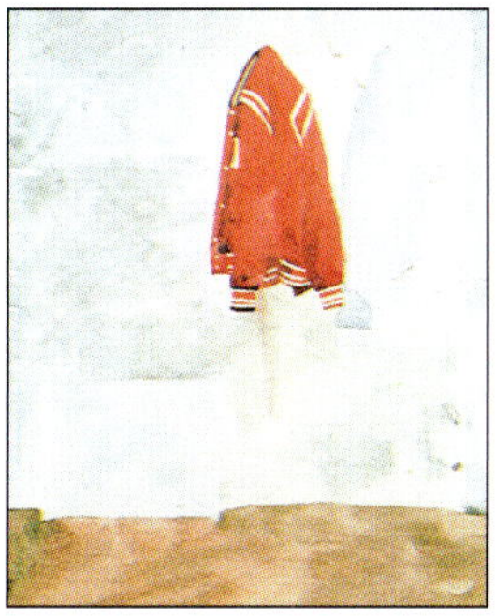

3 Mix a light brown from red and black and work over the red, showing folds and creases in the fabric and dark shadows. Lay a wash of brown across the foreground.

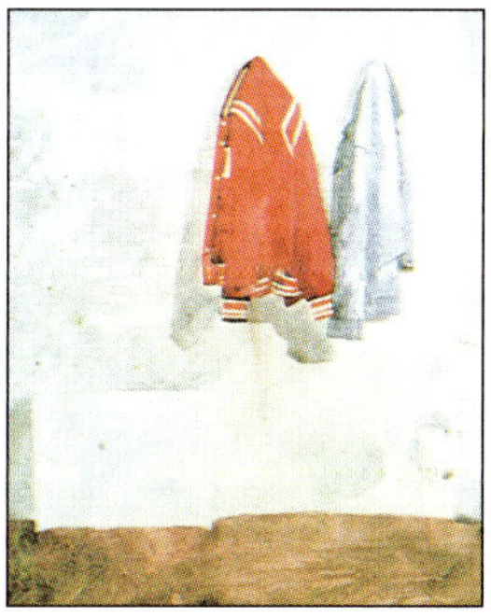

4 Work up shadows in the blue in the same way using a mixture of blue and black. Move over the whole painting putting in dark tones.

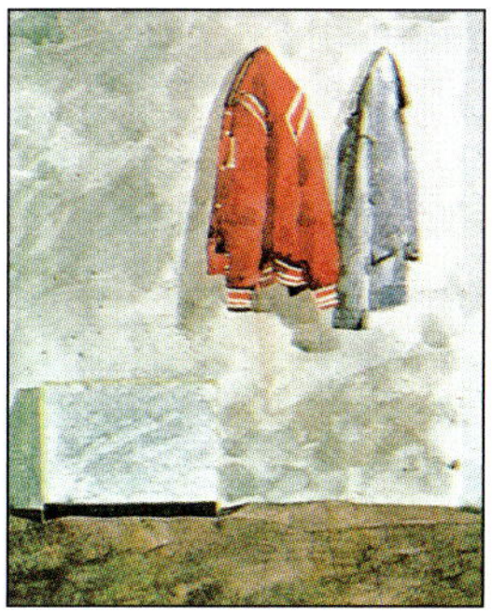

5 Strengthen all the colors, breaking up the shapes into small tonal areas. Bring out textural details by overlaying washes and spattering the paint lightly.

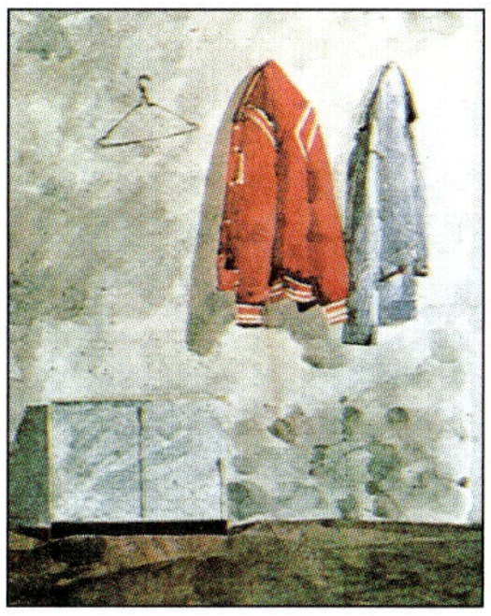

6 Intensify the dark brown in the foreground and use the same brown to indicate shadow on the wall behind. Vary the strength of the color.

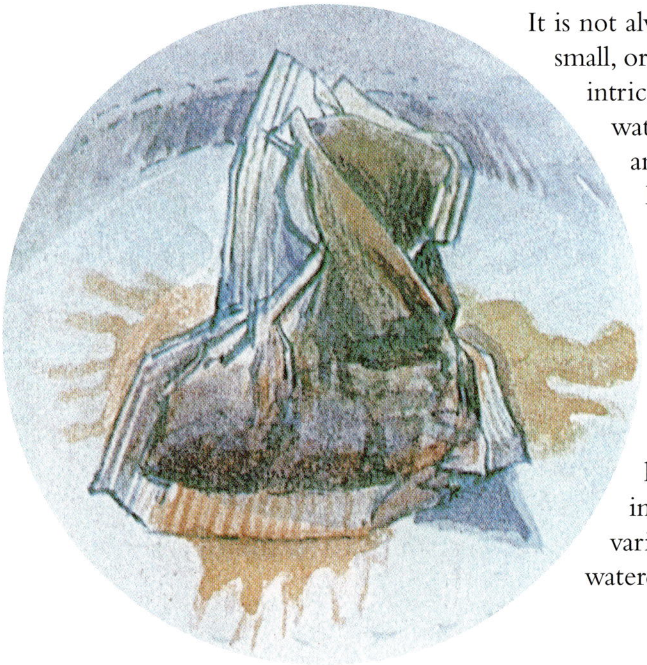

It is not always necessary to go to great lengths to assemble a still life as a small, ordinary object such as a teabag offers a complex structure and intricate range of tones and colors. As well, practice in quick watercolor studies develops keen perception and skills in drawing and painting, which are a sound basis for work in any medium. Here watercolor is used for a study which is essentially direct and immediate. The painting is rapidly completed, building up the form with a combination of line and thin washes of paint; the subject emerges through a careful interpretation of tiny shapes of color and tone.

In small paintings of this kind the paint should be wet but not overly so, ensuring that the marks are easy and fluid but controlled. The final effect is achieved by constantly checking lines and shapes; working wash over line; and drawing back into the washes. A limited range of color is used to create a variety of tones, demonstrating the rich versatility and potential of watercolors.

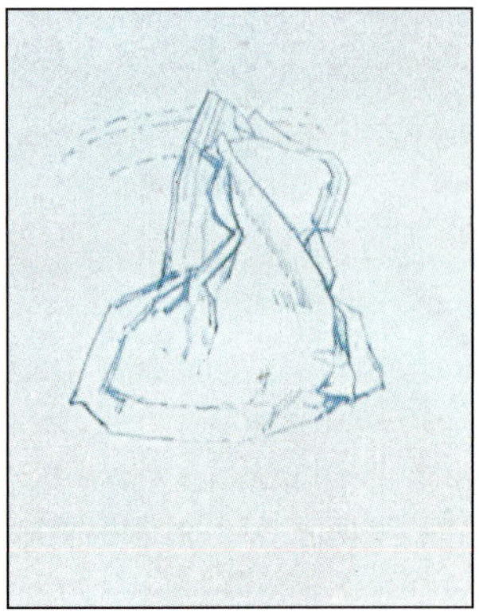

1 Load the brush with Prussian blue paint, well-thinned with water. Draw the outline of the shape and details of the form with the point of the brush.

2 Block in shadow areas with thin washes of cobalt blue. The color should not be too strong as this is the basis of a series of overlaid layers of paint.

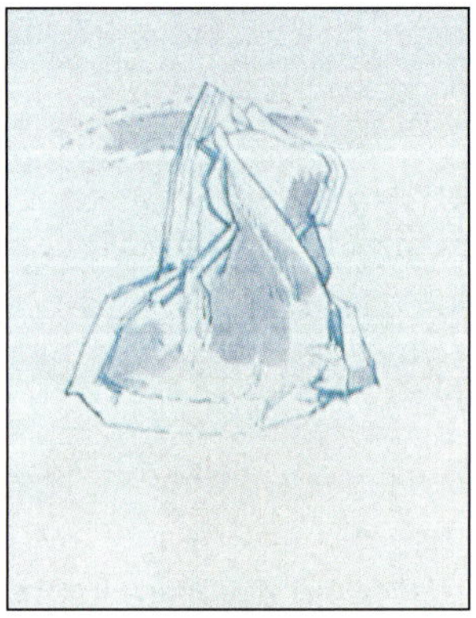

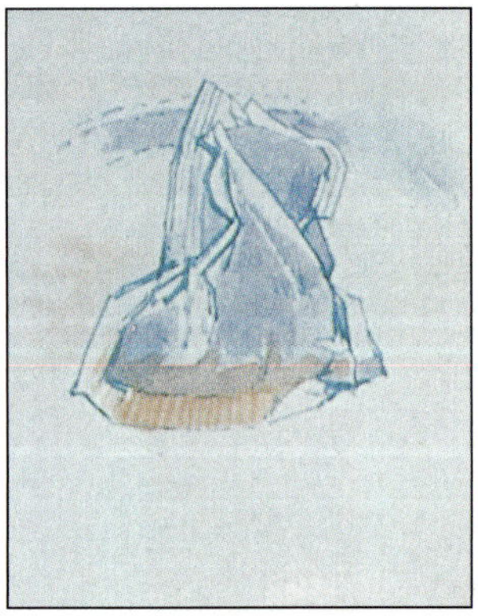

3 Let the painting dry and then start to define the shapes with washes of light red. Overlay red on blue to bring out the form.

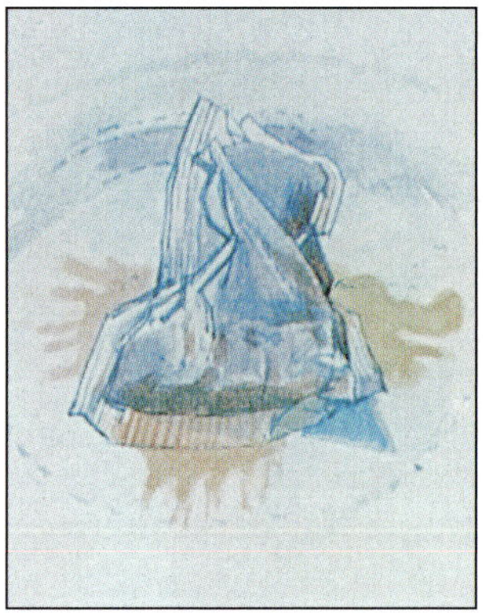

4 Continue to work with light red, cooling the tone where necessary with yellow ocher. Add definition to the shadows with blue washes in and around the outlines.

5 Draw into the washes of paint with a stronger tone of light red to describe creases in the surface. Indicate the shape of the plate with a light wash of viridian.

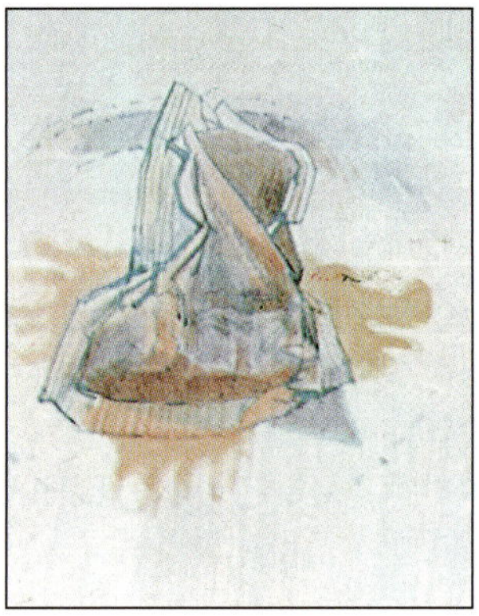

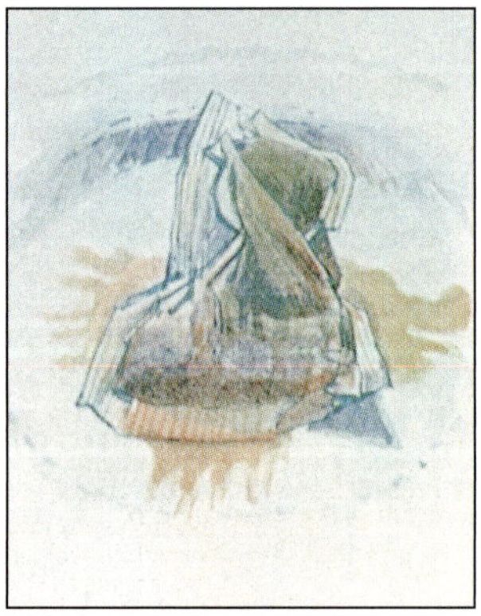

6 Where the color is too strong, lighten with a brush dipped in clean water. When the surface is dry, draw up the outlines again in blue with the point of the brush.

Still Life in Pastel

The still life can be an excellent way for the artist to explore various media and experiment with different ways of seeing. The choice of objects and their arrangement is virtually infinite; the artist can pick and choose, and arrange his subject to suit every need.

In this pastel painting, the artist chose to work with simple objects and a few bold colors. While this may at first seem the easier course to take – as opposed to complex subject matter and color schemes – to work with a few primary colors and a simple subject can often be a very difficult task.

The main problem in working with bold colors is how to control their intensities so that one does not overpower the other, although tones and hues may be altered and adjusted by blending, to retain the freshness and vibrancy of the individual colors demands that the artist carefully balance and weigh individual color areas. One way to ensure a balanced picture is to introduce a complementary color into a general color area. Thus in this picture there are small strokes of red within predominantly blue areas, and vice versa. This will also help to give the picture unity, as the observer's eye will pick up the individual colors as it moves around the picture.

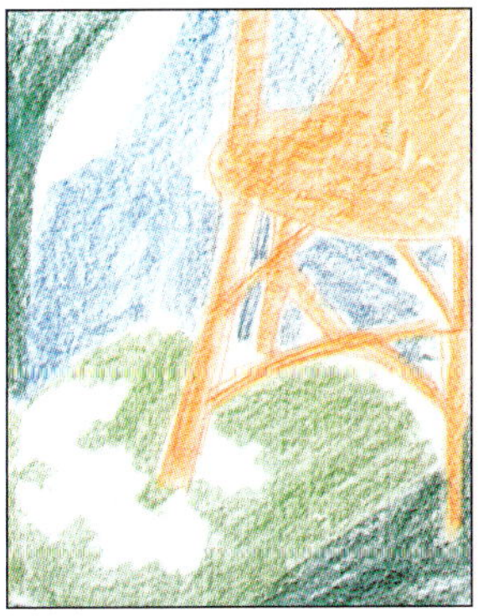

1 After lightly sketching the subject in with pencil, use the side of the crayon to put in the main color areas in blue, green, and orange.

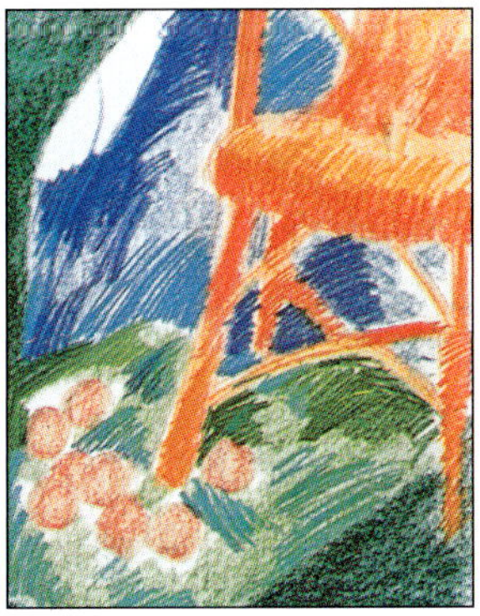

2 Using the end of the crayon, begin to work up stronger colors with sharp, directional strokes.

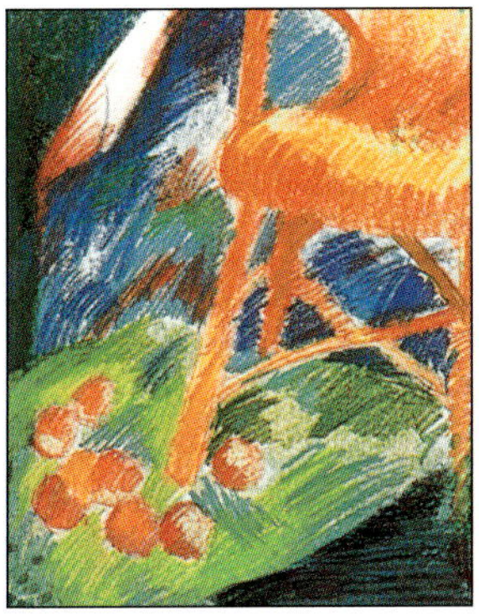

3 Begin to describe lights and darks in green areas by using various tones of green. Carry the red tone into the blue of the backdrop.

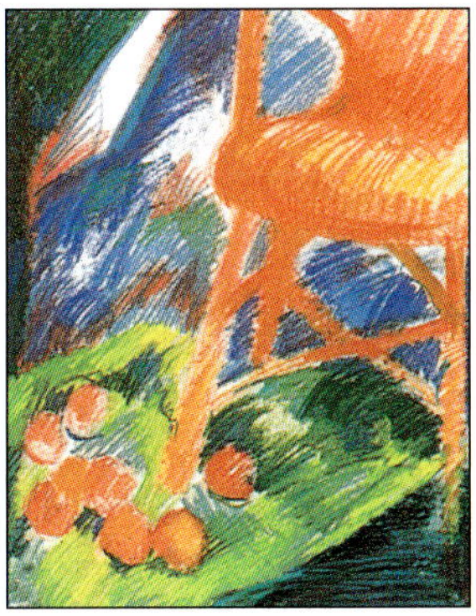

4 Intensify dark areas with dark green, Prussian blue, and dark red.

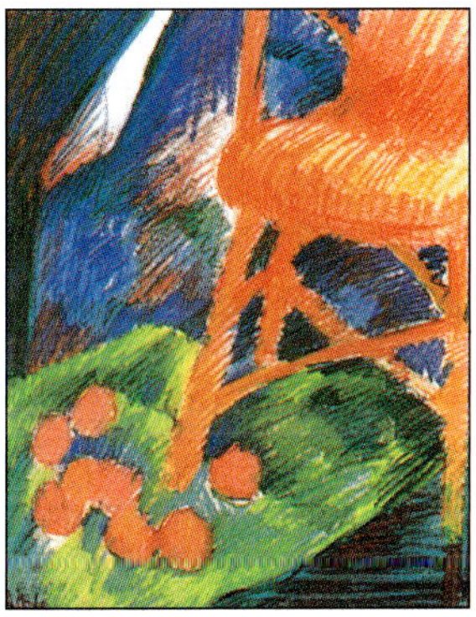

5 With pale blue, work into the foreground area as a highlight and tone down the background with the same color.

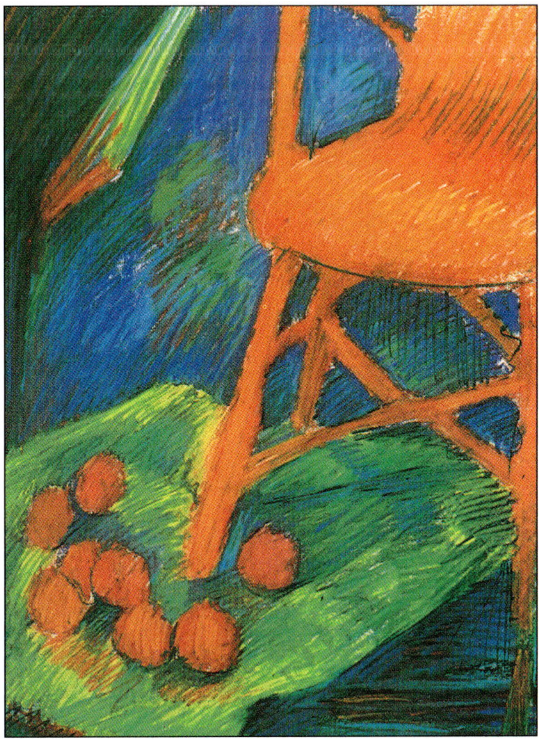

Still Life in Tempera

With a small surface and tempera paints, the artist can create a finished painting in a very short period of time. While the medium can be used with virtually any sized surface or type of subject, it is particularly well suited to small working areas and finely detailed work.

To create this picture, the artist worked on a small piece of hardboard, with the finished work resembling a miniature or enameled tile.

The scratching-back technique can give tempera painting textural interest. Although tempera dries to a sticky state fairly quickly, it remains workable for a short period of time. Scratching-back the surface with a sharp object to the original color of the paper or board and either leaving it or reglazing it will add luminosity and allow the artist to develop fine details. This process can be carried on almost indefinitely.

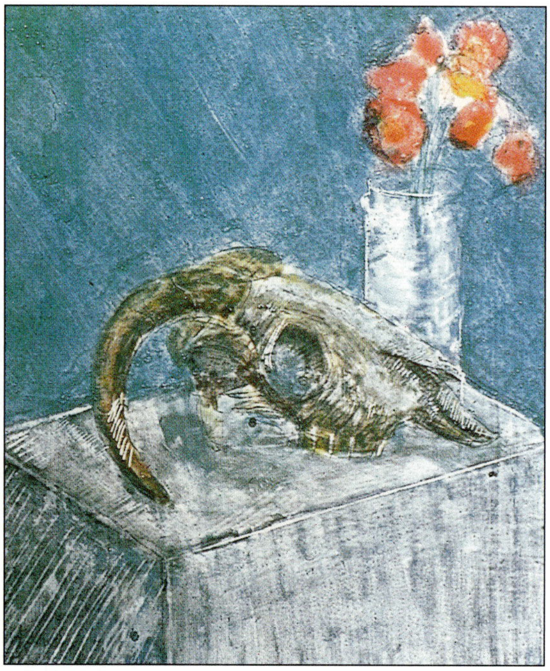

Pure, dry pigments can be very expensive, especially the inorganic colors such as the blues and reds, but it is worth acquiring and experimenting with the true tempera technique. On the other hand, it is perfectly acceptable to use commercial watercolors in tubes and mix these with a yolk medium for a less expensive method of tempera painting.

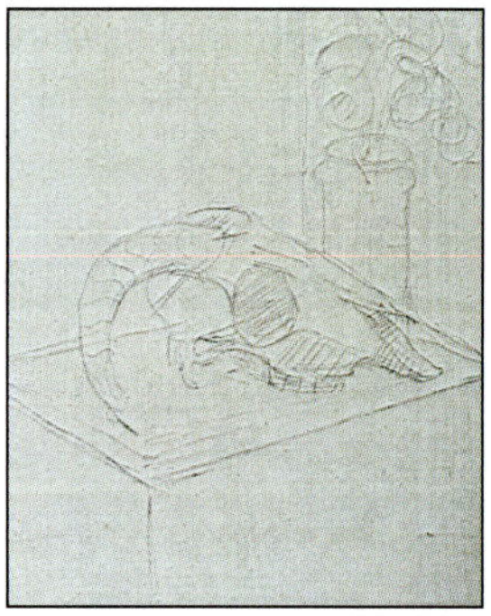

1 With fine sandpaper, sand a primed board until smooth. Put in the initial sketch with an HB pencil and sand again.

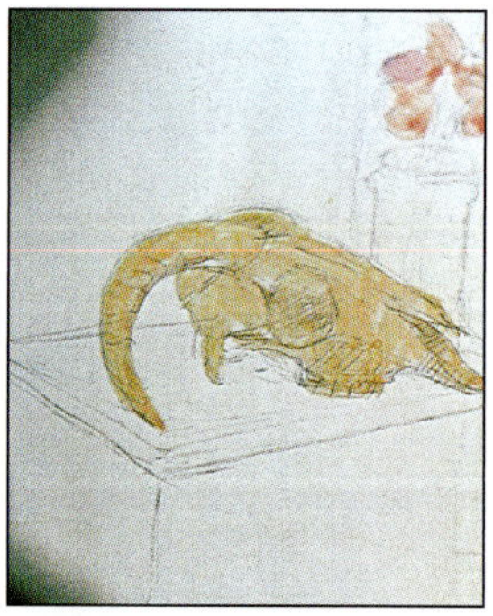

2 With a No. 2 sable brush, mix egg yolk with yellow ocher and put in the skull with short, vertical strokes. Do the same in cadmium red for the flowers.

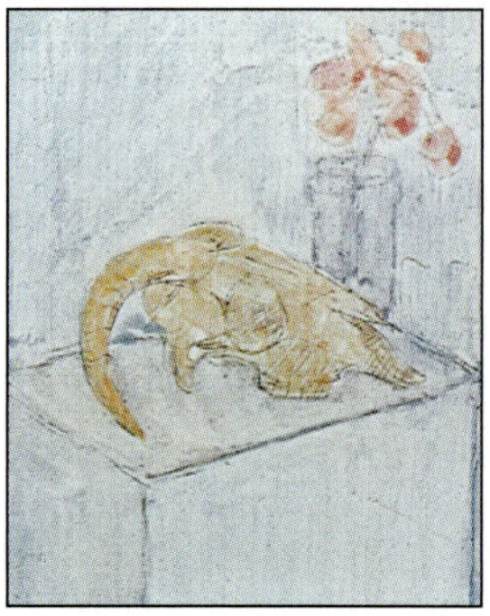

3 Mix cerulean blue and yolk and, with a No. 4 brush, put in the background. Add a touch of black and put in the shadow areas of the table.

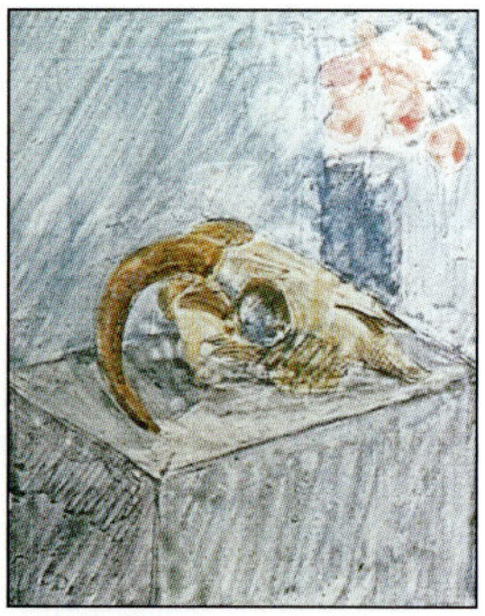

4 With more cerulean blue, block in the vase. Develop the shadows of the skull in burnt umber.

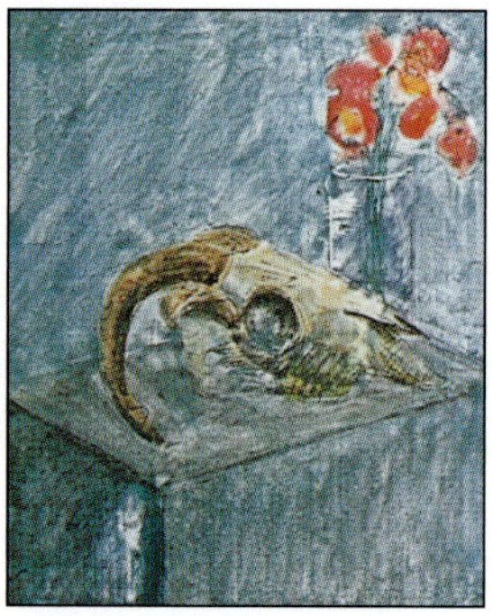

5 Mix black and cerulean blue in a darker tone and work back into the shadow areas with the No. 2 brush.

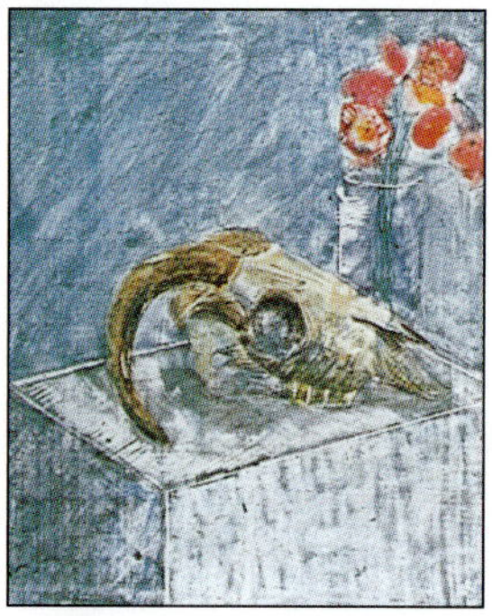

6 With a sharp tool, scratch-back the paint surface in the highlight areas, hatching with the point. Brush burrs of paint away with a rag or tissue.

Still Life in Pencil

A still life arrangement can be an excellent vehicle for the study of color, shape, and structure. The still life may take any form from the traditional subject of fruit and flowers to a jumble of objects randomly selected from whatever is at hand.

Choose objects which offer an interesting pattern of forms; develop contrasts and harmonies in the range of colors and between geometric and irregular shapes.

The final effect of this drawing is created by successive overlaying of lines in different colors, woven together to create a range of subtle hues. Each layer is described by lightly hatching and crosshatching to gradually build up the overall effect. Blue and purple form rich, deep shadows in the yellows; a light layer of red over yellow warms up the basic color without overpowering its character.

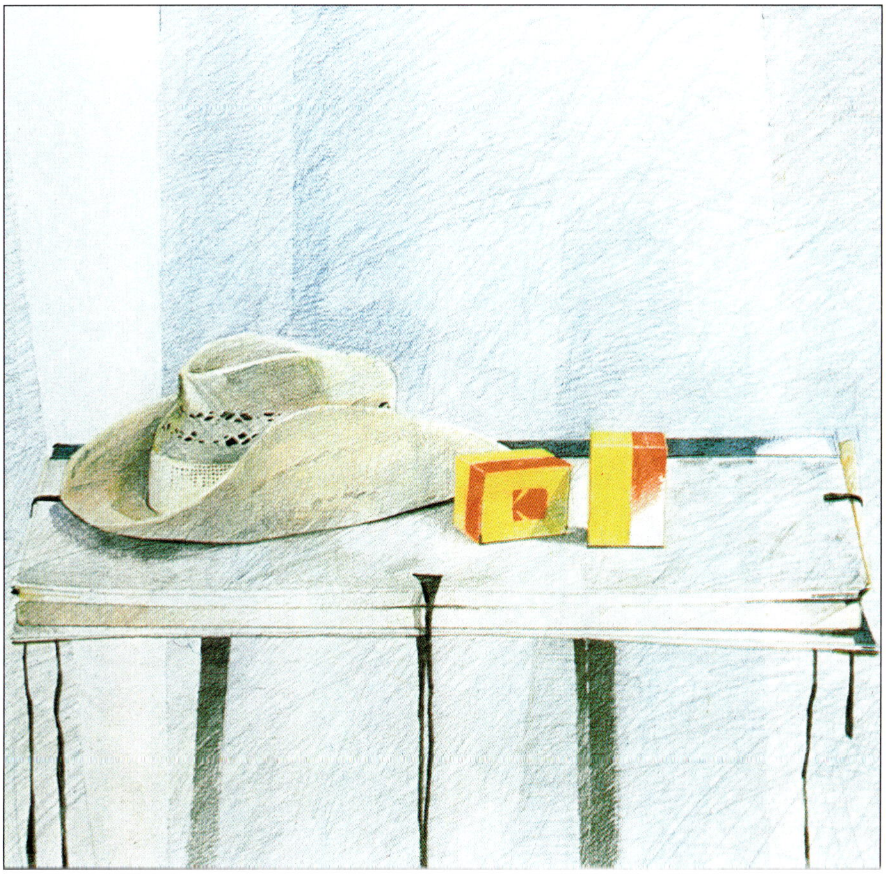

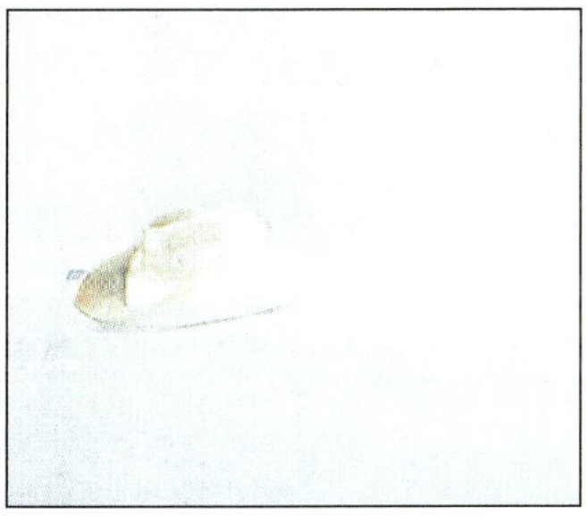

1 Lay in a block of light blue shading behind the hat, varying the direction of the pencil strokes. Use the same blue for shadows on and around the hat.

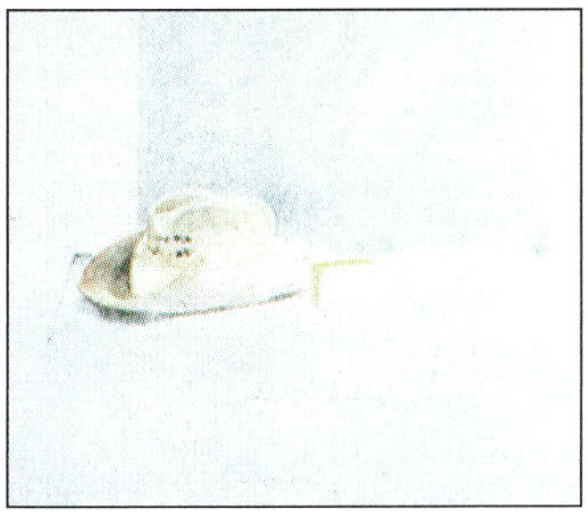

2 Strengthen and broaden the background color. Develop the shadows and pattern details of the hat. Draw in the shape of the boxes with yellow and red pencils.

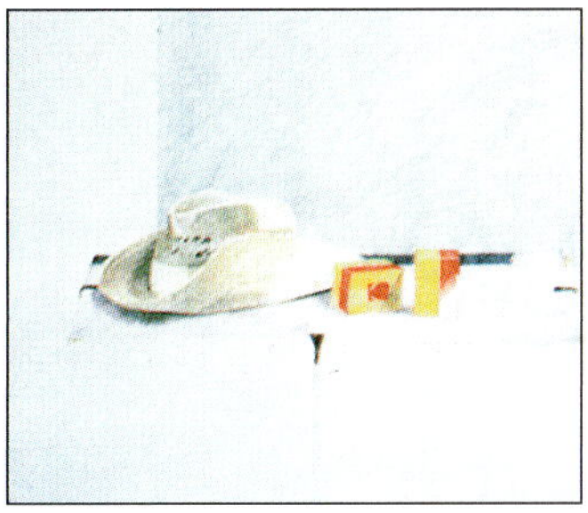

3 Build up the colors with contrasts of tone. Use purple in shadows under the hat, and darken blues to make the objects stand out from the background.

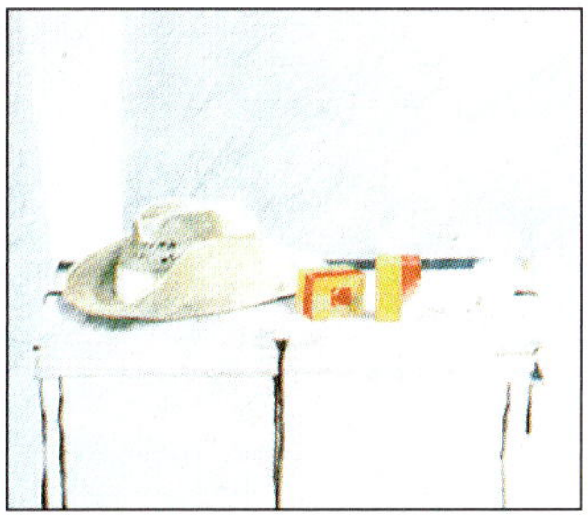

4 Outline the portfolio and sketchbook in black. Strengthen the bright colors against the neutral grays.

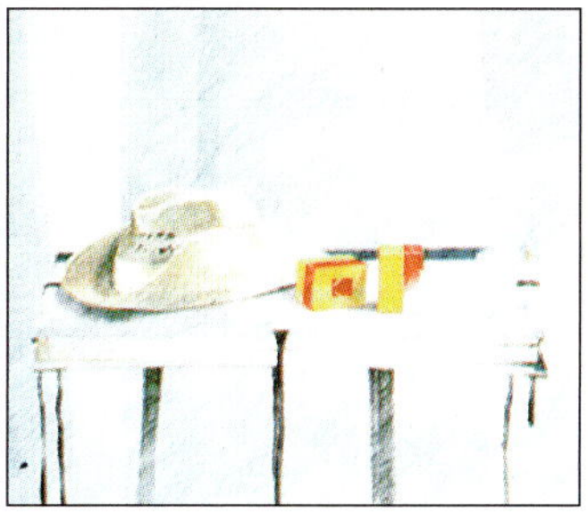

5 Lay in the rest of the background area in blue and vary the tones by heavily reworking. Build up details of line and tone with black and yellow ocher.

Still Life in Gouache

At first glance this painting may appear to be carefully detailed and realistic, but as the steps show, the technique is fluid and informal.

The first step for example, is not a meticulous drawing but a mass of vivid, liquid pools of color suggesting basic forms. As the paint is laid on in layers of loose streaks and patches, the impression of solidity and texture gradually emerges. Each object is described by carefully studying the subject colors and translating these into the painting.

In general, the technique used for this painting was to thicken the paint slightly with each application; but thin washes are laid in the final stage to indicate textures and shadows. The combination of thin washes with flat, opaque patches of color is most effective in capturing the reflective surface of the bottle and glass.

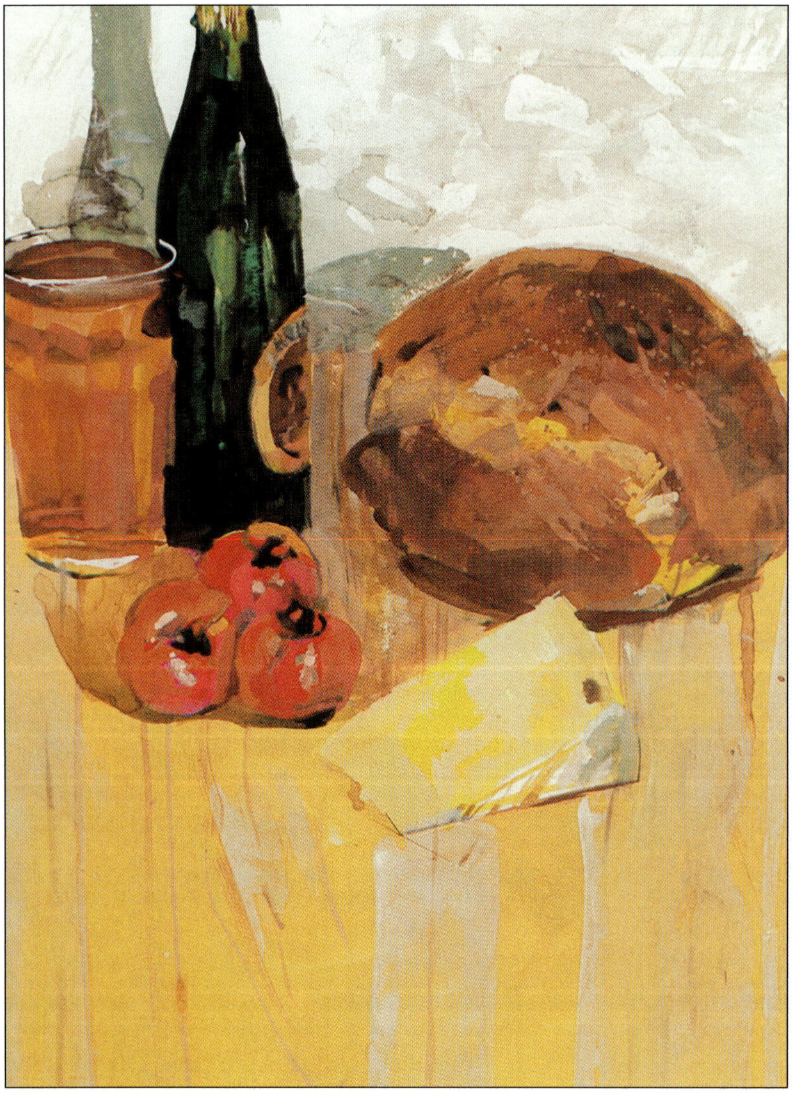

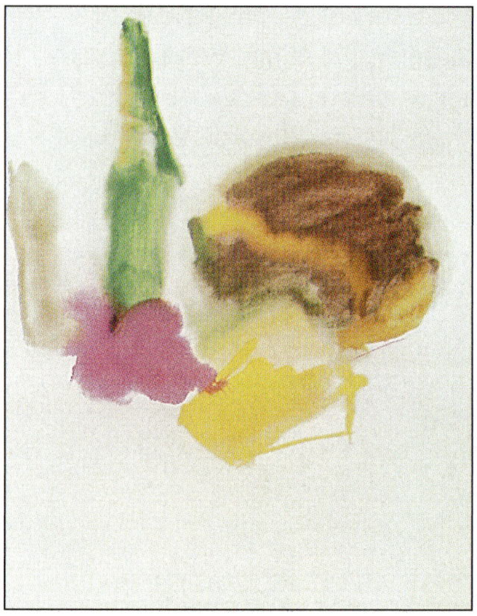

1 With a No. 8 sable brush lay in the basic shapes of the objects with thin, wet paint. Use burnt umber, sap green, magenta, and yellow and let the colors flow together.

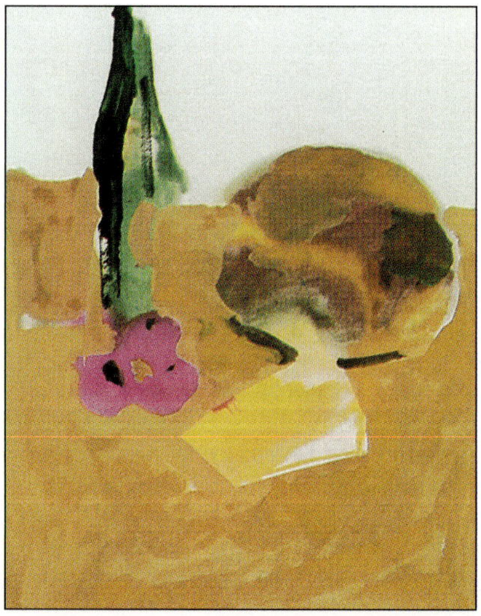

2 With a No. 5 brush, put in yellow ocher around the shapes and into the foreground. Work over the bottle and loaf of bread, painting in shadow details.

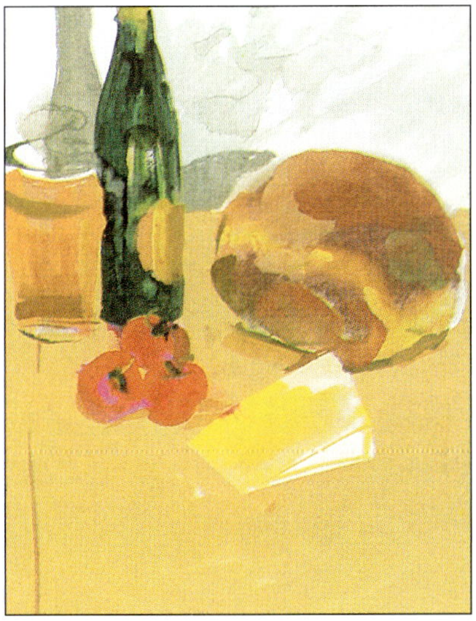

3 Indicate shadows in the background with a thin layer of green. Apply small patches of solid color to show form and surface texture in each object.

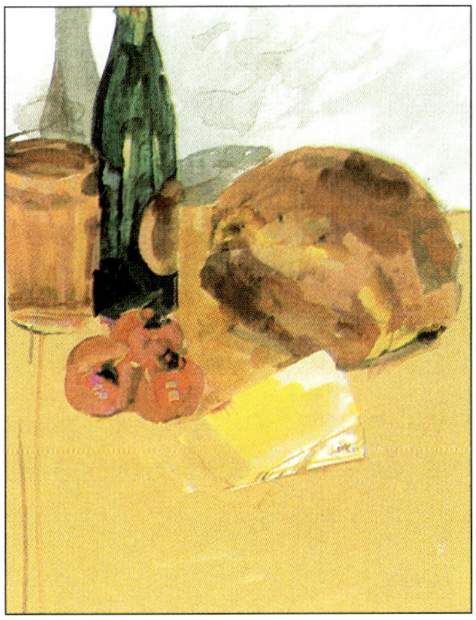

4 With a No. 12 brush, block in small dabs and streaks of color, developing the tones and textures.

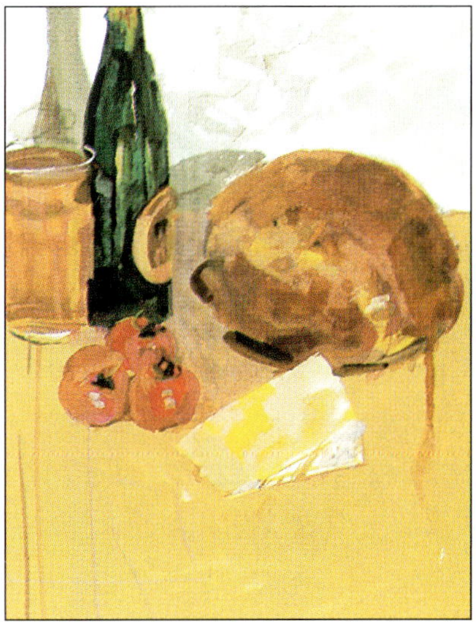

5 Intensify the contrast of light and dark with white highlights and brown shadows with the No. 5 brush. Work into the background with white.

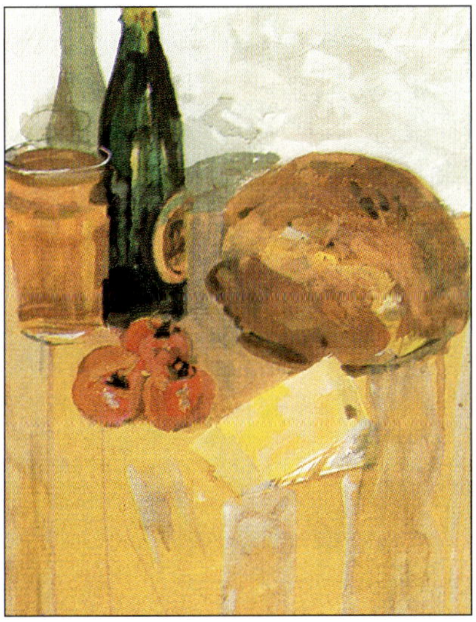

6 Work over the foreground and background with light tones of pink and yellow, keeping the paint thin. Spatter brown and black over the loaf.

Three methods were used in the painting of this picture – wet-into-wet, overpainting dry surface, and using paint straight from the tube.

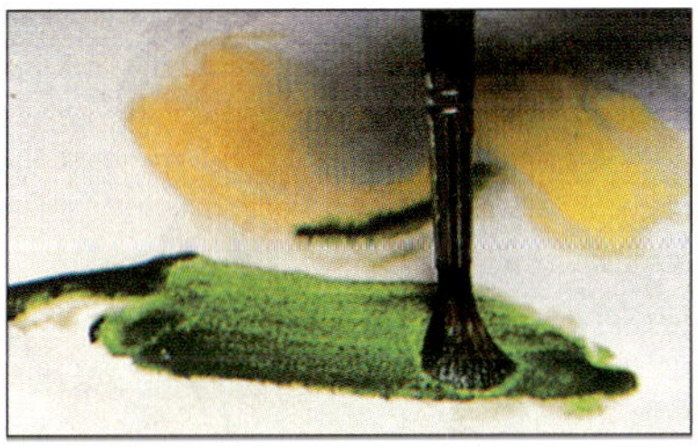

After dampening the paper in the shape of the object with water, the artist lays in a wash of color, allowing it to bleed over the damp area.

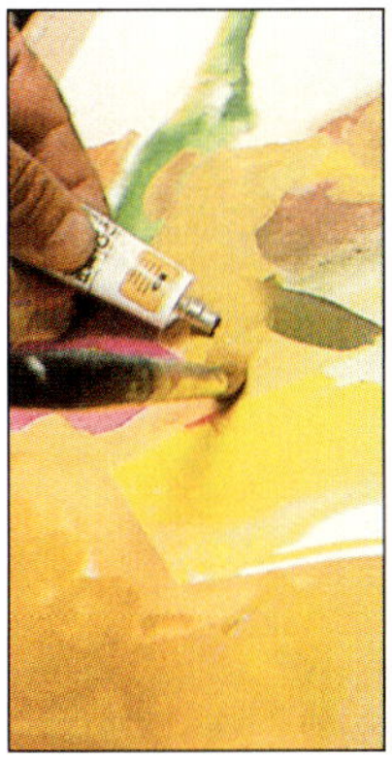

Over the dry underpainting, the artist here blocks in the label on the bottle with dryish paint.

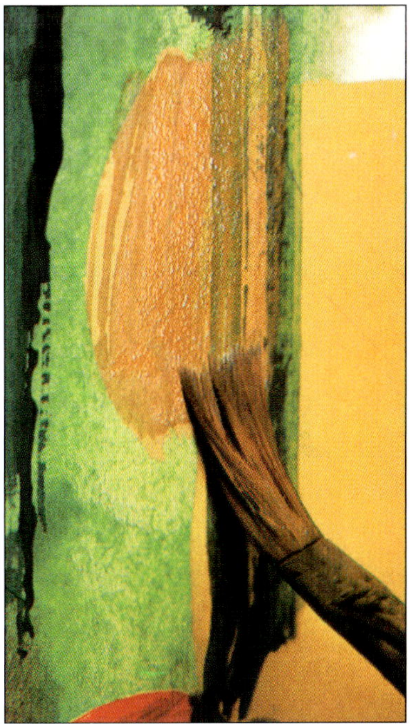

Using paint directly from the tube and a large brush well-loaded with water, the background is blocked in.

HOW TO PAINT: THE HUMAN FIGURE

The idealization of man has long been a preoccupation of art as has the description of man's miseries: the Greek sculptors with their "perfect form" or the agonies endured by Goya's subjects; Boucher's plump, seductive women, or the tense and anxious characters in a Giacometti. Nude or clothed, alone or in groups, the figure has always been a vehicle for expression, whether of tender compassion, or bitterness and anger.

Every picture which includes the human form invariably carries within it a dimension beyond other types of art, a comment or reflection upon the character of the individual or on the condition of man. It need not be deliberate, indeed, it often is not, but it is inescapable. Man describing man always involves visual interpretation and this can be used to the artist's advantage.

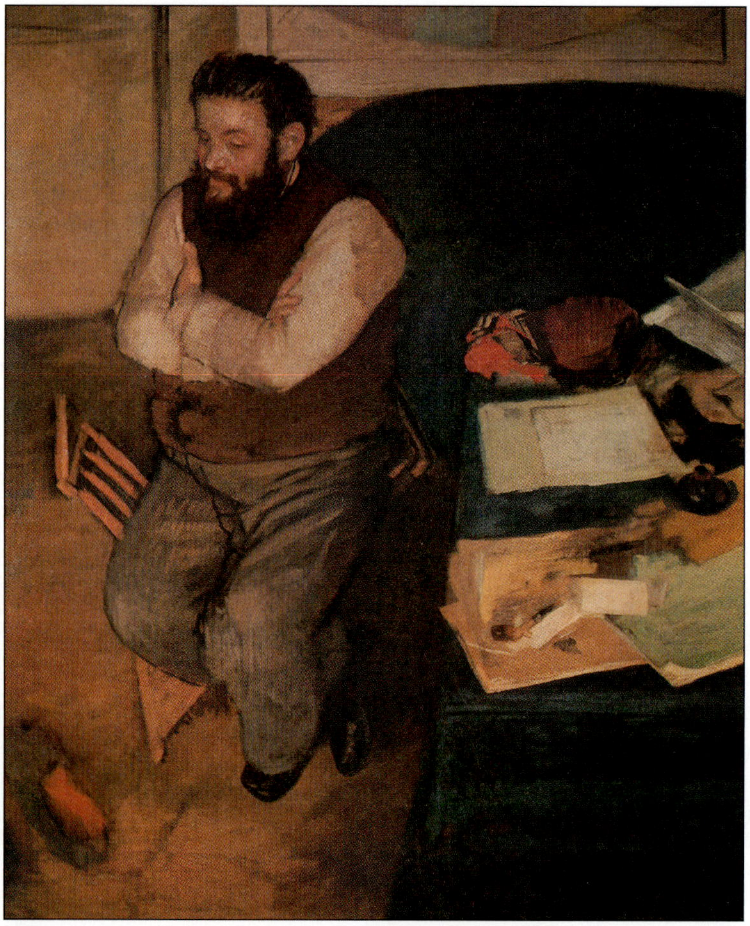

The Egyptians used the human form as symbols in the religious and social organization of their society. For centuries there was virtually no change in these figurative symbols which were instantly recognizable and unmistakable. The concept of foreshortening, which assumes a knowledge of perspective, escaped these early artists. Thus limbs were described as if seen in profile so that legs and feet appear in side view, attached to a frontal view of the torso. Heads turn to show a profile because this is the most characteristic shape.

The difference between Egyptian and Greek art was the result of fundamental philosophical and political divisions. The great advance in the depiction of the human form came with the Renaissance, and particularly with the close study of human anatomy. Figures were to become used in a thousand ways for as many different reasons; religious themes remained for centuries but, in due time, more secular needs were also met. The seventeenth century painter Rubens was a master at rendering the fleshy nudes fashionable in his day and indeed he ran a workshop/studio which produced large classical scenes and other subjects, with many a nude cavorting. The nineteenth century painter Fragonard dealt with the themes dear to the heart of the French courtiers – the shimmering world of high life at court. William Etty (1787–1849) was an English artist who painted virtually nothing but the figure, the fleshy surfaces of his nudes cunningly rendered. Into the nineteenth century the paintings of Courbet, magnificent in their composition and structure, contain supreme examples of figure painting, as do those of Millet.

Introduction

Drawing and painting the human figure obeys the same basic rules of drawing and painting as for any other subject matter. The problem still consists of translating what is three-dimensional onto a two-dimensional surface. But to most beginners, and even to artists of some experience, the problem of drawing the figure appears to be insurmountable.

It is often incorrectly thought that the artist requires years of detailed anatomical study and of practice in drawing the figure from life before any satisfactory result can be achieved. This tends to make beginners avoid inclusion of any figure in their drawings and paintings wherever possible. Children, however, are in no way inhibited when it comes to making a representation of their parents, brothers, sisters, or teachers, and they quite freely make images of people which, although not photographic images, can be stunning observations.

To introduce yourself to drawing the figure, do not at first try to make an accurate representation as you might do in still life. Accuracy of observation is certainly still required, but for drawing the figure the student must begin to develop a visual memory. Unlike still life, the human figure is animated and moving for most of the time, so some system of retaining and then recording the particularities of people is required. The character of a person is seen not only on the face but also in the way in which he or she stands, walks, and moves the arms and head. Someone who is reasonably well-known to you can be recognized from behind by the way in which he or she walks.

First practice drawing matchstick figures – but instead of drawing them in a childlike fashion, start considering where the joints of the arms and legs actually are. In this way, by observing people in their everyday activities and translating them into matchstick figures from memory, you will learn two of the most important elements in successful figure drawing. You will extend your visual memory and you will develop an understanding of animation. Artists such as Lowry developed the matchstick figure to a very high level of expression. On close examination of any of his paintings, what at first appears to be a matchstick figure turns out to be a highly

BELOW: *No matter how complex a figure drawing may at first appear, it is always possible to see the figure as a silhouette. Drawing one half and then the other, by arbitrarily drawing the subject at an angle, will help you to develop a sense of this two-dimensional aspect.*

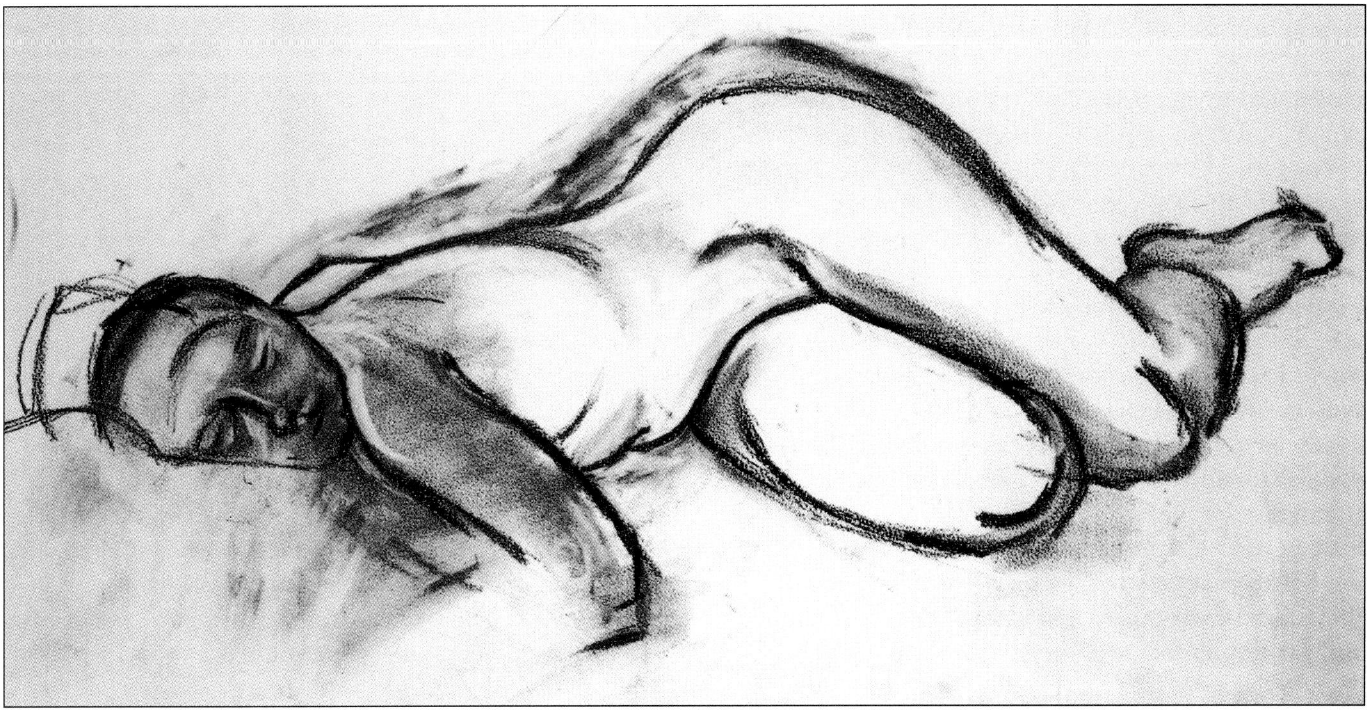

animated individual, with very little reference to any particular anatomical feature.

This approach is not dissimilar to that revealed in Aboriginal cave paintings, in which each individual character in the hunt can be seen playing an individual part in the action.

To help understand the way in which a figure is animated, it is useful for most beginners to make themselves a figure out of pipe cleaners and a bit of modeling clay, or obtain an artist's lay figure. By articulating the arms and legs where the joints occur, the figure can be set in a great variety of poses. It is usually obvious if the pose in which you have set the figure is incorrect. When satisfied with the pose, draw the matchstick figure from various angles. In this way, an understanding of how the arms and legs work in conjunction with one another can be appreciated. (You will probably find this exercise more difficult than you thought.)

After some practice, get a friend or member of your family to sit for you in as natural a pose as possible. Take into account non-professional models tend to be a little stiff and formal. Do not expect them to sit totally still for more than about ten minutes at a time, for it can become very uncomfortable and you could lose a potential model. After all, people are living and moving subjects, and you cannot make them static, like objects in a still life.

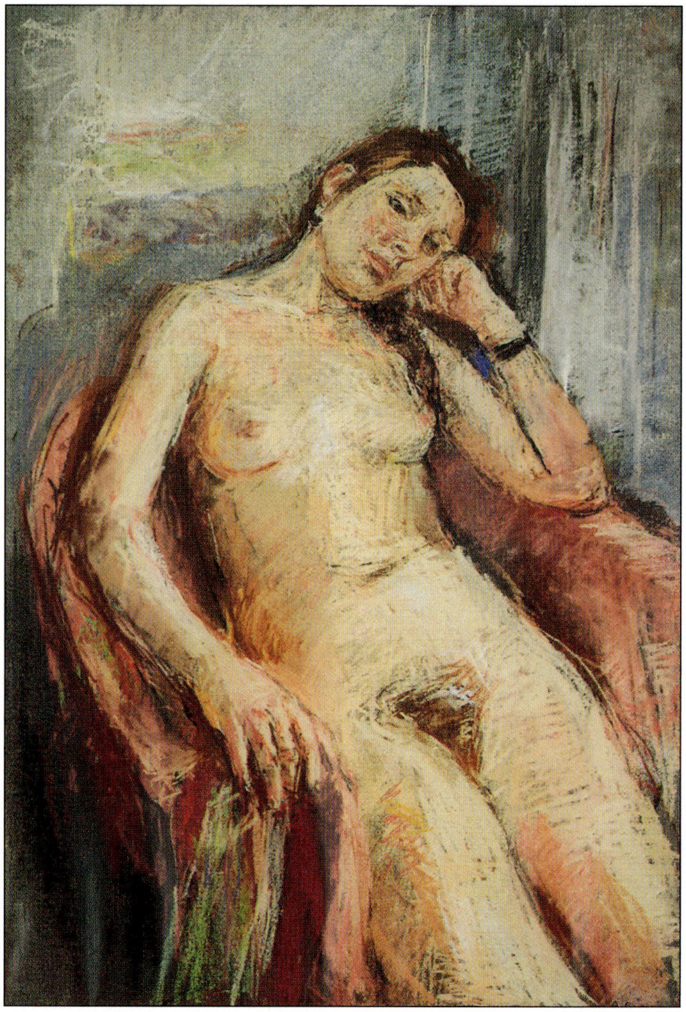

CRYSS IN A PINK CHAIR by Anthony Eyton

This is a large painting, just under 4 ft. (1.2 m) high, allowing the pastel strokes to display considerable energy right across the surface. The artist used fixative frequently throughout all stages of the painting, to help get the drawing right and create a ground to work on. It was drawn from life, requiring six or seven sittings to complete the image.

DRAWING FROM LIFE

Most of our experience of the figure takes place in a fully-clothed situation, and it is sometimes difficult for the beginner to appreciate fully that inside a jacket sleeve is an arm, and about halfway down the arm an elbow joint, and so on. Yet although it is helpful to draw from a nude model, it is by no means absolutely essential. If a life class or a life model is not immediately available, ask a fully-clothed friend to pose – but instead of drawing him or her, articulate a pipe cleaner figure or lay figure into the same pose as your model. With careful observation you will notice that even on a fully-clothed figure there are many indications as to where the points of articulation take place. The way in which a trouser leg falls, or the way it folds round the knee of a seated figure, clearly indicates the point of articulation.

The next time you are in a public place, look at the people around you and make some rapid sketches in matchstick form of how the figures are articulated, making particular notes of knees, ankles, elbows, and so on. For these matchstick figures really work. Remember: the points of articulation must be in the right relationship and proportion to one another.

PROBLEMS WITH FIGURE DRAWING

Although some major developments in the depiction of the human figure came about as a result of increased anatomical knowledge, it is not essential to know about anatomy in order to be a success at figure drawing. What is needed, however, as with drawing or painting any object, is a keen and analytical eye. Drawing the figure is often regarded as the supreme challenge. Many students who excel in other areas can do nothing with the figure and avoid drawing it. There are many reasons for this, but two are significant. First, more than with any other subject, it is difficult when drawing the figure not to have preconceived ideas about what you see. Subconsciously a

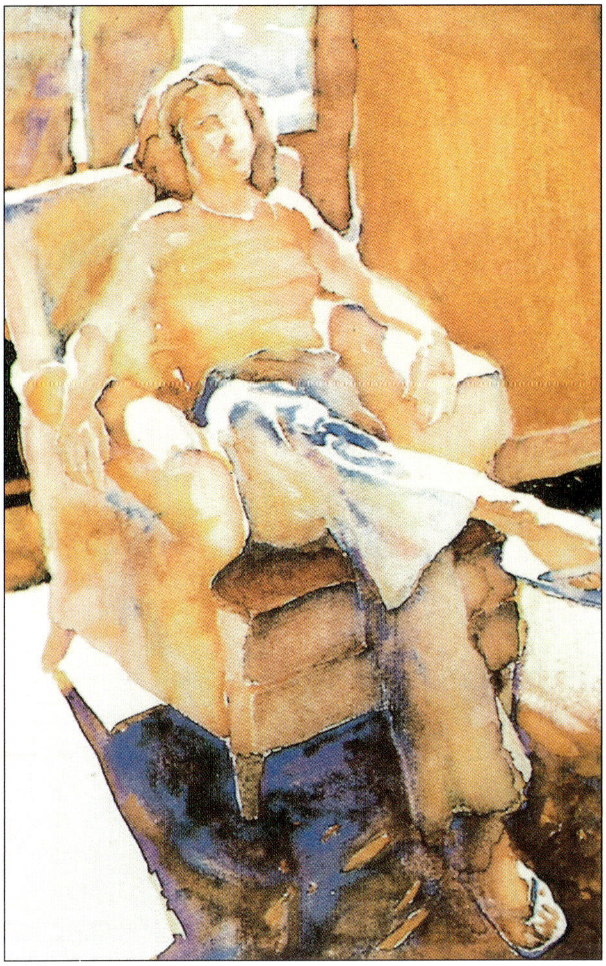

This artist was interested in light and color rather than in achieving a likeness of a particular person. The paint was kept fluid and free, with the minimum of detail, thus enhancing the relaxed mood of the light-flooded figure in the armchair.

particular pose may remind you of some admired drawing so that you begin to draw what you think ought to be in front of you rather than what is actually there. The second reason is that being human ourselves, we know much more about the human body than we do about, for example, animals or trees. You can pretend that a tree you have drawn is something like the actual tree, but it is much more difficult to ignore any defects when comparing a drawing of a figure with the actual person.

Whether drawing the nude or the clothed figure, the basic strategy should be the same. The figure must be seen in terms of simple forms that fit together. The proportions need to be accurately assessed and it is of the utmost importance that the balance of the figure is correct, particularly when drawing standing figures.

There is no better way of ensuring that the balance is right than by checking with a plumb line (a weight on the end of a thread, which provides an instant vertical) where the feet are positioned in relation to the head. Drawings by Degas show how, even in his maturity, he drew verticals on his drawings using a plumb line to check the balance of the figure.

Observe closely the subtle lack of tension in a sleeping face. Remember also that sleeping people move without warning, so work quickly to catch the pose.

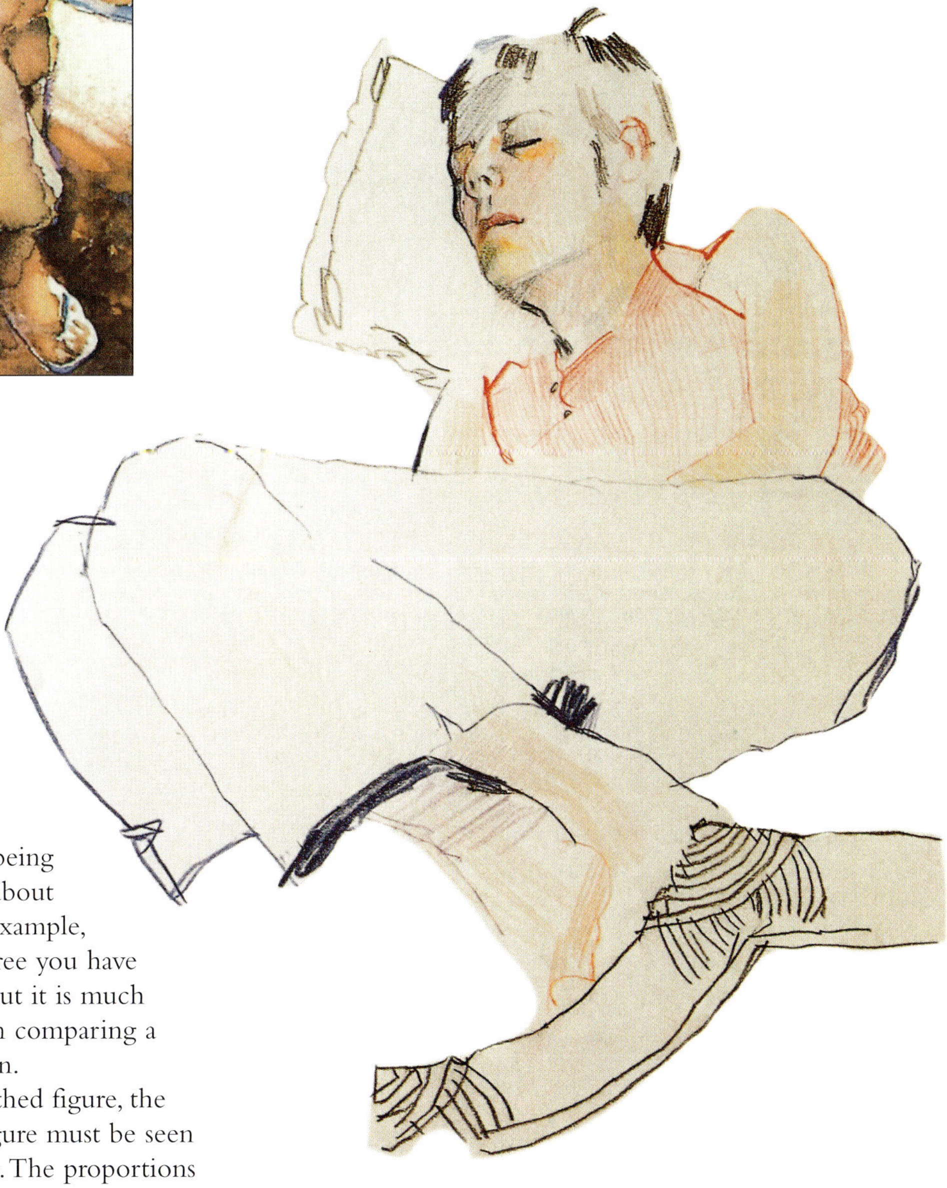

Standing Figures

Drawing the standing figure presents its own particular problems. It is much harder for even an experienced model to stand for a long period of time than it is to sit or recline.

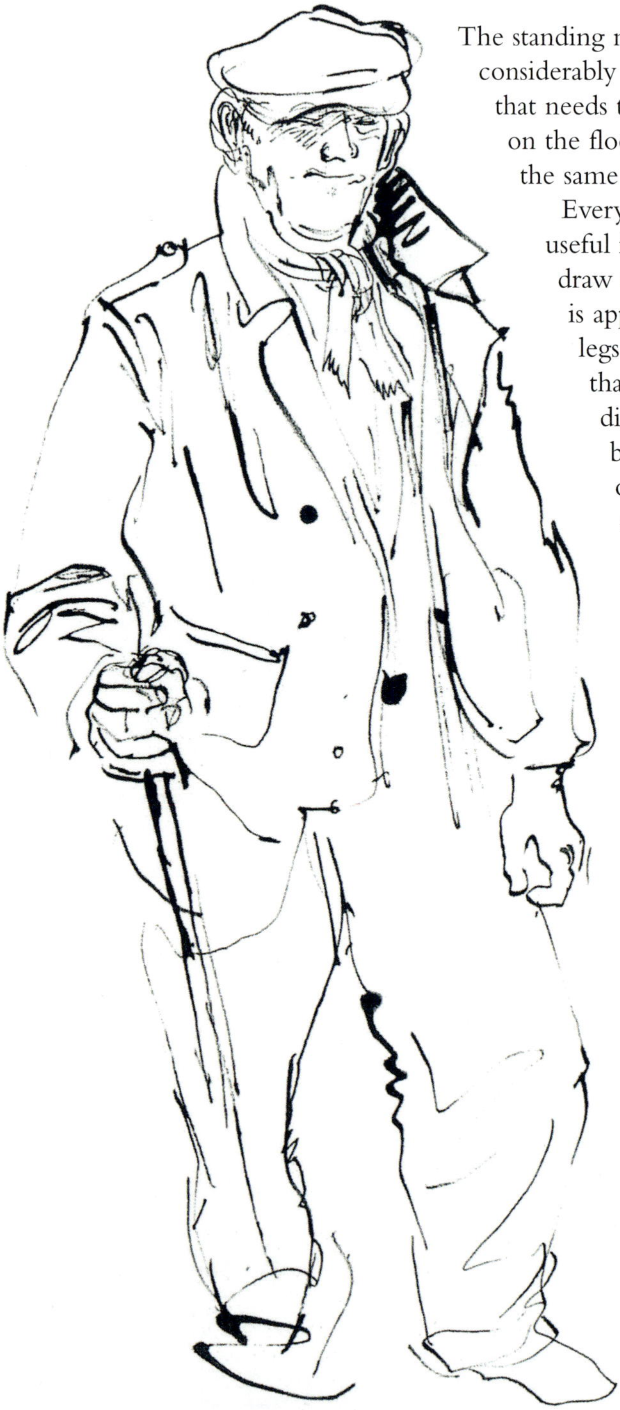

The standing model usually requires more frequent rests and may move considerably while posing. This movement, however slight, is the first problem that needs to be dealt with. Most artists mark the position of the model's feet on the floor (on a large piece of paper on which the model stands) so that the same basic position can be returned to after resting.

Every figure is slightly different from another, and measuring can be useful in getting one or two main dimensions correct. Students tend to draw the top part of the figure too large, failing to observe that the head is approximately one seventh of the height of the figure and that the legs are one half. The most important problem related to proportion is that of making the figure stand properly in the drawing. The distribution of the figure's weight – on one leg or on both – has to be established, and crucial to this is getting the vertical positioning of the neck, hips, and feet absolutely correct. In order to do so, the artist can use any vertical in the background (for example, the corner of a room or the frame of a window) as a reference, but much the most useful device is to use a plumb line to check the precise position of the key parts of the figure. Some artists attach the plumb line to a horizontal rod that is secured to the top of the drawing or easel and position it to make a single vertical reference line running through the model's neck and the ankle of the foot on which most weight is placed.

The silhouette (right) described in black ink shows clearly how careful selection of the main shapes of the figure produces a result that, although drawn as a pattern, still gives an impression of three dimensions.

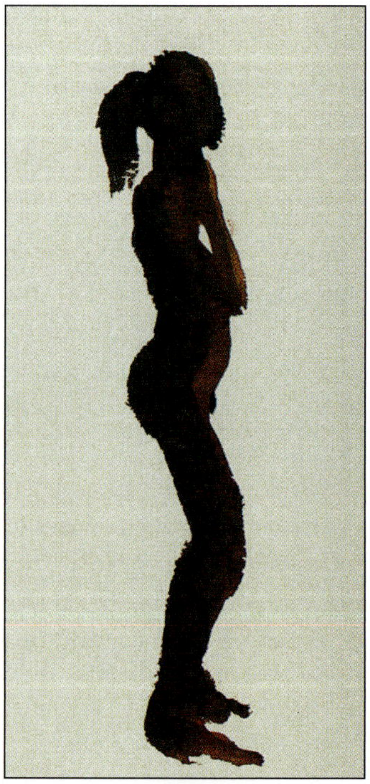

The artist has drawn this figure (left) with great freedom using pen and ink. Although the clothes are baggy, there is an excellent feeling of the structure of the figure underneath, and the tension of the hand gripping the stick has been beautifully realized. Note the variations in line and the way these help to give the figure its feeling of solidity.

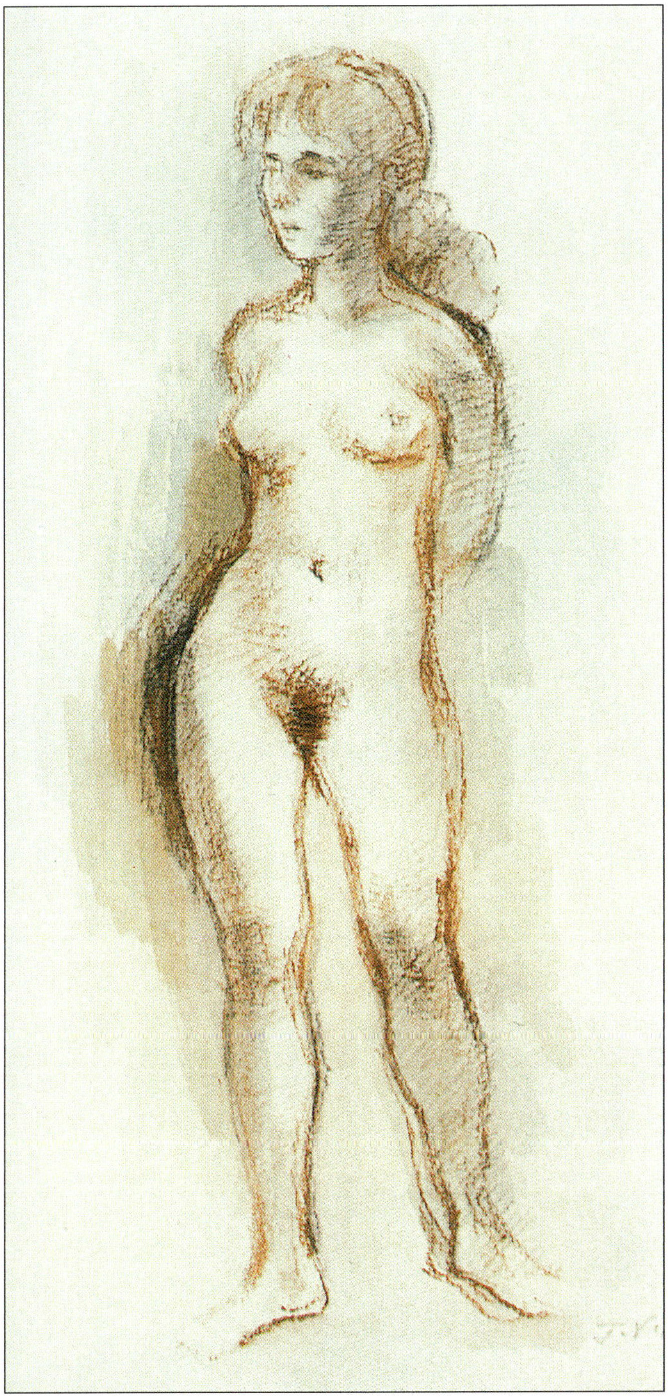

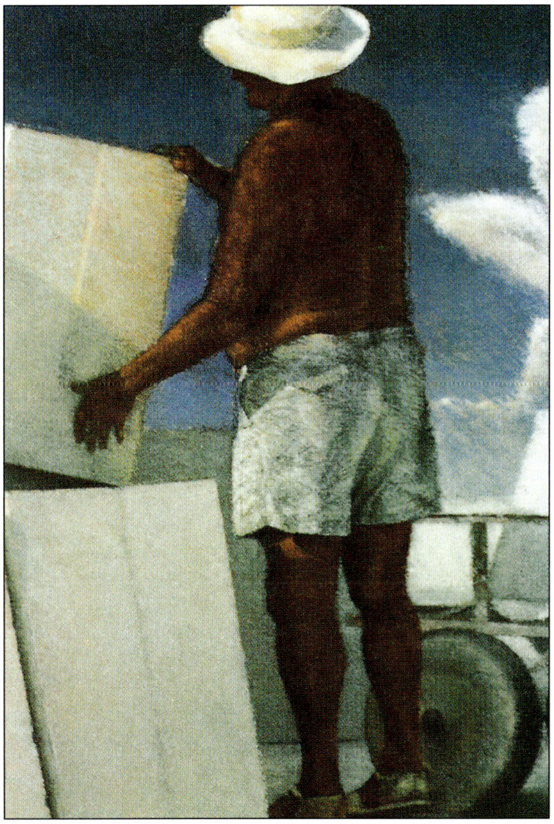

SPANISH QUARRY by Keith Bowen

The stocky shape of the stoneworker is seen as a virtual silhouette against the pale shades of the sky and stone, but each component is subtly modeled with light and shadow. The tilt of the body is seen in the repetitive, parallel stresses through the shoulders, waist, and alignment of the feet.

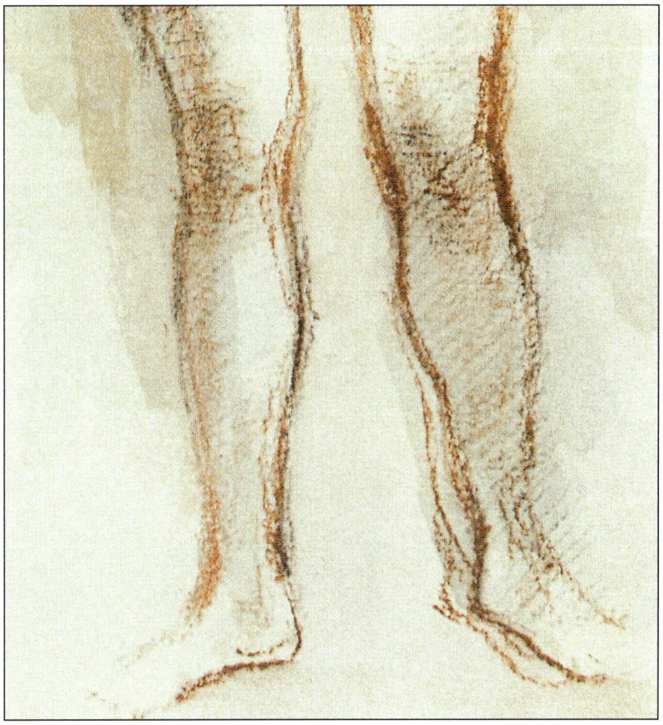

Different media were used together in this sketch of a standing figure. Outlines and contours were established with pencil and brown crayon, and pale washes of watercolor were added to darken the background. Watercolor and pencil hatching modeled the figure's form.

In the final stages of this drawing the artist used a pencil to refine the form. This can be seen clearly in the detail (right) where shading helps to strengthen the shadows and sets back one leg in relation to the other. Note how the position of the lower leg was corrected but the original outline was not erased. "Pentimenti," as these marks are known, actually add vitality to a drawing.

Seated and Reclining Figures

The most significant problem related to drawing seated or reclining figures is that of foreshortening. The brain will often not believe what the eye sees, so that when students first draw a figure that is lying down with the feet foremost they cannot believe how large the feet appear in comparison with the head. The secret is to use perspective to give an idea of what the relative scale of parts of the figure might be.

Objects associated with the figure being drawn can be extremely helpful guides. For example, if the figure is reclining on a bed, the rectangular plane of the bed assists in getting the correct degree of recession in the figure lying on it. If the figure is sitting on a chair, it is essential that the chair is constructed accurately (even if it is not drawn in great detail) before the figure is drawn in its correct place on the chair.

In almost any drawing or painting of a seated or reclining figure, there will be angles and planes that recede in space, often quite sharply, so the choice of viewpoint the artist takes is very important. It is best to avoid a viewpoint that presents the figure "flat on." Foreshortening, however, accurately assessed, looks unconvincing in certain poses, for example when the figure is lying flat and straight and is viewed from either the head or the feet. In a similar way, a formal seated pose may appear implausible when drawn from a head-on viewpoint, because the foreshortened thighs can look odd. In short, there are two golden rules: try to get at least an element of informality into the pose, and adopt a drawing position that avoids unconvincing foreshortening.

BELOW: *Pastel and chalk are often associated only with delicate drawing techniques. This dramatic life study shows how they can be manipulated in a bold and gestural manner. Smudging and hatching are combined to produce warm and colorful skin tones. The background of cool colors and strong black strokes makes a powerful contrast.*

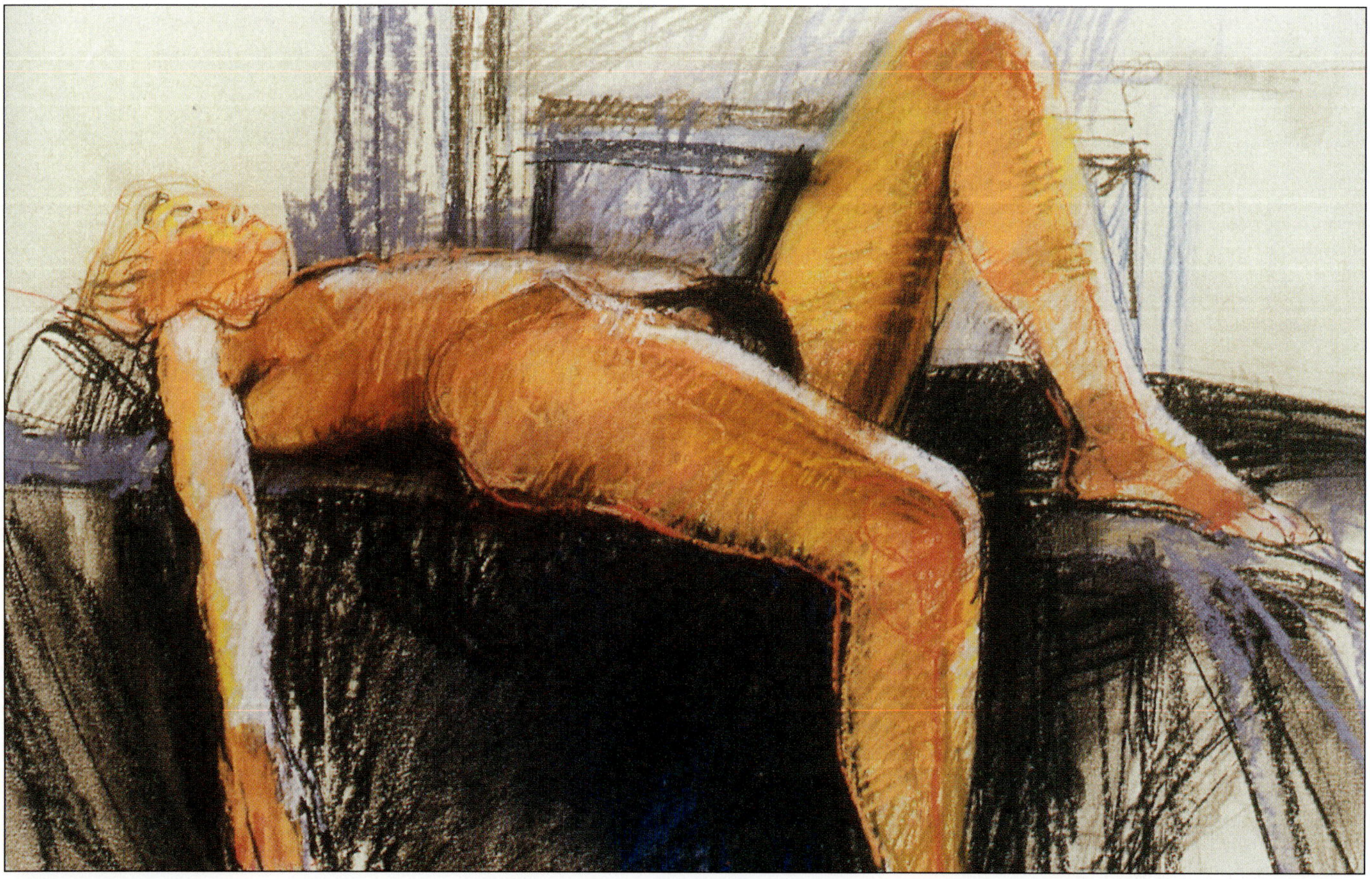

Figures in Action

The study of a person performing a specific task may be an opportunity to portray an unusual configuration of body and limbs, and to examine visual rhythms and tensions not expressed in formal poses.

There are different ways of conveying activity and movement, the two most common being a "freeze-frame" approach that focuses one aspect of the action, or a more abstract, sketchy approach that is often applied to rapidly moving figures.

Examples of the latter method are illustrated in the following section, while the compositions shown here take the first approach, a "snapshot" of the figure at work or play. In portraying the figure itself, it is important to notice the exact angle and direction of different parts of the body which contribute to the action, and also the way clothing and props help to explain the nature of the activity. Each of these images is carefully composed to convey the impression of the person's physical and mental concentration.

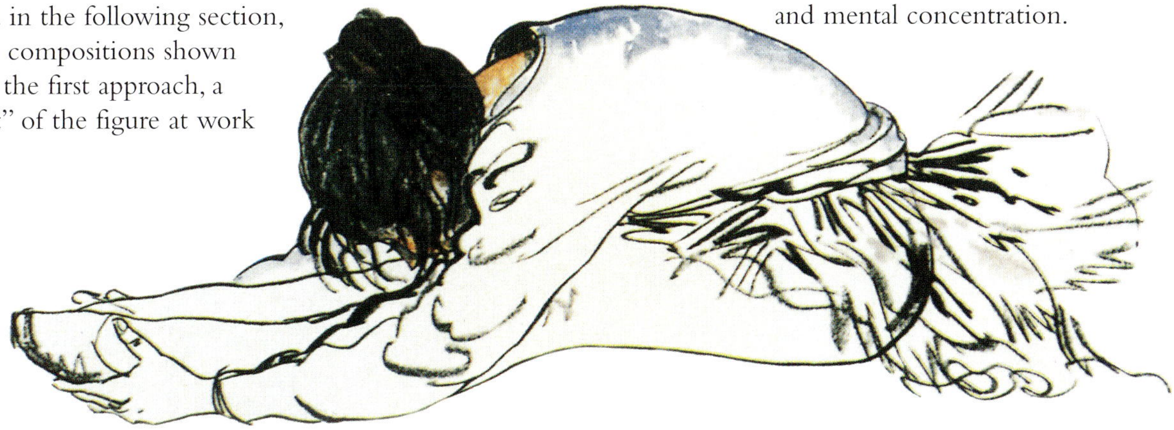

ABOVE: *Long unbroken lines made in charcoal pencil admirably capture the stretching action of the figure and are complemented by touches of watercolor for the flesh and the dancer's garment to give the drawing a more lifelike, three-dimensional feel.*

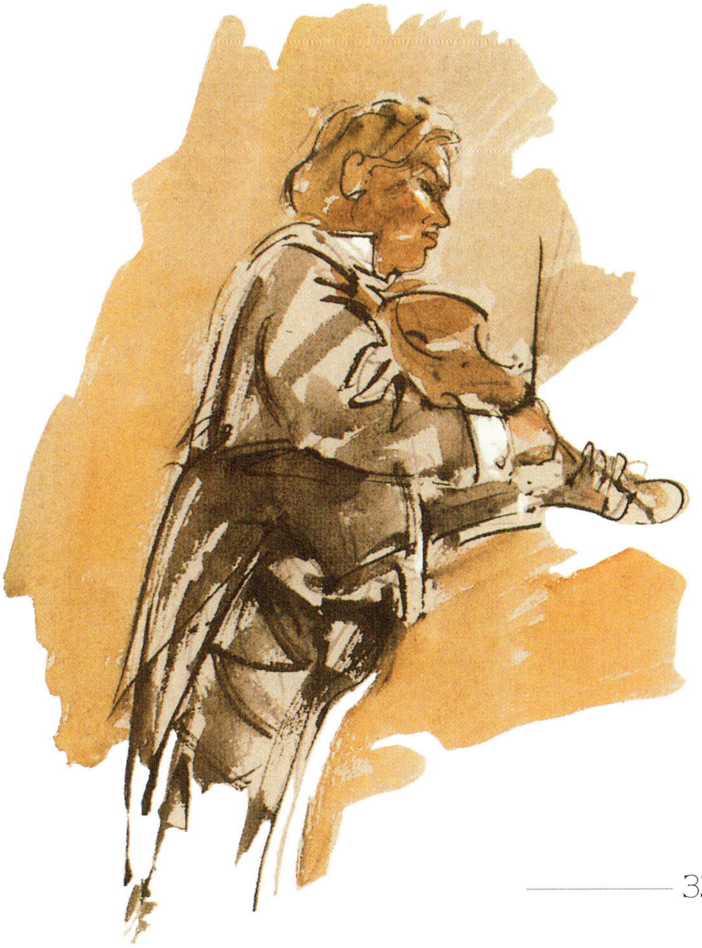

LEFT: *The artist has employed a variety of media and techniques in this freely drawn sketch of a violinist made on warm-toned paper. An initial watercolor wash was laid down using a fine brush, followed by the addition of warm background washes. The light areas on the face and forehead were then lifted out with a brush dipped in clear water. Finally, orange oil pastel provided a touch of color on the hand and white gouache was chosen for the dramatic highlight of cuff and collar.*

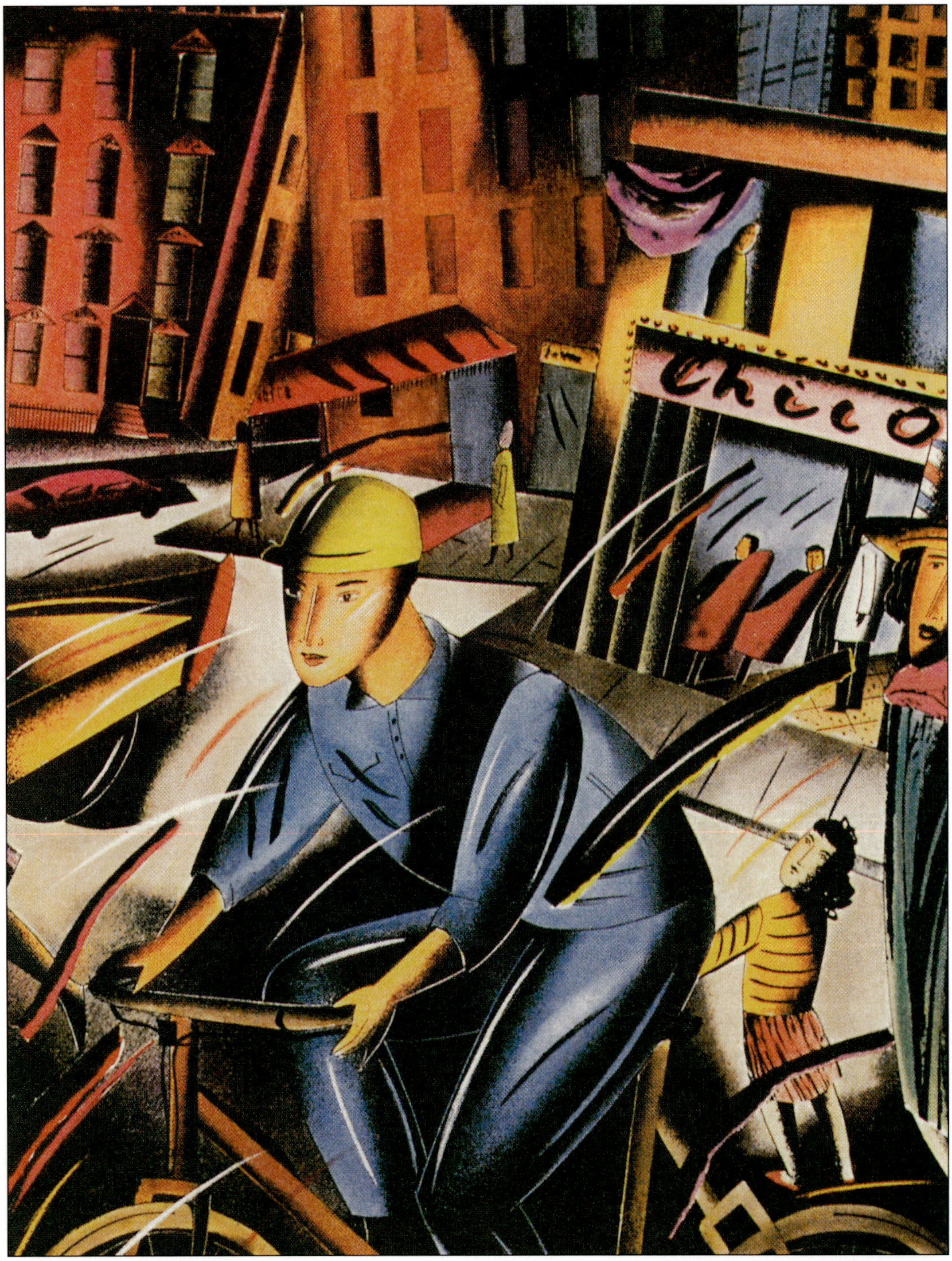

A successful combination of mixed media produced this energetic cyclist. Collage was the starting point; printed textures, shapes, and images were cut-out from magazines and assembled to make a composition. In the next step, a black-and-white photographic print was made of the collage. This print, worked over with pen, brush, ink, and watercolor, was then transformed into the final image. It would be possible when using this technique to make a number of prints and rework each one in a slightly different way.

The Ultimate Challenge – The Nude

Realistic representation of the figure did not develop further for several centuries until Giotto (1266–1337), Masaccio (1401–1428), and the Renaissance. The anatomical investigations of Leonardo da Vinci (1452–1519) and the drawings of the nude figure by him and by Raphaël (1483–1520) and Michelangelo (1475–1564) provided a basis for the representational drawings of today and firmly established the nude figure as an art form in itself.

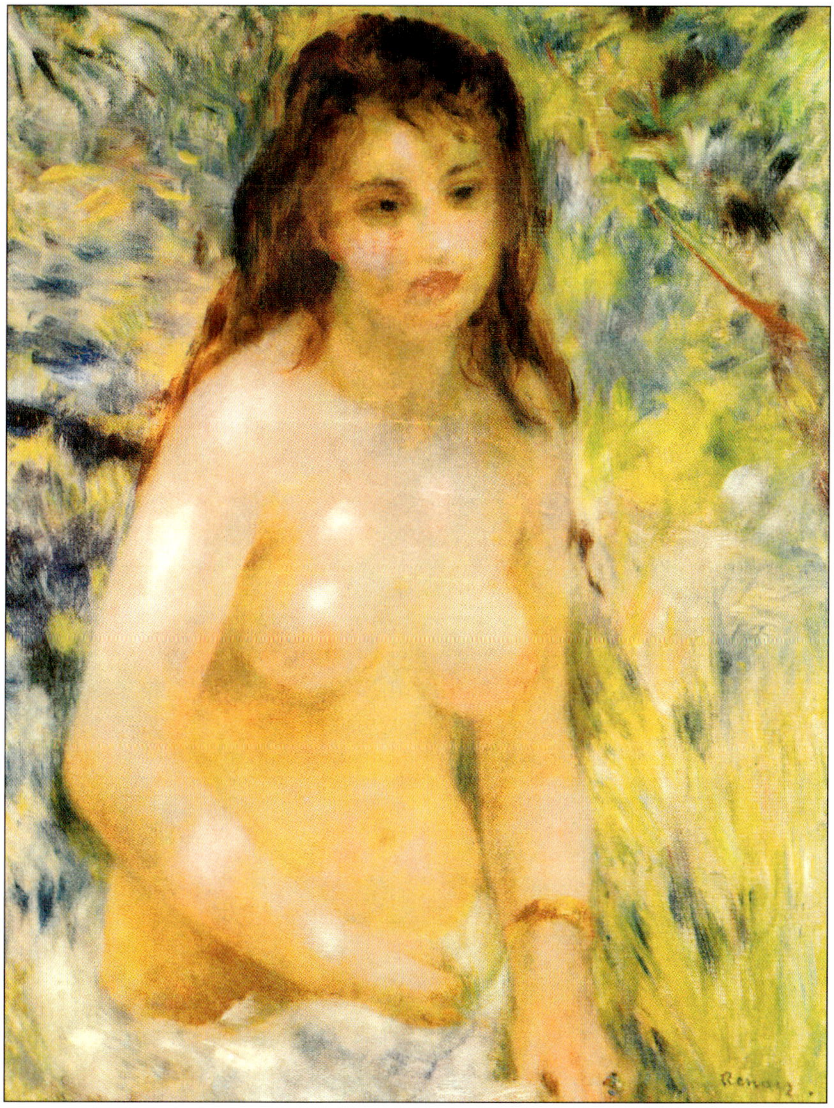

WOMAN'S TORSO IN SUNLIGHT by Auguste Renoir

Renoir is renowned for his sensuous nudes.

Nude figures had appeared in Roman and Greek art but it was in sixteenth-century Italy that the naked human figure was re-established as a form that could be used to invest stories with power and intense feeling. This use of the nude figure led over a period of time to the distinctive and dynamic figures of Rubens, the classical nudes of Ingres (1780–1867), and the dancing figures of Degas (1834–1917).

In the twentieth century, the nude drawings by Matisse (1869–1954) and Picasso, for example, have continued this tradition; and the survival of the life class in art schools indicates how firmly the drawing of the human figure has become established as an almost obligatory skill for the Western artist.

Outside the formal life class, it can be difficult to set up the right situation for this kind of figure study. But if you can find someone willing to pose for you at home, the more intimate atmosphere of a household setting gives an evocative character to the image. Nowhere is the formality of life drawing better integrated with a personal and social context than in Degas' pastel paintings of women bathing – and his inventiveness with technique and composition makes these images enduring models for pastel work.

Alongside these developments in the depiction of the nude figure, the clothed figure continued to be drawn and painted in many religious, allegorical, and historical pictures. Indeed, the increased refinement of nude representation brought higher standards of representation to the clothed figure. Portrait drawings and paintings have developed since Roman times, recording for posterity the appearances of the good and the great.

The Nude in Pastel

Pastel is a very versatile medium for painting figures, for the images you create can vary from quick sketches to highly finished, detailed, full-color compositions. Pastel's linear qualities can express contour, direction, and motion, while its painterly ones provide the means to interpret mass and color.

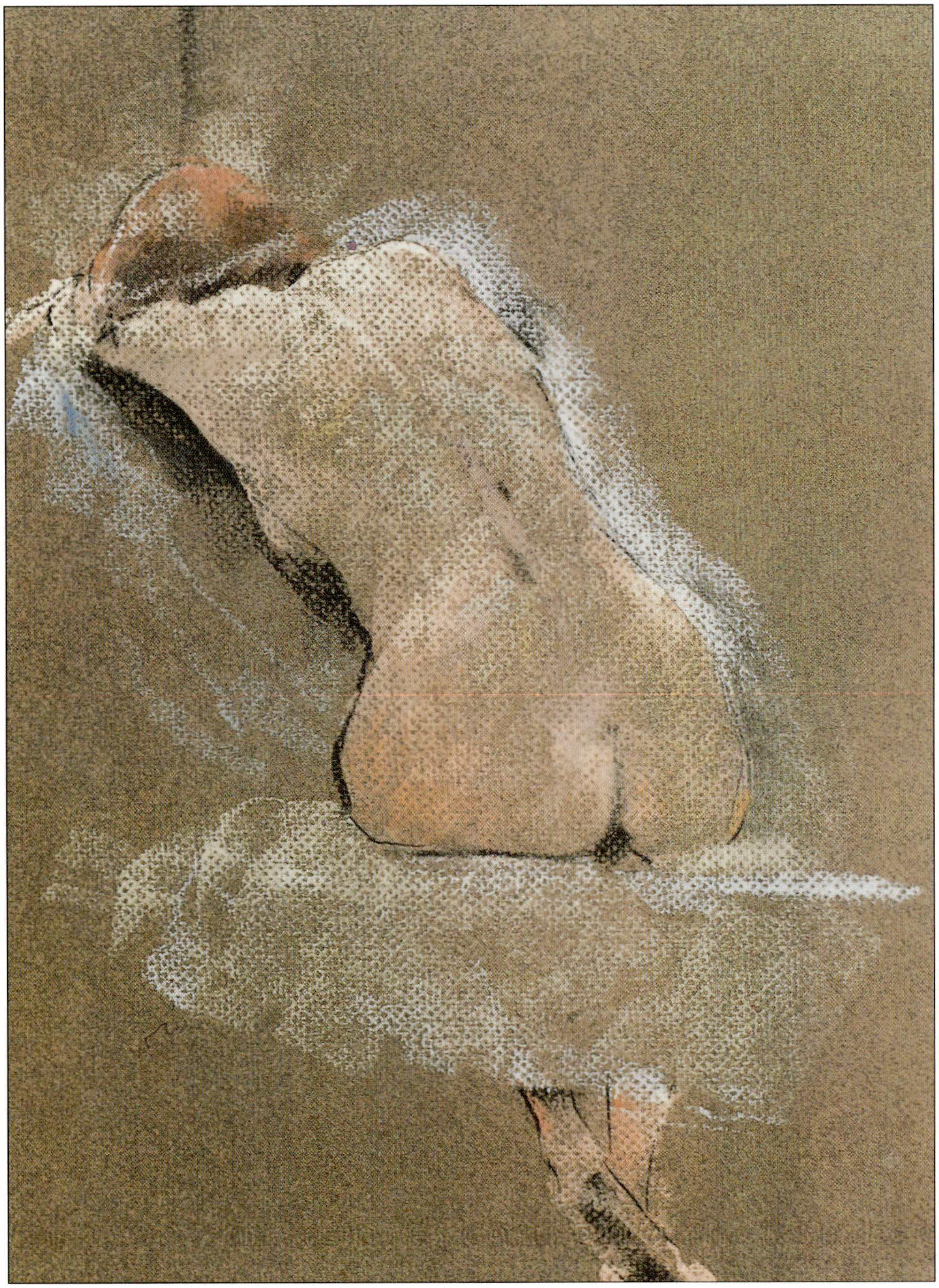

A LIFE STUDY by Clifford Hatts

The contour of the figure is sharply drawn with hard pastel, the delicate colors "brushed in" with gentle side strokes in soft pastel. The heavy grain of the textured ground breaks up the density of the pastel, providing a basic medium shade that accentuates the hints of strong color and gives the tints and highlights a special, shimmering vibrance.

The Nude in Colored Pencil

Much like crayons, colored pencils are often overlooked as an exciting drawing medium. As seen in this drawing, they are capable of producing brilliant colors and dramatic tones. The picture is interesting not only for the techniques used in describing the form, but for the unusual and striking composition as well.

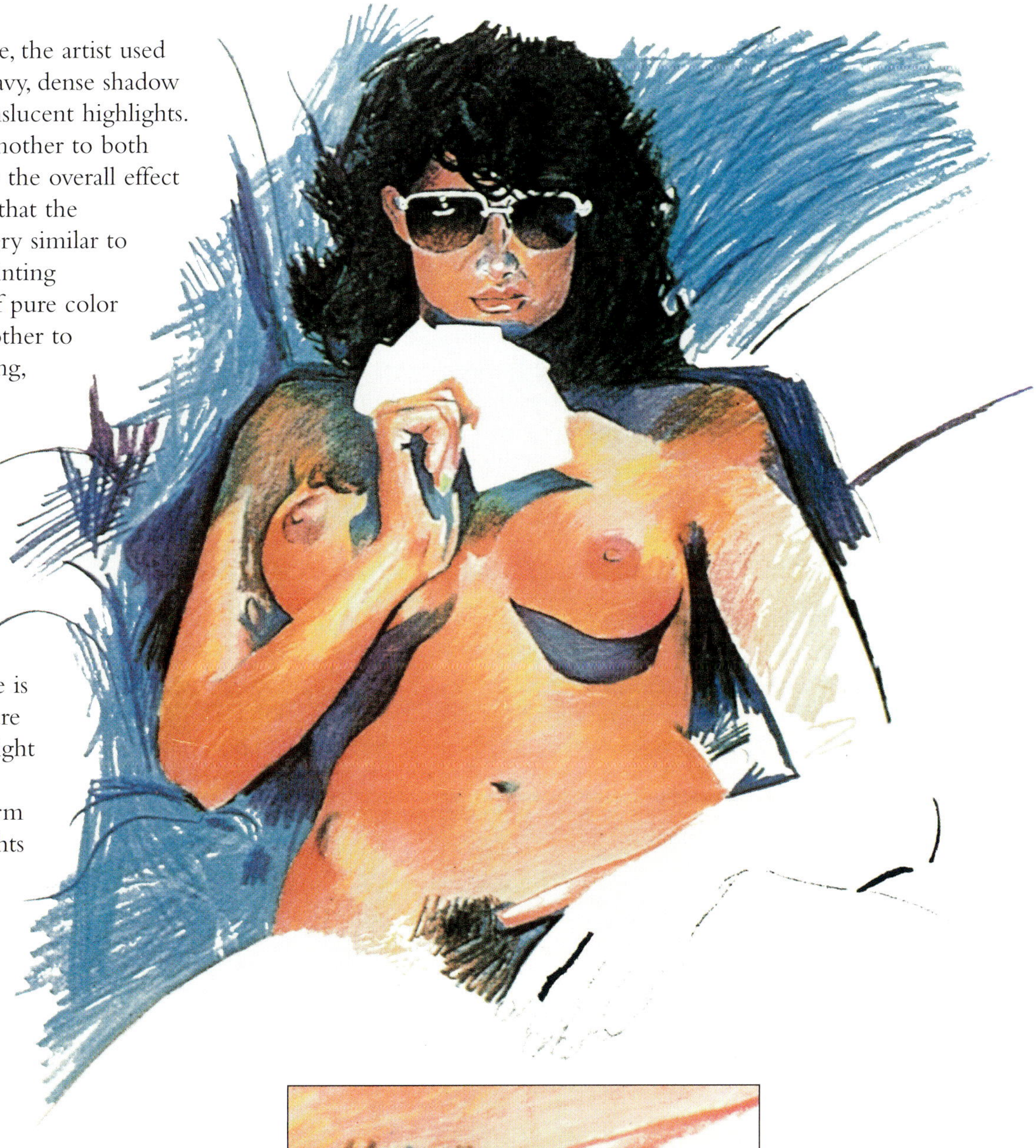

In terms of technique, the artist used a combination of heavy, dense shadow areas and lighter, translucent highlights. These play off one another to both heighten and modify the overall effect of the picture. Note that the drawing process is very similar to the traditional oil painting process; thin layers of pure color are laid over one another to build up a shimmering, translucent surface. While it appears that many individual tones and colors have been used, the artist has in fact used only a few warm and cool colors. The flesh tone is used all over the figure and altered for highlight and shadow areas by either overlaying warm red tones for highlights or cool blues for shadows.

Compositionally, the artist has exploited the white paper, using it to become part of the drawing as demonstrated in the playing cards and sunglasses. This is extremely effective in creating unity between the image and its environment, as well as strengthening the intensity of colored areas.

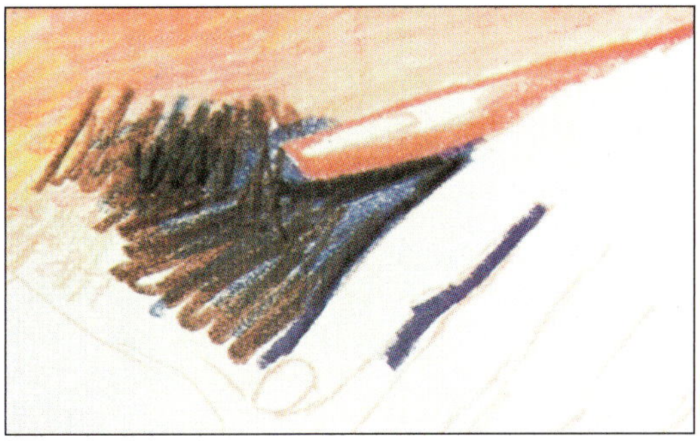

The detail on the left shows the use of the white paper, rather than color, to create the shape of the hand.

Skin Tones

Although skin appears predominantly pinkish or brownish, it is in fact made up of a great many different hues and tints, some very far removed from the tubes of color sold by paint manufacturers as "flesh tint." Even when you discount variations arising from light and shade on a form, the color and texture of skin is markedly different from one person to another, and it also varies according to the part of the body.

The presence of pigment darkens the skin, the extent according to racial origins and degree of exposure to the sun. All skin, however, is to some extent translucent, and much of its color comes from the blood in the capillaries below. This is responsible for the warm pink or red glow particularly noticeable on the face and hands. Sometimes, particularly with very pale-skinned people, you will also see tinges of blue from underlying veins.

Skin tends to appear as a collection of warm and cool colors, which can help to describe form, since the cool colors tend to recede and the warm ones to advance. The palette should therefore comprise a selection of both types. A suggestion for the cool primaries is cobalt blue, alizarin crimson, and lemon yellow, while the warm ones might be French ultramarine, cadmium red, and cadmium yellow. Other useful colors are yellow ocher, Naples yellow, burnt and raw sienna, and raw umber.

It is important to be decisive about the colors you apply to the painting. Keep mixtures clean and pure by limiting the number of colors in them to three or four, and take time over mixing or you will end up with a collection of random, unrelated hues.

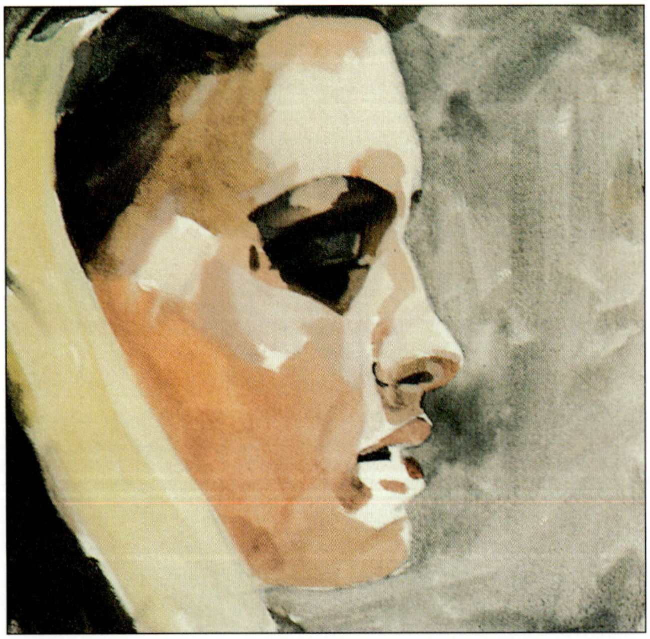

The techniques you use depend entirely on individual preferences, but certain skin qualities can be brought out by particular techniques, notably glazing over an underpainting. The translucency can be emphasized by

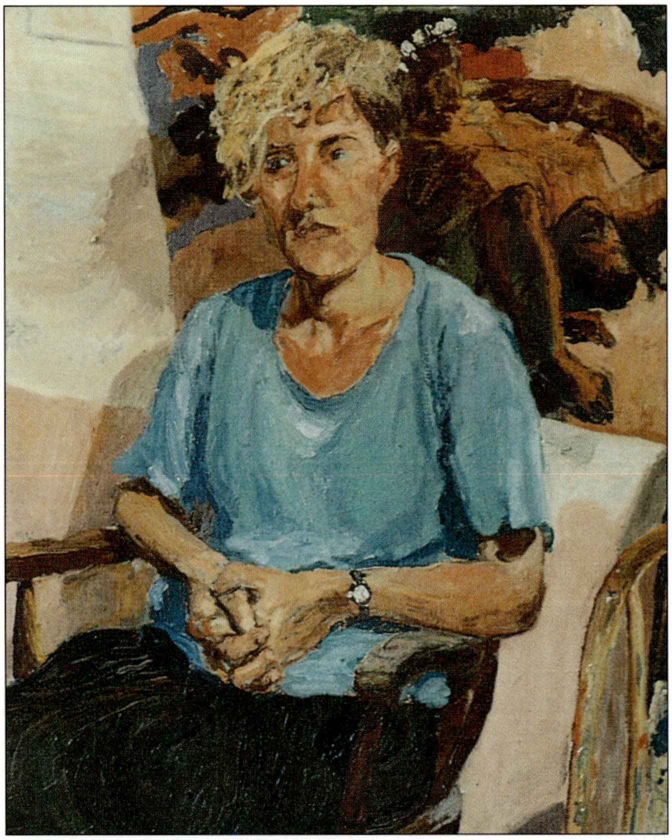

THE SPINAL INJURIES NURSE by Susan Wilson

The overall color of this sitter's skin appears as a brownish pink, but on close inspection you can see that this is made up of a variety of hues, from creams to browns and reds. Painting skin demands careful color mixing, as these colors are all closely related to one another, and a too-bright or over-dark patch of paint could have a disastrous effect.

LEFT: *The warm tones were established by using a mixture of yellow ocher and white for the hair, and burnt umber, cadmium red, and titanium white for the face.*

glazing dark over light as in the portraits of Rembrandt. A method widely used by Renaissance painters was to apply warmer skin colors thinly over a cool green, gray, or purple underpainting.

The best way to practice painting flesh tones is to make studies of your own hand under different lighting conditions. At first you may see pinks and reds only, but closer observation will soon reveal touches of yellow, gray, blue, brown, and even green.

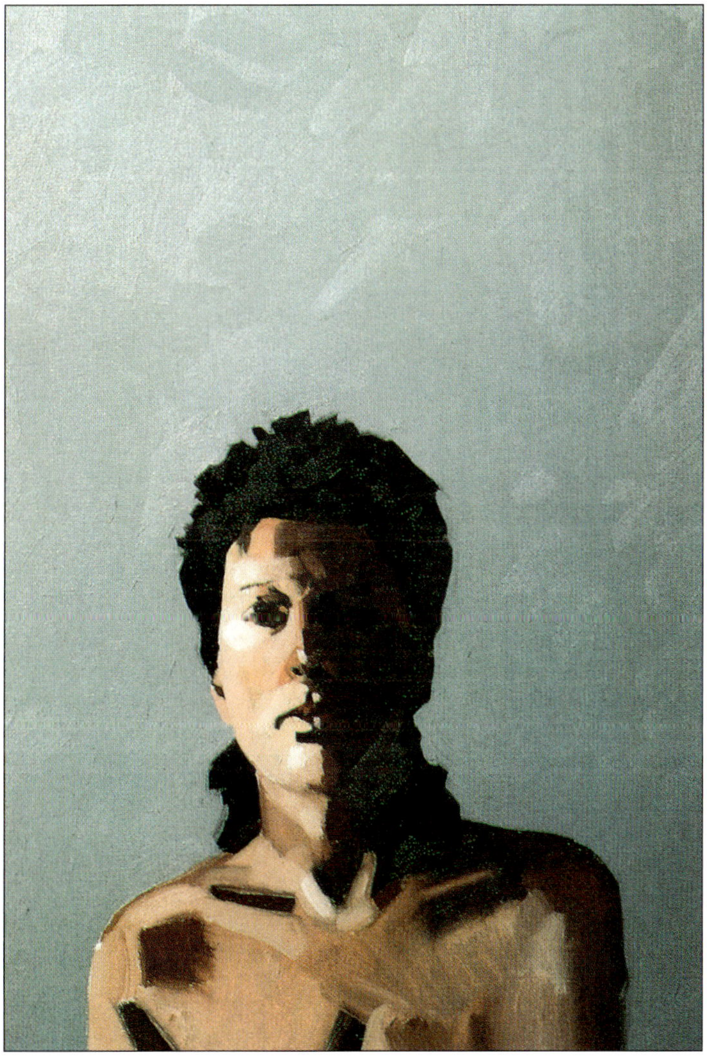

In complete contrast to the delicate transparency of watercolor, oil paints can be laid on with thick impasto to produce a heavily textured result. In this striking portrait, the artist worked alla prima*, applying all the paint in the same stage and working wet-into-wet over a beige ground. The paint was applied rapidly in large blocks of color which describe the planes of the figure in a bold, uncompromising manner. The painting has an almost sculptural form, accentuated by the strong side light which throws the figure into distinct planes of light and shadow.*

There is no single, all-embracing formula for painting flesh tones, and almost every artist has his or her own favorite palette of colors. It is best for you to decide which colors are best suited to your painting style.

BROWN SKIN

Because brown skin reflects light more than pale skin does, strong highlights and shadows have been used in the painting below. The colors used by the artist included cadmium red, cadmium orange, cadmium yellow, yellow ocher, raw umber, ivory black, and Payne's gray.

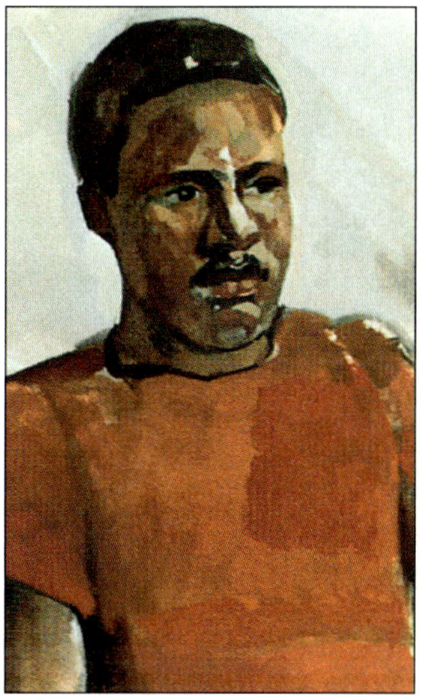

Because gouache is opaque it is possible to add light tones over much darker ones, as the artist has done here, adding highlights to the flesh over the darker base colors. When painting light over dark avoid diluting the paint too much and take care not to disturb the dried color beneath.

SKIN TEXTURE

Rendering the actual texture of the skin will depend very much on your own painting style, your chosen medium, and the particular character of your sitter. Oil paint is probably the medium most suited to portrait painting, having a richness and depth of tone that gives strength and solidity to the subject. There are a number of ways of using oils to interpret skin tones – you can start with a thin underpainting to establish form and bulk, overlaid with delicate glazes and scumbles to give sheen and translucency to the skin. The slow drying time of oils allows for subtle modulations of tone and color, achieved by blending with a fan brush. For a more direct, dynamic effect, try painting with bold slashes of broken color.

Watercolor has a reputation for being difficult to control when painting portraits and figures, but frequent practice will give you increasing confidence. You may choose to build up the flesh tones using glazes wet over dry, or you may prefer the more exciting method of applying pure colors and letting them blend wet-into-wet.

Hands and Arms

Hands are expressive indicators of emotions and states of mind, so it is worth taking time to understand their physical make-up. Put simply, fingers are all cylindrical and jointed in the same way, but they seem complicated because each moves independently of the others, creating its own shapes.

Their range of movement is, however, limited: they are either straight or bent, whether holding, gripping, pointing, or pressing. In contrast, arms pose fewer drawing problems than hands, for the most part, so long as you check their lengths. Make sure you observe individual variations, and pay attention to the flatter planes that are near the wrist in all but the fleshiest persons.

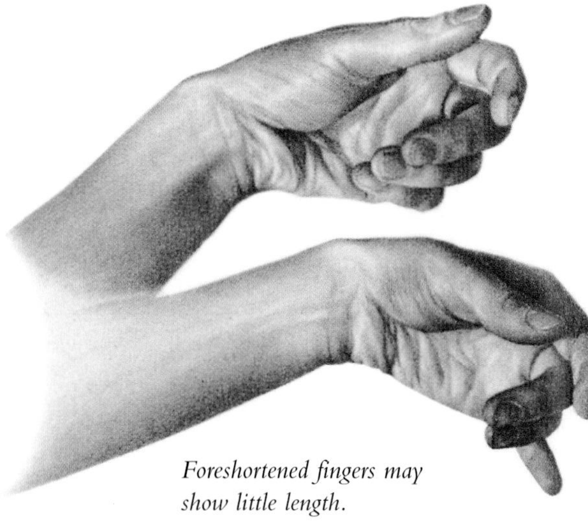

Foreshortened fingers may show little length.

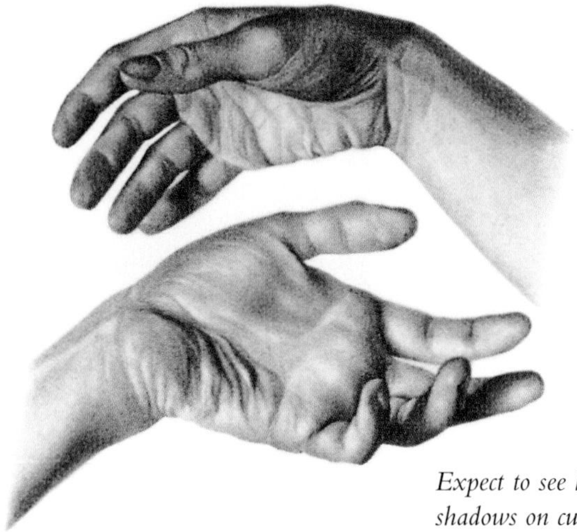

Expect to see heavy cast shadows on curved forms.

GETTING TO KNOW YOUR HANDS

As an exercise in familiarizing yourself with hands, examine your own. Are they tapered or spatulate, stubby or delicate, attenuated, broad-jointed, or dimpled? To show its form, place your non-drawing hand flat in directional light and draw the shadows cast by it. Then clench your fist and draw its triangular profile, completed by the thumb, with its larger, lower, offset joint. Open your hand again and note how the palm tapers toward the wrist, which is a flexible link to the columnar arm. Make a series of sketches of your hand in various positions, making sure that you observe the relationships between the fingers and noting their characteristics. Once you have established the solidity and proportions, you can add details, such as creases, hair, veins, and nails; including a wristwatch or one or more rings helps describe contours. When drawing other people, look for the relationships between pairs of hands or clasped hands, and be aware of their size in relation to the rest of the figure.

A complex series of joints in the hand make many combinations of movement possible. The flexible fingers of a healthy adult are capable of bending back some way over the top of the hand or of stretching across more than eight notes on a piano, while the other hand can simultaneously hold thin, fragile or moving objects of almost any shape, although there are limits as to size. When painting or drawing a figure, the artist soon becomes aware that hands are one of the most expressive features; Leonardo da Vinci was one of the first to notice and utilize this in his work. It is worth sketching them in different positions and from different angles to become familiar with the general form before incorporating them in paintings.

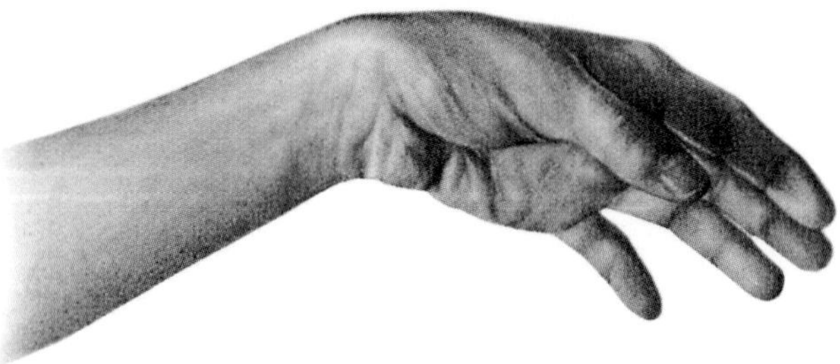

CLASPED HANDS

Until you have gained experience in making studies of two hands clasped together, expect to make changes and adjustments as you go along. Choose a fluid medium, such as gouache, that allows this to be done easily.

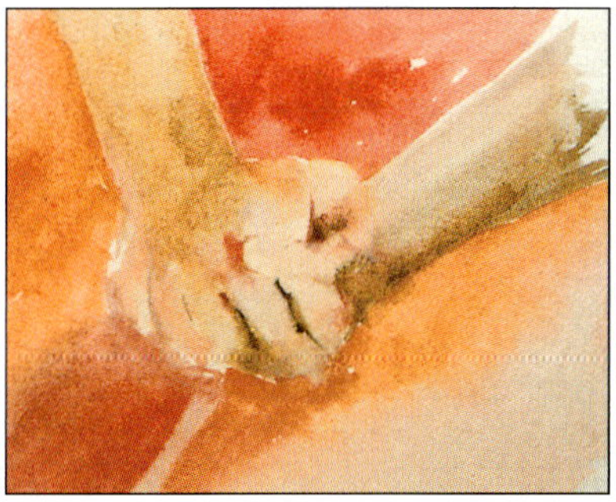

1 When starting a study, work loosely and give yourself plenty of room for adjustment. Draw freely, and manipulate the medium on the surface while it is still wet.

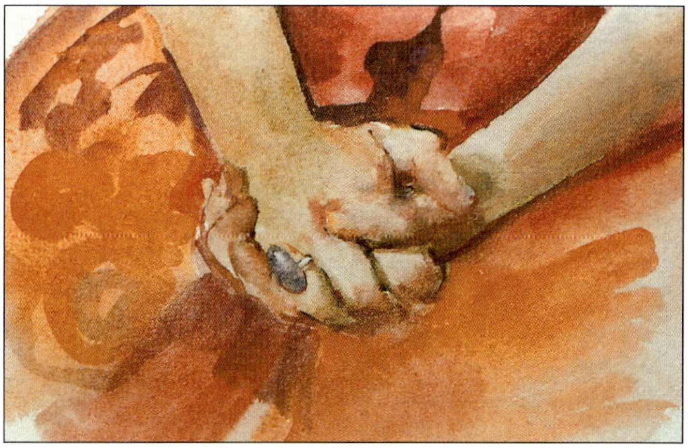

2 The covering power of gouache helps you to redefine drawings simply. You need only continue until you have realized the form, leaving the details until later.

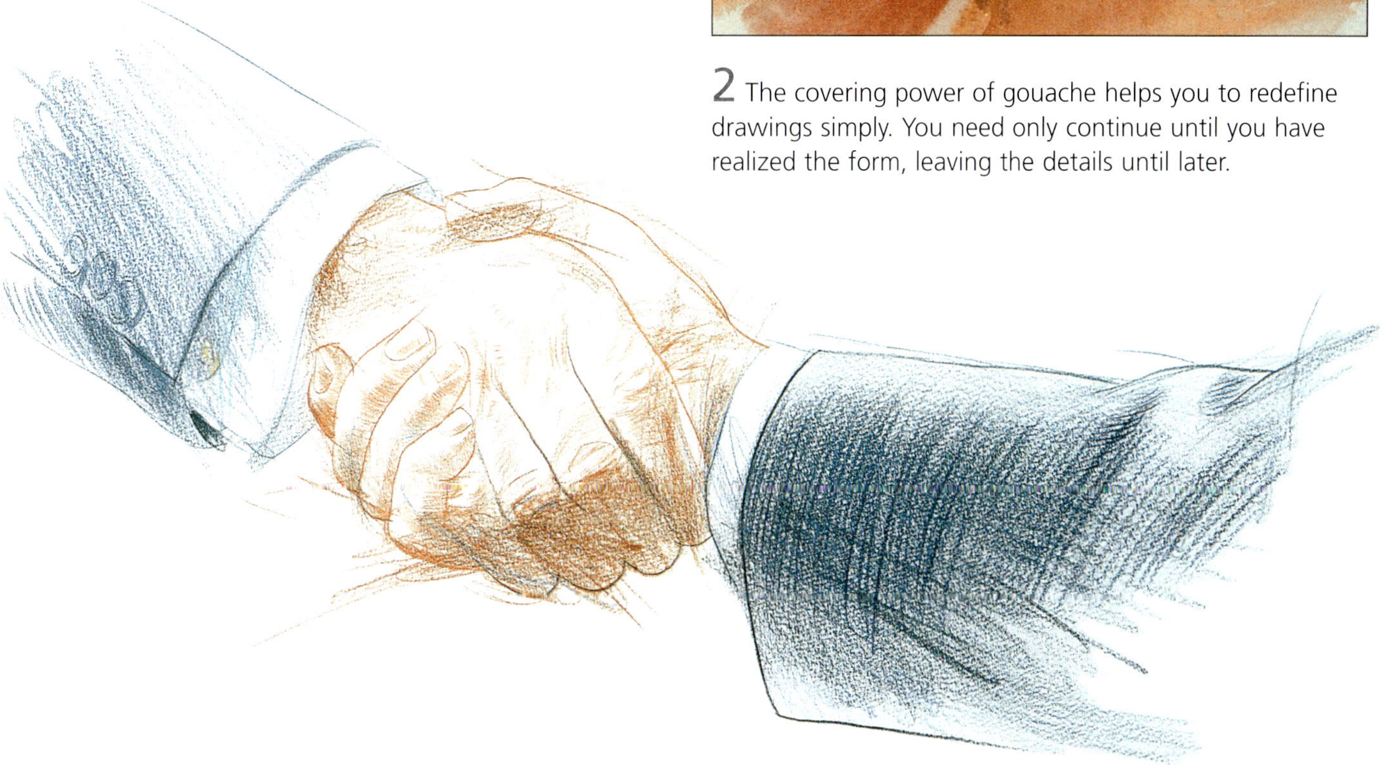

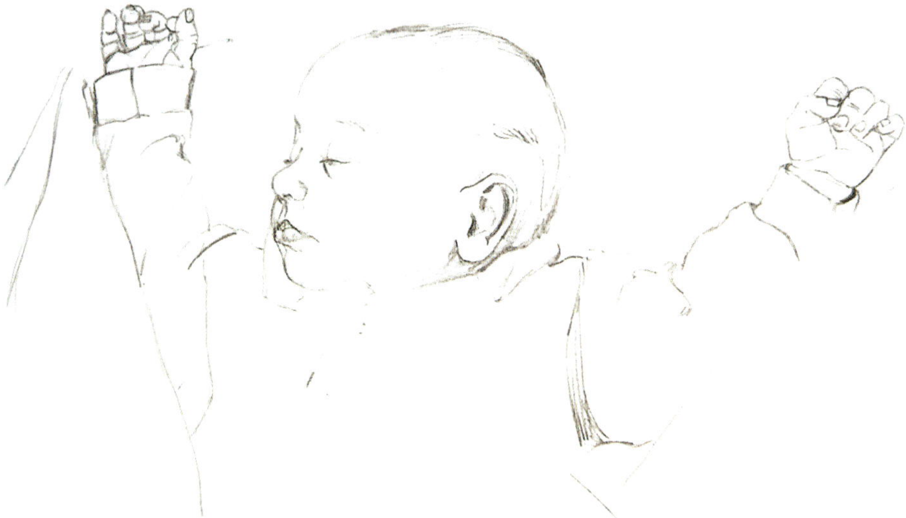

BABY HANDS

Drawing a sleeping baby's hands gives you the chance to explore the tiny proportions and details for longer spells than when the child is awake.

Feet and Legs

When drawing legs and feet, it is vital to make careful observation of their relative proportions compared to the rest of the body.

Don't fall into the elementary error of drawing legs the same size as arms – they are much larger limbs, designed to hold up the entire body, and their muscles are correspondingly bigger. In the same way, feet are longer extremities than hands; their bony arch and the shortness of toes, compared to fingers, gives them a more solid, substantial look. The ankle is a more robust joint than the wrist and again is larger. By keeping these facts in mind, and by making continual comparisons as you add information to your drawings, you can avoid errors and produce accurate depictions.

MAKING STUDIES OF FEET

Because you are less likely to find bare legs and feet to sketch, except in warm weather, use yourself as a first sitter. Prop up a mirror and make a thorough observation of your own feet and legs. Unless you have a low arch to your foot, you should see a rising instep abutting the ovoid ankle, which has protruding, bony sides. Make sure that you draw the correct dimensions of the curving big toe joint and the width of the ball of the foot, otherwise they may have a flipper-like appearance. Pay attention, too, to the toes; they share the columnar, circular form of fingers, but extend much less. Keep checking the entire foot for perspective, and do the same if you or your sitter are wearing shoes, which often have a shape very different from the feet that they are covering.

PAIRS OF LEGS AND FEET

If the feet and legs are together, draw them in perspective and in relation to each other, rather than attempting to draw each one as a separate entity. Look at them as a composite shape, and observe the relative dimensions within this.

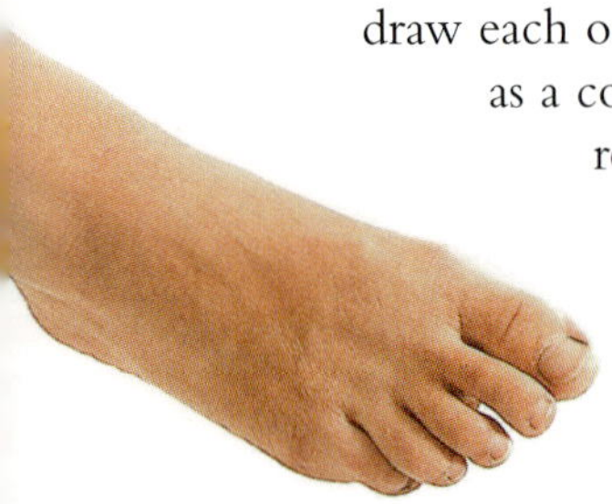

TOES

Most people's toes taper from the big toe in an arc to the little toe, but there are many individual variations. The second toe is sometimes comparatively long and protrudes beyond the others.

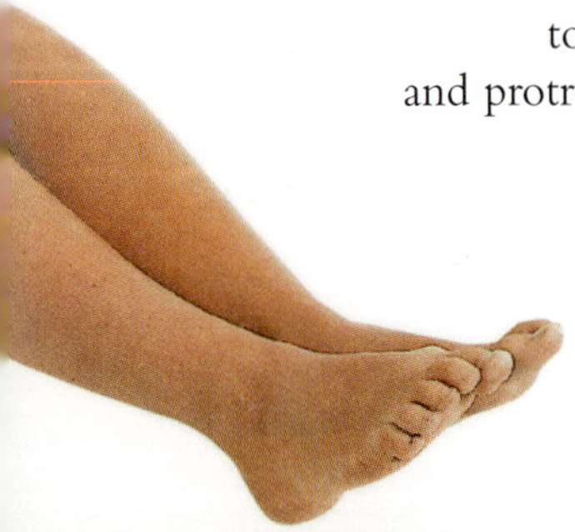

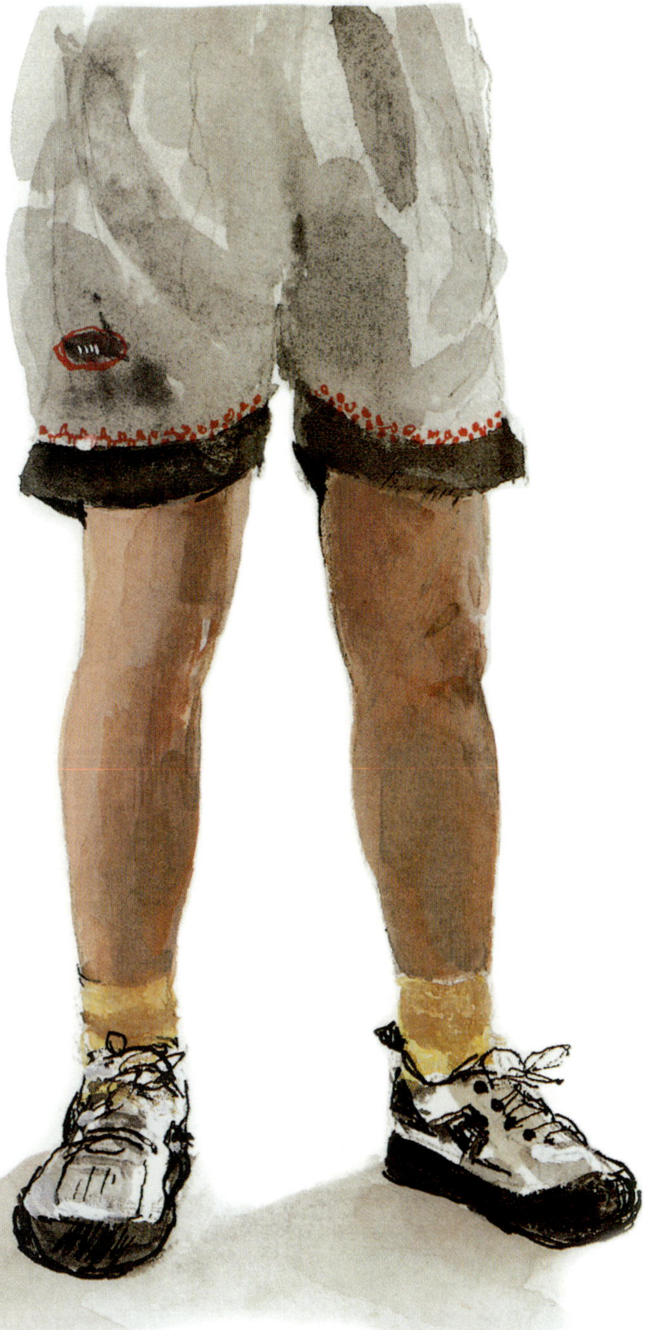

Shoes must curve with the feet and obey the laws of perspective.

BARE FEET AND SANDALS

When drawing bare feet or feet in sandals it is important to depict the curved taper of the toes and their joints, and the diminishing size of toenails.

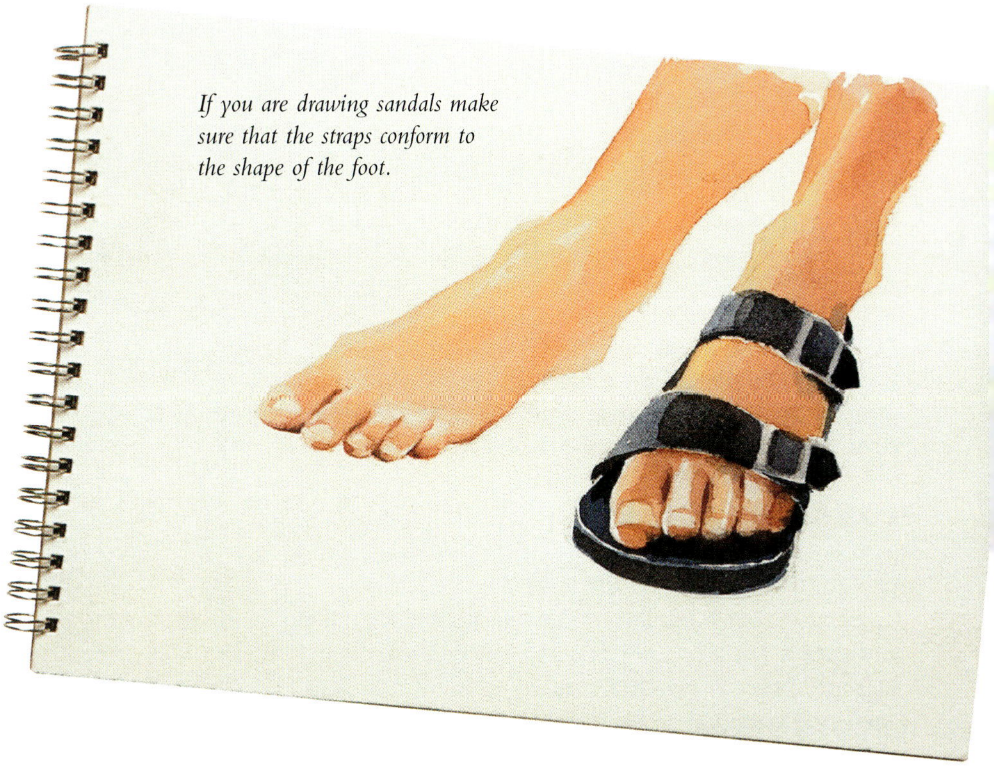

If you are drawing sandals make sure that the straps conform to the shape of the foot.

If legs are concealed by clothing with a different contour, make sure that the dimensions you draw allow for both the width of the leg and the clothing that hangs away from it.

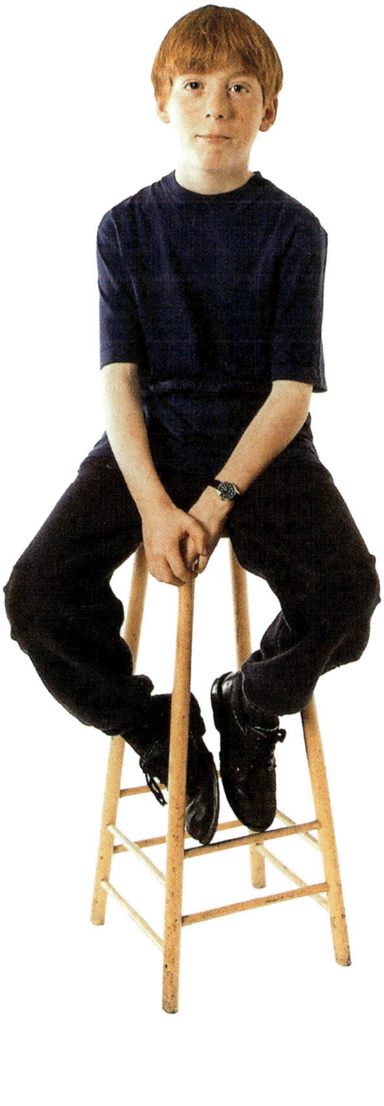

CROSSED LEGS

Crossed legs present complicated shapes and angles, so use a medium, such as gouache, which allows you to make alterations easily.

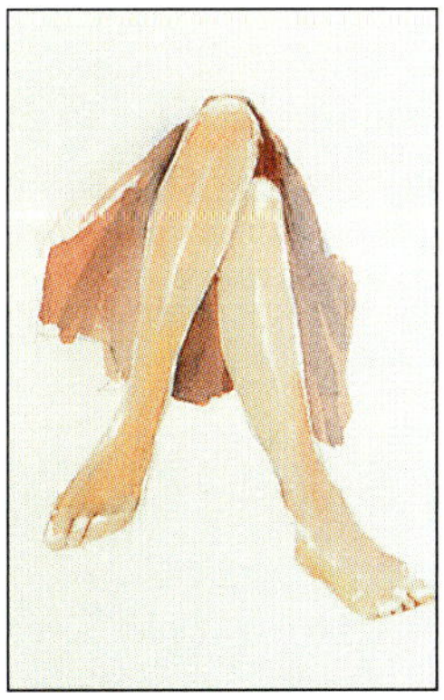

1 Where the thighs are concealed by a skirt, concentrate on the lower legs as a pair and use the negative space to set down their dimensions accurately.

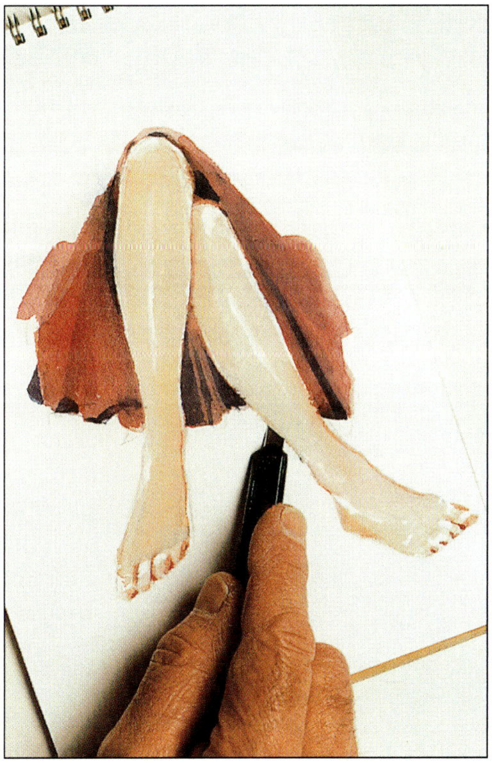

2 If you need to build up confidence, block in the basic shapes using a diluted wash, and sharpen the details later with fresh, full-strength washes. Errors may be scratched away carefully with a sharp blade.

Clothing

As well as protecting us from the elements and keeping us warm, clothes are an immediate guide to the image of ourselves we wish to convey. Bring an artist's observation of clothing into your sketches, and you will capture your subject's individuality more effectively.

For instance, clothing is a good indication of climate. To create an impression of cold weather, draw your sitter huddled in a winter coat; to show a hot temperature, draw him or her in tennis shorts and tennis shirt.

LOOKING CLOSELY

Think of clothing as "body wrapping" and use it to bring out the solidity of the wearer. A dressmaker's mannequin can be useful in showing how clothes hang and gather, but you can gain experience in sketching fabrics by examining clothes hung up in a closet. Pay particular attention to folds and creases. Light materials generally fall into small, fine creases, while thick or stiff fabrics have mostly broad folds, or stand away from the body. Look out, too, for the small surface changes that differentiate fresh, crisp clothing from worn or shabby clothes.

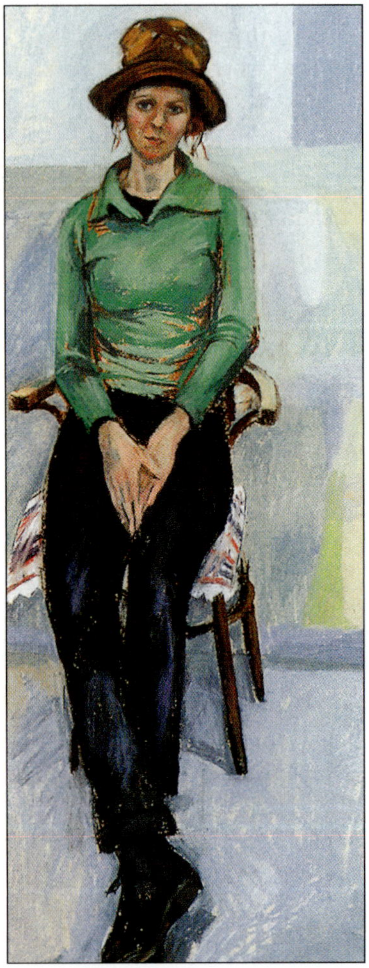

TEXTURES AND PROPS

Glossy materials are fascinating subjects: compare the glitter of gold lamé with the gleam of wet oilskin, or the sheen of satin, and bring out their differences in your sketches. Even impersonal work clothes and uniforms may incorporate plastic, in hard hats for example, and metal, in badges and accessories. Use hats, headscarves, and other headgear as special features. When drawing on location, include the "props" people carry or use, such as shopping bags, umbrellas, or shovels; these can unify a drawing.

Many items of clothing can act as props. Favorite hats, an old sweater, or a well-loved pair of shoes are often a part of the wearer. As a souvenir of a particular sitter during a distinctive period of their life, they can serve as a date marker.

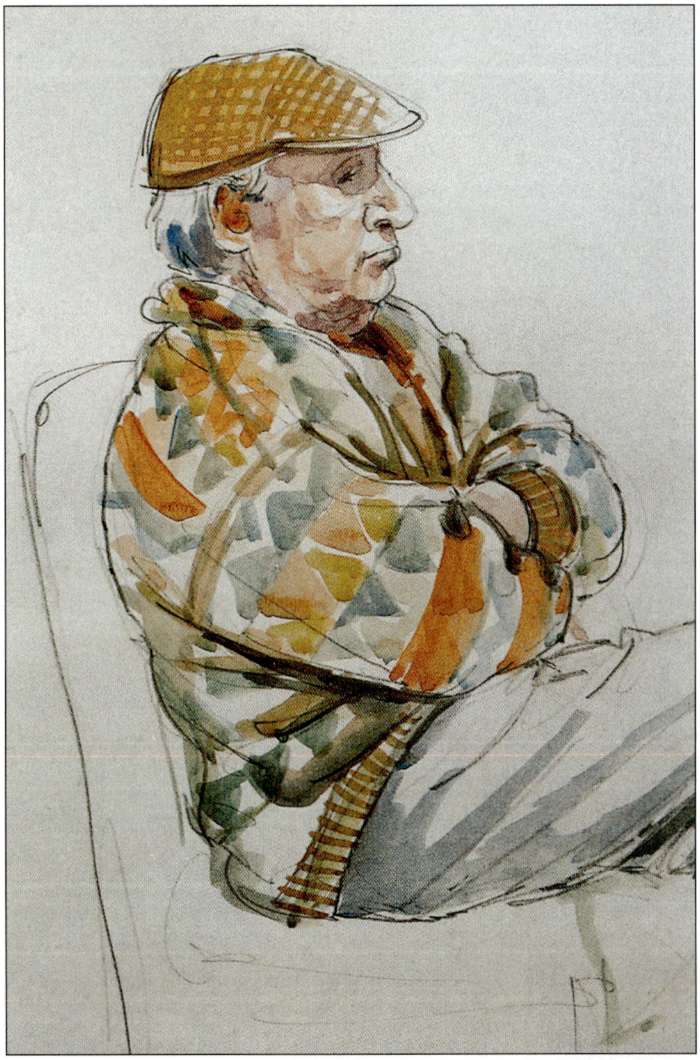

PATTERNS AND CONTOURS

There is no need to spend a lot of time slavishly drawing details of printed or knitted fabrics, unless this is vital. Look at how you can treat them economically. Use the direction of folds in garments to describe form. Use their size and depth to suggest the weight of the garment.

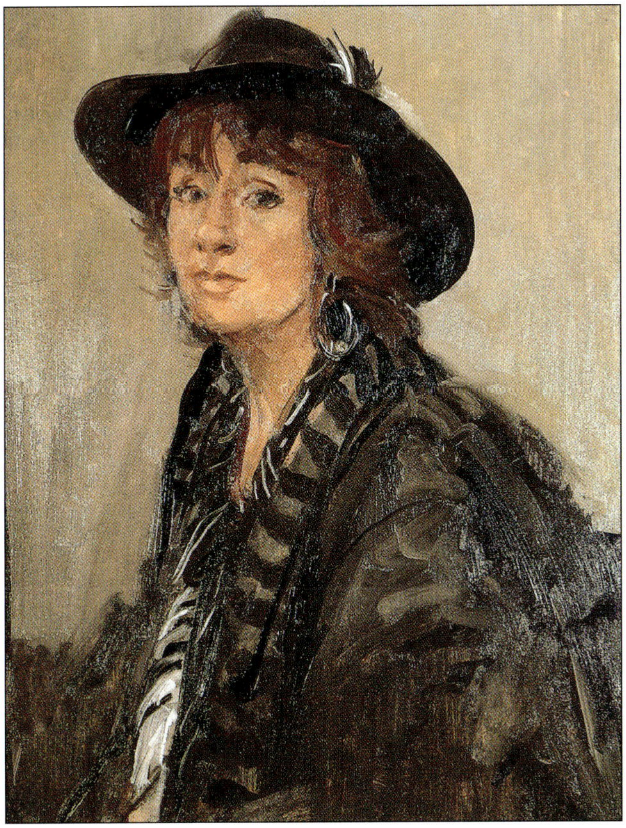

In this oil painting by Tom Coates, the clothing, particularly the area at bottom right, has been left vague so that it does not compete with the center of attention – the face.

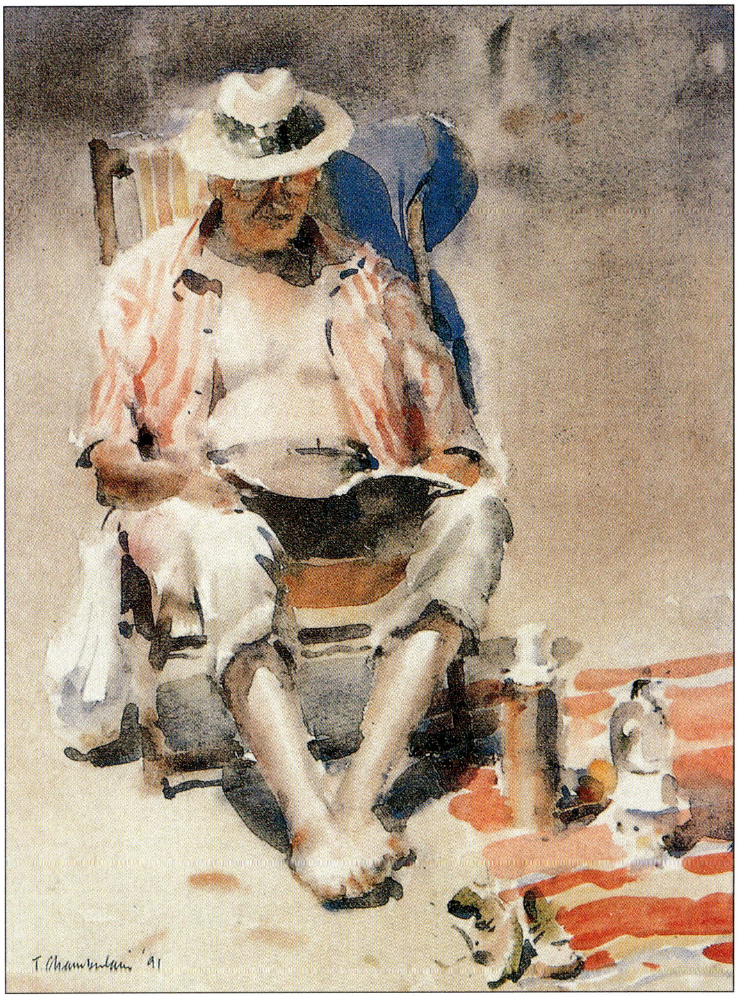

GRANDAD by Trevor Chamberlain

This watercolor painting is a fine example of how loose clothing gives the impression of a warm and sunny day.

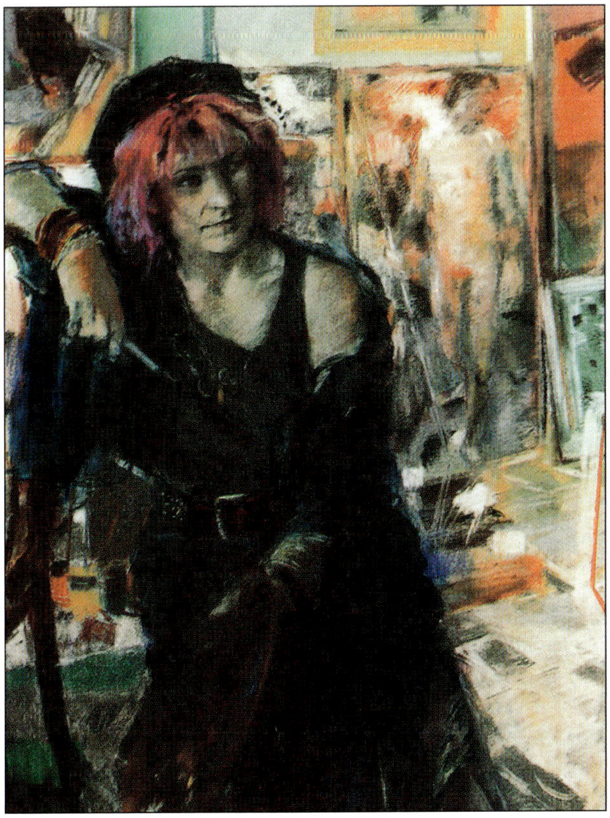

PORTRAIT OF A PAINTER by Barry Atherton

The informal pose and studio background give the figure both character and context. The dark clothing creates a solid shape, bringing the subject out clearly from the background, but even the darkest tones are alive with touches of vivid color, every mark playing an active role in modeling the forms and creating textural variety.

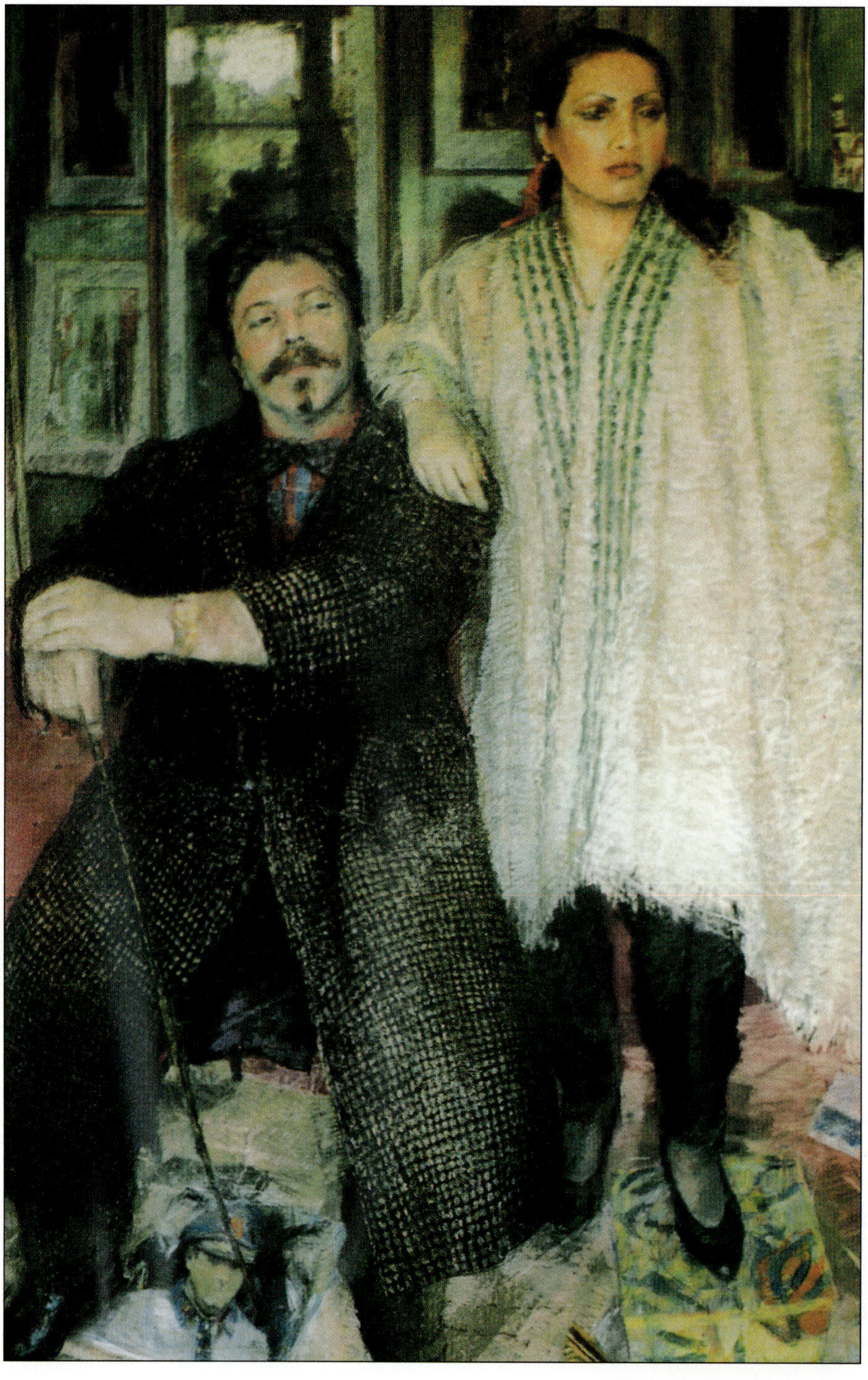

UNFINISHED by Barry Atherton

At 7 x 5 ft. (2.1 x 1.5 m) this is unusually large for a pastel painting, making the figures approximately life-size and enabling the artist to include a vast range of detail, especially in the faces and clothing.

Human Proportions

Poor drawing is the most common fault in figure painting, but this is usually the result of lack of observation rather than insufficient skill. You will certainly improve with practice, but initially it will help you to memorize a few simple rules about the proportions of the face and body.

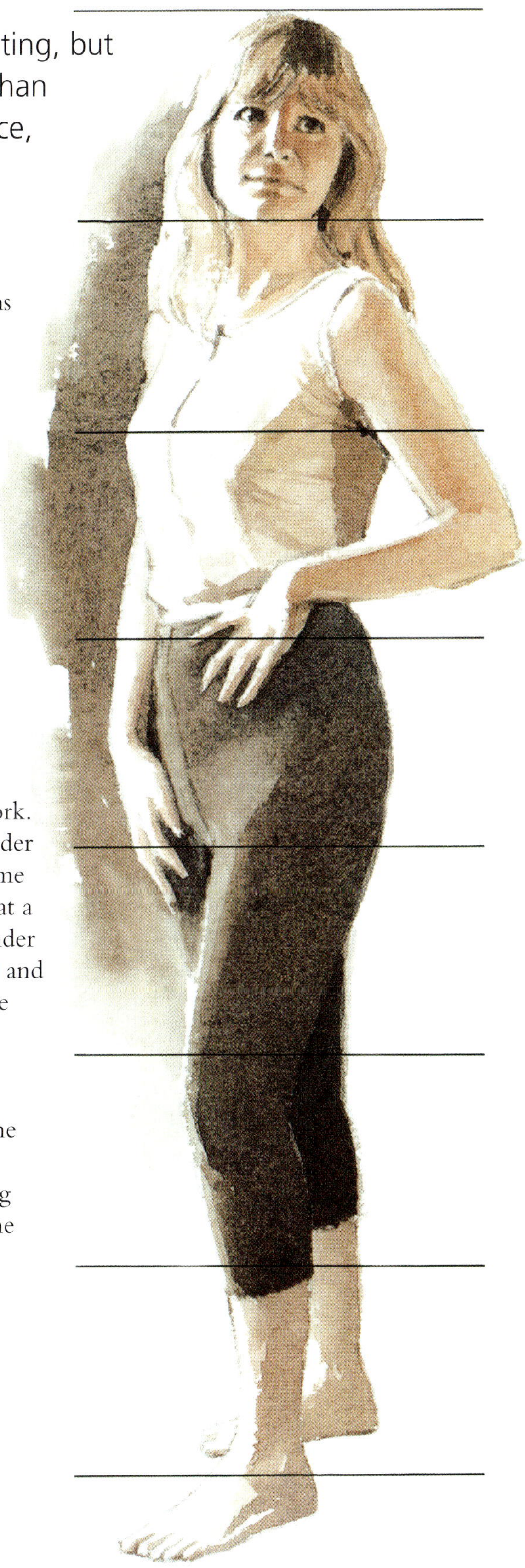

Taking as a basic proposition that six-and-a-half-to-seven head-lengths is the average, this distance can be divided into separate parts. From the top of the head to the pubic, just above the crotch, will be half the length of the total figure. When beginning a drawing or painting of the standing figure this formula is very useful; ticking off the distance between these points and then doubling it will make it obvious whether the full figure will fit on the sheet of paper.

In such an operation, however, the rule of thumb should operate. Avoid using a measuring device such as a ruler or other precision instrument. Never bhe a slave to the rules; the essence of good drawing is spontaneity and invention. Each artist decides and develops his own character and this includes selection and adjustment of human proportion.

OBSERVING THE DIFFERENCES

You can become aware of the differences in body shapes by looking out for the most obvious factors first and including them in your work. These include gender differences: males often have stronger arms, wider backs, and broader shoulders compared with female bodies of the same weight, which are usually broader at the hip and carry the forearms at a different angle. Age is a related factor – the childish figure, when gender differences are less manifest, is typified by a comparatively large head and light musculature. Although full adult height can be governed by race and gender, one of the effects of aging is to reduce this.

FORESHORTENING

The drawings below show how dramatically foreshortening affects the shape of a limb. The thigh appears much shorter and thicker in the bottom drawing, because it is coming toward the viewer, with the leg bent at the knee. When drawing foreshortened limbs, forget about the rules of proportion and trust your own eyes.

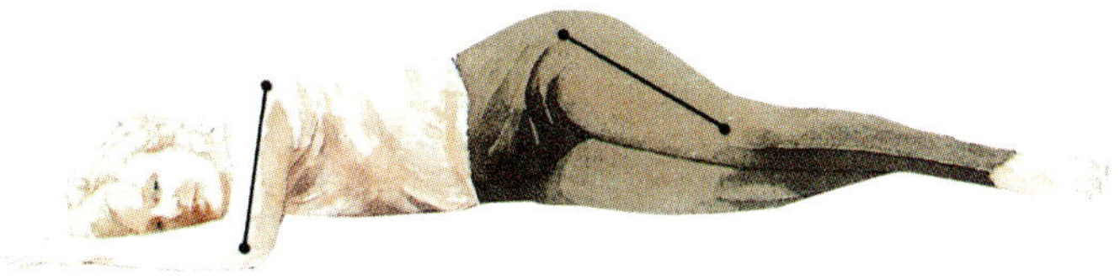

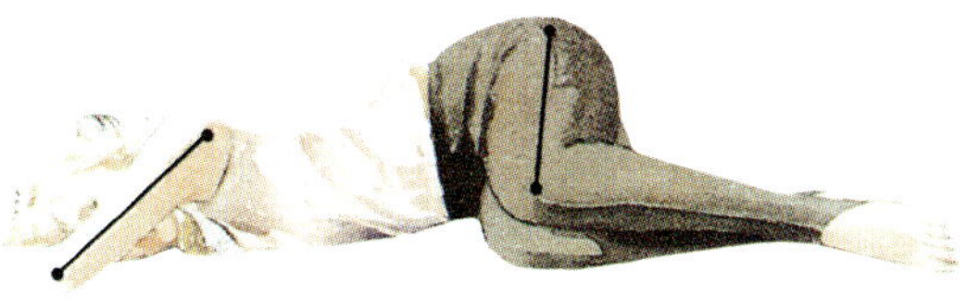

Children

The most common problem in drawing and painting children is identifying the precise characteristics that make them childlike – they are not mini-versions of adult people.

When you look at a child closely you will see that the head is larger in proportion to the body than in an adult; the limbs are mobile and flexible, but the chubbiness typical of young children disguises bone and muscle structure.

Children tend to look stiff and embarrassed if asked to pose for any length of time, which does not make for a good picture. Thus if you do intend completing a whole painting in front of the sitter you will have to be prepared to work quickly in short sessions. If you normally make an underpainting, it is helpful in such cases to use acrylic for this, as opposed to oil, as it dries in a matter of minutes.

One of the commonest mistakes is making the child look too old, which can happen if you even slightly overwork any dimples or shadows. It is best to keep the lighting soft, and avoid too much contrast of light and dark. The contours of the face are much gentler in children than in adults, so you may want to avoid obvious brush strokes – the finger painting method could be useful, at least in some areas of the picture.

Another difficulty is getting a child to pose. If you are working from life, you need to choose a style and technique that enables you to work quickly or can accommodate changes in the pose if the child becomes fidgety. If you are working on a more complex composition that needs prolonged attention to detail, you may need to work from photographic reference and, if possible, ask the child to pose briefly to check any elements of form and posture that are not clear from your reference pictures.

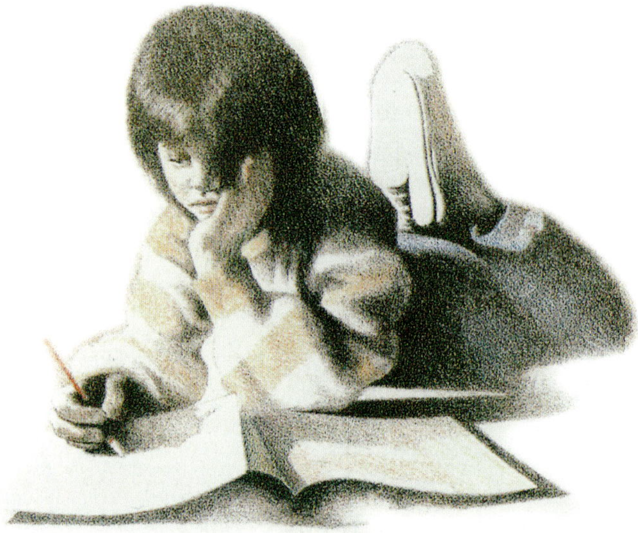

CHOOSING A MEDIUM

The "quick" media, such as charcoal, pastels, chalks, and brushes, are best, as they give wide color and tonal ranges fast. Using a pencil or pen is fine for drawing a sleeping child, but can be frustratingly slow when sketching a moving child. Whatever you use, aim to have more than one session of watching and catching brief notes.

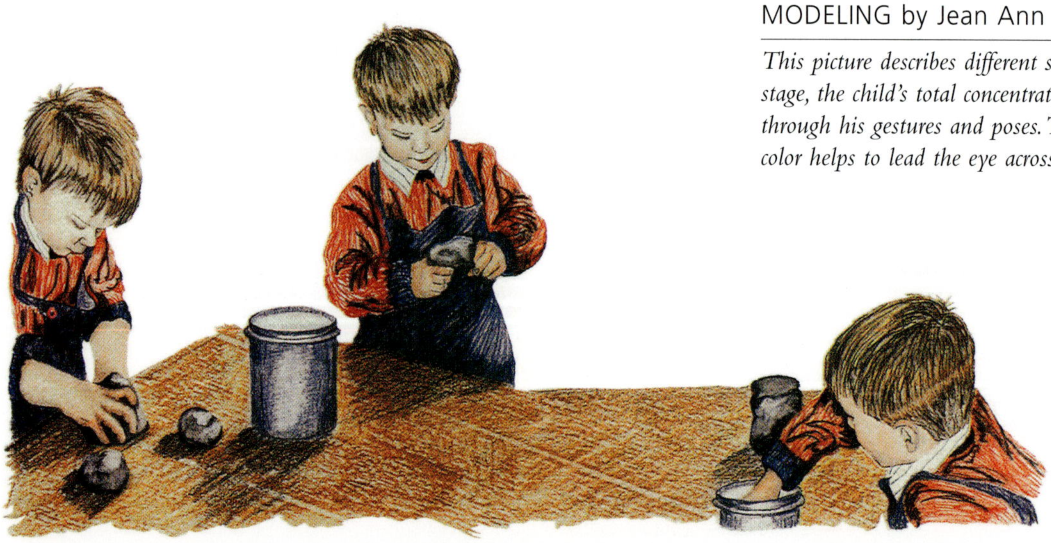

MODELING by Jean Ann O'Neill

This picture describes different stages of an activity. In each stage, the child's total concentration on the task is caught through his gestures and poses. The schematic arrangement of color helps to lead the eye across the image.

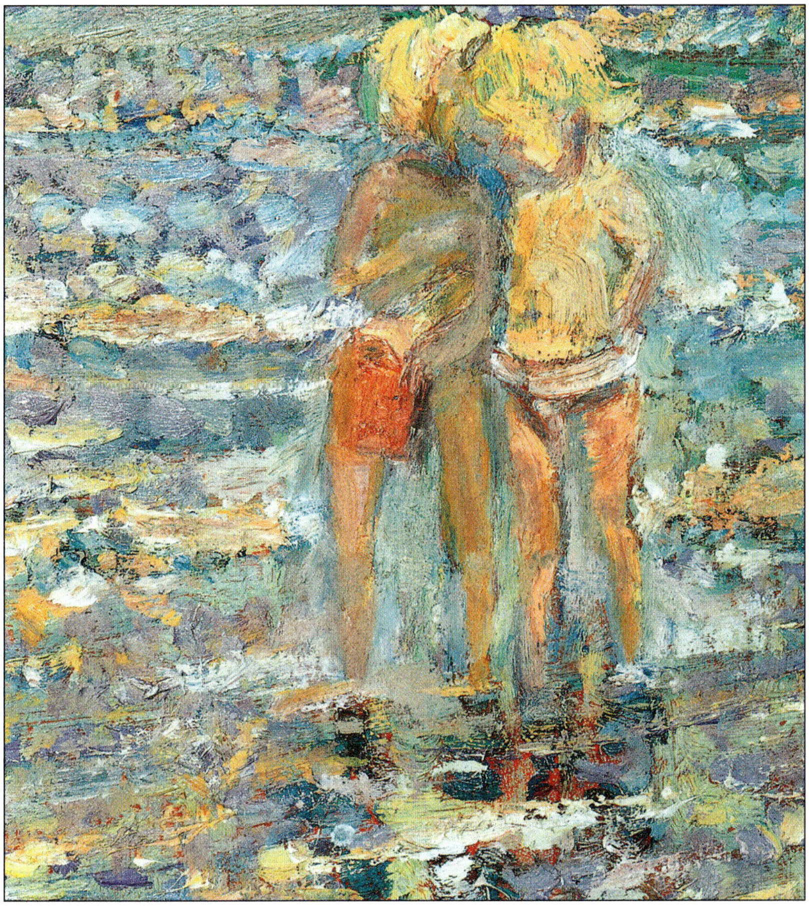

The pictures on this page show two completely different ways of capturing children at play on the beach.

BOY AND GIRL ON BEACH by Arthur Maderson (oil)

The placing of the children high in the picture enhances their slightness of build and also excludes the spectator from their private, whispering world by placing the water between them and us. Most of the painting is constructed of fat, slurred strokes of impasto over lean underpainting. A bright red colored ground left uncovered in many places is particularly noticeable in the foreground and the children's reflections.

CURIOSITY by Barry Freeman (pastel)

Children have an easy suppleness that enables them unconsciously to create graceful poses in the course of ordinary action and play. In this composition the two bodies are linked in a rhythmic, self-contained shape at the center of the picture, the more striking because detail of their surroundings is minimized. The natural color range and gentle technique express the simple pleasure of the subject. Broad, grainy pastel strokes juxtaposed and densely overlaid create defined areas of integrated light and color.

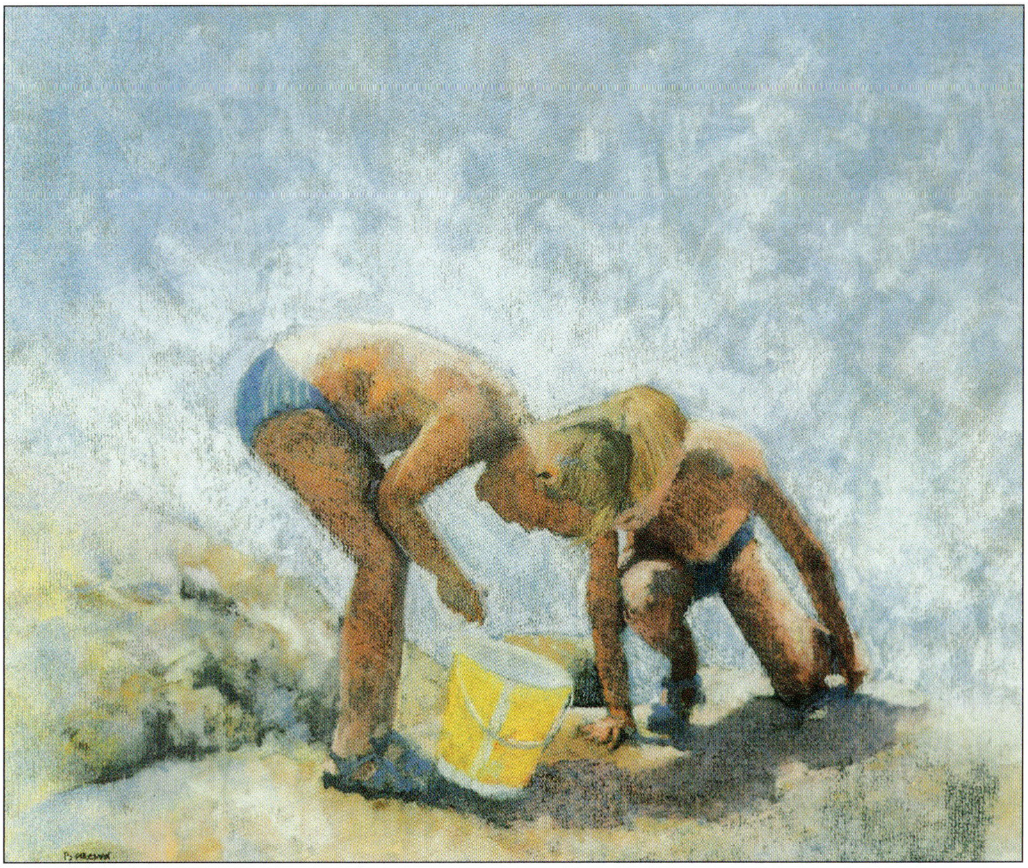

Groups

Any figure group, small or large, creates an interestingly dynamic image. There are complex rhythms and tensions in the way forms are interwoven and juxtaposed, caused by actual and implied movements in the figures.

The elements of pattern and texture can be varied and detailed – hair, clothing, accessories, background features. And as well as describing the physical facts of a group of people, you may also wish to convey a narrative context – a sense of the personal relationships between them, the common purpose or activity of the group.

Figure groups can represent all of the visual points of interest of the single figure, but their interactions are the keynote of the image. The elements of composition are as important as the details of individual form and character – alignment of the figures, the relationships of size and proportion, the space or closeness between them, and the relative distance from the viewer.

The grouping may be random, as with people on the street, or it may be due to a common purpose, of people come together to share an activity or form an audience. The active and passive relationships between the figures can be expressed in the composition, whether or not the group's full context and surroundings are portrayed.

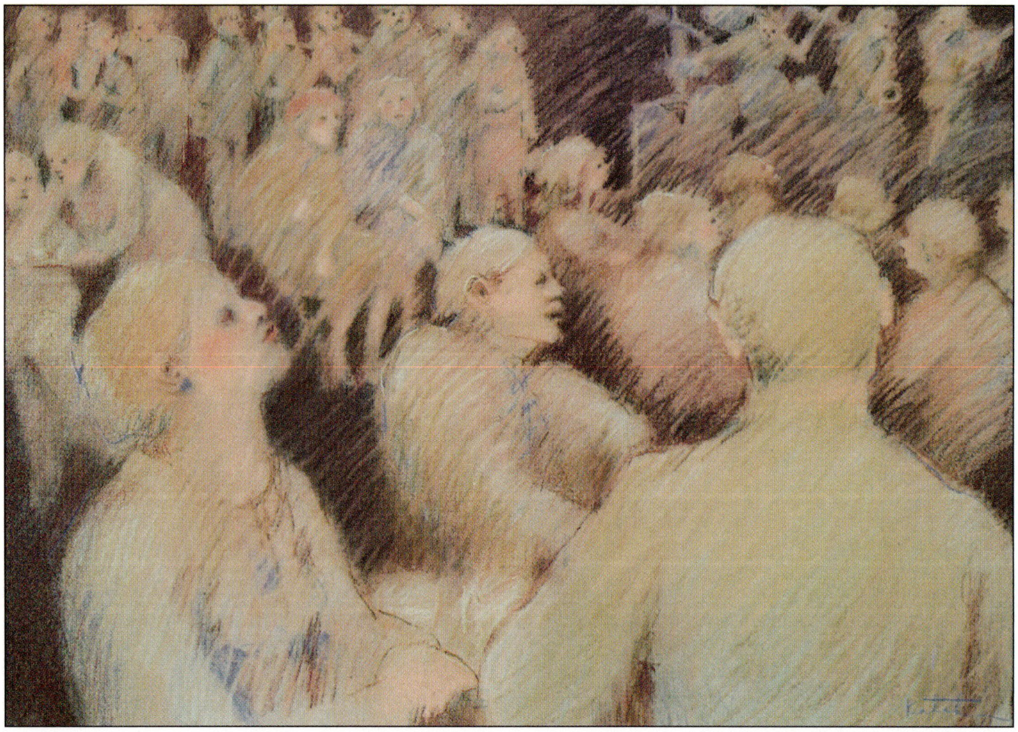

JAZZ AT THE MUSEUM by Carole Katchen

The consistency of style and technique in this composition is employed in emphasizing variations of form and character in the informal figure group. Individual body shapes and poses are broadly conveyed, but incorporate many subtle nuances of form and direction. The controlled color scheme effectively suggests a particular quality of interior light.

FIGURES IN A SETTING

The particular relationship between figure and background is most important. The lighting conditions may cause parts of the figure to appear to blend into the background, and much of the poetry of drawing is attained by softening an edge here and omitting a detail there, so as to leave something to the viewer's imagination. A common mistake made by beginners is to draw a hard outline around the figure, completely cutting it off from the background.

The setting, especially if it is an interior, often involves problems of perspective. But the perspective can be used to advantage to establish a clear ground plane; and the scale of the figure in relation to the objects in the setting can again be extremely helpful in creating a realistic representation of the figure itself. The background does not need to be drawn in elaborate detail, but the relationship between objects and setting is such a significant one that to ignore it is to deny one of the painting's most important features.

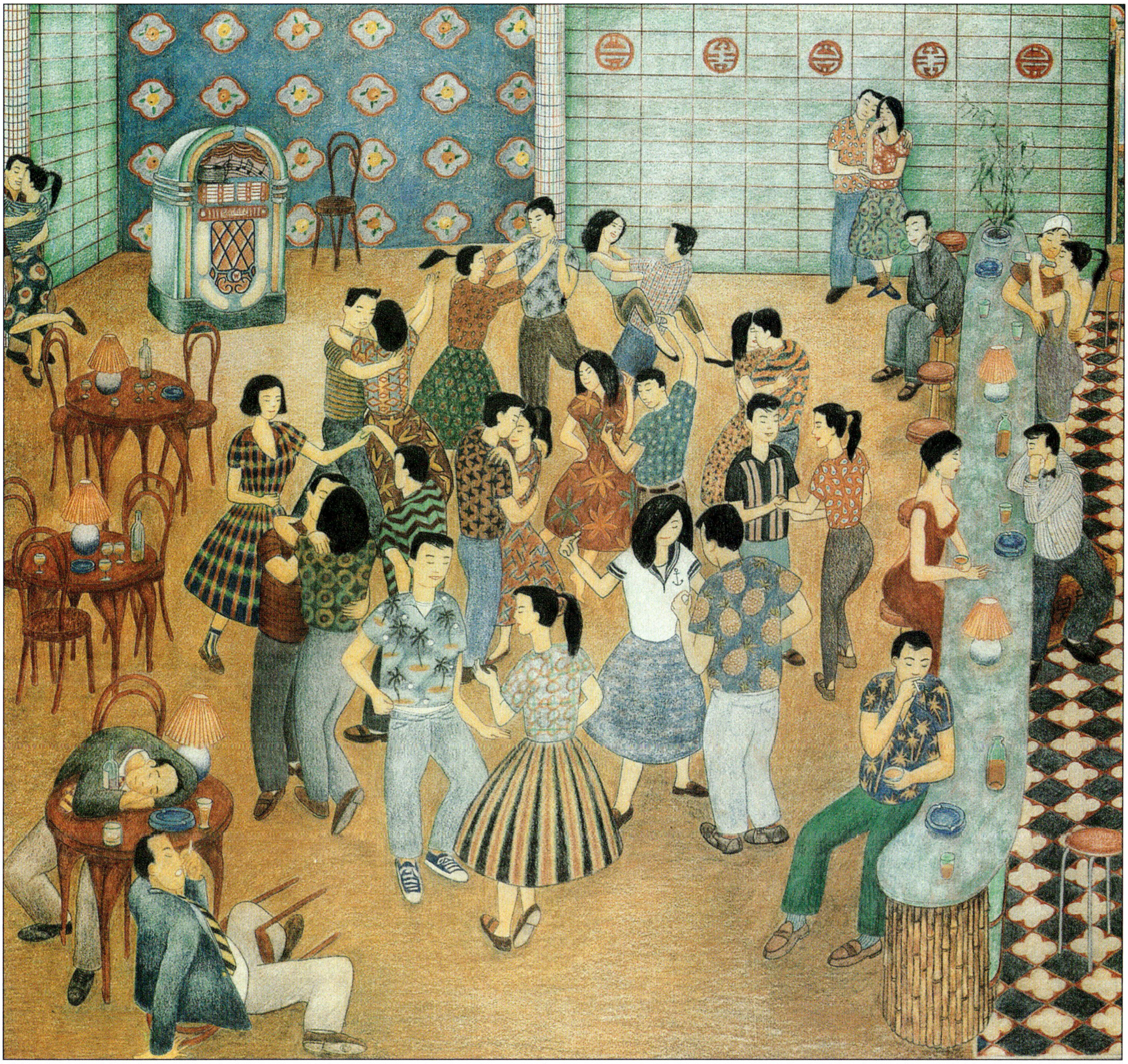

DANCE by David Buggins (colored pencil)

A strong thread of narrative runs through this composition, with the figures in the grouping mostly sorted into pairs, their attitudes suggesting different "stories" about their individual relationships and common enjoyment of the dancehall atmosphere. The artist has used simple shading to fill every shape with color and has added many interesting details of pattern and texture using a range of pencil marks.

Figure of a Young Man in Acrylic

This painting had to be done fairly quickly because standing poses are always tiring and cannot be kept up with any comfort for very long periods. The artist therefore gave the model a few minutes to settle thoroughly and comfortably into position, and also stopped for regular pauses for rest.

This procedure illustrates how important it is to remember that when painting the human form you are actually painting a person. You should not become so absorbed in paint and technique that you forget that your subject is human. Moreover, bearing this factor in mind can often help the finished picture. The breaks and movement constantly bring the artist back to the realization that something living is being painted and therefore calls upon the artist to ensure a lively rendering rather than a stagnant composition.

Using a large brush much of the time, the artist sketched in the main features rapidly. A lot of the original warm tint was left alone, to show through and act as a solid base for the lighter and darker planes painted on top. In order to allow the tint to show through, the artist applied the flesh colors – lighter and darker, warmer and cooler – quite thinly and transparently. He also used the "dry brush" method to give a layer of broken color.

Because the flesh-colored tint was chosen to establish a tone for the figure, it became necessary to re-establish the white wall before the artist could make the tones and colors of the figure work together.

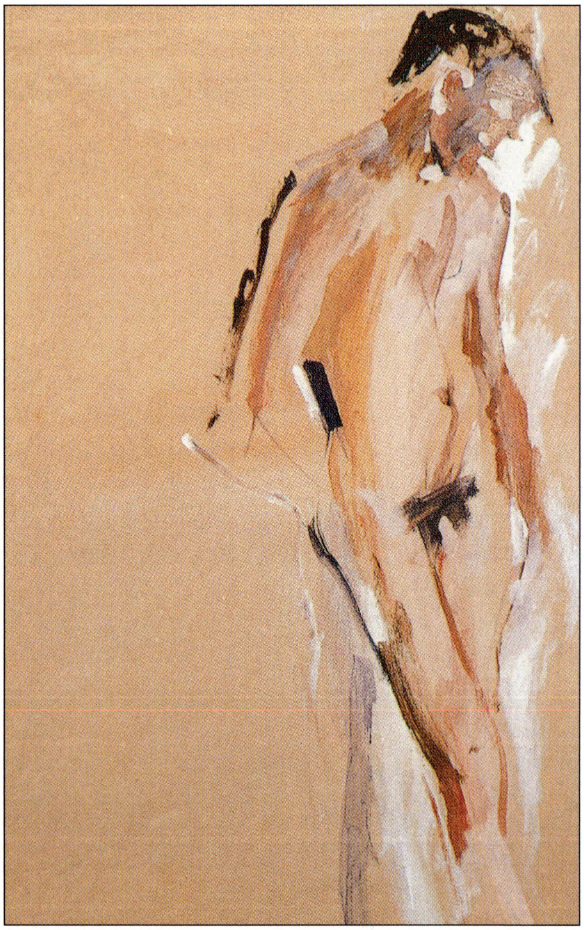

1 White emulsion mixed with raw sienna and cobalt blue is used to establish a middle tone over the whole canvas. This can now be lightened and developed with the rest of the painting. Using a small decorator's brush and working in sweeping strokes, the artist blocks in the figure with raw umber, red oxide, and Payne's gray.

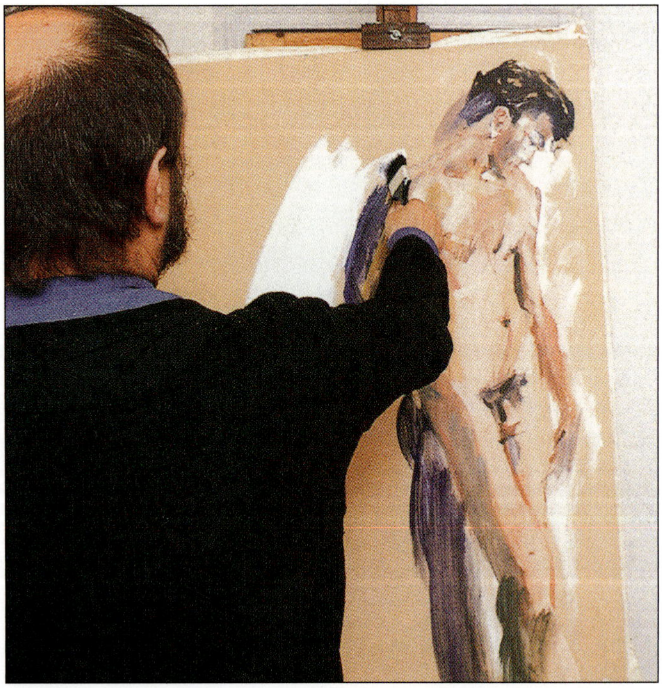

2 Background tones are blocked in around the figure. The new, light background color relates to those general tones already established on the subject.

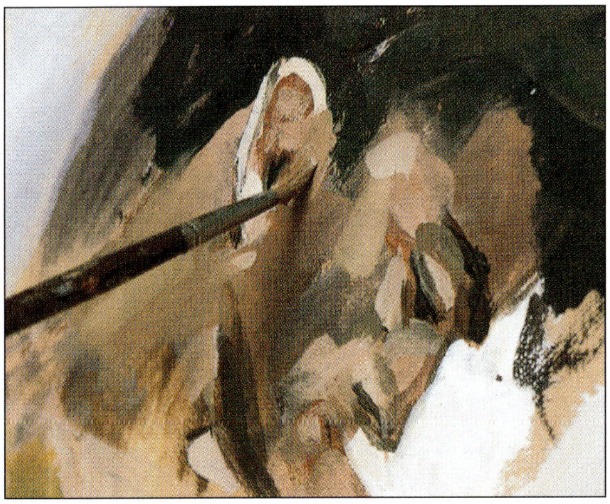

3 The head is treated in the same broad terms as the rest of the figure. Chromium oxide green is added to the basic flesh colors to establish the dark, cool, shadow areas.

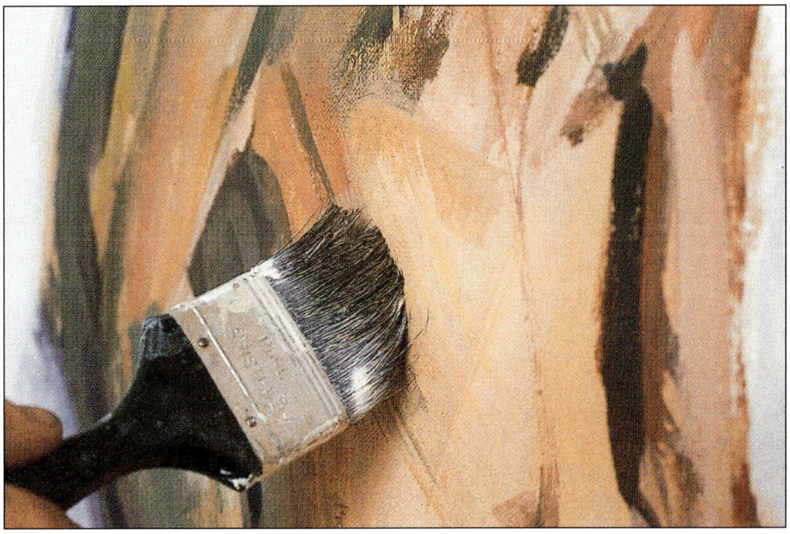

4 Broad planes of light across the abdomen are painted with a large decorator's brush. Working with a big brush encourages the artist to concentrate on the basic forms within the figure. It also produces a lively and spontaneous paint surface – something which is often sacrificed in very detailed and highly finished works.

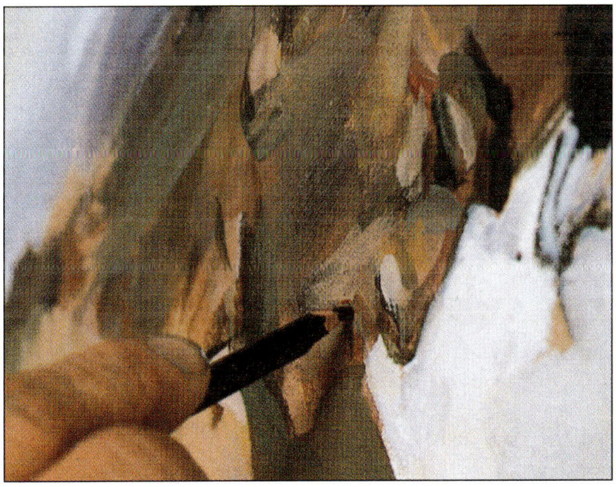

5 With a soft drawing pencil the artist works into the features, defining and strengthening the outlines to bring out the character of the young man's face. The loosely scribbled pencil lines introduce fresh texture into the work as well as tightening up the painting in these final stages.

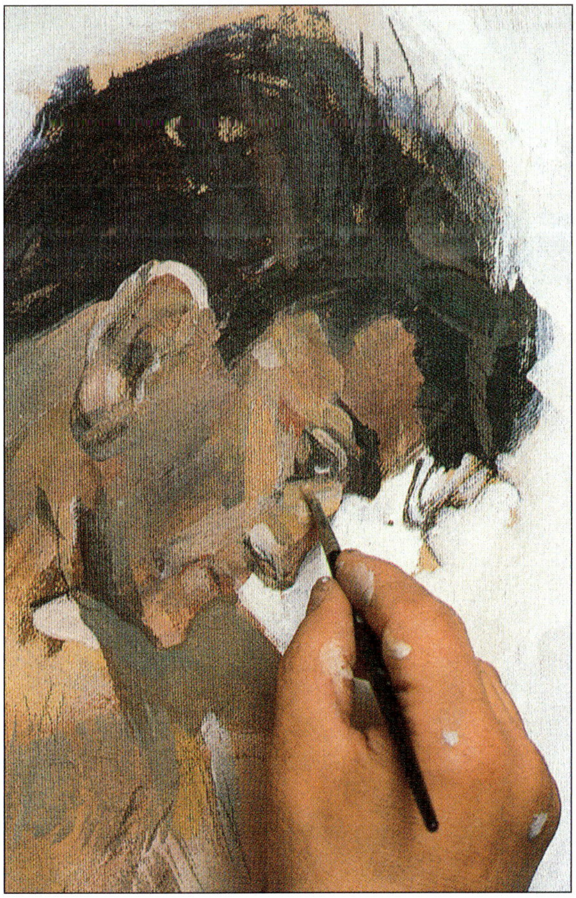

6 A small sable brush is used for some final touching up. Here the artist develops the fine planes around the eyes. These final touches should be kept to a minimum – it is not necessary to disguise and blend the larger brush strokes. Overworking will destroy the fresh, bold paintwork.

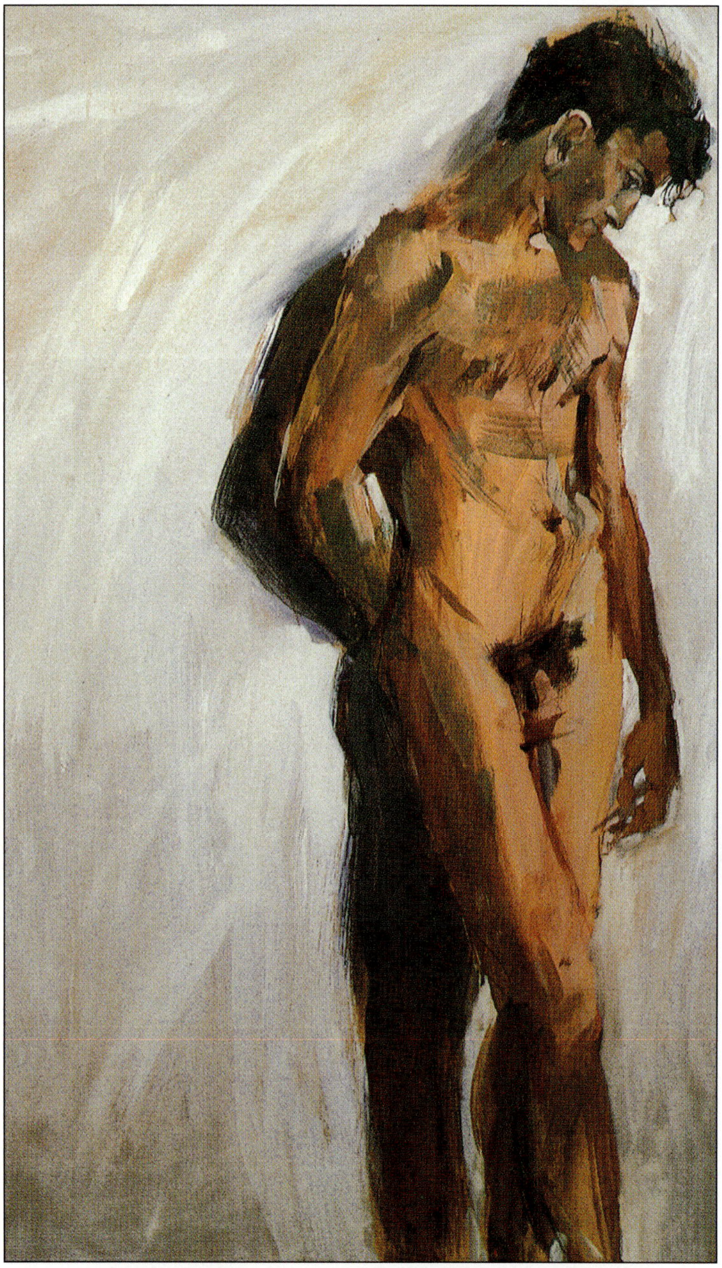

LEFT: The finished picture.

THE FIGURE SEEN DIFFERENTLY

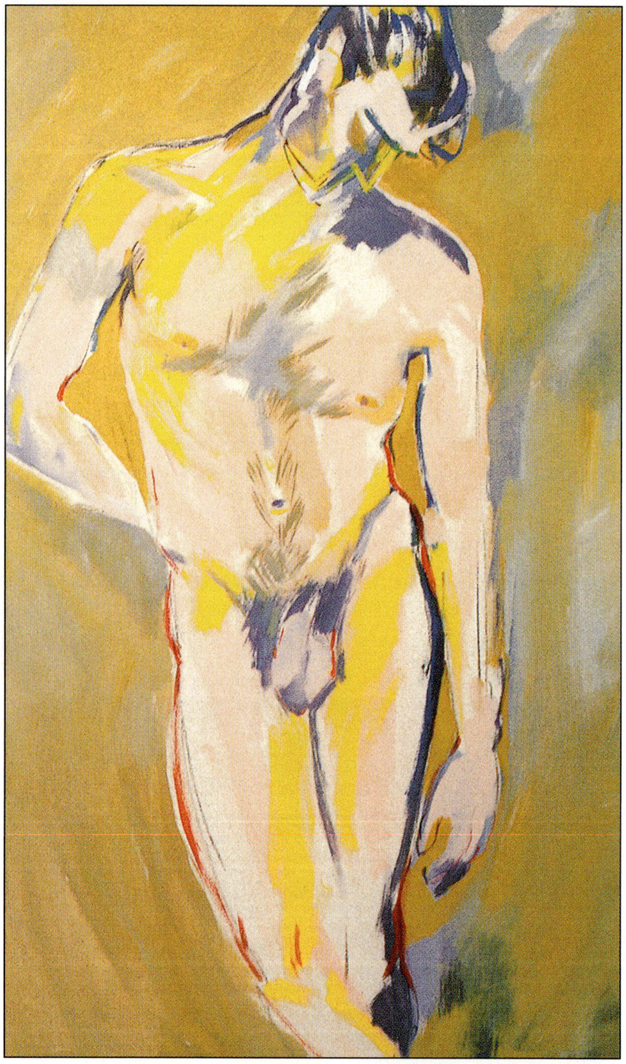

In the picture on the right, the artist used a different method, the negative and positive technique. Because she was working on a large scale, she used large brushes and confident strokes. She painted intuitively, without too much concern for light and shade. The danger here is that the painting will end up merely as lines and shapes without any real form, more like a flat pattern, whereas the objective was to achieve a more substantial representation of the living human form. One of the ways in which she overcame this problem was to vary the outlines. For instance, on the arms she used a bright and positive outline on one side, with a negative white line on the other. Thus the rounded arm is already given a three-dimensional form even before the final colors are applied. It could so easily have simply become a flat color between two lines on a flat surface, instead of an "arm."

She began by drawing the subject lightly in charcoal. The drawing looks casual, but she has in fact given herself quite a precise structure on which to work. It is a light drawing which will fade into insignificance during the ensuing stages of the work.

She did not use a rigidly systematic approach – that is, doing the outlines and then filling in the large areas of color or vice versa. Instead, she moved from one area to another, developing the outlines and the color across the whole image.

Offbeat colors were used in an impulsive way. Flesh pink, for instance, is not a color which most artists would take seriously, yet it is not used literally here but interacts spontaneously with yellows and blues; therefore it does not pretend to be "skin" color, but reflects the personal taste and technique of the artist.

A Baby in Oil

In this painting the artist has relied more on instinct than analysis and planning. This method requires self-confidence; it is not easy to boldly lay in free strokes without some anxiety over the outcome. With oil, however, if the artist lays down the wrong color or shape, this can be easily scraped away and worked over.

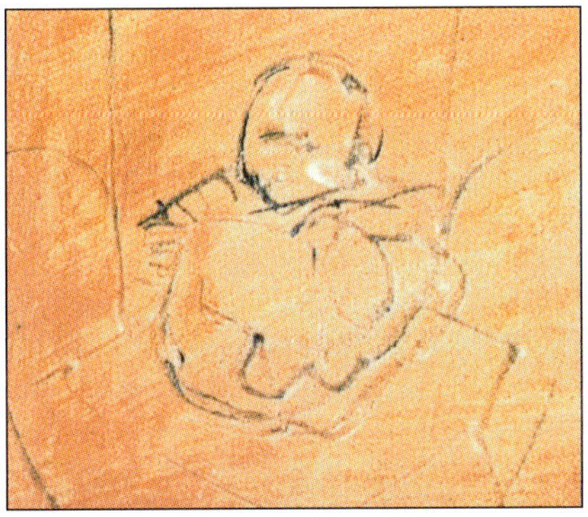

1 Mix burnt sienna and turpentine, and with a small rag, rub into the surface. Dip a small No. 2 sable brush in blue for outlines of figure and background.

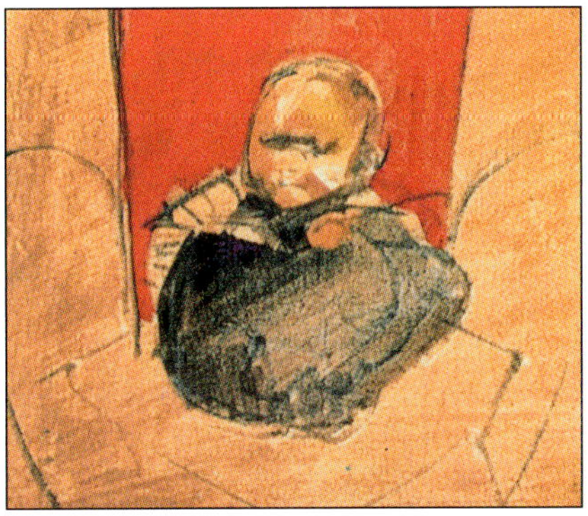

2 With a No. 4 bristle brush, block in the background with a thin wash of cadmium red. Use a thinned-down blue for the clothes, and red and ocher for the face.

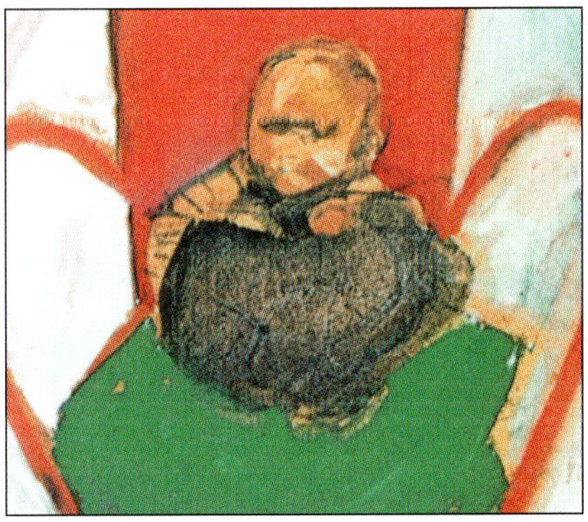

3 Using cadmium green, block in the chair seat with a No. 6 brush. Put in arms of chair in red with a No. 4 brush. Block in the white background and blend.

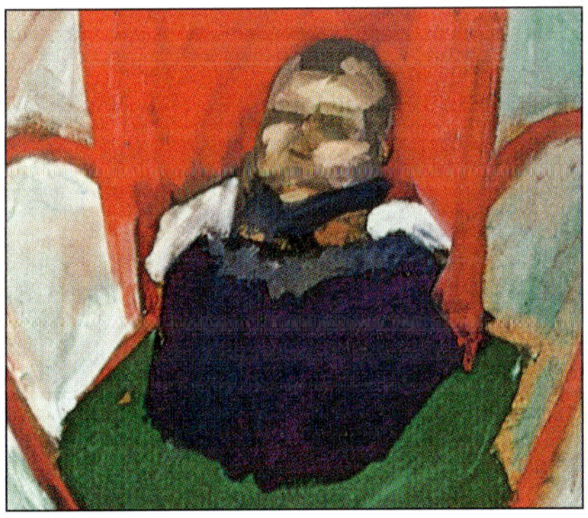

4 Block in blue clothes in ultra-marine. Use same white as for background to describe the arms. Rework the face with a mixture of ocher, white, and cadmium red.

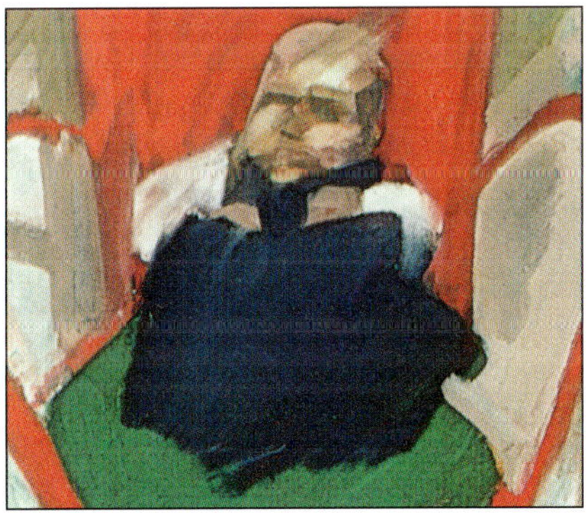

5 With the same color used for the face, put in the shadow of the chair. Mix white with cadmium red and put in chair highlights and blend with brush or rag.

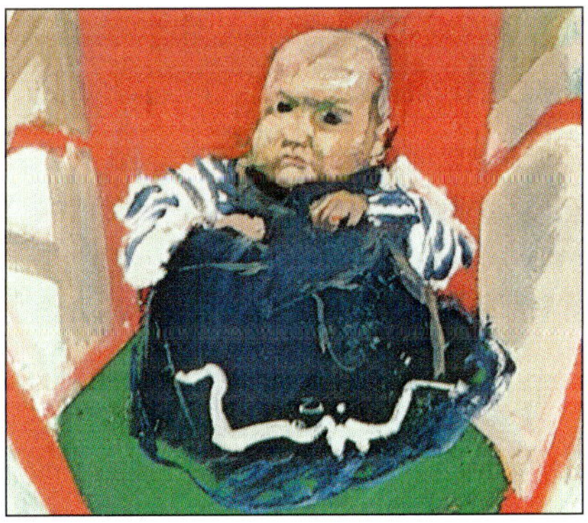

6 With a very loose stroke, put in white pattern at bottom of figure. With another brush, put in sleeve details with ultramarine blue and define the features.

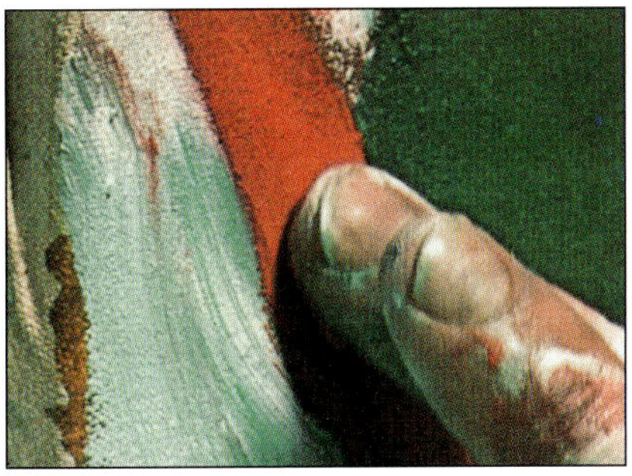

Fingers are often useful tools for creating an interesting texture and stroke. After applying paint directly from the tube the artist here smooths out the color with a finger.

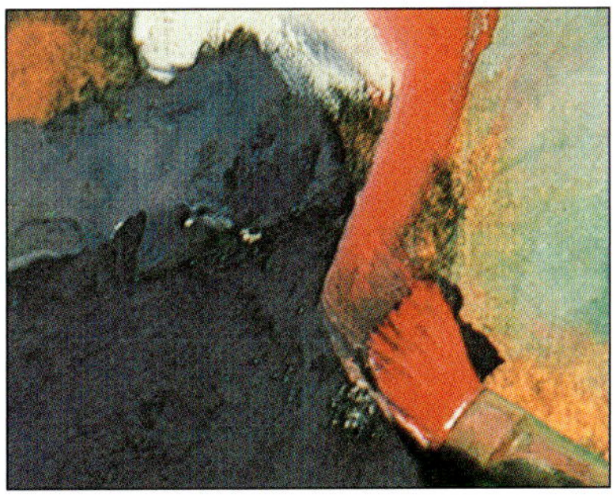

Working over the dry underpainting, the artist blocks in the arms of the chair beside the child's right elbow.

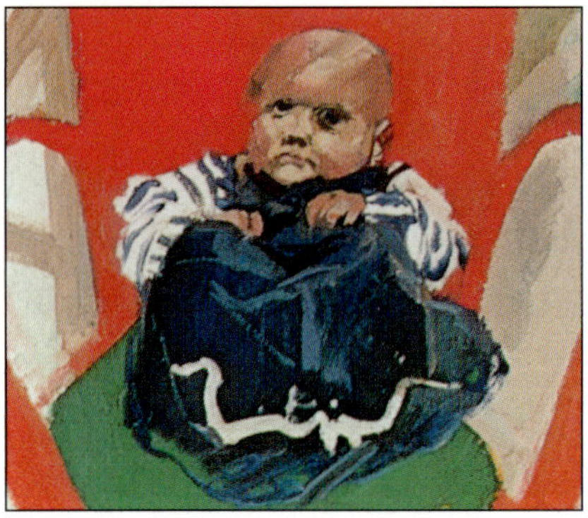

7 Work back into the clothes with the skin tone, indicating highlights. Add touches of red to the face and details in a greenish tone with a small brush.

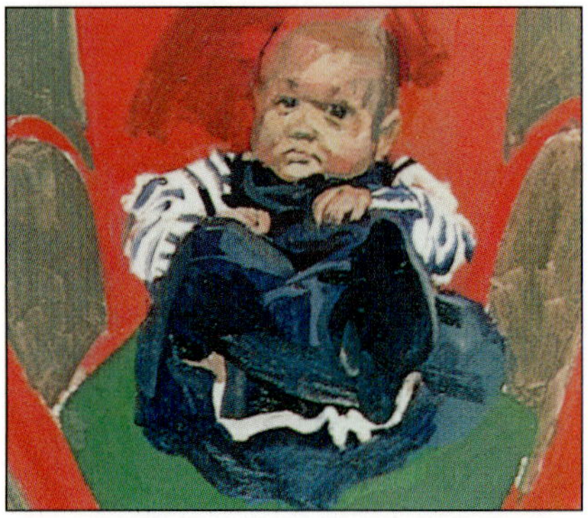

8 Mix burnt sienna, white, and red and cover the background. Use the same color in the face to strengthen shadow areas.

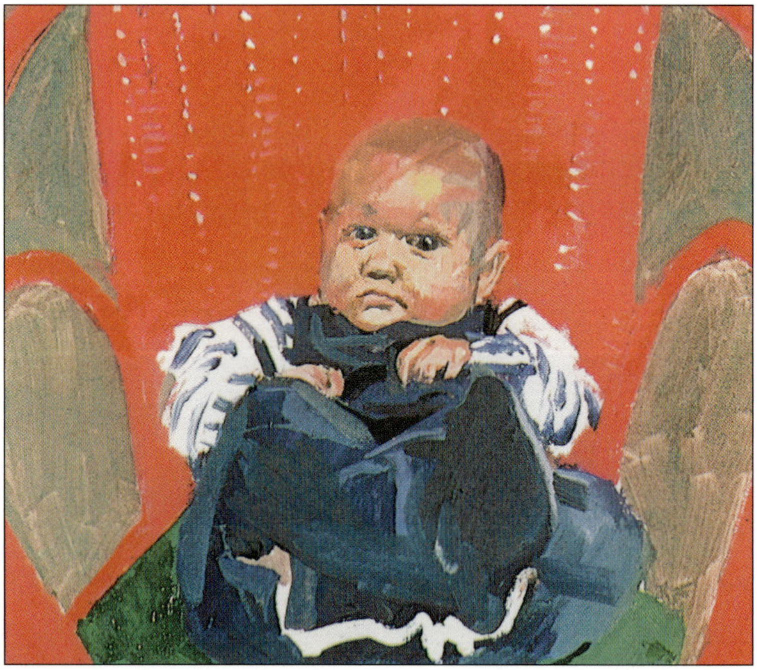

Besides employing a unique painting technique, the finished painting shows how much an interesting composition can add to any image. Especially in pictures of this type where the goal is to draw the viewer's eyes into the subject, attention should be paid to the placement of the figure.

The composition of this work is one of its outstanding features. The boldness of the colors and strokes and the oddly-shaped chair arms serve to subtly emphasize the smallness of the figure without overpowering it and draws the eye inward.

By changing the background from white to taupe the artist has allowed the highlights and features of the child's face to come forward. The loose, white stroke at the bottom of the child's feet is repeated in the sleeves, and the odd shape emphasizes the natural liveliness of the subject.

9 With a fine sable brush, the artist works back into the face to describe details. If the paint surface is still wet, these small lines of color can then be blended with a clean, dry brush.

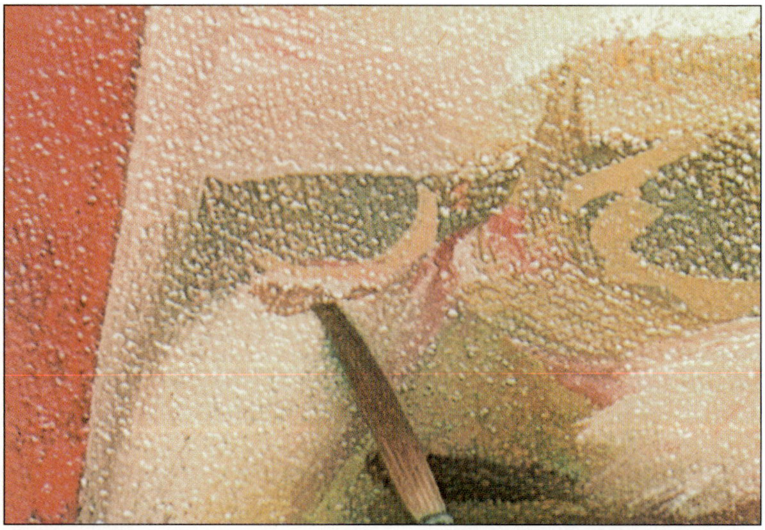

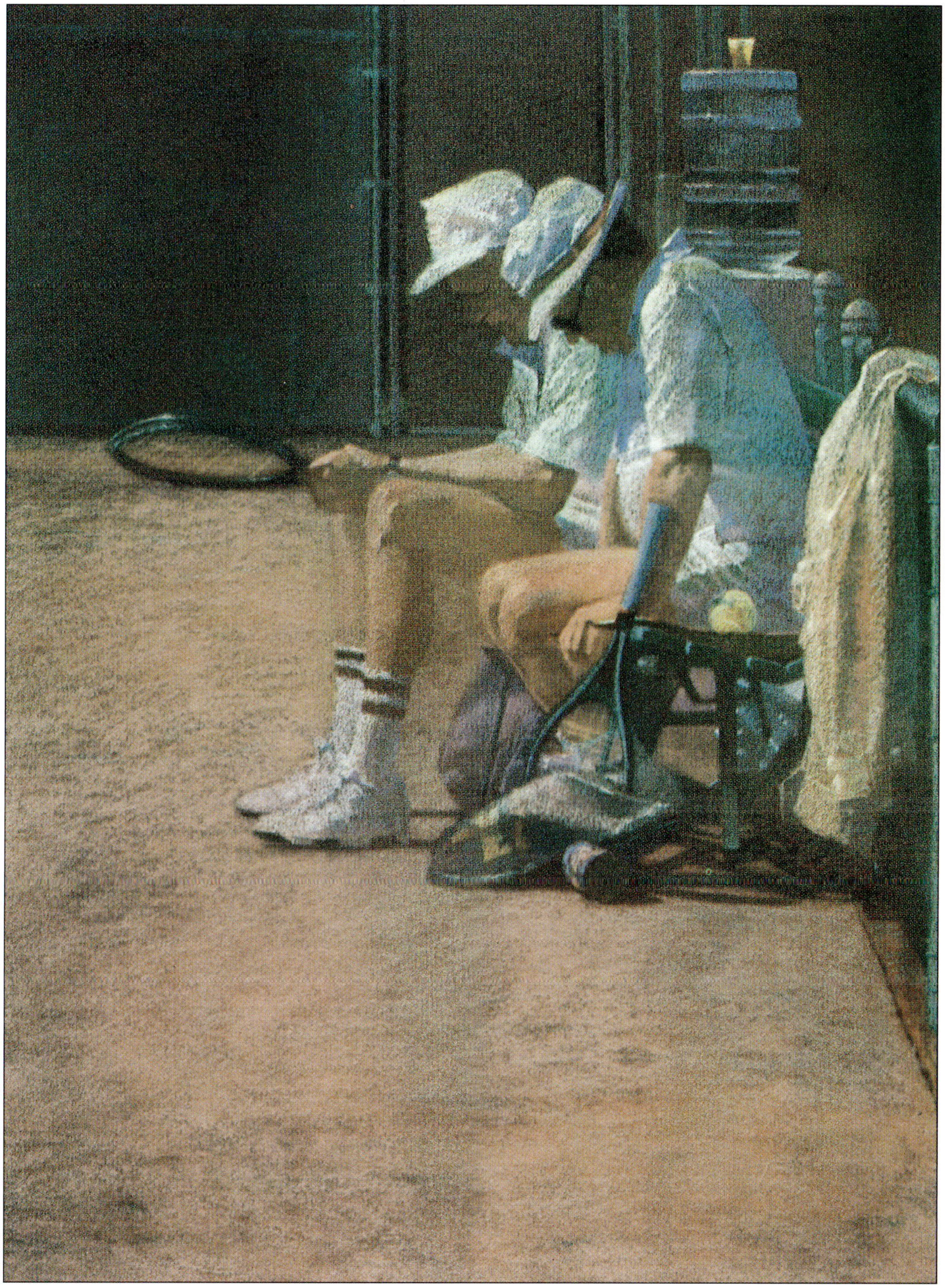

COURT BREAK by Sally Strand (pastel)

This artist achieves a remarkably precise sense of realism, yet the images are large and her technique allows a great deal of freedom. She first draws in charcoal on heavy watercolor paper, then rapidly brushes in watercolor washes to define basic shapes and forms. These washes are the opposite colors of what the pastel painting will be – for example she lays in warm ocher for an area that will ultimately be blue. The pastel overlays are built up with linear marks, working from dark to light and counterpointing the hues and tones. In later stages, side strokes and finger blending add to the weight and solidity of the forms. The quality of light is orchestrated by means of color. There is no white in this painting – the players' clothing is a brilliant combination of pale tints, including green, blue, mauve, pink, and yellow.

How to Paint: Birds and Animals

To some degree, animal painting is a specialized branch of art. There are painters and illustrators who make it their primary field, often as the result of a deep fascination with wildlife – some wildlife painters are also qualified zoologists or ornithologists who spend long hours observing and photographing their subjects before painting them.

But while it takes considerable skill, experience, and practice to produce paintings of scientific value, correct in every detail, many fine artists, notably Théodore Géricault (1791–1824) and Edgar Degas (1834–1917), included animals in their repertoire, and there is no reason why you should not do the same. Both these artists painted horses and jockeys, Géricault because he was a passionate horseman and Degas because he enjoyed the atmosphere of the racecourse and was fascinated by movement.

The main problem with animals is that they don't stay in one position for long, which makes it difficult or even impossible to complete a painting in one session. There are exceptions, such as cats sleeping in the sun; sheep, which don't move far unless you frighten them; and cows lying or grazing in a field. But in general you should get into the habit of sketching animals so that you can work your sketches up into a composition at home. You can also work from photographs, but this may give your painting a static quality unless you compensate by using the paint in an expressive and energetic way.

Pets are the easiest live models to start with, or farm or zoo animals, depending on accessibility. When studying the real thing, you may find it helpful at first to spend at least as much time watching the animal as you do drawing it. Give yourself time to get used to the continual movement so that you can start to identify the animal's characteristic details of form and texture.

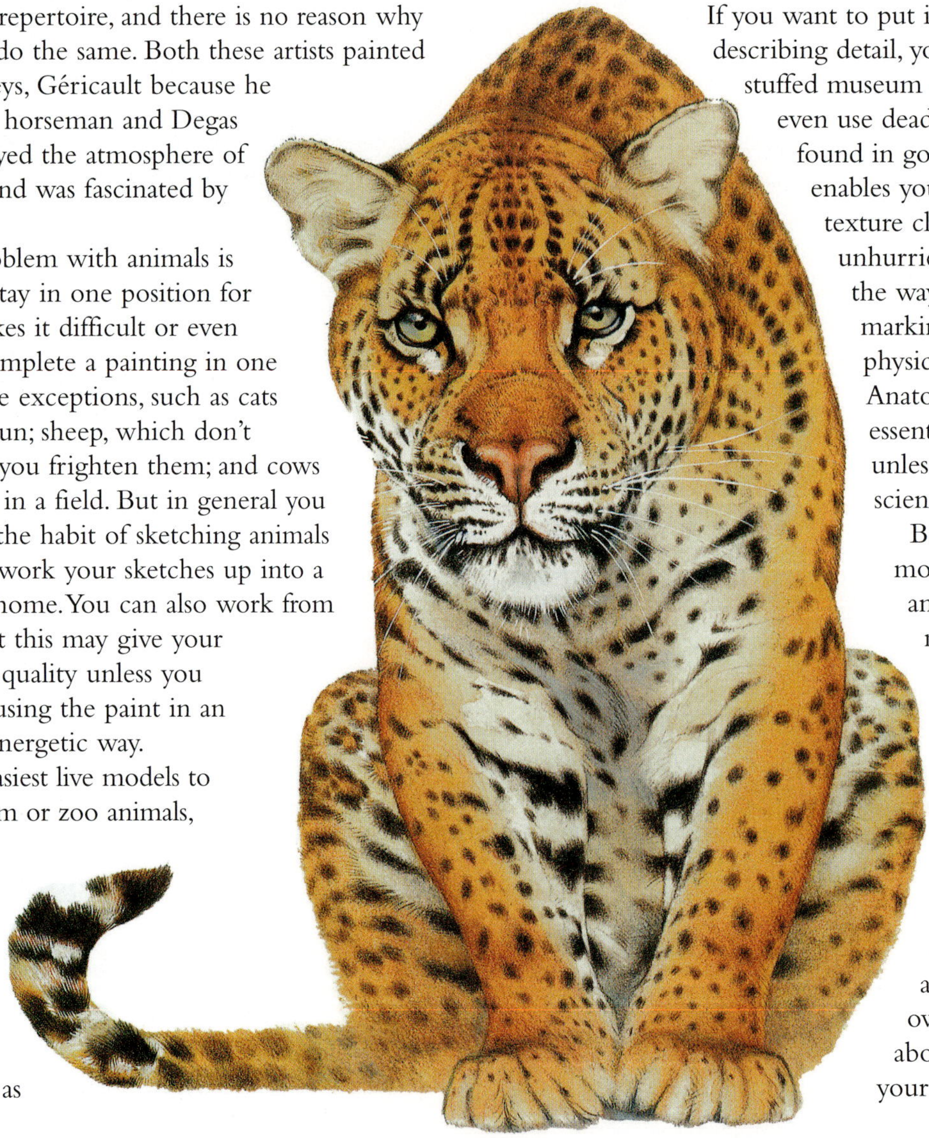

If you want to put in some practice on describing detail, you can work from stuffed museum exhibits; some artists even use dead animals and birds found in good condition. This enables you to study pattern and texture closely and unhurriedly, and to observe the ways a creature's markings relate to its physical structure. Anatomical studies are not essential to animal drawing, unless you want to take a scientific interest.

Bear in mind that the most detailed drawing of an animal is not necessarily the most realistic. When you look at a cat, a giraffe, or a bullfinch, you do not take in every hair, every color patch, every barb on a feather. A drawing or painting is always as much about your own perception as it is about the sum total of your subject.

Introduction

Animals as subject matter for the visual arts have a longer history than any other subject. The first images drawn by the human race depicted the animals that were hunted for survival – the prehistoric cave drawings at Niaux (Ariège), in France, are some of the best preserved examples.

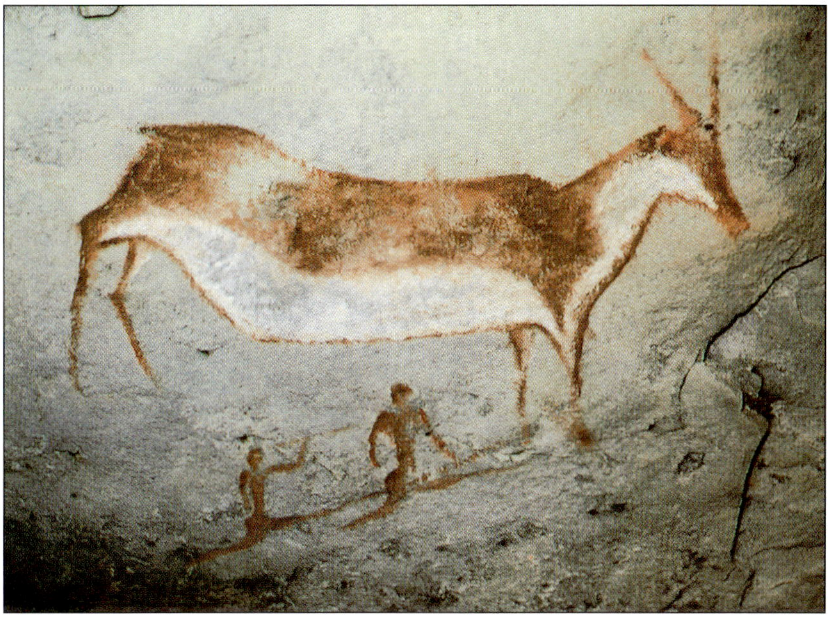

An eland painted by San Bushmen of South Africa. Note how large the animal is in comparison to the human figures. The eland was not merely an important source of food, but was also imbued with particular magical powers. Its relative size reflects its overwhelming importance to the artist. The white is powdered clay mixed with plant juices; the red is hematite with ox blood.

Lions, tigers, and hippopotamuses were frequent subjects for wall paintings in ancient Egypt and for relief carvings in ancient Syria. There are numerous Greek and Roman examples of animal images in mosaic, bas-relief, and sculpture. There is no period in art when animals have not played a major role.

In modern times, with the widespread use of mechanical transportation and with fewer people working on the land, everyday contact with animals has become more distant than at any other time in human history, so that first-hand experience of animals for many Western people comprises the particular relationship between man and his domestic pets.

Art has tended to reflect this change in social conditions with the result that many animals tend to be represented in art as cuddly and lovable, and the images are full of sentimentality. Even wild and savage animals observed at a zoo are often depicted as having all the ferocity of a large domestic cat. This has tended to turn animal representation into a secondary art form considered only fit as images for greetings cards. Our contemporary approach to this genre of painting is a far cry from the savagery and excitement depicted with such clarity in such works as the Syrian bas-relief of the lion hunt in the British Museum, London. It is not surprising that we find it difficult to draw animals with the directness with which our forebears saw them, for our sensibilities to and our relationship with the animal kingdom has changed so much.

William Blake, the eighteenth-century poet, engraver, and pamphleteer, might give us an indication of an approach to visual images of the animal kingdom more appropriate to today. His stunning engraving of a tiger with eyes burning bright to illustrate his poem, The Tyger depicts a primitive savage – but on reading the poem it is equally possible to come to the conclusion that the content is more about the conscious and unconscious savagery of humankind and that the tiger is used as a metaphor for the human condition. "What immortal hand or eye! Dare frame thy frightful symmetry" is a relevant question for today's artists, so isolated from the animal kingdom.

It is perhaps by taking this philosophical attitude to drawing the animal kingdom – portraying animals as a metaphor for the human character and condition – that it might be possible to break away from the sentimental imagery so often depicted. We are all familiar with animals being used as metaphor and in caricature by the political cartoonist, where the assumed character of a particular animal takes on the features of a person in the public eye. Many animals are associated with particular human traits – the courage of a lion, the infidelity of a monkey, the stupidity of a donkey, the wisdom of an owl, and a baying pack of jackals are commonly used as metaphorical images – and they have a long history of mythological (and religious) association.

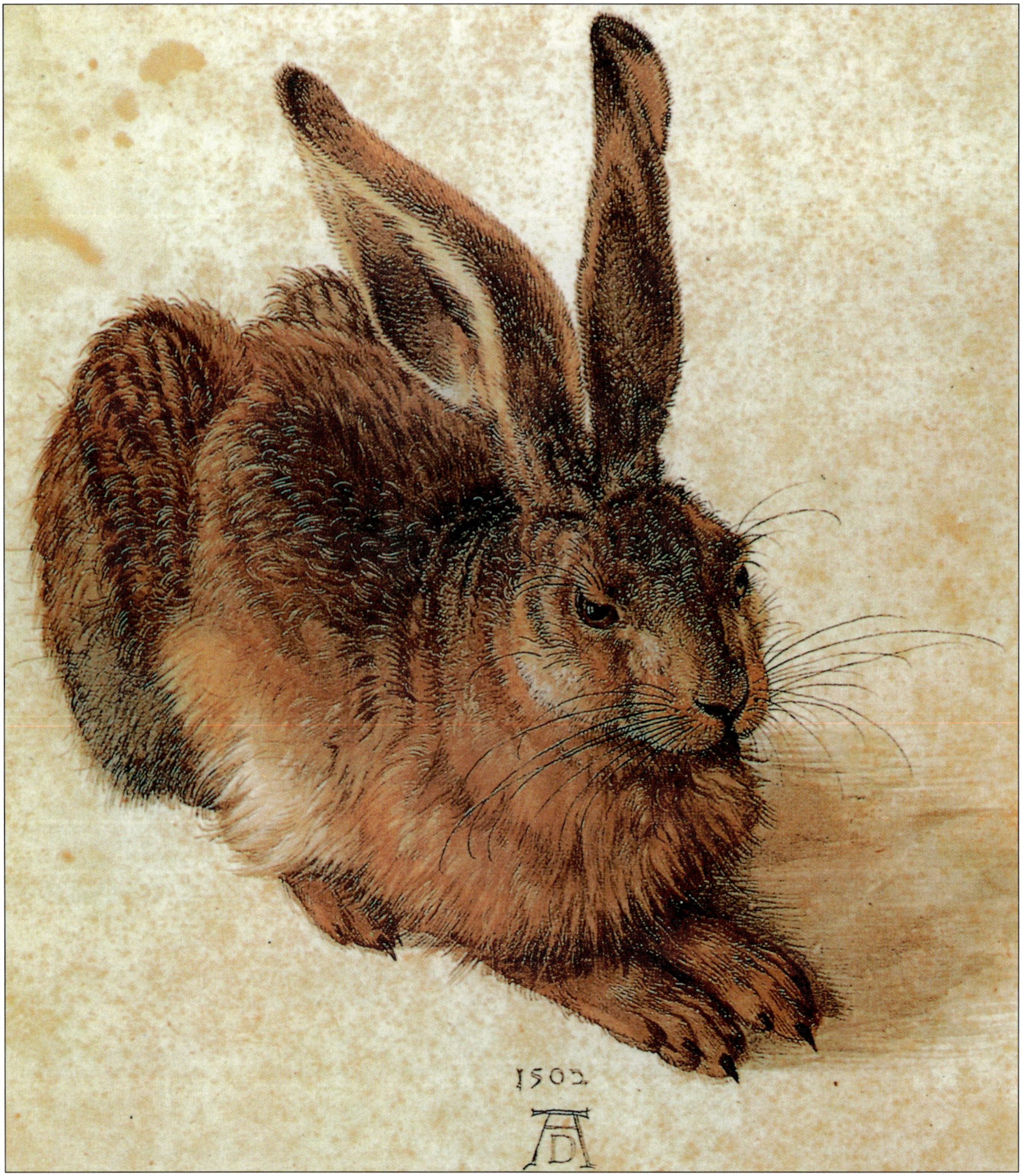

Dürer's marvelous brush drawing of a young hare is one of the best-known of all animal drawings. It is remarkable in the detail of its observation – every hair has been faithfully recorded. In the hands of a lesser artist this degree of detail could make for a lifeless drawing, but the hare is obviously an alert, living creature.

Choosing a Subject

Professional wildlife artists often specialize in this branch of painting because they are fascinated by animals and birds rather than because they love painting. When not painting they will be out "in the field" observing, making notes, and collecting visual information in the form of photographs and sketches.

But you don't have to devote your life to it in order to paint good animal pictures. However, painting wild animals will involve working from photographs or painting at a zoo. If you are interested in wildlife subjects look through nature magazines and other likely sources to amass a reference file of ideas.

There are two important things to bear in mind. First, basing a painting too closely on a photograph seldom produces good results and, second, there can be copyright problems. If you do a painting that is a recognizable copy of a photograph and try to sell it, you could find yourself in court.

It is probably best to stick to domestic animals that you can observe, sketch, or photograph first hand. If you live in the country you may have access to horses, cows, sheep, or goats, all of which make excellent subjects and will often obligingly stand still and graze quietly, allowing you to make sketches, or even complete a whole painting on-the-spot. For bird subjects you may be limited to ducks and geese on ponds and lakes, but don't dismiss them because they are so familiar – they are also highly paintable.

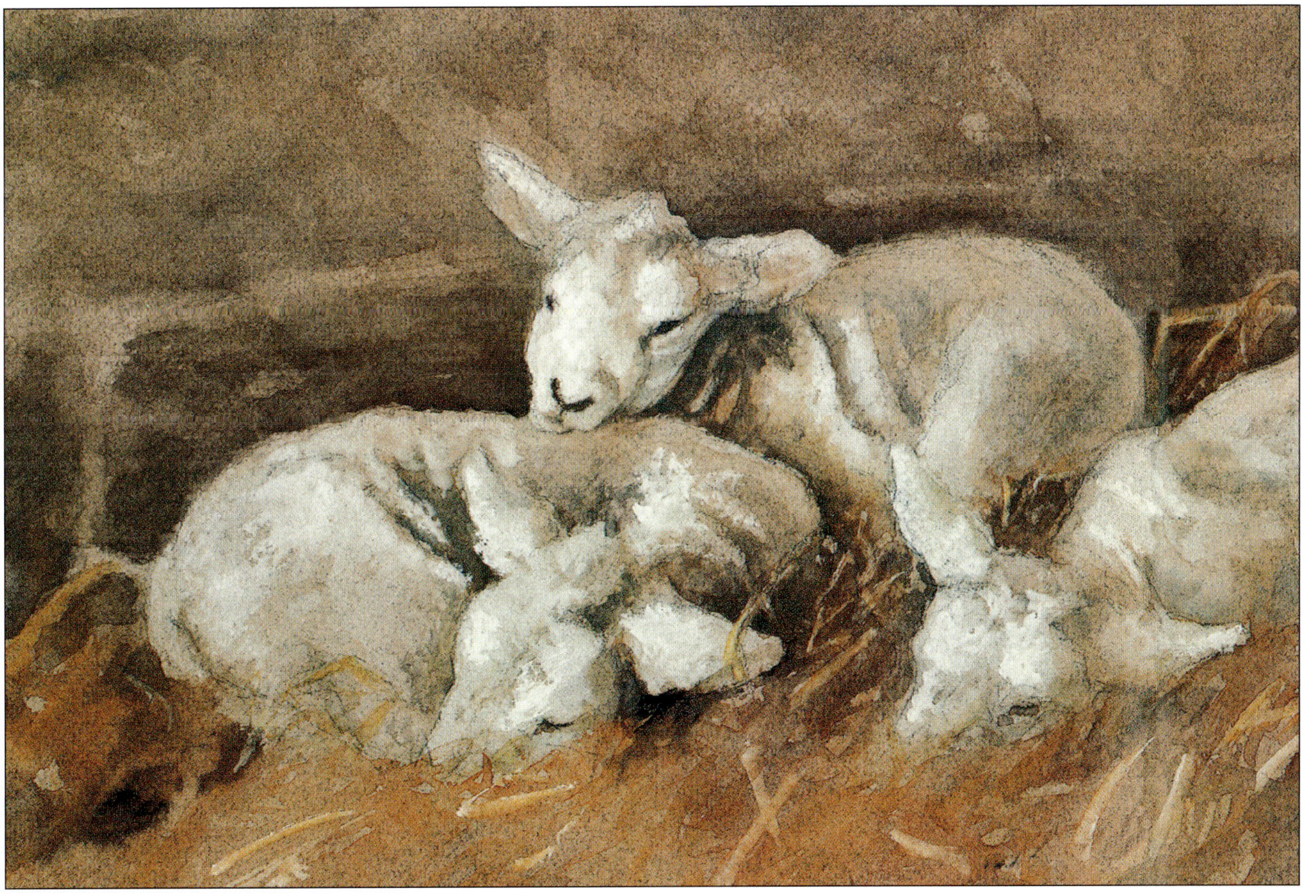

LAMBS RESTING by Gillian Carolan (watercolor)

For this beautifully observed study, the artist worked on a slightly tinted and textured paper, and mixed opaque white with the watercolor. She also used touches of soft pencil, most clearly visible around the ears of the lamb in the middle. The quiet color scheme and soft-edged quality suit the subject perfectly.

Animals in Motion

Although animals move most of the time, they tend to repeat characteristic movements. Cows in the corner of a field will, after moving, come back to the same position and eat in the same way as previously. A pet can often be drawn while it is eating; and birds in cages, or animals in the confines of a zoo often have a sequence of movements that they make around the cage, which enables the artist to depict them in certain characteristic positions. It is a good idea to work on several studies of a moving animal simultaneously, so that as it changes its position you can move to another drawing.

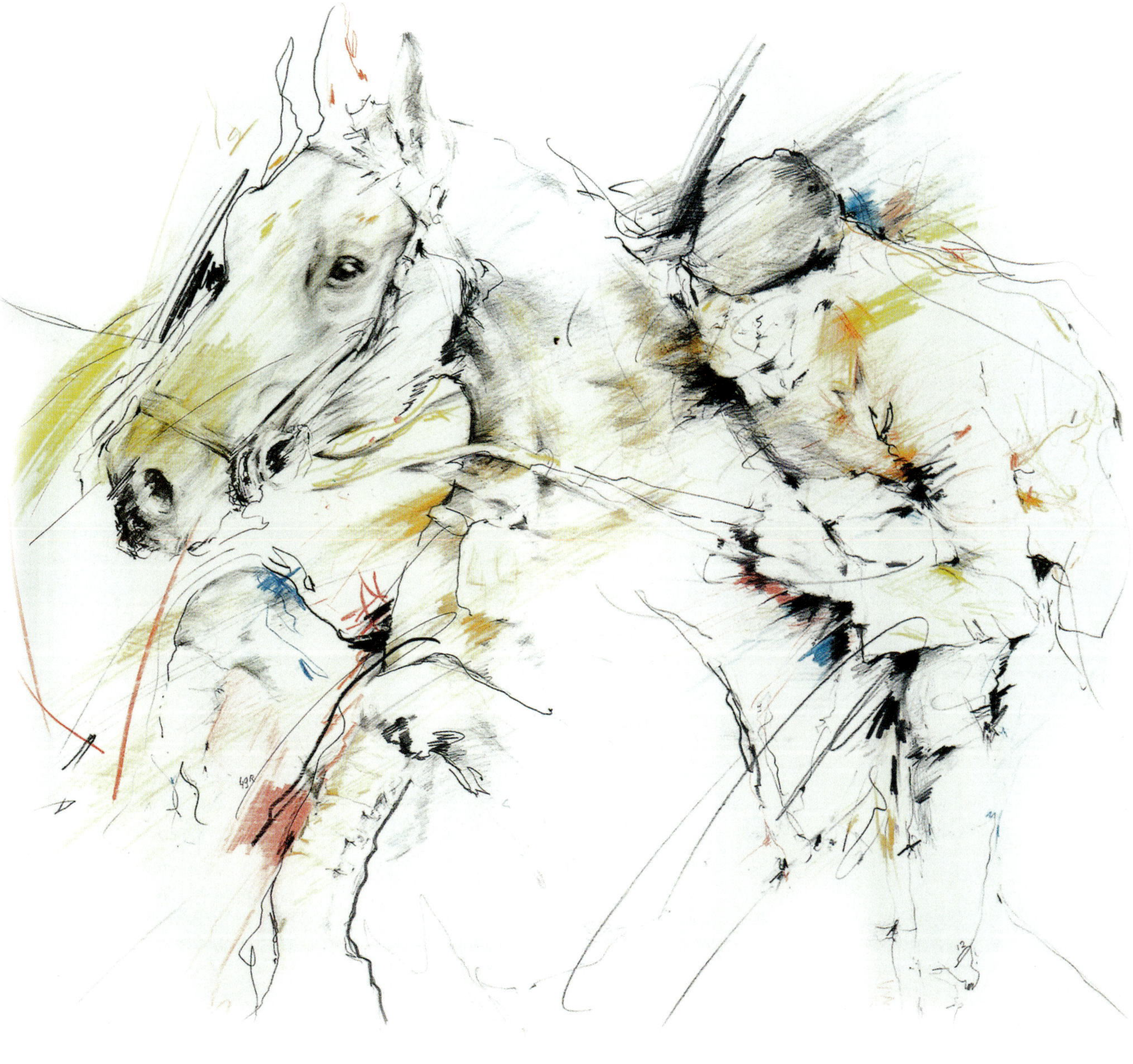

HORSE AND RIDER by Frank de Brouwer

The gestures of the artist's hand and arm can be seen from the rhythms of this drawing, giving it a sense of physical movement additional to that implied by the subject. The variations of line – emphatic black colored pencil over more tentative, shifting graphite pencil marks – enhance the vitality. The non-naturalistic primary colors that provide the mid-tones between black and white are also enlivening.

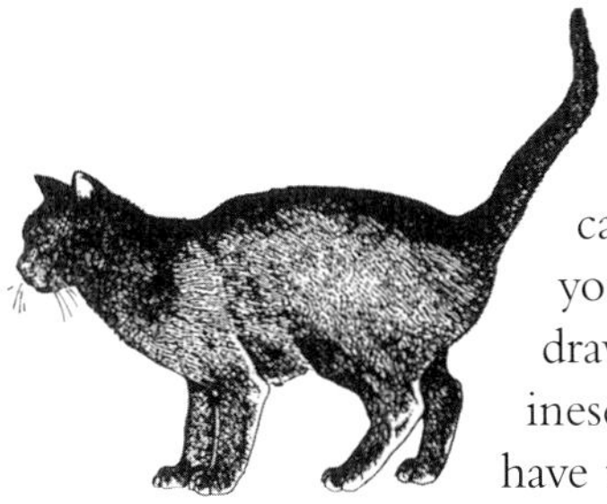

Animals are seldom still, and it is impossible to draw them posed as one can a human figure. So, unless you have an opportunity to draw a sleeping animal, it is an inescapable fact that you will have to contend with the difficult problem of drawing movement.

Movement can be portrayed in many different ways. Sometimes artists make the drawing itself convey a feeling of movement. They do not fix the object on the paper but give it an indistinct outline, or perhaps several outlines, to show that it is not static. A sense of movement can also be achieved through the style of drawing employed. Long, sweeping lines, gestures made by recording the movement of animal or bird with great speed, can imply motion. Generally, however, movement is represented by a single position that best characterizes the animal in motion. Usually you will be trying to select this typical position as the animal moves around. The secret is to observe the animal intensely and then to memorize what you have seen.

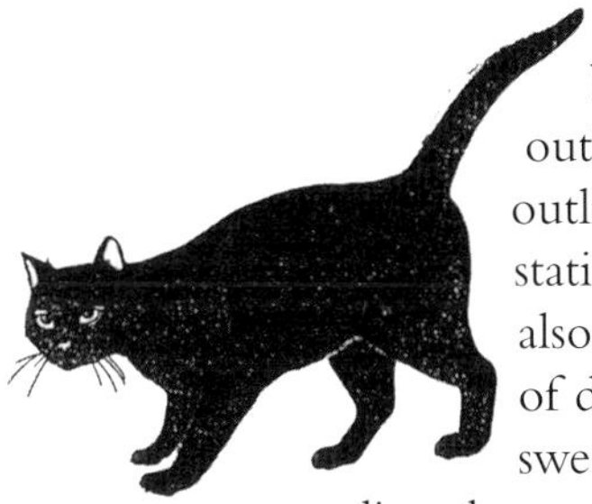

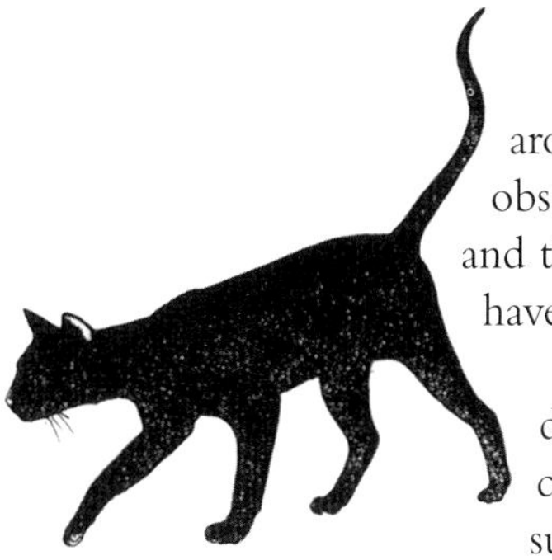

Now you will need to draw it quickly as far as you can. Refer back to the subject, waiting for it to be in the chosen position again, and then return to developing your drawing. Drawing in this way requires much patience and great concentration. It also necessitates a rapid, sketchy drawing style. This is not only so that you forget as little as possible, but also to help you capture – through the speed with which you produce the lines and marks – the elusive quality of movement.

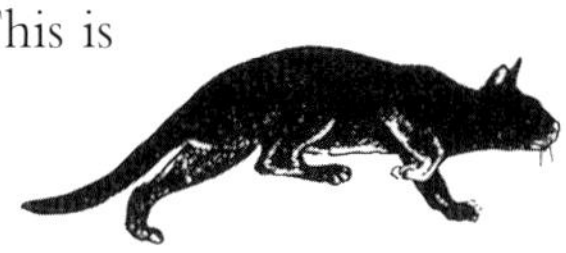

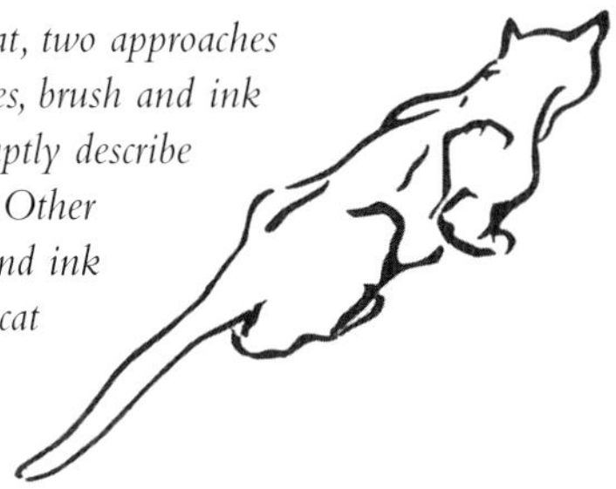

Among these five studies of a cat, two approaches are evident. In the lower sketches, brush and ink create rhythmical outlines that aptly describe the feline nature of the animal. Other sketches were executed in pen and ink and describe which parts of the cat were tense or relaxed.

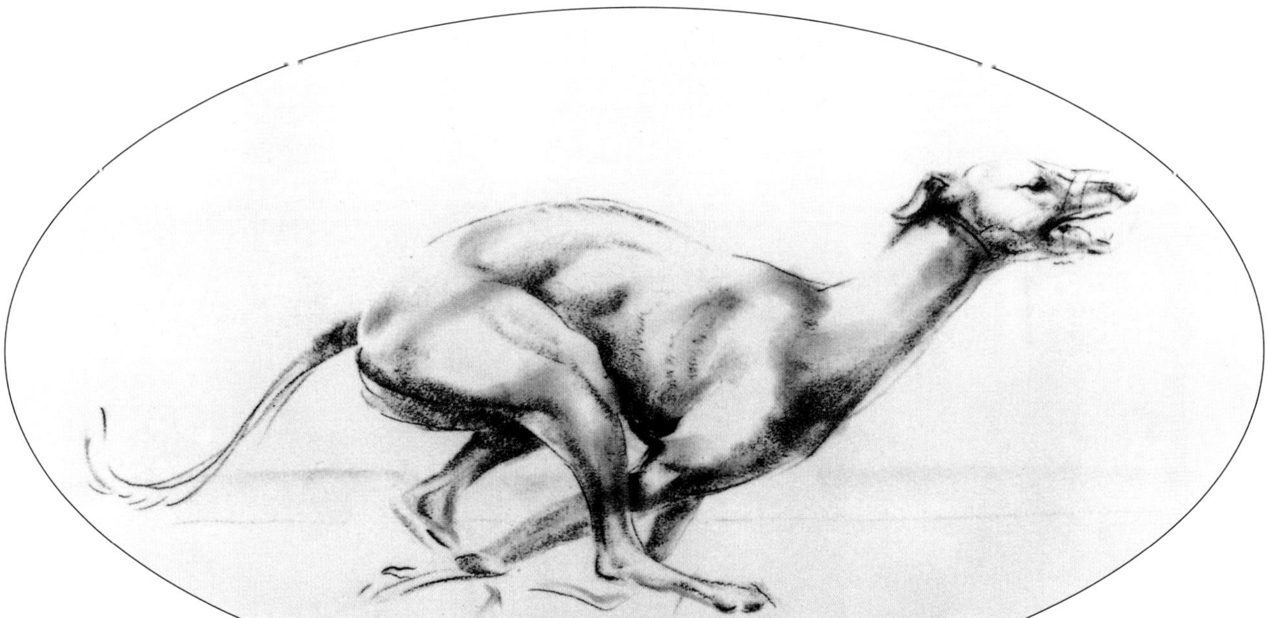

A racing greyhound is caught extended in mid-air. Yet (unlike many photographs) this pastel drawing does not appear static, even though the action is frozen. A sense of movement is created by the sensitive broken lines and dancing tones which animate the wave-like undulation along the muscular body, skillfully leading the eye from the dog's nose to the tip of his tail. The tail and paws are also slightly blurred as if moving fast.

Texture and Form

Not all drawings concentrate on textural aspects of an object, yet the fur of an animal or the feathers of a bird are so much an integral part of their form and character that it is difficult to portray such a subject and ignore its textures. As well as describing the feel of the animal, texture can reveal its underlying form. Drawing the texture as it follows the form of the animal gives the drawing a feeling of solidity.

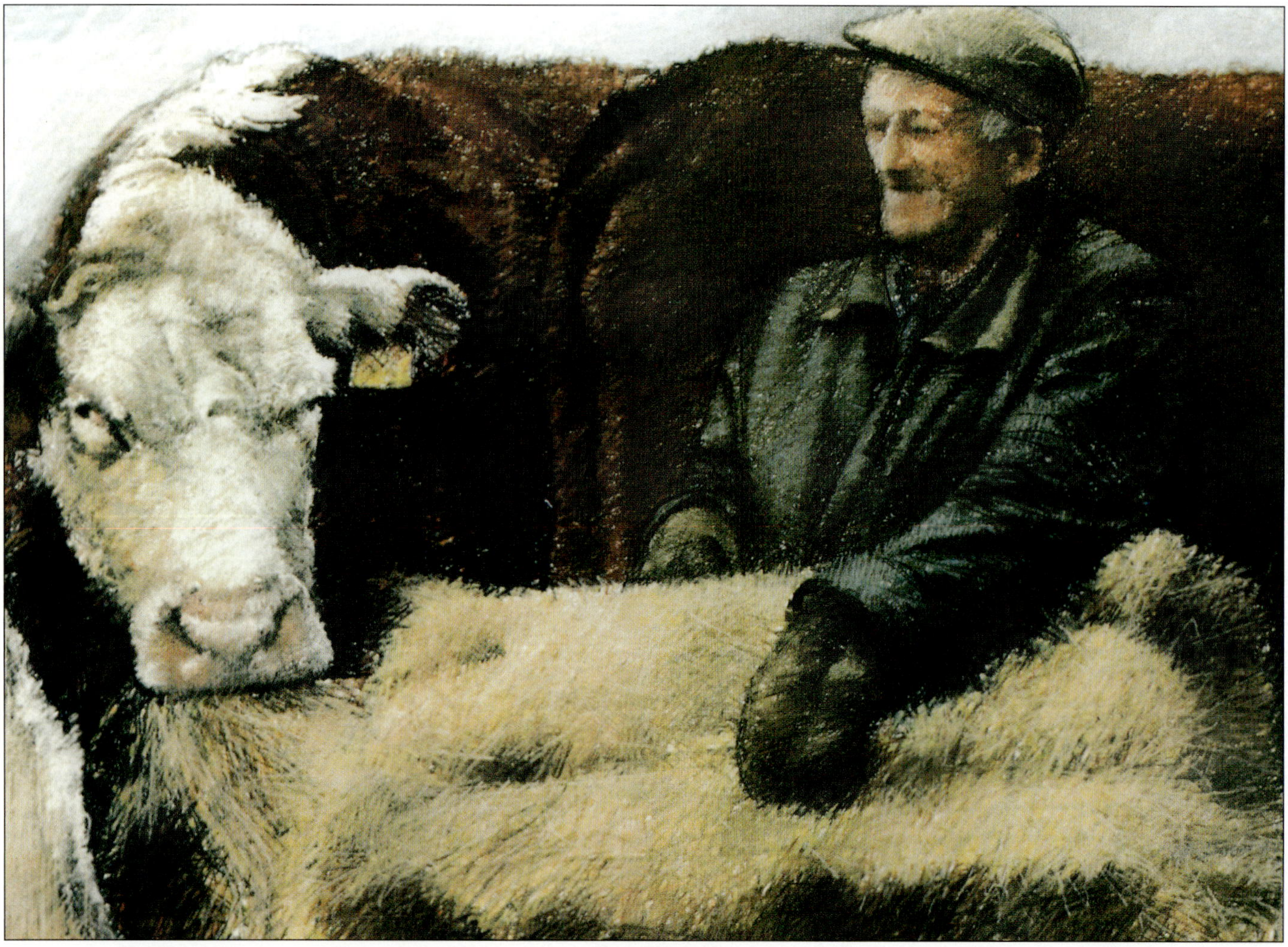

WINTER FEED by Keith Bowen

This combination of animal and human subjects conveys very clearly the context of the image and the scale of the massive beasts. The composition is interestingly divided into solid blocks of color by the strong vertical and horizontal stresses, but each color area is carefully modeled tonally, and given a distinctive texture built up with a dense network of individual pastel strokes. It is worked on heavy white paper, which shows through in tiny glints among the dark tones of the animals' tough hides.

Texture can also help to create a sense of depth in a drawing. In the case of drawing a brick wall, receding away from you, the bricks will get smaller the farther away they are. In the same way, even if the animal is small, the marks made to represent the texture of its coat will reduce in size the farther into the picture space they are meant to be, even over the length of the animal's body. Care has to be taken to choose a medium that will readily interpret the texture of the animal. Some media have inbuilt textural qualities. Chalk used on a coarse-grained paper will, for example, produce a broken, textured line naturally. Sometimes these ready-made textures can be adapted to suit a particular animal or bird.

A rule to observe when drawing animals or birds is to avoid trying to draw every hair or feather. Much can be suggested with very little. Make certain the outline shape of the animal expresses its texture, and look for distinctive marks or patterns that can be used to express the animal's underlying form.

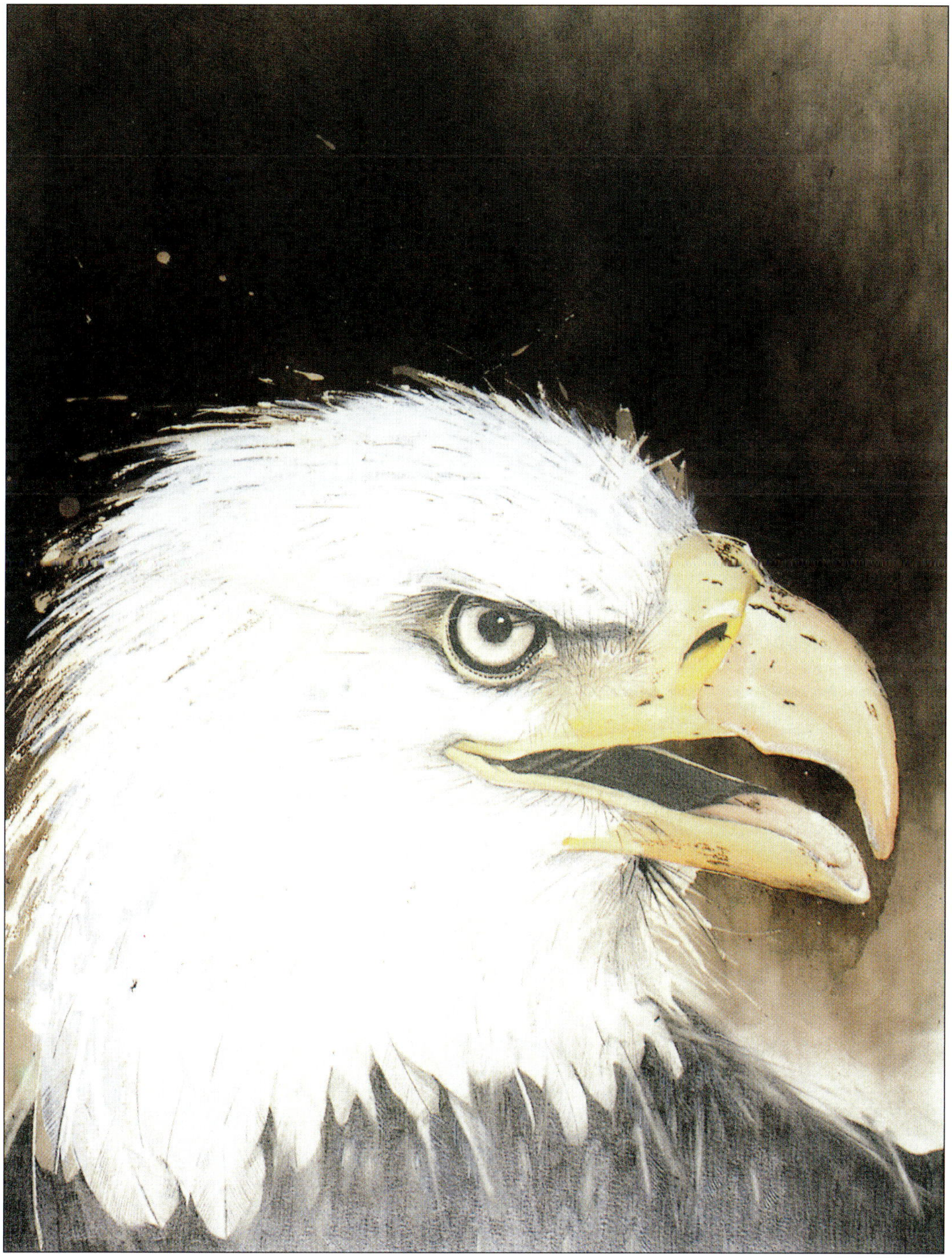

An unusual background texture was introduced into this drawing by smoking the sheet of paper, an accidental drawing method. The eagle's head was sketched in with pencil, and wax crayon added to take advantage of wax resist techniques. Next masking fluid and watercolor washes were used in combination to develop the texture of the feathers. Finally, the extremes of the tonal range were built up, with opaque white gouache forming the highlights – as can be seen on the tips of the feathers – and ink strengthening the darkest lines and tones.

Environment

If you are going to represent an animal in the context of its usual environment, you need to consider the degree of detail you wish to achieve, and the way your pastel techniques can construct an integrated image while appropriately describing separate aspects of the animal and its surroundings.

Unless an artist is making a study rather than a drawing or painting, animals need to be represented in an environment. This may be indicated only by a few lines or marks, merely to provide a hint of a background and give the drawing depth. Alternatively, it might be a feature of the drawing, showing the animal in relation to its human or natural environment.

With drawings of wild animals it is sometimes best to study the animals and the environment separately, bringing the two together in the completed painting. The only problem here can be that the two do not relate. The scale of animal to landscape may be wrong, or it may look as though one has been superimposed on the other. Experience helps to overcome this problem, but it is important when drawing the animal, in particular, that you indicate the relative sizes of significant environmental features.

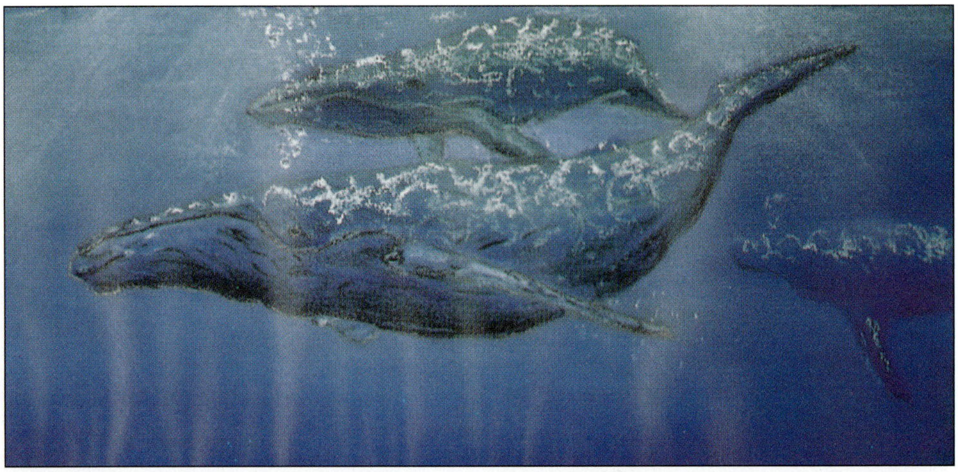

HUMPBACK WHALE COW AND CALF by Stephen Paul Plant

When the subject is marine mammals or fish, the character of their environment is highly influential on the form and coloring of the creatures. Here the artist interprets both elements as a composition of blended color gradations and fluid linear marks.

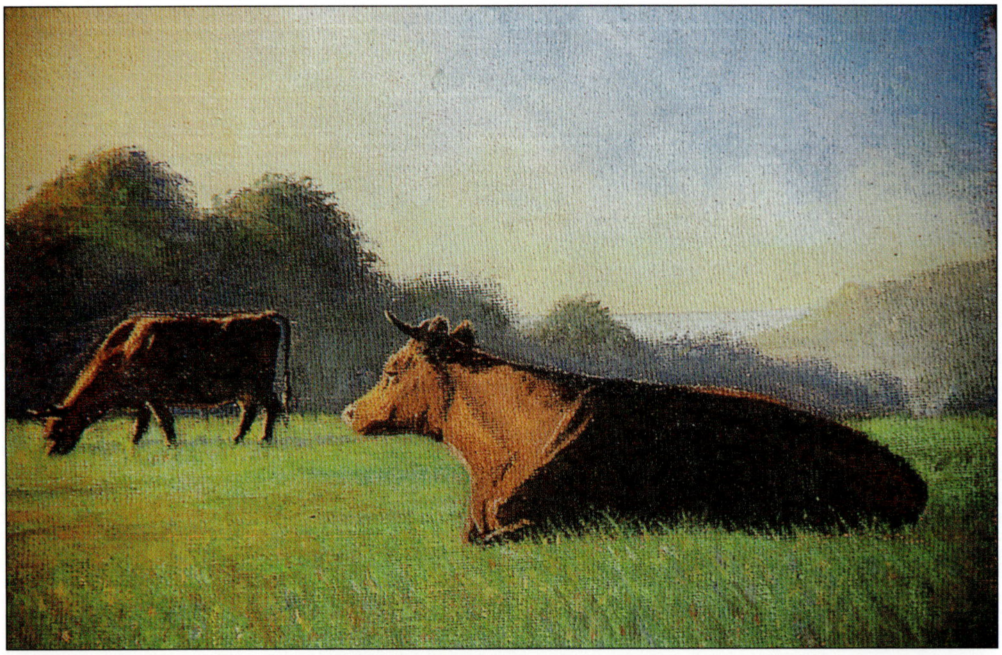

EVENING LIGHT by Bart O'Farrell

A more detailed approach has been taken to both the animals and their landscape setting in this tranquil painting, but the evening light silhouetting the forms has allowed for a degree of simplification. The painting surface is cheesecloth stuck onto hardboard, and the paint has been used thinly enough for the texture to be clearly visible.

Animals in cages are easier. It is possible to draw the cage and then fit the animal inside, so long as care is taken to observe the scale and relationship of the bars to the animal or the animal to the background.

Often animals are drawn in isolation and their environment largely ignored. But to produce realistic drawings of animals, it is necessary to draw them in natural groups and in relation to a typical environment of landscape, zoo, or farm.

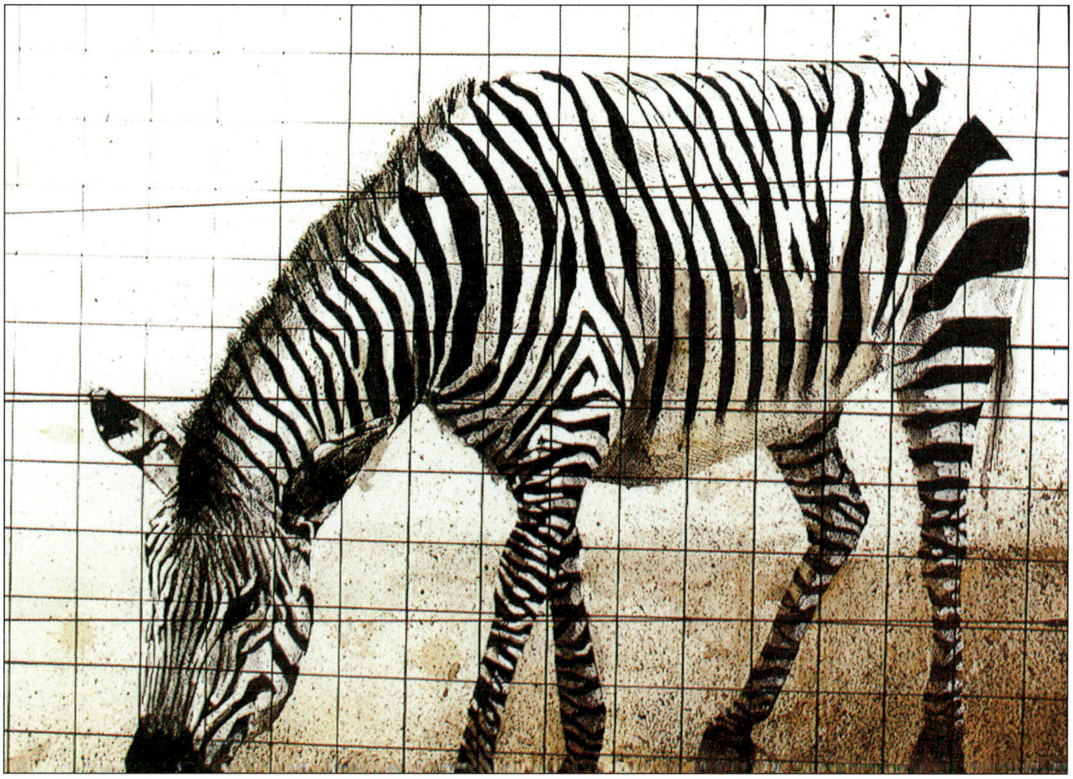

The animal above was drawn in a zoo. The striking beauty of the zebra's natural markings contrasts strongly with the regular pattern of its man-made enclosure fence. The zebra's stripes were brushed in with black Indian ink. Ink hatching, washes, and spatter techniques are exploited to develop this drawing.

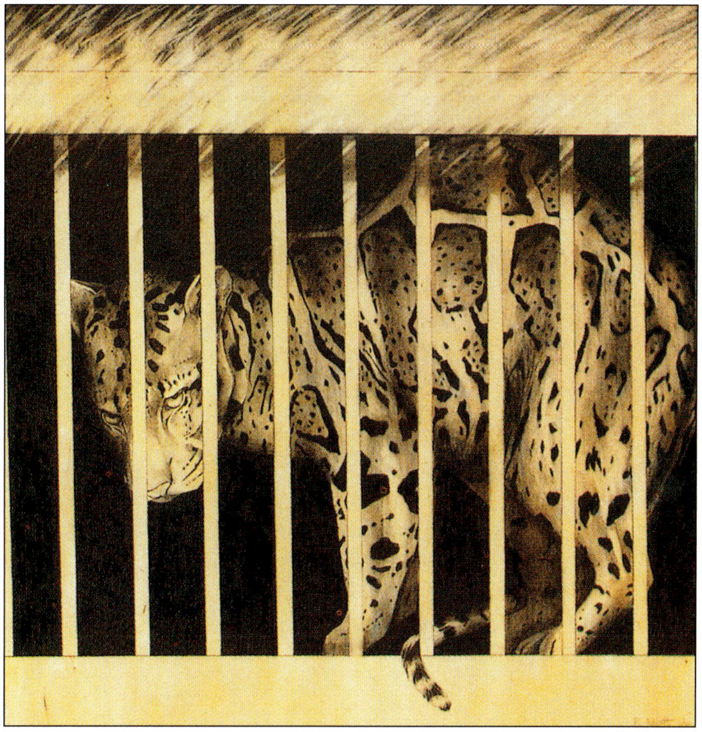

This poignant study of a big cat in a small, restricting cage was made with soft pencil on paper. The bars of the cage were masked out with tape before the dense tones of its shadowy interior were built up. Subtle shading was needed to portray the leopard's form and markings. An eraser was used to lift out the light across the top edge.

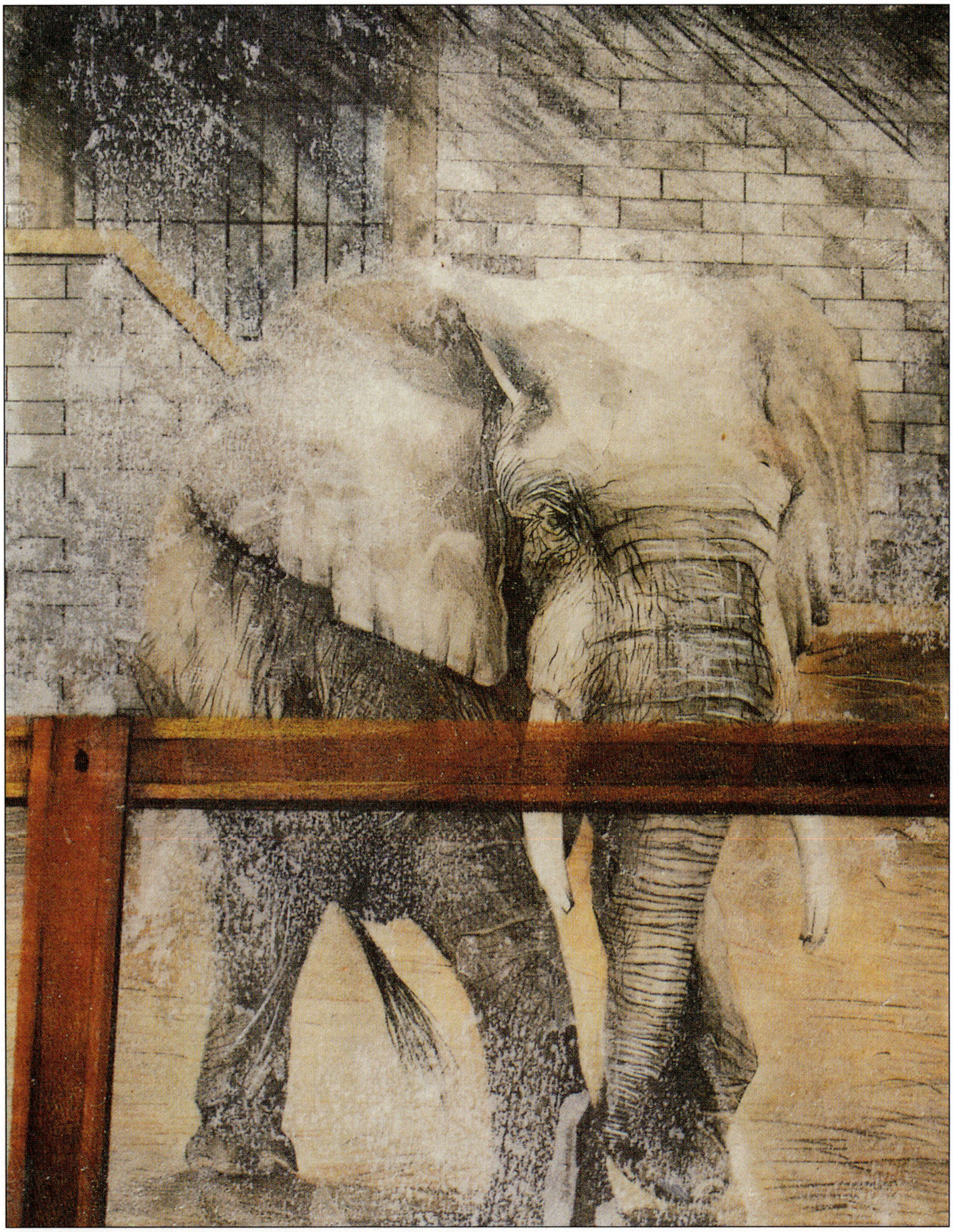

One important aspect of animal drawing is to convey the size and character of the subject. The elephant's massive bulk and potential power are expressed here by the mighty barrier needed to contain the animal. Pencils, crayons, and colored pencils have all been used in this drawing. The barrier was first drawn with crayon and pencil on a sheet of tracing paper. This was stuck in place, drawing side down, over the elephant drawing. The thinly transparent tracing paper acts as a veil, throwing the elephant back into the distance. At the same time, it has the effect of making the barrier appear very close to us.

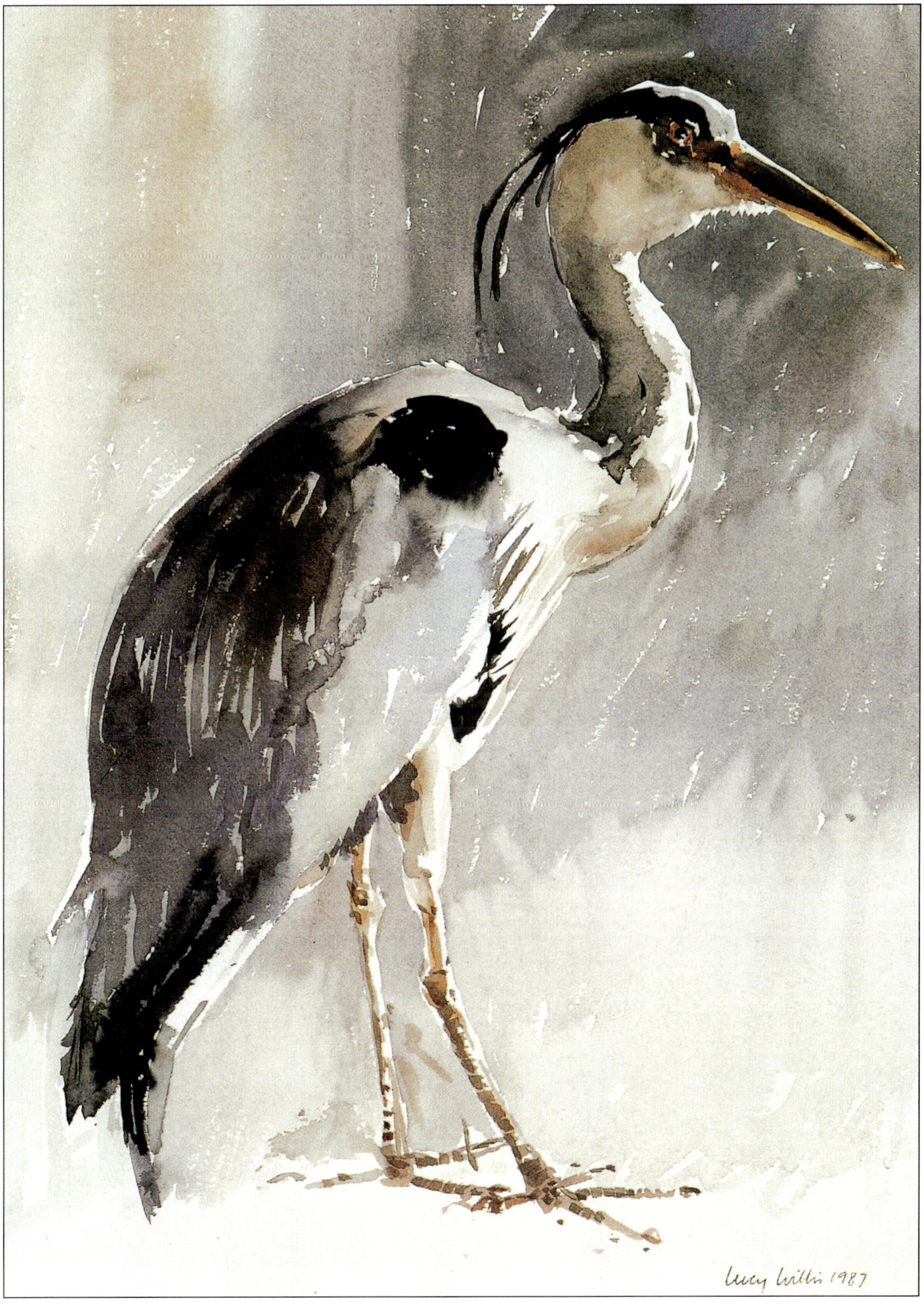

HERON by Lucy Willis (watercolor)

The form of the heron is described here through the counterchange of tones: light against dark and dark against light. In places where the tones are equal, there is often a subtle change of color which helps to define the shapes and adds interest to the background.

Birds and Fish

Birds and fish may present special problems, as they cannot usually be painted in their natural surroundings. There are notable exceptions – such as geese, ducks, and swans on lakes and ponds, or garden birds feeding from a bird table, all of which make attractive subjects – but for fish or birds in the wild, you may have to rely mainly on photographic reference.

There is nothing wrong with this – most wildlife artists make use of the camera – but it is important to observe the subject carefully as well as photographing it, or your paintings will lack the first-hand experience that gives them feeling and authenticity.

In order to familiarize yourself with the structure, colors, and plumage of birds, and the shapes and forms of fish, you could also try making studies from museum exhibits or consulting the drawings and paintings in natural-history books and magazines. The latter will also provide information on habitat.

Birds present the artist with an opportunity to test his or her drawing skills in recording a wide variety of sizes, shapes, and colors. Fortunately, there are many different places where birds can be studied. Many people have small birds in cages, and zoos usually have a selection of large and exotic birds on view. But, of course, wild birds can readily be coaxed down to your level if you have a bird table and some food to attract them or a vantage point which allows you to observe them unnoticed.

Often drawings are made from stuffed birds. Such an exercise can be a very useful way of gaining experience in drawing feather textures and discovering the main features of a particular bird. However, it is only by studying a bird

Every wildlife artist should consider keeping a sketchbook handy at all times. Over the years they develop into a vast store of information, there to be plundered for inspiration on days when it is lacking. In addition, a sketchbook is a good place to explore different media and techniques. Here the artist has sketched a wader using two different techniques: pencil and watercolor, and ink and watercolor.

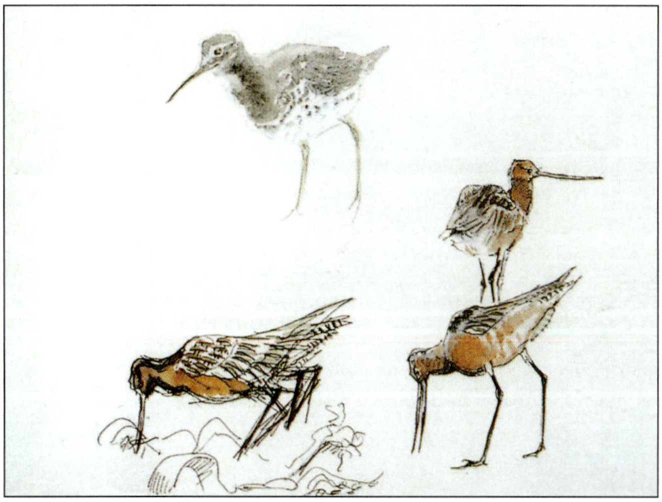

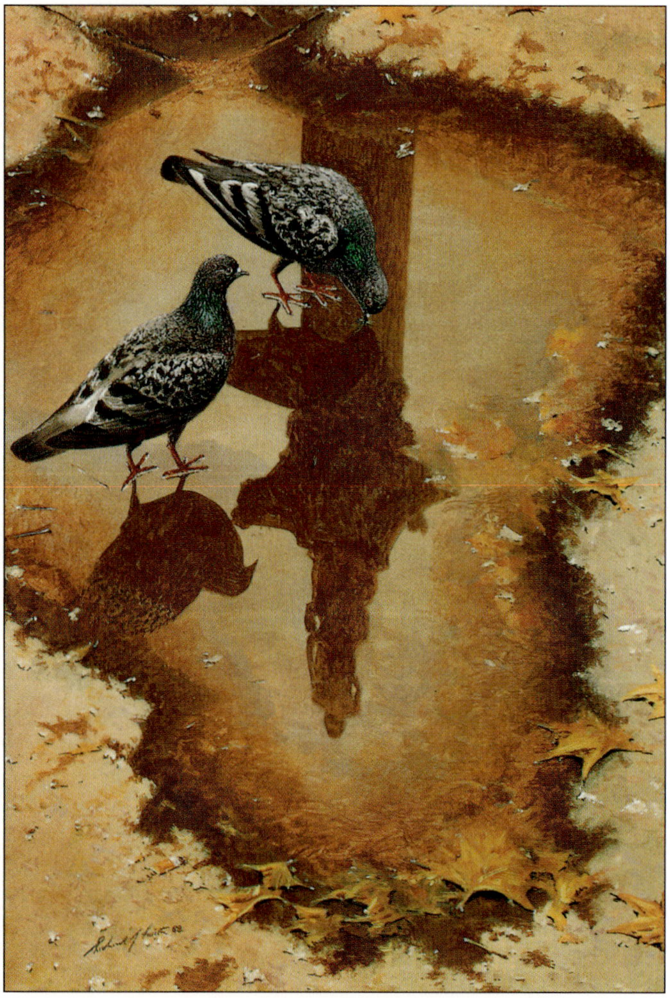

TRAFALGAR SQUARE by Richard J. Smith

A primed hardboard panel was also used for this painting, but here the colors were thinned with matt medium rather than gloss. Relatively thick paint has been used for the plumage of the birds – notice the individual brush strokes of white and near-black on a thinner, mid-toned underpainting. The puddles have been built up in a series of glazes, opaque in the center and becoming more transparent toward the edges.

moving in its natural habitat that one can really succeed in capturing its true character.

THE ANATOMY OF A BIRD

A thorough study of the anatomy and physical make-up of animals and birds will provide very useful information for drawing and painting them. In almost all animals, every part serves a purpose and it is important that the artist be aware of these aspects.

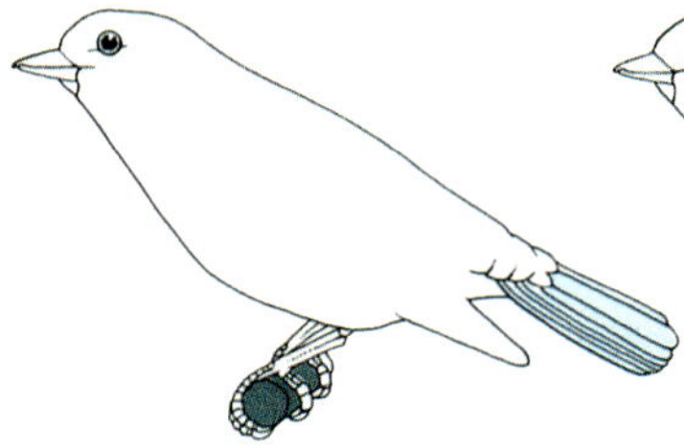

tail feathers

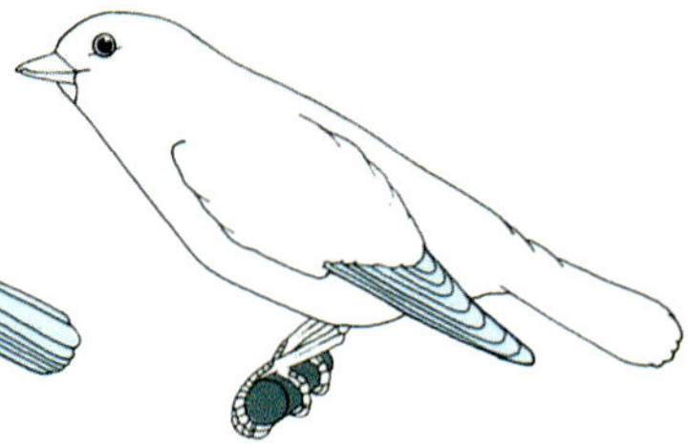

primaries

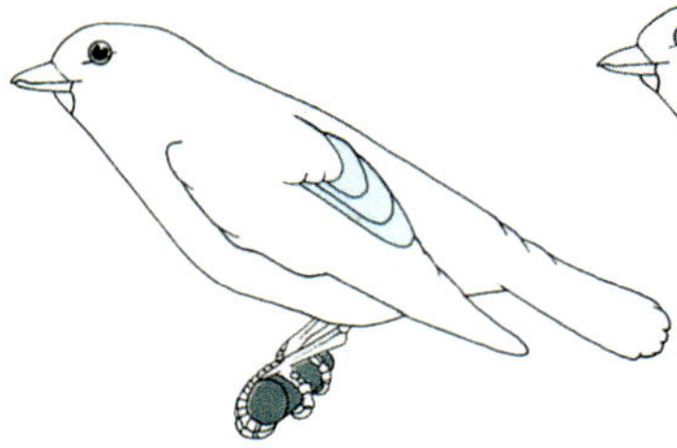

tertials

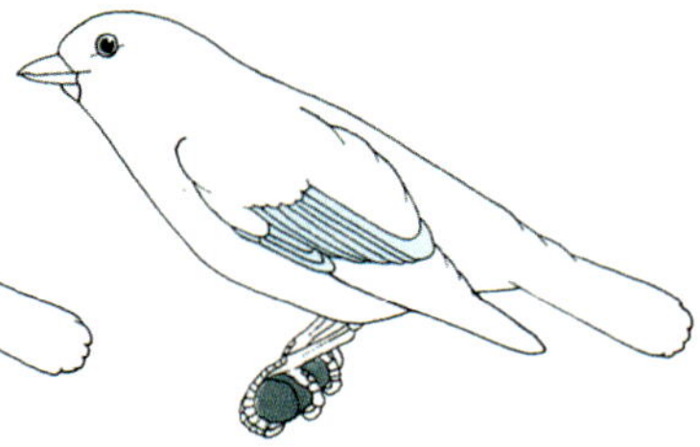

secondaries

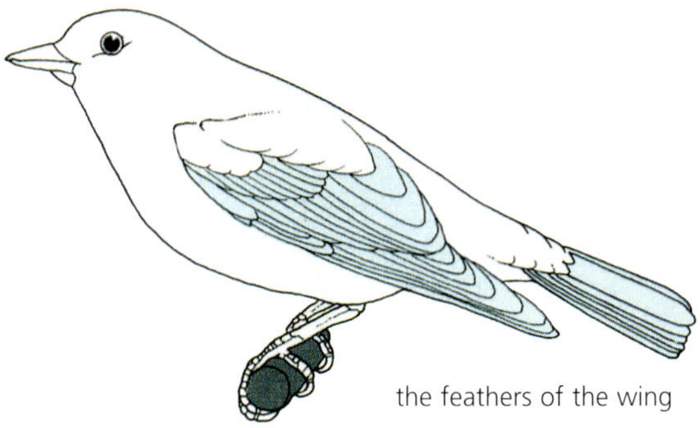

the feathers of the wing

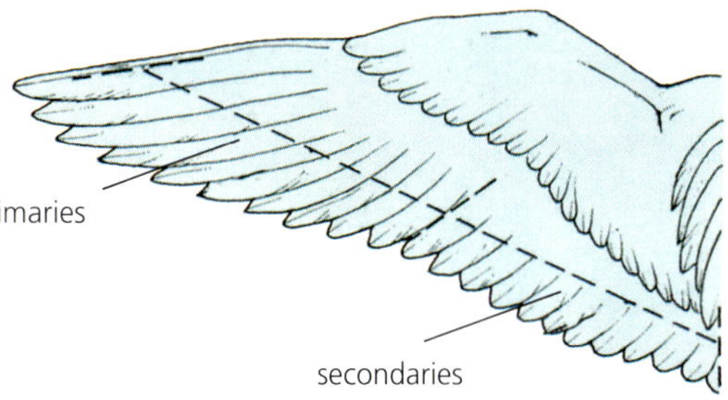

parts of an outstretched wing

A BIRD IN FLIGHT

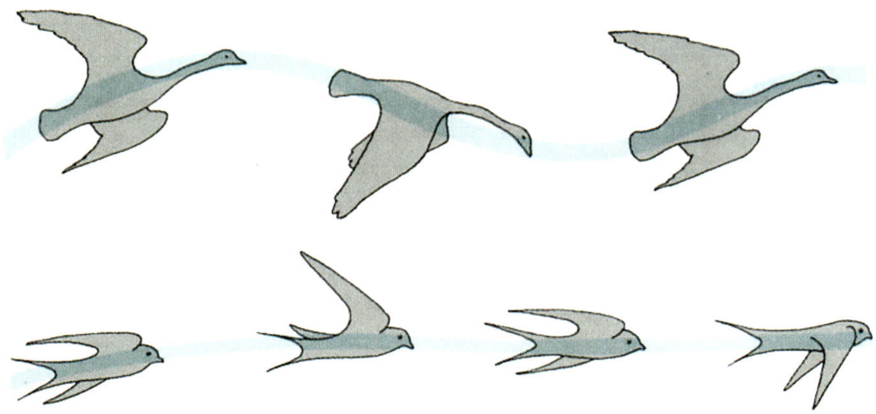

Animals are rarely still and it is to the artist's advantage to study their movements. The flight of a swan (*top left*) is contrasted with that of a swallow (*bottom left*). Note how the head and neck move in relation to the wings and the dipping motion of the swan's flight as opposed to the straight path of the swallow.

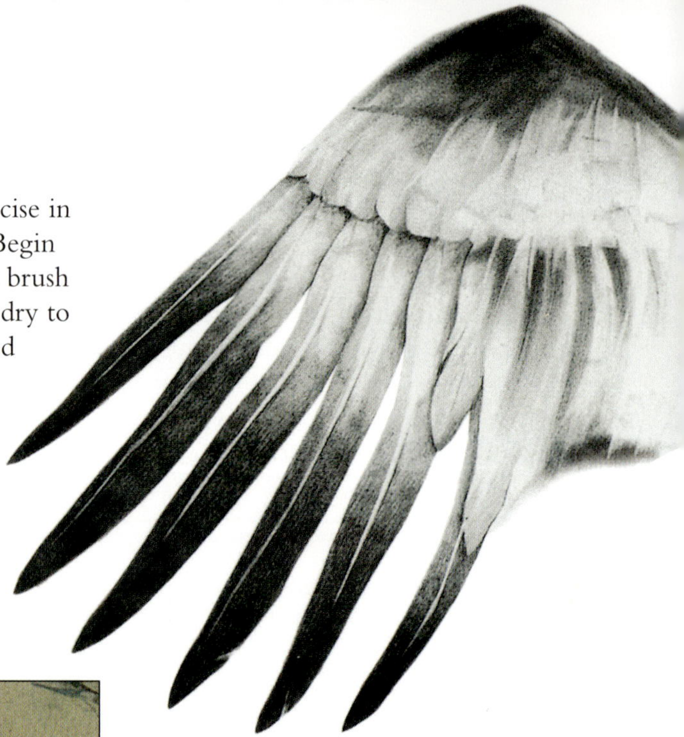

PAINTING FEATHERS

In most birds, the wing and tail feathers are quite smooth and precise in shape, while those on the neck and throat have a downy quality. Begin by painting the bird with a pale underwash. Then use a small, soft brush to delineate the markings of the main feathers, working wet over dry to achieve a precise pattern. The soft, downy feathers should be added last, using light, scumbled strokes.

USING PASTEL

Different types of pastel marks can be matched to the range of textures in a bird. The large sweeping strokes used in the picture below really express the character of the crane. He began with a rough outline in Payne's gray, working on sandpaper, which suits a bold direct approach. Next, the span of the wing was described, using a strong stroke with the side of a white pastel, and the basic blue of the body began to take on form. In the softer areas like the reds and blues of the head and neck, the colors are really pushed in, totally covering the support. In contrast, the radiating feathers of the crest have been built up from line drawn with the edge of the pastel and then smudged by sliding the pastel across the sheet.

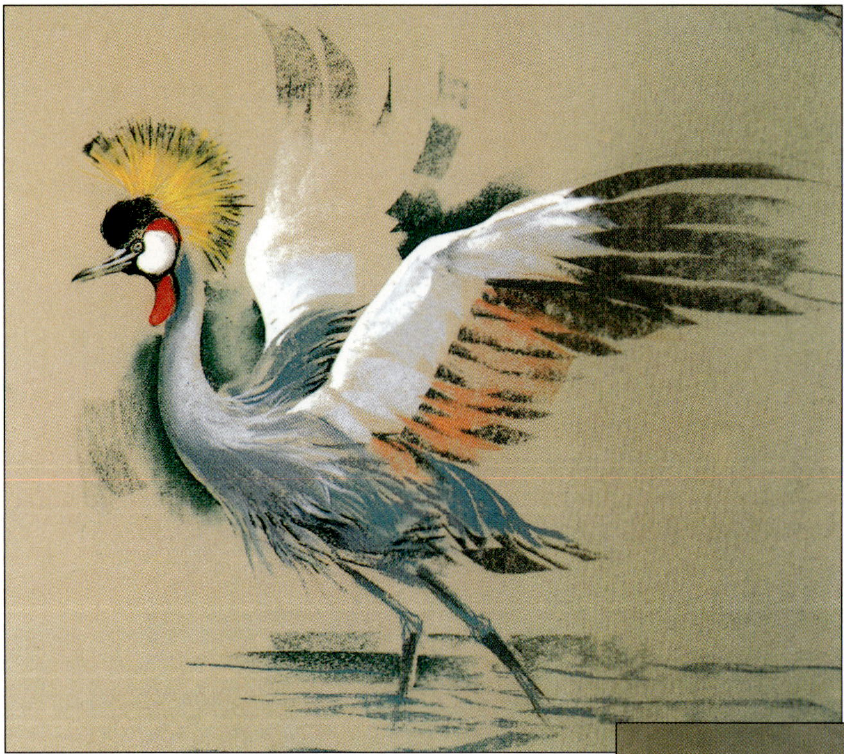

AFRICAN CROWNED CRANE by John Barber

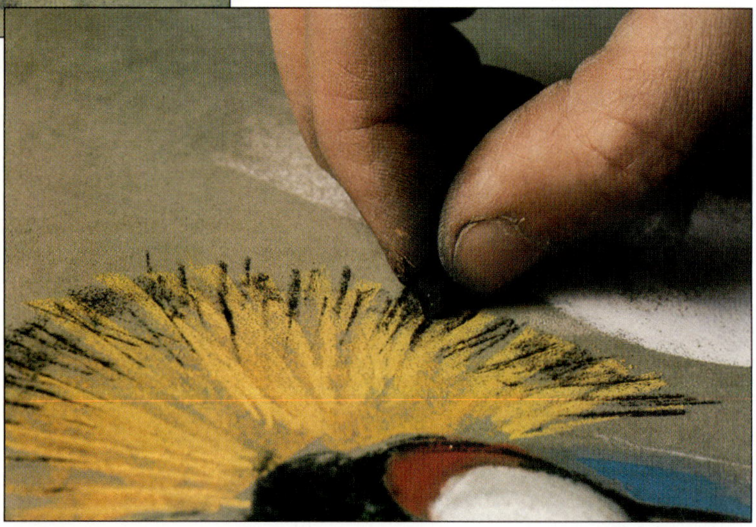

In this detail the soft feathers of the head are solidly blocked in, and now the artist uses small sharp strokes in pierre noire to pick out the radiating feathers of the crest.

USING WATERCOLOR

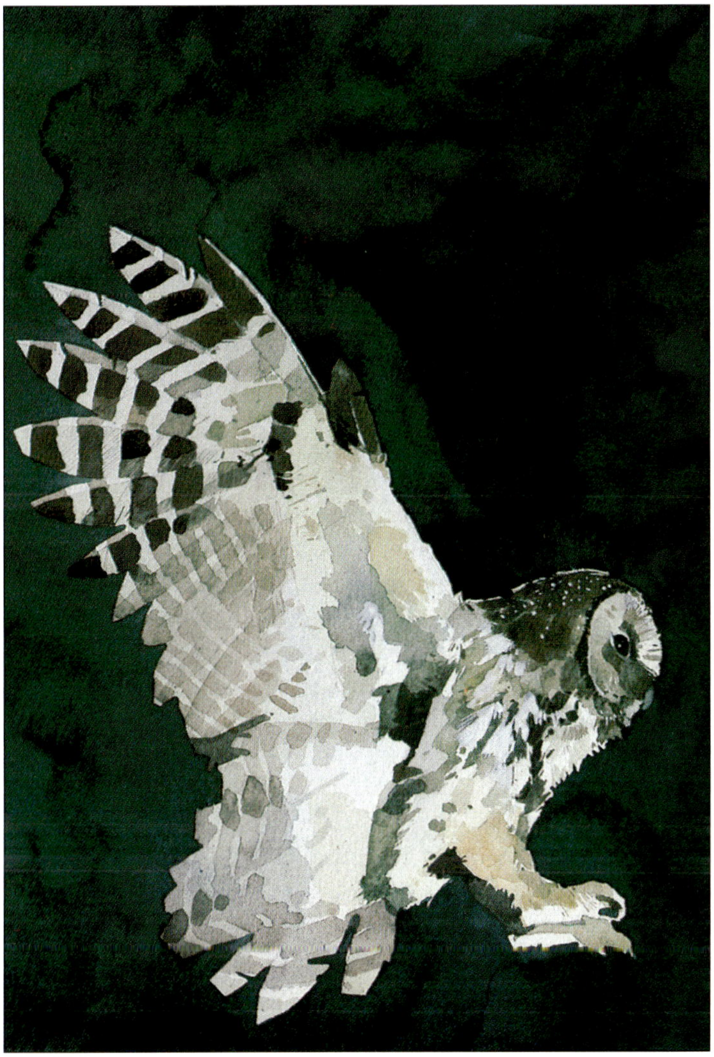

FEATHERS IN WATERCOLOR

In this dramatic study of an owl in flight, the artist uses very loose brushmarks, which not only capture the texture of the feathers but also accentuate the impression of flight.

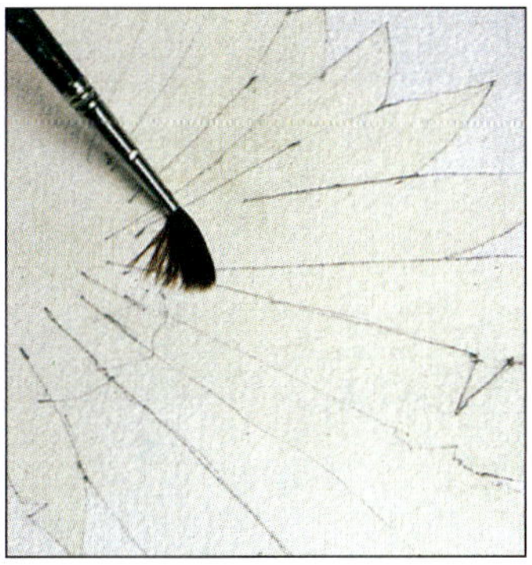

1 Detail from the wing feathers. The artist begins with a fairly accurate outline drawing of the bird and then blocks in the lightest tones of the wing feathers with a No. 4 sable brush and a very pale wash of yellow ocher.

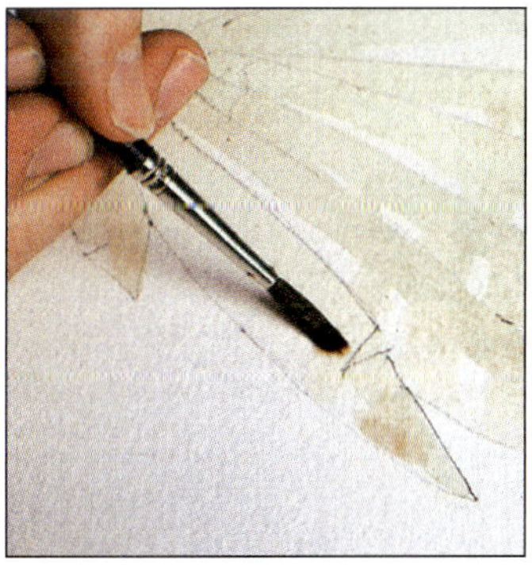

2 When the first wash is dry the artist begins to indicate the patterning on the feathers with a middle tone of burnt sienna and raw umber.

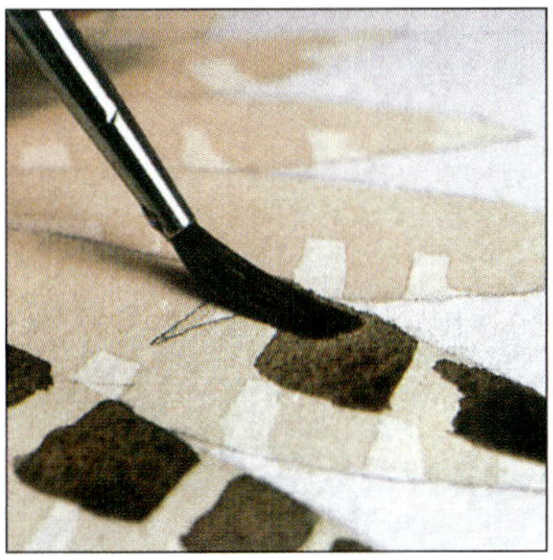

3 With a dark mixture of burnt sienna and ivory black, the darkest pattern on the feathers is blocked in.

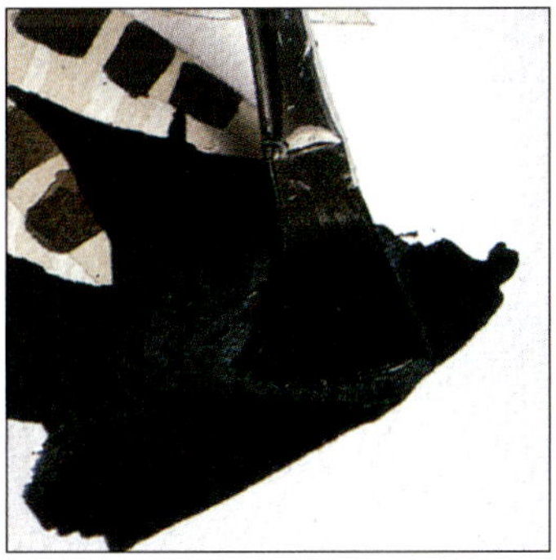

4 The drama of the painting lies in the clear, light shape of the owl against the inky black sky. Here the artist is blocking in the dark background with a very dark wash of Payne's gray. He first cuts carefully around the precise shapes of the feathers using a No. 2 sable brush. Once safely away from the edges of the feathers, he uses a ½ in. (1.27 cm) flat Dalon brush to complete the background.

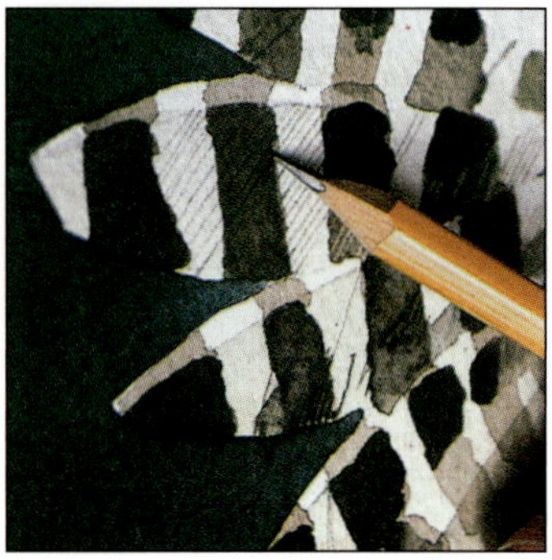

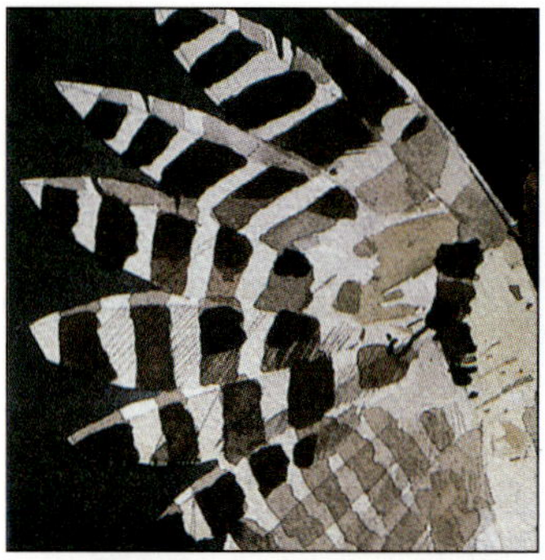

6 This close-up of the main wing feathers shows how the patterns and shapes have been built up, starting with the lightest tones and working up to the darks in the glazing technique. The process is very simple, but highly effective because it is so direct and to the point.

5 The artist now adds a hint of texture to some of the feathers by applying hatched lines with a sharp HB pencil.

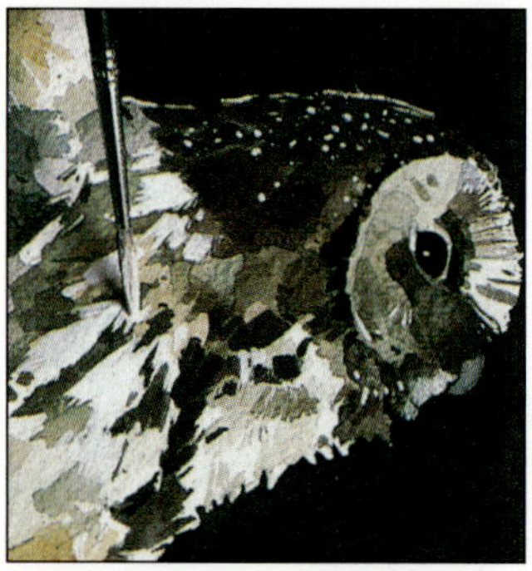

7 The feathers on the neck and the underside of the wing have a quite different quality from that of the sharply defined wing feathers. To indicate their thick, downy texture, the artist first applies various tones of Payne's gray, ivory black, and cadmium yellow with overlapping strokes. When these are dry, white gouache is applied with rapid brushmarks, overlapping the darker feathers in places. This semi-opaque color has the effect of softening the appearance of the feathers. Finally, white gouache is spattered lightly over the top of the head to give the characteristic markings (the rest of the picture was carefully masked off with newspaper to protect it from any stray droplets of paint).

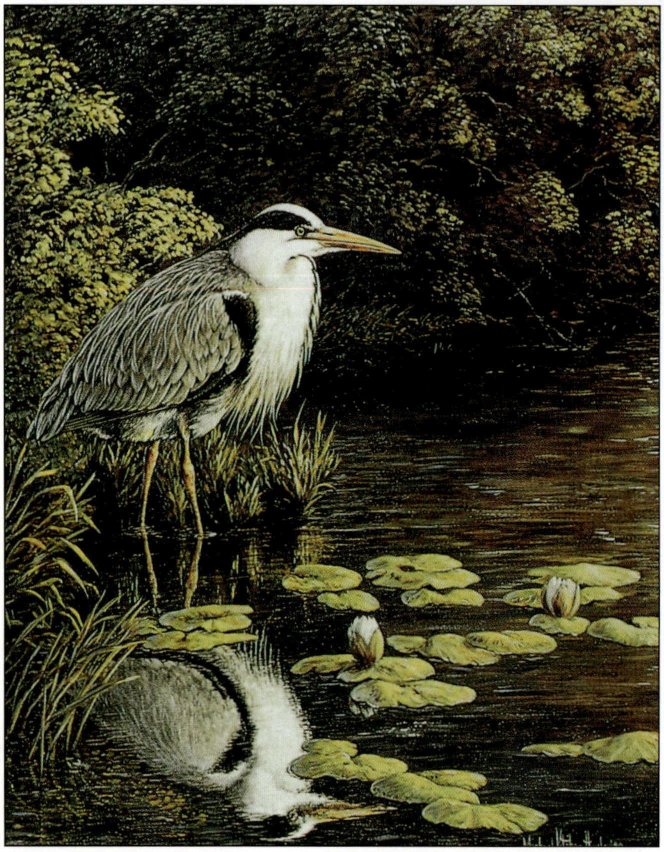

SILENT SENTINEL by Michael Kitchen-Hurle

This painting captures the color, texture, and characteristic stance of the heron, a bird which remains immobile for long periods while waiting for fish to catch – a habit that makes it easier to observe and paint than most other birds. The waterlilies in the foreground and the sunlit foliage on the left provide a compositional foil for the brilliant white of the bird's breast, repeated in the reflection.

This magpie has been skillfully drawn with intricate line and stipple work, executed with a pen and black Indian ink. The foliage and blossom alongside the bird add to the decorative quality of the drawing as well as describing the habitat.

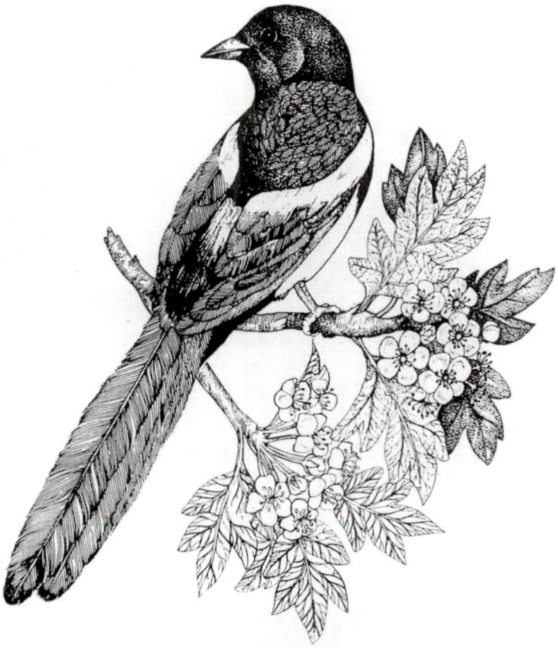

PAINTING AND DRAWING FISH

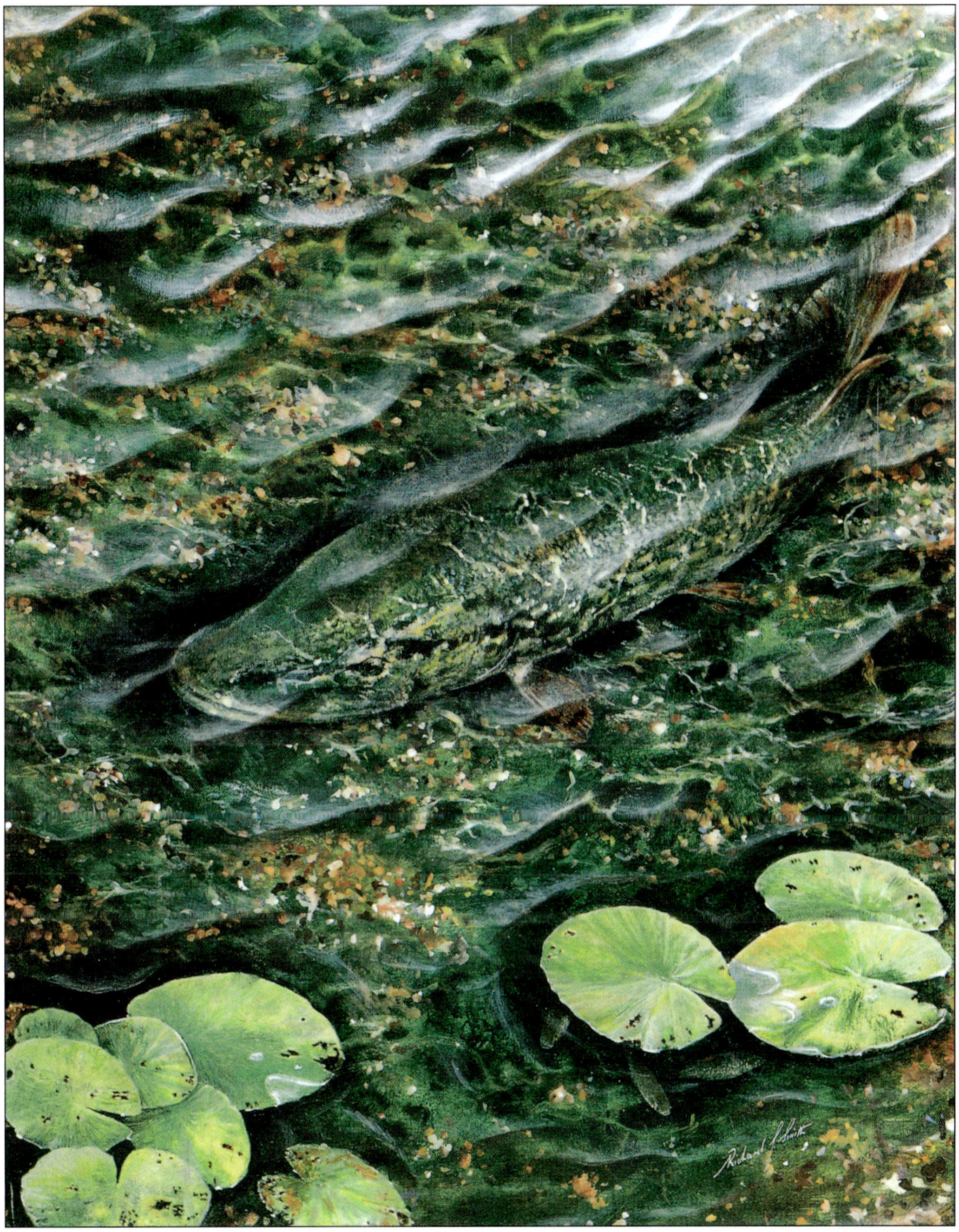

OVER THE SHALLOWS – PIKE by Richard J. Smith

Smith is a professional wildlife artist, and his paintings are evidence of how thoroughly he has observed his animal subjects and their habitats. The painting is on hardboard, primed with acrylic gesso to provide a smooth surface, and the paint has been diluted with gloss medium. The effect of the water surface reflecting light was achieved by brushing a thinned blue-white glaze over the surface with single strokes of a large household paintbrush.

FISH

The silvery, iridescent skin of fish makes them an excellent subject for painting, and they are particularly suited to the delicate, aqueous medium of watercolor. To portray the shiny, wet appearance of the skin, work with broad, loose washes of pale color on damp paper.

Allow the colors to merge wet-into-wet. While the paper is still damp, indicate the dark markings of the fish with dryish color, allowing the edges to bleed softly into the underlying wash. Do not attempt to indicate every scale on the fish's skin because the resulting appearance is too tight and stilted and destroys the essentially fluid form of the creature. Simply use a small, well-pointed brush to hint at the overlapping scales along the back. When the markings are dry, apply a final, thin wash of color over the fish's body. This creates a translucent effect, with the dark markings glowing through the final glaze of color.

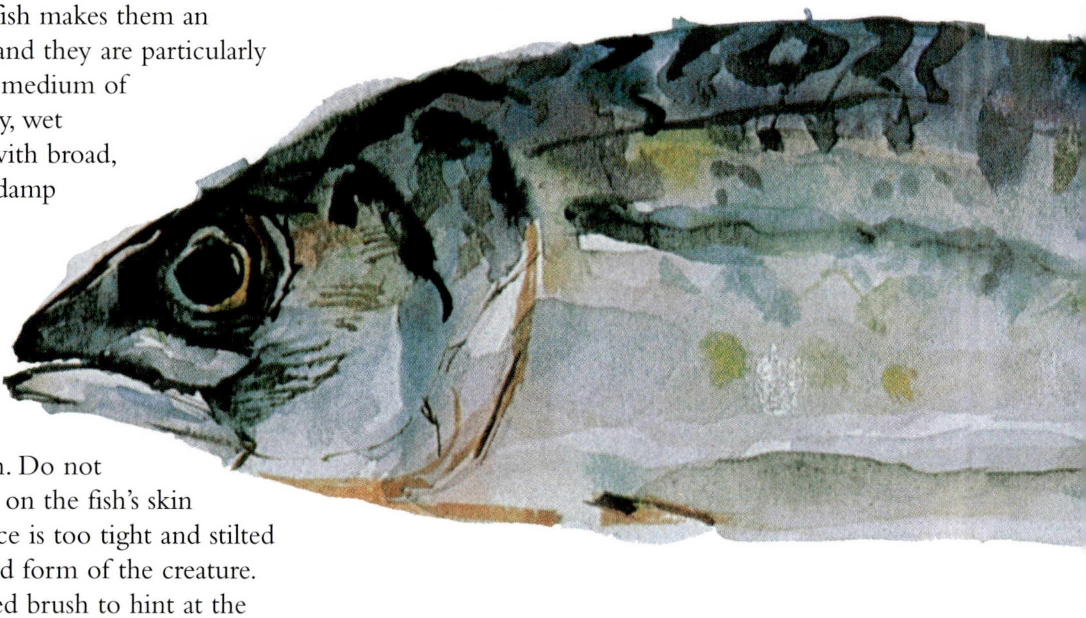

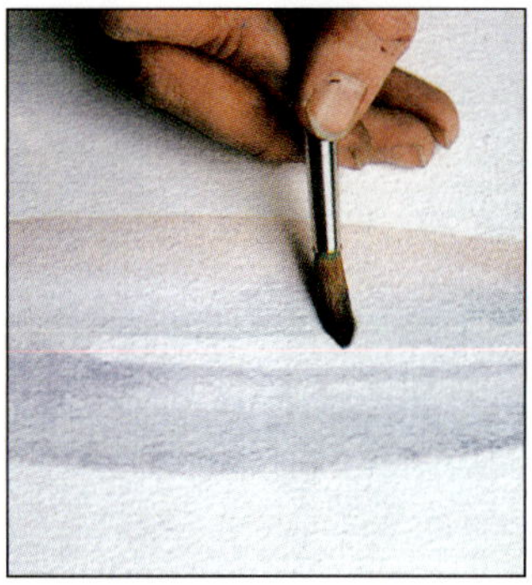

1 Working on a sheet of stretched paper, the artist begins by establishing the shape of the fish. He first dampens the area with water; then, using a round No. 10 sable brush, he applies pale washes of Payne's gray, turquoise, and cadmium red. It is best not to outline the shape in pencil, because this can inhibit the spontaneity of the succeeding washes of color. An outline should always be fluid enough to be altered during the painting process.

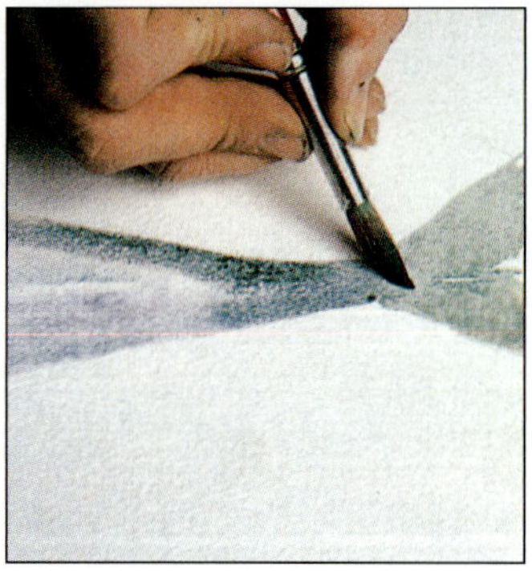

2 The dark shape of the tail is painted with Payne's gray. The artist has mixed gum arabic with the pigment on the palette: this gives a slight sheen to the color, which captures the shiny, lustrous appearance of the fish's skin.

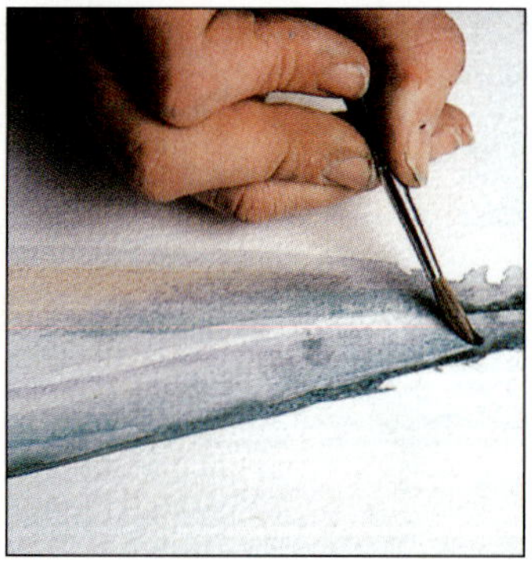

3 Switching to a No. 4 brush, the artist defines the head and spine of the fish with a darker wash of Payne's gray. Notice the broken quality of the line, which lends a sense of movement: a perfectly straight outline would look too static.

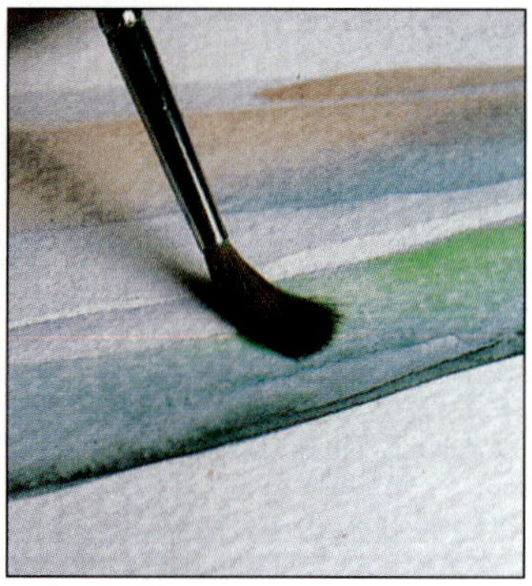

4 After allowing the previous colors to dry slightly, the artist starts to add further colors: sap green, turquoise, and brown madder alizarin are applied and allowed to bleed together wet-into-wet.

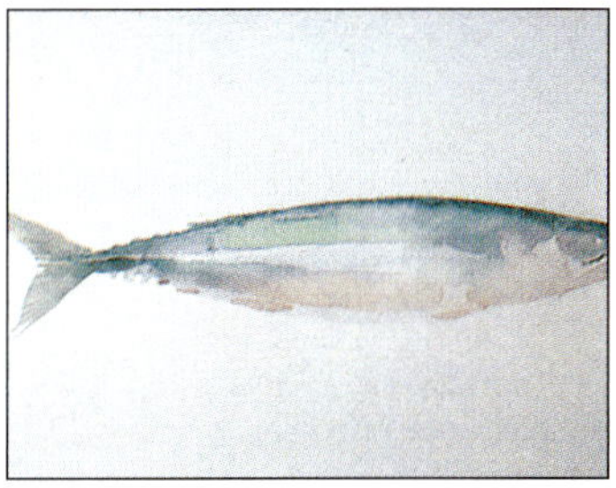

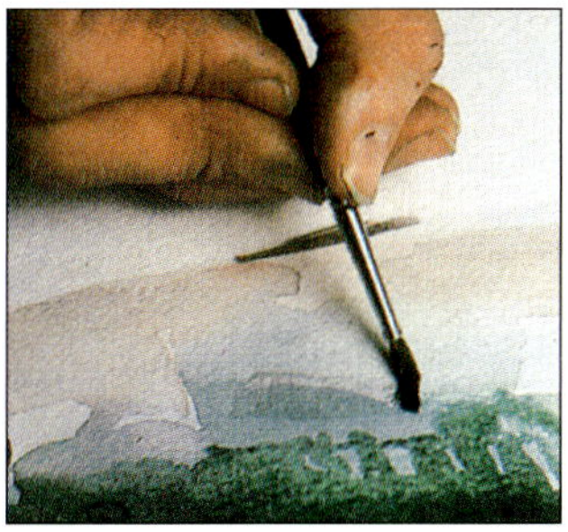

6 When the underlying washes are almost dry, the artist indicates the mottled pattern on the back, using a No. 4 sable brush and a dark, dryish mixture of Payne's gray and sap green. The bottom edge of the pattern is then flooded with water using a clean brush to make it bleed into the body of the fish.

5 At this stage, you can see how the underlying form of the fish has been established using wet washes. In places the colors were lightened by gently lifting out with a clean, moist brush, that helps to create the soft luster of the fish's skin.

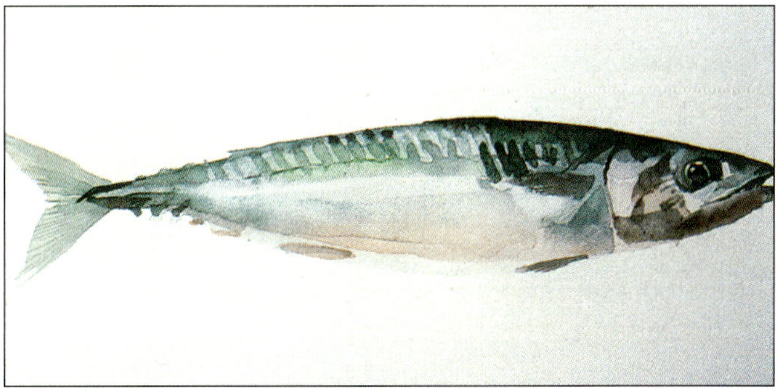

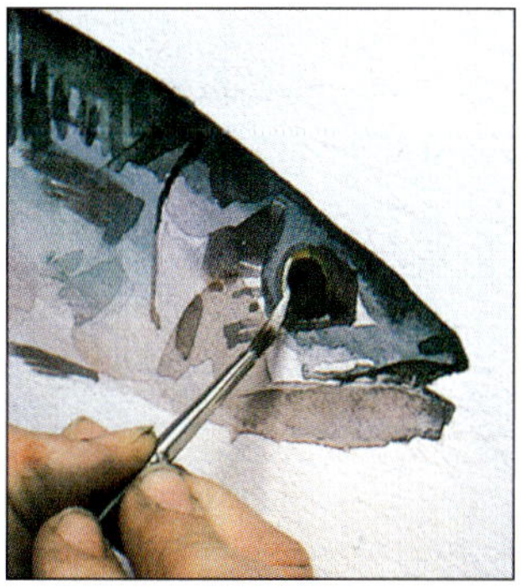

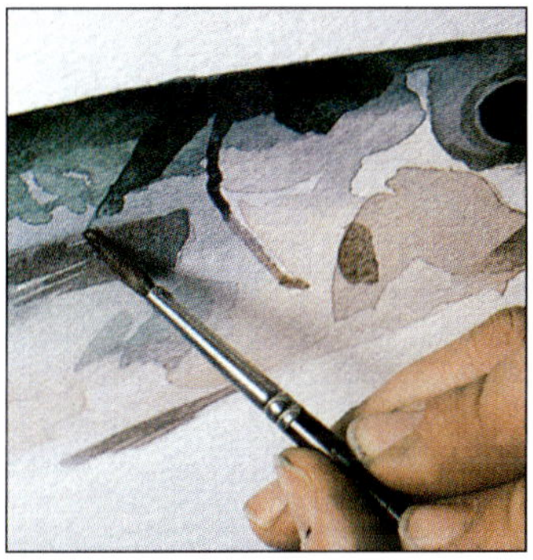

8 In developing this picture, the artist has exploited the fluidity and transparency of watercolor to the full, and the completed image captures the essence of the subject perfectly. It is the harmonious balance of loose, wet washes and darker, sharper details that gives freshness and vitality to the painting.

9 When the painting is dry, the artist adds a final touch: the highlights on the eye are painted with processed white.

7 The mouth and eye are defined with a dark mixture of Payne's gray and burnt umber, and a pale mixture of Payne's gray and sap green is used to paint the gills. You can see also where small, spontaneous strokes have been applied here and there over the dried underlayer, giving depth and luminosity to the colors.

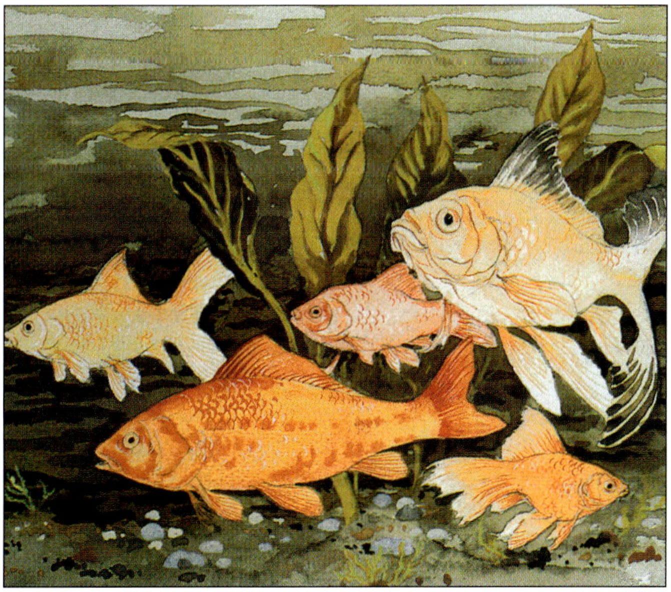

PAINTING SCALES
The artist paints uneven washes of lemon yellow and black in the background to create the effect of ripples in the water. After each layer dries she adds another to strengthen the color and so help define the shape of the fish. The fish scales are painted onto a weak wash of cadmium red and cadmium yellow pale with a No. 00 sable brush. The subtle blending of tones is achieved by applying the paint wet-into-wet. Around the gills and fins this is enriched by adding cadmium red and orange, giving the fish an iridescent quality.

Eyes

The eyes are often the most expressive feature of an animal or bird, so they are worthy of some attention. In creatures that are natural predators, for example, the eyes have a hard, watchful, imperious quality which should be emphasized with hard, crisply defined outlines.

Compare this quality to the soft, vulnerable appearance of the eyes of young animals and of non-predatory species such as horses, cows, and deer. Pale colors and a smudgy technique will portray the dewy, liquid look of these eyes.

The eyes of animals and birds have a pronounced spherical shape and their surface is glassy and highly reflective. Applying your colors in thin glazes is the best way to capture the subtle nuances of light and shade that give the eyes their depth and three-dimensionality. Pay attention also to the shapes of the highlights and shadows, which follow the convex contour of the eyeball.

PAINTING EYES IN WATERCOLOR

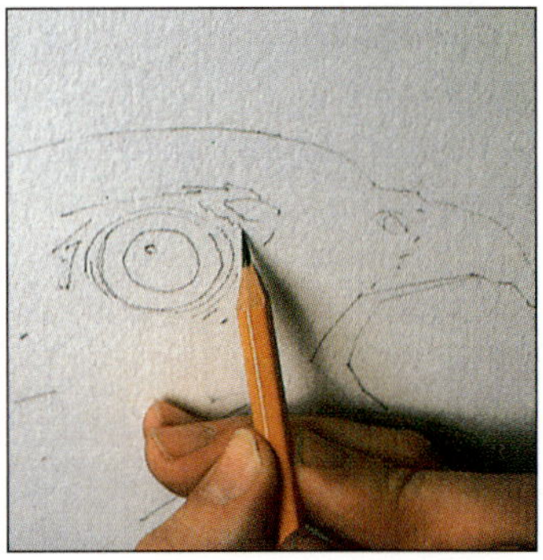

1 Working on a sheet of stretched 200 lb Bockingford watercolor paper, the artist sketches a simple outline shape for the eye with an HB pencil.

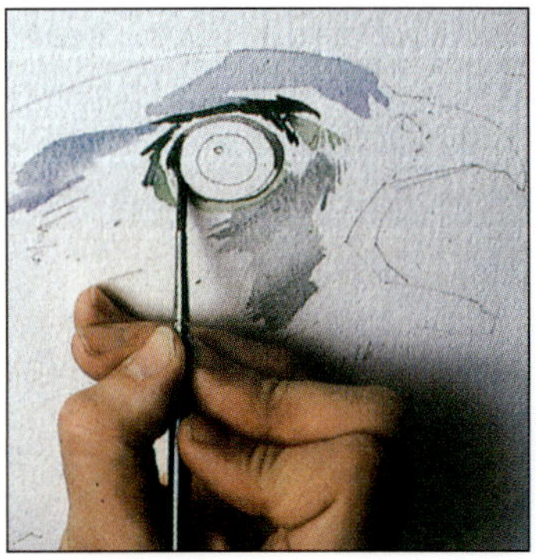

2 The artist begins by painting the area surrounding the eye with pale washes of Payne's gray and cobalt blue mixed with yellow ocher. Using a No. 2 round sable brush, he then defines the outer rim of the eye with ivory black.

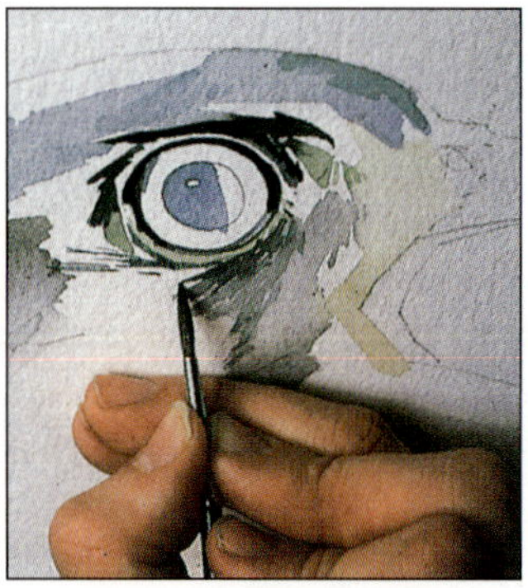

3 The feathers surrounding the eye are built up further with washes of cobalt blue and yellow ocher. Then the pupil of the eye is painted with cobalt blue, leaving a tiny dot of white paper for the brightest highlight.

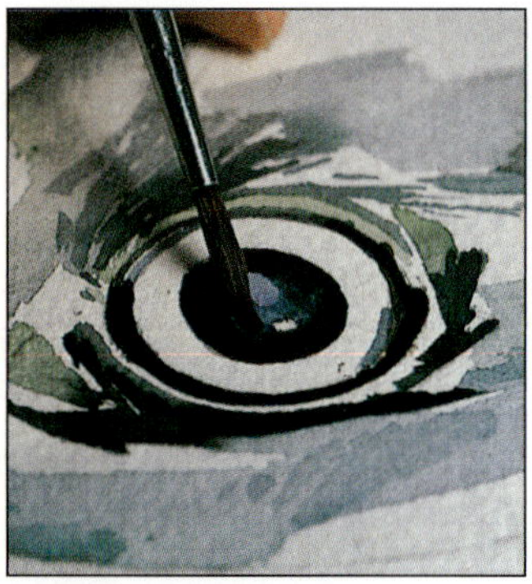

4 The darks of the pupil are gradually built up with repeated glazes of cobalt blue and Payne's gray. Because each glaze shines up through the next one, the color has a depth that captures the glassiness of the bird's eye. The darkest part of the pupil is painted with ivory black.

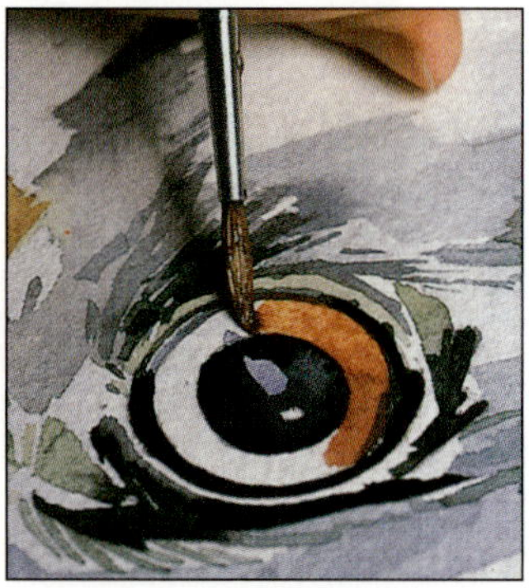

5 When the pupil is completely dry the artist paints the iris with a mixture of brown madder alizarin and cadmium orange. This is allowed to dry thoroughly before adding the next wash.

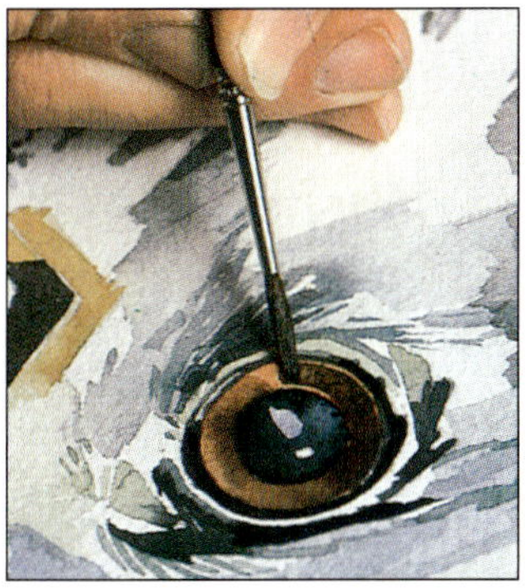

6 The rounded form of the eye is developed by adding a shadow wash over the iris with a mixture of burnt sienna and cadmium orange. In this close-up, notice how the artist has used a combination of hard and soft edges to define the form of the eye and prevent it from looking too static. The gradual build-up of washes helps to define the convex contour of the eyeball.

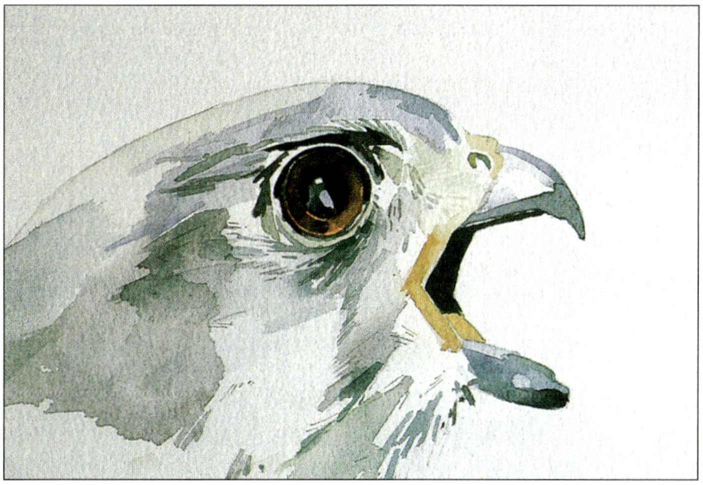

7 The clean, sharp, bright highlight of the eagle's eye conveys the fact that this bird is very much a predator.

TIGER'S EYES

The expression in this tiger's eyes is bold and unfaltering, accentuated by the small size of the pupils and the hard, glinting highlight.

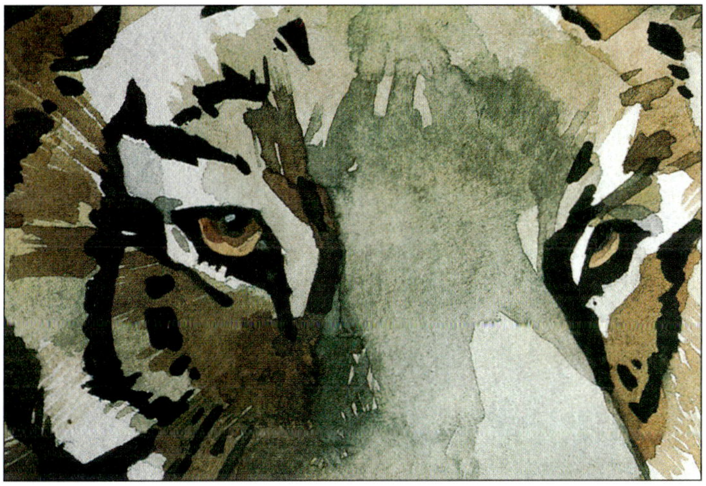

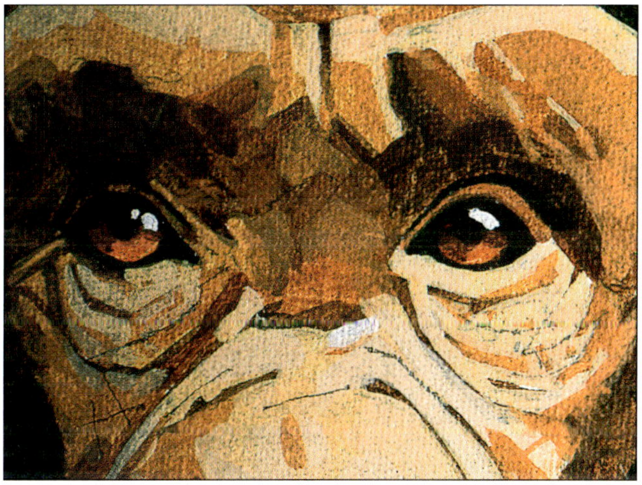

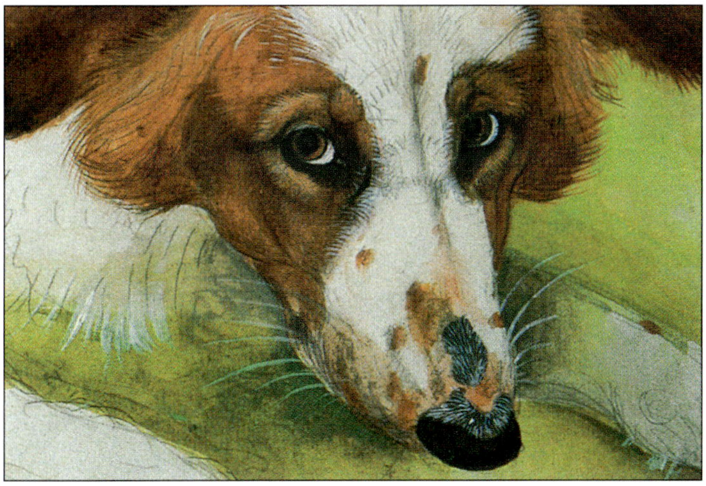

CHIMPANZEE'S EYES

The eyes of this young chimpanzee – a non-predator – are much softer. There is much more light in the eye, and the outer rim is less sharply defined.

DOG'S EYES

Using a very fine, No. 0 sable brush, the eyes were painted in layers of the same color, after each previous one had dried, to build up the density of color. The paint was laid on thinly to achieve a soft finish, leaving the paper white for the whites of the eyes.

Fur

Fur – just like human hair – comes in a wide variety of textures. How you render these depends on the type of animal you are portraying, the medium you are working with, and whether the animal is to be seen close-up or in the distance. On these next pages are some examples of suitable techniques, but it is wise to remember that you should always start by defining the outline of the animal, then suggest the pattern of light and shade on its body, and lastly, pay attention to the markings and individual features.

GLOSSY FUR

For animals with a sleek, glossy coat, use a wet-into-wet technique. Observe the patterns of light and shadow carefully, then paint them with fast, fluid brush strokes. Use as few strokes as possible, to accentuate the glossiness of the coat.

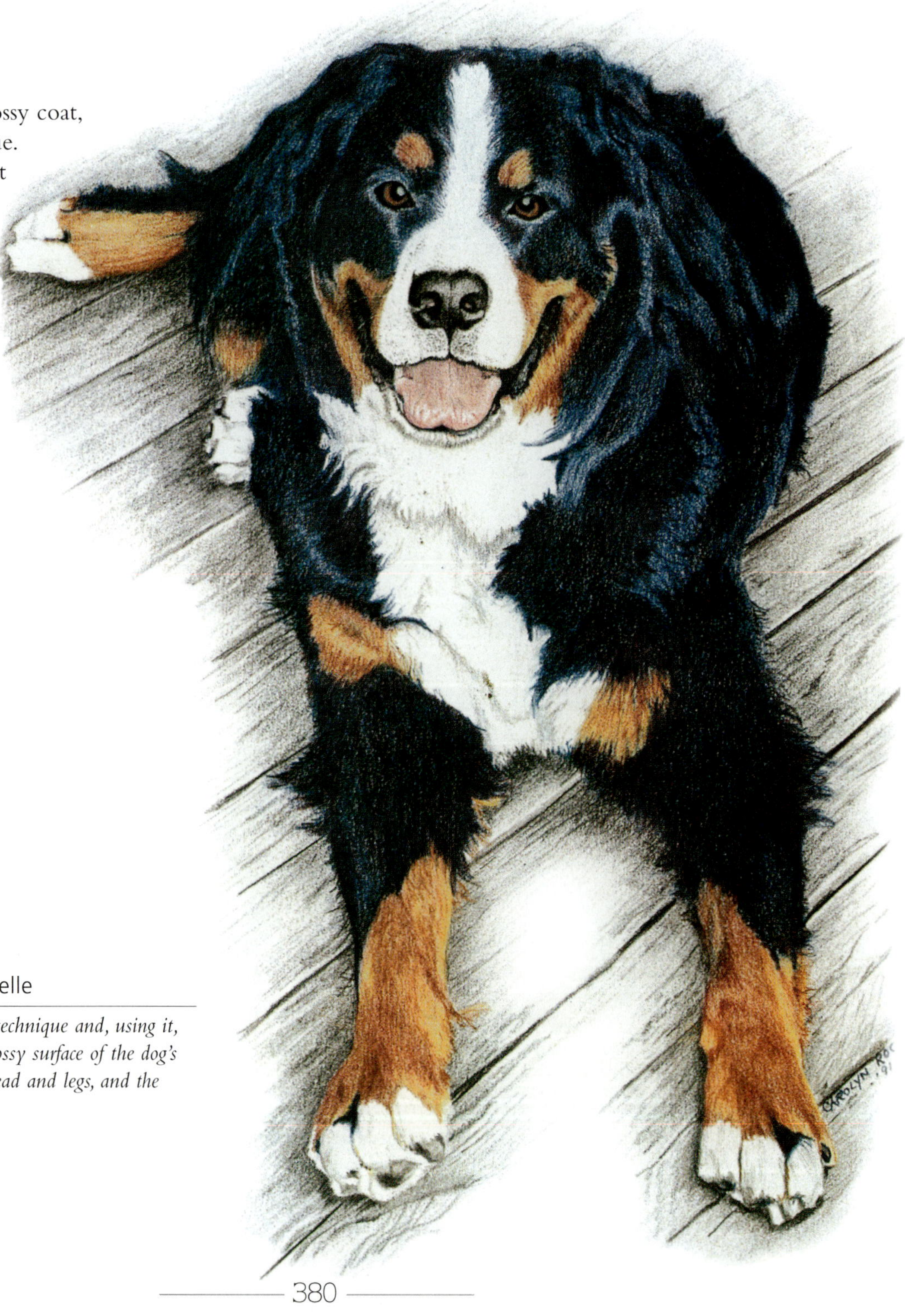

BARNABY by Carolyn Rochelle

Shading is an extremely versatile technique and, using it, the artist has here conveyed the glossy surface of the dog's coat, and the rougher fur on the head and legs, and the variations of color and tone.

SHAGGY COAT

For animals with a fluffy, shaggy, or wiry coat, use scumbling or dry brush with a bristle brush and fairly thick, dry paint. Another method, often used in watercolor and gouache, is to block in the colors and tones of the coat with broad washes; when this is dry, use the tip of the finely pointed brush to tick in tiny lines that follow the pattern of hair growth. This technique is effective for rendering short-haired animals such as dogs and foxes.

VELVETY HIDE

Some animals, such as horses, cows, deer, and smooth-haired dog breeds, have a short, sleek, and velvety coat. The muscular structure beneath the coat is much more pronounced than in long-haired animals, so attention must be paid to the subtle modeling of tones. You could start by defining the form with a series of watery washes, and then suggest the lie of the coat with very short strokes using a finely pointed brush.

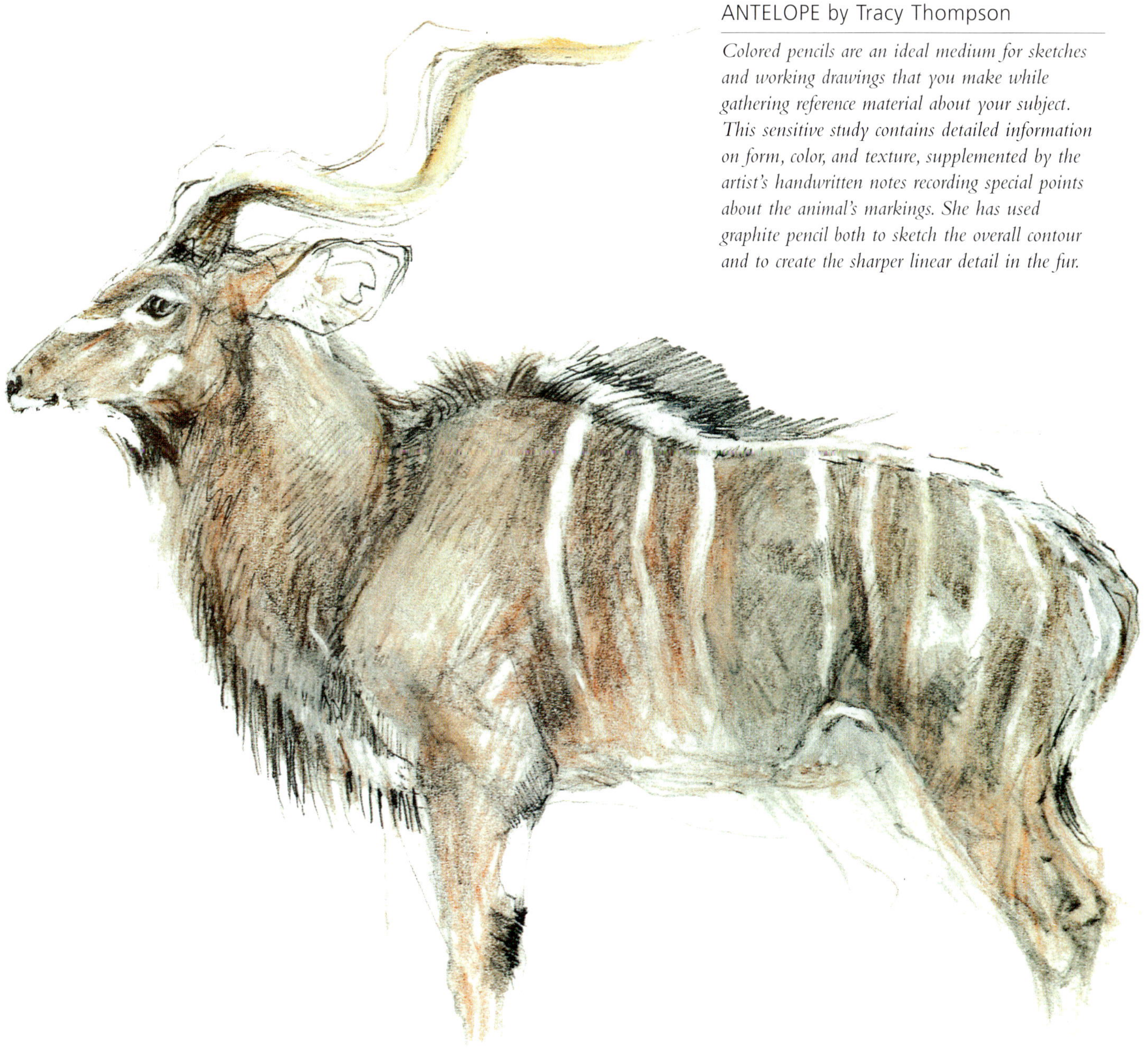

ANTELOPE by Tracy Thompson

Colored pencils are an ideal medium for sketches and working drawings that you make while gathering reference material about your subject. This sensitive study contains detailed information on form, color, and texture, supplemented by the artist's handwritten notes recording special points about the animal's markings. She has used graphite pencil both to sketch the overall contour and to create the sharper linear detail in the fur.

PAINTING FUR IN OIL

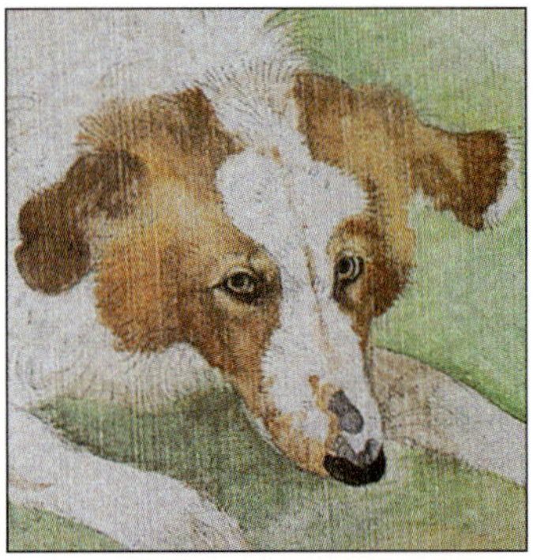

1 Layers of pigment have been applied thinly to build up the depth of color, and the details of the hairs are added on top, using a fine brush to smudge in the color.

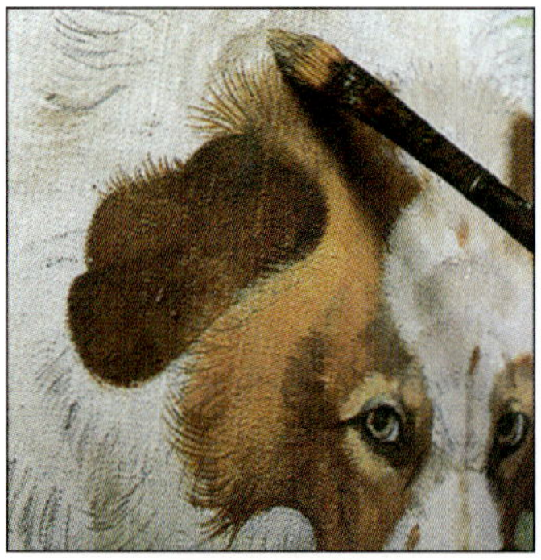

2 White hairs are added with a No. 0 sable brush, painting each individual hair slowly and methodically.

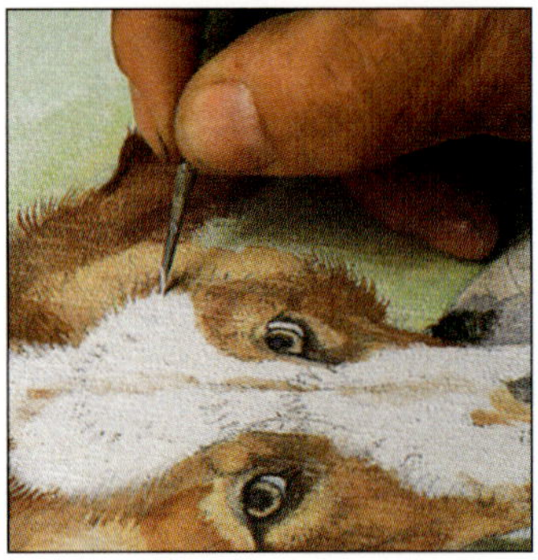

3 The pencil marks of the underdrawing indicate the folds of the dog's flesh and the way the fur stands out. In the final picture, right, the pencil marks are strengthened and flake white is added to pick out the fur against the background.

The finished effect.

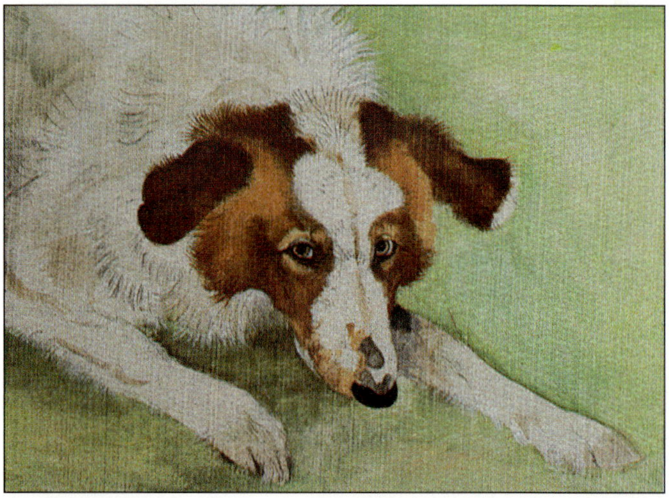

PAINTING FUR IN PASTEL

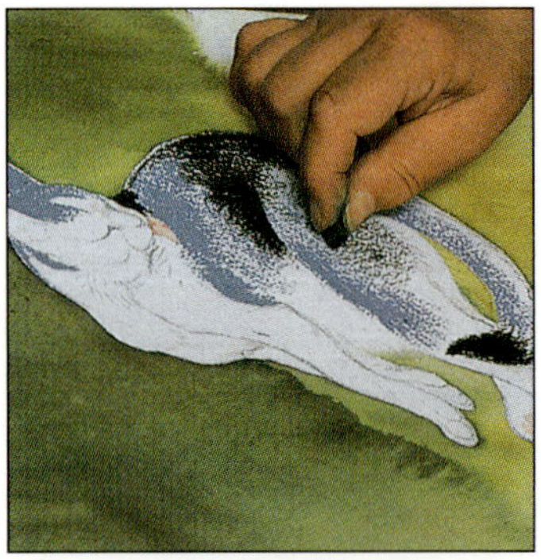

1 The background was laid in a watercolor wash because it is easier to apply over a large area than pastel is. A gray pastel is added and black is laid on top, to build up the depth of color of the cat's coat. The artist used the pastel stick on its side, because the result is more grainy than when the tip is used. The soft but dense color achieved is just right for the texture of fur.

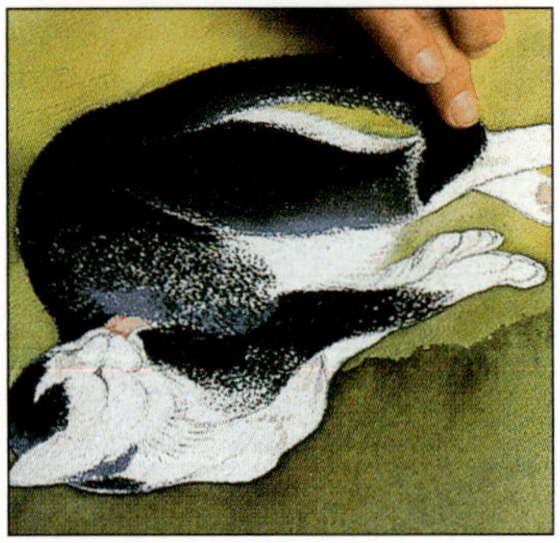

2 To increase the density of color the artist blends the black and gray pastels, working them into the grain of the paper.

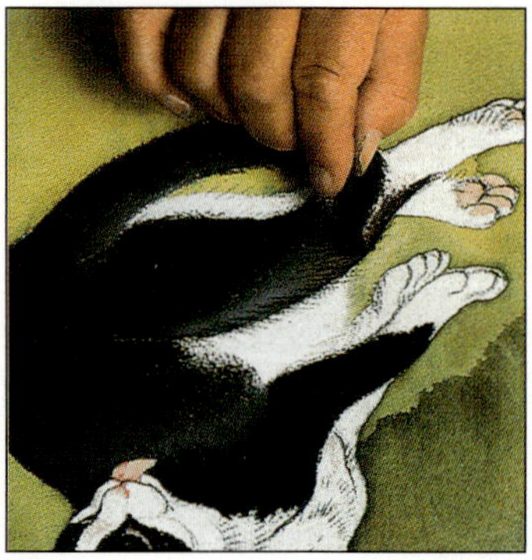

3 The fine black hairs are added individually using a black pastel stick, which has been broken in half to create a sharp drawing edge.

PAINTING FUR IN WATERCOLOR

1 A soft outline was drawn in pencil, using short strokes to convey the fur, and then a light wash was added. Once some of the details of the animal's hair had been drawn, the artist concentrated on the head. Here the artist applies the paint onto wet paper because he wants the edges to remain soft.

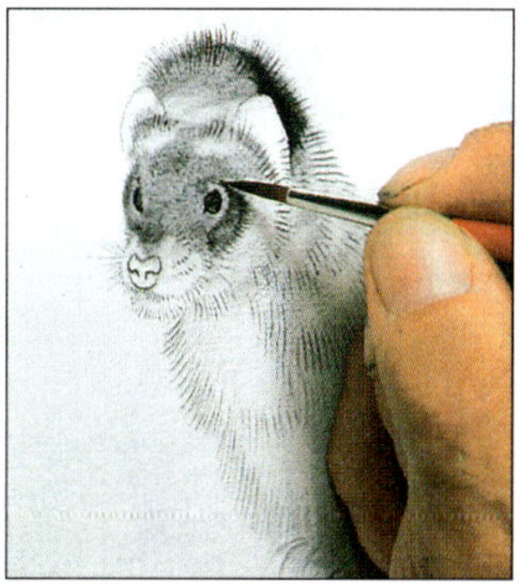

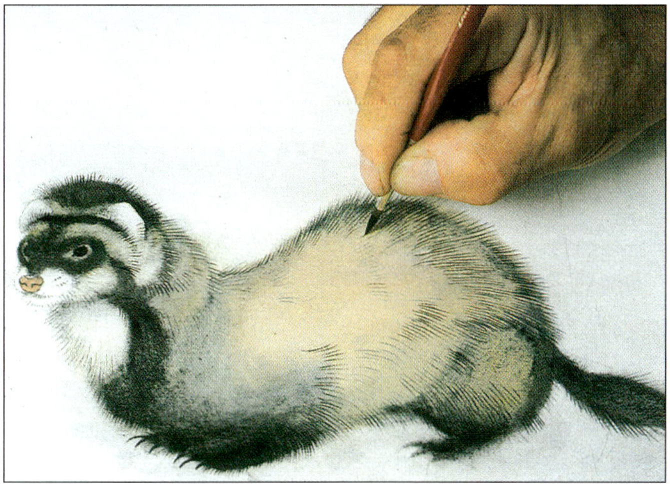

2 Having dried the picture using a hairdryer, the artist begins working on the body color. A pale mixture of cadmium yellow, cadmium red, and white is applied in a thin wash, with shadows added, in washes of black, where necessary. Remember that you can always soften the edges of a wash using a brush loaded with water.

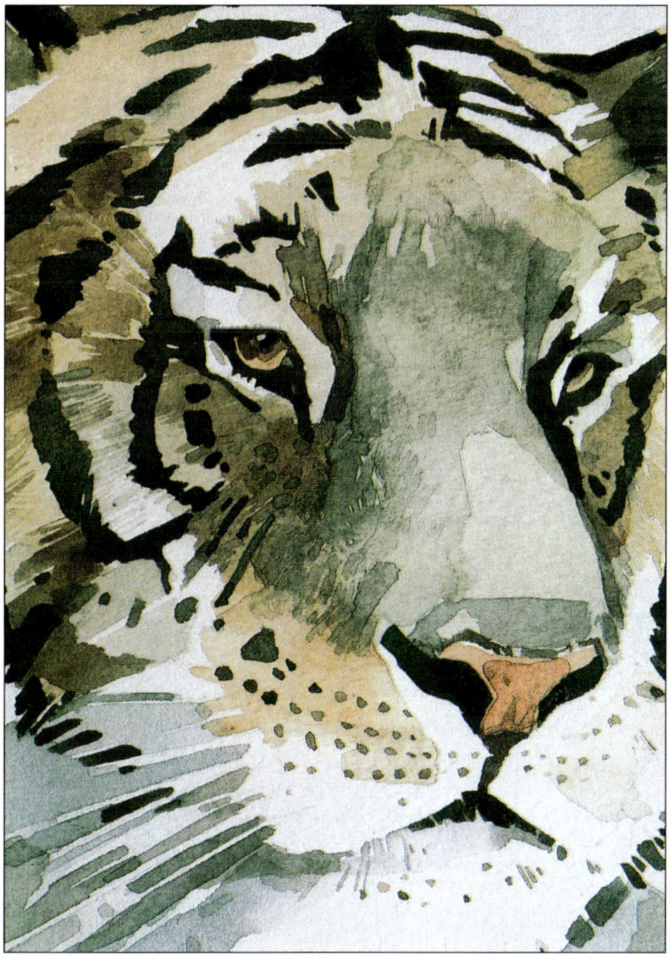

TIGER'S HEAD

In this close-up of a tiger's head, a combination of overlaid washes and linear work has been used to render the texture of the fur.

Working on a sheet of stretched 200 lb Bockingford paper, the artist begins by blocking in the middle tones of the fur with a No. 4 sable brush and varied mixtures of Payne's gray, ivory black, and burnt sienna. The lighter hairs are indicated by working these tones around negative white shapes. When the middle tones are completely dry, the tiger's black stripes are added, using a dryish mixture of ivory black and burnt sienna. Again, negative white shapes are left to indicate where lighter hairs cross over the stripes.

When the paper is dry, the tiger's golden-yellow fur is painted in. The artist begins by blocking in a pale tone of burnt sienna, once again leaving white spaces for the light hairs. This is allowed to dry. Switching to a well-pointed No. 2 brush, the artist uses burnt sienna, darkened with a touch of ivory black, to tick in individual hairs with long crisp strokes over the dried underwash. Tiny dots or "whisker holes" are painted on the muzzle, using the ivory black/burnt sienna mix. Here you can see how the negative white shapes now read as whiskers. The hairs on a tiger's nose are very fine, so very little modeling of individual hairs is required. The bridge of the nose is modeled with loose washes in various tones of Payne's gray, glazed wet over dry. Then the tip of the nose is painted with a pale wash of brown madder alizarin.

A Cat in Acrylics

The basis for this composition by Judy Martin was a black-and-white photograph, which allowed the artist freedom over the choice of colors. As a long-time cat owner she is familiar with feline subjects, and has studied and sketched her own cats extensively.

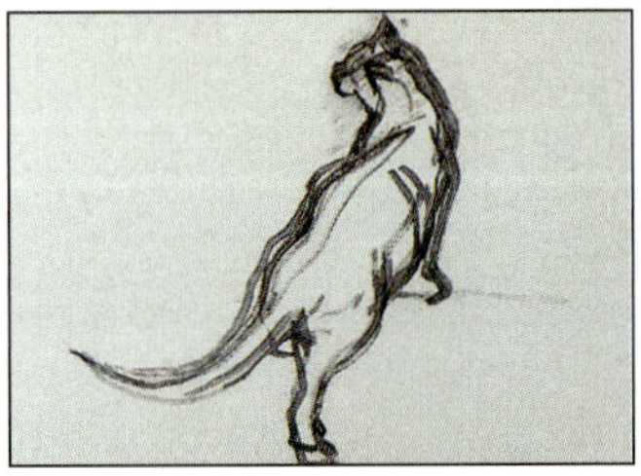

1 Working on watercolor paper, the artist begins with a brush drawing to establish the placing of the cat; the emphasis is on strong curves sweeping diagonally across the center of the picture.

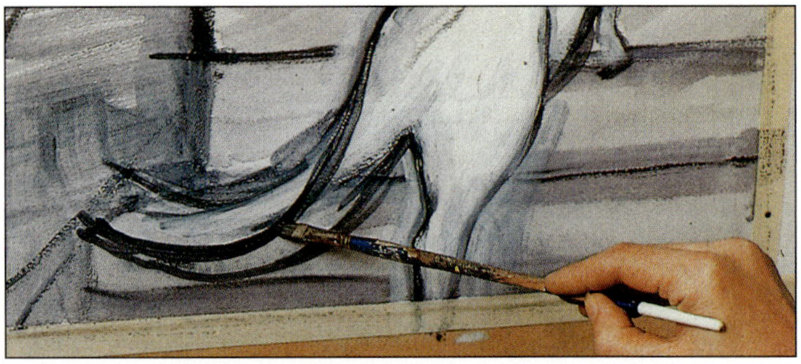

2 A monochrome underpainting is made next, and at this stage the drawing is amended by bringing the tail lower down and placing masking tape across the bottom of the picture to give a tighter crop. Previously, the leg had been cropped just above the foot, which looked awkward.

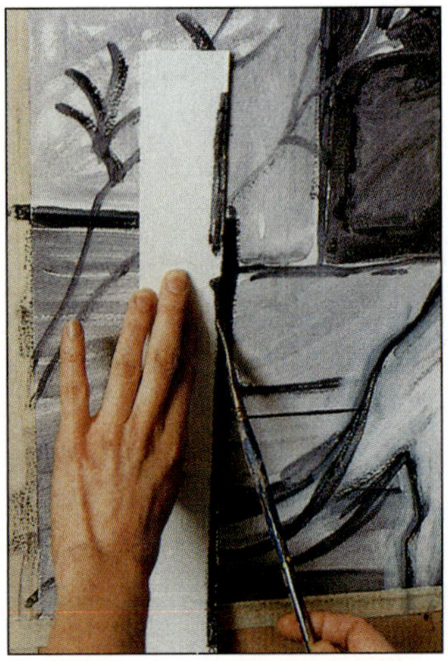

3 This vertical line is important, as it provides a balance for the diagonal formed by the body of the cat, so an edge of paper is used as a ruler to ensure that the line is straight.

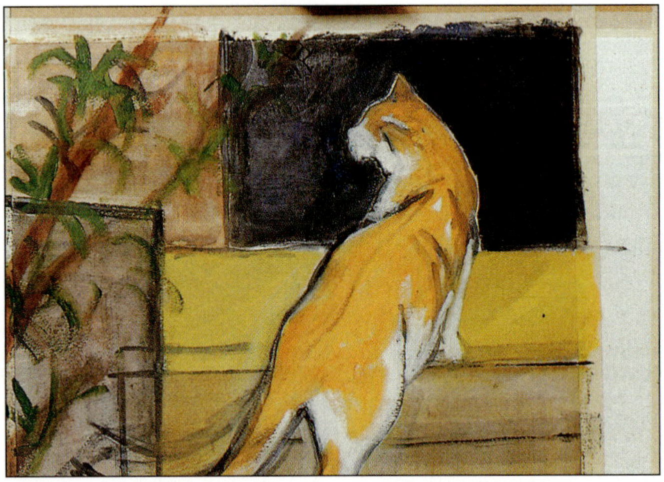

4 The first colors are now laid over the underpainting. The orange provides a key for the painting, but will be modified as the work progresses.

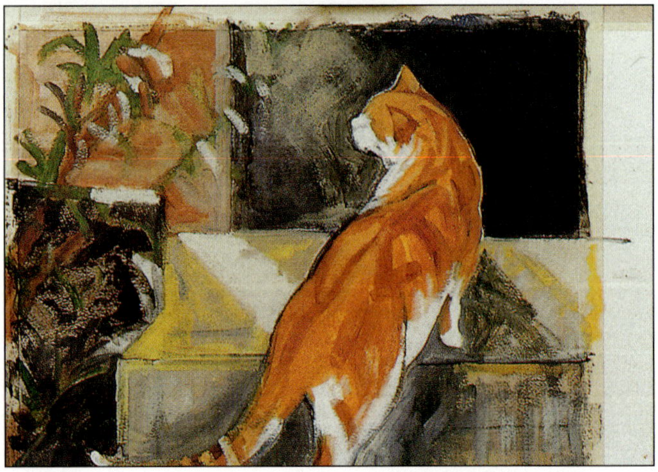

5 The colors of the cat are now built up more richly, beginning to define the forms of the animal, and grays and yellows have been lightly scumbled over the wall. This same broken-color effect has been applied to the background, contrasting with the crisper painting of the animal's head.

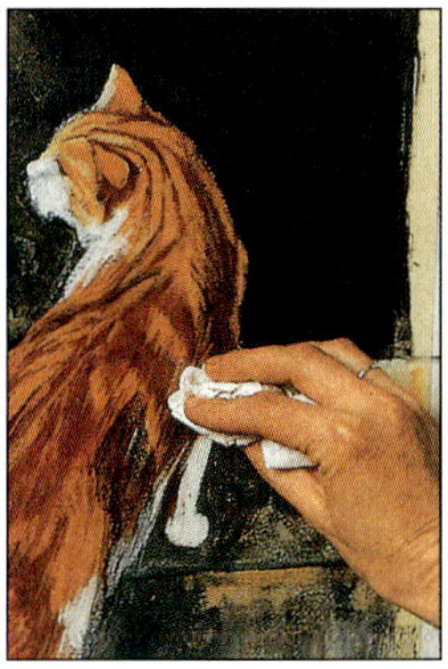

6 The markings and texture of the cat's fur have been accurately depicted by a combination of dry brush and lightly applied wetter paint. Further modeling is now given to the animal's body, with a rag used to push the dark paint into place and hold it away from the white area.

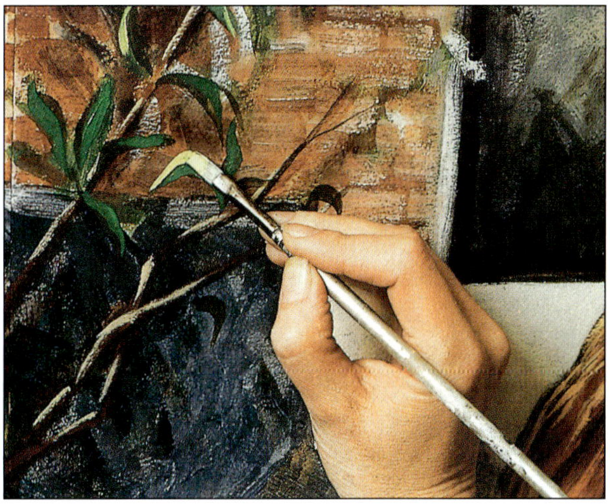

7 With the cat completed, the artist can now assess how much detail and definition is required elsewhere in the painting. Thick, light-colored paint is applied with a nylon brush to create highlights on the leaves and branches.

THE FINISHED PICTURE

The definition of the left-hand side of the painting plays an important part in the composition, as a focus is needed in the direction of the animal's gaze. The dark and light rectangles are equally vital in compositional terms, providing a geometric framework for the long curves of the body and tail.

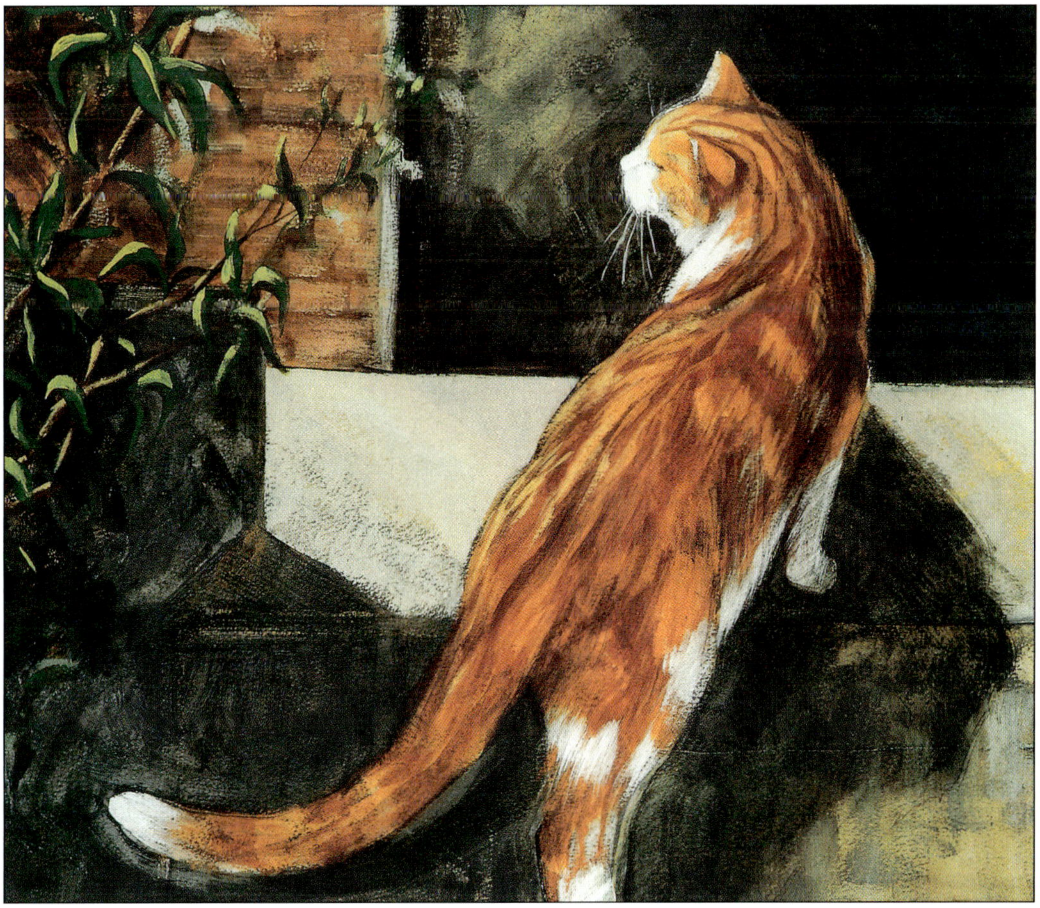

A Bird in Watercolor

The watercolor techniques used for this painting are particularly well-suited to the subject. A combination of loose transparent strokes with opaque white gouache produce an interesting contrast in both texture and tone.

The techniques used – working wet-into-wet and dry brush – require that the painting be executed quickly and confidently. The process involves working from dark to light and from the general to the particular.

Tinted paper was chosen since it has a unifying and reinforcing effect on the painting. When the color of the paper is used as a "color" within the subject, as demonstrated in the head of the bird, the contrast in color and texture both heighten the interest in the subject and link it to its environment.

The method of painting is largely intuitive: you should try and let the painting develop independently and take advantage of the various movements of the paint on the surface. A careful combination of control and a willingness to take chances is required and you should learn to take advantage of "accidents" and use them to express the unique qualities of the picture.

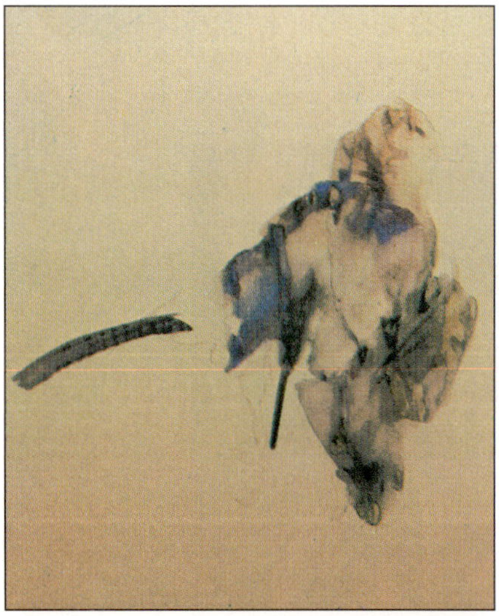

1 With a 2B pencil, lightly sketch in the subject. With a No. 2 sable brush, lay in a thin wash of burnt umber, blue, and alizarin crimson to define the shape of the bird.

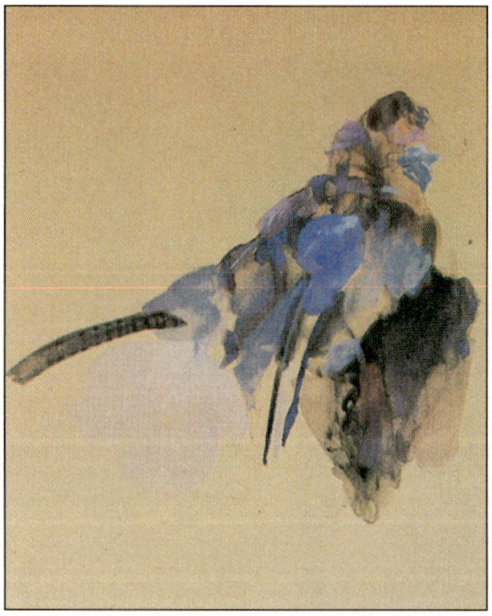

2 Mix a small amount of white gouache with blue and lay this over the undercolors, thinning with water. Put in dark areas with Payne's gray.

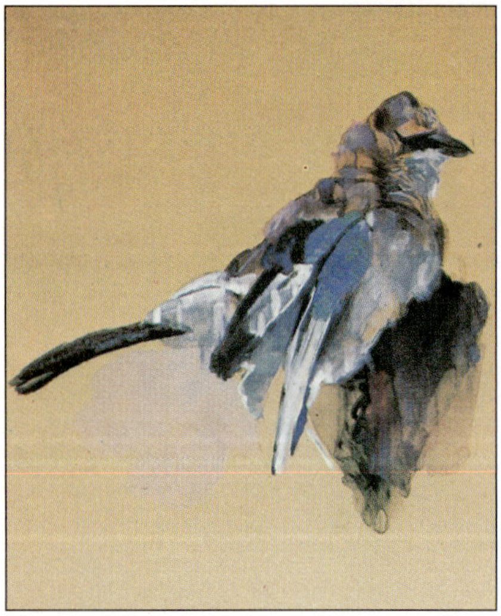

3 With a No. 1 brush, mix white gouache with blue and touch in feathers with a light, directional stroke. Add more blue and describe feather texture in the wing.

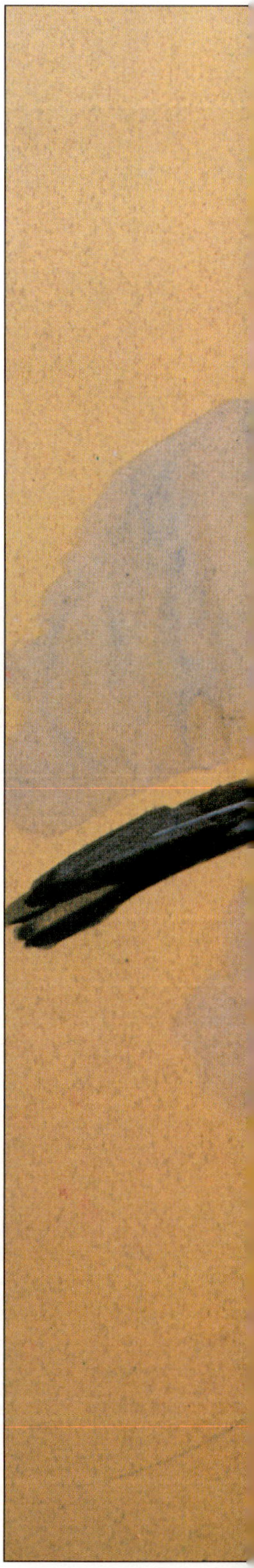

4 With the same brush mix an opaque mixture of Payne's gray and blue, and carefully put in dark details of the wings, tail, and head.

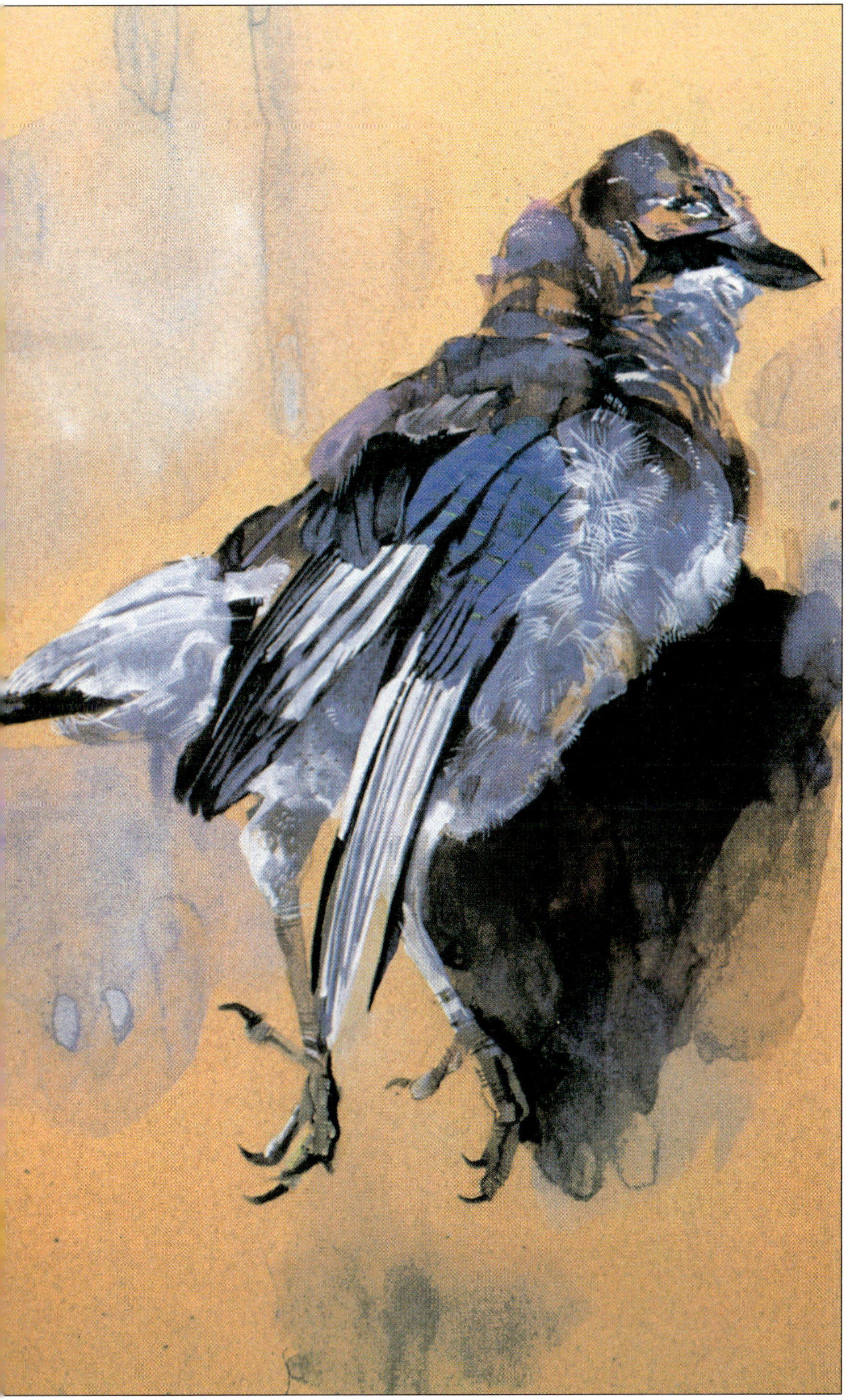

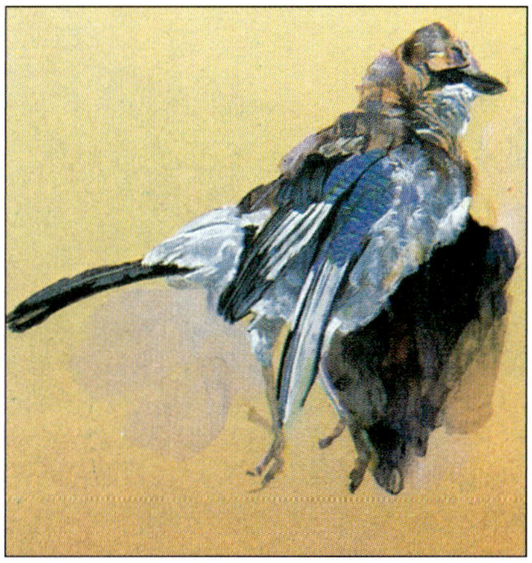

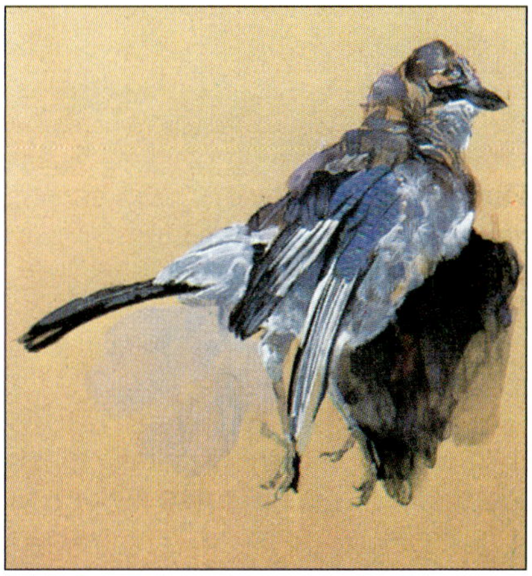

5 With a clean, dry No. 1 brush pick up a small amount of white gouache. Feather this onto the bird's breast and throat in a quick, flicking motion.

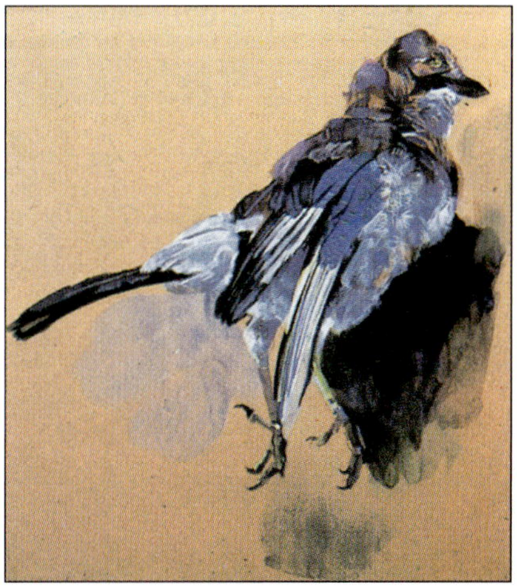

6 With a very thin wash of white gouache mixed with blue, quickly rough in the shadow area around the bird.

A Cheetah in Pastel

To draw an image of this kind from life is obviously impossible. The photograph used as reference was a very dynamic shot, and the incomplete pose, with tail and foreleg cropped, was retained as appropriate to the sense of movement conveyed by the image. The artist had previously studied cheetahs in sketches made at the zoo.

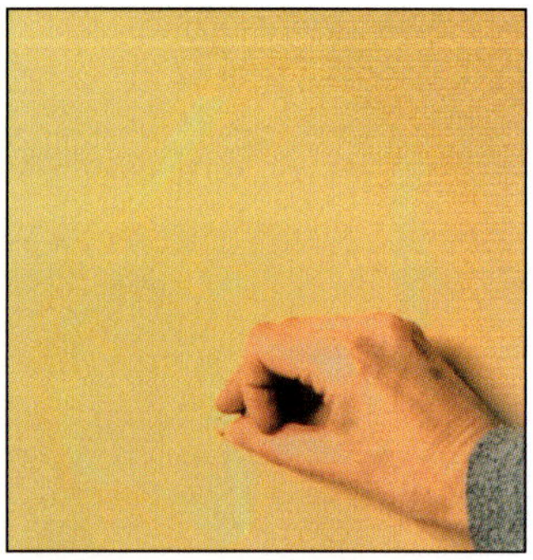

1 The artist is particularly interested in the camouflage patterns of animals. The sandy color of the paper forms the base color both of the cheetah's fur and the dry, earthy background. The contours are freely sketched in yellow ocher and the highlight areas blocked in with a paler yellow tint.

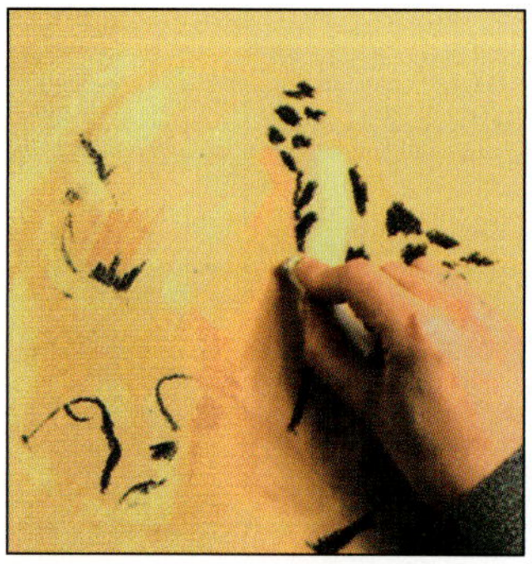

2 Some of the cheetah's markings are drawn in black pastel to key in the darkest tones. Yellow, orange, and brown tints in the fur are loosely indicated with rapid shading and broad, short side strokes.

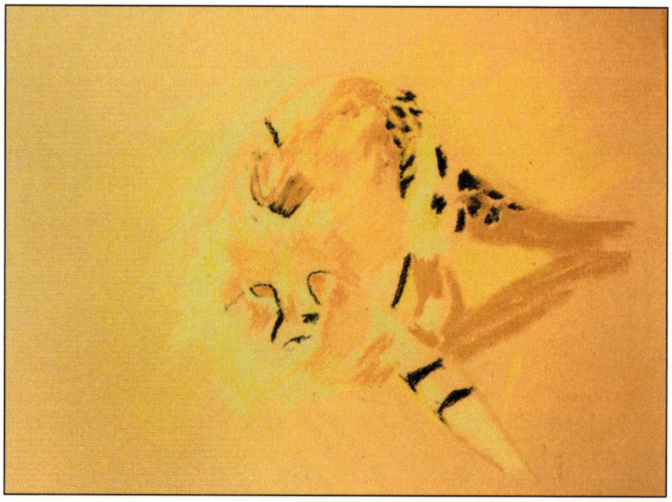

3 The patches of light and shade surrounding the animal are blocked in, and further tones and colors added to the fur, using gestural marks made with the pastel tip. The hints of color are overstated at this stage, but will become more integrated with gradual overworking.

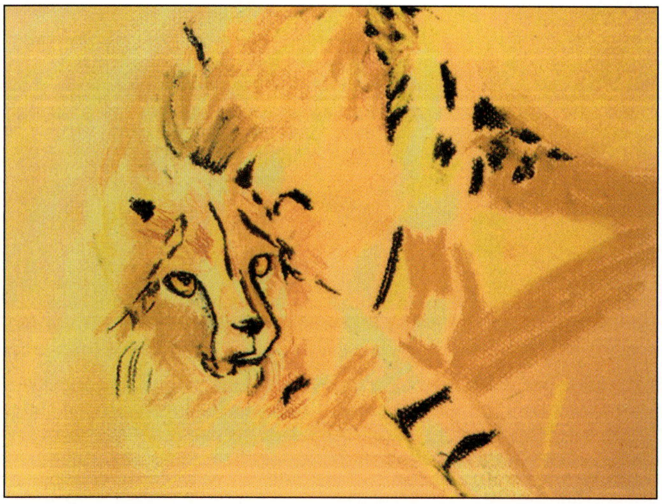

4 The artist begins to define the head, using the natural pattern of black lines around the eyes and nose, and the dark tufts behind the ears. With the stronger blacks in place, the color detail is reworked more heavily, including the orange and gold eyes.

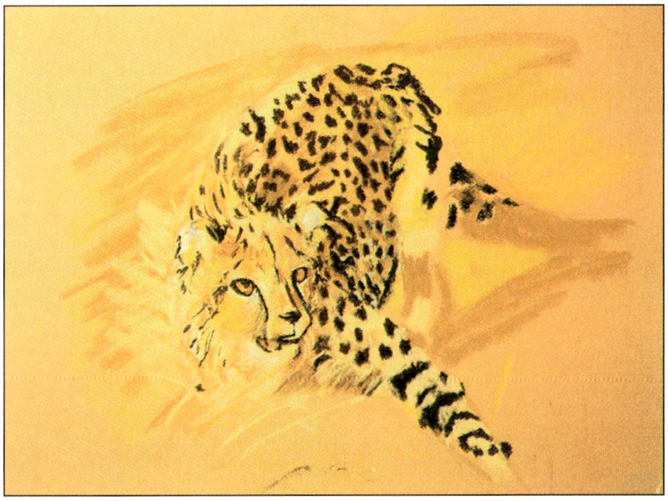

5 The pattern of spots on the cheetah's body and ringed markings on the foreleg are thickly worked with the pastel tip. Around the black spots, the color detail is developed with shading the linear marks, including the white fur highlighting the head and face.

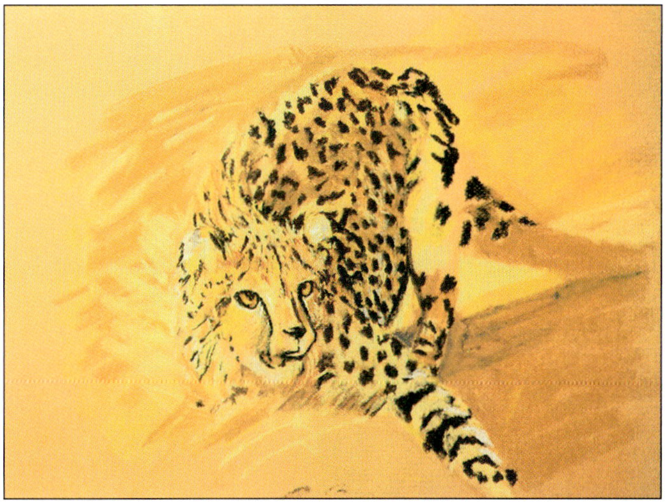

6 The cast shadow under the body and tail is emphasized with a cold gray that contrasts with the warm yellows. The sunlight reflecting on the ground plane is similarly strengthened with the same pale yellow tint previously applied to the fur.

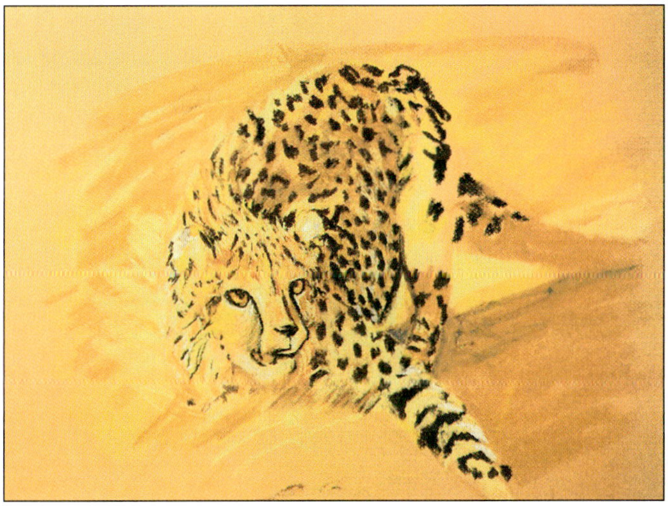

7 The final steps are to put finishing touches to the color detail. Because the yellows now appear a little flat, stronger orange and red ocher patches are laid into the body and tail, and the spot pattern is reworked in black and sepia. The ruff of fur around the head is more heavily textured.

CHEETAH by Judy Martin

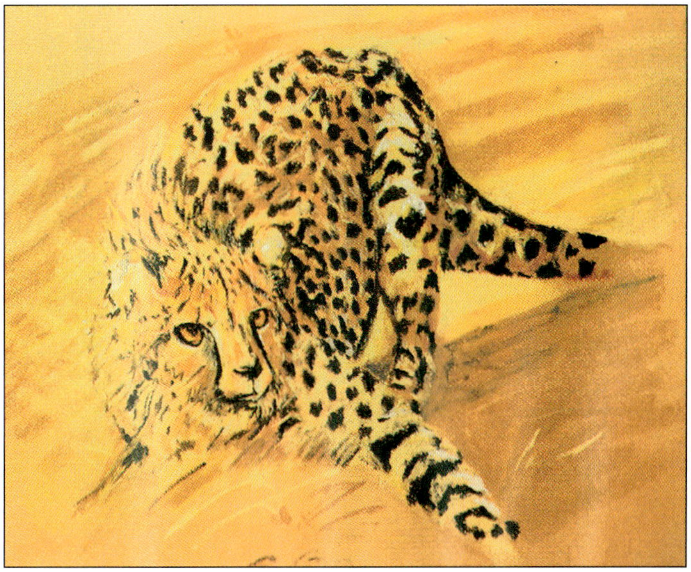

Chimpanzees in Oil

While the artist may use a natural-history subject to successfully capture the essential characteristics of the subject, it may also be used as a vehicle for creating a dramatic picture.

In this painting, the background colors are part of the range used to paint the animals. Although this provides a close harmony in the whole image, the tones must be handled carefully, or the figures will merge into the background. The dark colors of the animals are a rich texture compared with the solid black behind. The flat pink color of the floor is modified and enlivened with a pattern of shadowy color.

Oil paint is a particularly suitable medium for this subject, as it can be blended and streaked to create an impression of soft fur. It is important to study the color carefully. Dark brown fur will have tints and lights which can be used to enrich the painting.

As a starting point, sketch out the forms loosely with a broad bristle brush, but allow the overall shapes to emerge gradually in patches of color, treating each shape as a solid mass.

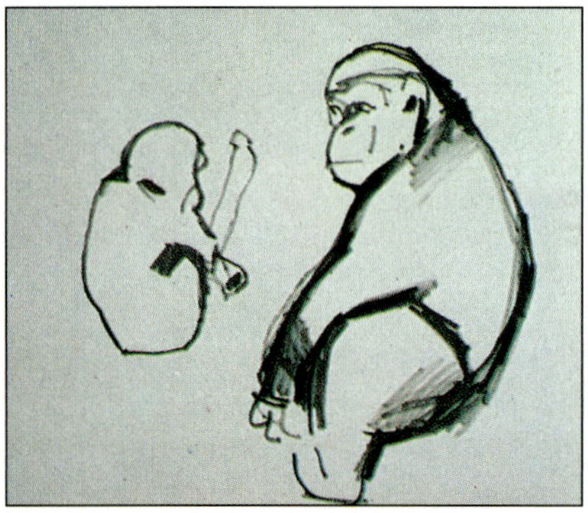

1 Draw up the outline of the animal with a dark brown mixed from raw umber and black. Use a long handled No. 6 bristle brush and work freely to lay in the shapes.

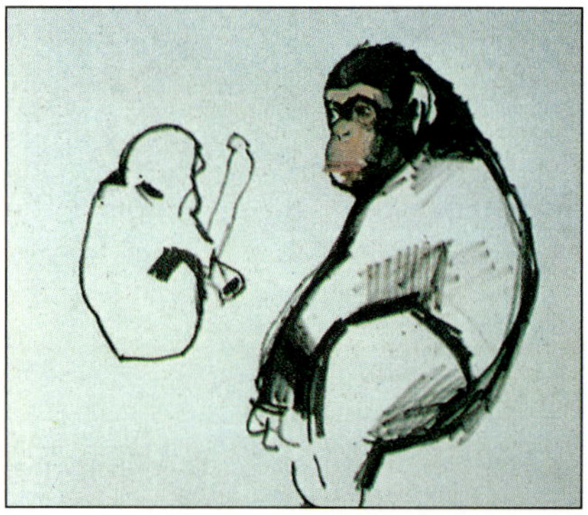

2 Start to work into the head, sketching in the features with the tip of the brush and blocking in the colors of skin and fur.

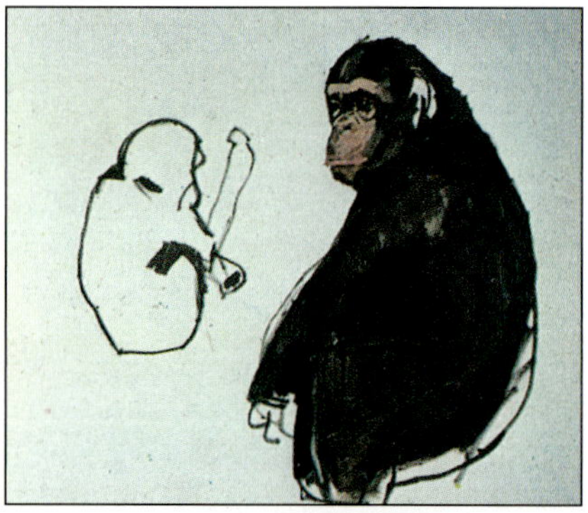

3 Use a sable brush to build up detail, developing the tonal structure of the head. Block in the whole shape of the body loosely with thin paint and a large brush.

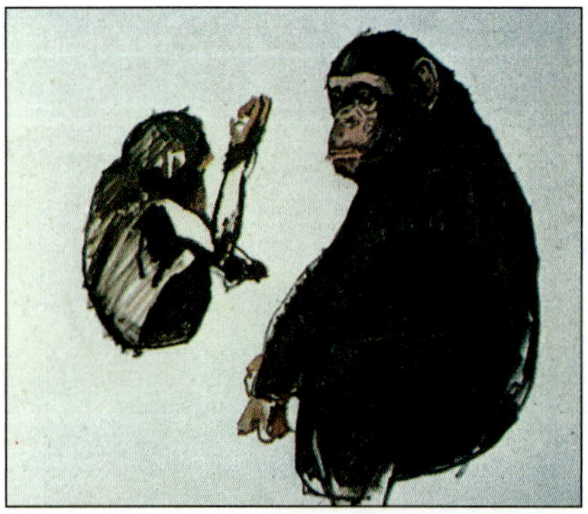

4 Work up the color over the image with pinks and browns, strengthening the dark tones. Lay a thin layer of paint over the shape of the second animal.

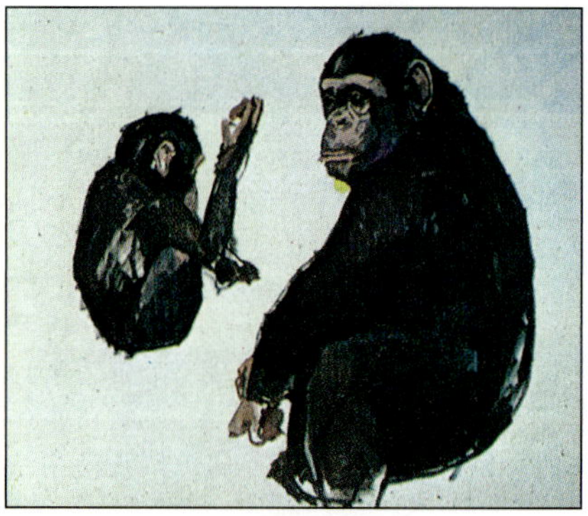

5 Paint freely into both shapes, gradually improving the details of the form and at the same time intensifying the tonal contrasts.

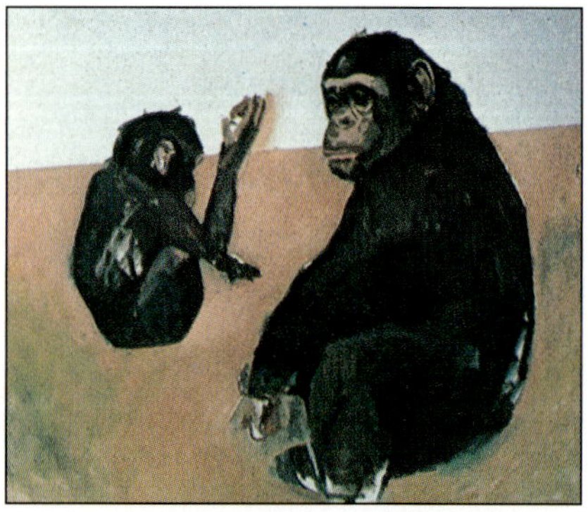

6 Fill-in background color with a layer of thin paint. Use masking tape to make a straight line across the canvas and paint into the outlines to correct the shapes.

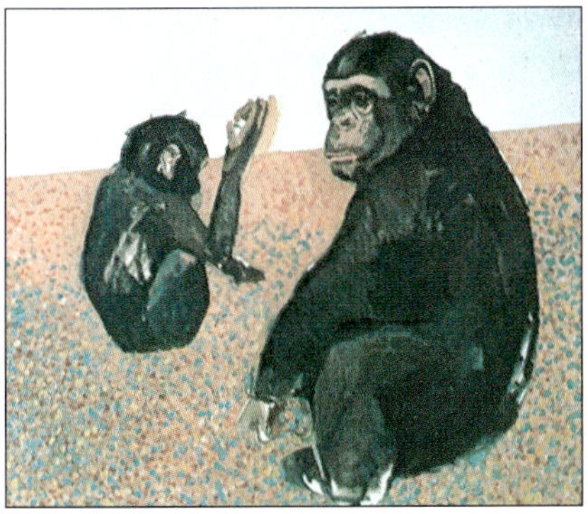

7 Dab in a multi-colored texture over the plain area of floor, overlaying dots of red, pink, blue, and yellow.

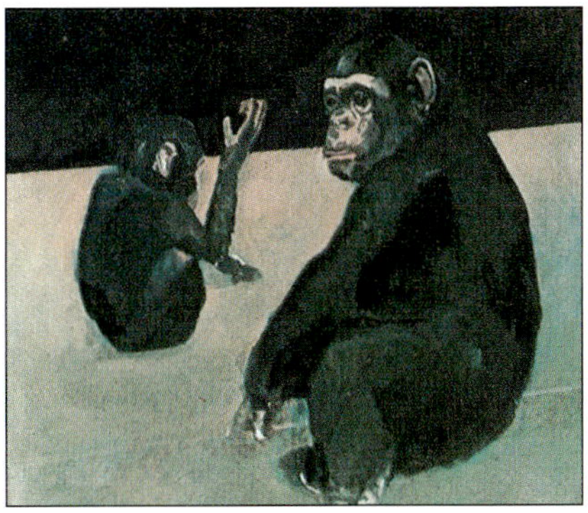

8 Scumble in a thin layer of color over the patterning and thicken it gradually so that some areas of colored dots show through. Brush in solid black across background.

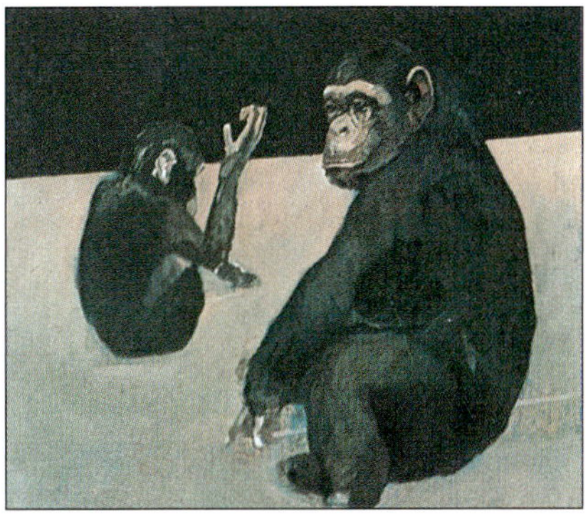

9 Draw back into the details of the face with a fine brush, adjusting the shapes and colors. Enrich the black and brown of the fur to give it texture and sheen.

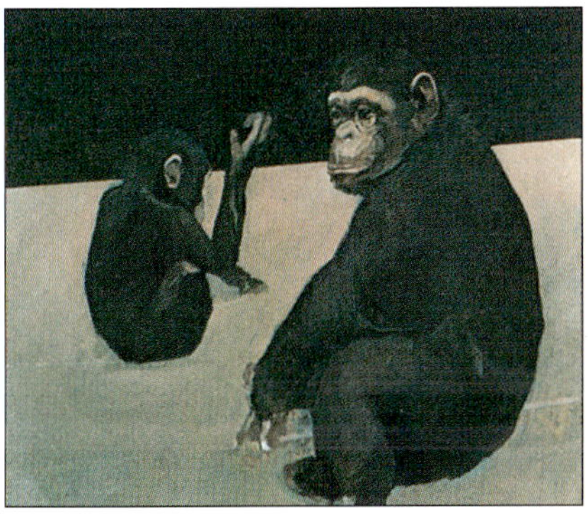

10 Mask off the black background and work across with another layer of color to intensify the dark tone.

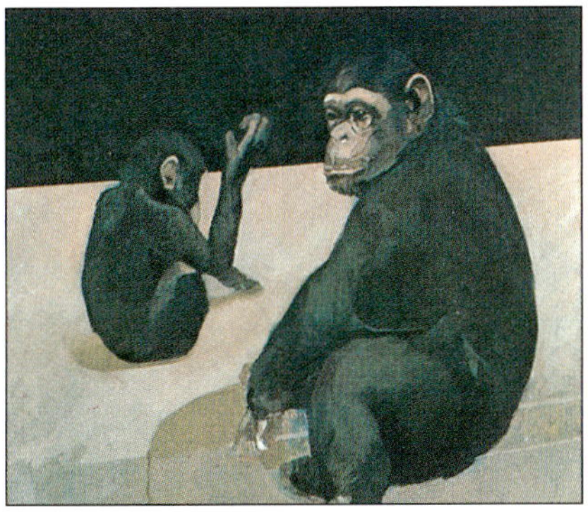

11 Draw up light brown shapes on the pink floor to suggest cast shadows. Finish off with white highlights in the fur.

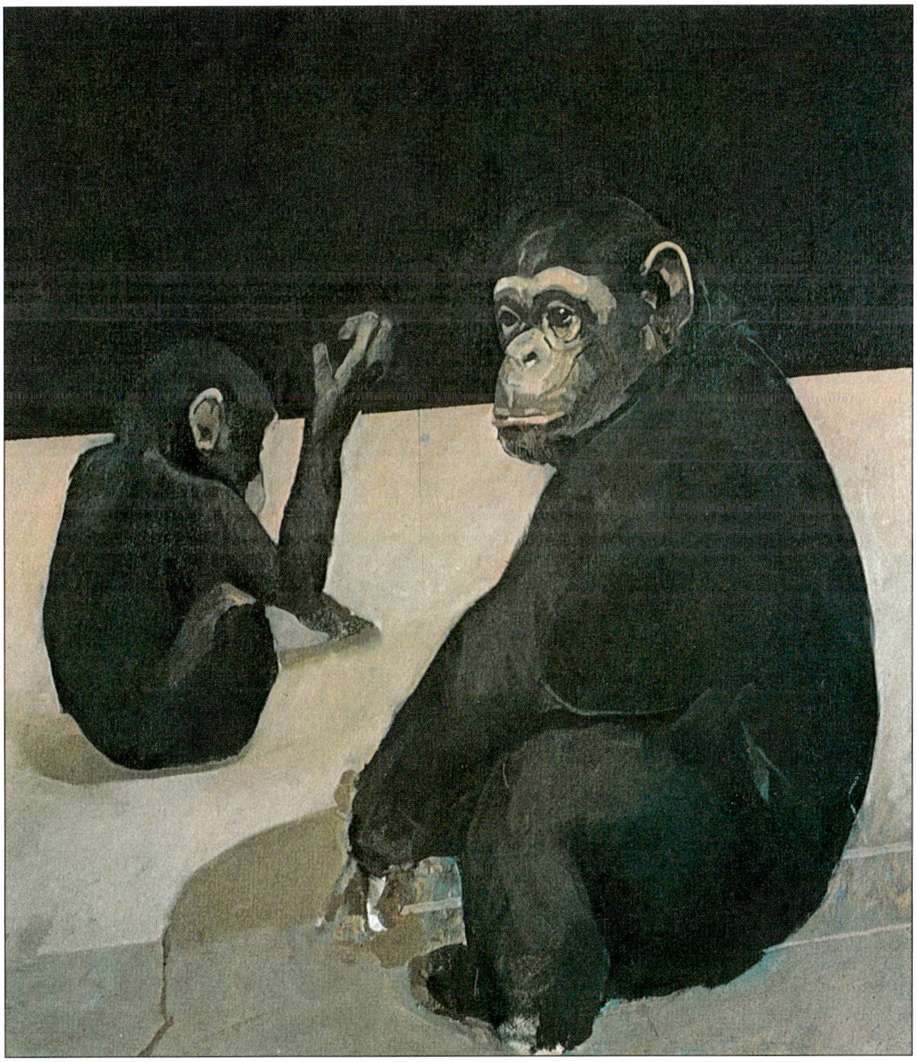

How to Paint: Buildings and Cities

Artists have always made drawings of their surroundings. There is evidence that prehistoric man made records of his home, but the earliest recognizable representational drawings of buildings appear in the backgrounds of early illuminated manuscripts. Sometimes these drawings are of natural places, sometimes they are of imagined cities, with Heaven portrayed as a place of magnificent cathedrals and beautiful palaces. Many important buildings that have long since disappeared are known only through the surviving drawings made of them.

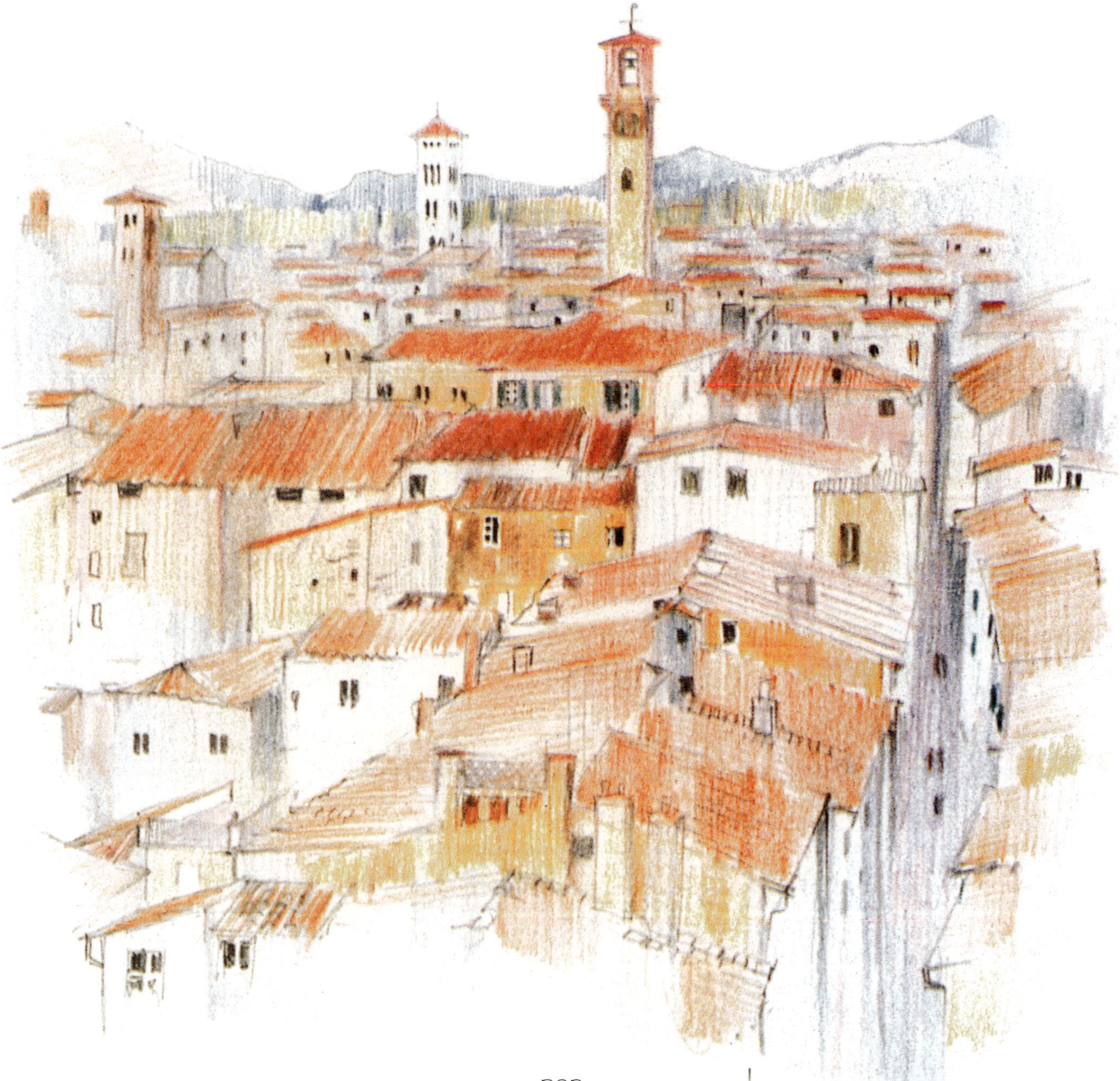

Introduction

Buildings and other man-made structures such as bridges, fences, and walls, attract the attention of painters because of their fascinating shapes, textures, and patterns. In the countryside these fixtures provide a good foil to the surrounding trees and fields; in the city or town the variety of architecture can suggest interesting contrasts, allowing the artist to play with shapes, moods, and tensions. In addition, the size and position of these structures within a composition lend a sense of scale to the scene, and add an element of human interest.

It goes without saying that buildings should always be accurately rendered in terms of scale and perspective, and be given a sense of volume and solidity. But the way they are treated depends on the picture being painted; for example, the flat tones and ruled lines of an architect's draft are inappropriate for a landscape painting but may be suitable for a cityscape. When painting a landscape the artist must approach man-made structures in exactly the same way as trees or clouds, using soft, flowing lines and a sensitive touch, so that they blend in with the surrounding elements of the image.

In rendering the solid, three-dimensional appearance of buildings, it helps if you can find an angle that takes a corner view and creates strong diagonals. Buildings viewed straight-on look much less interesting and more two-dimensional, rather like a flat piece of stage scenery. Remember also that strong contrasts of light and shadow accentuate the form and volume of buildings – long shadows cast in the late afternoon, for example, are particularly useful in this respect.

In order to simplify the process of painting buildings – particularly complex ones such as churches and castles – always start by reducing them to basic geometric shapes and paint these as flat areas of tone. Having laid the foundation, so to speak, you can work up gradually to the more specific details – but avoid overloading your painting with too much factual detail. Suggestion is the key: by giving an indication of texture of pattern here and there, you allow viewers to participate in the painting by filling in the rest of the detail themselves.

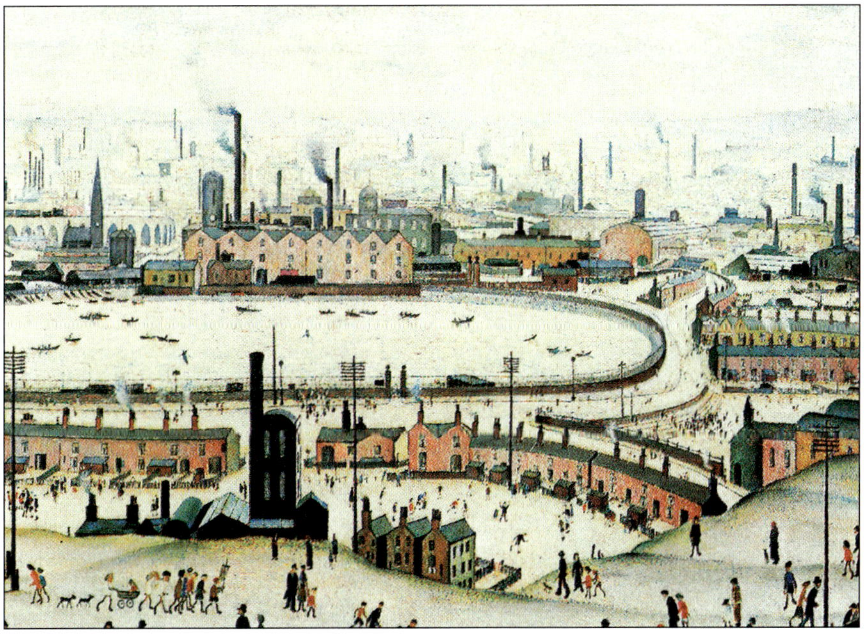

THE POND by L. S. Lowry

Lowry's approach to townscape differs from Canaletto (see page 394), in that the city acts as the environment for the ant-like inhabitants that Lowry makes the main theme of his paintings. He makes little attempt to glorify the buildings of the city. The Canaletto (on page 394) concentrates on the beauty of architecture, and the inhabitants play a secondary role. The aerial view in this painting enables the viewer to embrace a wide panorama. It is a very personal approach to perspective which does not offer any one dominant center of activity.

The romantic classical drawings of Piranesi (1720–1778) were a possible starting-point that allowed artists such as Hogarth (1697–1764) to portray a more realistic and accurate picture of the contemporary scene. By the time of the Impressionists, artists such as Pissarro (1831–1903) had become obsessed with making drawings and paintings of Paris or any other place they visited. More recently, artists have used their depiction of cities to make a social comment or convey a particular emotional quality. The paintings of Edward Hopper (1882–1967) are particularly evocative of the trivial detail of urban nightlife in America. The drawings

VIEW OF WHITEHALL LOOKING NORTH by Anatonio Canaletto

Canaletto is probably best-known for his views of the canals and buildings of Venice. He often painted at great speed for the tourist market. He was certainly skillful and, at his best, a thoughtful and objective observer in a realistic tradition. His earlier Venetian scenes were painted on-the-spot, which was unusual at the time, but he later worked both from drawings and with a camera obscura *in the studio. He worked in England for about ten years in the mid-eighteenth century.*

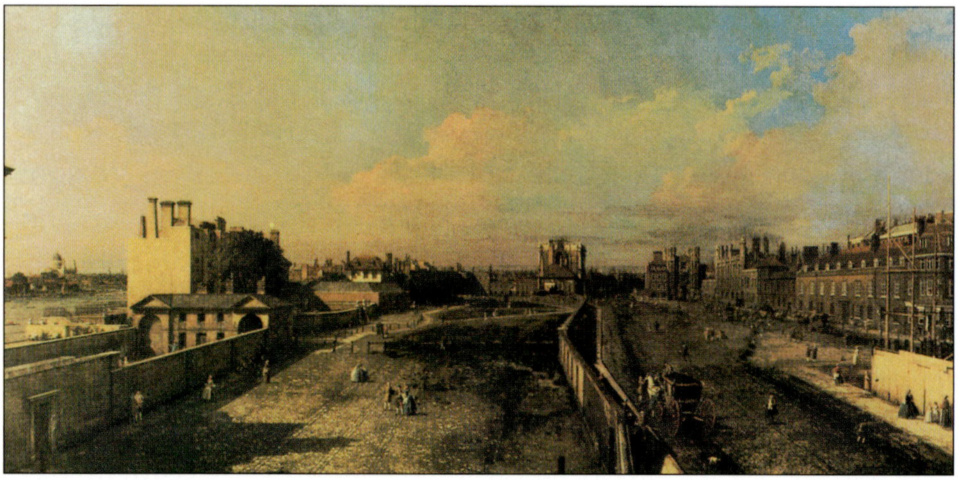

of L. S. Lowry (1887–1976) reveal the industrial north of England as a strange, misty, urban scene populated with stick-like figures. The paintings of European cities by Kokoschka (1886–1980), made from very high viewpoints, display a restless energy that characterizes the dynamism and sprawl of the modern metropolis.

CHOOSING A VIEWPOINT

Kokoschka's paintings, almost like bird's eye views, were made from the windows of very high buildings; and sketches made from windows offering excellent vantage points are one of the most effective ways of making architectural drawings. There are many public buildings, such as museums, that can be used as places in which to draw. The main difficulty in making architectural drawings is firstly, finding a suitable place to draw from – try making a drawing in Times Square, New York City, or in St Mark's Square in Venice – and secondly, deciding the degree to which you will either work "on-the-spot" or will recreate a drawing or painting from sketches, notes, and possibly photographs.

Canaletto made some use of a *camera obscura*, that had been invented in the sixteenth century although the basic principle was noted by Aristotle. The *camera obscura* is a box with a lens at the front, an inclined mirror inside, and a glass screen on top, over which is placed a sheet of thin paper. If the scene is sufficiently bright it will be projected onto the paper which can then be traced. In the early days of its use, when lenses were of relatively poor quality, the image was distorted at the edges and not all artists who used it as a drawing aid thought to correct this distortion. Among English painters to have used it are the Sandbys, Paul (1725/6–1809) and Thomas (1721–1798), de Loutherbourg (1740–1812), Thomas Girtin (1775–1802), and John Crome (1768–1821). Sir Joshua Reynolds (1723–1792) had a folding model, bound to look like a book on ancient history.

Working from direct observation almost always produces the best results. Working from photographs is difficult because generally they do not provide the information you expect. If the view you want depends on being at street level, then in many cities you may have to be at work at first light to be able to produce a drawing before your view is obscured by traffic and pedestrians. It is often very difficult in the high-density, modern city to be able to get far enough away from buildings to be able to see them from a single viewpoint. If you have to "scan up" or across a building in order to see it completely, your resulting drawing is highly likely to make the proportions, and therefore the perspective, appear very distorted.

In choosing a viewpoint at ground level or higher, it is wise to avoid the "flat-on" view of the façade of a building as a major element in your composition. This is because it is extremely difficult to give a building seen from this angle a feeling of solidity.

GEOMETRY AND DETAIL

Above all else, a sound knowledge of perspective is required in order to produce convincing drawings or paintings of architecture. In order to simplify the painting problems for complex buildings such as cathedrals and palaces, reduce them to basic geometric forms. Any building can be seen as a series of large blocks or cylinders, and once these have been lightly indicated, the building can be constructed, with the architectural detail gradually introduced. When you look at a building you get a general feel for it; you don't see the brick or stone patterns on the walls until you look at them separately. This overall impression needs to be retained in the drawing and the details of brick patterns or tiles must not become so prominent that they compete with more important architectural features.

Architectural drawings call in the main on the artist's skill in judging perspective, and in particular on his or her ability to create specific textures and depict the strong contrasts of light and shade.

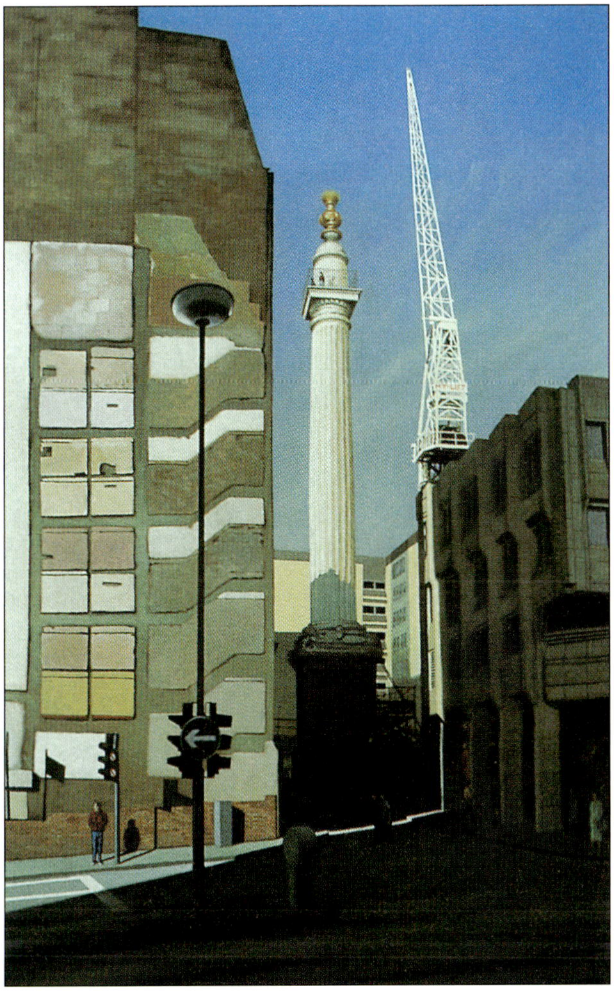

THE MONUMENT by Brian Yale

In this painting of London's Monument and the surrounding buildings, the approach is almost photographic, with minute attention paid to every detail and texture. The composition is beautifully worked out, with the diagonal line formed by the edge of the dark shadow leading the eye up the right-hand side of the building and the crane that forms a balance for the Monument itself.

MOOD AND ATMOSPHERE

All towns and cities have their own particular feeling, so if you are painting townscape rather than individual buildings, try to analyze what this feeling is and find ways of creating a sense of place by giving visual clues. In an exotic location, for example, people's clothing and characteristic postures will be strong indicators, while in a busy modern city you can make cars and typical "street furniture" part of the composition.

It is often possible to convey a sense of place through color or texture alone, making a play of light, bright colors or strong tonal contrasts in a sunny Mediterranean town, and exploiting "low-key" colors, such as grays and browns, in a northern industrial setting. Or you could make a feature of rough stone or peeling plaster on old buildings or the smooth or reflective surfaces of new ones.

A sense of mood derives from a complex interaction of factors, from simple physical characteristics to memories and associations brought to an image by artist or viewer. Some places have an inherent atmosphere relating to their appearance or function; some present a different character according to the weather or time of day. A straightforward record of a particular environment may in itself convey a mood, but you can also take a more deliberate approach and use formal elements of drawing and painting, such as color and composition, to develop your feeling for a subject and communicate more than just an immediate visual impression.

Your viewpoint and the extent and organization of your composition contribute to the mood of the subject. An individual building or a whole town can be made to appear isolated and remote by placing it centrally within a broader landscape. A low-level or flatly frontal view makes the building seem less accessible than an angled, eye-level view that emphasizes ways into and around the structure.

Harsh lighting or exaggerated colors can create a sense of alienation, while naturalistic color, even with strong lights and shadows, is more reassuring.

THE NEW CITY by Richard French

One of the most exciting visual phenomena of the modern city is that of reflections in the many large expanses of glass, often distorted in intriguing ways. Here the artist has mimicked the effect of such reflections by using multiple layers of acrylic glazes, working on a smooth-surfaced acid-free mountboard known as museum board. The painting is a large one, and to facilitate handling it was painted in three separate sections.

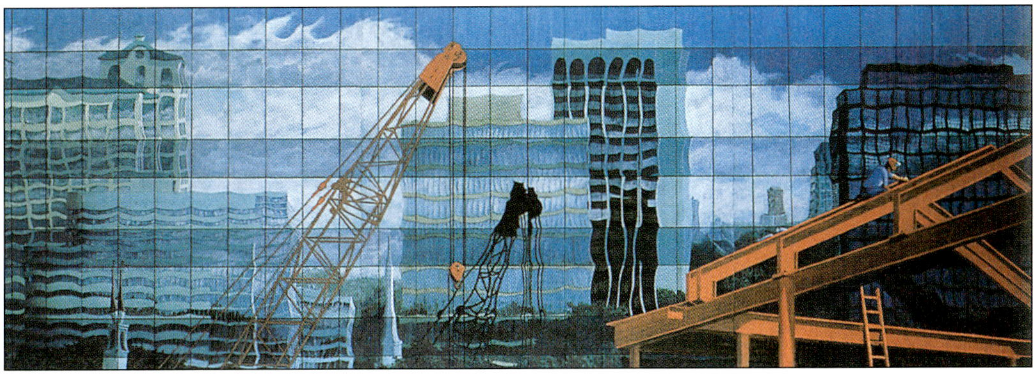

Brickwork

When you look closely at the walls of a building, you can see every brick and tile; but when you take in the overall look of a building, you don't see individual bricks – although you know they are there. This is the effect you should convey in your painting: by describing a few bricks here and there, you will suggest them all, without burdening your viewer with too much tiresome detail.

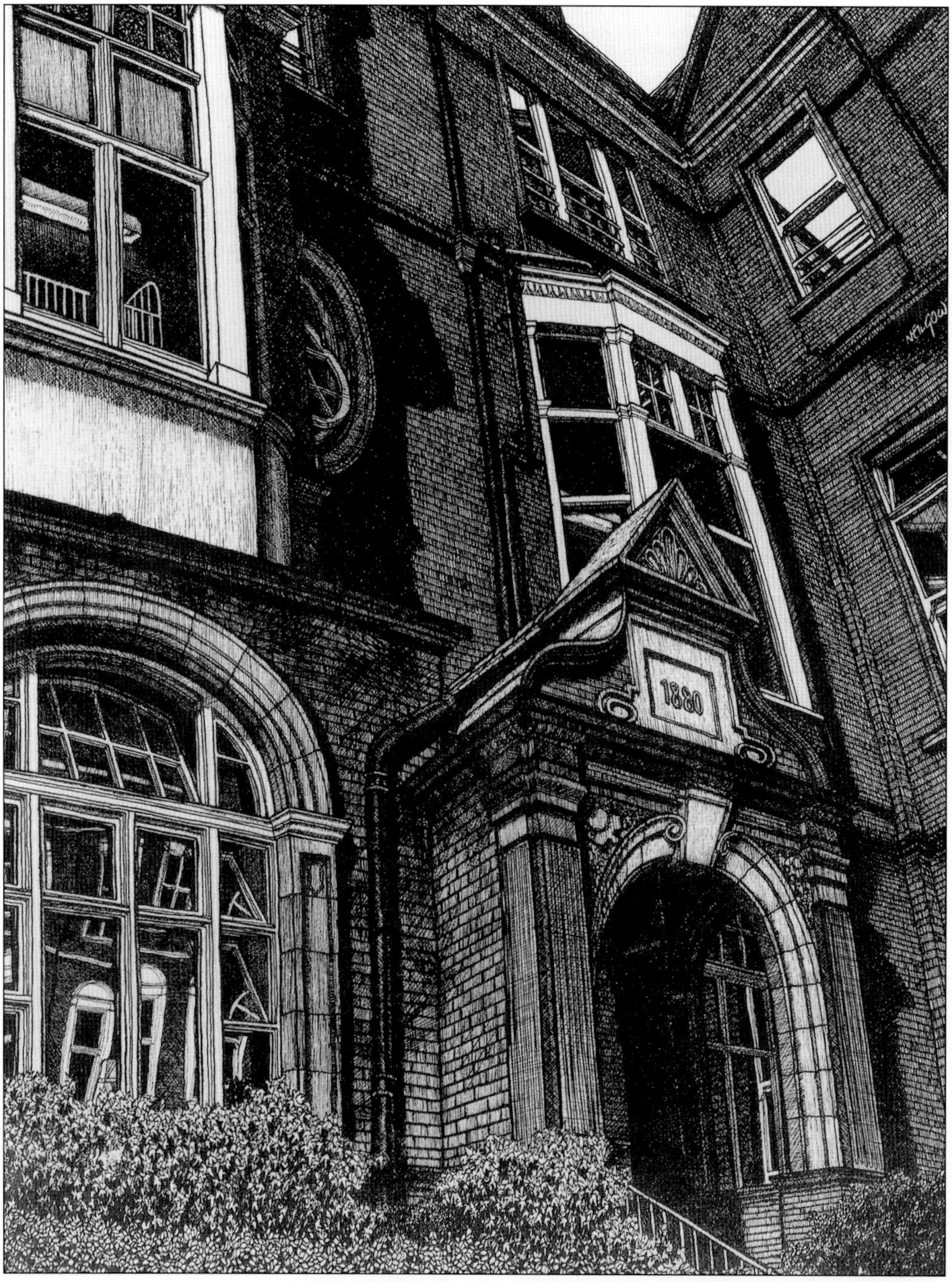

In reality, this imposing Victorian edifice must contain thousands of bricks, but the artist has not attempted to represent them all. By using horizontal and vertical hatching he has successfully conveyed the texture of the bricks, leaving the imagination to supply the details. Pen and ink linework has been used to create very dark areas of shadow by building up layers of crosshatching. Some spots of white paper break through these shadows, helping to retain a degree of luminosity and preventing them from looking dull and flat. The detail shows a lively use of hatching for the stonework of a large window arch.

Always begin by indicating the overall tone of the wall or roof, and the pattern of light and shade. Then add a suggestion of texture.

Beware of painting bricks and tiles too bright a color, and notice how the color can vary from brick to brick. Use warm, muted reds, plus greens, blues, and earth colors to describe them.

BRICK WALL

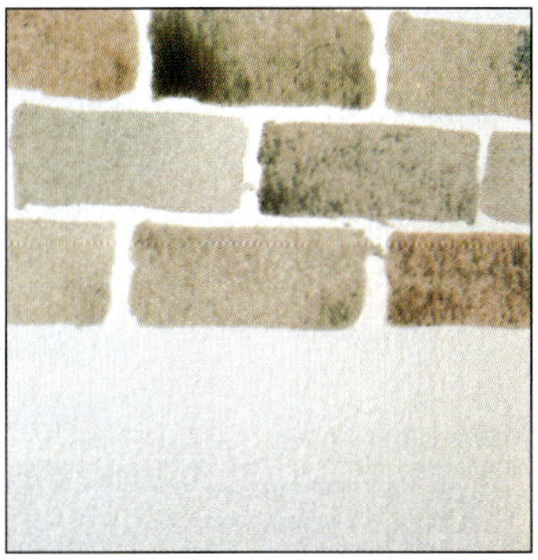

1 The artist begins painting the wall by laying in a pale wash of raw sienna to provide a background tone. When this is dry, a No. 6 chisel brush is used to paint the bricks, leaving uneven white spaces between the bricks to indicate light-colored mortar.

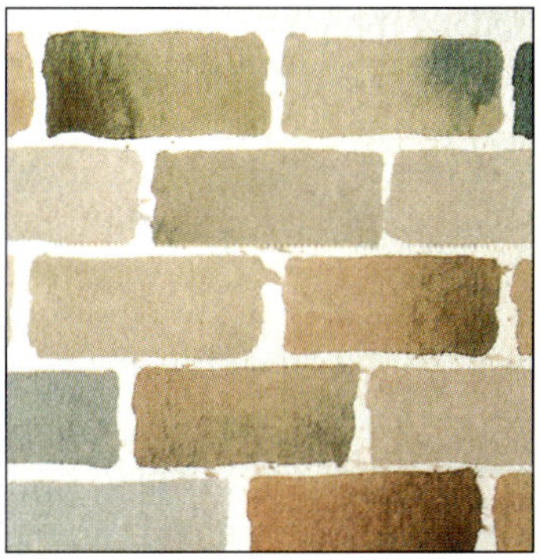

2 Notice the irregular shapes of the bricks, and the variety of colors and tones used. It is a good idea to have your colors mixed up ready on the palette rather than mixing them haphazardly, as you go along. This facilitates speed of handling, and you can be sure your colors will be clean and fresh. Wash the brush thoroughly between each application of color. The colors used here were raw umber, raw sienna, burnt sienna, and Payne's gray, used in varying strengths.

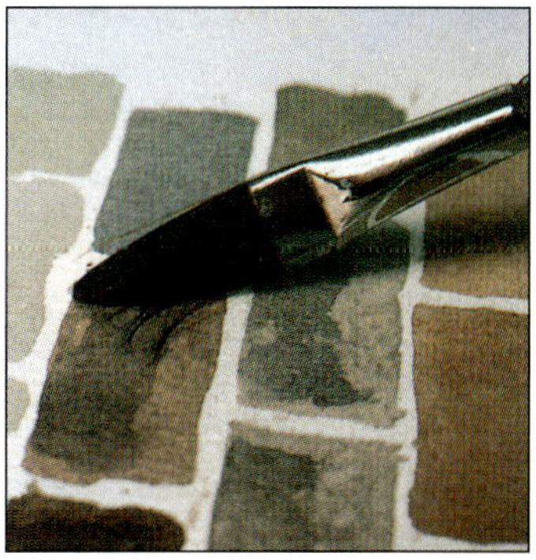

3 When the first colors are dry the artist adds shadow washes, wet over dry, with a weak solution of Payne's gray. This gives form and texture to the bricks.

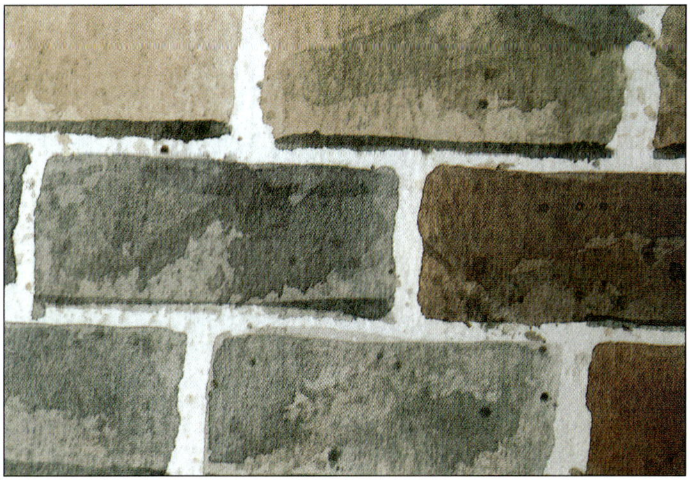

4 The shadows are developed further with washes and glazes to achieve a crisp, rugged look. Finally, a weak solution of Payne's gray and raw umber is mixed on the palette and then lightly spattered over the picture surface to accentuate the pitted, weathered character of the bricks.

PAINTING TIP

Special mediums are sold for texturing, but sand, chosen here, is equally effective for creating the texture of brick or stonework.

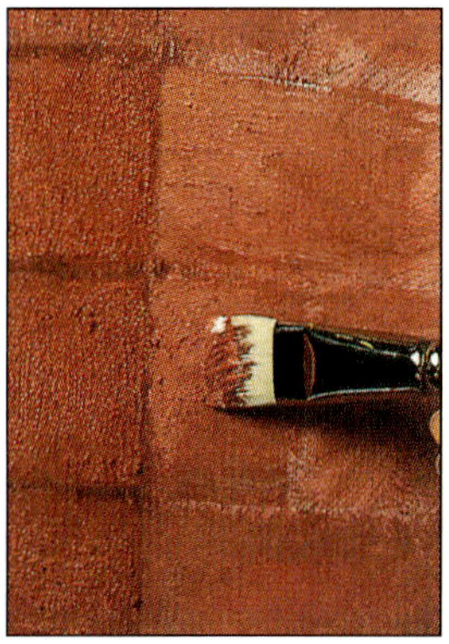

1 Begin with a base color in thinned paint. Then mix the color you want, add about half the quantity of sand, and apply it with a bristle brush.

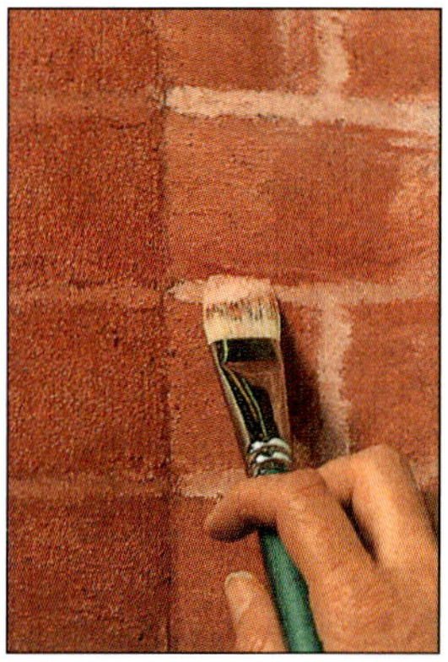

2 Use a little less sand for the lines of mortar between the bricks, since this has a smoother texture. Apply the paint with short downward strokes.

Stone

Walls and buildings made of stone are always an attractive feature, because of their hues and the interesting colors they take on as a result of the effects of weathering and the growth of moss and lichen on their surface.

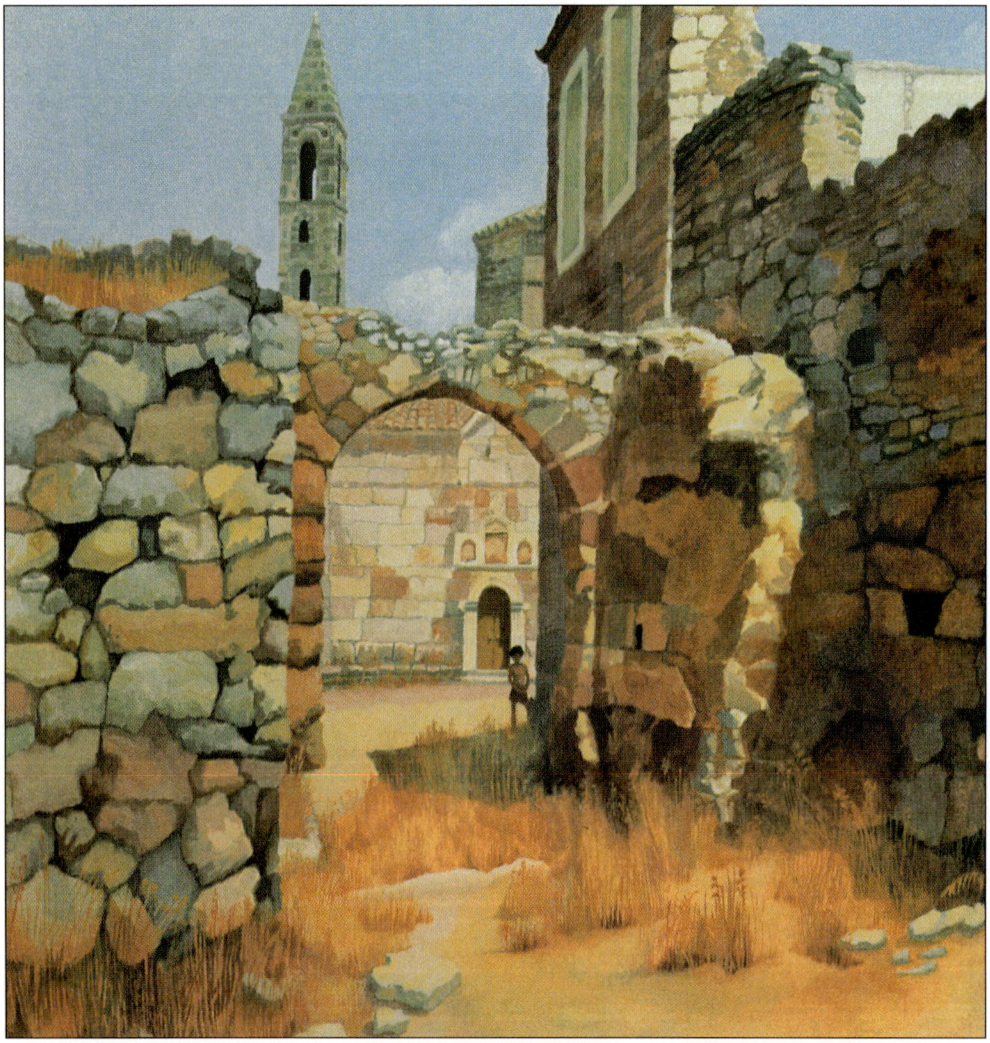

THE OLD VILLAGE OF KARDAMILI, PELOPONNESE by Jill Mirza

The varied colors and irregular shapes of the building stones and the strong shadows and highlights create a lively pattern throughout the painting. Acrylic can be used in transparent washes just like watercolor, but Mirza uses it very much like opaque gouache, laying light colors over dark and vice versa. The luminous quality of the shadowed walls on the left has been achieved by glazing thin paint over underlying colors.

Start with a pale wash of color to define the overall tone of the wall and then imply the texture of the stone's surface with dry brush strokes and/ or sgraffito techniques. Watercolorists frequently use spattering to indicate the pitted nature of stone; the addition of a few granules of salt while the paint is still wet adds an interesting weathered appearance.

When painting the dry stone walls often found on farms, it is usually best to begin by painting the wall as one mass rather than defining the individual stones. When the light and shadow planes have been established, you can then suggest individual stones – but without giving emphasis to every one. Use neutral tones – never black – to paint the cracks between the stones and the shadows cast by some stones protruding over the ones below.

PATTERN AND TEXTURE

Man-made structures provide as much variety of pattern and texture as the natural world, and it is often these that attract us to a particular building rather than its shape or proportion. Building materials vary hugely – there are houses with wooden boarding, great expanses of shimmering glass on modern office buildings, white-washed houses, mellowed brick mansions and great stone churches. It would be a great pity to ignore the inventiveness of generations of architects and builders, and, in any case, if you paint a wall or roof exactly the same color and tone all over, it will look like a cardboard cut-out.

Although in general old buildings provide the most

surface interest because the materials have become weathered, new ones also have texture or pattern of some kind, so always look for ways of suggesting these qualities.

There are many techniques ideally suited to painting texture. You could try, for example, the wax resist or scumbling methods. It is worth experimenting and you will then evolve your own personal variations.

DRY STONE WALL

The dry stone walls often seen in the countryside have a special character resulting from prolonged exposure to the elements. The stones lie unevenly, some protruding over the ones below and some indented, and their surface is pitted and cracked with age. Below is a step-by-step demonstration using watercolor paints.

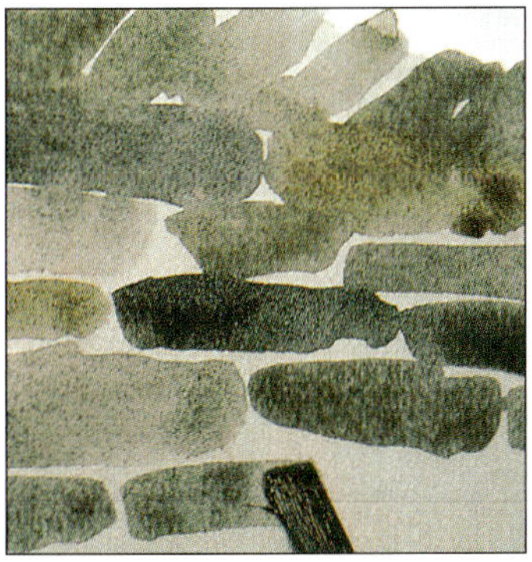

1 The first stage in painting the wall is to apply an all-over wash of raw umber, on a sheet of rough-textured paper. When this is dry, a chisel brush is used to indicate the rough shapes of the stones. The colors used here were raw umber, Payne's gray, and yellow ocher, mixed in various quantities to create a variety of sludgy tones and colors.

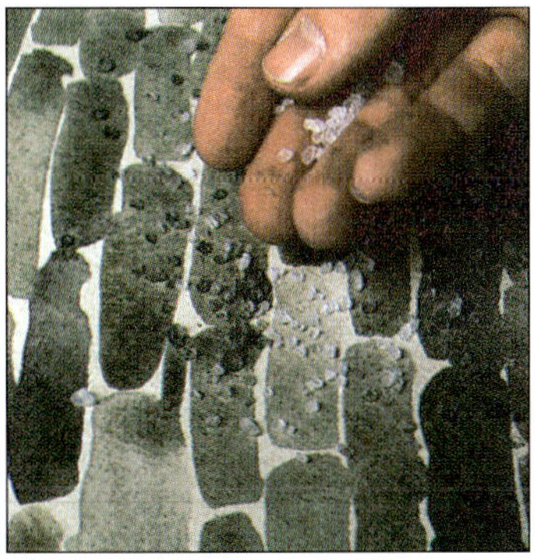

2 Just before the paint dries the artist sprinkles a few granules of rock salt over the painting and then leaves it to dry in a horizontal position.

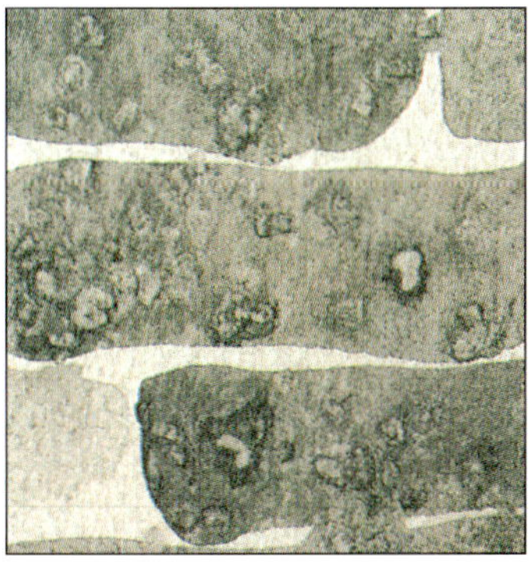

3 When the painting is dry the salt is brushed off. The salt granules have soaked up the paint where they landed, leaving tiny pale shapes which effectively simulate the pitted texture of the stones.

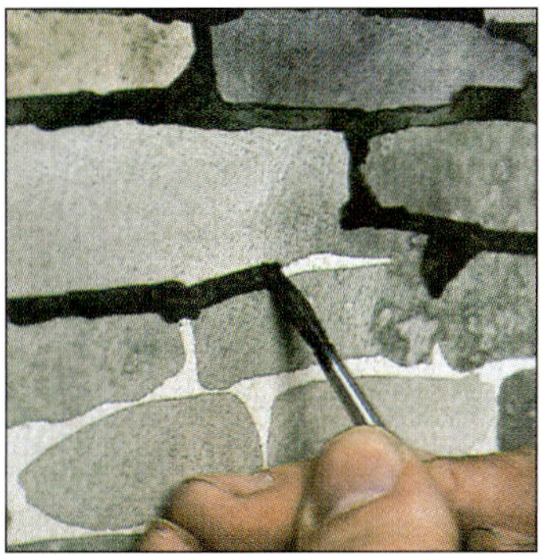

4 A strong mixture of Payne's gray and sap green is used to render the dark cracks between the stones. Introduce variety by making the cracks lighter in some places.

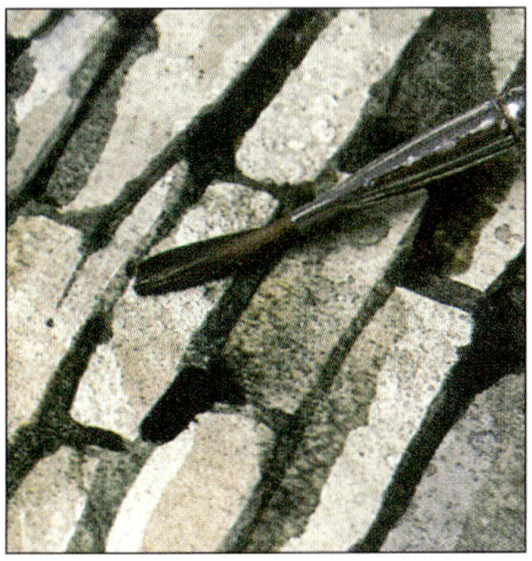

5 The painting is allowed to dry, then pale washes of raw sienna and Payne's gray mixed with sap green are used to add glazes that darken the wall in places.

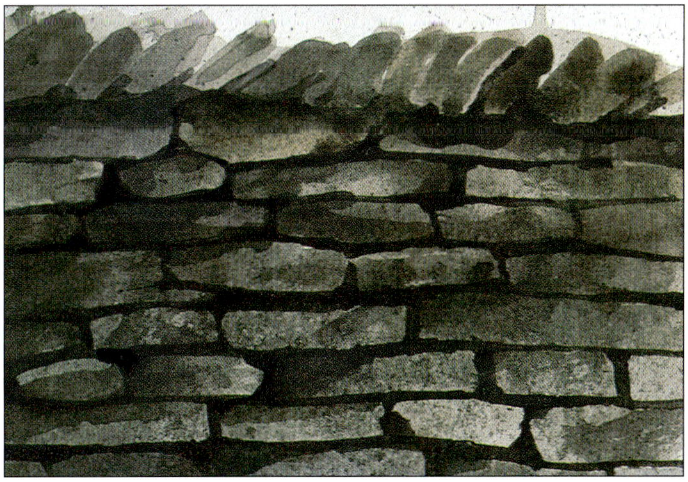

6 The same colors used in step 5 are lightly spattered over the picture surface. Here you can see how washes and glazes, spatter, and salt texture have been combined to give a suitably weathered look to the wall. The stones jutting out into the sunlight are sharply defined, whereas those farther back are blurred into the shadows.

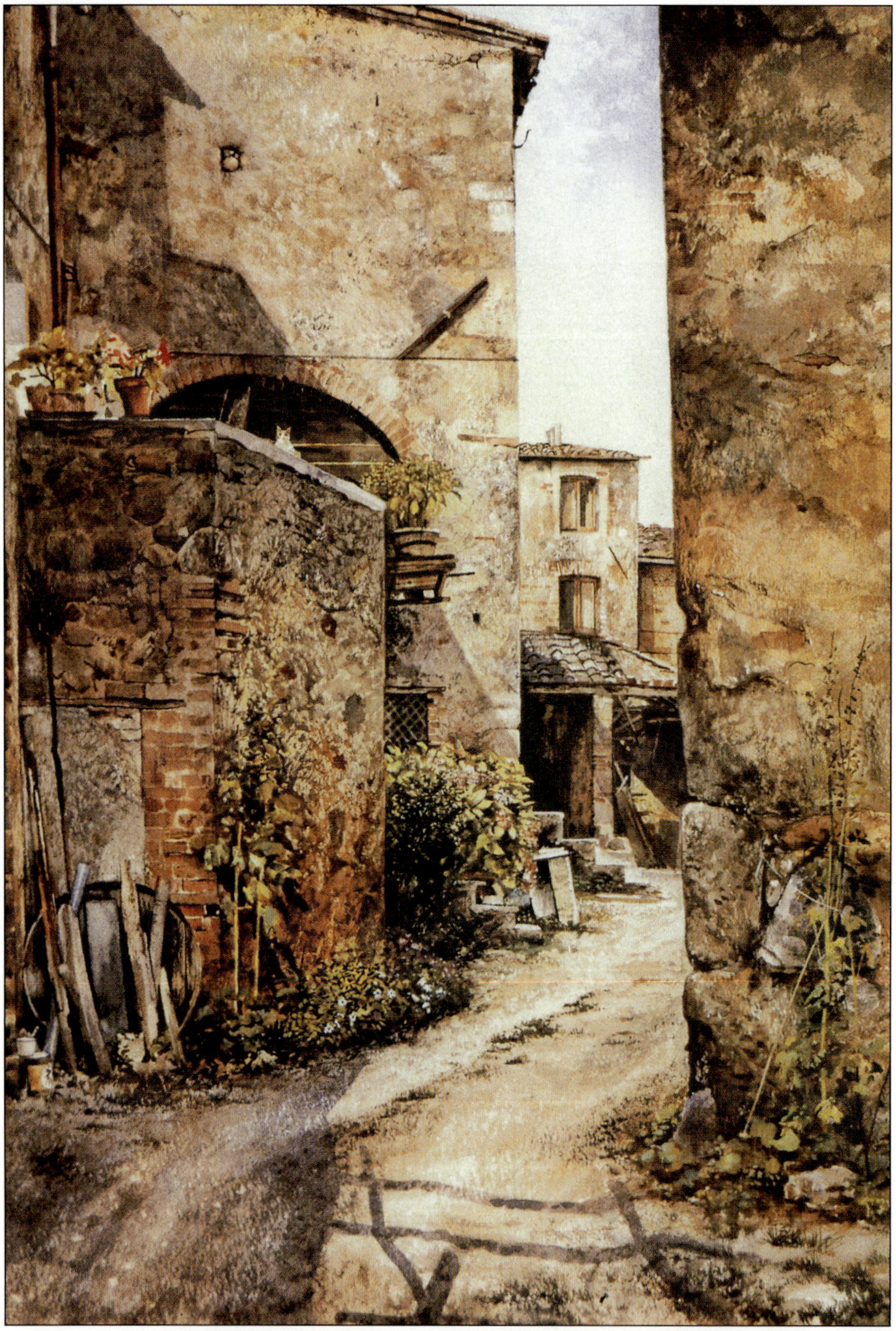

WITHIN THE CASTLE WALLS by Martin Taylor

Here Taylor has built up the richly textured surface of the old stonework by successive scumbling with a dry watercolor and acrylic mixture over transparent washes. In places he has scuffed the paper with the blade of a knife, applied paint on top, and then repeated the process. Good watercolor paper is surprisingly tough and can withstand a good deal of such treatment.

WEATHERED STONE

A painted stone wall might at first glance seem to be lacking in tonal variety, but closer examination will reveal a vast range of colors and textures which result from the effects of the climate. The pitted surface can be rendered with cool shadows to contrast with the warmth of the paler tones and can be textured with a combination of hard and soft edges.

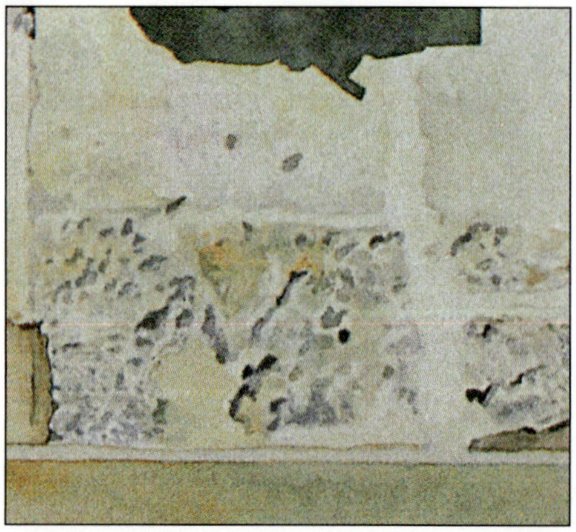

Details

A building derives much of its character from the details of its architecture, such as doors, windows, balconies, and decorative brick- and stonework, all of which make lovely painting subjects in themselves, as explained on the previous pages. An open shutter casting a shadow on a whitewashed wall, for instance, could make an exciting composition, providing a contrast of colors and an interplay of vertical and diagonal lines. This kind of subject can all too easily become static and dull, however, so try to keep your brushwork lively and varied, using a combination of fluid washes and crisp lines. You may find the line and wash technique adds this kind of extra dimension, or you could make texture the main theme of the painting, using, say, the wax resist method.

Try to relate the chosen detail to the structure of the building and be careful about the viewpoint you choose. If you paint a window from straight on, you will not be able to suggest the depth of the recess and hence the thickness of the wall, giving it the appearance of being stuck on rather than built in. Another common mistake when painting windows is to make them the same dark tone all over, but window glass takes its colors and tones from the prevailing light, often reflecting color from the sky or other buildings, or showing glimpses from the room behind. If you look carefully, you will see variations.

Once you begin to focus in on a building to see what it is that gives it its special character you will see a wealth of detail, such as balconies, cornices, window frames and sills, patterns of brickwork, and drainpipes twisting down a wall, and you will have to decide how much detail to include.

There is no reason why you should not put in everything you see, but equally there is no reason why you should. Remember that the painting is the important thing, and if the composition needs an accent of color in the form of a brightly painted door or a curtained window, then make the most of such things.

You might also consider taking a close-up approach and homing in on one small part of a building, such as an open door or a single window. Such subjects can make very exciting compositions, but you will have to plan the composition with care to avoid an over-symmetrical effect – symmetry is static and thus does not hold the viewer's interest.

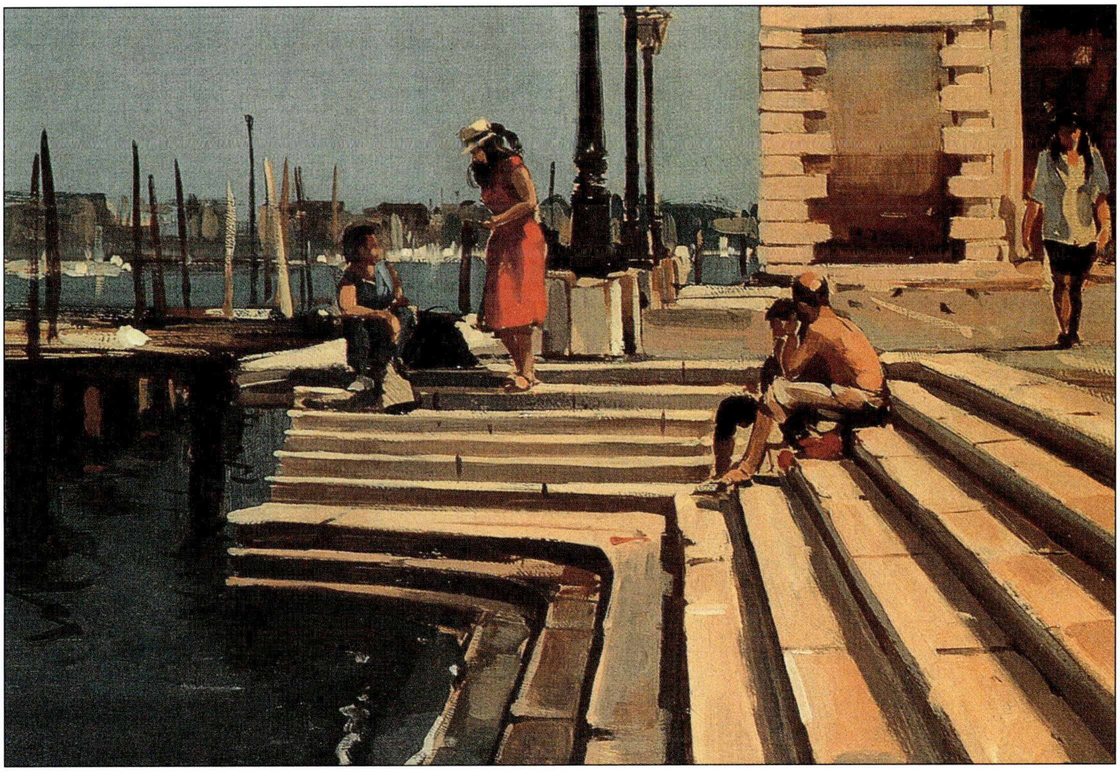

GIRL IN A RED DRESS by Raymond Leech

The vital ingredient of this unusual composition is the steps, whose form and repetitive shape lead the eye into the picture to the central lamppost and eye-catching red dress. They have been very carefully painted, as has the area of wall behind with its pattern of large slabs. This also plays an important part in the picture.

Façades

Concentrating on the façade of a building is like drawing its portrait. The three-dimensional depth and interior space become irrelevant; you focus on the details of the architecture that give the essence of the building's style and make it recognizable and memorable. You have to work out which details contribute to a true likeness of the building as you see it.

Since a direct, frontal viewpoint eliminates many elements of perspective, it simplifies your task in terms of identifying basic structures – but because there is no surrounding detail to distract the eye, the elements of the façade that you wish to portray need to be well-chosen and accurately rendered. The accuracy lies not in reproducing shape and proportion correctly as if from an architect's blueprint, but in defining the relationships of shape, form, color, and texture – the ways they interact and how each element functions within the whole. As can be seen from the examples here, this can be dealt with as an apparently detailed, naturalistic image or as a "portrait sketch" homing in on the bare essentials.

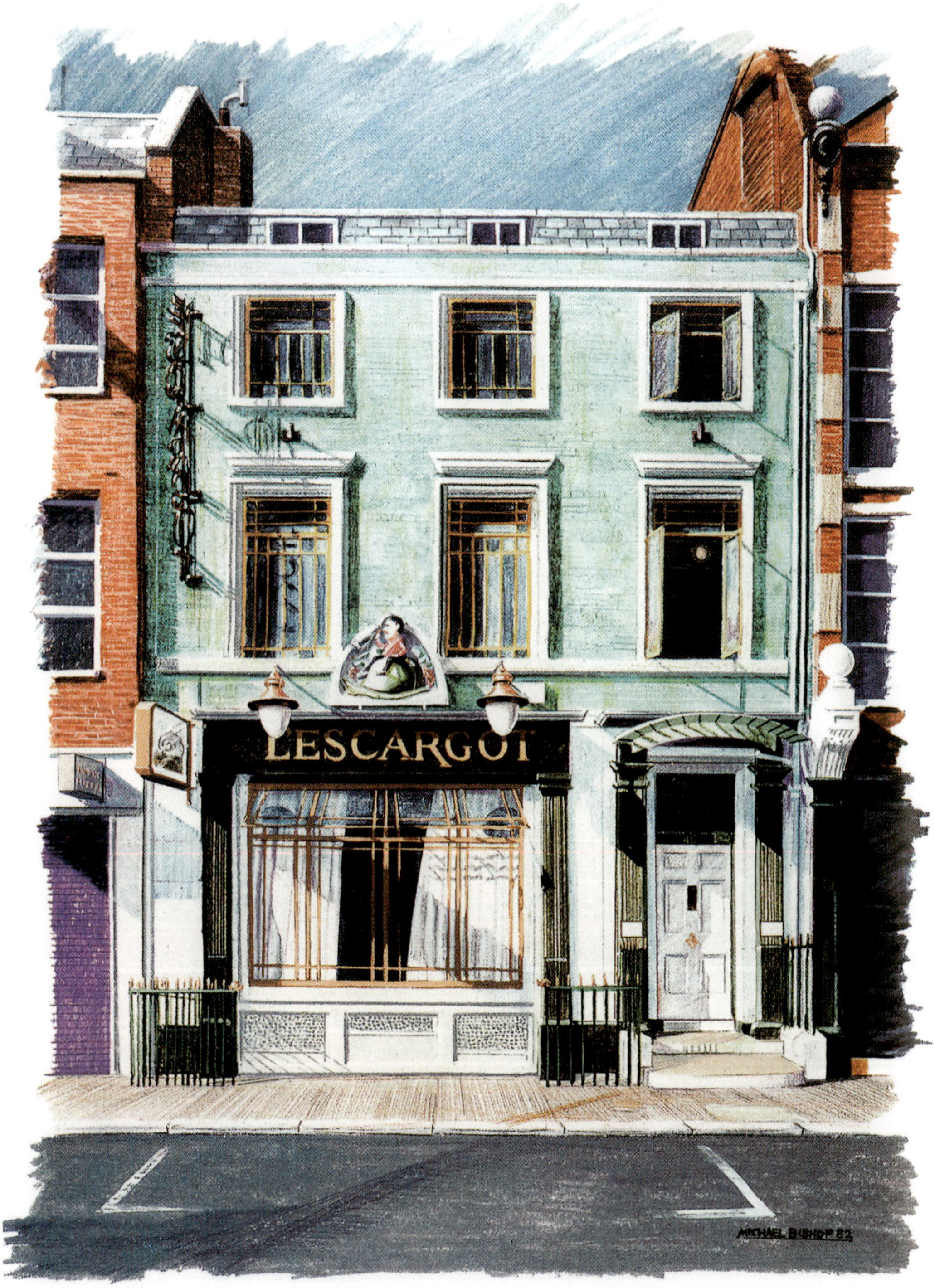

L'ESCARGOT by Michael Bishop

Many clever touches contribute to the detailed impression of this imposing façade. For example, in the brickwork, a few faint lines serve to convey the overall texture and the cast shadows on the flat surfaces emphasize the detail of the architecture. The quality of the pencil marks is varied to suggest different textures and the organization of color strongly underlines the structural framework.

Windows

Painting glass in windows is like painting reflections in water – glass is colorless, but reflects its surroundings. But because windows tend to be vertical, rather than horizontal, they reflect an even greater variety of things, and often look dark if they are not reflecting any of the sky. You can also see through glass, which makes the reflections even more complex. When painting glass windows, always use simple, flat areas of cool lights and darks.

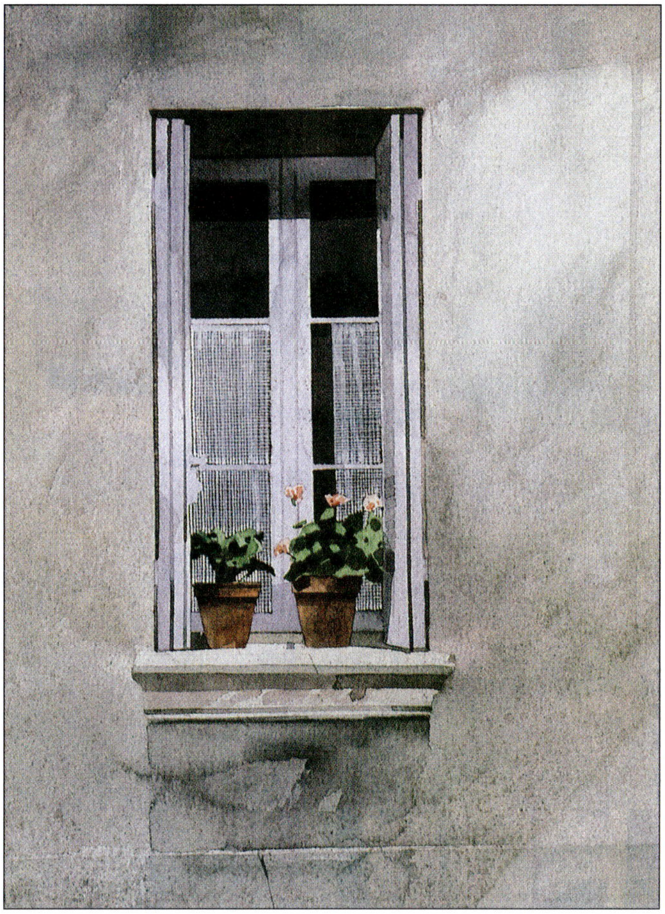

WATERCOLOR METHOD

1 Working on a sheet of stretched 200 lb Bockingford paper, the artist begins by lightly sketching the main shapes of the windows and shutters. The surrounding wall is then painted with a pale wash of raw sienna, lightly dry brushed and spattered with Payne's gray to give it some texture.

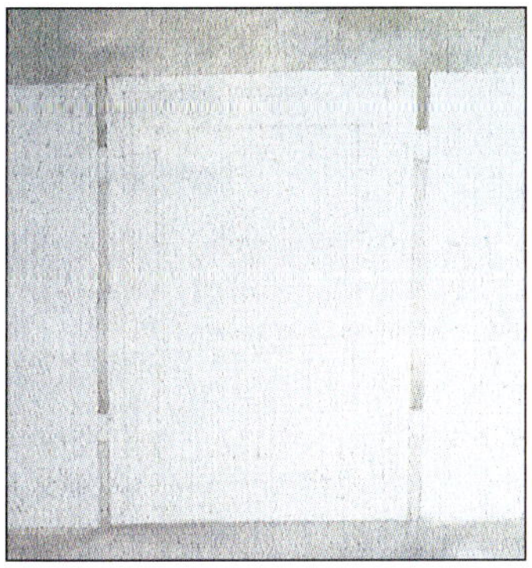

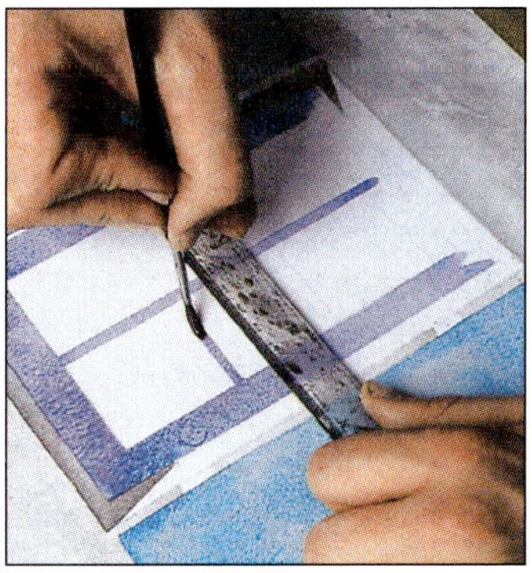

2 The window frame is painted with ultramarine blue. To make sure that the lines of the frame are perfectly straight, the artist uses the brushruling technique: holding the ruler at an angle to the paper, he carefully draws the brush along with the ferrule of the brush held firmly against the edge of the ruler.

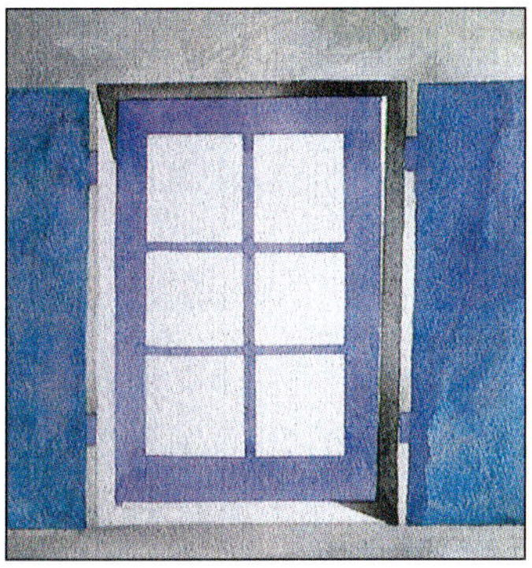

3 The cast shadow of the window frame is painted with Payne's gray. The wooden shutters are textured with glazes and scumbled strokes of cobalt blue and ultramarine. Notice how the colors granulate on the paper's surface: this texture provides the basis for the old and weatherbeaten appearance of the shutters.

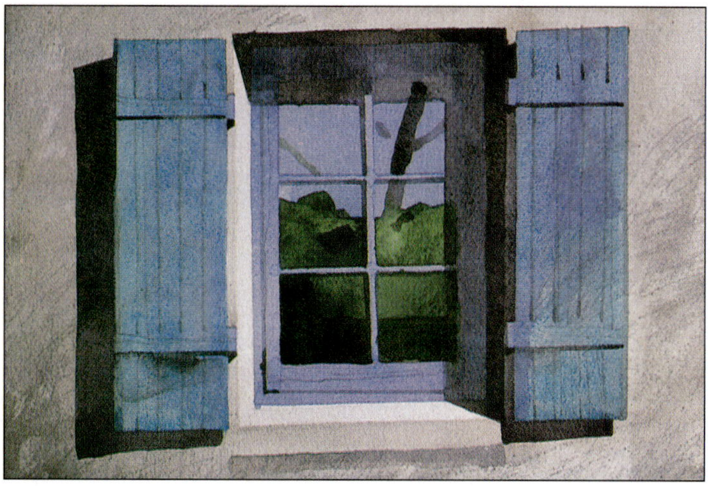

4 Now the artist paints the view through the window. A pale wash of cobalt blue is washed in for the sky, followed by washes of sap green and Payne's gray for the landscape. The landscape shapes are kept very simple, indicating their distance from the window. When this is dry a shadow wash of Payne's gray is blocked in around the window and behind the shutters. Finally, detail is added to the shutters with Payne's gray and a small, well-pointed brush.

ACRYLIC METHOD

1 Trying to paint straight edges is very difficult without the help of masking tape. In order to paint the window panes in this picture, the artist has used strips of masking tape.

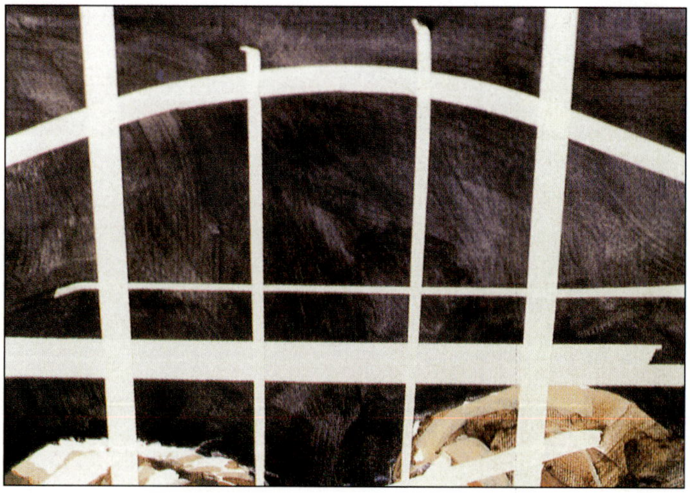

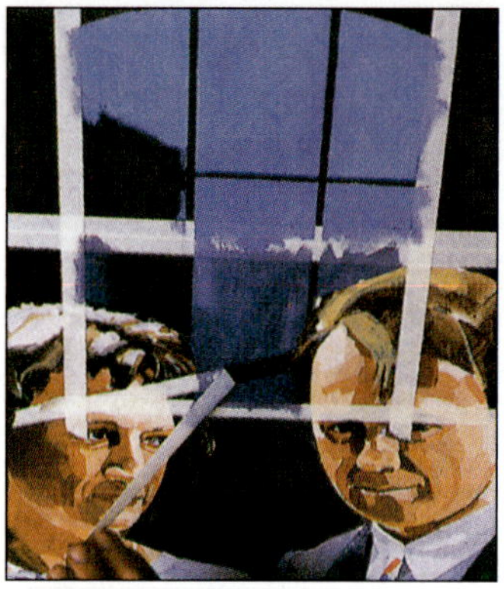

2 If the tape is pressed down firmly and the paint is used quite thickly, clean edges should result. When the paint is dry, remove the tape carefully.

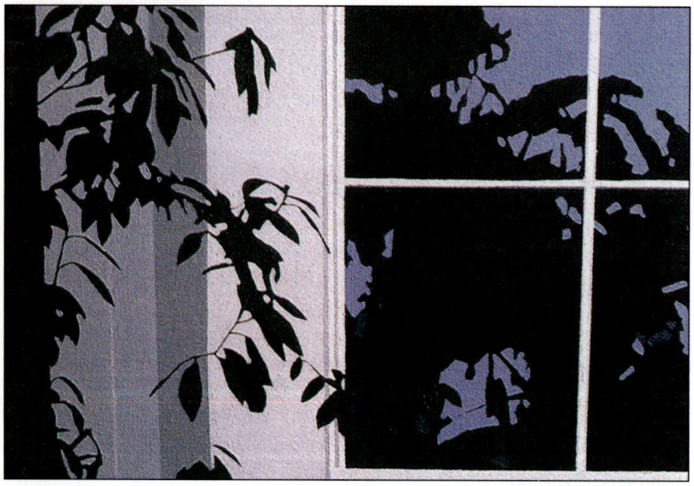

WINDOWS FROM THE INSIDE LOOKING OUT

Windows are a useful compositional device because they create intriguing "frames within a frame." This detail from a painting of a domestic interior makes an interesting composition in itself: the geometric shapes of the white window frame create a foil for the organic shapes of the plant and tree. There are fascinating echoes, too, between the leaves of the plant on the inside and the silhouetted foliage on the outside. This painting was executed in acrylics, the perfect medium for sharp-edged effects.

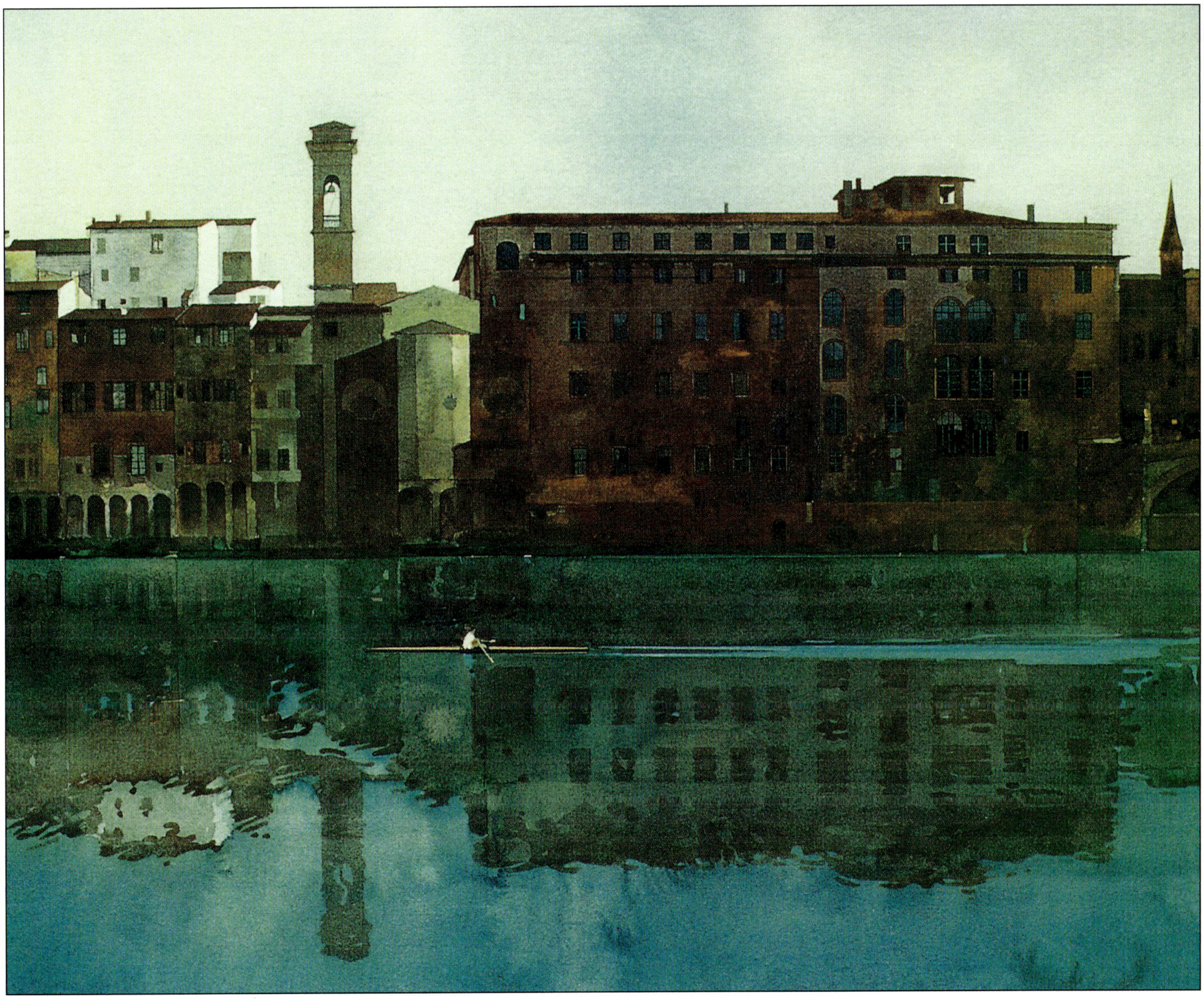

ROWING IN THE ARNO by Peter Kelly

There is lovely contrast between the solid, unmoving shapes of the buildings and their impermanent watery reflections. They could shift or disappear at any moment, and this feeling of transience is stressed by the boat streaking across the water leaving a long and dramatic wake.

Urban Scenes

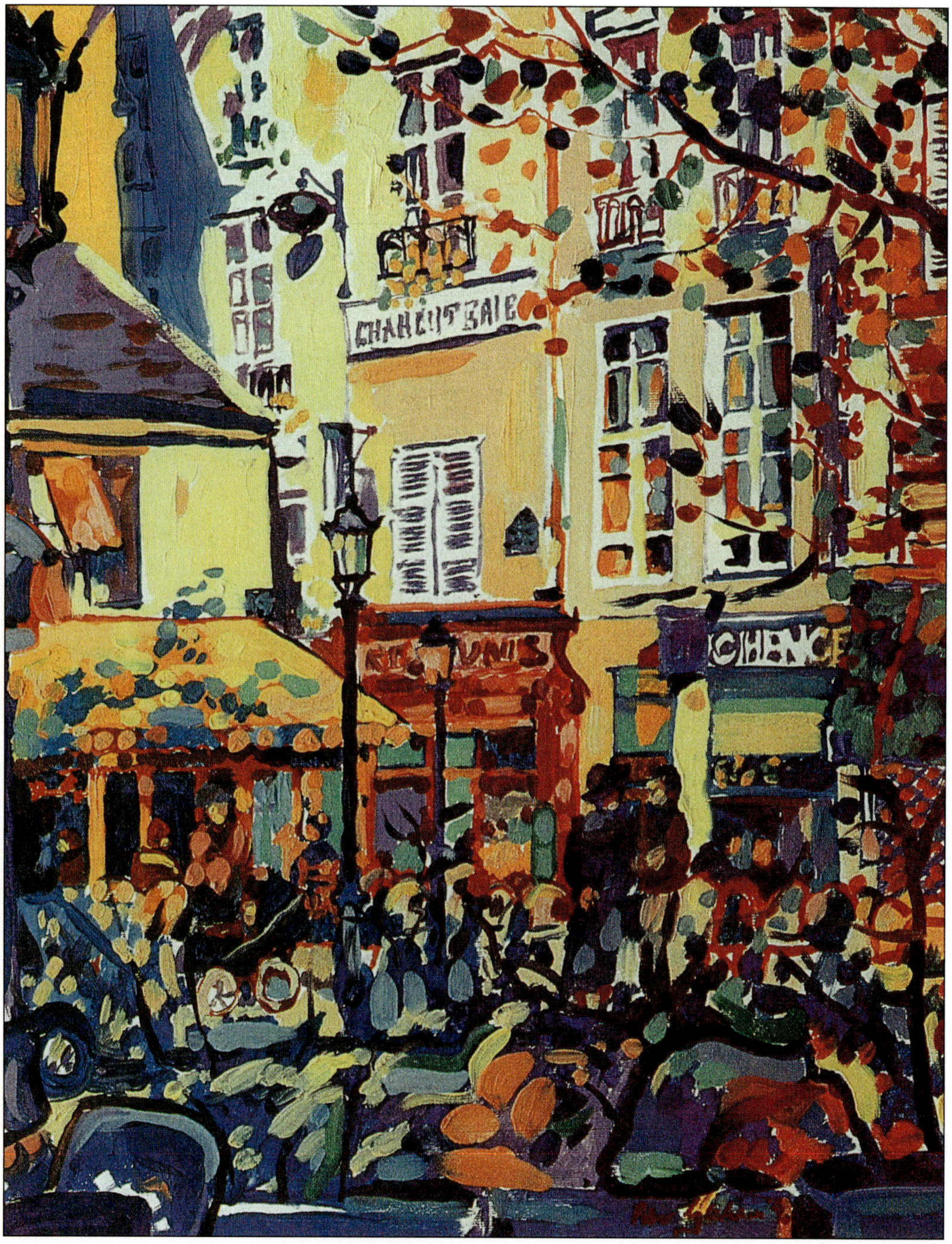

RUE SAINT-ANDRÉ DES ARTS by Peter Graham

The artist's flamboyant style has transformed an ordinary corner of Parisian life into an exciting and colorful composition.

City or townscapes can be marvelous painting subjects, but they are somewhat daunting to novices for a number of reasons. One is the thought of coping with so much detail – brickwork, balconies, doors and windows, roofs and chimneys – in one painting. And another is the complexity of the perspective when buildings are set at angles to one another, or on different levels. And, of course, there is the added problem of finding a suitable location in which to set up your easel.

It is probably wise to avoid very ambitious projects at first, as it is easy to become discouraged. Choose a small section of the scene, such as the corner of a street, which has fairly simple perspective, and remember to ignore details until the later stages, when you can see how many of them are really necessary to the painting.

The recurring verticals, horizontals, the squares and rectangles created by walls, windows, and doorways are powerful compositional tools. They can give a sense of stability or harmony to a picture and also guide the eye around its surface according to how they are placed. Diagonals, caused by receding horizontals, are excellent for leading the eye into a focal point, but be careful as they can become over-dominant. All these angles and shapes, of course, alter as you change your position, so choose your viewpoint carefully.

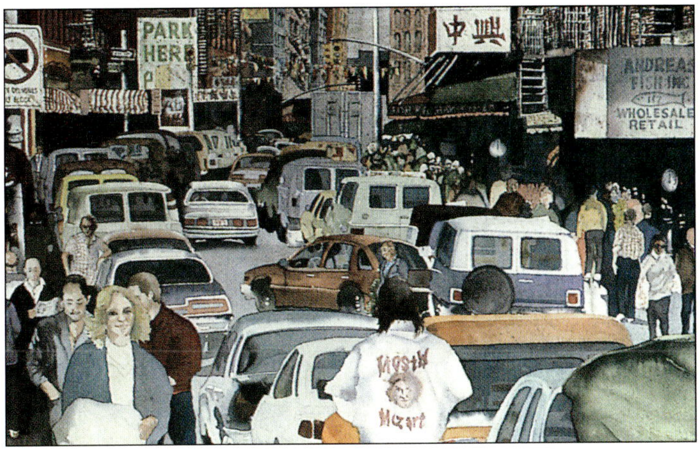

GRAND STREET by Sandra Walker (watercolor)

The sheer complexity of this New York cityscape, with its multitude of different shapes, colors, and forms, would be enough to daunt most painters. But Walker has been equal to the task, producing a busy and lively composition, in which there is no laboring of the paint, although every detail has received loving attention.

In industrialized countries, the rural populations are far outnumbered by those of towns and cities, and yet cityscapes do not rank high in popularity as painting subjects. This is perhaps not very surprising. Although most city dwellers can see a wealth of rich subject matter in their surroundings – colors, textures, shapes, and patterns – the prospect of painting them in a convincing manner seems daunting. There is perspective to contend with, not to mention the straight lines and the complex array of architectural details.

Towns and houses, however, are marvelous subjects. It is mainly a matter of deciding what interests you and making sure that your technique expresses it. An artist whose obsession is architecture may want to paint panoramic townscapes, using fine, precise brushwork to describe every detail, but another might be concerned exclusively with the interplay of geometric shapes or the quality of light, using a broad, more impressionistic technique.

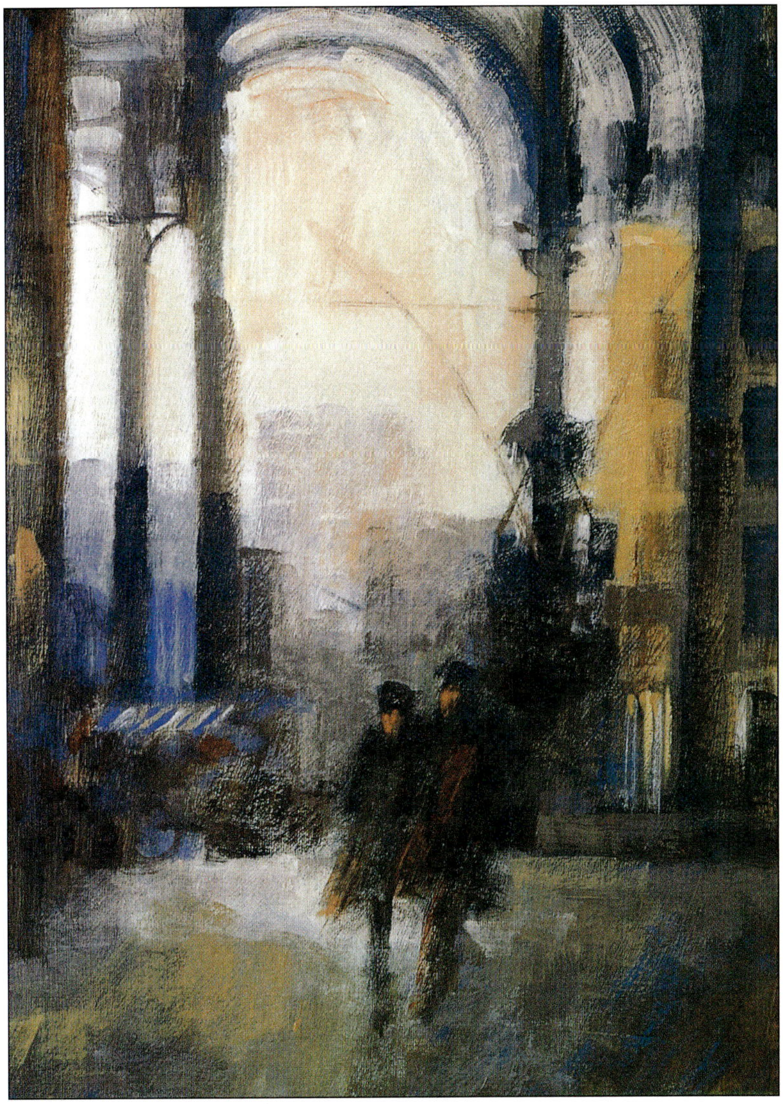

HAY'S GALLERIA by Debra Manifold (acrylic)

The artist was struck by the way the arches and columns framed the sky, making these pale shapes the dominant ones, and she photographed the scene for later use. The figures have been handled very cleverly so that they do not dominate the picture but are integrated into it, allowing us to read the composition as an interplay of shapes. This is partly due to the deliberate suppression of detail, but the limited color scheme, with blues and yellows repeated from one area to another, plays a part.

Cityscapes

Every large city has its own atmosphere, stemming in part from its historical background, which dictates the style of the buildings, and from climactic conditions.

A city such as Venice, with its lavish churches and palaces illuminated by bright or diffused sunlight, has a very different feeling from, say, Manhattan, or from an industrial town typically seen under lowering gray skies. The two paintings on this page convey a strong sense of place, which derives both from the inclusion of typical features – gondolas in one and automobiles in the other – and from the tonal key. This is somber in the picture on the right, and delicate in the one below.

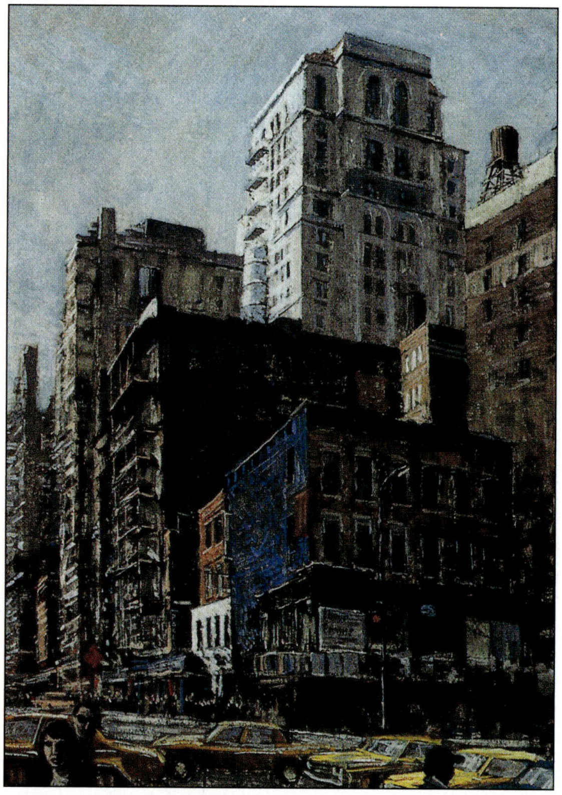

DOWNTOWN MANHATTAN by Gerald Cairns (acrylic)

The low-key approach was well suited to this cityscape, not only because it allowed the artist to express the atmosphere of this area of the city, but also because dark and middle tones give a sense of stability, anchoring the buildings solidly in space. The effect is enhanced by the careful control of color. Avoiding striking contrasts, the artist chose a range of harmonizing colors, giving additional richness and unity by painting on a red-brown ground. He used an oil-painterly technique, working on cardboard with mainly large brushes.

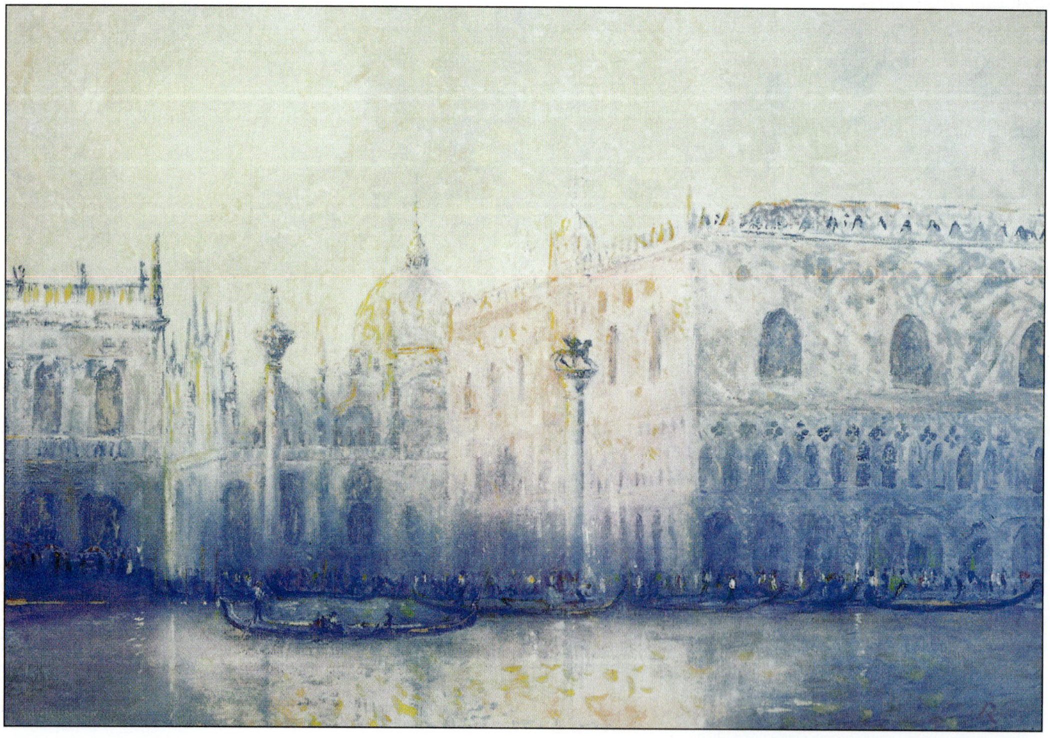

THE DOGE'S PALACE, VENICE by John Rosser

This is a high-key painting, in which the darkest tone would be located around the middle of a gray scale. The artist was especially interested in the effects of light, and captures perfectly the shimmering, misty sunlight often seen in this watery city. In contrast to the view of Manhattan, above, the buildings here seem insubstantial, almost as though carved from air itself. Harmonious colors were used here also, with touches of yellow counterpointing the dominant blues and setting up an understated complementary contrast. Additional contrast was achieved by varying the paint consistency from thin to thick.

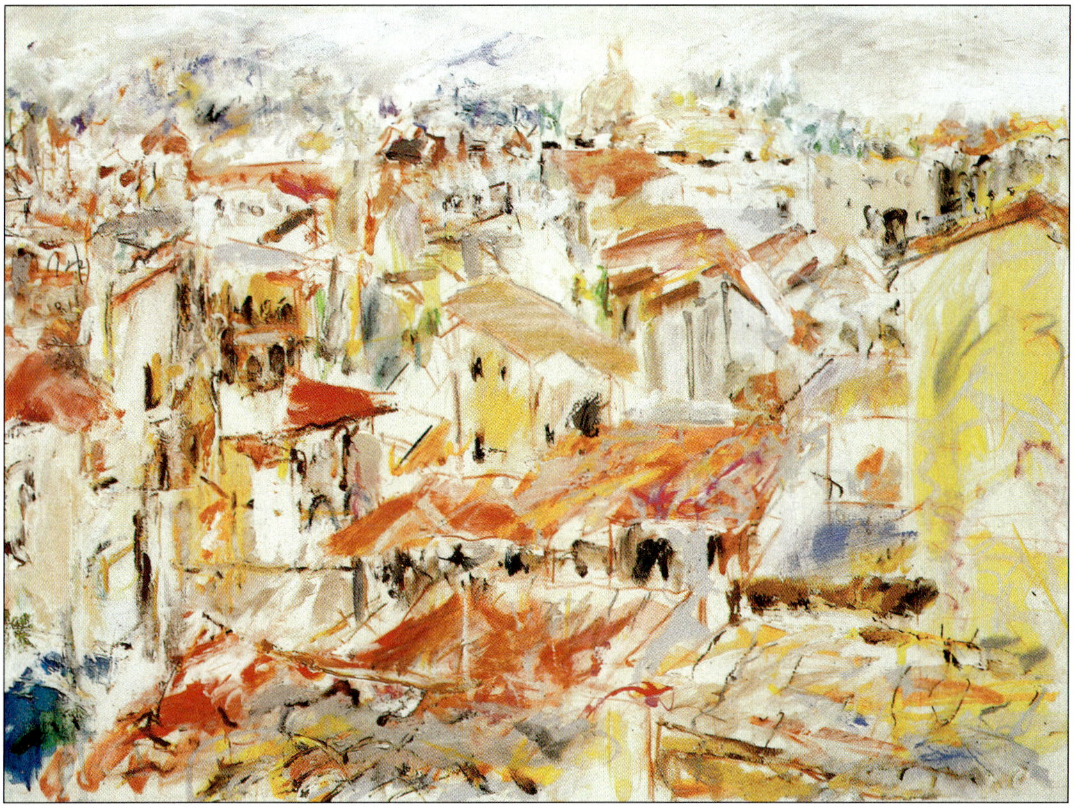

This mixed-media painting by Jacquie Turner is one of a series of the city of Florence, made from a church tower. High viewpoints such as this are much favored by painters of urban landscape, as they provide an exciting vista of rooftops and other features not visible from ground level. Although nothing is overly explicit and there has been no attempt to render the cityscape with the precision often associated with architectural painting and drawing, the picture conveys a powerful sense of place.

LONDON CITYSCAPE by Pip Carpenter (watercolor)

A crowded townscape presents a complex color range. Where there is a predominance of neutrals the artist has created "colored grays" by the interaction of blues, purples, yellow, and browns in thinly washed layers and sketchy, broken-color areas. The active brush-drawing technique enables her to introduce stronger colors discreetly and integrate linear marks with broad shapes, so the surface contains many variations of color and texture that enliven the rendering.

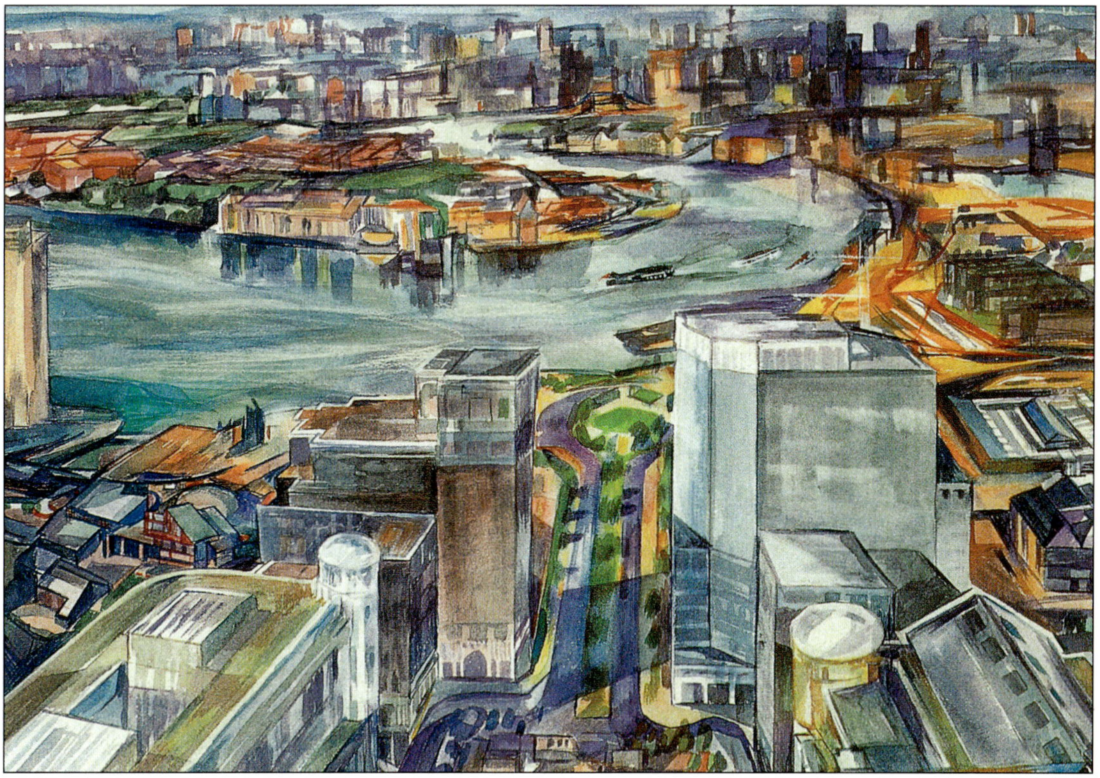

Using Light to Advantage

Cityscapes provide an excellent opportunity to study the play of light on shapes and surfaces. Observe the changes that take place in the city as the day progresses: from the hazy blue silhouettes of buildings in the early morning light, to the sharp, angular shadows and reflections under the midday sun, to the jumbled skyline etched in black against the evening sky. And don't forget the night-time world, which does not fade into darkness but comes brilliantly alive with a whole spectrum of artificial light.

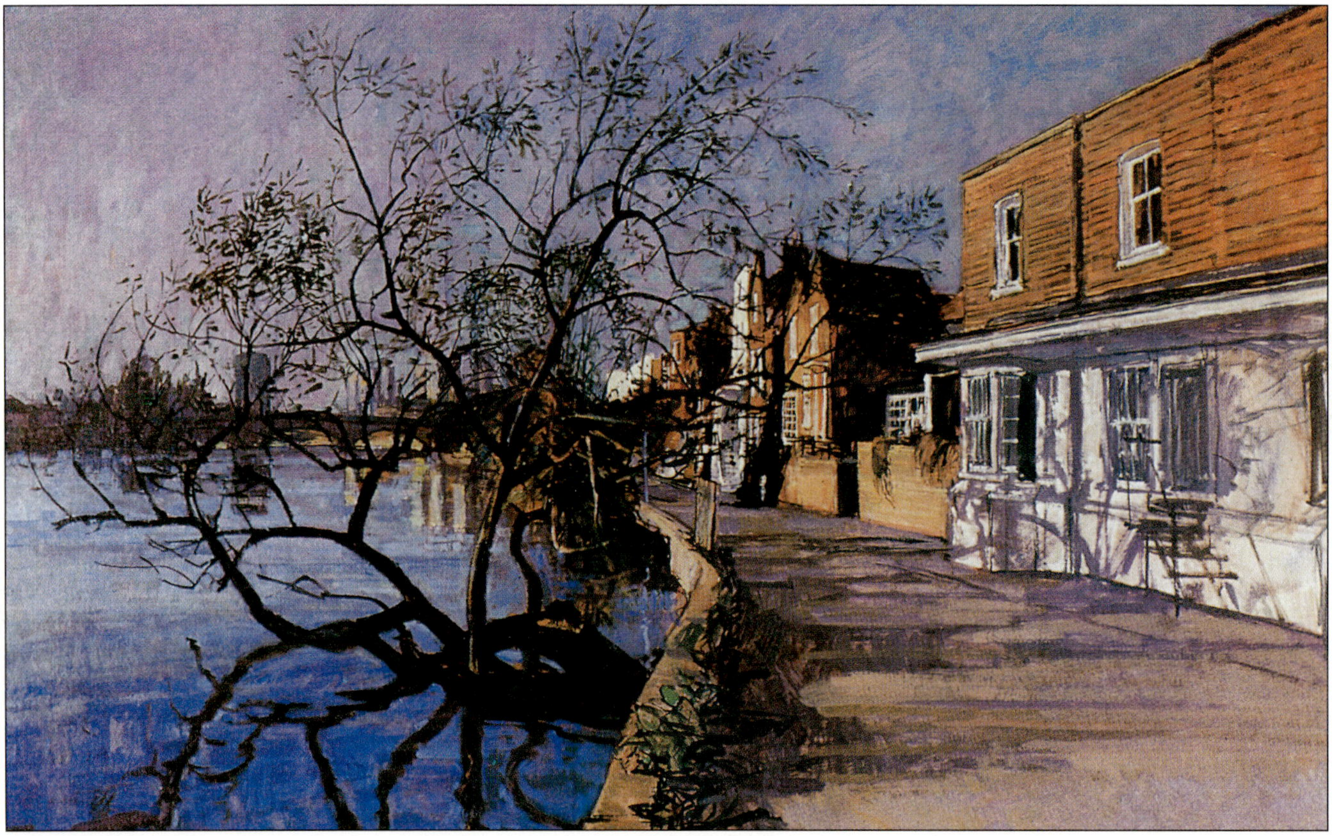

THE SUNKEN TREE, STRAND ON THE GREEN by William Bowyer (oil)

In the late afternoon, sunlight slants low across the landscape and creates dramatic contrasts of light and shade. Here the cool, dark colors of the tree and the water lend emphasis to the brilliant light striking the buildings.

Inclement weather, too, can invest a city scene with atmosphere and drama. Think of a dark winter's day, heavy with fog, when the gleam from office windows and car headlights shines in the gloom, or the way rooftops and pavements sparkle after a shower of rain. The magic comes not so much from the buildings themselves, but from the way light falls on them. Even a drab old brick wall comes alive when golden afternoon sunlight glances across it, or when the long, slanting shadows of a nearby building, or balcony, or fire escape, create graphic patterns across its surface.

It is, of course, impossible to set up your easel in a city street and paint on-the-spot, unless you wish to attract a crowd of curious onlookers. It is here that the training of your visual memory, aided by sketches and photographs, if you like, becomes vitally important. Jot down notes on any scrap of paper as you pass, to record any particular effects of color and light that have struck you. These can be enormously valuable when you come to recreate the scene later in your studio or home.

Although you cannot manipulate the lighting, you can choose the time of day that shows the buildings to the best advantage. This is important, because the direction and intensity of the light affects the colors, forms, and textures. When the sun is high in the sky, there will be fewest cast shadows, and these play a vital role in highlighting interesting details and textures, as well as providing an interplay of lights and darks. A low evening sun, on the other hand, casts long slanting shadows, picking out features you might not otherwise notice. It also enriches the colors, turning drab brick walls into molten gold.

So take a look at your subject at various times of day, and also in different weather conditions. If you want a brooding atmospheric effect – say, for an industrial townscape – an overcast day could be most suitable.

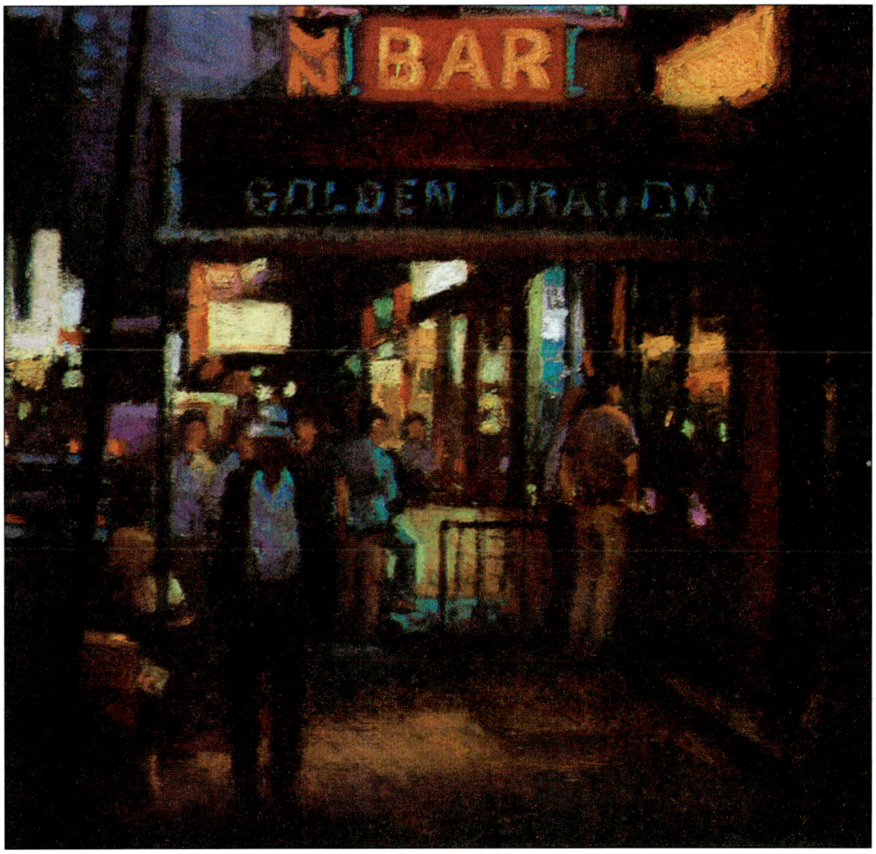

CHINA TOWN by Doug Dawson (pastel)

The vibrant colors in this pastel stand out brilliantly against the surrounding dark. This is a strongly suggestive image evoking all the excitement and mystery of the city at night.

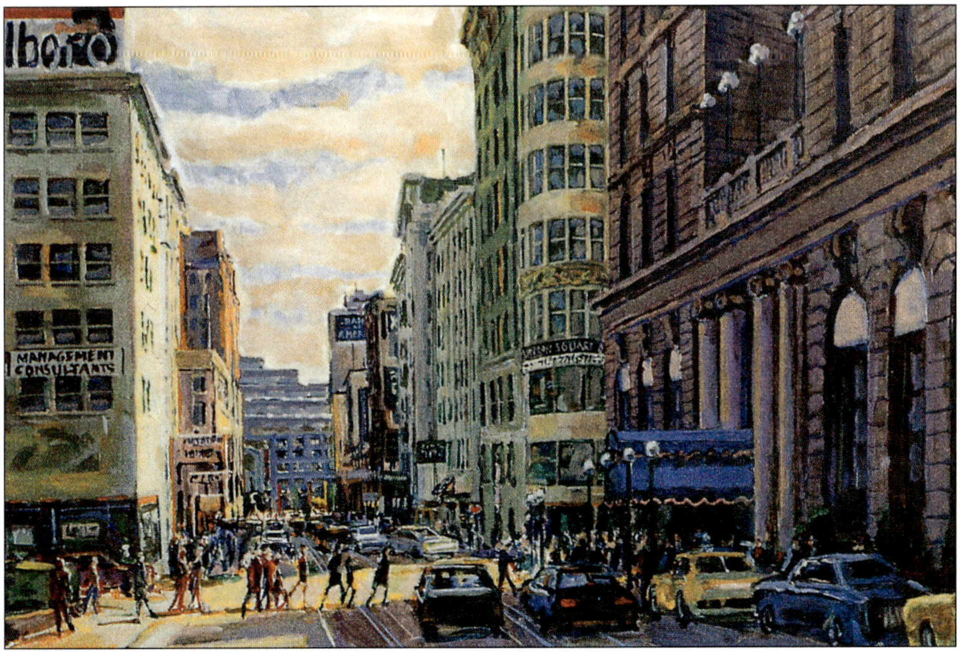

POWELL STREET by Benjamin Eisenstat (acrylic)

An attractive painting subject can sometimes be marred by the presence of cars and people, but they are an integral part of a daytime cityscape. Including vehicles, pedestrians, and other city features can also help the composition. Here the yellow cabs are important to the color scheme, balancing the yellows of the buildings and central patch of sunlight.

Night and Day

City streets are a fascinating subject for the study of light. Because the buildings are so closely confined, shadows fall from one to another, creating striking patterns of light and shade. For this project, find a convenient vantage point such as an upper-storey window which gives you a clear view of a city street. Make quick studies of the street, in any medium you like, at four different times of the day: morning, midday, late afternoon, and night. Your completed studies should provide a record of the changing temperature of the light as the day progresses, as well as the way shadows move and lengthen.

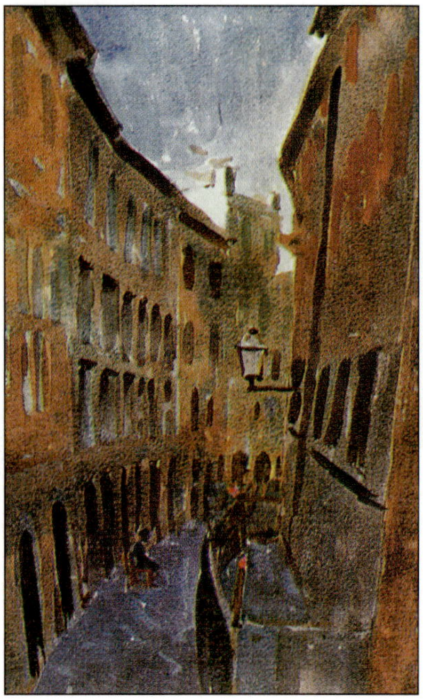

ABOVE: *Morning. Early in the morning, the scene was low-key with cool colors. The street was still in shadow, so there was little contrast in either color or tone except for the sunlit corner of the far building and the glow of the two hazard lamps in the foreground, where workmen had been digging up the road.*

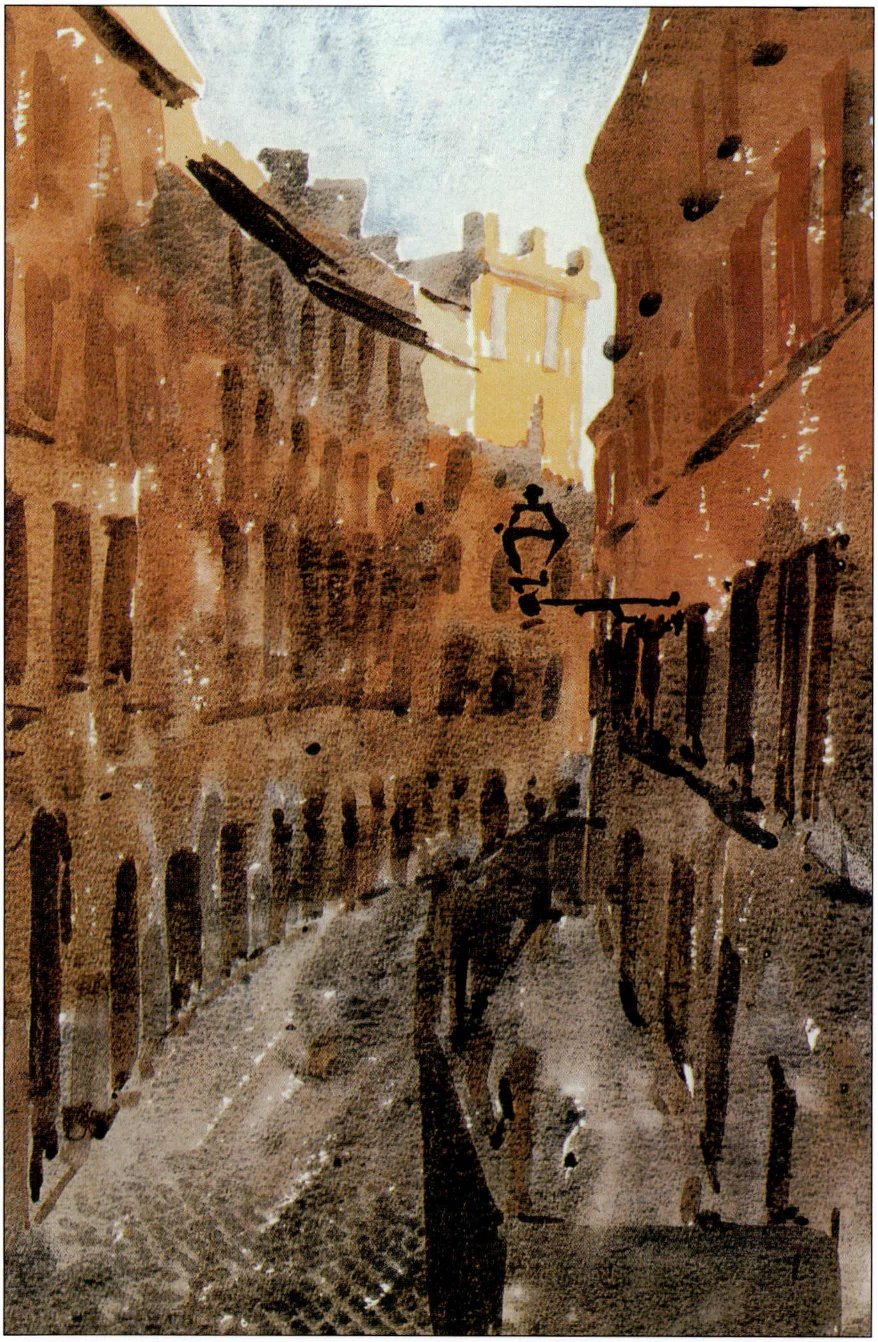

RIGHT: *Midday. Returning at midday from a shopping trip, the artist found that the sun had moved round but the street was still surprisingly shadowy. The sky was now a brilliant blue and the sun was beating strongly. Although still predominantly low-key, the colors were becoming warmer and the tonal contrasts stronger.*

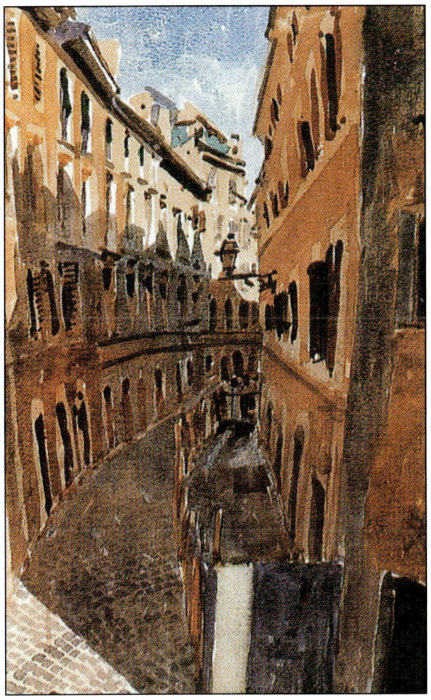

ABOVE: *Late afternoon. Returning in the late afternoon, the artist found at last there was some sunlight shining into the street. Though there was still a cool feeling in the shadows, the sunlight was reflected back onto the buildings on the left, clarifying the detail and warming the colors.*

RIGHT: *Night. By the time the artist came back from the restaurant that night the scene was transformed. Many of the windows, which had been dark and shuttered during the day, were now lit up, giving evidence of life and activity within. Slivers of light shone evocatively from open doorways. The central lamps, which had played a minor role in the daytime pictures, now became a focal point, while the far end of the street was cast into complete darkness.*

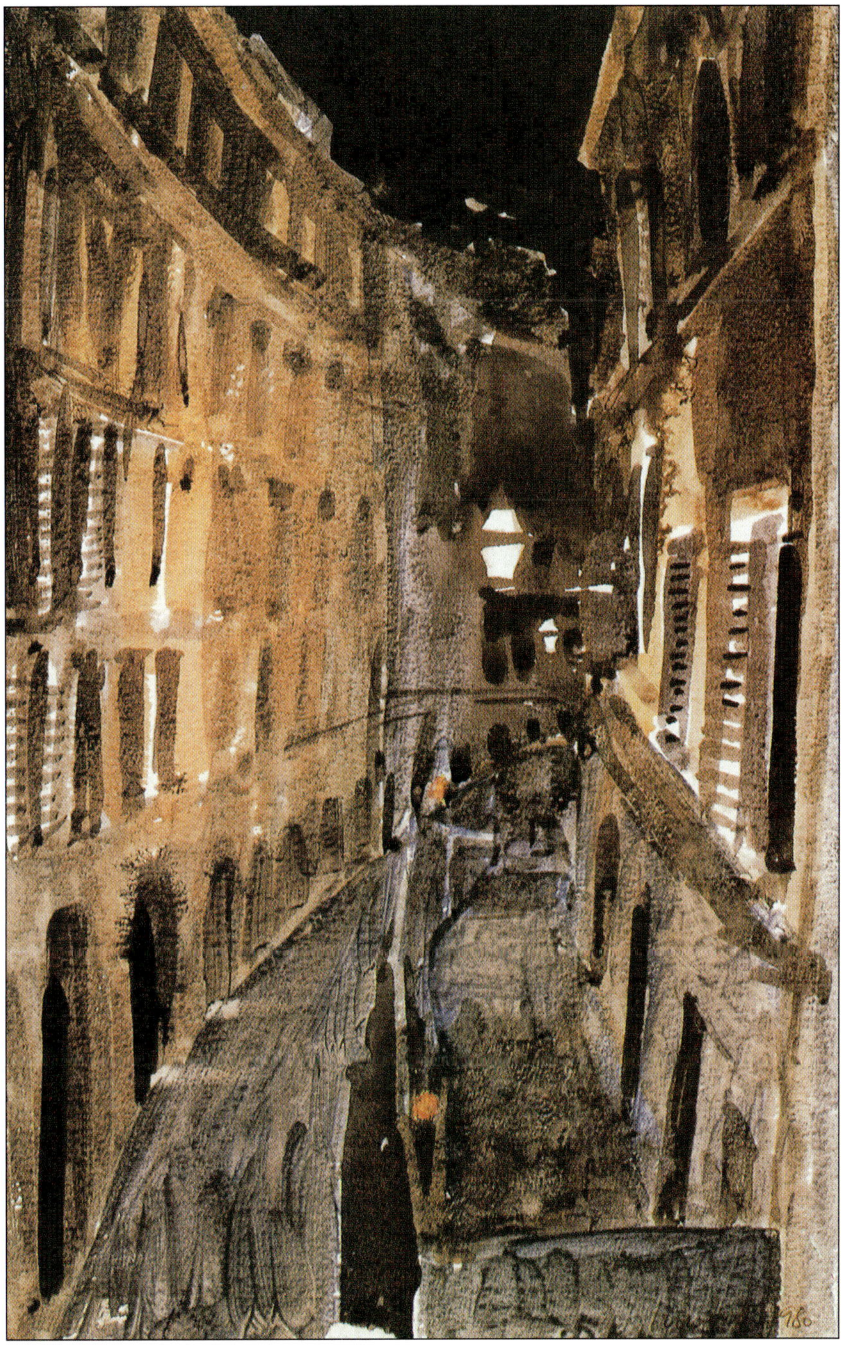

STUDIES OF A STREET IN TRASTEVERE by Lucy Willis (watercolor)

The artist painted these watercolor sketches while on holiday in Italy. She leaned precariously out of the window of her apartment, making studies of the quiet street below. She worked in watercolor, using a limited palette consisting of cobalt blue, Indian red, cadmium yellow, and Vandyke brown, mixing black and brown Indian ink with the paint in the shadow areas to give them more body.

Proportion and Character

A knowledge of perspective will help you to make buildings look convincingly solid, but it will not enable you to express their particular character. For that, you need to train your own powers of observation. If you want to achieve a recognizable likeness, an attention to proportion and detail are crucial.

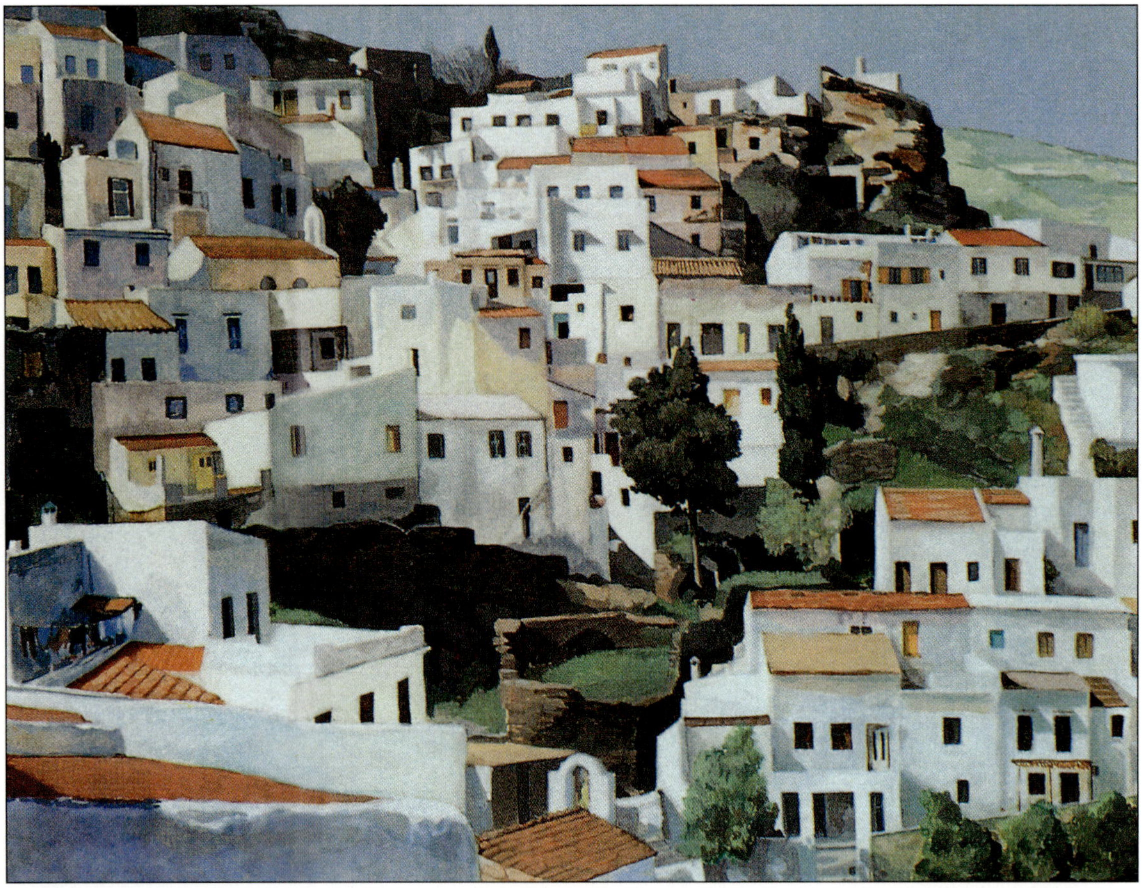

ACROSS THE TOWN, KEA by Jill Mirza

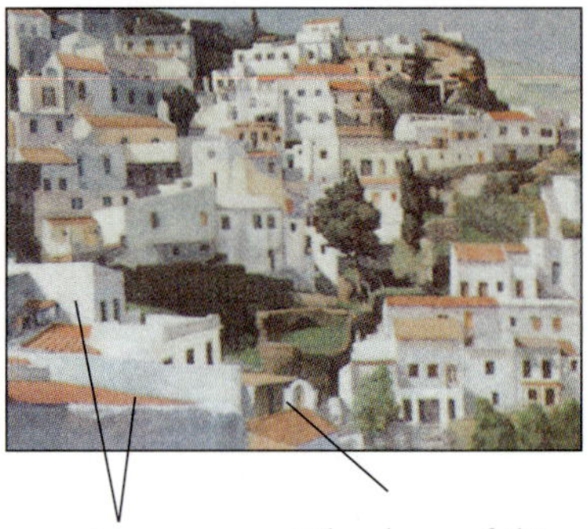

Thick walls are another characteristic of these houses, indicated here by the deep shadows.

The shape of this central building, with its upward-sloping wall, is clearly defined.

ATTENTION TO DETAIL

The small white or pastel-colored buildings set at seemingly random angles on a hillside are so typical of the Greek islands that little detail is needed, so long as the general shapes, proportions, and colors are correct. The artist paid careful attention to the shape of each house and the placing of the windows, and on the foreground wall gave a hint of the crumbly texture that is another feature of the whitewashed buildings.

Before thinking about perspective, analyze your subject and decide what its special features are. Is the building unusually tall or wide? Are the windows large or small, close together or widely spaced, or deeply recessed in thick walls? Are there any wrought-iron balconies or carved lintels, that will help you construct a portrait?

STYLES AND MATERIALS

Whether you are painting an urban or village scene, or an old barn set in landscape, you will want to give the impression of a specific place. Building styles often vary distinctly from one country and region to another, and so do the materials used. The skyscrapers of Manhattan and the flat-roofed houses of Greek villages are two obvious examples, but there are numerous others, such as the dark red brick of Victorian London, clapboard houses in parts of the United States, gray or sand-colored stone cottages in Britain and Ireland, and tall glass and concrete structures in many modern cities.

Old buildings, in particular, can provide intriguing textures to exploit in your painting. Do not overlook the possibilities of old wood, crumbling brickwork, and peeling whitewash, because the texture of a building is an integral part of its character.

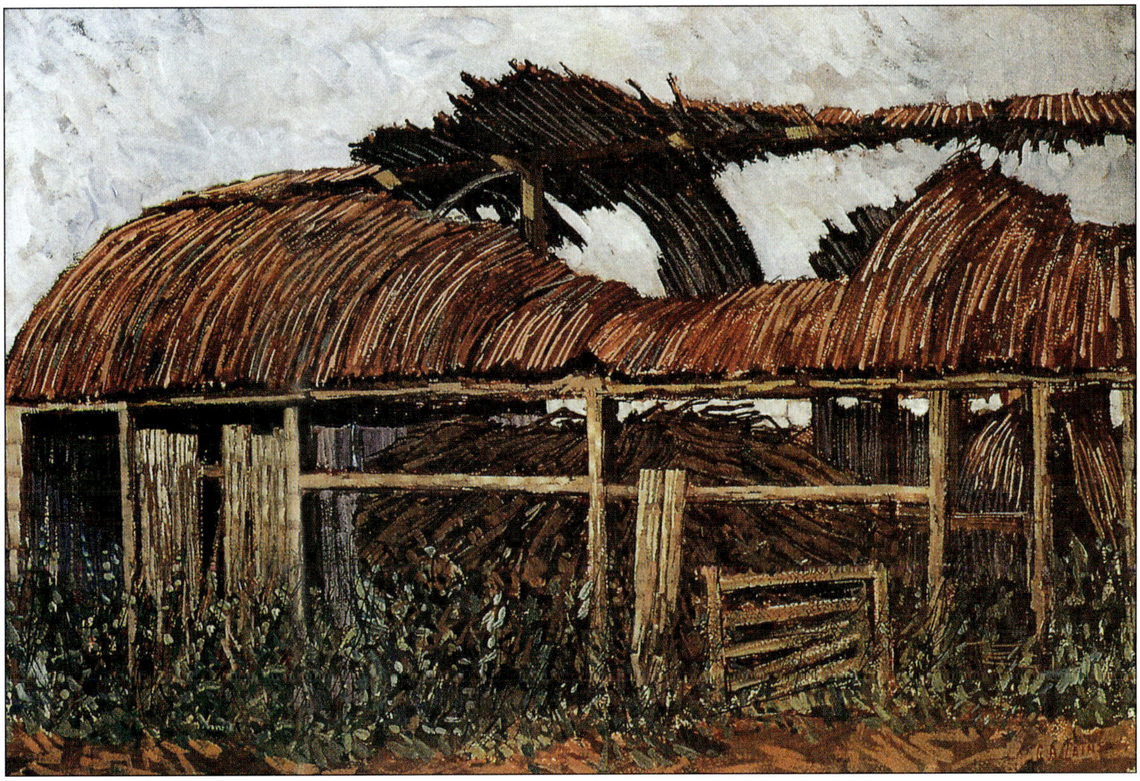

DERELICT BARN by Gerald Cains

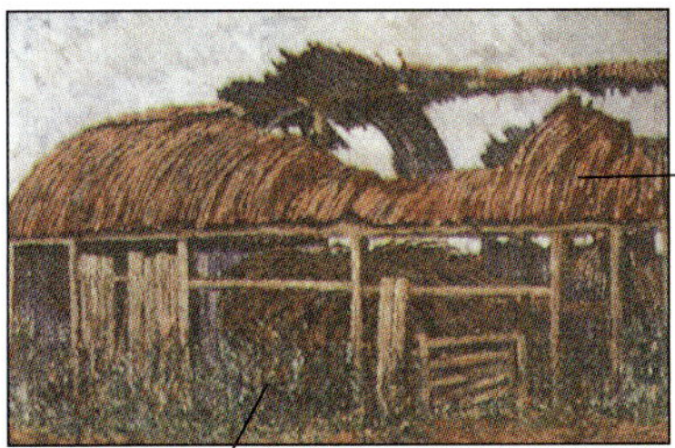

Fine linear brush strokes of light color were laid over brown to create the texture of the rusted corrugated iron.

The barn is the focal point of the painting, so the foreground is treated in less detail, with brush strokes suggesting grasses.

ATTENTION TO TEXTURE

Failing to exploit the rich textures of the wood and the rusted metal roof would have been a lost opportunity. They form an integral part of the subject, as exciting in their way as the dramatic shapes made by the broken roof outlined against the sky. The muted color scheme creates a somber atmosphere in keeping with the subject.

Watercolor Project: Church in France

This artist has worked in a very deliberate way, starting with a careful outline drawing made with a sharp pencil and ruler to map out the main areas, so that he is sure where to place his first wash. He then put on a series of flat washes, the first one being laid over the sky area and the second, very pale, over the building itself. Next he began to consider the best way of suggesting the stonework, and decided on masking fluid, applied in slightly uneven brush strokes. When this was dry he washed over the top with brownish gray paint and then removed the fluid, leaving lines of paint between and around the original brush strokes. Further texture was applied at a later stage by the spattering method, and crisp lines were given to details, such as the face and hands of the clock, by drawing with a sharp pencil. The whole painting has a pleasing crispness, produced by the very sharply defined areas of light and dark. No attempt has been made to blend the paint in the shadow areas, and very distinct tonal contrasts have been used – in the small round tree in front of the church, for example. The artist has also avoided the temptation to put in too much detail, which might have reduced the impact and made the picture look fussy and untidy. The tiled roof consists simply of a flat wash; although there is just enough variation in the sky to avoid a mechanical look, no attempt has been made to paint actual clouds.

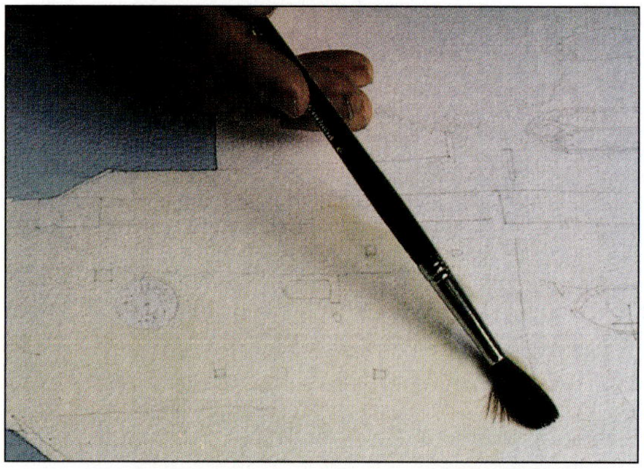

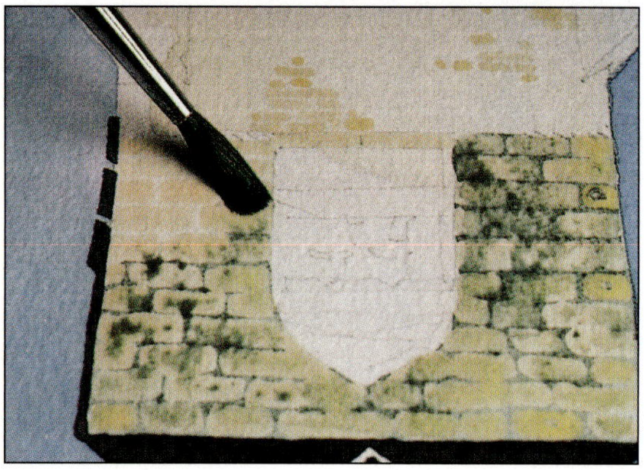

1 and **2** In a subject like this a careful outline drawing is essential. Once the drawing was complete the artist laid an almost flat wash over the sky and then a paler one over the building. These established his base mid-tones, enabling him to gauge the tonal strength of the steeple.

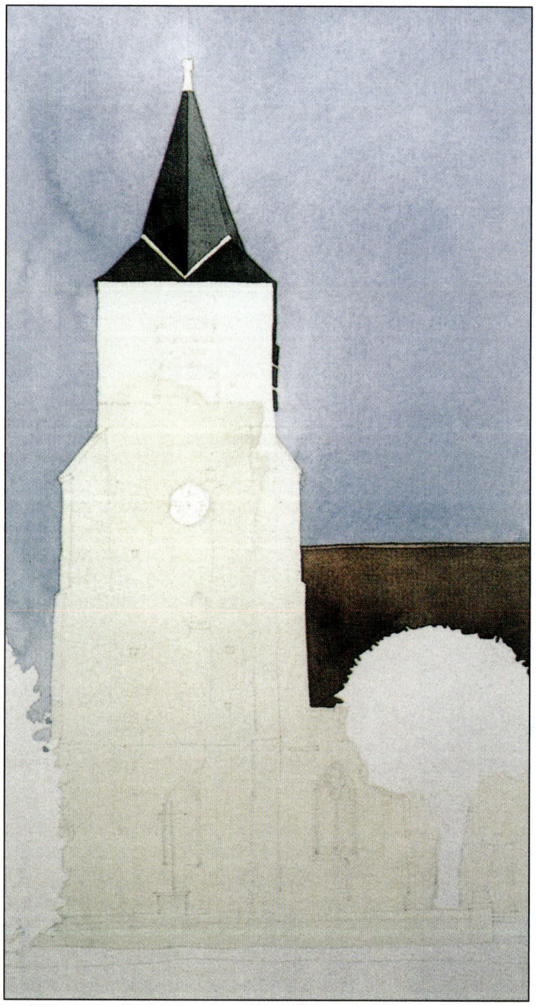

3 The steeple was painted and allowed to dry, after which masking fluid was put onto areas of the masonry, not as a flat wash but as individual brush strokes. Brownish paint was washed over this when dry so that it sank into the areas between the brush strokes.

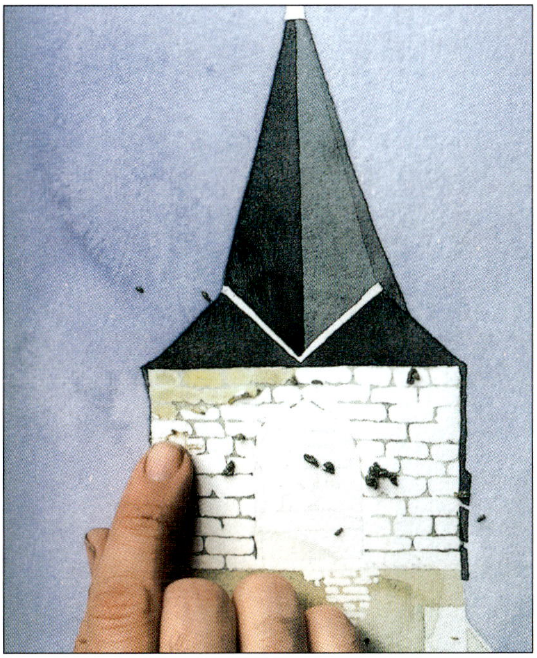

4 Here the masking fluid is being rubbed off with a finger, leaving the irregular lines of dark paint to suggest the edges of the stones. This is a more effective method than painting in the lines, and gives a much more natural look because the technique is a very slightly "random" one.

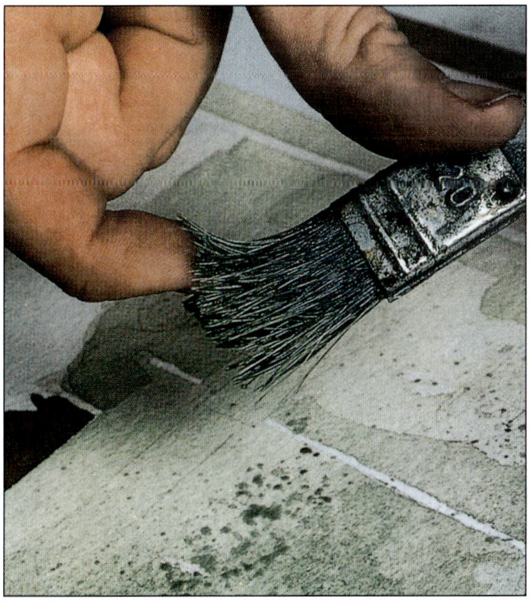

5 Here the spattering technique is being used to give further texture to the walls. It is sometimes necessary to mask off surrounding areas so that they do not get splashed, but this artist makes use of the method quite often, and is confident of his ability to control the paint.

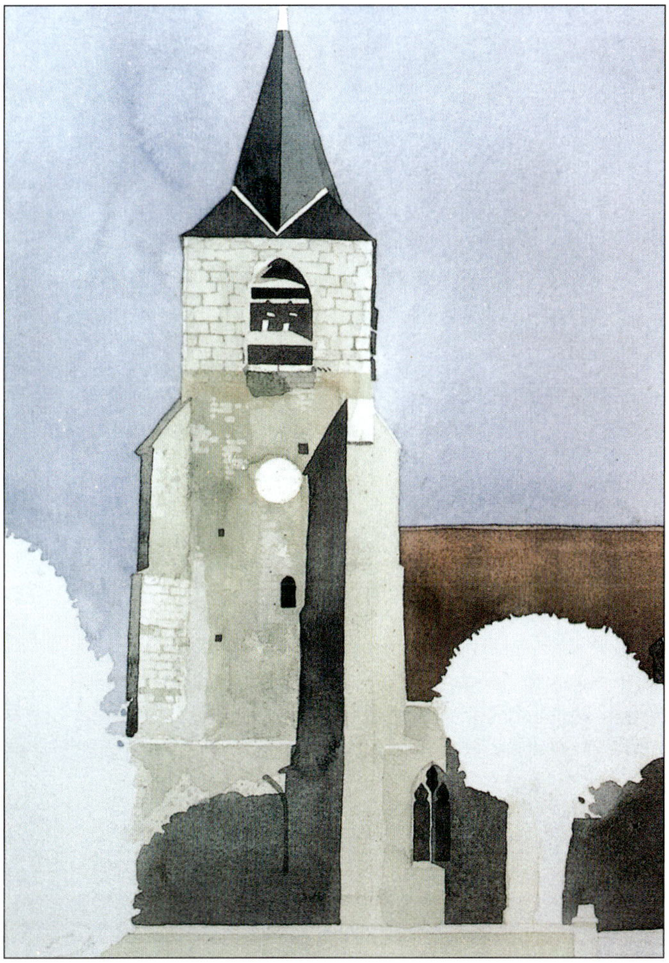

6 At this stage only the foreground, with the dark trees and bright grass, remain unpainted. The artist worked the painting piece by piece, as he found that having no overlapping layers of paint gave a crisper definition, but it is not a method recommended for beginners.

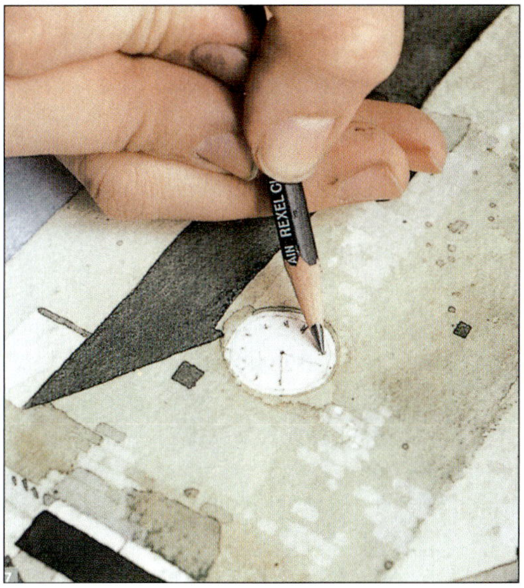

7 Here the hands and face of the clock are being carefully drawn in with a very sharp pencil over the original pale wash.

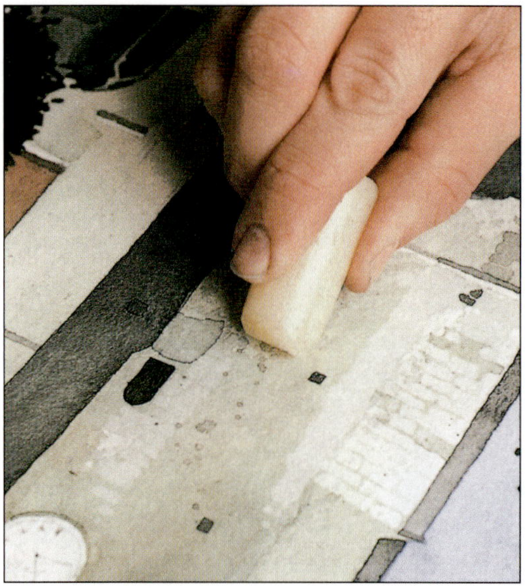

8 Further texture is given to the stonework by rubbing a candle over the paint. Candles or wax crayons can also be used as a resist method, like masking fluid, in which case they are applied before a final paint layer.

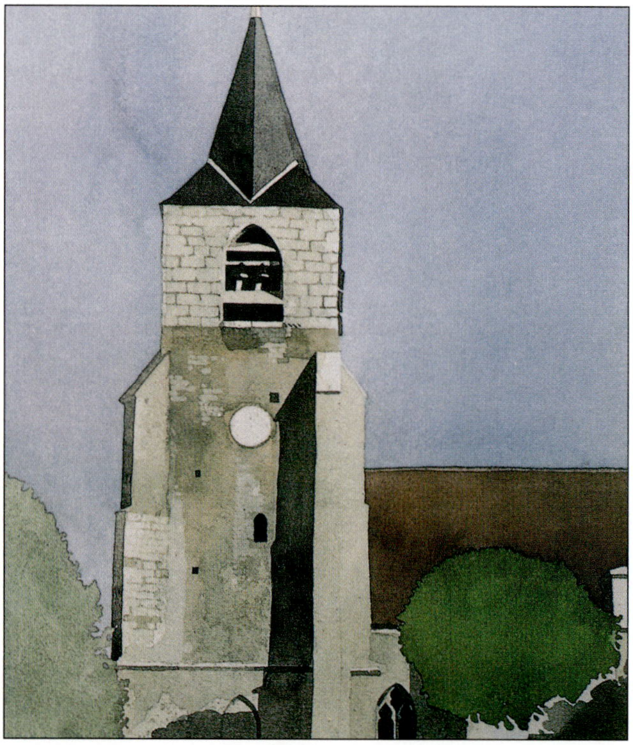

9 The mid-tones of the tree have now been laid in, providing a foil to the red-brown of the tiled roof.

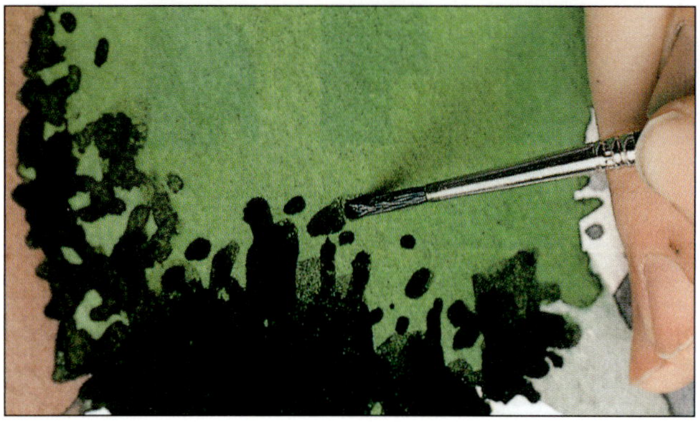

10 The artist now works carefully on the shadow side of the tree, using a fine brush and very dense dark green paint.

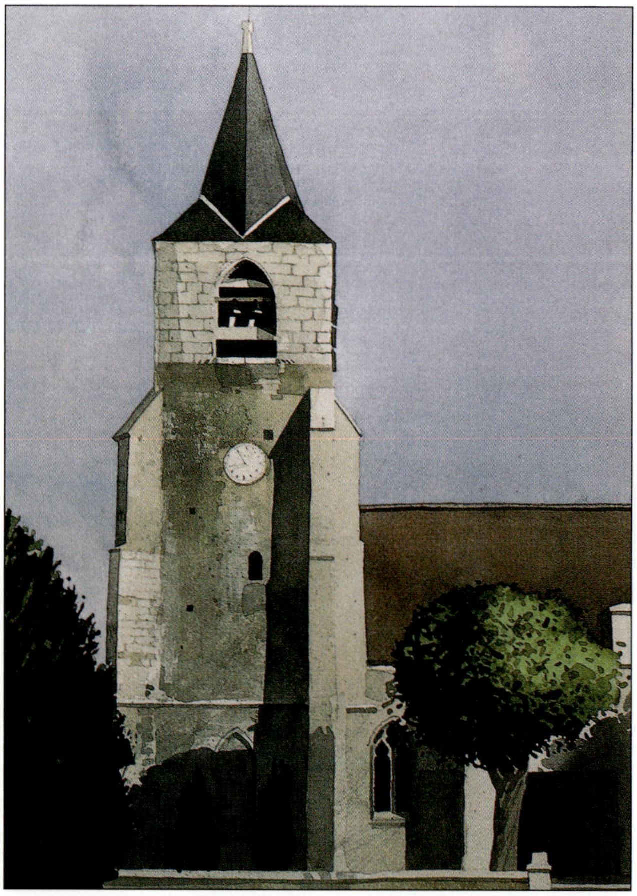

The final touches were to darken the left-hand tree and paint in the straight, dark shadow in the foreground. Two small trees were also added in the shadow area at the bottom of the church.

Colored Pencil Project

Colored pencils have a special relevance in drawing buildings and landscapes, especially when the artist wishes to depict the effects of sun and shadow. The variety of darks and lights which can be achieved with colored pencils allows the artist to either work with a very pale and delicate range of colors and tone, or with a very intense and bold palette. When the two are combined – a pale, loose stroke and an intense and colorful area – the effect is balanced yet dynamic. In this case, the combination of architecture and nature is well-suited to the medium, and vice versa.

Much like painting media, colored pencils allow the artist to build up layer upon layer of subtle color to create a transparent effect. For instance, crosshatching in different colors – overlaying one area of colored strokes over another color – can create an interesting tone and texture in the picture.

Drawing with colored pencil requires patience and thoroughness. The point of the pencil being relatively small, it is difficult to cover large areas with any evenness of tone and stroke. A smooth, hardish paper on board is normally used with pencil work, however, a roughly textured surface can create interesting white "gaps" and grainy effects.

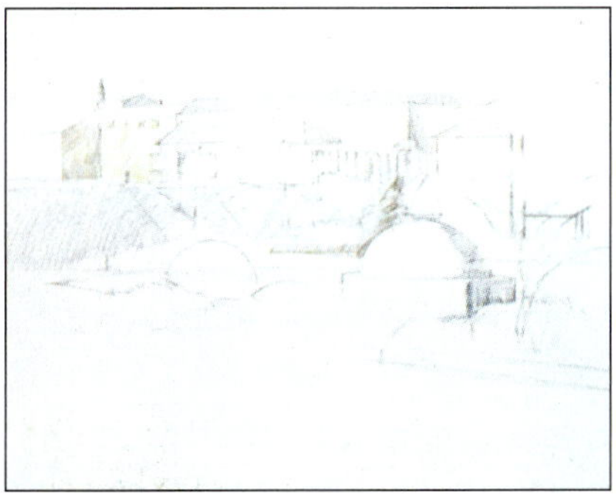

1 After sketching in general shapes with blue pencil, develop general shadow areas with blue and brown pencils.

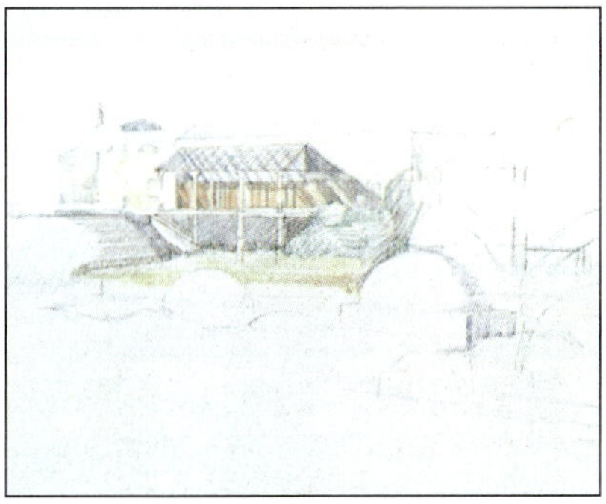

2 With a pale yellow pencil, begin to put in the lighter areas of the wooden structure. This "underpainting" will ensure a feeling of bright daylight.

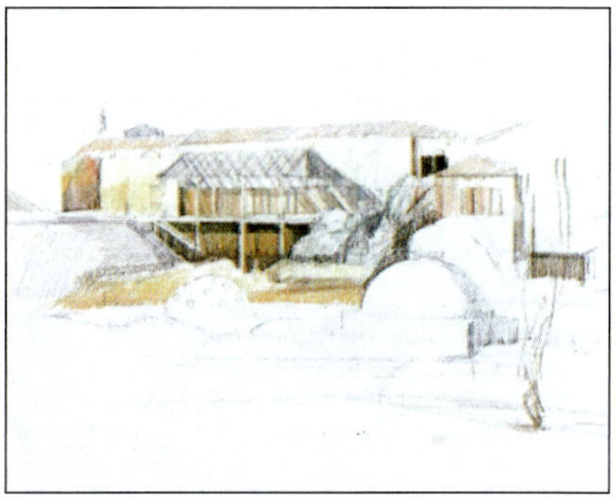

3 Put in dark areas with black and dark brown pencils. Crosshatch using different colors and directional strokes to create color and tone.

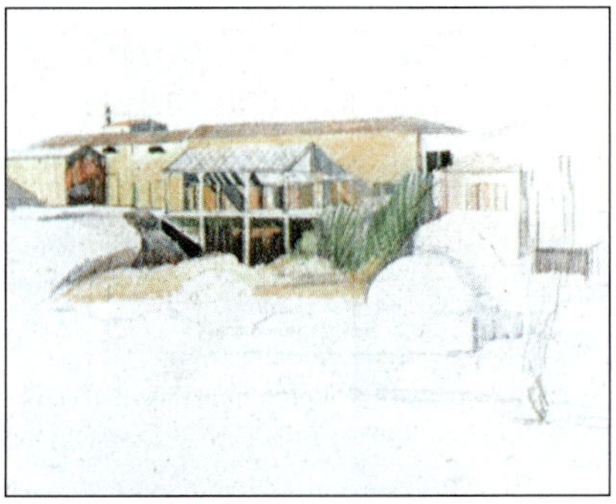

4 Work from the center outward to maintain the picture's focal point. Build up shapes using ultramarine blue for the darker areas.

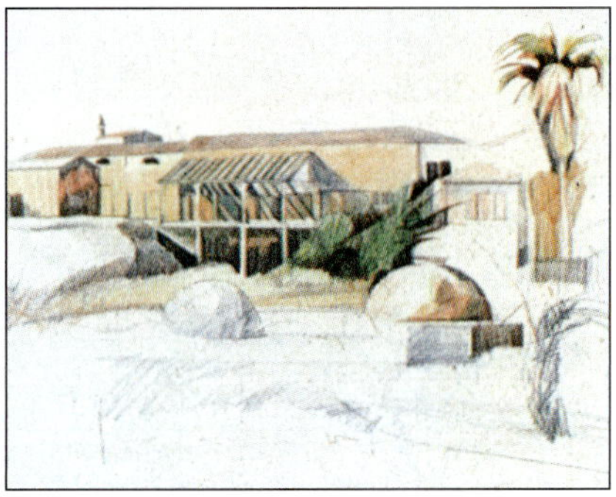

5 Carry the light yellow and ocher tones into the foreground and palm tree.

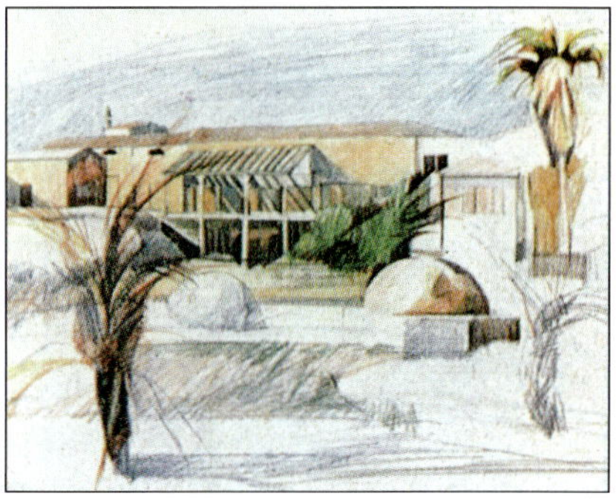

6 Build up a strong, detailed drawing of the foreground palm with pale and dark green tones.

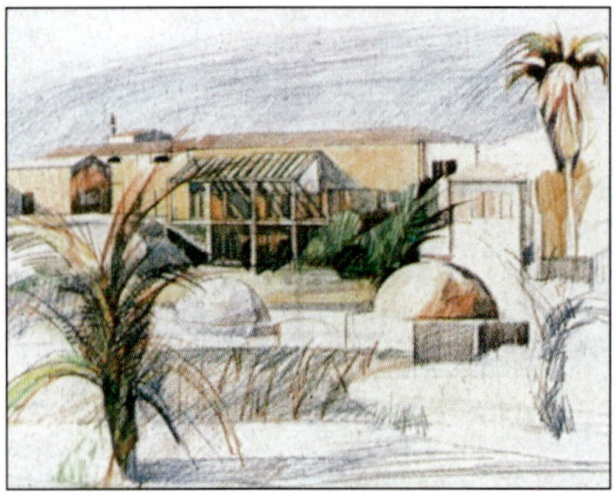

7 Put in very loose strokes of brown in the middle distance. With a strong stroke, develop the green of the foreground palm. Highlight very bright areas with white.

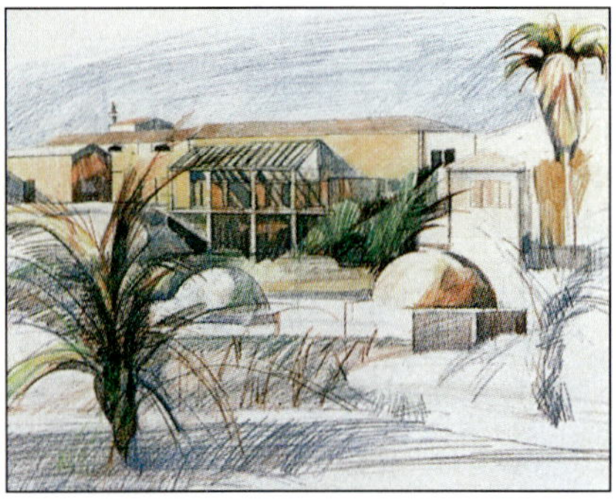

8 Carry loose, blue strokes over the foreground to indicate shadow.

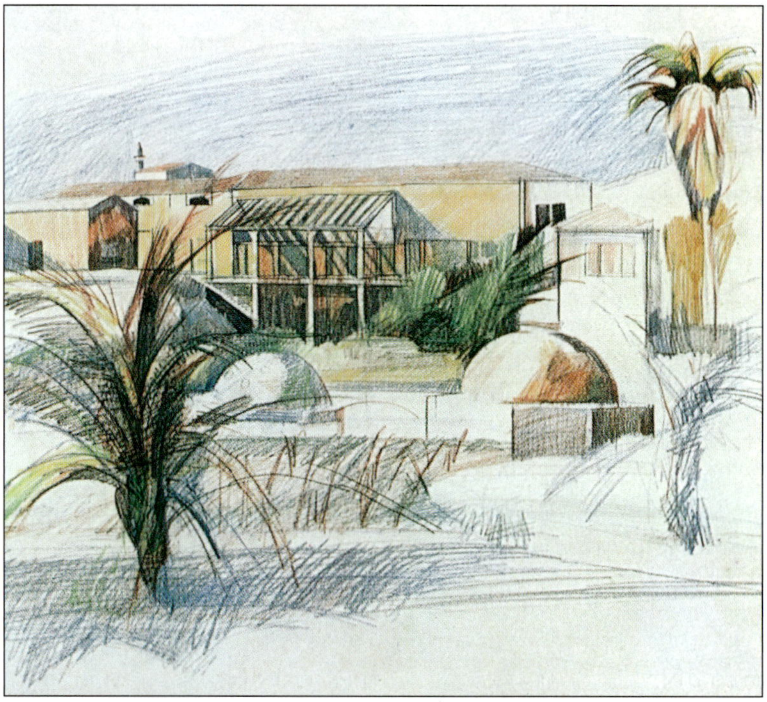

The finished picture.

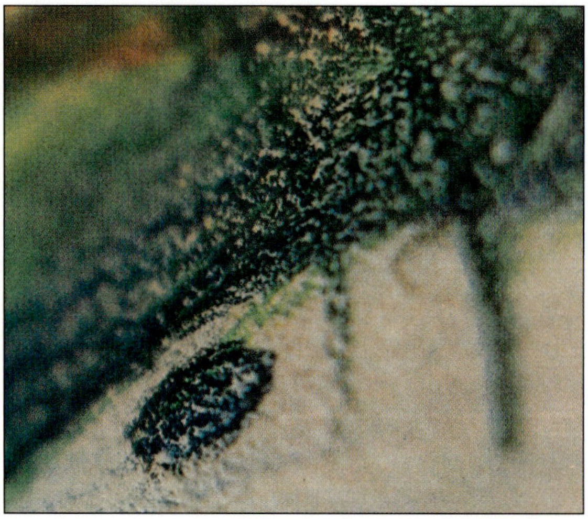

Working around the shape of the dome, the artist overlays a dark green area with light green strokes.

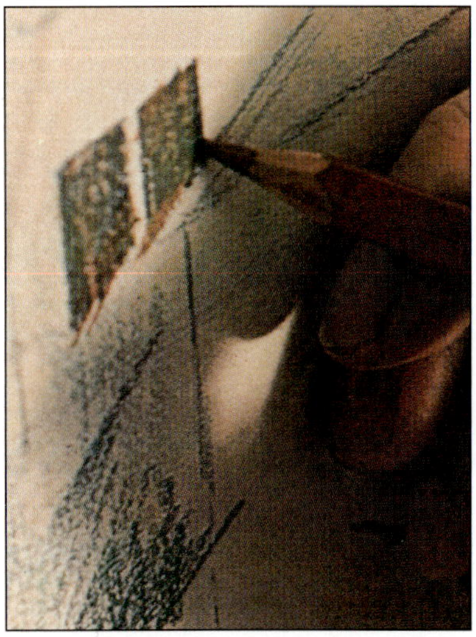

In the initial steps, the artist begins to block in areas of dark color as in the windows of the house.

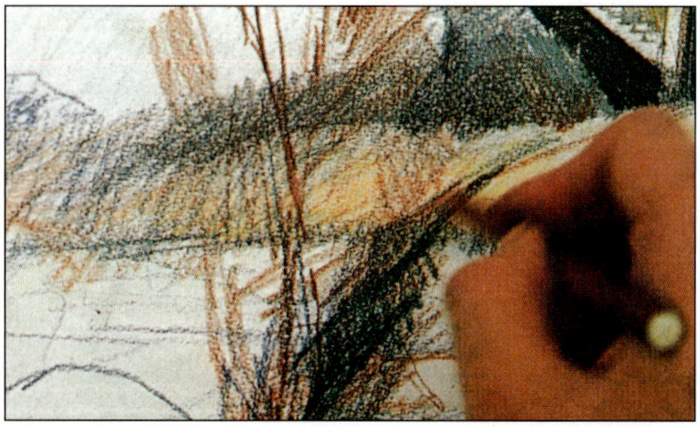

To create the texture of a palm tree, the artist overlays thin strokes of color.

Mixed Media Project

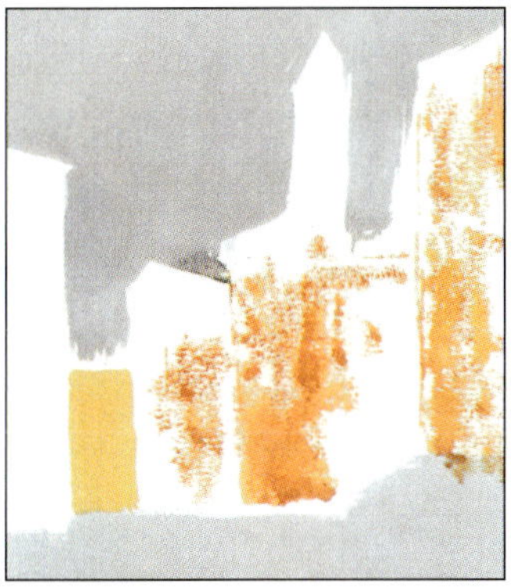

1 Moira Huntly uses watercolor, gouache, and pastel pencils for this painting. Having laid loose washes for sky and water, she applies texture by brushing watercolor onto a thick piece of paper and then pressing it firmly onto the working surface. The effect varies according to the texture of the paper and the wetness of the paint.

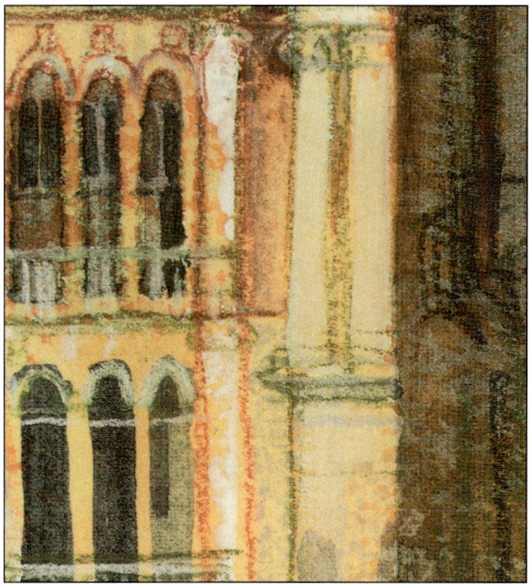

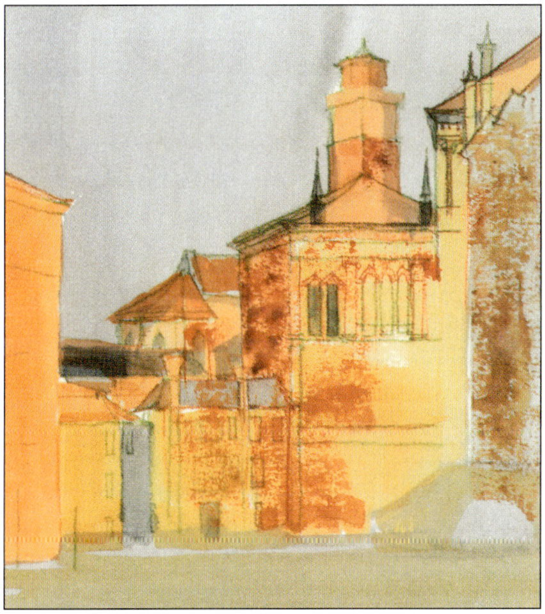

2 Flat washes of orange and raw sienna (the colors used for the printed texture) and the sky color are then brushed over the white shapes, in some areas superimposed over the textures. Detail is introduced by drawing with dark olive-green and red-brown pastel pencils, with the rough surface of the paper breaking up the line to give a grainy effect.

3 Darker shades are painted with watercolor washes of Payne's gray, echoing the sky color, which is the same gray with a small amount of crimson. Gouache is used to introduce further texture in the lighter-toned areas, again using the printing technique and opaque, cream-colored paint. A few final details are then added with white pastel pencil to complete the picture.

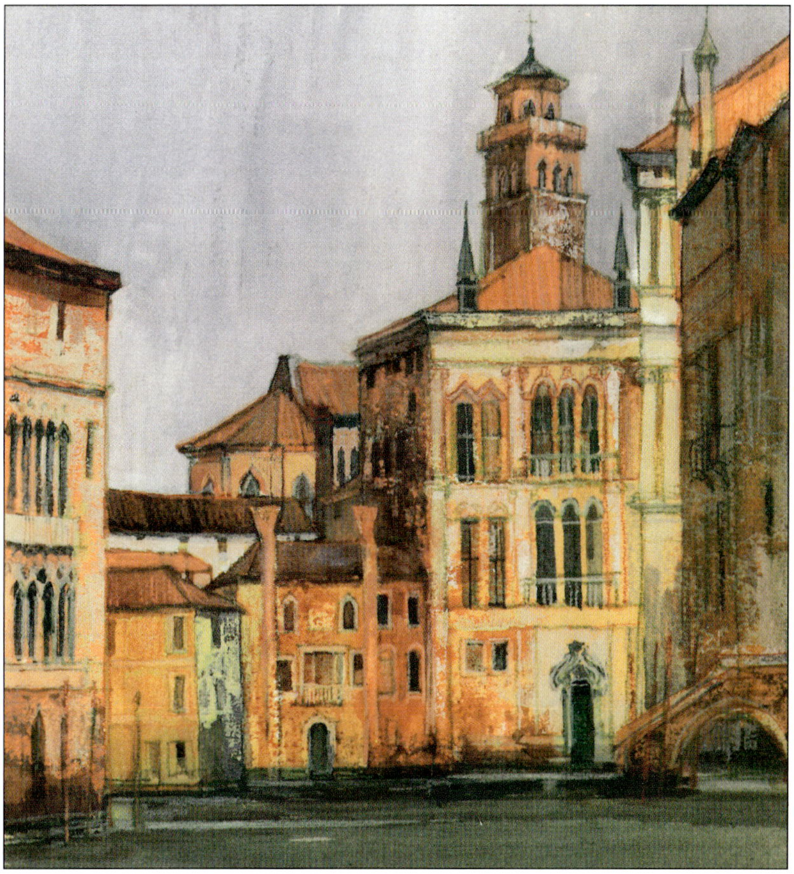

VENICE by Moira Huntly

Oil Project

This picture was based on a series of sketches and color studies made during a prolonged stay in the Greek islands. It was painted on hardboard with a white gesso priming, and was completed in one session.

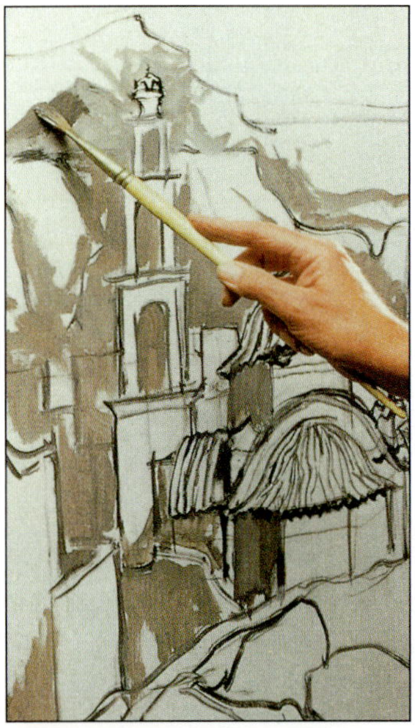

1 The foundations of the painting are laid in charcoal and then sprayed with fixative to prevent smudging. Some of the lines are reinforced with thinned black paint, which the artist often allows to show through in the finished work to give a linear emphasis in some areas. He now begins to block in broad areas with acrylic, which dries very rapidly.

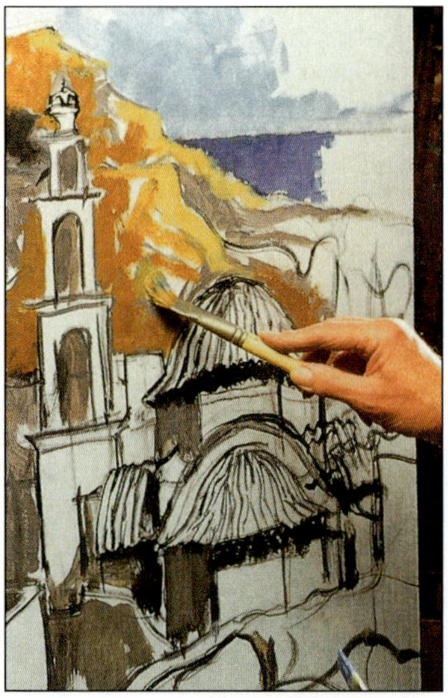

2 The background colors – yellow ocher and raw sienna mixed with varying amounts of white – are now applied in oils over the acrylic underpainting.

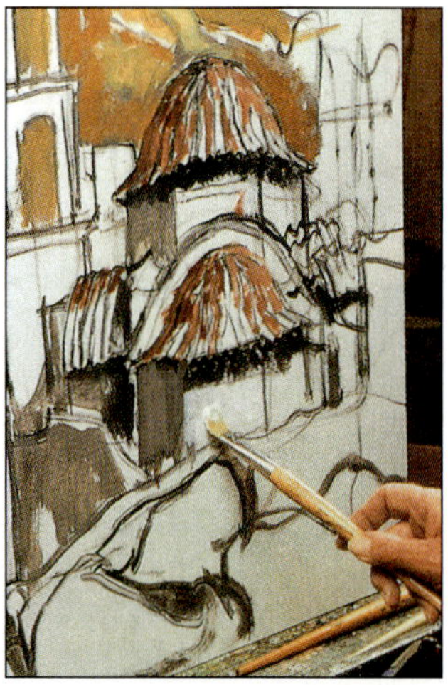

3 With the general color of the background established the artist is now able to judge the color relationships of the buildings. As nothing can be lighter than pure white, the painting of these whitewashed walls sets a tonal extreme against which other tones can be related.

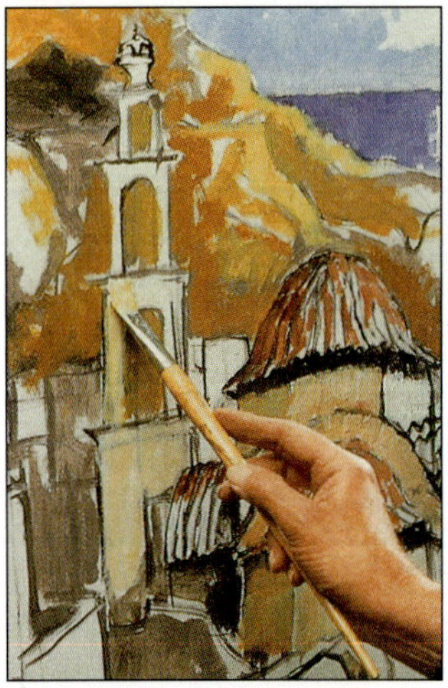

4 A pale ocher and white mixture is used for the bell tower. Large flat bristle brushes are ideal for straight-edged areas like this.

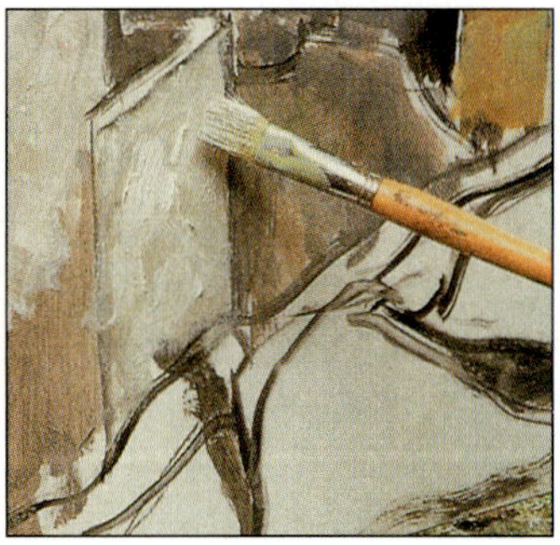

5 White paint, slightly thinned with a linseed oil and white spirit mixture, is applied with deliberately uneven brush strokes over the gray underpainting. This provides an interesting surface texture as well as suggesting the actual texture of the walls.

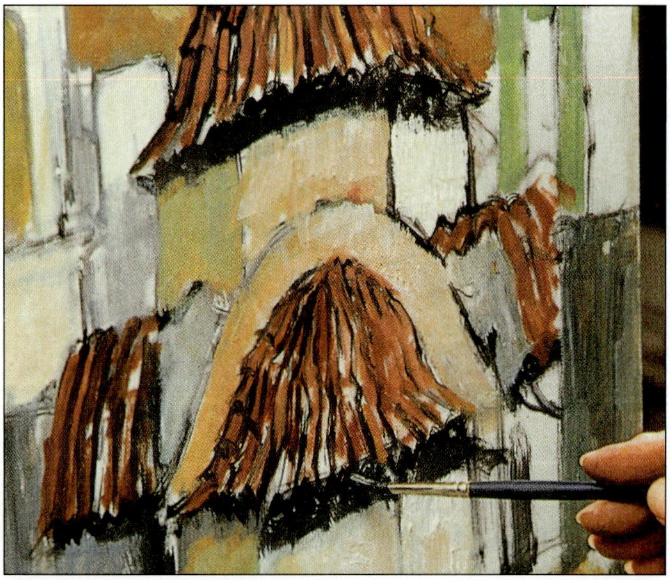

6 The shadows under the eaves are now sharpened up with a small sable brush and black paint. For these linear touches the artist uses somewhat thinner paint than the thick creamy impasto of the walls.

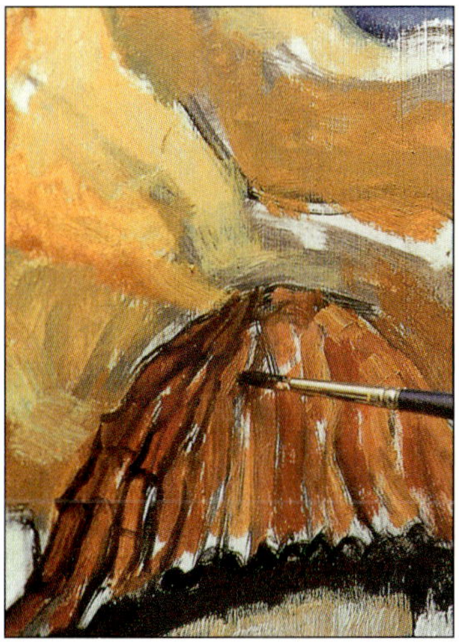

7 More linear work is carried out on the roofs, one of the main centers of attention in this picture. These warm reds and yellows play against the cooler gray of the underpainting.

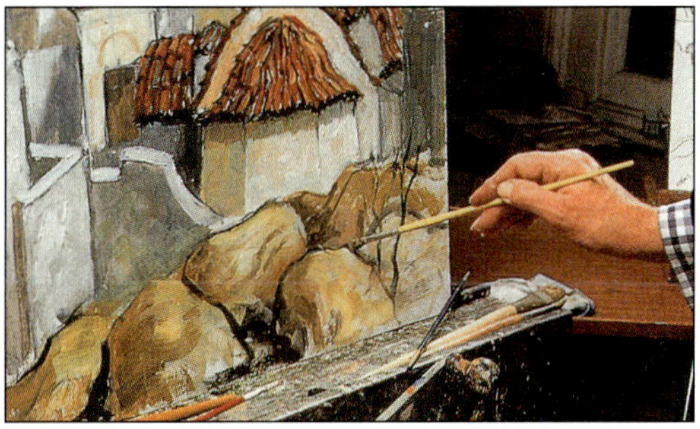

8 Throughout the painting process the artist has moved from one area of the picture to another rather than treating each in isolation. The foreground rocks are now being defined, with modeling given to their rounded forms and the black outlines reduced in intensity.

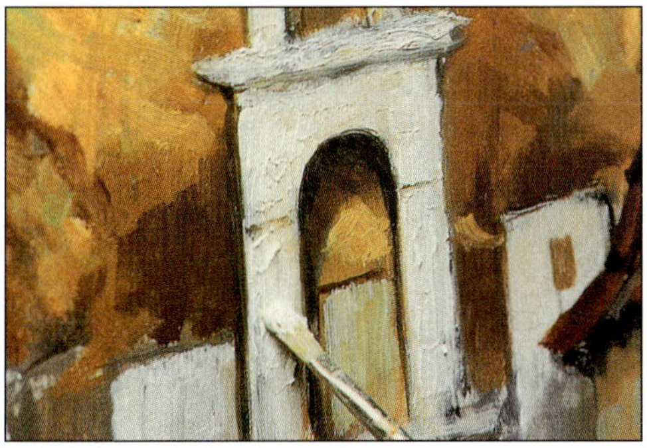

9 With the painting almost complete, the artist was able to assess what changes or additions should be made. The bell tower was sufficiently prominent, so he applied a further layer of thick white impasto, which was slightly modified by the still-wet layer of paint below.

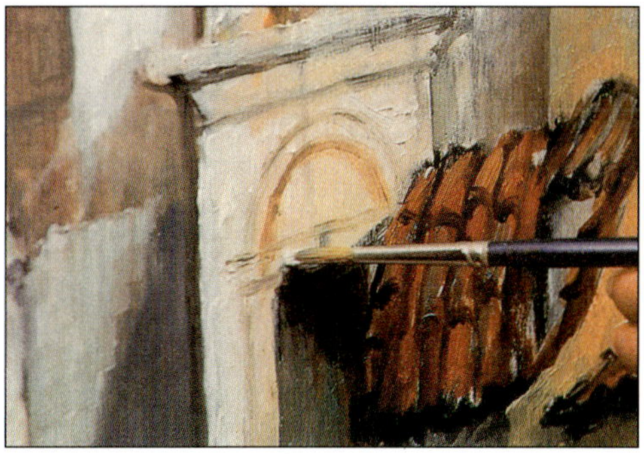

10 Small details like this arch, although vital to the painting, should be left until last. If you attempt to put them in too early they are likely to become spoiled by subsequent paint applications.

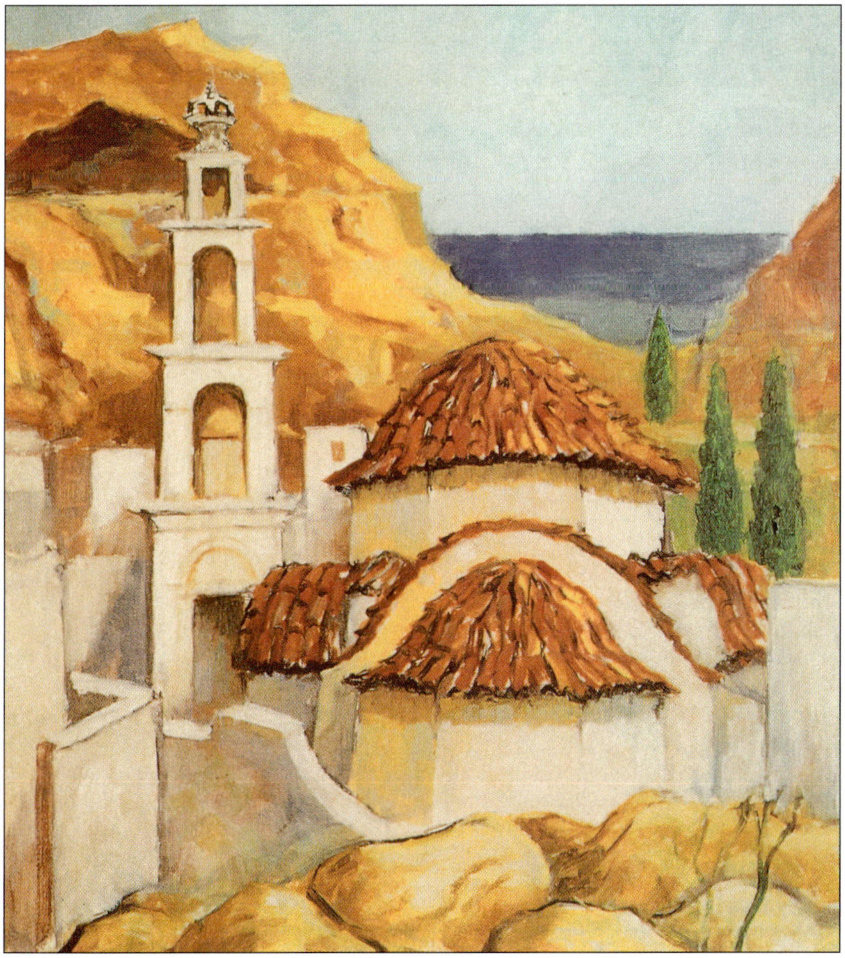

GREEK ISLAND VILLAGE by Gordon Bennett

How to Paint: Nature

The natural world is rich in fascinating material for the artist. Plants and flowers are obvious subjects and have the advantage of being available all year round. Your own garden will provide plenty of inspiration, and don't forget that plants and flowers make interesting compositions when painted *in situ*. The bits and pieces that you find lying around the garden or on a walk can be added to your collection – feathers, twigs, pebbles, leaves, mosses, and lichens can be assembled to create stimulating subjects rich in color and texture.

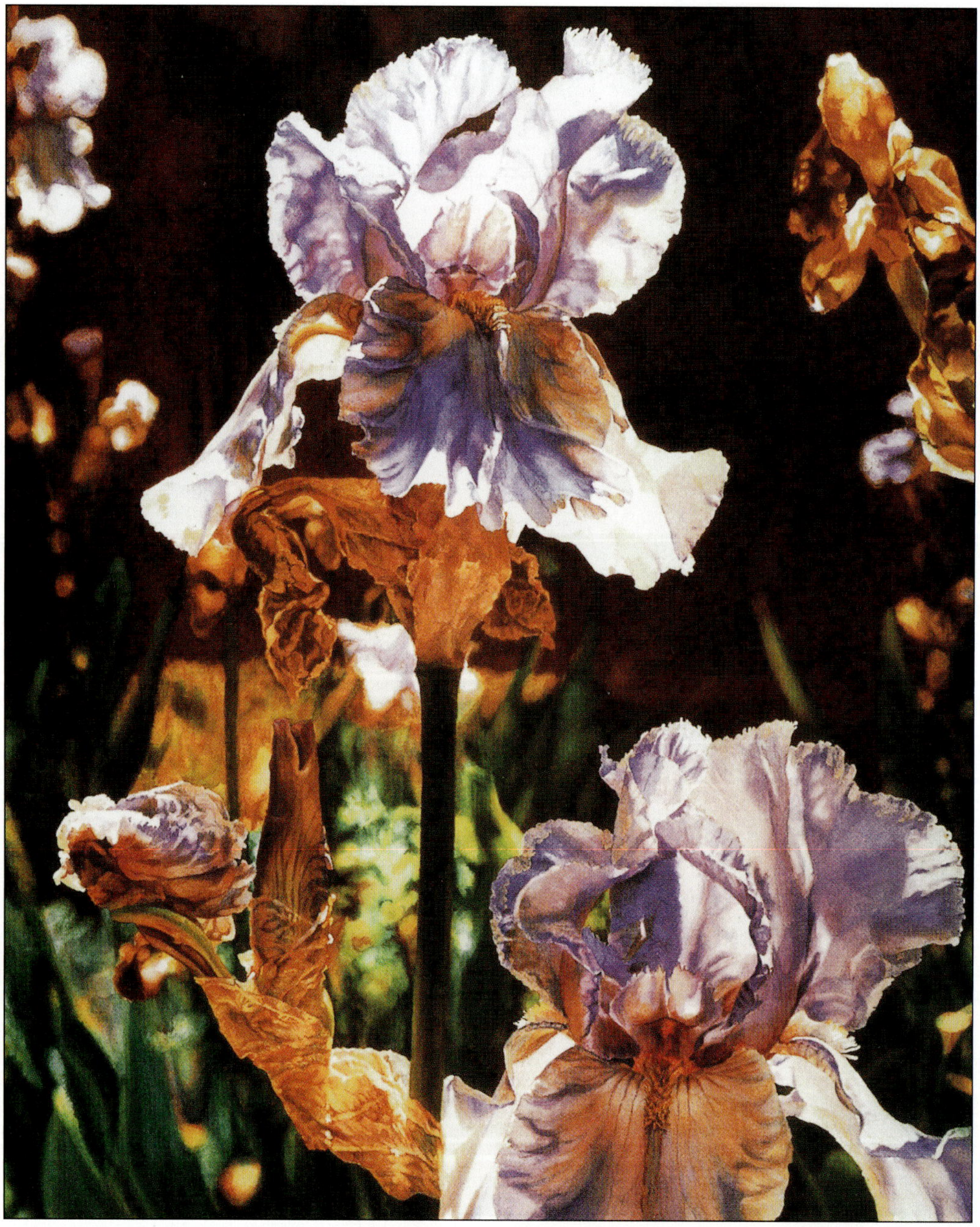

TWO KISLET IRISES by Nedra Tornay (watercolour)

Introduction

Artists of today are free of many of the conventions that placed limitations on painters of previous generations. "Working from nature" is a broad term that not only includes making literal pictures of plants, flowers, wildlife, and so on. In its wider sense it almost means studying structure and organic growth in all natural objects. Of course this wealth of opportunity and wide choice of subject can be confusing and bewildering, and no amount of freedom of expression or individuality can get away from the need for close observation and accuracy when working from nature.

Color is crucial and its contribution to the natural world cannot be overstated. To the artist the color, structure, mood, design, and texture cannot really be studied in isolation. In the painting below the artist has used a low-key palette and, although the color and tone have been freely interpreted, there is an underlying tautness – the result of careful attention to form and the underlying structure of the subject. Here the palette is deliberately restrained. Even if you delight in rich, vibrant colors, you should also sometimes experiment with a different color range to avoid the automatic repetition of too familiar colors. Use natural shapes as vehicles for investigation – as the artist has done here – and take an imaginative and interpretive approach to the subjects. This picture clearly demonstrates the fact that there are no rules in painting. As long as the final result works, the method – no matter how unusual – is justified.

Many natural forms are alive. Flowers and plants, for example, are growing organisms and are usually best left in their own surroundings while you paint or draw them. Potted plants are an easy and convenient source of subject matter, and providing you water them and keep them in a suitable temperature, can last for a long time.

Other natural forms, such as stones, pieces of driftwood or fossils, are inanimate and can be collected and taken home, thus enabling you to become completely familiar with them and to spend time studying their forms and shapes in the comfort of your own home or studio. Many artists have a huge selection of such things, standard favorites that they use time and time again, often as part of a larger composition.

A scientific curiosity about the things you draw and paint will often help you to understand why and how your subject came to be a certain color or shape. Of course, you do not need to be an expert in botany or geology to enjoy working from plants and rocks, but it often makes a subject more interesting if you know a little about its origins.

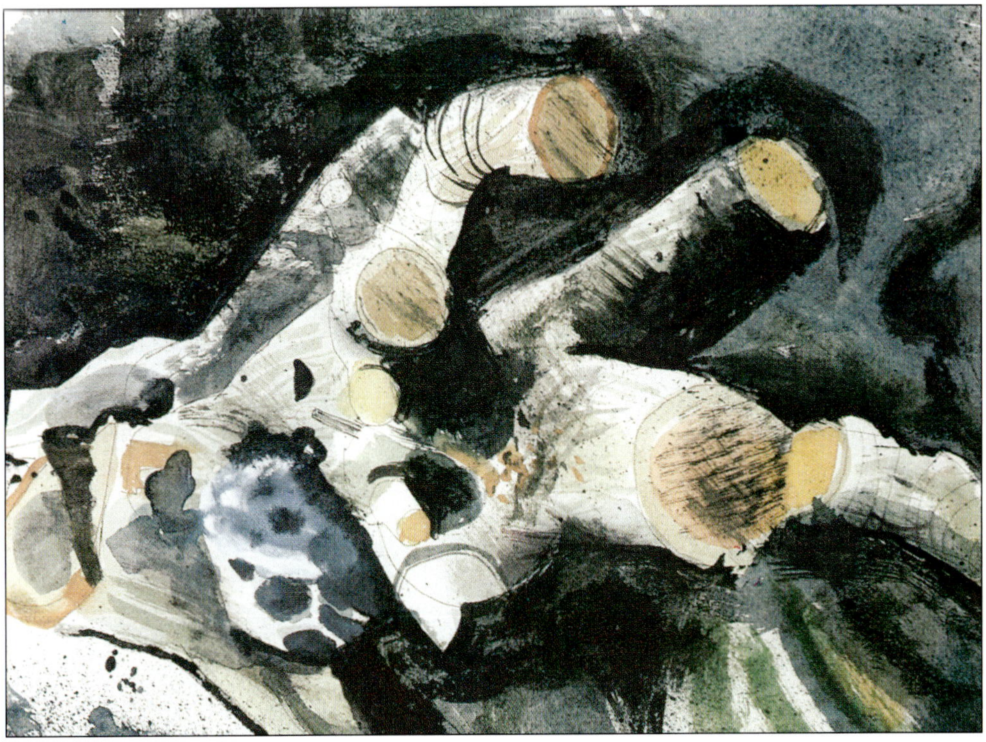

Flowers

For the beginner, flowers and their foliage provide an endless source of subject matter to practise on in any medium, even if you do not intend to specialize in them. From wild flowers to exotic, cultivated varieties, there is always something to paint, even in the dead of winter. They are also a good subject for the disabled or those who are housebound.

Flowers have been symbolic through the ages: life and death, the seasons, and your emotions can all be depicted through flowers. Artists use flowers and leaves for the message they can give, telling a story or sending a wish to a friend. For example, ivy is a fairly universal symbol for friendship and fidelity, and a red rose has the obvious implications of love. During the Renaissance, Mary, the mother of Jesus, was invariably painted with a white lily, the symbol of purity – this gave rise to the name, Madonna lily.

From the earliest times, artists have sought to capture the delicate and emotive designs of nature, as can be seen on pottery and jewelry found by archaeologists. A knowledge of herbs was vital to healers. The first dated examples of such "Herbals" comes from the Greeks and the Romans, and the oldest complete Herbal is the Codex of Dioscorides, which dates from AD 512, and was made on vellum.

Most great artists have depicted flowers in some form or other. In the seventeenth and eighteenth centuries, Dutch painters were renowned for their rich, glowing flower portraits. These depicted wonderfully elaborate arrangements, with meticulous attention given to a shining dewdrop or a snail, added to give emphasis to the composition. The fact that all the flowers in one painting could not have been in season at the same time does not seem to have mattered – perhaps the artists painted in each flower as it appeared through the seasons. The rich colors and gorgeous displays gave the Dutch pride of place in the flower-painting world, and this work is well-represented in many major collections.

There are basically two kinds of flower drawings or paintings. Botanical drawings are primarily intended to explain the construction of the flower and to show, almost diagrammatically, its botanical features. The flower drawings described earlier are drawings in which the pictorial possibilities of the flowers are explored and exploited. Some botanical drawings are beautiful by any standards and flower drawings can be botanically accurate, but the two kinds of drawings have distinctly different primary aims.

AN OBEDIENT SUBJECT

The most significant thing about painting flowers, as with making any still life painting, is that the artist is almost entirely in control. The subject can be arranged in any way the artist wishes. There is no problem in working from direct observation or spending periods working from memory or from sketches and then returning to the flowers for later reference.

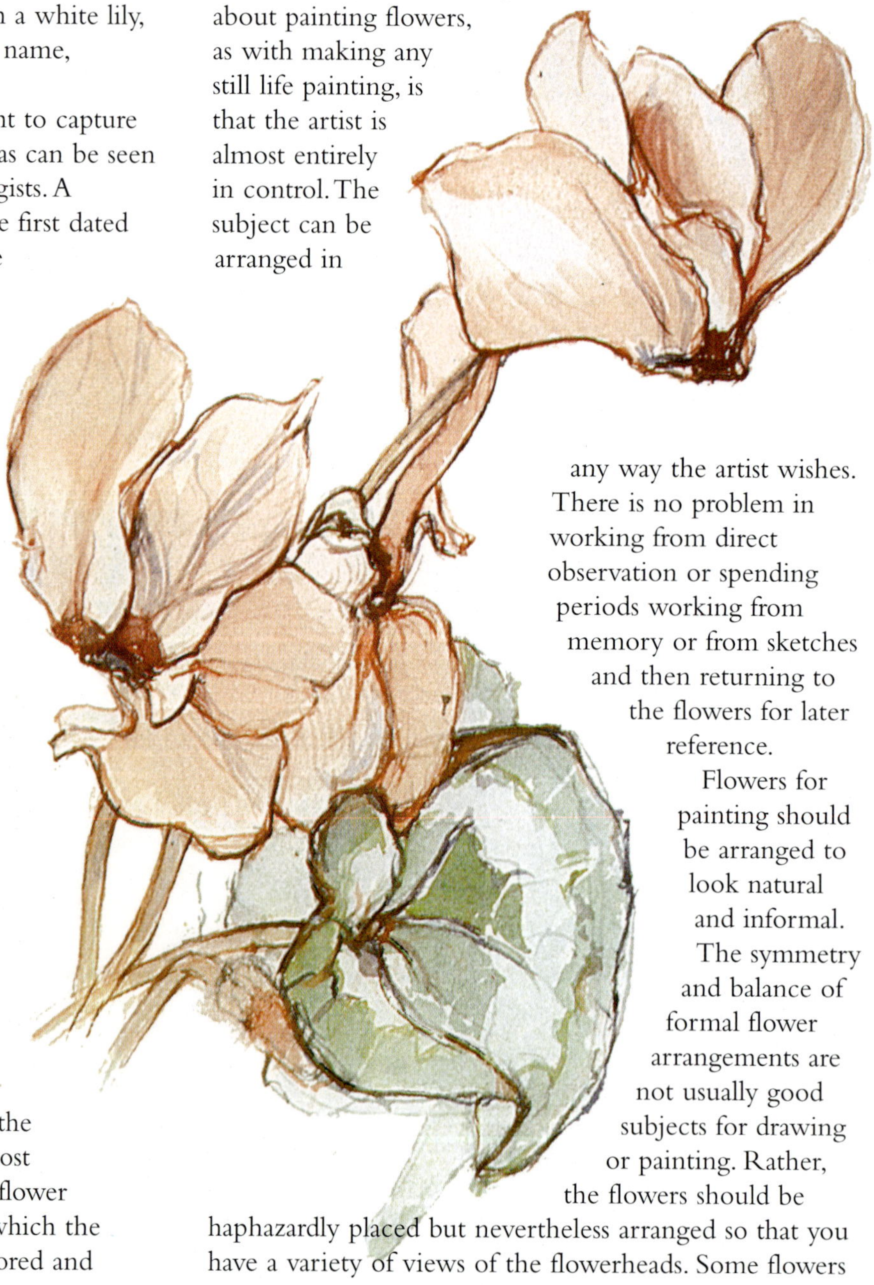

Flowers for painting should be arranged to look natural and informal. The symmetry and balance of formal flower arrangements are not usually good subjects for drawing or painting. Rather, the flowers should be haphazardly placed but nevertheless arranged so that you have a variety of views of the flowerheads. Some flowers

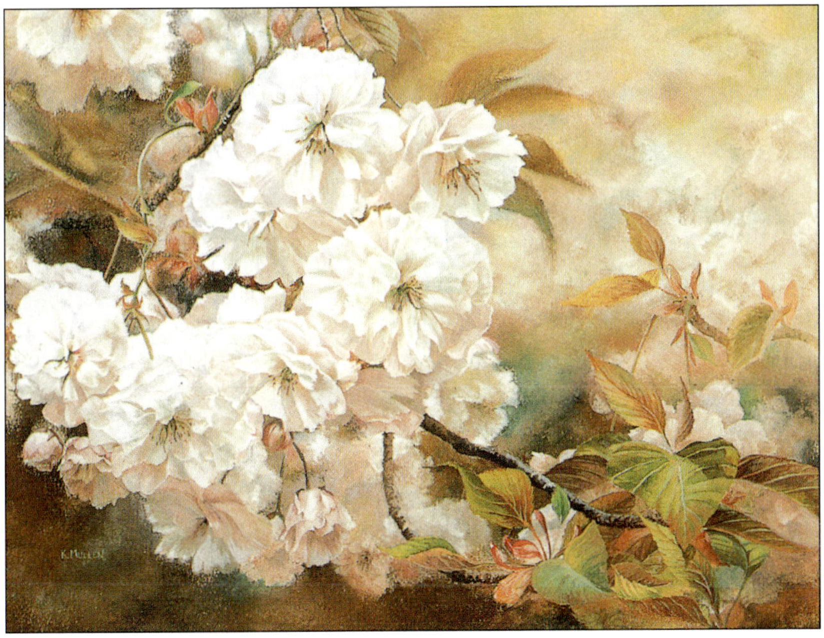

A soft pastel background lifts this cherry blossom painted in gouache. Dark stems and touches of pink and green help to restore focus, keeping the painting vibrant.

Most importantly, the whole arrangement of flowers must look round and three-dimensional and whatever attention is paid to an individual flower, it must not be at the expense of the flowers as a whole. Undue attention to detail and to flowers in isolation from the whole arrangement will almost inevitably lead to the production of a disappointing flat pattern, with little of the character that animated the original subject.

WHAT TO USE

Obviously, the most important aspect of any flower is its color, and watercolor paintings of flowers can produce the intense, luminous color that characterizes many flowers. Pastels and crayons are also popular and drawings in monochrome can represent the dramatic shapes of some flowers or illustrate the complex construction of others.

should overlap others, with the heads turned in different directions. If possible, the flowers should be at different stages of development with some in bud and others in full bloom.

Lighting is also important. Light from the side usually gives a strong contrast of light and dark, and assists in providing information that will help to create solid forms in the drawing. Whether this light is natural or artificial is immaterial, but remember that whereas artificial light can be controlled and provide sharper or softer shadows according to preference, it distorts the color of the flowers.

SUBDUING THE DETAIL

Possibly more than with any other subject, the danger in making paintings of flowers is that of being seduced by the detail. Flowers are intricate and incredibly beautiful but even so it is easy to make very boring pictures of them. Attention to detail has to be resisted until the painting is firmly constructed and detailed; even then it may be necessary only to select two or three flowers for explanation in great detail. The individual flower must not be seen in isolation but as a unit in the complex form of the whole arrangement. Once the form has been established against its background, the individual flowers can be drawn emerging from it. The flowers need to be drawn connected to their stems and the stems and foliage need to be drawn fitting into whatever kind of container is used.

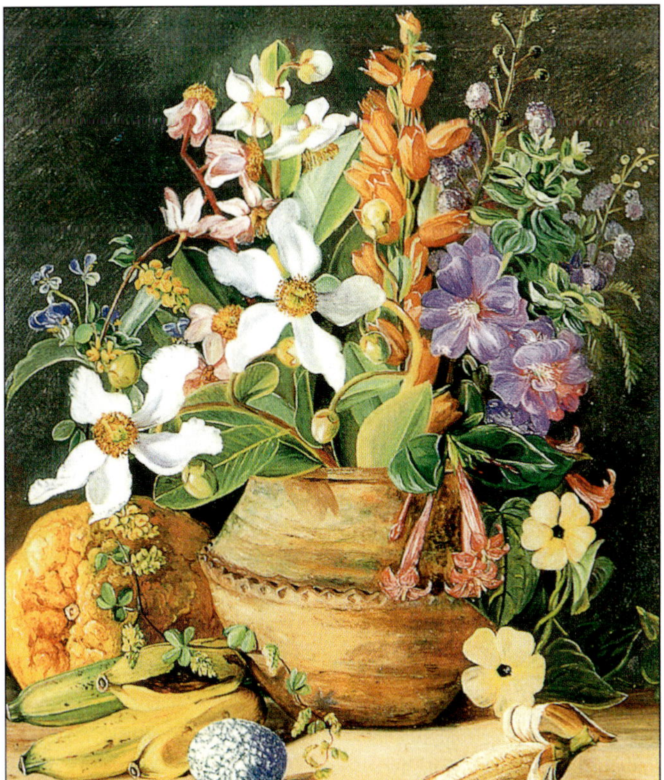

A group of "wild meadow flowers" from Brazil by Marianne North.

Irises in Watercolor

The two best-known methods of working in watercolor, wet-into-wet and wet on dry, are often regarded as separate techniques, but in fact most watercolor painters combine them in one painting, using wet-into-wet for certain areas and controlling the flow of paint so that it does not become unmanageable, as the artist has done in this painting. She has chosen hot-pressed paper rather than the more usual cold-pressed surface because the colors run into one another and form pools on the smoother surface, a tendency she likes to exploit.

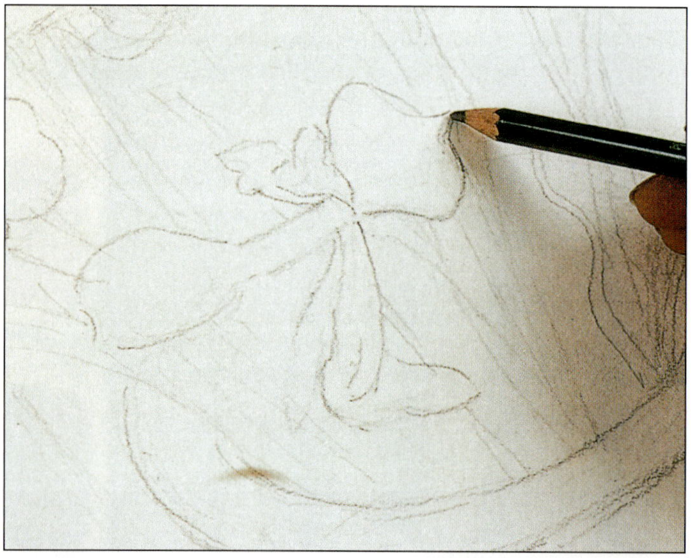

1 The composition is quite an elaborate one, so the artist began with a rough pencil sketch before making her preliminary drawing onto the working surface. She uses a soft (4B) pencil for this.

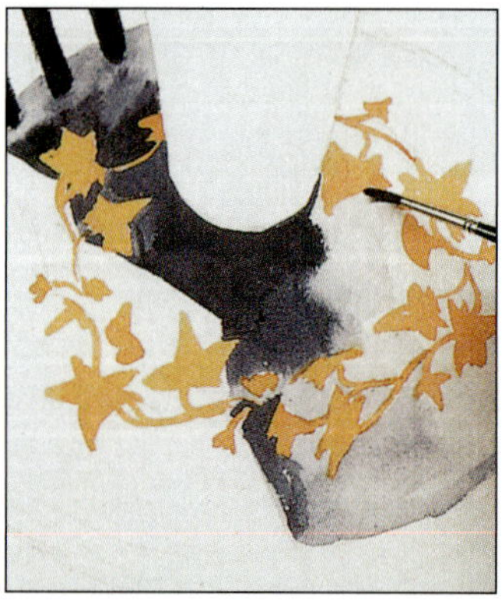

2 She has begun the painting with the ivy leaf decoration on the chair, which she felt needed to be taken into consideration early on. She now paints Payne's gray around them, working wet-into-wet so that puddles of light and dark paint are formed. These describe the irregular highlights on the chair very well, and were not altered.

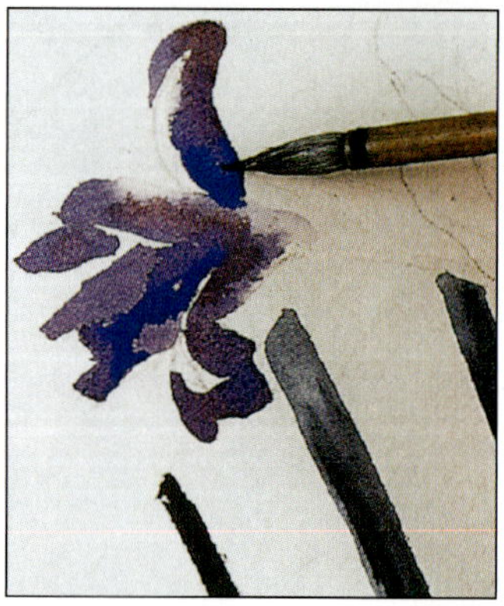

3 The chair back also needed to be tackled early, as it would work in with the flowers, so the struts were painted before the first of the flowers. For the iris, ultramarine blue is merged wet-into-wet with purple alizarin, the main flower color.

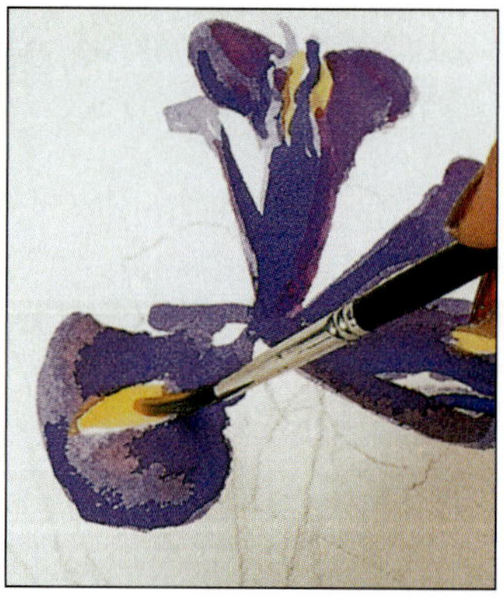

4 The flowerheads were worked wet-into-wet, with successive colors dropped in with a well-loaded brush so that they ran together and formed pools and tonal gradations. The yellow areas had to be crisp and clear, however, so the paper was left to dry before adding these.

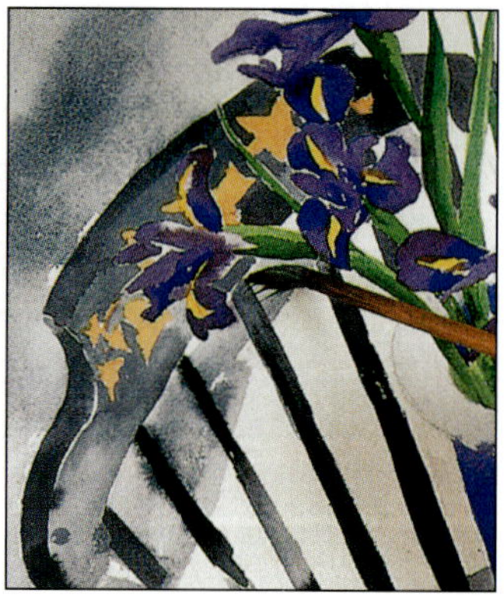

5 The chair back forms a background for the flowers, and was softened by keeping the paint very wet. A wet wash of the same gray as the chair is taken right over the chair struts and background, reducing the tonal contrasts.

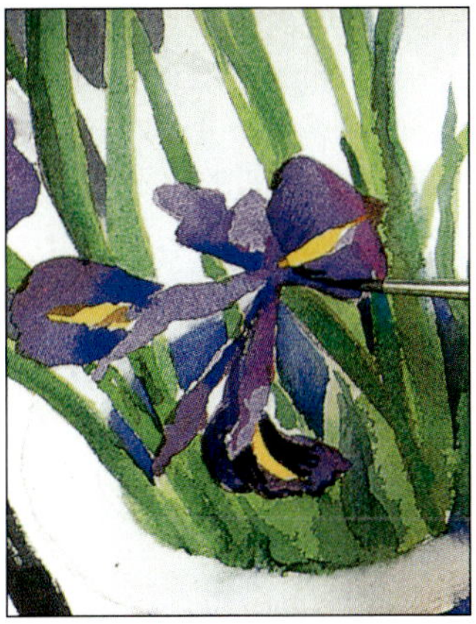

6 When the flowers and leaves were dry, final touches were added wet on dry, with the darkest flower tones picked up with mauve straight from the tube and a No. 4 round brush.

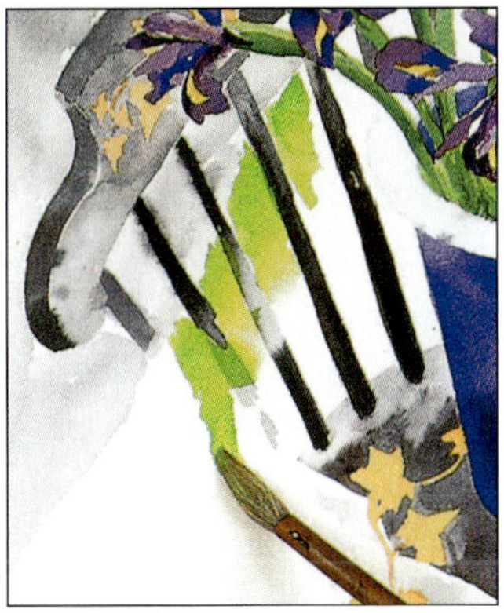

7 The last stage was to paint the filmy green cloth. The main color was a mixture of lemon yellow and Winsor green, chosen to contrast with the purple of the irises.

8 The best way to give unity to a painting is to restrict the colors and repeat similar ones from one area to another, creating a series of color links. Here the gray background links with the chair, the shadows on the cloth pick up the leaf colors, and the blue of the vase reappears on the lilies.

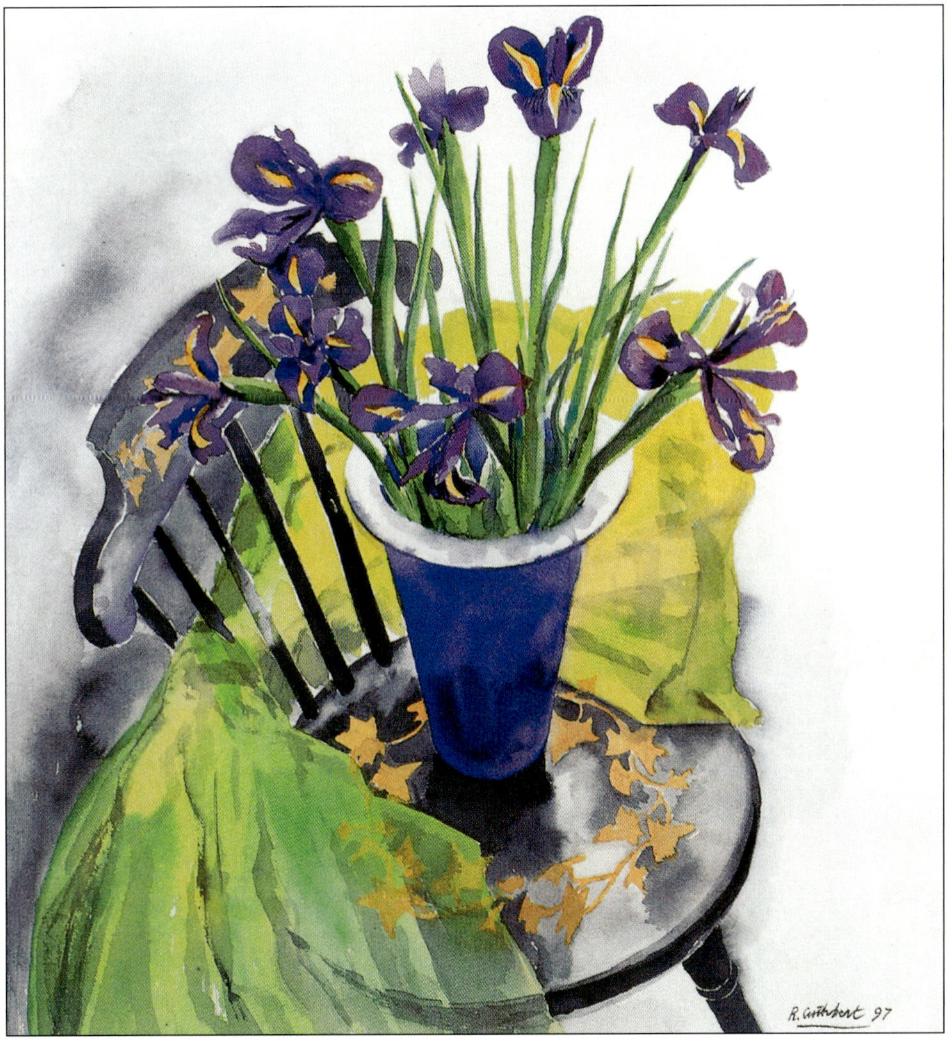

Botanical Studies

If you have ambitions toward professional botanical illustration, or simply admire the colors and shapes of flowers and want to engage with them in detail, remember you will need both time and patience.

The paintings shown here were the result of several sessions of work, and time spent studying and drawing plants. You also need a medium that can be thinned and controlled, and a smooth surface. To help blend the colors, you can wet one area, for example one leaf or petal, float the color onto it, and go over it again when dry to build up darker, richer colors.

To position flowers for botanical drawing, you should pay attention to shape and construction. Generally only one species is selected as an individual study, but depending on the type of flower, a stem with two flower-heads or blooms at different stages of development may be needed, so that two different characteristic views of the flower can be represented. It is difficult to prevent botanical drawings from appearing flat and lifeless because the artist conceives his or her work primarily as a scientific study of the object with all its features shown and explained so that it can be used for identification purposes. It must remain, therefore, uncluttered by unnecessary background information.

This is one area of drawing in which detailed knowledge of the object is a great advantage, and a sound knowledge of botany, along with painstaking observation and attention to detail, will produce the best results.

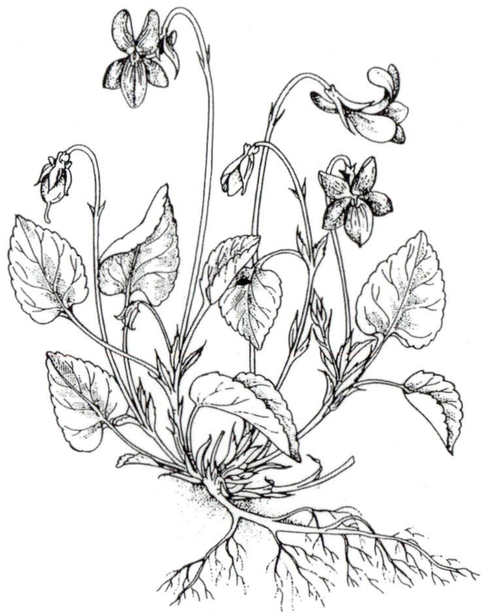

The pen and ink drawing above uses a stippling technique to convey a feeling of form and texture to the various parts of the flower. This shading cleverly follows the form of leaves and petals. As a result, although the artist has clearly described the shapes of leaves and flowers, the method of the shading saves them from looking flat.

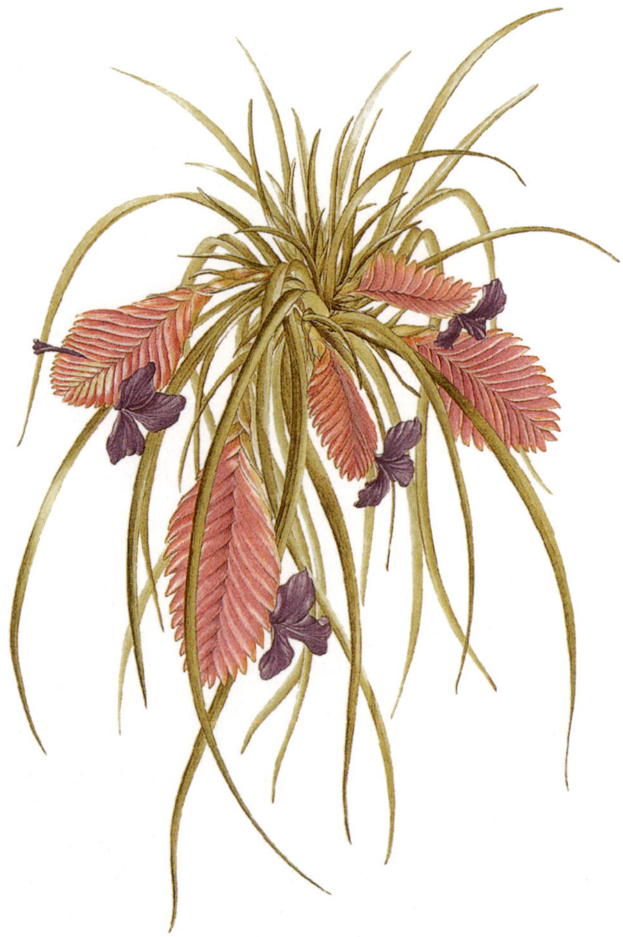

TILLANDSIA CYANEA by Pauline Dean

This is a perfect illustration of dry brush technique. The artist first made a drawing with a hard pencil (3H) on hot-pressed paper to make faint guide lines, and added color by "drawing" with a brush, making the strokes follow the flowing line of leaves. The placing on the paper gives space for the leaves.

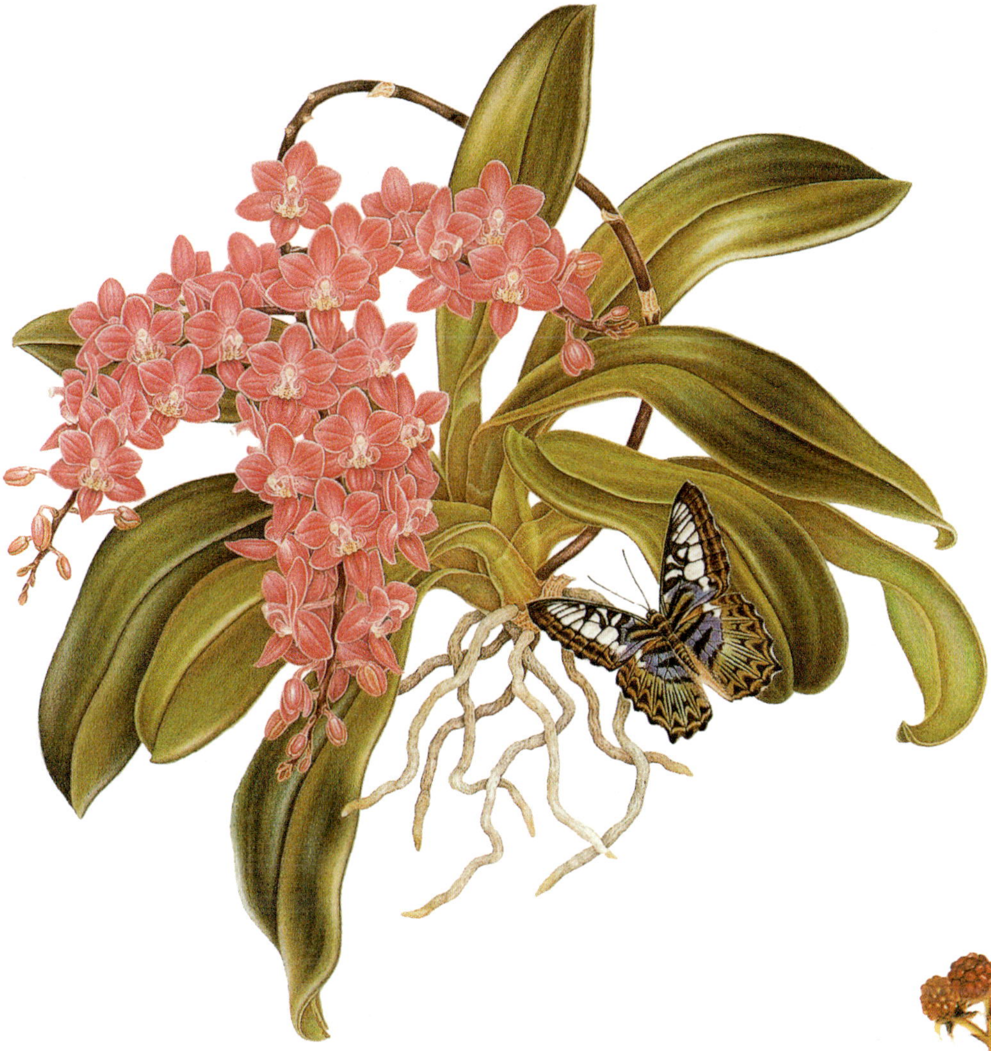

PHALAENOPSIS EQUESTRIS by Carol Woodin

This orchid has beautiful foliage which the artist has made the most of, using successive layered glazes to achieve their glossy, fleshy appearance and their slight mottling. They provide a perfect foil to the mass of small, brilliant flowers, which also have a slightly fleshy look to them. The butterfly adds a decorative touch and gives interest to an area which might have been dull.

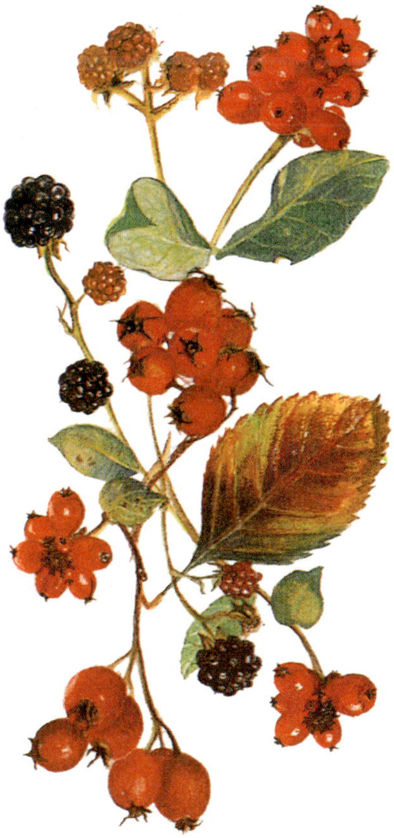

A detailed pencil outline was the first stage of this small drawing. Once satisfied with this, the artist blocked in the main colors and areas of shading with aquarelle pencils. Then, taking a small sable brush and clean water, she dissolved the applied color and blended carefully. By repeating the same procedure a number of times, the artist built up layers of strong color. Highlights, in addition to those created by leaving the white paper to show through the broken color, were dotted onto the drawing with a small brush and opaque white gouache. Aquarelle pencil used in this way makes it possible to build up beautifully subtle transitions of tone and color, as can be seen where green turns to brown on the large leaf.

Trees

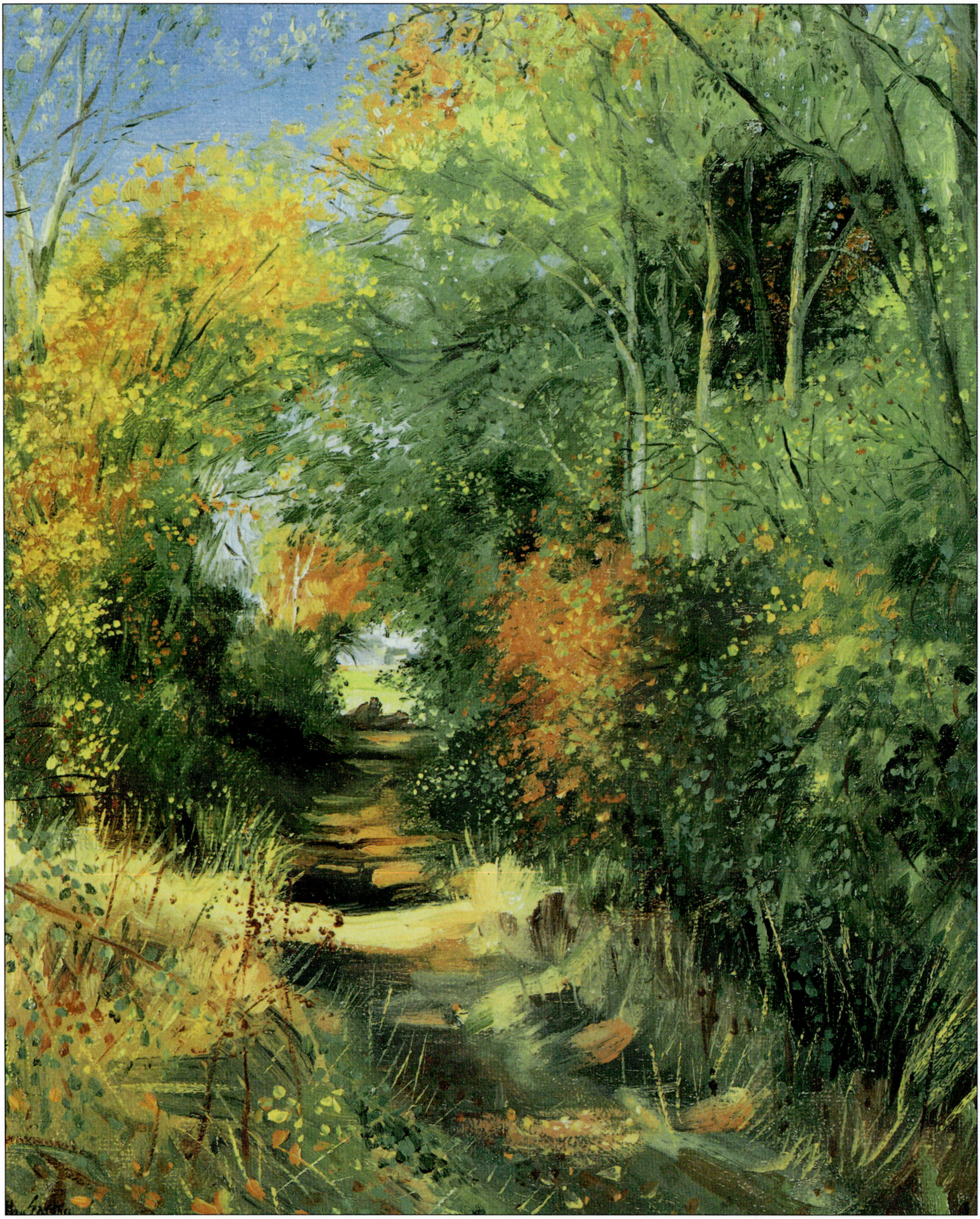

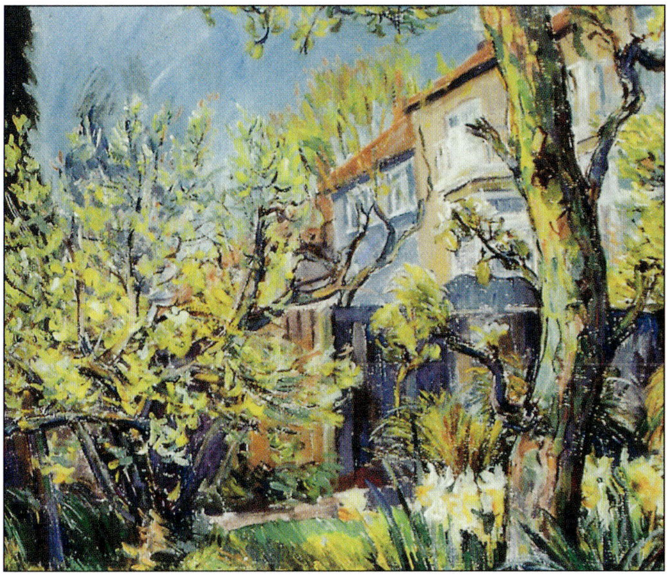

SPRING by Ted Gould (acrylic)

The tree trunk which forms a dramatic foreground to this painting on canvas has been beautifully observed and described – notice the variety of colors in this one area, and the fine marks made with a small brush to suggest the texture. The foliage of the left-hand tree has been painted with small brush strokes of impasto over thinner paint.

Trees can either be viewed as part of the general population of a landscape or as special features for close study. They have a fascinating amount of variation in their natural shapes, textures, and colors, according to the characteristics of the individual species and the seasonal changes they undergo.

While botanical identification is not an essential feature of tree studies, it is important to pay attention to specific visual qualities such as typical outline, branch structure, leaf shape, and color. The more you analyze the particular qualities, the more you can develop the richness and detail of a tree "portrait" or give definition and contrast to a study of massed trees.

Trees invite a number of different treatments. Tall trees in the foreground of a landscape, for instance, allow you to introduce a pattern element, contrasting verticals and horizontals, while massed trees in the middle distance create satisfying tall or bulky shapes and often an array of contrasting colors.

FAR LEFT: MID-DAY IN THE LANE by Timothy Easton (oil)

Small dabs of color over flatter layers of paint give the impression of dancing foliage. In the middle ground, the detail and tonal range are reduced.

Trees can also be appreciated for their varying textural qualities, and painted from a close viewpoint – tree barks, for example, provide a wealth of fascinating details as well as rich variations in color.

But however you choose to integrate trees into your painting, do study their shapes carefully or they will not look convincing. Each species of tree has its characteristic formation, some being tall and thin with upward-pointing branches, while others are almost as broad as they are tall, with the branches sweeping out into an umbrella shape.

WET MALVERN SPRING by Paul Powis (acrylic)

This artist does not restrict his outdoor work to the summer months, and these evergreen trees were painted on-the-spot during winter. There is a strong pattern element in the picture, done on Brazilian plywood, with an exciting interplay of diagonals and verticals offset by intricately shaped areas of bright and dark color. The clumps of foliage were defined by painting the sky around them last, light over dark.

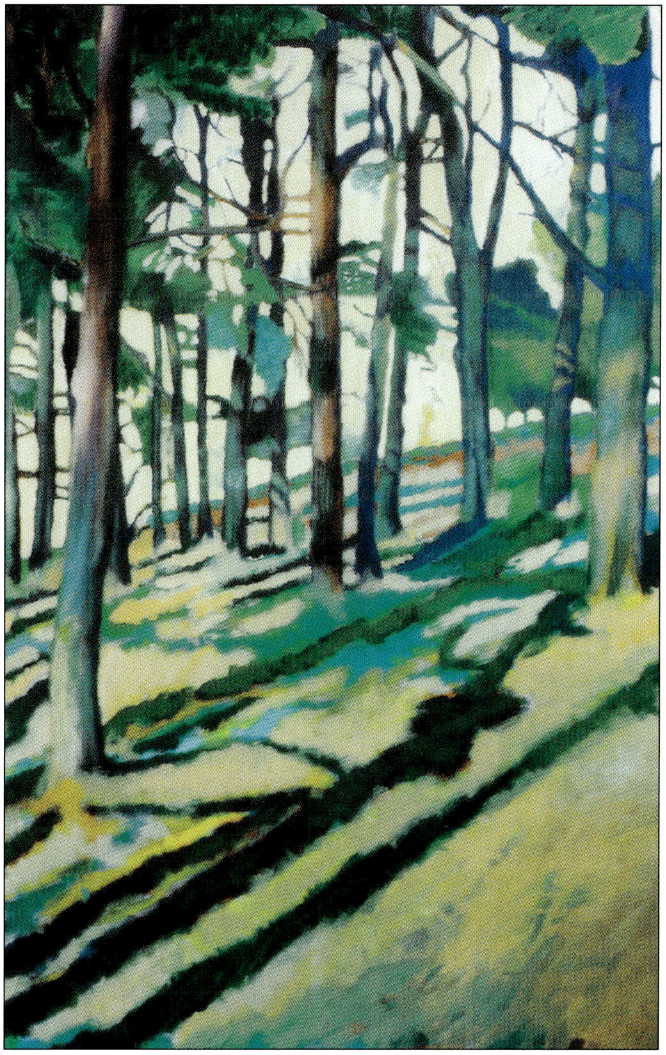

Identifying Tree Shapes

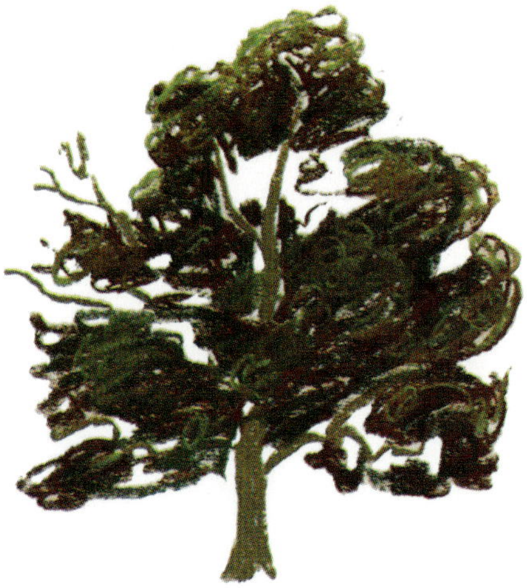

OAK (using pastel)

Colors used: red and yellow-browns, dark and bright greens. From dark to light, work into and around colors beneath.

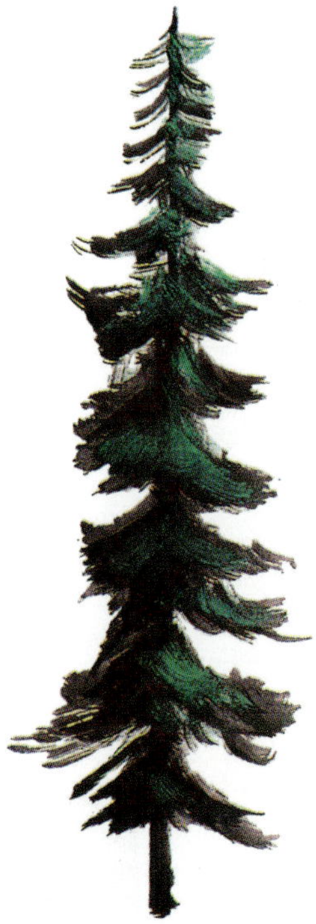

FIR (using gouache)

Colors used: ultramarine blue, carmine, viridian, and white.

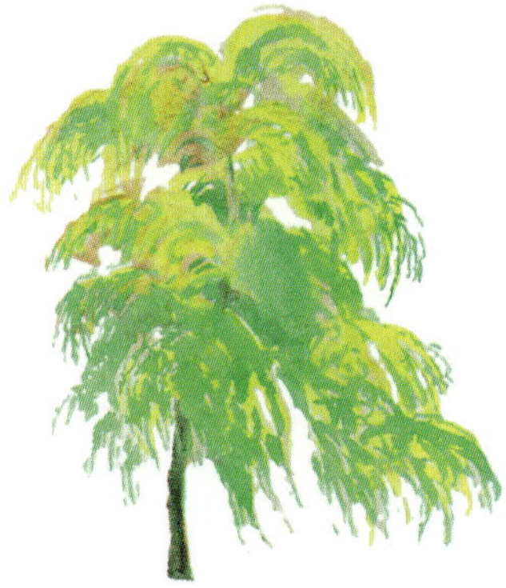

WEEPING WILLOW (using watercolor)

Colors used: cadmium yellow, raw umber, emerald green.

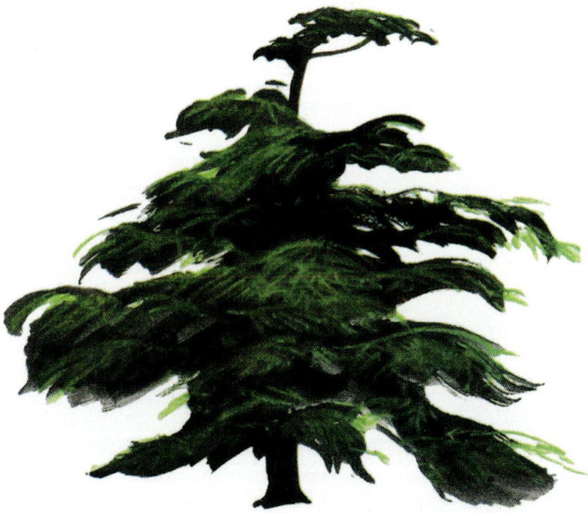

CEDAR (using gouache and pastel)

Colors used: black gouache under bright green pastel.

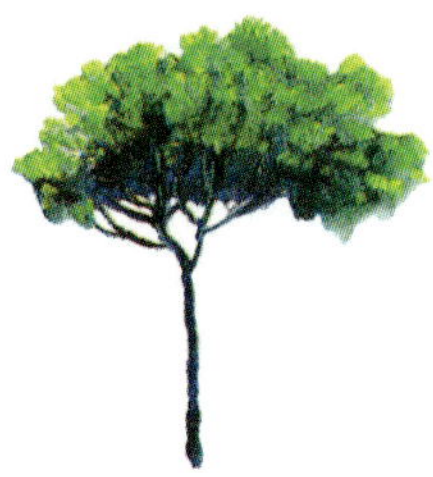

UMBRELLA PINE (using oil)

Colors used: cobalt blue, Hooker's green, cadmium yellow. Colors mixed and worked in wet-into-wet. Sgraffito detail added with end of brush.

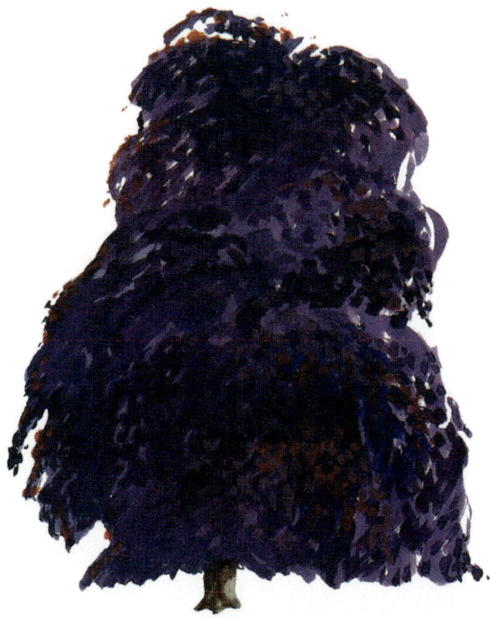

COPPER BEECH (using acrylic)

Colors used: ultramarine, carmine, white. Pale general wash, superimposed darks, dots of brighter reds.

Sponging Foliage

Many different types of sponge are available, from natural sponges to closely textured synthetic materials, all creating different effects. The medium you use and the dilution of the paint also varies the result. Watercolor and a small, natural make-up sponge are used here.

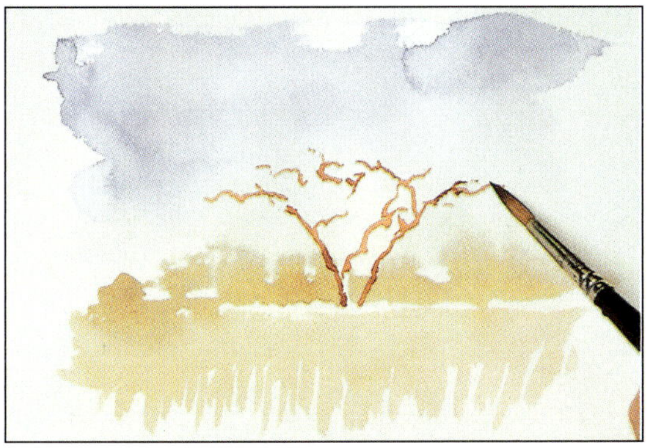

1 The painting is initially established with wet-into-wet washes, which are allowed to dry before the tree trunk is painted with a round sable brush.

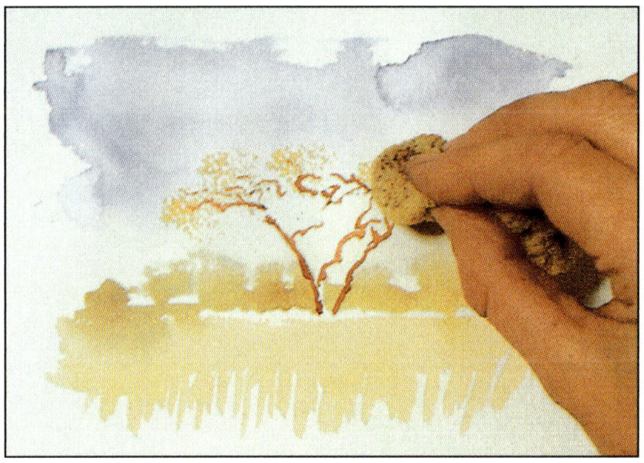

2 The sponge was dampened and then touched into a fairly dry mix of yellow ocher and cobalt blue, that is sponged delicately onto the paper.

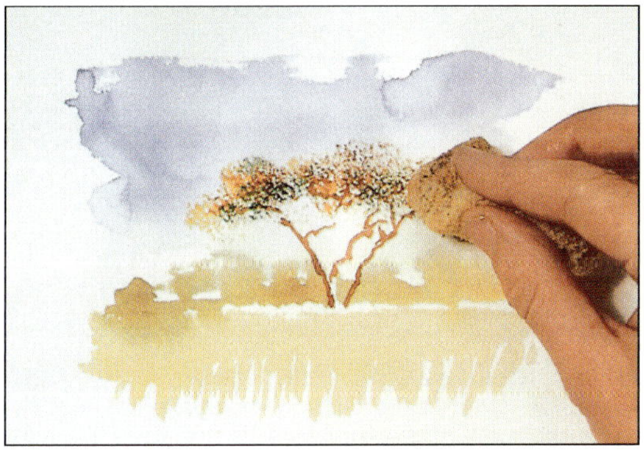

3 Two further layers of color are now superimposed over the first – alizarin crimson and then cobalt blue. The sponge is washed clean between colors and the paint kept as dry as possible.

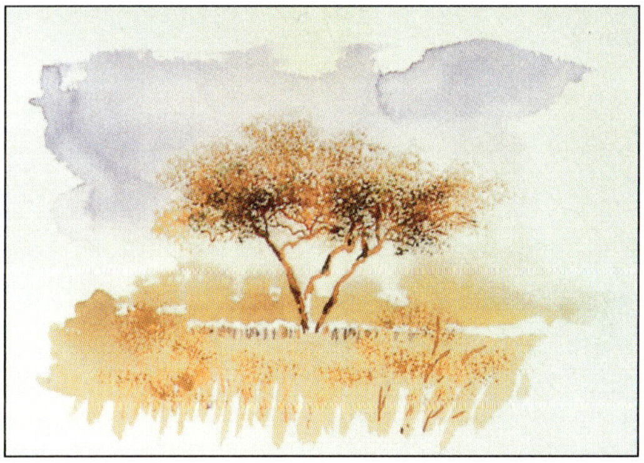

4 To preserve a unity of technique, the same method is used for the foreground grasses, with a touch of the sponge suggesting texture. Notice how the color on the tree varies in density, creating a soft edge.

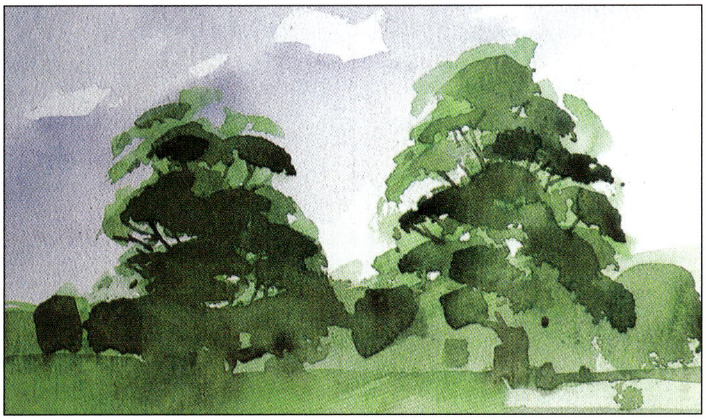

This painting has a refreshing spontaneity and feeling of light, and the sponged texture gives a convincing interpretation of heavy summer foliage.

Flowers in Their Natural Habitat

It is always an inspiring exercise to search out and draw a living plant. Flowers are at their best in their own surroundings, and seeking out wild flowers is a pleasurable occupation in itself. Indeed, it is often surprising where they crop up. Urban wastelands are scattered with the delicate colors of wild flowers. If you are unable to work on site, you can either make a quick sketch with color notes on-the-spot or take a photograph and work from this at home. Do not ignore the weeds; to the artist a humble dandelion is as intricate and beautiful as any cultivated bloom.

Working fast in oils, the artist builds up the paint with various customized painting knives, creating a thick impasto relief on the surface. As you can see, these knives are capable of achieving considerable detail.

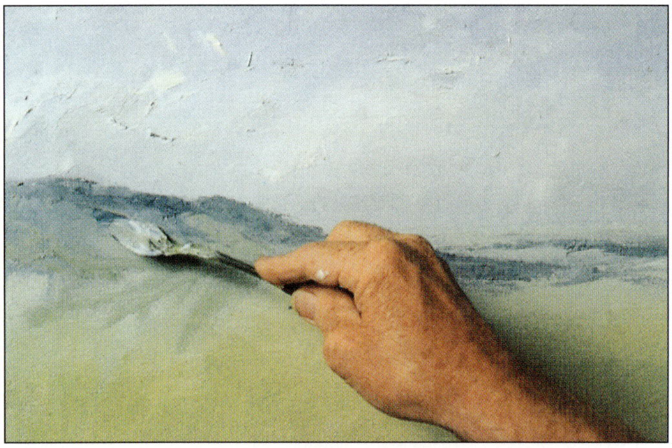

1 Having mapped out the painting, the artist starts from the top touching down the mix of color with the edge of the knife and then smoothing it out.

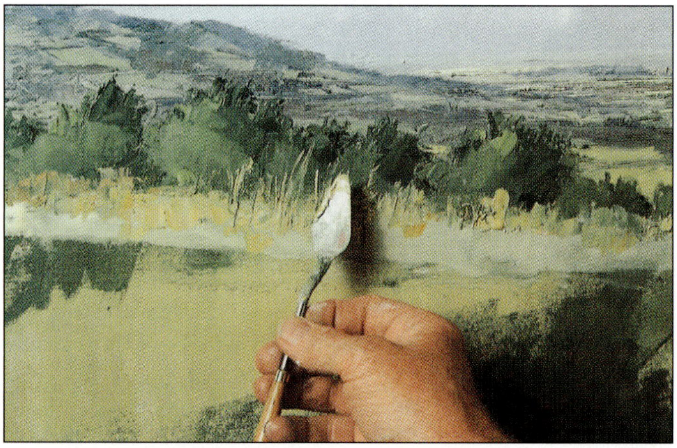

2 Now the middle ground area is developed carefully, although much of it will eventually be hidden by the foreground. The edge of the knife is used to create fine lines suggesting grasses.

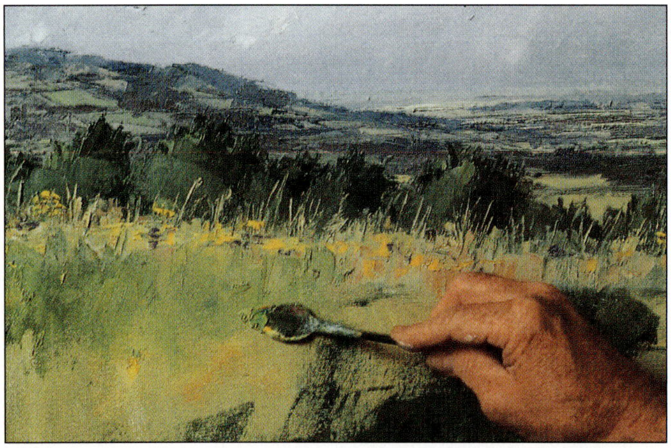

3 The foreground tones are now established, using greens mixed with indigo and chrome yellow. Touches of yellow ocher are added to lighten the mixture, and Winsor green to sharpen it.

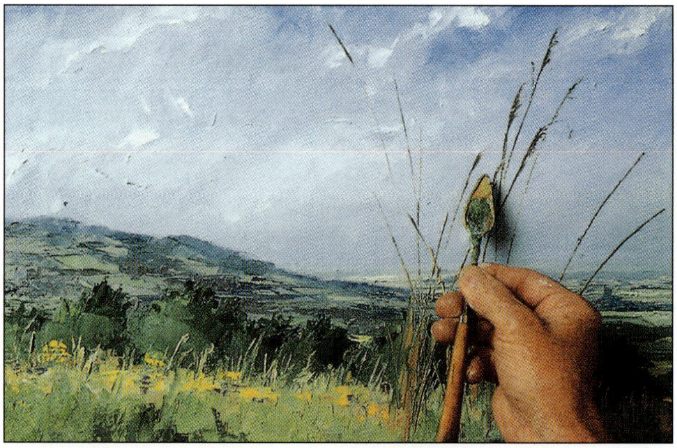

4 With a clean stroke, the artist "draws" the blade of grass with the edge of the knife, creating a varied line by altering the pressure along the edge as he proceeds.

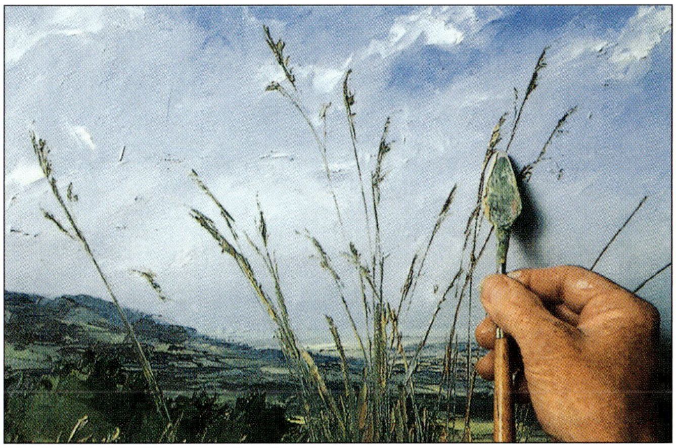

5 Seed heads are added with delicate sideway strokes made with the tip of the knife, using superimposed mixes of yellow ocher, white, and burnt umber.

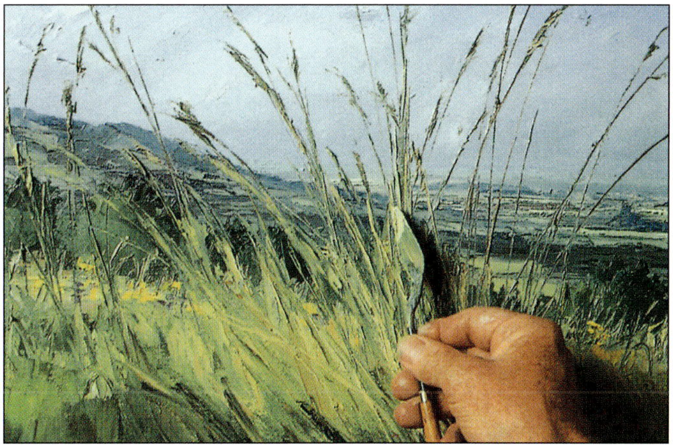

6 A sense of depth and movement in the foreground grass is created by strong directional knifemarks and a thick build-up of paint.

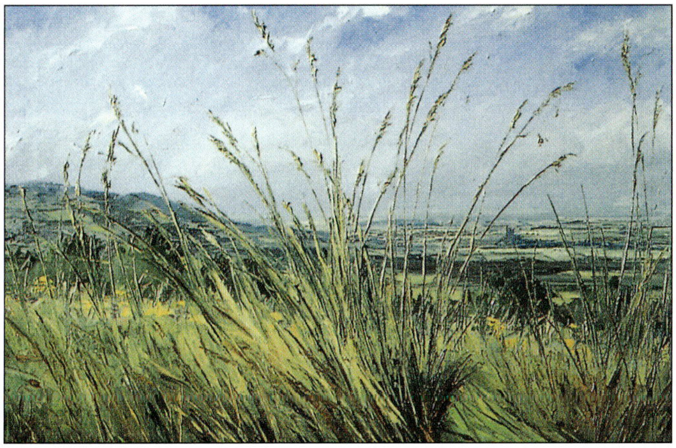

7 At the end of each "stage" the artist stands back and assesses the painting. A break in the grass has now been developed to form a "tunnel" in the foreground, leading the eye into the distance.

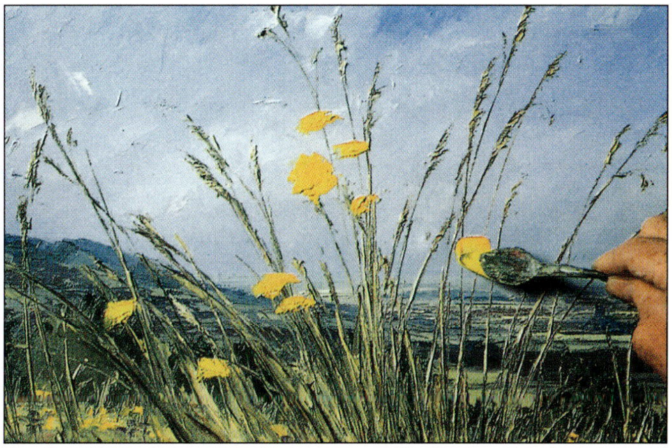

8 A loose mix of chrome and cadmium yellow is used for the flowerheads. Some of the underlying paint has been scraped away so that the yellow does not mix into the blue and become diluted.

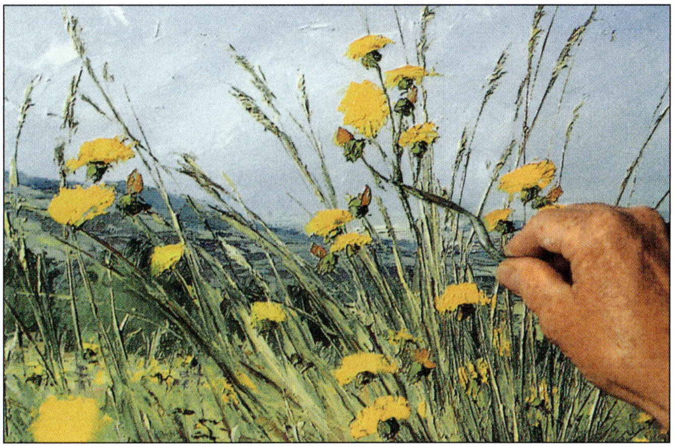

9 The yellow flowerheads are built up further and a few buds added with pure Mars yellow.

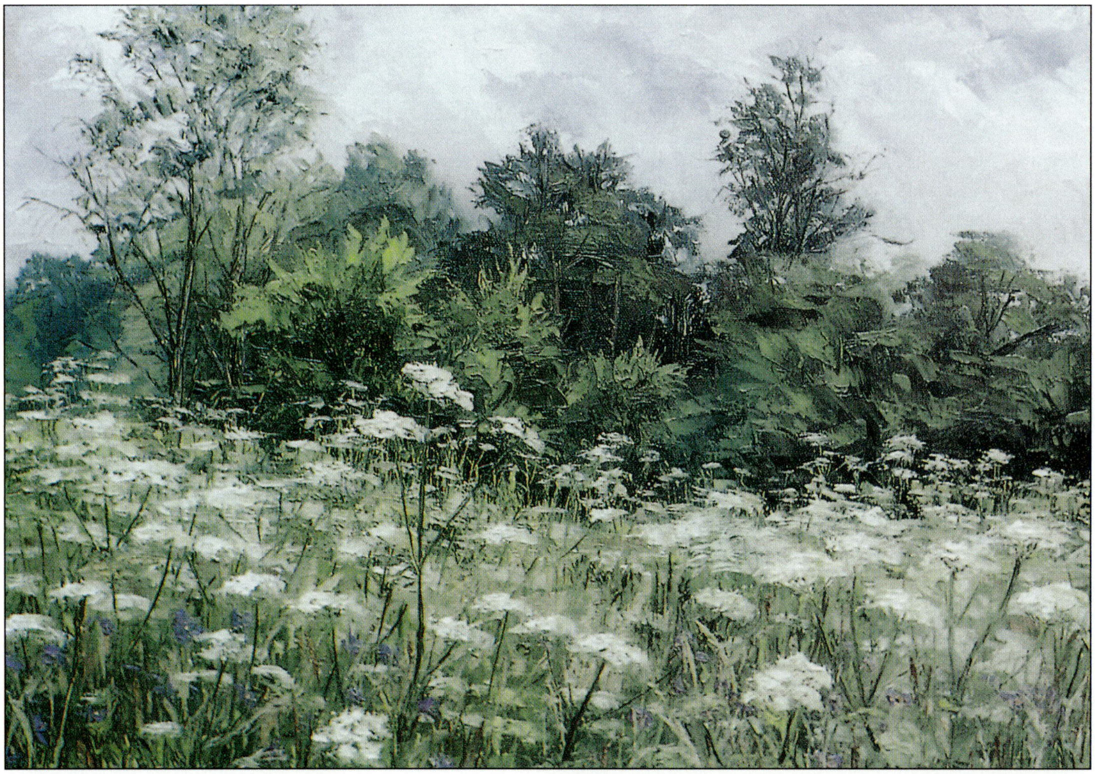

HOGWEED by Brian Bennett (oil)

The flowerheads have been built up with a succession of tiny brush strokes of thick paint in a semi-stippling technique to emphasize their texture. As it is a dull day, the tonal contrasts are not strong and the edges are soft except where the flowers are seen against the dark foliage of the middle ground.

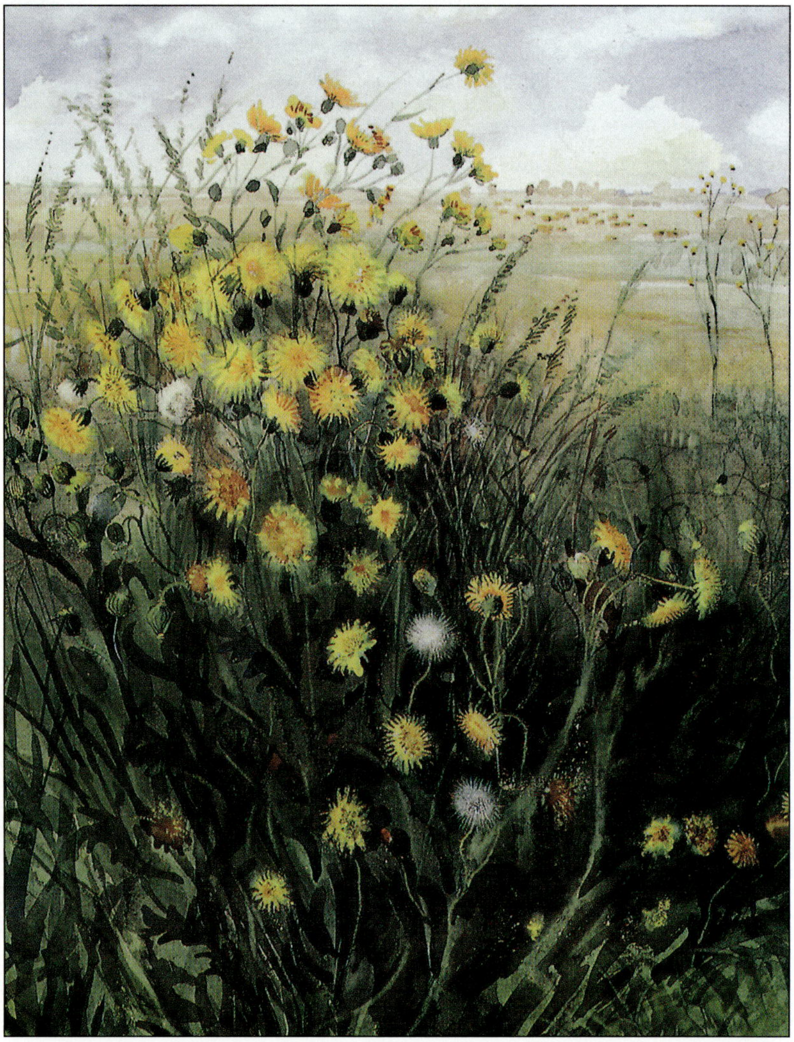

HOGWEED, NORFOLK by Maurice Read (watercolor)

Here is a different version of the same wild flower. When you look closely at the picture you can see how the artist has created an impression of the hogweed flowers with a few strokes of color. Even though the focus is on the flowers in the foreground, the view stretches out behind into the far distance.

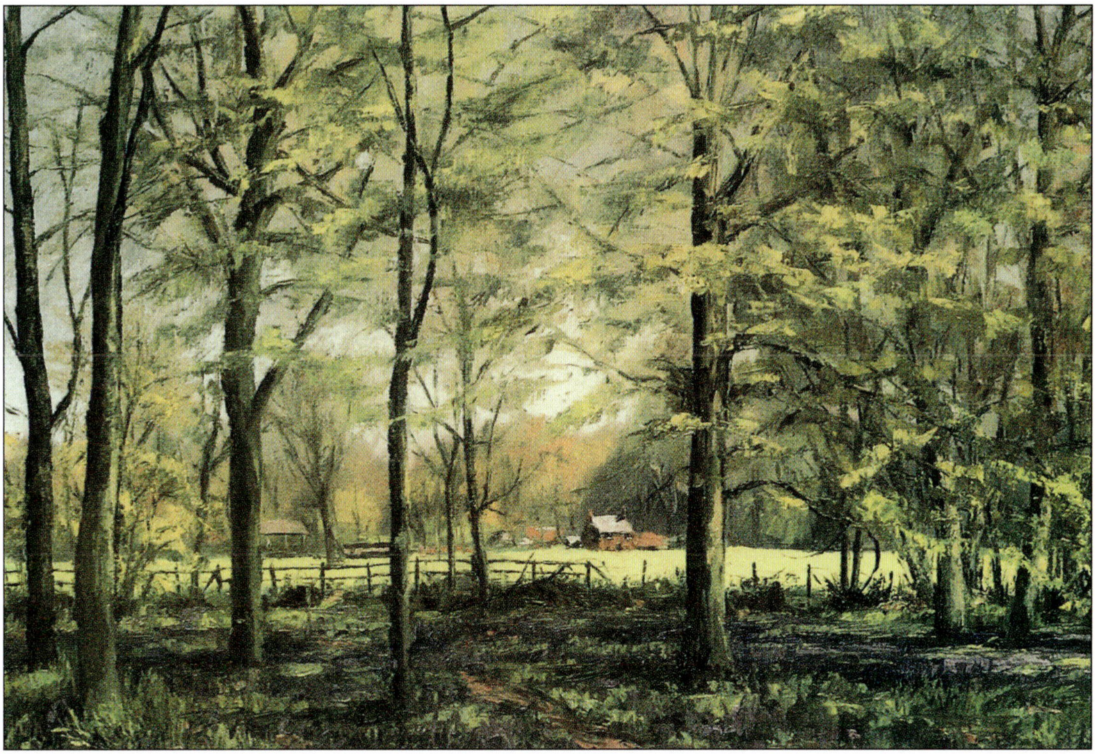

BLUEBELLS IN ASHRIDGE by Brian Bennett (oil)

You could not fail to recognize that this is a bluebell wood in springtime, yet no one flower is described literally. As long as sufficient clues are provided – in this case the wood and the color and distribution of the flowers – the mind is very easily persuaded.

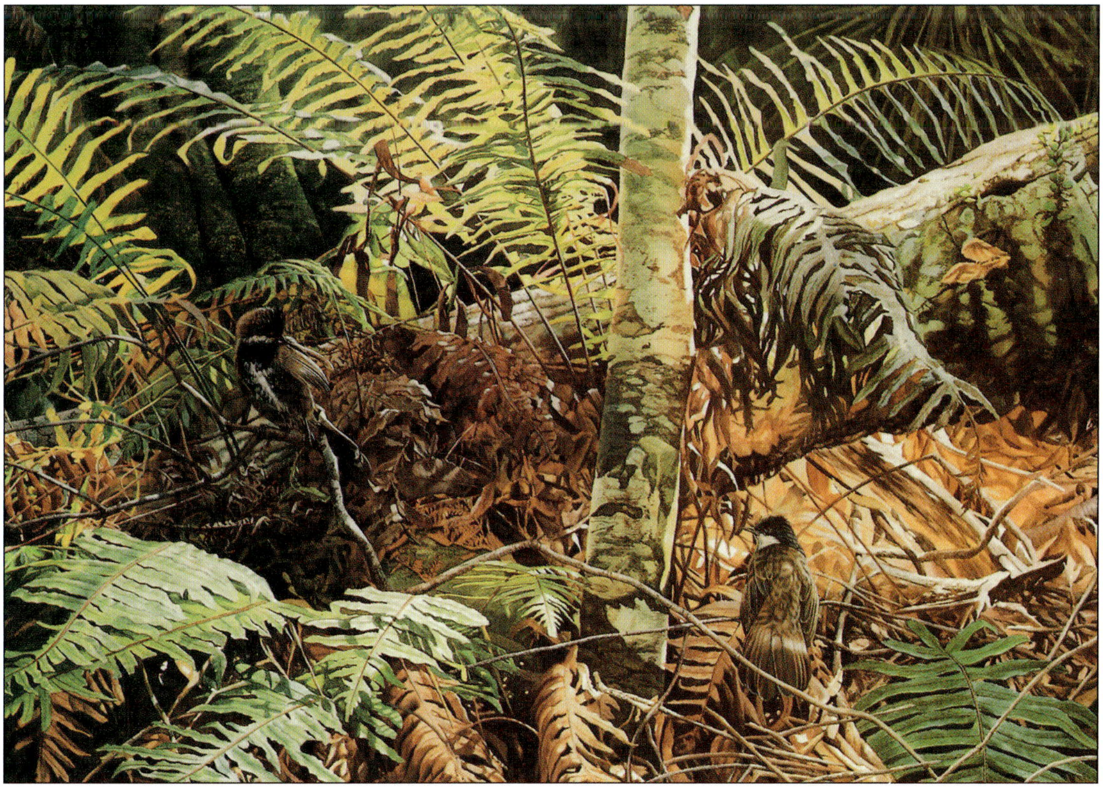

COACH WHIPS by James Luck (watercolor)

Notice how the artist controls the edges of the ferns and undergrowth where the two birds hide. If you run your eye down the outline of the birch trunk you can see how the edge is alternately lost and found through contrasts in tone and color between the trunk and the background.

Flower Study in Colored Pencil

Among a bunch of mixed flowers, the artist found this freshly-cut golden-yellow lily. The perfection of the large supple flowerhead seemed to warrant individual study. Placing the flower on a white surface, the artist set to work immediately with colored pencils. To make the most of the pattern created by the beautifully colored petals and ornate anthers, the artist decided to fill the paper with a close-up of the flowerhead. The choice of a high viewpoint means that the leaves, stems, and accompanying single bud combine to create an arresting and decorative linear design.

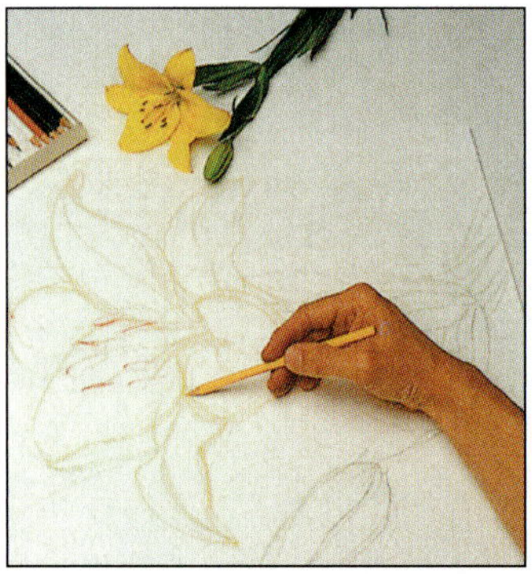

1 Pale contours and outlines of the flower, leaves, and stem are sketched in with corresponding local colors. The artist studies negative and positive shapes, keeping the drawing fairly loose to allow for adjustments as the image develops.

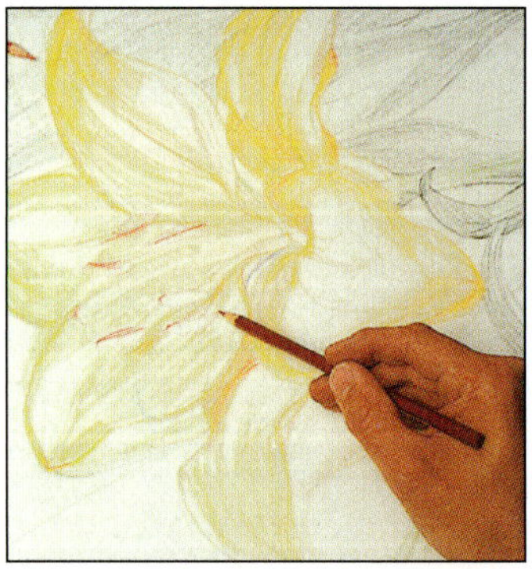

2 The mid-tones are now added and more colors introduced. Two different yellows and oranges are mixed to describe the subtle nuances of the petal color. Capturing the soft texture of the petals is of paramount importance and this is successfully achieved with languid strokes. These contrast with firmer hatching on the leaves.

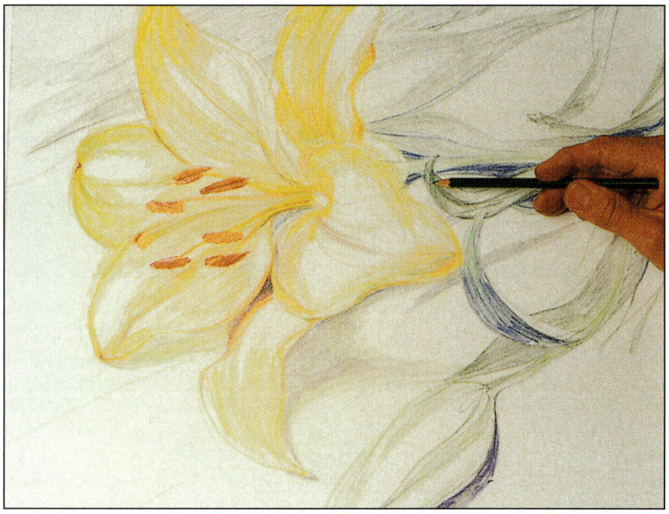

3 The artist begins to build up the rest of the drawing. The composition focuses on the flowerhead, which consequently is represented in brighter detail, but the leaves and stem play an important decorative role. The dark, linear patterns of the leaves and their shadows set off the delicate mass of yellow petals. Colder colors and deeper tones strengthen the shadows.

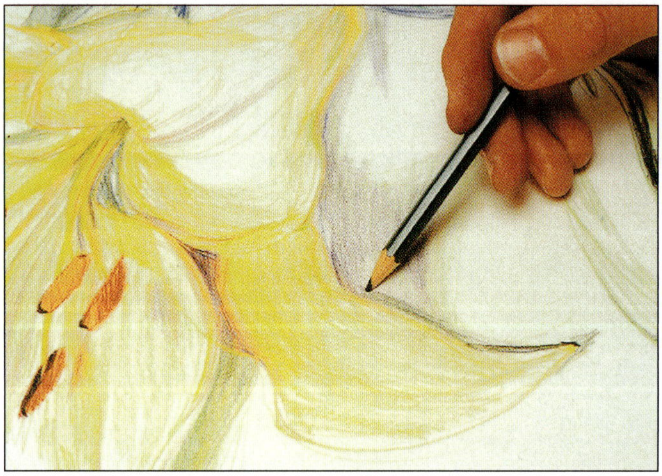

4 Finally a black pencil is used to pinpoint dark areas, that provide necessary contrast to enliven the drawing. Note the shadows cast onto some petals from the anthers. This well-observed detail adds an important sense of space (opposite).

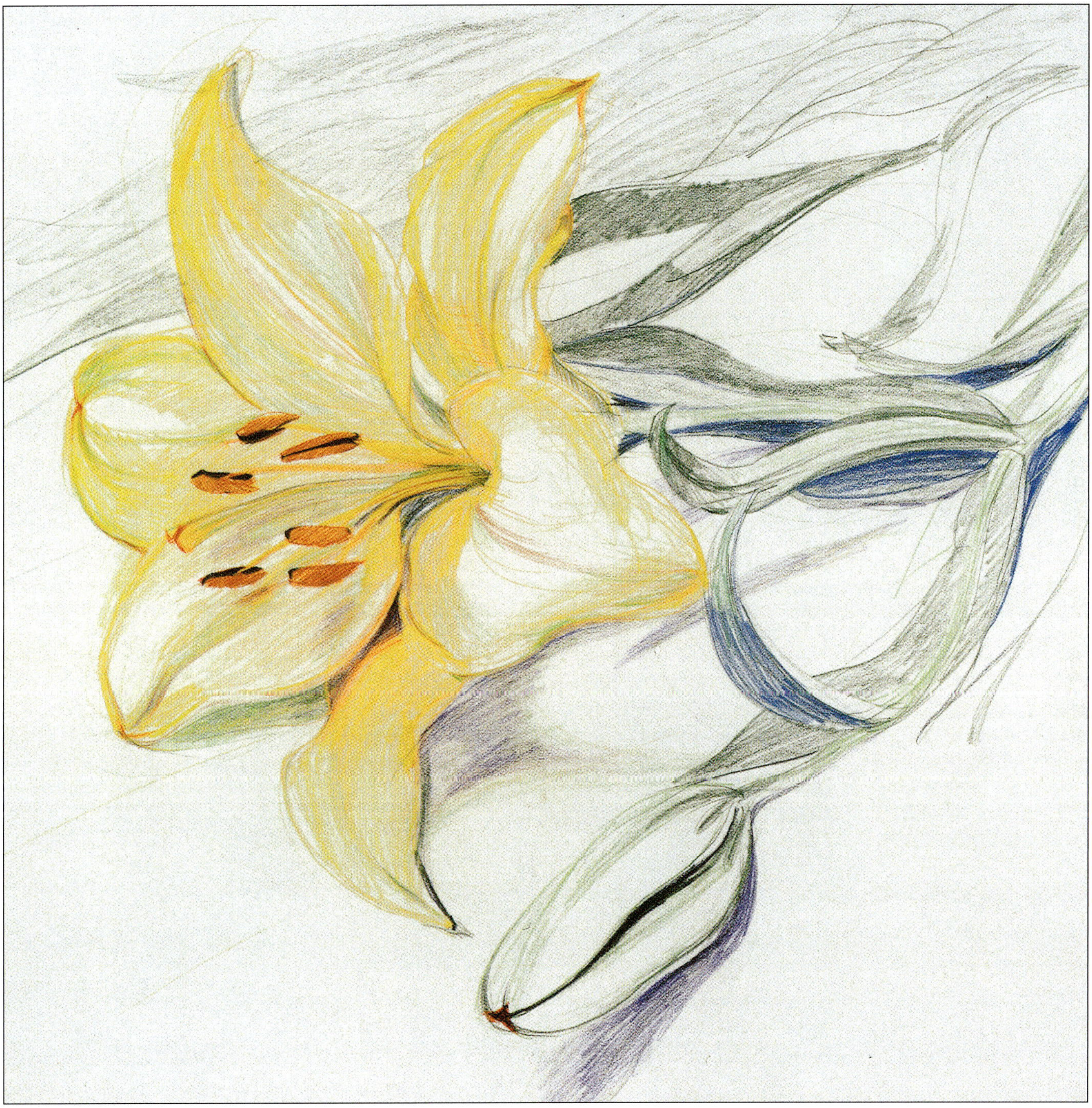

Natural Forms

This painting has a very natural look, partly because it features objects you would expect to see outdoors on a seashore. But, in fact, it was arranged with equal care to achieve a balance of colors, tones, and shapes, and an interesting composition. Notice how the dark tones of the metal waste in the center are echoed by those of the branch of heather at the top and the narrow dark shape on the right. The color scheme is based on the blue-yellow contrast, with the yellow of the foreground stone repeated on the shell and driftwood.

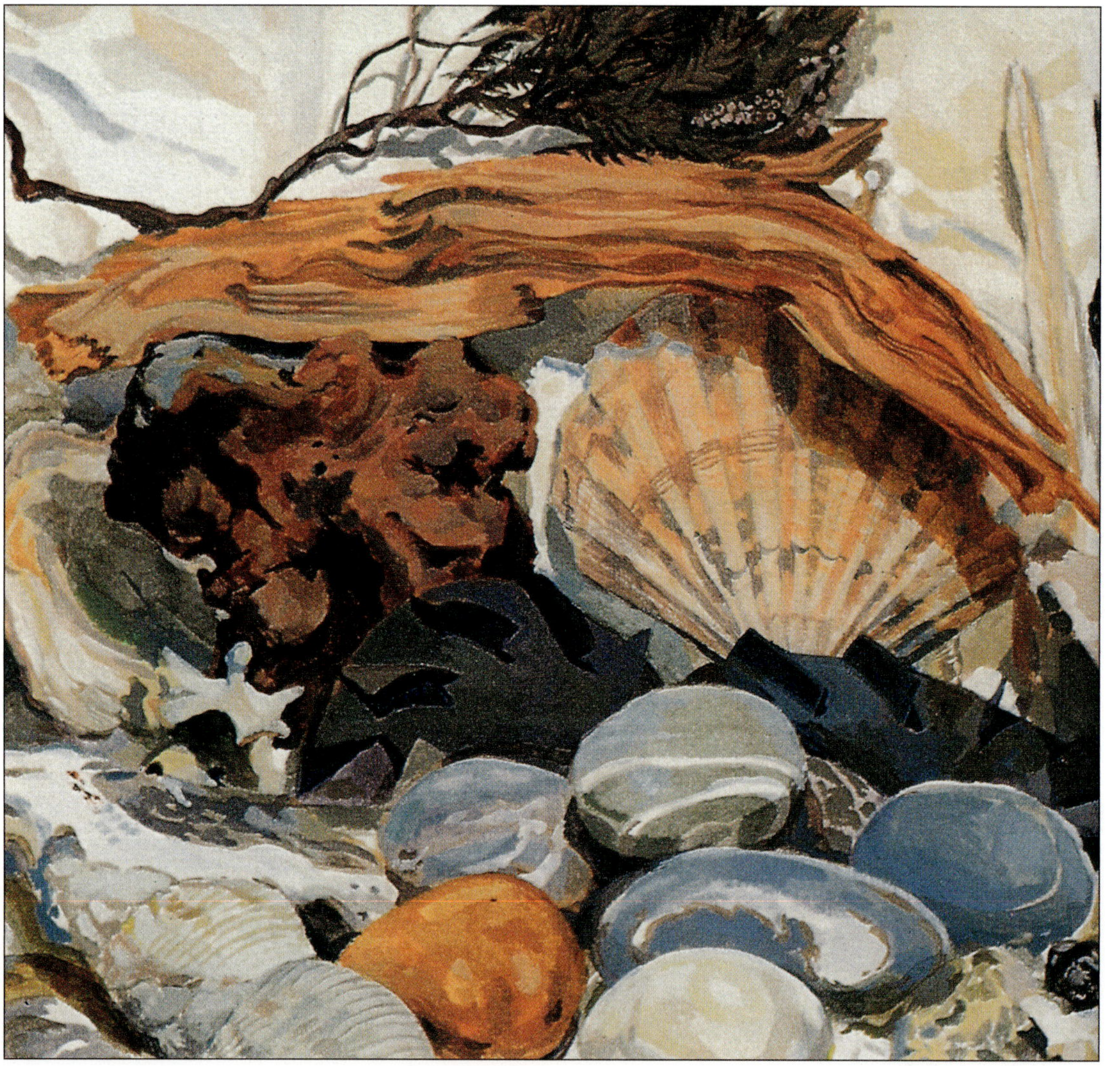

DRIFTWOOD WITH HEATHER by Jill Mirza

Small Shell and Cone

The smooth, mottled shell surface and jagged texture of the fir cone make these two small objects a challenging and interesting subject for a watercolor painting.

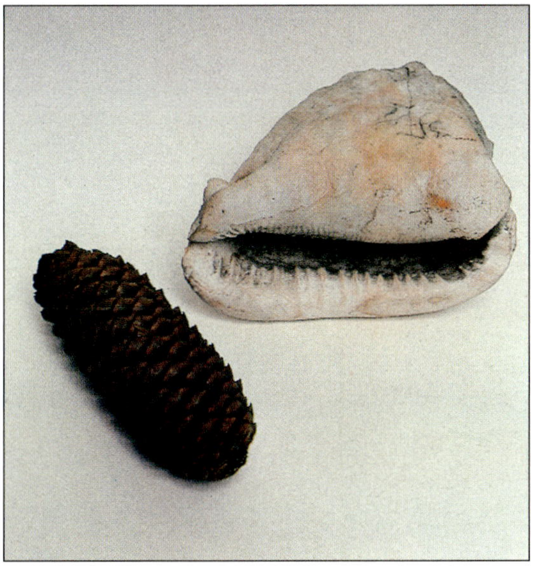

Using broad washes of color, the artist started by indicating the simple form and contour of the objects. By carefully copying each detail of texture and surface pattern, the diverse characters of the objects began to emerge. The shell is delicately tinged with red, yellow, and gray, and the subtle tonal changes which occur as the light falls over the undulating surface were carefully rendered. The mottled effect on the shell was achieved with the traditional watercolor technique of painting wet-into-wet. By laying one color on another before the first color is dry, the two colors fuse, thus avoiding a harsh edge to the paint.

The regular triangular shapes on the pine cone were drawn in with a fine sable brush, the color being used transparently and sparingly to prevent the linear pattern becoming too dominant. Here the artist waited for the yellow wash to dry to ensure a crisply defined line.

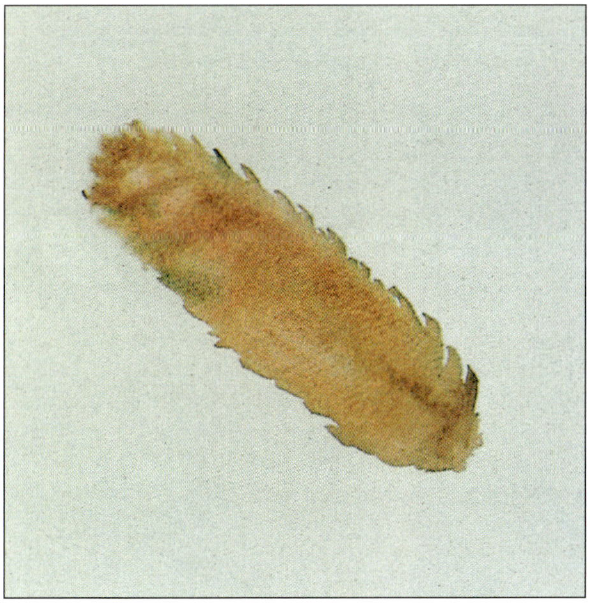

1 Lightly draw the shape of the cone using the tip of a No. 4 sable brush, blocking this in with a thin wash of burnt umber mixed with a little Payne's gray.

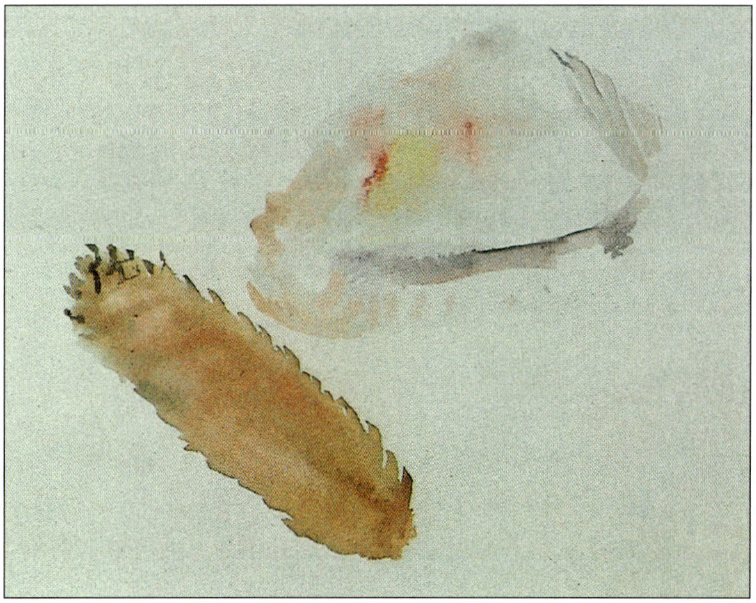

2 Use a diluted wash to lay in the subtle, mottled colors of the shell. Use the tip of the brush to pick out the surface details on both objects.

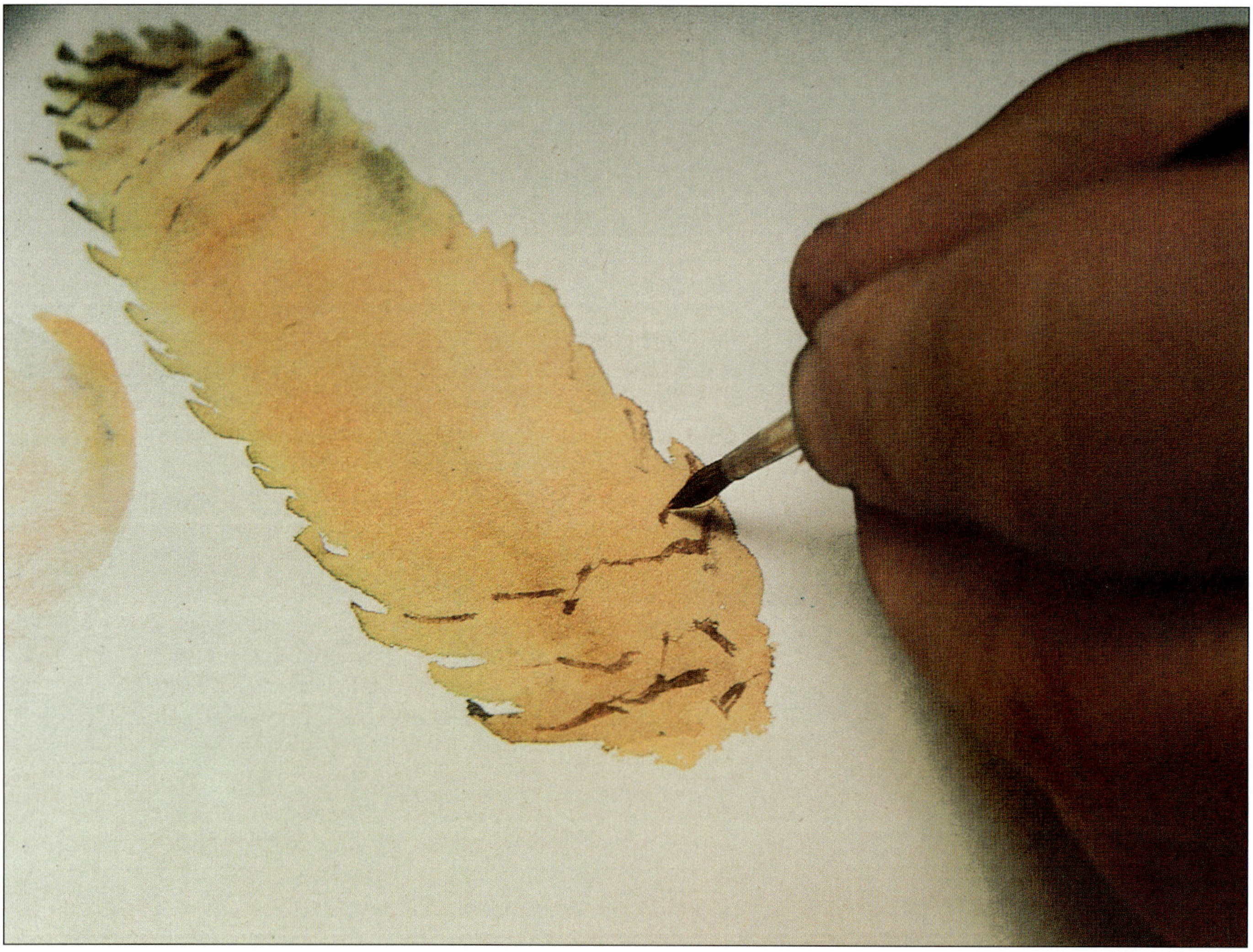

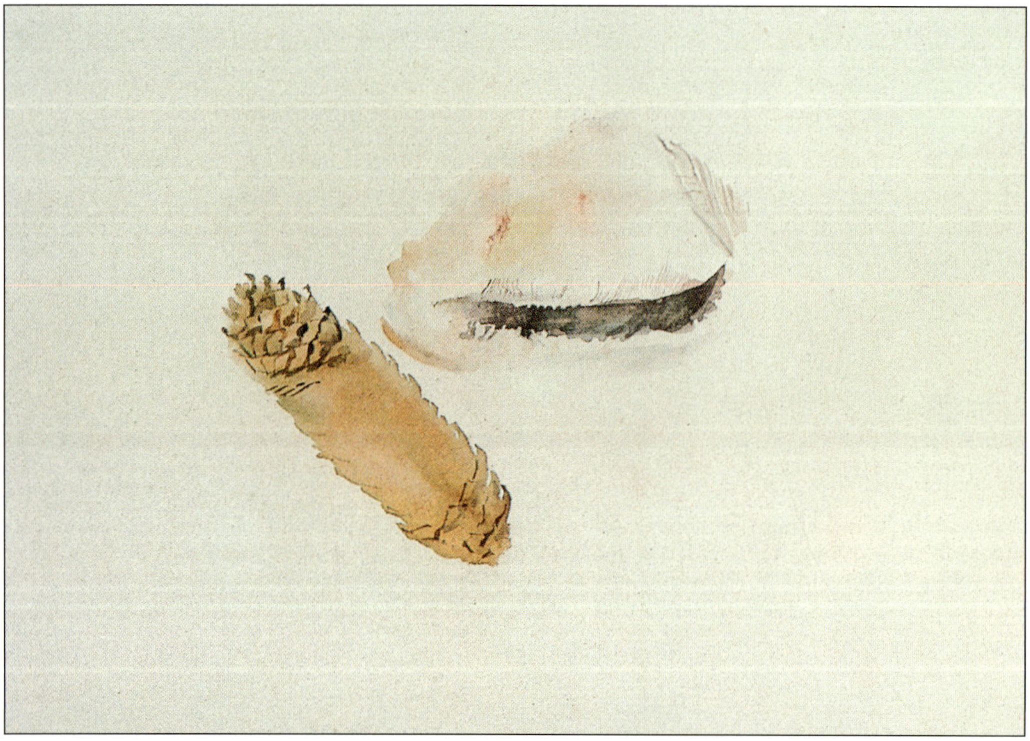

3 Use burnt umber on a very fine brush to describe the details on the pine cone over the dry underpainting (above). Continue to work over the cone, using the direction of the brush strokes to describe the form. Strengthen the dark tone inside the mouth of the shell (left).

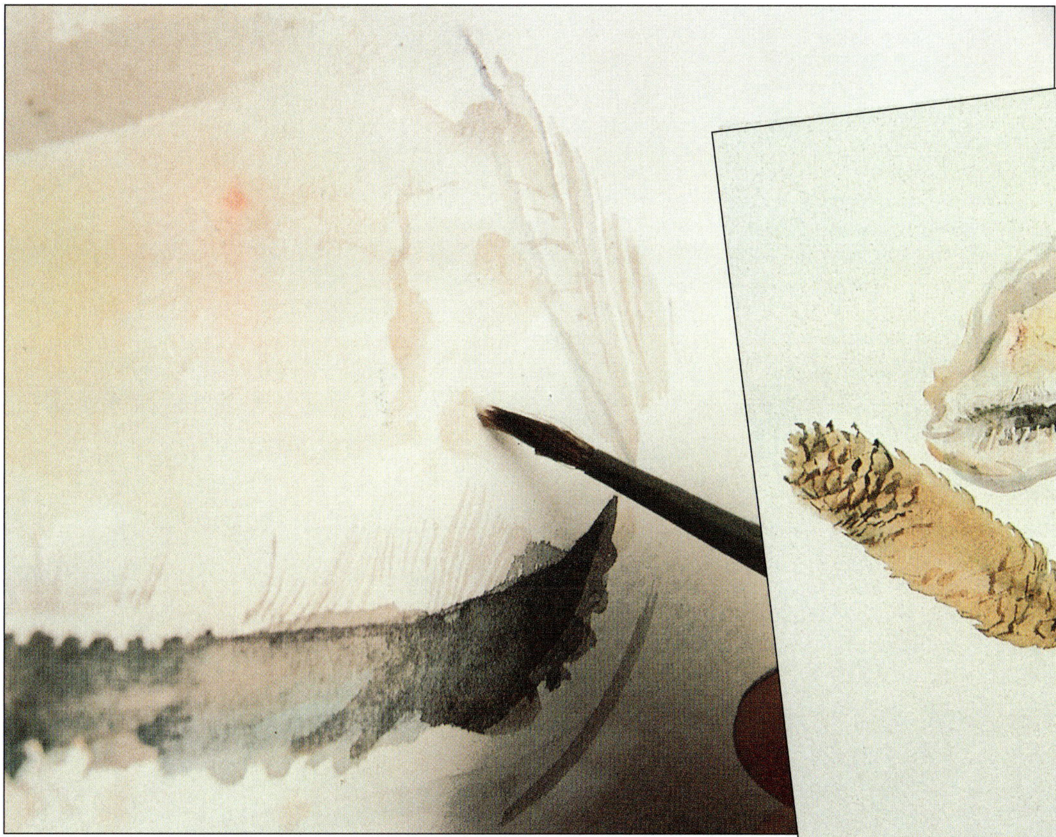

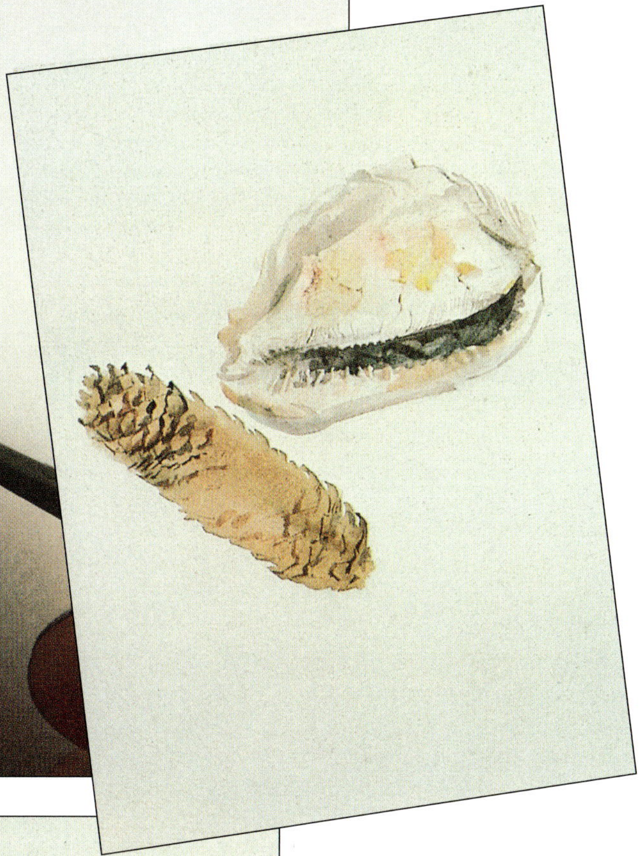

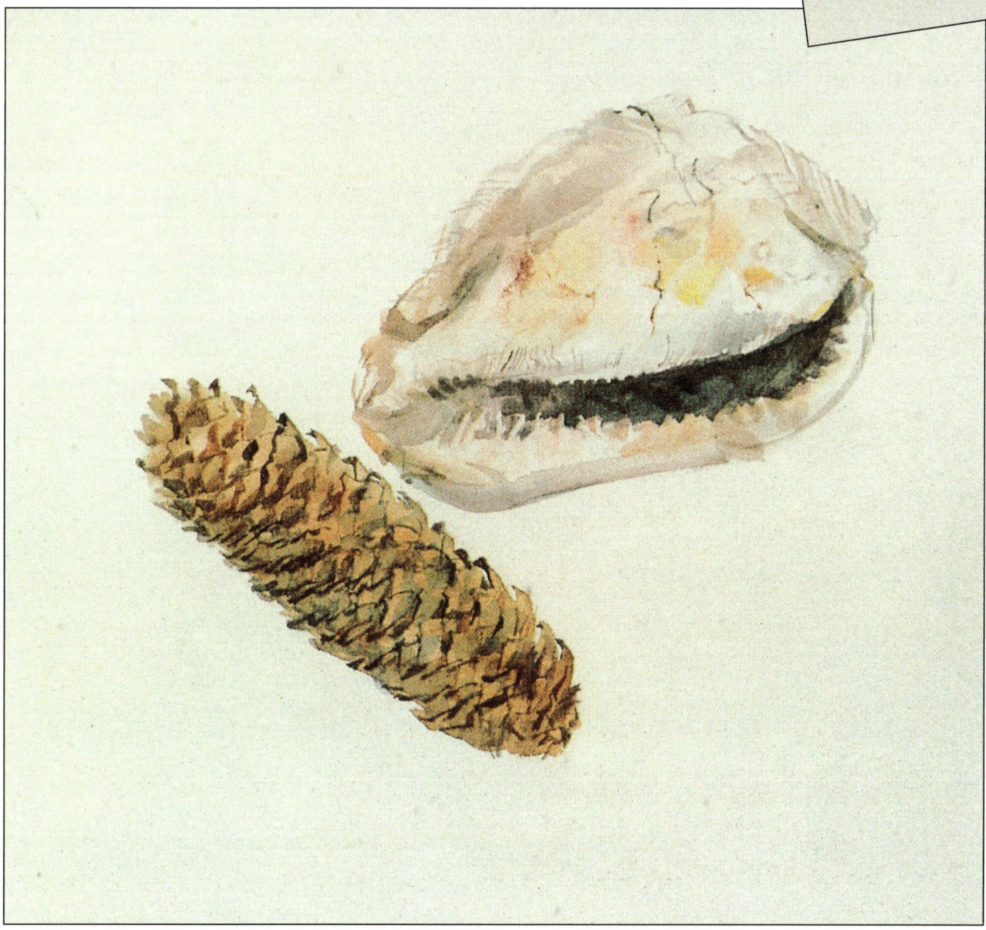

4 Continue to develop the subtle color of the shell with washes of gray, brown, and red. Use a very faint mixture of water and paint to start with (above left), gradually adding more color for the darker tones (above right). Complete the picture by working over both subjects with line and wash until the patterns are complete.

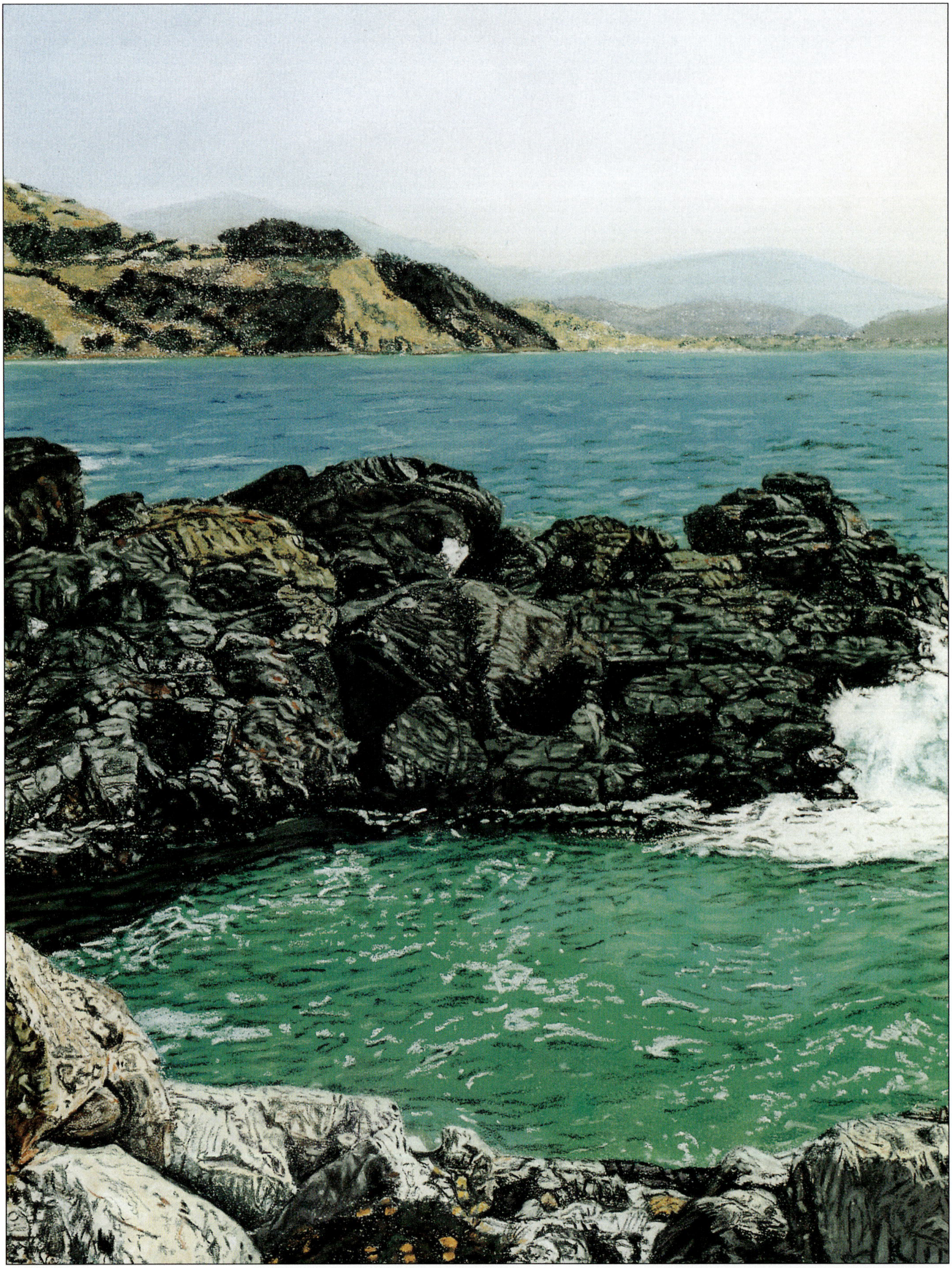

Water

Water is an alluring subject for those artists who look beyond themselves for subject matter. Its special characteristics of reflectivity and transparency and its ever-varied surface qualities pose a powerful challenge to artists of all abilities.

Yet the appeal of water goes beyond the purely visual – it plays tricks with the light. Some artists are put off by its reputation as being a "difficult subject." Yet, like any other subject, it can be approached either in a systematic way that reduces the chances of failure, or in an intuitive way that exploits the sensitivity of water to weather and light, and its potential for expressing human moods.

Water, wherever it is found, is unpredictable. A calm sea in a quiet cove can be whipped up into a monstrous swell with a change of wind direction or strength, or a deterioration in the weather. One day it gently laps the shore; on the next, it thunders with awesome power onto the rocks. Seen as a tidal wave or as part of a swollen, flooded river, such water represents nature at its most uncontrollable. It is this dark side of nature that draws many artists to water.

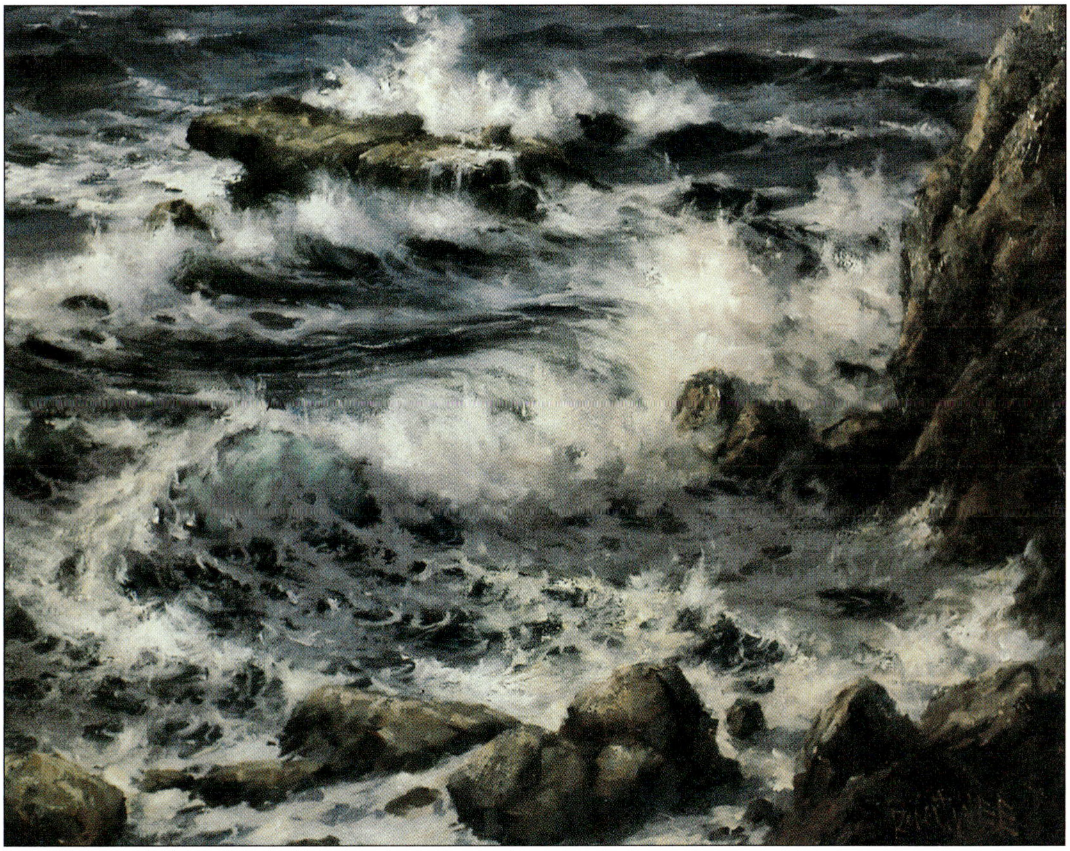

WAVE BATTERED ROCKS by Robert Wee (oil)

Using both the transparent and the opaque qualities of oils to build up the color of the water, superimpose with areas of white water at the crests of the waves and in the flying surf. The earlier applications are more diluted with turpentine, the later ones drier and thicker.

FAR LEFT: RESTLESS SEA by Milton Meyer (pastel)

In this picture, the artist has simplified the detail, giving the clues needed to read the pastel marks as a "restless sea."

CREATING A CONVINCING IMAGE

Water, like the sky, is an elusive subject, being constantly on the move: highlights and shadows appear and disappear; colors change; waves break and re-form before you even have a chance to put brush to canvas. The basic problem is how to pin down all this action and create a convincing image of it without losing the inherent sense of movement and spontaneity that makes it such an attractive subject in the first place. Don't try to "freeze" the motion, or render it with photographic precision, but allow a few, carefully placed brush strokes to convey a general impression of movement and fluidity. Water often contains myriad reflections and highlights, but if you try to paint them all the effect will be merely that of a patterned carpet. Always paint broadly and with a minimum of detail. The more decisively and simply you paint water, the wetter it looks.

Learn to harness the particular qualities of your chosen medium to depict the character of your subject. Oil and acrylic paints, for example, have a certain strength which suits the ruggedness of a stormy seascape. Watercolor and pastel, on the other hand, allow for a swift, spontaneous response to the feeling of light and running water.

Water is usually thought of as being blue, but in fact it is virtually colorless in itself, acquiring colors from the prevailing light in the sky and from its surroundings. Thus, the sea on a calm day will reflect the blue of the sky, whereas on a stormy day it may look brown-green. Seen at a distance, a river might reflect the cool gray of the sky, but seen at close range in the depths of a wood, it will reflect the dark greens of the nearby trees that obscure much of the light in the sky. In addition, algae, weeds, and sediment present in the water itself can add unexpected touches of greens, browns, and ochers.

GOLDEN IMAGE by John Sowers (watercolor)

Carefully building the image up from light to dark, the early washes are added wet-into-wet. Then darker, crisper-edged areas are added wet on dry.

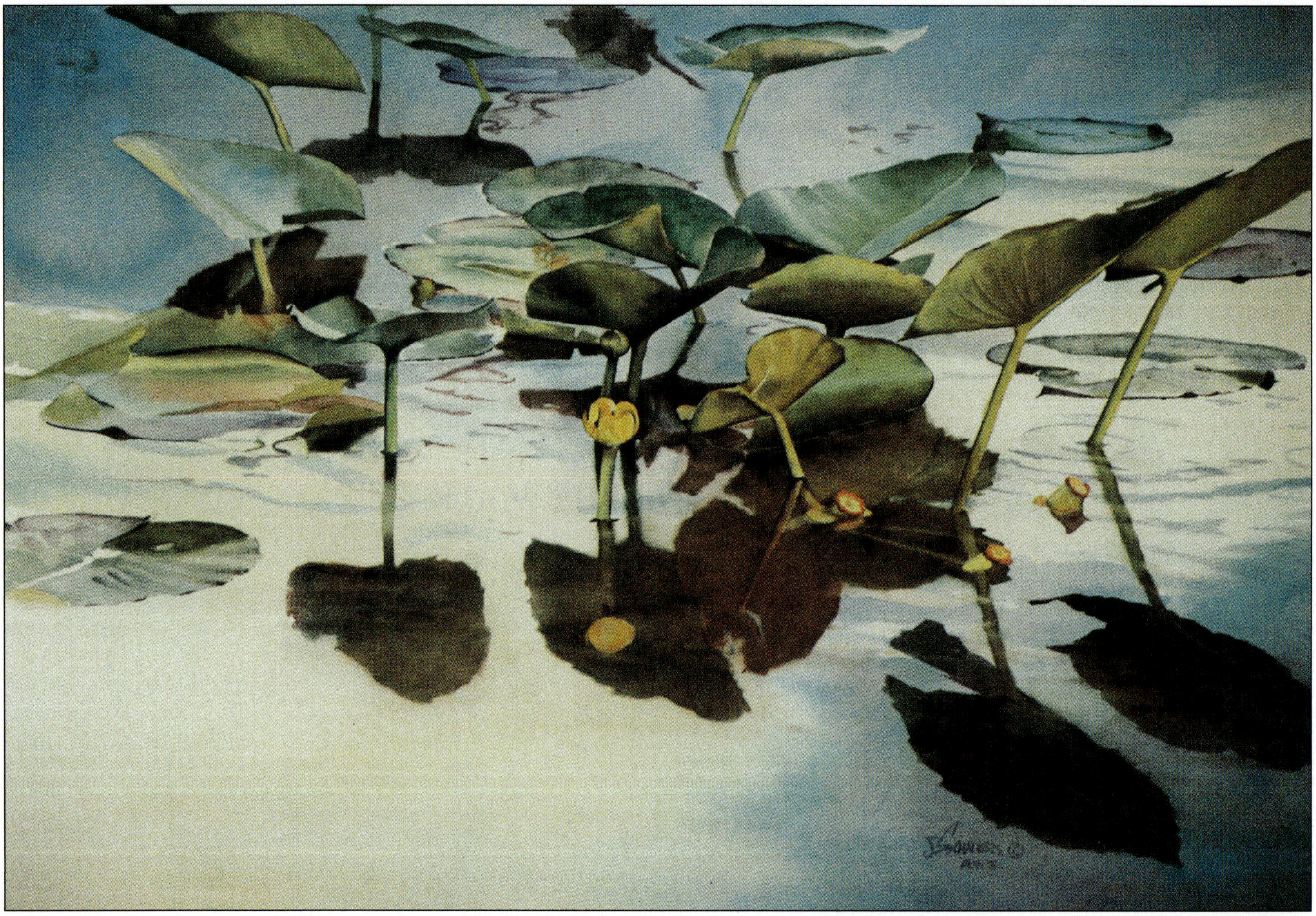

OBSERVE AND SIMPLIFY

To paint water successfully, it is necessary to simplify what you see, but you cannot hope to distill the essence of a subject until you are familiar with its complexities. So be prepared to spend time watching water – it is a pleasing pastime in itself. If you sit quietly by a river or on the seashore, you will begin to see that the movements of water, like its changing colors, follow certain patterns. Understanding, for instance, the way the sea swells to become a wave, before breaking into foam will enable you to paint it with assurance and freedom.

As soon as you begin to labor the paint, the effect of movement and fluidity will be destroyed. There are several techniques that are particularly suited to the subject, but, as a general rule, any method that involves much overlaying of paint should be avoided. Broad, flat, or broken washes are ideal for still lakes or calm sea, and a dry brush dragged across rough white paper is a wonderfully economical means of suggesting lines or patches of wind-ruffled water in the distance. Ripples and reflections can be described in a kind of shorthand by calligraphic brushmarks and squiggles, while the wet-into-wet method is marvelous for creating a soft, diffused impression. Everyone has their own way of painting, however, and ultimately the only way to find the best approach is by trial and error.

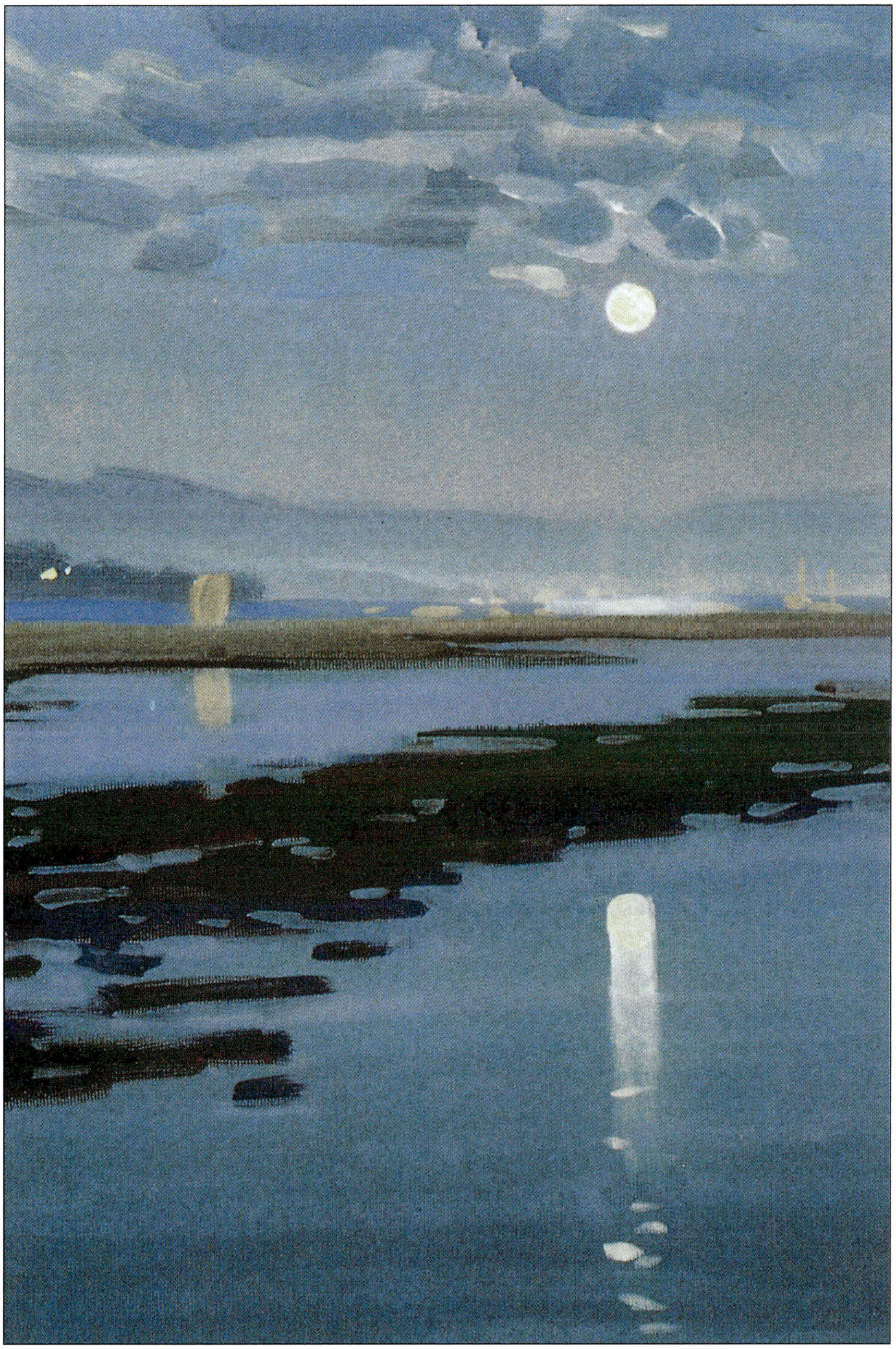

BLUE MOON by Marcia Burtt (acrylic)

Part of the impact of this painting stems from the omission of unnecessary detail. Broad horizontal brushmarks of darker blue suggest ripples that pull the moon's reflection downward, but the contrasts of tone were kept to a minimum in order to give prominence to the reflection itself.

LIGHT ON WATER

The effects of light on water are almost irresistible, particularly the more dramatic and fleeting ones caused by a changeable sky. Obviously they can seldom be painted on-the-spot; a shaft of sunlight suddenly breaking through cloud to spotlight an area of water could disappear before you lay out your colors. But you can recapture such effects in the studio as long as you have observed them closely.

When you begin to paint, remember that the effect you want to convey is one of transience, so try to make your technique express this quality. This does not mean splashing on the paint with no forethought – this is unlikely to be successful. One of the paradoxes of watercolor painting is that the most seemingly spontaneous effects are in fact the result of careful planning.

Work out the colors and tones in advance so that you do not have to correct them by overlaying wash over wash. It can be helpful to make a series of small preparatory color sketches to try out various techniques and color combinations. Knowing exactly what you intend to do enables you to paint freely and without hesitation. If you decide to paint wet-into-wet, first practice controlling the paint by tilting the board. If you prefer to work wet on dry, establish exactly where your highlights are to be and then leave them strictly alone or, alternatively, put them in last with opaque white used dryly.

As with any painting, before you begin it is a good idea to work out the direction of the light and the position of the sun in the sky. On a sunny day this is easy, but on a cloudy day, light appears to come from the whole sky creating a diffused, overall effect – dull if the cloud is thick, and bright if it is thin. The direction of the light will affect the highlights on the water and shadows.

There is a subtle difference between reflections of the sky and reflections of direct light from the sun. The sun lights up the sky which can be reflected on the surface of the water. If the water is broken in any way, direct rays of light will then create bright highlights so that reflections of a blue sky can be fragmented by "white" ripples catching brighter light from the sun.

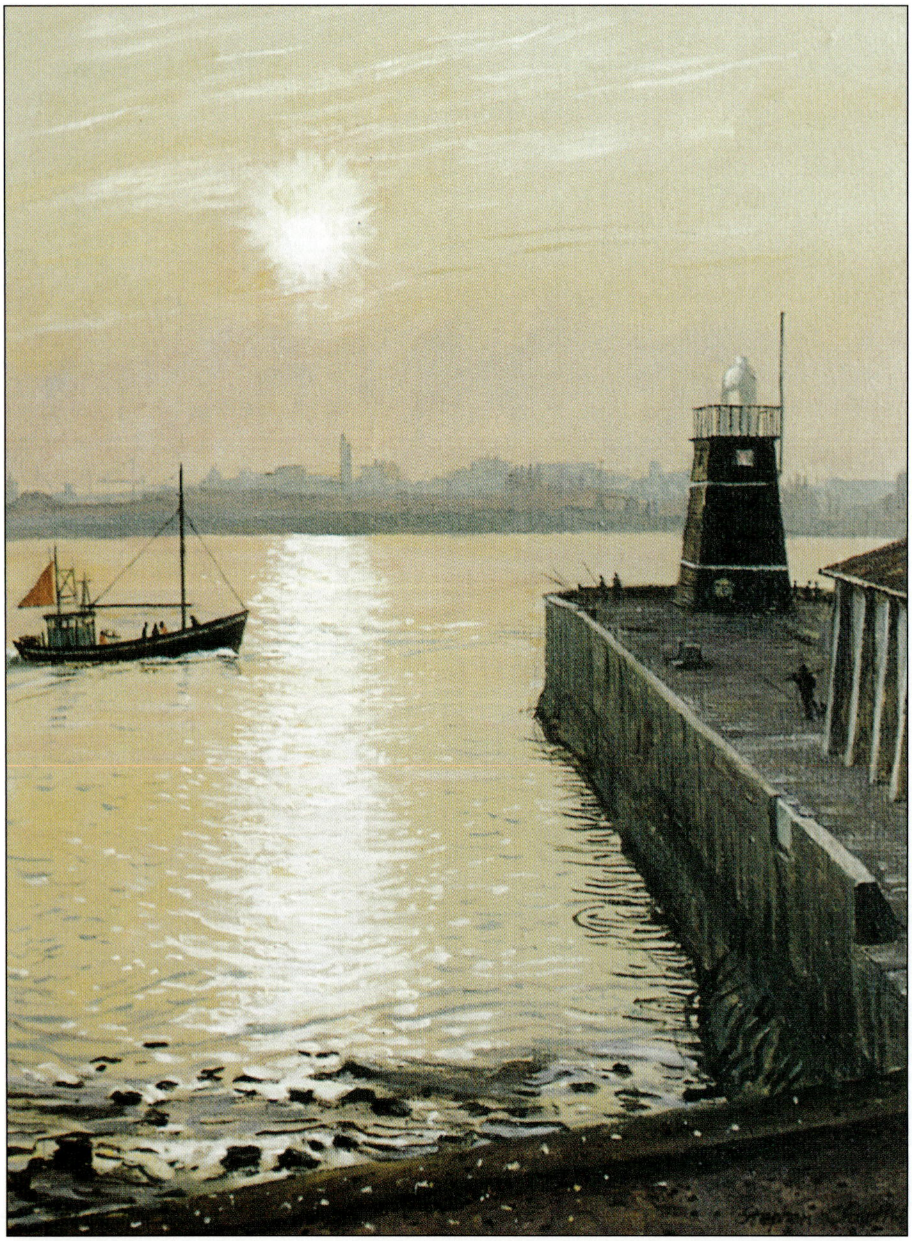

RETURN AT SUNSET by Stephen Crowther (oil)

When painting with oils, you can superimpose the bright pathway of the setting sun on the water at the end, in small impasto strokes that themselves reflect the light.

STRENGTH AND COLOR

On water that is flat and clear like a mirror, the stronger the light, the brighter and more distinct the reflections. In poor light, the water appears dark and only bright tones will be reflected. If the water is ruffled, the pattern of reflected light will then depend on where the sun is, whether the sun is behind you catching the sloping angles of each wavelet, or in front of you, highlighting the tops of each ripple.

The angle of the light makes a difference too, whether the sun is overhead as it is at midday or low as it is at sunrise or sunset. The season will make a difference as the sun never reaches great heights in the winter. With the sun high in the sky, the whole sky is bright and touches of direct reflected light are lost amongst the bright pattern of reflections. With the sun low in the sky, the colors are mellower and the tones deeper so that the reflections of the golden evening sun show up against the contrasting shadows.

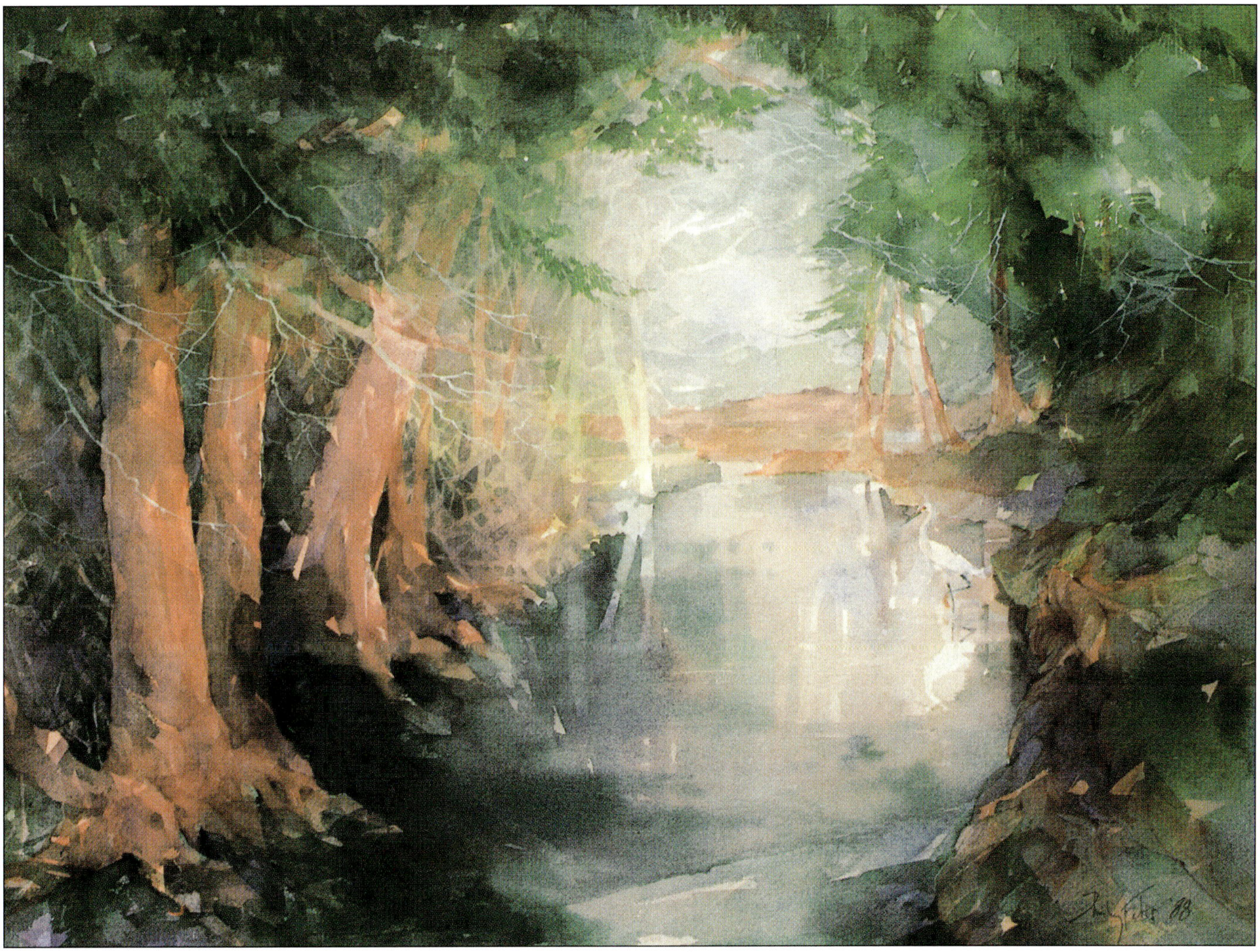

THE RIVER GUADALUPE by Shirley Felts (watercolor)

This lovely painting shows a breathtakingly skillful use of reserved highlights. Each pale reflection, tiny sunlit twig, and point of light has been achieved by painting around the area. This can result in tired, overworked paint, but here nothing of the luminosity of the watercolor has been sacrificed, and it remains fresh and sparkling.

FAST WATER

Painting fast-flowing water demands a keen eye and a sure hand. Once again, the trick is not to be overwhelmed by the apparent complexity of shadows and highlights. Look at the water through half-closed eyes and pick out the most obvious ripples and wavelets. Paint only these, with swift, decisive strokes.

To paint the rushing, white water of rapids and waterfalls, let the action of your brush suggest detail and movement. A few curving dry brush strokes, not too labored, are all that is needed to create an impression of water falling downward. Using a rough-textured paper or canvas helps, because the raised tooth of the surface catches and drags at the paint.

MOVING WATER IN OIL

In the following step-by-step sequence the artist is making a rapid oil sketch of the surface of a lake on a breezy day, when the water is ruffled by the wind and breaks up into tiny wavelets.

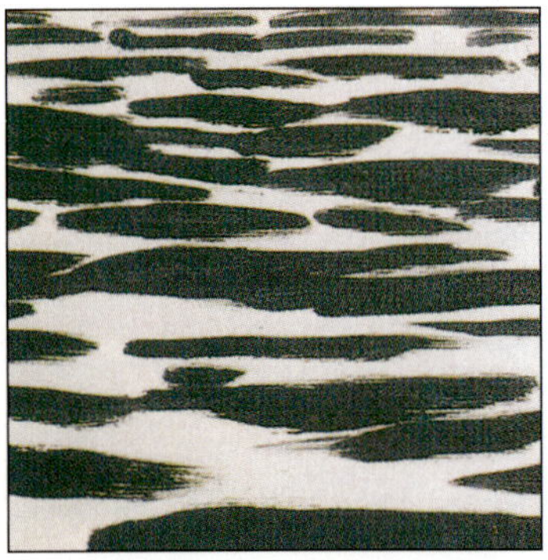

1 Using a No. 4 flat bristle brush, the artist paints the dark ripples with curving strokes of Payne's gray and ultramarine.

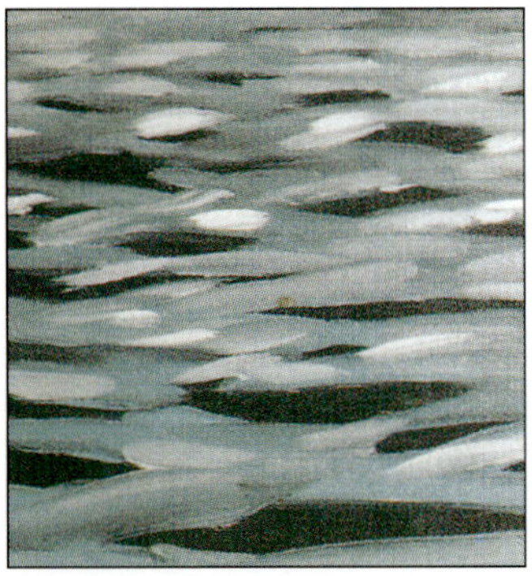

2 With a mixture of ultramarine and white, criss-cross strokes are now blocked in for the lighter ripples and the ruffled white highlights are put in last.

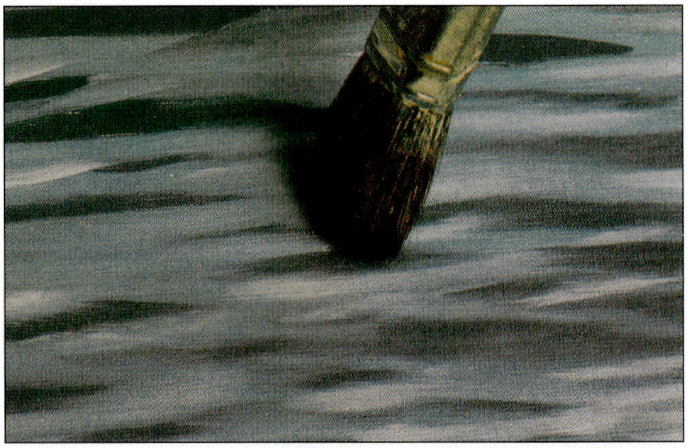

3 The paint is allowed to dry for about 15 minutes, then the artist blends the colors a little by brushing over the surface very lightly with a 1 in. (2.5 cm) decorator's brush.

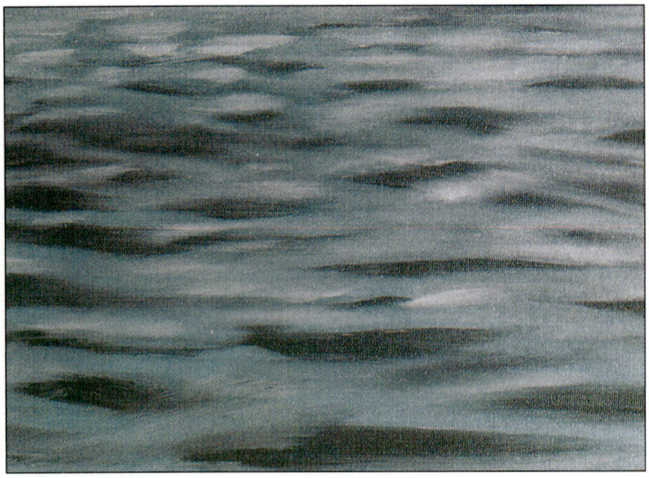

4 The finished study captures the impression of moving water that reflects the gray sky above.

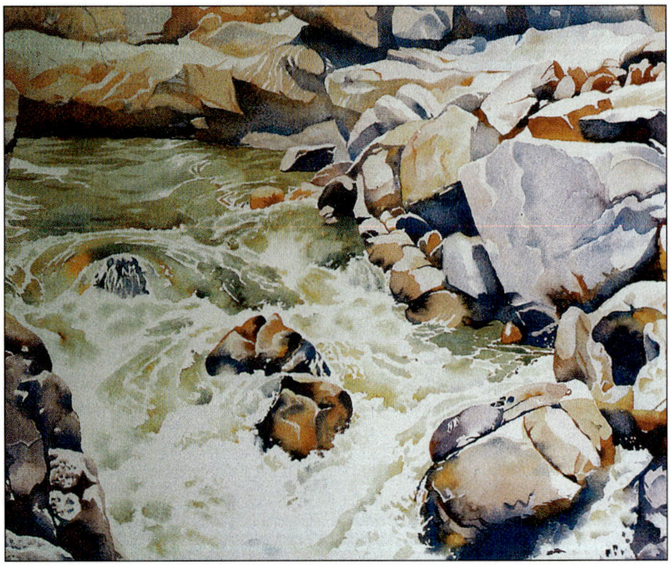

CASCADE BY HAZEL SOAN (watercolor)

WHITE WATER TECHNIQUES IN ACRYLIC

To begin with, areas of the canvas are left bare for the white water, and delicate shadow tones are added in the water with lively strokes. Then the raft is integrated into the boiling white water with dry brush and spattering.

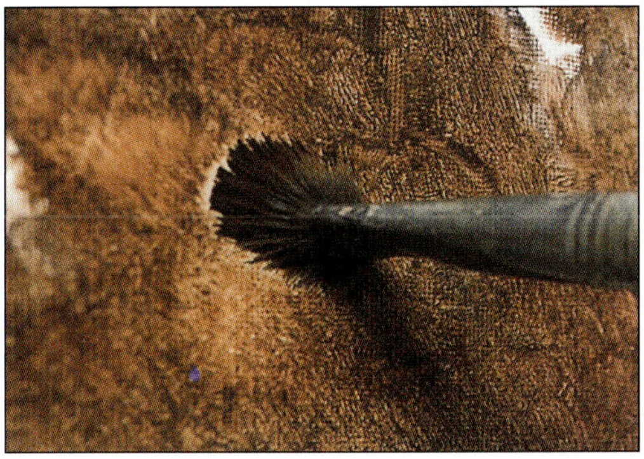

1 Block in the sheer rocky bank in the background using a coarse brush and a scrubbing motion. As the focus is on the water and raft, this area is left cursorily painted.

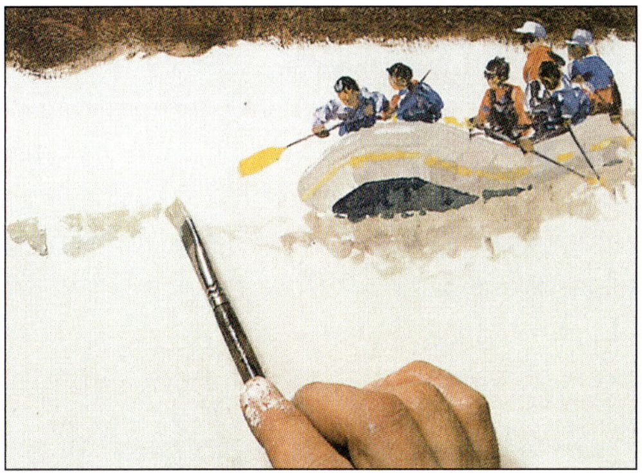

2 Block in the raft and crew with minimum detail, and then paint in the mid-tone shadows in the water with a pale gray mix. Try to map out the movement in the water using short, lively strokes.

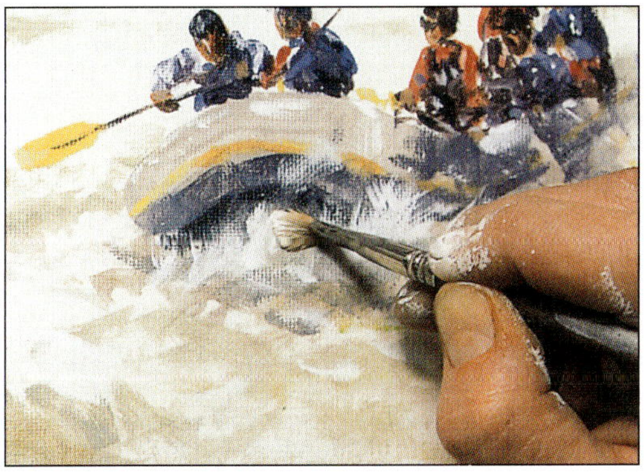

3 Add slightly darker, greener shadows to the water and then, with a dry brush, drag strokes of undiluted white up over the sides of the buffeted raft.

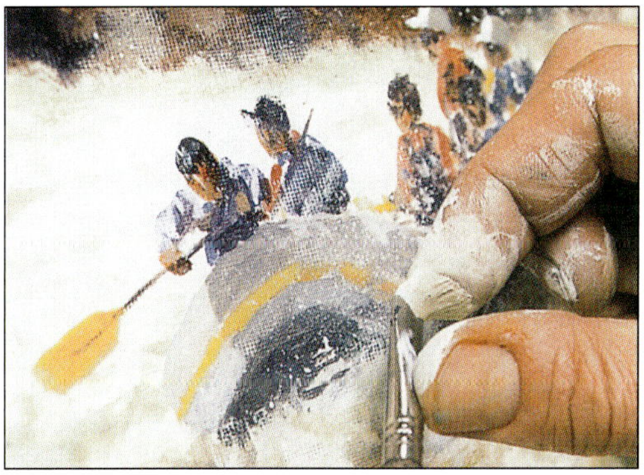

4 Now charge your brush with dilute white paint and spatter paint over the raft, bending back the bristles and then allowing them to spring forward to flick out the paint. You will need to experiment with the brush, the dilution of the paint, and the distance from the paper as they all affect the spatter.

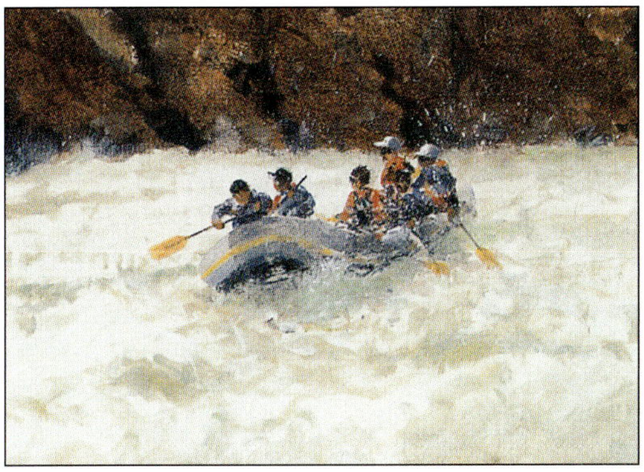

5 More spattering and dry brush work soften the waterline along the rocks in the background, further describing the turbulence of this white water. There is a real feeling of movement and excitement in this painting.

STILL WATER

When we imagine still water, we tend to think of inland water: enclosed, sheltered areas such as duck ponds; lakes small enough to be surrounded by woods; or stagnant canals set below ground level. Yet vast lakes and lochs, lazy summer rivers, and even the sea, can be as flat as the proverbial millpond, particularly in the evening when the wind drops. Distance has the effect of smoothing out water, too, so large expanses can appear calm even when they are not.

The factor common to all stretches of still water is that, because the surface is smooth and flat, it reflects everything around – and on – the water. Sky, buildings, trees, boats – all are pictured, mirror-like on the surface, and it can cause problems. Unless you introduce some visual clues to explain the water surface, the reflections will make no sense – they will simply look like an upside down version of the landscape. You can blur the reflections slightly in places, or introduce small ripples or some floating leaves. Having said this, still water also has depth. In some cases it is possible to see plants or pebbles on the bottom, or areas of sunlit sand. At other times you look down into a transparent darkness that seems to be unfathomable.

The most frequent reason for failure is simply poor observation. A calm expanse of water is seldom exactly the same color and tone all over, because it is a reflective surface. Even if there are no objects such as boats, rocks, or cliffs to provide clearly defined reflections, the water is still mirroring the sky and will show similar variations. These shifts in color and tone – often subtle – are also affected by the angle of viewing. Water looks darker in the foreground because it is closer to you and thus reflects less light.

It is also important to remember that a lake or area of sea is a horizontal plane. This sounds obvious, but has powerful implications for painting. A horizontal plane painted in an unvaried tone will instantly assume the properties of a vertical one because no recession is implied. It can sometimes be necessary to stress flatness and recession by exaggerating a darker tone or even inventing a ripple or two to bring the foreground forward.

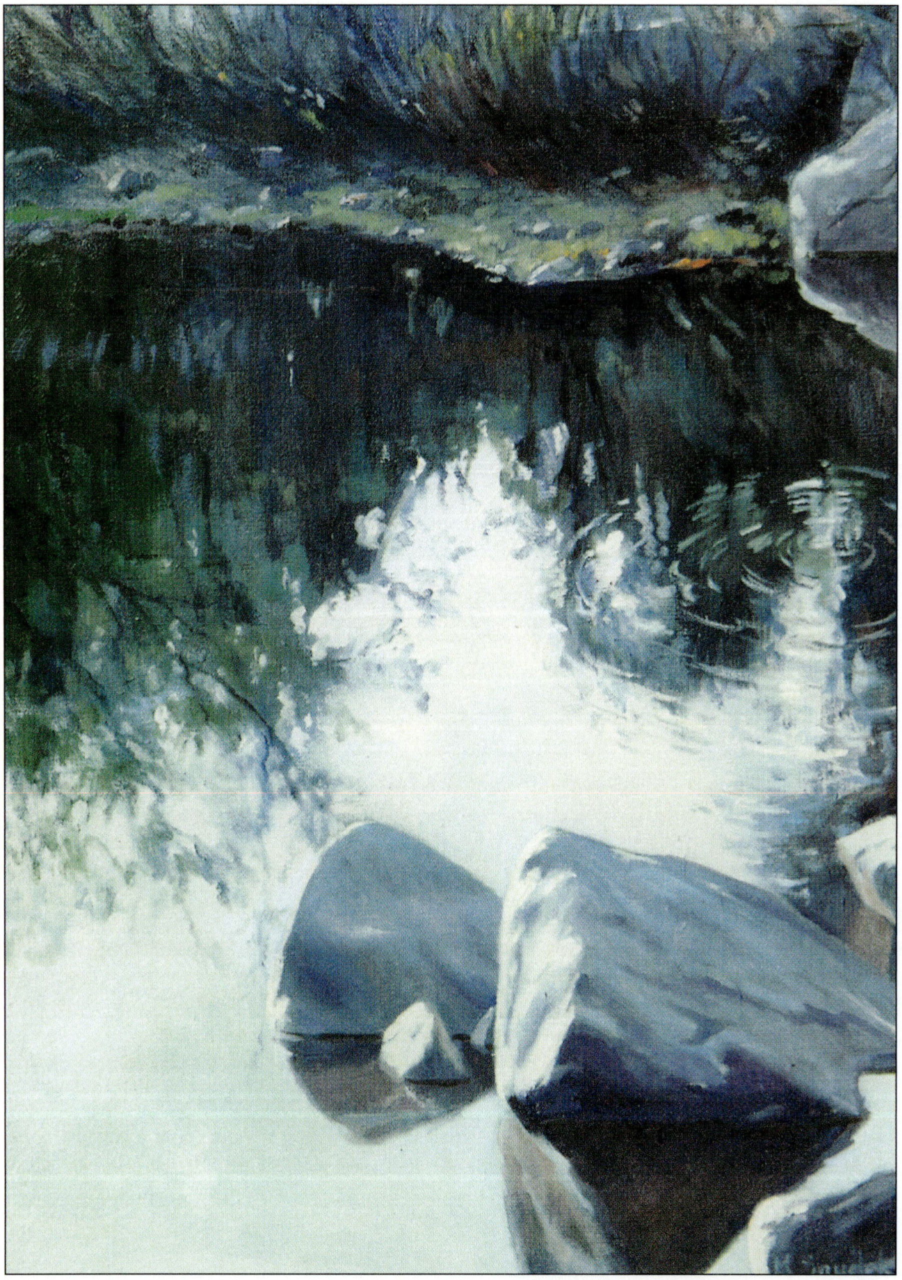

EVENING SOLITUDE by Martha Saudek (oil)

Reflections and shadows are used to map out the surface of this still pool, while the concentric ripples establish the surface as two-dimensional.

LAYING A WATERCOLOR WASH

The underlying color of this inlet of sea water is blue because it reflects the sky, but as the water varies in depth it is not a solid blue. In addition, although the water appears flat when seen from a distance, it has some movement. Because these details are not clearly visible from a distance the artist hints at them by varying the intensity of the wash.

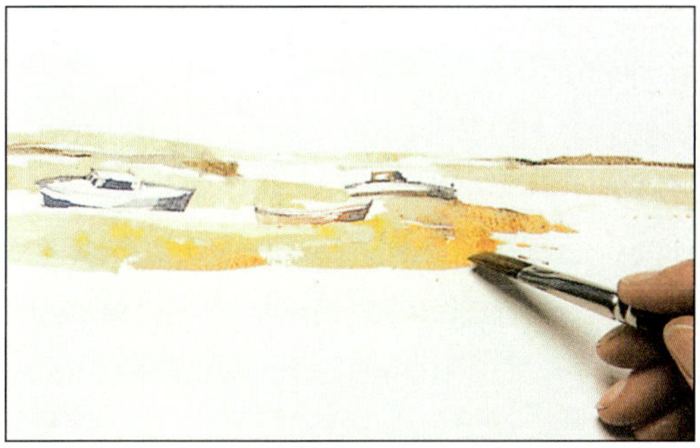

1 First paint in the boats with a fine brush, and then wash in the sand color around them.

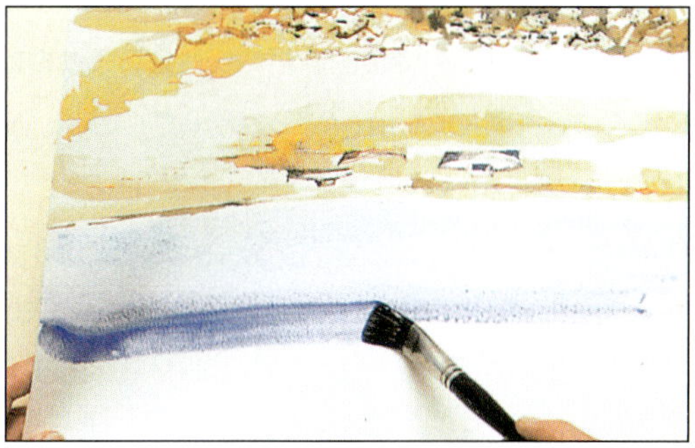

2 Turn the paper upside down and hold it in a vertical position. Wash in the sky adding more color as you work down the paper to give the idea of the sky receding toward the horizon. Turn the paper right way up again to create interesting backruns.

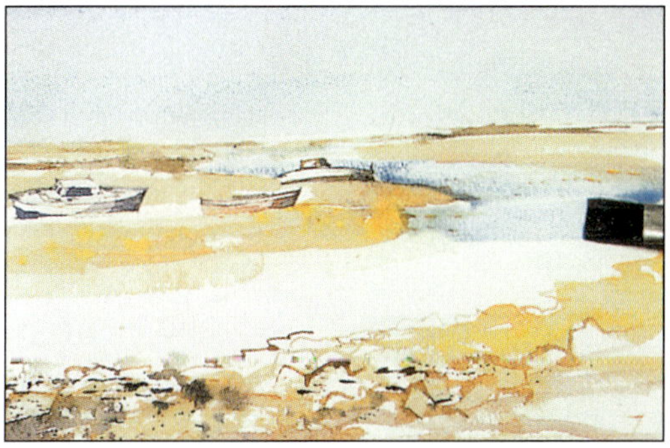

3 When the sand area is dry, mix plenty of dilute blue and quickly wash in the sea color using a large brush, taking the color over the edge of the sand. Vary the intensity of color in the wash and remember that it will dry paler.

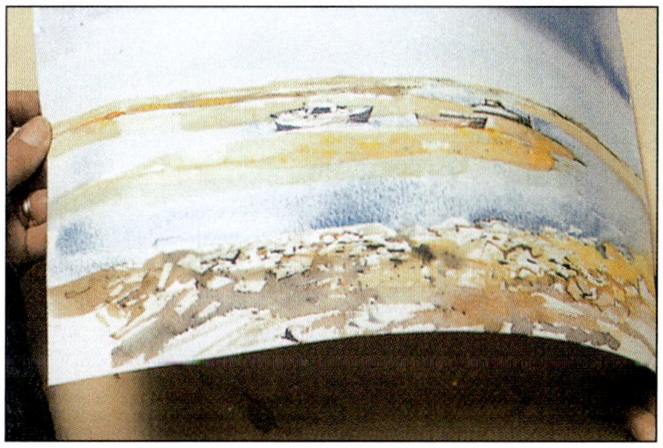

4 By bending and tipping the paper, you can control the direction in which the wash spreads. Here the artist breaks up the wash. Heavy watercolor paper, which need not be stretched, can be handled in this way without wrinkling.

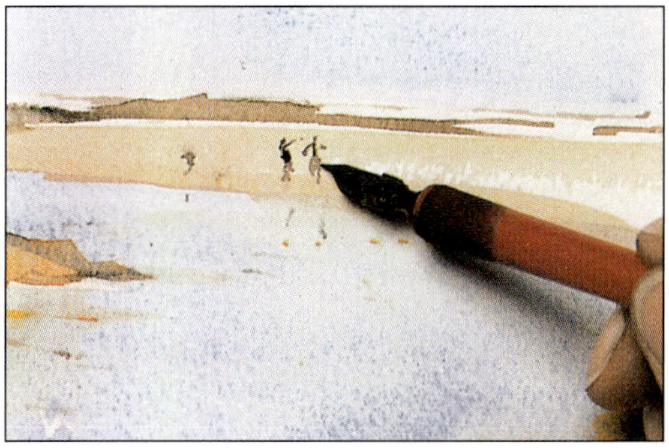

5 Using a pen and dilute watercolor (use a small brush to load the nib with paint), add in some small figures on the far shore for interest and to set the scale. Note how the sea wash has granulated, giving it an attractive texture.

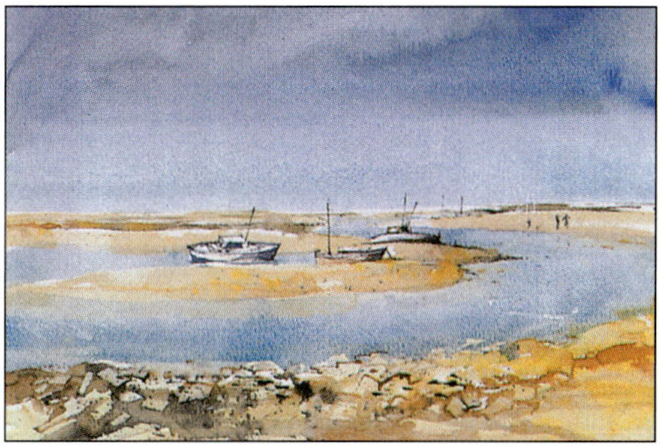

6 The variation in color and intensity of the wash used for the sea captures the changing color of the water, caused by variable factors such as shallows and turbulence.

How to Paint: Weather

The ability to generate a feeling of atmosphere and mood in a landscape painting is one of the hallmarks of a skilled artist. The prevailing light and weather conditions play an important part in establishing such a mood, and will often turn a perfectly ordinary scene into a memorable one. Strong sunlight makes the very air vibrate with color and gives rise to deep, dark shadows. Fog and mist act like a veil upon the landscape, turning hills and trees into eerie shapes that seem to float above the land. Storm clouds are particularly dramatic, especially when strong shafts of sunlight break through and spotlight the distant landscape. Lashing wind and rain set the landscape in motion as trees bend and leaves fly. And after a fall of snow, the whole landscape seems hushed and still, the dark shapes of trees and buildings looking in stark contrast to the whiteness of the land.

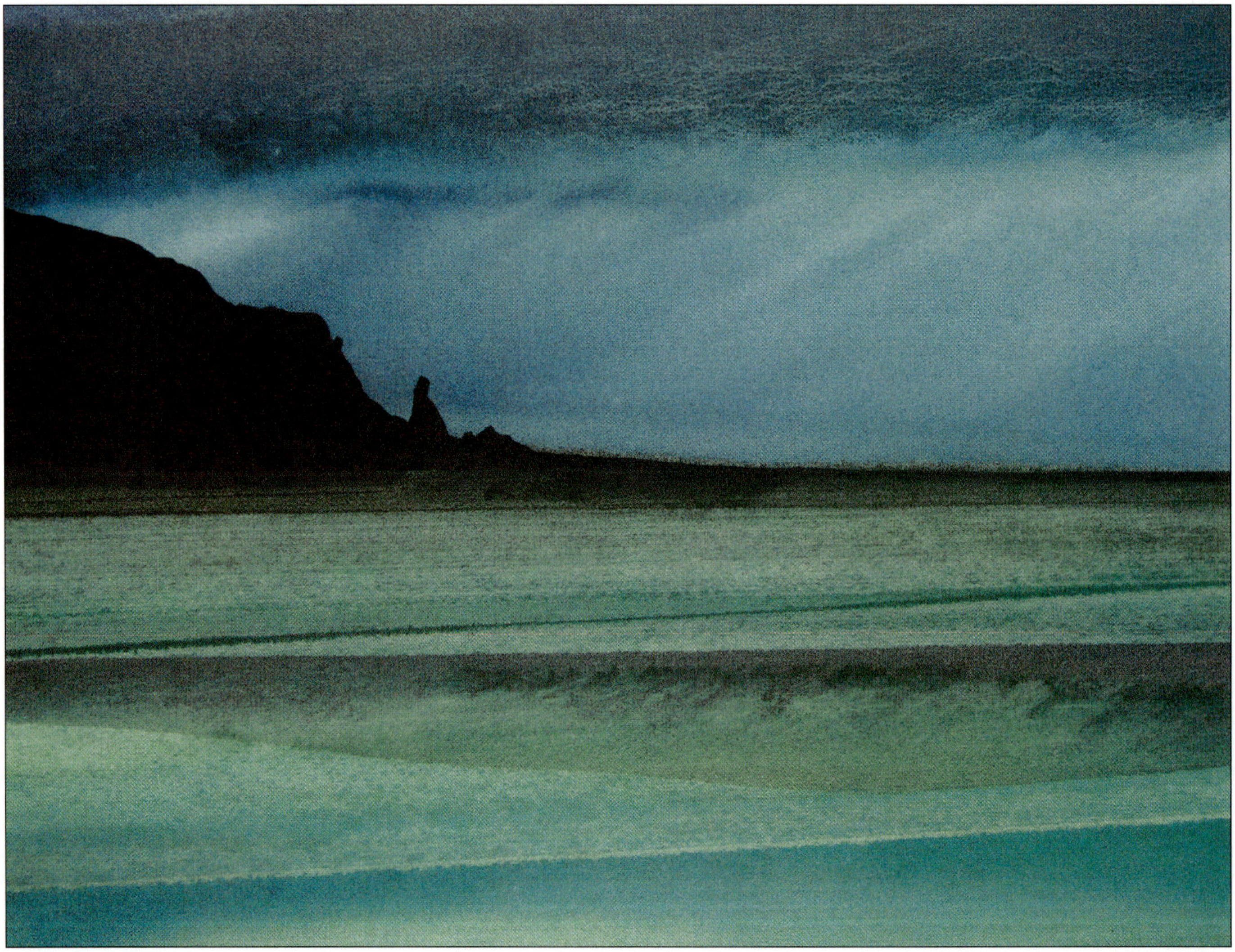

DISTANT TIDE, WINTER by Robert Tilling (watercolor)

The brooding, rain-streaked sky as well as the dark and cold colors give this painting a disturbing air which is intriguing.

Introduction

Though it is possible to recreate atmospheric effects from photographs, there is no substitute for actually getting out there among the elements. Other senses apart from sight have a part to play in painting; if you can smell the sun on the grass, hear the pounding of surf against the rocks, or feel the sharpness of a frosty day, these qualities will come through in your painting, almost without your being aware of it.

Even in a blizzard or a downpour, it is possible to work directly from nature by viewing the scene from your car window, or finding some other shelter. If you can't actually set up your easel, weather conditions can be recorded quickly in a watercolor or pencil sketch, so that a finished painting can be painted later in the studio. Indeed, working under adverse conditions often forces you to work directly and spontaneously, capturing the essence of the weather without danger of overworking your painting.

When painting weather, it is important to switch off the analytical side of your brain and be responsive to the feelings generated by a sparkling spring day or a crashing thunderstorm. Because atmospheric conditions are transitory and difficult to "pin down," the creative artist turns this to advantage by letting the paint itself suggest the power and drama of nature. The watercolorist has a distinct advantage here, since the medium's fluidity and spontaneity have often been compared to the behavior of nature itself. But every medium has its own special qualities, and it is worthwhile experimenting with unusual techniques to express the ever-changing moods of nature.

Both Constable (1776–1837) and Turner (1775–1851) were fascinated by weather effects, and made countless small color notes of this kind. Constable was particularly interested in rainbows, which offer a marvelous opportunity to contrast bright colors with a mass of dark grays.

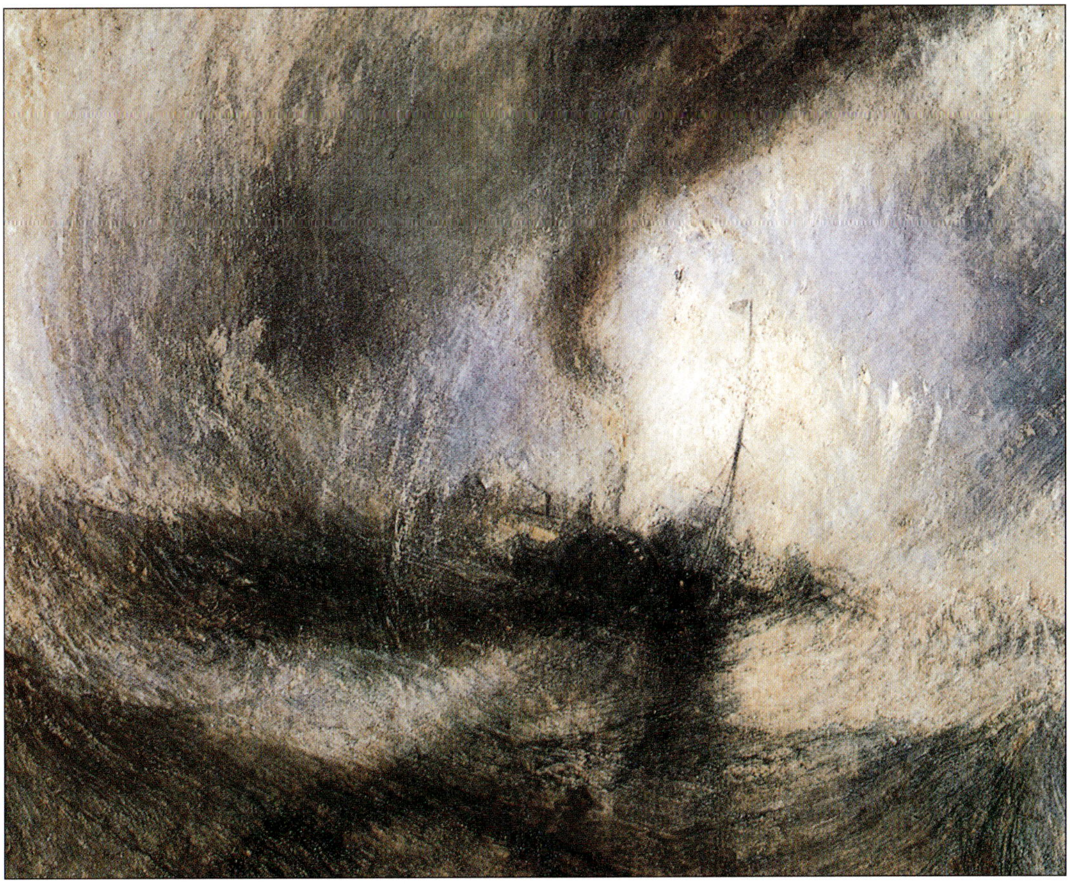

SNOWSTORM by William Turner (oil)

This painting demonstrates the wonderful atmospheric effects that Turner obtained by the use of transparent glazes of oil color.

Fog and Mist

A landscape that is shrouded in mist takes on a strange, haunting, unfamiliar aspect, and this indefinable quality has attracted artists for centuries. The great masters of traditional Chinese and Japanese painting delighted in rendering, with a few exquisite brush strokes, an impression of mountains and trees looking out of the mist. Of the European painters, Turner is the unequaled master of depicting the effects of sun, water, and light on landscapes and seascapes.

Because fog and mist are actually water vapor hanging in the air, it follows that a fluid medium such as watercolor lends itself particularly well to such a subject. Oil paints, too, can be used with great success, because their slow rate of drying allows for subtle wet-into-wet blendings. Pastel is another favorite medium, especially for on-the-spot studies; with a few rapid strokes, hastily smudged with the finger, the artist can capture a fleeting effect of hazy light before it disappears for ever. Finally, egg tempera is perfectly suited to the still, mysterious quality that pervades the landscape on a misty day.

Fog acts as a filter on the landscape, reducing forms to simple silhouettes, minimizing tonal contrast and eliminating textural detail. There are many techniques that

WINTER MORNING by Edward Seago (oil)

The artist has captured the misty chill of a winter morning with vigorous brushwork and an economical description of both cattle and landscape. The muted color scheme of blues and grays is enlivened by the flecks of warm sunlight glancing off the backs of the cattle.

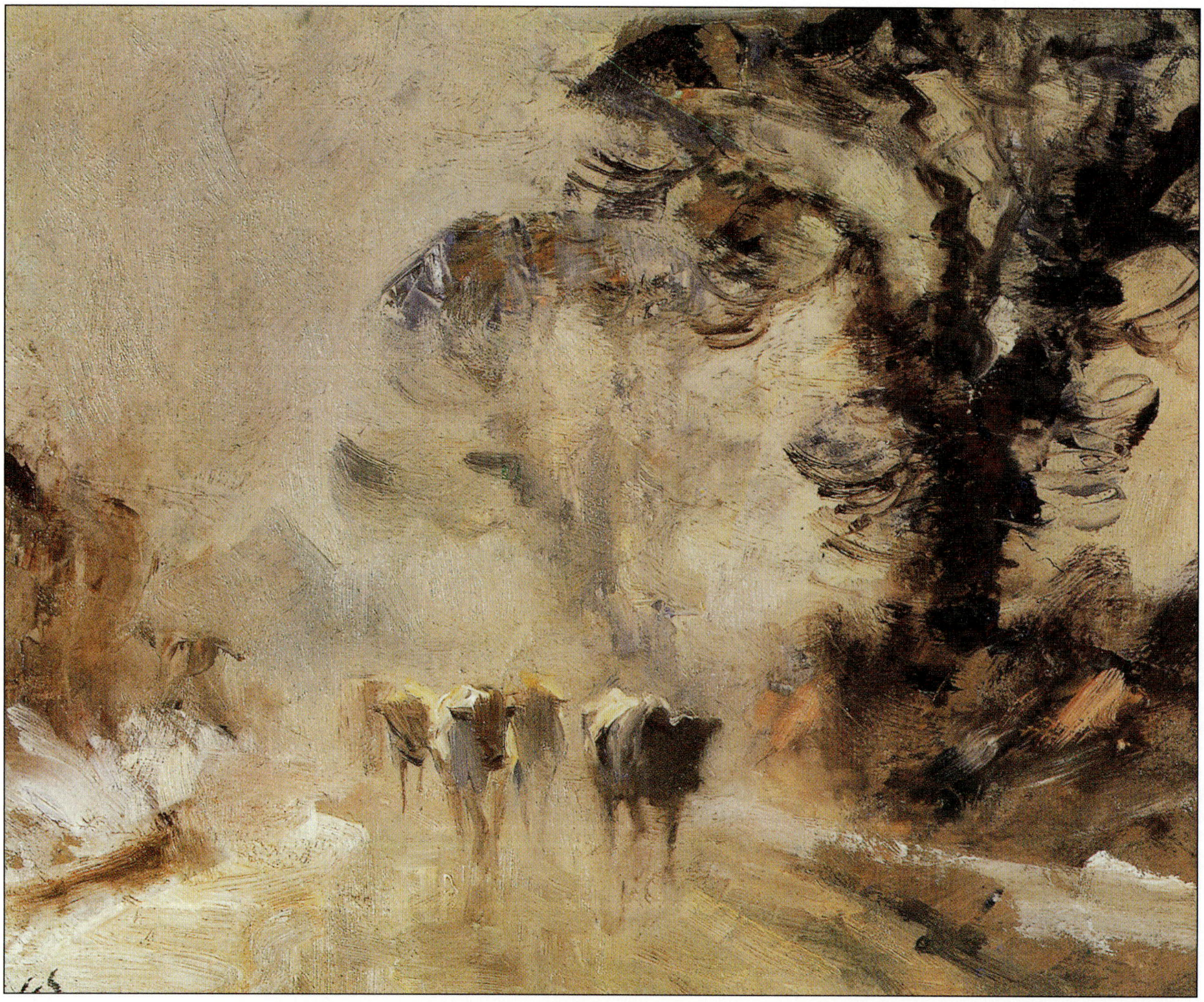

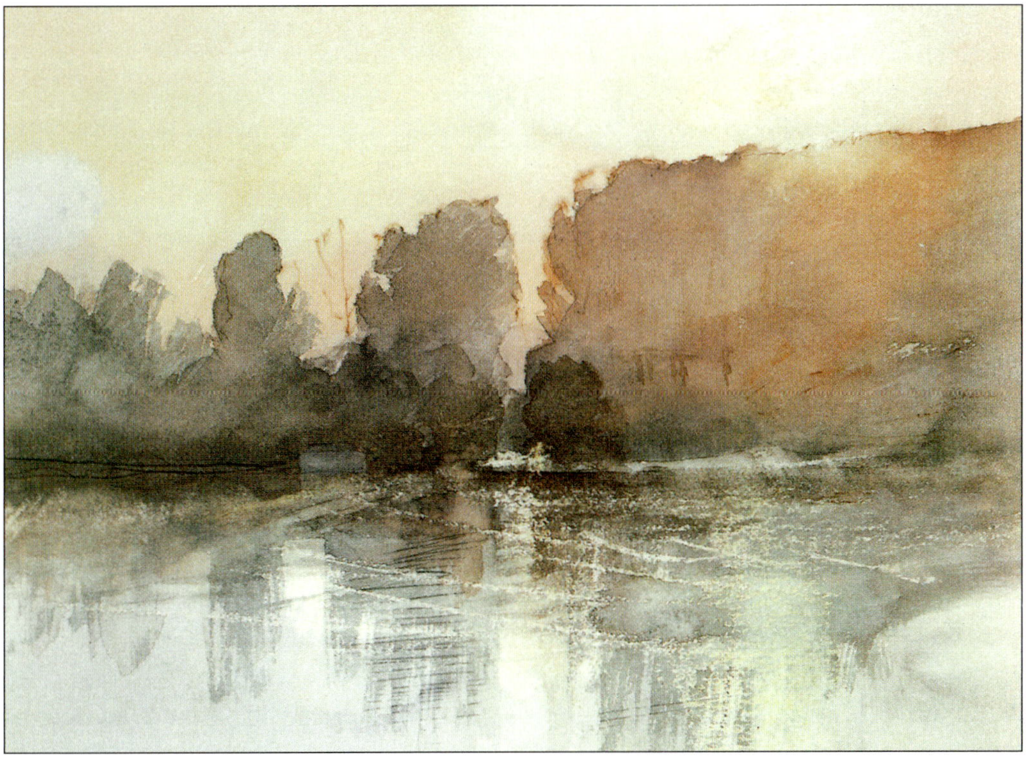

EVENING by Charles Knight (watercolor with wax and pencil)

The mist has been beautifully described by means of wet washes of pale colors. In the central tree area, the overlaying of washes has created lines, providing touches of definition. The effect of the setting sun behind the trees has been achieved by lightly sponging the area while lightly scribbled lines of wax crayon suggest ripples and highlights on the water.

you can use to render this effect in your paintings. In oil, an excellent method is to apply a toned ground of heavily diluted raw umber and then to render the muted tones and colors of the landscape with delicate scumbles that allow the ground color to show through. This technique produces a highly atmospheric, soft focus effect.

Another interesting technique is to "tonk" the painting with newspaper before the paint dries. This removes much of the color from the surface and has an overall softening effect on the painting.

Haziness is also achieved through the classic techniques of working wet-into-wet. The best way is to start with the middle tones and then work the darks and lights into the wet color, blending the edges of the forms into each other.

In watercolor, some artists prefer to soak the entire paper and work into the wet surface to produce a soft blending of tones. Others prefer to work on a dry surface, using a small sponge to wet those areas where a hazy effect is required. This method gives you more control over hard and soft edges and is excellent for depicting subjects that are only partially enveloped in mist.

In general, fog and mist reduce the intensity of colors, giving them a cold gray or gray-blue cast. The exception might be in the early morning or late afternoon, when the sun's rays color the mist a pale yellow. To achieve this muted effect, keep to a limited palette of harmonious colors.

Fog also reduces the intensity of tones, so tone values become very important when painting a misty scene. To achieve a sense of distance in your painting, always start with the pale, indistinct forms in the background. Then paint the middle ground, with slightly deeper tones. Finally, in the foreground, include accents of dark tone and sharp detail. This contrast makes the background look pale and more misty and lends a sense of depth and mystery to the scene.

Capturing the veiled and mysterious aspect of a foggy landscape requires sensitive observation and a certain amount of restraint in handling the paint. Use subdued, harmonious colors and closely-related tones; too many sharp contrasts will destroy the illusion of an all-enveloping mist. Reserve any clear details and dark tones for the foreground; these will enhance, through contrast, the mistiness in the background.

CREATING FOG IN WATERCOLOR

The softness and delicacy of watercolor makes it an excellent medium for rendering impressions of fog and mist. Here the artist uses a combination of hazy, indistinct washes and sharper, crisper detail to create a misty landscape which recalls the understated beauty of a traditional Oriental ink drawing.

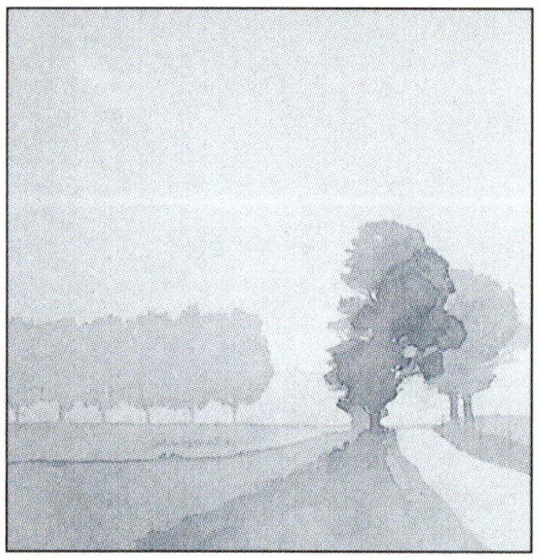

1 Working on a sheet of stretched 200 lb Bockingford paper, the artist begins by painting the field and the distant trees with a mixture of ivory black and Payne's gray, heavily diluted with water. When the first wash is dry the foreground trees are further developed by adding a slightly darker wash; this deeper tone gives depth to the scene by bringing the nearer trees forward and making the pale shapes in the background seem more distant by comparison.

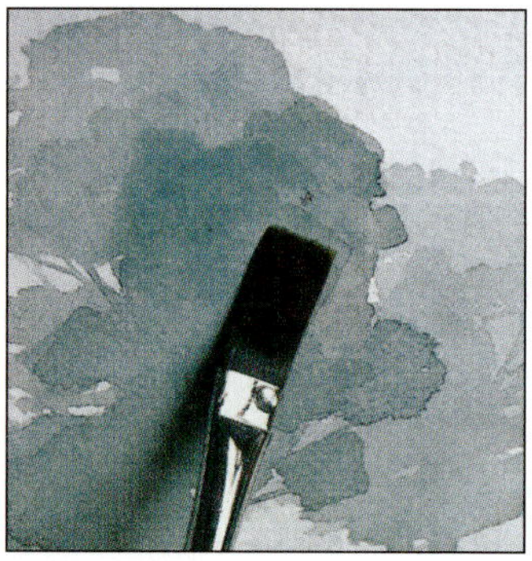

2 This detail shows how the washes are painted wet on dry to create crisp edges, which gives a suggestion of the foliage texture.

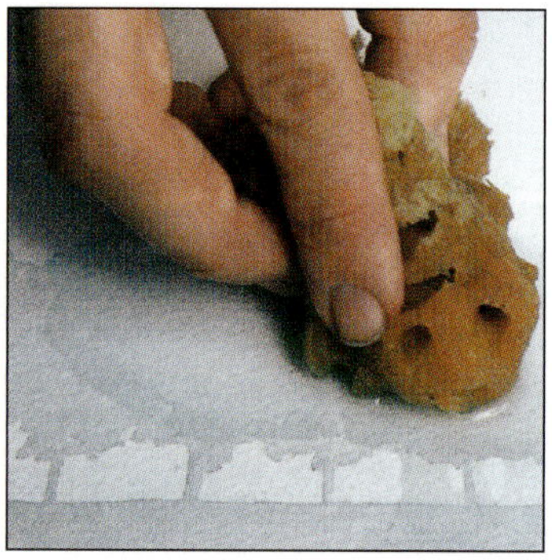

3 The painting is allowed to dry. The tops of the background trees are then flooded with clean water, applied with a soft sponge, and gently blotted with a tissue. This removes most of the pigment from the area, leaving just a slight hint of color. It is essential to allow the paint to dry *before* flooding it with water, so that the pigment has a chance to stain the paper.

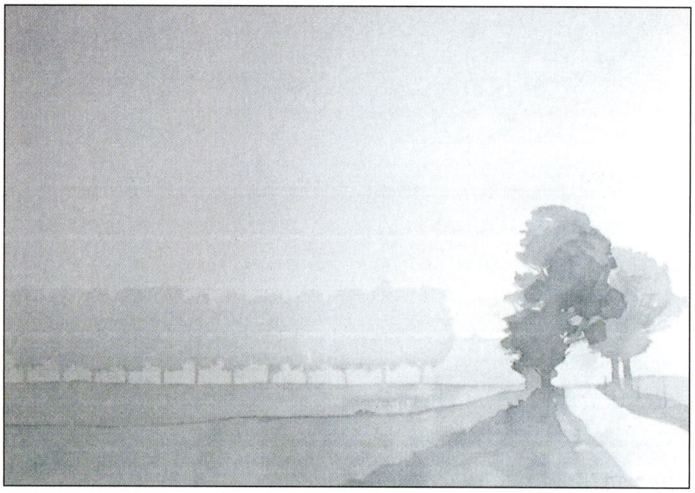

4 The background trees now have an intriguing lost-and-found quality, blending softly into the gray distance. The beauty of the painting lies in the delicate balance between crisp forms in the foreground and soft, hazy forms in the background.

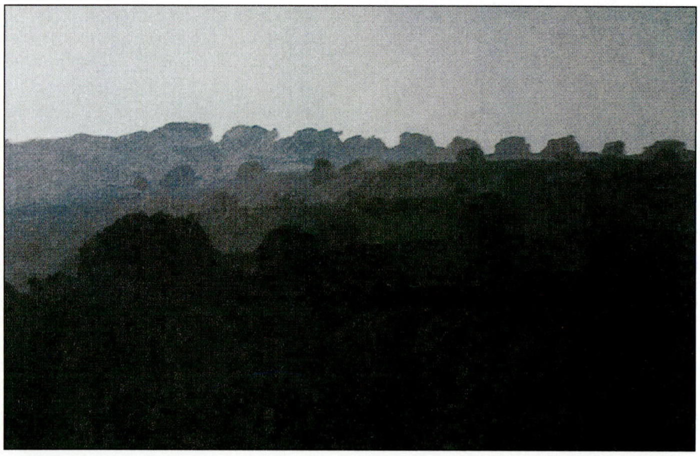

A landscape with rolling hills and fields stretching into the distance takes on a special atmosphere when shrouded in early morning mist. The effects of aerial perspective are heightened – foreground, middle ground, and background become more separate and distinct than usual, and the forms of the land become flattened silhouettes, almost like stage flats stacked one in front of the other. In this oil painting, the artist uses the direct, alla prima *technique, working the colors wet-into-wet to achieve the softness of tone characteristic of a misty day. He then finishes off by tonking the entire painting to soften the tones even more.*

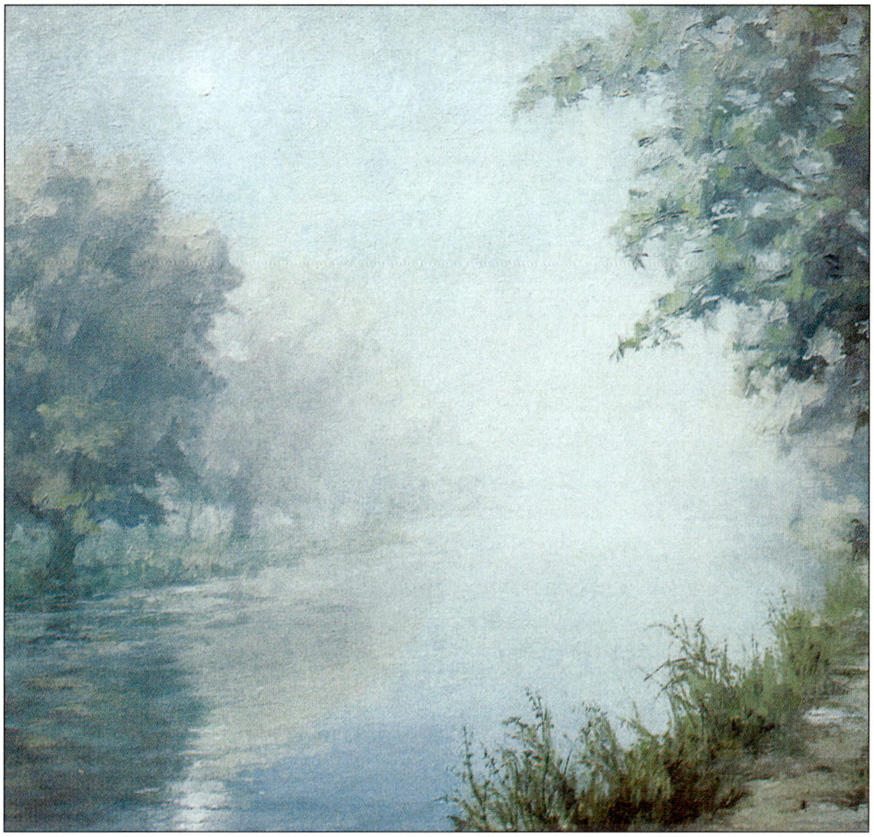

EARLY MORNING, RIVER GADE by Brian Bennett (oil)

In this high-key painting the artist has used the slow-drying properties of oils to full advantage, blending the forms into the surrounding atmosphere to give an impression of heavy mist on the river.

WELSH MOUNTAIN SHEEP by Trevor Chamberlain (oil)

Heavy cloud or mist on mountains is a perennially popular painting subject. Here the cloud plays as vital a role in the composition as the dark mountain, but the artist has stressed the different qualities of air and rock by painting the sky wet-into-wet to create a soft blurring. The sharper edges of the mountain are strengthened by contrast.

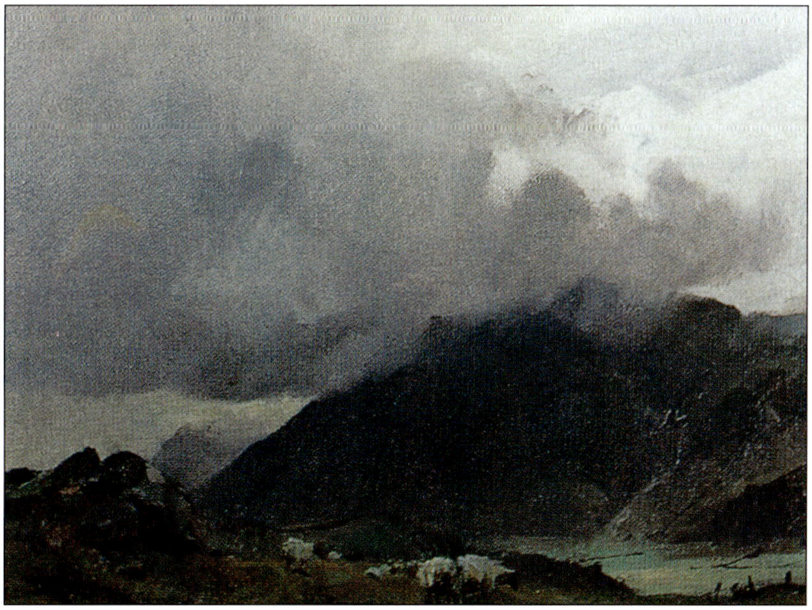

Rain

Painting an impression of a rainy day can be tackled in several ways. You can indicate falling rain by using diagonal or vertical brush strokes to build up the painting, or you can ignore the raindrops and choose instead to imply the effects of rain on the landscape by softly diffusing the images. To indicate the wetness of rooftops and roads, paint them very light in tone, and use a contrastingly dark tone for the sky. Puddles on roads and pavements, showing reflections of trees and buildings, also add to the atmosphere of a rainy day. The dominant color in a rainy scene is most likely to be gray, but make the grays interesting by mixing them from various combinations of blues, reds, and yellows, rather than just black and white.

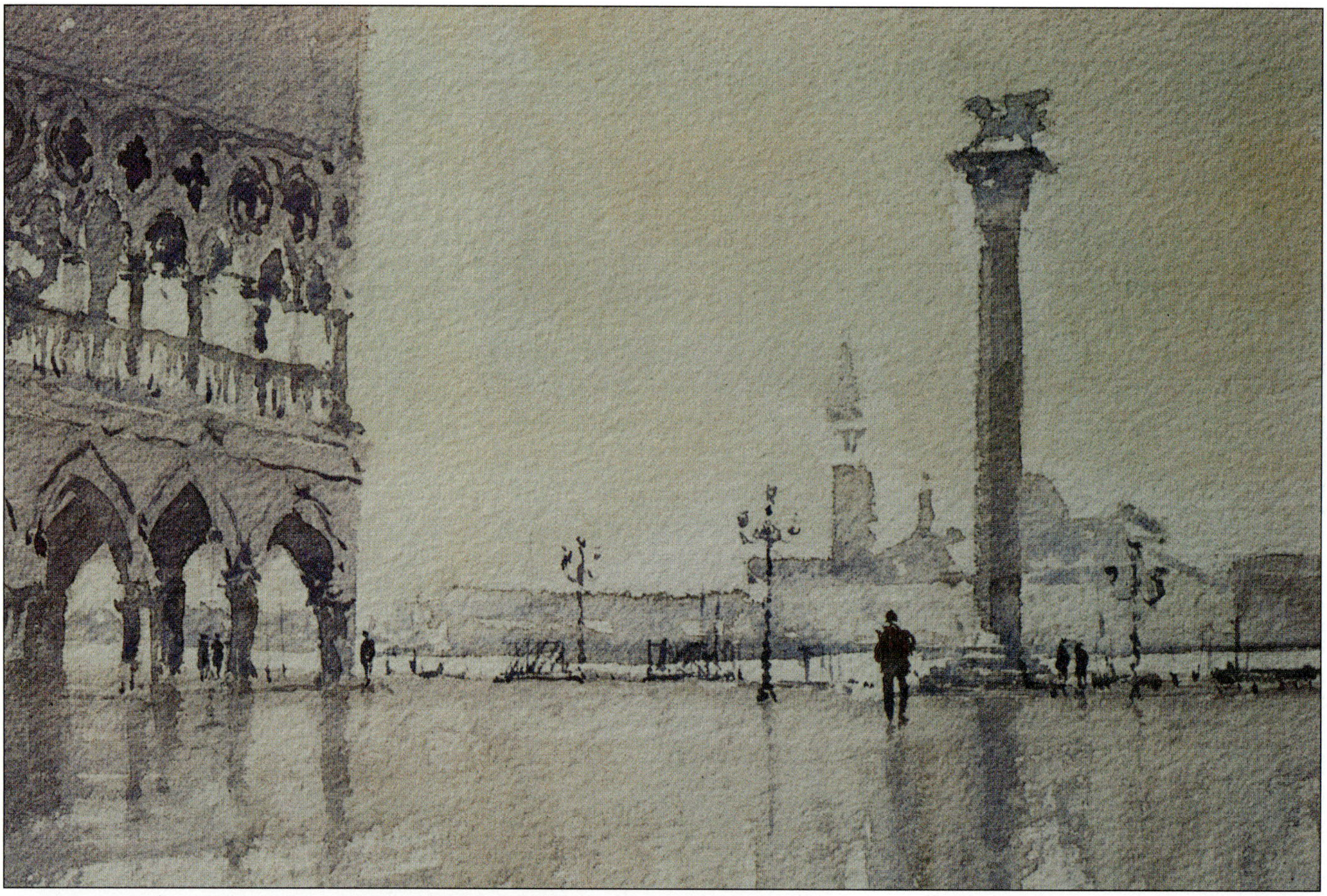

WET MORNING, ST MARK'S, VENICE by Alan Oliver (watercolor)

A simple, almost monochrome painting in which delicate washes represent the reflections caused by a diffused, pale yellow light.

Some of the most atmospheric and dramatic effects of light occur just before, during, or immediately after a downpour of rain. It is possible to represent rain itself in a graphic or symbolic way by manipulating the paint. This is particularly easy in a fluid medium like watercolor – try tilting your board downward so that the sky washes run toward the horizon. When the washes are dry, use spattering and dry brush strokes to indicate windblown rain. In both oils and watercolor you can scratch into the paint with a sharp point to indicate slanting rain. Don't overdo these effects though, just the merest indication of rain is all the viewer needs.

It is often more appropriate to paint not the rain itself, but some of the effects it can have. For instance, moisture in the air has a flattening effect on forms, and the effects of aerial perspective are evident over surprisingly short distances. Indicate this by painting features in the middle ground with pale, hazy tones and blending them into the surrounding atmosphere, while reducing distant features to a blur. Just after a rain shower, the sky brightens, and flat, wet surfaces will act as mirrors, reflecting the light. Indicate wet pavements and rooftops with pale, wet-into-wet washes and then overlay contrasting dark reflections when the underwashes are dry.

The approach of a storm, of course, offers great potential for dramatic effects. Suggest the brooding, threatening atmosphere by painting the land and the upper part of the sky with dark tones, leaving a strip of pale sky near the horizon.

CREATING RAIN WITH WATERCOLOR

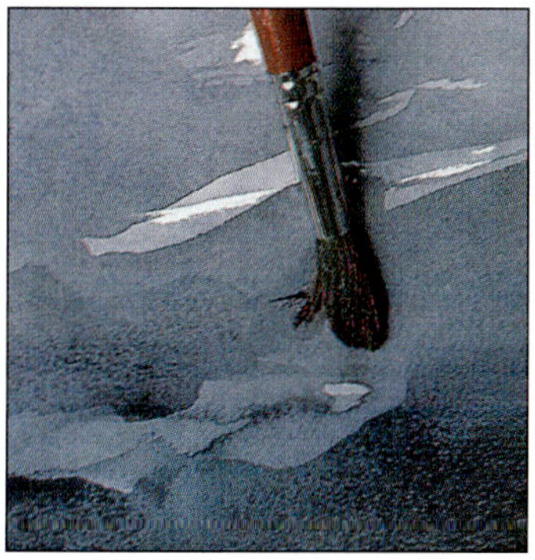

1 A sheet of 200 lb Bockingford paper is taped firmly to the drawing board and then wetted with clear water. A wash of Payne's gray is applied with broad strokes, leaving small areas of white paper which indicate bright light shining through gaps in the clouds. While this wash is still damp, a loose wash of Payne's gray and ivory black is flooded in, wet-into-wet, using a large sable brush.

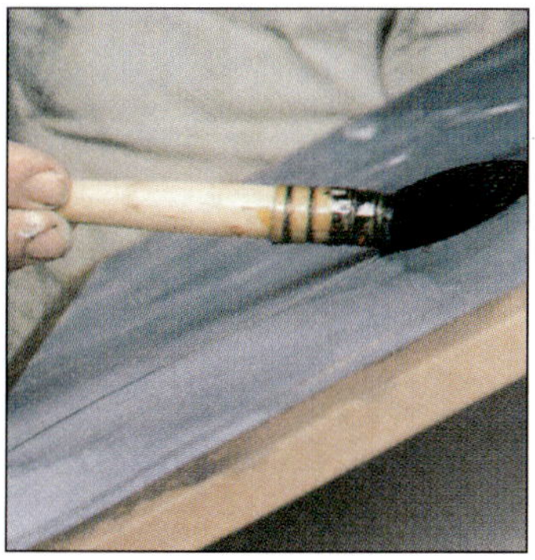

2 Tilting the board up at an angle, the artist allows the color to drift midway down the paper, using a large mop brush to guide the pigment where he wants it to go.

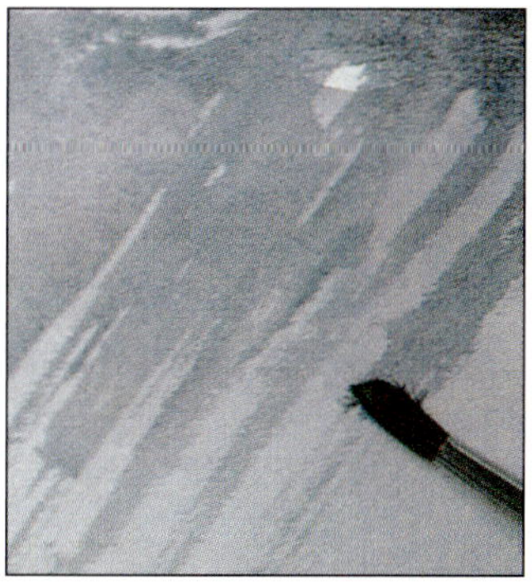

3 The color is then brought down toward the horizon with diagonal strokes, using a No. 6 sable brush. The artist works quickly and with a light touch, so that the color is broken up by the raised tooth of the paper.

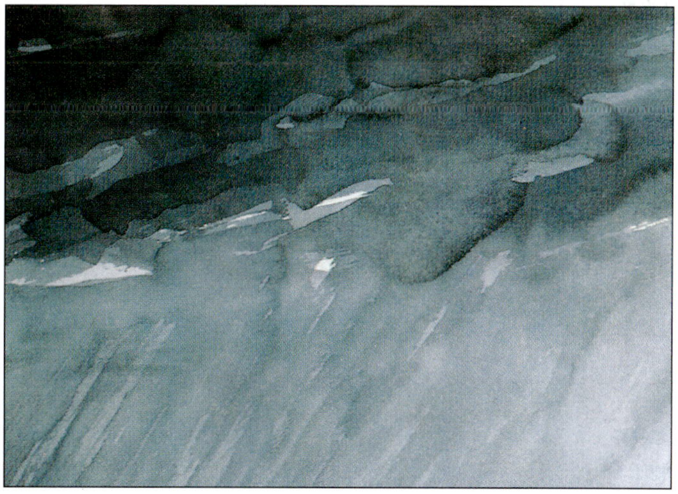

4 The diagonal strokes have softened slightly into the damp wash beneath, creating a subtle impression of drifting rain.

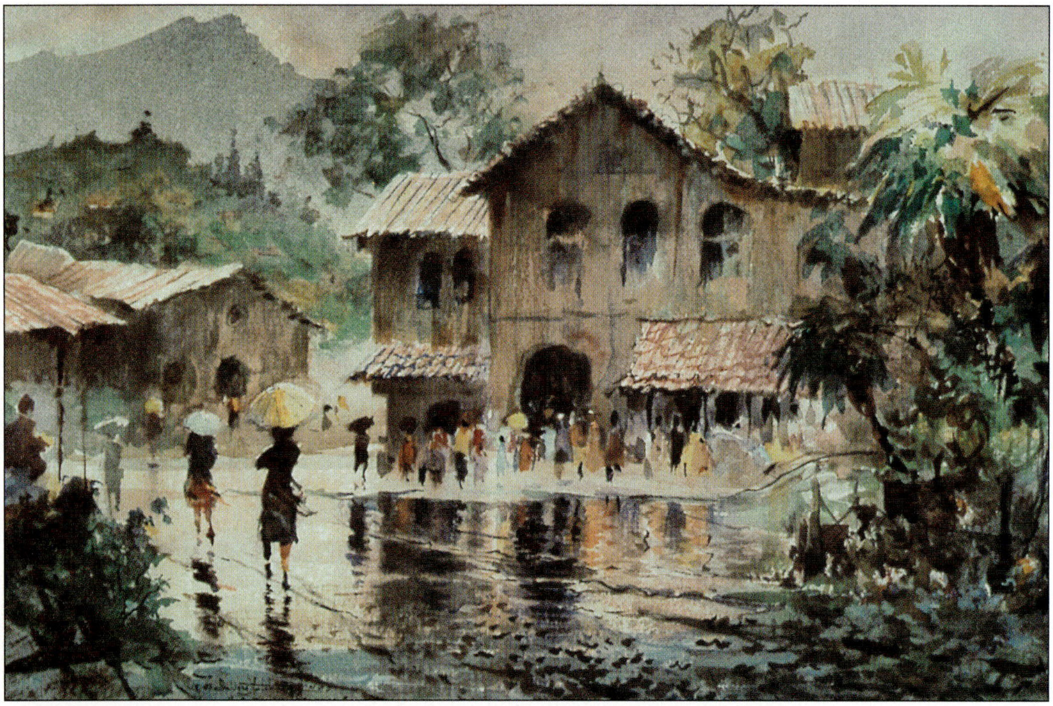

A TOUCH OF RAIN by LaVere Hutchings (watercolor)

Heavy rainfall floods the street and turns it into a patchwork of reflected color, captured with washes, wet-into-wet and then wet on dry.

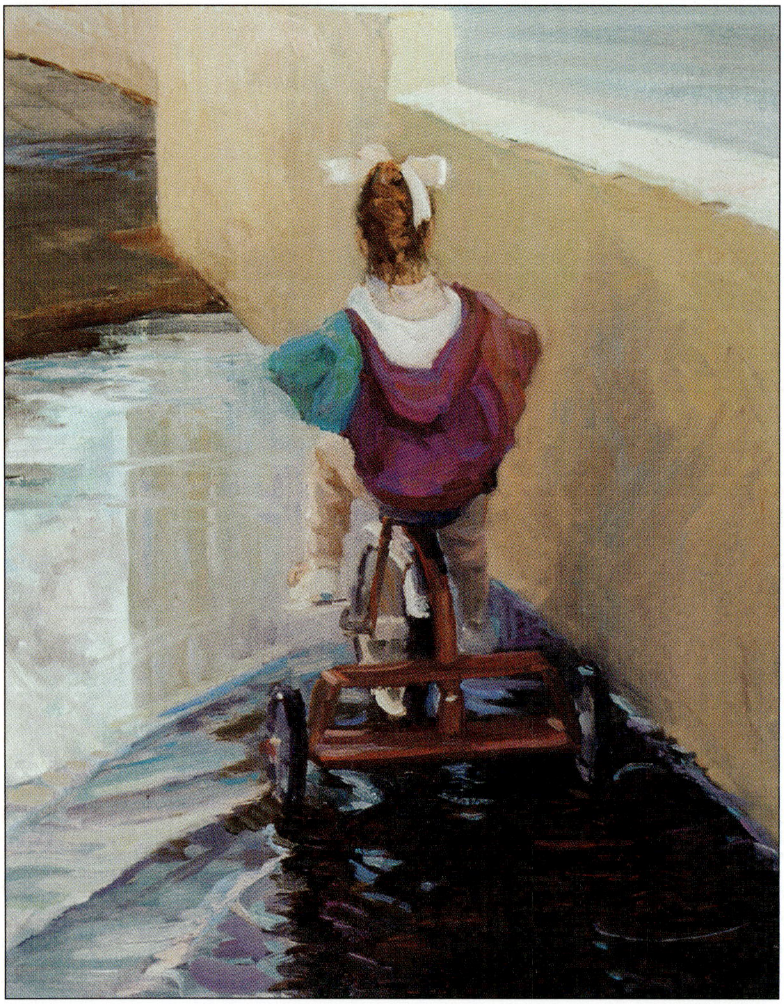

PUDDLE JUMPER by Denise Burns (oil)

In the small area of water the artist deals with reflections and shadows, broken water and movement, and establishes the integration of puddle and concrete.

WET STREETS

Rainwater remains on the surface of unabsorbent materials making slate roofs, pavements, and tarmac roads glisten in the brighter light after the clouds have passed. A wet street reflects light from the sky and street lights and, when it is truly wet, it will reflect other elements in the picture, such as people and street furniture.

Reflections in wet streets and puddles are often dominated by verticals snaking their way toward you. You need only look at the examples on these two pages. These snake-like strokes tell you that what you are looking at is a reflection in water rather than a shadow on dry land. With opaque media, you can run the brush through the built-up paint for these wiggling reflections, or use the brushend sgraffito style to create lighter reflections. For watercolor you will have to reserve pale reflections at the outset but darker ones can be added at the end. A painter may ask himself if the result does indeed look wet. Reflections on the streets and heightened contrasts will help to put across the wetness of the scene, as will scurrying rain clouds and people carrying umbrellas.

Puddles can make a subject in themselves, or they can be used to great effect in a composition, creating patches of reflected light along a dark road. For the city dweller, a puddle is a convenient way to study water and how it behaves in relation to light.

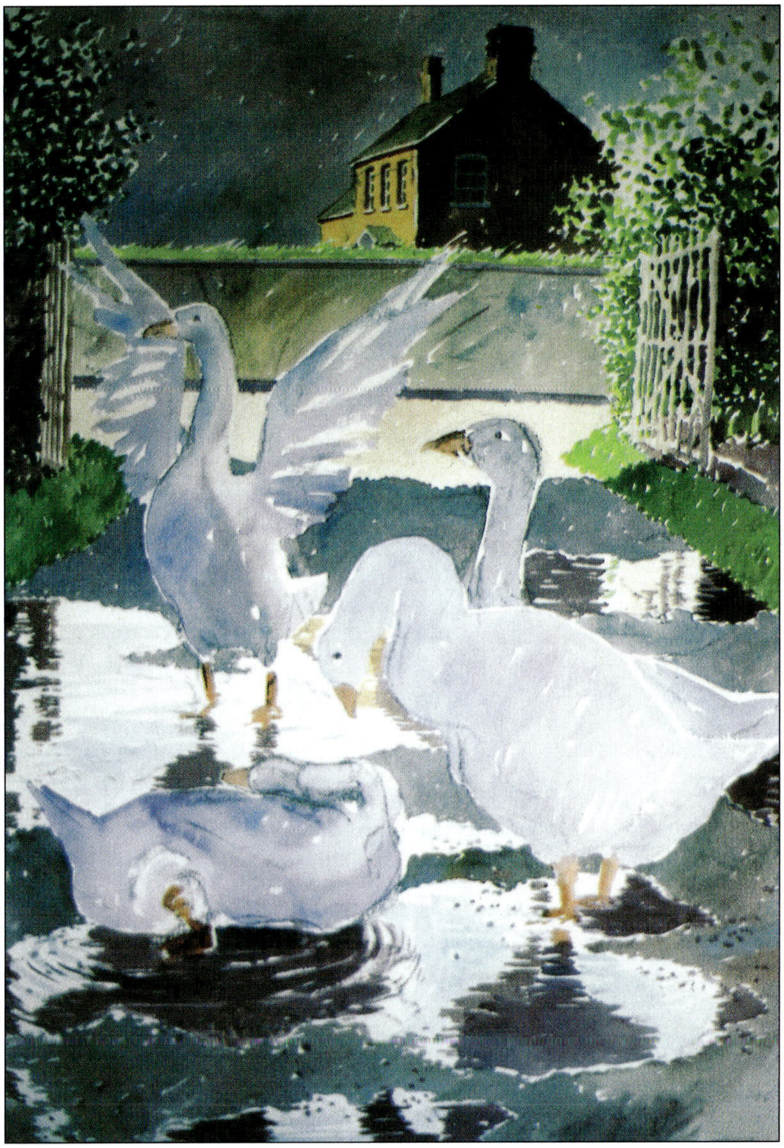

AFTER THE RAIN by Lucy Willis (watercolor)

Here Lucy Willis made use of light reflected on the wet ground to recreate that fresh, clear atmosphere that occurs after a rainstorm.

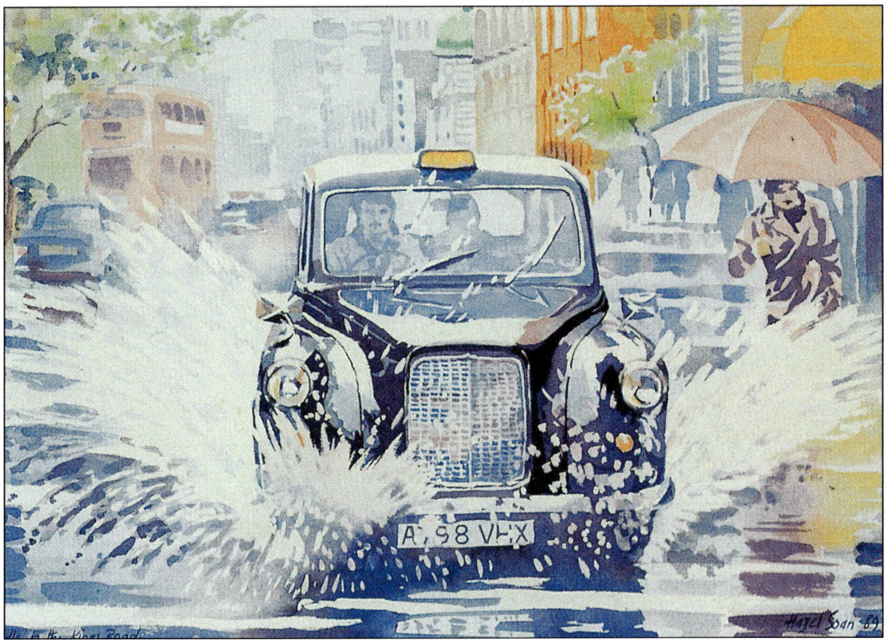

TAXI IN THE KINGS ROAD by Hazel Soan (watercolor)

Masking fluid is used to isolate the splashes, and the reflections are simplified into three basic, superimposed tones.

Snow and Ice

Having struggled through the summer months with green, which is the predominant and, arguably, the most difficult color in many landscapes, painting snow scenes comes as a welcome change. The interesting thing about snow scenes is that the landscape appears much more tonal. On an overcast day, the snow-covered land is, for once, lighter in tone than the sky, and the dark shapes of buildings and trees stand out in sharp contrast with the lighter tone of the snow. This can make for some very dramatic and exciting compositions, with a cool, moody atmosphere.

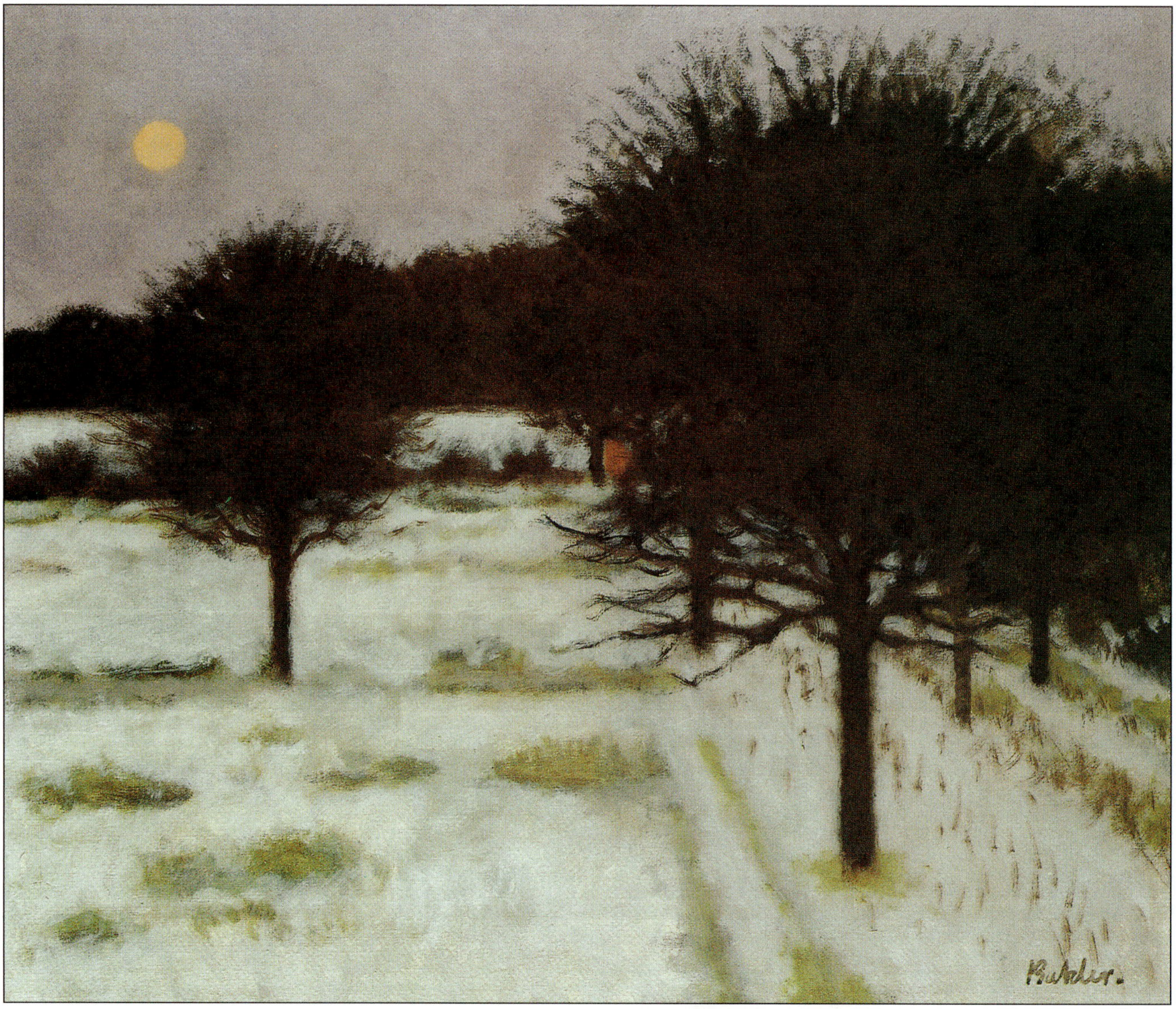

WINTER PARK, MOONLIGHT by Robert Buhler (oil)

In this low-key painting, Robert Buhler has caught the still, chill atmosphere of dusk on a snowy winter's evening. The closely-related tones, muted colors, and considered composition all combine to emphasize the mood of the picture.

Snow and ice are generally regarded as being white, but they are in fact rarely pure white, except in the brightest areas. Snow and ice are water in solid form, and, just like water, they reflect color from the sky and nearby objects. This is especially noticeable in the early morning and later afternoon, when the sun strikes the surface of the snow at a low angle and tinges it a delicate pink or yellow. In fact, these are the best times of the day for painting snow scenes; the light is far lovelier than it is during the middle of the day, casting warm pinks and golds in the highlights, and luminous blues and violets in the shadows. In addition, the long shadows cast by the sun at these times of the day add drama to the scene and help to define the snow-covered forms of the land.

Inexperienced artists tend to think that painting a snow scene means piling on endless layers of thick white paint. On the contrary, the most atmospheric snow scenes are those that contain a lot of shadow, with only small areas of bright, sunlit snow. The bright spots look dazzling because of the contrasting shadows, whereas if the whole picture were painted in bright white the effect would be flat and monotonous, with no feeling of light at all.

When painting a snow scene in opaque media, always begin with the light colors and gradually add the cool shadow colors. It takes less paint to darken a light color than it does to lighten a dark color. With transparent watercolor, the opposite applies. You must establish the position of the brightest highlights on the snow in advance, and paint around them, working from light to dark.

After a heavy fall of snow, the objects that it covers take on soft contours and curves. The light planes blur softly into the shadow planes, with no hard edges, so model these forms with wet-into-wet blending.

When painting shadows on snow, you will notice that they appear crisp near the object casting the shadow, but more diffused farther away. This is because a lot of reflected light enters the shadows from the sky or from nearby snowdrifts. Keep the shadows airy and transparent by using thin pigment and fresh, clean color.

FALLING SNOW

Falling snow cuts out much of the detail in background images, reducing them to faint silhouettes if the fall is heavy.

In opaque media, stippling and spattering are very effective in rendering falling snow. In watercolor painting, you can either spatter with opaque (Chinese) white or create an impression of snowflakes with the use of salt granules, as shown in Step 2, opposite.

USING GOUACHE AND WATERCOLOR

Use masking fluid to reserve white paper for the snow on the branches. Dip a toothbrush in white gouache mixed to a creamy consistency, hold it face down ½–1 in. (1–2.5 cm) above the painting and release speckles of paint by drawing your finger swifly back across the bristles.

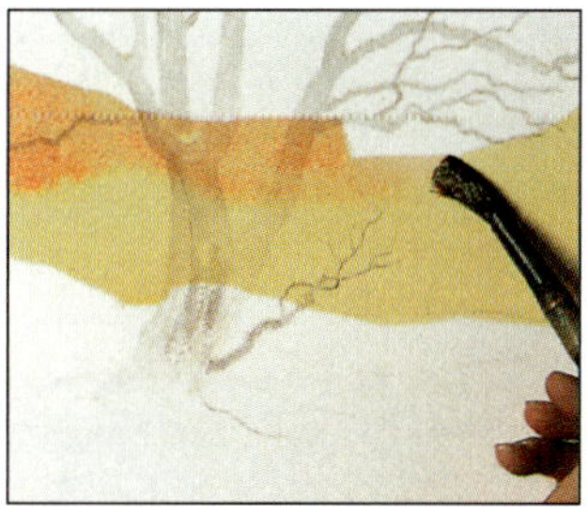

1 Sketch the tree form in light grey. Mask the snow-laden branches. Lay a streaky wash of ocher and light red over the sky and let it dry.

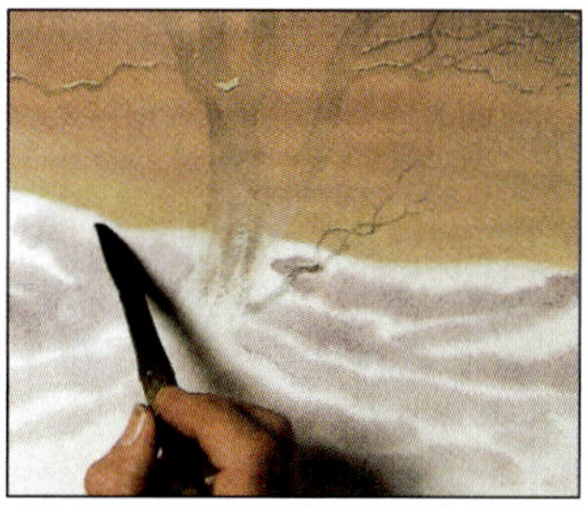

2 Dampen the sky and wash a mix of light red and cobalt blue over in streaks. Dampen the snow and use the same wash to draw in undulating shadows.

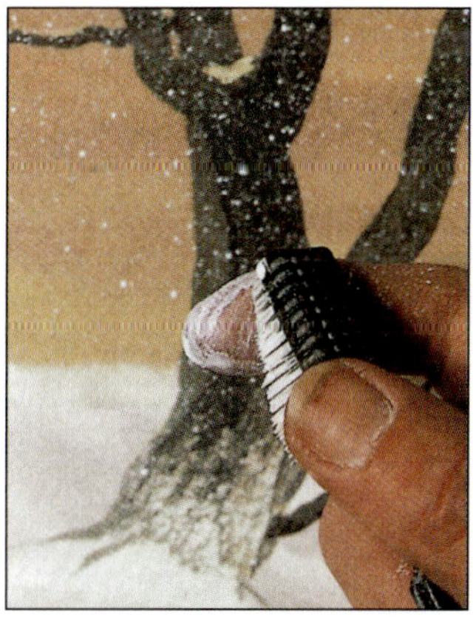

3 Darken up the tree, using dry brushwork at the base. Spatter thick white gouache over the top half of the painting with the toothbrush.

4 Rub off the masking fluid to reveal snow-laden branches. One wonderful wintry painting!

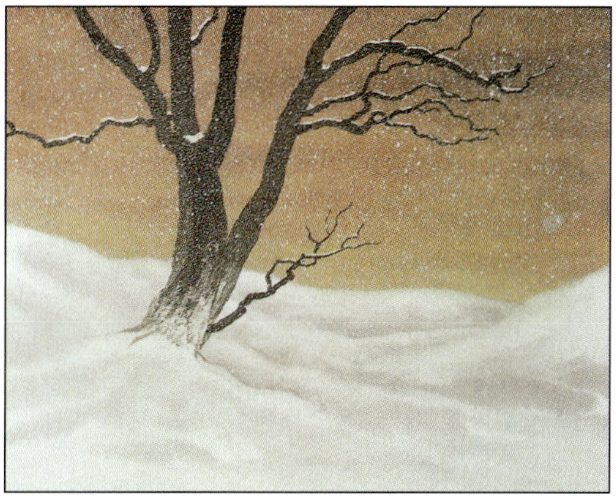

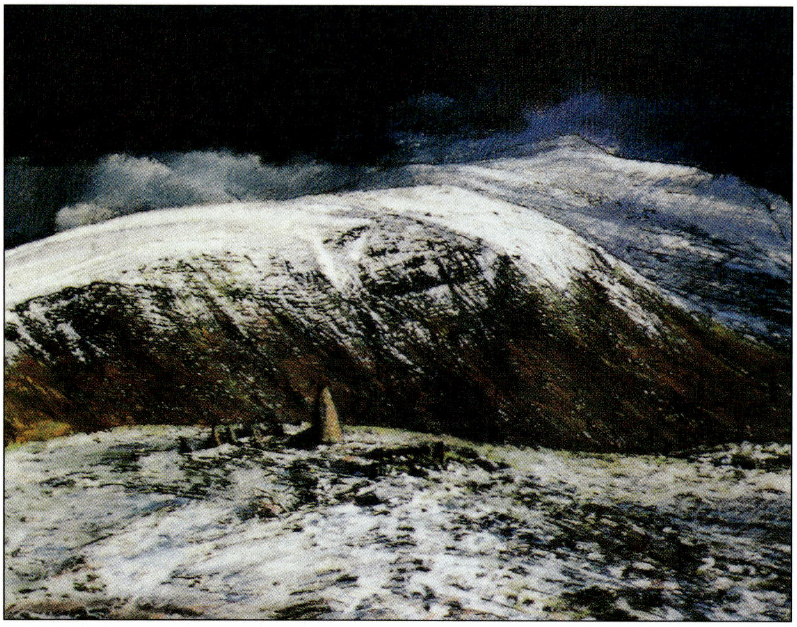

MOEL SIABOD by Keith Bowen (pastel)

The horizontal emphasis of this restrained composition underlines the bleak character of the open landscape. The color masses yield an immense amount of calligraphic activity, with the fine linear marks giving harsh texture to the snow-covered hills, and overlaid shading and hatching building the dense, blackened tones of the sky.

USING OILS

1 Once the basic colors for the sky and hills have been laid in cerulean blue and white, the artist paints in the long shadows with a mixture of cerulean blue and a small amount of white and black.

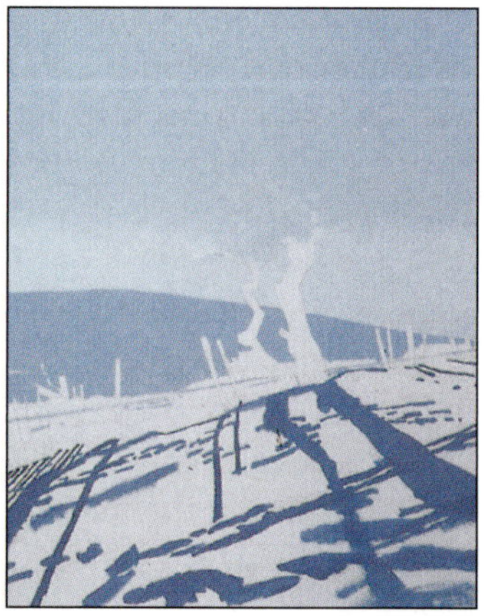

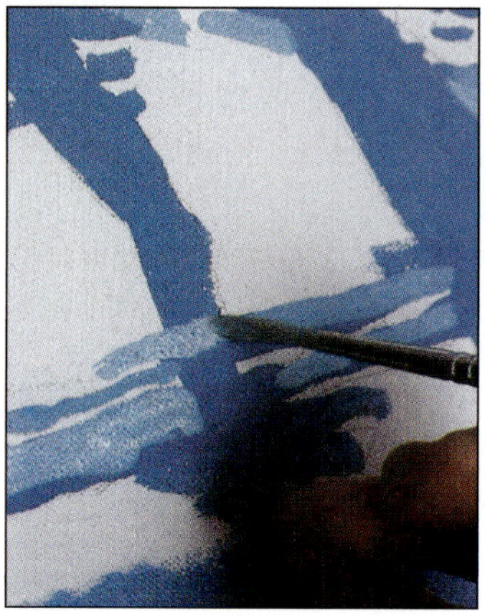

2 Then he adds the middle tones of the shadows, using a pale blue mixture.

3 As the painting develops the artist softens the hard lines of the snow and shadows by spattering white paint in the foreground to suggest falling snow.

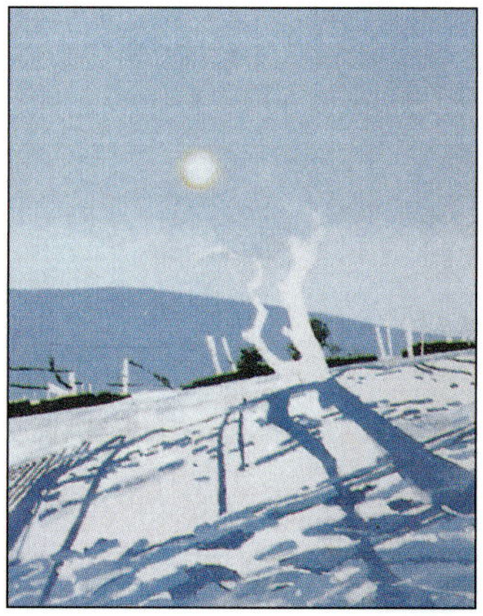

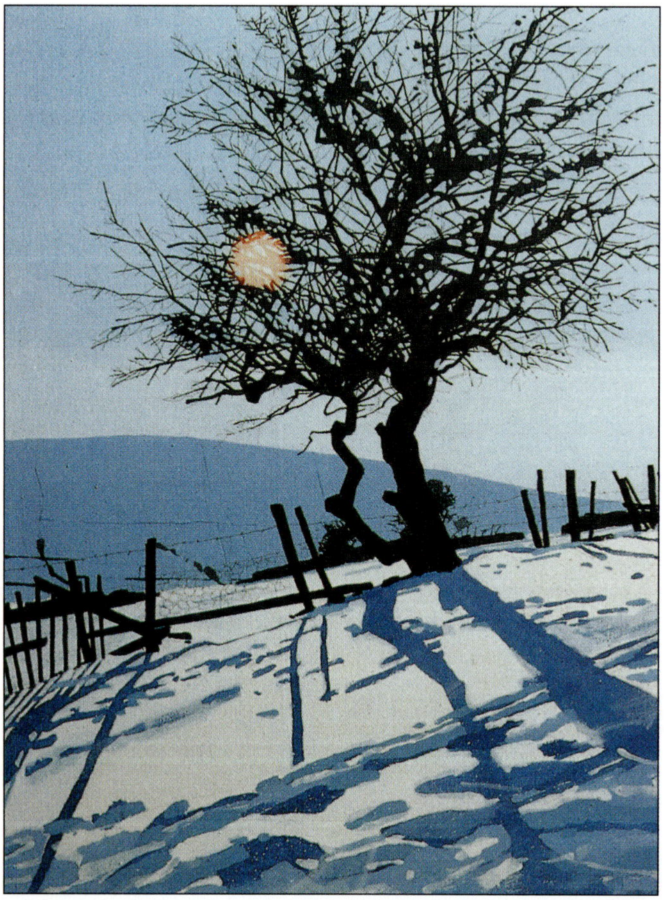

4 In the finished picture the artist has successfully created dramatic contrasts using simple forms and a limited palette for the dark silhouetted trees against the sky and the blue shadows against the snow.

PAINTING IN LOW TEMPERATURES

When painting outdoors in very low temperature, you may find that your washes will actually freeze as you apply them. Though this can sometimes result in attractive "snow crystal" effects, it very often means that you are pushing lumps of slush across the paper. To overcome this problem, make sure you have some gin or vodka with you. These are colorless alcohols and when added to your water act as an anti-freeze.

When painting in oils such interesting solutions are unnecessary because, of course, the paint will not freeze. It is a good idea to work on a pre-toned canvas, in a warm earth color such as yellow ocher, and allow the color to show through occasionally. Use a thicker impasto in the light-struck areas, smoothing the paint so it catches the light and appears more luminous.

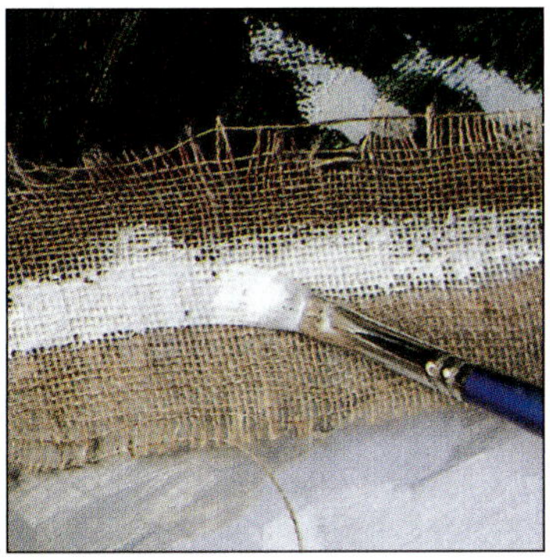

1 The fullness of snow is difficult to describe in paint but using a piece of burlap can achieve marvelous results. Tape the piece of burlap over the support and press a brush well-loaded with paint onto the burlap, forcing it through the fabric. The paint should not be pure white but tinged with the colors of the landscape.

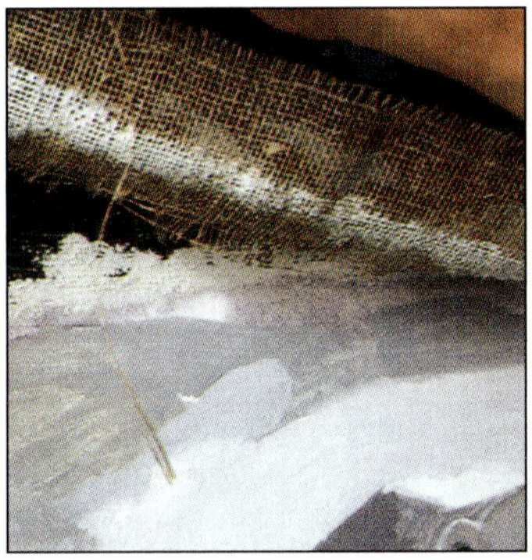

2 Lift the burlap from the painted surface carefully and you should reveal solid areas of paint with soft rather than hard edges.

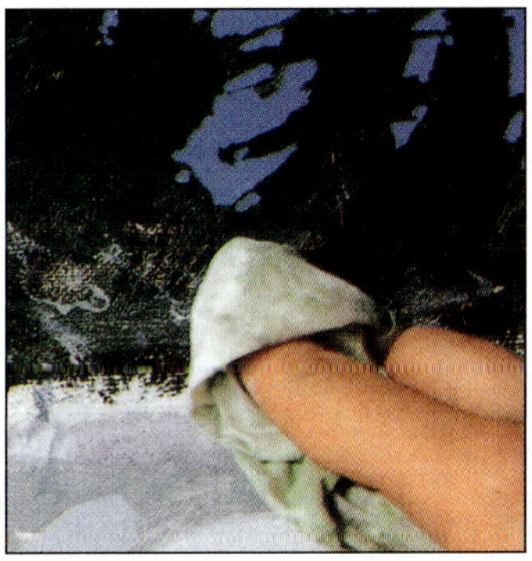

3 Sometimes too much paint gets pushed through the burlap – excess paint can be smudged with a rag.

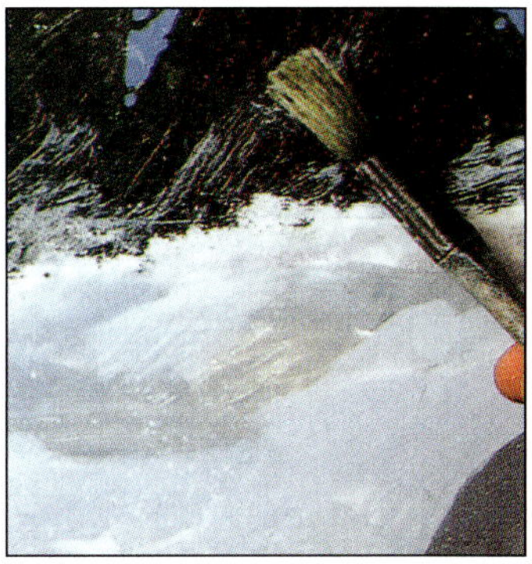

4 To create the effect of distant snow flurries, the artist spatters paint on the dark trees, using a 1 in. (2.5 cm) decorator's brush.

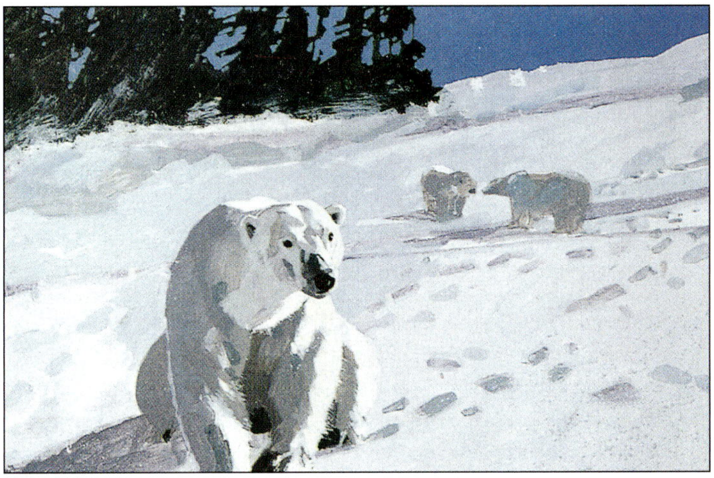

5 With this difficult subject of white on white, the artist has successfully built up the solid form of the bear against the fluffy white background.

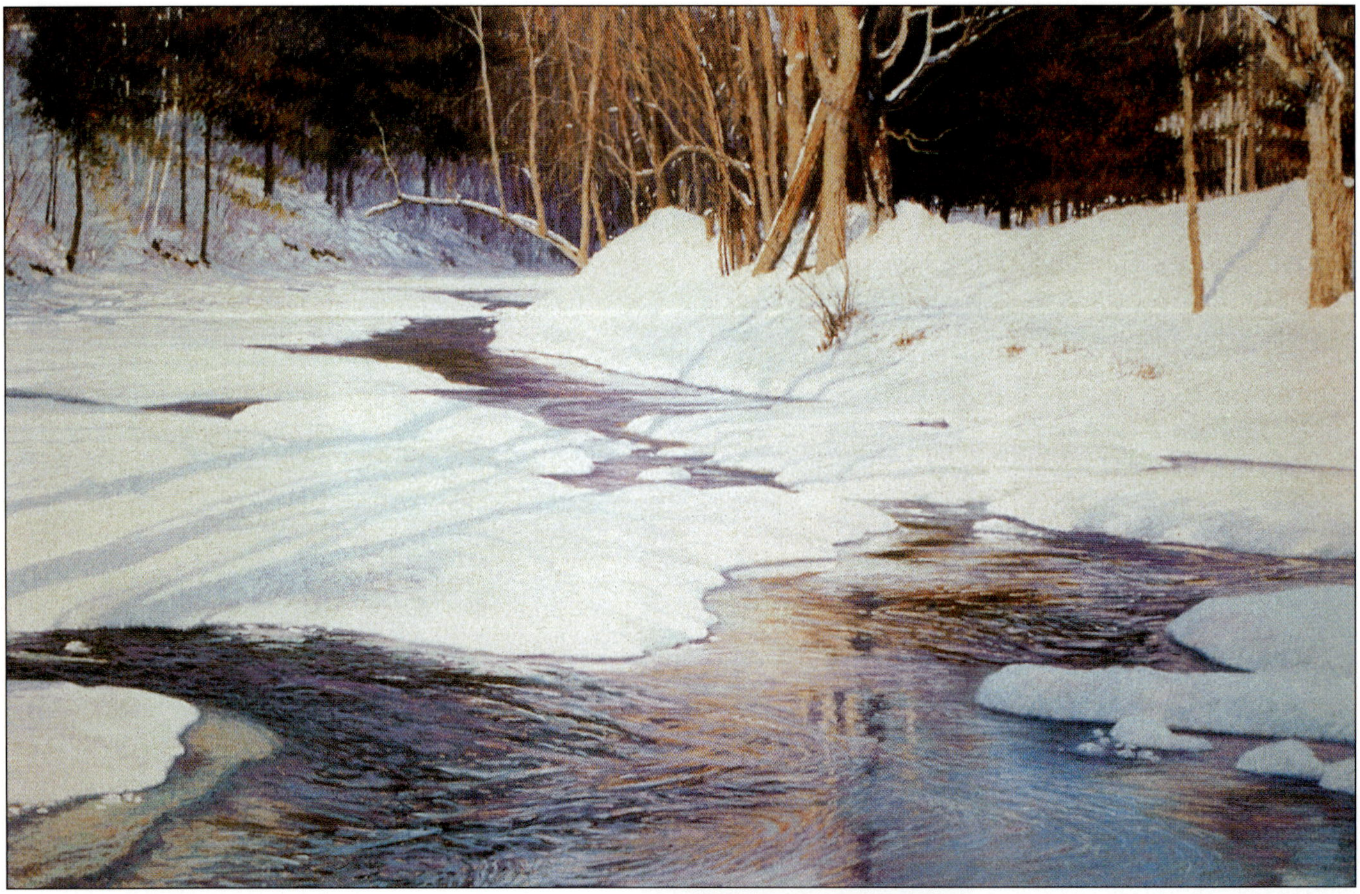

THE WHITE RIVER by Neil Drevitson (soft pastel)

The emphasis is on icy-cold blues reflected in the river and found in the shadows cast on the snow.

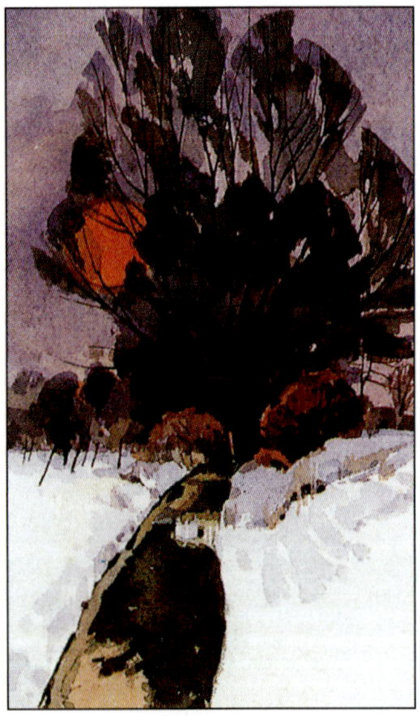

WINTER, SEDGE MOORE by Ronald Jesty RBA (watercolor)

In this bold composition, the dark tree and low, red sun counterpoint the brilliance of the white snow – the paper left uncovered. The brooding purple-gray sky often seen on a late winter afternoon has been exaggerated, both to make a more powerful statement and to provide a warm/cool contrast. The simplification of the tree into broad shapes accentuates the drama of the scene.

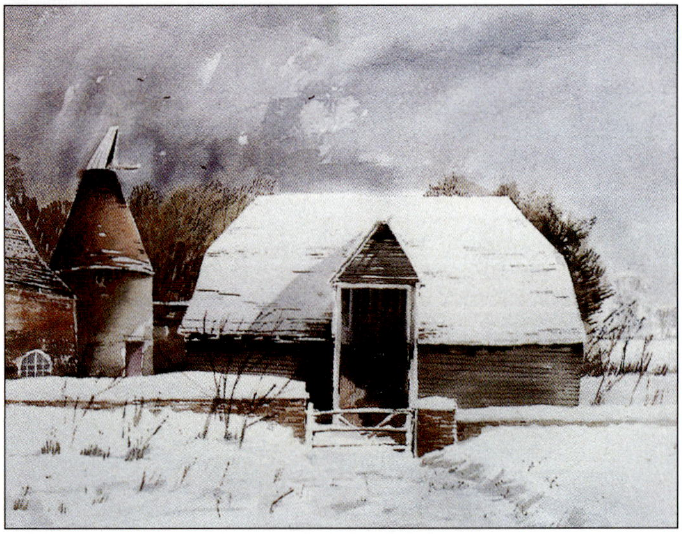

GROVE GREEN FARM by Michael Chaplin RE (watercolor)

We tend to think of snow as always being white, whatever the weather conditions, but the land always reflects color from the sky, and since white surfaces are more reflective than dark ones, snow is a direct mirror of the prevailing light. In this well-observed painting (done on-the-spot, wearing three pairs of socks) there are no whites, only pale and darker grays, emphasized by the warm red-browns of the buildings and trees. The impression of cold is palpable.

Stormy Weather

The tumultuous sky at the height of a storm, rain-drenched trees swaying under the force of the wind – these are exciting to watch and paint. Storms are energetic, so try to suggest movement with agitated brush strokes, or work wet-into-wet to convey the dynamism of clouds moving across the darkened sky.

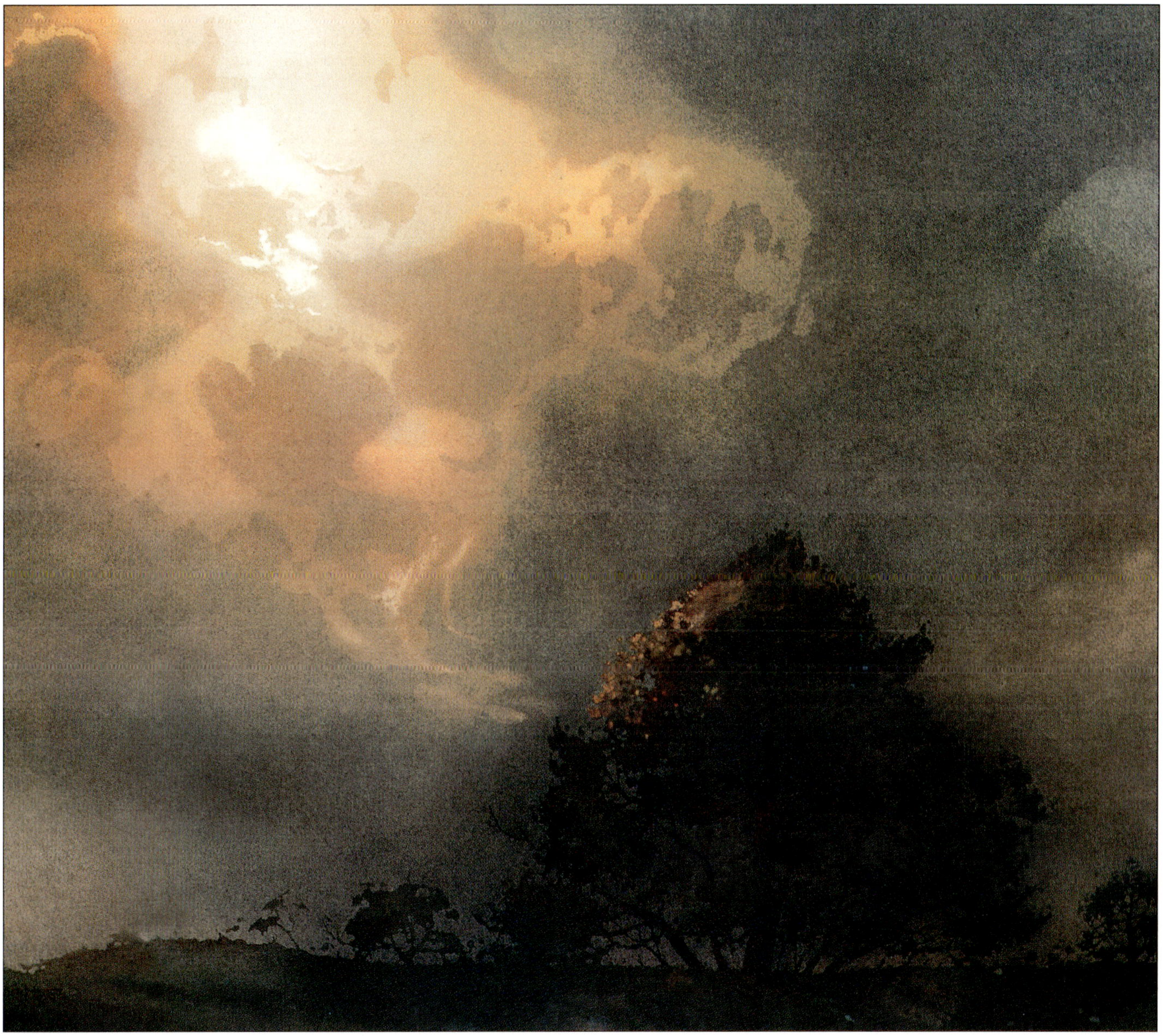

THE TEMPEST by Roland Roycraft (watercolor)

Besides being exciting to paint, skies also play a vital role in landscape composition. Here the sky is the main subject of the painting. Even when the sky occupies only a small part of a picture, you can use clouds (invent them if you wish) to give extra color and movement to a picture.

VARIEGATED WASH

Stormy skies shift and change with the speed of the wind, so a variegated wash is ideal, as the colors themselves move as you lay them. You need to work carefully to prevent a blurred muddle. Choose colors which will provide lights and darks and retain light passages between the dark clouds to create depth. A useful palette might be diluted raw sienna for the lights and mixtures of burnt umber, Indian red, Prussian blue, and indigo for the darks.

If the dark parts are drying too light, drop more pigment in while the wash is still wet. Blooms and backruns that develop may enhance the effect, but if they don't look right leave the wash to dry and lift out unwanted edges with a damp brush.

The following example of a variegated wash is laid on dry paper to maintain control of the light areas between the storm clouds until softening them at the end with opaque white. Strong dark colors are dropped into wet washes and allowed to spread.

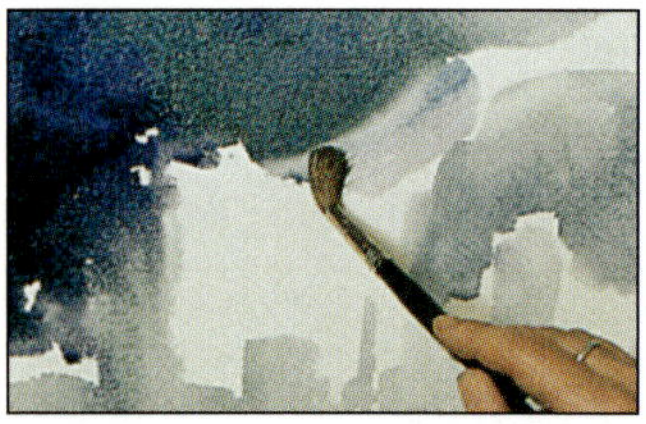

1 Mark in the outline of the buildings with blue-gray. Boldly wash in the clouds with a No. 10 round sable brush, leaving white lights in between.

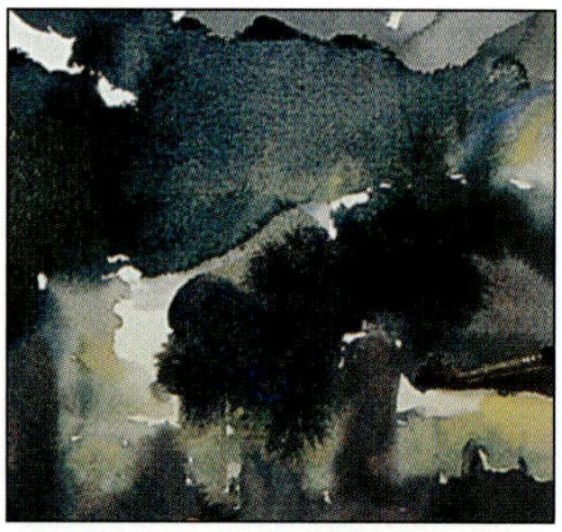

2 Paint a yellow wash into some of the light areas and drop darker color into the cloud bases, wet-into-wet. Strengthen the urban landscape below.

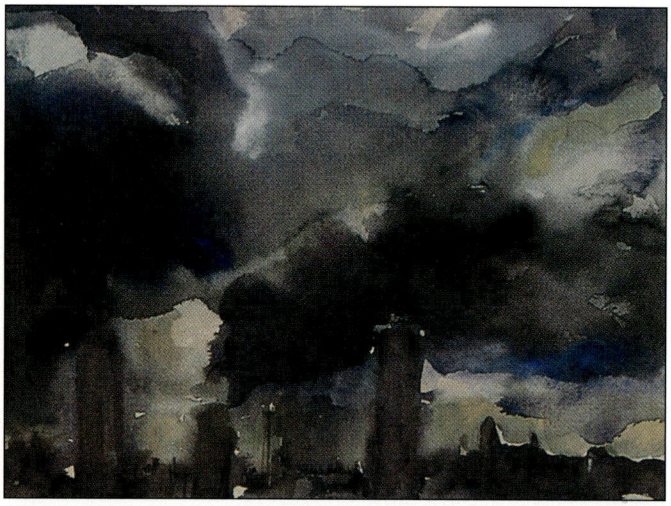

3 Use white bodycolor to create semi-translucent light areas between the clouds. Dab and blot freely throughout the paint, if required.

LIFTING/SCRATCHING OUT

To lighten clouds or suggest sunbeams, use a tissue or dry brush to lift out color while the wash is drying. You will probably need to do this several times, as the wet color will seep back into the shaft of light.

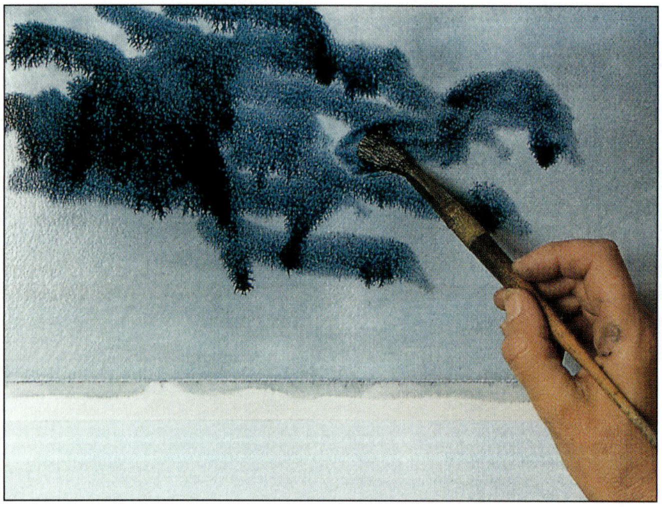

1 Lay a wash of Antwerp blue. Mask the shoreline with tape. Wet the sky area and flood in big sweeps of Payne's gray. Let it dry, and strengthen it in the same way.

Trees and foliage may be dark in the foreground and softly lit in the middle distance. This effect can also be created by lifting out with a tissue or sponge. Lightning streaks can be scratched out using the side of a single-edged razor blade. The darker the background, the brighter the revealed paper will appear.

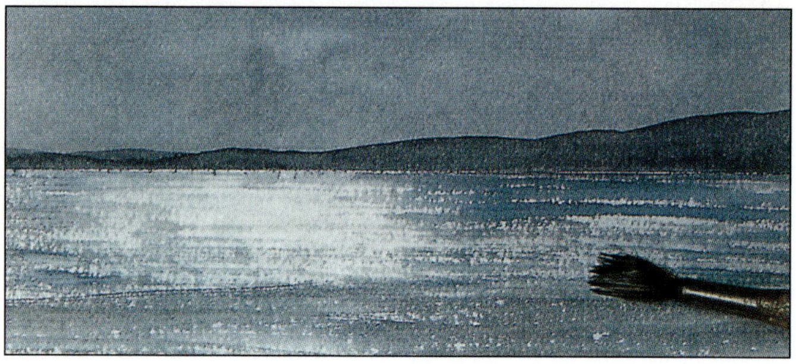

2 Paint the dark hills and create the sparkling water by dragging dry paint across in horizontal streaks.

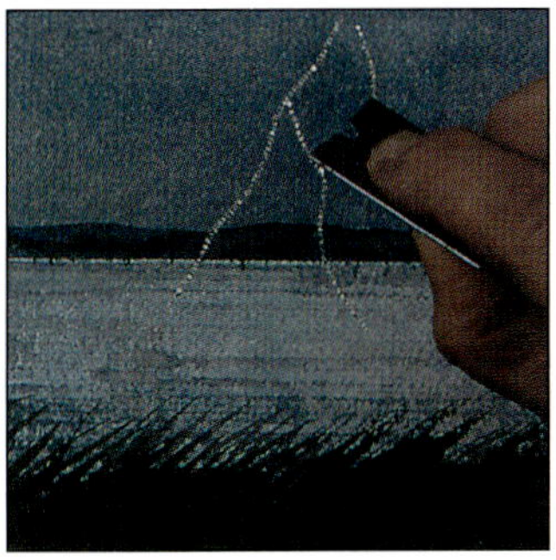

3 Brush in the foreground grasses. Make sure the paper is completely dry before scratching out the streaks of lightning with the edge of the razor-blade.

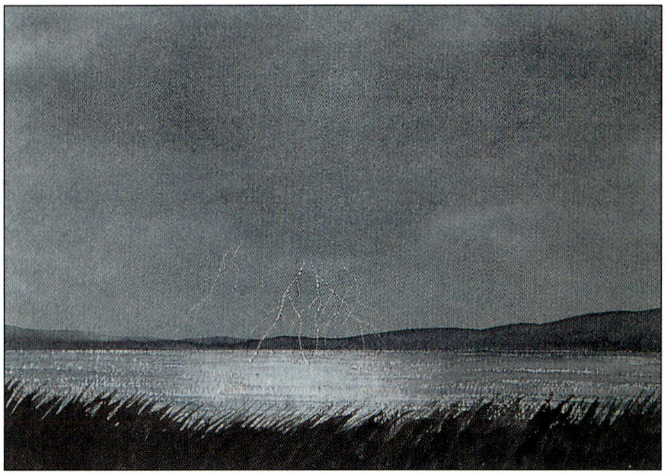

4 Be firm with the blade in order to reveal good, clear, white lines against the dark stormy sky.

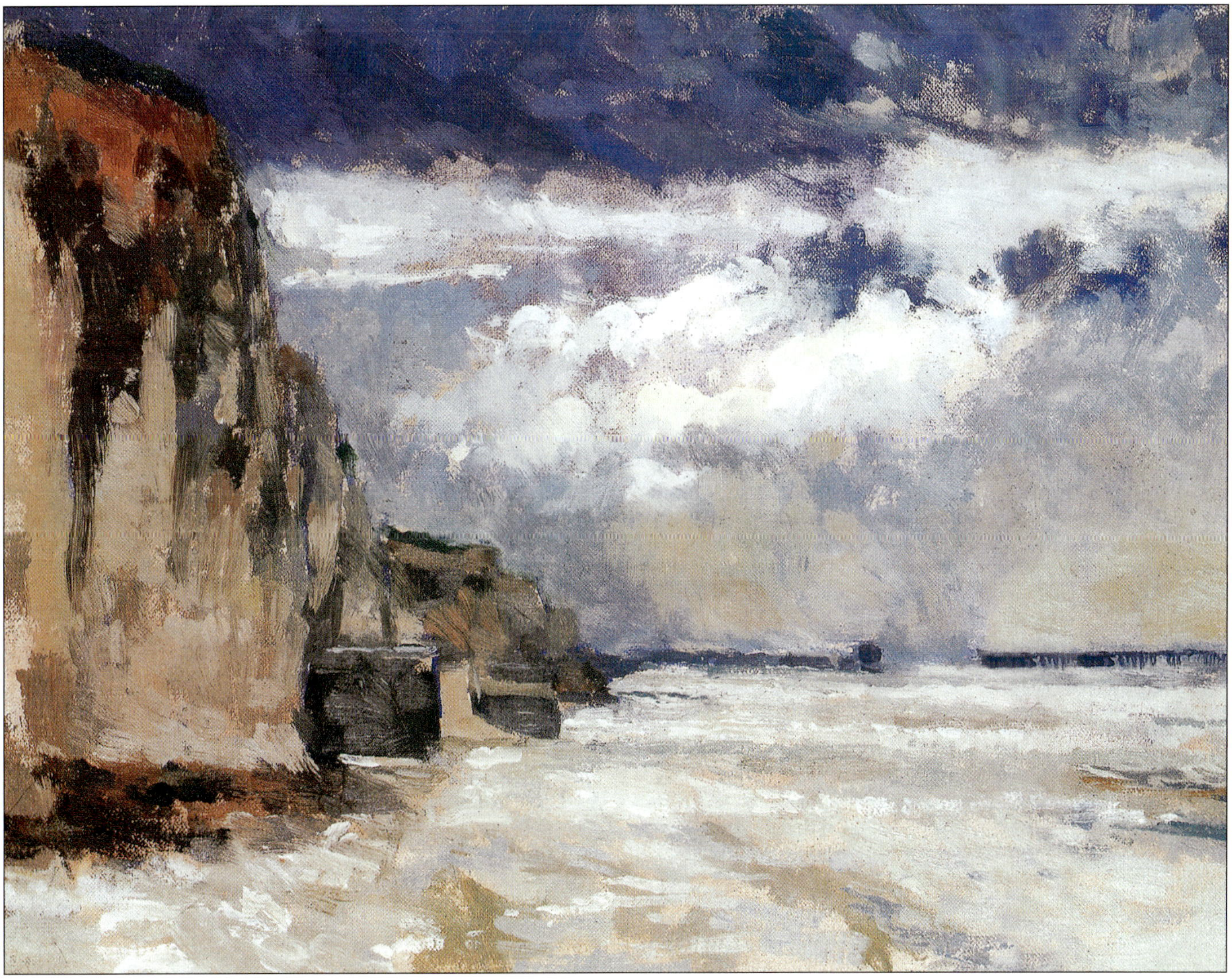

WALPOLE BAY, MARGATE by Pamela Kay (oil)

The artist worked quickly, using directional brush strokes, to create this vigorous image on a blustery day. Note the variety of color in the sky, ranging from white, through yellows, pinks, and blues to deepest indigo.

Skies and Clouds

Skies are a major subject in themselves and demand close observation and a degree of technical know-how. This is partly because of their infinite variety and partly because they are not subject to the same rules that govern the solid earth below.

A mountain, cliff, or tree will change in appearance under different lighting conditions, but its structure will remain stable, while clouds, seemingly solid but in fact composed of nothing but air and moisture, are constantly on the move, forming and re-forming in ways that can only partially be predicted and are never the same twice. Most important of all, the sky is the light source without which the landscape could not exist, and weather conditions above relate directly to the colors, tones, and prevailing mood of the land below. Thus, the surest way to spoil a landscape is by failing to analyze or express this interdependent relationship.

CLEAR SKIES

We tend to think of cloudless skies as simply blue, but in fact they vary widely according to the season and climate. A midsummer's sky in a hot country will be a warm blue, sometimes tending to violet and often surprisingly dark in tone, while a winter sky in a temperate zone is a paler and cooler blue. Nor is a clear sky the same color all over. A frequent mistake is to paint blue skies in one uniform wash, but there are always variations – sometimes slight, but often quite marked. As a general rule, skies are darker and warmer in color at the top and paler and cooler on the horizon, following the same rules of aerial perspective as the land. There is, however, an important exception to this. Sky directly over the sea will absorb particles of moisture, giving a darker band of color at the horizon, and a similar effect can often be seen in cities, where the dark band is caused by smoke, dust, or other pollution.

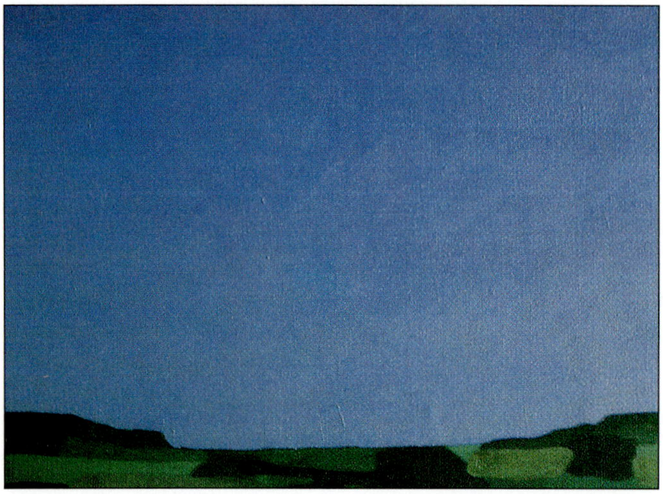

When painting a clear blue sky it is important to get the tones and colors right, in order to achieve a feeling of recession. Think of the sky as a dome, stretching over the landscape, rather than as a flat wall of color. In this oil painting, the artist began at the top of the canvas with a mixture of cerulean blue, titanium white, and a hint of alizarin crimson to give a warm tint to the foreground sky. Toward the horizon the blue becomes progressively cooler, with a hint of yellow ocher added to the color just above the distant hills.

PAINTING A CLEAR SKY USING PASTEL

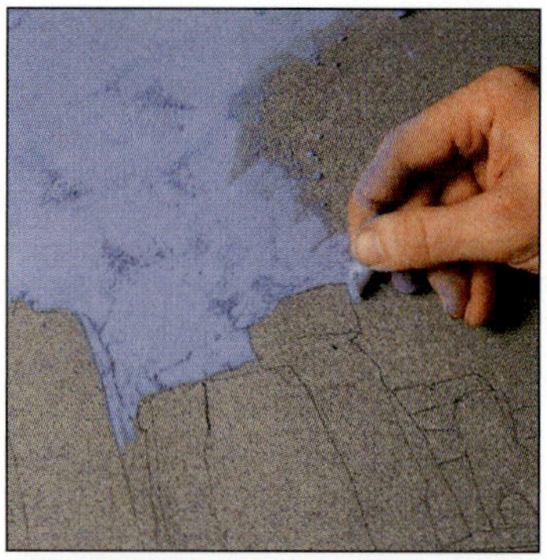

1 Once the pencil outline has been drawn the artist begins to block in the sky color. He is using a pale blue pastel, on its side, and is applying the color thickly.

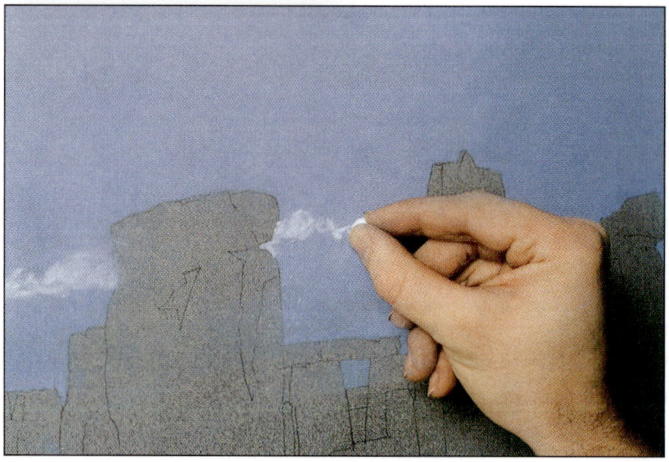

2 The artist then draws in the fluffy white clouds just above the horizon with a white pastel.

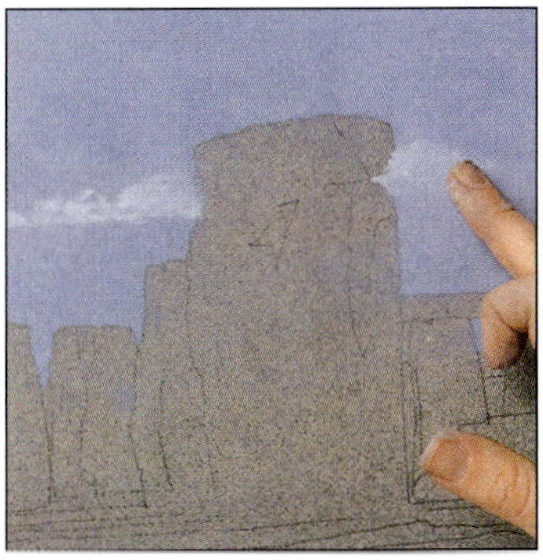

3 The white pastel of the cloud is smudged so that it does not stand out quite so much. In this second detail you can see how the artist has highlighted stone in fine lines, which he has then flicked with a cloth to reduce the sharpness of the line.

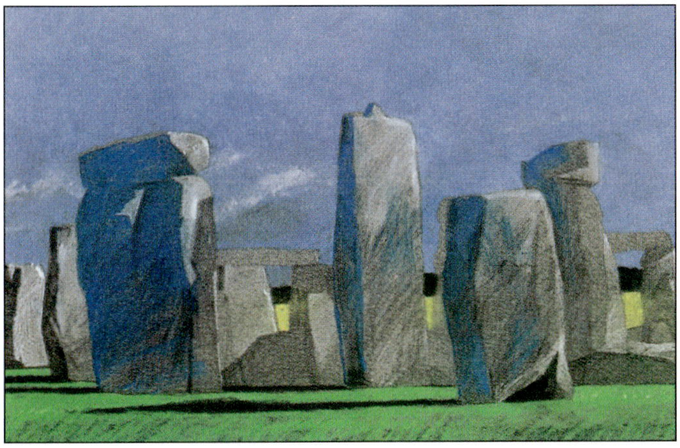

4 In the completed picture you can see how smoothly the blue pastel was applied. The sky contrasts with the texture of the grass and the strongly modeled shapes of the standing stones.

"LEARNING" CLOUDS

There are few people, whether they paint or not, who can fail to be enthralled by cloud effects – great dark thunderheads, delicate "mackerel" skies or the magical effects created by a low evening sun breaking through after a day's rain. Sadly, these effects are fleeting, so the landscape painter needs to be in constant readiness to watch, memorize, and sketch.

The British painter John Constable (1776–1837) was fascinated by skies and well understood their leading role in landscape painting. He made endless oil sketches of nothing but skies. Often these were done in a few minutes, but provided him with a storehouse of information that he drew on for his finished paintings. Such quick studies provide the ideal means of recording these transient effects: even a rapid pencil sketch of cloud shapes with written notes of the colors will act as an *aide-mémoire* and help you to observe constructively.

Photographs are also useful in this context, as long as you use them as part of a learning process and not as models to copy for a painting.

CIRRUS CLOUDS

Feathery streaks of white cloud, high in the sky, are associated with hot summer days. Handle these clouds with restraint, blending them slightly into the sky color so that they don't appear to be "pasted on." Scumbling and dry brush are perfect techniques for rendering this type of cloud.

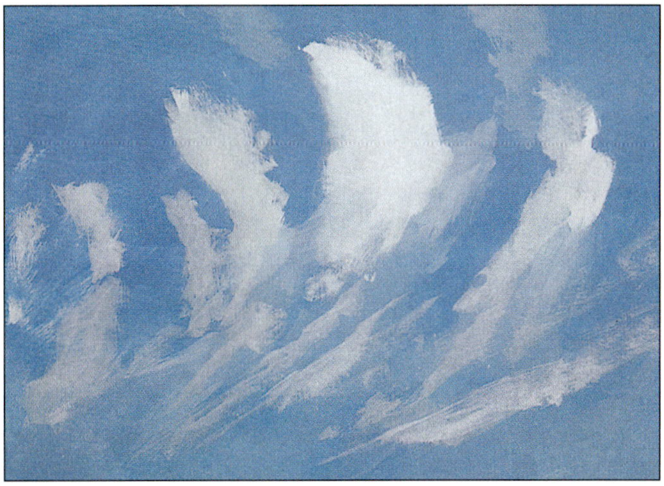

1 Oil paint is an excellent medium for rendering skies and atmospheric effects. In this painting the artist works wet-into-wet with thin veils of color to recreate the soft, vaporous nature of cirrus clouds.

If you are working outdoors, the drying time of oil paints can be reduced by mixing alkyd white or gel medium with your colors.

The artist begins by laying in the sky color with a mixture of cerulean blue and titanium white. When this is almost dry, the shapes of the cirrus clouds are blocked in roughly with a lighter version of the sky color, diluted to a thin consistency. Following the upward sweep of the clouds, the artist applies rapid dry brush strokes with a flat bristle brush. To create these semi-opaque veils of color, the artist keeps the brush starved of paint and works with a very light touch. The larger sunlit areas of cloud are then painted with titanium white, applied a little more thickly.

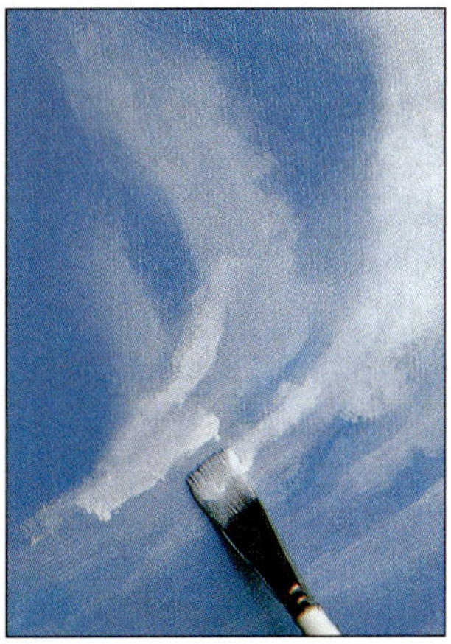

2 The artist now refines the shapes he has created. With a brush dipped in turpentine, he softens and blends the feathery clouds so that they merge with the sky tone to create a hazy appearance. Then the thicker, brighter areas of cloud are painted with opaque layers of titanium white.

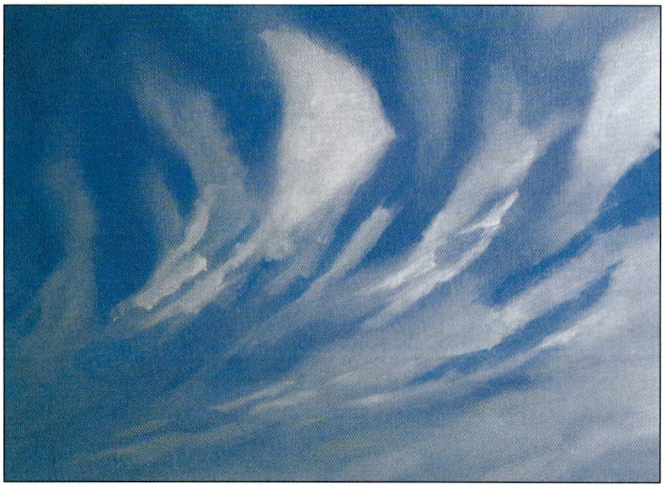

3 The completed study shows how softly blended passages create the effect of thin, vaporous clouds, whereas thicker strokes of color bring some clouds forward. The clouds appear as part of the sky, rather than painted on it. Cirrus clouds often have a powerful diagonal pattern which can be exploited to great effect in a painting.

CUMULUS CLOUDS

Those heaped, white clouds that often herald rain are called cumulus. Such clouds are wonderful to look at, and much can be learned by observing them closely and making sketches before attempting to paint them.

Cumulus cloud formations are usually well-defined, with distinct planes of light and shadow. During the day, the upper part of the cloud is bright and luminous, with a definite scalloped edge, whereas the underside is flatter and darker (at sunset the clouds are lit from below, so they glow underneath while being dark on top).

The three-dimensional appearance of clouds can be emphasized by modeling them with warm and cool colors. The lit planes of clouds are rarely a stark white; they may contain subtle hints of yellow, pink, and blue, depending on the weather and the time of day. Similarly, the shadows on clouds are not battleship gray, but contain a variety of blues, reds, browns, and violets.

Pay careful attention to the edges of the clouds, making sure that they appear to blend naturally into the atmosphere. This can be achieved by blending wet-into-wet, or by scumbling the cloud colors over the sky color, so that they melt softly together. Do, however, include a few hard edges for definition; otherwise the clouds tend to look like balls of cotton wool.

Another important point to remember is that the laws of perspective apply to clouds, just as they do to landscapes. Clouds appear to become smaller and closer together as they disappear toward the horizon; they also become cooler and more neutral in color and their forms soften.

USING WATERCOLOR

Cloud shapes can change very quickly and the fluidity of watercolor allows you to work with great spontaneity and achieve delightful, rapid effects.

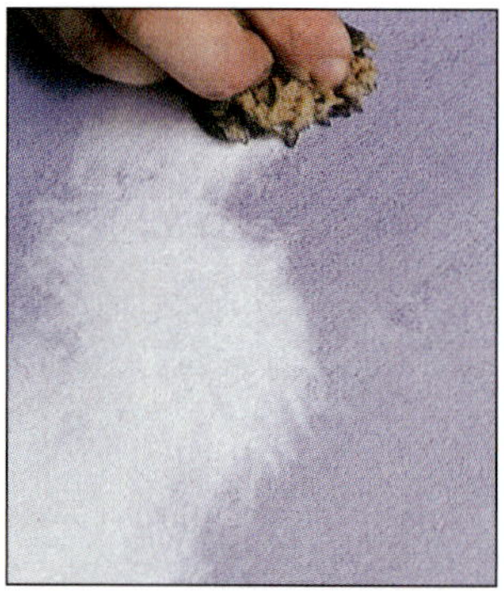

1 The artist works on a stretched sheet of 200 lb Bockingford paper, dampened with a sponge and clear water. He first lays a flat wash of cobalt blue for the sky, using a No. 8 Dalon brush. While the wash is still wet, a small natural sponge is used to lift out the cloud shapes.

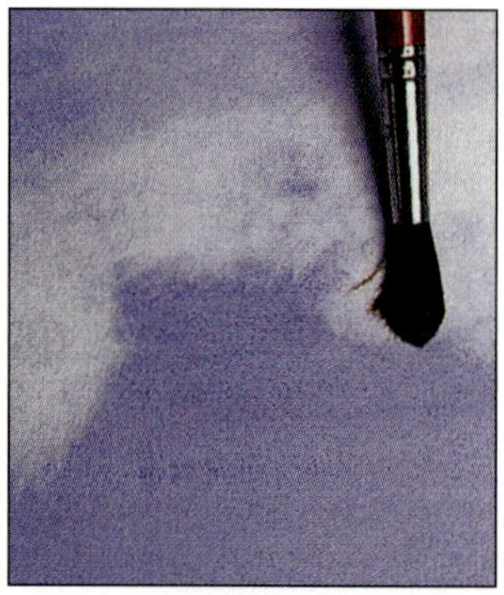

2 This detail shows the artist using a soft round brush to make scumbled strokes at the edges of the clouds.

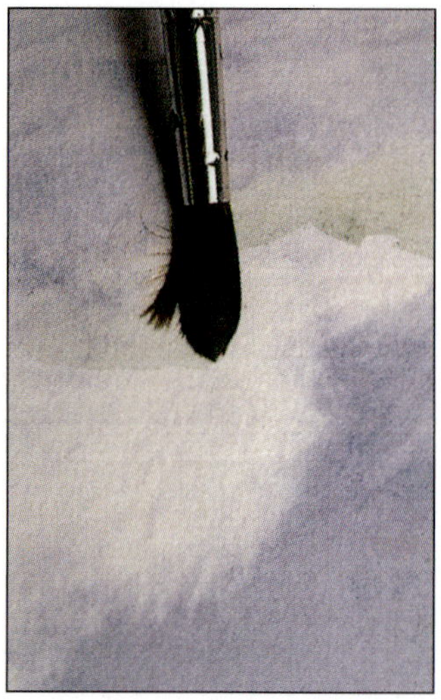

3 While the paper is still damp, a pale wash of Payne's gray and cadmium yellow is brushed into the lower, shadowed edge of the cloud, then softened and blended with clear water. The brush is rolled over the surface of the paper, suggesting the rhythm of the clouds and their heaped texture. When mixing the shadow color, remember to allow for the fact that it will dry much lighter in tone than when wet. Only the brightest, sunlit tops of the clouds are left as bare white paper.

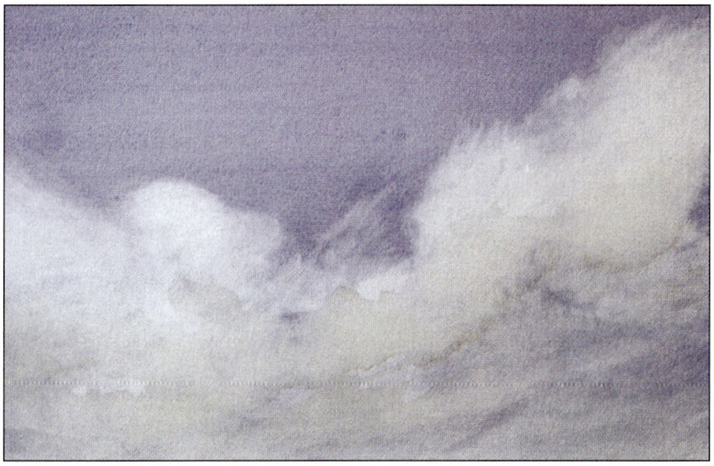

4 The finished effect. The upper part of the cloud is brighter and better defined than the lower part, which is darker and more ragged. The combination of warm and cool colors gives a rounded, three-dimensional feel to the clouds. Note, too, how the smaller clouds beneath give a suggestion of depth and perspective, and how the light scumbled strokes convey a sense of movement.

CLOUDS IN COMPOSITION

The possibilities of using clouds as an integral part of a composition are often ignored, which seems strange in view of the fact that skies are often the dominant element in a landscape. But the landscape painter must tackle this problem – clouds form exciting shapes in themselves, and these can be manipulated or exaggerated to add extra movement and drama to a subject. Shapes in the sky can also be planned to provide a balance for those in the foreground or middle distance, such as clumps of trees or rounded hills, and if colors as well as shapes are repeated from sky to land, the two parts of the painting will come together to form a satisfying whole. Since the sky is reflected to some extent in the land below, you will often see touches of blue or violet from the undersides of clouds occurring again in shadows or distant hills.

Not all paintings, of course, need this kind of sky interest. A mountain scene, for instance, or winter trees in stark silhouette, will be more successful if the sky is allowed to take second place, but a flat landscape can often be saved from dullness by an eventful sky, so keep a special sketchbook for recording cloud effects so that you can use them in landscapes painted indoors. Skies are very difficult to recreate from memory alone, so in addition to sketches, you could also use photographs of skies.

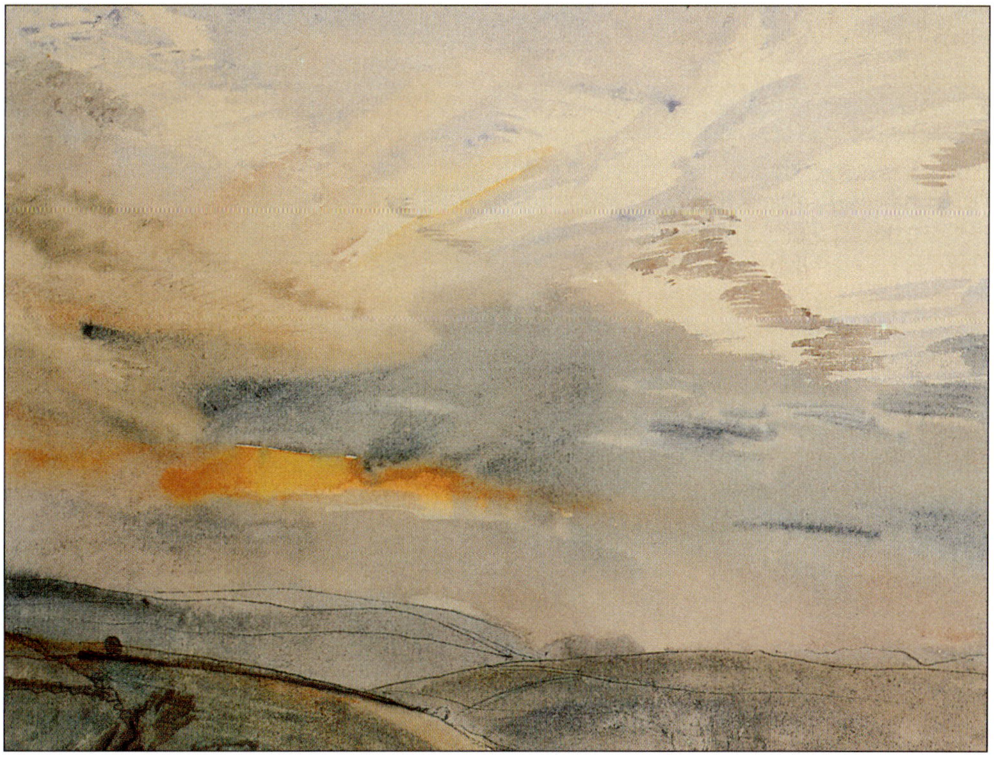

SUNSET, SOUTH DOWNS by Charles Knight (watercolor and pencil)

In this painting, the sky is virtually the whole composition, with the hills and fields serving as an anchor to the movement above. Much of the sky and foreground has been painted wet-into-wet, and in the central area the orange and gray washes have been allowed to flood together, giving a realistically soft effect. But the artist has not overdone the technique: below the orange patch there are clearer, harder edges, which are echoed by the crisp pencil lines defining the hills below, and the small clouds toward the top have been worked wet on dry.

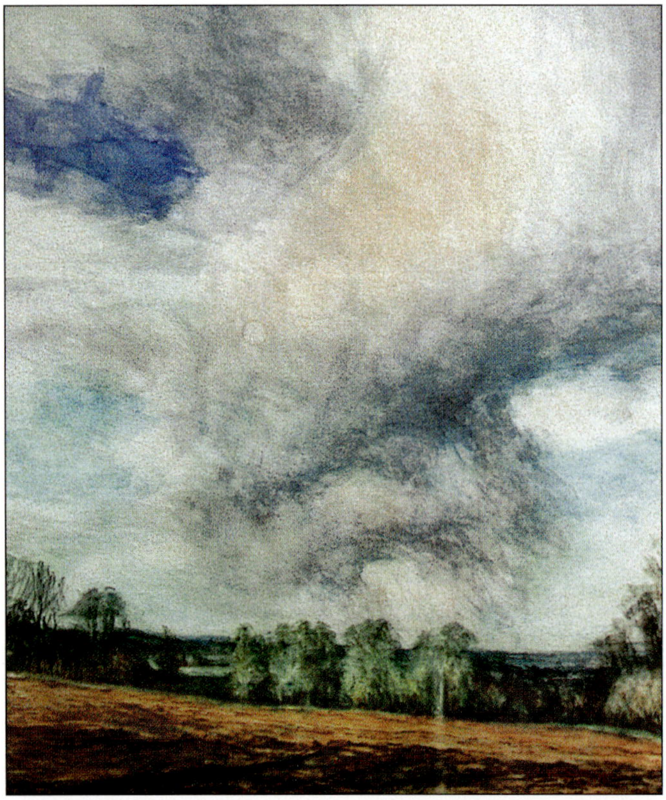

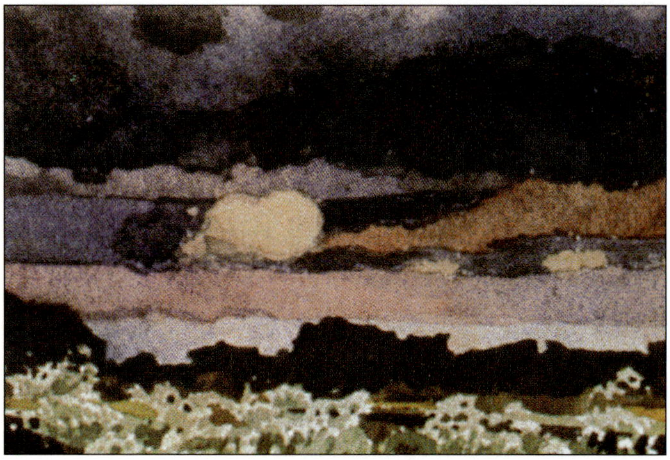

CLOUD STUDY by Ronald Jesty RBA (watercolor)

This dramatic painting, although giving the appearance of a planned and studio-composed piece, was in fact a study sketch made on-the-spot after a storm – which just goes to show that nature will do at least some of the composing if you are receptive enough to her suggestions. The painting is quite small and was done quickly, of necessity, with superimposed washes and the dark clouds at the top painted wet-into-wet. Wet paint was lifted out in places and the white cow parsley was suggested by stippling around the shapes with the point of a brush.

SPRING SHOWER by Donald Pass (watercolor)

This is the perfect example of clouds used as an integral part of a composition. The painting is full of movement, and our eye is encouraged to travel around it as we follow the direction of the dramatic, curving cloud – up to the right, around to the left, and then downward through the bright patches of blue to the sunlit trees. The artist has tied the sky to the land both by using the same kind of brushwork throughout the picture and by echoing shapes. The vertical cloud seems a logical extension of the central group of trees.

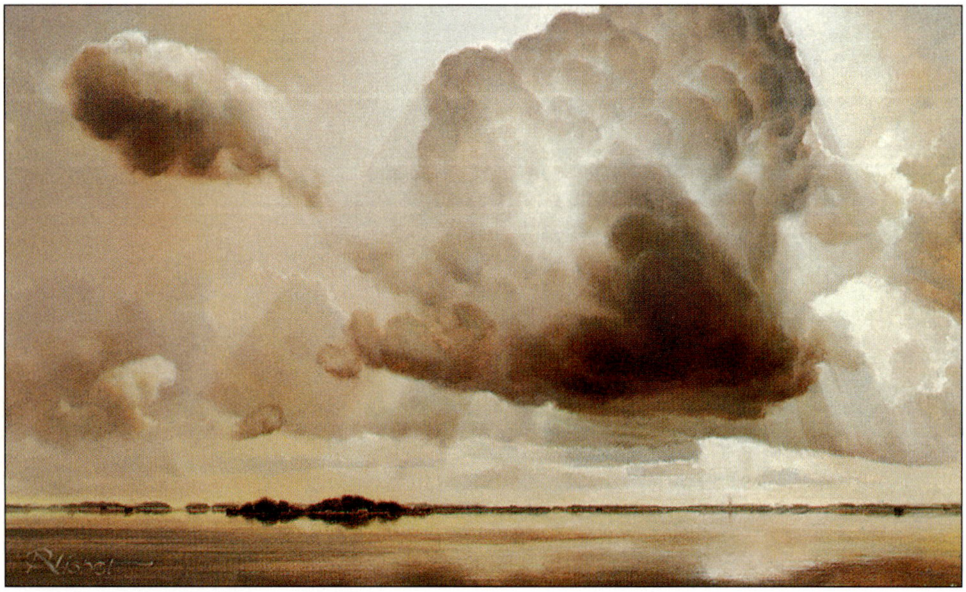

LIGHT WEIGHTS by P. A. Nisbet (oil)

Peter Nisbet has been fascinated by skies all his life and now spends much of his time painting them.

CLOUD FORMATIONS

Clouds are always on the move – gathering, dispersing, forming, and re-forming – but they do not behave in a random way. There are different types of cloud, each with its own individual structure and characteristics. It is not necessary to know the name of each and every type, but to paint clouds convincingly you need to recognize the differences. It is also helpful to realize that they form on different levels, because this affects their tones and colors.

Cirrus clouds (see page 475), high in the sky, are fine and vaporous, forming delicate, feathery plumes where they are blown by the wind. The two types of cloud that form on the lowest level are cumulus clouds (see page 476), with horizontal bases and cauliflower-like tops, and storm clouds (or thunderclouds) – great, heavy masses that rise up vertically, often resembling mountains or towers. Both these low-level clouds show strong contrasts of light and dark. A storm cloud will sometimes look almost black against a blue sky, and cumulus clouds are extremely bright where the sun strikes them and surprisingly dark on their shadowed undersides. Between these two extremes of high and low, there is often an intermediate level of cloud with gentler contrasts than the low layer, so a single sky with a mixture of all these types of clouds can present a fascinating ready-made composition of varied shapes and colors.

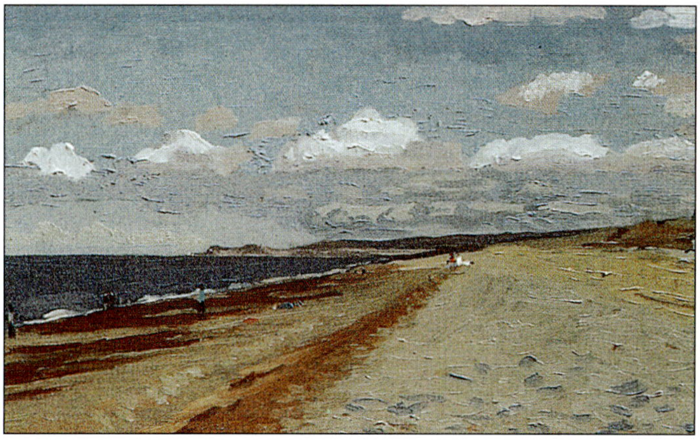

CLEY BEACH by Jeremy Galton (oil)

The regular, repeating pattern made by the little processions of white-capped cumulus drifting over the headland is so eye-catching that it might have completely dominated the picture. However, balance is provided by the near-central white figures and the touches of crisp impasto in the foreground.

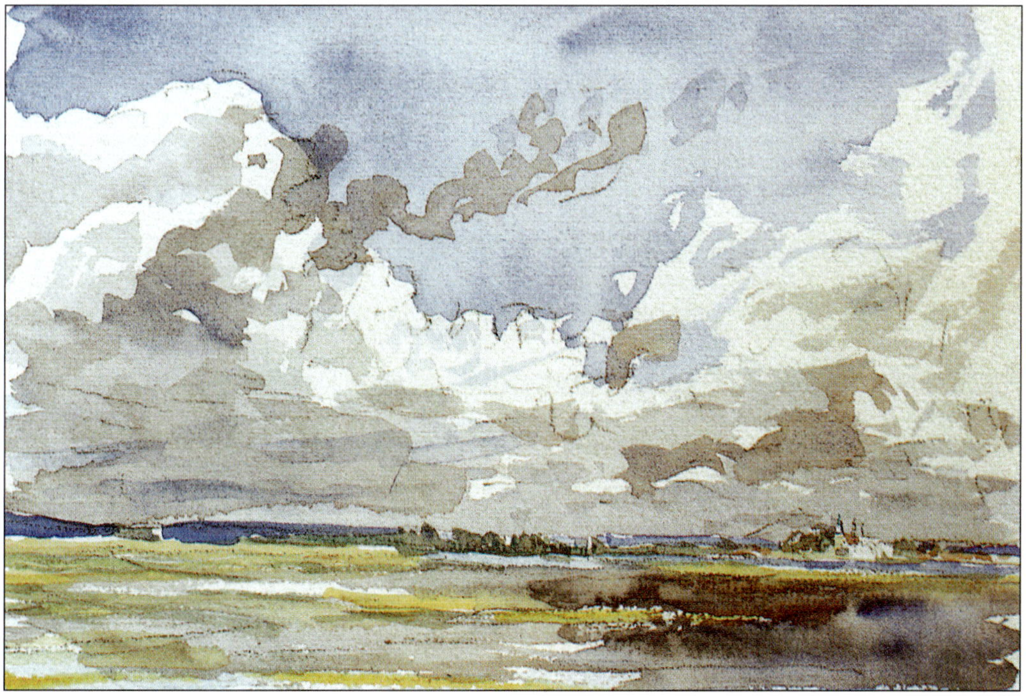

BOSHAM CLOUDS by Christopher Baker (watercolor and conté crayon)

The light conté-crayon drawing made to establish the main shapes has been deliberately used as part of the painting. Working on rag paper, which gives a pleasing texture to the picture surface, Baker has worked swiftly, with almost no overpainting. The subtle warm grays of the clouds were achieved by mixtures of ultramarine and light red, with some viridian and raw sienna in places.

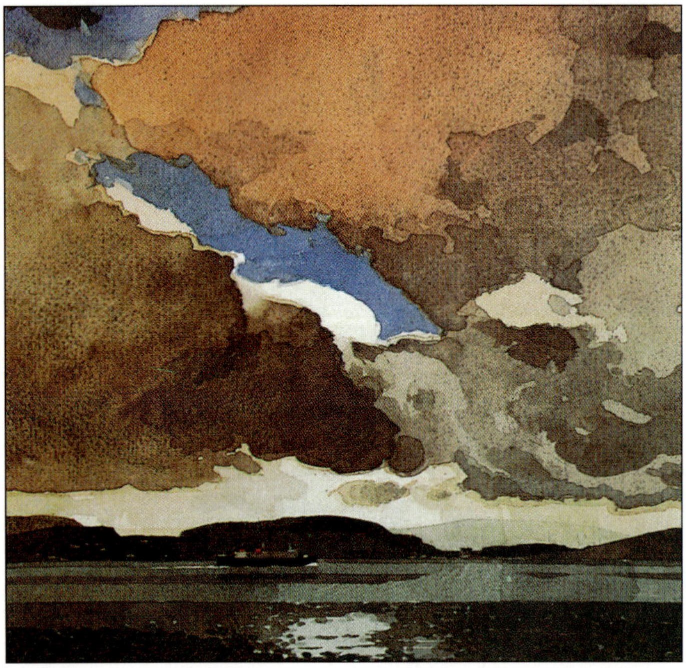

OUT OF OBAN by Ronald Jesty (watercolor)

This dramatic cloud study was painted in the studio from a pen sketch. Built up entirely by means of superimposed washes painted wet on dry, the colors are nevertheless fresh and clear. Although many watercolorists avoid overlaying washes for subjects such as these, which are easily spoiled by too great a build-up of paint, Jesty succeeds because he takes care to make his first washes as positive as possible. Notice the granulated paint in the clouds caused by laying a wet wash over a previous dry one, an effect often used to add extra surface interest.

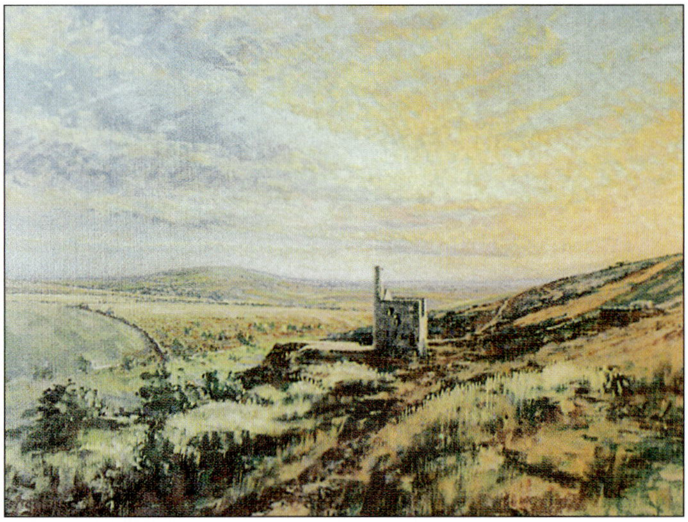

WHEAL BETSY, DARTMOOR by Lionel Aggett (pastel)

Pastel is a sympathetic medium for describing cloud formations, its softness contributing to the atmospheric elements and its range of luminous hues suited to capturing the varied qualities of natural light. The technique of using broken color enables the artist to deal with transient light effects.

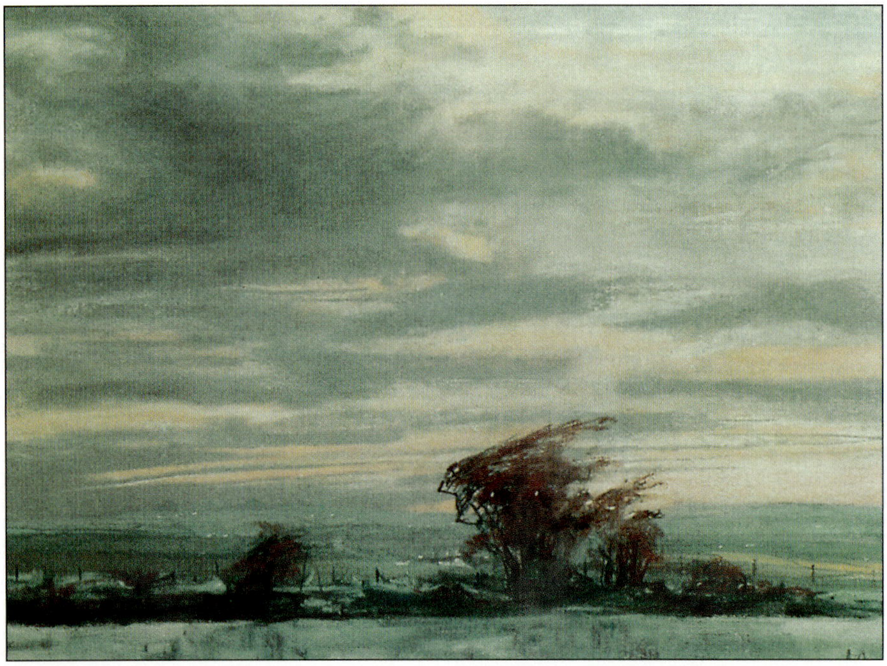

FEN LANDSCAPE by Geoff Marsters (pastel)

There is a grand impression of space in this landscape, partly due to the use of aerial perspective – the background trees are light compared with the central tree – and partly to the careful observation of the clouds. The largest cloud is at the top of the sky, with the horizontal bands of cloud becoming closer near the horizon.

Sunsets

The glorious descent of the sun is a subject that cannot fail to appeal, but it is a difficult time for the artist, as it all happens so fast.

The sunset doesn't end when the sun has gone down. The clouds turn redder and the whole sky glows. Rather than trying to capture the very moment when the sun is sinking, spend that time watching the sunset. Make a pencil sketch of the composition of the sky, with color notes about the lightest and darkest clouds, and the color they appear in front of the sun, then do the actual painting after the sun has gone. The arrangement of the clouds will remain similar.

When painting sunsets and sunrises, the most common mistake is to pile on too many pinks, oranges, and reds; this only results in the clichéd image often found on cheap postcards. The secret of success is to use your hot colors sparingly. Interwoven with the cool blues, grays, and violets in the rest of the sky, and offset by a shadowy landscape, the warm hues will take on a subtle, translucent glow.

Exercise restraint with your brushwork and be selective with your colors. It is tempting to put in every little streak of color – and more – but the result is fussy and amateurish. It is far better to understate the patterns in the sky, thereby creating an air of mystery and calm.

On this and the following page are three examples of how to create a realistic sunset.

LIFTING OUT

Soaking up color with a tissue, or loosening dry washes with a damp bristle brush and then dabbing them with a tissue, enables you to lift light clouds out of a darker wash without having to plan them beforehand.

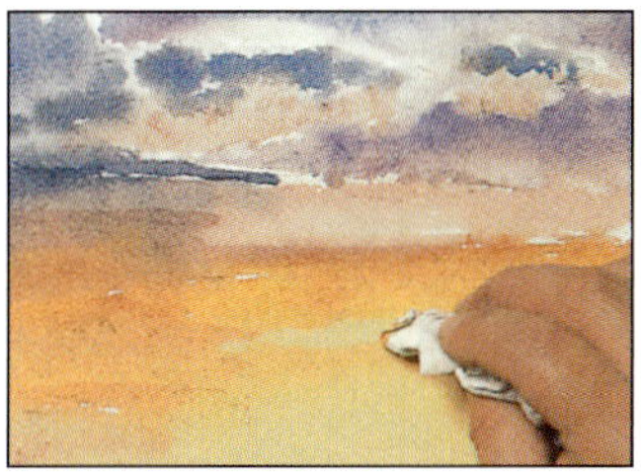

1 Loosely paint the cloud forms. Drop in darker color, wet-into-wet. Lift out cloud layers with a tissue before the wash dries.

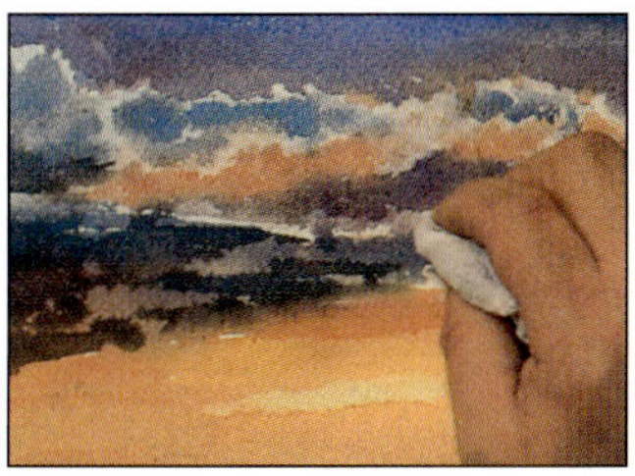

2 Loosen the edges of dried washes with a damp bristle brush before lifting out the color of background clouds with a tissue.

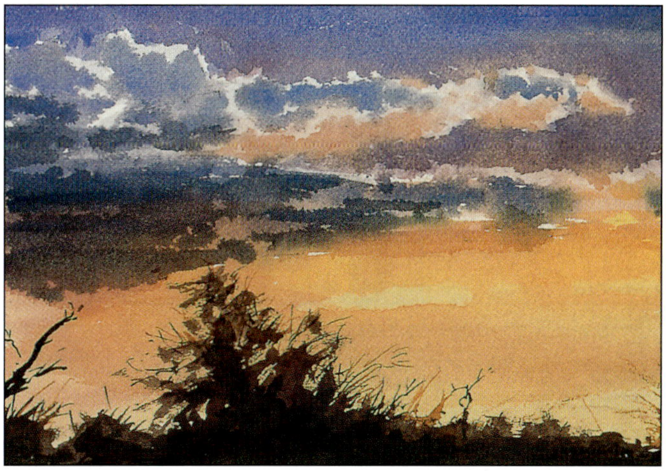

3 Touch in the landscape with indigo, but use Indian red for the branches that glow orange against the molten sky.

GRADUATED WASH

Mix up plenty of burnt sienna in the palette, and lay the wash on dampened paper. Grade the wash so that it is darker in the middle around the horizon, i.e. light, darker, lighter.

1 Mask out the sun and the reflection. Lay the graduated wash and, while damp, wash in some ultramarine blue to cool the color of the sea. Next, darken the horizon area, while wet, with more burnt sienna.

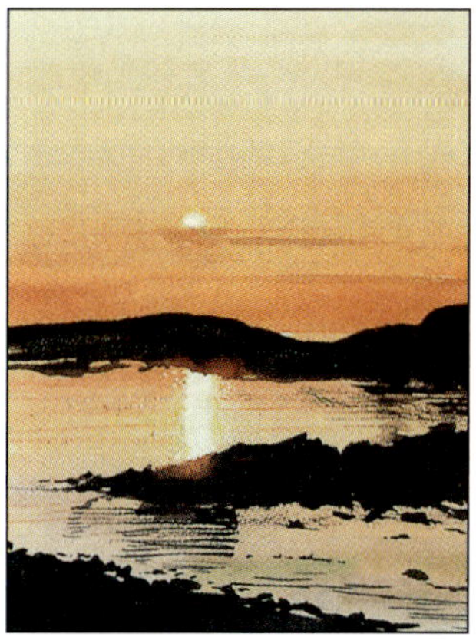

2 Touch a little burnt sienna into the dark rocks. Paint the ripples with horizontal dry brush strokes and, after rubbing off the masking, tint the edges of the reflection and the sun with yellow.

VARIEGATED WASH

Work down the paper with single applications of color and no reworking. Drop in narrow lines of cloud while wet, and lay rocks and foreground when dry. Note that the sea will reflect the color of the sky.

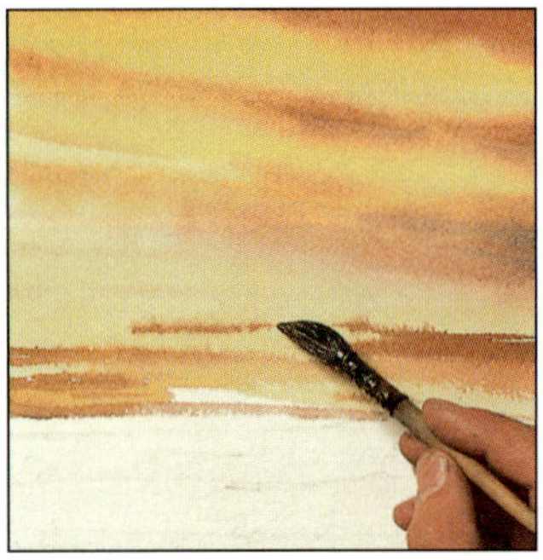

1 Dampen the paper and lay alternate bands of Indian red and Indian yellow, introducing violet. While wet, draw thin horizontal clouds with the tip of the brush.

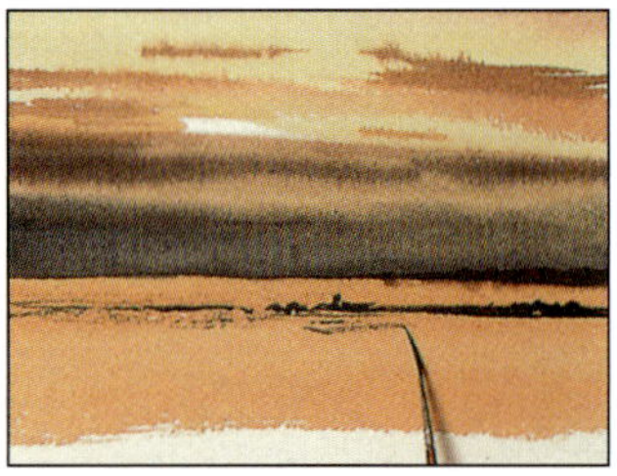

2 Create the cloud-bank on the horizon with a band of raw sienna and indigo, painted while the wash above is still wet. Only paint the sea wash when this is dry. Touch in the rocks with a rigger.

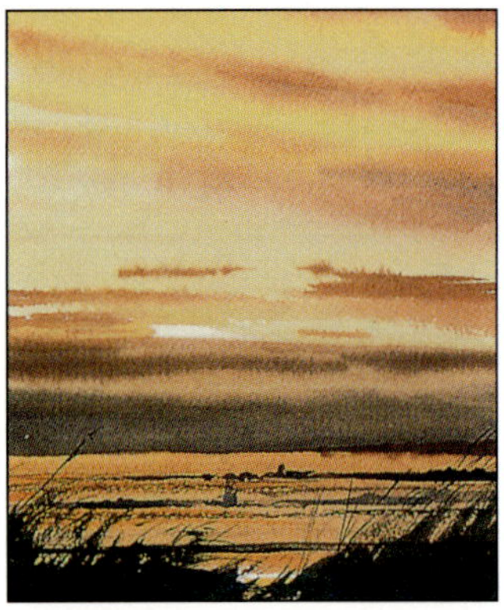

3 Paint the wavelines with a lighter tone than the rocks, and brush in the grasses with dry brush strokes.

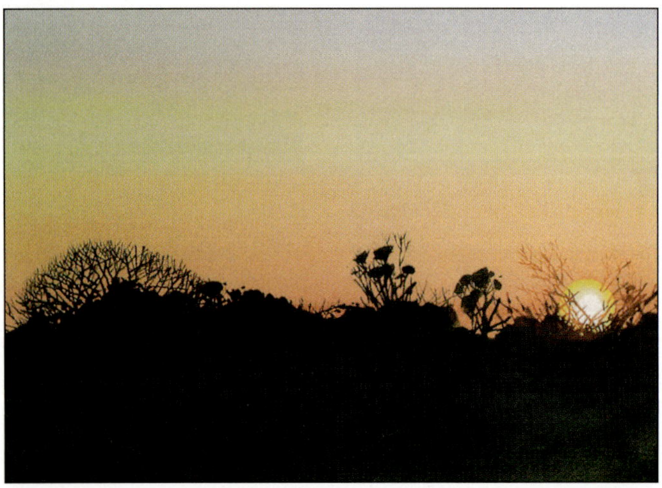

SUNSET IN WATERCOLOR

In the painting on the bottom left corner of this page, the artist uses delicate watercolor washes to describe the glowing, translucent quality of the sky at the point just before the sun sinks below the horizon. The dark silhouette of the landscape and trees helps to heighten the warm glow of the sky's colors.

The artist began by establishing the position of the horizon and the setting sun with very light pencil marks. He then used masking fluid to block out the round shape of the sun before painting the sky. When dry, the masking fluid would allow the sky washes to be brushed in freely, without the artist having to work carefully around the shape of the sun and possibly spoiling the clarity of the sky.

When the masking fluid had dried, the artist dampened the paper and covered the entire area with a graduated wash of color for the sky. Ultramarine (a warm blue) was brushed across the top of the paper, then a pale tint of lemon yellow beneath it, and finally a mixture of alizarin crimson and lemon yellow near the horizon. Each band of color was applied separately, leaving a narrow space between them. The colors spread outward and melted softly into each other where they met on the damp paper, but without running out of control.

When the sky wash was completely dry, the artist brushed in a loose wash of ivory black for the foreground, lifting out color here and there to create texture and tonal variety. Using the tip of a No. 2 brush, he then painted the delicate silhouettes of the trees against the sky.

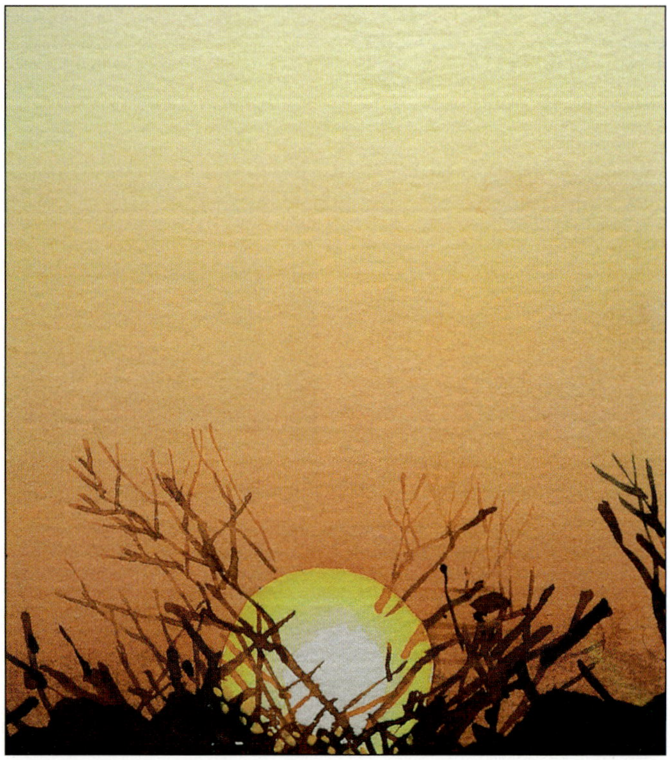

BRIGHT SUNSHINE

When painting a scene bathed in bright sunshine, it is all too easy to become "blinded" by the intensity of color and light. The result is that the painting becomes too high in key overall, lacks tonal contrast, and generally looks washed out. Interestingly, the secret of creating the effect of bright sunlight lies in painting the shadows. Light looks even brighter when surrounded by darks, which is why many artists employ the compositional device of throwing a shadow across the foreground and placing a small, brightly lit area in the middle ground. The viewer's eye instinctively focuses on that spot of bright light, and the scene looks sunny, even though most of it is in shadow.

When the sun is at its most intense, the color of the light itself affects the local colors of the objects it strikes, often quite dramatically. Everything the sun hits becomes lighter and warmer in tone, while shadows are correspondingly cool because they reflect the blue of the sky. Balance bright, warm colors with deep, cool shadows so that they intensify each other and create strong tonal contrasts that spell "sunshine."

Another important point to watch out for is the reflected light in shadows. On a sunny day, there is so much light about that it bounces from one object to another. Thus, the shadow side of a white house may look blue, reflecting the sky, or it may be tinged with green if there are trees nearby. Being aware of subtle points like this will lend greater luminosity to your painting.

Brushwork techniques also contribute to the atmosphere of the painting. In opaque media, always paint the shadows thinly and use thick impasto (which reflects a lot of light) for painting light-toned areas. In watercolor, the bleaching effect of the sun is rendered simply and effectively by leaving white shapes for highlights. Remember also that intense sunlight diminishes sharp details, so use softened brushwork in some areas.

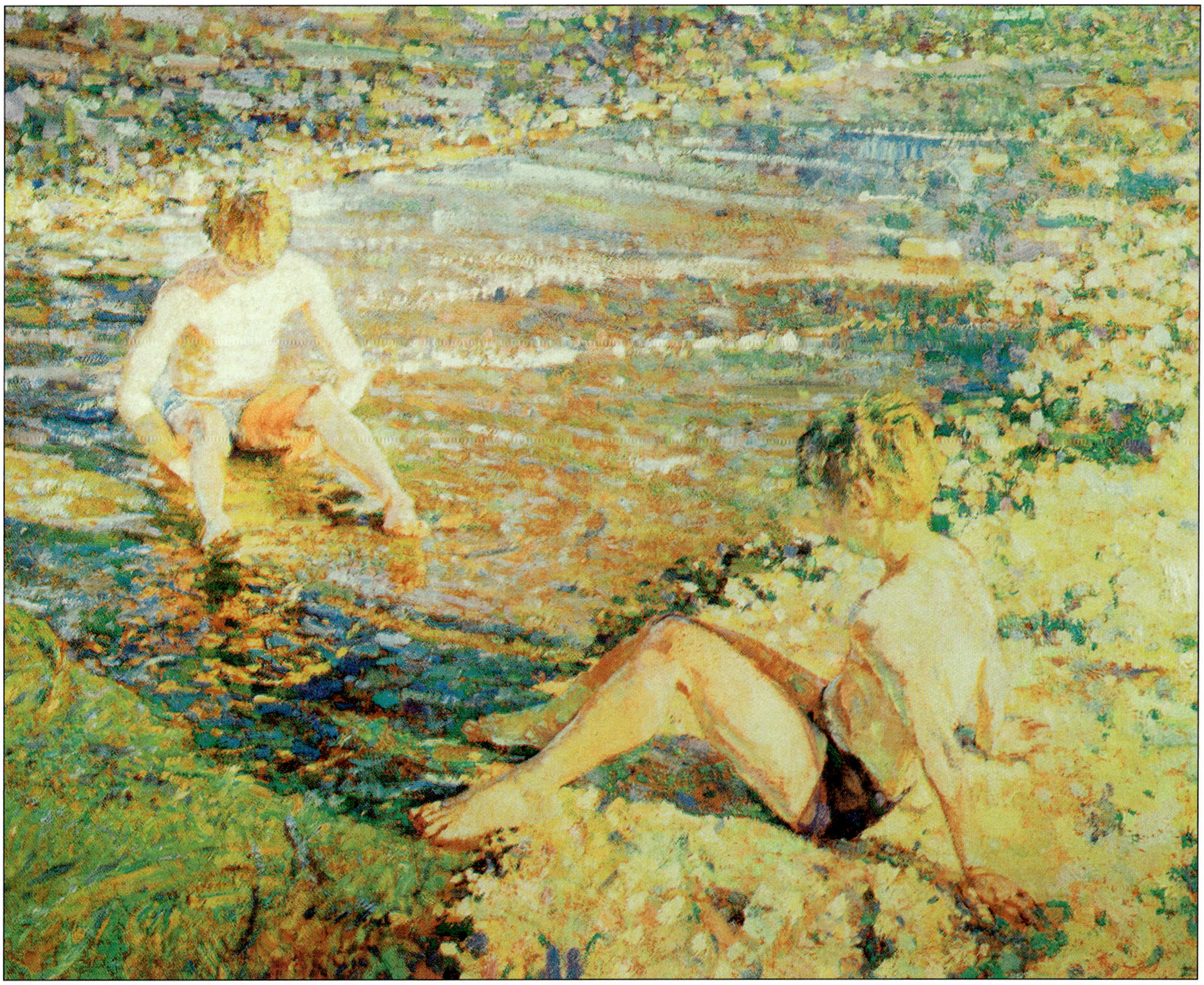

THE SUNSET HOUR, WEYMOUTH by Arthur Maderson (oil on canvas)

Sunlight and Shadows

There is probably no subject quite as appealing as sunlight and shadow, and it is most pleasant to paint outside on a warm sunny day under the shade of a tree.

Look carefully at the colors of shadows. They are rarely gray or black; they veer toward blue or mauve, crimson or green, as they are colored by both the surfaces on which they fall and by reflection from adjacent objects. Analyze their shapes; like clothes draping a person's body, shadows can be used to describe the forms over which they lie.

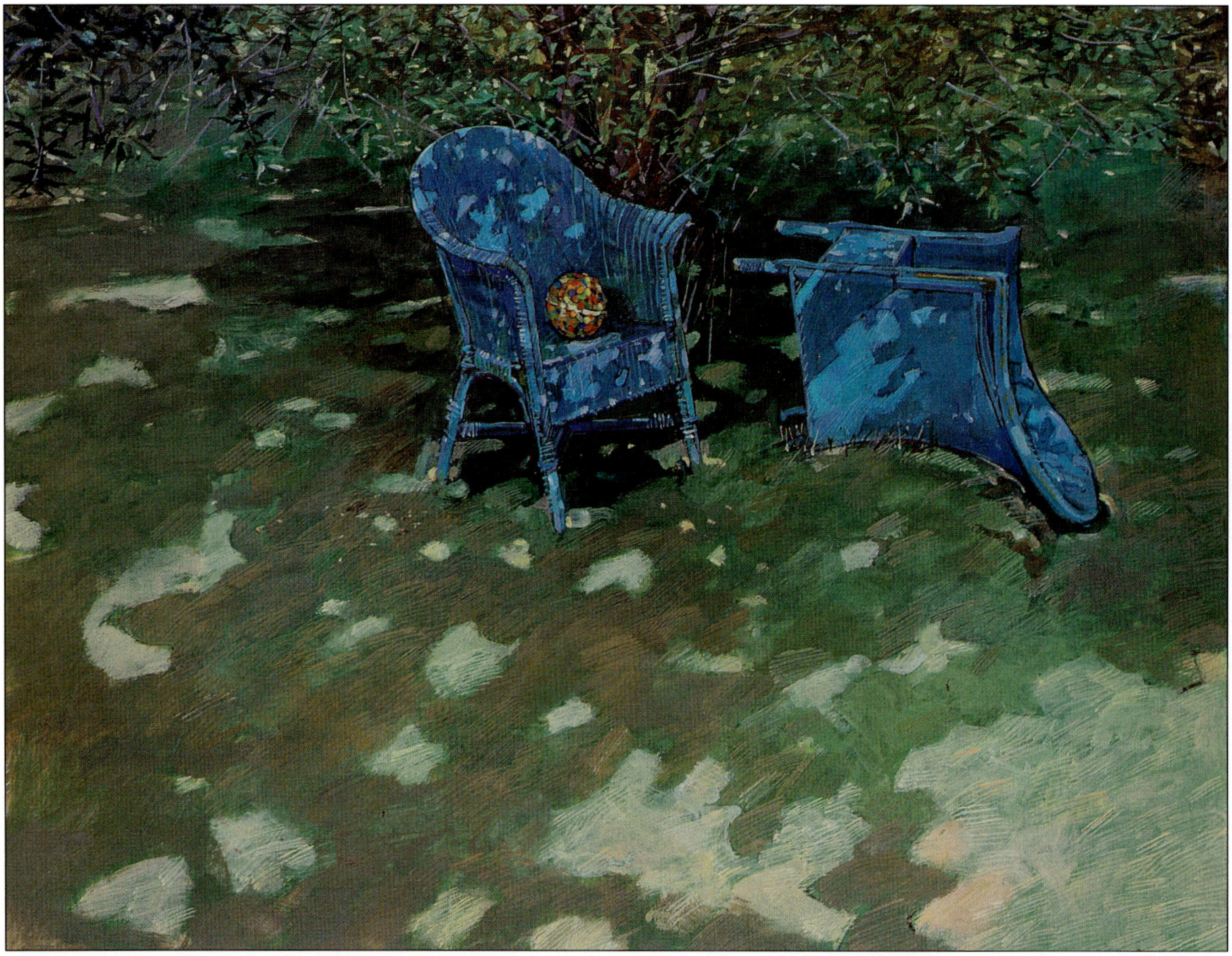

A DAY AT KELEEN by John Sprakes (tempera)

The impression of dappled light has great immediacy and charm, but the painting is technically complex. Shapes are full of detail and nuance, formed from layers of loosely brushed color, scumbling and vigorous hatching. The chairs, for example, reveal a busy network of widely varied blues and purples accented with yellow and white.

It is worth taking the time to make a study of shadows – there is more to them than meets the eye. For instance, why do some shadows have hard edges and others soft? One reason has to do with the actual source of light. If there is a single, bright light source, such as the sun or a desk lamp, the shadows cast by the object upon which the light falls will be strong and clear. If, however, the light comes from a large, diffuse source such as a window away from the path of direct sunlight, or the sky on an overcast day, the resulting shadows will be soft and blurred at the edges. Next time there is a sunny day, try looking for hard and soft shadows out of doors and resolve to recreate them in your paintings.

CREATING SHADOWS USING GLAZES

Thin glazes of greens, yellows, and pinks are built up in dabs so that the colors overlap and shine through from underneath. The shaded areas are washed over with a glaze of ultramarine blue. A fresh, lively effect of dancing color is created.

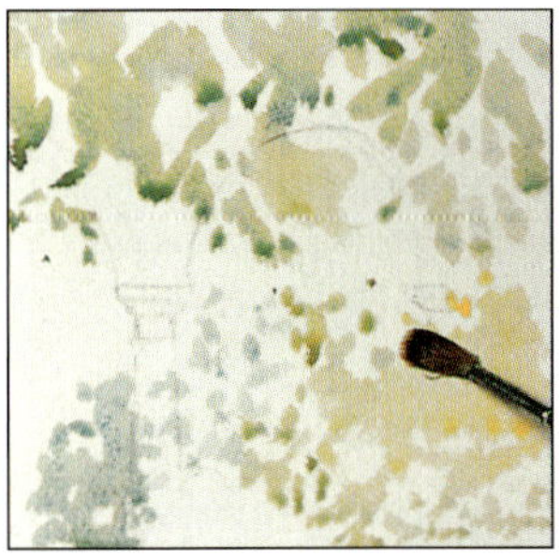

1 Build up the foliage with small, dabbed brushmarks in thin clear washes of color.

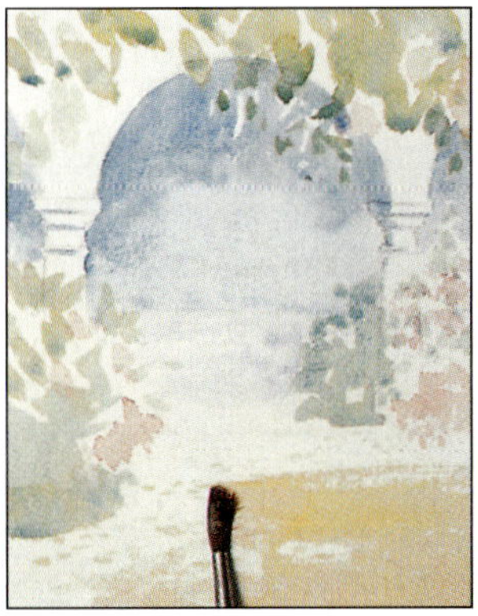

2 Lay colors over colors in transparent blobs. Wash in the foreground. As you paint the sky, take the blue into the shadows of the columns.

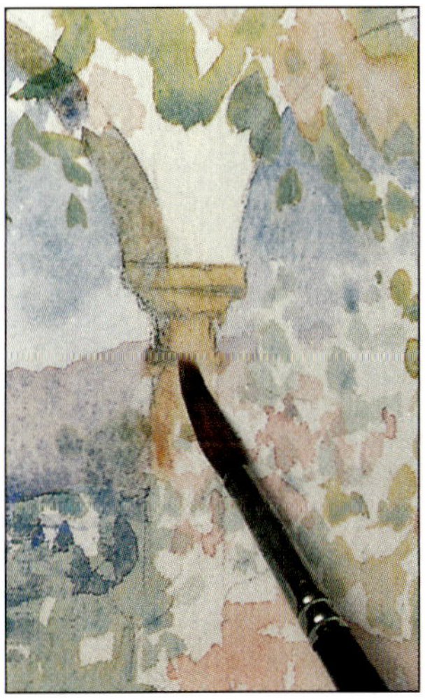

3 Paint a glaze of yellow ocher over the blue, shaded side of the columns. Build up the foliage with more dabs of color, one across another.

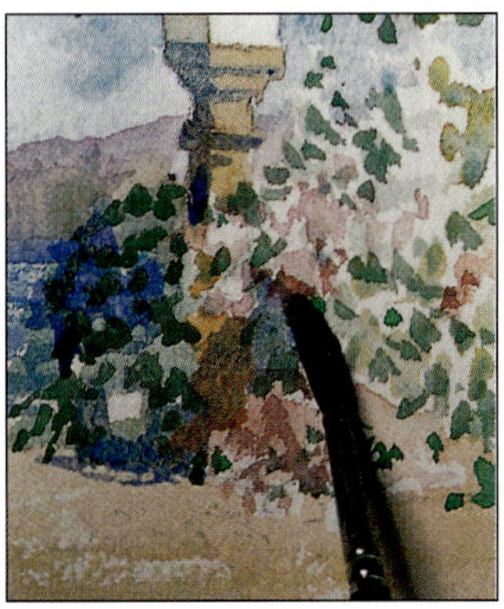

4 Wash a thin transparent glaze of ultramarine blue over the areas darkened by shadow, painting around the shapes of highlit leaves and flowers.

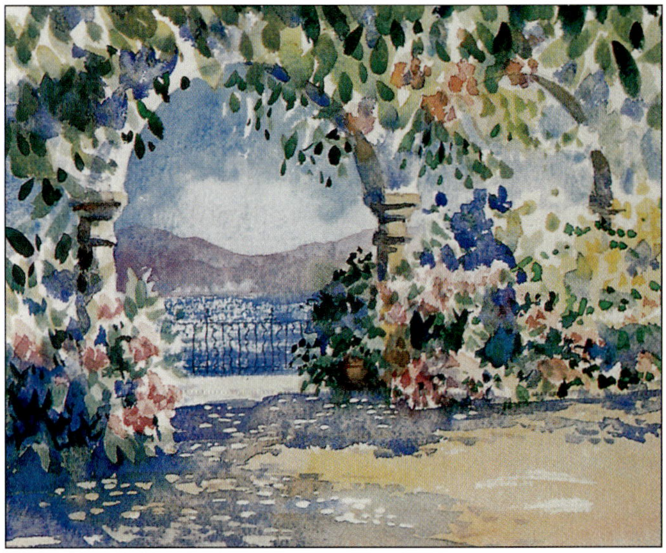

5 Brush in the foreground shadow, and strengthen the deeper shadows with Prussian blue.

RESERVING WHITE PAPER

The bright white paper left unpainted in the sunny landscape creates a strong contrast of light and shade. A light warm glaze of yellow is laid in patches to add to the glow.

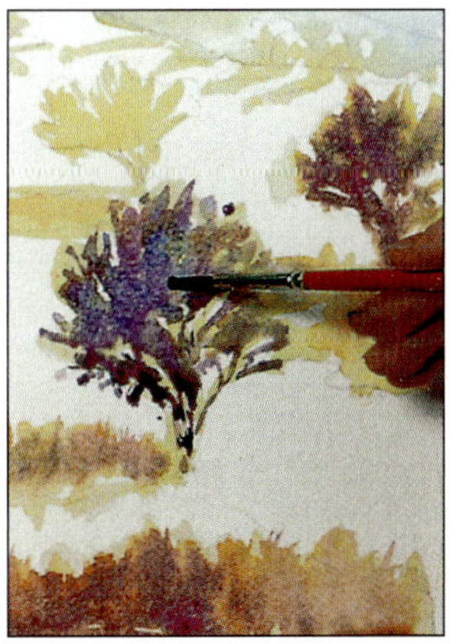

1 Draw out the dark tree shapes and shadows with an underwash of ocher and cadmium yellow to establish their positions. Paint very wet alizarin and ultramarine over the trees and shadows; then drop cerulean blue into the wet paint.

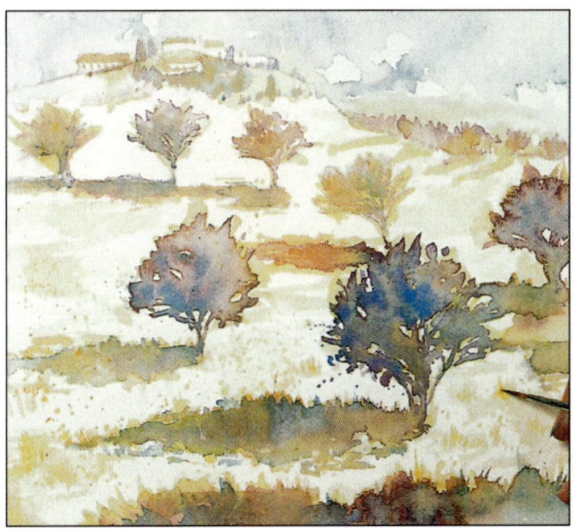

2 Drop spots of clean water onto the foliage masses to soften them. To make the white paper glow, touch in small washes and brush strokes of cadmium yellow.

Seasons

Each season of the year has its own characteristics, but since you cannot compare them at the same time, a clear sense of seasonal atmosphere comes from careful observation of actual qualities of light, color, and landscape structure.

Fall is a favored time for color studies; the colors of the trees can be sensational in themselves, and are often enhanced by a rich, warm light. Winter is a less inviting time to work outdoors, either drawing or observing the landscape, but it has its particular visual excitement in the skeletal forms of plants and the strange color range of lights and shadows on snow.

Seasonal character can also incorporate a mood, often relating to weather conditions – landscape rarely appears bleak under brilliant summer sunshine, but heavy storm clouds can make gentle pastoral land seem suddenly threatening.

FALL

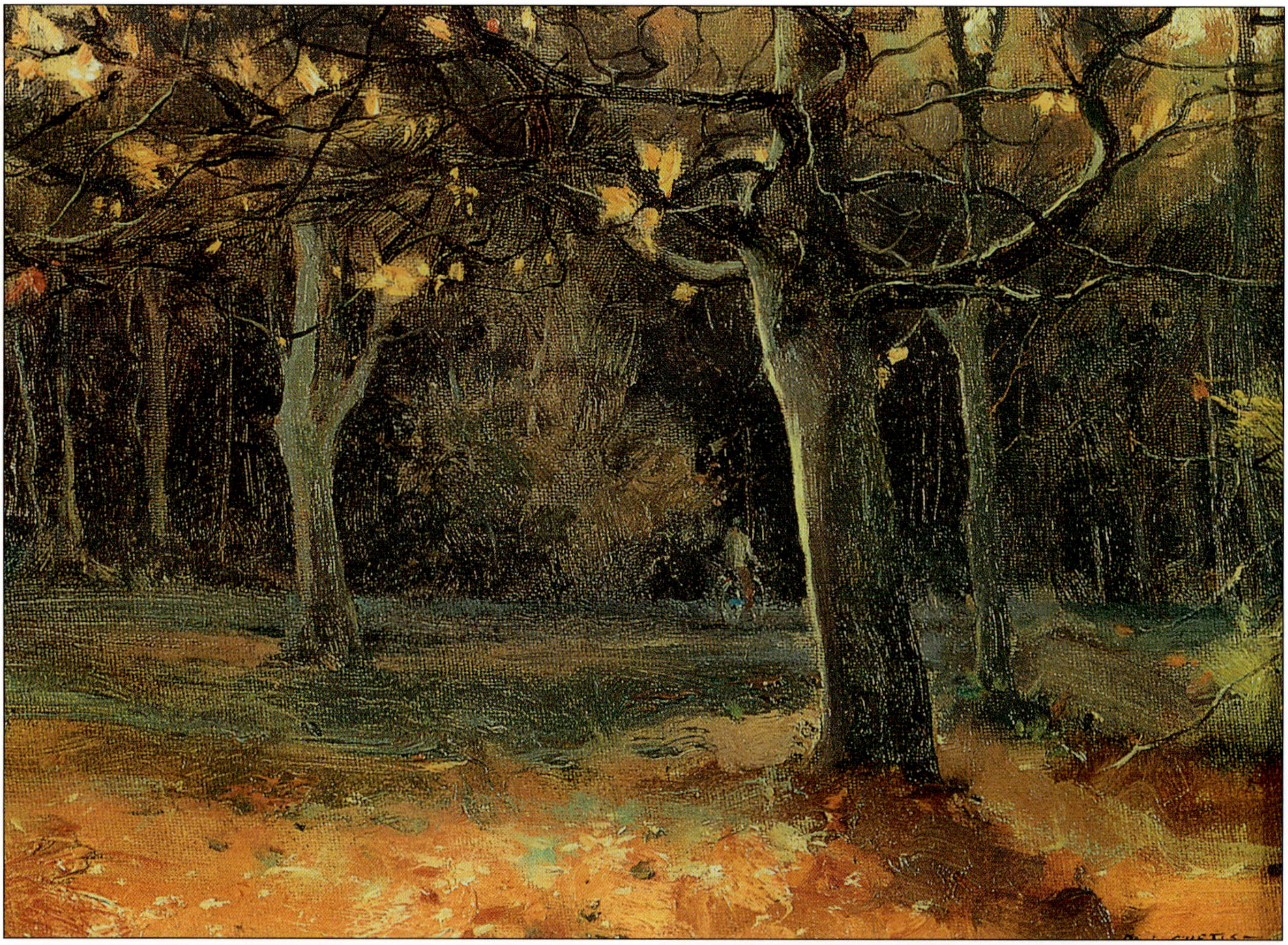

LATE AUTUMN, CLUMBER PARK by David Curtis (oil)

Fairly thin paint has been used for much of the picture, but the fallen leaves and the few golden leaves remaining on the trees are applied in thick impasto to great effect. Notice how all the branches of the nearest trees have been depicted in great detail, in contrast to the broader treatment of the distant forest. To achieve the effect of tiny lines of daylight in this area, the artist has scratched through the dark paint to reveal the white ground below (see sgraffito).

USING THE MASKING METHOD

The riot of color – with orange, yellow, and red instead of summer green – is the chief appeal of a landscape depicting fall. Protecting light details with masking fluid enables you to paint the composition freely and yet reserve the white paper underneath. Then you can rub off the masking fluid and touch in the details with light transparent glazes or leave white paper.

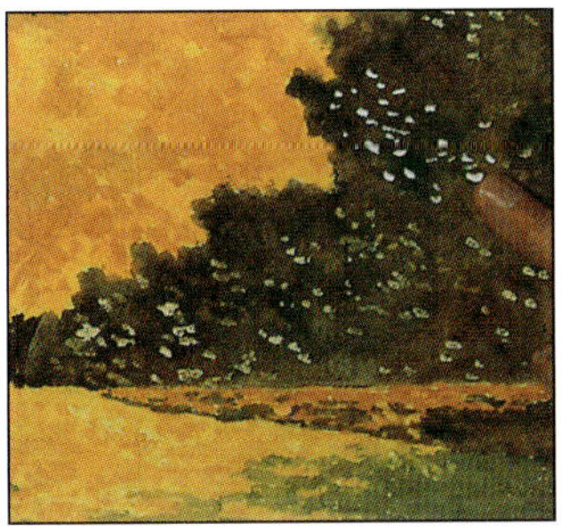

1 Before any color is laid, paint the fluttering leaves with dabs of masking fluid. When all the background washes have been put on, rub off the masking with your finger.

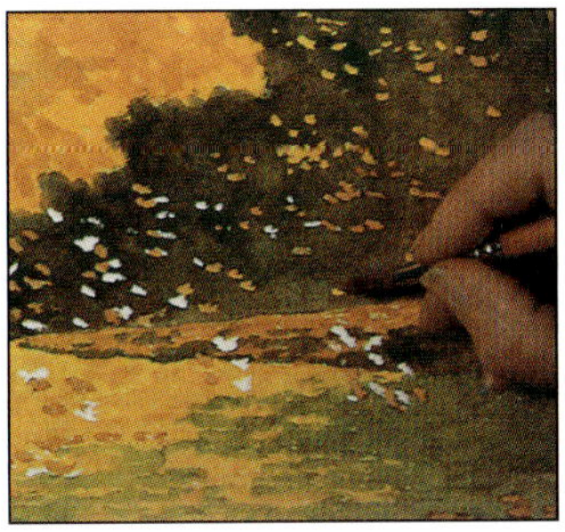

2 Glaze the unmasked leaves with transparent color. It will not matter if you overlap the dark background as you touch them in.

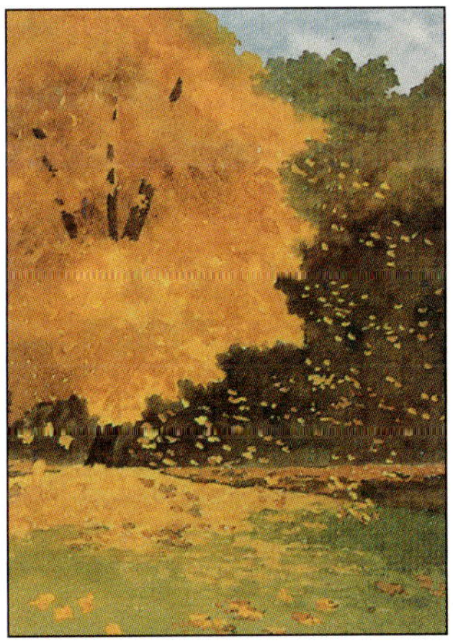

3 Paint small glazes over the leaves on the grass using new gamboge, yellow ocher, burnt sienna, and oxide of chromium (green).

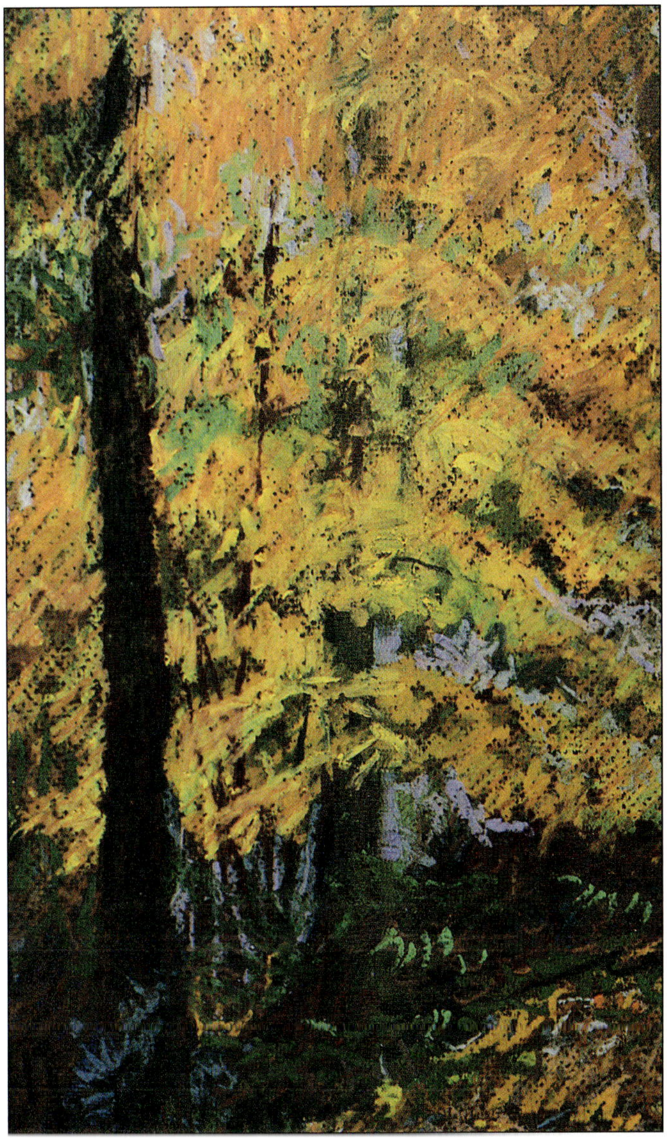

AUTUMN NEAR THE ARTIST'S STUDIO by John Elliot (oil pastel)

In pastel work it is often advisable to give full rein to the intensity of color, especially when the technique is free and bold. Oil pastel is used here to develop an active network of linear marks, where strong contrasts of color and tonal values allow the form and texture of the foliage to emerge. A dark, heavily-textured ground contributes to the broken color effects, although in places the pronounced grain of the paper is concealed by thick impasto dashes and streaks of color.

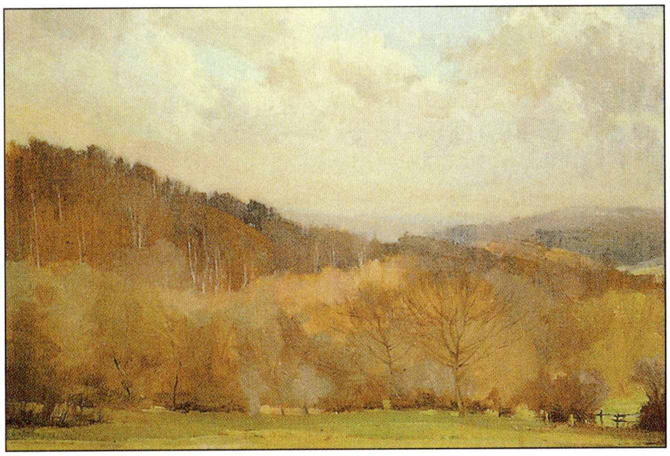

EARLY SPRING, CORDWELL VALLEY by David Curtis (oil)

The great variety of colors to be seen in winter trees is shown beautifully here, with pinks, browns, and purples neatly juxtaposed. Just a few trunks and branches have been picked out in detail, leaving the rest as suggestions.

PRESENTING YOUR WORK

Finished pictures need presentation. If they are to be hung for display, they should be backed and framed. If they are for commercial projects, submission to editors, or merely for sale unframed, they should be wet or dry mounted. All three methods can be practiced by the artist with the right tools, time, and care.

Mounting and framing your work can greatly enhance its appearance, and choosing the right color of mount, and the width and color of frame, needs careful consideration. A delicate and sensitive plant drawing would be overpowered by a flamboyant, gilded, heavy Victorian frame, and the choice must suitably enhance and reflect the subject matter. As a general rule, drawings are presented to their best advantage in frames with simple-shaped molding. For example, pencil drawings often look their best on a pale gray mount with a silver or metallic frame. The delicate and relatively negative quality of the pale gray mount and silver frame reflect and enhance the metallic nature of a pencil drawing.

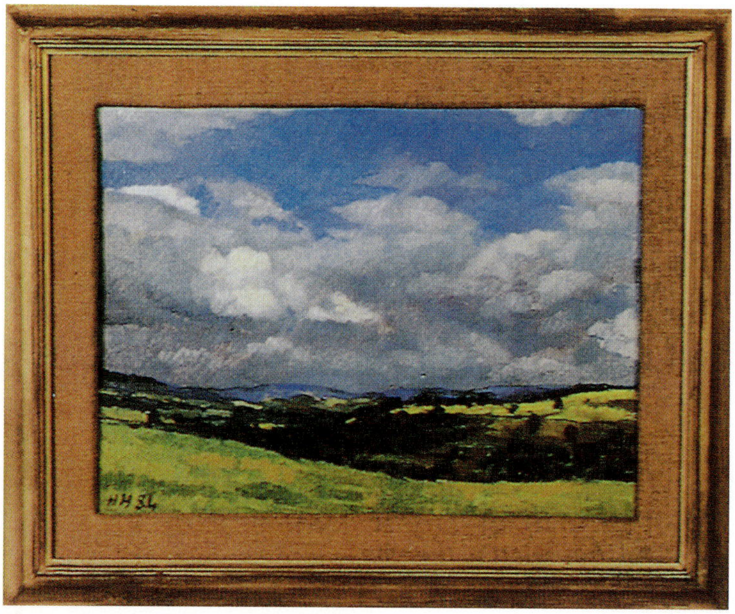

Beginners often make the mistake of cutting mounts for their work that are far too dark and heavy. A black mount may at first seem exciting placed against a pen drawing, but unfortunately in most cases the mount draws so much attention to itself that it presents a stronger image than the drawing. Darker-colored mounts, such as burgundy and olive green, should therefore be used with great caution in the framing and mounting of drawings. These strong colors really work only in conjunction with a robust piece of work.

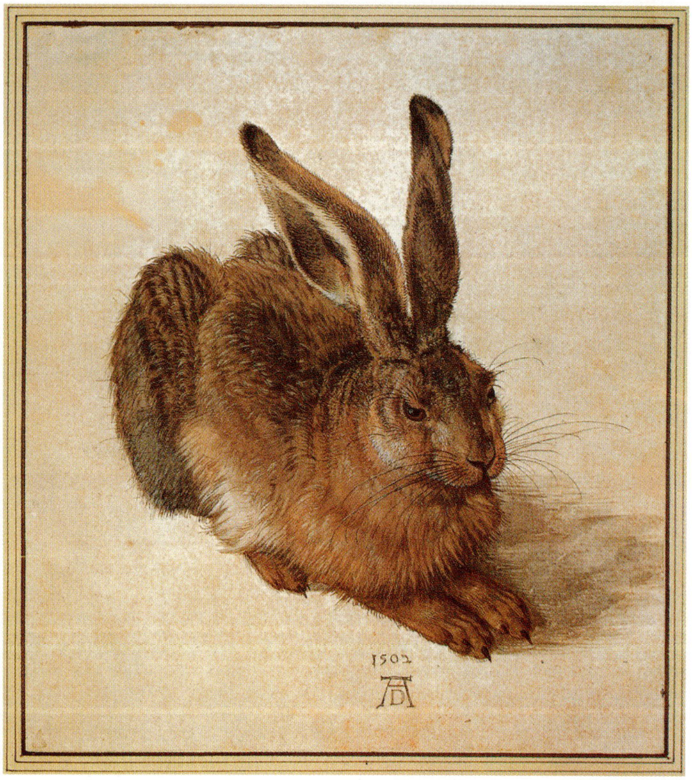

Drawings never look very satisfactory when framed to the actual size of the drawing without a mount; generally, therefore, all drawings and works of a graphic nature require a card mount to separate the image from the frame.

For the beginner, the advice of a good professional framer can be invaluable. Their experience can often enable them to intuitively choose the right mount and weight of frame for the work. For the more ambitious there is readily available a wide selection of wood and metal moldings and mounting card, and with the minimum of equipment and a little skill it should not be too difficult for the student to mount and frame his or her own work.

Mounts

The mounting and presentation of paintings and drawings is a craft in its own right. Every work of art needs a separator of some kind. It is essential to isolate a drawing or painting from its immediate surroundings, so that it can be seen clearly at full value.

Watercolors, gouaches, and drawings require window mounts with generous borders. White or cream or various-colored mounts can be matched against the painting. More often than not a neutral tint makes a better separator than a strong color, though in some instances a richly colored mount can enhance the work. Window mounts also serve the more practical purpose of keeping the painting or drawing from coming into contact with the glass. The window shape cut from the cardboard should be set above center so that the bottom margin is proportionally larger than the remaining sides. There are a number of mount-cutters, which are easy to use, currently on the market – they have an adjustable blade which can be angled to cut a beveled mount. If possible, always use an acid-free tape for fixing your drawing or painting to the mount. This prevents the work from becoming discolored at a later date. Acid-free mounting board is also recommended, but it can be very expensive.

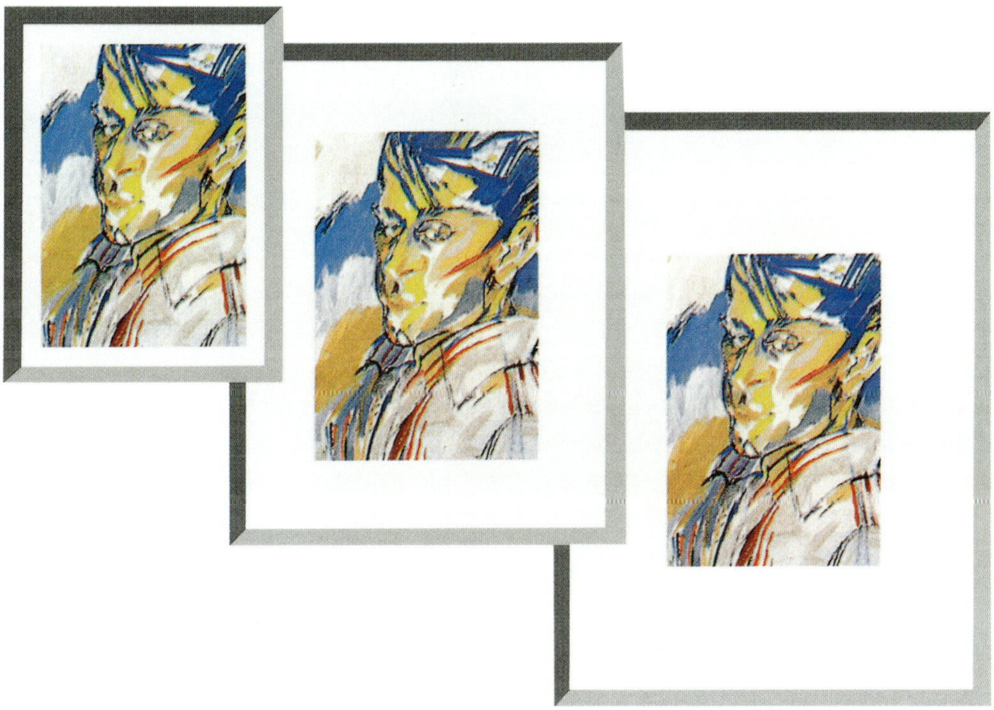

MOUNT WIDTHS

The width of the mount has an immediate effect on the framed picture as a whole. If the mount is too small, it can give the picture a cramped and restricted look. An equal all-round width works well with some images. If the mount is large in comparison with the picture, it is usually better if the picture "sits" high up in the frame – make sure the mount margin at the bottom of the picture is deeper than that of the other three sides.

It is important to differentiate clearly between the mount – the "window" which is placed upon the artwork – and the backing cardboard onto which the artwork is stuck before the process begins. Confusion arises because this backing is often referred to as the mount. The means by which the artwork is stuck to this backing is also referred to as "mounting." This section discusses the general principles of mounts and mounting.

THE BREATHING SPACE

Many artpieces are mounted as well as framed. In other words, the picture does not make direct contact with the frame but is surrounded by a wide margin which separates the picture from the frame. This is the mount. It is the "breathing space" between the picture content and the frame itself.

There are no rigid rules governing whether you should or should not have a mount within your frame but, as a basic guideline, consider the artpiece itself: does it, for instance, contain large areas of empty space in its composition, as in the case of a line drawing on a plain white background? This sort of picture would look

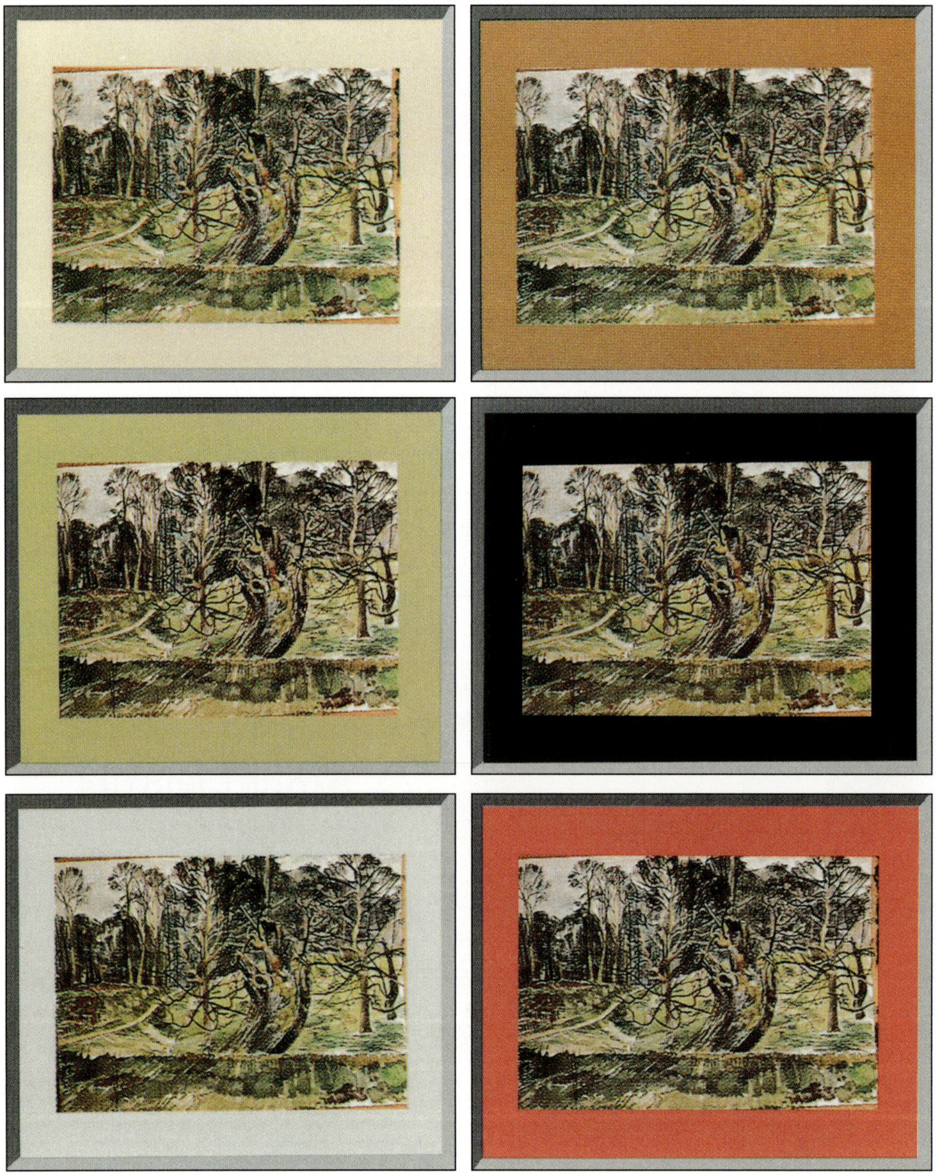

CHOOSING A COLOR

This landscape is painted in muted, earthy colors. With a picture like this, it is usually advisable to choose a color that harmonizes with the subject. The light beige mount makes the picture look darker; the dull olive green immediately picks out the green tones in the composition, while the black emphasizes the linear content. Sometimes a mount of an unrelated color works – the rich magenta contrasts attractively with the greens and browns in the picture.

effective with only a small amount of border, or possibly with none at all. On the other hand, a more crowded picture would benefit from a substantial border of space between the image and the frame.

The mount should be chosen before the frame, because it comes next to the artpiece. A great deal of mystery has been attached to the "proportions" of the mount – the amount of space which should be left at the bottom, sides, and top of the image. In fact, the choice is personal and there is nothing magical about the measurements.

The cutting of a good bevel-edged cardboard mount could be more difficult than the making of the actual frame, however, and the following suggested sequence may be useful to the beginner. It is best if you cut your own mount internally about one eighth of an inch smaller all round than your actual drawing, allowing on a small drawing about 2 in. (5 cm) between the mount and the frame. Fashions tend to change in relation to whether the mount should be an equal width all the way round or whether the bottom of the mount should be slightly wider. The original reason for the extra width was to allow space for a title or written description of the work to be shown on the mount. Visually, this title becomes part of the drawing, thus leaving an equal space to the other sides. Even when a title is not written, some artists prefer to have an extra weight of mount at the bottom, which can give the framed drawing a sense of stability.

Once the mount is finished, select the molding you require and cut the miters. However, do not attempt to cut without an accurate 45° miter block. When all four miters are cut, assemble the frame and pins. The size and number of pins depend very much on the size of molding and the weight of the drawing and glass. Do not attempt to drive in the pins without first drilling guide holes. Failure to do so almost inevitably results in the splitting and damaging of the molding.

Once the frame is assembled, cut the cardboard mount on the outer edges to fit the frame rebate snugly. Cut a backing to suit. At this point measure the internal dimensions of the rebate and get a piece of picture glass cut at your nearest glass-cutters.

This sequence has been suggested for a beginner when assembling a frame because there is nothing more infuriating than making a frame and then discovering that the glass or the mount is a fraction too small or too large to fit. By making all the final measurements to fit the frame, rather than the frame to fit a predetermined glass measurement, the beginner should avoid such frustration.

MAT CUTTING

In this demonstration, a ready-made clip frame is used. These come complete with glass, and all you need do is cut the mat.

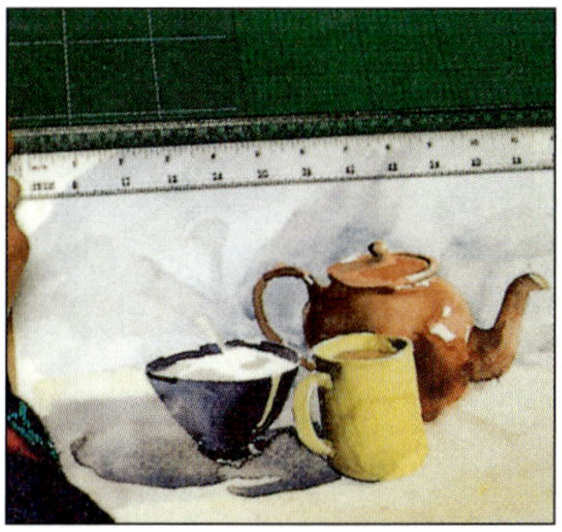

1 Measure the picture, deciding whether you want the mat to cover any of the edges.

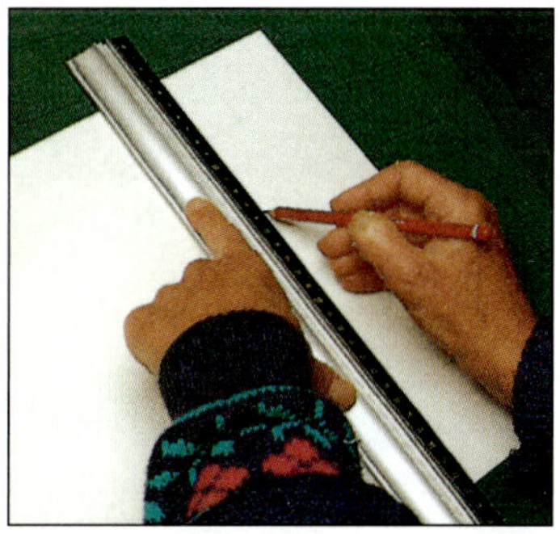

2 Cut the board to fit the glass of the frame, and then mark the measurements for the window.

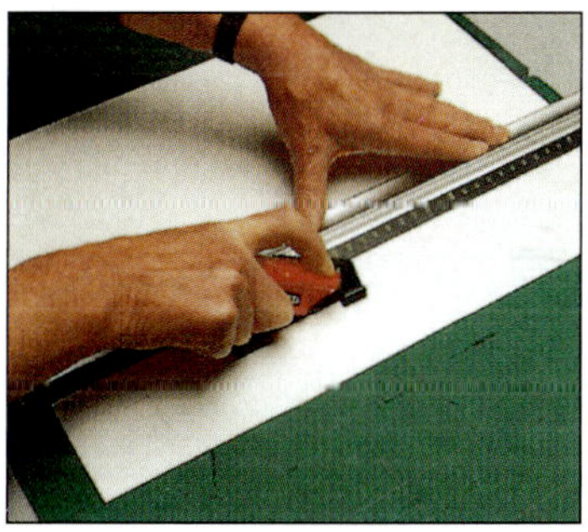

3 Like most mat cutters, this one is designed to cut on the back of the board. Cut carefully, exerting an even pressure.

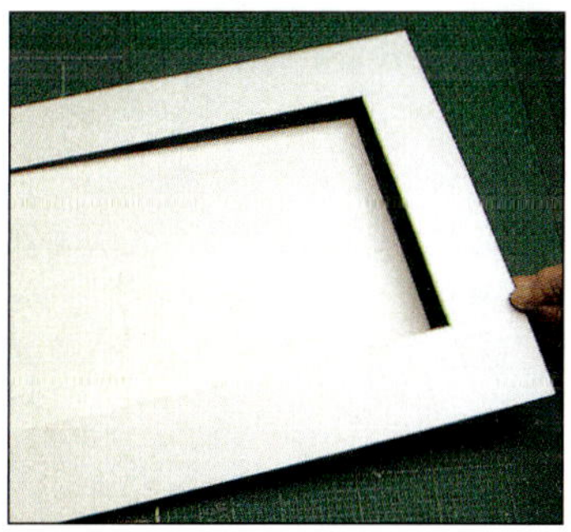

4 When all the edges and corners have been cut cleanly, lift the board by the edges and let the unwanted piece slip out.

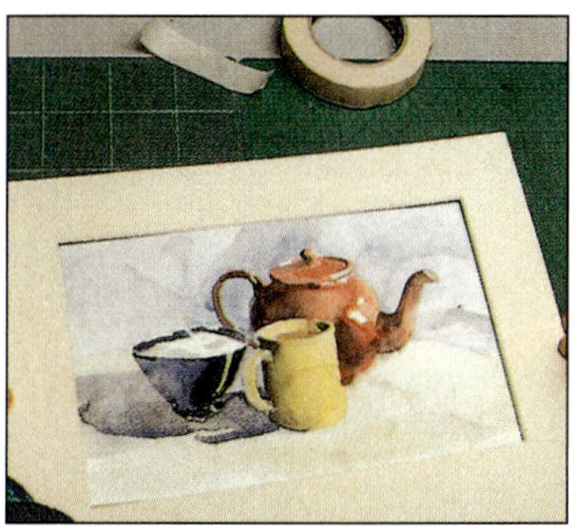

5 Position the mat, then fix the picture to it with a piece of masking tape attached to the back. Don't put tape around the edges, or the picture will buckle.

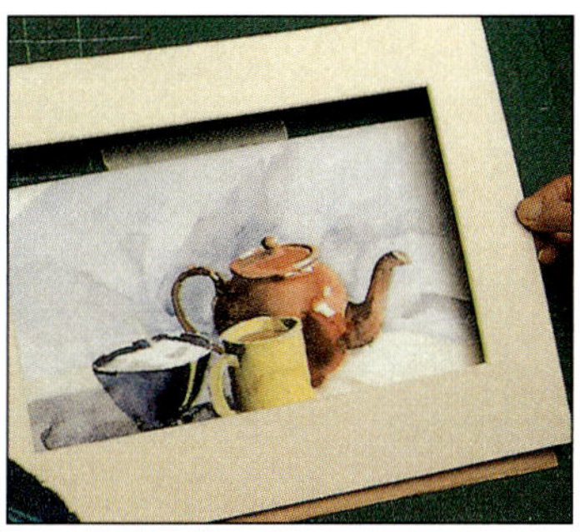

6 Place the picture and mat on the backing board.

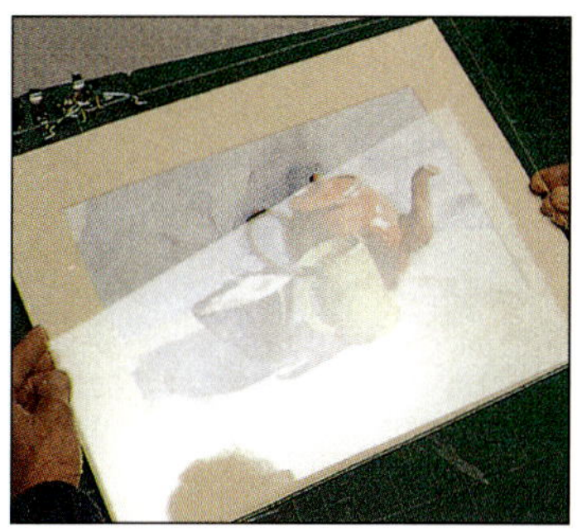

7 Put the glass on top, making sure it is clean. Finally, use the picture clips to secure board, picture, mat, and glass together.

Framing

Framing any painting needs careful consideration. An overly decorative gilt mounting, for instance, may be too overbearing on a simple landscape painting.

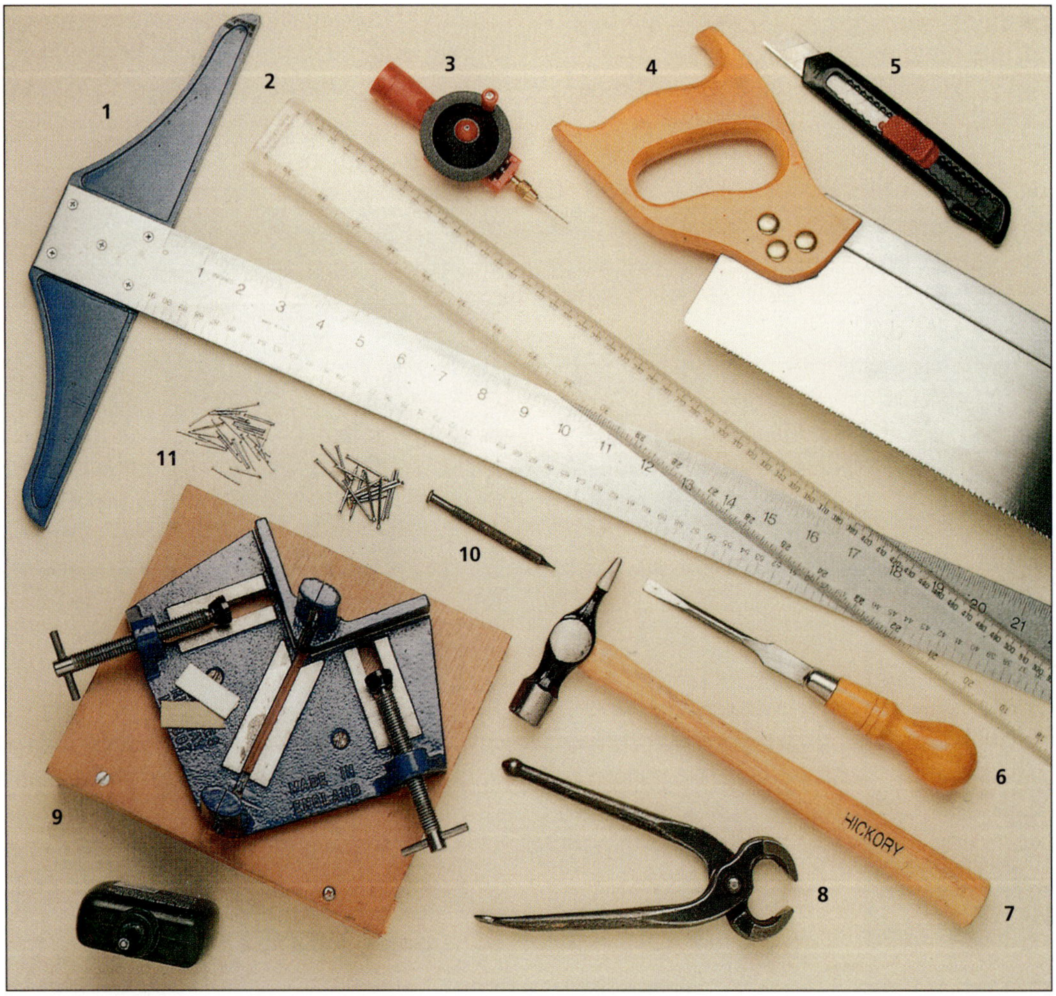

TOOLS FOR FRAMING
1 *Set square/ruler* **2** *Plastic ruler* **3** *Hand drill and bits* **4** *Tenon saw* **5** *Craft knife* **6** *Screwdriver* **7** *Pin hammer* **8** *Pincers* **9** *Miter box or clamp* **10** *Nail punch* **11** *Panel pins/tacks*

Most professional framers will allow you to test sample mitered corners of different types of molding against your own painting to gauge whether any of them is suitable. Prints and drawings work well in a stainless-steel or self-assembly aluminum frame. Charcoal and pencil drawings work best in a simple half-round or wooden box molding. Watercolors, if properly mounted, can be enhanced by narrow half-round gilt or silver wooden frames. Larger moldings are best for oil and acrylic paintings.

An artist is not always the best judge of how his work is best framed; he is often so close to the work that he finds it hard to make the right choice. For this reason I would suggest that much can be gained by seeking a second opinion, either from a frame-maker or from a fellow artist whose opinion you value. Remember that the main purpose of a frame is to act as a separator – it's better to be formal than flamboyant.

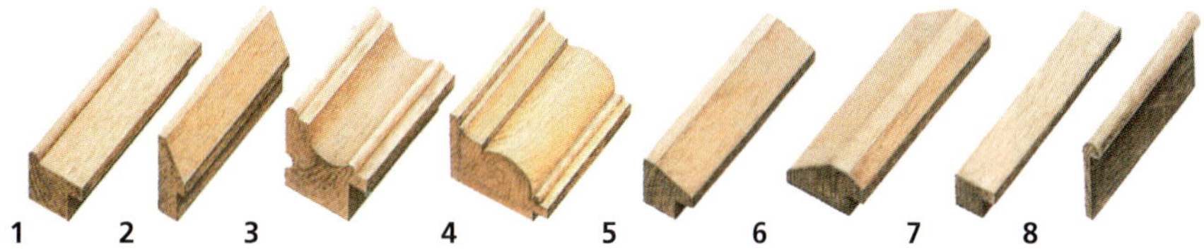

COMMON MOLDINGS

1 *Box* **2** *Reverse slope* **3** *Flat* **4** *Half-round* **5** *Raised bead and flat* **6** *Box* **7** *Spoon* **8** *Composite made from planed timber and architrave molding*

BOUGHT FRAMES AND MOLDINGS

A fine, grained frame with a raised inner edge stands complete at the top right of this section. The group of grained woods and veneers illustrates the range of frames and moldings available. At the bottom left-hand corner are two types of frame for an oval picture that would enhance a particularly treasured period miniature. A more formal style of room cries out for the more formal, polished frames that are typical of those grouped together here. Among the narrower frames is an elegant tortoiseshell and gold, two sides of which are illustrated at the top left. Next to it is a corner piece in antique walnut veneer. Some solid and grand frames lie across the center of the group, including one with fan-shaped wooden inlays. Take care when choosing frames of this sort – consideration should be given not only to the type of picture to be framed, but also to the suitability of the frame to the environment.

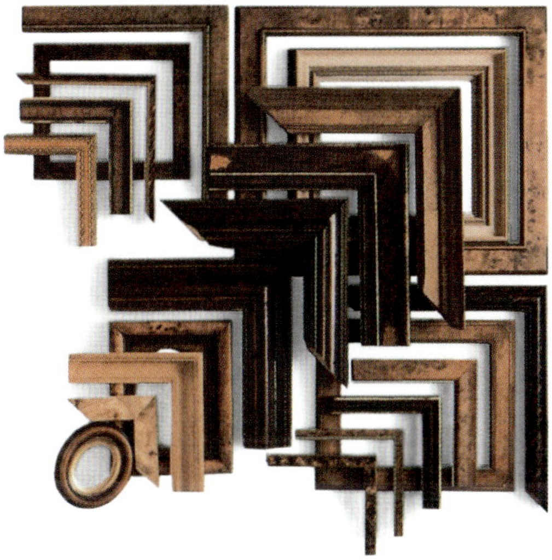

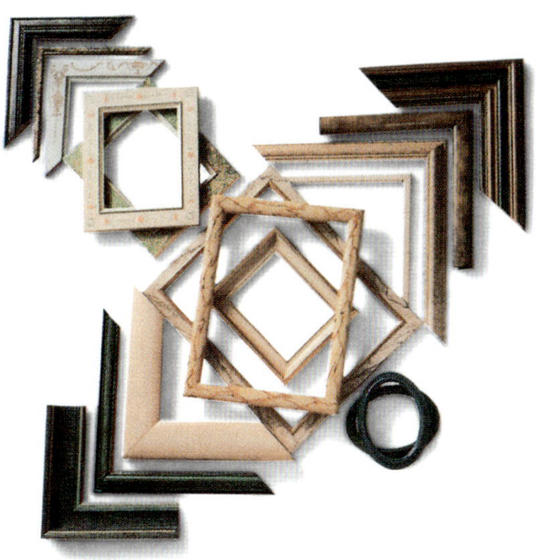

COLORFUL PAINT FINISHES

Some highly decorative paint finishes are featured in this group of moldings. All ready-cut frames, they continue a traditional period flavor with modern experimental finishes. The yellow marbled frame across the center is faked. Yet the result is a tasteful version of a traditional marbling technique. It contrasts strongly with the simple green and turquoise ovals that lie next to it in the group. To their bottom right is a series of specimens including a "faux" or "made" imitation malachite, and two elegant and narrow samples finished in stippled red and sponged blue. At the extreme top left of the whole group is a marbled dark blue frame, followed by frames sporting a variety of decorative finishes, including two rectangles with painted motifs and decoration over white and green stippled backgrounds.

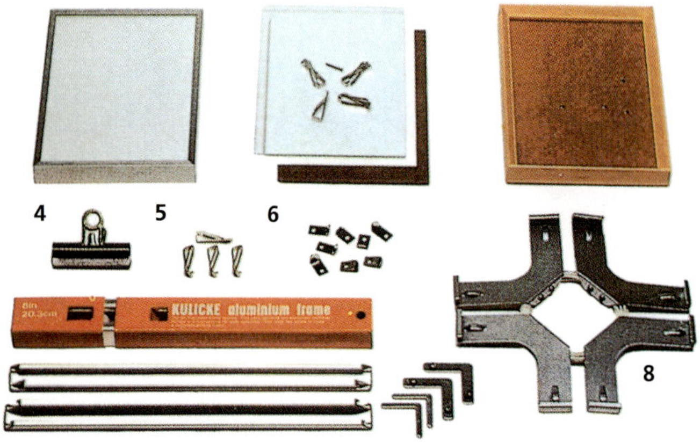

READY-MADE FRAMES AND CLIPS

1 *Emo interchangeable metal frame* **2** *Emo framers' pack, containing a piece of glass, a piece of fibreboard, and a number of small clips* **3** *Ready-made frame* **4 5** *and* **6** *Bulldog, spring, and mirror clips* **7** *and* **8** *Kulicke and Daler metal frame kits* **9** *Hang-it frame kit*

ASSEMBLING A FRAME

The first step in making a frame is to measure it. Do it not once, but twice, and, if necessary three times. Never cut until you are sure you have got it right. And remember, each length of the frame will be as long as the picture – plus twice the width of the frame. A canvas must always be given an extra $^1/_4$ in. (6 mm) all around to allow for expansion and contraction in temperature changes. Allow the space inside the rebate and cushion the canvas with cork spacers or veneer pins. If you are going to frame your favorite drawings, they will need glass at the front and a backing of hardboard.

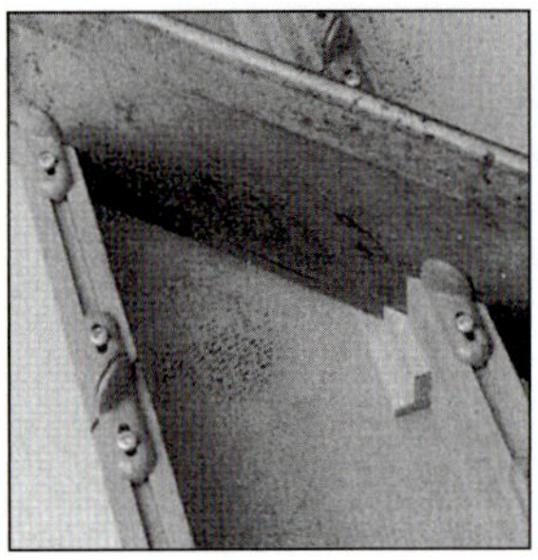

1 Secure a length of molding in a miter board or clamp. Position the saw and make the first cut.

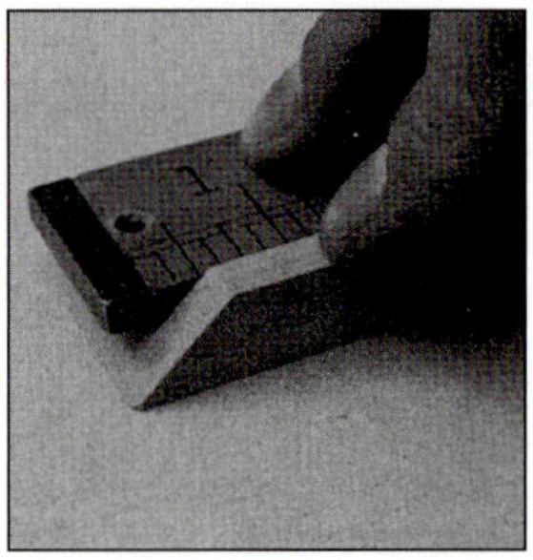

2 Measure the required length of molding along the inside of the rebate. Align the ruler with the mitered end of the wood.

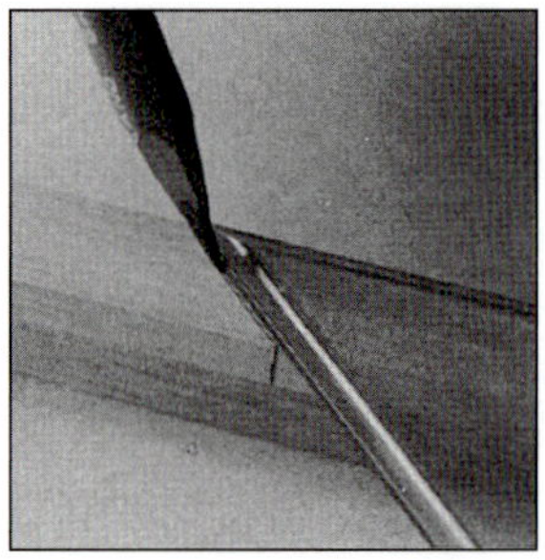

3 Mark up the other end of the section of molding using a set square to obtain the 45° angle of the miter.

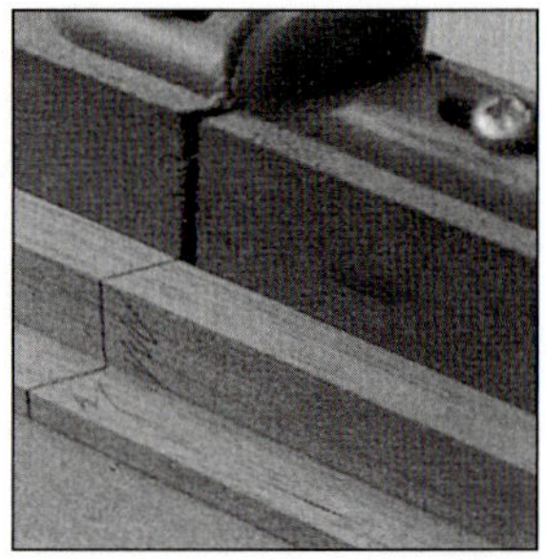

4 Mark the waste side of the cut, position the molding in the miter board, so that the cut is at the mark. Saw it through.

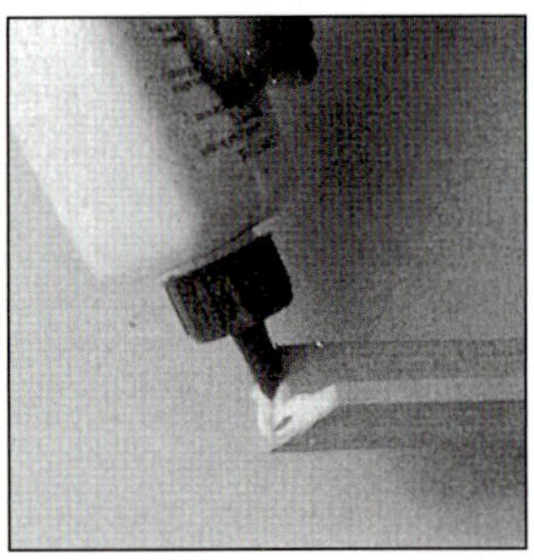

5 Cut all four sides of the frame. Apply adhesive to the mitered ends of the molding.

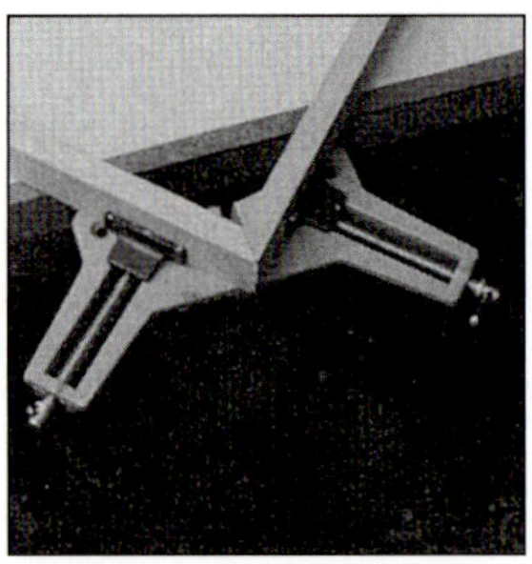

6 Secure two mitered ends together in a corner clamp, so that an L-shape is formed. Make sure that the molding lies flat.

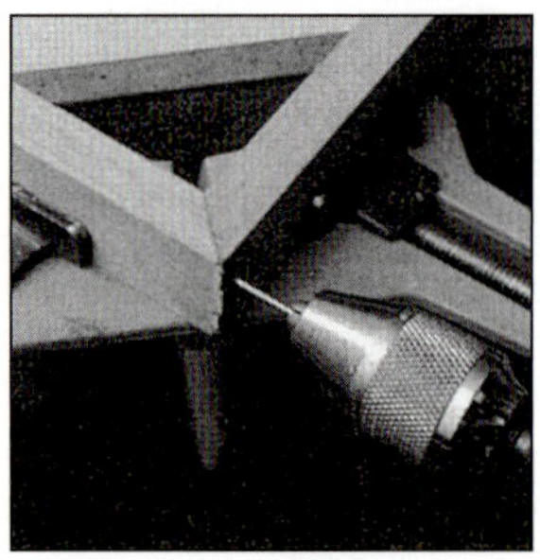

7 Drill small holes into each corner. Secure the pieces with panel pins. Repeat process, join two halves of the frame together.

DRY MOUNTING

This method is ideal for photographs and commercial art work. Cut a sheet of shellac tissue slightly bigger than the picture and, using the tip of a hot iron, fix the center of it to the back of your print or drawing. Turn the print over and trim off the edges of the shellac tissue. Lay the print, shellac tissue down, onto the mount. Place heat resistant paper over the picture and iron out with a medium hot iron. The mounting can be completed by gluing a window mount over the picture.

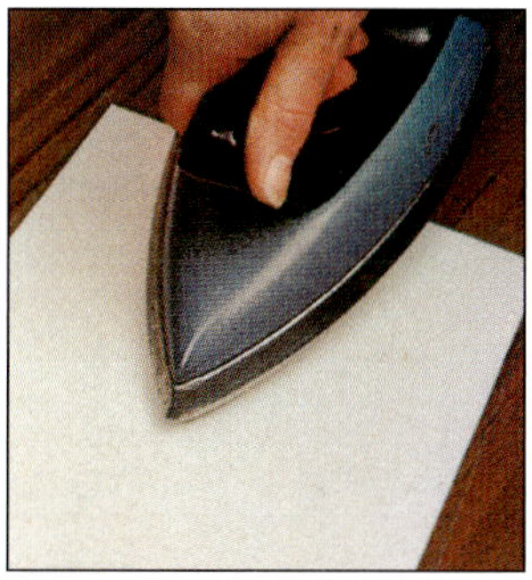

1 Tack a sheet of dry mounting tissue, slightly oversize, to the back of the print with an iron.

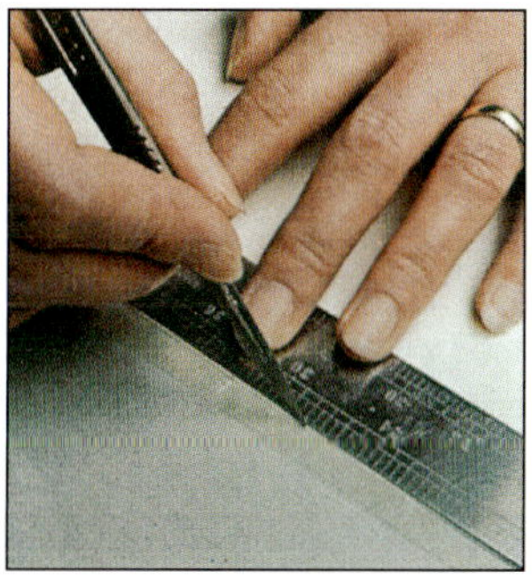

2 Trim the edges of the tissue with a scalpel along a steel ruler so that it is exactly the same size as the print.

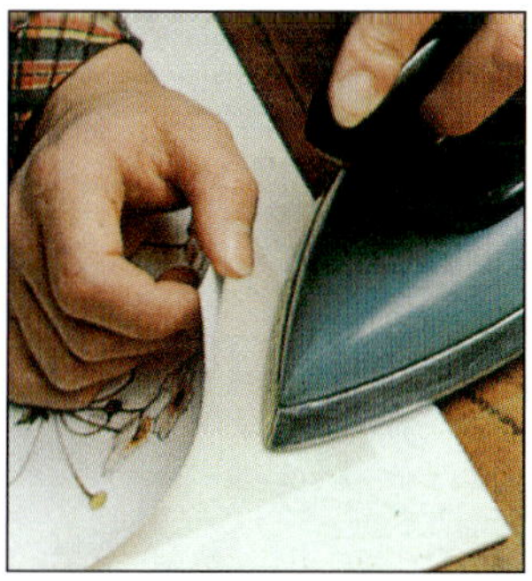

3 Place the print face up on a mounting card and tack the tissue to the card at each corner with the medium hot iron.

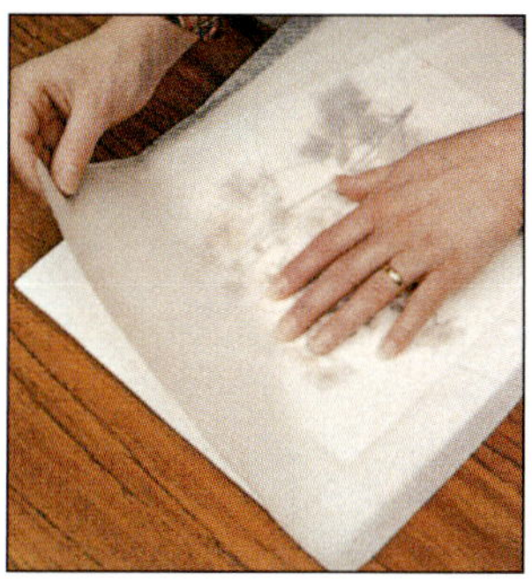

4 Lay a thin sheet of paper over the print to protect it from the hot iron.

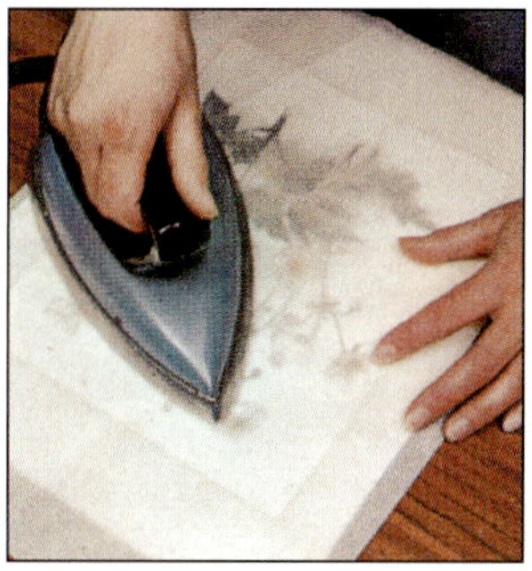

5 Run the iron evenly but firmly over the paper, working from the center outward. The heat adheres print to the card.

CUTTING GLASS

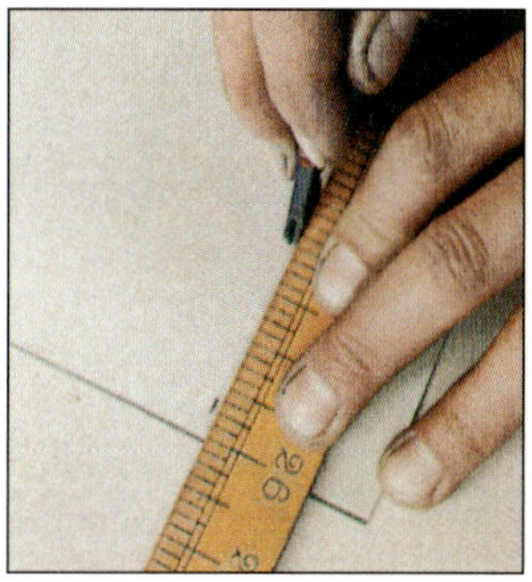

1 Measure from a straight edge of the piece of glass and mark the required dimensions with a felt tip pen. Place a ruler along the marks and draw the cutting tool firmly along the glass using the ruler to guide it down.

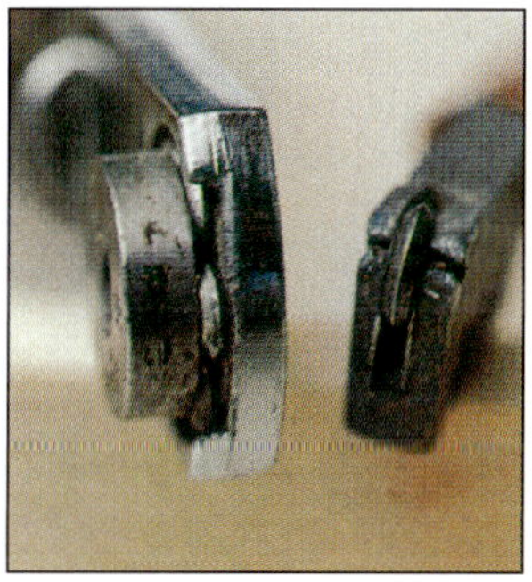

2 The cutting wheel on a glass cutting tool is centered and will be distanced slightly from the ruler when cutting. Allow for this.

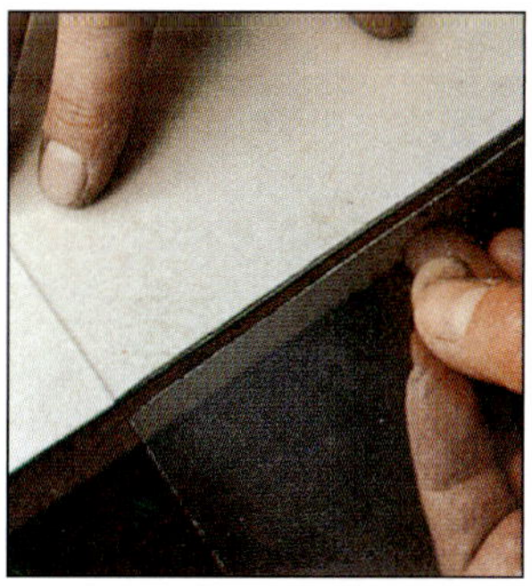

3 Place the scored mark directly over the edge of a table or board and let the glass drop gently, then snap it along the cut.

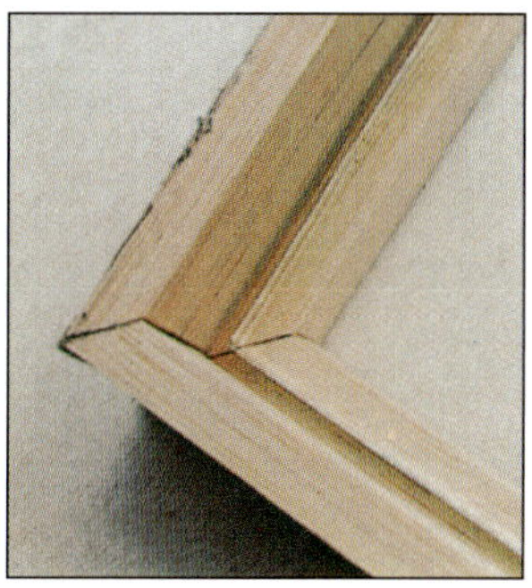

4 Glass for framing should always be cut smaller than the inside measurement of the frame so that it is not wedged inside the wood.

Caring for your Pastels

Unless you take steps to protect your finished work, it can easily become smeared and the paper damaged.

The best protection is provided by a frame and glass, but framing all your pictures would be expensive. A surface such as pastel board or sandpaper, which grips the pastel firmly, needs no fixing, but spray other work with fixative and let it dry thoroughly before putting it away. Pastels must be stored flat, not upright, to avoid damaging the edges of the paper. You can stack a good many paintings on top of one another, but they must be separated by tracing paper to prevent color transfer. Tracing paper is preferable to tissue paper, because it is heavier. The protective sheet should be fixed to the pastel paper, using any of the methods shown below, so that it does not move when you are looking through your work.

Pastels must be framed under glass to guard against accidental smearing and to protect them from damp and dust. The painting must never touch the glass. If you are having your work mounted professionally, ask the framer to insert a thick mat or small pieces of wood, known as slips, between the painting and the glass.

TAPE AND TRACING PAPER

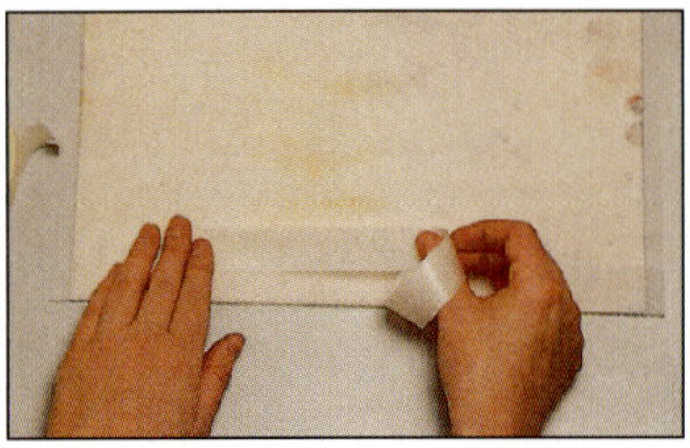

Cover the picture with tracing paper, fold about 1 in. (2.5 cm) over the back, and fasten down with masking tape.

MASKING TAPE HINGE

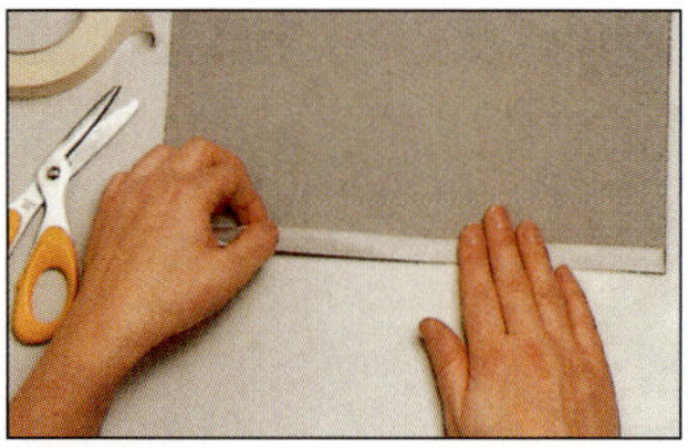

Or align the edges of tracing paper and picture, stick the tape onto the tracing paper, then fold over onto the back. You will need wider tape for this.

ATTACHING TO BOARD

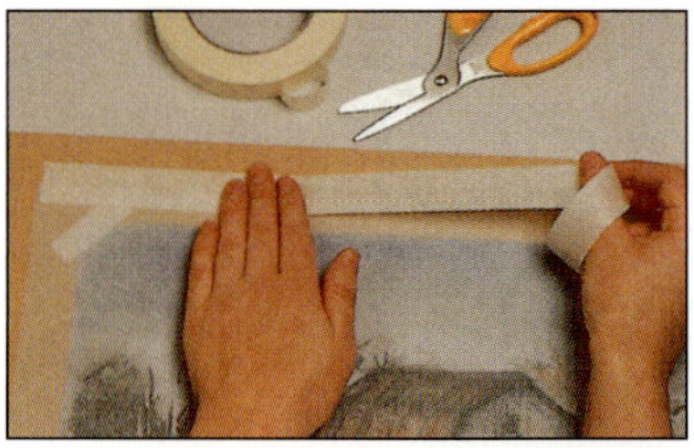

This method makes sure that the picture is kept flat. Fasten it to a piece of mat board larger than the painting, then cover with tracing paper and place tape along the top.

FRAMING TIPS

When framing work, the pastel must not touch the glass. If it does, moisture caused by condensation will make blotches on the picture surface.

USING A MAT

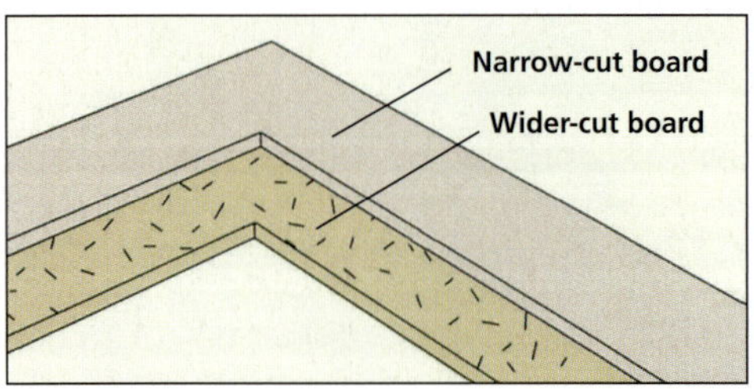

You can make a thick mat by gluing two pieces of mat board together and cutting to size. For a more decorative effect, cut one piece slightly smaller than the other, so that the edge of the bottom piece shows. Use identical or contrasting colors.

USING SLIPS

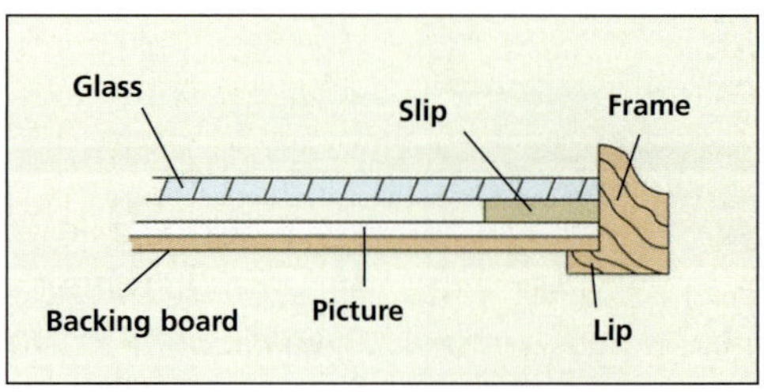

You can separate the glass from the picture by placing a thin piece of wood in the lip (the L-shaped groove on the inside edge of the frame molding). You need a frame with a deep lip.

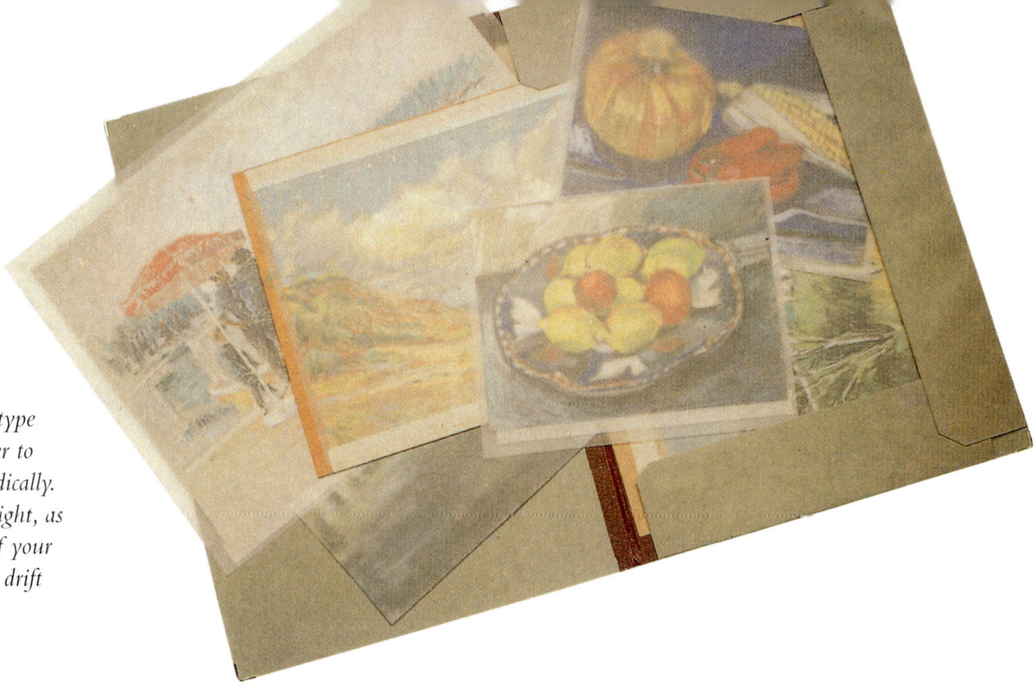

PORTFOLIOS

Keeping your pastels in a portfolio protects them from dampness and dust. The best type opens out flat, making it easier to look through your work periodically. Do not store the portfolio upright, as this could damage the edges of your work and cause pastel dust to drift downward.

ASSESSING YOUR WORK

Making a mat for your picture gives you a chance to reassess it, and you will sometimes find you can improve the composition simply by the way you place the mat.

If you have worked right to the edges of the paper, you will have to sacrifice a little of the picture – the edges must be covered by the mat and attached to it – but you can crop much more drastically than this. If you have placed the horizon too near the center, for example, you might lose some of the sky or foreground. Cut two "L" shapes as shown, and move them around on the picture to examine different options. You can use thick paper for this, or pieces of your mat board.

If you decide on a cropped version, cut the mat to these new dimensions, but don't cut pieces off the picture, because you may change your mind.

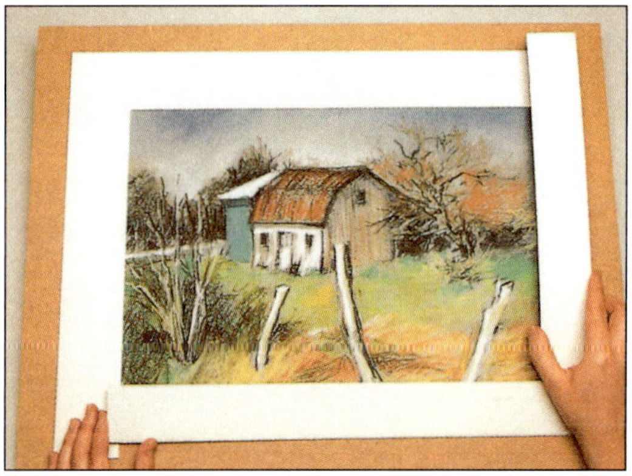

Picture might benefit from cropping foreground.

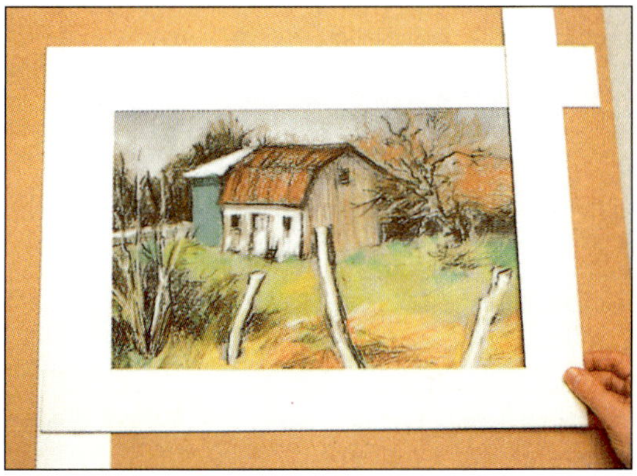

Cropping some sky focuses eye on house and foreground.

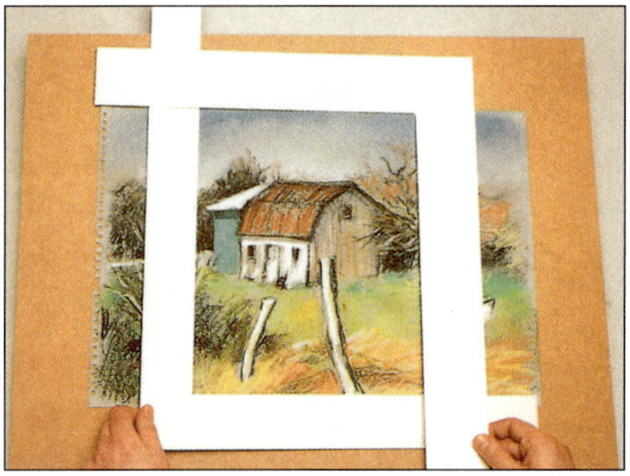

Central portion of picture makes an uncluttered composition.

GALLERY

Pastel

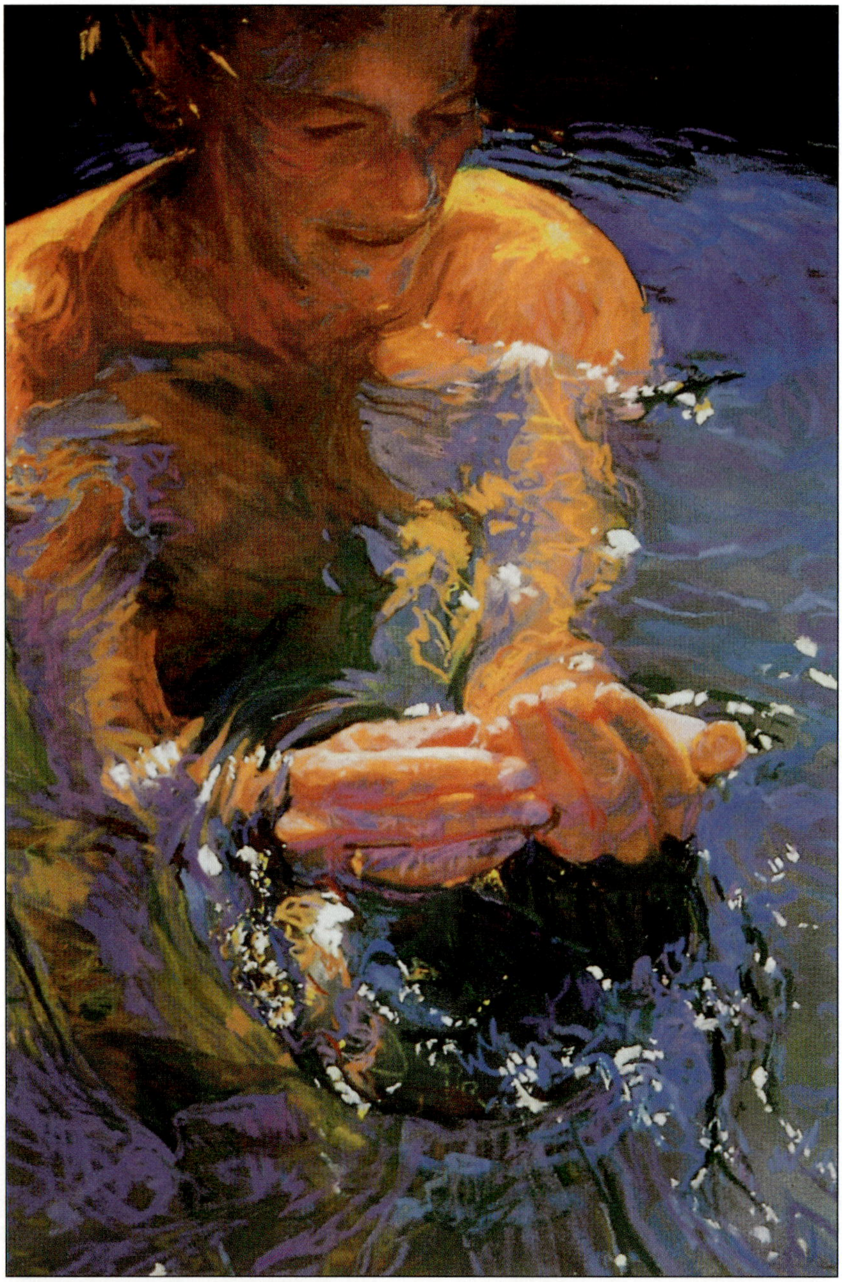

HOT TUB NO. 11 by Kitty Wallis

This artist particularly likes exploring the interaction of figures and water. She contrasted the solid bulk of the head and shoulders with the delicate, complex shapes where ripples of water distort the chest and arms. She achieved her rich colors by working over an acrylic underpainting on specially prepared sandpaper.

Acrylic

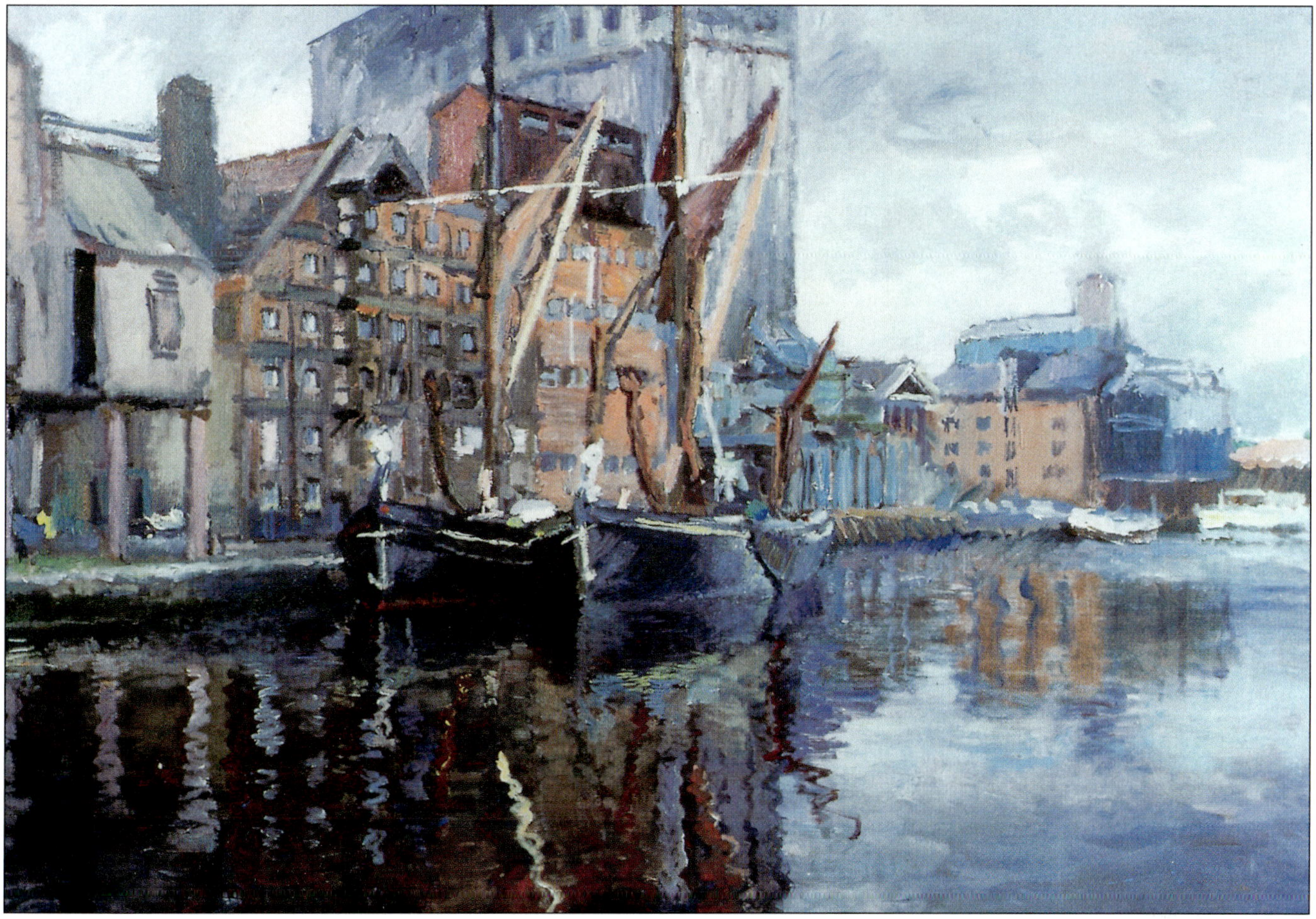

IPSWICH DOCKS by Gary Jeffrey

This lovely painting shows urban landscape at its most appealing – a true marriage of man-made and natural features. The artist has worked on canvas and his painting technique is similar to an oil-painter's, with the paint built up from thin to thick, and some use of wet-into-wet techniques, particularly in the reflections.

SELF-PORTRAIT WITH GULL by Brian Yale

The boat is painted in minute detail, so a similarly detailed feature was necessary in the foreground. Because the artist did not want to draw too much attention to the sand in the immediate foreground, he lightly suggested the texture in order to focus attention on the plank of wood.

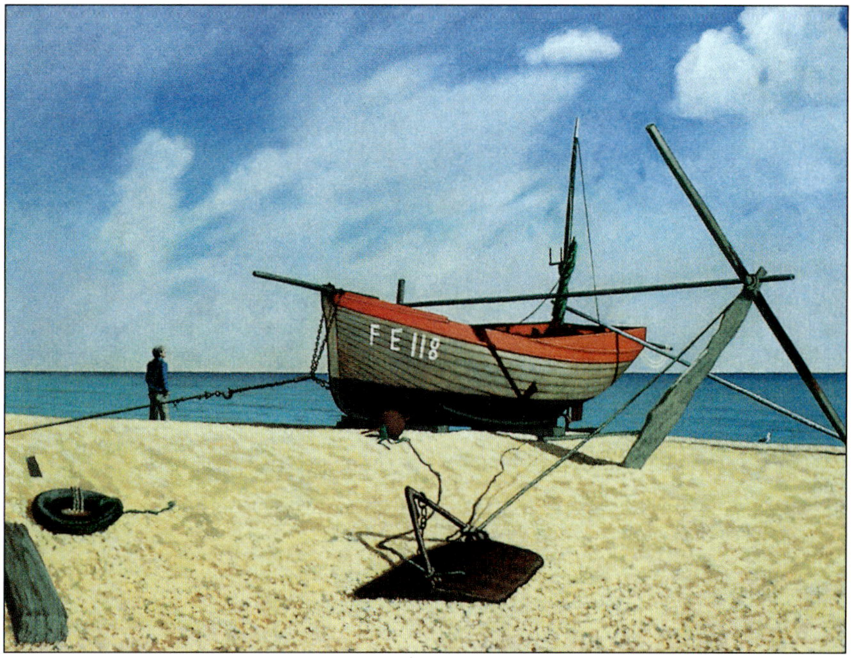

Colored Pencil

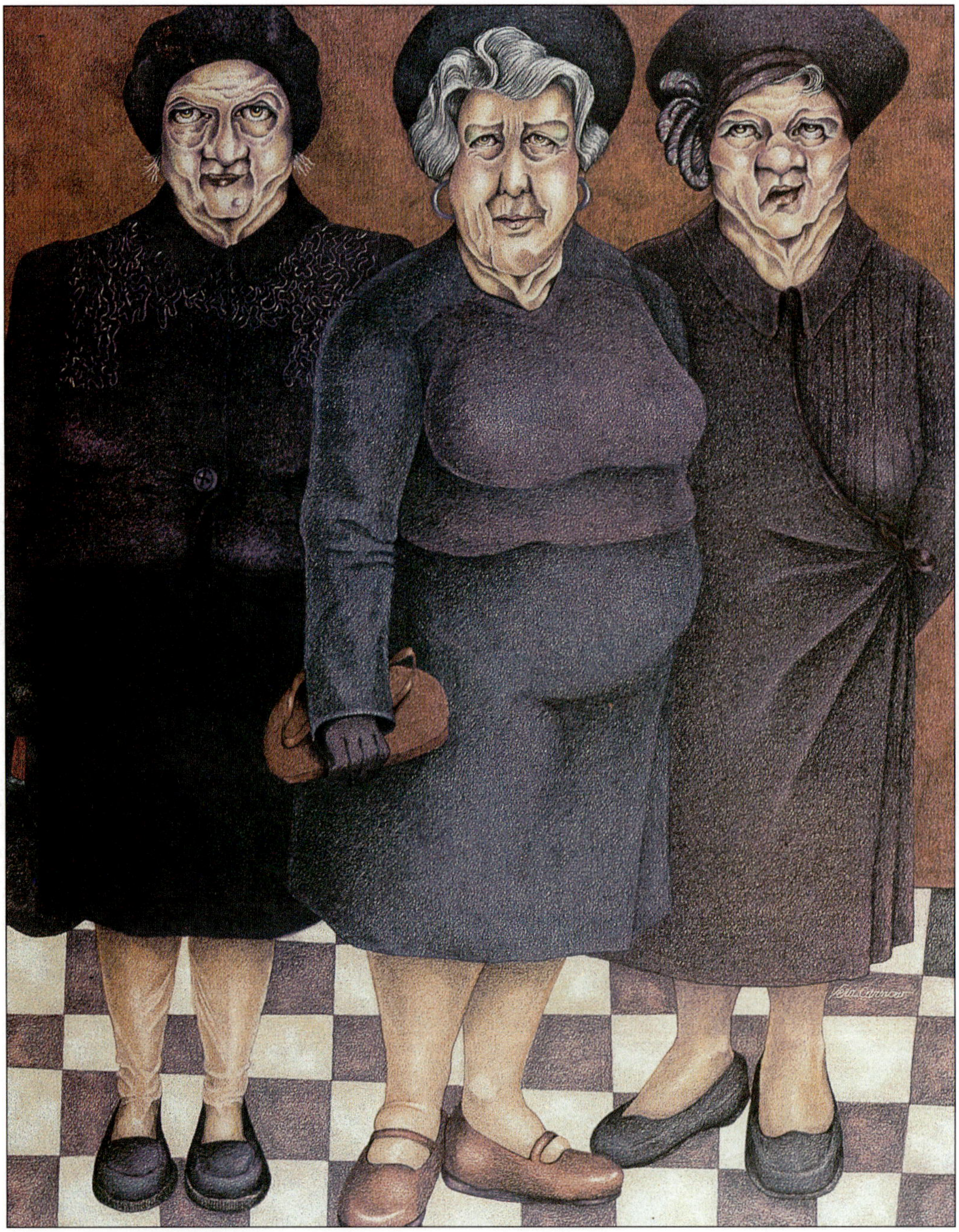

CLASS OF '44: THE CHEERLEADERS by Vera Curnow

The figures are affectionately caricatured in this stylized composition. The heavy shapes of the bodies are expressed with equally solid color applications, but, because the paper has a pronounced, pitted grain, the dark colors are relieved by tiny pinpoints of white. The artist employs this effect to help in modeling the tonal gradations, by varying the pressure of the pencil shading. Clean white line detail in the hair and clothing have been created by shading over impressed lines.

Watercolor

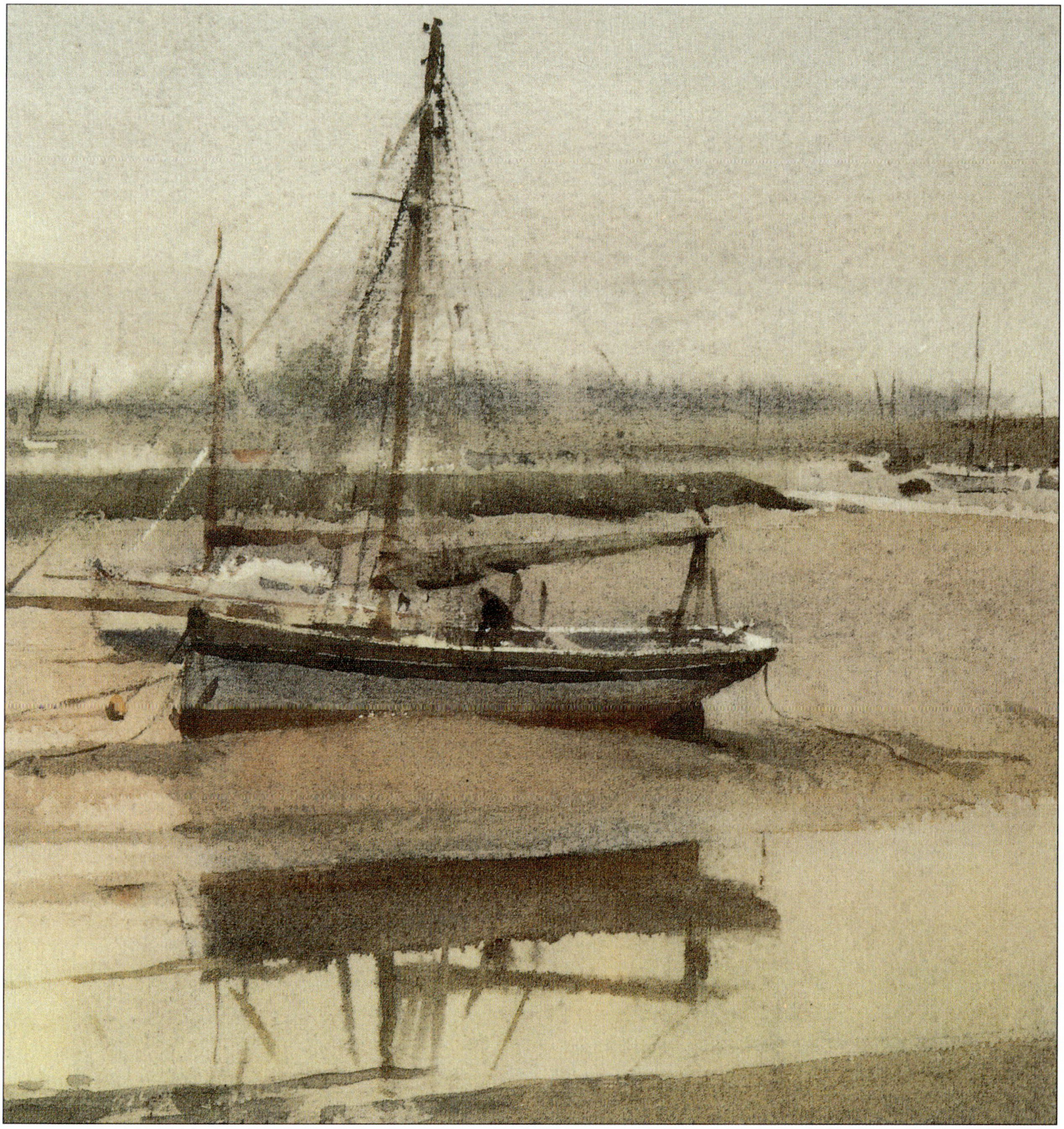

ON A SEA OF MUD, MALDEN by Trevor Chamberlain

This atmospheric painting expresses the quiet beauty of the scene as well as celebrating the unique qualities of watercolor.

Oil

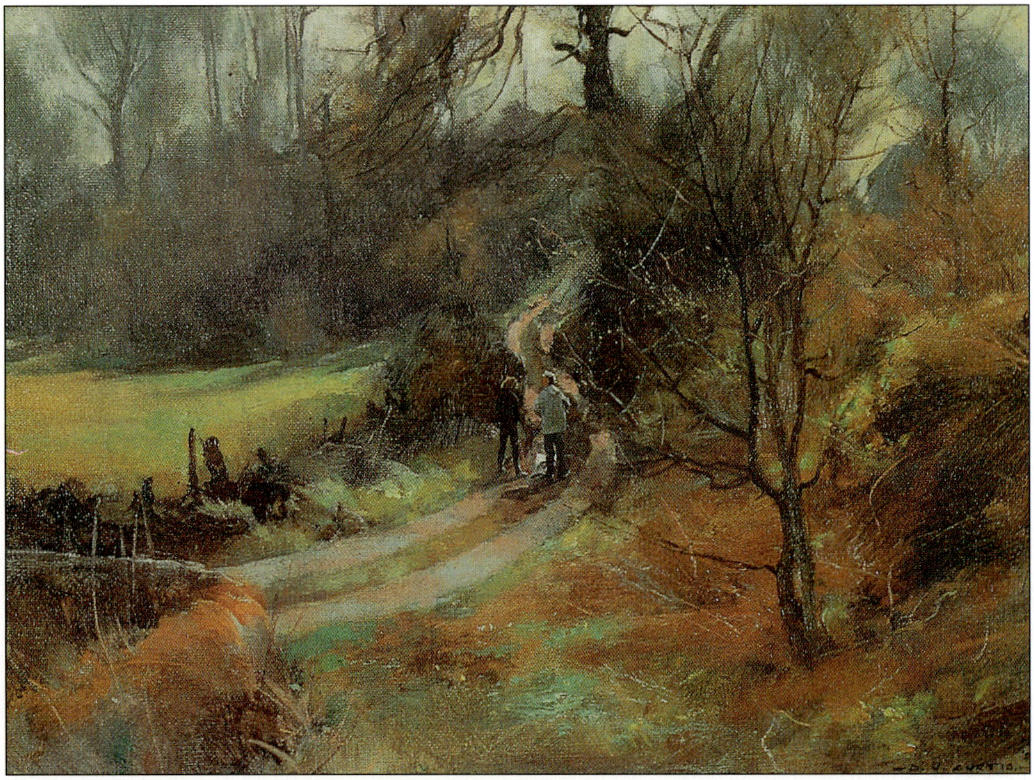

A MORNING WALK, STONE MILL by David Curtis

Figures naturally become the focal point in a landscape, simply because we identify with them, and here they are placed unequivocally center-stage. There are other, minor focal points in the picture, however, such as the distant house at the top right, the small tree at lower right, and the green field on the left disappearing into the distance, all of which hold our interest by inviting us to move from one part of the composition to another.

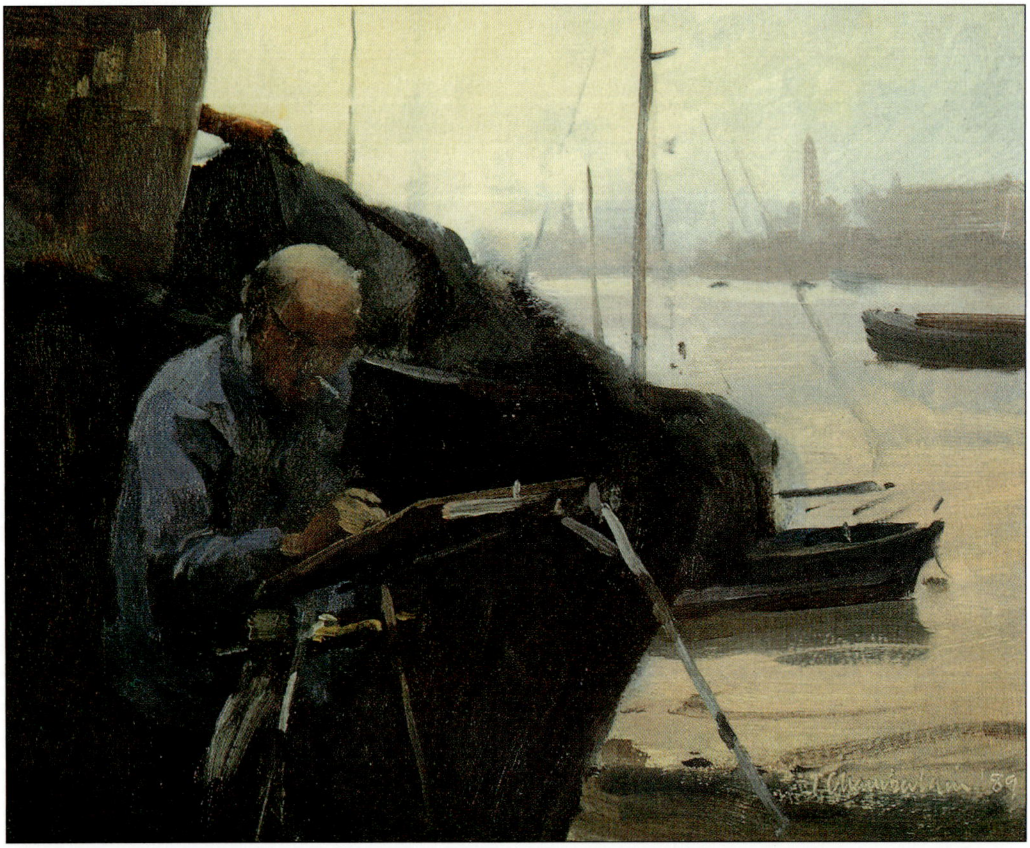

WORKING ON SITE, BUGSBY'S REACH by Trevor Chamberlain

A favorite subject for the painter is a fellow artist engaged in the same activity. The "model" is likely to remain more or less immobile as long as you are there, and can be shown in a setting which is wholly compatible with his or her occupation. Here the figure is the obvious center of interest, but our eyes are drawn from the foreground area to the delicate depiction of the distant river bank.

Gouache

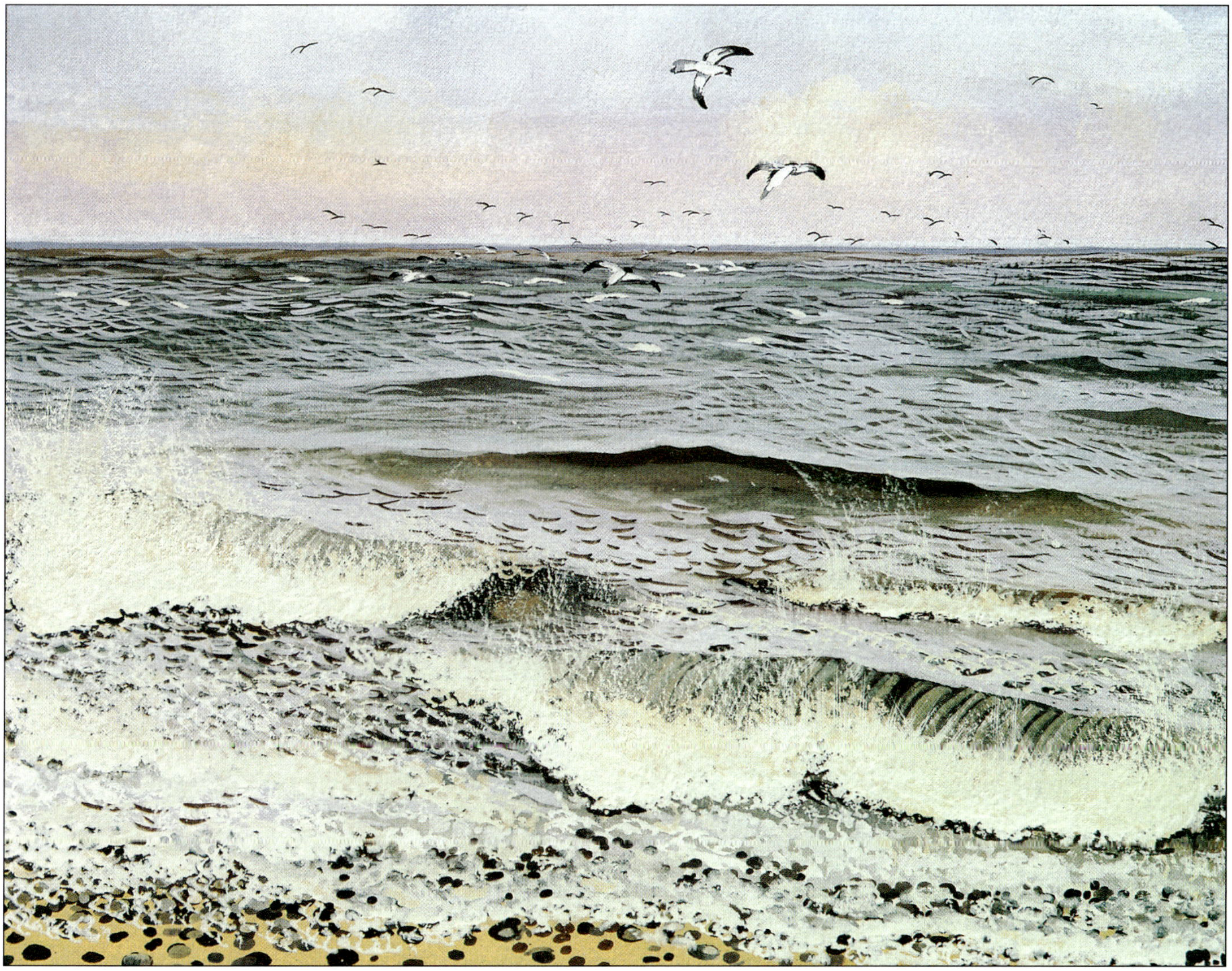

OUTGOING TIDE, KESSINGLAND by Michael Vincent

Dry brush textural techniques describe the foreground, contrasting with the flatter background. Note, too the use of the gulls to lead the eye into the distance.

GLOSSARY

Abstract Relying on color, pattern, and form rather than the realistic or naturalistic portrayal of subject matter.

Abstraction The creation of an abstract image by the simplification of natural appearances.

Action painting Splashing and dribbling paint on canvas. The technique is supposed to be derived from Leonardo's suggestion of using stains on walls as a starting point for a design.

Advancing colors Colors which appear to be near the viewer. Warm, strong colors seem to advance whereas cool colors recede.

Aerial perspective The use of color and tone to indicate space and recessions. Warm colors, clearly defined forms, and sharp contrasts of tone tend to advance toward the picture plane whereas cool colors, less clearly defined forms, and tonal contrasts appear further away.

Alla prima Completing the painting in one session with neither underdrawing nor underpainting.

Aqueous A term which refers to a pigment or medium soluble, or capable of being suspended in water.

Binder The adhesive which holds the powdered pigment together in a form suitable for painting. See Medium.

Blending Merging adjacent color areas so that the transition between the colors is imperceptible.

Blocking in The process of putting down roughly the main areas of tone and color in a composition before the work begins.

Body color Paint such as gouache, that has opacity and therefore covering power. Body color may be used to add highlights or color.

Broken color A term used in color theory to describe a color mixed from two secondary colors. These colors tend toward gray. It is also a method of painting in which colors are applied as areas of pure paint rather than being blended or mixed. These colors combine in the eye of the viewer to create new colors. The paint may be applied in small discrete patches, as in the Pointillist technique, or it may be applied in such a way that initial paint layers show through subsequent layers to create new colors.

Brushwork The personal handwriting of a painter. May be thick or thin, gentle or vigorous depending on the form of expression of the artist. It may be aesthetically pleasing in itself.

Calligraphic A term referring to a linear style of painting or drawing characterized by flowing, rhythmic marks.

Charcoal A drawing material made by reducing wood, through burning, to charred black sticks. All charcoal tends to powder but sticks are available in different thicknesses so the qualities in a charcoal drawing can be varied.

Chiaroscuro This term literally means "light-dark" and originally was used in reference to oil painting with dramatic tonal contrasts. It is now more generally applied to work in which there is a skillfully managed interplay of highlight and shadow.

Collage From the French word coller, meaning "to stick." A picture or design built up from pieces of colored paper. Devised by the Cubists. Any materials may be used likewise.

Complementary colors There are three basic pairs of complementary colors each consisting of one primary and one secondary color. These are opposite colors in that the primary is not used in mixing the secondary, thus blue and orange (red mixed with yellow) are complementary colors. On an extended color wheel, a warm red-orange is opposite green-blue.

Composition The arrangement of various elements in painting or drawing, for example, mass, color, tone, contour etc.

Covering power This term refers to the opacity or transparency of a paint. Some paints are transparent and are therefore more suitable for glazing whereas opaque paints are used for areas of dense color or where it is important to obliterate underlying color.

Crosshatching A technique of laying on areas of tone by building up a mass of criss-cross strokes rather than with a method of solid shading.

Design Roughly has the same meaning as composition, but applies also to artefacts and decorative objects, and functional equipment. Also has the same meaning as the Italian word *disegno* to mean drawing.

Diluent A liquid such as turpentine which is used to dilute paint. It evaporates completely and has no binding effect on the pigment.

Disegno An Italian word capable of many meanings, the simplest of which is drawing and the next simplest design.

Distemper Powdered color mixed with glue size. Because of its relative simplicity and cheapness was often used as a household paint for decoration, but since superseded by acrylic paints. Not to be confused with tempera.

Drawing The simplest way to plot out an image; to organize shapes and tones preparatory to painting or designing. To put down what is seen in an ordered way so that it is immediately understood. The way artists and designers think about their work. The artists' way of making notes and observations for future reference.

Dry brush In this technique a brush holding relatively dry paint is dragged across the surface giving a broken or feather effect.

Earth colors A range of pigments derived from inert oxides, for example, ochers, siennas, and umbers.

Ferrule The metal section of a paintbrush which holds the hairs.

Figurative This term is used in referring to paintings and drawings in which there is a representational approach to a particular subject, as distinct from abstract art.

Fixative A kind of thin varnish sprayed onto drawings and pastels to prevent their being rubbed (or picked up if overpainted).

Foreshortening The effect of perspective in a single object or figure, in which a form appears considerably altered from its normal proportions as it recedes from the artist's viewpoint.

Fresco Wall painting with a medium like watercolor (but without any binder) painted onto wet plaster which when dry acts as the binder by "locking-in" the paint. Absolutely permanent when favored by a dry and warm climate.

Fugitive This term describes pigments which fade on exposure to light.

Gesso Name of the ground used for tempera painting, and sometimes oil. Not recommended for acrylic.

Glazing The process of applying a transparent layer of paint over a solid one so that the color of the first is blended or modified by the second.

Gouache A water-based paint made opaque by mixing white with the pigments. Known variously as poster or designer's color.

Grain The texture of a support for painting or drawing. Paper may have a fine or coarse grain depending upon the methods used in its manufacture.

Graphite A form of carbon which is compressed with fine clay to form the substance commonly known as "lead" in pencils. The proportions of clay and graphite in the mixture determine the quality of the pencil, whether it is hard or soft, and the density of line produced. Thick sticks of graphite are available without a wooden pencil casing.

Ground The surface preparation of a support on which a painting or drawing is executed. A tinted ground may be laid on white paper to tone down its brilliance.

Gum arabic A water-soluble gum made from the sap of acacia trees. It is used as the binder for watercolor, gouache, and soft pastels.

Half tones A range of tones or colors which an artist can identify between extremes of light and dark.

Handling The name given to the most personal part of the work – the actual execution.

Hatching A technique of creating areas of tone with fine, parallel strokes following one direction.

Hot color Color which tends to be reddish in hue. The red end of the spectrum. Similarly, cool colors would tend to be blue, or at the blue end of the spectrum.

Hue This term is used for pure color found on a scale ranging through the spectrum, that is red, orange, yellow, green, blue, indigo, and violet.

Impasto Paint applied thickly so that it retains the mark of the brush or the knife.

Key Color is said to be high or low in key according to whether nearest to white (high-key) or black (low-key).

Lean A term used to describe oil paint which has little or no added oil. The expression "fat over lean" refers to the use of lean paint (thinned with turpentine or white spirit) under paint layers into which more oil is progressively introduced. This method of working prevents the paint surface from cracking as it dries.

Linear perspective A method of creating an illusion of depth and three dimensions on a flat surface through the use of converging lines and vanishing points.

Local color The actual color of the surface of an object unmodified by light, shade, or distance.

Mahl stick A cane used for steadying the painting arm when putting in fine detail. One end is covered with a soft pad to prevent the point from damaging the support.

Masking The technique of covering areas of the support (with either masking fluid or tape) in order to create a hard edge to the area being painted. The artist is free to use loose brush strokes, while at the same time protecting the covered area.

Medium 1 The liquid constituent of a paint in which the pigment is suspended. **2** Liquid with which the paint may be diluted without decreasing its adhesive, binding, or film-forming properties. **3** The mode of expression employed by an artist, e.g. painting, sculpture, or etching. **4** The actual instrument used by an artist; acrylic or oil paint, chisel, needle etc.

Mixed method Originally oil glazes over a tempera underpainting, but can also mean mixing compatible mediums like collage and paint; painting over drawing with inks, acrylic, and vice versa; adding three-dimensional objects to a flat surface.

Modeling In painting and drawing modeling is the employment of tone or color to achieve an impression of three-dimensional form, by depicting areas of light and shade in an object or figure.

Monochrome A painting executed in black and white, or black, white, and one other color.

Mural or wall painting is a term to describe any kind of wall decoration. Not interchangeable with fresco.

Negative space The spaces between and around the main elements of the subject – the background in a figure painting, for example.

Not A finish in high quality watercolor papers which calls between the smooth surface of hot-pressed, and the heavy texture of rough paper.

Ochers Earth colors derived from oxide of iron in a range from yellow to orange-red.

Opacity The quality of paint which covers or obscures a support or previous layers of applied color.

Optical color mixing Creating new colors by mixing pigments optically on the canvas rather than on the palette. The Pointillists placed small dots of unmixed color on the canvas so that viewed from a distance the dots are no longer visible and, for example, dabs of yellow and red would combine in the eye of the viewer to create orange.

Paint quality One of the desirable visual attributes of a finished painting. The term does not refer to good or bad ingredients. Paint quality is intrinsic for material beauty or successful surface effect. Something that comes with skillful handling, but often helped by the paint concerned.

Painting knife A knife with a thin flexible blade used for applying paint to a support. These knives generally have a cranked handle and are available in a range of shapes and sizes.

Palette The try or dish on which an artist lays out paint for thinning or mixing. This may be of wood, metal, china, plastic, or paper. By extension the term also refers to the range of colors used in making a particular image or a color scheme characteristic of work by one artist.

Palette knife A knife with a straight steel blade used for mixing paint on the palette, cleaning the palette, and for scraping paint from the support if necessary.

Pastel A drawing medium made by binding powder pigment with a little gum and rolling. The color mixtures are achieved by overlaying layers of pastel strokes or by gently blending colors with a brush or the fingers. Oil pastels have a waxy quality and less tendency to crumble, but the effects are not so subtle.

Perspective Systems of representation in drawing and painting which create an impression of depth, solidity, and spatial recession on a flat surface. Linear perspective is based on a principle that receding parallel lines appear to converge at a point on the horizon line. Aerial perspective represents the grading of tones and colors to suggest distance which may be observed as natural modifications caused by atmospheric effects.

Picking-up What happens when a color is laid over another incorrectly, so that the two colors combine and become muddy.

Picture plane The vertical surface area of a painting or drawing on which the artist plots the composition and arranges pictorial elements which may suggest an illusion of three-dimensional reality and a recession in space.

Pigment A substance which provides color and which may be mixed with a binder to produce paint or a drawing material. Pigments are generally described as organic (earth colors) or inorganic (mineral and chemical pigments).

Planes The flat surfaces of an object. These are revealed by light and can be seen in terms of light and dark. Even a curved surface can be regarded as an infinite number of small planes.

Plein air A French term meaning "open air" used to describe pictures painted out of doors.

Primary colors In painting the primary colors are red, blue, and yellow. They cannot be formed by mixtures of any other colors, but in theory can be used in varying proportions to create all other hues. This is not necessarily true in practise, as paint pigments used commercially are unlikely to be sufficiently pure.

Priming Also known as ground, this is the layer or layers of materials applied to a support to make it less absorbent or more pleasant to paint on. A suitable priming for canvas could consist of a layer of size, followed by an oil grounding.

Renaissance The cultural revival of classic ideals which took place in Europe from the 14th to the 16th centuries.

Resist This is a method of combining drawing and watercolor painting. A wash of water-based paint laid over marks drawn with wax crayon or oil pastel cannot settle in the drawing and the marks remain visible in their original color, while areas of bare paper accept the wash.

Retarder An additive to delay the drying process of acrylic paint.

Sable Small rodent-like animal, the fur of which goes to make fine, high-quality (and often expensive) brushes.

Saturated color Pure color, free of black and white and therefore intense.

Scumbling A painting technique in which opaque paint is dragged or lightly scrubbed across a surface to form an area of broken color which modifies the tones underneath.

Secondary colors These are the three colors formed by mixing pairs of primary colors; orange (red and yellow), green (yellow and blue), and purple (red and blue).

Size Used both as a noun and a verb. Size is the solution that is used to coat a support in order to render it less absorbent. To size is to carry out this process.

Spattering A method of spreading paint with a loose, mottled texture by drawing the thumb across the bristles of a stiff brush loaded with wet paint so the color is flicked onto the surface of the painting.

Staining power The color strength of a pigment and its ability to impart that color to white, or to a mixture. If a pigment has good staining power you will need only a little of it to impart color to a mixture.

Stippling The technique of applying color or tone as a mass of small dots made with the point of a drawing instrument or fine brush.

Study A drawing or painting, often made as preparation for a larger work, which is intended to record particular aspects of a subject.

Support The term applied to the material which provides the surface on which a painting or drawing is executed, for example, canvas, board, or paper.

Tempera Any kind of binder that will serve to temper powdered pigment and make it workable. In practise the term is usually confined to egg tempera only, yolk of egg being the binder. A unique but very slow medium to master.

Tone In painting or drawing, tone is the measure of light and dark as on a scale of gradations between black and white. Every color has an inherent tone; for example, yellow is light while Prussian blue is dark, but a colored object or a surface is also modified by the light falling upon it and an assessment of the variation in tonal values may be crucial to the artist's ability to indicate the three-dimensional form of an object.

Tooth A degree of texture or coarseness in a surface which allows a painting or drawing material to adhere to the support.

Transparency A quality of paint which means that it stains or modifies the color of the surface on which it is laid, rather than obliterating it.

Underdrawing The preliminary drawing for a painting, often done in pencil, charcoal, or paint.

Underpainting The preliminary blocking-in or the main forms, colors, and tonal areas.

Value The character of a color as assessed on a tonal scale from dark to light.

Vehicle A liquid used as the carrier of pigments in a paint. The term is interchangeable with medium, but is perhaps more properly applied to the liquid used as an ingredient in manufacture than to a liquid added during painting procedure.

Wash An application of considerably diluted paint to make the color spread quickly and thinly.

Watermark The symbol or name of the manufacturer incorporated in sheets of high quality paper. The watermark is visible when the paper is held up to the light.

Wet on dry The application of paint to a completely dry surface.

Wet-into-wet The application of wet paint to an already wet surface. Used in *alla prima* technique. Wet-into-wet allows the artist to blend colors and tones.

Whiting-out or repriming is the process of covering a painting or part of a painting that has "gone wrong" with a semi-transparent layer of white or tinted paint.

INDEX

U

V

W

Y

PICTURE CREDITS

The material in this book previously appeared in:

Painting with Watercolor
Watercolor School
Painting in Watercolor
The Artist's Manual
The Complete Watercolor Artist
The Watercolor Painter's Q&A Book
Water – How to See It – How to Paint It
The Complete Drawing & Painting Course
How to Draw & Paint in Watercolor and Gouache
How to Draw and Paint
The Complete Artist
How to Paint & Draw
The Encyclopedia of Illustration Techniques
The Encyclopedia of Watercolor Landscape Techniques
The Encyclopedia of Flower Painting Techniques
Painting in Watercolor
How to Draw & Paint Portraits
You Can Paint Portraits
Tonal Values – How to See Them, How to Paint Them
The Encyclopedia of Drawing Techniques
The Encyclopedia of Colored Pencil Techniques
The Encyclopedia of Watercolor Techniques
How to Draw & Paint Landscapes
How to Draw & Paint Still-Life
Light – How to See It, How to Paint It
The Encyclopedia of Pastel Techniques
Figure Sketching School
How to Draw in Pastels, Pencils and Pen & Ink
The Encyclopedia of Oil Painting Techniques
Painting Shapes & Edges
Acrylic School
How to Paint Trees, Flowers & Foliage
You Can Paint Flowers, Plants & Nature
The Encyclopedia of Acrylic Techniques
An Introduction to Drawing
Color – How to See It, How to Paint It
Drawing and Sketching
Pastel School
Painting with Oils
Painting with Acrylics
The Artist's Manual
Pastel Painting Techniques
Master Strokes Pastel
The Painting & Drawing Course